University Casebook Series

March, 1986

ACCOUNTING AND THE LAW, Fourth Edition (1978), with Problems Pamphlet (Successor to Dohr, Phillips, Thompson & Warren)

George C. Thompson, Professor, Columbia University Graduate School of Business.

Robert Whitman, Professor of Law, University of Connecticut.

Ellis L. Phillips, Jr., Member of the New York Bar.

William C. Warren, Professor of Law Emeritus, Columbia University.

ACCOUNTING FOR LAWYERS, MATERIALS ON (1980)

David R. Herwitz, Professor of Law, Harvard University.

ADMINISTRATIVE LAW, Seventh Edition (1979), with 1983 Problems Supplement (Supplement edited in association with Paul R. Verkuil, Dean and Professor of Law, Tulane University)

Walter Gellhorn, University Professor Emeritus, Columbia University.

Clark Byse, Professor of Law, Harvard University.

Peter L. Strauss, Professor of Law, Columbia University.

ADMIRALTY, Second Edition (1978), with Statute and Rule Supplement

Jo Desha Lucas, Professor of Law, University of Chicago.

ADVOCACY, see also Lawyering Process

AGENCY, see also Enterprise Organization

AGENCY—PARTNERSHIPS, Third Edition (1982)

Abridgement from Conard, Knauss & Siegel's Enterprise Organization, Third Edition.

ANTITRUST: FREE ENTERPRISE AND ECONOMIC ORGANIZATION, Sixth Edition (1983), with 1983 Problems in Antitrust Supplement and 1985 Case Supplement

Louis B. Schwartz, Professor of Law, University of Pennsylvania.

John J. Flynn, Professor of Law, University of Utah.

Harry First, Professor of Law, New York University.

BANKRUPTCY (1985)

Robert L. Jordan, Professor of Law, University of California, Los Angeles.

William D. Warren, Professor of Law, University of California, Los Angeles.

BUSINESS ORGANIZATION, see also Enterprise Organization

BUSINESS PLANNING, Temporary Second Edition (1984)

David R. Herwitz, Professor of Law, Harvard University.

BUSINESS TORTS (1972)

Milton Handler, Professor of Law Emeritus, Columbia University.

CHILDREN IN THE LEGAL SYSTEM (1983)

Walter Wadlington, Professor of Law, University of Virginia.
Charles H. Whitebread, Professor of Law, University of Southern California.
Samuel Davis, Professor of Law, University of Georgia.

CIVIL PROCEDURE, see Procedure

CLINIC, see also Lawyering Process

COMMERCIAL LAW (1983) with 1986 Bankruptcy Supplement

Robert L. Jordan, Professor of Law, University of California, Los Angeles.
William D. Warren, Professor of Law, University of California, Los Angeles.

COMMERCIAL LAW, CASES & MATERIALS ON, Fourth Edition (1985)

E. Allan Farnsworth, Professor of Law, Columbia University.
John Honnold, Professor of Law, University of Pennsylvania.

COMMERCIAL PAPER, Third Edition (1984)

E. Allan Farnsworth, Professor of Law, Columbia University.

COMMERCIAL PAPER (1983) (Reprinted from COMMERCIAL LAW)

Robert L. Jordan, Professor of Law, University of California, Los Angeles.
William D. Warren, Professor of Law, University of California, Los Angeles.

COMMERCIAL PAPER AND BANK DEPOSITS AND COLLECTIONS (1967), with Statutory Supplement

William D. Hawkland, Professor of Law, University of Illinois.

COMMERCIAL TRANSACTIONS—Principles and Policies (1982)

Alan Schwartz, Professor of Law, University of Southern California.
Robert E. Scott, Professor of Law, University of Virginia.

COMPARATIVE LAW, Fourth Edition (1980)

Rudolf B. Schlesinger, Professor of Law, Hastings College of the Law.

COMPETITIVE PROCESS, LEGAL REGULATION OF THE, Third Edition (1986), with Selected Statutes Supplement

Edmund W. Kitch, Professor of Law, University of Virginia.
Harvey S. Perlman, Dean of the Law School, University of Nebraska.

CONFLICT OF LAWS, Eighth Edition (1984)

Willis L. M. Reese, Professor of Law, Columbia University.
Maurice Rosenberg, Professor of Law, Columbia University.

CONSTITUTIONAL LAW, Seventh Edition (1985), with 1985 Supplement

Edward L. Barrett, Jr., Professor of Law, University of California, Davis.
William Cohen, Professor of Law, Stanford University.

CONSTITUTIONAL LAW, CIVIL LIBERTY AND INDIVIDUAL RIGHTS, Second Edition (1982), with 1985 Supplement

William Cohen, Professor of Law, Stanford University.
John Kaplan, Professor of Law, Stanford University.

CONSTITUTIONAL LAW, Eleventh Edition (1985), with 1985 Supplement (Supplement edited in association with Frederick F. Schauer, Professor of Law, University of Michigan)

Gerald Gunther, Professor of Law, Stanford University.

UNIVERSITY CASEBOOK SERIES—Continued

CONSTITUTIONAL LAW, INDIVIDUAL RIGHTS IN, Fourth Edition (1986), (Reprinted from CONSTITUTIONAL LAW, Eleventh Edition), with 1985 Supplement (Supplement edited in association with Frederick F. Schauer, Professor of Law, University of Michigan)

Gerald Gunther, Professor of Law, Stanford University.

CONSUMER TRANSACTIONS (1983), with Selected Statutes and Regulations Supplement

Michael M. Greenfield, Professor of Law, Washington University.

CONTRACT LAW AND ITS APPLICATION, Third Edition (1983)

The late Addison Mueller, Professor of Law, University of California, Los Angeles.
Arthur I. Rosett, Professor of Law, University of California, Los Angeles.
Gerald P. Lopez, Professor of Law, University of California, Los Angeles.

CONTRACT LAW, STUDIES IN, Third Edition (1984)

Edward J. Murphy, Professor of Law, University of Notre Dame.
Richard E. Speidel, Professor of Law, Northwestern University.

CONTRACTS, Fourth Edition (1982)

John P. Dawson, Professor of Law Emeritus, Harvard University.
William Burnett Harvey, Professor of Law and Political Science, Boston University.
Stanley D. Henderson, Professor of Law, University of Virginia.

CONTRACTS, Third Edition (1980), with Statutory Supplement

E. Allan Farnsworth, Professor of Law, Columbia University.
William F. Young, Professor of Law, Columbia University.

CONTRACTS, Second Edition (1978), with Statutory and Administrative Law Supplement (1978)

Ian R. Macneil, Professor of Law, Cornell University.

COPYRIGHT, PATENTS AND TRADEMARKS, see also Competitive Process; see also Selected Statutes and International Agreements

COPYRIGHT, PATENT, TRADEMARK AND RELATED STATE DOCTRINES, Second Edition (1981), with 1985 Case Supplement, 1986 Selected Statutes Supplement and 1981 Problem Supplement

Paul Goldstein, Professor of Law, Stanford University.

COPYRIGHT, Unfair Competition, and Other Topics Bearing on the Protection of Literary, Musical, and Artistic Works, Fourth Edition (1985), with 1985 Statutory Supplement

Ralph S. Brown, Jr., Professor of Law, Yale University.
Robert C. Denicola, Professor of Law, University of Nebraska.

CORPORATE ACQUISITIONS, The Law and Finance of (1986)

Ronald J. Gilson, Professor of Law, Stanford University.

CORPORATE FINANCE, Second Edition (1979), with 1984 Supplement

Victor Brudney, Professor of Law, Harvard University.
Marvin A. Chirelstein, Professor of Law, Columbia University.

CORPORATE READJUSTMENTS AND REORGANIZATIONS (1976)

Walter J. Blum, Professor of Law, University of Chicago.
Stanley A. Kaplan, Professor of Law, University of Chicago.

UNIVERSITY CASEBOOK SERIES—Continued

CORPORATION LAW, BASIC, Second Edition (1979), with 1983 Case and Documentary Supplement

Detlev F. Vagts, Professor of Law, Harvard University.

CORPORATIONS, see also Enterprise Organization

CORPORATIONS, Fifth Edition—Unabridged (1980), with 1984 Supplement

The late William L. Cary, Professor of Law, Columbia University.
Melvin Aron Eisenberg, Professor of Law, University of California, Berkeley.

CORPORATIONS, Fifth Edition—Abridged (1980), with 1984 Supplement

The late William L. Cary, Professor of Law, Columbia University.
Melvin Aron Eisenberg, Professor of Law, University of California, Berkeley.

CORPORATIONS, Second Edition (1982), with 1982 Corporation and Partnership Statutes, Rules and Forms

Alfred F. Conard, Professor of Law, University of Michigan.
Robert N. Knauss, Dean of the Law School, University of Houston.
Stanley Siegel, Professor of Law, University of California, Los Angeles.

CORPORATIONS COURSE GAME PLAN (1975)

David R. Herwitz, Professor of Law, Harvard University.

CORRECTIONS, SEE SENTENCING

CREDITORS' RIGHTS, see also Debtor-Creditor Law

CRIMINAL JUSTICE ADMINISTRATION, Third Edition (1986).

Frank W. Miller, Professor of Law, Washington University.
Robert O. Dawson, Professor of Law, University of Texas.
George E. Dix, Professor of Law, University of Texas.
Raymond I. Parnas, Professor of Law, University of California, Davis.

CRIMINAL LAW, Third Edition (1983)

Fred E. Inbau, Professor of Law Emeritus, Northwestern University.
James R. Thompson, Professor of Law Emeritus, Northwestern University.
Andre A. Moenssens, Professor of Law, University of Richmond.

CRIMINAL LAW AND APPROACHES TO THE STUDY OF LAW (1986)

John M. Brumbaugh, Professor of Law, University of Maryland.

CRIMINAL LAW, Second Edition (1986)

Peter W. Low, Professor of Law, University of Virginia.
John C. Jeffries, Jr., Professor of Law, University of Virginia.
Richard C. Bonnie, Professor of Law, University of Virginia.

CRIMINAL LAW, Third Edition (1980)

Lloyd L. Weinreb, Professor of Law, Harvard University.

CRIMINAL LAW AND PROCEDURE, Sixth Edition (1984)

Rollin M. Perkins, Professor of Law Emeritus, University of California, Hastings College of the Law.
Ronald N. Boyce, Professor of Law, University of Utah.

UNIVERSITY CASEBOOK SERIES—Continued

CRIMINAL PROCEDURE, Second Edition (1980), with 1985 Supplement

Fred E. Inbau, Professor of Law Emeritus, Northwestern University.
James R. Thompson, Professor of Law Emeritus, Northwestern University.
James B. Haddad, Professor of Law, Northwestern University.
James B. Zagel, Chief, Criminal Justice Division, Office of Attorney General of
Illinois.
Gary L. Starkman, Assistant U. S. Attorney, Northern District of Illinois.

CRIMINAL PROCESS, Third Edition (1978), with 1985 Supplement

Lloyd L. Weinreb, Professor of Law, Harvard University.

DAMAGES, Second Edition (1952)

Charles T. McCormick, late Professor of Law, University of Texas.
William F. Fritz, late Professor of Law, University of Texas.

DEBTOR–CREDITOR LAW (1984) with 1986 Supplement

Theodore Eisenberg, Professor of Law, Cornell University.

DEBTOR–CREDITOR LAW, Second Edition (1981), with Statutory Supplement

William D. Warren, Dean of the School of Law, University of California, Los
Angeles.
William E. Hogan, Professor of Law, New York University.

DECEDENTS' ESTATES (1971)

Max Rheinstein, late Professor of Law Emeritus, University of Chicago.
Mary Ann Glendon, Professor of Law, Boston College.

DECEDENTS' ESTATES AND TRUSTS, Sixth Edition (1982)

John Ritchie, Emeritus Dean and Wigmore Professor of Law, Northwestern
University.
Neill H. Alford, Jr., Professor of Law, University of Virginia.
Richard W. Effland, Professor of Law, Arizona State University.

DOMESTIC RELATIONS, see also Family Law

DOMESTIC RELATIONS, Successor Edition (1984) with 1985 Supplement

Walter Wadlington, Professor of Law, University of Virginia.

ELECTRONIC MASS MEDIA, Second Edition (1979)

William K. Jones, Professor of Law, Columbia University.

EMPLOYMENT DISCRIMINATION (1983) with 1985 Supplement

Joel W. Friedman, Professor of Law, Tulane University.
George M. Strickler, Professor of Law, Tulane University.

ENERGY LAW (1983)

Donald N. Zillman, Professor of Law, University of Utah.
Laurence Lattman, Dean of Mines and Engineering, University of Utah.

**ENTERPRISE ORGANIZATION, Third Edition (1982), with 1982 Corporation
and Partnership Statutes, Rules and Forms Supplement**

Alfred F. Conard, Professor of Law, University of Michigan.
Robert L. Knauss, Dean of the Law School, University of Houston.
Stanley Siegel, Professor of Law, University of California, Los Angeles.

ENVIRONMENTAL POLICY LAW 1985 Edition, with 1985 Problems Supplement (Supplement in association with Ronald H. Rosenberg, Professor of Law, College of William and Mary)

Thomas J. Schoenbaum, Professor of Law, University of Georgia.

EQUITY, see also Remedies

EQUITY, RESTITUTION AND DAMAGES, Second Edition (1974)

Robert Childres, late Professor of Law, Northwestern University.
William F. Johnson, Jr., Professor of Law, New York University.

ESTATE PLANNING, Second Edition (1982), with 1985 Case, Text and Documentary Supplement

David Westfall, Professor of Law, Harvard University.

ETHICS, see Legal Profession, and Professional Responsibility

ETHICS AND PROFESSIONAL RESPONSIBILITY (1981) (Reprinted from THE LAWYERING PROCESS)

Gary Bellow, Professor of Law, Harvard University.
Bea Moulton, Legal Services Corporation.

EVIDENCE, Fifth Edition (1984)

John Kaplan, Professor of Law, Stanford University.
Jon R. Waltz, Professor of Law, Northwestern University.

EVIDENCE, Seventh Edition (1983) with Rules and Statute Supplement (1984)

Jack B. Weinstein, Chief Judge, United States District Court.
John H. Mansfield, Professor of Law, Harvard University.
Norman Abrams, Professor of Law, University of California, Los Angeles.
Margaret Berger, Professor of Law, Brooklyn Law School.

FAMILY LAW, see also Domestic Relations

FAMILY LAW Second Edition (1985)

Judith C. Areen, Professor of Law, Georgetown University.

FAMILY LAW AND CHILDREN IN THE LEGAL SYSTEM, STATUTORY MATERIALS (1981)

Walter Wadlington, Professor of Law, University of Virginia.

FEDERAL COURTS, Seventh Edition (1982), with 1985 Supplement

Charles T. McCormick, late Professor of Law, University of Texas.
James H. Chadbourn, late Professor of Law, Harvard University.
Charles Alan Wright, Professor of Law, University of Texas.

FEDERAL COURTS AND THE FEDERAL SYSTEM, Hart and Wechsler's Second Edition (1973), with 1981 Supplement

Paul M. Bator, Professor of Law, Harvard University.
Paul J. Mishkin, Professor of Law, University of California, Berkeley.
David L. Shapiro, Professor of Law, Harvard University.
Herbert Wechsler, Professor of Law, Columbia University.

FEDERAL PUBLIC LAND AND RESOURCES LAW (1981), with 1983 Case Supplement and 1984 Statutory Supplement

George C. Coggins, Professor of Law, University of Kansas.
Charles F. Wilkinson, Professor of Law, University of Oregon.

FEDERAL RULES OF CIVIL PROCEDURE, 1984 Edition

FEDERAL TAXATION, see Taxation

FOOD AND DRUG LAW (1980), with Statutory Supplement

Richard A. Merrill, Dean of the School of Law, University of Virginia.
Peter Barton Hutt, Esq.

UNIVERSITY CASEBOOK SERIES—Continued

FUTURE INTERESTS (1958)

Philip Mechem, late Professor of Law Emeritus, University of Pennsylvania.

FUTURE INTERESTS (1970)

Howard R. Williams, Professor of Law, Stanford University.

FUTURE INTERESTS AND ESTATE PLANNING (1961), with 1962 Supplement

W. Barton Leach, late Professor of Law, Harvard University.
James K. Logan, formerly Dean of the Law School, University of Kansas.

GOVERNMENT CONTRACTS, FEDERAL, Successor Edition (1985)

John W. Whelan, Professor of Law, Hastings College of the Law.

**GOVERNMENT REGULATION: FREE ENTERPRISE AND ECONOMIC ORGANI-
ZATION, Sixth Edition (1985)**

Louis B. Schwartz, Professor of Law, University of Pennsylvania.
John J. Flynn, Professor of Law, University of Utah.
Harry First, Professor of Law, New York University.

HINCKLEY JOHN W., TRIAL OF: A Case Study of the Insanity Defense

Peter W. Low, Professor of Law, University of Virginia.
John C. Jeffries, Jr., Professor of Law, University of Virginia.
Richard C. Bonnie, Professor of Law, University of Virginia.

INJUNCTIONS, Second Edition (1984)

Owen M. Fiss, Professor of Law, Yale University.
Doug Rendleman, Professor of Law, College of William and Mary.

INSTITUTIONAL INVESTORS, 1978

David L. Ratner, Professor of Law, Cornell University.

INSURANCE, Second Edition (1985)

William F. Young, Professor of Law, Columbia University.
Eric M. Holmes, Professor of Law, University of Georgia.

**INTERNATIONAL LAW, see also Transnational Legal Problems, Transnational
Business Problems, and United Nations Law**

**INTERNATIONAL LAW IN CONTEMPORARY PERSPECTIVE (1981), with Essay
Supplement**

Myres S. McDougal, Professor of Law, Yale University.
W. Michael Reisman, Professor of Law, Yale University.

**INTERNATIONAL LEGAL SYSTEM, Second Edition (1981), with Documentary
Supplement**

Joseph Modeste Sweeney, Professor of Law, Tulane University.
Covey T. Oliver, Professor of Law, University of Pennsylvania.
Noyes E. Leech, Professor of Law, University of Pennsylvania.

**INTRODUCTION TO LAW, see also Legal Method, On Law in Courts, and
Dynamics of American Law**

INTRODUCTION TO THE STUDY OF LAW (1970)

E. Wayne Thode, late Professor of Law, University of Utah.
Leon Lebowitz, Professor of Law, University of Texas.
Lester J. Mazor, Professor of Law, University of Utah.

UNIVERSITY CASEBOOK SERIES—Continued

JUDICIAL CODE and Rules of Procedure in the Federal Courts with Excerpts from the Criminal Code, 1984 Edition

Henry M. Hart, Jr., late Professor of Law, Harvard University.
Herbert Wechsler, Professor of Law, Columbia University.

JURISPRUDENCE (Temporary Edition Hardbound) (1949)

Lon L. Fuller, Professor of Law Emeritus, Harvard University.

JUVENILE, see also Children

JUVENILE JUSTICE PROCESS, Third Edition (1985)

Frank W. Miller, Professor of Law, Washington University.
Robert O. Dawson, Professor of Law, University of Texas.
George E. Dix, Professor of Law, University of Texas.
Raymond I. Parnas, Professor of Law, University of California, Davis.

LABOR LAW, Tenth Edition (1986), with 1986 Statutory Supplement

Archibald Cox, Professor of Law, Harvard University.
Derek C. Bok, President, Harvard University.
Robert A. Gorman, Professor of Law, University of Pennsylvania.

LABOR LAW, Second Edition (1982), with Statutory Supplement

Clyde W. Summers, Professor of Law, University of Pennsylvania.
Harry H. Wellington, Dean of the Law School, Yale University.
Alan Hyde, Professor of Law, Rutgers University.

LAND FINANCING, Third Edition (1985)

The late Norman Penney, Professor of Law, Cornell University.
Richard F. Broude, Member of the California Bar.
Roger Cunningham, Professor of Law, University of Michigan.

LAW AND MEDICINE (1980)

Walter Wadlington, Professor of Law and Professor of Legal Medicine, University of Virginia.
Jon R. Waltz, Professor of Law, Northwestern University.
Roger B. Dworkin, Professor of Law, Indiana University, and Professor of Biomedical History, University of Washington.

LAW, LANGUAGE AND ETHICS (1972)

William R. Bishin, Professor of Law, University of Southern California.
Christopher D. Stone, Professor of Law, University of Southern California.

LAW, SCIENCE AND MEDICINE (1984)

Judith C. Areen, Professor of Law, Georgetown University.
Patricia A. King, Professor of Law, Georgetown University.
Steven P. Goldberg, Professor of Law, Georgetown University.
Alexander M. Capron, Professor of Law, Georgetown University.

LAWYERING PROCESS (1978), with Civil Problem Supplement and Criminal Problem Supplement

Gary Bellow, Professor of Law, Harvard University.
Bea Moulton, Professor of Law, Arizona State University.

LEGAL METHOD (1980)

Harry W. Jones, Professor of Law Emeritus, Columbia University.
John M. Kernochan, Professor of Law, Columbia University.
Arthur W. Murphy, Professor of Law, Columbia University.

LEGAL METHODS (1969)

> Robert N. Covington, Professor of Law, Vanderbilt University.
> E. Blythe Stason, late Professor of Law, Vanderbilt University.
> John W. Wade, Professor of Law, Vanderbilt University.
> Elliott E. Cheatham, late Professor of Law, Vanderbilt University.
> Theodore A. Smedley, Professor of Law, Vanderbilt University.

LEGAL PROFESSION, THE, Responsibility and Regulation (1985)

> Geoffrey C. Hazard, Jr., Professor of Law, Yale University.
> Deborah L. Rhode, Professor of Law, Stanford University.

LEGISLATION, Fourth Edition (1982) (by Fordham)

> Horace E. Read, late Vice President, Dalhousie University.
> John W. MacDonald, Professor of Law Emeritus, Cornell Law School.
> Jefferson B. Fordham, Professor of Law, University of Utah.
> William J. Pierce, Professor of Law, University of Michigan.

LEGISLATIVE AND ADMINISTRATIVE PROCESSES, Second Edition (1981)

> Hans A. Linde, Judge, Supreme Court of Oregon.
> George Bunn, Professor of Law, University of Wisconsin.
> Fredericka Paff, Professor of Law, University of Wisconsin.
> W. Lawrence Church, Professor of Law, University of Wisconsin.

LOCAL GOVERNMENT LAW, Second Revised Edition (1986)

> Jefferson B. Fordham, Professor of Law, University of Utah.

MASS MEDIA LAW, Second Edition (1982), with 1985 Supplement

> Marc A. Franklin, Professor of Law, Stanford University.

MENTAL HEALTH PROCESS, Second Edition (1976), with 1981 Supplement

> Frank W. Miller, Professor of Law, Washington University.
> Robert O. Dawson, Professor of Law, University of Texas.
> George E. Dix, Professor of Law, University of Texas.
> Raymond I. Parnas, Professor of Law, University of California, Davis.

MUNICIPAL CORPORATIONS, see Local Government Law

NEGOTIABLE INSTRUMENTS, see Commercial Paper

NEGOTIATION (1981) (Reprinted from THE LAWYERING PROCESS)

> Gary Bellow, Professor of Law, Harvard Law School.
> Bea Moulton, Legal Services Corporation.

NEW YORK PRACTICE, Fourth Edition (1978)

> Herbert Peterfreund, Professor of Law, New York University.
> Joseph M. McLaughlin, Dean of the Law School, Fordham University.

OIL AND GAS, Fourth Edition (1979)

> Howard R. Williams, Professor of Law, Stanford University.
> Richard C. Maxwell, Professor of Law, University of California, Los Angeles.
> Charles J. Meyers, Dean of the Law School, Stanford University.

ON LAW IN COURTS (1965)

> Paul J. Mishkin, Professor of Law, University of California, Berkeley.
> Clarence Morris, Professor of Law Emeritus, University of Pennsylvania.

UNIVERSITY CASEBOOK SERIES—Continued

PATENTS AND ANTITRUST (Pamphlet) (1983)

Milton Handler, Professor of Law Emeritus, Columbia University.
Harlan M. Blake, Professor of Law, Columbia University.
Robert Pitofsky, Professor of Law, Georgetown University.
Harvey J. Goldschmid, Professor of Law, Columbia University.

PERSPECTIVES ON THE LAWYER AS PLANNER (Reprint of Chapters One through Five of Planning by Lawyers) (1978)

Louis M. Brown, Professor of Law, University of Southern California.
Edward A. Dauer, Professor of Law, Yale University.

PLANNING BY LAWYERS, MATERIALS ON A NONADVERSARIAL LEGAL PROCESS (1978)

Louis M. Brown, Professor of Law, University of Southern California.
Edward A. Dauer, Professor of Law, Yale University.

PLEADING AND PROCEDURE, see Procedure, Civil

POLICE FUNCTION, Fourth Edition (1986)

Reprint of Chapters 1–10 of Miller, Dawson, Dix and Parnas's CRIMINAL JUSTICE ADMINISTRATION, Third Edition.

PREPARING AND PRESENTING THE CASE (1981) (Reprinted from THE LAWYERING PROCESS)

Gary Bellow, Professor of Law, Harvard Law School.
Bea Moulton, Legal Services Corporation.

PREVENTIVE LAW, see also Planning by Lawyers

PROCEDURE—CIVIL PROCEDURE, Second Edition (1974), with 1979 Supplement

The late James H. Chadbourn, Professor of Law, Harvard University.
A. Leo Levin, Professor of Law, University of Pennsylvania.
Philip Shuchman, Professor of Law, Cornell University.

PROCEDURE—CIVIL PROCEDURE, Fifth Edition (1984)

Richard H. Field, late Professor of Law, Harvard University.
Benjamin Kaplan, Professor of Law Emeritus, Harvard University.
Kevin M. Clermont, Professor of Law, Cornell University.

PROCEDURE—CIVIL PROCEDURE, Fourth Edition (1985)

Maurice Rosenberg, Professor of Law, Columbia University.
Hans Smit, Professor of Law, Columbia University.
Harold L. Korn, Professor of Law, Columbia University.

PROCEDURE—PLEADING AND PROCEDURE: State and Federal, Fifth Edition (1983), with 1985 Supplement

David W. Louisell, late Professor of Law, University of California, Berkeley.
Geoffrey C. Hazard, Jr., Professor of Law, Yale University.
Colin C. Tait, Professor of Law, University of Connecticut.

PROCEDURE—FEDERAL RULES OF CIVIL PROCEDURE, 1986 Edition

PRODUCTS LIABILITY (1980)

Marshall S. Shapo, Professor of Law, Northwestern University.

UNIVERSITY CASEBOOK SERIES—Continued

PRODUCTS LIABILITY AND SAFETY (1980), with 1985 Case and Documentary Supplement

W. Page Keeton, Professor of Law, University of Texas.
David G. Owen, Professor of Law, University of South Carolina.
John E. Montgomery, Professor of Law, University of South Carolina.

PROFESSIONAL RESPONSIBILITY, Third Edition (1984), with 1986 Selected National Standards Supplement

Thomas D. Morgan, Dean of the Law School, Emory University.
Ronald D. Rotunda, Professor of Law, University of Illinois.

PROPERTY, Fifth Edition (1984)

John E. Cribbet, Dean of the Law School, University of Illinois.
Corwin W. Johnson, Professor of Law, University of Texas.

PROPERTY—PERSONAL (1953)

S. Kenneth Skolfield, late Professor of Law Emeritus, Boston University.

PROPERTY—PERSONAL, Third Edition (1954)

Everett Fraser, late Dean of the Law School Emeritus, University of Minnesota.
Third Edition by Charles W. Taintor, late Professor of Law, University of Pittsburgh.

PROPERTY—INTRODUCTION, TO REAL PROPERTY, Third Edition (1954)

Everett Fraser, late Dean of the Law School Emeritus, University of Minnesota.

PROPERTY—REAL AND PERSONAL, Combined Edition (1954)

Everett Fraser, late Dean of the Law School Emeritus, University of Minnesota.
Third Edition of Personal Property by Charles W. Taintor, late Professor of Law, University of Pittsburgh.

PROPERTY—FUNDAMENTALS OF MODERN REAL PROPERTY, Second Edition (1982), with 1985 Supplement

Edward H. Rabin, Professor of Law, University of California, Davis.

PROPERTY—PROBLEMS IN REAL PROPERTY (Pamphlet) (1969)

Edward H. Rabin, Professor of Law, University of California, Davis.

PROPERTY, REAL (1984)

Paul Goldstein, Professor of Law, Stanford University.

PROSECUTION AND ADJUDICATION, Third Edition (1986)

Reprint of Chapters 11–26 of Miller, Dawson, Dix and Parnas's CRIMINAL JUSTICE ADMINISTRATION, Third Edition.

PSYCHIATRY AND LAW, see Mental Health, see also Hinckley, Trial of

PUBLIC REGULATION OF DANGEROUS PRODUCTS (paperback) (1980)

Marshall S. Shapo, Professor of Law, Northwestern University.

PUBLIC UTILITY LAW, see Free Enterprise, also Regulated Industries

REAL ESTATE PLANNING (1980), with 1980 Problems, Statutes and New Materials Supplement

Norton L. Steuben, Professor of Law, University of Colorado.

REAL ESTATE TRANSACTIONS, Second Edition (1985), with 1985 Statute, Form and Problem Supplement

Paul Goldstein, Professor of Law, Stanford University.

UNIVERSITY CASEBOOK SERIES—Continued

RECEIVERSHIP AND CORPORATE REORGANIZATION, see Creditors' Rights

REGULATED INDUSTRIES, Second Edition, 1976

William K. Jones, Professor of Law, Columbia University.

REMEDIES (1982), with 1984 Case Supplement

Edward D. Re, Chief Judge, U. S. Court of International Trade.

RESTITUTION, Second Edition (1966)

John W. Wade, Professor of Law, Vanderbilt University.

SALES, Second Edition (1986)

Marion W. Benfield, Jr., Professor of Law, University of Illinois.
William D. Hawkland, Chancellor, Louisiana State Law Center.

SALES AND SALES FINANCING, Fifth Edition (1984)

John Honnold, Professor of Law, University of Pennsylvania.

SALES LAW AND THE CONTRACTING PROCESS (1982)

Reprint of Chapters 1–10 of Schwartz and Scott's Commercial Transactions.

SECURED TRANSACTIONS IN PERSONAL PROPERTY (1983) (Reprinted from COMMERCIAL LAW)

Robert L. Jordan, Professor of Law, University of California, Los Angeles.
William D. Warren, Professor of Law, University of California, Los Angeles.

SECURITIES REGULATION, Fifth Edition (1982), with 1985 Cases and Releases Supplement and 1985 Selected Statutes, Rules and Forms Supplement

Richard W. Jennings, Professor of Law, University of California, Berkeley.
Harold Marsh, Jr., Member of California Bar.

SECURITIES REGULATION (1982), with 1985 Supplement

Larry D. Soderquist, Professor of Law, Vanderbilt University.

SECURITY INTERESTS IN PERSONAL PROPERTY (1984)

Douglas G. Baird, Professor of Law, University of Chicago.
Thomas H. Jackson, Professor of Law, Stanford University.

SECURITY INTERESTS IN PERSONAL PROPERTY (1985) (Reprinted from Sales and Sales Financing, Fifth Edition)

John Honnold, Professor of Law, University of Pennsylvania.

SENTENCING AND THE CORRECTIONAL PROCESS, Second Edition (1976)

Frank W. Miller, Professor of Law, Washington University.
Robert O. Dawson, Professor of Law, University of Texas.
George E. Dix, Professor of Law, University of Texas.
Raymond I. Parnas, Professor of Law, University of California, Davis.

SOCIAL SCIENCE IN LAW, Cases and Materials (1985)

John Monahan, Professor of Law, University of Virginia.
Laurens Walker, Professor of Law, University of Virginia.

SOCIAL WELFARE AND THE INDIVIDUAL (1971)

Robert J. Levy, Professor of Law, University of Minnesota.
Thomas P. Lewis, Dean of the College of Law, University of Kentucky.
Peter W. Martin, Professor of Law, Cornell University.

TAX, POLICY ANALYSIS OF THE FEDERAL INCOME (1976)

William A. Klein, Professor of Law, University of California, Los Angeles.

TAXATION, FEDERAL INCOME, Successor Edition (1985)

Michael J. Graetz, Professor of Law, Yale University.

TAXATION, FEDERAL INCOME, Fifth Edition (1985)

James J. Freeland, Professor of Law, University of Florida.
Stephen A. Lind, Professor of Law, University of Florida.
Richard B. Stephens, Professor of Law Emeritus, University of Florida.

TAXATION, FEDERAL INCOME, Volume I, Personal Income Taxation, Second Edition (1986), Volume II, Taxation of Partnerships and Corporations, Second Edition (1980), with 1985 Legislative Supplement

Stanley S. Surrey, late Professor of Law, Harvard University.
Paul R. McDaniel, Professor of Law, Boston College Law School.
Hugh J. Ault, Professor of Law, Boston College Law School.
Stanley A. Koppelman, Boston University

TAXATION, FEDERAL WEALTH TRANSFER, Second Edition (1982) with 1985 Legislative Supplement

Stanley S. Surrey, late Professor of Law, Harvard University.
William C. Warren, Professor of Law Emeritus, Columbia University.
Paul R. McDaniel, Professor of Law, Boston College Law School.
Harry L. Gutman, Instructor, Harvard Law School and Boston College Law School.

TAXATION, FUNDAMENTALS OF CORPORATE, Cases and Materials (1985)

Stephen A. Lind, Professor of Law, University of Florida.
Stephen Schwarz, Professor of Law, University of California, Hastings.
Daniel J. Lathrope, Professor of Law, University of California, Hastings.
Joshua Rosenberg, Professor of Law, University of San Francisco.

TAXATION, FUNDAMENTALS OF PARTNERSHIP, Cases and Materials (1985)

Stephen A. Lind, Professor of Law, University of California, Hastings.
Stephen Schwarz, Professor of Law, University of California, Hastings.
Daniel J. Lathrope, Professor of Law, University of California, Hastings.
Joshua Rosenberg, Professor of Law, University of San Francisco.

TAXATION, PROBLEMS IN THE FEDERAL INCOME TAXATION OF PARTNERSHIPS AND CORPORATIONS, Second Edition (1986)

Norton L. Steuben, Professor of Law, University of Colorado.
William J. Turnier, Professor of Law, University of North Carolina.

TAXATION, PROBLEMS IN THE FUNDAMENTALS OF FEDERAL INCOME, Second Edition (1985)

Norton L. Steuben, Professor of Law, University of Colorado.
William J. Turnier, Professor of Law, University of North Carolina.

TAXES AND FINANCE—STATE AND LOCAL (1974)

Oliver Oldman, Professor of Law, Harvard University.
Ferdinand P. Schoettle, Professor of Law, University of Minnesota.

TORT LAW AND ALTERNATIVES, Third Edition (1983)

Marc A. Franklin, Professor of Law, Stanford University.
Robert L. Rabin, Professor of Law, Stanford University.

UNIVERSITY CASEBOOK SERIES—Continued

TORTS, Seventh Edition (1982)

William L. Prosser, late Professor of Law, University of California, Hastings College.
John W. Wade, Professor of Law, Vanderbilt University.
Victor E. Schwartz, Professor of Law, American University.

TORTS, Third Edition (1976)

Harry Shulman, late Dean of the Law School, Yale University.
Fleming James, Jr., Professor of Law Emeritus, Yale University.
Oscar S. Gray, Professor of Law, University of Maryland.

TRADE REGULATION, Second Edition (1983), with 1985 Supplement

Milton Handler, Professor of Law Emeritus, Columbia University.
Harlan M. Blake, Professor of Law, Columbia University.
Robert Pitofsky, Professor of Law, Georgetown University.
Harvey J. Goldschmid, Professor of Law, Columbia University.

TRADE REGULATION, see Antitrust

TRANSNATIONAL BUSINESS PROBLEMS (1986)

Detlev F. Vagts, Professor of Law, Harvard University.

TRANSNATIONAL LEGAL PROBLEMS, Third Edition (1986) with Documentary Supplement

Henry J. Steiner, Professor of Law, Harvard University.
Detlev F. Vagts, Professor of Law, Harvard University.

TRIAL, see also Evidence, Making the Record, Lawyering Process and Preparing and Presenting the Case

TRIAL ADVOCACY (1968)

A. Leo Levin, Professor of Law, University of Pennsylvania.
Harold Cramer, of the Pennsylvania Bar.
Maurice Rosenberg, Professor of Law, Columbia University, Consultant.

TRUSTS, Fifth Edition (1978)

George G. Bogert, late Professor of Law Emeritus, University of Chicago.
Dallin H. Oaks, President, Brigham Young University.

TRUSTS AND SUCCESSION (Palmer's), Fourth Edition (1983)

Richard V. Wellman, Professor of Law, University of Georgia.
Lawrence W. Waggoner, Professor of Law, University of Michigan.
Olin L. Browder, Jr., Professor of Law, University of Michigan.

UNFAIR COMPETITION, see Competitive Process and Business Torts

UNITED NATIONS LAW, Second Edition (1967), with Documentary Supplement (1968)

Louis B. Sohn, Professor of Law, Harvard University.

WATER RESOURCE MANAGEMENT, Second Edition (1980), with 1983 Supplement

Charles J. Meyers, Dean of the Law School, Stanford University.
A. Dan Tarlock, Professor of Law, Indiana University.

WILLS AND ADMINISTRATION, Fifth Edition (1961)

Philip Mechem, late Professor of Law, University of Pennsylvania.
Thomas E. Atkinson, late Professor of Law, New York University.

WORLD LAW, see United Nations Law

University Casebook Series

EDITORIAL BOARD

THE LAW AND FINANCE
OF
CORPORATE ACQUISITIONS

By

RONALD J. GILSON

Professor of Law
Stanford University

Mineola, New York
THE FOUNDATION PRESS, INC.
1986

Library of Congress Cataloging in Publication Data

Gilson, Ronald J., 1946–
   The law and finance of corporate acquisitions.

   (University casebook series)
   Includes index.
   1. Consolidation and merger of corporations—United
States—Cases. 2. Corporations—Finance—Law and
legislation—United States—Cases. I. Title.
II. Series.
KF1477.A7G55 1986   346.73'06626   86–7589
ISBN 0–88277–280–5   347.3066626

Gilson Corp.Acquisitions UCB

[B]usiness is business!
And business must grow
regardless of crummies in tummies, you know.

Dr. Seuss, The Lorax (1971)

FOR NINA, CASSIE and BECCA

*

PREFACE

This book is an effort to fuse two innovations in corporate law scholarship and curriculum. The first, a transactional approach, treats the focus of interest as actual business phenomena rather than the traditional single academic subject matter. This direction was pioneered by David Herwitz in his 1966 casebook Business Planning: Materials on the Planning of Corporate Transactions. Its insight lay in both its problem orientation and its integration of corporate, tax and securities law in a single book. The second innovation, pioneered by Victor Brudney and Marvin Chirelstein in their 1972 Cases and Materials on Corporate Finance, was the recognition that financial theory was critically important to understanding traditional subjects of corporate law concern. Although each of these innovations—a transactional approach and a recognition of the importance of finance—has significant merit, their separation does not. The premise on which this book builds is that financial theory provides important insights not just for the familiar law and economics exercise of evaluating legal doctrine but, more importantly, for understanding the transactional process and, ultimately, for good lawyering.

Part One of the book (Chapters Two through Seven) provides the finance skills necessary to analyze corporate acquisitions from this perspective. Chapter Two introduces the idea of discounting and present value. Chapter Three lays the groundwork for development of capital asset pricing by examining how to measure risk and return. Consideration of the latter concept allows the introduction of subjective probability and decision tree techniques. Chapter Four then introduces the core of modern portfolio theory and capital asset pricing and Chapter Five examines the Efficient Capital Market Hypothesis with a special emphasis on identifying the mechanisms that influence the level of market efficiency observed.

Chapter Six—dealing with the value of information—is particularly important. Among other subjects, this Chapter introduces a statistical technique—cumulative abnormal returns—commonly used to measure whether a particular event alters the market's valuation of a security. This technique is at the core of an important empirical literature examining whether corporate acquisitions result in gains to the participants. Understanding the technique is thus critical to Part II's evaluation of the fit between theory and empirical evidence concerning gains from acquisitions. Part I ends with Chapter Seven, an examination of option pricing theory. The Chapter emphasizes that many common business relationships can be characterized as options and that understanding what factors determine the value of an option helps illuminate the incentives confronting the parties to a relationship.

All of the material in Part I should be understandable to readers who have had no prior exposure to financial theory, and the presentation requires no mathematical skills beyond simple arithmetic. What is important is that the insights underlying each aspect of financial theory covered be understood, not that any of the formal techniques (except, perhaps, for present value) be mastered in a computational sense. The book reflects the belief that transactional planning is in significant part a problem of understanding and manipulating the incentives of the parties to the transaction. A principal value of those aspects of financial theory covered in Part I is their ability to illuminate the nature of these incentives and to suggest ways of dealing creatively with them. Using financial theory in this way requires only an understanding at the conceptual level; it does not require mastery of the technical apparatus.

Building on the skills imparted in Part I, Part II (Chapters Eight through Twelve) then evaluates in separate chapters each of the commonly offered explanations for acquisitions: Financial accounting, diversification, displacement of inefficient management, synergy and taxes. Each Chapter follows a parallel approach: The explanation is described, its fit with the financial theory developed in Part I is evaluated, and the available empirical evidence bearing on the theory is described. Two chapters, Chapter Eight covering the claim that the financial accounting treatment of acquisitions explains why acquisitions take place, and Chapter Twelve covering the similar claim with respect to the tax treatment of acquisitions, also provide an opportunity to survey the technical elements of the financial accounting and tax aspects of acquisitions.

I have invested this much effort in examining alternative explanations for why acquisitions take place because I think it is important that a lawyer genuinely understand how a client believes it will gain from a transaction. But there is an additional explanation as well. I think it is important to reintroduce lawyers to the importance of empirical evidence in formulating legal arguments and public policy. This takes longer than might otherwise be the case because I want to be sure that the relevant empirical methodology is understood well enough that its results can be evaluated with the appropriate level of skepticism, something the original investigators sometimes have not done.

Part III (Chapters Thirteen through Fifteen) covers the corporate law issues bearing on the choice of transactional form and begins consideration of what I call the public ordering role of the business laywer: Structuring a transaction to minimize the cost of the potentially applicable regulatory apparatus. Chapter Thirteen examines, from the perspective of a planner, the mechanics of alternative acquisition techniques and such issues as what vote should be necessary to approve a negotiated acquisition, who should be allowed to vote, and the de facto merger doctrine. Chapters Fourteen and Fifteen address the corporate law concerns of the target company and the acquiring company, respectively. For the target company, the emphasis is on the problems of sale of control and of defensive tactics. For the acquiring company, the emphasis is on avoiding competitive bids and on freezing out minority shareholders. In both Chapters, financial theory is used both to illuminate the strategic value of alternative planning techniques and to evaluate the desirability of permitting the conduct in question. For example, Chapter Fourteen considers in detail both how to evaluate whether a particular defensive tactic will be effective and whether such tactics are consistent with what should be the role of target management in acquisition transactions.

Part IV (Chapters Sixteen through Eighteen) then covers non-corporate law subjects bearing on the structuring of a corporate acquisition. Chapter Sixteen surveys the securities law aspects of corporate acquisitions, with primary emphasis on the Williams Act. Chapter Seventeen considers the Hart-Scott-Rodino Premerger Notification Act, and Chapter Eighteen treats the problem of successor liability in corporate acquisitions, in particular focusing on products liability claims, obligations growing out of the target company's collective bargaining agreements, and successor employer problems under ERISA. Each of the areas considered in Chapter Eighteen falls within the broad subject matter boundaries of other law school subjects; however, each shares the common characteristic that it is usually given scant attention in the survey course covering that subject. Thus, the typical antitrust course gives little attention to Hart-Scott-Rodino problems; the typical securities law course, focusing on the Securities Act of 1933, gives little attention to the regulation of tender offers; and the typical labor law and torts courses give little attention to problems of carryover of collective bargaining agreements and of successor liability for defective or hazardous products.

While Part I focuses principally on financial theory, and Parts II, III and IV have primarily a transactional focus (albeit illuminated by financial theory), Part V (Chapter Nineteen) represents a self-conscious effort to integrate the perspective of financial theory with traditional professional tasks, more specifically, the preparation of an acquisition agreement. Chapter Nineteen presents the standard form of acquisition agreement as a series of solutions to problems inherent in capital asset pricing. The lesson of capital asset pricing theory is that a capital asset—including an acquisition—is valued on the basis of the riskiness of the returns associated with it. The theory is premised, however, on a set of perfect market assumptions, such as homogenous expectations, common time horizons, and costless information, which are obviously not valid in the real world. Chapter Nineteen builds on this fact to develop two related ideas. The first, and more general, is that the role of the business laywer is to create a transactional structure which allows the parties to act *as if*, for that transaction, the perfect market assumptions were valid. The second, more specific idea, is that the typical elements of an acquisition agreement are best understood from this perspective.

The end result of the analysis is to present the business lawyer as a transaction cost engineer whose task is to formulate transactional structures as near to "perfect" as possible. My goal in presenting an acquisition agreement (and, more broadly, the business lawyer's role) in terms of generic financial concepts is not only to improve lawyers' negotiation of acquisition agreements—focusing on, for example, representations as a device to overcome information assymetries changes the lawyer's task from one of distributive bargaining to one of joint problem solving—but also to improve their ability to respond creatively to "new" problems. Once one understands the standard set of transactional problems posed by asset pricing in an imperfect world, there are no new problems, only manifestations of the same problem in different contexts. The latter, I am persuaded, are significantly easier to deal with.

Having said something about what subjects the book covers, I should also say something about the manner in which those subjects are covered. To be straightforward, the book does not hide the ball; my views on the issues considered are made apparent, sometimes insistently so. I have taken this approach, in contrast to the traditional agnosticism typified by a series of unanswered questions at the end of a section, for two reasons—one pedagogic and one substantive. The pedagogic reason for giving the book an explicit point of view is that integrating not only different bodies of law, but a broad range of financial theory and an extensive empirical literature as well, is hard. My views are hardly the only ones possible (although I obviously prefer them to the alternatives, also discussed in the book), but they do illustrate the way in which the various elements interact and what matters would have to be taken into account in an alternative formulation. My own views thus serve both as an example and a target, each of which can be a useful pedagogic tool.

The substantive reason for the book's normative bent is the absence in the literature of an integrated treatment of the full range of legal issues raised by corporate acquisitions. The need for such a treatment is apparent in the recent performance of the Delaware Supreme Court. Since the development and legitimation of sophisticated hostile acquisition techniques and equally sophisticated defensive tactics, the Delaware courts have been subjected to a seemingly unending stream of difficult corporate law issues that have left little time for contemplation, for stepping back to see how the individual problems fit together. Like a beleaguered corporations student who is the object of a Socratic onslaught by an unyielding law professor, the Delaware Supreme Court simply has not had time to catch its breath. Just as the law professor continually serves up a new hypothetical, cleverly altering precisely the facts on which the student relied to dispose of the prior hypothetical, so have transaction planners almost immediately given the Delaware courts back their own justifications, but now taken just another step forward. Because of the high volume of acquisition activity, a significant number of transactions are in the planning or litigation stage whenever a Delaware court issues a new opinion; the planners then can reflect that opinion in their transactions almost immediately and the Chancery Court may have to confront the "next case" on a motion for preliminary injunction within a few weeks following the initial decision. This drastic telescoping of the common law process makes careful reconsideration of prior doctrine quite difficult; the demands of individual cases for prompt resolution (lest delay alone resolve the outcome of a transaction) are inconsistent with a slow and careful development of the common law. Thus, I have at least the hope that, in the best tradition of the legal treatise, this book can provide some of the contemplation and perspective, if not the reconceptualization itself, that the courts have lacked the leisure to undertake themselves.

Many people have provided invaluable help with this project. A number of friends and colleagues read drafts of one or more chapters and kept me from making too many embarrassing mistakes in substance or syntax. Victor Brudney, Reinier Kraakman, and Roberta Romano were especially generous with their time and comments. Bernard Black, Barry Newman and James Shorin provided valuable research assistance; in particular, Chapters Sixteen and Eighteen bear Black's mark and Chapter Seven that of Newman. Judy Dearing provided heroic service in producing the manuscript and in seeing to it that the text read better when she had finished with it than when I had given it to her. Most important, my wife Nina, and my daughters Cassie and Becca, gave me their patience. When the book interfered with family activities or vacations, or simply made me less attentive then I should have been, they never once asked the question that must have crossed their minds repeatedly: Who said this was easier than practice?

A final word about some mechanics. Case and statute citations, as well as footnotes in cases, articles and books have been omitted without so indicating. The original footnote numbering within such materials has been retained; footnotes added to such materials by the author are indicated by asterisks.

RONALD J. GILSON

Palo Alto, California
March, 1986

*

ACKNOWLEDGEMENTS

With appreciation, this acknowledgement is made for the publishers and authors who gave permission for the reproduction of excerpts from the following materials:

American Bar Association
  Armstrong, the Work and Workings of the FASB.
  Model Rules of Professional Responsibility.

American Bar Foundation Research Journal
  Carney, Fundamental Corporate Changes, Minority Shareholders, and Business Purposes.

American Institute of Certified Public Accountants
  APB Opinion No. 16, Business Combinations.
  APB Opinion No. 18, The Equity Method of Accounting for Investments in Common Stock.

American Law Institute
  Principles of Corporate Governance: Analysis and Recommendations.

Accounting Review
  Hong, Kaplan & Mandelker, Pooling vs. Purchase: The Effects of Accounting for Mergers on Stock Prices.

Bell Journal of Economics
  Amihud & Lev, Risk Reduction as a Managerial Motive for Conglomerate Mergers.

The Business Lawyer (ABA Section of Corporation, Banking and Business Law)
  Freund & Easton, The Three-Piece Suitor: An Alternative Approach to Negotiated Corporate Acquisitions.
  Maiwurm & Tobin, Creating Waves in the Market Place and Uncertainty in the Regulatory Framework.
  Nathan & Sobel, Corporate Stock Repurchases in the Context of Unsolicited Takeover Bids.
  Wachtell, Special Tender Offer Litigation Tactics.

Columbia University Press
  Aranow & Einhorn, Tender Offers for Corporate Control (1973).

The Dryden Press
  Davidson, Stockney & Weil, Financial Accounting (2d ed. 1979).

Financial Accounting Standards Board
  FASB Interpretation No. 35—Criteria for Applying the Equity Method of Accounting for Investments in Common Stock.

Financial Analysts Journal
  Lynch, Accounting for Investments by the Equity and Market Value Methods.
  Modigliani & Pogue, An Introduction to Risk and Return.

ACKNOWLEDGEMENTS

Foundation Press
Brudney & Chirelstein, Corporate Finance (2d ed. 1979).

The Free Press
Porter, Competitive Strategy.

G & C Merriam Co.
Sharpe, Investments (2d ed. 1981).

Georgetown Law Review
Loewenstein, Section 14(e) of the Williams Act and the Rule 10b–5
Comparisons.

Harvard Law Review
Andrews, The Stockholder's Right to Equal Opportunity in the Sale
of Shares.

Houghton-Mifflin Company
Scherer, Industrial Market Structure and Economic Performance
(2d ed. 1980).

Institutional Investor
Gurwin, The Scorched Earth Policy.

Journal of Accountancy
Beaver, What Should be the FASB's Objectives?

Journal of Accounting and Economics
Holthausen, Evidence on the Effect of Bond Covenants and Man-
agement Compensation Contracts on the Choice of Accounting
Techniques.

Journal of Business
Meeker & Joy, Price Premiums for Controlling Shares of Closely
Held Bank Stock.

Journal of Economic Behavior and Organization
Teece, Economies of Scope and the Scope of the Enterprise.

Journal of Economic Literature
Williamson, The Modern Corporation: Origins, Evolution, Attributes.

Journal of Finance
Levy & Sarnat, Diversification, Portfolio Analysis and the Uneasy
Case for Conglomerate Mergers.
Mason & Goudzwaard, Performance at Conglomerate Firms: A
Portfolio Approach.
Roberts, Stock Market Patterns and Financial Analysis: Method-
ological Suggestions.
Scott, On the Theory of Conglomerate Mergers.

Journal of Law and Economics
DeAngelo, DeAngelo & Rice, Going Private: Minority Freezeouts
and Stockholder Wealth.
Klein, Crawford & Alchien, Vertical Integration, Appropriable
Rents and the Competitive Contracting Process.

Schwert, Using Financial Data to Measure Effects of Financial Regulation.

Law and Business, Inc.
Fleischer, Tender Offers: Defenses, Responses, and Planning (2d ed. 1983).

Lexington Books
Feld, Tax Policy and Corporate Concentration (1982).

Little, Brown and Company
Cox, Financial Information, Accounting and the Law (1980).
Eisenberg, The Structure of the Corporation (1976).

The MacMillan Publishing Company
Salter & Weinhold, Diversification Through Acquisition (1979).

McGraw-Hill Book Company
Brealey & Myers, Principles of Corporate Finance (1981).
Sharpe, Portfolio Theory and Capital Markets (1970).

McGraw-Hill, Inc.
McGraw, A Reply to "Unconscionable" Action.

Mergers & Acquisitions
Haight, The Portfolio Merger: Finding the Company that Can Stabilize Your Earnings.

New York Times

Ohio State Law Journal and Coopers & Lybrand
DeFliese, Business Combinations Revisited: A Temporary Defense of the Status Quo.

Prentice-Hall, Inc.
Foster, Financial Statement Analysis (1978).
Holloway, Decision Making Under Uncertainty (1979).
Sharpe, Investments (1980).
Van Horne, Financial Management and Policy (5th ed. 1980).

Richard D. Irwin, Inc.
Bierman, Bonini & Hausman, Quantitative Analysis for Business Decisions (1981).
Lorie & Hamilton, The Stock Market: Theories and Evidence (1973).

Science
Tversky & Kahneman, Judgment under Uncertainty: Heuristics and Biases.

Sloan Management Review
Ruback, The Conoco Takeover and Stockholder Returns.

Stanford Law Review
Easterbrook & Fischel, Auctions and Sunk Costs in Tender Offers.
Gilson, A Structural Approach to Corporations: The Case Against Defensive Tactics in Tender Offers.
Gilson, The Case Against Shark Repellent Amendments: Structural Limitations on the Enabling Concept.

Gilson, Seeking Competitive Bids Versus Pure Passivity in Tender Offer Defense.

University of Michigan Press
Steiner, Mergers: Motives, Effects, Policies (1975).

Virginia Law Review
Gilson & Kraakman, The Mechanisms of Market Efficiency.
Note, Three Party Mergers: The Fourth Form of Corporate Acquisition.

Wachtell, Lipton, Rosen & Katz
Poison Pill Memorandum of Law.
Opinion Letter.

Wall Street Journal
American Express Gives Details of Plans to Buy McGraw-Hill in Filing With SEC.
Firm Withdraws Contested Offer for McGraw-Hill.
McGraw-Hill Directors Reject Takeover Move.
Meyer, Takeover Tremors: As Charges Intensify, Strategy Is Emerging in McGraw-Hill Battle.
Meyer, Cancelled Poll of McGraw-Hill Holders Signal End to American Express Bid.
Meyer & Abrams, McGraw-Hill Girds for Its Board Meeting Today to Act on Bid by American Express.

Warren, Gorham & Lamont, Inc.
Encyclopedia of Investments (1982) Scholes, Options—Puts and Calls.

Yale Law Journal
Easterbrook & Fischel, Corporate Control Transactions.
Gilson, Value Creation by Business Lawyers.
Manning, The Shareholder's Appraisal Remedy: An Essay for Frank Coker.

SUMMARY OF CONTENTS

PART V. PRIVATE ORDERING ASPECTS OF CORPORATE ACQUISITIONS

APPENDICES

TABLE OF CONTENTS

PART IV. NON–CORPORATE LAW PLANNING CONSIDERATIONS

TABLE OF CONTENTS

APPENDICES

TABLE OF CASES

**Principal cases are in italic type. Nonprincipal cases are in roman type.
References are to Pages.**

*

THE LAW AND FINANCE
OF
CORPORATE ACQUISITIONS

*

CHAPTER ONE. INTRODUCTION

A. The Professional Setting: Value Creation by Business Lawyers [1]

This book is an inquiry, set in the context of corporate acquisitions, into what business lawyers *really* do. By and large, critical study of the legal profession has displayed a myopic fixation with litigation—its frequency, complexity, expense and unequal availability—and with what can be done to "improve" it: clinical training, attention to methods of delivering legal services, emphasis on the administration of justice. Careful analysis of the function of the rest of the profession—business lawyers—has been absent.

At least among the critics, however, there has been some recent shift in attention. Spurred by the specter of declining American success in the international economy, and focused by Japan's remarkable success in the same arena, business lawyers have been criticized with increasing frequency as non-productive actors in the economy.[2] Derek Bok, the President of Harvard University, and former Dean of Harvard Law School, is perhaps the most prominent of this genre of critics. Bok notes that the total number of lawyers in Japan is less than one-half the number of lawyers that graduate from law school each year in the United States,[3] and that Japan annually trains 30 percent more engineers than does the United States despite a population half its size.[4] He then concludes that the United States' over-investment in a non-productive profession has an unavoidably negative impact on the American economy: "As the Japanese put it, Engineers make the pie grow larger; lawyers only decide how to carve it up." [5]

In the face of such criticism, it is surprising and just a little embarrassing that there seems to be no coherent answer to the question of what business lawyers *really* do.[6] That is not, of course, to say that answers have not been offered; there are a number of familiar re-

---

[1] Portions of this discussion draw heavily on Gilson, *Value Creation by Business Lawyers: Legal Skills and Asset Pricing,* 94 Yale L.J. 239 (1984).

[2] See, e.g., Bok, *The President's Report to the Board of Overseers of Harvard University for 1981–1982,* reprinted in 33 J.Leg. Educ. 570 (1983); Morita, *Do Companies Need Lawyers? Sony's Experiences in the United States,* 30 Japan Q. 2 (Jan.-Mar., 1983); Fried, *The Trouble with Lawyers,* The N.Y. Times, Feb. 12, 1984, § 6 (Magazine), at 56.

[3] Id. at 573. It has been pointed out frequently that Bok's statistics are misleading. While the number of lawyers actually admitted to the bar in Japan is quite small, there exists a much larger number of professionals who have formal legal training and who perform what in this country would be considered legal tasks. These individuals are not included in Bok's computation. For present purposes, however, the accuracy of Bok's data is less interesting than why he thinks it is relevant.

[4] Id. at 573–74.

[5] Id. at 574.

[6] The recent work of William Klein stands as an important exception. In *Business Organization and Finance* (1980) and *The Modern Business Organization: Bargaining Under Constraints,* 91 Yale L.J. 1521 (1982), he has made a major effort to bring to bear finance theory on understanding consensual—private—business arrangements.

sponses that lawyers have all heard or, what is worse, that lawyers have all offered at one time or another without really thinking very hard about them. The problem is that, for surprisingly similar reasons, none of them is very helpful.

Clients have their own, often quite uncharitable, view of what business lawyers do. In an extreme version, business lawyers are perceived as evil sorcerers who use their special skills and professional magic to relieve clients of their possessions. Kurt Vonnegut at least makes the point in an amusing way. A law student is told by his favorite professor that, to get ahead in the practice of law, "a lawyer should be looking for situations where large amounts of money are about to change hands." Though this advice is hardly different from standard professional suggestions about how to build a legal practice, the reasons offered for the advice lay bare a quite different view of the business lawyer's function:

> In every big transaction [the professor said], there is a magic moment during which a man has surrendered a treasure, and during which the man who is due to receive it has not yet done so. An alert lawyer will make that moment his own, possessing the treasure for a magic microsecond, taking a little of it, passing it on. If the man who is to receive the treasure is unused to wealth, has an inferiority complex and shapeless feelings of guilt, as most people do, the lawyer can often take as much as half the bundle, and still receive the recipient's blubbering thanks.[7]

Clients frequently advance another, more charitable but still quite negative, view of the business lawyer that also should be familiar to most practitioners. At best, business lawyers are seen as just a transaction cost, part of a system of wealth redistribution from clients to lawyers: Legal fees then represent simply a tax on business transactions that supports an income maintenance program for lawyers. At worst, lawyers are seen as deal killers whose continual raising of obstacles, without a commensurate effort at finding solutions, ultimately causes transactions to fail under their own weight.[8]

---

[7] K. Vonnegut, *God Bless You, Mrs. Rosewater* 9 (Dell ed. 1965).

[8] See, e.g., J. Donnell, *The Corporate Counsel: A Role Study* 57–58 (1970); Harris, *What an Investment Banker Looks for in a Lawyer*, 33 Bus.Law. 821, 822 (1978) (Partner, Salomon Brothers); Kelly, *Comment*, 33 Bus.Law. 825 (1978) (President, Esmark, Inc.). A lawyer turned journalist has captured the criticism nicely:

> What happens between lawyer and client today goes something like this: The lawyer sits at the elbow of the businessman while contracts are being negotiated, that is, while a deal is being made. Then, once the principals feel an agreement has been concluded, the lawyers assure them it has not. After further negotiation, the lawyers "draft a contract"—*reduce the deal to written law*—and pass it back and forth accompanied

in each passage by increasingly minute argumentation (e.g., "We believe in all fairness that the law of Luxembourg should govern in the event of non-performance under Para. V(e)(ii)" etc., etc.). Once they have decided that neither party can be further hoodwinked or bullied, the typist prepares many copies to make "doubly sure" (making doubly sure in this special fashion is 28 per cent of law practice), and the clients sign all of them. Then they smile at each other and shake hands, while glancing sidelong at their lawyers, who are still scowling (it's part of the fee-action). This little drama, in numerous manifestations, is the beginning of law—perhaps, even, the final heart of it as well.

Bazelon, *Clients Against Lawyers: A Guide to the Real Joys of Legal Practice*, Harper's

Lawyers, to be sure, do not share these harsh evaluations of their role. When this question—what do business lawyers *really* do—is put to business lawyers, the familiar response is that they "protect" their clients, that they get them the "best" deal. In the back of their minds is a sense that their clients do not appreciate them,[9] that clients neither perceive nor understand the risks that lawyers raise, and that, as a result, clients do not recognize that it is in their best interests when lawyers identify the myriad of subtle problems unavoidably present in a typical transaction.

A more balanced view is presented in the academic literature. Here the predominant approach has been functional. The lawyer is presented as counselor, planner, drafter, negotiator, investigator, lobbyist, scapegoat, champion and, most strikingly, even as friend.[10] Certainly the list of functions identified rings true enough. An experienced practitioner can quickly recall playing each of these roles.

Despite the surface dissimilarity of these characterizations of what a business lawyer does, they do share an important similarity and a common failure. To be sure, the unfavorable view ascribed to the client reflects the view that business lawyers *reduce* the value of a transaction, while both the quite favorable view held by business lawyers themselves, and the more neutral but still positive view offered by the academic literature, implicitly assume that business lawyers *increase* the value of a transaction. But both sides do seem to agree on the appropriate standard by which the performance of business lawyers should be judged: *If what a business lawyer does has value, a transaction must be worth more, net of legal fees, as a result of the lawyer's participation.* And the critical failure of all three of these views is not their differing conclusions. Rather, it is the absence of an explanation of the *relationship* between business lawyers' participation in a transaction and the value of the transaction to the clients. In other words, precisely *how* do the activities of business lawyers affect transaction value?

The goals of this book are to come to understand the relationship between what business lawyers do and transaction value, to develop analytical techniques that identify what activities have the potential for creating value, and to explore professional approaches that make

Magazine 104 (Sept., 1967) (emphasis in the original).

[9] See Mindes & Acock, *Trickster, Hero, Helper: A Report on the Lawyer Image,* 1982, Am.B.Found. Research J. 177, 193–98.

[10] See, e.g., L. Brown & A. Dauer, *Planning by Lawyers: Materials on a Nonadversarial Legal Process* (1978) (planning and counseling); Q. Johnstone & D. Hopson, Jr., *Lawyers and Their Work: An Analysis of the Legal Profession in the United States and England* Chap. 3 (1967) (litany of tasks performed by lawyers); Pashigian, *Regulation, Preventive Law, and the Duties of Attorneys,* in *The Changing Role of the*

Corporate Attorney 3 (W. Carney ed., 1982); Redmont, *Humanistic Law through Legal Counseling,* 2 Conn.L.Rev. 98, 98–99 (1969) (Lawyer as counsellor (or hallucinogenic drug): "The counsellor is an enabling agency of skill whose intuitive, reflective and prescriptive powers tend to move the party from a state of uncertainty or disagreeability to one of comparative, maximal or optimal well-being."); Simon, *Homo Psychologicus: Notes on a New Legal Formalism,* 32 Stan.L.Rev. 487 (1980) (criticism of psychological counseling approach); Fried, *The Lawyer as Friend: The Moral Foundation of the Lawyer-Client Relationship,* 85 Yale L.J. 1060 (1976).

business lawyers better at achieving this potential. Our emphasis will be on the two critical aspects of business lawyers' involvement with clients: the *public* ordering and *private* ordering aspects of business transactions. The public ordering aspect of business transactions results from the fact that in our mixed economy, most transactions are governed by significant regulatory apparatus. As simple a transaction as the transfer of real estate must be effected through a regulatory system that, in essence, actually determines ownership of the property.[11] A more complex transaction—such as a corporate acquisition—is the subject of a host of different regulatory systems, each of which can have an important impact upon the form taken by the transaction. As we will see, tax law,[12] corporations law,[13] securities law,[14] antitrust law,[15] products liability law,[16] labor law,[17] and pension law [18] all help determine the best form for a particular acquisition. As a result, a transaction that is private, in the sense that the government is not a party, has important elements of public ordering resulting from the need to comply with the relevant regulatory requirements and emanating from the issues of public policy that originally gave rise to the regulation.

The most important part of the public ordering aspect of private transactions, however, is not merely passive compliance—structuring a business transaction to meet the terms of seemingly applicable regulation. Rather, the business lawyer's task often is to actively design the structure of the transaction in order to minimize the number of rules that apply and the cost of complying with those that do. Regulation is thus a determinant of the structure of the transaction but, for the client, the goal may be minimizing cost, not maximizing compliance. Viewed from this perspective, what is important is that most regulatory systems express the boundaries of their application and the detail of their requirements in formal terms: Transactions that take a particular outward form are covered. So, for example, Subchapter C of the Internal Revenue Code treats corporate acquisitions that take the form of a statutory merger differently from those that take the form of a sale of assets,[19] and a similar distinction is drawn by many state corporation laws.[20] This approach to regulation inevitably permits a response. As

[11] See Baird & Jackson, *Information, Uncertainty and the Transfer of Property,* 14 J.Leg.Stud. 299 (1984).

[12] See Chapter Twelve infra.

[13] See Chapters Thirteen, Fourteen and Fifteen infra.

[14] See Chapter Sixteen infra.

[15] See Chapter Seventeen infra.

[16] See Chapter Eighteen B. infra.

[17] See Chapter Eighteen F. infra.

[18] See *id.*

[19] For example, Internal Revenue Code § 368(a)(1)(C) requires the use of essentially only voting stock as consideration in a "C" reorganization (an asset acquisition), while I.R.C. § 368(a)(1)(A) puts no limit on the form of consideration that can be used in an "A" reorganization (a statutory merger), and even Internal Revenue Service ruling standards require only that 50 percent of the consideration in a merger be voting stock to qualify as a reorganization. Rev.Proc. 77–37, ¶ 3.02, 1977–2 C.B. 568. Where either the buyer or the seller wishes to use some amount of cash as consideration, the difference is critical. Additionally, the determinants of reorganization and non-reorganization treatment generally are also expressed largely in formal terms. See Chapter Twelve infra.

[20] In Delaware, for example, shareholders of a corporation acquired in a merger typically have appraisal rights while those in a corporation that sells substantially all of its assets do not. Del.Code Ann. tit. 8,

will be developed in Part I,[21] the subject of most business transactions can be described generically as only a stream of future income with a particular level of risk. So long as actual cash flows are not altered, the formal trappings of the transaction can be manipulated extensively without altering its financial substance. The terms of the regulatory systems themselves then serve as an invitation to the targets of the regulation to structure transactions so that their form falls outside the terms of the regulation. This regulatory eternal triangle is completed by the courts which, in the end, must determine whether to credit the form in which the parties cast a transaction, or to look beyond the formal terms of the regulatory structure to its purpose, and through the formal structure of the transaction to its financial substance. This tension—between voluntary selection of transactional form and regulatory purpose—is really the central dilemma for most traditional business law. The form versus substance [22] and step transaction doctrines [23] in tax law and the de facto merger doctrine in corporate law [24] are only the most familiar examples.

The opportunity thus exists for business lawyers to create value by structuring a transaction so as to minimize the cost to the client of the variety of complex and conflicting regulatory systems that might otherwise touch on the transaction.[25] Parts III and IV of the book are directed at this opportunity: to understand both the regulatory systems that apply to corporate acquisitions and the public policy that gave rise to them, and to develop the facility to manipulate them to achieve a client's goals.

In addition to the public ordering aspects of business transactions, there are also important *private* ordering aspects: matters bearing on transactional structure that would be of importance even in a world with *no* regulation. To examine the lawyer's role with respect to these aspects of business transactions, however, it is important to be more specific about what it means to create value. Imagine that a client has had the good fortune to retain a very talented business lawyer when the other party to the transaction is represented by a dullard. Assuming that the lawyers can have any impact on the value of the transaction, we might anticipate that it would be to alter the allocation of gains from the transaction between the parties.[26] Here the claim is

§ 262 (Supp.1982). See Chapter Thirteen infra.

[21] See Chapters Two through Seven.

[22] See, e.g., Isenberg, *Musings on Form and Substance in Taxation,* 49 U.Chi.L. Rev. 859 (1982); Chirlstein, *Learned Hand's Contribution to the Law of Tax Avoidance,* 77 Yale L.J. 440 (1968).

[23] See, e.g., Chirlstein & Lopata, *Recent Developments in the Step Transaction Doctrine,* 60 Taxes 970 (1982); Paul & Zimet, *Step Transactions in Selected Studies in Federal Taxation* 200 (2nd Ser.1938).

[24] See Chapter Thirteen D infra.

[25] Determining whether manipulation of a regulatory system creates value in a soci- etal sense, as opposed to merely creating value for the particular parties, is straight-forward only if the social costs, if any, of the particular regulatory system not applying are taken into account. It is in this sense that issues of "public" policy enter into a private transaction.

[26] The assumption is that, pursuant to the Fundamental Theory of Exchange, "voluntary trade is mutually beneficial." J. Hirschleifer, *Price Theory and Applications* 164 (1976). A surplus thus results from a transaction that is subject to division between the parties. Note that, at least for now, there is no claim that any portion of this surplus results from the lawyers' participation.

merely that one lawyer's greater skill in distributive bargaining [27] results in that client receiving a greater share of the gain than would have been the case if the lawyers were more evenly matched. One might then argue that at least the performance of the more talented lawyer meets the value creation standard. From the perspective of that lawyer's client, the transaction is worth more than if that lawyer had not participated.

One reaches a quite different conclusion, however, if the transaction is viewed from the perspective of *both* clients. Then the value of the transaction has not changed as a result of participation by business lawyers; rather, resources have been expended to alter the *distribution* of gains that, by definition, would have been forthcoming even without the lawyers' participation. And for purposes of evaluating whether the participation of business lawyers in a transaction increases the transaction's value, the appropriate perspective is not that of the client with the more talented lawyer, but the joint perspective of both clients.

As in many other areas, evaluating whether a practice is beneficial, in this case participation by a business lawyer, depends on whether the issue is evaluated *ex ante* or *ex post*. If the evaluation is *ex post*—that is, if the transaction is one in which it has already been determined that both sides will retain a lawyer [28]—then a business lawyer whose skill in distributive bargaining results in his client receiving a larger portion of the gain from the transaction will be perceived as having increased the transaction's value to *that* client. If, however, the evaluation is *ex ante*—before either side has decided whether to retain a lawyer—the result is quite different. Both clients would determine jointly whether to retain lawyers for the transaction, recognizing that if either retained a lawyer, so would the other. In this situation, if all business lawyers offer is skill in distributive bargaining, the clients' joint decision would be to hire *no* lawyers at all because, net of lawyers' fees, the surplus from the transaction to be divided between the clients would be *smaller* as a result of the participation of lawyers, rather than larger. Only a client who believed that its lawyer would be better than the other party's with sufficient frequency that the expected gain from better distributive bargaining exceeded the cost of *both* lawyers would still use lawyers in the transaction. Given any reasonable assumption about the availability and distribution of legal talent among lawyers serving commercial clients, this disparity is unlikely to exist with any frequency.

Our focus with respect to the business lawyer's private ordering function thus will be on identifying how, without the crutch of regula-

---

[27] The intended distinction is between distributive bargaining in which the size of the pie is by definition fixed and any gain by one party comes at the expense of the other, and what may be called joint problem solving in which, through cooperation, the size of the pie, and hence the size of the piece received by both parties, can be increased. See generally H. Raiffa, *The Art and Science of Negotiation* (1982); R. Fisher & W. Ury, *Getting to Yes: Negotiating*

Without Giving In (1981). The dichotomy, while quite helpful, cannot be taken literally; any gain from cooperation must still be distributed between the parties.

[28] As long as one side has a lawyer, the other side also will get one if a lawyer could strengthen the hand of one party in distributive bargaining at the expense of an unrepresented party.

tion, a business lawyer can help private parties order their relationship in a way that increases the size of the entire pie, rather than merely increasing the size of one party's piece at the expense of the other's. We will approach this problem in Part V by carefully examining a standard corporate acquisition agreement to see if it evidences techniques that do hold the promise of creating value, and to see if these techniques fit a general pattern that can help explain more generally how business lawyers can create value through skill in designing the structure of private ordering.

Even at this early stage in the enterprise, a common theme should be emerging. The discussion thus far has focused on *value;* in particular, the central question is how business lawyers can increase the value of a transaction. The problem, however, is whether it is possible to tell if a business lawyer has accomplished this goal. How can we ever determine whether a transaction would have been more valuable if a lawyer had participated or, conversely, whether a transaction would have been worth less in his or her absence? A truly empirical approach to measuring the impact of a business lawyer's participation seems impossible for a number of reasons. It is unlikely that we could find data covering both a sample of transactions in which a business lawyer did participate and a control group of equivalent transactions which were accomplished without a lawyer. Even if the data-collection problem could somehow be solved,[29] serious methodological problems would nonetheless remain.[30] While we might know the dollar value attached to particular transactions by the participants, we would still face overwhelming problems in determining whether the transactions were really comparable so that any difference in value could be ascribed to the business lawyer's participation.

There is, however, an alternative approach to determining the potential for business lawyers to add value to a transaction. The first step is to understand how a transaction is valued in the absence of a business lawyer's participation. If this can be established—if the factors that generally determine transaction value can be identified—then the second step is relatively straightforward. By understanding

[29] For the difficulty in developing useful data bearing on what lawyers do, see Pashigian, *A Theory of Prevention and Legal Defense with an Application to the Legal Costs of Companies,* 25 J.L. & Econ. 247 (1982).

[30] Occasionally, researchers are fortunate enough to find actual settings where history has provided both the control group and the sample necessary to evaluate the impact of a single factor. Thus, for example, the simultaneous operation of both mutual and stock forms of savings and loan associations has allowed empirical study of the impact of form of ownership on performance. See O'Hara, *Property Rights and the Financial Firm,* 24 J.L. & Econ. 317 (1981); Nichols, *Stock versus Mutual Savings and Loan Associations: Some Evidence,* 57 Am.Econ.Rev. 2 (1967); see also Davies, *The Efficiency of Public versus Private Firms: The Case of Australia's Two Airlines,* 14 J.L. & Econ. 149 (1971) (comparison of performance of state and privately owned Australian airlines); Davies, *Property Rights and Economic Efficiency—Australia's Two Airlines Revisited,* 20 J.L. & Econ. 223 (1977) (same). Even then, however, it is still difficult to control for the impact of other factors. For example, while we can identify some states in which lawyers perform the title search in connection with real property transfers, and others in which title insurance companies provide this service, other differences between the states make it hard to isolate the role of just this difference. See generally Fisher, *Multiple Regression in Legal Proceedings,* 80 Colum.L.Rev. 702 (1980).

the relationship between the business lawyer's activities and the particular factors that determine transaction value, it should be possible to frame an hypothesis that directly links the application of legal skills to transaction value.

We begin this analysis by recognizing that the subjects of business transactions are typically capital assets: assets whose value is determined solely by the income, whether in cash flow or appreciation, they are expected to earn.[31] What we normally think of as a transaction, then, is simply the transfer of a capital asset from one party to another.[32] Characterizing transactions as transfers of capital assets is important because, over the last fifteen years, financial economists have developed a substantial body of theory to explain how capital assets are valued or, as a financial economist would put it, how capital assets are "priced." If capital asset pricing theory can identify the factors that determine transaction value, then these factors can be examined to determine whether business lawyers can influence them in a way that will alter transaction value. And if the systematic application of legal skills can affect transaction value, then two important results follow. First, we should be able to examine what business lawyers *really* do and determine if their activities are such that they could bear on transaction value. That is, it would be possible to inquire positively into the efficiency of the common "lawyer." Second, and more important, we should be able to make normative statements about what business lawyers *should* do in order to increase the value of a transaction—in order to *create* value. Here the prospect is really quite exciting: Theory will have been brought to bear not merely to criticize doctrine or urge public policy reform, but as a tool to improve the quality of legal practice.

The effort to understand what business lawyers do, and to learn how better to do it, then must begin with study of modern financial theory. Part I of the book introduces this theory. Part II applies the theory to evaluating why clients think making corporate acquisitions is a useful activity. Does the activity itself, without regard to the participation of business lawyers, hold promise for making money? If not, then there is little need to examine the business lawyer's role with respect to them. If so, however, it is critical for a business lawyer to

[31] This definition, while standard, is quite limited. In particular, any asset that has consumption value—i.e., its owner holds it for reasons other than (or in addition to) its potential for generating income—falls outside the definition. A familiar example would be a work of art that might be purchased in anticipation of appreciation, but that would still be enjoyed in the meantime. The exclusion, however, has broader application. For example, a sole proprietorship, clearly an income producing asset, may also have significant consumption value: the psychic value of being your own boss may explain why many owners of small businesses continue in their vocation even though the businesses earn less than the market value of their owners' services plus a return on invested capital.

[32] This is readily apparent in the simple case of a transaction consisting of the sale of tangible assets, for example, an apartment building. Then the value of the transaction is clearly the value of the asset transferred. The point remains equally valid, however, if the asset transferred is more ephemeral. In a lease or a joint venture, the asset transferred—the right to use real or personal property or the right to participate in an ongoing relationship—may be more difficult to visualize, but it still has value only because is has the potential to produce income.

understand how the client hopes to gain from a transaction. Understanding the client's motives is also a prerequisite to making the transaction more valuable. Parts III and IV review the various regulatory systems that bear on the opportunity to create value in connection with the public ordering aspects of corporate acquisitions. We return to private ordering concerns in Part V.

B. The Historical Setting

Having described the intended focus on the potential for business lawyers to create value, the next introductory step is to explain the choice of corporate acquisitions as a context in which to explore what business lawyers really do. It is, of course, criticial to look at the problem in some context. Bringing theory to bear on practice requires its careful application in a *real* setting so that its relevance actually can be evaluated. In our case, the theory to be applied is modern financial theory, with special emphasis on how capital assets are valued. Corporate acquisitions are a particularly appropriate setting for this theory for three important reasons.

First, a corporate acquisition is clearly the transfer of a capital asset. Indeed, valuation of corporate securities—the indicia of ownership of a corporation—has dominated the empirical tests of modern financial theory. Moreover, there is a growing body of empirical literature examining the impact on the security holders of both acquiring and target companies of both corporate acquisitions generally, and of a wide variety of the techniques and alternatives associated with corporate acquisitions. Thus, there is a body of theory *and* data against which both clients' beliefs about the private value of acquisitions, and public policy beliefs about the social impact of acquisitions and their regulation, can be measured.

Second, although corporate acquisitions are heavily regulated, they still provide substantial opportunity for private ordering. As a result, they allow examination of the potential for business lawyers to create value both through sophisticated manipulation of the regulatory regimes bearing on acquisition transactions and through structuring the private arrangement between the parties. And because the private ordering function is far more difficult for outsiders to observe, the fact that negotiation and preparation of the acquisition agreement is the business lawyer's principal charge in the transaction, so that there is a fairly complete record of the lawyer's activity, makes acquisitions a particularly useful setting in which to study what business lawyers do.

Third, corporate acquisitions are centrally important objects of study without regard to what they may tell us about how to be a business lawyer. In recent years, acquisition activity has been substantial and quite controversial. Critics have claimed that they have the potential to reshape the structure of the American economy, adding substantially to what are claimed to be already serious problems of concentration of economic and political power in the hands of large companies. In contrast, other commentators have argued that corporate acquisitions are a critically important element of the overall corporate governance structure, with particular significance for assuring that corporate management keeps the goal of profit maximization firmly in mind. Numerous Congressional hearings have been held on the question of whether particular types of corporate acquisitions, or acquisitions generally, should be curtailed, and it seems clear that significant portions of the changes in the corporate income tax enacted by the Tax Equity and Fiscal Responsibility Act of 1982 were motivated by concern over the level of acquisition activity, rather than concern over issues of pure tax policy.[33] Developing a detailed understanding of so controversial an activity is thus justifiable in itself.[34]

Despite the current controversy associated with corporate acquisitions, they are not, however, a new phenomenon. Apparent waves of acquisition activity, and controversy concerning them, have been a feature of the American economy since the late 1800's. But the character of the activity has changed dramatically over time, and understanding the current transactional pattern is aided by understanding something of the history of corporate acquisitions in the United States.

M. SALTER & W. WEINHOLD, MERGER TRENDS AND PROSPECTS FOR THE 1980s
2–27 (U.S. Dept. of Commerce 1980)

A BRIEF HISTORY OF CORPORATE MERGERS AND ACQUISITIONS IN THE UNITED STATES

Economists and students of industrial organization have identified three major merger waves which swept the American economy between 1890 and 1975. Figure 1 * * * outlines the scope and magnitude of these cycles. Each cycle has been well documented with extensive economic literature and policy debate.[7] To help put current merger

---

[33] The original legislation concerning taxation of corporate acquisitions that became part of TEFRA was introduced by Representative Stark as H.R. 6295, 97th Cong., 2d Sess. (1982), as The Corporate Takeover Tax Act of 1982. Martin Ginsburg describes the legislation as responding to the public impression "of a nation overwhelmed by a spreading rash of enormous corporate acquisitions motivated and financed in significant part by extraordinary tax avoidance." Ginsburg, *Taxing Corporate Acquisitions*, 38 Tax L.Rev. 171, 216 (1983). Federal tax treatment of corporate acquisitions is taken up in Chapter Twelve infra.

[34] On a more prosaic level, corporate acquisitions are transactions where, as Vonnegut put it, "large amounts of money are about to change hands;" and large legal fees are hardly possible when *small* amounts of money change hands. Thus, corporate acquisitions are an important source of business for major law firms. Students aspiring to be business lawyers

obviously can gain from an introduction to the substance of a significant area of their prospective employers' practice.

[7] Jesse W. Markham, "Survey of the Evidence and Findings on Mergers," in *Business Concentration and Price Policy*, National Bureau of Economic Research (Princeton: Princeton University Press, 1955), pp. 141–212; Ralph L. Nelson, *Merger Movements in American Industry, 1895–1956* (Princeton: Princeton University Press, 1955); Peter O. Steiner, *Mergers: Motives, Effects, Policies* (Ann Arbor: University of Michigan Press, 1975); William W. Alberts and Joel E. Segall, ed., *The Corporate Merger* (Chicago: University of Chicago Press, 1966); F.M. Scherer, *Industrial Market Structure and Economic Performance* (Chicago: Rand McNally College Publishing Co., 1970); and Jesse W. Markham, *Conglomerate Enterprise and Public Policy* (Boston: Division of Research, Harvard Business School, 1973) all provide excellent commentary on these merger waves.

and acquisition activity into proper perspective, it is useful to briefly review these three waves.

The first peak in merger and acquisition activity just prior to 1900 was reached in a period of rapid economic expansion following two decades of economic stagnation (industrial production, for instance, grew 100%). The wave of mergers between 1895 and 1905 involved an estimated 15% of all manufacturing assets and employees, and accompanied major changes in the nation's social and technological infrastructure. An important characteristic of this merger wave was the simultaneous consolidation of producers within numerous industries. These mergers, mostly horizontal integrations, were often made in search of market dominance. Many of today's industrial giants, including U.S. Steel, the several descendents of Standard Oil, General Electric, Westinghouse, United Fruit, Eastman Kodak, American Can, American Tobacco, U.S. Rubber, DuPont, PPG, International Harvester, and U.S. Gypsum, among others, trace their origins in this period. The tailend of this merger wave in 1903–1904 coincided with a severe economic recession and the *Northern Securities* decision which established that mergers could be successfully attacked under then existing antitrust law.

While George Stigler has characterized the first wave as "merging for monopoly," other economists have not been so bold. Many have noted that this merger wave accompanied a frenzied stock market and the aggressive promotional activities by bankers and brokers. J.P. Morgan, for example, is estimated to have earned over $60 million for his efforts in the consolidation of U.S. Steel. Others have argued that many of the consolidations failed in the following recession and that others did not even lead to market dominance. Nevertheless, as Markham concluded, "The conversion of approximately 71 important oligopolistic or near-competitive industries into near monopolies by merger between 1890 and 1904 left an impact on the structure of the American economy that fifty years have not yet erased."

The two decades following the 1903–04 market crash were relatively quiet ones in terms of merger activity. Only two notable combinations arose, General Motors in 1909, and International Business Machines in 1911. Much more important, however, was a relatively wide scale legal attack on the trusts formed in the previous wave. The year 1911 was the landmark, with the Supreme Court ordering the breakups of the Standard Oil and American Tobacco Companies. Market monopolies were clearly established as illegal. However, further judicial decisions, such as the 1920 U.S. Steel Decision, established that dominant firms would be subject to antitrust attack only if they abused their market position through aggressive and predatory attacks on their rivals. Since the Sherman Act only addressed issues of substantial monopoly power, Congress passed the Clayton Act in 1914 whose stated purpose was "to arrest the creation of trusts, conspiracies and monopolies in their incipiency and before consummation." [12]   The Federal

[12] Senate Report No. 698 to accompany H.R. 15,637 (63rd Congress, 2nd Session, 1914), p. 1.

Trade Commission was also established at this time to better control unrestrained corporate power. For the first time in antitrust history, specific business actions were declared illegal.

Figure 1
Number of Manufacturing and Mining Firms Acquired
1895–1978

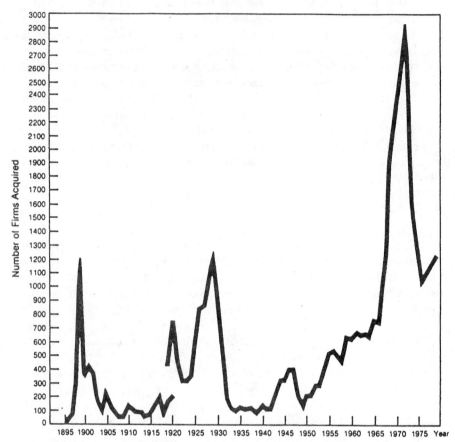

Source: Malcolm S. Salter and Wolf A. Weinhold, *Diversification Through Acquisition: Strategies for Creating Economic Value* (New York: Free Press, 1979), p. 10.

[D6543]

The second wave of merger and acquisition activity occurred during the 1920s and peaked in 1928. As with its predecessor, it too rode a period of economic growth and a stock market boom. All told, an estimated 12,000 firms disappeared during this period. Its impact on market structure, however, was much less noticeable for several reasons.

First, over one-third of this activity was in the banking and public utility sectors. Most significant was the rise of the giant utility holding company pyramids in the gas, electricity and water sectors, pyramids which were to collapse in the following depression. Since these sectors were already regulated, increased market concentration had little or no impact on economic power. Second, since the Clayton Act prevented large scale stock consolidations in search of market power, but not asset acquisitions, merger activity in the manufacturing sector was primarily limited to either small market share additions or to vertical integration. Worthy of special note, however, was the formation of strong "number two companies" in numerous industries previously dominated by one giant firm. The consolidations of Bethlehem Steel, Republic Steel and Continental Can all date from this era. This advent of oligopoly in many industrial sectors lead George Stigler to characterize this period of merger activity as "merging for oligopoly."

It was outside the previously consolidated heavy manufacturing industrial sectors where much of the merger activity was occurring. Mergers in the still fragmented food processing, chemicals, and mining sectors comprised 60% of all merger activity in manufacturing. Extensive vertical integration (in mining) and product extension moves (in food processing and chemicals) led to many major industrial enterprises. Kennecott, Anaconda, and Phelp's Dodge, Allied Chemical and DuPont (in chemicals outside explosives), and General Mills, General Foods, and Kraft all trace their emergence to this period.

While the merger wave of the 1920s was clearly as large or larger in absolute terms than the 1890–1904 wave, its relative impact was much less. In total, it apparently involved less than 10% of the economy's assets rather than the former wave's over 15%. Furthermore, in most industries, mergers embraced only a small proportion of the competing firms. Only in the food processing, metals, and chemicals sectors was industry structure substantially altered. Oligopoly, while clearly present, was, in fact, limited to a small fraction of all merger and acquisition activity.

The 1920's merger wave did, however, have several similarities with that of 1890–1905. Both occurred during a period of economic prosperity and a booming stock market. And, as before, it came to an end with a stock market crash and a severe economic slowdown. Internally, stock promoters once again seemed to have been a major driving force. Perhaps rightfully recognizing stock promotions as the principal avenue of abuse in this merger wave, legislation in the following years was aimed at securities regulation rather than at more rigorous antitrust controls.

The onset of a worldwide depression in 1929 brought merger activity to a halt. Throughout the 1930s and into World War II, acquisition activity remained at its lowest levels of the century. As the war ended, an upsurge in merger and acquisition activity began, once again accompanying economic prosperity and rising stock prices. The Federal Trade Commission, in its landmark 1948 report, concluded:

> No great stretch of the imagination is required to foresee that if nothing is done to check the growth in concentration, either giant corporations will ultimately take over the country, or the government will be impelled to step in and impose some form of direct regulation.[13]

[13] U.S. Federal Trade Commission, *The Merger Movement: A Summary Report*, Washington, 1948, pp. 25, 68. [Later studies challenge the FTC's conclusion that industrial concentration was increasing. See P. Areeda, *Antitrust Analysis* 844 n. 16 (2d ed. 1981) (collecting studies showing industrial concentration roughly constant after 1909). Ed.]

Table 1

Acquisition Activity Following the Celler-Kefauver Amendment

		Number of Acquisitions			Value of Assets Acquired (millions of dollars)	
Year	Total Recorded	All Manufacturing and Mining (M&M)	Large M&M Acquisitions *	Large M&M Acquisitions by 200 Largest Firms **	Large M&M Acquisitions	Large M&M Acquisitions by 200 Largest Firms
1950	NA	219	5	1	186	20
1951	NA	235	9	5	204	149
1952	NA	288	15	7	361	196
1953	NA	295	26	16	839	581
1954	NA	387	38	16	1,465	942
1955	NA	683	69	33	2,179	1,217
1956	NA	673	59	25	2,076	1,440
1957	NA	585	50	23	1,363	843
1958	NA	589	45	22	1,242	831
1959	NA	835	62	30	1,947	1,277
1960	1,345	844	64	32	1,279	1,013
1961	1,724	954	60	25	2,356	1,565
1962	1,667	853	70	33	2,448	1,301
1963	1,479	861	83	41	3,148	2,051
1964	1,797	854	91	38	2,728	1,248
1965	1,893	1,008	91	29	3,845	1,928
1966	1,746	995	101	35	4,171	2,468
1967	2,384	1,496	168	73	9,091	6,287
1968	3,932	2,407	207	94	13,297	8,209
1969	4,542	2,307	155	52	11,353	5,543
1970	3,089	1,351	98	30	6,346	2,672
1971	2,633	1,011	66	19	2,544	989

* Acquired firms with assets of $10 million or more.

** Ranked by 1970 total assets.

N.A. = not available.

Source: Federal Trade Commission, Bureau of Economics, *Current Trends in Merger Activity, 1970 and 1971,* Statistical Report Numbers 8 (March 1971) and 10 (May 1972).

Something was done, however, with the Celler-Kefauver Amendment substantially strengthening the anti-merger provisions of the Clayton Act in 1950. Horizontal or vertical acquisitions of significant size became virtually impossible to do. Beginning in 1947, acquisition activity fell drastically, reaching a low in 1950. This slump was due, however, to a falling stock market rather than these new public policy prescriptions. As the FTC and Department of Justice would find out in the subsequent wave, they too, like many generals, had planned for the last war.

By the mid-1950s, a third merger and acquisition wave had begun. Table 1 * * * detail[s] this growth in acquisition activity from the mid-1950s through 1961. This wave which, would prove to be longer and larger than either of the two preceding waves, was of an entirely new sort. This wave did not, in general, involve either large acquisitions or large acquirers. In fact, the larger the enterprise, the less important growth through acquisition would be. Despite its magnitude, this wave would witness little or no increase in intra-industry or market concentration and only a minor (and debatable) rise in aggregate economic concentration. What arose was a strategy of corporate diversification into new product markets.

Figure 3
Estimated Percentage of FORTUNE 500 Companies
in Each Category

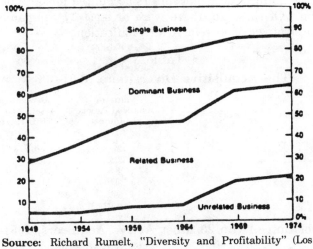

Source: Richard Rumelt, "Diversity and Profitability" (Los
Angeles: University of California at Los Angeles
Working Paper, 1977), p. 21.

[D6544]

This concept of unrelated diversification was pioneered by Textron, Litton, and ITT, and led to high rates of corporate growth. These fastgrowing firms, known as "conglomerates," were principally small- to medium-sized companies that emphasized acquisition activity outside their traditional areas of interest. Furthermore, their acquisitions were also of typically small- to medium-sized firms operating in either fragmented industries or on the periphery of major industrial sectors. As the stock market soared in the mid-sixties, this concept became more and more popular with both investors and corporate executives. [Earnings per share] growth and synergy were the bywords of this period. The dramatic increase in the number of companies following a diversification strategy during this period is seen in Figure 3, where "unrelated business" is roughly synonymous with conglomerate. Since this merger wave brought corporate growth but not increased market concentration, we have labeled this wave, to paraphrase George Stigler, "merging for growth."

At its peak in 1967–1969, several conglomerates were selling at 100 times earnings and were using their stock to devour acquisitions, often at the rate of one per week. Over 10,000 independent companies were acquired in the 1967–69 peak (over 6,000 in mining and manufacturing alone) and over 25,000 firms disappeared over the course of the entire wave (1960–1971). * * * [A]t the wave's peak over 70% of these acquisitions were conglomerate in nature and over 30% totally unrelated to the acquirer. Total assets acquired in the mining and manufacturing sectors exceeded $70 billion, or approximately 7–8% of all corporate manufacturing assets. In absolute terms this was by far the largest merger wave to occur in the U.S. economy.

Table 3 highlights the pacesetting role of conglomerates in this wave. The 200 largest manufacturing firms accounted for approximately one-half of all acquired assets during this period and among these 200, the 25 most active acquirers accounted for 59% or a total of $20.2 billion. Of these 25, there were at least 17 companies actively following a strategy of unrelated diversification. * * *

Table 3
The Acquisitive Diversifiers, 1961–1968

Most Active Acquiring Companies	Value of Acquired Assets ($ billions)	Percentage of Total Assets Acquired by the 200 Largest Companies	
		Group	Cumulative Total
First 25	20.2	59	59
Second 25	6.8	20	79
Third 25	3.6	11	90
Fourth 25	1.9	6	96
Second 100	1.6	4	100

Composition of the 25 Most Active Acquirers, 1961–1968

Number of Companies	Type of Company	Number of Acquisitions	Percentage of Acquisitions	Assets Acquired ($ millions)	Percentage of Assets Acquired
11	Conglomerates	479	68.9	10,867	53.6
6	Unrelated Diversifiers	70	10.1	4,371	21.6
5	Petroleum	34	4.8	3,302	16.3
3	Miscellaneous	112	16.2	1,724	8.5

Source: Bureau of Economics, Federal Trade Commission.

As with the two previous merger waves, this wave was also accompanied by aggressive stock promotion and rose and fell with the stock market. For conglomerates, the wave ended with the collapse of their stock prices following lowered earnings in the mild 1969–70 recession. For other acquirers it came to an end in 1973 with the advent of the nation's severest economic recession and stock market collapse since the 1930s.

At this stage it is useful to review what we know about the three merger waves that have occurred so far in U.S. history. Four similarities, all previously identified by Jesse Markham in 1955, apply to each of the three waves.[14] Briefly stated, these similarities are:

1. Contrary to popular opinion, relatively few mergers seem to have had market monopolization as their goal. Market power was most evident in the first wave but declined in each of the next two. The conglomerate wave of the 1960s had virtually no effect on either market concentration or aggregate economic concentration;

2. The most striking single motive for merger at each peak seems to have been the search for promotional profits. All three waves occurred during sustained periods of economic prosperity and rapidly rising levels of stock prices. Each merger wave peaked with the stock market and then quickly receded as stock prices fell and each wave was followed by a serious economic recession (the 1903–04 crash, the 1929–37 Great Depression and the 1974–75 recession). As

[14] Jesse Markham, op.cit., pp. 180–182.

each wave progressed, speculative stock activity and the formation of less viable enterprises became more evident. Stock promotion, of one form or another, eclipsed economic reality as each wave peaked. Thorp's comment on the 1920s wave is just as relevant to the other two waves: " * * * one businessman regarded it as a loss of standing if he was not approached once a week with a merger proposition. * * * A group of businessmen and financiers in discussing this matter in the summer of 1928 agreed that nine out of ten mergers had the investment banker at its core;" [15]

3. Many mergers were simply ordinary business transactions among entrepreneurs. Mergers and acquisitions provide one of the best means for entrepreneurs to exit an industry while reaping the maximum benefits of their work; and

4. Many mergers accompanied or were stimulated by massive changes in the economy's infrastructure. Typically, these radical changes in the economy lead to new market definitions and/or new production and distribution technologies. For example, the first wave followed rapid rail building, the advent of electricity and the rise of coal. The second was accompanied by automotive transportation and the radio. The last wave was accompanied by aircraft, television, and the use of liquid hydrocarbons. Whether a cause-and-effect relationship exists or whether it is coincidence has not been established.

The differences between the waves are surprisingly few. In essence, they concern the relative impact of each wave on the economy and their primary focus. While each wave was larger than the ones before it in both the number of companies involved and assets acquired, they consumed increasingly smaller proportions of the total economy. Either the size and diversity of the economy outgrew the capacity of corporations to grow through merger or, as some cynics have suggested, fewer and fewer attractive assets were left to acquire. In either case, relatively effective antitrust measures changed the focus of corporate merger and acquisition activity from that of market domination in the first wave to one of product market diversity in the third. Nevertheless, the fear of unrestrained market power, established in the public's mind in earlier years, still continued to influence economic and political debate on corporate mergers and acquisitions.

Merger and Acquisition Activity Since 1975

Since 1975 the characteristics of merger and acquisition activity have continued to evolve. Table 5 * * * provide[s] a comparative profile of acquisition activity during this most recent period, based on data compiled by the Federal Trade Commission. * * * In contrast to the surge in small- to medium-sized acquisitions during the 1967–1973 period, the number of large and very large acquisitions has increased dramatically since 1975. This is even more striking in light of the fall in the rate of acquisition activity to one-half of its earlier level.

---

[15] Willard L. Thorp, "The Persistence of the Merger Movement," *American Economic Review,* Supplement, March 1931, p. 86.

* * * [The trend toward diversifying acquisitions has continued with] many of the recent large and very large acquisitions have been unrelated diversification moves by the country's largest firms.

* * *

Table 5

Trend in Recorded Acquisitions

	All Acquisitions			Mining and Manufacturing Acquisitions		
	Number of Acquisitions	Number over $10 million	Number over $100 million	Number of Acquisitions	Number over $10 million	Number over $100 million
1951–55	NA	NA	NA	378/yr.	30/yr.	2/yr.
1956–60	NA	NA	NA	705/yr.	48/yr.	1/yr.
1961–66	1514/yr.	NA	NA	920/yr.	63/yr.	5/yr.
1967–69	3403/yr.	NA	NA	2070/yr.	150/yr.	27/yr.
1970	2854	NA	NA	1351	91	12
1971	2303	NA	NA	1011	59	5
1972	2758	NA	NA	NA	60	6
1973	1919	137	28	697	64	7
1974	1276	129	26	505	62	11
1975	889	112	16	355	59	11
1976	1081	159	23	461	81	14
1977	1182	195	38	619	99	19
1978	1350	260	45	NA	NA	31

Source: Salter and Weinhold, op. cit.

Table 9 helps place the most recent upsurge in merger and acquisition activity in much broader perspective. While total acquired assets in 1977–1979 exceeded the 1967–1969 peak in book value terms, the amount of acquired assets relative to *existing assets* was just approaching the average acquisition rate for the 1960–1966 period and still far below that of the frenzied 1967–1969 period. In fact, background data suggests that 1955–1956 and 1963–1971 as having as high or higher rates of merger and acquisition activity, relative to either new investment or total existing assets, than the more current 1977–1979 period.

* * *

Table 9

Comparison of Large Acquired Assets to New and Existing Investments for Manufacturing and Mining Companies

Year	New Investment * ($ billions)	Acquired Assets ** ($ billions)	Acquired Assets as percent of New Investment	Acquired Assets as percent of Existing Assets
1948–1953	$ 10.6/yr.	$ 0.3/yr.	2.8%	.18%
1954–1959	14.82/yr.	1.69/yr.	11.4	.80
1960–1966	20.2/yr.	2.93/yr.	14.5	.92
1967–1969	31.2/yr.	11.6/yr.	37.2	2.47
1970	33.8	6.6	19.5	1.14
1971	32.2	3.1	9.8	.51
1972	33.8	2.7	7.9	.41
1973	40.8	3.6	8.7	.50
1974	49.2	5.1	10.4	.69
1975	51.7	5.5	10.7	.68
1976	56.5	6.9	12.2	.79
1977	65.5	9.6	14.7	1.02
1978	73.2	12.3	16.8	1.19

* Total expenditures for new plant and equipment by manufacturing and mining firms.

** Acquired firms with assets of $10 million or more.

Source: Salter and Weinhold, op. cit.

The upswing in merger and acquisition activity beginning in 1975 has led many observers to announce a fourth wave of corporate marriages. This announcement reflects the fact that the aggregate annual value of all acquisitions in the late 1970s reached or exceeded the levels seen during the conglomerate wave of the late 1960s (though the total number of acquisitions was much lower). These observers typically argue that the U.S. economy is undergoing a radical transformation that will lead to further concentration in economic decision making and power.

Whether or not another major merger movement was launched in the late 1970s will only become possible to determine with the passage of time. Nevertheless, we feel that current merger activity can usefully be placed in an historical context. But this must be done with some care. An analysis based on gross comparisons between the total number of acquisitions made or the total asset values acquired will not be particularly enlightening. Both are static measures and fail to recognize the dynamic nature of the U.S. economy with its ever-growing size and complexity. In an expanding economy, comparisons based upon such static data will tend to suggest greater levels of merger activity than actually exist. Furthermore, rapid rates of inflation (such as what the U.S. has experienced over the last 15 years) will further distort any comparisons of merger activity based upon asset or market values. To establish reasonably consistent and truly comparable comparisons between current merger activity and that of earlier periods, the data on merger activity normally reported must be refined. Two adjustments are especially important: (1) merger volume should be measured in terms of constant or inflation adjusted dollars; and (2) merger activity should be measured in terms of the assets acquired *relative* to the total assets of the economy. Failure to make these adjustments prior to comparing the magnitude and extent of current merger activity with previous periods will inevitably lead to incorrect conclusions.

Table 10 looks at recent merger and acquisition activity on a constant dollar basis. It focuses on total consideration paid rather than assets acquired, since this best reflects the acquisition's perceived value in the marketplace. * * * What this analysis shows is that a substantial portion of recent acquisition activity reflects the high rates of inflation that have occurred over the last decade. In real terms, current acquisition activity is only running at about two-thirds of the rate of the 1967–69 peak in conglomerate acquisitions.

Table 10

Inflation Adjusted Consideration Paid in Acquisitions, 1967–1979

Year	Total Consideration * ($ billions)	GNP Implicit Price Deflator (1972 = 100)	Constant Dollar Consideration (1972 $ billions)
1967	18.0	$ 79.0	22.8
1968	43.0	82.6	52.1
1969	23.7	86.7	27.3

Table 10—Continued

Year	Total Consideration * ($ billions)	GNP Implicit Price Deflator (1972 = 100)	Constant Dollar Consideration (1972 $ billions)
1970	16.4	91.4	16.9
1971	12.6	96.0	13.1
1972	16.7	106.0	16.7
1973	16.7	105.8	15.8
1974	12.5	116.0	10.8
1975	11.8	127.1	9.3
1976	20.0	133.7	15.0
1977	21.9	141.7	15.5
1978	34.2	152.1	22.5
1979	43.5	165.5	26.3

* Reported by W.T. Grimm & Co., and based upon all reported acquisition offers where purchase price was available. This measure overstates actual consideration paid in U.S. acquisition by including certain foreign acquisitions, the effect of competing offers, and the impact of cancellations on deals announced but not completed by year end.

Tables 11 and 12 measure current acquisition activity in a slightly different manner. They attempt to measure acquisition volume relative to all other assets in the economy. This approach recognizes that the U.S. economy is continuing to grow and that what might be a high level of merger activity at one period in time may amount to only a modest level of activity a decade or two later. Table 11 measures acquisition volume relative to the value of all corporate securities. This data suggests that despite the extremely high aggregate value of acquisition payments made during 1975–79, it was not as great as in the mid-1960s relative to the market value of all other corporations. Table 12 looks at acquisition activity in terms of the book values of corporate assets rather than in terms of market values. While this measure does not reflect the impact of inflation, differences in asset productivity, or changes in economic and environmental conditions as fully as a market value measure, it does show that current acquisition activity is high relative to recent history, although not nearly as high as the 1967–69 conglomerate peak.

Table 11

Consideration Paid Relative to the Market Value of all U.S. Equities

Year	Consideration Paid * ($ billions)	Total Market Value of all Equities ** ($ billions)	Consideration Paid ÷ Market Value of all Corporations *** (%)
1965		$ 748	
1966		682	
1967	$ 18.0 Est.	868	2.1%

Table 11—Continued

Year	Consideration Paid * ($ billions)	Total Market Value of all Equities ** ($ billions)	Consideration Paid ÷ Market Value of all Corporations *** (%)
1968	43.0	1,034	4.2
1969	23.7	914	2.6
1970	16.4	906	1.8
1971	12.6	1,060	1.2
1972	16.7	1,198	1.4
1973	16.7	947	1.8
1974	12.5	675	1.8
1975	11.8	891	1.3
1976	20.0	1,106	1.8
1977	21.9	1,039	2.1
1978	34.2	1,086	3.1
1979	43.5	1,244	3.5

* W.T. Grimm & Co., and based upon all reported acquisition offers where purchase price was available. This measure overstates actual consideration paid in U.S. acquisitions by including some foreign acquisitions, cancellations, and competing offers.

** Federal Reserve Board, "Flow of Funds."

*** Since consideration paid includes acquisition premiums, this column will tend to overstate the capital market impact of acquisition activity by the relative level of the acquisition premiums.

Table 12

Comparison of Large Acquired Assets to Existing Assets for Large Mining and Manufacturing Companies

Year	Acquired Assets ($ billions)	Existing Assets ($ billions)	Acquired Assets as a % of Existing Assets
1960–66	$ 2.9/yr.	$ 263.3 (avg.)	1.1%
1967–69	11.6	402.7 (avg.)	2.9
1970	6.6	502.9	1.3
1971	3.1	537.8	.6
1972	2.7	574.2	.5
1973	3.6	627.7	.6
1974	5.1	660.1	.8
1975	5.5	690.6	.8
1976	6.9	749.6	.9
1977	9.6	830.4	1.2
1978 (est.)	12.3	903.6	1.3

Source: Federal Trade Commission, Statistical Reports on Mergers and Acquisitions.

What we can see, then, is that merger activity in the 1975–79 period has indeed been significant when looked at in absolute terms. However, relative to the size of the economy or the level of merger activity during the 1960s, the size and magnitude of the current merger activity is much less impressive. The 1970s witnessed rapid inflation and a growing economy, both of which served to diminish dramatically the relative impact of a given level of merger and acquisition activity. Table 13 summarizes current acquisition activity in comparison to the previous three merger waves. When viewed in terms of constant dollars or as a percent of total assets, merger and acquisition activity within the mining and manufacturing sectors during the 1975–1979 period does not look as significant as that during earlier periods.[16]

Table 13

Estimated Impact of Merger Activity on the U.S. Mining and Manufacturing Sectors: 1975–79 vs. the Three Previous Merger Waves

	Periods			
	1895–1902	1919–29	1960–70	1975–79 *
Total Acquisitions in and Manufacturing	2,600+	8,000	12,000	3,100
Total Mining and Manufacturing Assets Acquired ($ billions)	6.4+	12–15	70+	50
Assets Acquired in constant dollars 1967 = 100 ($ billions)	26+	24–30	69	30
Estimate of Assets Acquired as a % of Total Mining & Manufacturing Assets	15+	7–9	10+	6

* The current merger wave is not yet over so that these estimates will necessarily grow as the merger wave continues.

Note: This table is based upon authors' estimates. As noted elsewhere, reliable, consistent, and comprehensive data do not exist for even current acquisition activity let alone the earlier waves. It also does not reflect the increasing importance of service-based industries (and acquisitions within the service sector) in the post-WWII economy.

In addition to characteristics relating to the number, size, and diversity of transactions, other distinguishing characteristics of the current merger movement are emerging. Eight important ones stand out and are discussed below.

1. In contrast to the conglomerate buying spree of the 1960s, many of the acquiring companies in the late 1970s were well-established, conservative, old line giants. These acquirers typically had most of their assets concentrated in one or a few closely related

---

[16] What the data does not show is the increase in merger activity within the service sectors of the economy.

businesses. More often than not, these conservative giants were also facing maturing product markets in their major lines of business. General Electric, Johns Mansville, Mobil, Continental Group, Atlantic Richfield, R.J. Reynolds, Allied Chemical, United Technologies, and N.L. Industries all fall into this category.

This is not to say that these conservative giants were highly active acquirers during 1975–79, or that the conglomerates were not active acquirers. Both inferences are, in fact, misleading. * * * [T]he most active acquirers, in terms of the number of acquisitions made during the period, were companies following a strategy of either conglomerate diversification or companies within industries where environmental and competitive conditions were leading to substantial consolidation. On the other hand, the so-called conservative giants generally limited their merger activity to one or, at most, two acquisitions during this period. The important difference between these two groups, however, lies in the size of the acquisitions being made by the conservative giants. Despite little acquisition experience, they were the companies making the $300 million deals. * * * Ironically enough, in several instances, entire conglomerates (Eltra and Studebaker-Worthington) were themselves swallowed up by old line, conservative giants (Allied Chemical and McGraw Edison).

Table 15

Classification of Acquired Companies by Business Sectors, 1975–1979

Ranked by Net Announcements

Industry Classifications	Total Announcements, 1975–1979	Percentage of All Acquisitions
Finance, Banks and Insurance	1,608	14.6%
General Services	1,123	10.2
Wholesaler Retail	952	8.6
Food Processing and Agriculture	616	5.6
Machinery, Equipment, and Farm Equipment	527	4.8
Public Utilities	367	3.3
Chemicals, Paints and Coatings	357	3.2
Real Estate	353	3.2
Petroleum	326	3.0
Electronics	323	2.9
Total Acquisition Announcements	11,031	

Table 15—Continued

Ranked by Total Consideration Paid ($ millions)

Industry Classifications	Total Consideration Paid	Percentage of Consideration Paid in All Acquisitions
Finance, Banks and Insurance	$ 17,869	13.0%
Petroleum	14,666	10.7
Mining, Timber and Minerals	9,264	6.7
Food Processing and Agriculture	8,429	6.1
Wholesale and Retail	7,765	5.7
General Services	7,721	5.3
Machinery, Equipment and Farm Equipment	6,547	4.0
Chemicals, Paint and Coatings	4,423	3.2
Transportation	4,205	3.1
Public Utilities	4,164	3.0
Total, All Acquisitions	$137,400	

Source: W.T. Grimm & Co.

Virtually all of these large-scale acquisitions (outside continued consolidation within the petroleum sector) were unrelated to the acquirer in either classic economic or judicial senses. This pursuit of unrelated acquisitions undoubtedly reflects the antitrust constraints faced by most large U.S. companies. Their size and resource base virtually foreclosed either entry or expansion by acquisition in any market where they were a competitor or where they were perceived as a potential competitor. With growth slowing in their core markets, only large-scale unrelated diversification through acquisition offered these companies the chance to change their mix of the investment and profit opportunities.

2. Unlike the conglomerate merger movement of the 1960s where virtually every sector of the economy was affected, merger and acquisition activity since 1975 has been more severe in certain sectors than in others. Table 15 outlines those industries where acquisition activity has been most intense. The most active sectors—finance, bank, insurance, general services and wholesale and retail trade—are all service industries. Together they encompass over 30% of all acquisition activity. This activity reflects the increasing importance of services in the U.S. economy as well as the fact that these industries have a history of fragmentation.

The financial services sector has experienced the most extensive acquisition activity in recent years. Approximately 15% of all merger and acquisitions since 1975 has occurred here. * * * Of particular note is the number of acquisitions of major U.S. banks by foreign institutions. [Additionally,] many major industrial companies have also entered this field by acquiring nonbanking, financial services companies. * * * Here, large industrial companies with mature or declining product markets generally paid substantial acquisition premiums.

The second sector where significant acquisition activity has occurred is the natural resources area. This sector has witnessed relatively few acquisitions, but acquisitions which often dwarfed those done in any other industry. In 1979, the 5 largest participants have been the large oil companies which have acquired both additional oil reserves as well as companies with other natural resources reserves. At the same time, many industrial companies have also acquired natural resources companies as a way of securing a known set of inflation resistant, irreplaceable assets. Perhaps the most dramatic example of this strategy was General Electric's $2.1 billion acquisition of Utah International, a major coal producer with smaller activities in copper, uranium and other metals. Similarly, International Telephone and Telegraph, a pioneer of the conglomerate movement (which had been quiet since the antitrust proceedings following its 1968 acquisition of Hartford Insurance), acquired both a coal and an oil company. It is worth emphasizing that companies with their resource base in the United States or other safe, stable political environments have been those primarily sought after.

Since a Senate bill has been filed to limit acquisitions by the major oil companies, it is useful to outline their activities during the 1975–79 period.[19] Caught between escalating prices (leading to skyrocketing profits and cash flow) and limited numbers of attractive reinvestment opportunities, many of the major oil companies were led to either buying additional oil reserves or the reserves of natural resources outside the industry. * * * Other than Mobil's 1974/76 acquisition of Marcor, Sun's aborted diversification strategy, and Exxon's 1979 acquisition of Reliance Electric, these acquisitions have all remained within industries where the oil company's skills in finding, extracting, and producing investment intensive natural resources could be drawn upon.*

In many cases, foreign acquirers were content to take a substantial minority interest as in Friedrick Flick's 30% interest in W.R. Grace, or Robert Bosch's 9.9% interest in Borg-Warner. Minority participation

---

[19] "Oil Windfall Acquisition Act," Senate Bill 1246 (96th Congress, First Session, 1979).

* Interestingly, both the Marcor and Reliance Electric acquisitions have proven disastrous for the acquiring oil companies, with Exxon reportedly having lost in excess of $600 million on its purchase of Reliance. Berman, *Exxon's $600-Million Mistake,* 104 Fortune 68 (Oct. 19, 1981). [Ed.]

by foreign acquirers was particularly strong in industries such as semiconductors and data processing, where U.S. companies were technological leaders.

The primary difference between the large U.S. and foreign acquirers is in the type of diversification they pursued. Acquisitions by foreign acquirers were mostly related to their existing businesses, while their American counterparts tended to pursue unrelated acquisitions. Undoubtedly, a major factor behind this difference in diversification strategies was the antitrust freedom of most foreign acquirers relative to their U.S. counterparts. With generally few U.S. activities, these foreign acquirers could readily pursue acquisitions in business they already well knew. Only after becoming well-established in specific U.S. product markets were the foreign acquirers affected by U.S. antitrust law. For example, the 1970 merger of Ciba AG and J.R. Geigy, two major Swiss chemical companies, resulted in an extensive set of U.S. operations. Merger of these U.S. operations led to a consent decree with the Department of Justice whereby Ciba-Geigy agreed not to make any acquisitions for five years in its existing lines of businesses. Similarly, Nestle, the big Swiss food processor, had to sign a consent decree in order to acquire Libby McNeil & Libby, a major food canner. This antitrust limitation occurred because Nestle owned Stouffers (whose frozen foods and food management services both competed with and used Libby products) and had extensive operations itself in the U.S. Nestle's 1977 acquisition of Alcon Laboratories, a much larger acquisition than Libby McNeil & Libby, however, was readily cleared since Alcon's operations were in the health care industry and unrelated to Nestle's other U.S. activities.

Table 21

Payment Medium Used in Acquisitions *

Acquisitions of Private Companies

	1975	1976	1977	1978	1979
Cash	35%	38%	43%	31%	39%
Stock	42	42	39	44	41
Combination	22	19	17	24	20
Debt	1	1	1	1	—

Acquisitions of Public Companies

	1975	1976	1977	1978	1979
Cash	40%	53%	52%	57%	67%
Stock	47	42	38	23	14
Combination	12	5	8	19	19
Debt	1	—	2	1	—

* Based upon transactions reporting payment medium.
Source: W.T. Grimm & Co.

4. Another distinct characteristic of 1975–79 merger and acquisition activity is the widespread use of cash as a principal means of

payment. During the 1960s, by far the principal payment medium was common stock or equivalents such as convertible debt, convertible perferred, or debt plus warrants. The proliferation in the use of these common stock equivalents at the height of the conglomerate craze led many to call them "funny money" or "Chinese paper." Only rarely was a cash payment used during this acquisition spree; when used, it was usually as a sweetener to an already complicated package of securities.

In contrast, cash or a package of cash and equivalents was the payment medium in over [50] of the transactions from the mid-1970s onward. Figure 4 shows how the relative importance of cash, common stock, or a package of securities as the payment medium has changed over the last 10 years. It is worth noting that the use of cash for payment has had an inverse relationship to the general level of stock prices. Cash usage surged in 1973–74 as stock prices fell by over 40%.

*   *   *

Figure 4
Payment Medium Used in Corporate Acquisitions
1964–1969

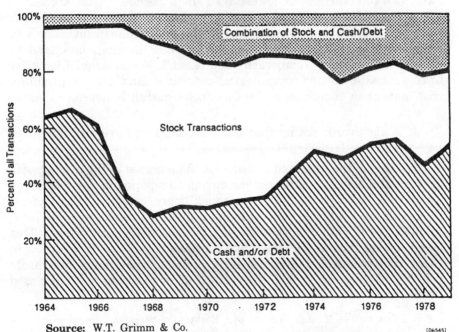

Source: W.T. Grimm & Co.   [D6545]

An additional observation about the "packaging" of acquisitions in 1975–79 is important. Since an acquisition may lead to a taxable transaction for both the buyer and the seller, tax considerations play an important part in structuring any deal. Marginal tax rates, the magnitude of capital gains, and the strength of the economy and the stock market are all significant forces in selecting an attractive securities package. Reflecting recent tax reforms and an unstable economy, many recent acquisitions have been structured to provide both taxable and tax free alternatives. In these cases, taxable cash payments are limited to less than half of the acquisition's purchase price. A package of common stock, preferred stock, convertible preferred, or debt instruments is then designed to preserve the transaction's tax status (generally tax-free or tax deferred to the seller) while meeting the acquirer's cash flow, tax and control requirements.

5. Closely linked to the use of cash as the primary payment medium for acquisitions during the 1975–79 period was the increase in the size of the average acquisition premium over market value. During the conglomerate merger wave of the 1960s, premiums on the order of 10% to 20% were common and only rarely did one exceed 40%.[20] However, in the merger movement of the late 1970s, premiums of 100% or more were not uncommon. Acquisition offers which were successful had an average premium over market of about 50%. Figure 5 shows how average acquisition premiums have changed since 1970.

The relative magnitude of the premium in a successful acquisition has been inversely related to the level of stock prices over this time period. The highest average premiums occurred in 1973–74 as the stock market reached its lowest level in a decade. That successful offers have higher premiums during periods of relatively poor stock price performance is quite natural. In this environment, investors will remember the recently higher values of their holdings and tend to consider their stocks "temporarily depressed." For an acquisition offer to be successful in this psychological context it must be at a premium that more than compensates for the stock's currently depressed value.

*   *   *

It is also worth noting that large acquisitions have also tended to have relatively large tender premiums.   *   *   *

6. One of the principal reasons for the increase in the average size of successful acquisition premiums during this period is that hostile or unwelcome takeovers have been much more common than before. Though there were only half as many acquisitions made in 1975/76 as in 1968, there were almost twice as many hostile tender offers. This trend toward hostile takeovers has continued.   *   *   * In addition to these visibly hostile takeovers, it is probable that many outwardly friendly mergers are, in fact, the vestiges of, or reactions to, undisclosed hostile overtures.

[20] S. Hayes and R. Tausig, "Tactics of Cash Takeover Bids," *Harvard Business Review* 45:2, March-April 1967, pp. 135–148, and John S.R. Shad, "The Financial Realities of Mergers," *Harvard Business Review* 47:6, November-December 1969, pp. 133–146.

Figure 5
Acquisition Premiums and the Level
of Stock Prices 1969–1979

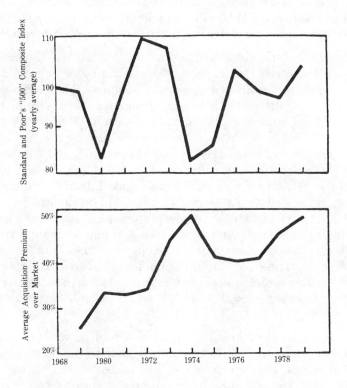

Source: W.T. Grimm & Co.   [D6546]

The number of hostile corporate takeovers became so numerous during the late 1970s that an entire supporting infrastructure grew up around it. Specialists on each side, with well-developed strategies and competitive tactics, are brought in at the slightest indication of a takeover. If the unwanted suitor cannot be driven off through adverse publicity or exhaustive litigation, the goal then shifts to extract the maximum purchase price possible. Often the target's incumbent management brings in a "white knight," or a company that is more friendly to its interests. Bidding wars and legal battles between the unwelcome suitor and the "white knight" then decide who wins. A classic example of this intercorporate warfare was the attempted takeover of Babcock & Wilcox by United Technologies in 1977. Following United's opening bid, J. Ray McDermott acquired stock in the open market and became a second unwanted suitor. As events unfolded, Babcock and Wilcox decided that McDermott would be the lesser of two evils. In the ensuing bidding battle, won by McDermott, the final price of Babcock and Wilcox was driven up by $200 million over United's initial overture, a bid which was itself at a $100 million premium over market value. In several other instances, three or even four corporate bidders entered the fray for a particularly desirable property. The 1979 divestiture of oil rich General Crude by International Paper saw Gulf, Mobil, Tenneco and Southland Royalty as bidders. International Paper took its proceeds (over $800 million) and, in turn, won a bidding battle with Weyerhaeuser for timber rich, privately owned Bodcaw.

Other takeovers were even more hostile than the General Crude situation. Two offers, one in late 1978 and the other in early 1979, set new standards for unlimited corporate warfare. The first was Mead Corporation's rebuff of Occidental Petroleum. Mead's counterattack was so thorough and complete in its exposure of Occidental's business affairs that it led to an investigation and censure by the SEC. Failing in the acquisition attempt, Oxy's president resigned and Armand Hammer, Oxy's chairman, commented that " * * * had we known of the bloodshed * * * we never would have gone into it." In early 1979, fireworks erupted with American Express' billion dollar offer for McGraw Hill. McGraw Hill's response spared no punches. Even the ethics and morals of American Express' top management was openly challenged in the business press. Leaving no stone unturned or word unsaid and implying self annihilation if unsuccessful in its defense, McGraw Hill's counterattack gave rise to what is now known in the trade as a "scorched earth" policy. Needless to say, American Express backed down.

The exact level of hostility in merger and acquisition activity is impossible to measure. Still, the hottest topic in the business press as the 1970s ended was not how to do a takeover, but rather how to defend/protect yourself (and, consequently, your company) from one. Many of the most vocal supporters of legislation aimed at limiting large-scale corporate acquisitions were not economists nor consumer activists, but rather corporate executives of middle-sized, prosperous companies that were quickly becoming the most attractive targets. It is somewhat ironic that many of these vocal critics of corporate takeovers, 1979 style, were themselves aggressive acquirers a few years earlier.[21]

7. A very distinctive and important characteristic of merger and acquisition activity in the late 1970s is that approximately one-half of all corporate acquisitions were also corporate divestitures. In contrast, during the conglomerate merger wave of the 1960s, divestitures made up only 10% to 15% of all acquisitions. Figure 6 details the ratio of divestments to acquisition activity over this period. The significance of this increased divestment activity is that a substantial portion of acquisition activity merely resulted in the "swapping" of assets by different companies. This means that acquisition activity as a driving force behind increasing aggregate economic concentration was probably

---

[21] See, for example, Walter Kissinger, "Against Forced Take-Overs," *The New York Times*, January 22, 1978, and William C. Norris in prepared testimony before the Senate Subcommittee on Antitrust and Monopoly, pp. 44–45.

a much smaller threat in the late 1970s than in the conglomerate wave of the 1960s.

The peak in divestment activity occurred in 1975–76 as many companies, both diversified and nondiversified, pruned their businesses following the severe 1974–75 recession. Product lines, operating units, and entire divisions were sold or shut down as companies attempted to rid themselves of weak or low potential units. N.L. Industries, for example, divested over 60 businesses in its shift from a lead recycler to a provider of oil well services. Many of these divestitures were businesses acquired during the conglomerate era of the 1960s, businesses that often had little relationship to the mainstream of the company's activities or whose financial and management needs were out of proportion with their performance. Others, such as General Motors' 1979 divestiture of Frigidaire, were of long-standing businesses that no longer fit the corporate image or which continued to absorb valuable assets. Finally, several companies such as W.R. Grace and Allegheny Ludlum, in a constant search for the "perfect" portfolio of businesses, developed divestiture programs that were almost as active as their acquisition programs.

8. In contrast to the modest increase in the number of acquisitions in the 1975–1979 period, there was a noticeable increase in the number of acquisitions of publicly held companies. This is shown in Table 23. While it is doubtful that this trend in itself qualifies as a distinctive characteristic of acquisition activity during the post-1975 period, it is closely related to several other characteristics previously identified. These other characteristics all provide a much clearer picture of 1975–1979 acquisition activity than does the notion of an increasing number of acquisitions of publicly held companies.

Table 23
Acquisitions of Publicly Held Companies, 1974–1979
Public Companies

Year	Announce-ments	Completed or Pending	Total Acquisitions Announcements	Public Acquisitions as a % of all Acquisitions
1974	133	68	2,861	4.7%
1975	174	130	2,297	7.6
1976	232	163	2,276	10.2
1977	267	193	2,224	12.0
1978	325	260	2,106	15.4
1979	343	248	2,128	16.1

Source: W.T. Grimm & Co.

There are three major links between the increased number of public acquisitions and the characteristics previously identified. First, publicly held companies tend to be several orders of magnitude larger than privately held companies and, therefore, it is only natural that the increasing number of public company acquisitions went hand in hand with the increasing size of acquisitions during the late 1970s. Second, since management and ownership are generally separated in public companies while closely linked in private companies, it was only natural that there were more tender offers involved in order to reach directly the public companies' owners. In addition, the so-called "hostility" surrounding these acquisitions was generally much higher since management had a limited ownership interest and any takeover would have severely effected its prerogatives. Third, since publicly held companies have a liquid market for their stock, their stockholders do not generally have as low a tax basis as shareholders in private companies for the stock. Payment packages for the acquisition of publicly held companies, therefore, tend to be biased toward the use of cash or cash equivalents, especially during periods of poor stock price performance, such as was the case during the 1970s.

Apart from these characteristics, an aspect of merger activity during the 1975–1979 period that has received considerable attention in the business press and in public policy debates is the purported preference of today's acquirers for "well-managed" companies. Corporate executives are often quoted as saying that they have neither the managerial resources nor the time to successfully undertake a turnaround. In contrast, many of the conglomerates of the 1960s argued that they brought new management talent and sophisticated management techniques to bear on poorly run companies.[22] Whether or not this preference for well-managed companies is a real and distinctive characteristic of the current merger movement is not entirely clear.

It may be that the apparent emphasis on good management is merely coincidental with the increasing scale of many acquisitions being made today. Many large companies, by virtue of their age and experience, have often established themselves as market leaders. And while market leadership and good management often go hand in hand, they are often confused by outside observers. On the other hand, the high proportion of divestments and the fact that several conglomerates (such as Gulf + Western Industries and Tyco Labs) have continued to acquire low performing companies with underutilized assets suggests that substantial opportunities for "turnarounds" still exist. Thus, it is not at all clear that current acquisition activity is as sharply focused on well-managed companies as many commentators would lead us to believe. What is more clear is that many highly visible, large public companies have been acquired, that these companies are often leaders in one or more product markets, and that due to their age, size, and market position, many have well-established, solid managements. Yet, it is also apparent that a large proportion of current merger activity involves divestitures of unwanted divisional operations whose performance does not meet the standards of the divesting parent. Thus, in the

---

[22] Hearings before Antitrust Subcommittee of the Committee on the Judiciary, U.S. House of Representatives, 91st Congress, May 13, 14, and 15, 1970.

presence of conflicting suppositions we feel that it is inappropriate to state that the acquisition of well-managed companies is a distinctive characteristic of current merger activity.

Figure 6
Corporate Divestitures or Partial Sales as a Percent of
Total Acquisition Activity
1969–1979

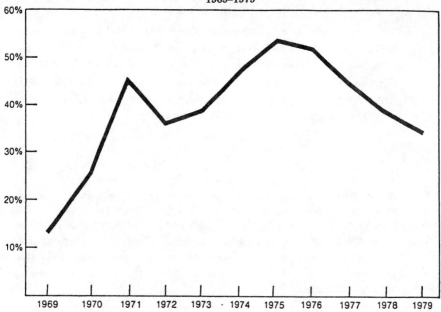

Source: W.T. Grimm & Co.

[D6547]

Summary

It is useful to summarize this merger movement's most important characteristics. Two important observations can be made from a study of aggregate merger data:

— Acquisition activity was substantial in nominal terms, but in terms of inflation-adjusted dollars it was only half as intense as in the late 1960s;

— Compared to previous merger waves, substantially fewer assets relative to existing assets in the mining and manufacturing sectors were involved. Naturally, the scale and scope of post-1975 merger activity may change with the passage of time.

Perhaps more interesting from a business policy point of view are those characteristics that emerge from a more detailed examination of merger data.

— Post-1975 acquisition activity can be characterized by both a large number of corporate divestitures and significant numbers of extremely large acquisitions in the over $100 million class.

— Acquisition activity was most intense in the service sectors. This reflects the fragmented nature of these sectors and their ever-increasing importance in the U.S. economy.

— Foreign acquirers were very active, making over 10% of all acquisitions and paying over 15% of the aggregate dollar volume.

— Cash, rather than the stock deals common of the 1960s, became the most widely used payment medium.

— Average acquisition premiums in the post-1975 period approached 50%, more than twice the premiums found in the 1960s. Premiums of 100% or more were not uncommon.

— Unfriendly takeovers were more common than in the 1960s. Intercorporate warfare, even among the conservative, old-line establishment, became widely accepted.

— Takeovers of public companies became increasingly common.

◆

Some recent work has questioned the conventional wisdom that acquisitions occur in waves. See Shughart & Tollson, *The Random Character of Merger Activity,* 15 Rand J.Econ. 500 (1984) (Annual data on U.S. mergers from 1958–1979 does not reject the hypothesis that merger levels are characterized by a white-noise process or by a stable autoregressive scheme).

C. The Modern Transactional Setting

While Salter and Weinhold's history of corporate acquisitions in the United States provides one perspective on current acquisition activity, another, less dispassionate, perspective is also important. Until 1975, no major investment banking firm would participate in a hostile takeover attempt. But once Morgan Stanley, the most conservative of the leading firms, legitimized hostile takeovers by participating in a hostile tender offer for International Nickel in 1975,[35] the conduct of parties to acquisitions have moved farther and farther from the image of "gentlemen" conducting business in a restrained and courteous fashion. Increasingly, the dominant metaphor was war: "battle" replaced "transaction" as a description of the event; "sneak attacks" by an offerer and "scorched earth" tactics by a target replaced "negotiation" as a description of the parties' activities. A useful sense of the changed character of many transactions appears from the following newspaper accounts of the unsuccessful 1979 offer by the American Express Company for McGraw-Hill, Inc.

[35] M. Salter & W. Weinhold, *Diversification Through Acquisition: Strategies for Creating Economic Value* 217–30 (1979).

AMERICAN EXPRESS GETS LOAN *

New York Times, January 12, 1979.

By ROBERT J. COLE

The American Express Company, determined to take over McGraw-Hill Inc., the giant publishing company, has borrowed $700 million to help finance the deal, well-placed industry sources disclosed yesterday.

Only three days ago, the company best known for its traveler's checks and credit cards, rocked the publishing industry when it offered to pay $830 million in cash to buy McGraw-Hill. Evidence began to build, however, that American Express was prepared to raise its bid to almost $1 billion in its determination to acquire the company.

This would mean that American Express would have to increase its $34-a-share offer to about $40. Wall Street professionals, who are gambling heavily that American Express will sweeten its bid or that another bidder will join the battle, are reported to have purchased most of the more than 750,000 shares traded Wednesday and were also heavy buyers again yesterday as the stock rose slightly to 31⅜. On Monday the stock stood at $26.

Although American Express is believed to have $1.5 billion in cash on hand, it was understood to have arranged the loan at least three weeks ago specifically for the McGraw-Hill takeover.

The money will come from a group of leading American banks, with the Morgan Guaranty Trust Company of New York playing a major role. The Chase Manhattan Bank is the traditional banker of American Express, while the First National Bank of Chicago and the Bank of California also have had long standing relationships with the company. It could not be determined, however, whether these banks were also among the lenders in this venture.

In a related development, telephone interviews with senior executives of both companies disclosed, among other things, that American Express had already devised a detailed plan to circumvent a problem that could seriously hinder its purchase of McGraw-Hill—the publishing company's ownership of four television stations.

Wall Street analysts, among others, contend that if McGraw-Hill is absolutely against the takeover, it could delay the venture for as long as a year by complaining to the Federal Communications Commission. The agency must approve any change in control of a broadcast station's ownership.

However, to avoid this problem, American Express is expected to follow a procedure already found effective by Northwest Industries in its $200 million takeover of the Coca-Cola Bottling Company of Los Angeles 15 months ago. Since that company owned a broadcasting property, Northwest is understood to have set up a voting trust under which the broadcasting operations would have their own management and board of directors—a move that did not meet with F.C.C. objection. American Express is believed to have been scrutinizing that device in the last few weeks.

The possibility that McGraw-Hill could also fight—if it chose to do so—by creating an antitrust problem is viewed as far-fetched, although such a tactic has worked in the past. However, if McGraw-Hill acquired a bank because American Express owns banks or a credit-card company because that would also create antitrust problems, McGraw-Hill most likely would face suits by stockholders for dissipation of assets on what arguably would be transactions specifically designed to frustrate a takeover.

In any case, American Express could be expected to say that if it took over McGraw-Hill, it would be prepared to divest itself of any venture that was deemed in violation of antitrust laws.

Meanwhile, as McGraw-Hill directors prepared for a meeting Monday morning—their first to consider their stance on the takeover bid—there were reliable reports that while Harold W. McGraw, Jr., chairman of McGraw-Hill, had told company insiders that he was stunned when American Express made its offer, he had in fact personally received informal overtures earlier.

The casual invitation to talk came to Mr. McGraw directly from James D. Robinson 3d, chairman of American Express, several months ago, a number of senior executives said. Mr. McGraw was understood to have pondered the proposal over a weekend and then to have told Mr. Robinson that he was not interested, but that if anyone made a hostile bid for the company, McGraw-Hill would turn to American Express to rescue the company.

While the possibility remains that McGraw-Hill will turn to another company, Wall Street analysts maintain that only a handful of companies have enough money to match the resources of such a determined bidder as American Express.

When McGraw-Hill directors meet on Monday, they could reject the offer outright or more likely may find it inadequate. They could also sue American Express to gain time. American Express then could increase its offer or, depending on circumstances, make a direct offer to the public, even perhaps at the $34 bid.

Mr. McGraw's cousin Donald, who was dismissed from the company for remarks that Mr. McGraw considered irreverent, said in an interview: "I don't think Harold would be interested if American Express offered $100 a share. He wants the independence."

There are signs, nevertheless, that other McGraws would be willing to sell for considerably less than that—along with dozens of major financial institutions that own most of the 75 percent of the stock in public hands.

McGRAW–HILL GIRDS FOR ITS BOARD MEETING TODAY TO ACT ON BID BY AMERICAN EXPRESS *

Wall Street Journal, January 15, 1979.

By PRISCILLA S. MEYER AND BILL ABRAMS

Staff Reporters of THE WALL STREET JOURNAL

NEW YORK—The curtain goes up this morning on an important scene in what promises to be one of the most fascinating corporate dramas of the year—American Express Co.'s attempt to take over McGraw-Hill Inc., publisher of Business Week magazine among other things.

Some of the nation's top corporate strategists will be pitted against one another, and the stakes could go to $1 billion or higher before it is over.

Over the weekend McGraw-Hill retained Martin Lipton, a partner in Wachtell Lipton Rosen & Katz, one of the nation's two best known legal specialists in hostile takeovers. The other is Joseph H. Flom of Skadden Arps Slate Meagher & Flom. He's working for American Express.

Morgan Stanley & Co., the investment banking firm hired by McGraw-Hill to help fend off the financial conglomerate, is said to have lined up more than 15 potential "white knight" companies ready to rush in with competitive offers for McGraw-Hill if the publishing concern's bid for independence fails. American Express is using two major investment bankers—Blyth Eastman Dillon & Co. and Lazard Freres & Co. One of the two Lazard partners working on the deal is Felix G. Rohatyn, one of the biggest merger-makers in the business.

"Dear Harold" Letter

This morning the 13 remaining members of McGraw-Hill's board must decide what to do about American Express's offer to buy the company for $34 a share, either in cash or a combination of cash and securities, totaling $830 million either way. Resignation of the 14th member was announced Friday. Roger H. Morley, American Express's president and a member of McGraw-Hill's board since early 1977, sent Harold W. McGraw Jr., chairman of McGraw-Hill, what a spokesman described as a "Dear Harold" letter.

Mr. McGraw already has reacted negatively to American Express's proposals, and sources in and out of the company assume that McGraw-Hill board will reject both American Express offers, probably quoting Morgan Stanley calling the offer "inadequate." But, as one investment banker put it, "there are 50 ways of saying no." And some large stockholders, including members of the McGraw family, have indicated willingness to sell at the right price. Board members are fiduciaries, meaning they must act in the best financial interest of the stockholders.

Should McGraw-Hill's board reject the offers, American Express could react by giving up and going away, which practically no one expects.

More likely the company would make several filings with regulatory agencies to get the project off the ground.

Tender Offer Possibility

First, American Express is apt to file with the Securities and Exchange Commission a tender offer proposal, possibly a cash offer for less than 50% of McGraw-Hill's common shares. It could offer $34 a share but there's speculation that it's more likely at that point to raise the amount. If successful, that would give American Express effective control of McGraw-Hill. Later it could make an exchange offer to acquire the shares it didn't already own with American Express securities valued at approximately the same amount, quite possibly some form of convertible preferred shares.

Second, American Express is expected to file with the Federal Trade Commission under the Hart-Scott-Rodino Act, a relatively new federal law that gives this agency time to study antitrust ramifications of "unfriendly" takeovers. This would provide a grace period of 15 days before American Express could complete any McGraw-Hill purchases. A 30-day grace period would occur before American Express could acquire the full interest in McGraw-Hill.

In addition American-Express would probably file with the New York State attorney general under the New York State takeover statute that gives the Attorney General the option of calling hearings and ruling on attempts to acquire publicly held New York-based companies such as McGraw-Hill. That could result in a 60-day delay. A test case challenging that law's constitutionality is pending before the U.S. Supreme Court.

Making Life Unbearable

At that point, assuming McGraw-Hill management decided it wouldn't acquiesce for the higher price, it would be up to Mr. McGraw, company management and its consulting wizards to pull enough tricks to make life unbearable for American Express. A number of strategies are possible and many have been at least considered in a flurry of meetings and consultations the past few days.

For one thing, there is the curious situation of Mr. Morley, who sat quietly as an outside director on McGraw-Hill's board while his own company's investment banking firm, for at least three months, was developing plans for a McGraw-Hill takeover. Indeed, Mr. Morley and Jonathan O'Herron, the Lazard partner in charge of the McGraw-Hill project, were Harvard Business School classmates and long-time friends.

Business Week said that several McGraw-Hill insiders believe Mr. Morley was scouting McGraw-Hill for his company during his two years on the board. And that, the McGraw-Hill publication says, angered Mr. McGraw.

American Express maintained: "Our legal counsel has concluded that there was nothing illegal or untoward in his being on that board."

One Scenario

Under one scenario developed in the McGraw-Hill camp over the weekend, Mr. Morley would be charged with breeching his fiduciary responsibilities to McGraw-Hill's shareholders by sitting on the Mc-Graw-Hill board and holding back information that might have permitted the company's holders to get a better price for their shares.

Under that scenario, the 21 prestigious members of the American Express board would be named as coconspirators in condoning Mr. Morley's fiduciary violations by approving the acquisition attempt. American Express's board includes such members as Archie R. Mc-Cardell, chief executive officer of International Harvester Co.; William W. Scranton, former U.S. Ambassador to the United Nations; William McChesney Martin Jr., former chairman of the Federal Reserve System; Vernon E. Jordan Jr., president of the National Urban League, and Rawleigh Warner Jr., chairman of Mobil Corp.

It's possible that even Morgan Guaranty Trust Co. of New York, McGraw-Hill's principal bank, could become embroiled as a coconspirator with Mr. Morley in such litigation, because Morgan Guaranty is the lead bank in standby lines of credit that American Express has lined up to generate funds for the takeover. American Express confirmed that it has already paid the fee for the credit lines. The amount hasn't been disclosed. Banking sources indicate, however, that these lines, if extended, could provide $900 million or more if needed in the takeover.

If the prospect of getting his bluechip board and bankers entangled in that does not cause enough problems for James D. Robinson III, American Express's chief executive, the enemy camp has some more ideas. Some would involve vigorous attempts in Washington to stir up interest in regulating some lightly regulated areas of American Express's business such as banking (its bank operations are international and fall outside the U.S. regulatory net) or traveler's checks. The collapse of a money-order-writing company in 1977 brought an outburst of federal interest in money-order and traveler's-check regulation. That interest dwindled when American Express and others contributed to the bailout.

Houghton Mifflin Example

McGraw-Hill also could consider the ploy successfully used by Houghton Mifflin Co., the Boston publishing concern, after Western

Pacific Industries Inc., parent of Western Pacific Railroad, purchased a 6.7% interest in it last year.

After several Houghton authors, representing about half the publishing company's annual revenue, threatened to "reexamine" their relations with Houghton if it were taken over by Western, Western backed out of its investment and sold its shares to Houghton.

"McGraw-Hill's assets go home in the elevator every night," said one takeover-fight veteran. "If the employes in a service business don't like the deal, forget it."

"Somebody here did suggest maybe the editors should put out a statement," said Lewis H. Young, editor-in-chief of Business Week. "But we talked about doing that and decided it would be as ineffective here as it was at New York magazine."

When Australian publisher Rupert Murdoch went after New York magazine, much of the staff threatened to quit, and did. He bought the magazine anyway and it continues.

"Great Worries"

"There is great concern among the editors and staff about this," Mr. Young said, adding, "I have great worries, but I'd like to see what American Express proposes, assuming the takeover is approved. If they promised no interference in the editorial product, perhaps it could work. But the first time they interfered I wouldn't stay. In all the years I've edited Business Week nobody has ever interfered in the editorial content."

"We strongly believe in the preservation of the independence of the communications media as well as the independence of securities-rating activities," Mr. McGraw said when he spoke last week against the American Express proposal. McGraw-Hill also owns Standard & Poor's Corp., a securities rating concern.

According to one merger expert at a big brokerage firm, American Express may have moved ahead expeditiously on its offer because of the threat of "antibigness" legislation in Washington. One top Justice Department official has indicated he'd like to see such legislation. One of his proposed tests of bigness, for example, is whether the resulting company would have sales of more than $2 billion.

In 1977, American Express sales were $3.4 billion; while McGraw-Hill had sales of $659 million.

This analyst expects anti-bigness legislation within the next two years and thus expects to see more supermergers in coming months.

Meanwhile, McGraw-Hill shares rose Friday to $33.50 apiece in New York Stock Exchange composite trading, up 62½ cents, indicating the investment community continues to believe either American Express or a white knight will end up with McGraw-Hill.

McGRAW–HILL'S DIRECTORS REJECT TAKEOVER MOVE *

Wall Street Journal, January 16, 1979.

Letter to American Express Blasts 'Lack of Intregrity'; Lawsuit Is Being Readied

---

By a WALL STREET JOURNAL Staff Reporter

NEW YORK—As expected, McGraw-Hill Inc. directors unanimously rejected American Express Co.'s offer to buy McGraw-Hill for $830 million.

In a letter to American Express directors, Harold W. McGraw, Jr., McGraw-Hill's chairman, president and chief executive officer, said the McGraw-Hill board had instructed management and legal counsel to "prepare and undertake all appropriate actions, including litigation, to protect McGraw-Hill against any improper and illegal attempts to take over McGraw-Hill or interfere with its normal business operations."

"American Express lacks the integrity, corporate morality and sensitivity to professional responsibility essential to McGraw-Hill publishing, broadcasting and credit-rating services relied upon by so many people," the letter charged.

American Express retorted that "we were disappointed in McGraw-Hill's response to our proposal. We were even more disappointed by the intemperate nature of the * * * response." James D. Robinson III, American Express's chairman, said his company would "proceed in a manner which it determined to be in the mutual interests of its shareholders and those of McGraw-Hill and wouldn't be dissuaded by Mr. McGraw's tactics."

Morley Is Attacked

McGraw-Hill specifically attacked Roger H. Morley, American Express's president and a McGraw-Hill director until he resigned from the diversified publisher's board late last week. Mr. Morley "clearly violated his fiduciary duties to McGraw-Hill and the stockholders of McGraw-Hill by misappropriating confidential information and conspiring with American Express, the members of the board of American Express and others to acquire McGraw-Hill at a price, in a manner and at a time that would be most beneficial to American Express, but to the detriment of McGraw-Hill's stockholders," the letter alleged.

Mr. McGraw said McGraw-Hill directors had authorized a suit against American Express, Mr. Morley, all other American Express directors "and every other person or entity participating with Ameri-

can Express and Mr. Morley in this conspiratorial breach of his fiduciary duty to McGraw-Hill's stockholders."

On that question, American Express's Mr. Robinson replied that
"the legal matters relating to American Express and Mr. Morley's
involvement had been fully considered by outside counsel." Mr. Robinson said he was "comfortable that American Express's proposal is legal
and proper."

McGraw-Hill's legal counsel advised, Mr. McGraw added, that
American Express's acquisition of McGraw-Hill "would raise serious
issues under the antitrust laws and can be expected to result in
litigation by the government to the detriment of both companies."

The letter also asserted that because some American Express
directors are directors of McGraw-Hill competitors, an acquisition could
prompt "multiple violations of" federal antitrust laws. Among the
directors cited was William McChesney Martin Jr., who also is a
director of Dow Jones & Co., publisher of The Wall Street Journal,
Barron's financial weekly and college textbooks. (Because of age limitations, Mr. Martin won't stand for reelection to the Dow Jones board
at the annual shareholders meeting in March, a Dow Jones spokesman
said.)

Other Conflicts Cited

The McGraw-Hill letter said the acquisition could give rise to other
conflicts of interest. "American Express holds more than $3 billion in
state and municipal securities and underwrites and insures additional
state and municipal securities—securities that must be rated independently by McGraw-Hill's Standard & Poor's division."

"Such insensitivity and disregard of integrity and corporate morality is inconsistent with the reputation many American Express directors
have enjoyed over the years," Mr. McGraw noted. "Perhaps it can be
explained as impulsive, precipitous, and immature actions taken by
younger members of management before the more experienced members of your board had ample opportunity to fully consider this reckless
proposal. * * *"

Meanwhile, McGraw-Hill released a memorandum from Lewis H.
Young, editor-in-chief of Business Week magazine, McGraw-Hill's most
visible publication, to Mr. McGraw. The memorandum expressed concern that ownership by American Express might compromise the independence of Business Week.

"The editors and I have five main concerns," Mr. Young said.

"That American Express would taboo certain story subjects, such
as the troubles in the entertainment credit card business or problems in
the casualty insurance industry, because it had major business activity
in them.

"That, if American Express allowed coverage of such subjects, our readers wouldn't believe what we published, thinking it was biased in favor of the owner of the magazine.

"That American Express wouldn't support the editors after they had written unpopular ideas or critical stories that unleashed corporate or government complaints.

Currying Favor a Concern

"That American Express would use the editorial columns of the magazine to sell its other products and services or to curry favor with government officials to aid its international businesses.

"That American Express, because of its financial orientation, wouldn't make the financial resources available for the staff to do the aggressive and comprehensive reporting job our readers expect.

"Although American Express is regarded as a well-managed financial conglomerate," Mr. Young wrote, "it has never been a commercial publisher of controversial subjects such as political economy, economic policy, financial news, labor, corporate strategies or government regulation. Its executives have never been exposed to the kinds of pressure their peers in corporations or in government can bring to bear when a story displeases such people. Yet, it is the ability to absorb such criticism without interfering in the journalistic process that makes for successful publishing, both journalistically and financially.

"I feel that Business Week wouldn't be able to retain or recruit good, talented journalists if the ownership of the magazine appeared to have other, more urgent commercial interests than the publication, and there was an inclination to use the editorial columns of the magazine to further those interests."

In a letter yesterday to Mr. McGraw, Mr. Robinson of American Express replied to some of Mr. McGraw's, and Mr. Young's concerns about the independence of Business Week.

"Editorial and media integrity and independence are as respected by, and as important to us as I know they are to you. . . . Not only do we regard . . . freedom as an important ethical principle but we believe that complete editorial freedom is the only business policy that makes sense in publications, broadcasting or rating agencies.

"Harold, I can state without equivocation that the editorial freedom and independence of McGraw-Hill's many activities, which you have fostered and supported so thoroughly and professionally, will be fully maintained after the combination of our businesses. We are prepared to work with you to reinforce your principles and we are confident that there are practical techniques for ensuring that is done."

Commenting separately on the McGraw-Hill response to the acquisition proposal, American Express said: "Rather than address the merits of the proposal, (the McGraw-Hill letter) consisted of unwarranted, unfounded attacks on American Express, its directors and management." Mr. Robinson accused Mr. McGraw of trying to "confuse the issues on personal and irrelevant grounds."

At a news conference, Mr. McGraw denied reports that there is dissension in the McGraw family over the American Express proposal. However, he said family members would have to vote "as any other individual shareholders" on any American Express offer that might be made and voted upon. Certain family members have indicated that their opposition to the takeover might soften if American Express raises its $34-a-share offer. The family is believed to own between 20% and 25% of McGraw-Hill's 24.2 million shares outstanding.

Mr. McGraw also was asked if he uses an American Express card.

"Yes," he replied, "but two weeks ago, in preparation for a trip to Japan, I obtained a Master Charge card and a Visa card. I'll leave to you to speculate which I will make primary use of."

AMERICAN EXPRESS GIVES DETAILS OF PLAN TO BUY McGRAW–HILL IN FILING WITH SEC *

Wall Street Journal, January 17, 1979.

By a WALL STREET JOURNAL Staff Reporter

NEW YORK—American Express Co. filed details of its proposed tender offer for McGraw-Hill Inc. with the Securities and Exchange Commission.

American Express says in the 150-page filing that it proposes to offer the previously disclosed $34 apiece for any and all of McGraw-Hill's 24.5 million shares, including both those outstanding and issuable on conversion. The company estimates this would cost $880 million, including related expenses.

But the filing doesn't prevent American Express from raising its offering price later or from changing the terms to cash and securities. If American Express "varies the terms of its offer before the expiration date by increasing the consideration to be paid for shares, (American Express) will pay such increased amount for all shares purchased pursuant to the offer, whether or not such shares have been tendered or purchased prior to such variation in the terms of the offer," the filing said.

It added, "The offer, if made, will be made only in compliance with applicable law. Until such time, American Express reserves the right to amend, modify or revoke the offer."

American Express explained in detail the regulatory filings it expects to make in connection with its tender offer and the amount of time each might take, delaying the start or finish of its proposed plan.

Such delays translate into money for traders, speculators or arbitragers who are buying McGraw-Hill shares with an eye toward making a marginal profit when they are tendered.

New York State Filing

American Express said it filed a registration statement with New York State's attorney general under the New York Security Takeover Disclosure Act. Early yesterday morning McGraw-Hill filed suit in New York state court to force American Express to make that filing, but that McGraw-Hill suit became academic when the SEC filing disclosed American Express had already filed with New York.

A tender offer can't be made for 20 days after the New York filing, and the attorney general has 15 days from the filing to schedule a public hearing. If a hearing is called, the company couldn't start its offer until it complied with any terms ordered by the attorney general. The hearing must begin within 40 days of the filing, and the attorney general would have 30 days after that to determine whether the company had complied with the act. In short, all this could take 70 days or more, if hearings are called.

In addition, prior approval of the Federal Communications Commission is needed before control of broadcast licenses may be transferred. McGraw-Hill owns four television stations. On Monday, McGraw-Hill requested that the FCC take action to prohibit American Express from making an offer to acquire control of McGraw-Hill without prior favorable action by the FCC on an application.

Petition to FCC

American Express said in its filing that it proposes to seek dismissal of that request because it intends to comply with communications laws. Conceding that normally such applications to transfer control "may take a substantial period," American Express said it would petition the FCC to consent to arrangements allowing it to complete the offer "within a relatively short time."

The FCC could prove a stumbling block, according to some lawyers. One way of expediting the merger would be to set up temporary trusts to hold the TV stations while American Express's applications were under way, but this hasn't been permitted in truly hostile takeover situations. And the Federal Reserve Board has rejected the trust route with hostile bank takeovers. Several years ago, some companies acquired TV stations as a method of discouraging unfriendly takeovers.

In addition, American Express said it plans to file with the Federal Trade Commission and the Antitrust Division of the Justice Department under the Hart-Scott-Rodino Antitrust Improvements Act, which would provide a variety of possible delays for filing or concluding the offer.

The longest potential delay, however, appears to involve a filing to be made in connection with a 45%-owned McGraw-Hill subsidiary, for which the waiting period expires on Feb. 15, with an additional 20-day delay if either the FTC or the Justice Department requests more information.

Lending Agreement Clues

That subsidiary, Rock-McGraw Inc., is a joint venture with a company owned by Rockefeller Center Inc., privately held by the Rockefeller family. The center houses McGraw-Hill's headquarters in New York.

In addition, there are clues to the timing American Express expects from terms of its bank lending agreement, disclosed in the SEC filing. It indicates that if $700 million isn't "taken down" by American Express by July 1, the company will have to pay an additional commitment fee on the unused amount at an annual rate of 5% of the prime lending rate of Morgan Guaranty Trust Co., the agent bank. Currently, Morgan's prime, or minimum, rate is $11\frac{3}{4}\%$.

McGraw-Hill closed at $33.125, off 37.5 cents, on the New York Stock Exchange composite tape yesterday, as 250,400 shares traded. The issue didn't trade on Monday when McGraw-Hill's board met and said that it "categorically rejected American Express's proposal as illegal, improper and unsolicited." Yesterday, McGraw-Hill said it has nothing to add as a result of American Express's SEC filing "other than to reiterate that it intends to spare absolutely no effort in protecting McGraw-Hill against this illegal takeover attempt."

American Express, in yesterday's filing, said once the offer is made it will accept all shares tendered. If it acquires more than 50%, under New York law it would have the power to elect all McGraw-Hill directors at the next annual meeting, the filing said. At any rate, it said, American Express would seek to get some members on the board, depending on how many shares were tendered.

Class Suit by Holder

If two-thirds were tendered, it said, it could proclaim a full merger without the affirmative vote of the holders of remaining shares.

Meanwhile, a McGraw-Hill holder brought a class-action lawsuit against McGraw-Hill in a New York state court late yesterday. The shareholder asked for unspecified compensatory damages from Mc-Graw-Hill and its board for holders of the concern. He alleged that McGraw-Hill and its board violated their fiduciary duty to holders by refusing to negotiate with American Express for the "highest price available" and instead retaining a law firm specializing in "defensive tactics."

A McGraw-Hill spokesman said he couldn't comment on the allegations in the class-action suit "because it's a matter that will be duly considered in the courts."

On Monday, McGraw-Hill's board authorized management and counsel to proceed with a suit against Roger H. Morley, president of

American Express and formerly a McGraw-Hill director, along with American Express and its directors, charging a "conspiratorial breach" of Mr. Morley's fiduciary duty to McGraw-Hill's holders. This action hasn't yet been filed.

American Express's filing with the SEC yesterday says Mr. Morley, who was a McGraw-Hill director between January 1977 and last Friday, "received nonpublic information from time to time about (McGraw-Hill), including 1978 estimates and 1979 projections of revenues and earnings received late in 1978." But, it adds, "none of the information received by Mr. Morley was material" to American Express's decision to make the offer.

A REPLY TO AN "UNCONSCIONABLE" ACTION
Wall Street Journal, January 19, 1979.

[McGraw-Hill Paid Advertisement]

In response to the concerns voiced by the many constituents served by McGraw-Hill—authors, journalists, business people around the world, employees, and shareholders of McGraw-Hill, Inc.—and to all those who are interested in the serious issues raised by the proposed illegal takeover of McGraw-Hill by American Express, the following letter, sent to the Board of Directors of American Express Company, is being published in its entirety.

To the Board of Directors American Express Company:

The McGraw-Hill Board of Directors has unanimously instructed me to categorically reject your request to discuss the illegal, improper, unsolicited, and surprising American Express proposal to take over McGraw-Hill.

Further, the McGraw-Hill Board, upon the advice of independent legal counsel, has directed management to vigorously protect the integrity and vital interests of this company against any takeover attempt you may launch.

You should understand that there are several significant and fundamental reasons that dictate this determination.

1. The *independence* and *credibility* of McGraw-Hill is vital to fulfilling its responsibilities to investors, the academic, educational, and scientific communities, as well as those who rely on the information and advisory services we offer.

It would be improper, inappropriate, and in direct violation of this responsibility to entrust McGraw-Hill's sensitive public interest activities (including Business Week and the Standard & Poor's credit rating services) to a company that pays virtually no federal income taxes on its hundreds of millions of dollars of annual income, operates in a manner that raises serious questions under the banking and securities laws, and pays no interest on the billions of dollars it derives from the issuance of travelers checks to the public.

One dramatic illustration of the potential for serious conflict of interest is the fact that, as a major investor in securities, American Express holds more than $3 billion in state and municipal securities and underwrites and insures additional state and municipal securities—securities that must be independently rated by McGraw-Hill's Standard & Poor's division!

The background and manner of your proposal demonstrates that American Express lacks the integrity, corporate morality, and sensitivity to professional responsibility essential to the McGraw-Hill publishing, broadcasting, and credit rating services relied upon by so many people.

Frankly, this surprises us. Such insensitivity and disregard of integrity and corporate morality is inconsistent with the reputation many American Express directors have enjoyed over the years. Perhaps it can be explained as impulsive, precipitous, and immature actions taken by younger members of management before the more experienced members of your board had ample opportunity to fully consider this reckless proposal and all of its implications to each company.

Mr. Roger H. Morley, President of American Express, was a director of McGraw-Hill when you formulated and made your proposal. He clearly violated his fiduciary duties to McGraw-Hill and the stockholders of McGraw-Hill by misappropriating confidential information and conspiring with American Express, the members of the Board of Directors of American Express, and others to acquire McGraw-Hill at a price, in a manner, and at a time that would be most beneficial to American Express, but to the detriment of McGraw-Hill's stockholders.

This breach of trust and conspiracy to subvert the interests of McGraw-Hill and its stockholders was initiated in the spring of 1978 by your Chairman, Mr. James D. Robinson, III. In seeking to solicit our interest in a merger with American Express, Mr. Robinson gave me his absolute word and assurance that if we were not interested in pursuing the matter, nothing further would be done. It was not in McGraw-Hill's best interest and so I made it clear that we were not interested in pursuing it. Yet, as recent events have shown, American Express continued in its plan and preparation. In light of this, Mr. Morley's remaining on the McGraw-Hill Board of Directors for several months following the rejection of Mr. Robinson's approach and our being assured that it would be dropped was insidious. The obvious conflict of interest created by your secret plan to pursue an acquisition of McGraw-Hill while Mr. Morley remained a director is an unprecedented breach of trust.

American Express' conspiratorial approach and lack of integrity is further emphasized by your obtaining the financing for acquisition of McGraw-Hill from Morgan Guaranty Trust Company which for more than 50 years, has been McGraw-Hill's principal bank—a fact well known to your Mr. Morley. Any company that would use its financial power to cause a bank to violate its relationship with a client lacks the integrity and morality essential to the business of McGraw-Hill.

2. Any combination of American Express and McGraw-Hill would be illegal.

The McGraw-Hill Board of Directors was advised by two independent law firms, White & Case and Wachtell, Lipton, Rosen & Katz, that, in their opinion, your acquisition of McGraw-Hill would raise serious issues under the antitrust laws and can be expected to result in litigation by the government to the detriment of both companies and their stockholders.

In addition, counsel has advised that the prior approval of the Federal Communications Commission and other regulatory agencies is required before American Express could acquire McGraw-Hill, and that any attempt by American Express to do so without such approval would be illegal.

Counsel also has advised that because many of American Express' directors are apparently directors of corporations which are competitors of McGraw-Hill, should American Express acquire McGraw-Hill, there could be multiple violations of United States Anti-Trust Laws and the Federal Communications Act (1934). For example:

• Howard L. Clark is a director of Xerox Corp., which is an educational publisher and also provides information systems;

• Henry H. Henley, Jr., is a director of General Electric Co., which owns and operates radio and TV stations;

• Vernon E. Jordan, Jr., is also a director of Xerox;

• William McChesney Martin, Jr., is a director of Dow Jones & Co., which is publisher of The Wall Street Journal and Barron's and which also owns Richard D. Irwin, publisher of college textbooks.

• William W. Scranton is a director of The New York Times Company which, in addition to newspapers, operates radio and TV stations and publishes consumer magazines and books.

The McGraw-Hill Board of Directors believes that the long-run interests of the stockholders of McGraw-Hill would best be served by McGraw-Hill remaining an independent company, and that a takeover of McGraw-Hill would have major adverse impact on the businesses and future profitability of McGraw-Hill.

Accordingly, the McGraw-Hill Board of Directors has instructed and authorized management and legal counsel to prepare and undertake all appropriate actions, including litigation, to protect McGraw-Hill against any improper and illegal attempts to take over McGraw-Hill or interfere with its normal business operations.

The McGraw-Hill Board of Directors also has authorized a lawsuit against American Express, Mr. Morley, each other director of American

Express, and every other person or entity participating with American Express and Mr. Morley in this conspiratorial breach of his fiduciary duty to McGraw-Hill's stockholders to recover the hundreds of millions of dollars of damages resulting from this wrongful conduct.

To permit American Express' unconscionable actions to succeed would jeopardize the underlying basis for public confidence in American Express as well as McGraw-Hill. For our part, we intend to spare absolutely no effort in protecting McGraw-Hill.

> Very truly yours,
> Harold W. McGraw, Jr.
> Chairman and President

AMERICAN EXPRESS SUES McGRAW–HILL *

New York Times, January 19, 1979.

Conspiracy to Avert Bid Cited

By ROBERT J. COLE

The American Express Company, in a blistering 22-page suit against McGraw-Hill Inc., accused the publishing company yesterday of using "libelous, false and misleading statements" to deprive investors of a "fair opportunity to evaluate" its $880 million takeover bid.

Part of an increasingly hostile takeover battle, the suit named both McGraw-Hill and Harold W. McGraw Jr., chairman of McGraw-Hill, as defendants and charged that they entered into a conspiracy to "oppose, obstruct, delay and defeat" and "interfere with American Express's right to make" an offer:

McGraw-Hill's management and directors were not named as defendants but were charged with having "aided and abetted" the alleged conspiracy. The suit further charged that they were "under the dominance and control" of Mr. McGraw.

McGraw Assails Suit

Responding to the suit, McGraw-Hill called it "a diversionary and spurious tactic designed to distract attention from the real issues." It called the bid illegal and an "improper surprise attack."

American Express maintained in its suit that McGraw-Hill had "falsely claimed" that Roger H. Morley, president of American Express and, until last week, a director of McGraw-Hill, had "violated his fiduciary duties" to McGraw-Hill and investors by "misappropriating confidential information and conspiring" with American Express. "No such breach of duty or misappropriation had occurred," American Express said.

The suit further contended that McGraw-Hill had "falsely claimed" that James D. Robinson 3d, chairman of American Express, had initiated a breach of trust and that he had given Mr. McGraw his "absolute word" in conversations six months ago that American Express would drop takeover plans unless McGraw-Hill approved. "No such representations were made," the suit said.

The rash of lawsuits in the contest for control of McGraw-Hill is spreading rapidly. McGraw-Hill has already filed one suit in New York and is expected to file others. It has also petitioned the Federal Communications Commission to intervene because McGraw-Hill owns four television stations. A McGraw-Hill stockholder, meanwhile, is suing McGraw-Hill for depriving him and other stockholders of a chance to make a profit.

Last week, in a letter personally delivered by Mr. Robinson to Mr. McGraw, the big financial-services company offered to pay $34 a share for McGraw-Hill stock at a time when the shares were selling for $26.

In further charges, American Express alleged that the defendants and others violated Federal and New York State laws by disseminating false and misleading statements, including those in a letter from McGraw-Hill to American Express reprinted as a paid advertisement in The New York Times and other newspapers. The suit said these and other statements were designed to induce investors to reject the company's offer and were circulated without first making filings with the Securities and Exchange Commission. McGraw-Hill said it had made all required filings.

"The public statements disseminated by defendants in furtherance of their unlawful conduct have gone far beyond the bounds of fair comment contemplated by the Federal securities laws," the suit continued. These statements, it said, were "intended to, and did, irreparably harm" American Express and "destroy the atmosphere necessary for businesslike discussions concerning a combination of the companies."

American Express said that it still remained hopeful that discussions could be undertaken "in a friendly and businesslike manner."

The suit further charged that Mr. McGraw and his company had formed a group, mostly members of the McGraw family owning nearly 12 percent of McGraw-Hill stock, to defeat American Express without filing papers with the S.E.C.

American Express asked the court to order McGraw-Hill to "take immediate corrective action," file its statements with the S.E.C. and supply the company with a stockholder list so that it could send investors corrective materials.

In a related development, Mrs. Elizabeth McGraw-Webster, whose husband, George, sits on the McGraw-Hill board, was reported to have sold 50,000 of her estimated one million McGraw-Hill shares last June at around $24 a share, $10 less than the American Express offer. Mrs Webster declined to comment.

TAKEOVER TREMORS *
AS CHARGES INTENSIFY, STRATEGY IS
EMERGING IN McGRAW–HILL BATTLE
Wall Street Journal, January 29, 1979.

American Express Considers Isolating of Publications; Roger
Morley's Defense

———

Split in the McGraw Family

———

By PRISCILLA S. MEYER

Staff Reporter of THE WALL STREET JOURNAL

NEW YORK—When American Express Co.'s two top officials
walked out of Harold McGraw's office three weeks ago after presenting
their $880 million plan to take over McGraw-Hill Inc., James D.
Robinson III, the American Express chairman, figured they had a deal.

"Robinson called me right afterward, and he was ecstatic," recalls
Felix G. Rohatyn, a partner in Lazard Freres & Co., which is managing
the deal for American Express. "He said they'd had a marvelous,
civilized, friendly discussion and that Harold McGraw said how much
he respected American Express. They even talked about issuing a joint
press release."

But the euphoria was short-lived. Right after that late-night
meeting, Mr. McGraw conferred with several key executives, who were
horrified by the proposal. Whatever openness the 61-year-old McGraw-
Hill chairman initially had to the deal soon turned to heated opposition. In short order, the company fired an angry barrage of letters and
lawsuits at American Express, charging lack of integrity, lack of
corporate morality, antitrust violations and conflict of interest. Most
of the interest conflict allegations have been focused on Roger H.
Morley, American Express's 48-year-old president, who has been accused of brewing plans for the takeover while he was sitting on the
McGraw-Hill board.

A Family Split

At this point, the Federal Trade Commission, the Securities and
Exchange Commission and a House Banking subcommittee are looking
into the takeover attempt. Issues related to the proposal have been
taken up by the Federal Communications Commission, the U.S. Comptroller of the Currency, the Federal Reserve Board, the New York State
attorney general and the New York State Banking Department.

Moreover, McGraw family members, who are said to hold some 20% of McGraw-Hill's shares, are widely split and are rowing in different directions. Five family holders, with 11% of the shares, have said they will support Harold McGraw.

But late last week, Donald C. McGraw, who holds 2.5% sent his cousin Harold a telegram recommending that Harold change his position and negotiate with American Express or any other company that might come along. Sources say some other McGraws are about to begin putting similar pressure on Harold McGraw.

Future Strategies

As attacks mount on both sides, observers say the new few weeks will be critical to the success or failure of what is turning out to be one of the most hotly contested takeover bids in recent time. Documents filed in support of various pieces of litigation and talks with officials on both sides indicate that the following strategies are likely to emerge in the days and weeks ahead:

—American Express is willing to consider setting up independent governing panels to insulate the editorial boards of Business Week and other McGraw-Hill publications from any editorial interference by American Express.

—Internally, at least, McGraw-Hill is taking the position that if American Express will simply go away, McGraw-Hill will gladly agree to drop everything, even the litigation over Mr. Morley's role. "I'd personally give (Morley) a big hug and forget the whole thing," says one insider.

—It appears that Mr. Morley's defense won't be that he wasn't involved in the takeover plan. Rather, he will apparently assert that he obtained outside opinion supporting each action taken by him and by American Express. And he will contend that such actions were based on information available to the public, not privileged inside information.

"Integrity Is Fundamental"

In describing the late-night meeting Jan. 8 with Harold McGraw, Mr. Robinson of American Express says, "We were prepared to be in there for five or 10 minutes and dodge an ashtray if need be. But we had a very constructive talk. If he'd come across hostile, we'd have backed off."

To his associates, Mr. McGraw has characterized the meeting somewhat differently. That Harold McGraw had so little rebuttal at the time and that the meeting itself lasted more than an hour are being attributed more to Mr. McGraw's shock over the $34-a-share takeover bid than to any responsiveness on his part, according to a McGraw-Hill insider.

Whatever the case, Mr. Robinson currently professes deep shock at Mr. McGraw's subsequent diatribes. "The most maddening thing is the extent to which he's taken off on our integrity," he says. "Integrity is fundamental to every business we're in. It's the kind of business where you make promises to pay and you keep those promises. Does he think we'd put hundreds of millions of dollars on the line and then tinker with the asset base? We're not idiots."

Mr. Robinson says that to counter the issues of editorial freedom raised by McGraw-Hill, he would be willing to set up an independent governing panel for Business Week. This would be similar to a plan under which a board of trustees insulates the editors of the Economist of London from its corporate owners. "Something like that shouldn't hurt the magazine's profitability," he says. "And if we went to the panel to say we felt the magazine should be doing this or that, they could always say they disagreed, and that would be the end of it."

Mr. Robinson is somewhat miffed that his experience with Travel & Leisure, American Express's travel magazine, isn't being considered by McGraw-Hill. "Our credit-card division will occasionally come up here yelling and screaming, 'Did you see that damn Travel & Leisure article on that hotel chain? Well, they're canceling their card agreement. When are you going to put a stop to it?' I tell them they can write what they feel they need to write, as long as they're doing their homework. That's what you're going to have to put up with."

For McGraw-Hill's big securities-rating unit, Standard & Poor's, Mr. Robinson envisons setting up some sort of oversight committee made up of independent outsiders who have wide credibility and prestige. But McGraw-Hill has adamantly refused to discuss any aspect of the takeover with American Express, terming the bid "illegal, improper and unsolicited." As a result, Mr. Robinson says that "whatever is appropriate and maximizes our chances we will do."

Though the evidently growing rift within the McGraw family would seem to help American Express's cause, there is one school of thought emerging that American Express just might surprise everyone and pull out of the deal, especially if McGraw-Hill in return would drop all litigation against the company and Mr. Morley, the American Express president.

"I may be the only analyst on the Street that thinks this, but I do think that (American Express's) odds of winning are less than even and that it may decide to withdraw," says J. Kendrick Noble Jr., an analyst at Paine Webber Mitchell Hutchins Inc. American Express could do so gracefully, Mr. Noble adds, simply by holding to its $34 bid and saying that to go any higher would be too costly. Mr. Robinson refuses to discuss under what circumstances he would be prepared to withdraw. But he adds, "I may be able to talk about that later this week."

An Approach in June

Much of McGraw-Hill's current rancor stems from the fact that last June, Mr. Robinson telephoned Harold McGraw to suggest a merger of the two companies. Mr. McGraw turned him down. According to McGraw-Hill, American Express indicated at the time that it wouldn't pursue the matter further.

Based on that assurance, Mr. Morley was permitted to remain on the McGraw-Hill board and on the financial policy and audit committees. "He continued to share the trust and confidence of McGraw-Hill directors and senior management and to have access" to confidential information, McGraw-Hill said in a filing in a New York state court. At the time, Harold McGraw even suggested that American Express might be a "white knight" if ever McGraw-Hill needed rescue in an unfriendly takeover attempt.

But documents filed by American Express in connection with the state-court proceeding indicate that months before the Jan. 8 meeting with Harold McGraw, American Express had settled on McGraw-Hill as a prospective "target" for a takeover attempt. The documents show that American Express was prepared for either a friendly or a "hostile" takeover.

The "Chinese Wall"

On Mr. Morley's behalf, American Express appears to be developing a "Chinese Wall" defense. According to testimony in a New York state court last week by an American Express attorney, Mr. Morley had set up procedures to keep all his McGraw-Hill papers "separately and under lock and key."

According to one source, Mr. Morley apparently intends to confirm that he was indeed central to the plan to acquire McGraw-Hill. Acquisitions, in fact, are one of Mr. Morley's specific responsibilities at American Express. But he is expected to argue that he never relied on any "inside information" and that he constantly obtained outside opinions from investment bankers such as Lazard Freres, who arrived at their conclusions from public information.

When American Express filed its proposed offer with the SEC, it contended that none of the information received by Mr. Morley in his role as a McGraw-Hill director was "material" to the decision of American Express to make its bid. But the SEC is known to be questioning the exact nature of the inside information he obtained and why American Express doesn't consider it "material."

Elaborating on that in state court last week, an American Express attorney said, "What that was meant to convey isn't that (inside information) was considered and then decided to be unimportant, but (people other than Mr. Morley) never received it. The information wasn't conveyed."

Observed Judge Martin B. Stecher, "He may not have disclosed (inside information) to his associates, but he certainly disclosed it to himself and wearing his hat as a director and officer of American Express." Both sides will have a chance to elaborate on that point on Thursday in the hearing before Judge Stecher to consider whether or not to enjoin American Express from the takeover bid.

FIRM WITHDRAWS CONTESTED OFFER FOR McGRAW–HILL *
Wall Street Journal, January 30, 1979.

But American Express Holds Out Option of 'Friendly' Merger
at $40 a Share

———

By a WALL STREET JOURNAL Staff Reporter

NEW YORK—American Express Co. said it is withdrawing its hotly contested offer for McGraw-Hill Inc. but still held out the option of a merger on "friendly" terms.

American Express said the "friendly" transaction would involve an offer of $40 a share for McGraw-Hill, up from the $34 a share it initially proposed, plus a promise to work out a system to protect the editorial independence of McGraw-Hill's publishing subsidiaries.

At $40 a share, American Express would be paying about $1.18 billion cash for McGraw-Hill including converted shares and expenses. That would be up from $880 million, on the same basis, in the earlier proposed tender offer. McGraw-Hill has about 24.4 million shares outstanding.

This is the first attempt by a big nonjournalistic corporation to buy a big national publication in the U.S., and among the attacks has been that the takeover would threaten editorial independence of Business Week and the other McGraw-Hill publications, as well as the credibility of Standard & Poor's Corp., its big securities-rating service.

American Express said it is prepared to work out suitable arrangements to ensure independence of these operations. It gave as an example arrangements at The Economist of London, which has a panel of trustees to insulate editors from the corporate owners.

In an eight-page letter sent to each McGraw-Hill board member yesterday, American Express said "no offer will be made without your board's recommendation of, or agreement not to oppose, such an offer."

But the proposed offer is conditioned on a response from the majority of McGraw-Hill's board "within a reasonable period of time" either that it won't oppose the offer, or at least that it won't oppose it by "propaganda, lobbying, litigation or otherwise."

Barrage of Litigation

Attorneys for both sides indicated this move by American Express probably makes "moot" most of the barrage of litigation filed against American Express to enjoin the takeover, since the offer in question has been withdrawn and the company has indicated it won't proceed in a hostile situation. That would include a suit in New York state court charging that Roger H. Morley, American Express's president, breached his fiduciary duty by sitting on the McGraw-Hill board while his company planned the takeover attempt.

All this puts the ball in McGraw-Hill's court and the publisher's board will hold its regular meeting tomorrow. Some sources say it's possible the board won't take any final action that quickly on the proposal.

McGraw-Hill, in a statement, said it was "gratified" that American Express has seen fit to withdraw "its unilateral proposed tender offer at $34 a share." And the statement reiterated that McGraw-Hill's board "has previously set forth its position as to the legality and appropriateness of any combination of McGraw-Hill and American Express.

McGraw-Hill has filed charges in state and federal court and with various regulatory agencies alleging the combination would violate federal antitrust and securities laws, and that it would violate numerous state statutes as well.

Some read that as an indication that McGraw-Hill would reject negotiating the proposed transaction with American Express on such grounds, even though the statement further said the board "would, of course, consider American Express's request."

Eagerness to Sell

An important consideration, however, will be the McGraw-Hill shareholders who have indicated an eagerness to sell to American Express, or anyone else, at prices higher than the $26 a share, quoted three weeks ago for McGraw-Hill shares, before word of the first American Express proposal.

"I believe it would be unfair not to have this proposal of $40 a share submitted to shareholders," said Maxwell M. Geffen, 82 years old, who says he holds about 100,000 McGraw-Hill shares. "But I'm afraid that isn't going to happen. Obviously Harold McGraw (McGraw-Hill's chairman) will react a different way," he said, adding that he had talked to Mr. McGraw during the week.

Mr. Geffen said he wasn't prepared to say whether he would consider bringing a class action lawsuit if the McGraw-Hill board doesn't cooperate with American Express. But he said he had acquired his shares as a result of having big holdings in Standard & Poor's and Medical World News, which were acquired by McGraw-Hill, and helped negotiate those sales.

"There were big questions then whether Standard & Poor's would lose its independence by being bought by a big company like McGraw-Hill," he observed.

Trading in McGraw-Hill shares was halted on the New York Stock Exchange yesterday. The issue closed last Friday at $31.75 a share.

The American Express letter said agreement by McGraw-Hill to the conditions in its latest proposal wouldn't preclude the McGraw-Hill board from recommending a higher offer from another company if a higher bidder comes along.

In the letter, James D. Robinson III, chairman of American Express, laid out for the McGraw-Hill board the reasons he had believed he was initially negotiating a friendly transaction, and rebutted various charges that American Express's decision to make the takeover involved inside information obtained through Mr. Morley.

"Late last year our investment bankers indicated that they believed that members of the McGraw family desired to sell their McGraw-Hill stock and suggested that we consider McGraw-Hill as a possible acquisition candidate. We did so, acting solely on the basis of publicly available information," Mr. Robinson said in the letter.

McGRAW SPURNS NEW OFFER *
New York Times, February 1, 1979.

But American Express Keeps $40 Bid Open

By EDWIN McDOWELL

The board of directors of McGraw-Hill Inc. unanimously rejected yesterday a $1 billion takeover offer from the American Express Company, saying that it was "not in the best interests of McGraw-Hill and its shareholders."

American Express, declaring that it was "disappointed and surprised at this precipitous action" that prevented McGraw-Hill's shareholders "from considering the merits of our proposal," said the offer would remain open until March 1.

After the initial American Express offer of $34 a share was rejected earlier this month by the 13-member McGraw-Hill board, James D. Robinson 3d, chairman of American Express, raised the offer to $40 on Monday of this week. He said then that the company would abandon its takeover attempt if a majority of the board still opposed it.

Issue of Independence Raised

The rejection appears to be a victory for Harold W. McGraw Jr., chairman and chief executive of the large publishing company. He has vehemently opposed the takeover, contending that it would compromise the editorial integrity and independence of such company properties as Business Week magazine and Standard & Poor's bond-rating service.

Some analysts credit Mr. McGraw with waging a brilliant counterattack by playing up precisely those issues of integrity and editorial independence, while giving only a passing nod to questions of possible antitrust or Federal banking law violations.

"If McGraw-Hill had been an industrial company, I'm sure American Express would have won," a close observer said.

But while Mr. McGraw apparently has the upper hand in the struggle between corporate giants, some close to the struggle believe that American Express is not yet out of the running. They believe that yesterday's decision to keep its offer open another month, coupled with the wording of its statement yesterday, is designed to give McGraw-Hill stockholders time to force the directors to change their minds. Earlier this month, a shareholder filed a class-action suit against McGraw-Hill for its failure to accept the original American Express offer.

McGraw-Hill stock last sold at $31.75 a share on the New York Stock Exchange when trading was suspended late last Friday. It sold for $26 a share when American Express made its $34 bid.

Meanwhile, McGraw-Hill management has taken steps that appear designed, at least in part, to mollify stockholder unhappiness. At yesterday's meeting, on the 49th floor of the McGraw-Hill building in mid-Manhattan, the directors declared a quarterly dividend of 32 cents a share, up from 25 cents. A news release announcing the 28 percent increase noted that the company had increased its dividend every year since 1974.

On Tuesday, McGraw-Hill reported record earnings and revenue for the fourth quarter and for 1978. Mr. McGraw announced that yearly earnings were up 24 percent to $63.7 million, or $2.57 a share, while revenue were up 16 percent to $761.2 million. And he confidently predicted even better results in 1979.

The question is whether these results will placate holders of the approximately 24.4 million shares of McGraw-Hill stock. The McGraw family owns about 20 percent of the stock in the company that James H. McGraw founded almost 100 years ago, while some 45 banks hold about 16 percent of it.

Family Divided on Merger

Donald C. McGraw Jr., a former McGraw-Hill officer and director, who was forced out of the company by his cousin Harold, has said that he is amenable to an American Express takeover at 40. He owns some 622,000 shares of stock, about 2.5 percent, although he serves as trustee for an unknown number of other shares.

But Donald's younger brother, John L. McGraw, a board member, who owns 609,000 shares of stock, apparently feels otherwise. Although he resigned as a company officer last May amid rumors of bad feelings between him and Harold McGraw, McGraw-Hill spokesman said that he attended yesterday's meeting and fully concurred with the decision. Efforts to reach John McGraw and other directors were unavailing.

Yesterday's apparent triumph has not noticeably lessened Harold McGraw's opposition to American Express. In a letter to Mr. Robinson yesterday, Mr. McGraw said that the sweetened offer of earlier this week "reflects the same disregard, as did your original offer, of the legal and regulatory problems involved in the takeover of McGraw-Hill by American Express, problems which have been confirmed rather than resolved since our rejection of your original offer of Jan. 8."

American Express said yesterday that it had "carefully reviewed" all those problems and had "complete confidence that there are no legal or regulatory reasons that would prevent us from making and consummating the offer."

'Serious Breach of Trust'

Mr. McGraw also said that Mr. Robinson's proposal this week "once again attempts to obscure the serious breach of trust committed by Mr. Roger H. Morley in simultaneously serving as a director of McGraw-Hill Inc. while participating in plans to take over the company."

Mr. Morley, president of American Express, resigned as a McGraw-Hill director shortly after the initial American Express offer. In a $500 million suit filed against American Express in mid-January, McGraw-Hill charged that Mr. Morley had divulged secret information to American Express that he obtained while on the McGraw-Hill board. American Express denied that Mr. Morley had acted as a "Trojan horse" in the takeover bid.

Irony of Recent Recovery

The irony in the takeover bid, in the view of some Wall Street analysts, is that, even taking into account whatever hyperbole accompanied McGraw-Hill's announcement of company earnings this week, the company finally appears to have straightened out the management problems that plagued it for more than 10 years, beginning in the middle of the 60's. From 1967 to 1971, earnings tumbled and stock prices plummeted from 56½ to 5⅜. The company's long-term debt climbed to almost $100 million.

Since then, McGraw-Hill has reoriented itself and diversified. Although it is still primarily a publishing company, with 29 magazines and 28 newsletters, which are mostly "spin-offs" from those magazines, it is increasingly emphasizing electronic data-based information systems customized for specialized industries.

Mr. McGraw recently told an interviewer that the company's future growth would come from the "information industry"—from being positioned to provide quick, accurate data to companies, individuals and government. He said that he regarded these services as not only potentially profitable but virtually recession-resistant.

CANCELED POLL OF McGRAW-HILL HOLDERS SIGNALS END TO AMERICAN EXPRESS BID *
Wall Street Journal, February 26, 1979.

By PRISCILLA S. MEYER
Staff Reporter of THE WALL STREET JOURNAL

NEW YORK—When Guy P. Wyser-Pratte threw in the towel last Friday on efforts to poll McGraw-Hill Inc.'s shareholders, Wall Street knew it was the end of any prospects that McGraw-Hill's board might be forced to consider American Express Co.'s $40-a-share takeover proposal.

McGraw-Hill stock dropped $2.50 a share to $26.375, pennies more than the market price Jan. 9 when American Express announced its takeover plans.

The 38-year-old Mr. Wyser-Pratte is an arbitrager, and by any account he's an unusual one. As an executive vice president and a director of Bache Halsey Stuart Shields Inc., he heads Bache's very profitable arbitrage department. Paid on a formula based on his department's profits, last year he earned $864,855, more than five times the salary of Bache's chief executive officer.

Arbitragers are the professional risk takers that, among other things, buy huge amounts of shares of target companies when a takeover appears likely. The idea is to make a quick killing in the stock. But sometimes they lose, often millions of dollars on one merger.

Shares Snapped Up

In the case of McGraw-Hill, Wall Street sources estimate that after American Express's takeover bid as much as 20%, or nearly five million, of McGraw-Hill's 24.4 million shares were snapped up by arbitragers.

With the exception of Ivan F. Boesky & Co. another of the Street's biggest arbitragers, and Mr. Wyser-Pratte, most of the largest arbitrage positions in McGraw-Hill are believed to be pretty well whittled down or liquidated—many at a loss. Selling by arbitragers, including the arbitrage department of Goldman Sachs & Co., over the past few weeks accounted for much of the high volume in McGraw-Hill.

Boesky is believed to hold more than 300,000 shares and possibly to have added a few shares to that position after word two weeks ago that Mr. Wyser-Pratte planned to poll McGraw-Hill's shareholders.

Mr. Wyser-Pratte has a small position by his company's standards. Bache waited a few days after the takeover bid and then bought 46,900 shares at $30 to $31.50. Mr. Wyser-Pratte waited a few days because, "I had to wait for 'piggy' to stop buying," he says. "Ivan the Pig" is the irreverent nickname some arbitragers give to Boesky, which generally comes in heavily when the market opens after a takeover bid. Boesky has enormous funds for investment—mostly from limited partnerships.

Buying After Boesky

Mr. Wyser-Pratte and other arbitragers claim that heavy buying sends the stock prices up until Boesky finishes, when prices fall slightly. Then others, like Bache, do their buying.

"I froze my position," Mr. Wyser-Pratte says, when he decided to get involved with a shareholders committee to poll McGraw-Hill holders. That decision was around Feb. 13, he says. "And I'm going to hold onto the shares for a while," he adds.

Traditionally arbitragers stay in the shadows, grumbling to themselves, when they lose. Not Mr. Wyser-Pratte.

Two years ago he became thoroughly angered at John C. Suerth, chairman of Gerber Products Co., who turned down a tender offer by Anderson, Clayton & Co. for Gerber. Mr. Wyser-Pratte journeyed to Fremont, Mich., where Gerber was holding its annual meeting in the local high school gymnasium. There he pelted Mr. Suerth with accusations until Mr. Suerth finally cut him off.

Mr. Wyser-Pratte says he plans to attend McGraw-Hill's annual meeting in April.

Mr. Wyser-Pratte also has been known to finance shareholder class-action lawsuits. "Wyser-Pratte's always been a sore loser," says one merger specialist advising McGraw-Hill.

"Out for Themselves"

Mr. Wyser-Pratte sees it differently. "Everyone in these things always claims they're doing what's in the best interest of the shareholders—the boards, the investment bankers, even the class-action lawyers. But everyone's really out for themselves. No one represents the interests of the shareholders," he says, claiming he could have jeopardized his own position because he froze his McGraw-Hill holdings when he attempted his McGraw-Hill shareholder poll. Beyond that, he expected to pay one-third of the costs of the polling effort that he estimates could have totaled $500,000.

Mr. Wyser-Pratte attributes withdrawal by his shareholders' committee to "subtle intimidation" by McGraw-Hill and its attorneys, and vows he's learned a lot for the next time he takes on directors and management that he figures aren't giving shareholders, including himself, a fair shake.

"For one thing, I'll get more shareholders involved," he says, saying that mud can only be slung in so many directions.

"My lawyers labeled it a children's crusade, and McGraw-Hill tried to take the children into the trenches," he claims.

Marshall Field Model

The Bache executive's plan, which he'd worked out with attorneys in an attempt last year to try to sway management of Marshall Field & Co., was a simple Securities and Exchange Commission filing by the three shareholder members of the committee that would then attempt to poll other McGraw-Hill shareholders. The approach hadn't been attempted before, as it wasn't ultimately used in the Marshall Field attempt. The results would be presented to McGraw-Hill management or the courts to help sway their opinion toward negotiating with American Express. The offer by American Express remains open until Thursday.

Things went downhill after the plan was made. McGraw-Hill's attorneys made clear they'd sue to force a more complicated, and expensive, proxy statement filing. They suggested Mr. Wyser-Pratte,

Bache, its directors, and the two other shareholders would quickly become targets of expensive litigation and other "scorched earth" tactics already used against American Express.

First, Donald C. McGraw Jr., holder of 622,000 McGraw-Hill shares and a former officer and director of McGraw-Hill, left for his yacht in the Bahamas. Then Maxwell Geffen, an 82-year-old holder of around 100,000 shares decided he'd had all he could take.

"We've decided this whole thing has become too complicated and there's too much risk of civil lawsuits to continue, so we're withdrawing any actions," Mr. Geffen said last Thursday on behalf of himself and Donald McGraw.

By that time the Bache board has determined to back its executive vice president's SEC filing anyway. But it was too late, and Bache too, issued a withdrawal statement.

*

PART I. MODERN FINANCIAL THEORY: THE REQUIRED ANALYTICAL TOOLS

Modern financial theory is commonly treated as beginning in the late 1950's. Prior to that time, leading finance texts, such as A. Dewing, *The Financial Policy of Corporations* (1934), were rich in institutional detail, but offered little in the way of comprehensive theory. As a result, their normative statements about the "correct" approach to issues like the proper capital structure for a corporation were sometimes logically inconsistent and, in any event, were not based on propositions whose accuracy could be empirically tested. They were thus ad hoc both theoretically and empirically.

The late 1950's marked a shift in scholarly emphasis from description to theory, and finance began its transmutation from a separate discipline oriented in large measure to practitioners, to a specialized application of microeconomics with the theoretical rigor and mathematical complexity associated with academic economics. This shift was facilitated by the initial availability in 1964 of computer tapes prepared by the Center for Research in Security Prices at the University of Chicago. These tapes contained monthly closing prices, dividends and changes in capital structure for all stocks listed on the New York Stock Exchange from 1926 forward, and daily closing prices on all stocks listed on the New York and American Exchanges since 1962. The availability of this data encouraged the development of statistical techniques that have made the theoretical statements of modern finance theory almost uniquely testable.[1]

This Part provides a survey of the aspects of modern financial theory necessary to understand how business transactions are valued. It thus provides a critical foundation for later analysis of how business lawyers might increase—create—transaction value. The gains from developing a facility with the tools of modern financial theory, however, are broader than that. Stated most generally, finance both provides guidance concerning the factors that determine the value of capital assets, and suggests analytic techniques that facilitate efforts to work with the factors in order to achieve a desired end. So, for example, it has been commonly claimed that the earnings a company reports for financial accounting purposes, regardless of whether these earnings reflect actual cash flows, is an important determinant of the value of its stock. And this assertion, in turn, has fueled a major controversy over the "right" way to account for acquisitions, both sides taking quite seriously the idea that reported, as opposed to real earnings, influence share price. At bottom, however, this conflict is over what factors determine the value of a capital asset—in this case, do reported earn-

---

[1] A more detailed history of modern financial theory is found in Jensen & Smith, The Theory of Corporate Finance: An Historical Overview, in *The Modern Theory of Corporate Finance* 2 (M. Jensen & C. Smith, eds. 1983).

ings influence the price of corporate stock. As a result, financial theory is directly relevant. Similarly, important elements of corporate law, such as whether acquiring company and target company shareholders get to vote on an acquisition transaction, depend on whether different forms of transactions are substantively similar. If similarity is taken to mean "of equal value," then understanding the factors that determine value is central to understanding when different forms of transactions should be treated as the same.

An important point thus emerges: Whether implicitly or explicitly, valuation is a central issue bearing on a wide variety of legal concerns. Understanding the techniques of modern financial theory is thus crucial to understanding and evaluating the applicable law.[2] A second point, somewhat less familiar but equally important, should also be stressed. Individuals maximize the value of their assets As a result, understanding how assets are valued provides a very useful way to predict, and to guide, private behavior. For example, imagine negotiating the terms of a loan agreement on behalf of the lender. How do you systematically anticipate what post-transaction behavior by the borrower the lender must be protected against? Financial theory, by specifying how the borrower would go about maximizing the value of its assets, provides a coherent framework in which to address the problem. This function of finance will be particularly evident in our examination of the valuation of options in Chapter Seven, and in our consideration of the private ordering aspects of corporate acquisitions in Part V.

Modern financial theory thus has application to both the public ordering and private ordering aspects of business transactions. Chapters Two and Three lay the groundwork for study of valuation. Chapter Two examines valuation in the simple world where there is no risk—in which the size and timely receipt of all future cash flows is certain. Chapter Three complicates matters by introducing the concept of risk and considering how the value of future cash flows can be expressed when their size and eventual receipt are uncertain. Chapter Four then confronts the problem of valuation under uncertainty and presents the Capital Asset Pricing Model—modern financial theory's paradigm of how assets should be priced under uncertainty. Chapter Five examines the Efficient Capital Market Hypothesis, a second paradigm of modern finance. Here the issue is what mechanisms cause market prices to approach those that capital asset pricing theory predicts. Chapter Six then moves to a more practical perspective. In an imperfect world, no decision-maker has perfect information. The question is how to evaluate, before the decision, whether to expend resources on acquiring additional information and, after the decision, whether the expenditure was worthwhile. Assistance with the pre-decision problem is offered through analysis of the concepts of the expected value of perfect information and sensitivity analysis; assistance with post-decision evaluation is offered through introduction to

[2] This theme is at the heart of the original groundbreaking effort of Victor Brudney and Marvin Chirlstein to bring to bear the techniques of modern financial theory on a variety of corporate problems. V. Brudney & M. Chirlstein, *Cases and Materials on Corporate Finance* (1st ed. 1972).

cumulative abnormal return statistical analysis. Finally, Chapter Seven focuses on valuation of a different kind of asset—an option—and introduces a final paradigm of modern finance: option pricing theory. We will return to each of the concepts examined in this Part—the time value of money, capital asset pricing, market efficiency, the value of information, and option pricing—throughout our analysis of corporate acquisitions and the business lawyer's potential for creating value.

CHAPTER TWO: VALUATION UNDER CERTAINTY

We begin learning how business transactions are valued by considering how assets would be valued in a world of complete certainty. In such a world, the only distinction between different assets is the quantity and timing of the future cash flows they generate. There is no risk (1) of not actually receiving the money, or (2) of the amount actually received differing from the amount expected, or (3) of receiving the money at a different time than anticipated.

This world of complete certainty, of course, is entirely artificial. Even so certain a cash flow as the interest payment on a short term Treasury bill is subject to the risk of inflation—the risk that the "real" amount received will be lower, will purchase less because of inflation, than the amount expected to be received. The value of the construct, however, is that it isolates one important determinant of value without complicating its analysis by the presence of other determinants. In this artificial world, value is determined only by the *time value of money*. Conceptually, the concept of time value is no more complicated than opportunity cost. The reason why a dollar now is worth more than one to be received in a year is because a dollar received now can be consumed now, rather than a year from now, or invested for a year. The mathematics of the concept are developed in Section A of this Chapter. In Section B, the concept and its application are considered in the context of capital budgeting: how to compare different streams of future income.

A. The Time Value of Money

J. VAN HORNE, FINANCIAL MANAGEMENT AND POLICY *

17–28 (5th ed. 1980).

In any economy in which time preferences of individuals, firms, and governments result in positive rates of interest, the time value of money is an important concept. For example, stockholders will place a higher value on an investment that promises returns over the next five years than on an investment that promises identical returns for years six through ten. Consequently, the timing of expected future cash flows is extremely important in the investment of funds. In essence, the methods proposed allow us to isolate differences in the timing of cash flows for various investments by discounting these cash flows to their present value.

Compound Interest

The notion of compound interest is central to understanding the mathematics of finance. The term itself merely implies that interest paid on a loan or an investment is added to the principal; as a result, interest is earned on interest. In this section, we examine a class of problems that can be solved using the same concept; these problems will be illustrated with a number of examples. To begin our discussion, consider a person who has $100 in a savings account. If the interest rate is 5 percent compounded annually, how much will he have at the end of a year? Setting the problem up, we solve for the terminal value of the account at the end of the year (TV_1)

$$TV_1 = \$100(1 + .05) = \$105$$

[If left for a second year, the $105 earns 5% interest again, and] becomes $110.25, as $5 in interest is earned on the initial $100 and $0.25 is earned on the $5 interest paid at the end of the first year. In other words, interest is earned on previously earned interest—hence the name compound interest. Therefore the terminal value at the end of the second year is $100 times 1.05 squared, or times 1.1025. Thus

$$TV_2 = \$100(1.05)^2 = \$110.25$$

At the end of three years, the individual would have

$$TV_3 = \$100(1 + .05)^3 = \$115.76$$

Looked at in a different way, $100 grows to $105 at the end of the first year if the interest rate is 5 percent, and when we multiply this amount by 1.05 we obtain $110.25 at the end of the second year. Multiplying $110.25 by 1.05, we obtain $115.76 at the end of the third year.

Similarly, at the end of n years, the terminal value of a deposit is
$$TV_n = X_o(1 + r)^n \qquad (2\text{--}1)$$
where X_o = amount of savings a the beginning
r = interest rate

While this equation may seem formidable, it is a simple matter to employ when using a calculator.

Table 2–1

Illustration of Compound Interest With $100 Initial Deposit and 5 Percent Interest

Period	Beginning Value	Interest Earned During Period (5 percent of Beginning Value)	Terminal Value
1	$100.00	$5.00	$105.00
2	105.00	5.25	110.25
3	110.25	5.51	115.76
4	115.76	5.79	121.55
5	121.55	6.08	127.63
6	127.63	6.38	134.01
7	134.01	6.70	140.71

Table 2-1—Continued

Period	Beginning Value	Interest Earned During Period (5 percent of Beginning Value)	Terminal Value
8	140.71	7.04	147.75
9	147.75	7.38	155.13
10	155.13	7.76	162.89

In Table 2–1, we show the terminal values for our example problem at the end of years 1 through 10. This table illustrates the concept of interest being earned on interest. Equation (2–1) is our fundamental formula for calculating terminal values. As can be visualized, the greater the interest rate r, and the greater the number of periods n, the greater the terminal value.

While our concern has been with interest rates, the concept involved applies to compound growth of any sort. For example, we might wish to determine the future earnings of a firm if they were expected to grow at a 10 percent compound rate. If earnings were $100,000 now, they would be the following at the end of years 1 through 5:

Year	Growth Factor	Expected Earnings
1	(1.10)	$110,000
2	$(1.10)^2$	121,000
3	$(1.10)^3$	133,100
4	$(1.10)^4$	146,410
5	$(1.10)^5$	161,051

Similarly, we can determine the level at the end of so many years for other problems involving compound growth. * * *

Tables of Terminal Values Using Eq. (2–1), one can derive tables of terminal values (also known as future values). An example is shown in Table 2–2 for interest rates of 1 to 10 percent. For the 5 percent column, we note that the terminal values shown for $1 invested at this compound rate correspond to our calculations in Table 2–1 for $100. Also, it is seen that for any rows involving two or more years, terminal value increases at an increasing rate with increases in the interest rate. This is particularly apparent for one hundred years in the future, where $1.00 deposited today will be worth only $2.70 if the interest rate is 1 percent, whereas it will be worth $13,780.59 if the interest rate is 10 percent. Behold the wonders of compound interest!

Compounding More Than Once a Year

Up to now, we have assumed that interest was paid annually. While it is easiest to work with this assumption, we consider now the relationship between terminal value and interest rates for different periods of compounding. To begin, suppose that interest is paid semi-annually [—that is, 2.5% is paid every 6 months.] If one then deposited $100 in a savings account at 5 percent, the terminal value at the end of six months would be

$$TV_{1/2} = \$100\left(1 + \frac{.05}{2}\right) = \$102.50$$

and at the end of a year it would be

$$TV_1 = \$100\left(1 + \frac{.05}{2}\right)^2 = \$105.0625$$

This amount compares with $105.00 if interest were paid only once a year. The $0.0625 difference is attributable to the fact that during the second six months, interest is earned on the $2.50 in interest paid at the end of the first six months. The more times during a year that interest is paid, the greater the terminal value at the end of a given year.

Table 2–2

Terminal Value of One Dollar at the End of N years

Year	1%	2%	3%	4%	5%	6%	7%	8%	9%	10%
1	1.0100	1.0200	1.0300	1.0400	1.0500	1.0600	1.0700	1.0800	1.0900	1.1000
2	1.0201	1.0404	1.0609	1.0816	1.1025	1.1236	1.1449	1.1664	1.1881	1.2100
3	1.0303	1.0612	1.0927	1.1249	1.1576	1.1910	1.2250	1.2597	1.2950	1.3310
4	1.0406	1.0824	1.1255	1.1699	1.2155	1.2625	1.3108	1.3605	1.4116	1.4641
5	1.0510	1.1041	1.1593	1.2167	1.2763	1.3382	1.4026	1.4693	1.5386	1.6105
6	1.0615	1.1262	1.1941	1.2653	1.3401	1.4185	1.5077	1.5869	1.6771	1.7716
7	1.0721	1.1487	1.2299	1.3159	1.4071	1.5036	1.6058	1.7138	1.8280	1.9487
8	1.0829	1.1717	1.2668	1.3686	1.4775	1.5938	1.7182	1.8509	1.9926	2.1436
9	1.0937	1.1951	1.3048	1.4233	1.5513	1.6895	1.8385	1.9990	2.1719	2.3579
10	1.1046	1.2190	1.3439	1.4802	1.6289	1.7908	1.9672	2.1589	2.3674	2.5937
11	1.1157	1.2434	1.3842	1.5395	1.7103	1.8983	2.1049	2.3316	2.5804	2.8531
12	1.1268	1.2682	1.4258	1.6010	1.7959	2.0122	2.2522	2.5182	2.8127	3.1384
13	1.1381	1.2936	1.4685	1.6651	1.8856	2.1329	2.4098	2.7196	3.0658	3.4523
14	1.1495	1.3195	1.5126	1.7317	1.9799	2.2609	2.5785	2.9372	3.3417	3.7975
15	1.1610	1.3459	1.5580	1.8009	2.0789	2.3966	2.7590	3.1722	3.6425	4.1772
20	1.2202	1.4859	1.8061	2.1911	2.6533	3.2071	3.8697	4.6610	5.6044	6.7275
25	1.2824	1.6406	2.0938	2.6658	3.3864	4.2919	5.4274	6.8485	8.6231	10.8347
50	1.6446	2.6916	4.3839	7.1067	11.4674	18.4201	29.4570	46.9016	74.3575	117.3907
100	2.7048	7.2446	19.2186	50.5049	131.5010	339.3014	867.7149	2,199.7569	5,529.0304	13,780.5890

The general formula for solving for the terminal value at the end of year n where interest is paid m times a year is

$$TV_n = X_o\left(1 + \frac{r}{m}\right)^{mn}$$

$$(2\text{–}2)$$

To illustrate, suppose that in our previous example interest were paid quarterly and that we wished again to know the terminal value at the end of one year. It would be

$$TV_1 = \$100\left(1 + \frac{.05}{4}\right)^4 = \$105.09$$

which, of course, is higher than that which occurs either with semiannual or with annual compounding.

The terminal value at the end of three years for the above example with quarterly interest payments is

$$TV_3 = \$100\left(1 + \frac{.05}{4}\right)^{12} = \$116.08$$

This compares with a terminal value with semiannual compounding of

$$TV_3 = \$100\left(1 + \frac{.05}{2}\right)^6 = \$115.97$$

and with annual compounding of

$$TV_3 = \$100\left(1 + \frac{.05}{1}\right)^3 = \$115.76$$

The greater the number of years, the greater the difference in terminal values that occur between two different methods of compounding.

If interest were compounded daily on the basis of a 365-day year, the terminal value of an X_o initial deposit at the end of n years would be

$$TV_n = X_o\left(1 + \frac{r}{365}\right)^{365n}$$

$$(2\text{--}3)$$

As m approaches infinity, the term $(1 + r/m)^{mn}$ approaches e^{rn}, where e is approximately 2.71828 and is defined as

$$e = \lim_{m\infty}\left(1 + \frac{1}{m}\right)^m$$

$$(2\text{--}4)$$

where ∞ is the sign for infinity. To see that e approaches 2.71828 as m increases, simply increase m in the above expression from, say, 5 to 10 to 20 and solve for e. The terminal value at the end of n years of an initial deposit of X_o where interest is compounded continuously at a rate of r is

$$TV_n = X_o e^{rn}$$

$$(2\text{--}5)$$

For our example problem, the terminal value at the end of three years would be

$$TV_3 = \$100(2.71828)^{(.05)(3)} = \$116.18$$

This compares with a terminal value with annual compounding of

$$TV_3 = \$100(1.05)^3 = \$115.76$$

and with semiannual compounding of

$$TV_3 = \$100\left(1 + \frac{.05}{1}\right)^6 = \$115.97$$

Continuous compounding results in the maximum possible terminal value at the end of n periods for a given rate of interest. As m is increased in Eq. (2–2), the terminal value increases at a decreasing rate until ultimately it approaches that achieved with continuous compounding.

Present Values

Suppose you wish to save for the future by putting aside a certain amount of funds today with the expectation that they will grow with interest to some larger amount in the future. To be more specific, suppose that you want to buy a stereo set which will cost $700 one year from now and that a local savings and loan association pays 6 percent on one-year deposits. How much must you put aside in order to have $700 one year hence? If we let A_1 represent the amount of money you wish to have one year from now, PV the amount saved, and k the annual interest rate, we have

$$A_1 = PV(1 + k) \qquad\qquad (2\text{–}6)$$

For our example problem, this becomes

$$\$700 = PV(1.06)$$

Solving for PV, we obtain

$$PV = \frac{\$700}{1.06} = \$660.38$$

Therefore $660.38 would need to be saved now in order to have $700 one year hence. Stated another way, $660.38 is the *present value* of $700 to be received at the end of one year when the interest rate involved is 6 percent.

The present value of a sum to be received two years from now is

$$PV = \frac{A_2}{(1 - k)^2}$$

$$\qquad\qquad (2\text{–}7)$$

which for our example problem would be

$$PV = \frac{\$700}{(1.06)^2} = \frac{\$700}{1.1236} = \$623.00$$

Thus $700 two years from now has a lower present value than $700 one year from now. Indeed, that is the whole idea of the time value of money.

In solving present-value problems, it is useful to express the interest factor separately from the amount to be received in the future. For example, our problem above can be expressed as

$$PV = \$700 \left[\frac{1}{(1.06)^2} \right] = \$623.00$$

In this way we are able to isolate the interest factor, and this isolation facilitates present-value calculations. In such calculations, the interest rate is known as the *discount rate,* and henceforth we will refer to it as such.

So far we have considered only present-value calculations for amounts of money to be received one and two years in the future. However, the principles are the same for amounts to be received further in the future. For example, the present value of $1 to be received at the end of n years is

$$PV = \frac{1}{(1 - k)^n} \tag{2-8}$$

To illustrate, suppose we wish to determine the present value of $1 to be received five years from now when the discount rate is 10 percent. Setting up the problem, we have

$$S1\left[\frac{1}{(1.10)^5}\right] = \$0.62092$$

This tells us that $1 five years from now is worth approximately 62 cents today if the discount rate is 10 percent.

Fortunately, present-value tables [or appropriately programmed calculators] exist that relieve us of having to make these calculations every time we have a problem to solve. Such a table is shown in Table A-1. Here, present values of $1, known as discount factors, are shown for discount rates from 1 percent to 40 percent and for periods 1 through 25 in the future. We see in the table that for a 10 percent discount rate, the discount factor for five years in the future is 0.62092, just as we calculated. For one year, two years, and three years in the future, we see that the discount factors are 0.90909, 0.82645, and 0.75131, respectively. These discount factors are merely the result of the following calculations: $1/(1.10)$; $1/(1.10)^2$; and $1/(1.10)^3$.

If we had an uneven series of cash flows—$1 one year hence, $3 two years hence, and $2 three years from now—the present value of this series, using a 10 percent discount rate, would be:

PV of $1 to be received at end of one
  year $1(0.90909) = 0.90909
PV of $3 to be received at end of two
  years $3(0.82645) = 2.47935
PV of $2 to be received at end of
  three years $2(0.75131) = 1.50262

              Present value of series $4,89106

Given a present-value table, we are able to calculate the present value for any series of future cash flows in the above manner.

Annuities However, the procedure can be simplified for a series if the cash flows in each future period are the same. A series of this sort is known as an *annuity*. Suppose that in a series of future cash flows, $1 was to be received at the end of each of the next three years. The calculation of the present value of this stream, using the above procedure, would be

  PV of $1 to be received in one year   =   0.90909
  PV of $1 to be received in two years   =* 0.82645
  PV of $1 to be received in three years =   0.75131

          Present value of series $2.48685

With an even series of future cash flows, it is unnecessary to go through these calculations. The discount factor, 2.48685, can be applied directly. We would simply multiply $1 by 2.48685 to obtain $2.48685.

Present-value tables for even series of cash flows have been developed that allow us to look up the appropriate compound discount factor. An example is shown in Table A–2.

We note that the discount factor for an even series of cash flows for three years, using a 10 percent discount rate, is 2.4868—as we calculated. Thus, for an even series of cash flows, we simply multiply the appropriate discount factor times the cash flow. If we wish to know the present value, using an 8 percent discount rate, of a future stream of $5 cash flows to be received at the end of each year over a four-year period, the calculation would be

$$\$5(3.3121) = \$16.56$$

Using the present-value tables shown in Tables A–1 and A–2 we are able to calculate the present value of various future streams of cash flows.

If we trace across any of the rows in Tables A–1 and A–2, we can see that the higher the discount rate, the lower the discount factor. However, we see that the relationship is not linear, but rather that the discount factor decreases at a decreasing rate with increases in the discount rate. Therefore the present value of an amount of money to be received in the future decreases at a decreasing rate as the discount rate increases. The relationship is illustrated in Figure 2–1. At a zero rate of discount, the present value of $1 to be received in the future is $1. In other words, there is no time value of money. As the discount rate increases, however, the present value declines but at a decreasing rate. As the discount rate approaches infinity, the present value of the future $1 approaches zero.

Figure 2–1
Relationship Between Present Value and the Discount Rate

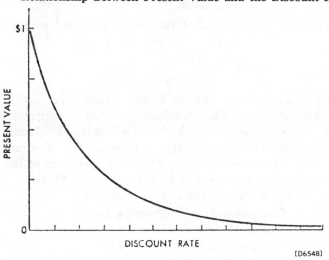

[D6548]

Present Value When Interest
Is Compounded More Then Once a Year

When interest is compounded more than once a year, the formula for calculating present values must be revised along the same lines as for the calculation of terminal value. Instead of dividing the future cash flow by $(1 + k)^n$ as we do when annual compounding is involved, the present value is determined by

$$PV = \frac{A_n}{\left(1 + \dfrac{k}{m}\right)^{mn}}$$

(2–9)

where, as before, A_n is the cash flow at the end of year n, m is the number of times a year interest is compounded, and k is the discount rate. The present value of $100 to be received at the end of year 3, where the discount rate is 10 percent compounded quarterly, is

$$PV = \frac{\$100}{\left(1 + \dfrac{.10}{4}\right)^{(4)(3)}} = \$74.36$$

The present value of $100 at the end of one year with a discount rate of 100 percent compounded monthly is

$$PV = \frac{\$100}{\left(1 + \dfrac{1}{12}\right)^{12}} = \$38.27$$

When interest is compounded continuously, the present value of a cash flow at the end of year n is

$$PV = \frac{A_n}{e^{rn}}$$

(2–10)

where e is approximately 2.71828. The present value of $100 to be received at the end of three years with a discount rate of 10 percent compounded continuously is

$$PV = \frac{\$100}{2.71828^{(.10)(3)}} = \$74.08$$

On the other hand, if the discount rate is compounded only annually, we have

$$PV = \frac{\$100}{(1.10)^3} = \$75.13$$

Thus the fewer times a year the discount rate is compounded, the greater the present value. This relationship is just the opposite of that for terminal values. To illustrate the relationship between present value and the number of times a year the discount rate is compounded, consider again our example involving $100 to be received at the end of three years with a discount rate of 10 percent. The following present values result from various compounding intervals.[1]

Compounding	Present Value
Annual	$75.13
Semiannual	74.62
Quarterly	74.36
Monthly	74.17
Continuous	74.08

[1] For semiannual compounding, m is 2 in Eq. (2–9) and mn is 6. With monthly compounding, m is 12 and mn is 36.

We see that the present value decreases but at a decreasing rate as the compounding interval shortens, the limit being continuous compounding.

Internal Rate of Return or Yield

The internal rate of return or yield for an investment is the discount rate that equates the present value of the expected cash outflows with the present value of the expected inflows. Mathematically, it is represented by that rate, r, such that

$$\sum_{t=o}^{n} \left[\frac{A_t}{(1 + r)^t} \right] = 0 \qquad (2\text{-}11)$$

where A_t is the cash flow for period t, whether it be a net cash outflow or inflow, n is the last period in which a cash flow is expected, and the capital Greek sigma denotes the sum of discounted cash flows at the end of periods o through n. If the initial cash outlay or cost occurs at time o, Eq. (2-11) can be expressed as

$$A_o = \frac{A_1}{(1 + r)} + \frac{A_2}{(1 + r)^2} + \cdots + \frac{A_n}{(1 + r)^n} \qquad (2\text{-}12)$$

Thus r is the rate that discounts the stream of future cash flows—A_1 through A_n—to equal the initial outlay at time O—A_o. [The higher the internal rate of return, the better the investment, other things (i.e., risk) equal.] Implicitly assumed is that the cash inflows received from the investment are reinvested to realize the same rate of return as r.*

*   *   *

To illustrate the use of Eq. (2-12), suppose that we have an investment opportunity that calls for a cash outlay at time O of $18,000 and is expected to provide cash inflows of $5,600 at the end of each of the next five years. The problem can be expressed as

$$18,000 = \frac{5,600}{(1 + r)} + \frac{5,600}{(1 + r)^2} + \frac{5,600}{(1 + r)^3} + \frac{5,600}{(1 + r)^4} + \frac{5,600}{(1 + r)^5} \qquad (2\text{-}13)$$

Solving for the internal rate of return, r, involves an iterative procedure using present values. Fortunately, there are computer programs for solving the internal rate of return; and these programs eliminate the arduous computations involved. To illustrate a manual method, however, consider again our example. The cash-flow stream is represented by an even series of cash flows of $5,600, to be received at the end of each of the next five years. We want to determine the discount factor that, when multiplied by $5,600 equals the cash outlay of $18,000 at time O. Suppose that we start with three discount rates— 14 percent, 16 percent, and 18 percent—and calculate the present value of the cash-flow stream. Using the different discount factors shown in Table A-2, we find:

---

* This assumption takes on substantial importance when the internal rate of return technique is used in choosing investments. See Section B of this Chapter, infra. [Ed.]

Discount Rate	Discount Factor	Cash Flow Each Year	Present Value of Stream
18%	3.1272	$5,600	$17,512.32
16	3.2743	5,600	18,336.08
14	3.4331	5,600	19,225.36

When we compare the present value of the stream with the initial outlay of $18,000, we see that the internal rate of return necessary to discount the stream to $18,000 falls between 16 and 18 percent, being closer to 16 than to 18 percent. To approximate the actual rate, we interpolate between 16 and 17 percent as follows:

	Discount Rate	Present Value
	16%	$18,336.08
	17	17,916.08
Difference	1%	$ 420.00

$$\frac{336.08}{420.00} = 0.80 \qquad 16\% + 0.80\% = 16.8\%$$

Thus the internal rate of return necessary to equate the present value of the cash inflows with the present value of the outflows is approximately 16.8 percent. It should be noted that interpolation gives only an approximation of the exact percent; the relationship between the two discount rates is not linear with respect to present value.

* * *

Table A-1

Present Value of One Dollar Due at the End of n Years

N	1%	2%	3%	4%	5%	6%	7%	8%	9%	10%	N
01	0.99010	0.98039	0.97007	0.96154	0.95238	0.94340	0.93458	0.92593	0.91743	0.90909	01
02	.98030	.96117	.94260	.92456	.90703	.89000	.87344	.85734	.84168	.82645	02
03	.97059	.94232	.91514	.88900	.86384	.83962	.81630	.79383	.77218	.75131	03
04	.96098	.92385	.88849	.85480	.82270	.79209	.76290	.73503	.70843	.68301	04
05	.95147	.90573	.86261	.82193	.78353	.74726	.71299	.68058	.64993	.62092	05
06	.94204	.88797	.83748	.79031	.74622	.70496	.66634	.63017	.59627	.56447	06
07	.93272	.87056	.81309	.75992	.71068	.66506	.62275	.58349	.54703	.51316	07
08	.92348	.85349	.78941	.73069	.67684	.62741	.58201	.54027	.50187	.46651	08
09	.91434	.83675	.76642	.70259	.64461	.59190	.54393	.50025	.46043	.42410	09
10	.90529	.82035	.74409	.67556	.61391	.55839	.50835	.46319	.42241	.38554	10
11	.89632	.80426	.72242	.64958	.58468	.52679	.47509	.42888	.38753	.35049	11
12	.88745	.78849	.70138	.62460	.55684	.49697	.44401	.39711	.35553	.31863	12
13	.87866	.77303	.68095	.60057	.53032	.46884	.41496	.36770	.32618	.28966	13
14	.86996	.75787	.66112	.57747	.50507	.44230	.38782	.34046	.29925	.26333	14
15	.86135	.74301	.64186	.55526	.48102	.41726	.36245	.31524	.27454	.23939	15
16	.85282	.72845	.62317	.53391	.45811	.39365	.33873	.29189	.25187	.21763	16
17	.84438	.71416	.60502	.51337	.43630	.37136	.31657	.27027	.23107	.19784	17
18	.83602	.70016	.58739	.49363	.41552	.35034	.29586	.25025	.21199	.17986	18
19	.82774	.68643	.57029	.47464	.39573	.33051	.27651	.23171	.19449	.16351	19
20	.81954	.67297	.55367	.45639	.37689	.31180	.25842	.21455	.17843	.14864	20
21	.81143	.65978	.53755	.43883	.35894	.29415	.24151	.19866	.16370	.13513	21
22	.80340	.64684	.52189	.42195	.34185	.27750	.22571	.18394	.15018	.12285	22
23	.79544	.63416	.50669	.40573	.32557	.26180	.21095	.17031	.13778	.11168	23
24	.78757	.62172	.49193	.39012	.31007	.24698	.19715	.15770	.12640	.10153	24
25	.77977	.60958	.47760	.37512	.29530	.23300	.18425	.14602	.11597	.09230	25

Table A-1

Present Value of One Dollar Due at the End of *n* Years (cont.)

N	11%	12%	13%	14%	15%	16%	17%	18%	19%	20%	N
01	0.90090	0.89286	0.88496	0.87719	0.86957	0.86207	0.85470	0.84746	0.84034	0.83333	01
02	.81162	.79719	.78315	.76947	.75614	.74316	.73051	.71818	.70616	.69444	02
03	.73119	.71178	.69305	.67497	.65752	.64066	.62437	.60863	.59342	.57870	03
04	.65873	.63552	.61332	.59208	.57175	.55229	.53365	.51579	.49867	.48225	04
05	.59345	.56743	.54276	.51937	.49718	.47611	.45611	.43711	.41905	.40188	05
06	.53464	.50663	.48032	.45559	.43233	.41044	.38984	.37043	.35214	.33490	06
07	.48166	.45235	.42506	.39964	.37594	.35383	.33320	.31392	.29592	.27980	07
08	.43393	.40388	.37616	.35056	.32690	.30503	.28478	.26604	.24867	.23257	08
09	.39092	.36061	.33288	.30751	.28426	.26295	.24340	.22546	.20897	.19381	09
10	.35218	.32197	.29459	.26974	.24718	.22668	.20804	.19106	.17560	.16151	10
11	.31728	.28748	.26070	.23662	.21494	.19542	.17781	.16192	.14756	.13459	11
12	.28584	.25667	.23071	.20756	.18691	.16846	.15197	.13722	.12400	.11216	12
13	.25751	.22917	.20416	.18207	.16253	.14523	.12989	.11629	.10420	.09346	13
14	.23199	.20462	.18068	.15971	.14133	.12520	.11102	.09855	.08757	.07789	14
15	.20900	.18270	.15989	.14010	.12289	.10793	.09489	.08352	.07359	.06491	15
16	.18829	.16312	.14150	.12289	.10686	.09304	.08110	.07078	.06184	.05409	16
17	.16963	.14564	.12522	.10780	.09293	.08021	.06932	.05998	.05196	.04507	17
18	.15282	.13004	.11081	.09456	.08080	.06914	.05925	.05083	.04367	.03756	18
19	.13768	.11611	.09806	.08295	.07026	.05961	.05064	.04308	.03669	.03130	19
20	.12403	.10367	.08678	.07276	.06110	.05139	.04328	.03651	.03084	.02608	20
21	.11174	.09256	.07680	.06383	.05313	.04430	.03699	.03094	.02591	.02174	21
22	.10067	.08264	.06796	.05599	.04620	.03819	.03162	.02622	.02178	.01811	22
23	.09069	.07379	.06014	.04911	.04017	.03292	.02702	.02222	.01830	.01509	23
24	.08170	.06588	.05322	.04308	.03493	.02838	.02310	.01883	.01538	.01258	24
25	.07361	.05882	.04710	.03779	.03038	.02447	.01974	.01596	.01292	.01048	25

Table A-2

Present Value of one Dollar Per Year. *n* Years at *r*%

Year	1%	2%	3%	4%	5%	6%	7%	8%	9%	10%	Year
1	0.9901	0.9804	0.9709	0.9615	0.9524	0.9434	0.9346	0.9259	0.9174	0.9091	1
2	1.9704	1.9416	1.9135	1.8861	1.8594	1.8334	1.8080	1.7833	1.7591	1.7355	2
3	2.9410	2.8839	2.8286	2.7751	2.7232	2.6730	2.6243	2.5771	2.5313	2.4868	3
4	3.9020	3.8077	3.7171	3.6299	3.5459	3.4651	3.3872	3.3121	3.2397	3.1699	4
5	4.8535	4.7134	4.5797	4.4518	4.3295	4.2123	4.1002	3.9927	3.8896	3.7908	5
6	5.7955	5.6014	5.4172	5.2421	5.0757	4.9173	4.7665	4.6229	4.4859	4.3553	6
7	6.7282	6.4720	6.2302	6.0020	5.7863	5.5824	5.3893	5.2064	5.0329	4.8684	7
8	7.6517	7.3254	7.0196	6.7327	6.4632	6.2098	5.9713	5.7466	5.5348	5.3349	8
9	8.5661	8.1622	7.7861	7.4353	7.1078	6.8017	6.5152	6.2469	5.9852	5.7590	9
10	9.4714	8.9825	8.5302	8.1109	7.7217	7.3601	7.0236	6.7101	6.4176	6.1446	10
11	10.3677	9.7868	9.2526	8.7604	8.3064	7.8868	7.4987	7.1389	6.8052	6.4951	11
12	11.2552	10.5753	9.9539	9.3850	8.8632	8.3838	7.9427	7.5361	7.1607	6.8137	12
13	12.1338	11.3483	10.6349	9.9856	9.3935	8.8527	8.3576	7.9038	7.4869	7.1034	13
14	13.0038	12.1062	11.2960	10.5631	9.8986	9.2950	8.7454	8.2442	7.7861	7.3667	14
15	13.8651	12.8492	11.9379	11.1183	10.3796	9.7122	9.1079	8.5595	8.0607	7.6061	15
16	14.7180	13.5777	12.5610	11.6522	10.8377	10.1059	9.4466	8.8514	8.3125	7.8237	16
17	15.5624	14.2918	13.1660	12.1656	11.2740	10.4772	9.7632	9.1216	8.5436	8.0215	17
18	16.3984	14.9920	13.7534	12.6592	11.6895	10.8276	10.0591	9.3719	8.7556	8.2014	18
19	17.2261	15.6784	14.3237	13.1339	12.0853	11.1581	10.3356	9.6036	8.9501	8.3649	19
20	18.0457	16.3514	14.8774	13.5903	12.4622	11.4699	10.5940	9.8181	9.1285	8.5136	20
21	18.8571	17.0111	15.4149	14.0291	12.8211	11.7640	10.8355	10.0168	9.2922	8.6487	21
22	19.6605	17.6580	15.9368	14.4511	13.1630	12.0416	11.0612	10.2007	9.4424	8.7715	22
23	20.4559	18.2921	16.4435	14.8568	13.4885	12.3033	11.2722	10.3710	9.5802	8.8832	23
24	21.2435	18.9139	16.9355	15.2469	13.7986	12.5503	11.4693	10.5287	9.7066	8.9847	24
25	22.0233	19.5234	17.4475	15.6220	14.0939	12.7833	11.6536	10.6748	9.8226	9.0770	25

Table A–2

Present Value of One Dollar Per Year. *n* Years at *r*% (cont.)

Year	11%	12%	13%	14%	15%	16%	17%	18%	19%	20%	Year
1	0.9009	0.8929	0.8850	0.8772	0.8696	0.8621	0.8547	0.8475	0.8403	0.8333	1
2	1.7125	1.6901	1.6681	1.6467	1.6257	1.6052	1.5852	1.5656	1.5465	1.5278	2
3	2.4437	2.4018	2.3612	2.3216	2.2832	2.2459	2.2096	2.1743	2.1399	2.1065	3
4	3.1024	3.0373	2.9745	2.9137	2.8550	2.7982	2.7432	2.6901	2.6386	2.5887	4
5	3.6959	3.6048	3.5172	3.4331	3.3522	3.2743	3.1993	3.1272	3.0576	2.9906	5
6	4.2305	4.1114	3.9976	3.8887	3.7845	3.6847	3.5892	3.4976	3.4098	3.3255	6
7	4.7122	4.5638	4.4226	4.2883	4.1604	4.0386	3.9224	3.8115	3.7057	3.6046	7
8	5.1461	4.9676	4.7988	4.6389	4.4873	4.3436	4.2072	4.0776	3.9544	3.8372	8
9	5.5370	5.3282	5.1317	4.9464	4.7716	4.6065	4.4506	4.3030	4.1633	4.0310	9
10	5.8892	5.6502	5.4262	5.2161	5.0188	4.8332	4.6586	4.4941	4.3389	4.1925	10
11	6.2065	5.9377	5.6869	5.4527	5.2337	5.0286	4.8364	4.6560	4.4865	4.3271	11
12	6.4924	6.1944	5.9176	5.6603	5.4206	5.1971	4.9884	4.7932	4.6105	4.4392	12
13	6.7499	6.4235	6.1218	5.8424	5.5831	5.3423	5.1183	4.9095	4.7147	4.5327	13
14	6.9819	6.6282	6.3025	6.0021	5.7245	5.4675	5.2293	5.0081	4.8023	4.6106	14
15	7.1909	6.8109	6.4624	6.1422	5.8474	5.5755	5.3242	5.0916	4.8759	4.6755	15
16	7.3792	6.9740	6.6039	6.2651	5.9542	5.6685	5.4053	5.1624	4.9377	4.7296	16
17	7.5488	7.1196	6.7291	6.3729	6.0472	5.7487	5.4746	5.2223	4.9897	4.7746	17
18	7.7016	7.2497	6.8399	6.4674	6.1280	5.8178	5.5339	5.2732	5.0333	4.8122	18
19	7.8393	7.3658	6.9380	6.5504	6.1982	5.8775	5.5845	5.3162	5.0700	4.8435	19
20	7.9633	7.4694	7.0248	6.6231	6.2593	5.9288	5.6278	5.3527	5.1009	4.8696	20
21	8.0751	7.5620	7.1016	6.6870	6.3125	5.9731	5.6648	5.3837	5.1268	4.8913	21
22	8.1757	7.6446	7.1695	6.7429	6.3587	6.0113	5.6964	5.4099	5.1486	4.9094	22
23	8.2664	7.7184	7.2297	6.7921	6.3988	6.0442	5.7234	5.4321	5.1668	4.9245	23
24	8.3481	7.7843	7.2829	6.8351	6.4338	6.0726	5.7465	5.4509	5.1822	4.9371	24
25	8.4217	7.8431	7.3300	6.8729	6.4641	6.0971	5.7662	5.4669	5.1951	4.9476	25

B. Time Value in a Transactional Context: Discounting in Project Choice

The discounting techniques developed in Section A of this Chapter are a means to recognize the impact of the time value of money on the valuation of a stream of income. In our assumed world of certainty, the result is a simple method to value an asset. The asset's value is the value of the income it generates over its life; the present value of that income is a summary statistic of the magnitude of that income stream taking into account when it will be received. The next step in developing the skills necessary to understand how transactions are valued is to apply the discounting techniques to the choice of investments, what is typically called "capital budgeting."

Put simply, capital budgeting is the analysis by which a firm decides how to invest its resources.[1] A number of different techniques are commonly used in capital budgeting, but all share the same three stages. First, the amount and timing of the income stream that will be generated by an investment opportunity are estimated. Second, a summary statistic of that income stream is calculated. Third, that

[1] While individuals also make investment decisions, the term capital budgeting is usually reserved for investments in real assets, like new plants or businesses, rather than investments in financial assets, such as stocks or bonds, typically made by individuals investing their personal resources. Although the firm-individual dichotomy is a familiar shorthand, the critical distinction is the character of the investment; a sole proprietor, just like a corporation, engages in capital budgeting with respect to the business' resources.

summary statistic is compared to an acceptance criterion that represents the least favorable investment the firm will accept. Investments that meet or exceed the acceptance criterion are made, those that do not are rejected.

Because we are still working in a world of certainty, the first step in capital budgeting—estimating the amount and timing of the investment's income stream—can be passed over. For now, we can assume that the precise amounts and timing of these cash flows are known.[2] It is with respect to the second stage—the calculation of a summary statistic of the income stream from the investment—that the different capital budgeting techniques most significantly diverge in their approaches to the problem. Most important, the techniques differ fundamentally in the extent to which the particular statistic used to summarize the investment's future cash flows takes into account the time value of money.

Average Rate of Return and Payback Period. Two frequently used techniques, the average rate of return and the payback method, do not adequately account for the time value of money. The average rate of return technique divides the average annual accounting net profit from a project by the project's average book value. The result is a measure of the average return on the amount invested in the project. Suppose a firm is considering a $9,000 investment in Project X that would result in a $5,000 book profit before depreciation in each of three years, with depreciation being taken on a straight line basis. The average annual net profit from the project is calculated as follows:

Project X

	Year One	Year Two	Year Three
Profit	$5,000	$5,000	$5,000
Depreciation	3,000	3,000	3,000
Net Profit	2,000	2,000	2,000

$$\text{Average Annual Net Profit} = \frac{\text{Total Net Profit}}{\text{Number of Years}} = \frac{\$6,000}{3} = \$2,000$$

The project's average book value is calculated as follows:

Project X

	Year One	Year Two	Year Three
Initial Investment	$9,000	$9,000	$9,000
Accumulated Depreciation	3,000	6,000	9,000
Net Book Value	6,000	3,000	0
Average Book Value	= $4,500[3]		

The average rate of return is then $2,000/$4,500, or 44.44%.

The problem with the average rate of return technique is that the time value of money is ignored; all cash flows are treated equally regardless of whether they are received in the first year or in the last.

---

[2] This assumption will be lifted in Chapter Three.

[3] When straightline depreciation is used, the average book value is always one-half the initial investment.

This can be seen by comparing Project X with Projects Y and Z, which also have a $9,000 initial investment and average rates of return of 44.44%, but which have quite different cash flow patterns.

Net Profit

	Project X	Project Y	Project Z
Year One	$2,000	$3,000	$1,000
Year Two	2,000	2,000	2,000
Year Three	2,000	1,000	3,000

The average rate of return technique treats all three cash flows as equivalent. If the time value of money is taken into account, even visual inspection of the cash flows suggests that Project Y is preferable.

The payback period approach is somewhat of an improvement in this regard. Here the idea is to calculate the number of periods necessary for the cash flows from a project to repay its initial investment. So, for example, the payback period of Project X above—the time necessary for the initial investment to be recovered—is less than two years.[4] All other things equal, a project whose cash flows come sooner is preferable to one whose cash flows come later. Nonetheless, the method still fails to adequately account for the time value of money. Most important, it gives no value to cash flows that are received after the project's initial investment is repaid. As a result, projects with identical payback periods and identical returns within the payback period would be deemed equivalent even if one had a large return in the year after the payback period ended while the other did not. In this sense, the payback period technique *over*-discounts future payments. Additionally, the payback period technique takes no account of differences in the timing of receipts within the payback period. So, for example, if the payback period for Projects X, Y, and Z were three years, the payback technique, like the average rate of return technique, would treat the three projects as equivalent, despite the difference in the timing of their receipts. In this sense, the payback period *under*-discounts future payments.

Both the average rate of return and the payback period techniques fail to provide appropriate guidance for capital budgeting decisions because they do not fully take into account the time value of money. We now turn to two techniques that do explicitly consider time value in their evaluation of potential investment projects.

The Internal Rate of Return and the Net Present Value Techniques. The mathematics of the internal rate of return and net present value techniques were described in the Van Horne excerpt in Section A of this Chapter. Both are discounted cash flow techniques that reduce future cash receipts to present value in determining the value of the asset giving rise to the payments. The internal rate of return technique solves for the discount rate—the internal rate of return—that

---

[4] Note that net profit *before depreciation* was used for this calculation. In this sense depreciation is itself a form of payback; including it within the calculation of the payback period would be double counting.

equates the present value of the investment in a project and the present value of the cash flows from the project. If the internal rate of return is high enough to meet the firm's acceptance criteria, the project is undertaken. The net present value rule discounts to present value each future cash outflow (including the original investment) and each future cash inflow, using the required rate of return, the firm's acceptance criterion, as the discount rate. If the sum of the present values, positive and negative, of all future cash outflows and inflows is positive, the project as a whole has a positive net present value and is undertaken.

Both techniques have substantial support in the financial community and, under most circumstances, will yield the same rankings of alternative projects. For our purposes, however, the most important difference is the discount rate each technique uses to reduce future cash flows to present value.[5] The internal rate of return technique in effect assumes that all intermediate cash flows can be reinvested during the life of the project at the same rate of return as earned from the project. Thus, the actual rate of return achieved by a project will equal the internal rate of return calculated in the capital budgeting decision *only* if the cash flows generated by the project can be reinvested in an equally profitable investment. A similar problem exists with the net present value technique. Here the assumption is that all intermediate cash flows can be reinvested at the chosen discount rate. Again, the actual return experienced will match the initial calculation *only* if opportunities for reinvestment at the discount rate actually exist at the time the cash flows are received.

It is often argued that the net present value technique is the more conservative because the discount rate chosen is presumably the external cost of capital, a market rate, while the discount rate implicit in the internal rate of return technique is the return associated with the particular project and, therefore, less likely to be duplicable on reinvestment.[6] For our purposes, however, the problem serves to highlight the artificiality of our assumption of a certain world, and the difficulty associated with using just these techniques in a world in which there exists even a very little uncertainty.

An example helps clarify the point.[7] Suppose you are the Vice President-Finance of an insurance company with $100,000 to invest. Your actuaries tell you that five years from now you must have on

---

[5] Among the difficulties with the use of the internal rate of return in contrast to net present value is the potential for a project to have multiple internal rates of return when cash flows change signs—positive or negative—more than once over the life of the project. While this may not seem a likely occurrence, imagine a project that requires a mid-stream investment of capital. See R. Brealey & S. Myers, *Principles of Corporate Finance* 73–75 (2nd ed. 1984). Problems also exist in taking into account differences in the scale of alternative projects. Because the internal rate of return is a relative measure, while net present value is an absolute measure, the rankings of projects will differ when there is a scale difference. So, for example, a small project may have a higher internal rate of return, but generate fewer dollars, and therefore have a lower net present value, than a larger project.

[6] J. Van Horne, supra, at 117.

[7] This example is drawn from Gilson, *Value Creation by Business Lawyers: Legal Skills and Asset Pricing,* 94 Yale L.J. 239, 299–300 (1984).

hand $190,000 to pay anticipated life insurance claims. A borrower then appears and offers to borrow that $100,000 for five years, with annual interest payments at 14%. Calculating the terminal value of the loan using the formula from Section A of this Chapter tells you that the transaction will be worth $192,541 in five years, just what is needed to meet expected claims. It will be recalled that the formula for calculating terminal value is:

$$TV = X(1 + r)^n \text{ where}$$

$$
\begin{aligned}
TV &= \text{terminal value} \\
X &= \text{principal} \\
r &= \text{interest rate per period} \\
n &= \text{the number of periods.}
\end{aligned}
$$

Therefore,
$$
\begin{aligned}
TV &= \$100,000(1 + .14)^5 \\
&= \$100,000(1.9251) \\
&= \$192,541.
\end{aligned}
$$

Similarly, the terminal value can be reduced to present value.

$$PV = \frac{X}{(1 + k)^n} \text{ where}$$

$$
\begin{aligned}
PV &= \text{present value} \\
k &= \text{interest rate per period.}
\end{aligned}
$$

Therefore,
$$
\begin{aligned}
PV &= \frac{\$192,541}{(1 + .14)^5} \\
&= \frac{\$192,541}{(1.9251)} \\
&= \$100,000
\end{aligned}
$$

What keeps you from leaving the office for a weekend at the beach is the knowledge that, even if there is no credit risk, no risk that the borrower's payments will be made other than in the amount and at the time specified, a substantial risk nonetheless remains that you will not have on hand in five years the amount necessary to meet anticipated claims. The reason is that the terminal and present value calculations assume that the 14% annual interest payments can be reinvested at the same 14% rate. The risk is that this assumption will prove wrong. If interest rates drop sometime during the five years, your actual reinvestment rate will be lower than 14% and your company will be insolvent when the anticipated claims are presented for payment in five years. The calculations simply do not take into account the risk that interest rates may change over the term of the loan.

The point of the example is that even where there is no credit risk, valuation techniques that are designed for a certain world fail when risk is introduced. This is not to say that the discounting techniques examined in this Chapter are not helpful. Rather, they are designed to deal with one aspect of valuation—the time value of money. More accurate valuation requires adding another factor—risk—and devising other techniques to take account of it.

CHAPTER THREE.   VALUATION UNDER UNCERTAINTY: RISK AND RETURN

It is time now to relax the assumption of certainty on which our examination of the importance of the time value of money was based. So long as there is no uncertainty concerning future cash flows, the net present value technique is an adequate means to value an investment provided that we are sensitive to the assumed reinvestment rate. What happens, however, if we are not entirely certain about the amount and timing of the cash flows that will be forthcoming from an asset? Suppose, for example, that the profit we expect from a proposed project depends on whether a particular technological problem can be solved. How do we express this uncertainty about future returns in a fashion that then allows the application of discounting techniques to take into account the time value of money?

The problems that result from the introduction of uncertainty into the valuation process, however, are not limited to devising a means of expressing our expectation of a project's returns in light of our inability to accurately predict the precise pattern of returns that will be forthcoming. In addition, different projects will present more or less uncertainty about their future returns. Where future profit from a project depends on solving a technological problem, and where we also are unsure whether the problem can be solved at all and, if it can, how costly the solution will be, a wide variety of possible future cash flows are possible. In contrast, an investment grade bond presents uncertainty concerning the available reinvestment rate and the rate of inflation, but little variation in the expected pattern of payments. How can we take into account in valuation the different degrees of uncertainty associated with different assets?

In this Chapter we first consider techniques to take uncertainty into account both in expressing expectations of the returns from an asset, and in expressing the extent of the uncertainty associated with those expected returns. We then turn to how the extent of uncertainty associated with an asset's returns—what financial economists mean when they use the term *risk*—should be taken into account in choosing among assets.

A.   Expressing Returns Under Conditions of Uncertainty

1.   Expected Values and Decision Trees

H. BIERMAN, C. BONINI & W. HAUSMAN, QUANTITA-TIVE ANALYSIS FOR BUSINESS DECISIONS *

51–69 (6th ed. 1981).

EXPECTED VALUES AND DECISION TREES

[We now] consider * * * the application of probability concepts to business decisions which must be made under conditions of uncertainty. We shall develop a means for making consistent decisions and for estimating the cost of uncertainty. We shall propose expected monetary value as an appropriate criterion for decision making. Later we will describe the limitations of expected monetary value and suggest modifications in the analysis.

Conditional Value

Suppose a grocer is faced with a problem of how many cases of milk to stock to meet tomorrow's demand. Assume that any milk that remains unsold at the end of the day will represent a complete loss to the grocer. Also, any unsatisfied demand bears no cost except the cost of the lost sale; the disappointed customer will come back in the future. This example is highly simplified but illustrates the basic principles of conditional and expected value.

In our analysis of the grocer's problem, it would be helpful if we knew something about past sales, on the assumption that this experience may serve as a guide to what may be expected in the future. Suppose the grocer has maintained records such as those shown in Table 3–1.

With a purchase price (variable cost) of $8 per case and a selling price of $10 per case, the table of conditional values (Table 3–2) is a description of the problem facing the grocer.

The possible actions (number to buy) facing the grocer are listed across the top of the table. It is, of course, possible to buy 24 or 29 cases, and so on; but if in the last 200 days, sales were in the range of 25–28 cases, the grocer might view a stock of greater than 28 or less than 25 as not worthy of consideration. We shall make this assumption. The possible (conceivable) events—in this example the possible sales—are listed in the far left column. If the grocer is willing to assign probabilities in accordance with the historical data, then events (sales) other than those listed will carry zero probabilities; they are considered impossible events.

* Copyright © 1981. Reprinted by permission of Richard D. Irwin, Inc.

Table 3–1

Historical Demand

Total Demand Per Day	Number of days each demand level was recorded	Probability of each event
25 cases	20	0.10
26 cases	60	0.30
27 cases	100	0.50
28 cases	20	0.10
	200	1.00

Table 3–2

Conditional Values

Event: Demand	Possible actions			
	Stock 25	Stock 26	Stock 27	Stock 28
25 cases	$50*	$42	$34	$26
26 cases	50	52*	44	36
27 cases	50	52	54*	46
28 cases	50	52	54	56*

* Best act for the event.

Table 3–2 can be thought of as a conditional value or conditional profit table. Corresponding to each action the grocer takes, and each event that happens, there is a given conditional profit. These profits are conditional in the sense that a certain profit results from following a specific course of action (act) and having a specific demand (event) occur. All the possible combinations are shown in Table 3–2. The best act for each possible event is indicated by an asterisk.

Looking at the act column, "Stock 27," let us trace through the calculations of each dollar amount. This is done in Table 3–3. Similar computations have to be made for acts "Stock 25," "Stock 26," and "Stock 28."

The calculations of Table 3–3 reflect the fact that if 27 cases are stocked, only 27 can be sold, even if the demand turns out to be 28 cases. Hence the profit reaches a maximum of $54 for the sale of 27 units, and levels off at that figure despite the demand for 28 units.

Table 3–3

Conditional Profits of Act "Stock 27"

Event: Demand	Selling price	Total revenue	Cost of 27 cases (27 × $8)	Conditional profit of act "Stock 27"
25 cases	$10	$250	$216	$34
26 cases	10	260	216	44
27 cases	10	270	216	54
28 cases	10	270	216	54

*   *   *

It should be emphasized that a conditional profit (or loss) relates to a profit conditional on:

1. An event happening.

2. A given action.

We do not know which event is going to occur; there is uncertainty. Therefore the conditional profit for a decision is not one number but a table of profits (or losses) associated with possible events. Profit is $44 only on condition of both stocking 27 units and an actual demand of 26 units. If the demand is different than 26 units, the actual profit will be different than $44.

Expected Monetary Value

Even though the conditional values * * * help characterize the problem facing the grocer, it is not yet possible to offer an optimum solution. The grocer could choose the best act with advance knowledge of tomorrow's demand but this information is not available in our example. The problem facing the grocer is to make some forecast of the event and then choose an act that is consistent with the forecast. Suppose a forecast is made by assigning probabilities to the possible events and then analyzing the action alternatives. If the probabilities are based on historical information (see Table 3–1), they would be as shown in Table 3–5. If the grocer believes that for some reason tomorrow's demand will vary somewhat from the observed pattern, the probability assignment should be modified.

The next step is to bring the assigned probabilities into the analysis. We accomplish this by *weighting the conditional values of each event in the conditional-value table by the probability of the event occurring, and adding the products.* The resulting number is the **expected monetary value** for the act; the optimum act is the one with the highest expected monetary value. The calculations are given in Table 3–6 for the acts of stocking 26 and 27 units. The calculations for 25 and 28 units would be similar.

Table 3–5

Event: Demand	Probability of event
25 cases	0.10
26 cases	0.30
27 cases	0.50
28 cases	0.10
	1.00

In Table 3–6 the expected monetary value *(EMV)* is calculated by multiplying each conditional value by its probability and then adding the weighted conditional values. Table 3–7 shows the expected monetary values for all acts.

Table 3–6

Calculations of Expected Monetary Values

Event: Demand	Probability of Event	Act: Stock 26		Act: Stock 27	
		Conditional value (CV)	Expected value: CV weighted by probability of event	Conditional value (CV)	Expected value: CV weighted by probability of event
25 cases	0.10	$42	$4.20	$34	$3.40
26 cases	0.30	52	15.60	44	13.20
27 cases	0.50	52	26.00	54	27.00
28 cases	0.10	52	5.20	54	5.40
Expected monetary value			$51.00		$49.00

Table 3–7

Summary of Expected Monetary Values

Act	Expected monetary value
Stock 25	$50
Stock 26	51 (optimum act)
Stock 27	49
Stock 28	42

The grocer calculates for act "Stock 26" an expected monetary value of $51, the highest *EMV*. Therefore, based on expected monetary value, 26 cases should be stocked.

Note that the *EMV* of $51 will not be the profit on any one day. It is the expected or average profit. If the decision were repeated for many days (with the same probabilities) the grocer would make an average of $51 per day by stocking 26 cases of milk. Even if the decision were not repeated, the action with the highest *EMV* is the best alternative that the decision maker has available.

To summarize, our plan for solving the grocer's problem is as follows:

1.   Construct a payoff (conditional value) table listing the acts and events that are considered to be possibilities, and the outcomes for each act and event. In listing the events, be sure that each event is mutually exclusive (i.e., make sure that no two or more events can occur simultaneously) and that all events considered together are exhaustive (i.e., that the events listed cover all the possibilities). This table includes the economics of the problem (costs and revenues) by presenting a conditional value (or loss) for each act and event combination.

2.   Assign probabilities to the events.

3.   Calculate an *EMV* for each act by weighting (multiplying) the conditional values by the assigned probabilities and adding the weighted conditional values to obtain the *EMV* of the act.

4.   Choose the act with the largest *EMV*.

Sensitivity Analysis of Subjective Probabilities

Estimating probabilities is one of the most difficult steps in applying the expected-monetary-value decision criterion. Sometimes it is possible to avoid this step, at least partially, by leaving the estimation of probabilities to the last. For each act, a range of probabilities can be found over which the given act is optimal. The decision maker then determines in which interval the probabilities lie.

Example:

We will illustrate this using a previous example. * * * Consider again the example of the grocer deciding how many cases of milk to stock. From Table 3–7 we determined that the optimum act was to stock 26 cases. This result was obtained using the probabilities in the first column in Table 3–14 below. You can easily check that the action "Stock 26" remains optimal for all the various sets of probabilities shown in Table 3–14. Hence, the decision maker can see that the decision is not *sensitive* to the variations in the probabilities that are given in Table 3–14. Other variations could cause a change in decision. For example, if the probability attached to the event "demand of 25 cases" is greater than 0.20, then the optimal decision changes to ordering 25 cases.

The general approach suggested by this example is called sensitivity analysis. The decision maker makes a preliminary set of estimates (for probabilities or for payoffs). Variations in these estimates are then made. If the variations do not change the optimal decision, one need go no further. If, on the other hand, the decision is sensitive to the changes, the manager must refine the preliminary estimates in order to arrive at a decision.

Table 3–14

Alternative Possible Sets of Probabilities

Event: Demand	Sets of probabilities			
	1	2	3	4
25 cases	0.1	0.2	0.05	0.1
26 cases	0.3	0.3	0.15	0.1
27 cases	0.5	0.4	0.40	0.3
28 cases	0.1	0.1	0.40	0.5

*   *   *

Decision Trees

The previous sections * * * developed the decision criterion of expected monetary value, and analyzed simple decisions using conditional-value tables. This section describes a general approach for more complex decisions that is useful both for *structuring* the decision problem as well as finding a solution. The approach utilizes a **decision tree**, a graphic tool for describing the actions available to the decision maker, the events that can occur, and the relationship between these actions and events.

Decision Tree for Grocer's Problem

To illustrate the basic ideas, let us first develop the decision tree for the grocery problem of the last section. Recall that the decision involves how many cases of milk to order. The decision point is represented by a *square box* or *decision node* in Figure 3–1. The alternatives are represented as *branches* emanating from the decision node.

Figure 3–1
Grocer's Alternatives

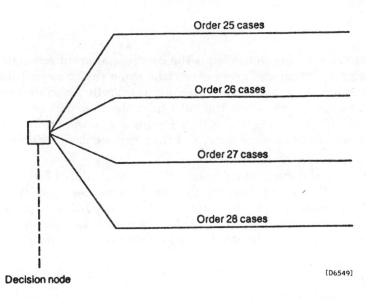

Order 25 cases

Order 26 cases

Order 27 cases

Order 28 cases

Decision node

[D6549]

Suppose the grocer were to select some particular alternative, say order 28 cases. There are several possible events that can happen, each event representing a number of cases of milk that customers might demand. These are shown in Figure 3–2 as branches emanating from a round node. (We are using the convention of a square box for a decision node and a circle for an event node). Note that these branches represent uncertain events over which the decision maker has no control. However, probabilities can be assigned to each event and are entered under each branch in parentheses.

FIGURE 3–2   Events for alternative "order 28 cases"

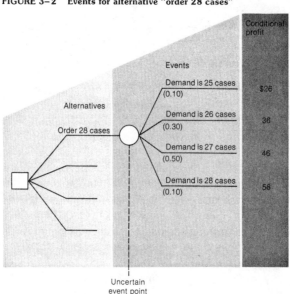

At the end of each branch is the conditional profit associated with the selected action and given event (the same values as in Table 3–2). The conditional profit thus represents the profit associated with the decisions and events along the path from the first part of the tree to the end. For example, the $26 in Figure 3–2 is the profit associated with ordering 28 cases of milk, and then experiencing a demand of 25 cases.

The expected monetary value (*EMV*) is calculated for each event node exactly as was done in the previous section (see Table 3–6). That is, probabilities are multiplied by conditional profits and summed. The *EMV* is placed in the event node to indicate that it is the expected value calculated over all branches emanating from that node.

Figure 3–3 shows the complete decision tree for the grocer's problem. Note that it is not necessary to list every possible event separately for all decisions. Thus, when 26 cases are ordered, there are only really two events that lead to different conditional profits: demand is 25 cases with profit $42; and demand is 26 or more (that is, demand is 26, 27, or 28 cases) with profit $52. If the grocer orders 25 cases, as another example, there is only one outcome, namely the sale of all 25 cases with conditional profit of $50.

FIGURE 3–3   **Complete decision tree—grocer's problem**

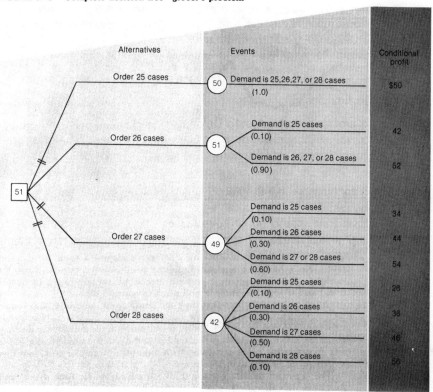

In Figure 3–3, the expected monetary values are shown in the event nodes. The grocer must then choose which action to take, and this choice is to select the one with the highest *EMV*, namely order 26 cases with *EMV* = $51. This is indicated in the tree by putting 51 in the decision node (square box) at the beginning of the tree. In addition, the mark ‖ is drawn across the nonoptimal decision branches, indicating that they are not to be followed.

In summary, the decision tree uses the same idea of maximizing expected monetary value developed in the previous section. For this simple example, the use of a table, such as Table 3–2, may seem easier. However, as the decision problem becomes more complex, the decision tree becomes more valuable in organizing the information needed to make the decision. This is especially true if the manager must make a *sequence* of decisions, rather than a single decision, as the next example will illustrate.

Decision Tree Example

Suppose the marketing manager of a firm is trying to decide whether or not to market a new product and at what price to sell it. The profit to be made depends upon whether or not a competitor will introduce a similar product and upon what price the competitor charges.

Note that there are two decisions: (1) introduce the product or not, and (2) the price to charge. Likewise, there are two events: (1) competition introduces a competitive product (or not), and (2) the competitor's price. The timing or sequence of these decisions and events are very important in this decision. If the marketing manager must act before knowing whether or not the competitor has a similar product, the price may be different than with such knowledge. The decision tree is useful in this type of situation since it displays the order in which decisions are made and events occur.

Suppose in our example that the firm must announce or decide to scrap its new product shortly. However, the price decision can be made later. If the competitor is going to act, it will announce its product within a month. In three months, our firm will establish and announce its price. After that, the competitor will announce its price. This can be diagrammed in the decision tree in Figure 3–4. Note that this is a sequential decision problem. Our firm must make a decision *now* about introduction and *subsequently* set price, *after* learning about the competitor's action.

The decision tree shows the structure of the decision problem. To complete the analysis, conditional profits must be estimated for every combination of actions and events (that is, for every path through the tree). Suppose our marketing manager has done this, and the profits are shown in Figure 3–4 at the ends of the tree. These profit values include the costs of introducing the product and the profits made from its sale. Negative values indicate that introduction costs exceeded subsequent profit from sales.

Also, the probabilities for each event must be assessed by the decision maker; for our example they are shown under the event branches in Figure 3–4. Note that these probabilities may depend upon prior actions or events.

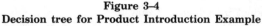

Figure 3–4
Decision tree for Product Introduction Example

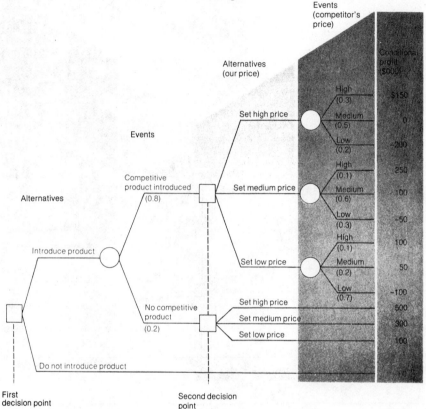

Thus, the probabilities for the competitor's price behavior in Figure 3–4 are different when our price is high than when our price is low.

Analysis of the Decision Problem

To analyze a decision tree we begin at the end of the tree and work backwards. For each set of event branches, the *EMV* is calculated as illustrated, and for each set of decision branches, the one with the highest *EMV* is selected. This is illustrated in Figure 3–5 for our example. First, the *EMV*s are calculated for the event nodes associated with the competitor's price. For example, the *EMV* of $5,000 in the topmost right circle in Figure 3–5 represents the sum of the product of probabilities for high, medium, and low prices times the respective conditional profits:

Figure 3–5
Completed Decision Tree for Product Introduction Example

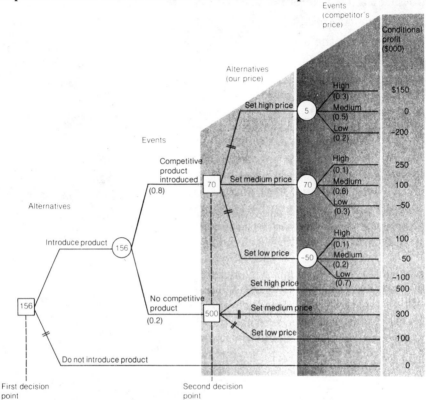

$$EMV = (0.3)(150) + (0.5)(0) + (0.2)(-200) = 5$$

The other values are computed similarly.

Now if we move back on the decision tree to the second decision point, we are faced with two decision situations. The first—when a competitive product has been introduced—involves setting a high, medium, or low price with expected profits of $5,000, $70,000, and –$50,000, respectively. Assume the choice is the one with highest expected profit—the medium price. A mark ‖ is placed on the lines related to the other alternatives, indicating that they are nonoptimal, and the expected profit of $70,000 is attached to the upper box of the second decision point.

When no competitive product is introduced, the best choice is a high price, with profit of $500,000.

At the event point to the left, an expected value of $156,000 is computed by multiplying the expected profit given a competitive product ($70,000) by its probability, 0.8, and adding the profit given no competitive product ($500,000) times its probability of 0.2. The *EMV* in thousands is:

$$EMV = (0.8)(70) + (0.2)(500) = 156.$$

Finally, the decision to market the product is made since the expected net profit of $156,000 is greater than the zero profit from not marketing the product.

Note that the decision that results from an analysis of the decision tree is not a fixed decision, but rather a *strategy:* introduce the product and charge a high price if there is no competitive entry; but charge a medium price if there is competition.

Developing the Decision Tree

The decision tree is a model of a decision situation, and like all models it is an abstraction and simplification of the real problem. Only the important decisions and events are included; otherwise the tree becomes too "bushy." And judgment is required, not only about what to include, but also to assess probabilities.

In drawing a decision tree, certain rules must be observed:

1. The branches emanating from any node must be all of the same type, either events or alternatives, and never a mix of the two.

2. The events associated with branches from any event node must be mutually exclusive and all events included, so that the sum of the probabilities is one.

3. The alternatives associated with a decision node must include all the alternatives under consideration at that point.

It is generally helpful to develop the tree in chronological sequence, so that the proper order of decisions and events is maintained.

*   *   *

2. Problems With Subjective Probability

The decision tree technique, and the expected monetary value measure it seeks to maximize, is based on a particular concept of probability. One use of the term probability—commonly referred to as *objective*—focuses on the inherent uncertainty of a physical process. Examples of this use include predictions of the outcome of the flip of a coin or the uncertainty principle in physics. In this sense, probability is a fact, a physical property of a thing or process that can be discovered and that will not differ depending on the identity of the observer. The grocer's estimation of how many cases of milk will be purchased, or the marketing manager's decisions regarding the introduction of a new product, however, do not use probability in this way. Rather, they refer to *subjective* probability: a description not of a physical property of the external world—that a properly weighted and flipped coin has a 50/50 chance of landing on either side—but of an individual's belief about the outcome of a future uncertain event that does not depend on immutable physical properties. An easy rule of thumb by which to distinguish between the two forms of probability is to ask yourself whether rational people could differ about the assessment. If the answer is yes, then the probability in question is likely subjective, reflecting the observer's view of the world rather than a physical property of the world.

Despite the subjective basis of the form of decision analysis described by Bierman, Bonini & Hausman, it has had very substantial acceptance as a decisionmaking technique. Indeed, in one variant it has been described as "the major paradigm in decision making since the Second World War." [1] Viewed most favorably, the use of subjective probability in decision analysis is an optimization technique that answers the following question: Taking as given the quality of your information about the likely shape of future events, how do you make the best decisions with what you have? Thus, subjective probability and decision trees provide a structure that allows you to better utilize your beliefs about the future, whatever they are, than do the purely intuitive techniques to which we would otherwise resort.

Marc Victor, a pioneer in the application of this form of analysis to legal decision making,[2] has illustrated this point in a particularly vivid fashion. Victor asked a group of people to think about the following kinds of questions: What does it mean to say that there is "a significant possibility" that an event—like a judge issuing a favorable jury instruction—will occur and how does it differ from the statement that the same event is "likely to occur"? Victor then asked the group to assign numerical probabilities to these and similar terms. He found that the results varied so widely that even when the terms were expressed as a range—for example, defining "likely" to refer to a 51% to 70% likelihood of occurrence—the ranges specified by different people often did not even overlap. A particular instance drives this point home. A lawyer attended one of Victor's lectures with his businessman client. Together with the rest of the audience they were asked to write down the percentage range that they assigned to the phrase "significant possibility." When asked to compare the ranges they had selected, they discovered that theirs did not overlap at all. In the context of a lawyer-client relationship, this disparity in estimates suggests that it is entirely possible [3] for the lawyer and client to believe that they have agreed on a matter when their agreement is only linguistic and, in fact, camouflages a substantial disagreement. It is not difficult to imagine a client taking action, like continuing a challenged business practice, because when the lawyer told him that there was a substantial likelihood of the practice being upheld, the client interpreted that probability to be 70% while the lawyer meant it to be no more than 30%.

If we complicate the problem somewhat, although still leaving it artificially simple by comparison to the real world, by making the

---

[1] Schoemaker, *The Expected Utility Model: Its Variants, Purposes, Evidence and Limitations,* 20 J.Econ.Lit. 529, 529 (1982) (referring to the expected utility variation).

[2] See, e.g., Victor, *The Proper Use of Decision Analysis to Assist Litigation Strate-*gy, 40 Bus.Law. 617 (1985); Victor, *Predicting the Cost of Litigation,* 6 Planning Review # 6 (1978).

[3] What probability should be assigned to this phase?

probability conditional—i.e., what is the probability of a favorable verdict when that depends on the probability that the judge will give a favorable instruction and on the likelihood that the jury will find a particular fact—the difficulty of systematically dealing with intuitive formulations of probability is underscored. How, after all, do you express the product of a possibility times a conundrum times a conjecture? In short, the case for the use of subjective probability and structured decision analysis is that it allows a decision maker to systematically exploit the information available and meaningfully communicate the result. It is not so much that your analysis is "right", it's just that it's better.

Note, however, that thus far we have paid scant attention to the accuracy of the subjective probabilities that form the heart of the technique. A common criticism voiced by lawyers when exposed to subjective decision analysis for the first time is that it is too exact; that by expressing uncertainty using a cardinal scale we give the impression that we can systematically justify assigning to a future event a probability of occurrence of 33% rather than 32%. This objection usually fades with exposure, as the critics become more familiar with the technique and misleading impressions are overcome. There is, however, a far more telling criticism of subjective probability for consideration.

In recent years, a number of social scientists, particularly cognitive psychologists, have gathered substantial amounts of empirical evidence suggesting that the process by which we assign subjective probabilities is subject to a variety of systematic biases that can lead to verifiably incorrect estimates and, ultimately, decisions. The nature of the problem and a sample of the available empirical evidence is set out in the following excerpt from the work of two leading scholars in the field.

JUDGMENT UNDER UNCERTAINTY: HEURISTICS AND BIASES *

AMOS TVERSKY AND DANIEL KAHNEMAN

185 Science 1124 (1974).

Many decisions are based on beliefs concerning the likelihood of uncertain events such as the outcome of an election, the guilt of a defendant, or the future value of the dollar. These beliefs are usually expressed in statements such as "I think that * * *," "chances are * * *," "it is unlikely that * * *," and so forth. Occasionally, beliefs concerning uncertain events are expressed in numerical form as odds or subjective probabilities. What determines such beliefs? How do people assess the probability of an uncertain event or the value of an uncertain quantity? This article shows that people rely on a limited number of heuristic principles which reduce the complex tasks of assessing probabilities and predicting values to simpler judgmental operations. In general, these heuristics are quite useful, but sometimes they lead to severe and systematic errors.

* * *

Representativeness

Many of the probabilistic questions with which people are concerned belong to one of the following types: What is the probability that object A belongs to class B? What is the probability that event A originates from process B? What is the probability that process B will generate event A? In answering such questions, people typically rely on the representativeness heuristic, in which probabilities are evaluated by the degree to which A is representative of B, that is, by the degree to which A resembles B. For example, when A is highly representative of B, the probability that A originates from B is judged to be high. On the other hand, if A is not similar to B, the probability that A originates from B is judged to be low.

For an illustration of judgment by representativeness, consider an individual who has been described by a former neighbor as follows: "Steve is very shy and withdrawn, invariably helpful, but with little interest in people, or in the world of reality. A meek and tidy soul, he has a need for order and structure, and a passion for detail." How do people assess the probability that Steve is engaged in a particular occupation from a list of possibilities (for example, farmer, salesman, airline pilot, librarian, or physician)? How do people order these occupations from most to least likely? In the representativeness heuristic, the probability that Steve is a librarian, for example, is assessed by the degree to which he is representative of, or similar to, the stereotype of a librarian. Indeed, research with problems of this type has shown that people order the occupations by probability and by similarity in exactly the same way.[3] This approach to the judgment of probability leads to serious errors, because similarity, or representativeness, is not influenced by several factors that should affect judgments of probability.

Insensitivity to prior probability of outcomes

One of the factors that have no effect on representativeness but should have a major effect on probability is the prior probability, or base-rate frequency, of the outcomes. In the case of Steve, for example, the fact that there are many more farmers than librarians in the population should enter into any reasonable estimate of the probability that Steve is a librarian rather than a farmer. Considerations of base-rate frequency, however, do not affect the similarity of Steve to the stereotypes of librarians and farmers. If people evaluate probability by representativeness, therefore, prior probabilities will be neglected. This hypothesis was tested in an experiment where prior probabilities were manipulated.[4] * * * Subjects were shown brief personality descriptions of several individuals, allegedly sampled at random from a group of 100 professionals—engineers and lawyers. The subjects were

[3] Kahneman & Tversky, *On the Psychology of Prediction*, 80 Psych.Rev. 237 (1973).   [4] Id.

asked to assess, for each description, the probability that it belonged to an engineer rather than to a lawyer. In one experimental condition, subjects were told that the group from which the descriptions had been drawn consisted of 70 engineers and 30 lawyers. In another condition, subjects were told that the group consisted of 30 engineers and 70 lawyers. The odds that any particular description belongs to an engineer rather than to a lawyer should be higher in the first condition, where there is a majority of engineers, than in the second condition, where there is a majority of lawyers. * * *. [Nonetheless,] the subjects in the two conditions produced essentially the same probability judgments. Apparently, subjects evaluated the likelihood that a particular description belonged to an engineer rather than to a lawyer by the degree to which this description was representative of the two stereotypes, with little or no regard for the prior probabilities of the categories.

The subjects used prior probabilities correctly when they had no other information. In the absence of a personality sketch, they judged the probability that an unknown individual is an engineer to be .7 and .3, respectively, in the two base-rate conditions. However, prior probabilities were effectively ignored when a description was introduced, even when this description was totally uninformative. The responses to the following description illustrate this phenomenon:

Dick is a 30 year old man. He is married with no children. A man of high ability and high motivation, he promises to be quite successful in his field. He is well liked by his colleagues.

This description was intended to convey no information relevant to the question of whether Dick is an engineer or a lawyer. Consequently, the probability that Dick is an engineer should equal the proportion of engineers in the group, as if no description had been given. The subjects, however, judged the probability of Dick being an engineer to be .5 regardless of whether the stated proportion of engineers in the group was .7 or .3. Evidently, people respond differently when given no evidence and when given worthless evidence. When no specific evidence is given, prior probabilities are properly utilized; when worthless evidence is given, prior probabilities are ignored.

Insensitivity to sample size

To evaluate the probability of obtaining a particular result in a sample drawn from a specified population, people typically apply the representativeness heuristic. That is, they assess the likelihood of a sample result, for example, that the average height in a random sample of ten men will be 6 feet (180 centimeters), by the similarity of this result to the corresponding parameter (that is, to the average height in the population of men). The similarity of a sample statistic to a population parameter does not depend on the size of the sample. Consequently, if probabilities are assessed by representativeness, then the judged probability of a sample statistic will be essentially independent of sample size. Indeed, when subjects assessed the distributions of average height for samples of various sizes, they produced identical distributions. For example, the probability of obtaining an average height greater than 6 feet was assigned the same value for samples of 1000, 100, and 10 men.[5] Moreover, subjects failed to appreciate the role of sample size even when it was emphasized in the formulation of the problem. Consider the following question:

> A certain town is served by two hospitals. In the larger hospital about 45 babies are born each day, and in the smaller hospital about 15 babies are born each day. As you know, about 50 percent of all babies are boys. However, the exact percentage varies from day to day. Sometimes it may be higher than 50 percent, some-times lower.

For a period of 1 year, each hospital recorded the days on which more than 60 percent of the babies born were boys. Which hospital do you think recorded more such days?

The larger hospital (21)

The smaller hospital (21)

About the same (that is, within 5 percent of each other) (53)

The values in parentheses are the number of undergraduate students who chose each answer.

Most subjects judged the probability of obtaining more than 60 percent boys to be the same in the small and in the large hospital, presumably because these events are described by the same statistic and are therefore equally representative of the general population. In contrast, sampling theory entails that the expected number of days on which more than 60 percent of the babies are boys is much greater in the small hospital than in the large one, because a large sample is less likely to stray from 50 percent. This fundamental notion of statistics is evidently not part of people's repertoire of intuitions.

* * *

Misconceptions of chance

People expect that a sequence of events generated by a random process will represent the essential characteristics of that process even when the sequence is short. In considering tosses of a coin for heads or tails, for example, people regard the sequence H–T–H–T–T–H to be more likely than the sequence H–H–H–T–T–T, which does not appear random, and also more likely than the sequence H–H–H–H–T–H, which does not represent the fairness of the coin.[6] Thus, people expect that the essential characteristics of the process will be represented, not only globally in the entire sequence, but also locally in each of its parts. A locally representative sequence, however, deviates systematically from chance expectation: it contains too many alternations and too few runs. Another consequence of the belief in local representativeness is the well-known gambler's fallacy. After observing a long run of red on the roulette wheel, for example, most people erroneously believe that black is now due, presumably because the occurrence of black will result in a

---

[5] Kahneman & Tversky, *Subjective Probability: A Judgment of Representativeness*, 3 Cognitive Psych. 430 (1972).

[6] Kahneman & Tversky, supra note 5.

more representative sequence than the occurrence of an additional red. Chance is commonly viewed as a self-correcting process in which a deviation in one direction induces a deviation in the opposite direction to restore the equilibrium. In fact, deviations are not "corrected" as a chance process unfolds, they are merely diluted.

Misconceptions of chance are not limited to naive subjects. A study of the statistical intuitions of experienced research psychologists [7] revealed a lingering belief in what may be called the "law of small numbers," according to which even small samples are highly representative of the populations from which they are drawn. The responses of these investigators reflected the expectation that a valid hypothesis about a population will be represented by a statistically significant result in a sample—with little regard for its size. As a consequence, the researchers put too much faith in the results of small samples and grossly overestimated the replicability of such results. In the actual conduct of research, this bias leads to the selection of samples of inadequate size and to overinterpretation of findings.

Insensitivity to predictability

People are sometimes called upon to make such numerical predictions as the future value of a stock, the demand for a commodity, or the outcome of a football game. Such predictions are often made by representativeness. For example, suppose one is given a description of a company and is asked to predict its future profit. If the description of the company is very favorable, a very high profit will appear most representative of that description; if the description is mediocre, a mediocre performance will appear most representative. The degree to which the description is favorable is unaffected by the reliability of that description or by the degree to which it permits accurate prediction. Hence, if people predict solely in terms of the favorableness of the description, their predictions will be insensitive to the reliability of the evidence and to the expected accuracy of the prediction.

This mode of judgment violates the normative statistical theory in which the extremeness and the range of predictions are controlled by considerations of predictability. When predictability is nil, the same prediction should be made in all cases. For example, if the descriptions of companies provide no information relevant to profit, then the same value (such as average profit) should be predicted for all companies. If predictability is perfect, of course, the values predicted will match the actual values and the range of predictions will equal the range of outcomes. In general, the higher the predictability, the wider the range of predicted values.

Several studies of numerical prediction have demonstrated that intuitive predictions violate this rule, and that subjects show little or no regard for considerations of predictability.[8] In one of these studies, subjects were presented with several paragraphs, each describing the

---

[7] Tversky & Kahneman, *The Belief in the "Law of Small Numbers,"* 76 Psych. Bull. 105 (1971).

[8] Kahneman & Tversky, supra note 3.

performance of a student teacher during a particular practice lesson. Some subjects were asked to *evaluate* the quality of the lesson described in the paragraph in percentile scores, relative to a specified population. Other subjects were asked to *predict*, also in percentile scores, the standing of each student teacher 5 years after the practice lesson. The judgments made under the two conditions were identical. That is, the prediction of a remote criterion (success of a teacher after 5 years) was identical to the evaluation of the information on which the prediction was based (the quality of the practice lesson). The students who made these predictions were undoubtedly aware of the limited predictability of teaching competence on the basis of a single trial lesson 5 years earlier; nevertheless, their predictions were as extreme as their evaluations.

The illusion of validity

As we have seen, people often predict by selecting the outcome (for example, an occupation) that is most representative of the input (for example, the description of a person). The confidence they have in their prediction depends primarily on the degree of representativeness (that is, on the quality of the match between the selected outcome and the input) with little or no regard for the factors that limit predictive accuracy. Thus, people express great confidence in the prediction that a person is a librarian when given a description of his personality which matches the stereotype of librarians, even if the description is scanty, unreliable, or outdated. The unwarranted confidence which is produced by a good fit between the predicted outcome and the input information may be called the illusion of validity. This illusion persists even when the judge is aware of the factors that limit the accuracy of his predictions. * * *

The internal consistency of a pattern of inputs is a major determinant of one's confidence in predictions based on these inputs. For example, people express more confidence in predicting the final grade-point average of a student whose first-year record consists entirely of B's than in predicting the grade-point average of a student whose first-year record includes many A's and C's. Highly consistent patterns are most often observed when the input variables are highly redundant or correlated. Hence, people tend to have great confidence in predictions based on redundant input variables. However, an elementary result in the statistics of correlation asserts that, given input variables of stated validity, a prediction based on several such inputs can achieve higher accuracy when they are independent of each other than when they are redundant or correlated. Thus redundancy among inputs decreases accuracy even as it increases confidence, and people are often confident in predictions that are quite likely to be off the mark.[9]

[9] Id. [Is it so clear that the people who feel more confident about predicting the performance of the consistent student are wrong? What if it was very important not to be wrong; for example, suppose you were hiring a summer clerk for your law firm? Ed.]

Misconceptions of regression

Suppose a large group of children has been examined on two equivalent versions of an aptitude test. If one selects ten children from among those who did best on one of the two versions, he will usually find their performance of the second version to be somewhat disappointing. Conversely, if one selects ten children from among those who did worst on one version, they will be found, on the average, to do somewhat better on the other version. More generally, consider two variables X and Y which have the same distribution. If one selects individuals whose average X score deviates from the mean of X by k units, then the average of their Y scores will usually deviate from the mean of Y by less than k units. These observations illustrate a general phenomenon known as regression toward the mean, which was first documented * * * more than 100 years ago.

In the normal course of life, one encounters many instances of regression toward the mean, in the comparison of the height of fathers and sons, of the intelligence of husbands and wives, or of the performance of individuals on consecutive examinations. Nevertheless, people do not develop correct intuitions about this phenomenon. First, they do not expect regression in many contexts where it is bound to occur. Second, when they recognize the occurrence of regression, they often invent spurious causal explanations for it.[10] We suggest that the phenomenon of regression remains elusive because it is incompatible with the belief that the predicted outcome should be maximally representative of the input, and, hence, that the value of the outcome variable should be as extreme as the value of the input variable.

The failure to recognize the import of regression can have pernicious consequences, as illustrated by the following observation.[11] In a discussion of flight training, experienced instructors noted that praise for an exceptionally smooth landing is typically followed by a poorer landing on the next try, while harsh criticism after a rough landing is usually followed by an improvement on the next try. The instructors concluded that verbal rewards are detrimental to learning, while verbal punishments are beneficial, contrary to accepted psychological doctrine. This conclusion is unwarranted because of the presence of regression toward the mean. As in other cases of repeated examination, an improvement will usually follow a poor performance and a deterioration will usually follow an outstanding performance, even if the instructor does not respond to the trainee's achievement on the first attempt. Because the instructors had praised their trainees after good landings and admonished them after poor ones, they reached the erroneous and potentially harmful conclusion that punishment is more effective than reward.

Thus, the failure to understand the effect of regression leads one to overestimate the effectiveness of punishment and to underestimate the effectiveness of reward. In social interaction, as well as in training, rewards are typically administered when performance is good, and punishments are typically administered when performance is poor. By

[10] Id.   [11] Id.

regression alone, therefore, behavior is most likely to improve after punishment and most likely to deteriorate after reward. Consequently, the human condition is such that, by chance alone, one is most often rewarded for punishing others and most often punished for rewarding them. People are generally not aware of this contingency. In fact, the elusive role of regression in determining the apparent consequences of reward and punishment seems to have escaped the notice of students of this area.

Availability

There are situations in which people assess the frequency of a class or the probability of an event by the ease with which instances or occurrences can be brought to mind. For example, one may assess the risk of heart attack among middle-aged people by recalling such occurrences among one's acquaintances. Similarly, one may evaluate the probability that a given business venture will fail by imagining various difficulties it could encounter. This judgmental heuristic is called availability. Availability is a useful clue for assessing frequency or probability, because instances of large classes are usually reached better and faster than instances of less frequent classes. However, availability is affected by factors other than frequency and probability. Consequently, the reliance on availability leads to predictable biases, some of which are illustrated below.

Biases due to the retrievability of instances

When the size of a class is judged by the availability of its instances, a class whose instances are easily retrieved will appear more numerous than a class of equal frequency whose instances are less retrievable. In an elementary demonstration of this effect, subjects heard a list of well-known personalities of both sexes and were subsequently asked to judge whether the list contained more names of men than of women. Different lists were presented to different groups of subjects. In some of the lists the men were relatively more famous than the women, and in others the women were relatively more famous than the men. In each of the lists, the subjects erroneously judged that the class (sex) that had the more famous personalities was the more numerous.[12]

In addition to familiarity, there are other factors, such as salience, which affect the retrievability of instances. For example, the impact of seeing a house burning on the subjective probability of such accidents is probably greater than the impact of reading about a fire in the local paper. Furthermore, recent occurrences are likely to be relatively more available than earlier occurrences. It is a common experience that the subjective probability of traffic accidents rises temporarily when one sees a car overturned by the side of the road.

[12] Tversky & Kahneman, *Availability: A Heuristic for Judging Frequency and Probability*, 5 Cognitive Psych. 207 (1973).

Biases due to the effectiveness of a search set

Suppose one samples a word (of three letters or more) at random from an English text. Is it more likely that the word starts with *r* or that *r* is the third letter? People approach this problem by recalling words that begin with *r* (road) and words that have *r* in the third position (car) and assess the relative frequency by the ease with which words of the two types come to mind. Because it is much easier to search for words by their first letter than by their third letter, most people judge words that begin with a given consonant to be more numerous than words in which the same consonant appears in the third position. They do so even for consonants, such as *r* or *k*, that are more frequent in the third position than in the first.[13]

Different tasks elicit different search sets. For example, suppose you are asked to rate the frequency with which abstract words (*thought, love*) and concrete words (*door, water*) appear in written English. A natural way to answer this question is to search for contexts in which the word could appear. It seems easier to think of contexts in which an abstract concept is mentioned (*love* in love stories) than to think of contexts in which a concrete word (such as *door*) is mentioned. If the frequency of words is judged by the availability of the contexts in which they appear, abstract words will be judged as relatively more numerous than concrete words. This bias has been observed in a recent study [14] which showed that the judged frequency of occurrence of abstract words was much higher than that of concrete words, equated in objective frequency. Abstract words were also judged to appear in a much greater variety of contexts than concrete words.

* * *

Adjustment and Anchoring

In many situations, people make estimates by starting from an initial value that is adjusted to yield the final answer. The initial value, or starting point, may be suggested by the formulation of the problem, or it may be the result of a partial computation. In either case, adjustments are typically insufficient.[15] That is, different starting points yield different estimates, which are biased toward the initial values. We call this phenomenon anchoring.

Insufficient adjustment

In a demonstration of the anchoring effect, subjects were asked to estimate various quantities, stated in percentages (for example, the percentage of African countries in the United Nations). For each quantity, a number between 0 and 100 was determined by spinning a wheel of fortune in the subjects' presence. The subjects were instructed to indicate first whether that number was higher or lower than the value of the quantity, and then to estimate the value of the quantity by

---

[13] Id.

[14] Galbraith & Underwood, *Perceived Frequency of Concrete and Abstract Words,* 1 Memory & Cognition 172 (1973).

[15] Slovic & Lichtenstein, *Comparison of Bayesian and Regression Approaches to the Study of Information Processing in Judgment,* 6 Org.Behav. & Human Perf. 649 (1971).

moving upward or downward from the given number. Different groups were given different numbers for each quantity, and these arbitrary numbers had a marked effect on estimates. For example, the median estimates of the percentage of African countries in the United Nations were 25 and 45 for groups that received 10 and 65, respectively, as starting points. Payoffs for accuracy did not reduce the anchoring effect.

Anchoring occurs not only when the starting point is given to the subject, but also when the subject bases his estimate on the result of some incomplete computation. A study of intuitive numerical estimation illustrates this effect. Two groups of high school students estimated, within 5 seconds, a numerical expression that was written on the blackboard. One group estimated the product

$$8 \times 7 \times 6 \times 5 \times 4 \times 3 \times 2 \times 1$$

while another group estimated the product

$$1 \times 2 \times 3 \times 4 \times 5 \times 6 \times 7 \times 8$$

To rapidly answer such questions, people may perform a few steps of computation and estimate the product by extrapolation or adjustment. Because adjustments are typically insufficient, this procedure should lead to underestimation. Furthermore, because the result of the first few steps of multiplication (performed from left to right) is higher in the descending sequence than in the ascending sequence, the former expression should be judged larger than the latter. Both predictions were confirmed. The median estimate for the ascending sequence was 512, while the median estimate for the descending sequence was 2,250. The correct answer is 40,320.

Biases in the evaluation of conjunctive and disjunctive events

In a recent study by Bar-Hillel [16] subjects were given the opportunity to bet on one of two events. Three types of events were used: (i) simple events, such as drawing a red marble from a bag containing 50 percent red marbles and 50 percent white marbles; (ii) conjunctive events, such as drawing a red marble seven times in succession, with replacement, from a bag containing 90 percent red marbles and 10 percent white marbles; and (iii) disjunctive events, such as drawing a red marble at least once in seven successive tries, with replacement, from a bag containing 10 percent red marbles and 90 percent white marbles. In this problem, a significant majority of subjects preferred to bet on the conjunctive event (the probability of which is .48) rather than on the simple event (the probability of which is .50). Subjects also preferred to bet on the simple event rather than on the disjunctive event, which has a probability of .52. Thus, most subjects bet on the less likely event in both comparisons. This pattern of choices illustrates a general finding. Studies of choice among gambles and of judgments of probability indicate that people tend to overestimate the probability of conjunctive events and to underestimate the probability

[16] Bar-Hillel, *On the Subjective Probability of Compound Events,* 9 Org.Behav. & Human Perf. 396 (1973).

of disjunctive events. These biases are readily explained as effects of anchoring. The stated probability of the elementary event (success at any one stage) provides a natural starting point for the estimation of the probabilities of both conjunctive and disjunctive events. Since adjustment from the starting point is typically insufficient, the final estimates remain too close to the probabilities of the elementary events in both cases. Note that the overall probability of a conjunctive event is lower than the probability of each elementary event, whereas the overall probability of a disjunctive event is higher than the probability of each elementary event. As a consequence of anchoring, the overall probability will be overestimated in conjunctive problems and underestimated in disjunctive problems.

Biases in the evaluation of compound events are particularly significant in the context of planning. The successful completion of an undertaking, such as the development of a new product, typically has a conjunctive character: for the undertaking to succeed, each of a series of events must occur. Even when each of these events is very likely, the overall probability of success can be quite low if the number of events is large. The general tendency to overestimate the probability of conjunctive events leads to unwarranted optimism in the evaluation of the likelihood that a plan will succeed or that a project will be completed on time. Conversely, disjunctive structures are typically encountered in the evaluation of risks. A complex system, such as a nuclear reactor or a human body, will malfunction if any of its essential components fails. Even when the likelihood of failure in each component is slight, the probability of an overall failure can be high if many components are involved. Because of anchoring, people will tend to underestimate the probabilities of failure in complex systems. Thus, the direction of the anchoring bias can sometimes be inferred from the structure of the event. The chain-like structure of conjunctions leads to overestimation, the funnel-like structure of disjunctions leads to underestimation.

Anchoring in the assessment of subjective probability distributions

In decision analysis, experts are often required to express their beliefs about a quantity, such as the value of the Dow-Jones average on a particular day, in the form of a probability distribution. Such a distribution is usually constructed by asking the person to select values of the quantity that correspond to specified percentiles of his subjective probability distribution. For example, the judge may be asked to select a number, X_{90} such that his subjective probability that this number will be higher than the value of the Dow-Jones average is .90. That is, he should select the value X_{90} so that he is just willing to accept 9 to 1 odds that the Dow-Jones average will not exceed it. A subjective probability distribution for the value of the Dow-Jones average can be constructed from several such judgments corresponding to different percentiles.

By collecting subjective probability distributions for many different quantities, it is possible to test the judge for proper calibration. A judge is properly (or externally) calibrated in a set of problems if exactly II percent of the true values of the assessed quantities falls below his stated values of X_n. For example, the true values should fall below X_{01} for 1 percent of the quantities and above X_{99} for 1 percent of the quantities. Thus, the true values should fall in the confidence interval between X_{01} and X_{99} on 98 percent of the problems.

Several investigators * * * have obtained probability disruptions for many quantities from a large number of judges. These distributions indicated large and systematic departures from proper calibration. In most studies, the actual values of the assessed quantities are either smaller than X_{01} or greater than X_{99} for about 30 percent of the problems. That is, the subjects state overly narrow confidence intervals which reflect more certainty than is justified by their knowledge about the assessed quantities. This bias is common to naive and to sophisticated subjects, and it is not eliminated by introducing proper scoring rules, which provide incentives for external calibration. This effect is attributable, in part at least, to anchoring.

To select X_{90} for the value of the Dow-Jones average, for example, it is natural to begin by thinking about one's best estimate of the Dow-Jones and to adjust this value upward. If this adjustment—like most others—is insufficient, then X_{90} will not be sufficiently extreme. A similar anchoring effect will occur in the selection of X_{10}, which is presumably obtained by adjusting one's best estimate downward. Consequently, the confidence interval between X_{10} and X_{90} will be too narrow, and the assessed probability distribution will be too tight. In support of this interpretation it can be shown that subjective probabilities are systematically altered by a procedure in which one's best estimate does not serve as an anchor.

Subjective probability distributions for a given quantity (the Dow-Jones average) can be obtained in two different ways: (i) by asking the subject to select values of the Dow-Jones that correspond to specified percentiles of his probability distribution and (ii) by asking the subject to assess the probabilities that the true value of the Dow-Jones will exceed some specified values. The two procedures are formally equivalent and should yield identical distributions. However, they suggest different modes of adjustment from different anchors. In procedure (i), the natural starting point is one's best estimate of the quality. In procedure (ii), on the other hand, the subject may be anchored on the value stated in the question. Alternatively, he may be anchored on even odds, or 50–50 chances, which is a natural starting point in the estimation of likelihood. In either case, procedure (ii) should yield less extreme odds than procedure (i).

To contrast the two procedures, a set of 24 quantities (such as the air distance from New Delhi to Peking) was presented to a group of subjects who assessed either X_{10} or X_{90} for each problem. Another group of subjects received the median judgment of the first group for each of the 24 quantities. They were asked to assess the odds that each of the given values exceeded the true value of the relevant quantity. In the absence of any bias, the second group should retrieve the odds specified to the first group, that is, 9:1. However, if even odds or the stated value serve as anchors, the odds of the second group should be less extreme, that is, closer to 1:1. Indeed, the median odds stated by this group, across all problems, were 3:1. When the judgments of the two groups were tested for external calibration, it was found that subjects in the first group were too extreme, in accord with earlier studies. The events that they defined as having a probability of .10 actually obtained in 24 percent of the cases. In contrast, subjects in the second group were too conservative. Events to which they assigned an average probability of .34 actually obtained in 26 percent of the cases. These results illustrate the manner in which the degree of calibration depends on the procedure of elicitation.

Discussion

*   *   *

The reliance on heuristics and the prevalence of biases are not restricted by laymen. Experienced researchers are also prone to the same biases—when they think intuitively. For example, the tendency to predict the outcome that best represents the data, with insufficient regard for prior probability, has been observed in the intuitive judgments of individuals who have had extensive training in statistics.[17] Although the statistically sophisticated avoid elementary errors, such as the gambler's fallacy, their intuitive judgments are liable to similar fallacies in more intricate and less transparent problems.

It is not surprising that useful heuristics such as representativeness and availability are retained, even though they occasionally lead to errors in prediction or estimation. What is perhaps surprising is the failure of people to infer from lifelong experience such fundamental statistical rules as regression toward the mean, or the effect of sample size on sampling variability. Although everyone is exposed, in the normal course of life, to numerous examples from which these rules could have been induced, very few people discover the principles of sampling and regression on their own. Statistical principles are not learned from everyday experience because the relevant instances are not coded appropriately. For example, people do not discover that successive lines in a text differ more in average word length than do successive pages, because they simply do not attend to the average word length of individual lines or pages. Thus, people do not learn the relation between sample size and sampling variability, although the data for such learning are abundant.

The lack of an appropriate code also explains why people usually do not detect the biases in their judgments of probability. A person could conceivably learn whether his judgments are externally calibrated by keeping a tally of the proportion of events that actually occur among those to which he assigns the same probability. However, it is not natural to group events by their judged probability. In the absence of such grouping it is impossible for an individual to discover, for example, that only 50 percent of the predictions to which he has assigned a probability of .9 or higher actually come true.

[17] Kahneman & Tversky, supra note 3; Tversky & Kahneman, supra note 7.

The empirical analysis of cognitive biases has implications for the theoretical and applied role of judged probabilities. Modern decision theory * * * regards subjective probability as the quantified opinion of an idealized person. Specifically, the subjective probability of a given event is defined by the set of bets about this event that such a person is willing to accept. An internally consistent, or coherent, subjective probability measure can be derived for an individual if his choices among bets satisfy certain principles, that is, the axioms of the theory. The derived probability is subjective in the sense that different individuals are allowed to have different probabilities for the same event. The major contribution of this approach is that it provides a rigorous subjective interpretation of probability that is applicable to unique events and is embedded in a general theory of rational decision.

* * *

The inherently subjective nature of probability has led many students to the belief that coherence, or internal consistency, is the only valid criterion by which judged probabilities should be evaluated. From the standpoint of the formal theory of subjective probability, any set of internally consistent probability judgments is as good as any other. This criterion is not entirely satisfactory, because an internally consistent set of subjective probabilities can be incompatible with other beliefs held by the individual. Consider a person whose subjective probabilities for all possible outcomes of a coin-tossing game reflect the gambler's fallacy. That is, his estimate of the probability of tails on a particular toss increases with the number of consecutive heads that preceded that toss. The judgments of such a person could be internally consistent and therefore acceptable as adequate subjective probabilities according to the criterion of the formal theory. These probabilities, however, are incompatible with the generally held belief that a coin has no memory and is therefore incapable of generating sequential dependencies. For judged probabilities to be considered adequate, or rational, internal consistency is not enough. The judgments must be compatible with the entire web of beliefs held by the individual. Unfortunately, there can be no simple formal procedure for assessing the compatibility of a set of probability judgments with the judge's total system of beliefs. The rational judge will nevertheless strive for compatibility, even though internal consistency is more easily achieved and assessed. In particular, he will attempt to make his probability judgments compatible with his knowledge about the subject matter, the laws of probability, and his own judgmental heuristics and biases.

◆

Tversky & Kahneman offer what seems like a serious indictment of the accuracy of our assessments of subjective probabilities. What is the impact of the failures they identify on the usefulness of the decision tree technique? The problem, of course, is an application of the theory of the second best: If our estimates of subjective probabilities are biased, then are our decisions really made better by systematic, rather than merely intuitive, reliance on them?

The answer appears to be yes, and the explanation rests on the distinction between the positive and normative implications of the empirical evidence Tversky and Kahneman marshall. The data suggests that there are important biases in our intuitive assessments of probabilities. This conclusion, in turn, has important implications for debates concerning the appropriate level of governmental paternalism in regulating different types of hazards as by consumer labeling. See Slovic, Fischoff & Lichtenstein, *Facts Versus Fears: Understanding Perceived Risks* in *Societal Risk Assessment: How Safe is Safe Enough?* (R. Schwing & W. Albers eds., 1980). But understanding what biases we have also has important normative implications for how we should make decisions. First, the very process of systematically approaching the specification of subjective probability reduces our reliance on the shorthand techniques which are the source of the bias in the first place. We are simply less likely to make the same mistakes if we think about the problem more carefully. Second, learning to recognize the biases, a process that should be part of learning to use the decision tree technique, goes a long way toward eliminating them, whether in yourself or in the client whose assessment of particular subjective probabilities you wish to elicit. In this regard, the dialogue between a decision analyst and an uninitiated subject constructed in J.M. Jones, *Introduction to Decision Theory* 314–38 (1977), is instructive in showing how a client can be taken through the process. Finally, education in statistical techniques provides an alternative to the heuristics which Tversky and Kahneman describe as a means to process information. Note, however, that not all decisions are important enough to warrant avoiding the heuristic techniques and their attendant biases. The techniques, after all, persist precisely because, in most situations, they work. And even in the situations where bias is possible, there will be many decisions which are simply not worth the time, energy or money necessary to apply more systematic decision techniques. See R. Nisbett & L. Ross, *Human Interference: Strategies and Shortcomings of Social Judgment* 273–94 (1980).

The research in this area has continued at an accelerated pace since the date of the Tversky & Kahneman article. For more recent (and exhaustive) surveys see, e.g., *Judgment Under Uncertainty: Heuristics and Biases* (D. Kahneman, P. Slovic & A. Tversky eds. 1982); R. Nisbett & L. Ross, supra; Shoemaker, *The Expected Utility Model: Its Variants, Purposes, Evidence and Limitations*, 20 J.Econ.Lit. 529 (1982).[4]

On an applications level, the problem raised by Tversky and Kahneman has significant implications for economic analysis generally. The economist's model assumes rational (i.e., maximizing) behavior by individuals. What happens to the analysis if we acknowledge that although individual maximizing is undertaken, the information on which decisions are based may be systematically biased? For an

[4] There have also been efforts to explain some of the empirical evidence of heuristic biases in terms which are consistent with expected utility theory. See, e.g., DeMeza & Dickinson, *Risk Preferences and Transaction Costs*, 5 J.Econ.Beh. & Org. 223 (1985) (incorporation of transaction costs into expected utility theory).

interesting beginning at incorporating this form of "irrationality" into the economist's model, see Ackeroff & Dickens, *The Economic Consequences of Cognitive Dissonance,* 72 Am.Econ.Rev. 307 (1982); see also Arrow, *Risk Perception in Psychology and Economics,* 20 Econ.Inquiry 1 (1981); Loomes and Sugden, *Regret Theory: An Alternative Theory of Rational Choice under Uncertainty,* 92 Econ.J. 805 (1982). There have also been recent efforts to consider the relevance of research on the cognitive aspects of decisionmaking to a particular setting in which the relationship between information and decisions is particularly critical to regulatory efforts: the setting of financial accounting standards. One function of financial accounting is to provide information. Information has value only to the extent it alters behavior. Thus, the manner in which information is actually used in decision making is important to determining what information should be provided. The research in this area is surveyed in M. Gibbons & P. Brennan, *Behavioral Research and Financial Accounting Standards,* in P. Griffin, *Usefulness to Investors and Creditors of Information Provided by Financial Reporting: A Review of Empirical Accounting Research* 99–134 (1982).

B. Expressing Risk

The expected monetary value of a range of expected returns allows us to describe an important aspect of that range. It is a measure of the central tendency—in statistical terms, the mean—of that distribution. Consider Investment A, whose expected returns are estimated as follows:

Investment A

Probability	Expected Return ($)	Probability x Return ($)
.10	−10	−1.00
.25	0	0
.30	10	3.00
.25	20	5.00
.10	30	3.00
	Expected Monetary Value =	$10.00

But while the expected monetary value describes the central tendency of this distribution of future returns, it does not capture another important aspect of the uncertainty of the distribution. Consider Investment B, whose expected returns are estimated as follows:

Investment B

Probability	Expected Return ($)	Probability x Return ($)
.15	−10	−1.50
.22	0	0
.26	10	2.60
.22	20	4.40
.15	30	4.50
	Expected Monetary Value =	$10.00

Investment B also has an expected monetary value of $10.00. Its pattern of expected returns, however, differs significantly from that of Investment A, as can be seen in the following bar graph:

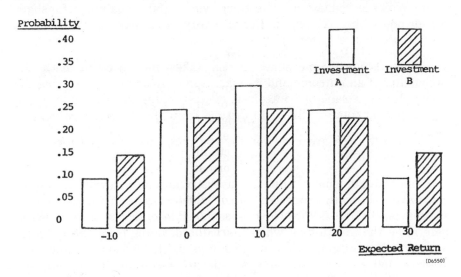

In particular, Investment B has a higher likelihood than Investment A of losing money, and of earning the highest return, even though both have the same expected monetary value. We still need a way to express this aspect of uncertainty—the shape or dispersion of the expected returns around the mean. This dispersion—the likelihood that the actual return will differ from the expected monetary value—is what financial economists treat as the risk of an investment. The greater the likelihood that the actual return will differ from the expected return, the riskier the investment.

Professor William Sharpe develops this concept and the statistical measure of dispersion in the following:

W. SHARPE, INVESTMENTS
119–22 (2nd ed. 1981) *

The *Webster's New Collegiate Dictionary* definition of risk includes the following meanings: "* * * possibility of loss or injury * * * the degree or probability of such loss." [1] This conforms to the connotation put on the term by most investors. Professionals often speak "downside risk" and "upside potential" on the grounds that risk has to do with bad outcomes; potential with good ones.

As formal measures of risk, such notions can be criticized on two grounds: vagueness and excessive simplicity. One might measure risk by the probability that return will fall below the expected value. But this could characterize many different investments as equally risky.

---

* Copyright © 1981. Reprinted by permission of Prentice-Hall, Inc., Englewood Cliffs, N.J.

Merriam Co., Publishers of the Merriam-Webster dictionaries.

[1] By permission. From *Webster's New Collegiate Dictionary* ©1980 by G. & C.

(For example, the probability in question is .50 for all symmetric distributions.) A more common procedure would focus on the probability of any *negative* return. But even this is an extremely blunt measure. Which is riskier: an investment with a .30 probability of a slight loss or one with a .29 probability of a very large loss? Most investors would specify the latter.

A more useful measure of risk takes into account both the probability of an outcome and its magnitude. Instead of measuring the probability of a range of outcomes, one estimates the extent to which the actual outcome is likely to *diverge* from the expected value.

Two measures are used for this purpose: the average (or mean) absolute deviation and the standard deviation.

Table 6–2(a) shows how the average absolute deviation can be calculated. First the expected return is determined in the usual way. In this case it is 6.50%. Next, each possible outcome is analyzed to determine the amount by which its value deviates from the expected amount. These figures, shown in column (5) of the table, include both positive and negative values. As shown in column (6), a weighted average, using probabilities as weights, will equal zero. This is a mathematical necessity, given the way the expected value is calculated. To assess risk, the signs of the deviations can simply be ignored. As shown in column (7), the weighted average of the absolute values of the deviations, using the probabilities as weights, is 7.65%. This constitutes the first measure of "likely" deviation.

The second measure is slightly more complex but preferable analytically. As shown in Table 6–2(b), the deviations are squared (making the values all positive); then a weighted average of these amounts is taken, using the probabilities as weights. The result is termed the *variance*. We convert it to the original units by taking the square root. The result (in Table 6–2(b), 9.3675%) is termed the *standard deviation*.

In the examples shown in Tables 6–2(a) and (b) any single measure of likely deviation would provide at best a very crude idea of the possibilities. But in the more common case in which a portfolio's prospects are being assessed, either of the measures described earlier may prove to be a very good guide to the analysts' degree of uncertainty. The clearest example arises when the situation can be reasonably well represented by the familiar bell-shaped curve: that is, the analyst is willing to use a *normal probability distribution*. This is often considered a plausible assumption for analyzing returns on diversified portfolios when the holding period being studied is relatively short (say a quarter or less). For longer holding periods, a more appropriate procedure assumes that the portfolio's *continuously compounded rate of return* is distributed in this manner (equivalently: that the return itself follows a "log-normal" distribution). Such an approach may be applied for any holding period; but for short holding periods, since actual return differs little from the continuously compounded return, either procedure may be used.

Table 6–2(a)

Calculating the Mean Absolute Deviation

(1) Event	(2) Probability	(3) Return (%)	(4) = (2) × (3) Probability x Return
a	.20	−10	−2.00
b	.35	5	1.75
c	.45	15	6.75
		Expected return =	6.50

(5) = (3) − 6.50 Deviation	(6) = (2) × (5) Probability x Deviation	(7) Probability x Absolute Deviation
−16.50	−3.300	3.300
− 1.50	−.525	.525
8.50	3.825	3.825
	0	
	Average absolute deviation =	7.65

Table 6–2(b)

Calculating the Standard Deviation

(1) Event	(2) Probability	(3) Deviation	(4) = (3) Deviation Squared	(5) = (2) × (4) Probability x Deviation Squared
a	.20	−16.50	272.25	54.45
b	.35	−1.50	2.25	.7875
c	.45	8.50	72.25	32.5125
	Variance = probability weighted average squared deviation =			87.75
	Standard deviation = square root of variance =			9.3675

For a normal distribution the standard deviaion is about 125% of the average absolute deviation. Either value may thus be determined, once the other is known. In general, a list of portfolios ordered from highest to lowest on the basis of the standard deviation of return would differ little if at all from a list ordered on the basis of average absolute deviation.

But why count happy surprises (those above the expected value) at all in a measure of risk? Why not just consider the deviations *below* the expected return? Measures that do so have much to recommend them. But if a distribution is symmetric, the results will be the same, since the left side is a mirror image of the right! And in general, a list of portfolios ordered on the basis of "downside risk" will differ little if at all from one ordered on the basis of standard deviation. A similar statement can be made about many other reasonable measures of risk.

* * *

Table 6-3

Probabilities of Divergence for a Normal Distribution

Divergence, in Terms of Standard Deviation Units	Probability that Divergence Will Be Less than This Amount
0	0
.10	.08
.20	.16
.30	.24
.40	.31
.50	.38
.60	.45
.70	.52
.80	.58
.90	.63
1.00	.68
1.10	.73
1.20	.77
1.30	.81
1.40	.84
1.50	.87
1.60	.89
1.70	.91
1.80	.93
1.90	.94
2.00	.95
2.10	.96
2.20	.97
2.30	.98
2.40	.98
2.50	.99

* * *

Let us emphasize the meaning of this measure of risk:

The standard deviation is an estimate of the likely divergence of an *actual* amount from an *expected* amount.

For working purposes, the returns are often assumed to follow a normal distribution, giving the relationships shown in Table 6-3. Thus the odds are thought to be about 2 out of 3 that the actual outcome will lie within one standard deviation of the expectation and about 95 out of 100 that the actual outcome will lie within two standard deviations of the expectation.

When an analyst predicts that a stock will return 12% next year, he or she is presumably stating something comparable to an expected value. If asked to express the *uncertainty* about the outcome, the analyst might reply that the odds are about 2 out of 3 that the actual return will be within 8% of the estimate (i.e., betwen 4% and 20%). The standard deviation is a formal measure of uncertainty, or risk, expressed in this manner, just as the expected value is a formal measure of a "best guess" estimate. Most analysts make such predictions directly, without explicitly assessing probabilities and making the requisite computations. No matter. The point is to consider uncertainty or risk and to measure its extent as best one can.

———————◆———————

C.   Criteria for Choice

Taken together, the mean and standard deviation of the expected returns from an investment describe the uncertainty associated with it. But an understanding of how that investment is valued requires as well understanding something about the desirability of each of these characteristics. In the previous section, Investments A and B had identical means, but Investment A had a standard deviation of $\sqrt{11.4}$ while Investment B had a standard deviation of $\sqrt{12.81}$.[5] How should this difference be taken into account in evaluating the two investments? To further complicate matters, suppose you have a choice between two investments that differ both as to risk and return. One investment has both a higher expected monetary value than the other, *and* a higher standard deviation. Put differently, one investment has a higher return, the other a lower risk. Understanding the relationship between risk and return is the central core of how assets are valued under uncertainty. The following discussion lays part of the foundation for our focus on this relationship in Chapter Four.

———————◆———————

W. SHARPE, PORTFOLIO THEORY AND CAPITAL MARKETS
26–31 (1970).[*]

Investors' Preferences

The desirability of a portfolio is expressed by the values of E_p and σ_p.[**] Two portfolios with quite different probability distributions might nonetheless have the same E_p and the same σ_p. The theory assumes that any investor would consider such portfolios equivalent— he would just as soon have one as the other. This may not be strictly true in every instance. As always, abstraction may lead to error. But the chance of error may be small; and the error, if made, may not be serious.

Any portfolio can be represented by a point on a graph such as that shown in Fig. 2–4. Standard deviation of rate of return is plotted on

---

[5] Technically, this is completely correct only on the assumption of a normal distribution and quadratic utility functions.

[*] Copyright © 1970. Reprinted by permission of McGraw-Hill Book Company.

[**] Ep stands for expected value (or expected return, an equivalent term) and σ_p stands for the standard deviation of return. [Ed.]

the horizontal axis, and expected rate of return is plotted on the vertical axis.

How does an investor choose among alternative portfolios? The following rules are assumed to apply for any investor:

1. If two portfolios have the same standard deviation of return and different expected returns, the one with the larger expected return is preferred.

2. If two portfolios have the same expected return and different standard deviations of return, the one with the smaller standard deviation is preferred.

3. If one portfolio has a smaller standard deviation of return and a larger expected return than another, it is preferred.

Figure 2–4

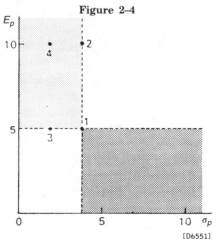

[D6551]

The rules may be summarized succinctly:

4. E_p is *good*: other things equal, more is preferred to less.

5. σ_p is *bad*: other things equal, less is preferred to more.

Assumption 5 is often termed *risk aversion*. A large body of evidence indicates that almost everyone is a risk averter when making important decisions. Clear counterexamples are rarely found. A day at the horse races provides something besides risk and probable loss, and even the ardent fan seldom takes his entire earnings to the track.

Figure 2–5 shows the distributions of rate of return for four portfolios; their E_p and σ_p values are plotted in Fig. 2–4. Among other things, the assumptions about investor preferences imply that:

Portfolio 2 is preferred to portfolio 1 (rules 1, 4).

Portfolio 3 is preferred to portfolio 1 (rules 2, 5).

Portfolio 4 is preferred to portfolio 1 (rules 3, 4, and 5).

Graphically, the rules assert that for any investor:

Portfolios represented by points lying to the northwest of the point representing a portfolio are better (i.e., preferred).

Portfolios represented by points lying to the southeast of the point representing a portfolio are worse (i.e, the original portfolio is preferred).

Portfolios represented by points lying in the lightly shaded area in Fig. 2–4 are preferred to portfolio 1, but portfolio 1 is preferred to all those represented by points lying in the darkly shaded area.

The major results of portfolio theory follow directly from the assumption that investors like [return and dislike risk.] * * * Of course, more can be said about the preferences of any *given* investor. How strong is his dislike for σ_p vis-à-vis E_p? How much uncertainty is he willing to accept to enhance his prospects for a likely rate of return?

Figure 2–5

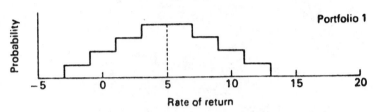

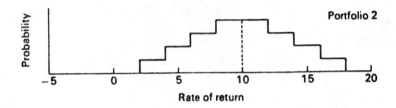

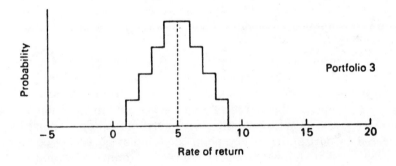

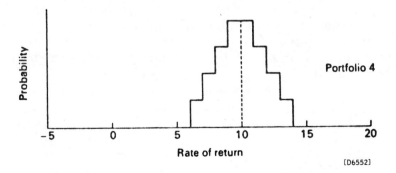

[D6552]

The feelings of a particular investor can usefully be represented by a family of *indifference curves*. Consider Fig. 2–6. The lightly shaded area contains all the points representing portfolios that Mr. *T* prefers to portfolio 1. The darkly shaded area contains all the points representing portfolios that he considers inferior to portfolio 1. The curve that divides the region contains all the points representing portfolios that he considers equivalent to portfolio 1; he has no preferences among them—he is *indifferent* about the choice.

Figure 2–6

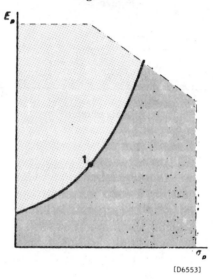

[D6553]

As long as E_p is desired and σ_p is not, every indifference curve will be upward-sloping. Generally, each curve will become steeper as E_p and σ_p increase.

The indifference curve in Fig. 2–6 captures some of Mr. *T*'s feelings. But to represent the manner in which he would make choices in a great variety of circumstances, many more curves are required. Figure 2–7 repeats the curve of Fig. 2–6 as I_1. In addition it shows another curve derived by starting with portfolio 2. Since portfolio 2 is preferred to portfolio *I*, every point on I_2 must be preferred to every point on I_1. This follows from the concept of indifference and minimal requirements for rational choice.[1] Indifference curves may not cross.

The number of indifference curves is almost limitless. Only a selected few are shown in graphical examples. It is conventional to label those shown in order of preference. Thus points on I_2 are preferred to those on I_1; points on I_3 are preferred to those on I_2, etc.

A set of indifference curves summarizes the preferences of a given individual. Figure 2–8 shows two extreme cases. Mr. Fearless is oblivious to risk; Mr. Chicken is oblivious to everything except risk. Figure 2–9 shows more common cases. Mr. Birch is relatively conservative, requiring substantial increases in E_p to induce him to accept

---

[1] I.e., transitivity of preferences.

greater uncertainty (σ_p). Mr. Flynn is more adventuresome. Neither
likes uncertainty, but Mr. Birch dislikes it more (relative to his preference for E_p).

Figure 2–7

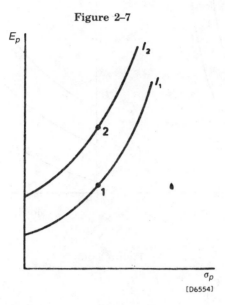

[D6554]

Choosing a Portfolio

Consider Mr. Z. His preferences are shown by the indifference
curves in Fig. 2–10. Many portfolios are available to him. Their E_p
and σ_p values may be shown by a group of points in the figure. Such
points will entirely fill the shaded area. Which will Mr. Z prefer?
Obviously the one shown by point B [which lies on the most preferred
indifference curve given this array of possible investments.]

Figure 2–8

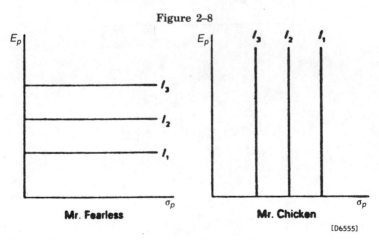

[D6555]

Figure 2–9

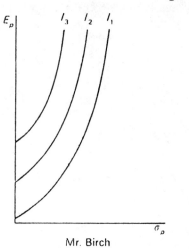

Mr. Birch

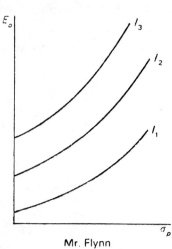

Mr. Flynn

Figure 2–10

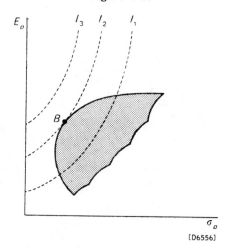

[D6556]

CHAPTER FOUR. PORTFOLIO THEORY

In Chapter Three, we saw that the mean and standard deviation of the distribution of expected returns from an investment were sufficient to describe the uncertainty associated with the investment. This description then provided the beginning of a way to choose among investments: All other things equal, more return and less risk is preferable. At this point, however, we need to complicate things somewhat. An alternative to selecting a single investment is to select a number of investments—a portfolio. But the problem is that the risk associated with a portfolio of investments differs from the simple sum of the risks associated with the individual investments. It depends as well on the relationship *among* the returns of the investments in the portfolio, what is called covariance. The importance of diversification—holding a number of investments rather than a single investment—as a means of reducing risk is examined in Section A of this Chapter. Section B then considers the factors bearing on how to select a portfolio of investments and Section C builds on this analysis to introduce the Capital Asset Pricing Model, modern financial theory's paradigm of how assets should be valued under uncertainty. Section D then applies the insights derived from the Capital Asset Pricing Model to the task of capital budgeting.

A. The Value of Diversification

The insight of portfolio theory is that by holding a portfolio of assets, as opposed to a single asset, the risk borne by an investor, the likelihood that actual returns will differ from expected returns, can be reduced *without* reducing expected returns. The idea can be made clear with an example. Imagine that a lawyer is considering making the investment in human capital necessary to become either a securities lawyer, specializing in venture capital placements, or a bankruptcy lawyer, specializing in reorganizations.[1] Further imagine that the investment in human capital necessary to achieve either specialty is identical, and that they are mutually exclusive. The lawyer believes that the expected return on an investment in becoming a securities lawyer will depend on the performance of the stock market. His expectations of that return and its relationship to stock market performance are as follows:

Stock Market Performance	Probability of Occurrence	Additional Earnings as a Securities Lawyer
Bull market	⅓	$200,000
Flat market	⅓	$100,000
Bear market	⅓	$0

[1] This discussion is based on Gilson & Mnookin, *Sharing Among the Human Capitalists: An Economic Inquiry into the Corporate Law Firm and How Partners Split Profits,* 37 Stan.L.Rev. 313, 327–28 (1985).

Similar analysis of the expected returns from a bankruptcy specialty shows that these will also vary with stock market performance but in exactly the opposite direction, presumably because, in contrast to a securities practice, bad economic times—resulting in a bear market—means good times for a bankruptcy lawyer.[2] Accordingly, the lawyer believes the returns associated with an investment in bankruptcy skills would be as follows:

Stock Market Performance	Probability of Occurrence	Additional Earnings as a Bankruptcy Lawyer
Bull market	$\frac{1}{3}$	$0
Flat market	$\frac{1}{3}$	$100,000
Bear market	$\frac{1}{3}$	$200,000

Analysis of both tables indicates that an investment in either securities law or bankruptcy law expertise has an identical expected return: earnings of $100,000. Both investments, however, present substantial risk; there is a $\frac{1}{3}$ probability that the lawyer would earn no return at all on either investment.

This risk, however, could be diversified away, as demonstrated in the following table, if the lawyer somehow could put one-half of his investment in each specialty.

Stock Market Performance	Probability of Event	Half Additional Earnings as a Securities Lawyer	Half Additional Earnings as a Bankruptcy Lawyer	Portfolio Earnings
Bull market	$\frac{1}{3}$	$100,000	$0	$100,000
Flat Market	$\frac{1}{3}$	$50,000	$50,000	$100,000
Bear Market	$\frac{1}{3}$	$0	$100,000	$100,000

Because the returns on an investment in expertise in securities law and bankruptcy law respond in exactly opposite ways to the performance of the stock market, the risks associated with future stock market performance are entirely eliminated—diversified away—by holding a portfolio composed of equal investments in both forms of human capital.[3]

As the example of the lawyer's investment in specialization illustrates, the risk of a portfolio is determined by the covariance of the returns of the investments in the portfolio—the extent to which the returns vary together, rather than independently. If the returns move

---

[2] The inverse relationship between earnings from venture capital and bankruptcy practices described in the text, while rhetorically helpful, may in reality be inaccurate. Earnings from a bankruptcy practice may well lag the business cycle because only as poor conditions continued would businesses be forced into bankruptcy. In contrast, a venture capital practice may anticipate an upturn in the business cycle so that, in fact, movements in the earnings from the two types of practice at times might well be parallel. Certainly the 1982–83 boom in both specialties lends credence to this analysis.

[3] Gilson & Mnookin, supra, use this analysis to provide an explanation for the existence of law firms. If an investment in being a securities lawyer and in being a bankruptcy lawyer are mutually exclusive, and if there is no market in which a lawyer can sell a portion of his returns from one specialty and use the proceeds to purchase an interest in the returns from the other, forming a law firm in which lawyers with different specialties combine their income may be the one way by which the risks associated with investments in specialized human capital can be diversified.

in exactly opposite directions in exactly the same amounts, as is the case with respect to the lawyer's investments, all risk is eliminated; the portfolio's return is always $100,000. Nor is the point limited to settings of perfect negative covariance. As long as the returns from two investments do not vary in exactly the same manner, the risk of holding both will be lower than the risk of holding either alone.

The next point in the development of portfolio theory involves a closer look at what kind of risk is reduced by diversification. The overall risk associated with an investment's return is made up of two components, typically referred to as *systematic* and *unsystematic* risk. Systematic risk is that associated with holding *any* asset. Broad changes in economic conditions, such as increases or decreases in GNP or a change in the level of inflation, to some extent affect the value of all assets. By contrast, unsystematic risk is that associated with a particular investment. For example, if the investment is in the lawyer's specialized knowledge of securities law, the risk that changes in the market for new issues will reduce the demand for securities lawyers is unsystematic. By diversifying one's portfolio, an investor can elilminate all unsystematic risk. To stay with the example of the law firm, so long as it has invested in a sufficient number of specialties, the impact of an event that affects a particular specialty will be balanced by both the same event's different impact on other of the firm's specialties, and by the occurrence of other events affecting other specialties, such that, on balance, there will be no effect on the value of the portfolio as a whole. In other words, a fully diversified portfolio is simply not subject to unsystematic risk. The only risk that remains in a diversified portfolio, then, is systematic risk: the risk of events that will alter the value of all assets, including legal skills.

The relationship between diversification and portfolio risk is illustrated in the following graph.

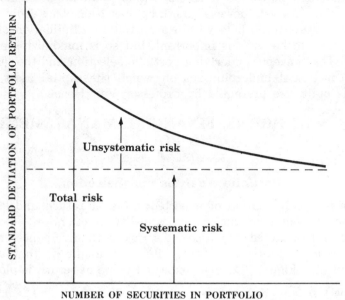

As the number of assets in the portfolio increases, the total risk and the unsystematic risk of the portfolio decrease until, at some point, further increases in the number of assets held yield no significant decrease in risk. While the level of optimal diversification will depend on the cost of acquiring and holding additional securities, it has been estimated that the number of different securities necessary to achieve significant diversification is as low as 15 or 20. See R. Brealey, An Introduction to Risk and Return from Common Stocks, 111–12 (2nd ed. 1983).

The fact that the unsystematic risk associated with an asset can be eliminated by diversification has an important implication for the way in which assets are valued. Investors will not be paid to bear risk that can be avoided. As a result, the return on, and therefore the price of, a capital asset should depend only on the amount of *systematic* risk associated with it, without regard to the amount of unsystematic risk associated with it.

To see that differences in unsystematic risk will not affect the value of an asset, suppose that a public utility intends to issue common stock on the basis of competitive bids: The highest bid—i.e., the lowest return to the investor—will succeed. Further suppose that there are two bidders, one that already holds a diversified portfolio of investments and one that does not. Because the diversified investor would bear less risk than the undiversified investor but would still receive the same return, the stock would be worth more to the diversified investor: He would be able to offer a higher bid. The value of an asset is thus set on the basis of its value to a diversified investor. As a result, the undiversified investor will receive no return for bearing unsystematic risk.

B. Selecting a Portfolio

Thus far, we have seen that portfolio theory dictates that individuals should hold portfolios of assets, rather than an investment in a single asset. As yet, however, nothing has been said about how to select the assets to be held within a portfolio. Elimination of unsystematic risk, to be sure, is important, but so is maximizing expected return. The concepts underlying portfolio selection and the last piece of the conceptual underpinnings on which the capital asset pricing model is built, are presented by Professor Van Horne.

J. VAN HORNE, FINANCIAL MANAGEMENT AND POLICY
54–59 (5th ed. 1980).*

Portfolio Analysis and Selection

The best combination of expected value of return and standard deviation depends upon the investor's utility function. * * * If an investor is risk-averse and associates risk with divergence from expected value of return, his utility function might be that depicted graphically by Figure 3–2. The expected value of return is plotted on the vertical axis, while the standard deviation is along the horizontal. The curves are known as *indifference curves;* the investor is indifferent between any combination of expected value of return and standard deviation on a particular curve. In other words, a curve is defined by those combinations of expected return and standard deviation that result in a fixed level of expected utility.[3]

* * *

Figure 3–2
Hypothetical Indifference Curves

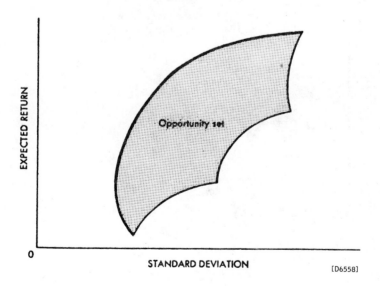

Figure 3–3
Hypothetical Opportunity Set

[3] For further discussion and proof that indifference curves for a risk-averse investor are concave, see Eugene F. Fama and Merton H. Miller, *The Theory of Finance* (New York: Holt, Rinehart & Winston, 1972), pp. 226–28.

The greater the slope of the indifference curves, the more averse the investor is to risk. As we move to the left in Figure 3–2, each successive curve represents a higher level of expected utility. It is important to note that the exact shape of the indifference curves will be different for different investors. While the curves for all risk-averse investors will be upward sloping, a variety of shapes are possible depending on the risk preferences of the individual.

The individual investor will want to hold that portfolio of securities that places him on the highest indifference curve, choosing it from the opportunity set of available portfolios. An example of an opportunity set, based upon the subjective probability beliefs of an individual investor, is shown in Figure 3–3. This opportunity set reflects all possible portfolios of securities as envisioned by the investor. In other words, every point in the shaded area represents a portfolio that is attainable by the investor. The dark line at the top of the set is the line of efficient combinations, or the efficient frontier. It depicts the tradeoff between risk and expected value of return. According to the Markowitz mean-variance maxim, an investor should seek a portfolio of securities that lies on the efficient frontier.[4] A portfolio is not efficient if there is another portfolio with a higher expected value of return and a lower standard deviation, a higher expected value and the same standard deviation, or the same expected value but a lower standard deviation. If an investor's portfolio is not efficient, he can increase the expected value of return without increasing the risk, decrease the risk without decreasing the expected value of return, or obtain some combination of increased expected value and decreased risk by switching to a portfolio on the efficient frontier.

Figure 3–4
Selection of Optimal Portfolio

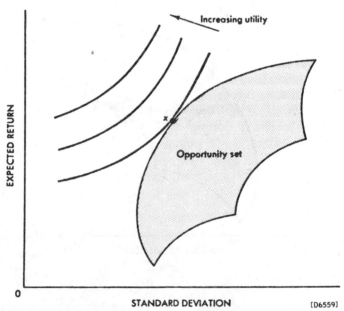

[4] Harry M. Markowitz, *Portfolio Selection: Efficient Diversification of Invest-* *ments* (New York: John Wiley, 1959), Chaps. 7 and 8.

As can be seen, the efficient frontier is determined on the basis of dominance. Portfolios of securities tend to dominate individual securities because of the reduction in risk obtainable through diversification.

*   *   *

The objective of the investor is to choose the best portfolio from those that lie on the efficient frontier. The portfolio with the maximum utility is the one at the point of tangency of the opportunity set with the highest indifference curve. This tangency is illustrated in Figure 3–4, and the portfolio represented by the point of tangency is the optimal one for an investor with those expectations and utility function.

Presence of Risk-Free Security

If a risk-free security exists that yields a certain future return, the portfolio selection process described above must be modified. This security might be a U. S. Treasury security that is held to maturity. Although the expected return may be low relative to other securities, there is complete certainty as to return. Suppose for now that the investor is able not only to lend at the risk-free rate but to borrow at it as well. (We relax this assumption later on.) To determine the optimal portfolio under these conditions, we first draw a line from the risk-free rate, *i*, through its point of tangency with the opportunity set of portfolio returns, as illustrated in Figure 3–5. This line then becomes the new efficient frontier. Note that only one portfolio of risky securities—namely, *m*—would be considered. In other words, this portfolio now dominates all others. *   *   *

Any point on the straight line tells us the proportion of the risky portfolio, *m*, and the proportion of loans or borrowings at the risk-free rate. To the left of point *m*, the investor would hold both the risk-free security and portfolio *m*. To the right, he would hold only portfolio *m* and would borrow funds, in addition to his initial investment funds, in order to invest further in it. The farther to the right in the figure, the greater borrowings will be. The optimal investment policy is determined by the point of tangency between the straight line in Figure 3–5 and the highest indifference curve. As shown in the figure, this point is portfolio *x* and it consists of an investment in both the risk-free security and the risky security portfolio, *m*. If borrowing were prohibited, the efficient frontier would no longer be a straight line throughout but would consist of line *i-m-n.*. The optimal portfolio would be determined in the same manner as before—namely, the tangency of the efficient frontier with the highest indifference curve.

Capital Market Line

Assuming both borrowing and lending at the risk-free rate, the straight line passing through the risk-free rate on the vertical axis and the expected return-standard deviation point for the market portfolio is known as the *capital market line*. It is shown in Figure 3–5, but we illustrate it separately in Figure 3–6. This line describes the tradeoff between expected return and risk for various holdings of the risk-free security and the market portfolio. Thus two things are involved—the price of time and the price of risk. The former is depicted by the intercept of the capital market line and the vertical axis. The risk-free rate, then, can be thought of as the reward for waiting. The slope of the capital market line represents the market price of risk. It tells us the amount of additional expected return that is required for an increment in standard deviation. Thus the capital market line depicts the *ex ante* equilibrium relationship between return and risk.

Figure 3–5
Selection of Optimal Portfolio When Risk-Free Asset Exists

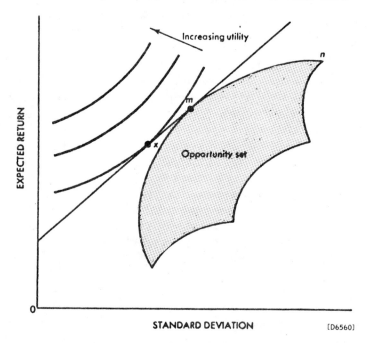

Separation Theorem. Note that in the construct of the capital market line, the utility preferences of the individual affect only the amount that is borrowed or loaned. They do not affect the optimal portfolio of risky assets. Turning to Figure 3–5, the investor would select portfolio *m* of risky assets no matter what the nature of his indifference curves. The reason is that when a risk-free security exists, and borrowing and lending are possible at that rate, the market portfolio dominates all others. Thus the individual's utility preferences are independent or separate from the optimal portfolio of risky assets. This condition is known as the *separation theorem.*[6] Put another way, it states that the determination of an optimal portfolio of risky assets is independent of the individual's risk preferences. Such a determination depends only on the expected returns and standard deviations for the various possible portfolios of risky assets. In essence, the individual's approach to investing is two phased. First he determines an optimal portfolio of risky assets, and then he determines the most desirable combination of the risk-free security and this portfolio. Only the second phase depends on his utility preferences.

[6] This theorem was originally stated by J. Tobin, "Liquidity Preference as Behavior towards Risk," Review of Economic Studies, 25 (February 1958), 65–86.

Figure 3–6
The Capital Market Line

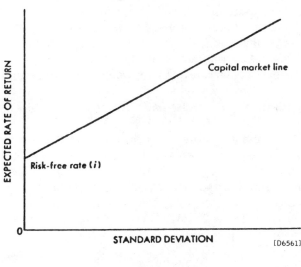

C. The Capital Asset Pricing Model: The Relationship of Risk and Return

Our study of valuation has to this point led to two important conclusions. First, the unsystematic risk associated with an investment can be eliminated by holding that investment as part of an adequately diversified portfolio. Second, because of the separation theorem, individual preferences do not affect the value of a security. The result is that the only factors that remain to determine value are systematic risk and expected returns. Specifying the relationship between these factors—between risk and return—and how they determine the price of an asset is the subject of the Capital Asset Pricing Model (CAPM), the current paradigm of how assets are valued in the market. We begin with the development of the model, and then consider the empirical support for it. This evidence, while supportive, is not conclusive, and leads to discussion of the validity and usefulness of the CAPM if some of its perfect market assumptions are relaxed, and in light of important questions that have been raised about whether the CAPM can be tested empirically at all. Consideration of the CAPM closes with a brief description of the leading alternative, the Arbitrage Pricing Theory developed by Professor Stephen Ross.

1. The Model

MODIGLIANI & POGUE, AN INTRODUCTION TO RISK AND RETURN

30 Fin.Anal.J. 68 (March-April, 1974); Fin.Anal.J. 69 (May-June, 1974).

5. The Risk of Individual Securities

[T]he systematic risk of an individual security is that portion of its total risk (standard deviation of return) which cannot be eliminated by combining it with other securities in a well diversified portfolio. We now need a way of quantifying the systematic risk of a security and relating the systematic risk of a portfolio to that of its component securities. This can be accomplished by dividing security return into two parts: one dependent (i.e., perfectly correlated), and a second independent (i.e., uncorrelated) of market return. The first component of return is usually referred to as "systematic", the second as "unsystematic" return. Thus we have

Security Return　=　Systematic Return
　　　　　　　　　　+ Unsystematic Return.　　　　　　(4)

Since the systematic return is perfectly correlated with the market return, it can be expressed as a factor, designated beta (β), times the market return, R_m. The beta factor is a market sensitivity index, indicating how sensitive the security return is to changes in the market level. The unsystematic return, which is independent of market returns, is usually represented by a factor epsilon ($\acute{\varepsilon}$). Thus the security return, R, may be expressed

$$R = \beta\ R_m + \acute{\varepsilon}.\qquad(5)$$

For example, if a security had a β factor of 2.0 (e.g., an airline stock), then a 10 per cent market return would generate a systematic return for the stock of 20 per cent. The security return for the period would be the 20 per cent plus the unsystematic component. The unsystematic component depends on factors unique to the company, such as labor difficulties, higher than expected sales, etc.

The security returns model given by Equation (5) is usually written in a way such that the average value of the residual term, ϵ, is zero. This is accomplished by adding a factor, alpha (α), to the model to represent the average value of the unsystematic returns over time. That is, we set $\acute{\varepsilon} = \alpha + \varepsilon$ so that

$$R = \alpha + \beta\ R_m + \varepsilon,\qquad(6)$$

where the average ε over time is equal to zero.

The model for security returns given by Equation (6) is usually referred to as the "market model". Graphically, the model can be depicted as a line fitted to a plot of security returns against rates of return on the market index. This is shown in Exhibit 7 for a hypothetical security.

The beta factor can be thought of as the slope of the line. It gives the expected increase in security return for a one per cent increase in market return. In Exhibit 7, the security has a beta of 1.0. Thus, a ten per cent market return will result, on the average, in a ten per cent security return. The market-weighted average beta for all stocks is 1.0 by definition.

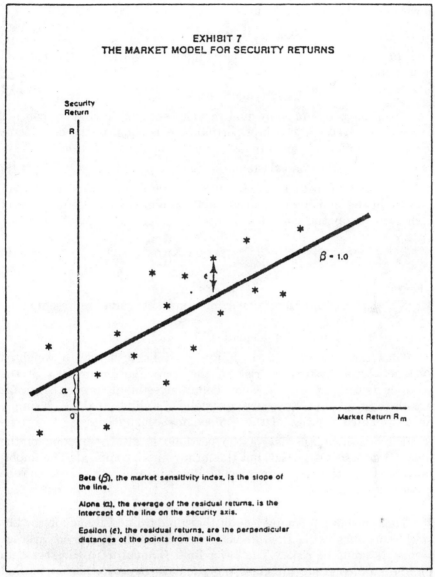

EXHIBIT 7
THE MARKET MODEL FOR SECURITY RETURNS

Beta (β), the market sensitivity index, is the slope of the line.

Alpha (α), the average of the residual returns, is the intercept of the line on the security axis.

Epsilon (ϵ), the residual returns, are the perpendicular distances of the points from the line.

[D6562]

The alpha factor is represented by the intercept of the line on the vertical security return axis. It is equal to the average value over time of the unsystematic returns ($\tilde{\epsilon}$) on the stock. For most stocks, the alpha factor tends to be small and unstable. (We shall return to alpha later).

Using the definition of security return given by the market model, the specification of systematic and unsystematic risk is straightforward—they are simply the standard deviations of the two return components.

The systematic risk of a security is equal to β times the standard deviation of the market return:

$$\text{Systematic Risk} = \beta \ \sigma_m \qquad\qquad (7)$$

The unsystematic risk equals the standard deviation of the residual return factor ϵ:

$$\text{Unsystematic Risk} = \sigma_\epsilon. \qquad\qquad (8)$$

Given measures of individual security systematic risk, we can not compute the systematic risk of portfolio. It is equal to the beta factor for the portfolio, β_p, times the risk of the market index, σ_m:

$$\text{Portfolio Systematic Risk} = \beta_p \ \sigma_m. \qquad\qquad (9)$$

The portfolio beta factor in turn can be shown to be simply an average of the individual security betas, weighted by the proportion of each security in the portfolio, or

$$\beta_p = \sum_{j=1}^{N} X_1 \ \beta_1. \qquad\qquad (10)$$

where

    X_1 = the proportion of portfolio market value represented by security j

    N = the number of securities.

Thus the systematic risk of the portfolio is simply a weighted average of the systematic risk of the individual securities. If the portfolio is composed of an equal dollar investment in each stock (as was the case for the 100–security portfolio of Exhibit 2), the β_p is simply an unweighted average of the component security betas.

The unsystematic risk of the portfolio is also a function of the unsystematic security risks, but the form is more complex. The important point is that with increasing diversification this risk can be reduced toward zero.

* * *

Table 2 shows a comparison of the standard deviations for the 20–stock portfolios with the predicted lower limits based on average security systematic risks. The lower limit is equal to the average beta for the quality group ($\bar{\beta}$) times the standard deviation of the market return (ϵ_m). The standard deviations in all cases are close to the predicted values. These results support the contention that portfolio systematic risk equals the average systematic risks of the component securities.

The main results of this section can be summarized as follows: First, * * * roughly 40 to 50 per cent of total security risk can be eliminated by diversification. Second, the remaining systematic risk is equal to the security β times market risk. Third, portfolio systematic risk is a weighted average of security systematic risks.

The implications of these results are substantial. First, we would expect realized rates of return over substantial periods of time to be related to the systematic as opposed to total risk of securities. Since the unsystematic risk is relatively easily eliminated, we should not expect the market to offer a risk premium for bearing it. Second, since security systematic risk is equal to the security beta times σ_m (which is common to all securities), beta is useful as a *relative* risk measure. The β gives the systematic risk of a security (or portfolio) relative to the risk of the market index. Thus it is often convenient to speak of systematic risk in relative terms (i.e., in terms of beta rather than beta times σ_m).σ

Table 2

Standard Deviations of 20–Stock Portfolios and Predicted Lower Limits

June 1960—May 1970

(1) Stock Quality Group	(2) Standard Deviation of 20–Stock Portfolios σ %/mo	(3) Average Beta Value for Quality Group β	(4) Lower Limit * $\beta\ \sigma_m$ %/mo
A+	3.94	0.74	3.51
A	4.17	0.80	3.80
A−	4.52	0.89	4.22
B+	4.45	0.87	4.13
B	6.27	1.24	5.89
B− & C	6.32	1.23	5.84

*σ_m = 4.75% per month.

6. The Relationship Between Expected Return and Risk: The Capital Asset Pricing Model

[We have] developed two measures of risk: one is a measure of total risk (standard deviation), the other a relative index of systematic or nondiversifiable risk (beta). The beta measure would appear to be the more relevant for the pricing of securities. Returns expected by investors should logically be related to systematic as opposed to total risk. Securities with higher systematic risk should have higher expected returns.

The question to be considered now is the form of the relationship between risk and return. In this section we describe a relationship called the "Capital Asset Pricing Model" (CAPM), which is based on elementary logic and simple economic principles. The basic postulate underlying finance theory is that assets with the same risk should have the same expected rate of return. That is, the prices of assets in the capital markets should adjust until equivalent risk assets have identical expected returns.

To see the implications of this postulate, let us consider an investor who holds a risky portfolio with the same risk as the market portfolio (beta equal to 1.0). What return should he expect? Logically, he should expect the same return as that of the market portfolio.

Let us consider another investor who holds a riskless portfolio (beta equal to zero). The investor in this case should expect to earn the rate of return on riskless assets such as treasury bills. By taking no risk, he earns the riskless rate of return.

Now let us consider the case of an investor who holds a mixture of these two portfolios. Assuming he invests a proportion X of his money in the risky portfolio and $(1 - X)$ in the riskless portfolio, what risk does he bear and what return should he expect? The risk of the composite portfolio is easily computed when we recall that the beta of a portfolio is simply a weighted average of the component security betas, where the weights are the portfolio proportions. Thus the portfolio beta, β_p, is a weighted average of the beta of the market portfolio and the beta of the risk-free rate. However, the market beta is 1.0, and that of the risk-free rate is zero. Therefore

$$\beta_p = (1 - X) \cdot 0 + X \cdot 1,$$
$$= X. \tag{11}$$

Thus, β_p is equal to the fraction of his money invested in the risky portfolio. If 100 per cent or less of the investor's funds is invested in the risky portfolio, his portfolio beta will be between zero and 1.0. If he borrows at the risk-free rate and invests the proceeds in the risky portfolio, his portfolio beta will be greater than 1.0.

The expected return of the composite portfolio is also a weighted average of the expected returns on the two-component portfolios; that is,

$$E(R_p) = (1 - X) \cdot R_F + X \cdot E(R_m). \tag{12}$$

where $E(R_p)$, $E(R_m)$, Σ and R_F are the expected returns on the portfolio, the market index, and the risk-free rate. Now, from Equation (11) we know that X is equal to β_p. Substituting into Equation (12), we have

$$E(R_p) = (1 - \beta_p) \cdot R_F + B_p \cdot E(R_m),$$

or

$$E(R_p) = R_F + \beta_p \cdot (E(R_m) - R_F). \tag{13}$$

Equation (13) is the Capital Asset Pricing Model (CAPM), an extremely important theoretical result. It says that the expected return on a portfolio should exceed the riskless rate of return by an amount which is proportional to the portfolio beta. That is, the relationship between return and risk should be linear.

The model is often stated in "risk-premium" form. Risk premiums are obtained by subtracting the risk-free rate from the rates of return. The expected portfolio and market risk premiums (designated $E(r_p)$ and $E(r_m)$ respectively) are given by

$$E(r_p) = E(R_P) - R_F, \tag{14a}$$

$$E(r_m) = E(R_m) - R_F. \tag{14b}$$

Substituting these risk premiums into Equation (13), we obtain

$$E(r_p) = \beta_p \cdot E(r_m). \tag{15}$$

In this form, the CAPM states that the expected risk premium for the investor's portfolio is equal to its beta value times the expected market risk premium.

We can illustrate the model by assuming that short-term (risk-free) interest rate is 6 per cent and the expected return on the market is 10 per cent. The expected risk premium for holding the market portfolio is just the difference between the 10 per cent and the short-term interest rate of 6 per cent, or 4 per cent. Investors who hold the market portfolio expect to earn 10 per cent, which is 4 per cent greater than they could earn on a short-term market instrument for certain. In order to satisfy Equation (13), the expected return on securities or portfolios with different levels of risk must be:

Expected Return for Different Levels of Portfolio Beta

Beta	Expected Return
0.0	6%
0.5	8%
1.0	10%
1.5	12%
2.0	14%

The predictions of the model are inherently sensible. For safe investments ($\beta = 0$), the model predicts that investors would expect to earn the risk-free rate of interest. For a risky investment ($\beta > 0$) investors would expect a rate of return proportional to the market sensitivity (β) of the investment. Thus, stocks with lower than average market sensitivities (such as most utilities) would offer expected returns less than the expected market return. Stocks with above average values of beta (such as most airline securities) would offer expected returns in excess of the market.

In our development of CAPM we have made a number of assumptions that are required if the model is to be established on a rigorous basis. These assumptions involve investor behavior and conditions in the capital markets. The following is a set of assumptions that will allow a simple derivation of the model.

(a) The market is composed of risk-averse investors who measure risk in terms of standard deviation of portfolio return. This assumption provides a basis for the use of beta-type risk measures.

(b) All investors have a common time horizon for investment decision making (e.g., one month, one year, etc.). This assumption allows us to measure investor expectations over some common interval, thus making comparisons meaningful.

(c) All investors are assumed to have the same expectations about future security returns and risks. Without this assumption, the analysis would become much more complicated.

(d) Capital markets are perfect in the sense that all assets are completely divisible, there are no transactions, costs or differential taxes and borrowing and lending rates are equal to each other and the same for all investors. Without these conditions, frictional barriers would exist to the equilibrium conditions on which the model is based.

While these assumptions are sufficient to derive the model, it is not clear that all are necessary in their current form. It may well be that several of the assumptions can be substantially relaxed without major change in the form of the model. A good deal of research is currently being conducted toward this end.

While the CAPM is indeed simple and elegant, these qualities do not in themselves guarantee that it will be useful in explaining observed risk-return patterns.

R. BREALEY & S. MYERS, PRINCIPLES OF CORPORATE FINANCE *

143–50 (1981).

A Proof of the Capital Asset Pricing Model

We have given you a bald statement of the capital asset pricing model.   *   *   *   Now you need to understand where that formula came from.

One investment strategy is to decide how much money you wish to put at risk and then to invest this sum in the market portfolio. If you have any money left over, you can *lend* it at a fixed rate of interest; if you don't have enough money, you can *borrow* the balance at a fixed rate of interest.   *   *   *

Suppose that you decide to invest proportion x of your money in the market portfolio and that you can lend or borrow the balance $1 - x$ at r_f, the risk-free rate of interest.[9] Then the beta of your investment is simply a weighted average of the beta on the market ($\beta_m = 1.0$) and the beta on the risk-free loan ($\beta_f = 0.0$):

$$\text{Beta of investment} = \left(\begin{array}{c} \text{proportion} \\ \text{in market} \end{array} \right) \left(\begin{array}{c} \text{beta of} \\ \text{market} \end{array} \right) + \left(\begin{array}{c} \text{proportion} \\ \text{in loan} \end{array} \right) \left(\begin{array}{c} \text{beta of} \\ \text{loan} \end{array} \right)$$

$$\beta = x(1.0) + (1 - x)0$$
$$= x$$

The beta of your investment is, therefore, equal to x, the proportion invested in the market portfolio.

The *expected risk premium* on your investment is also a weighted average of the expected risk premium on the market ($r_m - r_f$) and the risk premium on the risk-free loan (zero):

[9] If you invest less than all your wealth in the market, $1 - x$ is positive; i.e., you *lend* the balance. If you invest more than all your wealth in the market, $1 - x$ is negative; i.e., you need to *borrow* the balance.

$$\text{Expected risk premium on investment} = \begin{pmatrix} \text{proportion} \\ \text{in market} \end{pmatrix} \begin{pmatrix} \text{expected} \\ \text{risk premium} \\ \text{on market} \end{pmatrix}$$

$$+ \begin{pmatrix} \text{proportion} \\ \text{in loan} \end{pmatrix} \begin{pmatrix} \text{expected} \\ \text{risk premium} \\ \text{on loan} \end{pmatrix}$$

$$r - r_f = x(r_m - r_f) + (1 - x)0$$

$$= x(r_m - r_f)$$

But we have already seen that the *beta* of your investment is equal to x. So we can rewrite the expected risk premium as

$$r - r_f = x(r_m - r_f)$$
$$= \beta(r_m - r_f)$$

In other words, investors can always obtain an expected risk premium of $\beta(r_m - r_f)$ just by holding a mixture of the market portfolio and a risk-free loan. They will, therefore, be willing to hold other investments only if they offer an equally good return. Therefore the required risk premium on *any* investment is

$$r - r_f = \beta(r_m - r_f)$$

Let us go through this argument again more slowly. Figure 8–9 depicts the consequences of four possible investment policies:

Policy 1. Suppose you just hold the market portfolio. Then the diagonal line in figure 8–9 shows the relationship between the risk premium on your investment and the risk premium on the market. Not surprisingly, the risk premium on your investment $(r - r_f)$ is always equal to the market risk premium $(\tilde{r}_m - r_f)$. (Note that Figure 8–9 shows a range of possible outcomes for the market. The vertical scale shows expected risk premiums *given* particular outcomes for the market.)

Policy 2. Now suppose instead that you invest all your money in risk-free bills. Regardless of what happens to the market, you will just earn the rate of interest r_f. The risk premium on your investment is always zero. It is, therefore, represented by the horizontal axis in Figure 8–9.

Policy 3. Another possibility is to divide your money evenly between the market portfolio and risk-free bills. In that case, your risk premium will always be midway between the market risk premium and the rate of interest.

Policy 4. If you are more daring, you might choose to borrow funds at the risk-free interest rate and invest these and an equal amount of your own money in the market portfolio. In this case the risk premium on your investment will be twice as high as on the market portfolio.

Of course these are not the only possible policies. By holding an appropriate mixture of the market portfolio and borrowing or lending, an investor can achieve *any* of the positions that can be represented by a straight line passing through the origin in Figure 8–9. If the portfolio involves borrowing, it has above-average risk and the slope of the line is *greater* than 1.0. If the portfolio involves lending, it has below-average risk and the slope of the line is *less* than 1.0.

Figure 8–9
These Lines Show how the Expected Risk Premium on Your Investment is Related to the Actual Risk Premium on the Market. If you Borrow and Invest in the Market Portfolio, the Line Will be Steep; if you Lend and Invest in the Market Portfolio, it Will Be Relatively Flat.

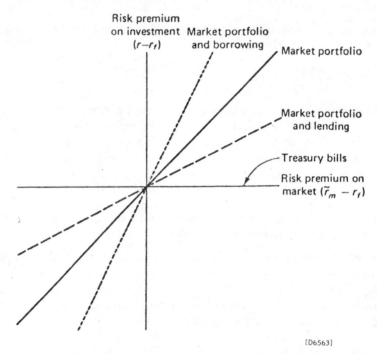

[D6563]

Now look at Figure 8–10*a*. The lighter line is known as a **characteristic line.** It shows the relationship between the expected risk premium on a security and the market risk premium. You can see that this security is unaffected by the market. Therefore it has a beta of zero. It also has a negative expected risk premium. What would you do if such a stock were offered to you? We hope you would not buy it—if you want an investment with a beta of zero, you should invest in Treasury Bills. If everybody shares your view of the stock's prospects, the seller will have to cut the offering price.

Suppose now that someone offers you the stock shown by the lighter characteristic line in Figure 8–10*b*. It has a beta of 1.0. But, if that is the risk you want, you would do better with the market portfolio which offers a higher expected risk premium whatever the market does. Once again the seller will have to cut the offering price.

Our third hypothetical stock is represented by the lighter characteristic line in Figure 8–10*c*. It has a beta of 0.5. But you can expect to do better in all circumstances by investing half your funds in Treasury bills and half in the market portfolio. So nobody is going to want to buy the stock. Finally, Figure 8–10*d* shows a stock with a beta of 2.0. This time you could expect to do better in all circumstances by borrowing at the interest rate r_f and investing in the market portfolio.

Figure 8–10

(*a*) **Nobody Loves Security A: the Treasury Bill Gives a Higher Expected Return Regardless of What Happens to the Market.** (*b*) **Nobody Loves Security B: the Market Portfolio Gives a Higher Expected Return Regardless of What Happens to the Market.** (*c*) **Nobody Loves Security C: a Mixture of the Market Portfolio and Lending Gives a Higher Expected Return Regardless of What Happens to the Market.** (*d*) **Nobody Loves Security D: a Mixture of the Market Portfolio and Borrowing Gives a Higher Expected Return Regardless of What Happens to the Market.**

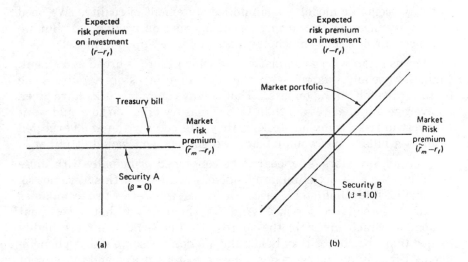

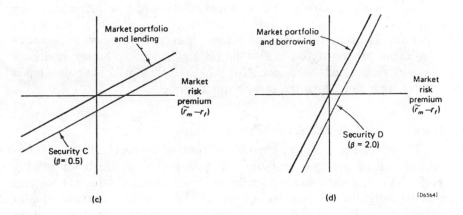

We think we have made our point. An investor can always obtain an expected risk premium of $\beta(r_m - r_f)$ by holding a mixture of the market portfolio and a risk-free loan. So in well-functioning markets nobody will hold a stock that offers an expected risk premium of *less* than $\beta(r_m - r_f)$. But what about the other possibility? Are there stocks that offer a higher expected risk premium? If we take all stocks together, we have the market portfolio. Its beta is 1.0 and its expected risk premium is:

$$\text{Expected market risk premium} = \beta(r_m - r_f) = r_m - r_f$$

Since stocks *on average* offer an expected risk premium of $\beta(r_m - r_f)$ and since none offers a *lower* expected risk premium, then there can't be any that offer a *higher* premium. The expected risk premium on each and every stock is:

$$r - r_f = \beta(r_m - r_f)$$

Validity and Role of the Capital Asset Pricing Model

Any economic model is a simplified statement of reality. We need to simplify in order to interpret what is going on around us. But we also need to now how much faith we can place in our model.

Let us begin with some matters on which there is broad agreement. First, few people quarrel with the idea that investors require some extra return for taking on risk. That is why common stocks have given on average a higher return than U. S. Treasury bills. Who would want to invest in risky common stocks if they offered only the *same* expected return as bills? We wouldn't and we suspect you wouldn't either.

Second, investors do appear to be concerned principally with those risks that they cannot eliminate by diversification. If this were not so, we should find that stock prices increase whenever two companies merge to spread their risks. And we should find that investment companies which invest in the shares of other firms are more highly valued than the shares they hold. But we don't observe either phenomenon. Diversifying mergers don't increase stock prices and investment companies are no more highly valued than the shares they hold.

The capital asset pricing model captures these ideas in a simple way. That is why many financial managers find it the most convenient tool for coming to grips with the slippery notion of risk. And it is why economists often use the capital asset pricing model to demonstrate important ideas in finance even when there are other ways to prove these ideas. In years to come economists will develop better models of risk and return, but it is doubtful whether they will ever develop a simpler and more intuitively appealing model.

* * *

Tests of the Capital Asset Pricing Model

The ultimate test of any model is whether it fits the facts. Unfortunately there are two problems in testing the capital asset pricing model. First, it is concerned with *expected* returns, whereas we can observe only *actual* returns. Second, the market portfolio should include all risky investments, whereas most market indexes contain only a sample of common stocks.[11]

No study has properly tackled the second problem, but a paper by Fama and MacBeth avoids the main pitfalls that come from having to work with actual rather than expected returns. Fama and MacBeth

---

[11] See e.g., R. Roll, "A Critique of the Asset Pricing Theory's Tests; Part 1: On Past and Potential Testability of the Theo- ry," *Journal of Financial Economics*, 4 (March 1977), 129–176.

grouped all New York Stock Exchange stocks into 20 portfolios. They then plotted the estimated beta of each portfolio in one 10-year period against the portfolio's average return over a subsequent 5-year period.[12] Figure 8–11 shows what they found. You can see that the estimated beta of each portfolio told investors quite a lot about its future return.

If the capital asset pricing model is correct, investors would not have expected any of these portfolios to perform better or worse than a comparable package of Treasury bills and the market portfolio. Therefore, the expected return on each portfolio, given the market return, should plot along the sloping lines in Figure 8–11. Notice that the *actual* returns on Fama and MacBeth's portfolios do plot *roughly* along these lines. That is encouraging, but we should like to know why the portfolios don't plot *exactly* along the lines. Is it because the capital asset pricing model is only a rough approximation to real markets? Or is it because the tests are not appropriate? (Remember that Fama and MacBeth are looking at *actual* returns, whereas the capital asset pricing model is concerned with expectations; also, Fama and MacBeth did not include *all* risky assets in their market index.) Unfortunately nobody knows which explanation is correct. It looks as if the capital asset pricing model is telling us *something* about expected returns, but we can't be sure how much.

Figure 8–11

The Capital Asset Pricing Model States That the **Expected** Return From Any Investment Should Lie on the Market Line. The Dots Show the **Actual**—Returns from Portfolios With Different Betas.

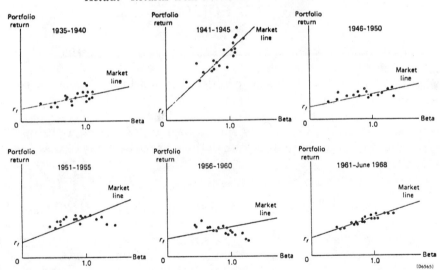

[Source: Results supplied by E.F. Fama and J.D. MacBeth. See their paper, "Risk, Return and Equilibrium: Empirical Tests," *Journal of Political Economy*, 81:607–636 (May 1973).]

———————◆———————

[12] Fama and MacBeth first estimated the beta of each stock by using the returns in each odd month. They then formed portfolios on the basis of the odd-month betas. Finally, they reestimated the beta of each portfolio by using only the returns in each even month. This rather ingenious trick ensured that the estimated betas for each portfolio were largely unbiased and free from error. E. F. Fama and J. D. MacBeth, "Risk, Return and Equilibrium: Empirical Tests," *Journal of Political Economy*, 81:607–636 (May 1973).

2. Evaluation and Alternatives

Evaluation of the accuracy of the CAPM in predicting how assets are valued is particularly important because of its claim that only an asset's return and its systematic risk—its beta—determine the asset's price. That claim has important implications for investment decisions by firms and individuals, including decisions concerning whether acquisitions have the potential to increase firm value.[4] If, however, the CAPM's claims are not entirely valid, then room remains for unsystematic risk to play a role in valuation, and investment strategies must be altered accordingly.

Evaluation of the CAPM has taken place at a number of levels. First, efforts have been made to evaluate the validity of the model when one or more of the perfect market assumptions which allow its derivation—for example, that investors can borrow or lend at the same rate, that investors have homogeneous expectations, or that information is costlessly available to everyone—are relaxed. Second, questions have been raised concerning the validity of the empirical tests of the CAPM's claims and, indeed, whether the CAPM can be tested at all. These concerns have given rise to an alternative model, Professor Stephen Ross' Arbitrage Pricing Model,[5] which also warrants attention.

a. Relaxing the Assumptions

J. VAN HORNE, FINANCIAL MANAGEMENT AND POLICY
69–71 (5th ed. 1980).*

[T]he capital-asset pricing model serves as a useful framework for evaluating financial decisions. The basic tenets of the model hold even when assumptions are relaxed to reflect real-world conditions. Given that investors tend to be risk-averse, a positive tradeoff exists between risk and expected return for efficient portfolios. Moreover, expected returns for individual securities should bear a positive relationship to their marginal contributions of risk to the market portfolio (i.e., systematic risk).

*   *   *

Let us turn now to modifying some of the assumptions. * * *

Relaxing Assumptions in the Model

In this section, we briefly examine the effect of relaxing some of the earlier assumptions of the capital-asset pricing model. The first is that the investor can both borrow and lend at the risk-free rate. Obviously, the investor can lend at this rate. If the borrowing rate is higher, however, an imperfection is introduced, and the capital market line is no longer linear throughout. As shown in Figure 3–10, it is straight through market portfolio M_l. This segment represents combi-

---

[4] The implications of the CAPM for corporate acquisitions are considerd in Part II, Motivations for Acquisitions.

[5] Ross, *The Arbitrage Theory of Capital Asset Pricing*, 13 J.Econ. Theory 341 (1976).

nations of the risk-free asset and the market portfolio M_l. Because the
borrowing rate is higher, another tangency point is introduced, namely
M_b. The relevant portion of this line is from point M_b to the right; it
represents borrowing to invest in the market portfolio M_b. The segment of the capital market line between M_l and M_b is curved and is
simply a portion of the efficient frontier of the opportunity set of risky
securities. As is evident from the figure, the greater the spread
between the borrowing and the lending rates, the greater the curved
segment in the capital market line.[14] Different borrowing rates for
different investors complicates the picture even more because the
equilibration process involves an interaction among investors.

Figure 3–10
Effect of Differing Borrowing and Lending Rates

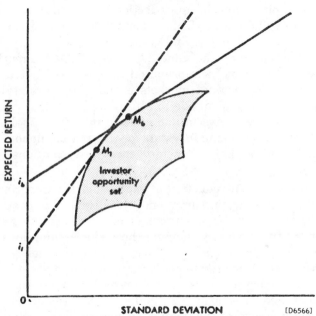

[D6566]

Relaxation of another major assumption, homogeneous expectations, complicates the problem in a different way. With heterogeneous
expectations, a complex blending of expectations, wealth, and utility
preferences across individual investors emerges in the equilibrating
process. In essence, each investor has his own capital market line.
This complex equilibrating process has been examined by the author
elsewhere and will not be presented here.[15] The principal implication
is that precise generalizations are not possible; the overall capital
market line becomes fuzzy. With only moderate heterogeneity in
expectations, however, the basic tenets of the capital-asset pricing
model still hold and rough estimates of the expected return-risk trade-

---

[14] Even with different borrowing and
lending rates, essentially the same risk-
return conclusions are possible as with the
capital-asset pricing model if investors are
able to engage in unrestricted short sales.
Using a zero beta portfolio in place of a
risk-free asset, Fischer Black, "Capital
Market Equilibrium with Restricted Borrowing," *Journal of Business*, 45 (July

1972), 444–54, provides a model for the
equilibrium risk-return relationship for
risky securities when borrowing at the
risk-free rate is not possible.

[15] James C. Van Horne, *Financial Market Rates and Flows* (Englewood Cliffs, N.
J.: Prentice-Hall, 1978), Chap. 3.

offs for portfolios and individual securities are possible. Still, the lack of precise description must be recognized.[16]

Transaction costs also affect market equilibrium. The greater these costs, the less investors will undertake transactions to make their portfolios truly efficient. Rather than all portfolios being on the efficient frontier or capital market line, some may be on one side or the other because transaction costs more than offset the advantages of being right on the line. In other words, there may be bands on either side of the capital market line within which portfolios would lie. The greater the transaction costs, the wider the bands might be. Similarly, when securities are not infinitely divisible, as is the case in the real world, investors are able to achieve an efficient portfolio only up to the nearest share of stock or the nearest bond.

Another capital market imperfection is the differential tax on dividends and capital gains. This imperfection makes dividend-paying stocks less attractive than "capital gains" stocks, which pay little or no dividends, all other things the same. * * * The last imperfection we consider is imperfections in information to investors.[17] Recall that an assumption of perfect capital markets is that all information about a firm is instantaneously available to all investors without cost. To the extent that there are delays in and costs to information, there will be differing expectations among investors for this reason alone. The effect here is the same as that for heterogeneous expectations, which we discussed earlier.

In summary, the introduction of capital market imperfections and the relaxation of other assumptions complicate the generalizations possible with the capital-asset pricing model.[18] A number of authors have expanded the model by relaxing the major assumptions and have found the theory to be fairly robust even with such relaxation.[19] However, while the basic relationship between expected return and risk for individual securities holds, this relationship is not as clear or as exact as described previously. In general, the greater the imperfections, the more important the unique, or unsystematic, risk of the firm. Recall that the capital-asset pricing model assumes that this risk can be diversified away. If it cannot, certain implications of the model do not entirely hold. * * *

———————◆———————

[16] Another assumption is that the probability distributions of possible returns on all portfolios are normal. As long as the distributions are close to symmetric, however, this condition is met in a practical sense.

[17] For an analysis of the effect of short-sale restrictions and other imperfections, see Stephen A. Ross, "The Capital Asset Pricing Model (CAPM), Short-Sale Restrictions and Related Issues," *Journal of Finance*, 32 (March 1977), 177–83.

[18] For an excellent overview of the capital-asset pricing model and its limitations, see Stephen A. Ross, "The Current Status of the Capital Asset Pricing Model (CAPM)," *Journal of Finance*, 33 (June 1978), 885–901.

[19] For a review of these studies, see Michael C. Jensen, "Capital Markets: Theory and Evidence," *Bell Journal of Economics and Management Science*, 3 (Autumn 1972), 371–91; and Richard J. Rogalski and Seha M. Tinic, "Risk-Premium Curve vs. Capital Market Line: A Reexamination," *Financial Management*, 7 (Spring 1978), 73–84.

b. *Evaluation of the Empirical Evidence*

Evaluation of the empirical evidence concerning the accuracy of the CAPM's specification of asset prices involves two different levels of inquiry. The first, and most straightforward, is whether the data confirms that returns do lie on the capital market line—that the level of systematic risk does determine returns. As the evidence described by Brealey & Myers reflects, systematic risk alone explains a good deal of an asset's returns, but by no means all of it. Further, recent studies suggest that the portion of returns that are not explained by the CAPM may be explained by adding other factors in addition to systematic risk, such as dividend yield or firm size. See T. Copeland & J. Weston, *Financial Theory and Corporate Policy* 204–09 (2nd ed. 1983) (summarizing findings). There is controversy, however, with respect to whether some of the empirical anomalies are real, or merely result from statistical problems with the measurement techniques used by the investigators. For example, Reinganum, *Misrepresentation of Capital Asset Pricing: Empirical Anomalies Based on Earnings' Yields and Market Values,* 9 J.Fin.Econ. 19 (1981), found that returns on the securities of small firms seem higher than the returns on the securities of large firms, even adjusted for risk. In turn, Roll, *A Possible Explanation for the Small Firm Effect,* 36 J.Fin. 879 (1981), argued that the "small firm effect" may be no more than a mirage created by the use of a risk measure that, because the stock of small firms trades less frequently than that of large firms, understates the risk of holding a portfolio composed of small firms. The issue remains far from settled. Further empirical study seems to show an anomaly in return levels for different size firms that thus far cannot entirely be explained either by methodological deficiencies or by any economic explanation, such as higher transaction costs or tax selling, as yet offered. See Schwert, *Size and Stock Returns and Other Empirical Irregularities,* 12 J.Fin.Econ. 3 (1983) (surveying literature). In short, the CAPM seems to explain a significant portion of asset returns, but not all. Precisely how much of an asset's returns the CAPM does not explain and, in turn, what factors might explain the balance, are among the subjects at the cutting edge of research in financial economics.

The second level of inquiry concerns the difficulty of conducting *any* empirical test of the CAPM's validity. One problem in testing the CAPM was described by Brealey & Myers earlier in this Chapter: The model concerns expected returns while empirical studies by necessity use actual returns because of the near impossibility of actually measuring expectations.[6] But while this problem has been controlled, at least operationally, a second problem, originally raised by Richard Roll,[7] has not been satisfactorily resolved. Empirical tests of the CAPM typically compare the returns from a particular portfolio of assets with those

---

[6] The problem is typically avoided by assuming that returns on assets are a fair game so that actual returns will not differ systematically from expected returns. For a detailed description of how this is accomplished, see T. Copeland & J. Weston, *Financial Theory and Corporate Policy* 204–07 (2nd ed. 1983).

[7] Roll, *A Critique of Asset Pricing Theory's Tests, Part 1: On Past and Potential Testability of the Theory,* 4 J.Fin. 129 (1977).

from a portfolio composed of Treasury bills and the market portfolio in such proportions that it has the same beta as the particular portfolio of assets. If the returns from the asset portfolio are the same as those from the Treasury bill/market portfolio combination, the results are treated as supporting the hypothesis that the CAPM correctly describes how asset prices are set. The difficulty with this empirical test, however, is that the market portfolio theoretically specified by the CAPM includes *all* assets: stocks, bonds, real estate, commodities, human capital, etc. For obvious reasons, returns from the real market portfolio cannot be calculated; instead a more tractable proxy—for example, the Standard & Poor's 500 stock index, or the New York Stock Exchange index—is used for empirical testing. Roll argues that because there is no way to predict the relationship between the real market portfolio and its empirical proxy, *any* empirical result achieved is ambiguous. If returns on the asset portfolio differ from those on the comparable proxy market portfolio, they nonetheless may be the returns that would be predicted if the real market portfolio were used. Similarly, if the returns from the asset portfolio are the same as those of the comparable proxy market portfolio, they nonetheless may differ from the returns that would be predicted if the real market portfolio were used.

c.   *An Alternative: The Arbitrage Pricing Theory*

The leading alternative to the CAPM is the Arbitrage Pricing Theory (APT) which avoids the particular problems identified with the CAPM. The APT posits that, rather than a single factor determining returns as in the CAPM, a number of factors interact to determine returns. The return to an asset is thus determined by its sensitivity to each factor—i.e., there is a "beta" for each factor. So, for example, if return were a function of systematic risk and liquidity, the security market line becomes a security market plane,[8] as in the following figure.

Possible Relationship between Expected Return,
Beta, and Liquidity [9]

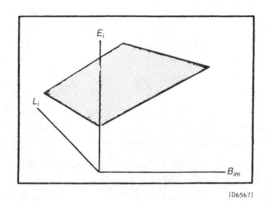

E_i = expected Return

L_i = Liquidity

B_{im} = Beta

[D6567]

---

[8] The term "security market plane" is a trademark of Wells Fargo Bank.

[9] This figure is taken from W. Sharpe, Investments 175 (2nd ed. 1981).

If a security is priced somewhere off the security market plane,[10] arbitrage by investors, either buying or selling the asset depending on the direction of its divergence from the plane, push the security's price back towards the plane. Thus, empirical evidence that return is determined by factors in addition to systematic risk, so troublesome for the CAPM, is expressly contemplated by the APT. Indeed, in this sense the CAPM is only a special case of the APT—one where just a single factor determines returns.[11] As well, the APT is not subject to Roll's methodological criticism because, unlike the CAPM, it does not require investors to form efficient portfolios, thereby eliminating the need to consider the market portfolio at all.

The generality of the APT, however, is not achieved without a substantial price. While the CAPM tells us that systematic risk determines returns, the APT itself provides no economic explanation for what factors are relevant; we know only the character of the relationship between them—whatever they are—and return. The usefulness of the APT will depend on whether future research allows specification of what factors, in addition to systematic risk, interact to determine returns, and the sensitivity of an asset's returns to each. As yet, empirical efforts at resolving these questions remain at a preliminary stage and subject to controversy.[12]

d.   Conclusion

Professor Van Horne has concluded that "a stock's beta still has a positive and very substantial effect on explaining returns, but estimates are improved with the addition of" some other factors.[13] But this qualification is less troublesome for our purposes than it may be for those who require empirical precision. The potential for other factors to also play a role requires us to be careful in considering the value of what lawyers do in connection with a particular transaction; we need always ask what, in addition to systematic risk, may be operative. However, if lawyers can act to influence *any* factor bearing on asset value, the potential for value creation is present. Thus, the present inability of financial theory to specify all factors the sensitivity to which determines an asset's returns does not interfere with our project here.[14]

[10] If more than two factors are involved, the relationship cannot be shown visually, limited as we are to three dimensions. Id. at 176.

[11] T. Copeland & J. Weston, supra at 214.

[12] See, e.g., J. Van Horne, *Financial Management and Policy* 70–71 (6th ed. 1983); Brealey & Myers, *Principles of Corporate Finance* 156–57 (2nd ed. 1984); Dhrymes, Friend & Gultekin, *A Critical Reexamination of the Empirical Evidence on the Arbitrage Pricing Theory*, 39 J. Fin. 323 (1984); Roll & Ross, *A Critical Reex-* amination of the Empirical Evidence on the Arbitrage Pricing Theory: A Reply, 39 J.Fin. 347 (1984); Shanken, *The Arbitrage Pricing Theory: Is it Testable?* 37 J.Fin. 1129 (1982).

[13] J. Van Horne, supra at 71.

[14] To be sure, the more we know about the factors that determine value, the greater the potential for value creation; however, so long as we know that beta, and the CAPM, is an important, if perhaps not exclusive, determinant of price, our inquiry can proceed.

D. Capital Budgeting and the Capital Asset Pricing Model

In our discussion of capital budgeting in Chapter Two B., an important assumption was made implicitly that now both should be made explicit and relaxed. There the stress was on the importance of taking into account the time value of money in evaluating the returns from a prospective investment. Implicit in this discussion was the assumption that there was no risk associated with the investment's returns—that the required rate of return (the discount rate) reflected *only* the time value of money. In this Chapter and in Chapter Three, however, we introduced the concept of risk. In the CAPM, the required return for a project is composed of two elements: a payment that reflects the time value of money; and a payment for bearing the systematic risk associated with the project. The latter is represented by the slope of the security market line; the former is represented by its intercept. Now that the importance of risk in the valuation of an investment has been made explicit, it is time to relax the assumption of certainty that controlled our earlier discussion of capital budgeting techniques. How do we take risk into account in capital budgeting? Put somewhat differently, how do we determine the appropriate discount rate for a project? The accepted approach to this question is developed by Professors Brealey and Myers in the following.

R. BREALEY & S. MYERS, PRINCIPLES OF CORPORATE FINANCE
157–60 (1981).[*]

Long before the development of capital asset pricing theory, smart financial managers adjusted for risk in capital budgeting. They realized intuitively that, if other things are equal, risky projects are less desirable than safe ones. Therefore they demanded a higher rate of return from risky projects or they based their decisions on conservative estimates of the cash flows.

Various rules of thumb are often used to make these risk adjustments. For example, many companies estimate the rate of return required by investors in its securities and use this **company cost of capital** to discount the cash flows on all new projects. Since investors require a higher rate of return from a very risky company, such a firm will have a higher company cost of capital and will set a higher discount rate for its new investment opportunitites.

You can use the capital asset pricing model as a rule of thumb for estimating the company cost of capital. For instance, * * * the stock of Digital Equipment Corporation (DEC) had a beta of 1.22 at the end of 1978. The corresponding expected rate of return was about 20.0 percent. Therefore, according to the company cost of capital rule, DEC should have been using a 20.0 percent discount rate in order to compute project net present values.

This is a step in the right direction. Even though we can't measure betas or the market risk premium with absolute precision, it is still reasonable to assert that DEC faced more risk than the average firm and, therefore, should have demanded a higher rate of return from its capital investments.

But the company cost of capital rule can also get a firm into trouble if the new projects are more or less risky than its existing business. Each project should be evaluated at *its own* opportunity cost of capital. This is a clear implication of the value-additivity principle. For a firm composed of assets A and B, firm value is

Firm value = PV(AB) = PV(A) + PV(B) = Sum of separate asset values

Here PV(A) and PV(B) are valued just as if they were mini-firms in which stockholders could invest directly. Note: Investors would value A by discounting its forecasted cash flows at a rate reflecting the risk of A. They would value B by discounting at a rate reflecting the risk of B. The two discount rates will, in general, be different.

If the firm considers investing in a third project C, it should also value C as if it were a mini-firm. That is, it should discount the cash flows of C at the expected rate of return investors would demand to make a separate investment in C. *The true cost of capital depends on the use to which the capital is put.*

Figure 9–1

A Comparison Between the Company Cost of Capital Rule and the Required Return Under the Capital Asset Pricing Model. DEC's Company Cost of Capital is 20.0 Percent. This is the Correct Discount Rate Only if the Project Beta is 1.22. In General, the Correct Discount Rate Increases as Project Beta Increases. DEC Should Accept Projects With Rates of Return Above the Market Line Relating Required Return to Beta.

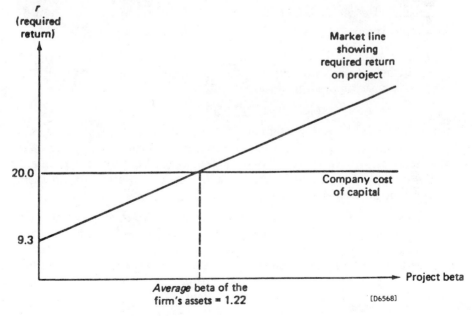

[D6568]

Capital asset pricing theory tells us to invest in any project offering a return that more than compensates for the *project's beta*. This means that DEC should have accepted any project above the upward-sloping market line in Figure 9–1. If the project had a high beta, DEC needed a higher prospective return than if the project had a low beta. Now contrast this with the company cost of capital rule, which is to accept any project *regardless of its beta* as long as it offers a higher return than the *company's* cost of capital. In terms of Figure 9–1 it tells DEC to accept any project above the horizontal cost-of-capital line—that is, any project offering a return of more than 20.0 percent.

It is clearly silly to suggest that DEC should demand the same rate of return from a very safe project as from a very risky one. If DEC used the company cost of capital rule, it would reject many good low-risk projects and accept many poor high-risk projects. It is also silly to suggest that, just because AT&T has a low company cost of capital, it is justified in accepting projects that DEC would reject. If you followed such a rule to its seemingly logical conclusion, you would think it possible to enlarge the company's opportunities by investing a substantial sum in Treasury bills. That would make the common stock relatively safe and create a low company cost of capital.[2]

The notion that each company has some individual discount rate or cost of capital is widespread, but far from universal. Many firms require different returns from different categories of investment. The following discount rates might be set, for example:

Cagetory	Discount Rate, Percent
Speculative ventures	30
New product	20
Expansion of existing business	15 (company cost of capital)
Cost improvement, known technology	10

[The main problem in using] beta and the capital asset pricing model to help cope with risk in practical capital-budgeting situations * * * is to estimate the discount rate:

$$r = r_f + \text{(project beta)} (r_m - r_f)$$

And in order to do that you have to figure out the project beta. It is a difficult problem: so much so that many people hope it will go away if they ignore it. They may go away but unfortunately the problem won't—any investment decision that is made contains an *implicit* assumption about project risk.

We will start by reconsidering the problems you would encounter in using beta to estimate a company's cost of capital. It turns out that beta is difficult to measure accurately for an individual firm: much greater accuracy can be achieved by looking at an average of similar companies. But then we have to define *similar*. Among other things we fill find that a firm's borrowing policy affects its stock's beta. It would be misleading, for example, to average the betas of Chrysler, which is a heavy borrower, and General Motors, which is not.

The company cost of capital is the correct discount rate for projects that have the same risk as the company's existing business but *not* for those that are safer or riskier than the company's average. The problem is to judge the relative risks of the projects available to the firm. In order to handle that problem, we will need to dig a little deeper and look at what features make some investments riskier than others. After you know *why* AT&T stock has less market risk than, say, Youngstown Sheet and Tube, you will be in a better position to judge the relative risks of capital investment opportunities.

There is still another complication: project betas can shift over time. Some projects are safer in youth than in old age, others are riskier. In this case, what do we mean by *the* project beta? There may be a separate beta for each year of the project's life. To put it another way, can we jump from the capital asset pricing model, which looks out one period into the future, to the discounted-cash-flow formula [used] for valuing long-lived assets? Most of the time it is safe to do so, but you should be able to recognize and deal with exceptions.

As you have no doubt guessed, capital asset pricing theory supplies no mechanical formula for measuring and adjusting for risk in capital budgeting. These tasks of financial management will be among the last to be automated. The best a financial manager can do is to combine an understanding of the theory with good judgment and a good nose for hidden clues. Therefore don't be discouraged if we dwell on the problems of using the theory. Do you want to be a dilettante who is interested solely in the theory, or a professional who looks to theory for help but not always a final answer?

CHAPTER FIVE. THE EFFICIENT CAPITAL MARKET HYPOTHESIS *

In the preceding Chapters, we surveyed the teachings of financial theory with respect to how capital assets are valued. The survey culminated with the Capital Asset Pricing Model—the insight that the return on an asset, and hence its price, bears a linear relation to the asset's systematic risk. At this point, however, an important question arises. What enforces the pricing relationship the CAPM posits? Suppose that the capital market is in equilibrium so that all asset prices are as predicted by the CAPM. Further suppose that an event then occurs that alters the expected returns associated with a particular asset. How does the market price of that asset change to reflect the new level of returns?

This question raises the issue of the Efficient Capital Market Hypothesis (ECMH). Under standard formulations, a market is efficient if prices "fully reflect all available information." In such a market, the impact of each new event that bears on the expected risk or return of an asset is reflected in the asset's price virtually instantaneously. If a particular market has this quality, important practical and policy implications follow. On the practical level, if new information about an asset is incorporated into an asset's price this quickly, then it would be very difficult at best to make a living by searching out new information about an asset with the intent of buying or selling the asset, depending on whether the information is good or bad, *before* the rest of the market learned of it. In an efficient market, there simply is no before. The implications for choice of investment strategy are apparent.

The implications of the ECMH are no less significant on the policy level. Much of the current regulation of the capital market is really an effort to remedy perceived shortcomings in the quality and accuracy of the information that is available to the capital market. The Securities Act of 1933, for example, requires the distribution of a prospectus—a lengthy document filled with detailed historical information about a proposed issuer of securities—before that issuer can sell its securities. Similarly, the Securities Exchange Act of 1934 mandates continual disclosure by publicly traded companies of a wide range of information concerning their activities. Both pieces of legislation obviously rest on the assumption that, at least with respect to the particular information required to be disclosed, the capital market is *not* efficient. Thus, understanding the concept of market efficiency has important implications for the shaping of public policy. If the market is efficient, then this regulation is at very best wasteful. If the market is not efficient, then understanding market efficiency—why does the market work when it does—may help in designing an effective remedy.

* The discussion of market efficiency in this Chapter draws heavily on Gilson & Kraakman, *The Mechanisms of Market Efficiency*, 70 Va.L.Rev. 549 (1984). While a lengthy excerpt from this article is reproduced later in the Chapter, the entire Chapter reflects the article and, of course, what I learned with and from Professor Kraakman in the course of its writing. [Ed.]

The ECMH has been the leading success story of modern finance theory in both its practical and policy guise. It has been tested so frequently and with such apparent success that Professor Michael Jensen has stated that "there is no other proposition in economics which has more empirical evidence supporting it than the efficient markets hypothesis." [1] Moreover, these results have been sufficiently influential that investment strategies based on its precepts, such as the "index fund," [2] have become important forces in the investment community. At the level of public policy, the ECMH has structured debate over the future of securities regulation both within and without the Securities and Exchange Commission, [3] and has served as the intellectual premise for a major revision of the disclosure system administered by the Commission. [4] It has even begun to influence judicial decisions [5] and the actual practice of law. [6]

Thus, there are a number of important reasons to understand the ECMH. As noted at the outset, it is the final piece of our effort at understanding how assets are valued; it is market efficiency that polices asset prices. Moreover the remarkable success of the ECMH in influencing both the investment community and policy makers is justification enough for understanding the concept. In the remainder of this Chapter we will explore the ECMH in two steps. First, we will review the history and survey the empirical support for the ECMH. While this may seem like putting the cart before the horse—examining support for a hypothesis before examining the hypothesis itself—the order of presentation actually matches the unusual history of the

[1] Jensen, *Some Anomalous Evidence Regarding Market Efficiency,* 6 J.Fin.Econ. 95, 96 (1978).

[2] An index fund is designed not to outperform the market, but to achieve results that parallel those of the stock market as a whole. This is accomplished by holding a portfolio of securities that is weighted to correspond to one or another market index, such as the Standard & Poor's Composite Index (S & P 500). The result is that the value of the portfolio will move in lock-step with the value of the index. See Schulman, *Index Funds,* in Encyclopedia of Investments (M. Blume & J. Friedman eds., 1982). An investment strategy whose goal is to do only as well as the market (but never worse) reflects the assumption that the market is efficient enough that a portfolio manager cannot consistently outperform it over time.

[3] See, e.g., H. Kripke, *The SEC and Corporate Disclosure 83–142; Report of the Advisory Committee on Corporate Disclosure of the Securities and Exchange Commission,* 95th Cong., 1st Sess. (House Comm. Print 95–29, 1977).

[4] In the Release proposing its new integrated disclosure system, the Commission stated that "the concept of integration also proceeds from the observation that information is regularly [the] being furnished to the market through periodic reports under Exchange Act. * * * To the extent that the market accordingly acts efficiently, there seems to be little need to reiterate this information in a prospectus. Securities Act Release No. 6235, *Proposed Comprehensive Revision to the System for Registration of Securities Offerings,* [1980 Trans. Binder] Fed.Sec.L.Rep. (CCH) ¶ 82,649 (1980); See also *Executive Summary of Securities Act Release Nos. 6331–6338* ("Proposed Form S–3 relies on the efficient market theory * * *.").

[5] See, e.g., Blackie v. Barrack, 524 F.2d 891, 907 (9th Cir.1975); Panzirer v. Wolf, 633 F.2d 365 (2d Cir.1981); Seaboard World Airlines v. Tiger International, 600 F.2d 355, 362 (2d Cir.1979); Teamsters Local 282 Pension Trust Fund v. Angelos, 762 F.2d 522 (7th Cir.1985); Metlyn Realty Corp. v. Esmark, Inc., 763 F.2d 826 (7th Cir.1985); In re LTV Securities Litigation, 88 F.R.D. 134 (N.D.Tex.1980); In re Ramada Inn Securities Litigation, 550 F.Supp. 1127, 1131 (D.C.Del.1982).

[6] See, e.g., Fischel, *Use of Modern Finance Theory in Securities Fraud Cases,* 38 Bus.Law. 1 (1982); Pickholz & Horahan, *The SEC's Version of the Efficient Market Theory and Its Impact on Securities Law Liabilities,* 29 Wash. & Lee L.Rev. 943 (1982).

ECMH itself. By and large, the vast outpouring of empirical research demonstrating market efficiency greatly outpaced efforts to explain what caused the phenomenon. As Professor Beaver recently commented, theory was needed "to complement the predominantly empirical tradition of efficient market research * * *. The empirical findings have largely preceded a formal, conceptual development of market efficiency." [7]

Our second step will be to pursue the inquiry Professor Beaver suggests: What makes the market efficient? This effort is necessary to completely understand the ECMH; it is also necessary to thoroughly pursue the practical and policy implications of the ECMH. Only by understanding what makes the market efficient generally is it possible to determine whether there are situations where it is inefficient and where, as a result, unusually lucrative investment opportunities might lie. In the same vein, when the empirical fact of market efficiency serves as the basis for changes in the regulation of the capital market, as has been the case with recent changes in the SEC's disclosure requirements, without a clear understanding of the mechanisms that make the market efficient in the first place, efforts at reform risk interfering with the very conditions that originally made it desirable. On a more positive note, understanding the mechanisms of market efficiency should allow the design of more effective reform.

A.   An Introduction to Empirical Testing of the ECMH

J. LORIE & M. HAMILTON, THE STOCK MARKET: THEORIES & EVIDENCE
70–97 (1973).*

THE EFFICIENT MARKET HYPOTHESIS

INTRODUCTION

During the decade of the 1960s, there was a curious and extremely important controversy about the process which determines the prices of common stocks. Initially, the controversy focused on the extent to which successive changes in the prices of common stocks were independent of each other. In more technical terms, the issue was whether or not common stock prices follow a random walk. If they do, knowledge of the past sequence of prices cannot be used to secure abnormally high rates of return.

* * *

As the controversy and related work have progressed through the years, students have come to distinguish three forms of the efficient-

---

[7] Beaver, *Market Efficiency*, 56 Accounting Rev. 23 (1981); see Verrecchia, *On the Theory of Market Information Efficiency*, 1 J. Acct'g & Econ. 77 (1979) ("Despite the substantial empirical evidence in support of the efficient market hypothesis, information efficiency has proved difficult to interpret in a compelling way."); Figlewski, *Market "Efficiency" in a Market with Heterogeneous Information*, 26 J.Pol.Econ. 581, 596 (1978) ("Discussions of the efficient-markets model seldom specify precisely how the market processes information to produce a price that accurately discounts it."). These commentators refer to the lack of a *causative* theory of market efficiency.

* Copyright © 1973. Reprinted by permission of Richard D. Irwin, Inc.

market (formerly, the random-walk) hypothesis: (1) the weak form; (2) the semistrong form; and (3) the strong form. The weak form asserts that current prices fully reflect the information implied by the historical sequence of prices. In other words, an investor cannot enhance his ability to select stocks by knowing the history of successive prices and the results of analyzing them in all possible ways. The semistrong form of the hypothesis asserts that current prices fully reflect public knowledge about the underlying companies, and that efforts to acquire and analyze this knowledge cannot be expected to produce superior investment results. For example, one cannot expect to earn superior rates of return by reacting to annual reports, announcements of changes in dividends, or stock splits. The strong form asserts that not even those with privileged information can often make use of it to secure superior investment results.

* * *

SOME HISTORY

Early Beginnings

The term "random walk" has been of interest to statisticians for almost seventy years. It is believed that the term was first used in an exchange of correspondence appearing in *Nature* in 1905. The exchange provided the proper answer to a common, vexing problem: If one leaves a drunk in a vacant field and wishes to find him after a lapse of time, what is the most efficient search pattern? It has been demonstrated that the best place to start is the point where the drunk was left. That position is an unbiased estimate of his future position, since the drunk will presumably wander without purpose or design in a random fashion.

Even before the correspondence in *Nature,* Louis Bachelier had studied commodity prices and concluded that they followed a random walk, though he did not use the term. Bachelier asserted and presented convincing evidence that commodity speculation in France was a "fair game." This meant that neither buyers nor sellers could expect to make profits. In other terms, the current price of a commodity was an unbiased estimate of its future price. Or, still again, if the *expected* price on each day were subtracted from the *actual* price, the sum of those differences, on the average, would be zero.

Bachelier's earlier work was pregnant with meaning for investors, but the gestation period was one of the longest on record. * * * [T]he burgeoning of modern work on this subject did not begin until 1959. In that year, two original and provocative papers were published.

In one, Roberts indicated that a series of numbers created by cumulating random numbers had the same visual appearance as a time series of stock prices.[8] An observer with a predisposition to see familiar patterns in these wavy lines could detect the well-known head-and-shoulders formations and other patterns both in the series representing stock prices and in the random series. Roberts also pointed out the

---

[8] Roberts, *Stock Market Patterns and Financial Analysis: Methodological Suggestions,* 14 J.Fin. 1 (1959).

first differences of the numbers generated by the random process looked very much like the first differences of stock prices. Roberts' interesting pictures are given in figures 4–1 and 4–2. * * *

Figure 4–1
Actual and Simulated Levels of Stock Market Prices for 52 Weeks

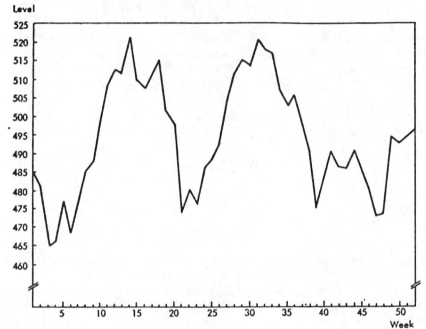

Friday closing levels, December 30, 1955–December 28, 1956, Dow Jones Industrial Average

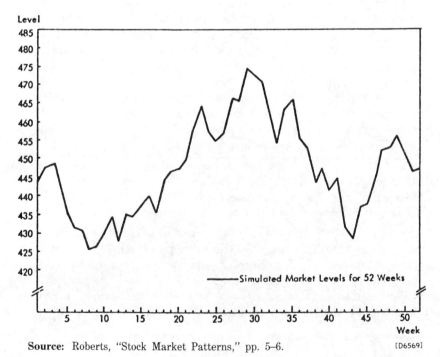

Simulated Market Levels for 52 Weeks

Source: Roberts, "Stock Market Patterns," pp. 5–6.   [D6569]

Figure 4–2
Actual and Simulated Changes in Weekly Stock Prices for 52 Weeks

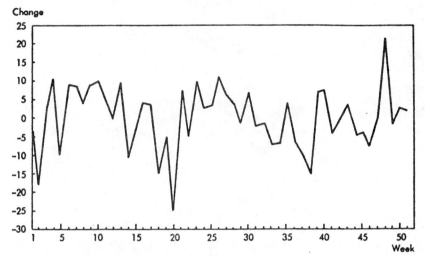

Changes from Friday to Friday [closing] January 6, 1956–December 28, 1956, Dow Jones Industrial Average

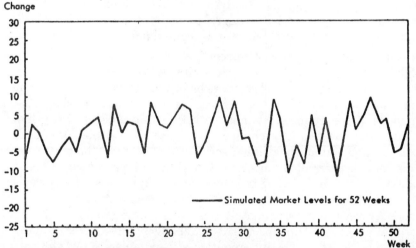

Source: Roberts, "Stock Market Patterns," pp. 5–6.
Friday closing levels, December 30, 1955–December 28, 1956, Dow Jones Industrial Average

The second work appearing in 1959 which provoked controversy and stimulated research was by Osborne.[9] He was a distinguished physicist with the Naval Research Laboratory in Washington, D. C. when the article was published. Although Osborne has learned a great deal about the stock market since 1959, he professed (probably incorrectly) to be ignorant about the market at that time. He chose to look at the numbers representing stock prices to see whether they conformed to certain laws governing the motion of physical objects. In particular, he was interested in seeing whether the movements of prices were of the sort that characterizes the movements of very small particles suspended in solution—so-called "Brownian motion." He

[9] Osborne, *"Brownian Motion in the Stock Market,"* 7 Oper.Res. 145 (1959).

found a very high degree of conformity between the movements of stock prices and the law governing Brownian motion. Specifically, the variance of price changes over successively longer intervals of time increases as the square of the length of time. This implies that the logarithms of price changes are independent of each other. Although Osborne's point of view is different, his findings are consistent with Roberts'.

Early Tests of the Weak Form

The work by Osborne and Roberts at first was taken seriously only by a small group of academicians. Both pieces of work suggested, on the basis of preliminary and tentative investigation, that changes in stock prices were random. The first reactions in the academic community were to devise various ingenious tests of this randomness using bodies of data considerably more extensive than those used by either Osborne or Roberts. These tests * * * provided substantial support for the tentative conclusions of Osborne and Roberts. On the basis of measurements of serial correlations between price changes, through investigation of the number of successive changes of given sign, and in other ways, these workers tested the statistical independence or the randomness of successive changes in stock prices. They uniformly found only insignificant departures from randomness.

Since there is general agreement, we will present only a few highlights. Moore [10] was one of the first to look at the serial correlation between successive price changes of individual stocks. The interpretation of this sort of test is that a low coefficient suggests that previous price changes cannot be used to predict future changes. Moore examined weekly changes of 29 randomly selected stocks for 1951–58 and found an average serial correlation coefficient of —0.06. This value is extremely low, indicating that data on weekly changes are valueless in predicting future changes. Fama [11] studied the daily proportionate price changes of the 30 industrial stocks in the Dow Jones Average for approximately five years, ending in 1962. The serial correlation coefficients for the daily changes are all very small, the average being 0.03. The investigation was extended to test the possibility that lagged price changes show some dependence. Again, the coefficients do not differ substantially from zero. Fama's results are shown in table 4–1. The correlation coefficients are very low. While the evidence is impressive, correlation coefficients have an unfortunate attribute. They may be dominated by a few extreme and unusual observations.

[10] Moore, *Some Characteristics of Changes in Common Stock Prices in The Random Character of Stock Market Prices* 139 (Cootner ed. 1964).

[11] Fama, *The Behavior of Stock Market Prices,* 38 J.Bus. 34 (1965).

Table 4–1

Daily Serial Correlation Coefficients for
Lags of 1, 2, . . ., 10 Days

Stock	1	2	3	4	5	6	7	8	9	10
Allied Chemical	.017	-.042	.007	-.001	.027	.004	-.017	-.026	-.017	-.007
Alcoa	.118*	.038	-.014	.022	-.022	.009	.017	.007	-.001	-.033
American Can	-.087*	-.024	.034	-.065*	-.017	-.006	.015	.025	-.047	-.040
A.T.&T.	-.039	-.097*	.000	.026	·.005	-.005	.002	.027	-.014	.007
American Tobacco	.111*	-.109*	-.060*	-.065*	.007	-.010	.011	.046	.039	.041
Anaconda	.067*	-.061*	-.047	-.002	.000	-.038	.009	.016	-.014	-.056
Bethlehem Steel	.013	-.065*	.009	.021	-.053	-.098*	-.010	.004	-.002	-.021
Chrysler	.012	-.066*	-.016	-.007	-.015	.009	.037	.056*	-.044	.021
Du Pont	.013	-.033	.060*	.027	-.002	-.047	.020	.011	-.034	.001
Eastman Kodak	.025	.014	-.031	.005	-.022	.012	.007	.006	.008	.002
General Electric	.011	-.038	-.021	.031	-.001	.000	-.008	.014	-.002	.010
General Foods	.061*	-.003	.045	.002	-.015	-.052	-.006	-.014	-.024	-.017
General Motors	-.004	-.056*	-.037	-.008	-.038	-.006	.019	.006	-.016	.009
Goodyear	-.123*	.017	-.044	.043	-.002	-.003	.035	.014	-.015	.007
International Harvester	-.017	-.029	-.031	.037	-.052	-.021	-.001	.003	-.046	-.016
International Nickel	.096*	-.033	-.019	.020	.027	.059*	-.038	-.008	-.016	.034
International Paper	.046	-.011	-.058*	.053*	.049	-.003	-.025	-.019	-.003	-.021
Johns Manville	.006	-.038	-.027	-.023	-.029	-.080*	.040	.018	-.037	.029
Owens Illinois	-.021	-.084*	-.047	.068*	.086*	-.040	.011	-.040	.067*	-.043
Procter & Gamble	.099*	-.009	-.008	.009	-.015	.022	.012	-.012	-.022	-.021
Sears	.097*	.026	.028	.025	.005	-.054	-.006	-.010	-.008	-.009
Standard Oil (Calif.)	.025	-.030	-.051*	-.025	-.047	-.034	-.010	.072*	-.049*	-.035
Standard Oil (N.J.)	.008	-.116*	.016	.014	-.047	-.018	-.022	-.026	-.073*	.081*
Swift & Co.	-.004	-.015	-.010	.012	.057*	-.017	.012	-.043	.014	.001
Texaco	.094*	-.049	-.024	-.018	-.017	-.009	.031	.032	-.013	.008
Union Carbide	.107*	-.012	.040	.046	-.036	-.034	.003	-.008	-.054	-.037
United Aircraft	.014	-.033	-.022	-.047	-.067*	-.053	.046	.037	.015	-.019
U.S. Steel	.040	-.074*	.014	.011	-.012	-.021	.041	.037	-.021	-.044
Westinghouse	-.027	-.022	-.036	-.003	.000	-.054*	-.020	.013	-.014	.008
Woolworth	.028	-.016	.015	.014	.007	-.039	-.013	.003	-.088*	-.008

* Coefficient is twice its computed standard error.

Source: Fama, "The Behavior of Stock Market Prices," p. 72.

To test this, Fama looked at the signs rather than size of successive changes to see if runs tended to persist. The daily changes in the prices of each of the 30 Dow Jones stocks were classified as zero, positive, or negative. A sequence of + + − + + + − − 0, for example, would be made up of five runs. If runs do tend to persist (i.e., if there are trends), the total number of runs will be less and the average length of a run longer than if the series were random. Fama's findings are in table 4–2. In general, the actual number of runs conforms very closely to the numbers expected, although there is a slight tendency for runs in daily changes to persist. This is also suggested by the predominately positive correlation coefficients for daily changes. The departure from randomness is negligible, however, and the evidence is strong support for the random-walk hypothesis. The financial community seemed to be unaware of or indifferent to this work.

Some advocates of technical analysis argued that these tests were unfair because they were too rigid and that possible complicated dependencies in successive price changes must be investigated. This led to an interesting effort to refute the implications of the work of Roberts, Osborne, Fama, and the others. Alexander [13] tried to devise trading rules based solely on price changes which could produce abnormally high rates of return. If he could find such rules, they would imply that price changes followed patterns and were not random. Alexander's trading rule was of the following form: Wait until stock prices have advanced by x percent from some trough and then buy stocks; next, hold those stocks until they have declined y percent from some subse-

---

[13] Alexander, *Price Movements in Speculative Markets: Trends and Random Walks,* 2 Indus.Mgmt.Rev. 7 (1961).

quent peak and then sell them or sell them short. Continue this process until bankrupt or satisfied.

Alexander's first efforts to refute the assertions of randomness appeared to be successful, since his results implied the existence of trends or persistence of movements in stock prices. His so-called filter technique produced enormous rates of return. On the basis of corrections in his work * * * the profits disappeared. The major shortcomings of Alexander's early work were the failure to realize that dividends were a cost rather than a benefit when stocks were sold short, the failure to take transaction costs into account, and the assumption that stocks could be bought or sold at the precise price at which the signal to buy or sell was given. Fama and Blume [15] demonstrated that filter schemes cannot, in general, provide returns larger than a naive policy of buying and holding stocks. Very small filters can generate larger profits before commissions, suggesting some persistence in short-term price movements. This is corroborated by some of the evidence presented earlier. However, the trends are so short that the profits are wiped out by commissions. The only ones to be enriched by using filter techniques to buy and sell stocks would be the brokers; the investors themselves would be bankrupt.

* * *

Table 4–2

Total Actual and Expected Numbers of Runs for One-, Four-, Nine-, and Sixteen-Day Periods

Stock	Daily		Four-Day		Nine-Day		Sixteen-Day	
	Actual	*Expected*	*Actual*	*Expected*	*Actual*	*Expected*	*Actual*	*Expected*
Allied Chemical	683	713.4	160	162.1	71	71.3	39	38.6
Alcoa	601	670.7	151	153.7	61	66.9	41	39.0
American Can	730	755.5	169	172.4	71	73.2	48	43.9
A.T.&T.	657	688.4	165	155.9	66	70.3	34	37.1
American Tobacco	700	747.4	178	172.5	69	72.9	41	40.6
Anaconda	635	680.1	166	160.4	68	66.0	36	37.8
Bethlehem Steel	709	719.7	163	159.3	80	71.8	41	42.2
Chrysler	927	932.1	223	221.6	100	96.9	54	53.5
Du Pont	672	694.7	160	161.9	78	71.8	43	39.4
Eastman Kodak	678	679.0	154	160.1	70	70.1	43	40.3
General Electric	918	956.3	225	224.7	101	96.9	51	51.8
General Foods	799	825.1	185	191.4	81	75.8	43	40.5
General Motors	832	868.3	202	205.2	83	85.8	44	46.8
Goodyear	681	672.0	151	157.6	60	65.2	36	36.3
International Harvester	720	713.2	159	164.2	84	72.6	40	37.8
International Nickel	704	712.6	163	164.0	68	70.5	34	37.6
International Paper	762	826.0	190	193.9	80	82.8	51	46.9
Johns Manville	685	699.1	173	160.0	64	69.4	39	40.4
Owens Illinois	713	743.3	171	168.6	69	73.3	36	39.2
Procter & Gamble	826	858.9	180	190.6	66	81.2	40	42.9
Sears	700	748.1	167	172.8	66	70.6	40	34.8
Standard Oil (Calif.)	972	979.0	237	228.4	97	98.6	59	54.3
Standard Oil (N.J.)	688	704.0	159	159.2	69	68.7	29	37.0
Swift & Co.	878	877.6	209	197.2	85	83.8	50	47.8
Texaco	600	654.2	143	155.2	57	63.4	29	35.6
Union Carbide	595	620.9	142	150.5	67	66.7	36	35.1
United Aircraft	661	699.3	172	161.4	77	68.2	45	39.5
U.S. Steel	651	662.0	162	158.3	65	70.3	37	41.2
Westinghouse	829	825.5	198	193.3	87	84.4	41	45.8
Woolworth	847	868.4	193	198.9	78	80.9	48	47.7
Averages	735.1	759.8	175.7	175.8	74.6	75.3	41.6	41.7

Source: Fama, "The Behavior of Stock Market Prices," p. 75.

All of these early investigations were tests of the so-called "weak form" of the random-walk hypothesis. That is, they tested the statistical properties of price changes themselves without reference to the relationship of these changes to other kinds of financial information. The evidence strongly supports the view that successive price changes are substantially independent. It also indicates that knowledge of the negligible dependencies cannot be used to enhance profits because of transaction costs.

[15] Fama & Blume, *Filter Rules and Stock Market Trading*, 39 J.Bus. 226 (1966, Suppl.).

* * *

Tests of the Semistrong Hypothesis

Investigations of the semistrong form of the hypothesis are concerned with market efficiency and the extent to which prices fully reflect public knowledge. The focus of the empirical tests is the speed of adjustment to new information. Fama, Fisher, Jensen, and Roll [25] looked at the effect of stock splits on stock prices. The folklore with respect to stock splits was that the total value of an issue of common stocks was increased by increasing the number of shares. Efforts to explain this apparent irrationality were numerous and untested. The various explanations seemed to have in common the belief that investors, for various reasons, preferred stocks with low prices per share and that this preference led to an increased demand for stocks at low prices, even though the level of earnings, volatility of earnings, and other underlying economic variables remained unchanged.

Believers in the efficiency of markets and the rationality of investors were skeptical about the folklore. There would seem to be no reason why splitting a stock should change its aggregate value unless the split implied something about the company. Fama, Fisher, Jensen, and Roll subjected the folklore to its first comprehensive and rigorous scientific test. Their hypothesis was that splits, which are usually accompanied by dividend increases, were interpreted by the market as a predictor of a dividend change. A dividend change can convey information about management's confidence about future earnings. In an efficient market, the only price effects of a split would be those associated with the information implied by a possible dividend change.

Both the methods and the findings of the investigators are of considerable interest. They examined all stock splits of 25 percent or more on the New York Stock Exchange from January 1927 through December 1959. The investigators did not try to find out whether prices went up or down after stock splits; they tried to find out whether stock prices went up or down more than could have been expected. This required that they abstract from the influence of general market conditions during months surrounding the time of the split.

Their first step was to determine the relationship between rates of return on individual stocks in the study and rates of return on the market as a whole except for the period around the split. For each of the 622 securities in the study, they estimated statistically the relationship of the monthly rates of return of individual stocks to the rates of return on all listed stocks on the New York Stock Exchange. The estimated relationships are based on the 420 months during the 1926–60 period with the exception of the 15 months before and the 15 months after the month of the split. These months were excluded because unusual price behavior in months surrounding the split would obscure the long-term relationship.

The market would be judged to have been efficient if the split did not alter this relationship, except to the extent that the split contained

[25] Fama, Fisher, Jensen & Roll, *The Adjustment of Stock Prices to New Information*, 10 Int'l Econ.Rev. 1 (1969).

information which altered expectations about rates of return on the stocks which split. New information would be reflected in deviations of rates of return from normal relations to the market rates.

* * *

[The authors found] that rates of returns for stocks that split tend to be high, relative to the market as a whole, by comparison with their longer term historical relationship. After the split, however, the rates of return on these stocks, on the average, have the normal relationship to rates of return on the market as a whole. * * * [The result] for stocks which had dividend increases within a year of the time when the stocks were split [was similar.] A dividend increase (or decrease) occurred, by definition, if the ratio of dividends paid in the year following the split to those paid in the year preceding the split was larger (or smaller) than the ratio for the exchange as a whole. Following the split, there is a very slight upward drift in the rates of return on stocks with dividend increases relative to the market by comparison with the normal relationship. By the end of 30 months, however, the normal relationship has been resumed. Of particular interest is the fact that the rise in average rates of return begins well before the split. Since information about a split is received on the average only two to four months in advance, the rise cannot be accounted for by the split. A more likely explanation is that splits occur after periods of unusual prosperity for the company which is reflected in the prices of the stocks. * * * [S]tocks that did not have a subsequent dividend increase [after a split] had declining rates of return relative to the market by comparison with the normal relationship. The authors interpret these findings as indicating that the announcement of a stock split implies the strong likelihood of a subsequent increase in dividends. The likelihood is substantial but not certain. When these expectations are fulfilled by a subsequent dividend increase, there is a slight feeling of relief on the part of investors and a slight enhancement in the rates of return on the affected stocks relative to what could be expected in the absence of the stock split and accompanying dividend increase. When expectations are disappointed, there is a decline in rates of return relative to the market, reflecting the disappointment of investors.

In summary, the authors regard their work as providing strong support for the hypothesis that the market is efficient. Stock splits have no effect on rates of return, independent of the effect created by the presumption that the stock split contains information regarding future dividend changes and therefore earnings potential. In Fama's words, "* * * apparently the market makes unbiased forecasts of the implications of a split for future dividends, and these forecasts are fully reflected in the price of the security by the end of the split month." [26]

* * *

A [different] kind of public announcement was studied by Ball and Brown.[28] For the period of 1946–66, the deviations from "normal" rates of return for 261 firms were examined to detect the effect of annual earnings announcements. The authors classified the firms into two

---

[26] Id. at 17.

[28] Ball & Brown, *An Empirical Evaluation of Accounting Income Numbers*, 6 J. Acctg. Res. 159 (1968).

groups: those whose earnings for a given year increased relative to the market and those whose earnings decreased relative to the market. They found that the average rates of return for stocks with "increased earnings" rose throughout the year preceding the announcement. For stocks with "decreased earnings," the opposite was true. In other words, most of the information in the earnings announcement had been anticipated by the market.

* * *

Tests of the Strong Form of the Hypothesis

* * *

Now it is time to examine the strong form of the hypothesis—namely that prices of stocks reflect not only what is generally known through public announcements but also what may not be generally known. Certain groups have monopolistic access to information. Also, the ardent quest of legions of security analysts for original insights and small revealing clues could confer superior ability to predict the future course of stock prices. Tests of the strong form consist of analyses of the performance of portfolios managed by groups which might have special information.

These tests consist of an examination of the performance of professionally managed portfolios. The argument is that performance by professionally managed portfolios that was consistently superior to the performance of the market as a whole or to relevant subsets of stocks in that market would indicate an element of inefficiency in the price-making process. Consistent superiority would suggest that some people have superior access to relevant information not reflected in the prices of stocks.

The most visible of the professionally managed portfolios are the mutual funds. They are required by law to present all of the information necessary to compute rates of return on their portfolios. Fortunately for the brevity of this discussion, the results of investigations of mutual fund performance are rather uniform. * * *

[For example, a] study of mutual fund performance by Michael Jensen [36] covered the performance of 115 mutual funds for the period 1955–64. He followed Sharpe in that he did not take account of rates of return alone. Recognizing that variations in fund performance could be expected on the basis of differences in the degree of risk assumed, Jensen compared the performance of individual mutual funds with the performance that could have been expected from randomly selected portfolios of equal riskiness. * * *

Within the context of the "capital asset pricing model," it is possible by artificially constructing portfolios consisting of varying proportions of riskless assets—generally government debt securities—and a portfolio of all stocks listed on the New York Stock Exchange, to create portfolios of different riskiness that would have been selected on the average by random selection. These have a range of riskiness covering that experienced by the mutual funds. Since the riskiness of these randomly selected portfolios depends only upon the proportion

---

[36] Jensen, *The Performance of Mutual Funds in the Period 1945–64*, 23 J.Fin. 389 (1968).

invested in the riskless asset and the proportion invested in the market
portfolio, the portfolios representing different degrees of riskiness lie on
a straight line. The market portfolio in Jensen's work is defined as the
Standard & Poor's Composite Index. The measure of risk which he
uses is a measure of the sensitivity of a fund's return to changes in the
return on the market as measured by the index. Jensen's major results
are illustrated in the figure 4–7.

In figure 4–7, the straight line represents the risk and return on
randomly selected portfolios, and the individual dots represent the
performance of individual mutual funds, * * * on the assumption
that mutual funds had no expenses other than brokerage commissions.
It can be observed that about half of the dots lie above the line and
about half below. This is the result that would be expected if the
market were highly efficient with market prices fully reflecting all that
was knowable through public announcement or ascertainable through
the efforts of individual security analysts.

Figure 4–7

Scatter Diagram of Risk and (Gross) Return for 115 Open-End Mutual Funds in the Period 1955–64

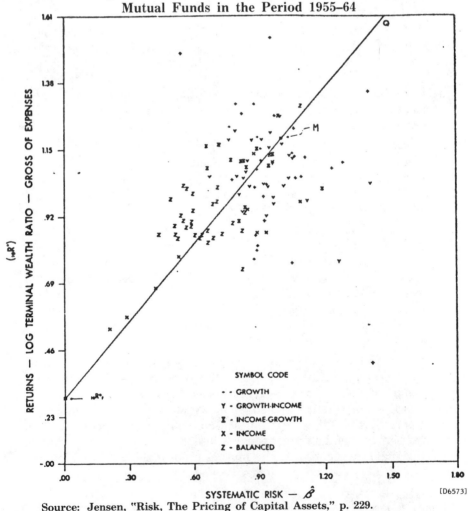

Source: Jensen, "Risk, The Pricing of Capital Assets," p. 229.

Figure 4–8 indicates comparisons between mutual fund performances and randomly selected portfolios of equal riskiness after mutual funds are charged with the expenses which they incurred. Naturally, a much smaller proportion of the mutual funds did as well as the randomly selected portfolios. In fact, only 43 out of 115 mutual funds had superior performance. On the average, for the ten-year period, the terminal value of the mutual funds, assuming reinvestment of dividends, would have been about 9 percent less than the terminal value of the randomly selected portfolios, assuming reinvestment of dividends and interest. When loading charges are taken into account, the comparisons are even more adverse from the point of view of mutual funds. At the end of the ten-year period, the average terminal value of the funds was 15 percent less than that of the randomly selected portfolios.

Figure 4–8

Scatter Diagram of Risk and (Net) Return for 115 Open-End Mutual Funds in the Ten-Year Period 1955–64

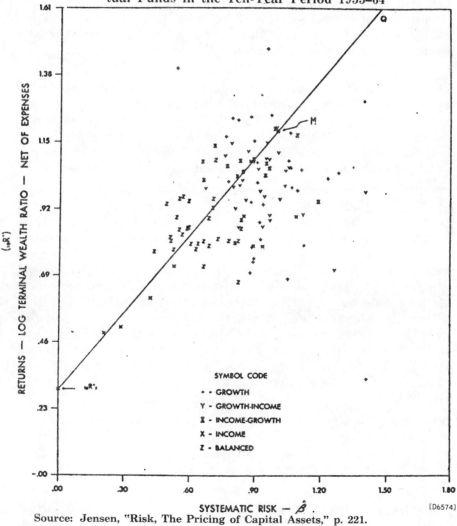

SYMBOL CODE

+ - GROWTH
Y - GROWTH-INCOME
Z - INCOME-GROWTH
X - INCOME
Z - BALANCED

SYSTEMATIC RISK — $\hat{\beta}$.   [D6574]

Source: Jensen, "Risk, The Pricing of Capital Assets," p. 221.

Although Jensen's results indicate that mutual funds on the average did not outperform randomly selected portfolios of equal riskiness, there remains the possibility that some mutual funds consistently outperform randomly selected portfolios. Such a finding would represent a partial invalidation of the strong form of the random walk hypothesis. Jensen, in his study, looked into this matter to some degree, though he admitted that further investigation is warranted. On the basis of his preliminary inquiry, Jensen found that a mutual fund which was superior to a randomly selected portfolio in one period was superior to a randomly selected portfolio in a subsequent period about half the time. Obviously, about half the time the performance of the mutual fund in the subsequent period was inferior to the randomly selected portfolio. Jensen also sought to determine whether any fund was more frequently superior to randomly selected portfolios during the ten-year period than would be expected on the basis of chance alone. He found no evidence of such superiority. In sum, Jensen's investigation of mutual fund performance provided additional support for the strong form of the random-walk hypothesis. Mutual fund managers did not appear to have monopolistic access to information. Moreover, large expenses were not associated with high rates of return.

*   *   *

One can readily imagine that findings such as [these] did not create strong euphoria in the mutual fund industry. The least happy interpretation of the findings cited above was that mutual fund managers were incompetent. Even if one avoided that *misinterpretation*, it was possible to conclude—although erroneously—that mutual funds provided no useful function. In fact, neither charges of incompetence nor of uselessness are justified.

The fact that mutual funds did not outperform randomly selected portfolios could mean, and probably does mean, merely that mutual fund managers compete in an efficient market with other portfolio managers of approximately equal competence. Mutual fund managers must compete with the managers of trust departments of commercial banks, with professional individual investors, and with other professionals in investment counseling firms, insurance companies, and elsewhere. Since mutual fund managers must maintain a portfolio of at least 20 securities, and since these are usually widely diversified, it is not at all surprising or indicative of incompetence that on the average these portfolios do not do significantly better or worse than portfolios of equal riskiness selected from the market as a whole.

*   *   * Thus, we can conclude that evidence on mutual fund performance supports the strong form of the random-walk hypothesis but does not indicate either lack of competence by mutual fund managers or the foolishness of individual investors who use mutual funds as an outlet for their savings.

Investigations of the investment behavior of investors other than managers of mutual funds who might have access to monopolistic information are less numerous. There is some evidence, however, that inside information is a potential source of inefficiency in the market.

Niederhoffer and Osborne [40] examined the trading of specialists on major exchanges. They concluded that information on unexecuted orders can be used profitably. The finding that the price declines following a secondary offering are larger if the vendor is a corporation or corporate officer indicates that insiders may benefit from privileged information.[41] Lorie and Niederhoffer [42] also found evidence of profitability in insider trading. They analyzed insider trades from January 1950 to December 1960 of 105 New York Stock Exchange companies. They conclude that:

> proper and prompt analysis of data on insider trading can be profitable. * * * When insiders accumulate a stock intensively, the stock can be expected to outperform the market during the next six months. Insiders tend to buy more often than usual before large price increases and to sell more often than usual before price decreases.[43]

They also found that a change in direction of trading activity can be an important clue to insider expectations concerning their stock.

These findings, while meager in comparison to the evidence in support of the efficient market hypothesis, do suggest there are minor departures from complete efficiency. There is no evidence however, that groups other than specialists or corporate insiders can use special information to earn above normal profits.

◆

B. The Mechanisms of Market Efficiency

Although empirical verification of the fact of market efficiency preceded a thorough explication of the mechanisms that accounted for that result, in recent years financial economists have found the absence of an explanation for market efficiency increasingly troubling. To be sure, the phenomenon of market efficiency is easily explained under perfect market assumptions—for example, that information is immediately and costlessly available to all participants in the capital market. But this explanation is, in the words of a joke commonly directed at both lawyers and economists, "absolutely accurate and totally useless." [8] In commenting on Fama's seminal review article on market

---

[40] Niederhoffer & Osborne, *Market Making and Reversal on the Stock Exchange*, 61 J.Am.Stat. Assoc. 897 (1966).

[41] Scholes, *The Market for Securities: Substitution versus Price Pressure and the Effects of Information on Share Prices*, 45 J.Bus. 179 (1972).

[42] Lorie & Niederhoffer, *Predictive and Statistical Properties of Insider Trading*, 11 J.L. & Econ. 35 (1968)

[43] Id. at 52.

[8] The story usually begins with two people in a hot air balloon who discover they

have lost their way. They notice someone on the ground and call out, "Where are we?"

Unhesitatingly the ground observer responds, "You're in a balloon."

At this point one balloonist turns to the other and says, "He must be a lawyer (economist)."

"How can you tell?" the second passenger asks.

"It's easy," the first responds. "What he said was absolutely accurate and totally useless."

efficiency,[9] Professor Sharpe made precisely this point. "Simply put, the thesis is this: in a well-functioning market, the prices of * * * securities will reflect predictions based on all relevant and available information. This seems almost trivially self-evident to most professional economists—so much so, that testing seems almost silly." [10] What makes the ECMH non-trivial, of course, is its prediction that, even though information is *not* immediately and costlessly available to all participants (and it is the "even though" that is critical), the market will act *as if* it were.

The challenge of explaining why the market can behave efficiently despite the fact that information—even publicly "available" information—is costly to obtain and process, has led financial economists to formulate models of different market mechanisms each of which, under carefully specified circumstances, could cause the capital market to act *as if* everyone were costlessly informed when, in fact, they were not.

In the following, the authors propose a general explanation of the factors that lead to—and limit—market efficiency. Their focus is on integrating not only the different capital market mechanisms that appear in the financial economics literature, but also the interaction between these mechanisms and the information market.

GILSON & KRAAKMAN, THE MECHANISMS OF MARKET EFFICIENCY
70 Va.L.Rev. 549, 554–613 (1984).

We begin in Section I with a necessary preliminary: the clarification of precisely what is meant by market efficiency.

* * *

I. PRELIMINARY DEFINITIONS

The language of efficient capital market theory reveals its origins as a vocabulary of empirical description. The common definition of market efficiency, that "prices at any time 'fully reflect' all available information," is really a shorthand for the empirical claim that "available information" does not support profitable trading strategies or arbitrage opportunities. Similarly, Eugene Fama's landmark 1970 review article first proposed the now-familiar division of the ECMH into "weak," "semi-strong," and "strong" forms as a device for classifying empirical *tests* of price behavior.[24] Weak form tests examined the claim that the histories of securities prices could not yield lucrative trading opportunities. Semi-strong form tests probed the same prediction about categories of publicly available information of obvious inter-

[9] Fama, *Efficient Capital Markets: A Review of Theory and Empirical Work*, 25 J.Fin. 383 (1970).

[10] Sharpe, *Discussion*, 25 J.Fin. 419 (1970). Professor Beaver has made a similar point more recently: "Why would one ever expect prices *not* to 'fully reflect' publicly available information? Won't market efficiency hold trivially?" Beaver, *Market Efficiency*, supra at 32.

[24] Fama, *Efficient Capital Markets: A Review of Theory and Empirical Work*, 24 J.Fin. 383, 388 (1970). Fama credited Harry Roberts with distinguishing weak and strong form tests. Id. at 383 n.1.

est to investors.[26] Finally, strong form tests examined the extension of the hypothesis to information that was available only to particular groups of privileged investors.[27] In this usage, the weak, semi-strong, and strong form categories have proved both useful and precise. The hypothesized dearth of arbitrage opportunities, whatever its explanation, clearly grows in strength with each successive genre of test. The more private the information, the more intuitively reasonable the proposition that one might profit by trading on it, and so the stronger the opposing claim that such profitable trading is impossible.

Over time, however, scholars have pressed the weak, semi-strong, and strong form categories beyond their original service as a classification of empirical tests into more general duty as a classification of market responses to *particular kinds of information.* For example, prices might be said to incorporate efficiently one genre of information that is semi-strong or public, but fail to reflect another that is strong form, or non-public. Indeed, taken a step further, scholars sometimes describe markets themselves as weak, semi-strong, or strong form efficient. Without ever being quite explicit, this powerful shorthand implies that different market dynamics are involved in the reflection of different kinds of information into price, and that varying degrees of market efficiency might well be the consequence.

The recognition that different market mechanisms operate on different types of information is central to our analysis of market efficiency. But before we explore this conclusion in greater detail, it is

[26] Studies of semi-strong form efficiency are tests of *how long* market prices require to adjust to price-relevant information that is released to the public. These studies typically ask whether trading activity that follows the release of such information can earn investors abnormally high returns and focus on the security's price history before and after the test period. The discovery of abnormal returns indicates trading opportunities and, therefore, possible market inefficiency. The results thus far indicate efficient price responses to a wide variety of publicly released information, ranging from earning reports and dividend announcements to accounting changes, stock splits, press evaluations, and even changes in Federal Reserve Board policy.

* * *

[27] Unlike weak and semi-strong form tests, which probe for trading opportunities that might arise from particular *kinds* of information, strong form studies cannot test for analogous opportunities arising from the generation of non-public information because investigators are unlikely to learn about such information (or if they do, they are unlikely to employ it for research purposes). For this reason, strong form tests must probe indirectly for trading opportunities arising from non-public information. Such tests seek to identify investors who are likely to possess non-public

information and to determine whether these traders consistently earn net returns higher than the market average. The results have been mixed. Corporate insiders, such as officers, directors and affiliated bankers, systematically outperform the market. So do specialists on the major stock exchanges who possess non-public information about unexecuted investor orders. See, e.g., Baesel & Stein, *The Value of Information: Inferences from The Profitability of Insider Trading,* 14 J.Fin. & Quantitative Analysis 553 (1981) (corporate insiders); Lorie & Niederhoffer, *Predictive and Statistical Properties of Insider Trading,* 11 J.L. & Econ. 35, 52–53 (1968) (corporate insiders); Niederhoffer & Osborne, *Market Making and Reversal on the Stock Exchange,* 61 J.Am.Stat. A. 897 (1966) (exchange specialists). Mutual funds, however, appear to outperform the market only well enough to cover administrative and trading costs. See Jensen, *The Performance of Mutual Funds in the Period 1945–1964,* 23 J.Fin. 389, 418 (1968); Mains, *Risk, the Pricing of Capital Assets, and the Evaluation of Investment Portfolios: Comment,* 50 J.Bus. 371, 384 (1977) (reanalyzing Jensen data and noting that Jensen's conclusion that mutual funds were inferior performers should be revised to call them neutral performers).

first necessary that we define the key terms of the ECMH, and that we do so conceptually rather than operationally. * * * Two of these are encompassed within the operational definition of market efficiency: that prices "fully reflect" all "available" information. [A] third inheres in the expanded use of the weak, semi-strong, and strong form categories to describe price response to different kinds of information. We need a concept of "relative efficiency" that distinguishes among and ranks the different market dynamics according to how closely they approximate the ideal of ensuring that prices *always* fully reflect all available information.

It is our good fortune here, as at several junctures in this analysis, to have at hand prior work that provides major elements of the theoretical structure required by our discussion. The ambiguities inherent in the loose operational terminology of efficient market theory have led several commentators, including Beaver,[29] Rubinstein,[30] and Fama himself,[31] to propose restatements of the basic price-oriented definition of market efficiency. Their efforts have focused on clarifying the first two concepts, that prices "fully reflect" all "available information." Following Beaver's analysis, the requirement that prices "fully reflect" information means that prices must behave "*as if* everyone knows" the relevant information. Full reflection of information, then, entails a hypothetical identity between two equilibria in the same market: the equilibrium that would result if everyone knew the information, and the equilibrium that is actually observed. The market is efficient if (and when) the two equilibria are identical. * * *

By contrast, the second basic concept embodied in the operational definition of market efficiency, that prices mirror all available information, is less in need of reformulation than of expansion. The availability of information is a function of its distribution among traders in a given market. Different "bits" of information are more or less "available" depending on how many traders are aware of them. Thus, the strength of the claim that prices fully reflect *all* available information hinges in large part on where one sets the minimum threshold of information distribution. Strong form market efficiency tacitly sets the threshold as low as possible, by describing information as "available" if it is accessible to only a single individual even if no one actually trades on it. The consequence, as Fama has observed, is an "extreme null hypothesis" that cannot literally be true. Weak form market efficiency, on the other hand, implicitly sets the distributional threshold as high as possible. Information about prices in the recent past, for example, is likely to be distributed to all traders in a single market.
* * *

Because different distributions may place information anywhere between these extremes of high and low "availability" to traders, our concern must be with particular categories or "sets" of information rather than with information in general. An efficient market response

[29] Beaver, *Market Efficiency*, 56 Acct. Rev. 23, 27–31 (1981).

[30] Rubinstein, *Securities Market Efficiency in an Arrow-Debreu Economy*, 65 Am. Econ.Rev. 812, 812 (1975).

[31] E. Fama, supra note 24, at 384–88.

to one information set does not necessarily mean that the market will respond efficiently to a different set. *   *   *

In clarifying the operational definition of market efficiency—that prices fully reflect all available information—we have suggested that different market mechanisms may be responsible for the reflection in price of differentially available categories of information. Differences among market mechanisms will matter, however, only if these mechanisms operate with unequal results. We still require a measure of success—a yardstick of "relative efficiency"—in order to assess the importance of differences in the mechanisms of price formation.

The formal definition of informationally efficient prices does not provide such a yardstick. To say, without more, that sooner or later prices will reflect certain information only describes the endpoint of a process that by itself is not very interesting or surprising. We learn something by fixing this endpoint, of course: that the price *dis*equilibrium generated by new information ultimately evolves to a new equilibrium with the same efficient prices that would result if all traders initially possessed the new information. But this description of the restoration of efficient prices ignores all aspects of the process itself, including the most critical: *How long* does it take?

The operational definition of market efficiency tightly restricts the speed of the market's response to new information by requiring prices to reflect such information "always"—i.e., very promptly. It is a short step from this emphasis on the rapidity of price response to a definition of "relative efficiency." The market, and the mechanisms that operate to reflect new information in price, are more or less efficient depending on how quickly they yield efficient equilibrium prices; relative efficiency is a measure of the speed with which new information is reflected in price. Similarly, the relative efficiency of market mechanisms determines the magnitude of arbitrage opportunities that new information creates for the fortunate traders who "know" it first. The requirement that prices *always* reflect new information means, in effect, that these mechanisms must function rapidly enough to foreclose any exploitable trading opportunities. This result is the benchmark against which claims of market efficiency are ordinarily measured. Thus, when we speak simply of the "efficiency" with which market mechanisms incorporate information into price, we will use this term in its relative sense.

*   *   *

II. MECHANISMS OF MARKET EFFICIENCY

Review of the basic vocabulary of efficient market theory reveals a missing link: an account of the mechanisms of market efficiency that its terms foreshadow but do not explicitly detail. Once the "full reflection" of information into price is reformulated as an identity between an existing equilibrium price and a fully informed equilibrium price, the general contours of these mechanisms become clear. They must be trading processes that, with more or less promptness (or "relative efficiency"), force prices to a new, fully informed equilibrium. Moreover, clarifying the meaning of informational "availability" also reveals the chief obstacle to any mechanism that serves to push prices toward a fully informed equilibrium. New information is "available" to the capital market under an extraordinary variety of circumstances, ranging from the extreme of near-universal initial distribution of information—when everyone really does know the information—to the opposite extreme of initial distribution to only a very few traders. A satisfactory account of the mechanisms of market efficiency must describe their operation over this entire continuum of availability, including those circumstances in which the initial distribution is extremely limited or incomplete. Finally, and most important, the insight implicit in the extended application of the weak/semi-strong/ strong form categories to information sets and markets suggests how one can explain distinct levels of relative efficiency over the entire continuum of informational availability. We must search for *several different mechanisms,* each of which can operate over an information set of particular availability to market traders, and each of which can generate its own dynamics of price equilibration.

Fortunately, the most difficult step in this search—the identification of a basic repertoire of mechanisms to explain the incorporation of new information into equilibrium securities prices—has already been taken. Over the past dozen years, financial economists have proposed four general forms of mechanisms, which may be termed "universally informed trading," "professionally informed trading," "derivatively informed trading," and "uninformed trading." In accordance with the economists' rigorous conventions of formal exposition, each of these mechanisms has thus far been modeled in isolation, as if it singlehandedly could explain the dynamics of price equilibration. Yet from the perspective of policy formulation, the precise operation of these mechanisms *in vacuo* is of less interest than the fact that all four shape the formation of prices in the same securities markets. Moreover, they do so in a fashion that can account for the reflection of information in price over the entire range of informational availability. We shall present these four mechanisms as components of a single complex repertoire of market responses.   *   *   *

Three features of the relation among the market mechanisms are critical. First, only one of the market mechanisms at a time can ordinarily operate to cause a particular bit of new information to be reflected in price. Second, which mechanism will dominate the dynamics of price change at any time depends on how widely the particular information is distributed in the market. Third, each of the mechanisms operates with a characteristic level of relative efficiency that depends on how widely information must be distributed in order to trigger it. The wider the initial distribution of information that a mechanism requires, the more rapidly that mechanism operates.

Together, these characteristic interrelationships permit us to array the four market mechanisms on a continuum based on the initial distribution of information among traders, that is, on *how many* traders learn of the new information. Although all four mechanisms can ultimately lead to efficient equilibrium prices, the dynamics of equilibration will take longer as one moves from wide to narrow distribution mechanisms. Thus, just as the extended use of the weak/semi-strong/ strong form categories implies, less "available" information will require more time for "full reflection" in price because its narrower distribution will force a qualitatively more circuitous form of price equilibration. Correlatively, the individual trader who initially learns of new information can capture an increasing portion of its trading value as the initial distribution of the information narrows and the dominant market mechanism shifts accordingly.

A.   Universally Informed Trading

The simplest efficiency mechanism that causes prices to behave "as if" all traders knew of information is a market in which all traders are, in fact, costlessly and simultaneously informed. To be sure, universally informed trading in its purest sense results in efficient prices tautologically, and may seem more a statement of a sufficient condition for market efficiency than an active mechanism. But several varieties of price-relevant information at least approximate the ideal of universal dissemination. "Old" information, embedded in securities prices, is one example. Ongoing market activity assures its distribution to all interested traders, and precisely because all know it, we do not expect it to reveal arbitrage opportunities in the form of lucrative screens or trading rules that all alike could exploit. Another example is important news items—from presidential election results, which most citizens learn almost instantaneously, to changes in Federal Reserve Board policy, which are announced after trading hours precisely in order to ensure widespread dissemination.[59] Thus, the universally informed trading mechanism ranges over all "old" price information and much that is new. It lumps together traditional "weak-form" information about price histories with information about current events into a single information set that prices reflect rapidly and with near perfect dynamic efficiency.

[59] In practice, of course, much of the trading impact of routine press announcements is often registered *before* publication, presumably as the result of either accurate forecasting or inside trading. See, e.g., Morse, *Wall Street Journal Announcements and the Securities Markets,* Fin. Analysts J., Mar.-Apr. 1982, at 69, 69, 75–76 (company-specific information announced in Wall Street Journal largely anticipated); Waud, *Public Interpretation of Federal Reserve Discount Rate Changes:* Evidence on the "Announcement Effect," 38 Econometrica 231, 248–49 (1970) (Federal Reserve decisions anticipated 5–7 days in advance); SEC's Inquiry Widens As It Questions Broker, Others in Journal Case, Wall St. J., Apr. 2, 1984, at 1, col. 6 (Wall Street Journal reporter admitted leaking market-sensitive information to investors). Yet the residual price response that follows publication is extremely rapid. See, eg., Lloyd-Davies & Canes, *Stock Prices and the Publication of Second-Hand Information,* 51 J.Bus. 43, 55 (1978) (Wall Street Journal columns affect prices too rapidly to support trading profits).

Note that, even *after* the "universal" dissemination of reliable trading facts, some portion of the resulting price impact may be channelled through other market mechanisms, especially "professionally informed" and "uninformed" trading. This will occur if the quality of trader expectations about "how much" good or bad news affects value differs substantially. * * * Under these circumstances, one would expect universal trading to account for the bulk of post-dissemination price movements and expert trading to provide fine tuning. Arguably, this phenomenon explains the "technical corrections" that are often said to follow close on the heels of initial market responses to dramatic trading news.

B.   *Professionally Informed Trading*

In contrast to news about price and current events, however, much so-called "public" information is not universally disseminated among traders.   Many traders are too unsophisticated to make full use of the technical accounting information contained in mandated disclosure reports;   much disclosure data is accessible in the first instance only through documents on file with government agencies;   and much information about a firm's prospects may be announced initially only to small groups of securities analysts and other market professionals. How, then, do prices come to reflect this semi-public information?   The answer, as identified in general terms by Fama [64] and many others,[65] is that rapid price equilibration does not require widespread dissemination of information, but only a minority of knowledgeable traders who control a critical volume of trading activity.   From this perspective, the universally informed trading mechanism is actually only a special case of price formation through the activity of traders who are direct recipients of information.   Subgroups of informed traders, or even a single knowledgeable trader with sufficient resources, can also cause prices to reflect information by persistent trading at a premium over "uninformed" price levels.   The rapidity of such price adjustments depends on the volume of informed trading.   And although a precise account of that process has yet to be offered, it seems plausible that the relative efficiency of price adjustment to new information that proceeds through professionally informed trading declines only gradually as initial access to the information narrows to a threshold minority of traders, after which it declines rapidly.[67]

---

[64] Fama, supra note 24, at 387–88.

[65] E.g., R. Brealey, *An Introduction to Risk and Return from Common Stocks* 17 (2d ed. 1983); J. Lorie & M. Hamilton, supra note 7, at 86–88.

[67] This account still begs the question of exactly *how* informed minority trading can lead to the rapid price reflection of new information even when the minority is too small to dominate trading volume. If *un*informed traders held widely divergent beliefs about the value of a security, a short answer would be "price pressure": trading by informed investors that alters the demand or supply for particular securities, and raises or lowers their prices accordingly.   This answer is almost certainly incomplete, however.   It rejects wholesale the homogeneous expectations postulate of the Capital Asset Pricing Model, as well as the depiction of securities as fungible commodities with large numbers of near-perfect risk-return substitutes.   A far more plausible answer is that suggested by Myron Scholes, who demonstrated that secondary offerings affect securities prices primarily through the release of information rather than through price pressure. Scholes, *The Market for Securities: Substitution versus Price Pressure and the Effects of Information on Share Prices*, 45 J.Bus. 179, 182–84, 206–08 (1972).

Similarly, intense trading by an informed minority will trigger temporary fluctuations in price and volume that may, in turn, alert an uninformed majority to the existence of new information.   Cf. Kraus & Stoll, *Price Impacts of Block Trading on the New York Stock Exchange*, 27 J.Fin. 569 (1972) (temporary liquidity and transaction-cost price fluctuation from block trading).   The ways in which uninformed traders may "learn" from price changes are discussed [in Section IIC].   The involvement of uninformed traders in the professionally informed trading mechanism would help explain the need for a threshold number of informed traders to assure the rapid reflection of new information in price.   Rapid learning by uninformed traders requires a clear price signal and, therefore, a *critical volume* of informed trades.

In today's securities markets, the dominant minority of informed traders is the community of market professionals, such as arbitrageurs, researchers, brokers and portfolio managers, who devote their careers to acquiring information and honing evaluative skills. The trading volume in most securities that these professionals control, directly or indirectly, seems sufficient to assure the market's rapid assimilation into price of most routine information.[69] Of course, the relative efficiency of the assimilation is never perfect. Since informed trading is costly, market professionals must enjoy some informational advantage that permits them to earn a commensurate return. But given competitive arbitrage and the market for analyst services, we would not expect the long-run returns of individual professionals to exceed the market average by very much, especially in exchange markets where professionals dominate trading. This expectation is largely confirmed by empirical studies of mutual fund returns.

In sum, the professionally informed trading mechanism explains why any information that is accessible to significant portions of the analyst community is properly called "public," even though it manifestly is not. Such information is rapidly assimilated into price, with only minimal abnormal returns to its professional recipients. And it is these characteristics, we submit, that largely convey the meaning of a "semi-strong form" market response.

C. Derivatively Informed Trading

Yet not all information is public, even within the narrow confines of the professional analyst community. Corporate insiders and exchange specialists, for example, enjoy easy access to information that would be prohibitively costly for anyone else to obtain,[73] while professional analysts conduct in-depth research that generates occasional informational monopolies.[74] In these and similar instances of monopolistic access, information first enters the market through a very small number of traders whose own resources are not large enough to induce speedy price equilibration. But reflection of this information in price does not depend exclusively on the trading efforts of these insiders. Derivatively informed trading enhances relative efficiency and erodes the insider's advantage by capitalizing on the "informational leakage" associated with trading itself.

[69] * * * Direct estimates of *how* rapidly prices reflect information after it becomes widely accessible to market professionals are difficult to come by, but one indication may be the market's response to news of block trades. According to one study, it requires a mere 15 minutes—too short an interval for post-trade arbitrage—for prices to stabilize after such trades. Dann, Mayers & Raab, *Trading Rules, Large Blocks and the Speed of Price Adjustment,* 4 J.Fin.Econ. 3, 18–21 (1977). * * *

[73] The strong form efficiency tests, supra note 27, amply document the systematic informational advantage enjoyed by corporate insiders and other "insider" groups. Indeed, if anything, these tests radically underestimate the magnitude of this advantage by relying on data about trades that are registered or otherwise public. Because trading on inside information is both unlawful and easily hidden, data limited only to publicly disclosed trading by insiders systematically excludes the trades most likely to reflect important informational advantages. See Keown & Pinkerton, *Merger Announcements and Insider Trading Activity: An Empirical Investigation,* 36 J.Fin. 855, 856–57 (1981).

[74] For a dramatic example, see SEC v. Dirks, 103 S.Ct. 3255 (1983). * * *

Informational leakage can assume many forms. Pure leakage—inadvertent, direct communication of trading information to outsiders—doubtlessly plays a significant role in rendering markets more efficient,[76] even if its effects remain erratic. But beyond such direct disclosure by accident or "theft," two forms of *indirect* leakage also contribute to market efficiency. These are trade decoding and price decoding.[77]

Trade decoding occurs whenever uninformed traders glean trading information by directly observing the transactions of informed traders. Myron Scholes' classic study of secondary distributions documents a common example of this phenomenon by demonstrating that only some large block sales of stock lead to substantial, permanent declines in share price. The declines are especially pronounced when sellers are officers or other insiders of the issuer; moderate when sellers are investment companies and mutual funds (which act on the advice of research staffs); and barely noticeable when sellers are individuals, bank trust departments, and other traders who may liquidate their holding for reasons other than investment gain. The clear implication is that uninformed traders use the identities of large sellers to deduce whether the latter are likely to possess valuable information, and then proceed to trade accordingly.[80] Moreover, incidental evidence suggests that trade decoding is pervasive well beyond the limited context of block trades.[81] Indeed, the Federal Securities Acts themselves provide prime opportunities for trade decoding by the uninformed by forcing insiders and other informationally-advantaged traders to disclose their activities, if not their motives.[82]

[76] A professional in a major tender solicitation firm explains the "pure" informational leakage that precedes public announcement of tender offers as follows:

You start with a handful of people, but when you get close to doing something the circle expands pretty quickly * * *. You have to bring in directors, two or three firms of lawyers, investment bankers, public-relations people, and financial printers, and everybody's got a secretary. If the deal is a big one, you might need a syndicate of banks to finance it. Everytime you let in another person, the chance of a leak increases geometrically.

Klein, *Merger Leaks Abound, Causing Many Stocks To Rise Before the Fact*, Wall St.J., July 12, 1978, at 1, col. 6, at 31, col. 1.
* * *

[77] We owe this latter term to Robert Verrecchia. See Verrecchia, *Consensus Beliefs, Information Acquisition, and Market Information Efficiency*, 70 Am.Econ.Rev. 874, 881 n.12 (1980).

[80] Id. at 202. The absence of any relationship between distribution size and the magnitude of longterm price change further supports a trade-decoding interpretation of Scholes' findings. Id. at 207.

[81] Brokers are particularly well-placed to engage in trade-decoding. Consider the ease with which employees of E.F. Hutton & Company detected trading on inside tender-offer information by a partner in a major Wall Street law firm: "employees at Hutton are understood to have noticed a pattern in [the partner's] account where, as one source put it, 'He got too lucky * * *.' " Cole, Wachtell Lawyer is Out in Insider-Trading Case, N.Y. Times, Sept. 12, 1981, at D29, col. 1 at D36, col. 3.
* * *

[82] E.g., § 13(d) of the Securities Exchange Act of 1934, 15 U.S.C. § 78m(d) (1982) (requiring reporting, within 10 days, of boilerplate information regarding the purchase of any security that gives the owner more than 5 percent of that class of security); § 16(a) of the 1934 Act, 15 U.S.C. § 78p (1982) (requiring directors, officers, and 10% beneficial owners to report purchases and subsequent changes in ownership of issuer's equity securities within 10 days after initial acquisition and 10 days "after the close of each calendar month thereafter").

Pervasive though it may be, however, trade decoding remains limited by a significant constraint: uninformed traders must be able to identify informed traders individually and observe their trading activities directly. By contrast, the second form of indirect leakage, price decoding, does not require uninformed traders to discover the identity of their informed cohorts. It merely requires uninformed traders to observe and interpret anonymous data on price and trading volume against the backdrop of other information or expectations that these traders possess.

In theory, at least the logic of price decoding is simple. When trading on inside information is of sufficient volume to cause a change in price, this otherwise inexplicable change may itself signal the presence of new information to the uninformed. * * * But beyond the "weak" learning involved in identifying the presence of new information, uninformed traders may also succeed in decoding the actual content of the information.[84] The trick here, and admittedly it is no mean feat, is the uninformed trader's ability to employ knowledge of the informational constituents of the old price to deduce which possible accretion of new information would successfully explain observed price changes.[85] Yet, probabilistically, such "strong" learning may be less difficult than it at first appears; consider, for example, how frequently increases in price signal the presence of inside information about impending tender offers.[86]

The theory of "weak" learning from prices is standard economic fare, traditionally linked with the contributions of Friedrich Hayek. Attempts to model "strong" learning, however, are comparatively recent and are still in a developmental stage in which they must radically

[84] What we term "weak" learning from price, then, does *not* involve the active extraction of information from price, but only the more modest recognition that unanticipated price changes may signal the *existence* of new information. This reflects the "rational expectation" that other traders, like oneself, buy or sell securities on the basis of their expected returns. If market prices change unexpectedly, the reason must be that other traders have acquired new facts or forecasts that alter their assessments of expected returns. * * *

[85] Thus, unlike screening rules or other attempts to discover trading opportunities in price data alone, price decoding relies principally on the interaction *between* price changes and independent information about firms. The more widespread this independent information is among traders, of course, the more widely distributed correct deductions from price changes will be, and the less likely it is that price decoding will yield trading profits. But if incipient price changes can only be interpreted by a few traders who have already acquired detailed knowledge about the firm, or if unexpected price changes lead a handful of traders to research the firm, these price changes may well yield trading profits.

* * *

[86] See Keown & Pinkerton, supra note 73, who report not only accelerating price increases during the three weeks that precede tender offers, but also

that 79, 60, and 64 *percent* of the acquired firms exhibited higher volume one, two and three weeks prior to the announcement date than they had three months earlier with the weekly average volume over this three week period 247, 112, and 102 percent higher than it was three months earlier.

Id. at 863.

It is impossible to determine how much such crescendos of trading activity owe to pure leakage, trade decoding, or price decoding, respectively. The very strength of the incipient price and volume changes, however, suggests that "strong" price decoding plays a major role, especially as the other forms of informational leakage amplify the strength of the price signals.

simplify the learning processes of real markets.[88]   Nevertheless, they not only provide the best available account of this commonplace market phenomenon,[89] but they also raise a question that cuts to the core of efficient market theory. Why would anyone incur the cost and risk of acquiring restricted-access information, if hair-triggered "decoders" will extract the bulk of its value? The answer must be that prices are not fully informative and, indeed, that the acquisition effort is made precisely because they are not. As Grossman and Stiglitz[90] recently demonstrated, a market in which price decoding was both costless and accurate could not support an efficient equilibrium in which prices fully reflect trading information. Rather, such a market would be doomed to an oscillating dynamic of enlightenment and ignorance. Traders would initially acquire information because, in an inefficient market, they could earn returns on their investment in acquisition. As more traders became initially informed, however, the price system would convey more information to uninformed traders, thereby lowering the returns to informed traders. At the point at which the market became fully efficient, there would be no return to informed traders for having acquired the information, and, as a result, information acquisition would cease. The market would sink into informational inefficiency once more, only to repeat the cycle as soon as some traders again found information acquisition profitable.

Perhaps it is fortunate, then, that fully-effective price decoding remains a theoretical concept rather than a market reality. It is only because uninformed traders cannot infer *all* information from price— i.e., because prices are "noisy"—that informed traders enjoy a return on their information up to the point at which further trading moves prices beyond the noise threshold. Thus, the reflection of non-public information into price is a two-stage process; it is first triggered by initially informed "inside" trading, but, at a critical threshold, it rapidly accelerates as a result of reactive trades. This much ensures

---

[88] On the use of simplifying assumptions, see, e.g., Grossman & Stiglitz, *On the Impossibility of Informationally Efficient Markets*, 70 Am.Econ.Rev. 393, 395 (1980) (proving conjectures regarding non-existence of fully-informative prices under simplified assumptions). Some scholars have criticized * * * rational expectations "micro-theorists" for relying on implausible, regression-like accounts of individual forecasting. See, e.g., Frydman, *Towards an Understanding of Market Processes: Individual Expectations, Learning, and Convergence to Rational Expectations Equilibrium*, 72 Am.Econ.Rev. 652, 664–65 (1982). In our view, however, neither the complexity of real markets, nor the difficulties of providing a wholly satisfactory theoretical account of individual forecasting behavior, diminish the central insights of the price decoding theorists. * * *

[89] The history of market manipulation is replete with persuasive, if back-handed, evidence of trader reliance on price decoding.

To the extent that such venerable scams as "wash sales" and "matched orders" trick uninformed traders into bidding up share prices through misleading price and volume data, they succeed for precisely the same reason that stock touting succeeds: namely, they transmit misinformation through a usually reliable information channel. See Kryzanowski, *Comment: Misinformation and Security Markets*, 24 McGill L.J. 123, 124–26 (1978). Indeed, the fact that such deceptions can create "manipulation bubbles" of considerable duration (1–12 months) on thinly-traded exchanges, id. at 130–31, suggests not only the extent of investor reliance on price information but also a link between price decoding and the volatility of securities prices generally. * * *

[90] Grossman & Stiglitz, supra note 88; Grossman & Stiglitz, *Information and Competitive Price Systems*, 66 Am.Econ. Rev. 246, 250–51 (1976).

that price reflects each "bit" of decoded information with a moderate degree of relative efficiency—less, to be sure, than a wider initial distribution might provide, but far more than the trades of initially informed investors alone could produce. For the price system as a whole, background noise implies an "equilibrium degree of disequilibrium." [94] Noise levels regulate the numbers of informed traders much like returns on initially informed trading regulate entry into the community of market professionals in the context of professionally informed trading. The number of informed traders, in turn, determines the volume of limited-access information that influences prices at any particular moment, and the end result is perpetual, if constrained, disequilibrium.

In short, derivatively informed trading, whether it operates through trade- or price-decoding, is self-limiting. It guarantees neither full efficiency nor inefficiency, but rather a level of relative efficiency that is jointly determined by the effort required to acquire information and the decoding possibilities that limit its exploitation. Derivatively informed trading thus explains how prices can come to reflect much information that is truly "non-public," even while suggesting the inevitable limits to the process.

D.   Uninformed Trading

The three trading mechanisms that we have considered thus far each describe processes by which prices come to reflect particular key trading facts. Such pieces of information have strong and straightforward implications for price. * * * [H]owever, information is not limited to hard facts; it also includes soft information, the stuff of forecasts and predictions, that is at least as critical to trading as key trading facts. Both in developing forecasts of future events and in making a master forecast of value, traders employ, in addition to key facts, a wide variety of secondary facts, differing beliefs, and diverse levels of predictive skills. This heterogeneity of information, beliefs, and skills adds additional uncertainty to that stemming from the inherent indeterminancy of the future. The uncertainty arises from the sheer impossibility of acquiring both the full range of secondary facts and the complete repertoire of skills necessary to frame optimal forecasts. [Thus,] a hypothetical fully informed trader would form optimal forecasts as a result of access to the aggregate information, beliefs, and skills of *all* traders in the market, but individual traders would remain ignorant of this optimal forecast information. Such information is "available" to the market, but it nonetheless lies at the extreme pole of the continuum depicting the initial distribution of information to traders. In extreme contrast to the virtually complete distribution of information that underlies universally informed trading, optimal forecast information is not available to any *individual* trader. At this juncture, the basic question of market efficiency resurfaces. What is the mechanism by which the market comes to reflect the

[94] Grossman & Stiglitz, supra note 88, at 393.

diverse and imperfect forecasts of individual traders into the aggregate forecast of price, and how well does this mechanism function as measured against the yardstick of optimal forecast data?

The final market efficiency mechanism, uninformed trading, permits prices, in some circumstances, to reflect aggregate—or consensus—forecasts that are more nearly optimal over the long run than those of any individual trader. In this sense, prices can reflect information about which *all* traders are uninformed.[100] * * *

If each trader's forecast about the likelihood of a future event is informed in part by secondary facts and evaluations to which only he has access, then an aggregation of all forecasts draws on an information pool much larger than that possessed by any individual trader. Although each trader's own forecasts are skewed by the unique constraints on his or her judgment, other traders will have offsetting constraints. As trading proceeds, the random biases of individual forecasts will cancel one another out, leaving price to reflect a single, best-informed aggregate forecast. Uninformed trading, then, resembles a regression in which the dependent variable is price, the independent variables are the "bits" of information bearing on an unbiased forecast, and the weights attached to each bit are determined by the buy-sell decisions of individual traders. Although individual traders will attach biased weights because each knows only a fraction of the relevant information, the cumulative weights will be unbiased unless trading volume is itself skewed toward the views of one set of uninformed traders. In this respect, unsystematic bias "washes out" over trading in the same way that unsystematic risk "washes out" in a diversified portfolio. Moreover, if any bias persists, it does so because the "errors" of individual traders are perversely correlated, just as unsystematic risks might be in a poorly diversified portfolio.[104]

Robert Verrecchia [105] has modeled the conditions under which the regression-like behavior of uninformed trading aggregates all forecast information available to the market—but not to all individual traders—into a consensus best estimate of value. Of course, real markets at best can only approximate these conditions, but the interesting issue here, as with the other market mechanisms, is the identification of the

[100] Note, however, that uninformed trading *never* leads to prices that reflect wholly optimal forecast data. Rather, this mechanism can lead to prices that reflect a *better approximation,* over the long run, of such hypothetical optimal forecasts than can the parallel assessments made by individual traders. For this reason, the uninformed trading mechanism has the lowest relative efficiency of any of the four market mechanisms. As measured against the yardstick of the target information—i.e., optimal forecast data—it can never assure fully informed prices, even though it may reflect consensus forecasts in price much more rapidly than, say, derivatively informed trading will reflect inside information in price.

[104] Any widespread mistake, forecasting error, or breakdown in the acquisition of key facts can generate bias with respect to the "true" distribution of probabilities associated with contingent outcomes. For example, widespread, if unjustified, optimism about the virtues of conglomeration represents an apparently common form of trader bias in poorly informed markets. The existence of forecasting bias, however, does not necessarily indicate that individual traders are acting irrationally. Forecasting methods that were accurate in the past, including reliance on the information content of price, may prove inadequate in light of altered circumstances.

[105] See Verrecchia, supra note 77.

factors that determine when and how well uninformed trading operates. Verrecchia's model requires traders to make independent assessments of the value of risky securities based on their own facts and forecasts, which in the aggregate form a bounded, unbiased distribution around the hypothetical price that a fully informed trader would assign the security. The first of these conditions, that trader assessments be independent, requires an absence of collusion, "learning," or shared prejudice among traders that would render individual forecasting errors mutually reinforcing. Complete independence, of course, is unlikely in real markets, but so is widespread mutual dependence where it contradicts the independent judgments of many traders. * * * The second condition of uninformed trading, that trader assessments be "bounded," merely requires that all such assessments fall in the same ball park. Traders with wildly-skewed personal assessments will impede price convergence—reduce the relative efficiency of the uninformed trading mechanism—and may even preclude it entirely in thinly-traded markets.[109] Again, however, market discipline in the form of heavy trading losses will restrain idiosyncratic traders and may even eliminate them through a "Darwinian" process of natural selection.[110]

It is the third condition of uninformed trading, that aggregate trader assessments remain unbiased with respect to the optimal price estimate of a fully informed trader, that may be the most demanding. This condition embraces the preceding two requirements, since either widely-shared forecasting errors or idiosyncratic trading can bias the aggregate-level distribution of trader assessments. But, in addition, the "no-bias" condition carries implications for the acquisition of new key trading facts that can significantly alter individual assessments. Until the market fully incorporates such key information into price the independent assessments of uninformed traders—traders who do not know of the new information—are inevitably systematically biased. Once *any* trader acquires a new key fact that renders hitherto uncertain contingencies more (or less) likely, the consensus forecast of uninformed traders, as embodied in existing price, is biased relative to the

---

[109] The analogy for purposes of our regression metaphor, see supra text accompanying note 103, is wildly skewed "outliers" in data sets. These outliers can have a dramatic and often unwarranted effect on the predicted magnitude and variance of the dependent variable (here market price), especially when the data set is small. Precisely because of this effect, Verrecchia suggests that smaller firms with fewer shareholders will have a comparatively greater incentive to release information and reduce the dispersion of trader forecasts that might otherwise lead to skewed share prices. Verrecchia, *On the Theory of Market Information Efficiency*, 1 J.Acct. & Econ. 77, 89–90 (1979). * * *

[110] Verrecchia, supra note 109, at 82. Cootner provides the classic early discus-

sion of "natural selection" (or wealth redistribution) and how it contributes to the uninformed trading mechanism:

> Given the uncertainty of the real world, many actual and virtual investors * * * will have many, perhaps equally many, price forecasts * * *. If any group of investors was consistently better than average in forecasting stock price, they would accumulate wealth and give their forecasts greater and greater weight * * *. Conversely, investors who were worse than average in forecasting ability would carry less and less weight.

P. Cootner, *The Random Character of Stock Market Prices* 80 (1964). * * *

newly-available information. Moreover, it remains so until the market fully incorporates the new key information into price, through one of the three "informed" trading mechanisms previously described.

This complementary relationship among the market mechanisms can be viewed either from the perspective of uninformed trading or from that of the three informed trading mechanisms. When viewed from the perspective of uninformed trading, the informed market mechanisms are "shortcuts" to the elimination of sudden informational bias in consensus prices. They rely on the speedy transmission of information to traders rather than on the much slower and less certain process of market discipline. By contrast, when uninformed trading is viewed from the perspective of the three informed market mechanisms, it represents an interstitial mechanism that operates between the appearances of new key trading facts. Uninformed trading "fine-tunes" equilibrium price and assures that price registers any gradually developing consensus about future contingencies.

The example of a truly innovative investment contract, such as a radically novel form of bond indenture, further illustrates the complementary nature of the market mechanisms. When an issuer first announces such an innovative security, all traders will be uncertain about its worth. Although the issuer may make good-faith representations about value, most traders will discount these as self-interested puffery. Absent convincing assurances, the initial pricing of the innovative security will be left to the uninformed trading mechanism, which will tend to "undervalue" it relative to the information possessed by the good-faith issuer—but not, of course, relative to the aggregate forecasts of the uninformed traders. Thus, the security's uninformed equilibrium price will be "biased," and relatively inefficient. Efficiency is possible only if the issuer succeeds in making its representations credible, or if an enterprising trader independently acquires the key facts that establish their accuracy. In the first case, subsequent price equilibration would proceed rapidly through the universally informed or professionally informed trading mechanisms; in the second, it would proceed more slowly through derivatively informed trading.

Yet this depiction of the relationship between uninformed and informed trading mechanisms still remains incomplete in one important respect: it ignores the fact that traders themselves are acute observers of market behavior. If prices successfully aggregate all available information, including consensus forecasts and secondary facts, traders will begin to condition their trading activity on price as well as on their individual assessments of value. This conditioning on price adds "learning" to the basic aggregation mechanism of uninformed trading and is precisely the "weak learning" from price that we previously contrasted with the "strong learning" of price decoding. Weak learning in this sense occupies a middle ground between uninformed and derivatively informed trading. Unlike price decoding, which transmits key trading facts, weak learning conveys refracted data about consensus opinion that is already fully impounded in price and has comparatively little potential for revising individual traders' facts and forecasts.   In many instances, the simple aggregation process of uninformed trading will obscure the sources of weak or gradual price changes and so preclude any deduction about their meaning other than the obvious one—that a shift has occurred in consensus market expectations.   But even where traders are able to associate price and volume signals with shifts in *particular* aggregate forecasts, such as an altered consensus forecast about future Federal Reserve Board policies, they will only acquire an indication of whether the market disagrees with them, not of why it does.   The force of such an indication depends on each trader's level of confidence. Individual estimates of value will move toward existing prices, and individual forecasts toward consensus predictions, in rough proportion to how highly each trader assesses the comparative quality of his or her own collection of information.

The existence of weak learning from price itself indicates that, on average, such learning improves the quality of individual trading decisions.   To the extent that it succeeds, it will also have a beneficial "feedback" effect on the core aggregation processes of uninformed trading by decreasing unwarranted dispersion in individual assessments of value.[119]   The amount and importance of weak learning that occurs, however, are also constrained by the level of price noise—the same random fluctuation in price that masks the transmission of key trading facts through price decoding.   Price noise, then, regardless of its source, establishes the limits on the ultimate efficiency of uninformed trading.[121]   On the other hand, the instances in which the market has "guessed" right are an index of the success of uninformed trading.   The paradigmatic examples are the many occasions on which publication of Federal Reserve Board policy decisions, fluctuations in money supply, and similar data of interest to investors have resulted in no discernable effect on prices.   Not surprisingly, these examples differ from the case of the novel innovative security in that they concern

[119] If traders rely on price in roughly inverse proportion to the quality of their independent assests, the most poorly informed traders will rely most on price, thereby reducing the number of wildly skewed "outlier" trades.   In this sense, weak learning from price can function as a short-cut to the elimination of bias, just as do the informed trading mechanisms. On the other hand, weak learning can also generate inefficiency in uninformed trading by amplifying any systematic bias reflected in price.   Weak learning cannot *create* biased prices, but if the forecasts of confident investors who trade heavily on their independent assessment are already biased, weak learning by less confident traders may transmit the bias and "freeze" it into price.   This phenomenon parallels the transmission of misinformation through price decoding.   In all likelihood, schemes to defraud investors through "churning" and "matched orders" depend on the joint operation of both price decoding and weak learning.

* * *

[121] Stated differently, it limits the extent to which price can converge to a single best estimate that reflects not only key trading facts, but also optimal forecasts of all residual uncertainties affecting a security's value.

future events about which all traders are likely to possess well-specified, reasonably exact forecasts.

In sum, the formulation of expectations in response to uncertainty
will always constitute a major portion of the task of valuing securities.
Over much of this domain, the uninformed trading mechanism will
bear the burden of reflecting these expectations in price.

E. Summary

The uninformed trading mechanism completes the array of capital
market mechanisms that, in our view, constitutes an essential element
of efficient market theory. For any initial distribution of information
in the market, including an initial distribution to no one in the case of
optimal aggregate forecasts, one or more efficiency mechanisms facilitate the eventual "reflection" of information into price.[124] Moreover,
the four efficiency mechanisms are complementary; each functions
over a characteristic segment of the continuum of initial distributions
of information among traders.

As Figure One illustrates, if the mechanisms are portrayed in this
fashion, they parallel the criterion for partitioning information sets
that implicitly informed Fama's trichotomy of weak/semi-strong/strong
form tests of market efficiency. Universally informed trading extends
over all widely-disseminated information, including the price-history
information that underlies weak form tests. Professionally informed
trading operates on all publicly available information, but it is particularly active where information is "semi-public"—i.e., initially distributed or useful to only a minority of sophisticated trading professionals.
Professionally informed trading thus links the information sets sampled by semi-strong form tests and by those strong form tests, including
studies of mutual fund performance, that aggregate returns to sophisticated traders over time. By contrast, derivatively informed trading
acts most prominently on key trading facts over which very small
numbers of traders exercise monopolistic access. It dominates the
remaining strong form tests that routinely demonstrate substantial
market inefficiency, such as those involving corporate insiders and
market specialists. Finally uninformed trading acts on the "soft"
information of forecasts and assessments that is not directly sampled by
any of the other tests.

*   *   *

[124] This is not to say that all information
will be fully reflected in price, regardless of
its initial distribution or trading import.
Some inside information may never trigger
a sufficiently powerful price signal to alert
uninformed traders. Nor is it likely that
uninformed trading will ever *fully* reflect
optimal forecast data in price, no matter
how rapidly it operates.

Figure 1.

Capital Market Efficiency Mechanisms

Much work remains to be done in further illuminating the operation of the four market efficiency mechanisms. Not only is the modeling of each mechanism, considered independently, still in its developmental stage, but attempts to model the synergistic interaction of the mechanisms are even more preliminary. Research of the latter type may help explain puzzling discrepancies between the actual response of price to new information and the response that any one of the mechanisms considered alone might lead one to expect. Why, for example, does informed trading appear to operate with little loss in relative efficiency down to a quite narrow initial distribution of information among traders, a critical threshold floor of initially informed traders? One answer might be that a threshold number of traders is required to emit a strong price signal. In this case, derivatively informed trading may "amplify" professionally informed trading by alerting the entire analyst community to the existence of new semi-public information. Similarly, uninformed trading, by reducing price noise levels, may help accelerate price decoding and so contribute to the relative efficiency of derivatively informed trading.

Finally, the cycle is complete when uninformed trading generates prices that reflect high-quality forecasts about future events or facts that are as yet unknown to the market. Such anticipation minimizes the discrepancies between ex ante "uninformed" and ex post "informed" equilibrium price levels and thereby enhances the relative efficiency of all three informed trading mechanisms. However, because uninformed trading works best when large numbers of traders form well-specified assessments about future facts and future events, it will be most efficient when traders are well aware of the importance of such contingencies in advance. That is, uninformed trading works best for "known" uncertainties: those future events that are likely to be widely anticipated before they are known, and widely known when they occur. Such "future facts" are rapidly assimilated into price by the universally informed and professionally informed trading mechanisms.[129] Conversely, when key trading facts that bear on the forecasting of future events are rapidly disseminated, they help minimize the bias of individual trader assessments and thereby enhance the relative efficiency of uninformed trading. Thus, the efficiency mechanisms discriminate jointly as well as separately among information sets. Some types of information, such as Federal Reserve Board announcements and routine disclosure reports, are efficiently reflected in price in two ways: ex ante in the form of accurate anticipation, and ex post in the form of rapid assimilation through the most efficient informed trading mechanisms. Other types of information, of which data about innovation is the best example, may be subject to relatively inefficient assimilation both ex ante and ex post.

The exact nature and magnitude of such interaction among mechanisms, which presumably contributes to total market efficiency across *all* available information sets, must await future investigation. At this juncture, we must content ourselves with the more limited observation that the four capital market mechanisms function with decreasing

---

[129] Uninformed trading works best for "known" uncertainties for two reasons. Many traders will form careful, independent forecasts about these contingencies, thus expanding the information base that is aggregated by price; and, because these contingencies are familiar to the market, trader forecasts will fall within a bounded distribution of expected outcomes, thus increasing the predictive quality of the assessments reflected into price.

relative efficiency. Thus, we expect the breadth of the initial distribution of information among traders to determine the relative efficiency of the market's response.

III. THE INFORMATION MARKET

In the previous section we suggested that the capital market's relative efficiency depends on the initial distribution of information, and that the various capital market mechanisms are not equally effective for all distributions of information. We illustrated these points by arraying both the mechanisms and Fama's original trichotomy of weak, semi-strong and strong form efficiency along a continuum representing the breadth of initial distribution of trading information. Fama's trichotomy, we suggested, was really an approximation of an underlying relationship between how broadly information is initially distributed, and the particular market mechanism—and level of market efficiency—with which it is reflected in price. But while this analysis explains how (and how much) efficiency is achieved given the initial distribution of information among traders, it tells only half the story. Given the operative capital market mechanisms, the relative efficiency of the market's response to particular information depends on the initial distribution of that information among traders. The question now is, what determines that initial distribution?

To answer that question, the focus of our analysis shifts to the operation of a different market: the market for information. Although the distribution of information determines which capital market mechanism will operate and, therefore, how efficient the capital market will be, it is the information market that determines how information is initially distributed. Analysis of the overall process of market efficiency thus requires careful consideration of the structure of the information market.

A. *The Central Role of Information Costs*

Since efficiency in the capital market depends on the distribution of information, it is ultimately a function of the cost of information to traders. The lower the cost of particular information, the wider will be its distribution, the more effective will be the capital market mechanism operating to reflect it in prices, and the more efficient will be the market with respect to it. Understanding market efficiency, then, requires detailed analysis of the nature and dynamics of information costs.

1. *A Taxonomy of Information Costs*

Information costs may be divided into three categories. ＊ ＊ ＊ The first category is costs of *acquisition*. These costs will differ in character depending on whether one is the originator of the information or only its subsequent recipient. For the originator, acquisition costs are the costs of producing the information in the first place (as with a discovery or innovation). For the subsequent recipient, acquisition costs are those of securing access to information produced by

someone else. This may be done either with the originator's cooperation, as through purchase, or despite the originator's efforts to prevent
access, as, at the extreme, through industrial espionage.

The second category is the cost of *processing* information once it is
acquired.[132] For both the originator and a subsequent recipient,
processing costs are best exemplified by investment in human capital.
Evaluation of information, whether self-produced or acquired from
others, requires special skills, such as a facility in accounting, finance
or securities analysis, that can ordinarily be obtained only through
investment in expensive professional training. The cost of such training is reflected in the wages of the skilled employee or in the opportunity costs of his or her principal.

The third category of information costs arises from the problem of
verification. Here the task is to determine the quality of information.
How does the acquirer of information determine its accuracy? Like
aquisition costs, the expense of verification manifests itself differently
depending on whether one is the originator of the information or a
subsequent recipient. For the originator, verification costs take the
form of further investments to determine the accuracy of the existing
information by, for example, hiring an expert to evaluate it. A subsequent recipient may undertake similar efforts, but its principal verification cost is that of determining the veracity of the originator. The
originator will have an incentive to act opportunistically by misrepresenting the accuracy, and therefore the value, of the information. In
this case, verification costs may take the form of a direct investigation
by the subsequent recipient, similar in character to the efforts undertaken by an originator, or of alternative verification techniques such as
bonding or the use of third party experts.[135]

2. Market Responses to Information Costs

Market participants shape the cost structure of the information
market by their efforts to reduce each category of information costs.
Consider, for example, how a general contractor who bids on a construction contract might respond to verification costs. The size of the
contractor's bid depends on, among other things, the accuracy of information provided by a subcontractor about the completion date for its
portion of the project. If the general contractor believes that there is a
fifty percent chance that this information is incorrect and that the

---

[132] When information is acquired by purchase, the acquisition and processing categories of information costs merge to some
extent. For example, purchasers must incur processing costs before they can set a
price for the information they seek to acquire. The same problem also arises with
respect to verification costs. Despite the
potential blurring of our categories when
information is acquired by purchase, they
remain analytically useful. Moreover, not
all information is acquired by purchase.

[135] "Bonding" occurs when the originator
of information puts at risk an asset that is
forfeited if the information is less accurate
than represented. * * * The general
problem of verification costs, in relation to
products as well as information, is surveyed in Barzel, Measurement Cost and
the Organization of Markets, 25 J.L. &
Econ. 27 (1982).

resulting delay will increase overall costs by $100,000, the general contractor's bid must be $50,000 higher to reflect the potential inaccuracy. The general contractor therefore has an incentive to invest in verification, because more accurate information—a lower probability that the information is incorrect—allows it to make a lower and more competitive bid.

But some forms of verification will be more costly than others, in that they will assure less accuracy for a given expenditure. One approach to the verification problem is "pre-purchase verification" by the recipient of information. In this case, the general contractor would itself investigate the subcontractor by, for example, speaking with others for whom the subcontractor has worked or with the subcontractor's bank. This approach is costly, however, not only because the general contractor must expend resources to acquire the verifying information, but also because the information itself is of limited usefulness. The fact that the subcontractor has completed other projects on time in the past may not be sufficient assurance that it will do so again. An incentive exists not only to verify but to obtain high quality verification as economically as possible.

For this purpose, an alternative form of pre-purchase verification that requires the sub-contractor's cooperation may prove far more successful. The subcontractor may simply warrant that its information is of the represented quality; i.e., that it will complete the project by the promised date. This allows the general contractor to spend less on verification, because its bid may be made as if the subcontractor's information were completely accurate. If the information proves inaccurate, the subcontractor bears the cost.[139] The general contractor can then learn the true accuracy of the information costlessly as the project proceeds. As a result, its total information costs are reduced, and its bid is more likely to succeed.[140]

[139] Of course, the general contractor must still incur some verification costs to determine whether the subcontractor can satisfy its monetary obligation if it breaches its warranty. * * *

[140] This technique not only responds to the verification problem, but does so in a way that minimizes the cost of the response. The burden of verification is put on the subcontractor, the party for whom information costs are the lowest. It is simply cheaper for the subcontractor to gather information bearing on the probabilities of his own performance. See Barzel, supra note 135, at 28–32.

Figure 2.

The Cost Structure of the Information Market

Type of Information Cost	Market Response				
Verification	Pre-existing investment in Reputation	Collective Signalling Civil and Criminal Penalties	Seller Signalling Investment in Firm Specific Capital Bonding Warranties Hostage	Financial Intermediaries Investment Bankers Mutual Funds Insurance/Guarantees Information Intermediaries Rating Agencies	Buyer Verification Buyer Use of Experts
Processing	Financial Press	Information Intermediaries	Economies of Scale and Scope Information Intermediaries Third Party Experts		Individual Human Capital Investment Investment in Support Facilities
Acquisition	Financial Press — Distribution by Originator	Information Intermediaries	Collectivization Public Private Federal Analyst Securities Trade Acts Associations		Espionage Surveillance Investigative Analysis
Level of Information Costs	LOW ⟶ HIGH				

[D6576]

Economizing on verification costs, moreover, is not limited to a particular technique. Indeed, warranties may prove to be wholly ineffective where the information in question is not the prediction of a single future event—that a project will be completed on time—but is rather a subjective probability distribution of future results.[141] Here, subsequent events would not necessarily reveal the accuracy of information; a party who received a warranty would thus have to expend substantial resources to determine whether its warranty had been violated. In such settings, alternative economizing techniques are more effective. For example, the parties may use information intermediaries who offer economies of specialization, scale, and scope in verification that are not available to the individual acquirers of information.[142]

B.   Information Costs and Market Efficiency

Our special interest in the information market's economizing process is its relationship to capital market efficiency. If, as we argue, capital market efficiency is a function of information costs, then economizing on information costs pushes the capital market in the direction of greater efficiency. Because the information market determines the breadth of initial distribution of information to the capital market, our approach suggests that the inefficiencies of the information market— particularly inefficiencies in the distribution of information that arise from transactions costs—should be the focus of analysis.

The overall relationship between information costs, information cost economizing techniques, and the distribution of information, can be effectively depicted in graphic form. Figure Two displays the three categories of information costs, and the market economizing techniques that have developed to reduce each category of costs, along a continuum of absolute costs. Consider first the expense of acquiring information. Where an originator desires to protect its product, the cost of acquisition by a subsequent recipient will be quite high. Information about the product will not be for sale at all or, at best, its sale price will be high. The market will respond to the high cost of the information through economizing techniques such as investigative analysis, careful surveillance of the originator's behavior, or industrial espionage.

These techniques will reduce, to some extent, the acquisition cost to subsequent recipients. In absolute terms, however, cost will remain high for at least two reasons. First, these economizing techniques are themselves quite expensive. Over and above the direct costs how does one evaluate, for example, the indirect expense to the Japanese computer companies recently indicted for purchasing stolen IBM business secrets?[144] Second, the accuracy of the information acquired is subject to substantial uncertainty. Verification therefore becomes a critical concern; yet the acquirer cannot use most of the conventional market

---

[141] An example is a prediction of the likelihood of a borrower defaulting on an outstanding debt.

[142] See, e.g., Leland & Pyle, *Information Asymmetries, Financial Structure and Financial Intermediaries*, 32 J.Fin. 371 (1977). Information intermediaries arbitrage information asymmetries with the same beneficial effect on markets as in any other arbitrage setting.

[144] See Tinnin, *How IBM Stung Hitachi, Fortune*, Mar. 7, 1983, at 50 ("After the arrests, one of Hitachi's foremost objectives in its legal maneuvers was to avoid a trial in which this embarrassing material would be displayed for the world to see and hear.").

techniques for economizing on verification costs because these require the cooperation of the information's originator. One could hardly expect the originator and involuntary transferor of information to assist in its verification, if only because most of the techniques for acquiring information from such a recalcitrant originator depend on the originator's ignorance of the effort.[145]

Other examples of market economizing on acquisition costs occur when the originator makes no effort to protect the information, but merely decides not to incur the full costs of distributing it. We then see market efforts to economize on acquisition costs through collectivization at both the private and public levels. At the private level, for example, organizations of securities professionals hold cooperative programs in which high company officials speak to many analysts at once, thus reducing the cost of access for any individual analyst. Indeed, the very existence of information intermediaries such as financial and securities experts reflects, in part, the potential for economies of scale and scope [147] in efforts to economize on information costs.

At the collective level, legislation such as the Securities Exchange Act of 1934, which requires continual disclosure of extensive current information by public companies, eliminates the repetitive cost of individual acquisition of information by each analyst. This form of mandatory disclosure collectivizes information acquisition by requiring the originators of information to distribute it and, in some cases, even requiring them to create it.[150]

Market efforts to reduce acquisition costs also occur at the lower end of the cost continuum. For example, a company that wishes to distribute information indicating favorable corporate prospects may do so at little cost merely by issuing a press release. The financial press as an institution functions to reduce the acquisition costs of information recipients, in large part by reducing the costs of voluntary distribution to the originators of information.

Figure Two also shows how markets economize on the costs of processing information. Perhaps the most pervasive example is the specialized business of securities analysis itself, which permits substantial economies of scale and scope in utilizing human capital. Similar

[145] If the originator were aware of the surveillance, he could take steps either to falsify the information, or to stop the surveillance.

[147] The fact that substantial capital may be needed to acquire and store information generates the potential for economies of scale in this context. Economies of scale in general arise where increased volume allows operation at a lower portion of a declining average cost curve.

[150] Collectivization of production and distribution costs also exploits the economies of scope that exist when the company is already producing similar information and has an established means of distributing it.

* * *

This is consistent with a "public choice" approach to the regulatory process, which posits that "regulations will tend to favor (subsidize) relatively small and well organized groups that have a high per capita stake in the regulations * * *." S. Phillips & J. Zecher, *The SEC and the Public Interest* 22 (1981). The financial analyst community, which most directly benefits from a reduction in the cost of producing information about publicly traded companies, is precisely the type of group that would be expected to lobby for the adoption of such regulations. Id. at 22–23.

economies are available in the use of the support equipment, such as computer hardware and software, that is increasingly necessary for performance of the analyst's task. As a result, there are specialists in information processing such as research firms and the research departments of brokerage firms, whose functional advantage is their ability to process information more cheaply than non-specialists.[152]

The category of verification costs, however, yields the most interesting array of market techniques for reducing information costs. Consider the producer of a new financial product. The producer has an obvious incentive to supply the market with information indicating that the product is worth its asking price. Indeed, the product can be described generally as only an uncertain stream of future income; information concerning the risk and timing of that stream is part of the product itself. But even if distribution by the seller eliminates the cost of acquiring information, a would-be purchaser is still subject to an information cost problem. How does it know whether the information the producer supplies is accurate? After all, the information's producer will often stand to benefit by leading the recipient to overvalue the product. Where the quality of the information is difficult to determine, its buyer has little choice but to assume that it, and the product it concerns, are of lower quality than represented. Only by discounting the information's accuracy can the buyer be certain that he or she has not unknowingly overpaid. The result is that sellers have too little incentive to provide better information, because "it won't be believed anyway." Poor quality information drives higher quality information from the market,[154] and individual buyers who wish to obtain more accurate predictions of a security's value can do so only by making substantial individual investments in verification.. Better products will be mispriced because the capital market will not efficiently reflect information about their superior quality.

A broad range of market techniques has developed to deal with this problem by reducing verification costs. At the most costly end of the continuum are solutions that rely solely on buyer verification without the assistance of the originator. For example, buyers may employ experts, such as accountants, lawyers, or business consultants, to examine the offered information. Although these techniques still require each buyer to verify the information individually, they do achieve economies of scale with respect to the skills necessary for verification.

Yet these and other buyer verification techniques that function without the seller's cooperation are very costly. Substantial additional savings in verification costs are achieved if the seller itself verifies the

---

[152] The financial press plays a similar role, offering almost continual analysis of corporate and economic prospects. Such collectivization of the processing function reduces costs, but it may discourage independent efforts by traders to process the information more quickly, thoroughly, or creatively. Assuming that the economic advantage to be derived from individual efforts is relatively small, a trader would have to engage in a substantial volume of trading to justify such expenditures. This again suggests a role for intermediaries who, through aggregation, control a volume of trading large enough to make the effort profitable.

[154] This is an example of the "lemon problem." E.g., Akerlof, *The Market for "Lemons": Quality Uncertainty and the Market Mechanism*, 84 Q.J. Econ. 488 (1970).

accuracy of the information. One such approach relies on the efforts of information sellers, unaided by intermediaries, to "signal" in a believable fashion that they offer high quality information. Signaling in this context means the distribution of a particular type of information. In general, parties signal when they desire to convey information about an attribute that is not otherwise discernible. In our case, that attribute is the seller's propensity to misrepresent the accuracy of the offered information. For the signal to be effective, the seller must show that its interests do not lie in misrepresenting accuracy. The signal therefore contains no new information about the accuracy of the original information in the absence of something that demonstrates that the signal itself is accurate.

A typical but costly form of signaling is the investment by sellers in firm-specific capital, such as reputation and advertising, whose value would be reduced if the quality of the product were lower than represented. In situations where this form of investment is not feasible, sellers may employ hostage techniques; for example, a seller may post a bond that is forfeited to the buyer if the information is of lower quality than represented.[158]

In other situations, however, the costs of signaling or bonding by the seller will simply be too high; the seller will lack the capital and time to invest in reputation or the funds to post a bond.[159] In many such cases, outside specialists acting as information intermediaries will offer their own reputation in lieu of the sellers' as a bond of quality.[160] Examples of such specialists in the products market are the Underwriter's Laboratory and the Good Housekeeping Seal; in the financial markets, the most obvious example is the role played by rating agencies such as Standard & Poor's and Moody's. A less obvious but similar role is also played by financial intermediaries, although the verification technique used by these information agents differs. Rather than dem-

---

[158] See Williamson, *Credible Commitments: Using Hostages to Support Exchange*, 73 Am.Econ.Rev. 519 (1983).
* * *

[159] One example involves the role of the investment banker in the mergers and acquisition context. The investment banker acts as an information seller who must verify the accuracy of the information (the acquisition opportunity) it offers for sale to its client. Gilson, *Seeking Competitive Bids Versus Pure Passivity in Tender Offer Defense*, 35 Stan.L.Rev. 51 (1982). One way to reduce the client's verification costs is for the client to "pay" some portion of the investment banker's fee by allocating to the banker some of the client's post-transaction investment banking services. If the information proves to be inaccurate, the client can penalize the investment banker by obtaining these services from another source. This is, however, a very expensive verification technique; it is

available only to a diversified information seller, like an investment banker, who can offer post-transaction services to the client. Id. at 59.

[160] In some situations a third party is critical to the verification process. Where, for example, the verification problem concerns information provided by the issuer of corporate debt, the issuer's reputation is already at stake and the promise to repay the debt commits the entire financial resources of the issuer. Any additional issuer warranty or bond concerning the accuracy of the information would be superfluous, and some signaling by third parties is necessary. See generally Thakor, *An Exploration of Competitive Signalling Equilibria with "Third Party" Information Production: The Case of Debt Insurance*, 37 J.Fin. 717 (1982) (insurance coverage on corporate debt issue can signal its probability of default). * * *

onstrating confidence in the accuracy of the seller's information by staking their reputation on it, these financial intermediaries signal their belief by purchasing the seller's offering for their *own* account, thereby staking *their* future directly on the accuracy of the seller's information.[163]

A collective, and therefore potentially less expensive, solution to the problem is the legislative imposition of civil and criminal penalties on low quality producers. By imposing costs only on those producers who would exploit high buyer verification costs by falsely pretending to provide quality information, such legislation makes it more costly for producers of low quality goods to mimic the behavior of high quality producers. At the extreme, well-defined and energetically enforced legislation of this type turns the lemon problem on its head and drives low quality producers from the market. This process may explain in part why trade associations that are dominated by high quality firms often lobby for *more* stringent legislative standards and greater enforcement of those standards.[164]

Finally, we should briefly consider the low cost end of the verification cost continuum. What residual verification costs attend the sale of information by sellers who have preexisting investments in reputation, such as AT&T, or accompany the sale of information where collective responses to verification costs, such as legislatively imposed penalties for misrepresentation, have already effectively limited entry by low quality producers? Here the residual costs associated with verification should be quite small.

Figure Two summarizes the cost structure of the information market. Levels of cost associated with particular information differ depending on the extent of acquisition, processing, and verification costs, as well as on the availability of economizing techniques. With this structure in place, we are now in a position to complete the inquiry with which this section began, by examining the relationship between information costs, on the one hand, and the "availability" of information to the capital market, on the other.

Figure Three superimposes Fama's original weak/semi-strong/ strong form classification scheme, and the relative efficiency continuum that underlies it, on Figure Two's depiction of the cost structure of the

---

[163] It is precisely this type of behavior that facilitates the trade decoding mechanism.

[164] Section 11 of the Securities Act of 1933, 15 U.S.C. § 77k(a) (1982), which imposes liability on underwriters and others for misstatements or omissions in a registration statement, may fit this model. Certainly fairness does not compel imposing liability on underwriters in amounts substantially in excess of their profit from engaging in the transaction. Nor is the imposition of liability on underwriters the best means of spreading costs among potential victims. Rather, imposing substantial liability on the underwriters, but with a defense that relieves it of liability if it has made a diligent investigation of the issuer, is better explained by a belief that the behavior of the *issuer,* the ultimate object of the legislation, is constrained more effectively by imposing liability on the issuer's agent than by increasing the penalties imposed on the issuer itself. See Kraakman, *Corporate Liability Strategies and the Costs of Legal Controls,* 93 Yale L.J. 857, 895–96 (1984).

information market. This juxtaposition reveals that the relative efficiency continuum substantially parallels the information cost continuum. A market is strong form efficient if its prices reflect inside information that is privately held; by definition, the originator of such information wishes to prevent its dissemination. Not surprisingly, all three categories of information costs in this region of Figure Three are at the high end of the cost continuum. Acquisition costs are high because they involve such costly techniques as monitoring the originator's behavior or engaging in commercial espionage. Processing costs are high because the information is less intelligible than it would be if the originator had voluntarily cooperated with the recipient, and because the often surreptitious methods of acquiring such information prevent pooling or other cooperative means of achieving scale economies in processing information. Finally, many of the most effective techniques for economizing on verification costs are unavailable because of the originator's unwillingness to cooperate.

Fama's semi-strong form category also corresponds to a particular range of the information cost continuum in Figure Three. Cooperative efforts frequently reduce the total costs of acquiring information in this region and also achieve economies of scale and scope in processing costs, often through the services of information intermediaries such as financial analysts. Moreover, the availability of verification techniques that rely on the cooperation of originators of information now make economizing on verification costs more effective. These techniques include bonding and hostage strategies, the use of third party verifiers like certified public accounts,[166] and the good offices of intermediaries such as rating services and financial intermediaries.

[166] While part of their value lies in their ability to exploit economies of scale and scope, third-party verifiers such as certified public accountants also function as reputational intermediaries. Central to this function is the accountant's reputation for independence; only if the accountant can be expected to treat the client at arm's length is its message of verification believable. This explains the emphasis on independence both in public regulation, see 17 C.F.R. § 210.2–01(b)–(c) (1983) (requirement of independence for recognition as certified public accountant by Securities and Exchange Commission), and in studies of the demand for public accounting services. See, e.g., Benston, *The Market for Public Accounting Services: Demand, Supply and Regulation,* 2 Acct. J. 2 (1979).

Figure 3.

Information Costs and Market Efficiency

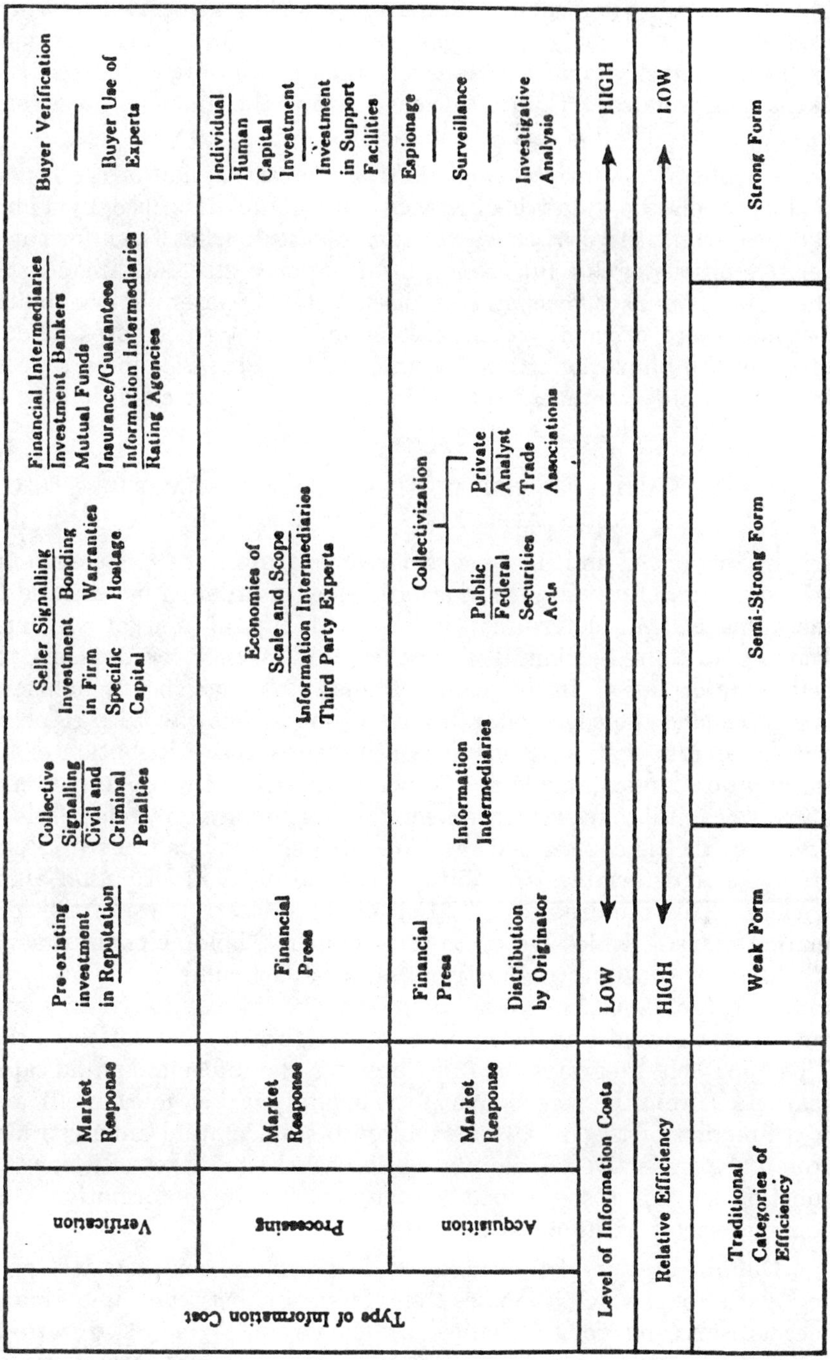

Type of Information Cost		Market Response				
Verification	Market Response	Pre-existing investment in Reputation	Collective Signalling Civil and Criminal Penalties	Seller Signalling Investment in Firm Specific Capital — Bonding Warranties Hostage	Financial Intermediaries Investment Bankers Mutual Funds Insurance/Guarantees Information Intermediaries Rating Agencies	Buyer Verification — Buyer Use of Experts
Processing	Market Response	Financial Press	Information Intermediaries	Economies of Scale and Scope Information Intermediaries Third Party Experts		Individual Human Capital Investment — Investment in Support Facilities
Acquisition	Market Response	Financial Press — Distribution by Originator	Information Intermediaries	Collectivization: Public Federal Securities Acts / Private Analyst Trade Associations		Espionage Surveillance Investigative Analysis
Level of Information Costs		LOW →		→ HIGH		
Relative Efficiency		HIGH →		→ LOW		
Traditional Categories of Efficiency		Weak Form		Semi-Strong Form		Strong Form

[D6577]

Fama's final category, weak form efficiency, parallels cost conditions at the low end of the cost continuum in Figure Three. In this region, acquisition costs are minimal and the marginal costs of producing and distributing information are low. Such conditions are perfectly consistent with the form of information typically associated with weak form efficiency, namely, historical price information. This information is an ordinary byproduct of market trading: the organized securities exchanges produce it as a routine service, and the financial press serves to collectivize its low cost dissemination.

An important insight emerges from the discussion of the correlation between the relative efficiency continuum described by Fama's categories and the cost characteristics of the market for information: relative efficiency is a function of information costs. Holding constant the capital market mechanisms discussed in Section II, the market becomes more efficient as the cost of information decreases. Put in terms of the Fama definition, the information *available* to be reflected in price by the capital market is determined by cost conditions in the information market.

IV. THE CAPITAL MARKET AND THE INFORMATION MARKET: THEORETICAL APPLICATIONS OF THE SYNTHESIS

In Sections II and III we considered separately the two elements of the common definition of market efficiency in order to understand the mechanisms that determine the level of capital market efficiency. Looking first in Section II at the capital market mechanisms that reflect information in price, we argued that which mechanism is operative, and the concomitant efficiency of the market with respect to particular information, is a function of the initial distribution of that information among traders. A wider distribution triggers a more effective capital market mechanism and thus makes for greater relative efficiency in the capital market. We then shifted our focus in Section III to what determines the initial distribution of information among traders. This required examination of the cost structure of the information market, which led us to conclude that, holding capital market mechanisms constant, the distribution of a particular piece of information is a function of its cost. If information is less costly, it is more widely distributed and more efficiently reflected in securities prices. This approach integrates the functioning of the information and capital markets. From the perspective of the capital market, market efficiency is a function of the initial distribution of information among traders; from the perspective of the information market, market efficiency is a function of the costs associated with particular information. The common factor is information costs.

Our integration of the capital and information markets is depicted in Figure Four, which combines the relationship between capital market mechanisms and relative efficiency shown in Figure Two with the relationship between cost conditions in the information market and relative efficiency shown in Figure Three. As in Figures Two and Three, the level of market efficiency appears on the capital market side as a function of the initial distribution of information among traders, and on the information market side as a function of the information costs attending that information. The juxtaposition of these two relationships demonstrates the link between the capital and information markets. The information cost continuum, lying immediately above the measure of relative efficiency, parallels the distribution of information continuum, lying immediately below a similar index of efficiency. As information costs decline, more—and better—information is available to more traders, and the market becomes more efficient, both because the information is better and because its wider distribution triggers a more effective capital market mechanism. The intuition underlying this relationship is also reflected in Figure Four. Consider the most efficient range of the relative efficiency continuum that associated with the weak form portion of the Fama trichotomy. The acquisition cost of information in this range can be as low as the price of a newspaper. Such information is also easy to process and nearly costless to verify.[169] As a result, it is widely distributed. Indeed, it almost meets the sufficient condition for market efficiency reflected in the perfect market assumption: that the information be costlessly available to all traders.

Figure 4.

Integrating the Capital and Information Markets

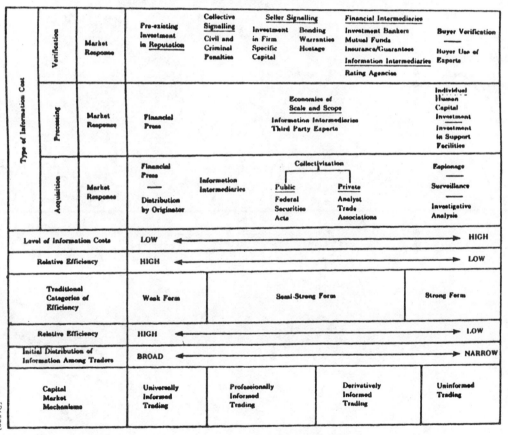

---

[169] A possibility of price manipulation always exists, but the costs of policing against this danger suggest a collective rather than an individual response, consistent with the anti-manipulation provisions of the Securities Exchange Act. From this perspective, the prohibitions in section 9 of the Exchange Act against, for example, creating "actual or apparent active trading in [any] * * * security or raising or depressing the price of such security, for the purpose of inducing the purchase or sale of such security by others," 15 U.S.C. § 78i(a)(2) (1982), are a collective effort to preserve the integrity of the trading information upon which the capital market mechanisms, particularly derivatively informed trading, depend. So understood, the Securities Exchange Act makes it illegal to create "noise" intentionally or to employ price and volume to disseminate misleading signals that reduce the informativeness of price.

The core of our analysis, then, is that the cost of information critically determines market efficiency because it dictates not only the amount of information attending a particular security but also the distribution of that information among traders, which in turn determines the operative capital market mechanism. This focus on information costs also identifies the invisible hand that moves the market toward greater informational efficiency. Information market incentives lead to economizing on information costs and thus to the availability of more effective capital market mechanisms. The result is an integrated understanding of the mechanisms of market efficiency that we believe provides both theoretical insights and new opportunities for employing the market efficiency concept to inform regulatory policy.

* * *

CHAPTER SIX. THE VALUE OF INFORMATION

The development of the Efficient Capital Market Hypothesis in Chapter Five focused on the central role of information costs. How much information is produced—and the capital market's relative efficiency—turns on how expensive that information is to acquire, process and verify. But knowledge of the *costs* associated with the production of particular information is not in itself a sufficient basis on which to decide whether to produce the information. It is also necessary to know something about the *benefits* that would result from having the information: the *value* of the information. In this Chapter we examine techniques designed to measure the benefits of particular information in two important decision making settings. The first setting arises when an individual must decide whether to invest in the acquisition of particular information. Section A presents techniques for estimating the value of information *ex ante*—before the information is actually acquired. The second setting is evaluative. Suppose a decision was made that the production of particular information would be beneficial. How can you evaluate, after the fact, whether the decision was correct? The question has particular importance with respect to public policy evaluation. For example, for a period of time the SEC took the position that disclosure of payments by a company to officials of foreign governments was required because the information was material to investors.[1] Disclosure of wrongdoing, of course, was not costless to the disclosing company; among other problems, disclosure increased the likelihood of foreign prosecution as well as potentially damaging the company's future ability to do business in the particular country. In this setting, the problem is how to determine whether the policy decision that information about foreign payments was valuable to investors was correct. Section B presents techniques for measuring the value of information *ex post*—after the information has been acquired.

A. Ex Ante: The Expected Value of Information

Chapters Three and Four stressed the importance of taking uncertainty into account in valuation. The problem was that we do not know with certainty what will be an asset's future returns. The greater that uncertainty—the higher the standard deviation of our best estimate of the distribution of future returns—the riskier the asset. Additional information has value if it allows us to better predict future returns and, as a result, reduce the risk of an asset. What is needed is a way to estimate the impact of information on our predictions of the size and distribution of future returns. In the following discussion, Professor Charles Holloway introduces techniques designed to facilitate such estimates that build on our discussion of decision analysis in Chapter Three A.

[1] See Report of the Securities and Exchange Commission on Questionable and Illegal Corporate Payments and Practices, 94th Cong. 2d Sess. (Comm. Print 1976).

C. HOLLOWAY, DECISION MAKING UNDER UNCERTAINTY

348–59 (1979).*

Value of Information

What is the value of information in a particular setting? The basic principle is that *information only has value in a decision problem if it results in a change in some action to be taken by a decision maker.* Even though some data or statements from an expert provide new knowledge, it may not have any value in the context of a particular decision problem.

The value of information can be calculated using the [decision] techniques already developed. An *information alternative* is created and included in the decision diagram like any other alternative. The *cost* that makes the information alternative equivalent to the *best alternative without information* is called the *value* of the information.

Two cases are usually considered:

Expected Value of Perfect Information

Definition: The Expected Value of Perfect Informa-tion (EVPI) =

(expected value if perfect information could be obtained) − (expected value of the best alternative without information)

Expected Value of Sample Information

Definition: The Expected Value of Imperfect or Sample Information (EVSI) =

(expected value of the information alternative) − (expected value of the best alternative without information)

Information alternatives are treated like any other alternative on a decision diagram. In determining the EVPI or EVSI, no information costs are included on the diagram. After rolling back the tree, the difference between the information alternative and the best alternative without information is directly available.

Some calculational short cuts and interpretations are demonstrated by the examples that follow.

Expected Value of Perfect Information (EVPI)

Perfect information about a given event means complete elimination of all uncertainty about the event's outcomes. That is, *after* receiving the information, you will know exactly which outcome will occur. In some cases perfect information *is* obtainable. For instance, if the uncertain event involved the decision of a customer to let a contract, it might be possible to find out what the decision is by offering the customer an incentive for telling you. In other cases perfect information is not possible but is a useful concept. It is useful because it provides an *upper bound* on the value of information in a particular decision, and because the calculations usually can be done easily.

There are several ways to visualize and calculate the EVPI. To illustrate the methods, consider the following example.

A construction contract must be completed prior to June 1, 1978 to avoid a significant penalty. There are three different plans that can be used for the construction. The plans differ primarily in their ability to provide flexibility in the face of varying weather conditions. Plan 1 will be the most profitable if good weather exists during the construction period; however, it is the worst under other conditions. Plan 2 is adequate under all conditions. Plan 3 is good under two weather types but poor under the other two possible weather types. The plans and their net contribution in thousands of dollars for the four possible weather types are shown in Table 14.1 along with the assessed probabilities for the weather possibilities.

Table 14.1

Net Contribution

Weather	Plan 1	2	3	Probability
Type n_1	48	24	40	0.4
Type n_2	16	24	16	0.2
Type n_3	16	32	24	0.2
Type n_4	16	24	16	0.2
EMV	28.8	25.6	27.2	1.00

Alternatives involving information can be included just like any other alternative on a decision diagram. In this example, if we include the option of obtaining perfect information we have the diagram shown in Figure 14.2. From the diagram we see that the expected monetary value of the alternative *perfect information* is $35,200. Note that the decision to obtain perfect information does *not* eliminate all uncertainty. You are still (until the perfect information is received) uncertain about what the information will reveal. Without perfect information plan 1 will yield the maximum expected monetary value of $28,800. Therefore, the value of the perfect information must be the difference between $35,200 and $28,800, or $6,400.

This calculation can also be done using tables. Table 14.1 provides the expected monetary value for the best plan without perfect information. The expected monetary value with perfect information can be calculated using Table 14.2.

* * *

Figure 14.2

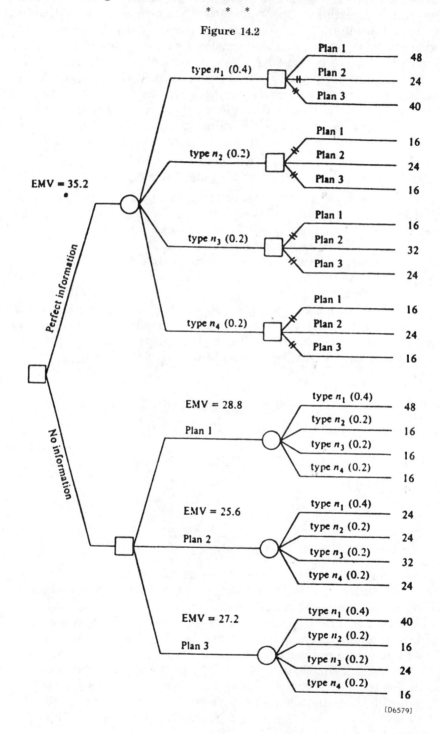

[D6579]

Table 14.2

Weather	Choice with Per-fect Information	Payoff	Probability
Type n_1	Plan 1	48	.04
Type n_2	Plan 2	24	.02
Type n_3	Plan 2	32	.02
Type n_4	Plan 2	24	.02
	EMV	35.2	

*   *   *

Another method of visualizing EVPI is to consider how much perfect information would be worth to you for each possible weather state. For instance, what if the information transmitted were that weather *type* n_1 would occur? Without this information you would choose Plan 1. With this information you would still choose Plan 1. Therefore, the information *weather type* n_1 would result in no change in your choice and it would not be worth anything to you. However, if the signal were *weather type* n_2 you would switch to Plan 2, increasing your payoff by $24,000 - $16,000 = $8,000.

Table 14.4

Weather	Current Choice	Choice if Information Specified Given Weather State	Change in Payoff	Probability
Type n_1	Plan 1	Plan 1	0	0.4
Type n_2	Plan 1	Plan 2	8	0.2
Type n_3	Plan 1	Plan 2	16	0.2
Type n_4	Plan 1	Plan 2	8	0.2

Table 14.4 displays your actions and the difference in payoff for each state of weather.

Now place yourself back at a point in time before the information on which weather state will occur has been transmitted, and ask: "How much would I be willing to pay for the information?" The amount clearly depends upon which signal (i.e., weather type) is transmitted. All you have available are the probabilities of various weather types, and therefore you can calculate the EVPI as $(0 \times 0.4) + ($8,000 \times 0.2) + ($16,000 \times 0.2) + ($8,000 \times 0.2) = $6,400$.

Expected Value of Imperfect or Sample Information

When the information available is not perfect but still offers the potential for reducing the uncertainty associated with a decision problem, its expected value can sometimes be calculated.   *   *   *

Example 14.3

Faced with a difficult technological problem, the manager of an engineering and development laboratory was considering bringing in an outside expert to help determine whether the process under development would be a technological success. It was impossible to know for sure if the process would be a success until the research was completed. However, the expert he had in mind was more knowledgeable than anyone on his staff on the crucial part of the project. If the process turns out to be a success, the payoffs will be large—approximately $10,000,000. On the other hand, a failure will result in a substantial loss, estimated to be $5,000,000. The manager currently assesses the chances of success at only 30%. When considering the expert, he feels confident the assessment provided after the investigation will be a probability of success of 60%, 40%, 20%, or 0%. Moreover, he feels that each possibility is equally likely. As a matter of fact, this assessment on the expert's response, which corresponds to an overall probability of success of 30% [$(0.25) \times (0.06) + (0.25) \times (0.40) + (0.25) \times (20) + (0.25) \times (0) = 0.30$], just confirms his opinion about the success of the project. Nevertheless, since it is a potentially profitable project, he still wants to consider the possibility of hiring the expert.

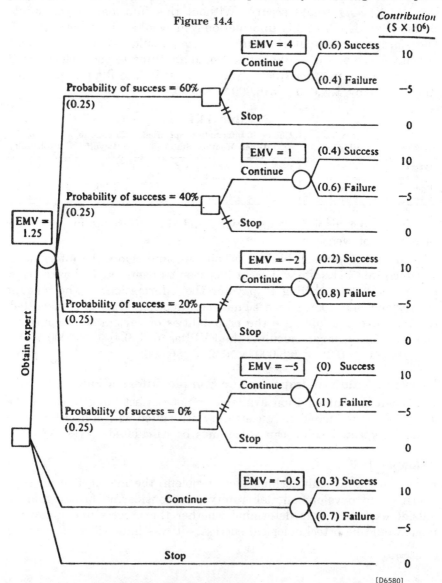

Figure 14.4

Contribution
($ X 10⁶)

The diagram facing the manager is shown in Figure 14.4. The *obtain expert* alternative has the highest expected monetary value. The next best alternative based on expected contribution is to stop, which yields a contribution of $0. Therefore, without the expert's help, the project will be stopped with an expected incremental contribution of $0. Consequently, the expected value of the expert's information is $1.25 − $0 = $1.25 million.

- **The Relationship Between Value of Information and Amount of Uncertainty**

The value of information depends on both the amount of uncertainty (or the prior knowledge available) and the payoffs. To demonstrate, consider the following simplified example.

Example 14.4

As an investor you are convinced that XYZ Company's earnings have an equal chance to be either $2 per share or $2.50 per share for last year. Furthermore you believe the stock price will be 10 times last year's earnings per share (EPS) in either case. The stock is now selling for $22 per share and the earnings are to be reported in 1 month. Your cash flow position allows you to invest for only 2 months (assume that there are no market effects and no transaction charges). You now own no XYZ stock and if you buy you will buy 1,000 shares. Furthermore, assume that you decide to make your decision based on expected contribution. Although you are not sure if you can obtain "perfect" information, you realize that it would be possible to get close to perfect information by talking with company officials. Since this would be a time-consuming and expensive process, you want to get a feel for the value of the information. Figure 14.5 shows your problem, assuming you could obtain perfect information.

Figure 14.5

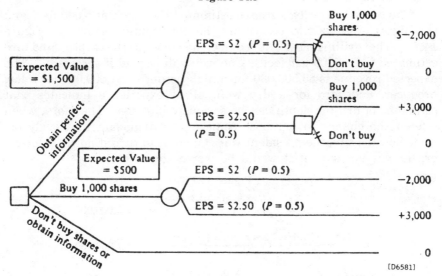

The EVPI is $1,500 − $500 = $1,000. This value is based on the prior assessment $P(\text{EPS} = \$2) = 0.5$, $P(\text{EPS} = \$2.50) = 0.5$. If the prior probabilities were changed from 0.5, the EVPI would change. Figure 14.6 displays how EVPI changes for this particular problem as

P(EPS = $2.50) varies from 0 to 1.0. At either extreme the EVPI is low because the *amount* of uncertainty is not great. In the middle ranges the additional uncertainty is reflected in a higher EVPI.

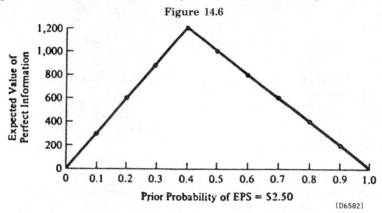

Figure 14.6

[D6582]

Sensitivity Analysis

Sensitivity analysis provides a simple but powerful tool for investigating the value of information. If the decision maker's actions are the same for any possible value of a random variable, then even knowing the exact value that will occur has no value to the decision maker. Under these conditions the expected value of perfect information is seen to be zero without further calcuations. As an illustration, consider the following problem.

Example 14.5

The president of a petroleum exploration company is trying to decide whether a wildcat well should be drilled. His geologists have provided him with assessments relating to the likely quantities of oil, as shown in Figure 14.7.

The company geologists have estimated the depth at 5,000 feet, and this figure was used to determine the contribution shown in Figure 14.7. (The drilling costs, of course, depend on the depth, and are estimated to be $100 per foot.) The well will be sold if successful. The expected revenue is $3,500,000 for a high producer, $1,500,000 for a low producer, and zero for a dry well. Past experience indicates that estimates of drilling depth can be seriously in error. Therefore, when offered the chance to purchase some exploration data previously obtained on the site, the president was reluctant to turn it down. However, he was not sure if it would be worth the price.

Figure 14.7

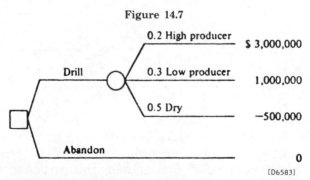

[D6583]

Sensitivity analysis can be used to analyze the president's problem. Assume that the president will chose the alternative with the highest expected value. The expected contribution can be written in terms of well depth as follows.

Expected Contribution for Drill $= (3,500,000 - 100 \times \text{depth}) \times 0.2$
$+ (1,500,000 - 100 \times \text{depth}) \times 0.3$
$+ (-100 \times \text{depth}) \times 0.5$
$= 1,150,000 - 100 \times \text{depth}$

For the estimated depth level of 5,000 feet, the expected contribution for drill is $650,000. The relationship between expected contribution and depth is shown in Figure 14.8. From the curve we see that the decision will not change as long as the depth is believed to be less than 11,500 feet. Therefore, although the expected contribution may be sensitive to depth, the decision in this case is not particularly sensitive. If the president asked the geologists for a maximum depth figure and was given 10,000 feet, he would know that the exploration data would be of no value to him for this particular decision.

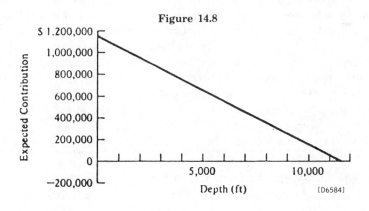

Figure 14.8

B. Ex Post: Measuring the Impact of Information—
The Cumulative Abnormal Returns Technique

Professor Holloway states that "information only has value in a decision problem if it results in a change in some action to be taken by a decisionmaker." That suggests, in turn, a standard against which to measure the accuracy of our *ex ante* beliefs about the value of information in determining the price of an asset. To return to the example of required disclosure of company payments to foreign officials, the SEC's *ex ante* belief was that this information has value to investors. The accuracy of that belief could be tested by seeing whether investors altered their valuation of the company's stock after the disclosure was made. If there was no change in the price of the stock, then the argument would be that the information disclosed had no value to investors.

While this concept is hardly remarkable, in the past there has been a fundamental barrier to actually applying it. Asset value is a result of the simultaneous impact of a large number of events; the difficulty is how to hold everything else constant in order to isolate the impact on asset value of just a single event, such as the disclosure of a foreign bribe. Recently, however, financial economists have developed a statistical technique—cumulative abnormal return analysis—that, in appropriate circumstances, allows us to do precisely that. The idea is if we can accurately predict what the returns from holding an asset would have been in the absence of the information in question, the predicted returns then can be compared to the actual returns. The difference reflects the impact of the information in question. At least with respect to one important category of assets, publicly traded securities, financial theory gives us the means to make the required prediction.

The power of this empirical technique is substantial. In the context of mandatory disclosure regulation like that of the Securities Exchange Act of 1934, it allows empirical evaluation of whether particular disclosure has any impact on securities prices. In the context of a different form of mandatory disclosure regulation, the determination of financial accounting standards, it allows empirical investigation of whether choice of financial accounting method has any impact on securities prices. The technique's use, however, is not limited to evaluating the impact of regulatory activity. It also can be used to evaluate the impact on securities prices of voluntary actions. Of particular relevance to our concerns here, the technique can be used to measure the impact of the announcement of an acquisition on the value of the stock of the acquiring and the target companies. There is thus the potential to make empirical statements about whether particular actions by a company increase or decrease the wealth of its shareholders.

In the following excerpts, the cumulative abnormal return technique is both explained and an example of the mechanics of its calculation provided. Thereafter, we consider the problems associated with evaluating the data provided by cumulative abnormal returns analysis of the recent acquisition of Conoco by DuPont.

1. The Technique

SCHWERT, USING FINANCIAL DATA TO MEASURE EFFECTS OF FINANCIAL REGULATION
24 J. Law & Econ. 121–58 (1981).*

I. INTRODUCTION

The positive analysis of government regulation—measuring the actual rather than the intended effects of regulation—is an increasingly popular topic of research. Often this analysis concentrates on the "wealth effects" of regulation. At one extreme the "public-interest" or consumer-protection hypothesis predicts that regulation confers net benefits on consumers at the expense of regulated firms. At another extreme the "capture" or producer-protection hypothesis predicts that regulated firms receive net benefits at the expense of consumers. Yet another possibility is that regulators themselves receive net benefits at the expense of both consumers and regulated firms. All of these hypotheses make predictions about the effects of regulation on the value of the regulated firm.[1] * * *

The efficient-markets * * * hypothesis posits that security prices reflect all available information. Hence, unanticipated changes in regulation result in a current change in security prices, and the price change is an unbiased estimate of the value of the change in future cash flows to the firm. This hypothesis underlies a variety of methods for estimating the effects of unanticipated regulatory change on shareholder wealth.

The efficient-markets * * * hypothesis also implies that it is impossible to test the effects of existing or anticipated regulation by using security returns. If regulation has implications for the value of securities, the effects of regulation are impounded into prices at the time when they are first anticipated. Subsequent security returns only reflect the equilibrium expected returns to assets of comparable risk, unless the actual effects of regulation deviate from the originally anticipated effects.

* * *

II. Tests of Changes in the Regulation of Individual Firms or Industries

The main difficulty with measuring the effects of regulatory change on security prices is identifying when the market first anticipates the effects of the change on future profitability. In an efficient market any regulatory change, including new regulation or different enforcement of existing regulations, that affects future cash flows will cause a change in asset prices as soon as the regulatory change is anticipated by the market.

* * *

In general, it is difficult to separate the effects of regulatory change on the expected value and the risk of future cash flows, especially if the discount rate is not the same for all future periods. Nevertheless, an efficient capital market sets the prices of assets equal to the present value of the expected future cash flows, thus reflecting the total impact of regulatory change on shareholder wealth.

To estimate the effects of unanticipated changes in regulation it is necessary to measure the change in stock prices before and after the change in regulation. * * * [T]he before and after stock prices, *P* and *P* *, cannot be measured at the same time. Instead, the effect of regulation is estimated by comparing the stock return over the mea-

---

[1] George J. Stigler, *The Theory of Economic Regulation*, 2 Bell J. Econ. & Management Sci. 3 (1971); Richard A. Posner, *Theories of Economic Regulation*, 5 Bell J. Econ. & Management Sci. 335 (1974); and Sam Peltzman, *Toward a More General Theory of Regulation*, 19 J. Law & Econ. 211 (1976), discuss some of the prominent hypotheses about government regulation.

surement interval, $R_{it} = (P_{it} + d_{it} - P_{it\text{-}1})/P_{it\text{-}1}$, [where P_{it} is the price of asset i at the end of period t, d_{it} is the cash flow of asset i during period t, and $P_{it\text{-}1}$ is the price of asset i at the end of period t–1] with a "normal" return to the stock which would be expected in the absence of the regulatory change. The "abnormal" return to the stock then measures the change in the stock price relative to the before-regulation stock price. The next section of the paper describes some models of "normal" stock returns which have been developed in the finance literature.

A. Review of Capital Market Theory and Evidence

* * *

1. The Efficient-Markets * * * Hypothesis.   * * *

Market efficiency *   *   * implies that asset prices are set to reflect all available relevant information; there is no opportunity to make economic profits by buying (selling) assets whose prices are too high (low).

[T]he efficient-markets model [predicts] that deviations of returns to asset i, $\tilde{R}_{it}$, from their equilibrium expected values, $E(\tilde{R}_{it}\backslash\phi_{t\text{-}1})$, conditional on the information set available at time $t - 1$, $\phi_{t\text{-}1}$, are not systematically different from zero. In other words, the "fair game" variable

$$\tilde{\epsilon}_{it} = R_{it} - E(\tilde{R}_{it}\backslash\phi_{t\text{-}1})$$

has a mean of zero. Given an economic model of equilibrium expected returns to assets, which might incorporate risk premia, term premia, or other differences among assets, market efficiency can be tested by examining the statistical properties of the fair-game variable, $\tilde{\epsilon}\phi_{it}$. [That is, if we know what the return should be, a variation in actual return from predicted return indicates *either* that the market is to that extent inefficient *or* that information not available at t–i became available and was incorporated into the price by time t.   Ed.]

* * *

The "market model" posits that there is a common factor in the returns to all assets, which can be represented by the regression model

$$\tilde{R}_{it} = \alpha_i + \beta_i\tilde{R}_{mt} + \tilde{\epsilon}_{it}, \qquad (4)$$

where $\tilde{R}_{mt}$ is the return on a value-weighted portfolio of all marketable assets. Conditional on the information set, $\phi_{t\text{-}1}$, and the contemporaneous return on the market portfolio, $\tilde{R}_{mt}$, the equilibrium expected return to asset i is

$$E(\tilde{R}_{it}\backslash\phi_{t\text{-}1}, R_{mt}) = \alpha_i + \beta_i R_{mt},$$

so that the disturbance $\tilde{\epsilon}_{it}$ in (4) is a fair-game variable. [That is, it has an expected mean of zero.] This model has been used to analyze the effects of firm-specific events (such as stock splits, secondary distributions of securities, or announcements of accounting data) on the prices of the firm's securities. Using the market model (4) to control for the marketwide variation in returns to all assets yields more precise estimates of the firm-specific effects on asset returns. There is substantial evidence that the market model is a well-specified time-series regression model when monthly returns to NYSE stocks are analyzed. Thus, the market model provides a basis for measuring abnormal returns to securities which will generally be more precise than the estimates from the random-walk model.

2. *The Capital Asset Pricing Model.*   *   *   *

The CAPM predicts that the expected return to asset i is linearly related to the risk of the asset in the portfolio of all marketable assets:

$$E(\tilde{R}_{it}) = R_{ft} + \beta_i[E(\tilde{R}_{mt}) - R_{ft}], \tag{5}$$

where R_{ft} is the return on the risk-free asset, such as a treasury bill, $E(\tilde{R}_{mt})$ is the expected return on the value-weighted market portfolio, and β_i *   *   * is *   *   * the risk of asset i relative to the risk of the market portfolio.   *   *   *

According to the CAPM, the only differences among the equilibrium expected returns to assets are attributable to differences in "systematic risk," β_i.

The market model in (4) and the CAPM in (5) are related. The slope coefficient, β_i, in the market model is equal to the systematic risk in the CAPM; therefore, the CAPM implies that the intercept of the market model is $\alpha_i = (1 - \beta_i)R_{ft}$. Thus, the economic model of capital market equilibrium (the CAPM) places a constraint on the parameters of the statistical model for returns (the market model). Empirical evidence generally supports the proposition that expected returns are linearly related to risk as measured by β_i, at least for NYSE common stock returns.

*   *   *

Although there have been numerous refinements of the CAPM, the important result for the purpose of measuring the effects of regulation is that the CAPM provides an estimable relationship between risk and expected return. The CAPM can be viewed as a specific model of equilibrium expected returns which, along with market efficiency, can be used to measure abnormal changes in asset values in association with unanticipated regulatory changes.

The CAPM can also be used to determine how regulation affects the risk of firms. If regulation changes the risk of the firm, it is possible to estimate the risk change by estimating [return] using samples from both before and after the regulatory change. In this way, it is possible to separate out the effects of regulation on the expected value and the risk of future cash flows.*

*   *   *

B. *Changes in Regulation That Affect Firms Simultaneously*

1. *Methodological Issues.* Many legislative regulations affect a large number of firms at the same point in time. Also, major legal precedents that change the enforcement of existing legislation can

---

* It should be emphasized again that the use of this technique necessarily assumes the validity of the CAPM. If the CAPM is less than completely accurate, the informa-tion derived concerning the effect of regulatory change will also be inaccurate. [Ed.]

affect a large number of firms simultaneously. In such cases, the common effect of regulation on a set of firms can be measured by analyzing the returns to a portfolio of affected assets. * * *

In order to measure the full effect of an unanticipated regulatory change on the value of the regulated firm, it is necessary to measure the rates of return to all of the firm's securities. Because market price data are not readily available for most corporate debt securities, most studies to date have concentrated on common stock returns. Nevertheless, unless the regulatory change substantially alters the probability that the regulated firm will default on its debt commitments, it seems unlikely that the concentration on common stock returns causes misestimation of the effect on firm value (although the effect on firm value is usually understated when only analyzing stock returns).

There are important statistical reasons for using portfolio returns instead of analyzing the returns to each individual asset in association with a regulatory change. There is substantial evidence that returns to NYSE common stocks are * * * correlated, and this is probably true for other assets as well. Thus, * * * individual asset returns for the same time period are not independent, and there is no simple way to combine the single-asset tests into a joint probability statement about the entire set of assets. * * *

* * * [T]he capital asset pricing model (5) can be used to control for marketwide changes in asset values that occur at the same time, but that are unrelated to the regulatory change. By controlling for variation in R_{it} that is unrelated to the regulatory change, it is possible to get a more precise estimate of the impact of regulation on shareholder wealth.

There is an important problem which has been glossed over in this stylized illustration: It is often difficult to determine when a regulatory change is first anticipated by the market. Many regulatory changes result from a series of public hearings, or a study, or some other prolonged process. The market will use this information to determine the probability that regulatory change will occur, and every time these probabilities are revised the market will adjust security prices accordingly. Hence, in many instances it is necessary to look at abnormal security returns many periods before the actual implementation of the regulatory change in order to measure the full effect of regulation. For example, in the hypothetical example above, if hearings were held during the six months prior to the imposition of the profits tax, it would be appropriate to measure the abnormal return to the affected securities over the entire six-month period. Of course, when the effects of regulation are spread over longer time intervals it becomes more difficult to measure them, because the random variability in security returns increases with the length of the measurement interval.[17] Therefore, it is important to specify as accurately as possible the timing of changes in expectations about regulation.

Finally, it is important to note that the efficient-markets hypothesis does not imply that investors have perfect foresight about the future

---

[17] For example, the variance of the six-month return to the portfolio is six times as great as the variance of the one-month return. This means that the standard error increases by $\sqrt{6}$, thus reducing the precision of the estimate.

effects of regulation (or anything else). Security prices change to reflect the most accurate unbiased prediction of what will happen in the future, but it is entirely possible that the actual effects of regulation will turn out to be very different from what was expected at the time of the regulatory change. In principle, it should be possible to determine whether the actual effects of regulation deviate substantially from the expected effects by measuring the returns to affected securities after the regulatory change. For example, if a sequence of identifiable events provides successively more information about the effects of a particular regulation, it would be necessary to sum the abnormal returns associated with all of these events in order to measure the actual impact of regulation.

*   *   *

C. Regulatory Changes That Affect Firms at Different Times

1. *Methodological Issues.* Some changes in public regulation occur through case law, or administrative law, or because of decisions by governmental regulatory agencies. In many instances a specific type of regulatory change will affect different firms at different times. For example, antitrust suits filed by the Justice Department or the Federal Trade Commission usually only affect the market value of the defendant firm. Even if every antitrust suit has the same impact on the defendant firm when it is filed, the impact of regulation occurs in different periods for different firms. This is beneficial because it randomizes the effects of other events which also affect security returns.

Fama, Fisher, Jensen, and Roll pioneered the analysis of abnormal security returns in "event time." [28] For example, the effect of filing an antitrust suit can be measured by averaging the abnormal returns to all defendant firms' securities in the period of the event

$$\tilde{\epsilon}_t = \frac{1}{N} \sum_{i=1}^{N} \epsilon_{it},\qquad(6)$$

where the event time, *t*, will generally be a different calendar date for each firm in the sample. The pattern of effects can be analyzed by computing an average abnormal return for several periods before and after the event occurs. This is especially important if there is some doubt about the time when the regulatory change is first anticipated by the securities market, since some of the effects may occur before or after the designated event period. The total effect of the regulatory change can be measured by summing the average abnormal returns for the event dates when expectations were revised (Fama *et al.* refer to this as "cumulative average abnormal returns").

If all the firms in a particular sample have regulatory events on different calendar dates, the individual-firm abnormal returns should not be correlated, and the variance of the average abnormal return is proportional to the sum of the variances of the individual abnormal returns

[28] Eugene F. Fama, Lawrence Fisher, Michael C. Jensen, & Richard Roll, The Adjustment of Stock Prices to New Information, 10 Int'l Econ.Rev. 1 (1969).

$$\text{Var}(\tilde{\epsilon}_t) = \frac{1}{N} \cdot \sum_{i=1}^{N} \text{Var}(\epsilon_{it}).$$

However, if some firms have regulatory events on the same date, it is more difficult to get a direct measure of the variability of the average abnormal return, because the returns that occur on the same date are likely to be correlated.

Another technique to analyze the impact of regulation that occurs at different times for different firms is to form a portfolio composed of all affected firms at each calendar date. This can be thought of as a trading strategy where the investment rule is to buy securities that are likely to be positively affected by regulation and to sell short those likely to be negatively affected. The return to this strategy, properly adjusted for risk, provides a measure of the impact of the regulatory change. The average of the time series of abnormal returns of the trading-strategy portfolio is conceptually similar to the cross-sectional average abnormal return in (6). In fact, if the trading-strategy portfolio never contains more than one security at any calendar date, the two measures will be identical. The trading-strategy portfolio method can be used to analyze anticipation or lag effects by including all firms with regulatory events in a span of several months either side of the event date.

* * *

G. FOSTER, FINANCIAL STATEMENT ANALYSIS
362–65 (1978).*

Estimating the Abnormal Returns of a Security
* * *

The most appealing theoretical framework for the CAR [cumulative abnormal returns] technique is within the context of a capital asset pricing model. Consider the [CAPM]:

$$E(\tilde{R}_{it})=R_{ft}+\beta_i[E(\tilde{R}_{mt})-R_{ft}], \tag{11.7}$$

where R_{it} = return on asset i in period t,
R_{ft} = return on a risk-free asset in period t,
R_{mt} = return on the market portfolio in period t,
β_i = relative risk of asset i.

Using (11.7) in an empirical study means replacing expected returns by realized returns:

$$\tilde{R}_{it}=R_{ft}+\hat{\beta}_i(\tilde{R}_{mt}-R_{ft})+\hat{U}_{it}, \tag{11.8}$$

where $\hat{U}_{it}$ is a residual whose expectation is zero. Equation (11.8) is usually rearranged as follows when estimating β_i:

$$\tilde{R}_{it}-R_{ft}=\hat{\beta}_i(\tilde{R}_{mt}-R_{ft})+\hat{U}_{it}. \tag{11.9}$$

Equation (11.9) can be estimated with ordinary least squares (usually with the intercept suppressed to zero). Given the OLS estimate of β_i, the abnormal return of security i in period t ($\hat{U}_{it}$) is

$$\hat{U}_{it} = (\tilde{R}_{it} - R_{ft}) - \hat{\beta}_i(\tilde{R}_{mt} - R_{ft}). \qquad \textbf{(11.10)}$$

It is important to note that when using (11.10) to (say) examine the capital market reaction to an earnings announcement, *we are jointly testing the hypothesis that the [CAPM] is a descriptively valid model of asset pricing and that the earnings have information content.*

An Example

Data for *Jos. Schlitz Brewing Company* will be used to illustrate the computation of the cumulative abnormal return measure for the 12 months up to and including the 1973 annual earnings announcement. The preliminary 1973 earnings of \$53,675,000 (1972 earnings = \$37,539,000) was announced in the *Wall Street Journal* on February 12, 1974. Thus the 12 months of interest are March 1973–February 1974. Table 11.4 contains details of $\tilde{R}_i$ [column (1)], $\tilde{R}_m$ [column (2)], and R_f [column (3)] over the March 1973–February 1974 period. The proxy for R_f is the return on government bonds with 1 month to maturity. A value-weighted index of all NYSE stocks is the proxy for R_m. Table 11.4 also contains the excess returns for *Schlitz* [$\tilde{R}_{it} - R_{ft}$: column (4)] and the market [$\tilde{R}_{mt} - R_{ft}$: column (5)].

Table 11.4

CAR Estimation for Jos. Schlitz Brewing Company

Month	R_{it} (1)	R_{mt} (2)	R_{ft} (3)	$R_{it} - R_{ft}$ (4)	$R_{mt} - R_{ft}$ (5)
March 73	.095	−.004	.005	.090	−.009
April 73	−.055	−.044	.005	−.060	−.049
May 73	.064	−.019	.006	.058	−.025
June 73	−.044	−.009	.005	−.049	−.014
July 73	.082	.051	.006	.076	.045
August 73	−.025	−.031	.008	−.033	−.039
September 73	−.114	.051	.006	−.120	.045
October 73	.096	−.001	.007	.087	−.008
November 73	−.188	−.117	.005	−.193	−.122
December 73	.107	.014	.006	.101	.008
January 74	−.040	−.001	.006	−.046	−.007
February 74	−.028	.004	.006	−.034	−.002

$$\sum_{t=1}^{12} = -.123 \qquad \sum_{t=1}^{12} = -.177$$

KEY: R_{it} = monthly return on *Jos. Schlitz Brewing Company*,
R_{mt} = monthly return on market index,
R_{ft} = monthly return on a risk-free asset.

Excess returns for the 60 months prior to March 1973 were used to estimate $\beta_i=1.087$ for this period. This β_i implies, for instance, that when the excess return on the market $(\tilde{R}_{mt} - R_{ft})$ is 1%, the "normal" excess return on *Schlitz* $(\tilde{R}_{it} - R_{ft})$ is 1.087%. The abnormal returns for each month in the 12-month period are estimated as follows:

$$\hat{U}_{it}=(\tilde{R}_{it} - R_{ft}) - 1.087\times(\tilde{R}_{mt} - R_{ft}). \tag{11.11}$$

Thus, for March 1973,

$$\hat{U}_{it}=.090-1.087\times(-.009)=.100.$$

For April 1973,

$$\hat{U}_{it}=.060-1.087\times(-.049) - .007.$$

Similarly, for May 1973,

$$\hat{U}_{it}=.058-1.087\times(-.025)=.085.$$

The cumulative abnormal return is estimated as follows:

$$\text{CAR} = \sum_{t=1}^{12} \hat{U}_{it}$$
$$= .100+(-.007)+.085\ldots=.069. \tag{11.12}$$

The cumulative excess return for the market over this 12-month period was $-.177$. Given a $\hat{\beta}$ of 1.087, *Schlitz's* "normal" cumulative excess return would have been $-.192$. However, *Schlitz's* actual excess return was only $-.123$. Thus, the cumulative abnormal return was .069. Note that this positive cumulative abnormal return was also associated with a positive earnings change for 1973 earnings vis-à-vis 1972 earnings.

◆

Although Schwert focuses on the use of the CAR technique to evaluate the impact of government regulation on the return to a security, the technique works equally well with respect to voluntary actions. Suppose we want to test the impact of a particular voluntary activity—such as the announcement of an acquisition—on the returns to the parties. The approach is the same as that described by Schwert, only the event date in question is the day on which the acquisition is announced. Additionally, it is possible to use the technique to measure the impact of events related to only a single company, as exemplified by Professor Ruback's study in the following section.

2. Introduction to Problems of Evaluation

RUBACK, THE CONOCO TAKEOVER AND STOCK-HOLDER RETURNS, SLOAN MANAGEMENT REVIEW

13–33 (Winter, 1982).*

On August 5, 1981, Du Pont announced that its takeover of Conoco had been successful. This announcement concluded one of the most dramatic takeovers in history: Du Pont initially offered an average price of $79.52 for each share of Conoco, but it revised the offer three times over a two-month period in response to bids by Seagram and Mobil. The successful bid involved a cash payment of $98 a share for 45 percent of Conoco and 1.7 shares of Du Pont for each of the remaining Conoco shares. The total value of this final offer was $7.54 billion, making it the largest takeover in American business history. This article examines this takeover in detail by evaluating the stock price changes associated with the bids and other information releases.

Empirical Results

Background of the Conoco Takeover

In March and April of 1981, Dome Petroleum Ltd. approached Conoco to discuss the purchase of Conoco's 52.9 percent interest in Hudson Bay Oil and Gas Company. On May 6, 1981, Dome announced a tender offer for 13 percent to 20 percent of Conoco's common stock at $65 a share. The expressed intention of the offer was to negotiate an exchange of Conoco shares for Conoco's interest in Hudson Bay Oil and Gas Company.[7] On May 12, 1981, Conoco announced that its board of directors opposed the Dome bid. The Dome offer was, however, successful. On May 27, Dome announced that it had received tenders for about 50 percent of Conoco's common stock and that it would purchase 20 percent of Conoco. Finally on June 1, 1981, Dome and Conoco announced that Conoco would exchange its interest in Hudson Bay Oil and Gas Company for Dome's 20 percent of Conoco's common stock and $245 million. The exchange was completed on June 10, 1981.

These events precipitated the bidding for Conoco by Seagram, Mobil, and Du Pont for at least two reasons. First, Conoco's management, in an attempt to thwart Dome's offer, sought out other bidders. These discussions started the chain of events which eventually led to the takeover offers that are described in the next section. Second, the success of the Dome offer suggested that control of Conoco could be obtained at only a modest premium. Compared to Conoco's stock price of $49.875 on May 5, 1981, the day before the Dome offer was announced, the premium implicit in the Dome offer was 30 percent. This premium is within the range of average premiums reported in prior takeover studies. It appears that the combined effect of these two phenomena led firms to consider seriously the profitability of acquiring Conoco.

Stock Market Reactions to Major

Announcements in the Conoco Takeover

Before presenting the abnormal returns associated with major announcements in the Conoco takeover, several factors that affect their interpretation are worth highlighting.

---

[7] Dome structured its bid for Conoco's interest in Hudson Bay Oil and Gas in this manner so that Conoco could avoid capital gains tax. For more details, see: L. Smith, "The Making of the Megamerger: An Inside View of the $7.6 Billion Conoco Takeover," Fortune, 7 September 1981, pp. 58–64;

S. Brill, "Conoco: Great Plays and Errors in the Bar's World Series," The American Lawyer (November 1981), pp. 39–52.

First, there were many news reports relating to the Conoco takeover during June, July, and August of 1981. The contents of these reports * * * vary substantially and thus the definition of a "major announcement" is ambiguous. In this section, the stock market reaction to twelve different announcements is described. The announcements, presented in Table 1, primarily include bid announcements. * * * (The dates in the figures indicate the last trading day for each week.)

* * *

[Second,] stock market prices incorporate the expected value of future uncertain opportunities. Thus, measured abnormal returns reflect the unanticipated percentage changes in expected value. This means that abnormal returns can only be unambiguously interpreted for unanticipated events. Fortunately, the initial bid by Du Pont seems to have been unanticipated. The initial bids by Seagram and Mobil were anticipated since they followed public announcements of the bidders' intention to seek control of Conoco. These public announcements, however, appear to have been unanticipated, and thus the cumulative abnormal returns from the first public announcement through the bid announcement can be interpreted unambiguously.[8] After the initial bid, the interpretation of a given daily abnormal return involves speculation about changes in expectations.

[Third,] when two pieces of information are released, only their combined effect can be measured.

With these considerations in mind, the analysis of the Conoco takeover begins on *June 19, 1981* when Conoco announced that it rejected a bid from an unidentified firm to purchase about 25 percent of Conoco for $70 a share. Table 1 presents the abnormal stock returns associated with the major events for Conoco, Seagram, Du Pont, and Mobil. The first event of Table 1 shows that the rejection of the takeover bid is associated with an abnormal return of 6.55 percent for Conoco. The *t*-statistic of 3.68 indicates that this positive abnormal performance is statistically significant. This initial increase in the value of Conoco could be attributed to either the expectation of a forthcoming takeover bid or the revaluation of Conoco, based on the information that another firm valued Conoco at $70 a share. Also, the first event of Table 1 suggests that the market did not know the identity of the future bidders, since their abnormal returns are not statistically different from zero.

On *June 23, 1981,* the unidentified bidder was identified as Seagram, and Seagram announced its intention to purchase shares of Conoco in the open market. Ironically, in light of subsequent events,

---

[8] The first bid by Du Pont and the first public announcements of Seagram and Mobil appear to have been unanticipated for two reasons. First, there was virtually no accurate speculation in the *Wall Street Journal* prior to the public announcements. Second, the abnormal returns do not indicate any leakage prior to the events; the abnormal returns vary around a value of zero, and on the date of the event, a substantial abnormal return is observed.

Seagram revealed that its rejected offer included a "standstill agreement," in which Seagram had agreed not to seek control of Conoco. The announcement that Seagram would purchase shares in the open market led to a statistically significant abnormal return of 8.85 percent for Conoco and a statistically insignificant abnormal return of 1.71 percent for Seagram.

16   Ruback   Conoco Takeover

Table 1
Major Events in Conoco Takeover and Corresponding Abnormal Returns of Participating Firms
(t-statistics in parentheses)

Event	Abnormal Returns			
	Conoco	Seagram	Du Pont	Mobil
June 19, 1981: [b] Conoco rejects offer by unidentified foreign corporation to buy about 25% of its stock for $70 a share.	6.55% (3.68)	1.77% (0.50)	–0.11% (–0.06)	1.53% (0.55)
June 23, 1981: [c] Seagram identified as Conoco's foreign suitor. Seagram announces intention to buy shares in open market.	8.85 (4.97)	1.71 (0.49)	1.00 (0.56)	0.84 (0.30)
June 25, 1981. [d] Seagram announces tender offer for 41% of Conoco at $73 a share.	5.37 (3.02)	7.65 (2.18)	–0.75 (–0.42)	0.97 (0.35)
July 6, 1981: Du Pont offers to merge with Conoco. Du Pont would pay $87.50 for 40% of Conoco and exchange 1.6 Du Pont shares for remaining shares.	11.87 (9.42)	–3.88 (–1.56)	–8.05 (–6.32)	1.07 (0.54)
July 13, 1981: Seagram revises tender offer to $85 a share for 51% of Conoco. Mobil signals intention to bid for Conoco.	9.14 (7.27)	–0.29 (–0.12)	–0.20 (–0.16)	–0.44 (–0.22)
July 15, 1981: Du Pont increases its merger bid for Conoco to $95 a share for 40% of Conoco and 1.7 Du Pont shares for remaining 60% of Conoco.	1.46 (1.16)	–0.47 (–0.19)	–1.29 (–1.01)	–1.23 (–0.62)
July 17, 1981: Mobil mails offer of $90 a share for 50% of Conoco. The offer, if successful, would be followed by exchange of $90 worth of Mobil preferred stock or debentures.	–0.55 (–0.44)	–0.83 (–0.33)	–1.94 (–1.52)	–1.43 (–0.72)
July 23, 1981: Seagram revises bid to $92 a share for 51% of Conoco.	3.93 (3.12)	–2.34 (–0.94)	–0.77 (–0.60)	0.82 (0.42)
July 27, 1981: Du Pont raises bid to $95 a share for 45% of Conoco and 1.7 Du Pont shares for Conoco's remaining stock. Mobil changes bid to $105 a share for 50% of Conoco and $85 worth of Mobil preferred stock or debentures for rest of Conoco.	0.35 (0.28)	–1.90 (0.76)	–1.31 (–1.03)	–1.09 (–0.55)
August 3, 1981: Mobil raises cash portion of its Conoco offer to $115 a share. Seagram starts purchasing Conoco shares at $92. Du Pont-Conoco merger is conditionally approved by Justice Department.	5.58 (4.43)	7.49 (3.02)	0.73 (0.57)	1.26 (0.64)
August 4, 1981: Du Pont raises cash portion of its Conoco offer to $98 a share. Justice Department grants antitrust clearance for Du Pont-Conoco merger.	–4.75 (–3.78)	–1.87 (–0.75)	–0.60 (–0.47)	–0.97 (–0.49)
August 5, 1981: [e] Du Pont receives tenders for 55% of Conoco and is apparent victor. Mobil tenders its Conoco shares to Seagram. Seagram extended its offer for Conoco.	–2.09 (–1.66)	–1.89 (–0.76)	2.24 (1.76)	1.70 (0.86)

[b] Conoco's board of directors rejected the offer on June 17, 1981, but it was not announced until June 19, 1981. Abnormal return for Conoco of 4.01% on June 18 suggests news was partially released before its official announcement. Thus the abnormal return for this information release includes June 18 and June 19, 1981.

[c] On June 22, 1981 Seagram notified regulating authorities that it might acquire more than 25% of Conoco's common stock. Conoco announced on June 23 that it received notification of Seagram's filing and identified Seagram as bidder whose bid was rejected. Since filing by Seagram could have been known on filing date, abnormal returns include both June 22, and 23, 1981.

[d] Seagram tender offer was announced on June 25, 1981. Trading in Conoco was suspended, thus stock price did not include information until trading was resumed on June 26, 1981. Reported abnormal returns for all firms are measured over June 25 and 26, 1981.

[e] Abnormal return for Conoco is based on shares of Conoco not tendered to Du Pont.

[D8040]

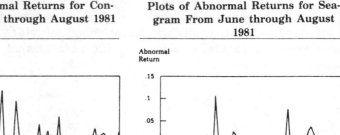

Figure 1
Plots of Abnormal Returns for Conoco From June through August 1981

Figure 2
Plots of Abnormal Returns for Seagram From June through August 1981

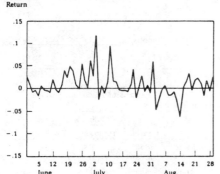

Figure 3
Plots of Abnormal Returns for Du Pont From June through August 1981

Figure 4
Plots of Abnormal Returns for Mobil From June through August 1981

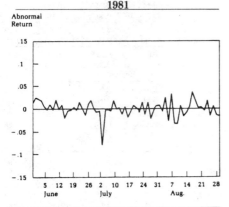
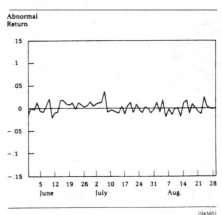

(D6585)

On *June 25, 1981,* Seagram announced its first tender offer of $73 a share for 41 percent of Conoco. Conoco's shareholders realized an abnormal return of 5.37 percent on that day. Since the takeover attempt was anticipated because of the earlier announcements made on June 19 and June 23, the correct measure of the abnormal return is the cumulative performance from all three announcements, which is 22.2 percent and which is within the range reported in the earlier studies of takeovers. Somewhat surprising, however, was the large positive abnormal return of 7.65 percent for Seagram on June 25, 1981. A glance at Figure 2, which presents a plot of the daily abnormal returns for Seagram, shows that this is the largest abnormal return that Seagram stock realized during June through August of 1981. This is surprising since most studies report small or no abnormal returns for bidders. The positive abnormal return for Seagram on June 25 suggests that the market viewed Seagram's tender offer as a value increasing investment. Seagram's cumulative abnormal performance over the three announcements was 11.42 percent, which translates into an increase in its equity value of $213,270,000, or approximately $6.08 a share.

The tender offer by Seagram was opposed by Conoco's management and Conoco sought out other takeover bids. This search resulted in an agreement with Du Pont, and a takeover of Conoco by Du Pont was announced on *July 6, 1981*. This offer, which was supported by Conoco's management, involved the payment of $87.50 a share for 40 percent of Conoco's stock and an exchange of 1.6 shares of Du Pont for each of the remaining Conoco shares. An unusual feature of the agreement between Conoco and Du Pont was that Du Pont received an option to buy 15.9 million shares of Conoco at $87.50 a share until March 31, 1982. This option provided Du Pont a partial hedge against failure of its takeover bid. If another bidder offered a price in excess of $87.50 for each share of Conoco, Du Pont could exercise its option and tender its Conoco shares and thereby realize a profit. Also, the option increased the probability that Du Pont's offer would be successful. Under Delaware law, the merger required the approval of a majority of Conoco shares. The option, if exercised, would give Du Pont 15.6 percent of Conoco's outstanding shares and would increase the likelihood of obtaining majority approval.

The effect of Du Pont's July 6, 1981 offer on Conoco's common stock price was positive and dramatic. As Table 1 indicates, the abnormal return of Conoco was 11.87 percent on July 6, or approximately $711 million. The *t*-statistic of 9.42 indicates statistical significance, and inspection of Figure 1 shows that it is the largest abnormal return during the period. Equally dramatic was Du Pont's negative abnormal performance of –8.05 percent on July 6 which has a corresponding *t*-statistic of –6.32. Figure 3 shows that this abnormal return is large even for this turbulent three-month period. This negative abnormal return translates into a one-day reduction of $641 million in the equity value of Du Pont. This loss in Du Pont's equity value is roughly equal to the dollar value of Conoco's gain.[9] The market, therefore, apparently did not expect the merged firm to be more valuable than the separate firms, and thus the premium seems to be just a wealth transfer to Conoco's shareholders from Du Pont's shareholders. Also, note that Seagram's stockholders incurred an abnormal loss of –3.88 percent, which is consistent with the view that Seagram's initial tender offer was a good investment for them; Du Pont's offer raised the price of acquiring Conoco and thereby both reduced the likelihood that Seagram would be successful and reduced the profitability of the takeover.

Seagram responded to the Du Pont offer by increasing its offer to $85 a share for 51 percent of Conoco on *July 13, 1981*. Compared to Seagram's earlier offer, the revised offer involved the purchase of more shares at a higher offer price. Conoco's stock responded to this revised offer and shareholders realized a significant abnormal return of 9.14 percent on July 13, 1981. The two active bidders for Conoco, Seagram and Du Pont, realized relatively small negative abnormal returns of

[9] The gain to Conoco exceeded Du Pont's loss by about $69.5 million, which is small in comparison to the performance of the individual firms. In other words, the holder of a value weighted portfolio of Du Pont and Conoco common stock would have realized an abnormal return of about 0.5 percent.

–0.29 percent and –0.20 percent respectively. For Du Pont, this small negative abnormal return is somewhat surprising in light of the substantial decline in its equity value that was associated with its first bid for Conoco. The revised Seagram offer provided a convenient means for Du Pont to abandon its takeover attempt and perhaps reverse its stock price decline. One interpretation of the small negative abnormal return is that the market anticipated subsequent bids by Du Pont for Conoco.

On *July 15, 1981*, Du Pont increased the cash portion of its bid for Conoco to $95 a share from $87.50 a share for 40 percent of Conoco and also increased the exchange ratio for the remaining shares of Conoco to 1.7 a share from 1.6 shares of Du Pont. Again, Conoco's stock price rose, although the abnormal return of 1.46 percent was considerably smaller than the market reaction to the earlier bids and was statistically insignificant. Each of the bidders incurred abnormal losses: the abnormal return for Seagram was –0.47 percent; for Du Pont the abnormal return was –1.29 percent; and for Mobil the abnormal return was –1.23 percent. While these losses are not significantly different from zero, the point estimates indicate that the market anticipated a decline in the profitability of the takeover for the bidders. For Du Pont the negative market reactions to each of its bids indicate that the market viewed Du Pont's takeover bid as an unprofitable investment.

Mobil entered the bidding for Conoco on *July 17, 1981* with an offer of $90 a share for 50 percent of Conoco and an exchange of $90 worth of Mobil securities upon completion of a merger with Conoco. In contrast to the impact of previous offers, the abnormal return for Conoco was negative, but it was very small in relation to the previous large positive abnormal returns and was not significantly different from zero. All three of the active bidders incurred abnormal losses. Seagram responded to Mobil's offer by raising its bid for 51 percent of Conoco to $92 a share from $85 a share on *July 23, 1981*. Conoco's stock rose and the abnormal return was 3.93 percent, with a *t*-statistic of 3.12. Seagram incurred an abnormal loss of –2.34 percent, suggesting a reduction in value of the takeover for Seagram's shareholders.

Du Pont and Mobil revised their offers for Conoco on *July 27, 1981* and the pattern of negative abnormal returns for bidding firms was repeated. Mobil revised its offer a third time on *August 3, 1981* by increasing the cash portion of its bid to $115 a share from $90 a share. The familiar pattern of negative abnormal returns for bidders was not repeated: Seagram realized a positive abnormal return of 7.49 percent, with a *t*-statistic of 3.02, and the other bidders, Mobil and Du Pont, realized small positive abnormal returns. This abnormal performance cannot, however, be attributed to Mobil's offer since there were three other important announcements that occurred on the same day. First, Seagram announced that it had received tenders for 15.5 million shares of Conoco and that they would begin purchasing them at $92 a share. Second, the Justice Department said that its only antitrust concerns in a Du Pont-Conoco merger involved a joint venture between Conoco and Monsanto Company. Du Pont announced plans to file a consent decree which would eliminate this problem. Third, the Justice Department requested more information from Mobil, which postponed Mobil's purchase of Conoco's stock by at least ten days. The abnormal returns for

August 3 incorporate the effects of the Mobil bid and the three other announcements.

On *August 4, 1981,* Du Pont raised the cash portion of its offer to $98 a share and the Justice Department announced antitrust clearance for a Du Pont-Conoco merger. The three bidders incurred abnormal losses on August 4. The abnormal return for Conoco, in contrast to earlier announcements, was –4.75 percent. This abnormal return is based on a closing price of $96 a share on August 3. According to the *Wall Street Journal*, there are suspicions that this $96 a share closing price may have been manipulated; only 1,400 shares were traded on the Pacific Coast Exchange at this price before its close. Using the NYSE closing price for Conoco of $93.75 a share on August 3, the abnormal return for Conoco on August 4 was –1.60 percent, with a *t*-statistic of –1.26.

The takeover battle for Conoco ended with the announcement by Du Pont on *August 5, 1981* that it had received tenders for 55 percent of Conoco's common stock. In calculating the abnormal return to Conoco shareholders on August 5, it is important to distinguish those Conoco shares tendered to Du Pont from those that were not. Since the withdrawal deadline was August 4, the shares tendered to Du Pont could not have been sold by the shareholders. Also, after August 4, Du Pont was no longer willing to pay $98 for each share of Conoco. The market price on August 5 and thereafter reflects the value of those shares that were not tendered to Du Pont. Table 3 details the calculation of Conoco's equity value on August 5, 1981, which was approximately $8,028 million. This implies an average price per share of $93.35. The abnormal return for Conoco, based on this average price, was –0.43 percent; whereas the abnormal return, based on the market price, of Conoco shares on August 5 was –2.09 percent.

The abnormal return for Du Pont on August 5, 1981 was 2.24 percent, with a *t*-statistic of 1.76, and the abnormal return for those Conoco shares not tendered to Du Pont was –2.09 percent, with a *t*-statistic of –1.66. This is in contrast to previous abnormal returns associated with bid announcements where Conoco realized positive abnormal returns and bidders incurred abnormal losses. One interpretation of these results is that prior to Du Pont's announcement of success, the market anticipated additional bids for Conoco. These anticipations were reflected in market prices on August 4. The announced Du Pont victory on August 5 meant that the bidding was over. Thus, Conoco's stock price went down because no higher bids would have been made, and Du Pont realized a positive return because it would no longer be making higher unprofitable bids. For Mobil, the positive abnormal return of 1.70 percent suggests that its takeover proposal was unprofitable, and thus its takeover failure was good news for Mobil's shareholders.

The abnormal return of –1.89 percent on August 5 for Seagram is difficult to interpret. Du Pont's success meant that Seagram's offer would not succeed, and thus the negative abnormal return seems to imply that Seagram lost a profitable investment opportunity. However, the initial market reaction to Seagram's last bid on July 23, 1981 was negative. Ignoring the market's expectations, the pattern of abnormal returns suggests the nonsensical interpretation that Seagram's bid was a negative net present value investment, but that the loss of this investment opportunity reduced shareholder wealth. Of course, the four bids by Du Pont and Mobil that occurred between July 24 and August 5 could have increased the market's estimate of Conoco's value so that, as of August 4, the market viewed Seagram's last bid as profitable. Other interpretations are also plausible. For example, Seagram's July 23 bid might have been profitable, but not as profitable as the market had expected it to be. This demonstrates the difficulty of interpreting the abnormal returns on individual days when expectations change. In the next section, the cumulative abnormal returns, which include all of the expectation changes, are examined.

Summary of Abnormal Returns

Table 4 summarizes the abnormal returns associated with each firm's involvement in the Conoco takeover. The most dramatic effect of the takeover was on the value of Conoco's common stock. The cumulative abnormal return for Conoco, measured from June 17, 1981, the day Conoco's board rejected Seagram's first offer, through August 5, 1981, the day Du Pont's success was announced, was 71.24 percent.[10] In dollar terms, the equity value of Conoco rose by over $3 billion as a result of the takeover.

Table 3

Measuring the Value of Conoco's Common Stock on August 5, 1981

Class of Conoco	Number of Shares (Millions)	Per Share Value (Value on August 5, 1981)	Total Value of Class (Millions)
Shares tendered to Du Pont and bought for cash	38.7	$98.00	3792.60
Shares tendered to Du Pont and ex-changed for Du Pont stock	9.4	80.1125 [a]	753.06
Remaining shares outstanding	37.9	91.875	3482.06
All shares	86.0	93.35[b]	8027.72

[a] The per share value of shares to be exchanged is based on an exchange ratio of 1.7 Du Pont shares for each share of Conoco and a closing price of Du Pont on August 5, 1981 of $47.125.

[b] This is the average price per share.

[10] The cumulative abnormal return for Conoco incorporates the purchase of Conoco shares by Du Pont on August 5, 1981. See Table 3 for details of this calculation.

The successful bidder, Du Pont, realized cumulative abnormal returns of –9.90 percent from its involvement in the Conoco takeover. The negative abnormal return for Du Pont translates into an abnormal decline in equity value of $789 million. If the stock market is assumed to be efficient in the sense that it correctly values firms, this evidence means that the acquisition of Conoco was a negative net present value investment. Furthermore, the market's response to each of Du Pont's bids was negative (see Table 1), implying that each successive Du Pont bid reduced the value of Du Pont's common stock.

The two unsuccessful bidders, Seagram and Mobil, exhibited different abnormal returns. For Seagram, the cumulative abnormal return associated with its attempted takeover of Conoco was 1.13 percent. This small positive abnormal return indicates that Seagram's attempted takeover did not have a substantial impact on its equity.[12] From a Seagram shareholder's viewpoint, it was as if the takeover attempt never occurred. For Mobil, negative abnormal returns of –3.05 percent are associated with its attempted Conoco takeover. The origin of this reduction in Mobil's stock price is unclear. While the reduction incorporates the loss of legal fees and other transaction costs, it is hard to attribute the entire loss of over $400 million to transaction costs. A plausible source of these losses involves Mobil's antitrust difficulties. Mobil asserted that its acquisition of Conoco did not present any substantial antitrust problems. However, the Justice Department's policy toward horizontal mergers was and still is unclear. The Justice Department's request for more information from Mobil on August 3, 1981 substantially raised doubts that the takeover would be approved and thus increased the cost of the acquisition of Conoco by postponing Mobil's purchase of Conoco shares. Also, this action signaled an increase in the probability that the Justice Department would oppose the takeover. Thus, the negative abnormal returns for Mobil could be attributed to the expectation that the Justice Department would oppose Mobil's future acquisition attempts.

Some Explanations

The empirical results of this article indicate that the takeover of Conoco by Du Pont resulted in a 71 percent increase in the equity value of Conoco and a decrease in the equity value of Du Pont by almost 10 percent. Furthermore, these effects were consistent throughout the bidding process; each bid announcement was associated with positive abnormal returns for Conoco and negative abnormal returns for Du Pont. These results raise two puzzling questions. First, what caused the substantial revaluation of Conoco? Second, why did Du Pont pursue an acquisition that decreased the wealth of its stockholders?

[12] Seagram's takeover attempt was not entirely unsuccessful. Seagram obtained 28 million shares of Conoco for $92 each. These shares were tendered to Du Pont for 47.6 million shares of Du Pont's common stock, which represents 20 percent of Du Pont's equity. This enabled Seagram to obtain some control over Du Pont. For the details of the agreement between Du Pont and Seagram, see L. Kraar, "Seagram Tightens Its Grip on Du Pont," *Fortune,* 16 November 1981, pp. 75–78. Based on Du Pont's stock price as of August 5, 1981, Seagram paid a premium of 14.8 percent for its Du Pont shares, which was a relatively small control premium.

Table 4
Summary of Abnormal Returns for Firms Involved in Conoco Takeover

Firm	Holding Period [a]	Cumulative Abnormal Return (Percent)	Cumulative Abnormal Equity Value Change (Millions) [c]
Conoco	June 17–Aug. 5, 1981	71.24%	$3201.2
Seagram	June 17–Aug. 5, 1981	1.13	20.6
Du Pont	July 6–Aug. 5, 1981	−9.90	−789.1
Mobil	July 13–Aug. 5, 1981	−3.05	−405.4

[a] The holding period is from the first indication that the firm would become involved in the takeover through Aug. 5, 1981 the date Du Pont announced that it had won.

[c] The cumulative abnormal equity value change for each firm is calculated by multiplying the equity value for the firm on the day before the holding period starts times the firm's cumulative abnormal return over the holding period.

* * *

Economies of Scale

Economies of scale in production do not appear to be the source of the revaluation mainly because Conoco and Du Pont are in different industries. Also, according to public information, no explicit combination of assets was intended. Of course, some economies of scale may be realized in research and development, accounting, data processing, etc. But it is unlikely that these economies of scale are sufficient to explain the magnitude of the revaluation.

Monopolization of Product Markets

Similarly, monopolization of product markets does not explain the revaluation. The merger was carefully scrutinized by the Justice Department, and, after Conoco's purchase of Monsanto's share of a joint venture, no antitrust objections remained. There is no factual basis to support the hypothesis that the merger increased the market power of either Du Pont or Conoco. Thus, synergy in the form of vertical integration, economies of scale, or monopolization of product markets does not explain the revaluation of Conoco and Du Pont's continued pursuit of Conoco.

Departure from Wealth Maximization

The hypothesis of managerial departures from stockholder wealth maximization would attribute the revaluation of Conoco to the elimination, after the completion of the merger, of inefficient management. Also, Du Pont's pursuit of Conoco, in spite of the market's signal that the takeover was a negative net present value investment, could be explained by asserting that Du Pont's management had an objective function different from that of shareholder wealth maximization. Both aspects of this hypothesis are difficult to test because methods to assess objectively the efficiency of management and to infer the objective function of a firm's management are unavailable. However, the magnitude of the revaluation of Conoco ($3.2 billion) seems inconsistent with this hypothesis, especially since Conoco did not have a reputation for being a poorly managed firm.

Similarly, Du Pont's loss of $789 million seems too large to be explained by the hypothesis of management departures from the objective of stockholder wealth maximization. Also, it is unlikely that Du Pont's management benefited from the takeover. The directors and officers of Du Pont had beneficial ownership or rights to acquire approximately 6.3 percent of Du Pont's common stock before the acquisition of Conoco. Thus they incurred losses of about $50 million as a result of the acquisition. The hypothesis of management departures requires an increase in managerial compensation or perquisites to offset these losses. Du Pont's incentive compensation plan is a function of its reported net income and the maximum amount of incentive compensation would increase by roughly 53 percent as a result of its acquisition of Conoco.[17] However, since the acquisition also increases the number of executives, an increase in per capita executive compensation is not apparent.[18] While perquisites may increase as a result of the acquisition, it seems likely that Du Pont's management could have obtained the same level of perquisites from acquiring another firm without incurring the substantial reduction in its stockholder wealth. Thus, while it is difficult to reject the hypothesis of management departures from stockholder wealth maximization, the magnitude of Conoco's revaluation and the lack of evidence that Du Pont's management benefited from the acquisition seem inconsistent with the hypothesis.

New Information

The third general hypothesis in the takeover literature is that revaluation of target firms is due to the release of positive information

[17] The maximum contribution to Du Pont's Incentive Compensation Fund is given by: .20 [net income — .06 (average stockholder's equity in the current and previous year)] where net income and stockholder equity are adjusted for payments to the fund. Details of Du Pont's compensation plans are reported in Du Pont's Proxy statement dated March 9, 1979. The percentage increase in the maximum contribution is based on information in Du Pont's prospectus dated July 15, 1981. Ignoring the adjustments, the maximum contribution to the fund in 1980 was about $74 million; $70 million was actual-ly allocated to the fund. Using the net income reported in the Pro Forma Combined Consolidated Income Statement for 1980 and the stockholder's equity reported in the Pro Forma Combined Consolidated Balance Sheet for March 31, 1981 as a measure of the average stockholder's equity in the current and previous year, the maximum contribution to the fund would have been about $114 million in 1980.

[18] The incentive compensation plan is subject to change. Also, other forms of executive compensation, such as stock options, are discretionary.

about its value. One frequently advanced piece of information was that Conoco's natural resource holdings were substantially undervalued by the stock market. The proposition evolves from an appraised value of Conoco at $160 per share by John S. Herold, Inc.[19] Stock prices below their appraised value are not unique to Conoco. Using stock prices of July 1, 1981 and John S. Herold, Inc.'s 1981 appraised values, the stock prices of oil refining and producing firms are, on average, about 45 percent of their appraised value.[20] While testing the hypothesis that the market value of oil companies does not reflect the present value of their natural resource holdings is beyond the scope of this article, several considerations suggest that this is not a valid explanation for the revaluation of Conoco and Du Pont's pursuit of Conoco. First, if the sole purpose of the acquisition of Conoco was to invest in natural resource reserves, Du Pont could have avoided the premium, which is usually required when control is sought, by investing in a portfolio of natural resource firms. Second, even if control was required to realize the benefits from the investment, this hypothesis does not explain why Conoco was pursued so vigorously when other "undervalued" natural resource firms were available.[21] Third, since the market was aware of the Herold valuation estimates, Du Pont's abnormal return of –8 percent on July 6, 1981 indicates that the market valued Conoco's natural resource holdings less than the average offer price of $79.52 a share.

Inside Information

An alternative explanation for Conoco's revaluation is that Du Pont possessed information about the value of Conoco that was not available to the market. This explanation for the revaluation of Conoco, if correct, also provides a rationale for Du Pont's pursuit of Conoco. The market consistently signaled that it perceived Du Pont's bids as negative net present value investment. These signals, however, did not incorporate the inside information that led Du Pont to value Conoco so highly because the information was not available to the market. Also, if the information was not specific to Du Pont, it would not be in Du Pont's best interests to reveal this information since it would raise the cost of acquiring Conoco. Furthermore, while Conoco could have released inside information to the entire market, it might not have been in the best interests of its shareholders to do so. For example, publishing research and development directions, marketing and production plans, and other types of inside information could have reduced Conoco's value to the successful bidder, and thereby would have reduced the premium paid to Conoco's stockholders. Note that

[19] See J.S. Herold, Inc., *Oil Industry Comparative Appraisals* (July, 1981) p. 40.

[20] See A.A. Lappen, "Appraised Value: The Stuff of Dreams," *Forbes*, 12 May 1980, pp. 145–153. Here the author compares the stock prices of natural resource firms with their appraised values (supplied by John S. Herold, Inc.). These data indicate that the stock prices of oil refining and producing firms were about 7 percent of their appraised value on average in May, 1980.

[21] On July 1, 1980, Conoco stock price was 43 percent of its appraised value. Of the nineteen oil refining and producing firms examined, nine firms had equity prices that were less than 43 percent of appraised value.

upon completion of the merger, information of this type would not be revealed, except in very general character by the successful bidder, since it would reduce the value of the newly acquired assets. Two additional facts support this explanation. First, Conoco did allow Du Pont to examine inside information. Second, on August 18, 1981, the day after Du Pont's shareholders met to vote on the merger, Du Pont's abnormal return was 3.4 percent, with a *t*-statistic of 2.67. This suggests that Du Pont's management released some information at that meeting which resulted in a revision in the market's estimate of the value of Conoco to Du Pont. Nevertheless, the hypothesis that some information that was not available to the market caused both Conoco's revaluation and Du Pont's bids cannot be confirmed since the nature of this information remains unknown.

* * *

---◆---

Note: Interpretive Problems

Professor Ruback's study of the impact of the bidding contest for Conoco on the value of the participants' stock serves as an excellent example of the difficulties in interpreting cumulative abnormal return ("CAR") data. But before considering the way in which the Ruback study illustrates particular problems, a more general point is worth emphasis: CAR data is of little use standing alone. The statistical technique merely states that abnormal returns were or were not earned during a specified period; *it does not explain why.* Developing an explanation for the presence of positive or negative abnormal returns requires a detailed understanding of the substance of the events and the institutions under study. Put most simply, if the market's response was based on a strategy of which the investigator is unaware, or does not understand, the CAR results, though technically accurate, will be used to support a nonetheless inaccurate explanation of what occurred. The availability of the CAR statistical technique does not substitute for traditional methods of assessing cause through deductive reasoning; it only—although this is substantial—helps delineate precisely what is in need of explanation.

With respect to particular interpretative problems, both Schwert and Ruback point out that the CAR technique measures only abnormal returns associated with *unexpected* events. Suppose, for example, we are trying to determine the impact on an ongoing merger contest of a new Justice Department position, and that the CAR's for the parties on the date the new position is publicly announced is zero. One explanation for this result is that the market believed that the Justice Department's action would have no effect at all on the participants. An alternative explanation, equally consistent with the data, is that the Justice Department's action had a very substantial effect, but one that had been anticipated prior to public announcement and, thus, would have caused abnormal returns at an earlier time. It is, therefore, critical to identify when the event under study first became known, a problem that can be quite difficult if, as with acquisitions, much of the information concerning the event is transmitted informally, independent of formal public announcements. In the case of acquisitions, mistakes in specifying the relevant events date were not uncommon in early studies. For example, Mandelker, *Risk and Return: The Case of Merging Firms,* 1 J.Fin.Econ. 303 (1974); Ellert, *Mergers, Antitrust Law Enforcement and Stockholder Returns,* 3 J.Fin. 715 (1976) and Langetieg, *An Application of a Three-Factor Performance Index to Measure Stockholders' Gains from Mergers,* 6 J.Fin.Econ. 365 (1978), all used as the event date, the date on which an acquisition was legally effective, rather than the much earlier date on which it was first publicly announced.

Even when the event date—that is, the date on which the new information would have been incorporated into the price of the security—can be unambiguously specified, it may still be quite difficult to explain entirely the relationship between the event and the abnormal returns associated with the corresponding date. Ruback shows that Conoco's June 19, 1983 announcement that it had rejected an offer of $70 a share for 25% of its stock was associated with a positive abnormal return of 6.55%. The question then becomes why *rejection* of a premium offer resulted in increased value for Conoco. Ruback suggests alternative explanations: either (i) the rejection of the first offer caused the market to believe that there was an increased probability that a subsequent premium offer would succeed; or (ii) the fact that an unnamed bidder valued Conoco so highly was new information that led the market to revalue Conoco without regard to the likelihood of a future takeover.[2] To further complicate matters, there seems to be no reason why both explanations could not have played a role.

If it is important to be able to differentiate between the competing explanations, then further investigation, and creativity, is necessary. For example, Ruback suggests that Conoco became a serious prospect for acquiring firms when, on May 27, 1981, Dome Petroleum announced that its bid for 13 to 20 percent of Conoco's stock, at a 30% premium, had resulted in tenders of some 50% of Conoco's stock. This response signaled that control of Conoco could be acquired for a "reasonable" premium. But if this signaled to potential acquiring companies that Conoco was available, would not the same fact also have signaled to the rest of the market that Conoco was a likely target? And if this is correct, then the relevant date with respect to Ruback's first explanation—that the abnormal returns resulted from the market's reassessment of the probabilities of an eventual takeover of Conoco by someone—would be May 27th, not June 19th. This hypothesis might be tested by determining the abnormal returns associated with Conoco on May 27th, the date Dome announced the results of its offer. A positive abnormal return for that date would suggest that the market had

---

[2] We will devote substantial attention in Part II, Motivations for Acquisitions, to analysis of what expectations about possible gains from acquisitions might account for the pattern of abnormal returns described in the numerous CAR studies of the impact of acquisitions on shareholder wealth.

already taken into account the expectation of a subsequent tender offer by the time that the 25% offer was rejected three weeks later. This would leave a general revaluation as an explanation for the later abnormal return.[3]

Even if analysis of the abnormal returns on May 27, the date the results of the Dome offer were announced, confirmed this hypothesis, the mystery would still be far from solved. The June 19th offer might have further altered the market's estimate of the probability of a subsequent offer, thereby leaving ambiguous the abnormal returns associated with rejection of this offer.

A similar interpretive problem exists with respect to the market's evaluation of Seagram's losing the bidding contest over Conoco to Du Pont. Ruback points out that the announcement of Seagram's final bid resulted in its stock experiencing negative abnormal returns, suggesting that the market viewed Seagram's making the bid as having a negative impact on the value of the firm; i.e., that a Conoco acquisition would not be beneficial for Seagram's shareholders. This, in turn, suggests that the subsequent failure of the Seagram bid should have resulted in an offsetting positive abnormal return to reflect the elimination of an event expected to reduce firm value. The actual result of Seagram's losing the contest, however, was a small *negative* abnormal return that is subject, as Ruback suggests, to a wide variety of explanations. One explanation that Ruback does not consider involves the market's expectations concerning what Seagram would do with its Conoco stock now that Du Pont had won. If Seagram might decide—as it ultimately did—to exchange its large number of Conoco shares for Du Pont shares in the merger, then the negative abnormal returns may have reflected the market's perception of the value of the Du Pont stock Seagram would receive in light of Du Pont's winning the contest. In this regard, note that Du Pont experienced a slightly higher negative abnormal return on the occasion of its victory than did Seagram on the occasion of its loss.

In addition to difficulties in interpreting the resulting data, the CAR technique has also given rise to quite sophisticated statistical debates over which of a number of different computational variations yields the most accurate measurement of abnormal returns. These problems are thoroughly surveyed in Brown & Warner, *Measuring Security Price Performance*, 8 J.Fin.Econ. 205 (1980). For our purposes, however, the problems of determining the appropriate event time and the difficulties in interpreting the resulting data loom far larger than conflicts over the most accurate statistical methodology. Brown & Warner state this conclusion explicitly:

"A 'bottom line' that emerges from our study is this: * * * there is no evidence that more complicated methodologies convey

[3] The Dome offer itself, independent of the Conoco shareholders' response to it, might not have suggested that Conoco was a likely target. Dome's offer had as its purpose acquiring only Conoco's Canadian assets, a strategy prompted by regulatory efforts of the Canadian Government intended to prompt the return of ownership of Canadian energy sources to local hands.

any benefit. [E]ven if the researcher doing an event study has a strong comparative advantage at improving existing methods, a good use of his time is still in reading old issues of the *Wall Street Journal* to more accurately determine event dates."

Id. at 249.[4]

---

[4] This conclusion concerned the use of *monthly* stock price data in CAR studies. Brown & Warner extended their analysis and their conclusion to daily stock price data in *Using Daily Stock Returns: The Case of Event Studies*, 14 J.Fin.Econ. 14 (1985).

CHAPTER SEVEN. THE OPTION PERSPECTIVE

A. The Traditional Context

In both practical and theoretical terms, some of the most important recent developments in financial theory have concerned valuation not of assets, but of options to acquire or dispose of assets. The growing importance of options is vividly illustrated by the fact that the world's second largest securities market, measured by dollar volume of securities traded, is *not* the American Stock Exchange, nor that of London or Tokyo. Rather it is the Chicago Board of Option Exchange, founded only in 1973.[1] Not surprisingly, the growth of an organized market for options led to a strong academic interest in how this peculiar form of security should be priced. This attention resulted in the specification of an option pricing model by Fischer Black and Myron Scholes [2] that has come to represent one of the major paradigms in modern financial theory. But while the practical and theoretical significance of option pricing warrant attention in their own right, what is of principal interest to us here is somewhat different. Although examining the characteristics of exchange listed options on common stock is a necessary first step, our focus will be on the insight, also originating with Black and Scholes,[3] that much can be learned about a variety of corporate settings by recasting the participants' various interests in terms of their having given or having received an option. One can then consider what the determinants of option pricing suggest about the incentives of the participants: What behavior by each participant would maximize the value of his or her interest? It is necessary to begin, however, with consideration of options in their familiar context. The following excerpt by one of the pioneers in the field provides an excellent introduction.

M. SCHOLES, OPTIONS—PUTS AND CALLS, in ENCYCLOPEDIA OF INVESTMENTS
559-78 (M. Blume & J. Freidman eds. 1982).

BASIC CHARACTERISTICS

Definitions

A call option is the right to buy an asset—for example, 100 shares of common stock—at a fixed price, on or before a date in the future. A put option is the right to sell the asset to another investor. The fixed price of the option is called its "striking price" or its "exercise price";

---

[1] R. Brealey & S. Myers, *Principles of Corporate Finance* 429 (2nd ed. 1984). Options are also now traded on the American, Philadelphia and Pacific Stock Exchanges. Prior to 1973, options were traded over-the-counter.

[2] Black & Scholes, *The Pricing of Options and Corporate Liabilities*, 81 J.Pol.Econ. 637 (1973); see also Merton, *Theory of Rational Option Pricing*, 4 Bell J.Econ. 141 (1973).

[3] Black & Scholes, supra note 1.

the date of expiration of the contract is called its "maturity date" or its "expiration date"; the asset itself is called the "underlying security." The sellers of options are known as option writers and the buyers of options are known as option buyers. The price of an option is called the "option premium."

Similarity to Other Securities

Since 1973, call options and, more recently, put options have been trading on organized secondary markets. Investors have become familiar with the characteristics of these contracts, which are relatively simple contracts with set maturity dates and exercise prices. They may be unaware, however, that other commonly traded securities are first cousins to options. Warrants, executive stock options, and even the common stock and bonds of a corporation are examples of securities that are closely related to put and call options.

The common stock of a corporation with bonds in its capital structure is an option because the shareholders have the right to buy back the assets of the firm from the bondholders by paying off the face amount of the debt (its fixed price) at the maturity of the bond (the expiration date of the contract). Since many financial instruments have characteristics similar to those of put and call options, a detailed knowledge of put and call options may be helpful in understanding these other contracts, and vice versa.

* * *

How an Option Differs From Similar Investments

Buyers exercise their options only if it is in their economic interest to do so. Unlike investors in other securities, investors in call options do not have to buy the shares, and investors in put options do not have to sell the shares of the underlying common stocks on which they hold these options. On expiration of the contract, call options are exercised only if the price of the underlying stock is above the striking price; put options are exercised only if the price of the underlying stock is below the striking price. Buyers of options may find it in their interest to exercise prior to the expiration of the contract.

An option contract is similar to an insurance policy. The asset being insured is the underlying common stock. Investors insure against possible loss in return on the holdings of common stock by buying put options on their stock; a put option with the same exercise price as the current stock price insures against a decline in the stock price for the term of the put option. Loss, like a fully deductible insurance policy, is limited to the premium paid for the put option; on a fall in price the investor puts the stock to the put seller, the insurer, and receives the exercise price in return. Naturally, if the stock increases in price, the put is not exercised; the insurance is not used. * * * As an insurance policy on a home insures against the loss from a fire, holding put options on common stock insures against the loss from a drop in the price of the stock. Using options, investors can sell off part of the risk—insure part of the risk of common stock investments. The sellers of options, like insurers generally, expect that the option premiums will cover the costs of the insurance they sell to the buyers of the options.   If actuarially fair, neither the buyer nor the seller expects to earn an above-normal rate of return at the expense of the other side of the trade.

Although options are similar to insurance contracts, options have been confused with futures contracts and with forward contracts.   The confusion arises because the terms are similar.   Several concepts used in the marketing of futures contracts were adopted by the CBOE * for use in the trading of options.   Buyers of futures contracts for July wheat have bought the July wheat, although they will not take delivery until July.   The buyer of a forward contract for delivery of an asset in July—such as a house—has bought the asset.   The futures contract is marked to market, settled for cash each day, whereas the forward contract will change in value with changes in the value of the asset. Buyers of options for July IBM, in contrast, have not bought IBM, but only the right to buy IBM at a fixed price.

* * *

Since buyers match sellers and no new money is raised by corporations, [future and option] contracts have been compared to side bets and to gambling, contracts without an economic purpose.   Futures and options both have economic purposes; they help investors with portfolio planning, thereby facilitating the functioning of the primary and secondary markets in the commodities or securities.

* * *

ATTRACTIVE FEATURES

Reduction of Risk in Investment Portfolios

The attractive characteristics of options become evident when options are combined with other securities.   Combining options with other securities transforms the returns and risks of an option into the returns and risks of an investment strategy: options combined with other investments to produce patterns of returns for a portfolio of investments.   There are several important ways to limit the risk of investing in securities.   Diversification is one of the main ways to limit the risk of holding securities.   The larger the number of assets held in a portfolio, the smaller will be an investor's exposure to the risks of any one of the securities within the portfolio; the risk of the portfolio approaches the risk of the market portfolio.   Another approach to limiting the risk of holding securities is to invest a percentage of the assets in bonds.   By holding a larger fraction of the portfolio in bonds or money market funds, the investor unlevers the portfolio.   The percentage changes in the value of the total portfolio will be less than the percentage changes in the value of the risky securities.

With options, investors can limit risk by insuring against adverse changes in the prices of their holdings of securities, or against adverse changes in the value of a portfolio of assets.   Options provide patterns

* Chicago Board of Option Exchange
[Ed.].

of returns that cannot be duplicated at reasonable cost by combining securities in various ways to try to produce the same result.

Increased Efficiency of Securities Market

Options trading has made the market for securities more efficient. In an efficient market, the prices of securities adjust quickly to changes in the economic prospects of the firm and the economy. Investors who want to adjust their holdings of securities have the protection of a competitive market; they expect neither to buy nor to sell at too high or too low a price. When equilibrium values of a security change, its price should be allowed to move immediately to the new equilibrium value. If not, investors trading in the interim will lose money to more knowledgeable investors.

Increased Liquidity of Secondary Market

One impediment to the operation of a well-functioning securities market is the limited ability of specialists and other market makers to buy or to sell large blocks of stock because of limited capital and the strictures on market makers obtaining participations in the block by outside investors. Market makers can reduce the risk of their holdings by selling options: The buyers of options assume some of the risk; they participate in the trade. This increases the liquidity of the secondary market for securities by providing the market maker with some depth needed to make better trading markets. Option trading may reduce the price variability in the secondary market and may allow investors to obtain better execution prices on their trades.

Lower Costs of Short-Selling

Many investors evaluate the prospects of firms and act on these evaluations. This process is one way in which security prices reflect the value of information. Although investors acting on information profit from this trading, the profits are not large given the costs of the trade and of gathering the information. Moreover, other investors discover the same information at about the same time; therefore, competition forces the price to the new equilibrium value. Unfortunately, it is more difficult to act on unfavorable information than on favorable information; investors must abide by the short-selling rules of the various exchanges. Short-selling rules impose costs on investors. Investors must wait for an increase in the price of the stock before making a short sale, and they do not earn full interest on the proceeds of short sales. Selling call options is one method of doing what amounts to borrowing shares for short sales without these costs.

Use as Investment Insurance

Put options as insurance. A put option is like a term insurance policy in which the term or maturity is the length of time between the purchase of the put and its expiration date; the item being insured is the value of the underlying stock. The face value of the policy, or the maximum claim that is paid in the event that the underlying stock becomes worthless, is equal to the number of shares specified in the contract times the exercise price. For partial losses, the amount received is equal to the number of shares times the difference between the exercise price and the market price of the underlying security at the time that the put is exercised.

Moreover, depending upon the relation between the striking price and the price of the underlying stock when the put is purchased, the put option will have features quite similar to an insurance policy with a deductible amount. If investors own 100 shares of stock with a market value of $100 per share, and if they buy a put with a striking price of $100, they insure totally against any decline in the price of the stock during the life of the option. If, however, investors buy instead a put on the stock with an exercise price of $90 per share, they are not insured against the first 10 point decline (i.e., the first $1,000 in losses), although they are covered against any additional losses resulting from a decline below $90; therefore, the put has a $1,000 deductible. It is even possible to buy the insurance with a negative deductible: The investor purchases a put option with an exercise price of $110, thereby insuring against the event that the stock price does not appreciate by at least 10 percent. Unlike traditional insurance, however, the investor can buy the insurance without owning the asset.

Call options as insurance. Call options are also akin to insurance policies. Consider the following investment strategy: (1) Buy one share of a non-dividend-paying security; (2) take out a term discount loan promising to pay $E, the striking price, at the maturity of the option, T months in the future. The loan, if prepaid, is prepayable at face value; (3) buy a put option on one share of the stock with a striking price of $E and an expiration date T months in the future. If, at the end of T months, the stock were selling for $S per share, the value of the position would be as follows. If S were less than E, the put would be exercised, the stock delivered, for $E. The face amount of the loan, $E, however, must be repaid. The net value of the position is zero. On the other hand, if S were greater than E, the put would expire, the stock would be sold for $S, and the loan repaid from the sale of the stock. The net value of the position would be $(S − E). In abbreviated form, the payoff to the net value of the position is the $MAX [0, S − E].

Suppose the investment strategy consisted of buying a call option on one share of the stock with an exercise price of $E and an expiration date T months in the future. If, at the end of T months, the stock were selling for $S per share, with S less than E, the call would expire unexercised; the value of the position would be zero. If S, however, were larger than E, the call would be exercised, paying $E for the stock, selling the stock for $S; the value of the position would be $(S − E). In abbreviated form, the payoff to the net position is the $MAX [0, S − E].

Since the payoffs to both strategies are the same for every possible price of the underlying security at the maturity of the contracts, the two are functionally equivalent: Call options are equivalent to a long position in the underlying security levered by a term loan with a face value of $E plus an insurance policy against declines in the stock price below $E per share. While the leverage component of a call option is its most commonly known characteristic, the insurance characteristic distinguishes call-option strategies from simple stock strategies such as buying stocks on margin.

For two call options with the same maturity, the one with the higher striking price will have more leverage; also, it will have a larger insurance component. A call option on a volatile stock is more valuable than a call option on one that is less volatile; the source of this greater value is the insurance component.

Conversion strategies. Strictly speaking, this exact relation holds for put and call options that can be exercised at maturity only. With the right to exercise early, puts have greater value than implied by the above parity theorem. Many brokers use these relations to convert puts into calls and to convert calls into puts. To convert puts into calls, they buy the security, while selling a call option and buying a put option. To convert calls into puts, they sell the underlying security short, while buying a call option and selling a put option. These positions have low risk and will earn a return close to the short-term rate of interest.

Analyzing returns. The procedure of analyzing the payoffs on a strategy at the end can be used to analyze the functional characteristics of various option strategies. The naked option-writing strategy is simply a short sale of a call option. The characteristics of this strategy are equivalent to: (1) selling the stock short; (2) lending money on a term basis; and (3) insuring the buyer against declines in the stock below the exercise price. If the naked strategy is combined with buying 100 shares of the underlying security, the strategy is called a "fully covered option-writing strategy," a strategy used by many pension fund managers. The stock purchase offsets the implicit short sale of shares associated with the naked strategy; therefore, a fully covered writing strategy is functionally equivalent to lending money on a term basis and to issuing an insurance policy against declines in the stock below the exercise price. Moreover, as the fully covered writing strategy is applied to options with higher striking prices to stock price ratios, the insurance component becomes a larger component of the investment. On the other hand, if the options written in a fully covered strategy have striking prices well below the stock price, the essential characteristic of the strategy is to lend money with a small amount of insurance.

Consider investors who choose the option strategy of buying a call option and investing in low-risk, fixed income securities such as money market instruments. Depending on the amount allocated to the fixed income securities, the strategy will be functionally equivalent to a long position in the stock plus an insurance policy against declines in the stock; the strategy is similar to insuring a stock by buying put options on the stock. A strategy of buying call options and bonds can make option buying into a more and more conservative investment by buying more and more bonds relative to options.

Buying call options and bonds is similar to buying put options on stock, a conservative investment strategy. Writing call options against a stock investment is similar to selling insurance and to lending money, investing in bonds. Although this does not seem as conservative as buying options and bonds, the fully covered strategy is thought to be more conservative. Investors, however, should realize what they are doing when they use the fully covered strategy; namely, that they are doing something akin to selling a put option naked and escrowing the exercise payment in bonds. If the stock goes down, the investor will have the put premium and interest to offset part of the loss on the stock; if the stock goes up, the investor will have the put premium plus interest only. By using fully covered writing strategies, investors are selling insurance on securities.

* * *

GLOSSARY

actuarial value—Value of a contract computed using the probabilities and payoffs on an outcome.

AMEX—American Stock Exchange.

arbitrage—Buying an asset and selling another asset to make a sure profit.

Black-Scholes—Pricing model for options used by practitioners.

call option—Right to buy a security for a fixed price on or before a given date.

CBOE—Chicago Board Options Exchange; first options exchange formed in 1973.

clearing corporation—Guarantor and maker of all option contracts.

clearing margin—Money deposited by a clearing member with the clearing corporation.

clearing member—Broker allowed to deliver contracts to the clearing corporation.

exchange—Place to trade standardized contracts with set terms and conditions.

exercise value—Value of the option if it was to be exercised.

expiration cycle—Three-month trading cycle for a listed option.

expiration date—Last day on which the option can be exercised.

fully covered—Writing an option on stock held by the writer.

futures contract—Buying an asset today for delivery in the future.

hedging—Reducing risk by selling an asset similar to the one held.

insurance contract—Protects against a contingent event such as a fire.

interest rate—Rate subtracted from the reciprocal of the price of a pure discount government Treasury bill.

in-the-money call—Stock price is above the striking price of the option.

in-the-money put—Stock price is below the striking price of the option.

leverage—Borrowing money to buy an asset.

limit order—An order not to buy or not to sell unless possible at a set price or better.

listed call option—Right to buy 100 shares from clearing corporation in a set month and for a set price.

listed put option—Right to sell 100 shares to clearing corporation in a set month and for a set price.

market maker—An exchange member trading on its own account on the floor of the exchange.

market order—An order to trade at the current market price of the option.

naked option—Writing an option to deliver a security that is not owned.

open interest—Number of contracts held by option buyers on a security.

option buyer—One who has the right to exercise the option.

option writer—Person who sells the right of exercise to the buyer of the option.

out-of-the-money—For a call option, the stock price is below the striking price; for a put option, the stock price is above the striking price.

premium—Price paid for the option to the writer by the buyer.

put option—Right to sell a security for a fixed price on or before a given date.

spreading—Buying a call option and writing a call option on the same security but with a different expiration date or striking price.

striking price—Price at which the option can be exercised.

time value—Value of the option attributable to the discount loan.

underlying security—Common stock on which the option holder has the right to exercise the option.

volatility—A measure of the dispersion of the percentage price fluctuations in the price of the underlying security.

* * *

B. Determinants of Option Value

Having surveyed the institutional setting of option trading and the variety of investment strategies that can be pursued on an organized options exchange, we can turn to consideration of the factors that determine the value of an option. Bear in mind that our concern is *not* with the value of the option *on the expiration date*, because that value is obvious. If the value of the underlying security at maturity is less than the exercise price, then the option is worthless. Certainly no one would pay for the privilege of buying a share of IBM for $70 when it is trading at $63. Alternatively, if the value of the underlying security at maturity is greater than the exercise price, then the value of the option is equal to the excess. Thus, at maturity the value of the right to purchase one share of IBM for $63 when it is trading at $70 per share, would be $7. The valuation problem is interesting only when the value of the underlying asset at expiration of the option is uncertain, and when time remains between the date on which valuation is attempted and the option's expiration. Valuing an option prior to maturity thus presents elements both of the time value of money and of uncertainty that have characterized the asset valuation problems examined in earlier chapters.

There are five fundamental determinants of option value:

(1) The value of the underlying security at the time the option is to be valued (the current value);

(2) The exercise price;

(3) The time value of money;

(4) The variability in the value of the underlying security; and

(5) The time remaining until the option expires.

1. Current Value

It should hardly be surprising that the value of an option increases with an increase in the value of the underlying security. Assume that the option can be exercised at any time before the expiration date.[4] Because the option holder can always exercise, if the price of the option is less than the amount by which the option's current value exceeds its exercise price—in the IBM example above, for example, if the price of the option were less than $7—arbitrageurs will buy the option, exercise it, and sell the underlying security, thereby earning a riskless return. The increase in demand for the option, in turn, will increase the option price until the discrepancy is eliminated. Therefore, so long as the current value exceeds the exercise price, the option value cannot be less than the excess. It follows that any further increase in the current value necessarily results in an increase in the option value.

This relationship is not limited, however, to situations in which the current value exceeds the exercise price. All other things equal, an increase in the current value will also result in an increase in the value of the option even if the current value is *less* than the exercise price. To see this, however, requires that we first consider the other determinants of option value.

2. Exercise Price

The impact of the exercise price on the value of the option is simply the other side of the current value relationship. What is critical is the difference between current value and exercise price. Just as an increase in current value affects this amount, so does a decrease in the exercise price.

3. Time Value of Money

One way of analyzing the purchase and ultimate exercise of an option is to treat it as the purchase of the underlying security at the exercise price using borrowed funds with repayment required on the exercise date.[5] Because there is no separately stated interest rate, the

---

[4] This point distinguishes an American from a European option, the latter being exercisable only on the expiration date.

[5] From an investor's perspective, owning an option is quite like owning the underlying security itself because one can sell the

exercise price necessarily includes not only payment for the underlying security, but also an interest component. To determine the "real" purchase price of the underlying security, the exercise price must be discounted to present value. In Chapter Two we learned that the longer the discount period and the higher the discount (interest) rate, the lower the present value. Thus, the longer the period until expiration, and the higher the prevailing interest rate, the lower the present value of the exercise price and, therefore, the greater the value of the option.[6]

4. Variability in Value

The most important determinant of the value of an option is the variability in value of the underlying security [7]: The *greater* the expected variability in the value of the underlying security, the greater the value of the option. At first glance, this relationship seems counter-intuitive. When the asset itself is being sold, an increase in variability—the measure of *risk* that an investor must be paid to bear in connection with real assets—results in a *decrease* in the price of the asset. But when an option on that asset is being sold, an increase in variability results in an *increase* in the price of the option. The logic underlying this relationship becomes clear when we consider the impact of an increase in variability on the relationship that we have already identified between the value of the underlying security and the value of an option to acquire the security—that option value increases with an increase in the value of the underlying security.

The two curves in the following figure represent the probability distribution of the future price of the stock of two companies, Stable Co. and Variable Co. The heavy black line represents the payoff to an option—the gain on exercise of the option and sale of the underlying security—at any share price.

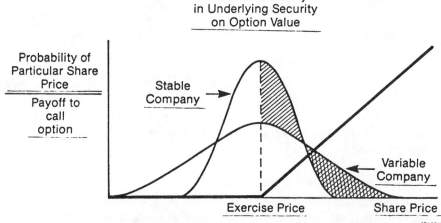

Effect of Variability in Underlying Security on Option Value

option just as one can sell the security. See R. Brealey & S. Myers, supra, at 434.

[6] Because the exercise price is paid only if the option is exercised, the effect of interest rates on the value of the option depends as well on the likelihood of exercise. The more likely an option is to be exercised, the greater the impact of a change in interest rate on its value. See M. Scholes, supra, at 34–6.

[7] J. Van Horne, *Financial Management and Policy* 84 (6th ed. 1983).

If both Stable Co. and Variable Co. stock sold at the same price, Stable Co. stock would be more attractive than Variable Co. stock because, despite equivalent mean prices, Variable Co. has greater risk—more upside potential and more downside potential. Because investors prefer less risk to more given equivalent return, they will prefer the stock of Stable Co. to that of Variable Co. Put differently, if there is more risk associated with Variable Co., investors will pay a lower price for its stock than for that of Stable Co.

Holding an option on the stock, rather than the stock itself, reverses this relationship. An increase in the risk of a security increases the upside potential and downside potential of a security equally. The effect of holding only an option, however, is to eliminate the impact of the increase in the downside potential. In the figure, the exercise price of an option on either company's stock is set at the mean value of the probability distribution of future values and the heavy black line traces the gain to the option holder depending on the price of the stock on the exercise date. Obviously there is no gain if the share price is below the exercise price; however, there is also no loss because, in that event, the option will not be exercised. As the share price exceeds the exercise price, the heavy black line rises at a 45 degree angle to reflect the fact that each $1 increase in the share price above the exercise price results in a $1 gain to the option holder.

The result is that, in valuing an option, the only portion of the probability distribution that matters is that to the right of the exercise price. Increasing the variability of the value of the underlying security shifts that portion of the distribution to the right, thereby increasing the probability of a higher stock price and, therefore, the gain to the option holder.

This result can also be seen from the figure. While the increased volatility of Variable Co. as compared to Stable Co. increases the likelihood of both high and low values for Variable Co. stock, the increase in the likelihood of a low value is irrelevant since, in that event, the option holder would not exercise; option value is bounded by zero. The increase in upside potential, however, *is* valuable to the option holder. Because the mean of the distributions of the two companies is identical, the areas to the right of the exercise price under both curves are also identical. However, if one calculated the mean of *just* those portions of the probability distributions to the right of the exercise price, the mean of the Variable Co. curve is greater by an amount that reflects the size of the striped area under the Stable Co. curve and the cross-hatched area under the Variable Co. curve. While both represent equivalent probabilities, the cross-hatched area is at a higher price than the striped. Thus, in the relevant range Variable Co. simply has a higher expected price than Stable Co., which results, as we saw in 1. above, in an increased value for the option. In short, an increase in upside potential, with no increase in the downside, increases the value of an asset and, thus, the value of an option on that asset.

This relationship between increased variability and option value yields an insight that will be of substantial value when we consider the relevance of the option perspective in non-traditional contexts. Suppose you are a major stockholder of Stable Co. and have to decide whether it will make a major acquisition. After studying the issue in the manner suggested in Chapter Four D, you conclude not to make the acquisition because the return associated with it is insufficient to compensate Stable Co. for the associated risk. Would your conclusion change if you held an option on Stable Co.'s stock rather than the stock itself? The point to keep in mind is that a change in risk has a very different impact on an option holder than it does on the holder of the underlying security. We will return to this point in Section C of this Chapter.

5. Time Remaining Until Expiration

While the discounting aspect of this determinant has already been considered, the time remaining until expiration, in conjunction with the variability in the value of the underlying security, affects option value in yet another way. The longer the period that remains before expiration, the more time there is for one of the more favorable results on the probability distribution curve to occur. Thus, for example, even if the current value of the underlying security is below the exercise price, so long as any part of the curve describing the distribution of future values of the underlying security is to the right of the exercise price, the option will have a positive value because some possibility exists that, at maturity, the underlying security will have a value greater than the exercise price. The longer the time remaining until expiration, the higher the option value because there is greater opportunity for a favorable result to occur.

C. Non-Traditional Applications

Understanding the factors which bear on the value of options can be of substantial value in understanding a far broader range of events than just how an option covering common stock should be priced. In fact, many common relationships can be recharacterized as involving the grant and receipt of an option. The value of doing so is that analysis of such "option" relationships in terms of the determinants of option value can provide insights into what factors bear on the value of the interests held by each party to the relationship and, as a result, the incentives each party faces. While the range of settings in which this approach can be useful is substantial, and will be a recurrent theme in later chapters, two examples will serve to illustrate its application: (1) the conflict between bondholders and stockholders; and (2) the conflict between management and stockholders.

1. An Option Perspective on the Conflict Between Debt and Equity

Assume that Company X has a capital structure made up of only debt and equity, and that the debt has a specified face value and is repayable on a specified date in a single lump sum. The value of the equity is then the Company's total value less the value of the debt. If the debt is not repaid on the required date, the Company will go into reorganization with the result that the holders of the equity will be eliminated and the holders of the debt will become the sole owners of the Company. Thus, the value of the debt on the repayment date will be its face value if it is repaid, or the value of the Company's assets if the debt is not repaid and its holders take over the Company. The issue now is what incentives are likely to influence the parties' behavior while the debt is outstanding.

This arrangement can be recharacterized as an option. The equity holders can be seen as having sold the assets of the Company to the debtholders in return for the face value of the debt, a management contract and, most importantly, a call option to repurchase the Company's assets for the repayment price of the debt (face value plus interest). On the date for repayment, the equity holders will "exercise their option" to repurchase the Company's assets if the value of the assets exceeds the repayment price. If the value of the assets is less than the repayment price, the equity holders presumably will not exercise their option, and will default on the debt.[8]

Given the recharacterization of the relationship between debtholders and equity holders as an option, what do the determinants of option value tell us about the incentives bearing on the behavior of both parties? In a static world, we would expect the debtholders to negotiate an interest rate that reflected their view of the risk of non-payment at the time the terms of the debt were negotiated. What would the equity holders then do? Because a major determinant of the value of an option is the variability in the future value of the assets subject to the option, the equity holders have an incentive to undertake projects which increase the risk associated with the value of the Company's assets. In other words, they would cause the Company to make *riskier* investments than it had before. Since all of the increased upside potential goes to the option holders, who do not share in the increase in risk, while all of the increased risk goes to the holders of the underlying asset, who do not share in the increase in upside potential, the effect of this change in investment policy is to increase the value of the equity holders' option at the expense of the value of the debt.[9]

The world is not static, however. The potential for such behavior would be anticipated by debt holders when the terms of the debt were negotiated, and they would demand an interest rate commensurate with the anticipated increase in risk. In turn, if the equity holders did not intend to alter the riskiness of the Company's investments, and therefore did not wish to pay an interest rate which reflected that possibility, they would seek to convince the debt holders of this by offering to enter into covenants prohibiting the Company from, for example, substantially altering its investment portfolio, incurring additional debt, or other actions that would increase the variability of the Company's income and, hence, the risk of default.[10] Analysis from the

---

[8] Black & Scholes, supra note 2.

[9] Put differently, the increase in risk acts to reduce the risk-adjusted interest rate of the debt. See Jackson & Kronman,

Secured Financing and Priorities Among Creditors, 88 Yale L.J. 1143 (1979).

[10] See Jensen & Meckling, *Theory of the Firm: Managerial Behavior, Agency Costs*

option perspective, by focusing on the importance of variability in the value of the underlying asset, highlights the incentives of the equity holders and, hence, the debt holders' need for protection, whether by contract or by a higher interest rate.[11]

The benefits to lawyers from developing facility with this form of option analysis are substantial. It is typically lawyers who are charged with devising the contractual constraints on opportunistic behavior by parties to a relationship. Understanding the determinants of option value provides a systematic method to identify the actions that should be prohibited.[12] Similarly, it is typically lawyers who bear responsibility for explaining why particular conduct has violated a fiduciary responsibility because of conflicts of interest. Option analysis can be quite helpful in understanding the incentives a fiduciary faces and the impact of actions taken on other parties. For example, a decision to increase dividends, typically an unreviewable business judgment of directors, may take on a different light where convertible debentures are outstanding. If by removing assets from the corporation the dividend reduces the value of the underlying security, the value of the option—the conversion right—also decreases.[13]

and Ownership Structure, 3 J.Fin.Econ. 305 (1976); Smith & Warner, *On Financial Contrasting: An Analysis of Bond Covenants,* 7 J.Fin.Econ. 117 (1979); Black, Miller & Posner, *An Approach to the Regulation of Bank Holding Companies,* 51 J.Bus. 379 (1978).

One response to this explanation for the presence of protective indenture provisions is that, so long as the bondholders were fairly compensated through a higher interest rate for opportunistic behavior by the equity holders, both would be indifferent as between a high interest rate loan that allowed opportunistic behavior, or a low interest rate loan that did not. In fact, however, the problem is not zero sum. Because an option holder can gain from increasing risk even if it is accomplished by causing the company to make negative present value investments—the option holder, it will be recalled, gets only the increase in the upside potential and is not penalized if the increase in the downside potential is even greater—prohibiting opportunistic behavior by the equity holders should increase the value to both.

[11] The same analysis is possible with respect to the conflict between preferred and common stockholders. See Gilson, *The Case Against Shark Repellent Amendments: Structural Limitations on the Enabling Concept,* 34 Stan.L.Rev. 774, 834 n. 228 (1982).

[12] See Ho & Singer, *Bond Indenture Provisions and the Risk of Corporate Debt,* 10 J.Fin. 375 (1982) (effort to model the effect of alternative bond indenture provisions on

allocation of risk among claimants); John & Kalay, *Costly Contracting and Optimal Payout Constraints,* 37 J.Fin. 457 (1982) (development of most effective forms of constraint); Kalay, *Stock-Bondholder Conflict and Dividend Constraints,* 10 J.Fin. 211 (1982) (evaluation of American Bar Foundation, Commentaries on Indentures (1971)).

While a large part of such protective provisions are treated as boilerplate, opportunity for innovation remains. For example, high interest rate securities typically have provisions limiting the extent to which they can be refinanced in order to assure their holders of receipt of high expected returns for the negotiated period. Franklin Life Insurance Co. v. Commonwealth Edison Co., 451 F.Supp. 602 (S.D.Ill. 1978), affirmed *per curiam* 598 F.2d 1109 (7th Cir.), cert. denied 444 U.S. 900 (1979), and Morgan Stanley & Co., Inc. v. Archer Daniels Midland Co., 570 F.Supp. 1529 (S.D.N.Y.1983), held that high interest rate securities—preferred stock in *Franklin Life* and bonds in *Morgan Stanley*—could be refinanced by the issuer more promptly after a drop in interest rates than the language in the preferred stock contract and bond indenture suggested. Moreover, the drop in the market price of the preferred following announcement of the redemption in *Franklin Life* strongly suggests that the market had not anticipated that such refinancing was allowable.

[13] See, e.g., Harff v. Kerkorian, 347 A.2d 133 (Del.1975).

2. An Option Perspective on the Conflict Between Stockholders and Management

Although more complicated, an option perspective can also be useful in examining the conflict between management and stockholders. It has become common place to recognize that management and shareholders may have different incentives with respect to firm decisions. Stockholders desire profit maximization. Managers, however, desire that combination of salary, perquisites—like luxurious offices—and profit maximization that yields *them* the most value.[14] The analysis need go no further to see that, absent corrective forces, management will engage in less profit maximization than the stockholders would prefer. A typical response to this divergence is to offer management stock options on the theory that management's incentives will then be identical to the stockholders' so that management will choose the correct amount of profit maximization.

In light of the determinants of option value, would you expect the incentives of management holding stock options to be the same as the stockholders who, in effect, own the underlying security? Taken this far, management might well have an incentive to choose riskier investments than would the stockholders, because the stockholders bear all of the downside risk, but only share the upside potential with management.

How could this problem be solved? What would be the effect on managerial incentives if the grant of the stock options were coupled with a right on the part of the stockholders to repurchase the stock covered by the options (a put) at a price that denied management any increase in value resulting from post-grant increases in the risk associated with the company? In other words, what would be the effect of a contractual ceiling imposed on the value of the option? For an interesting effort at developing option packages which control the types of incentives discussed here, see Haugen & Senbet, *Resolving the Agency Problems of External Capital Through Options*, 36 J.Fin. 629 (1981). See also Diamond & Verrecchia, *Optimal Managerial Contracts and Equilibrium Security Prices*, 37 J.Fin. 275 (1982).

Keep in mind, however, that even when management holds only stock options, other incentives bear on their inclination to increase the riskiness of the company. For example, management will typically have a greater investment in the company through their human capital than through the value of their options. Thus, if a management decision to increase the riskiness of the company was perceived by the market for managers as evidence of incompetence, so that the value of management's human capital would decline as a result, an incentive toward conservatism is created that might offset the incentive toward risk preference resulting from management's stock option holdings. See Fama, *Agency Problems in the Theory of the Firm*, 88 J.Pol.Econ. 288 (1980). Additionally, management typically will not hold a diversified portfolio if their human capital is taken into account. See Chapter

[14] E.g., Gilson, *A Structural Approach to Corporations: The Case Against Defensive* *Tactics in Tender Offers*, 33 Stan.L.Rev. 819, 835–36 (1981).

Nine C. 3. infra. As such, management may have an incentive, not held in common with the stockholders, to reduce the variability of the company's value so as to reduce the risk associated with their investment in human capital. While stockholders can diversify the risk that the company will go into bankruptcy and they will lose their capital, it may be that the principal way management can reduce the risk that their human capital will be depreciated through the company's bankruptcy is to decrease the variability of the company's income stream.

PART II. MOTIVATIONS FOR ACQUISITIONS

In this Part, we survey a number of explanations for why corporate acquisitions take place. From the perspective of the target company, of course, the explanation for why acquisitions take place is perfectly straightforward. Typically an acquirer offers to pay a premium above the market price for the target company. For target company shareholders, the gain from the transaction is measured by the size of the premium received.

For the acquiring company, however, the question is much more difficult. In order for the acquisition to produce a gain for acquiring company shareholders, the post-transaction value of the combined companies must increase by an amount in excess of the sum of the premium paid to target shareholders plus the transaction costs associated with the acquisition. The question, then, is from where might this increase in value come?

The common thread that joins our evaluation of each of the explanations for acquisitions considered in this Part is "the principle of value additivity."[1] It means simply that "if we have two streams of cashflow, A and B, then the present value of A + B is equal to the present value of A plus the present value of B."[2] Coupled with the concept of market efficiency, value additivity posits that the mere act of combining two corporations cannot result in a value for the combined entity greater than the sum of the pre-combination values of the separate entities. If a premium is paid to target company shareholders, then the principle of value additivity holds that the transaction results in no more than a wealth transfer from shareholders of the acquiring company to shareholders of the target company.

Each of the explanations for acquisitions we consider in this Part is an effort to identify circumstances in which the principle of value additivity does not hold—when 2 + 2 can equal 5 or more. The first two explanations examined—the manner of financial accounting for acquisitions in Chapter Eight and diversification in Chapter Nine—are financial in character. The idea is that firm value can be increased either by altering the manner in which financial information about the firm's economic performance is disclosed to the public, or by altering the ownership of the firm, without any alteration in the firm's real economic performance. Other purely financial explanations for acquisitions focus not on whether the value of the entire firm increases as a result of an acquisition, but on whether an acquisition can increase the value of some interests in the corporation even though at the expense of other interests. For example, acquisitions may benefit managers at the expense of shareholders, or shareholders at the expense of creditors.

---

[1] R. Brealey & S. Myers, *Principles of Corporate Finance* 128 (2nd ed. 1981).

[2] Id. at 353.

This type of explanation for acquisitions is also considered in Chapter Nine.

In contrast to these purely financial explanations for acquisitions, the remaining three explanations considered in this Part—displacement of inefficient management in Chapter Ten, synergy and strategy in Chapter Eleven, and the federal income tax treatment of acquisitions in Chapter Twelve—all contemplate an improvement in the firm's real economic performance either as a result of better management, more effective use of assets, or more favorable tax treatment.

Our approach will be the same in each Chapter, albeit with occasional digressions to explain the basic rules governing financial accounting for acquisitions and their federal tax treatment. First, the theory itself is explained: Why is it claimed that the principle of value additivity is overcome? Next, the theory is evaluated in light of what we learned about modern finance in Part I: Is it consistent with how financial economists believe the capital market works? Finally, the available empirical evidence is surveyed: Does the data support the theory in question?

Such intensive evaluation of the various explanations for why acquisitions take place is important for purposes of both public policy and private lawyering. Although public policy toward corporate acquisitions might also take into account noneconomic considerations such as the desirability of large concentrations of economic power in a democracy, a critical influence on that policy will be whether we believe corporate acquisitions result in better economic performance. If acquisitions motivated by some theories do hold out promise of economic gains, while those motivated by other theories do not, then the question is whether we can identify which are which and thereby improve upon present constraints on inefficient acquisitions. From the perspective of private lawyering, it is critical to understand how your client seeks to gain from an acquisition. Whatever his or her motivation, the structure of the transaction must be designed to facilitate it.

CHAPTER EIGHT. FINANCIAL STATEMENT ALCHEMY

Among the variety of motivations for acquisitions, the legal and accounting professions have paid the most attention to one based on how an acquisition is reflected in the acquiring company's financial statements. The logic of this theory of acquisitions, at least at first glance, is fairly straightforward. If the acquiring company has a choice of how to account for the transaction, it is hardly surprising that the company would choose the method that it perceives as most favorable. Nor is it surprising that, all other things being equal, the accounting method which produced the highest earnings per share would generally be perceived as most favorable. As we learned in Part I, the value of a company is determined by the size and certainty of its future earnings, and current earnings are an important source of information concerning future earnings. The higher the current earnings reported, the higher the future earnings anticipated by the market, and the higher the company's value. It would then follow that if freedom to choose the most desirable accounting method was constrained—the availability of the more favorable method limited to particular circumstances—transactions that could be reported by the more favorable method would be more attractive than those that could not, and would occur more frequently in both relative and absolute terms.

At second glance, however, evaluation of the logic of this theory of acquisitions is much more complicated. Suppose two transactions were of equal value except that one could be accounted for by a method that would report higher earnings for financial accounting purposes. Would a difference in accounting earnings, without a difference in the actual cash flows produced by the transactions, result in a difference in the value of the firm? This is the issue presented by the controversy over the appropriate method of accounting for corporate acquisitions. Two principal methods of accounting—purchase or pooling of income for complete acquisitions, and equity or cost for minority investments—are available and, depending on the circumstances, one method or the other can be accurately predicted to result in higher reported earnings. The rules governing the availability of each method have changed over time, but it remains the case that by carefully structuring the transaction, an acquiring company can choose, albeit at some cost, which accounting method will be required. Do such accounting choices have an effect on the value of the company? If so, then the standards that govern the choices have important public policy implications because they influence real economic activity. And the implications for private lawyering are even more apparent: A lawyer must understand and be able to manipulate the accounting rules in order to structure a transaction that meets the client's goal.

The terms of the debate concerning the proper method of accounting for acquisitions, and the conventional wisdom, assume that there is a relationship between how an acquisition is accounted for and the value of the company. In this view, to the extent lawyers or accountants cannot successfully manipulate the accounting rules, some acquisitions take place or do not take place depending on the rules governing the availability of a particular accounting method. This Chapter explores that assumption and, more generally, the relationship between financial accounting methods and firm value. It begins by examining the different methods of accounting for acquisitions and the rules governing their availability, and then considers the theory that links the choice of accounting method to firm value. The consistency of this theory with both the financial theory discussed in Part I and with the available empirical evidence is next considered. Finally, we turn to the insights that financial theory offers for how financial accounting standards should be set.

A. Financial Accounting for Acquisitions and Investments

1. Accounting for Complete Acquisitions: Purchase Versus Pooling

The conceptual debate over the relative merits of the purchase and pooling methods of accounting for a complete acquisition on the books of the acquiring company historically has taken the form of a search for a Platonic ideal. One ideal form of transaction occurs when a company simply buys an asset; principles of historical cost accounting require the asset to be recorded on the books of the acquiring company at cost. Asset value then serves as a repository of cost waiting to be charged (through depreciation or amortization) against the income the company earns from the asset. This is the core of the purchase method of accounting for acquisitions. The other ideal form of transaction was thought to occur when assets were acquired through a true "merger"— when two companies combined, or "pooled" their operations, but the shareholders remained the same. In this case, the argument goes, there is no occasion to alter the historical cost of either of the companies' assets. Because the task is to measure the economic performance of the same entities after the merger as before it, there is no reason to change the amounts charged against income to reflect the assets' cost. This is the core of the pooling method of accounting for acquisitions.

For transactional purposes, the problem was how to tell which ideal form a particular acquisition transaction most resembled. The principle actors in this process of line drawing were public accountants and, to a much lesser degree, lawyers, both of whom were understandably interested in facilitating their client's goals, so long as the result could be justified in the context of the traditional debate.

Lawyers will hardly be surprised at how this type of standard setting worked out: Each transaction could be seen as sufficiently like a previous transaction that the desired outcome always could be justified. The ultimate result was a general collapse of standards that finally culminated in both pooling and purchase being treated as alternative methods for accounting for the same transaction, with the choice resting in the virtually unlimited discretion of the acquiring company. This result led, in turn, to a response—the adoption in 1970 of Accounting Principles Board Opinion No. 16 by the American Institute of Certified Public Opinion, the then authoritative accounting standard setting body [1]—that substantially restricted the availability of the pooling of interests method.

The following describes the mechanics of both methods of accounting for complete acquisitions—in essence, the stakes of the debate—and then examines the terms in which the debate was carried out, and the substance of the resolution: the determinants of accounting method set forth in APB No. 16.

a. The Mechanics

S. DAVIDSON, C. STICKNEY & R. WEIL, FINANCIAL ACCOUNTING
477–87 (2d ed. 1979).[*]

CORPORATION ACQUISITIONS

Purchase Method—Central Concepts

The purchase method follows normal historical-cost accounting principles for recording acquisitions of assets and issuances of stock. Three particular principles are central to the purchase method.

First, assets acquired under historical costing are recorded at their cost. Cost is generally the amount of cash given in exchange for the asset acquired. If a firm acquires a building for $100,000, the entry is

Building	100,000	
Cash		100,000

Second, cost is measured by the fair market value of any noncash consideration given in exchange for an asset acquired. If a firm gives 5,000 shares of its $2-par-value common stock for a building and the common stock currently sells for $20 a share, the cash-equivalent value of the shares given is $100,000 (= 5,000 shares × $20 per share). The entry is

Building	100,000	
Common Stock—$2 Par Value		10,000
Additional Paid-in Capital		90,000

Building acquired for shares with current market value of $100,000.

Third, when more than one asset is acquired in a single transaction, the total cost must be allocated to each of the assets acquired according to their market value. * * *

---

[1] The process in which accounting standards are set is discussed in Section E. of this Chapter, infra.

[*] From FINANCIAL ACCOUNTING, Second Edition by Sidney Davidson, Clyde P. Stickney, and Roman L. Weil. Copyright © 1979 by The Dryden Press. Reprinted by permission of CBS College Publishing.

Assume the preceding transaction involved the acquisition of land with a market value of $25,000 and of a building with a market value of $75,000. The entry is

Land	25,000	
Building	75,000	
Common Stock—$2 Par Value		10,000
Additional Paid-in Capital		90,000

The purchase method may require two extensions of the historical-cost model. In most business combinations, the amount of the consideration given by the acquiring company exceeds the sum of the market values of the identifiable assets acquired. This excess generally represents items not shown in the balance sheet such as a good reputation with customers, a well-trained labor force, superior managerial talent, or the fruits of internal research and development efforts. The excess is caused by the failure in accounting to record all future benefits as assets and the requirement that assets be shown at cost, not current value. Under the purchase method, the excess of cost over the fair market value of the identifiable net assets acquired is called "goodwill."

Assume that the preceding transaction involved the acquisition of land with a market value of $25,000 and a building having a market value of $75,000, and that these were the only assets of the firm acquired. Now assume that 6,000 (rather than 5,000 as before) shares are required to persuade the previous owner to sell. The value of the shares given up is $120,000 (= 6,000 shares × $20 per share). The market value of the identifiable assets acquired is $100,000 (= $25,000 + $75,000). The goodwill is $20,000 (= $120,000 − $100,000). The entry would be

Land	25,000	
Building	75,000	
Goodwill	20,000	
Common Stock—$2 Par Value		12,000
Additional Paid-in Capital		108,000

$120,000 of shares given for a firm with assets having market value of $100,000.

The valuations assigned to the land and building by the purchaser are their current fair market values. The valuations shown on the books of the seller will rarely, if ever, reflect current fair market value. Thus, they are not useful for establishing the valuation on the books of the purchaser.

The second extension of the historical-cost model occurs when liabilities of an acquired company are assumed by the acquiring company. The liabilities assumed will be stated at the present value of the future cash payments at the date of acquisition. The payments are discounted at a *current* rate of interest appropriate for the risk of the borrowing company. This present value is the current market value of the liabilities. Assume in the preceding transaction that liabilities having a present value of $20,000 were assumed by the acquiring company but still 6,000 shares were given up. The entry would be

Land	25,000	
Building	75,000	
Goodwill	40,000	
Liabilities		20,000
Common Stock—$2 Par Value		12,000
Additional Paid-in Capital		108,000

$120,000 of shares given for a firm with assets having current value of $100,000 and liabilities having current value of $20,000.

These three central components of the purchase method are summarized as follows:

1 Consistent with the historical-cost model, assets acquired are recorded at their cost on the acquisition date.

2 Cost is equal to the amount of cash given plus the market value of any noncash consideration exchanged.

3 The aggregate acquisition cost amount is allocated to all identifiable assets acquired (less liabilities assumed) based on the fair market values of each. Any excess of acquisition cost over the market values of the identifiable net assets acquired is considered goodwill.[6]

Example—Merger

To illustrate the application of the purchase method, consider the balance sheet amounts for P Company and S Company shown in Exhibit 12.4.*

P Company and S Company have agreed to merge. P Company will give 40,000 shares of its $5 par-value common stock for all of the outstanding common shares of S Company. The S Company shares will then be canceled and S Company will be legally dissolved. The current market price of P Company stock is $20 per share. The market value of the shares given is $800,000 (= 40,000 shares × $20 per share). Company P makes the following entry to record the acquisition of the S Company shares:

Current Assets	250,000	
Fixed Assets—Net	600,000	
Patent	50,000	
Goodwill	70,000	
Current Liabilities		80,000
Long-Term Liabilities		90,000
Common Stock—$5 Par Value		200,000
Additional Paid-in Capital		600,000

[6] In cases where the market value of the consideration given is less than the market values of net identifiable assets acquired, Accounting Principles Board *Opinion No. 16* (1970) provides that the "values otherwise assignable to noncurrent assets acquired (except long-term investments in marketable securities) should be reduced by a proportionate part of the excess to determine assigned values." [This subject is considered in greater detail in Section A. 1.c. of this Chapter, infra. Ed.]

* In this discussion, the acquiring corporation is referred to as "P" and the acquired corporation as "S". [Ed.]

Exhibit 12.5 shows the effects of recording the merger on the books of P Company. Note the following aspects of the purchase method:

1. All assets are recorded on P Company's books at their cost. P Company gave consideration for the patent and goodwill and these assets are therefore recorded, even though they did not appear on the records of S Company. (Recall that costs incurred for internally developed patents are expensed.)

2. The book value of P Company, after the merger, exceeds the sum of the book values of P Company and S Company before the merger. This is caused by the fact that the recorded assets and liabilities of S Company were restated to current market values and the patent and goodwill were recognized.

3. The goodwill arising from a purchase is a long-lived asset, and generally accepted accounting principles require that this asset be amortized over a period of no more than 40 years.[7] * * * If less than 100 percent of the subsidiary's stock is acquired, the goodwill recognized is calculated as the acquisition price minus the product of the fraction of the outstanding stock acquired times the fair market value of the net assets.

Exhibit 12.4

Illustration Data for P Company and S Company

Assets	P Company Book Value	S Company Book Value	S Company Market Value
Current Assets [a]	$ 500,000	$200,000	$250,000
Property, Plant, and Equipment (net) [a]	2,000,000	500,000	600,000
Patent	0	0	50,000
Total Assets	$2,500,000	$700,000	
Equities			
Current Liabilities [a]	$ 300,000	$ 80,000	$ 80,000
Long-Term Liabilities	400,000	100,000	90,000
Common Stock—$5 Par Value	1,000,000	100,000	—
Additional Paid-in Capital . .	200,000	200,000	—
Retained Earnings	600,000	220,000	—
Total Equities	$2,500,000	$700,000	

---

[a] Individual assets and liabilities have been aggregated to simplify the illustration.

[7] *APB Opinion No. 17,* 1970.

Exhibit 12.5

Effects on P Company's Books of Recording the Merger of S Company Under the Purchase Method

		Acquisition and Merger		
Assets	**Before Merger**	**Debit**	**Credit**	**After Merger**
Current Assets	$ 500,000	$250,000		$ 750,000
Fixed Assets (net)	2,000,000	600,000		2,600,000
Patent	0	50,000		50,000
Goodwill	0	70,000		70,000
Total Assets	$2,500,000			$3,470,000
Equities				
Current Liabilities	$ 300,000		$ 80,000	$ 380,000
Long-Term Liabilities	400,000		90,000	490,000
Common Stock—$5 Par Value	1,000,000		200,000	1,200,000
Additional Paid-in Capital	200,000		600,000	800,000
Retained Earnings	600,000			600,000
Total Adjustments		$970,000	$970,000	
Total Equities	$2,500,000			$3,470,000

Pooling of Interests—Central Concepts

The key elements of the pooling concept are as follows:

In a pooling of interests, the *form* in which the entities conduct their operations has changed (that is, a new combined firm replaces the previously separate firms) but the *substance* has not—each business entity has the same assets and liabilities and carries out the same business activities as before.

* * *

Since no acquisition has taken place, no new basis of accounting arises. The book values of the assets and liabilities of the former companies are carried over to the new combined company.

* * *

The pooling-of-interests concept is somewhat unusual in accounting because current market values are ignored in the accounting for a negotiated trade.

* * *

Illustration of the Pooling-of-Interests Method

The balance sheet data for S Company and P Company, as presented in Exhibit 12.4, will be used to illustrate the pooling-of-interests method.

Gilson Corp.Acquisitions UCB—11

P Company exchanges 40,000 shares of its common stock for all of the outstanding common shares of S Company. The S Company shares will then be canceled and S Company will be legally dissolved. The current market price of the P Company is $20. The entry to record the acquisition of the S Company shares is

Current Assets	200,000	
Fixed Assets (Net)	500,000	
Current Liabilities		80,000
Long-Term Liabilities		100,000
Common Stock—$5 Par Value		200,000
Additional Paid-in Capital		100,000
Retained Earnings		220,000

Exhibit 12.7

Effects on P Company's Books of Recording the Merger of S Company Under the Pooling-of-Interests Method

	Combination and Merger			
	Before			After
Assets	Merger	Debit	Credit	Merger
Current Assets	$ 500,000	$200,000		$ 700,000
Fixed Assets (net)	2,000,000	500,000		2,500,000
Total Assets	$2,500,000			$3,200,000
Equities				
Current Liabilities	$ 300,000		$ 80,000	$ 380,000
Long-Term Liabilities	400,000		100,000	500,000
Common Stock—$5 Par Value	1,000,000		200,000	1,200,000
Additional Paid-in Capital	200,000		100,000	300,000
Retained Earnings	600,000		220,000	820,000
Total Adjustments		$700,000	$700,000	
Total Equities	$2,500,000			$3,200,000

Exhibit 12.8

Illustration of the Effects of the Purchase and Pooling-of-Interests Methods on Net Income

	Before Combination		Combined Operations After Merger	
	P Company	S Company	Purchase	Pooling of Interests
Sales	$2,000,000 +	$400,000 =	$2,400,000	$2,400,000
Cost of Goods Sold	(1,200,000) +	(200,000) =	(1,400,000)	(1,400,000)
Selling and Administrative Expenses	(300,000) +	(50,000) =	(350,000)	(350,000)
Additional Cost of Goods Sold			(50,000)	—
Additional Depreciation Expense ($100,000/10 years)			(10,000)	—
Patent Amortization Expense ($50,000/10 years)			(5,000)	—
Goodwill Amortization Expense ($70,000/40 years)			(1,750)	—
Net Income Before Taxes	$ 500,000	$150,000	$ 583,250	$ 650,000
Income Taxes at 40 Percent	(200,000)	(60,000)	(260,000)*	(260,000)
Net Income	$ 300,000	$ 90,000	$ 323,250	$ 390,000
Total Assets on Merger Date			$3,470,000	$3,200,000
All Capital Earnings Rate (Based on Totals on Merger Date)			9.3%	12.2%
Total Owners' Equity (Based on Merger Date)			$2,600,000	$2,320,000
Rate of Return on Owners' Equity (Based on Merger Date)			12.4%	16.8%

* The choice of pooling or purchase accounting will not normally affect income for tax purposes; hence taxes are the same under either method. [Ed.]

From the standpoint of the combined firm, the shares of P Company merely replace the shares of S Company. S Company contributed capital is shown on its books at $300,000 (= $100,000 + $200,000). The shares issued by P Company are stated at this amount. The $300,000 is allocated to common stock and additional paid-in capital of P Company based on the par value of the shares issued. (That is, 40,000 shares × $5 par value = $200,000. This amount is allocated to common stock at par value. The remainder is allocated to Additional Paid-in Capital.)

Exhibit 12.7 shows the effects of recording the merger on the books of P Company. Note the following aspects of the pooling-of-interests method:

> 1.   The amounts for the individual assets and liabilities after the merger are merely the sum of the amounts for each firm before the merger.

2. The total contributed capital after the merger ($1,200,000 + $300,000) is equal to the sum of the contributed capital accounts of the two companies before the merger.

3. Retained earnings after the merger is the sum of the retained earnings of the two firms before the merger.

Effect of Purchase and Pooling of Interests on Net Income

The asset amounts recorded under the purchase method in Exhibit 12.5 exceed the corresponding amounts under the pooling-of-interests method in Exhibit 12.7. Such an excess usually occurs. The market values of assets acquired usually exceed their book values. What are the effects of these two methods of recording the business combination on net income of subsequent years?

Net income under the purchase method will be lower than under pooling. The higher amounts for inventory, buildings, and equipment recorded in a purchase lead to larger amounts for cost of goods sold and depreciation. In addition, any previously unrecorded assets that are recognized in a purchase, such as patents and goodwill, must be amortized. The extra amortization expense after a purchase lowers the income as compared to that after a pooling.

To illustrate the effects of these methods on net income subsequent to the combination, assume that the $50,000 excess of market value over book value of S Company's current assets is attributable to an undervaluation of inventory. A FIFO cost-flow assumption is made. The fixed assets and patents have a 10-year life remaining on the date of the combination. The goodwill is to be amortized over 40 years, the longest period allowed in generally accepted accounting principles.[10] The straight-line method of depreciation (for fixed assets) and amortization (for patents) is to be used.

Exhibit 12.8 shows the calculation of net income for the first year after the merger assuming that the levels of income for the two firms before the merger are maintained afterwards. We assume that there are no savings in operating costs as a result of merging the two firms.

The pretax net income under the pooling method of $650,000 is higher than under the purchase method, since the additional cost of goods sold, depreciation, and amortization expense are not recognized after a pooling. Coupling this higher net income with the lower book value of assets and owners' equity under pooling leads to significant differences in the rates of return on both assets and owners' equity.

* * *

Pooling of interests not only keeps reported income from decreasing after the merger, it may also allow management of the pooled companies to manage the reported earnings in an arbitrary way. Suppose, as has happened, that Company P merges with an old, established firm, Company F, which has produced commercial movie films. These films were made in the 1940s and 1950s and were amortized so that by 1970 the book value of these films is zero or close

[10] *APB Opinion No. 17,* 1970.

to zero. But the market value of the films is much larger than zero, because television stations find that old movies please their audiences. If Company P purchases Company F, then the old films will be shown on the consolidated balance sheet at the films' current fair market value. If Company P merges with Company F using the pooling-of-interests method, the films will be shown on the consolidated balance sheet at their near-zero book values. Then, when Company P wants to bolster reported earnings for the year, all it need do is sell some old movies to a television network, and a handsome gain can be reported. Actually, of course, the owners of Company F enjoyed this gain when their stock was "sold to" (or exchanged with) Company P for current asset values, not the obsolete book values.

* * *

---

b.   Determinants of Choice of Method

The debate leading up to the adoption of APB No. 16 was quite lengthy and controversial. As early as 1963, Wyatt, *Accounting Research Study No. 5: A Critical Study of Accounting for Business Transactions* (1963), recommended eliminating or severely curtailing the availability of the pooling of interest method. Controversy continued, including testimony by an SEC official before a congressional committee that the SEC would act to establish accounting standards for business combinations unless the Accounting Principles Board (APB) acted. This led to an initial APB proposal that would have effectively prohibited pooling. In response to negative reaction from the business community, the direction of the regulatory effort shifted to setting stringent standards for when the pooling method would be available. This approach was equally controversial. An initial proposal to prohibit pooling if the acquiring firm was more than three times the size of the target was weakened to a 10:1 prohibition, and the size test was ultimately eliminated entirely when APB No. 16 was issued in August, 1970.[2]

APB Opinion No. 16

BUSINESS COMBINATIONS *

AUGUST, 1970

* * *

Appraisal of Accepted Methods of Accounting

15. The pooling of interests method of accounting is applied only to business combinations effected by an exchange of stock and not to those involving primarily cash, other assets, or liabilities. Applying the purchase method of accounting to business combinations effected by

---

[2] The events leading up to the adoption of APB No. 16 are summarized in Leftwich, *Evidence on the Impact of Mandatory Changes in Accounting Princi-* ples *on Corporate Loan Agreements*, 3 J.Acctng & Econ. 3, 15–16 (1981).

* Copyright © 1970 by the American Institute of Certified Public Accountants, Inc.

paying cash, distributing other assets, or incurring liabilities is not challenged. Thus, those business combinations effected primarily by an exchange of equity securities present a question of choice between the two accounting methods.

16. The significantly different results of applying the purchase and pooling of interests methods of accounting to a combination effected by an exchange of stock stem from distinct views of the nature of the transaction itself. Those who endorse the pooling of interests method believe that an exchange of stock to effect a business combination is in substance a transaction between the combining stockholder groups and does not involve the corporate entities. The transaction therefore neither requires nor justifies establishing a new basis of accountability for the assets of the combined corporation. Those who endorse the purchase method believe that the transaction is an issue of stock by a corporation for consideration received from those who become stockholders by the transaction. The consideration received is established by bargaining between independent parties, and the acquiring corporation accounts for the additional assets at their bargained—that is, current—values.

Purchase Method

17. The more important arguments expressing the advantages and disadvantages of the purchase method and some of the practical difficulties experienced in implementing it are summarized in paragraphs 18 to 26.

* * *

19. *A bargained transaction.* Proponents of purchase accounting hold that a business combination is a significant economic event which results from bargaining between independent parties. Each party bargains on the basis of his assessment of the current status and future prospects of each constituent as a separate enterprise and as a contributor to the proposed combined enterprise. The agreed terms of combination recognize primarily the bargained values and only secondarily the costs of assets and liabilities carried by the constituents. * * *

20. Accounting by the purchase method is essentially the same whether the business combination is effected by distributing assets, incurring liabilities, or issuing stock because issuing stock is considered an economic event as significant as distributing assets or incurring liabilities. A corporation must ascertain that the consideration it receives for stock issued is fair, just as it must ascertain that fair value is received for cash disbursed. Recipients of the stock similarly appraise the fairness of the transaction. Thus, a business combination is a bargained transaction regardless of the nature of the consideration.

21. *Reporting economic substance.* The purchase method adheres to traditional principles of accounting for the acquisition of assets. Those who support the purchase method of accounting for business combinations effected by issuing stock believe that an acquiring corporation accounts for the economic substance of the transaction by applying those principles and by recording:

a. All assets and liabilities which comprise the bargained cost of an acquired company, not merely those items previously shown in the financial statements of an acquired company.

b. The bargained costs of assets acquired less liabilities assumed, not the costs to a previous owner.

c. The fair value of the consideration received for stock issued, not the equity shown in the financial statements of an acquired company.

d. Retained earnings from its operations, not a fusion of its retained earnings and previous earnings of an acquired company.

e. Expenses and net income after an acquisition computed on the bargained cost of acquired assets less assumed liabilities, not on the costs to a previous owner.

22. *Defects attributed to purchase method.* Applying the purchase method to business combinations effected primarily by issuing stock may entail difficulties in measuring the cost of an acquired company if neither the fair value of the consideration given nor the fair value of the property acquired is clearly evident. Measuring fair values of assets acquired is complicated by the presence of intangible assets or other assets which do not have discernible market prices. Goodwill and other unidentifiable intangible assets are difficult to value directly, and measuring assets acquired for stock is easier if the fair value of the stock issued is determinable. The excess of the value of stock issued over the sum of the fair values of the tangible and identifiable intangible assets acquired less liabilities assumed indicates the value of acquired unidentified intangible assets (usually called goodwill).

23. However, the fair value of stock issued is not always objectively determinable. A market price may not be available for a newly issued security or for securities of a closely held corporation. Even an available quoted market price may not always be a reliable indicator of fair value of consideration received because the number of shares issued is relatively large, the market for the security is thin, the stock price is volatile, or other uncertainties influence the quoted price. Further, the determinable value of one security may not necessarily indicate the fair value of another similar, but not identical, security because their differences affect the value—for example, the absence of registration or an agreement which restricts a holder's ability to sell a security may significantly affect its value.

24. Those who oppose applying the purchase method to some or most business combinations effected by stock also challenge the theoretical merits of the method. They contend that the goodwill acquired is stated only by coincidence at the value which would be determined by direct valuation. The weakness is attributed not to measurement difficulties (direct valuation of goodwill is assumed) but to the basis underlying an exchange of shares of stock. Bargaining in that type of transaction is normally based on the market prices of the equity securities. Market prices of the securities exchanged are more likely to be influenced by anticipated earning capacities of the companies than

by evaluations of individual assets. The number of shares of stock issued in a business combination is thus influenced by values attributed to goodwill of the acquirer as well as goodwill of the acquired company. Since the terms are based on the market prices of both stocks exchanged, measuring the cost of an acquired company by the market price of the stock issued may result in recording acquired goodwill at more or less than its value determined directly.

25. A related argument is that the purchase method is improper accounting for a business combination in which a relatively large number of shares of stock is issued because it records the goodwill and fair values of only the acquired company. Critics of purchase accounting say that each group of stockholders of two publicly held and actively traded companies evaluates the other stock, and the exchange ratio for stock issued is often predicated on relative market values. The stockholders and management of each company evaluate the goodwill and fair values of the other. Purchase accounting is thus viewed as illogical because it records goodwill and values of only one side of the transaction. Those who support this view prefer that assets and liabilities of both companies be combined at existing recorded amounts, but if one side is to be stated at fair values, they believe that both sides should be recorded at fair values.

26. Criticism of the purchase method is directed not only to the theoretical and practical problems of measuring goodwill in combinations effected primarily by stock but also to accounting after the combination for goodwill recorded by the purchase method. Present accounting for goodwill, which often has an indeterminate useful life, is cited as an example of lack of uniformity because selecting among alternative methods of accounting is discretionary.

Pooling of Interests Method

27. The more important arguments expressing the advantages and disadvantages of the pooling of interests method and some of the practical difficulties experienced in implementing it are summarized in paragraphs 28 to 41.

28. *Validity of the concept.* Those who support the pooling of interests method believe that a business combination effected by issuing common stock is different from a purchase in that no corporate assets are disbursed to stockholders and the net assets of the issuing corporation are enlarged by the net assets of the corporation whose stockholders accept common stock of the combined corporation. There is no newly invested capital nor have owners withdrawn assets from the group since the stock of a corporation is not one of its assets. Accordingly, the net assets of the constituents remain intact but combined; the stockholder groups remain intact but combined. Aggregate income is not changed since the total resources are not changed. Consequently, the historical costs and earnings of the separate corporations are appropriately combined. In a business combination effected by exchanging stock, groups of stockholders combine their resources, talents, and risks to form a new entity to carry on in combination the previous

businesses and to continue their earnings streams. The sharing of risks by the constituent stockholder groups is an important element in a business combination effected by exchanging stock. By pooling equity interests, each group continues to maintain risk elements of its former investment and they mutually exchange risks and benefits.

* * *

30. Each stockholder group in a pooling of interests gives up its interests in assets formerly held but receives an interest in a portion of the assets formerly held in addition to an interest in the assets of the other. The clearest example of this type of combination is one in which both groups surrender their stock and receive in exchange stock of a new corporation. The fact that one of the corporations usually issues its stock in exchange for that of the other does not alter the substance of the transaction.

31. *Consistency with other concepts.* Proponents of pooling of interests accounting point out that the pooling concept was developed within the boundaries of the historical-cost system and is compatible with it. Accounting by the pooling of interests method for business combinations arranged through the issuance of common stock is based on existing accounting concepts and is not an occasion for revising historical costs. Both constitutents usually have elements of appreciation and of goodwill which are recognized and offset, at least to some extent, in setting a ratio of exchange of stock. The bargaining which occurs usually reflects the relative earning capacities (measured by historical-cost accounts) of the constituents and frequently recognizes the relative market values of the two stocks, which in turn reflect earning capacity, goodwill, or other values. Accounting recognizes the bargaining by means of the new number of shares outstanding distributed in accordance with the bargained ratio, which has a direct effect on earnings per share after the combination.

* * *

34. Some proponents of pooling of interests accounting support a restriction on the difference in size of combining interests because a significant sharing of risk cannot occur if one combining interest is minor or because a meaningful mutual exchange does not occur if the combination involves a relatively small number of shares. Most, however, believe that there is no conceptual basis for a size restriction and that establishing a size restriction would seriously impair pooling of interests accounting.

* * *

36. Indeed, many opponents of the pooling of interests method of accounting believe that effective criteria [distinguishing a pooling from a purchase] cannot be found. The concept of a uniting or fusing of stockholder groups on which pooling of interests accounting is based implies a broad application of the method because every combination effected by issuing stock rather than by disbursing cash or incurring debt is potentially a pooling of interests unless the combination significantly changes the relative equity interests. However, so broad an application without effective criteria results in applying the pooling of

interests method to numerous business combinations which are clearly in economic substance the acquisition of one company by another.

* * *

39.   The most serious defect attributed to pooling of interests accounting by those who oppose it is that it does not accurately reflect the economic substance of the business combination transaction.   They believe that the method ignores the bargaining which results in the combination by accounting only for the amounts previously shown in accounts of the combining companies.   The acquiring corporation does not record assets and values which usually influence the final terms of the combination agreement with consequent effects on subsequent balance sheets and income statements.   The combined earnings streams, which are said to continue after a pooling of interests, can continue unchanged only if the cost of the assets producing those earnings is identical for the acquiring corporation and the acquired company.   That coincidence rarely occurs because the bargaining is based on current values and not past costs.

* * *

Applicability of Accounting Methods

42.   The Board finds merit in both the purchase and pooling of interests methods of accounting for business combinations and accepts neither method to the exclusion of the other.   The arguments in favor of the purchase method of accounting are more persuasive if cash or other assets are distributed or liabilities are incurred to effect a conbination, but arguments in favor of the pooling of interests method of accounting are more persuasive if voting common stock is issued to effect a combination of common stock interests.   Therefore, the Board concludes that some business combinations should be accounted for by the purchase method and other combinations should be accounted for by the pooling of interests method.

43.   The Board also concludes that the two methods are not alternatives in accounting for the same business combination.

* * *

44.   The Board believes that accounting for business combinations will be improved significantly by specifying the circumstances in which each method should be applied and the procedures which should be followed in applying each method.   The distinctive conditions which require pooling of interests accounting are described in paragraphs 45 to 48. * * *

Conditions for Pooling of Interests Method

45.   The pooling of interests method of accounting is intended to present as a single interest two or more common stockholder interests which were previously independent and the combined rights and risks represented by those interests.   That method shows that stockholder groups neither withdraw nor invest assets but in effect exchange voting common stock in a ratio that determines their respective interests in the combined corporation.   Some business combinations have those features.   A business combination which meets *all* of the conditions

specified and explained in paragraphs 46 to 48 should be accounted for by the pooling of interests method. The conditions are classified by (1) attributes of the combining companies, (2) manner of combining interests, and (3) absence of planned transactions.

46. *Combining companies.* Certain attributes of combining companies indicate that independent ownership interests are combined in their entirety to continue previously separate operations. Combining virtually all of existing common stock interests avoids combining only selected assets, operations, or ownership interests, any of which is more akin to disposing of and acquiring interests than to sharing risks and rights. It also avoids combining interests that are already related by substantial intercorporate investments.

The two conditions in this paragraph define essential attributes of combining companies.

    a. Each of the combining companies is autonomous and has not been a subsidiary or division of another corporation within two years before the plan of combination is initiated.

A plan of combination is initiated on the earlier of (1) the date that the major terms of a plan, including the ratio of exchange of stock, are announced publicly or otherwise formally made known to the stockholders of any one of the combining companies or (2) the date that stockholders of a combining company are notified in writing of an exchange offer. Therefore, a plan of combination is often initiated even though consummation is subject to the approval of stockholders and others.

* * *

A wholly owned subsidiary company which distributes voting common stock of its parent corporation to effect the combination is also considered an autonomous company provided the parent corporation would have met all conditions in paragraphs 46 to 48 had the parent corporation issued its stock directly to effect the combination.

* * *

    b. Each of the combining companies is independent of the other combining companies.

This condition means that at the dates the plan of combination is initiated and consummated the combining companies hold as intercorporate investments no more than 10 percent in total of the outstanding voting common stock of any combining company.

* * *

47. *Combining of interests.* The combining of existing voting common stock interests by the exchange of stock is the essence of a business combination accounted for by the pooling of interests method. The separate stockholder interests lose their identities and all share mutually in the combined risks and rights. Exchanges of common stock that alter relative voting rights, that result in preferential claims to distributions of profits or assets for some common stockholder groups, or that leave significant minority interests in combining companies are incompatible with the idea of mutual sharing. Similarly, acquisitions of common stock for assets or debt, reacquisitions of outstanding stock

for the purpose of exchanging it in a business combination, and other transactions that reduce the common stock interests are contrary to the idea of combining existing stockholder interests. The seven conditions in this paragraph relate to the exchange to effect the combination.

> a. The combination is effected in a single transaction or is completed in accordance with a specific plan within one year after the plan is initiated.

Altering the terms of exchange of stock constitutes initiation of a new plan of combination unless earlier exchanges of stock are adjusted to the new terms.

A business combination completed in more than one year from the date the plan is initiated meets this condition if the delay is beyond the control of the combining companies because proceedings of a governmental authority or litigation prevent completing the combination.

> b. A corporation offers and issues only common stock with rights identical to those of the majority of its outstanding voting common stock in exchange for substantially all of the voting common stock interest of another company at the date the plan of combination is consummated.

The plan to issue voting common stock in exchange for voting common stock may include, within limits, provisions to distribute cash or other consideration for fractional shares, for shares held by dissenting stockholders, and the like but may not include a pro rata distribution of cash or other consideration.

Substantially all of the voting common stock means 90 percent or more for this condition. * * *

* * *

Condition 47–b relates to issuing common stock for the common stock interests in another company. Hence, a corporation issuing stock to effect the combination may assume the debt securities of the other company or may exchange substantially identical securities or voting common stock for other outstanding equity and debt securities of the other combining company. An issuing corporation may also distribute cash to holders of debt and equity securities that either are callable or redeemable and may retire those securities. * * *

A transfer of the net assets of a combining company to effect a business combination satisfies condition 47–b provided all net assets of the company at the date the plan is consummated are transferred in exchange for stock of the issuing corporation. However, the combining company may retain temporarily cash, receivables, or marketable securities to settle liabilities, contingencies, or items in dispute if the plan provides that the assets remaining after settlement are to be transferred to the corporation issuing the stock to effect the combination. Only voting common stock may be issued to effect the combination unless both voting common stock and other stock of the other combining company are outstanding at the date the plan is consummated. The combination may then be effected by issuing all voting common stock or by issuing voting common and other stock in the same proportions as the outstanding voting common and other stock of the other combining company. * * *

    c. None of the combining companies changes the equity interest of the voting common stock in contemplation of effecting the combination either within two years before the plan of combination is initiated or between the dates the combination is initiated and consummated; changes in contemplation of effecting the combination may include distributions to stockholders and additional issuances, exchanges, and retirements of securities.

Distributions to stockholders which are no greater than normal dividends are not changes for this conditions. Normality of dividends is determined in relation to earnings during the period and to the previous dividend policy and record. Dividend distributions on stock of a combining company that are equivalent to normal dividends on the stock to be issued in exchange in the combination are considered normal for this condition.

    d. Each of the combining companies reacquires shares of voting common stock only for purposes other than business combinations, and no company reacquires more than a normal number of shares between the dates the plan of combination is initiated and consummated.

Treasury stock acquired for purposes other than business combinations includes shares for stock option and compensation plans and other recurring distributions provided a systematic pattern of reacquisitions is established at least two years before the plan of combination is initiated. A systematic pattern of reacquisitions may be established for less than two years if it coincides with the adoption of a new stock option or compensation plan. The normal number of shares of voting common stock reacquired is determined by the pattern of reacquisitions of stock before the plan of combination is initiated.

Acquisitions by other combining companies of voting common stock of the issuing corporation after the date the plan of combination is initiated are essentially the same as if the issuing corporation reacquired its own common stock.

    e. The ratio of the interest of an individual common stockholder to those of other common stockholders in a combining company remains the same as a result of the exchange of stock to effect the combination.

This condition means that each individual common stockholder who exchanges his stock receives a voting common stock interest exactly in proportion to his relative voting common stock interest before the combination is effected. Thus no common stockholder is denied or surrenders his potential share of a voting common stock interest in a combined corporation.

    f. The voting rights to which the common stock ownership interests in the resulting combined corporation are entitled are exercisable by the stockholders; the stockholders are neither deprived of nor restricted in exercising those rights for a period.

This condition is not met, for example, if shares of common stock issued to effect the combination are transferred to a voting trust.

g.   The combination is resolved at the date the plan is consummated and no provisions of the plan relating to the issue of securities or other consideration are pending.

This condition means that (1) the combined corporation does not agree to contingently issue additional shares of stock or distribute other consideration at a later date to the former stockholders of a combining company or (2) the combined corporation does not issue or distribute to an escrow agent common stock or other consideration which is to be either transferred to common stockholders or returned to the corporation at the time the contingency is resolved.

An agreement may provide, however, that the number of shares of common stock issued to effect the combination may be revised for the later settlement of a contingency at a different amount than that recorded by a combining company.

48.   *Absence of planned transactions.*   Some transactions after a combination is consummated are inconsistent with the combining of entire existing interests of common stockholders.   Including those transactions in the negotiations and terms of the combination, either explicitly or by intent, counteracts the effect of combining stockholder interests.   The three conditions in this paragraph relate to certain future transactions.

a.   The combined corporation does not agree directly or indirectly to retire or reacquire all or part of the common stock issued to effect the combination.

b.   The combined corporation does not enter into other financial arrangements for the benefit of the former stockholders of a combining company, such as a guaranty of loans secured by stock issued in the combination, which in effect negates the exchange of equity securities.

c.   The combined corporation does not intend or plan to dispose of a significant part of the assets of the combining companies within two years after the combination other than disposals in the ordinary course of business of the formerly separate companies and to eliminate duplicate facilities or excess capacity.

Subsidiary Corporation

49.   Dissolution of a combining company is not a condition for applying the pooling of interests method of accounting for a business combination.   One or more combining companies may be subsidiaries of the issuing corporation after the combination is consummated if the other conditions are met.

*   *   *

Application of Purchase Method

*   *   *

Recording Assets Acquired and Liabilities Assumed

87. An acquiring corporation should allocate the cost of an acquired company to the assets acquired and liabilities assumed.

* * *

First, all identifiable assets acquired, either individually or by type, and liabilities assumed in a business combination, whether or not shown in the financial statements of the acquired company, should be assigned a portion of the cost of the acquired company, normally equal to their fair values at date of acquisition.

Second, the excess of the cost of the acquired company over the sum of the amounts assigned to identifiable assets acquired less liabilities assumed should be recorded as goodwill. The sum of the market or appraisal values of identifiable assets acquired less liabilities assumed may sometimes exceed the cost of the acquired company. If so, the values otherwise assignable to noncurrent assets acquired (except long-term investments in marketable securities) should be reduced by a proportionate part of the excess to determine the assigned values. A deferred credit for an excess of assigned value of identifiable assets over cost of an acquired company (sometimes called "negative goodwill") should not be recorded unless those assets are reduced to zero value.

Independent appraisals may be used as an aid in determining the fair values of some assets and liabilities. Subsequent sales of assets may also provide evidence of values. The effect of taxes may be a factor in assigning amounts to identifiable assets and liabilities.

* * *

Excess of Acquired Net Assets Over Cost

91. The value assigned to net assets acquired should not exceed the cost of an acquired company because the general presumption in historical-cost based accounting is that net assets acquired should be recorded at not more than cost. The total market or appraisal values of identifiable assets acquired less liabilities assumed in a few business combinations may exceed the cost of the acquired company. An excess over cost should be allocated to reduce proportionately the values assigned to noncurrent assets (except long-term investments in marketable securities) in determining their fair values (paragraph 87). If the allocation reduces the noncurrent assets to zero value, the remainder of the excess over cost should be classified as a deferred credit and should be amortized systematically to income over the period estimated to be benefited but not in excess of forty years. The method and period of amortization should be disclosed.

92. No part of the excess of acquired net assets over cost should be added directly to stockholders' equity at the date of acquisition.

* * *

> The Opinion entitled "Business Combinations" was adopt-
> ed by the assenting votes of twelve members of the Board.
> Messrs. Broeker, Burger, Davidson, Horngren, Seidman,
> and Weston dissented.

Messrs. Broeker, Burger, and Weston dissent to issuance of this Opinion because they believe that it is not a sound or logical solution of the problem of accounting for business combinations. They believe that, except for combinations of companies whose relative size is such as to indicate a significant sharing of ownership risks and benefits, business combinations represent the acquisition or purchase of one company by another and that accounting should reflect that fact. While they agree that the criteria specified in this Opinion for the pooling of interests method represent, in most cases, an improvement over present criteria in practice, this action does not, in their opinion, represent a substantive response by the Accounting Principles Board to the overall problem.

Messrs. Davidson, Horngren, and Seidman dissent to the Opinion because it seeks to patch up some of the abuses of pooling. The real abuse is pooling itself. On that, the only answer is to eliminate pooling. Paragraphs 35 to 41 set forth some of the defects of pooling. The fundamental one is that pooling ignores the asset values on which the parties have traded, and substitutes a wholly irrelevant figure—the amount on the seller's books. Such nonaccounting for bargained acquisition values permits the reporting of profits upon subsequent disposition of such assets when there really may be less profit or perhaps a loss. Had the assets been acquired from the seller for cash, the buyer's cost would be the amount of the cash. Acquisition for stock should make no difference. The accounting essence is the amount of consideration, not its nature. Payment in cash or stock can be a matter of form, not substance. Suppose the seller wants cash. The buyer can first sell stock and turn over the proceeds to the seller, or the seller can take stock and promptly sell the stock for cash.

The following deal with some arguments made in the Opinion for pooling: (1) Pooling is described in paragraph 28 as a fusion resulting from "pooling equity interests." But it is the sort of fusion where a significant exchange transaction takes place. The seller parts with control over its assets and operations. In return the buyer issues stock representing an interest in its assets and operations. That interest has value and is a measure of the cost of the acquisition to the buyer. (2) [The Opinion] declares that pooling is really a transaction among the stockholders. That just is not the fact. The buyer is always a company. (3) Paragraph 25 decries purchase accounting because it results in a write-up of only seller's assets. There is no write-up. There is only a recording of cost to the buyer. That cost is measured by the value of the assets acquired from the seller. (4) Pooling is said to avoid the difficulty of valuing assets or stock (paragraph 22). Difficulty of valuation should not be permitted to defeat fair presentation. Besides, the parties do determine values in their bargaining for the amount of stock to be issued.

Some say that to eliminate pooling will impete mergers. Mergers were prevalent before pooling, and will continue after. Accounting does not exist to aid or discourage mergers, but to account for them fairly. Elimination of pooling will remove the confusion that comes from the coexistence of pooling and purchase accounting. Above all, the elimination of pooling would remove an aberration in historical-cost accounting that permits an acquisition to be accounted for on the basis of the seller's cost rather than the buyer's cost of the assets obtained in a bargained exchange.

◆

Note. Is APB No. 16 Really a Constraint? The critical issue from the perspective of both public policy and private lawyering is whether APB No. 16 significantly constrains the use of the pooling of interest method. As was stressed in Section A of Chapter One, the requirements for the use of the pooling of interest method set forth in APB No. 16, whatever their purpose, also serve as an explicit road map for planners who want to structure their transaction so that it *can* be accounted for by the desired method. A constraint exists *only* if structuring the transaction to comply with the terms of APB No. 16 is costly. As an exercise, assume that you represent the acquiring company in a transaction that your client wants to account for by the pooling of interest method. Which of the requirements are merely formal and which impose significant compliance costs? [3] What if your client wants to account for the transaction by the purchase method? Is this choice costly? Your judgment about how serious an impediment APB No. 16 is to choice of accounting method should be compared to the Board's conclusion, in Paragraph 43, "that the two methods are not alternatives in accounting for the same business combination."

Some limited evidence exists with respect to this issue. Rayburn, *Another Look at the Impact of Accounting Principles Board Opinion No. 16—An Empirical Study,* 10 Mergers and Acquisitions 7 (Spring, 1975), reports that some 76 percent (832 out of 1,087) of the mergers between New York Stock Exchange listed companies occurring in the *pre*-APB No. 16 period between November 1968 and October 1969 were accounted for by the pooling of interest method while some 81 percent (567 of 703) of such mergers occurring in the *post*-APB No. 16 period between November 1971 and October 1972 were accounted for by that method.[4]

c. *Negative Goodwill in Purchase Accounting—The Preferred Accounting Method in a Down Market*

The controversy at which APB No. 16 was primarily directed—the ability of an acquiring corporation to increase its reported earnings by use of pooling of income accounting—was, in some respects, a product of its times. Only if the purchase price of the acquired company exceeds

---

[3] For example, how important is the prohibition in Paragraph 43-g of the use of an earn-out: an acquisition price that depends on the subsequent performance of the acquired business? One experienced practitioner has stated that this prohibition substantially reduced the frequency of use of earn-outs. J. Freund, *Anatomy of a Merg-er: Strategies and Techniques for Negotiating Corporate Acquisitions* 205 (1975). The value of this technique is examined in detail in Chapter Nineteen, infra.

[4] What is the relevance of the decrease in the total number of transactions in the post-APB No. 16 period?

its book value does the purchase method result in a reduction in earnings because of an increase in depreciation charges and the amortization of goodwill. During the late 1960's—the "go-go years" on Wall Street [5]—a rapidly rising stock market resulted in companies trading, and being acquired, at amounts substantially above book value. Therefore, APB No. 16, adopted in 1970, focuses on restricting the use of pooling because of fears of artificially inflated earnings. As more recent times have demonstrated, however, there is no guarantee of a stock market in which companies trade above book value. For example, in the transaction giving rise to Singer v. Magnavox,[6] a case which has received substantial attention for other reasons,[7] the book value of Magnavox's net assets exceeded the consideration paid by North American Phillips Corporation (NAPC) for the company by almost $22 million,[8] a condition that presented a strikingly different problem from that which gave rise to ABP No. 16. If the acquisition was accounted for by the pooling of interests method, the result would be straightforward. Magnavox's assets would be brought on to NAPC's books at the same value at which they were carried on Magnavox's books. But what if purchase accounting were used? Under this method, when the purchase price *exceeds* book value, the excess serves to increase the value of the assets acquired and, perhaps, create goodwill. This, in turn, serves to increase depreciation and amortization charges, and thus, *reduces* net income. In the Magnavox type of situation, however, there is a deficiency—book value exceeds the purchase price—rather than an excess, an amount sometimes referred to as "negative goodwill." What happens to this amount?

Paragraph 91 of APB 16 treats the problem essentially as the mirror image of the pooling problem and again requires a purchase type of treatment. The carrying values of noncurrent assets are reduced to their market value (which serves to reduce the deficit), and any remaining portion of the deficit is treated as a deferred credit that is amortized, in this case *added,* to income over an appropriate period. The income statement effect is to *increase* net income (as a result of reducing depreciation and amortizing the deferred credit) when compared to the result if pooling was used. In the Magnavox example, the net income of NAPC was increased by some $3.5 million, or 12.5%, by the use of purchase as compared to pooling accounting.

Thus, while pooling is the most favorable accounting method for the acquiring company in an up market, purchase accounting becomes more desirable when the market is down. The following discussion explores the potential for abuse of purchase accounting in the latter situation.

[5.] See J. Brooks, *The Go-Go Years* (1973).

[6] 380 A.2d 969 (Del.1977).

[7] See Chapter Fifteen B. infra.

[8] North American Phillips Corporation 1975 Annual Report, Notes to Consolidated Financial Statements, Note 2, Acquisitions.

BUSINESS COMBINATIONS REVISITED: A TEMPORARY DEFENSE OF THE STATUS QUO

By Philip L. Defliese *
35 Ohio State L.J. 393–94, 403–06 (1974).

HERE WE GO AGAIN!

Bowing to the demands of a small number of long-standing critics of the pooling-of-interests method of business combinations, the Financial Accounting Standards Board [FASB] has placed on its growing agenda the entire subject of business combinations for reconsideration. In addition to the requests stemming from conceptual disagreement, a considerable number of requests had also been received for clarification and interpretation of specific minor issues that had arisen in the area. Thus, the decision to reopen the subject was taken in lieu of handling these matters separately.

It is now more than three years since the Accounting Principles Board [APB] of the American Institute of Certified Public Accountants [AICPA] approved Opinion No. 16, *Business Combinations*, and No. 17, *Intangible Assets*. The issuance of these Opinions came after a two-year open struggle of unprecedented intensity. (At various times, lawsuits were even threatened by members of industry and Board members.)

* * *

It is well-known that Opinions 16 and 17 were derived from a single proposed opinion that could not gain the necessary two-thirds vote of the Board needed for approval, such was the diversity of views among the 18 members. Many members (including this writer) accepted Opinion No. 17 only because it was necessary for compromise, and because they believed that the effect upon business of the 40-year amortization requirement would be minimal (and, in many cases, avoidable, by carefully subscribing to the new pooling criteria). The drawbacks were a small price to pay for the overall gain, principally the restoration of pooling to its original posture.

* * *

THE PROBLEMS OF PURCHASE ACCOUNTING

Opinion 16 did away with the freedom to choose between the pooling method and the purchase method. In effect, the method is now dictated by the terms of the exchange. Any combination not meeting the strict criteria for a pooling must be recorded as a purchase. Of course, it is a simple matter to structure the combination as either, if both groups of shareholders are open-minded regarding the manner in which the merger or acquisition is to be effected. When stock is used in a purchase, however, and market values are high, the accounting

* Managing Partner, Coopers & Lybrand; Past Chairman of the Accounting Principles Board, presently serving as a member of the Advisory Council to the Financial Accounting Standards Board. Copyright 1974 by Coopers & Lybrand, reprinted with permission.

consequences of the purchase method are awesome, because of the required restatement of asset values of the acquired company to market value and the consequent amortization of goodwill. Under these conditions, pencils are sharpened if the pooling method is not available. In the final analysis, there is every reason to believe that the new rule has made for sounder mergers.*

When the purchase method is brought into play by the use of cash or debt, the costs (fair value) ascribed to the assets purchased are presumed to be readily measurable in the aggregate (the total purchase price), and there remains only the task of allocation. Most accountants agree that the excess of such aggregate value over the values ascribed to tangibles and specific intangibles is an indefinite intangible representing many factors—an excess commonly described as "goodwill." But when stock or assets instead of cash or debt are used in the purchase of an operating company, the determination of the purchase price or "cost" as used in accounting is not so easy. *   *   *

It is no secret that share values may bear little or no relation to the underlying asset values at certain times. In an exchange of stock for stock of two publicly traded stocks, the exchange rates are usually predicated on the relative market quotes (plus a "sweetener"). Using the market values of the shares issued as a basis of valuation, the accounting result can thus be horrendous under the purchase method. If the aggregate market value of the shares issued is less than the book value of the acquired company, a condition common in bear markets, the assets will be written down, producing an increase in earnings (from lower depreciation) that would not reflect economic reality. If the market value of the shares is *greater* than the book value acquired, a condition associated with bull markets, the resultant lower earnings (from increased depreciation and amortization of goodwill) would be equally misleading. In view of the fact that a bear market seems to be the order of the day, this consideration has immediate relevance.

At present, the stocks of many companies are being traded at values far below book value. A good example is American Airlines, which, at December 31, 1972, had a book value of about $21 per share. In December 1973, it was trading in the neighborhood of $8 per share. An aggressive and enterprising company could offer its shares at an exchange value of $10-11 per share (assuming CAB permission is granted) and effect a pooling. Under the purchase method, the net assets of American Airlines would have to be written down approximately 50 percent (about $290 million), and future earnings would be raised by a consequent reduction of about $25 million in depreciation. Thus, a losing company might suddenly become a profitable company! This is unrealistic from either an accounting or an economic standpoint. It should be apparent that depressed market values have no

* Note that this assumes the answer to the question with which we began this Chapter: Does a difference in financial ac- counting method, in the absence of a corresponding difference in cash flow, alter the value of a transaction? [Ed.]

relationship to the value of underlying assets; and the same is true of inflated market values.**

To further demonstrate the fallacy of the purchase method, some examples of poolings that took place during the bull market of the late sixties are given in the Appendix. These examples, involving mergers between publicly traded companies, show how the mergers would have been reflected under the purchase method and what they would look like if current stock values were used. The examples were specially selected because it is believed that they conform to the more important pooling criteria contained in Opinion 16—this was rare in the sixties. Thus, they represent exchanges of voting common stock for voting common stock of publicly traded companies at exchange ratios reflecting the relative stock values at the time, plus a small sweetener to induce stockholders to accept the offer.

In each case, it is clear that if the purchase method had been applied and market quotations used as the measurement of underlying asset value, there would have been a need to inflate both tangible and intangible assets by amounts ranging from $12 to $151 million. There is every indication that it would have been impossible to avoid ascribing large portions of these excess amounts to goodwill and amortizing them over a 40-year period in accordance with Opinion 17. The combination of such amortization and the increased depreciation on written-up tangibles would have depressed their earnings severely. If the shares that were originally issued are now valued on the basis of November 30, 1973, stock prices, these same assets would require adjustments ranging from a *deficiency* of $22 million (actual write-down from original book values) to an excess of only $45 million. Of course, this shows what a bear market can do to stock values, but, more to the point, it shows that the use of the purchase method coupled with stock market values that can fluctuate severely can be distorting.

Referring specifically to the first illustration in the Appendix, one can visualize the effect of applying market values in the application of the purchase method. The merger between Litton Industries and Stouffer Foods on March 31, 1967, was effected at a time when Litton common was selling at $104 per share, Stouffer was selling at $27 a share, and an exchange ratio of .312 of Litton for 1 of Stouffer was used. If purchase accounting had been applied, the net assets of Stouffer would have had to be written up by $66 million, or 218 percent. At November 30, 1973, Litton was selling for $9 per share (adjusted). While many subsequent factors may have a bearing on this depreciation in market value, it would appear that the Litton value in 1967 was inflated (as was Stouffer's) and that placing such a value on the Stouffer assets would have been unrealistic. When the market values of both constituents are inflated (as was the case in this illustration), pooling preserves some reasonableness in the accounting.

** How does this view compare to the Efficient Capital Market Hypothesis considered in Chapter Five? [Ed.]

Admittedly there is one major flaw in this exercise: It is doubtful that the mergers would have taken place if purchase accounting had been mandatory. "As if" research in accounting is always subject to this sort of consideration, especially since it is well known that management is unwilling to enter into a transaction if the accounting result proves unrealistic. *   *   *

APPENDIX

COMPARISON OF ACCOUNTING FOR BUSINESS COMBINATIONS ON POOLED BASIS,
PURCHASE BASIS AND NEW–ENTITY BASIS (NOTES 1 AND 2)

Issuing company Other combining company	LITTON INDUSTRIES, INC. STOUFFER FOODS CORP.		TELEDYNE, INC. RODNEY METALS, INC.	
Combination valuation due	March 31, 1967		December 1, 1967	
	No. of Common Shares Outstanding	Market Quotation Per Share	No. of Common Shares Outstanding	Market Quotation Per Share
At combination valuation date (Note 3):				
Issuing company	21,460,100	$104.25	8,470,000	$134.00
Other combining company	2,956,590	27.00	925,000	36.63
Shares to be issued in combination	922,456		290,000	
Exchange ratio	.312 for 1		.31351 for 1	
Issuing company's market quotation per common share at November 30, 1973 (Note 3)	$9.21		$24.78	

	In Dollars (000 omitted)	%	In Dollars (000 omitted)	%
Net assets acquired on pooled basis (Note 4):				
Issuing company	$402,500	93	$153,090	94
Other combining company	30,250	7	10,150	6
	$432,750	100	$163,240	100
If combination accounted for on a purchase basis, excess (deficiency) of cost over carrying basis of other combining company's net assets based on market quotations at (Note 3):				
Combination valuation date	$65,920	218	$28,710	283
November 30, 1973	(21,750)	(72)	(2,960)	(29)
Net change	($87,670)	(290)	($31,670)	(312)
If combination accounted for on a "new-entity" basis (Note 5), excess (deficiency) of cost over carrying basis of both constituents' net assets based on market quotations at (Note 3):				
Combination valuation date	$1,913,700	442	$1,011,190	619
November 30, 1973	(213,480)	(49)	54,400	33

	Aggregate (000 omitted)	Per Common Share	Aggregate (000 omitted)	Per Common Share
Net assets attributable to common equity (Note 6): pooled bases	$302,050	$13.49	$143,510	$16.38
Based on market quotations at combination valuation date (Note 3):				
Purchase basis	367,970	16.44	172,220	19.66
New-entity basis	2,215,750	98.99	1,154,700	131.82

(12/27/73)

NOTES:

1. Combinations represent (a) acquisitions involving common for common or common for net assets and business, and (b) constituents both publicly held.
2. Dollars approximated to the nearest ten-thousandths, except for per share amounts.
3. Market quotations represent (a) at combination valuation date, the closing sales price on the day preceding public announcement of the proposed combination or day approximating date of acquisition agreement, and (b) at November 30, 1973, the closing sales price adjusted for stock splits and stock dividends since date of combination.
4. Net assets acquired on pooled basis derived from pro forma financial data included in proxy statement relating to proposed combination.

APPENDIX

COMPARISON OF ACCOUNTING FOR BUSINESS COMBINATIONS ON POOLED BASIS,
PURCHASE BASIS AND NEW–ENTITY BASIS (NOTES 1 AND 2)

TRANSAMERICA CORP. TRANSINTERNATIONAL AIRLINES CORP. January 17, 1968		AMFAC, INC. FRED HARVEY March 15, 1968		FOREMOST-McKESSON, INC. "21" BRANDS, INC. September 2, 1969	
No. of Common Shares Outstanding	Market Quotation Per Share	No. of Common Shares Outstanding	Market Quotation Per Share	No. of Common Shares Outstanding	Market Quotation Per Share
23,643,663	$53.63	2,466,184	$39.62	11,033,412	$27.12
6,276,768	25.38	484,800	36.00	2,678,275	9.25
3,138,384		533,280		1,004,353	
1 for 2		1.1 for 1		.375 for 1	
$19.97		$28.88		$11.63	

In Dollars (000 omitted)	%	In Dollars (000 omitted)	%	In Dollars (000 omitted)	%
$565,470	97	$82,050	90	$190,990	94
17,250	3	9,170	10	13,120	6
$582,720	100	$91,220	100	$204,110	100
$151,050	876	$11,960	130	$14,120	108
45,440	263	6,230	68	(1,440)	(11)
($105,610)	(613)	($5,730)	(62)	($15,560)	(119)
$910,920	156	$27,630	30	$207,820	102
9,680	2	(4,610)	(5)	21,240	10

Aggregate (000 omitted)	Per Common Share	Aggregate (000 omitted)	Per Common Share	Aggregate (000 omitted)	Per Common Share
$525,270	$19.61	$91,220	$30.41	$118,700	$9.86
676,320	25.25	103,180	34.40	132,820	11.03
1,436,190	53.63	118,850	39.62	326,520	27.12

5. "New-entity" basis, as used here, refers to use of market quote of *each* constituent to a combination as the basis for asset revaluation of the respective constituents (not a generally accepted accounting principle), following the logic that if one constituent is so valued so should the other be. It should not be confused with a new-entity approach sometimes advocated, in which both sides revalue (to current value) all tangible and specific intangible assets, and goodwill is ignored.

6. "Net assets attributable to common equity" gives effect to involuntary liquidation value of preferred stock where applicable.

◆

d. The Status of the Controversy

As the Defliese article indicates, the adoption of APB No. 16 did not put an end to the controversy over the appropriate method of accounting for acquisitions. The reconsideration that Defliese describes resulted in the preparation of a lengthy analysis of the problem, *Financial Accounting Standards Board, FASB Discussion Memorandum: Accounting for Business Combinations and Purchased Intangibles* (August, 1976), and the scheduling of a public hearing on the problem, but no further action. A later survey of academic and practicing accountants as well as financial executives suggests that, with the possible exception of the academics, the FASB's immediate constituents were satisfied with (or resigned to) the current rules. Hermanson & Hughes, *Pooling vs. Purchase and Goodwill: A Longstanding Controversy Abates,* 15 Mergers & Acquisitions 15 (Fall, 1980).

The explanation for the truce may well be the increased attention being paid to current value accounting, generally, as a result of the heightened inflation experienced in the recent years. See, e.g., Siegel, *Accounting and Inflation: A Analysis and A Proposal*, 29 U.C.L.A.L. Rev. 271 (1981). From this perspective, an acquisition is only one of a great variety of events that might appropriately trigger revaluation of a company's assets.[9]

2. Accounting for Minority Interests: Equity Versus Cost

Not all acquisitions are accomplished in one or even two steps. Frequently a company purchases a small stake in the target corporation as an initial step, thereby allowing the potential acquiring company to retain substantial flexibility concerning whether, when and how to proceed with an acquisition[10] Moreover, such a stake serves to hedge the risk that a competitive bidder may overbid for the target company. In that event, the initial investor earns a substantial return on its investment.[11] In the first quarter of 1980, for example, there were reports of 419 such "toe-hold" acquisitions,[12] and the rate seems to have held steady, with 1570 such transactions in 1981 and 1169 through early August, 1982.[13]

As with complete acquisitions, there are alternative methods of accounting for minority acquisitions that have significantly different effects on the reported earnings per share of the acquiring company. The equity method allows the acquiring company to include in its income statement the same percentage of the target company's income as it owns of the target company's stock, while the cost method allows the acquiring company to report income from its investment only when the target company actually pays a dividend. As with complete acquisitions, the standards that determine which method must be used have been the subject of controversy. The following describes the mechanics of both methods of accounting for minority investments, the standards governing their availability, and the potential for abuse.

[9] Homer Kripke made precisely this argument prior to the issuance of APB No. 16. Kripke, *Accounting for Corporate Acquisitions and the Treatment of Goodwill: An Alert Signal to All Business Lawyers*, 24 Bus.Law. 89 (1968).

[10] The non-accounting advantages of such acquisitions and the problems they present under a variety of regulatory systems are canvassed in Tobin & Maiwurm, *Beachhead Acquisitions: Creating Waves in the Marketplace and Uncertainty in the*

Regulatory Framework, 38 Bus.Law. 419 (1983).

[11] The subject of competitive bidding in acquisitions is considered in Chapter Fifteen A., infra.

[12] "More Firms are Buying 'Toehold' Stakes in Others as Pace of Acquisitions Declines," Wall St.J., April 7, 1980, at p. 15.

[13] Tobin & Maiwurm, supra.

a. The Mechanics

S. DAVIDSON, C. STICKNEY & R. WEIL, FINANCIAL ACCOUNTING
454–59 (2d ed. 1979).*

MINORITY INVESTMENTS

When a firm owns less than 50 percent of the voting shares of another company, the firm is called a *minority* investor. Investors account for minority investments using one of two methods, depending on the fraction of shares owned. These two methods are the *lower-of-cost-or-market method* and the *equity method.*

Lower-of-Cost-or-Market Method

When a corporation, P, holds less than 20 percent of the stock of another corporation, S, P will use the lower-of-cost-or-market method to account for its investment under current generally accepted accounting principles. * * *

Suppose that P acquires 1,000 shares of S for $40,000. This is P's only investment in an equity security, so the single investment is its "portfolio" for purposes of applying the lower-of-cost-or-market method. The entry to record the acquisition would be

Investment in Equity Securities	40,000	
Cash		40,000
Acquisition of equity shares as investment.		

If the purpose of the purchase were merely a short-term investment to use idle cash, the debit would be to Marketable Securities.

If, while P holds this stock, S declares a dividend of $2 per share, P would make the following entry:

Dividends Receivable	2,000	
Dividend Revenue		2,000
Dividend declared on shares held as an investment.		

When the dividend is collected, P will debit Cash and credit Dividends Receivable.

If, at the end of the period, the market value of the investment has dropped to $30,000, the journal entry would be

Unrealized Loss on Investment in Equity Securities	10,000	
Allowance for Excess of Cost of Investment in Equity		
Securities over Market Value		10,000
Entry to write investment down to market value.		

The credit is to a contra account, known as a *valuation account.* * * * The Unrealized Loss account does not appear on the income statement for the period, but appears in the owners' equity section of the balance sheet as an amount reducing owners' equity.

If, at the end of the next period, the market value of the investment has increased to $36,000, the entry would be

Allowance for Excess of Cost of Investment in Equity
    Securities over Market Value 6,000
        Unrealized Loss on Investment in Equity Securities   6,000
To write the investment up to current market value.

This entry does not affect reported income for the period. The Unrealized Loss on Investment account is a balance sheet account, not an income statement account. The Allowance account can never have a debit balance. That is, once the market value has recovered to original cost, no additional debits to the Allowance account are permitted. The investment will continue to be shown at original cost.

When the investment is sold, or otherwise disposed of, a realized gain or loss is recognized in an amount equal to the difference between selling price and the *original cost* (not current book value) of the securities. Assume that the investment is sold at the end of the third period for $39,000. Then the holding loss during the time the investment is held is $1,000 (= $40,000 − $39,000). The entire loss is recognized in the period when the investment is sold:

Cash 39,000
Realized Loss on Investment in Equity Securities   1,000
    Investment in Equity Securities   40,000
To recognize sale of investments at a loss.

Since this was P's only investment in marketable equity securities, an entry must also be made at the end of the period to eliminate amounts in the Allowance account and in the Unrealized Loss account:

Allowance for Excess of Cost of Investment in Equity
    Securities over Market Value 4,000
        Unrealized Loss on Investment in Equity Securities   4,000
At the end of the period, the Allowance account has a
credit balance of $4,000; this entry removes the Allowance account and the Unrealized Loss account from
the balance sheet.

Suppose that the investment were sold for $42,000. The investment would be

Cash 42,000
    Investment in Equity Securities   40,000
    Realized Gain on Investment in Equity Securities   2,000
To recognize sale of investments at a gain.
Allowance for Excess of Cost of Investment in Equity
    Securities over Market Value 4,000
        Unrealized Loss on Investment in Equity Securities   4,000
To close the Allowance account and the Unrealized Loss
account, since there are no equity securities at the end
of the period.

To summarize, when Company P accounts for its long-term investment in Company S using the lower-of-cost-or-market method:

    1. Company P reports as income each period its share of the dividends declared by Company S.

2. Company P reports on the balance sheet the lower-of-cost-or-market value of the shares in Company S.

    a. Declines in market value below cost are debited directly to an owners' equity account such as "Unrealized Losses on Investments" and credited to an asset contra account.

    b. Subsequent increases in price up to, but not exceeding, the original cost of the investment are debited to the asset contra and credited to the balance sheet account for unrealized losses.

3. Company P recognizes gains or losses on the income statement from holding the stock of Company S only at the time the shares are sold. The gain or loss is the difference between selling price and original cost.

Equity Method: Rationale

Under the lower-of-cost-or-market method, P recognizes income or loss on the income statement only when it becomes entitled to receive a dividend or sells all or part of the investment. Suppose, as often happens, that S follows a policy of financing its own growing operations through retention of earnings and consistently declares dividends substantially less than its net income. The market price of S's shares may increase. Under the lower-of-cost-or-market method, P will continue to show the investment at original cost and P's income from the investment will be only the modest dividends it receives. If P holds a substantial fraction of the shares of S, then P can influence the dividend policy of S. Under these conditions, the lower-of-cost-or-market method may not reasonably reflect the earnings of S generated under P's control. The equity method is designed to provide a better measure of P's earnings and its assets for investments where it can control the operations of S because of substantial holdings.

When Company P can exercise significant influence over operating and financial policies of Company S, generally accepted accounting principles require that the investment by P in S be reported using the *equity method*.[2] To determine when significant influence can be exercised involves judgment. For the sake of objectivity, generally accepted accounting principles presume that P can influence S and should use the equity method when P owns 20 percent or more of the common stock of S, but not more than 50 percent of it. It may be required even when less than 20 percent is owned, but in those cases management and accountants must agree on whether or not Company P exercises significant influence over Company S. (The equity method is also required when more than 50 percent of the shares are owned and consolidated statements are not issued.) *

[2] *APB Opinion No. 18*, 1971.

* The standards for consolidation are considered in Section A.3. of this Chapter, infra. [Ed.]

Equity Method: Procedure

Under the equity method, the initial purchase of an investment is recorded at cost, the same as under the lower-of-cost-or-market method. Company P treats as income (or revenue) each period its proportionate share of the periodic earnings, not the dividends, of Company S. Dividends declared by S are then treated by P as a reduction in its Investment in S.

Suppose that P acquires 30 percent of the outstanding shares of S for $600,000. The entry to record the acquisition would be

(1) Investment in S 600,000
        Cash   600,000
        Investment made in 30 percent of Company S.

Between the time of the acquisition and the end of P's next accounting period, S reports income of $80,000. P, using the equity method, would record

(2) Investment in S 24,000
        Revenue from Investments   24,000
        To record 30 percent of income earned by investee
        accounted for using the equity method. Revenue
        account title often used in practice is Equity in
        Income of Unconsolidated Affiliates.

If S declares a dividend of $30,000 to holders of common stock, P would be entitled to receive $9,000 and would record

(3) Dividends Receivable 9,000
        Investment in S   9,000
        To record dividends receivable from investee ac-
        counted for using the equity method and the result-
        ing reduction in the investment account.

Notice that the credit is to the Investment in S account. P records income earned by S as an *increase* in investment. The dividend becomes a return of capital or a *decrease* in investment.

Suppose that S subsequently reports earnings of $100,000 and also declares dividends of $40,000. P's entries would be

(4) Investment in S 30,000
        Revenue from Investments   30,000
(5) Dividends Receivable 12,000
        Investment in S   12,000
        To record revenue and dividends from investee,
        accounted for using equity method.

P's Investment in S account now has a balance of $633,000 as follows:

Investment in S

(1)	600,000	9,000 (3)
(2)	24,000	12,000 (5)
(4)	30,000	
Bal.	633,000	

If P now sells one-fourth of its shares for $152,000, P's entry to record the sale would be

(6)	Cash	152,000	
	Loss on Sale of Investment in S	6,250	
	Investment in S		158,250

(¼ × $633,000 = $158,250.)

* * *

[A] complication in using the equity method arises when the acquisition cost of P's shares exceeds P's proportionate share of the book value of the net assets (= assets minus liabilities), or stockholders' equity of S, at the date of acquisition. For example, assume that P acquires 25 percent of the stock of S for $400,000 when the total stockholders' equity of S is $1 million. The excess of P's cost over book value acquired is $150,000 (= $400,000 – .25 × $1,000,000) and is called *goodwill*. Goodwill must be amortized over a period not greater than forty years. * * *

On the balance sheet, an investment accounted for on the equity method is shown in the Investments section. The amount shown will generally be equal to the acquisition cost of the shares plus P's share of S's undistributed earnings since the date the shares were acquired. On the income statement, P shows its share of S's income as a revenue each period. (The financial statements of the investee, S, are not affected by the accounting method used by the investor, P.)

b. *Determinants of Choice of Method*

APB Opinion No. 18

THE EQUITY METHOD OF ACCOUNTING FOR INVESTMENTS IN COMMON STOCK *

MARCH, 1971

* * *

7. Under the cost method of accounting for investments in common stock, dividends are the basis for recognition by an investor of earnings from an investment. Financial statements of an investor prepared under the cost method may not reflect substantial changes in the affairs of an investee. Dividends included in income of an investor for a period may be unrelated to the earnings (or losses) of an investee for that period. For example, an investee may pay no dividends for several periods and then pay dividends substantially in excess of the earnings of a period. Losses of an investee of one period may be offset against earnings of another period because the investor reports neither in results of operations at the time they are reported by the investee. Some dividends received from an investee do not cover the carrying costs of an investment whereas the investor's share of the investee's earnings more than covers those costs. Those characteristics of the cost method may prevent an investor from reflecting adequately the earn-

ings related to an investment in common stock—either cumulatively or in the appropriate periods.

* * *

10.   Under the equity method, an investor recognizes its share of the earnings or losses of an investee in the periods for which they are reported by the investee in its financial statements rather than in the period in which an investee declares a dividend.   An investor adjusts the carrying amount of an investment for its share of the earnings or losses of the investee subsequent to the date of investment and reports the recognized earnings or losses in income.   Dividends received from an investee reduce the carrying amount of the investment.   Thus, the equity method is an appropriate means of recognizing increases or decreases measured by generally accepted accounting principles in the economic resources underlying the investments.   Furthermore, the equity method of accounting more closely meets the objectives of accrual accounting than does the cost method since the investor recognizes its share of the earnings and losses of the investee in the periods in which they are reflected in the accounts of the investee.

* * *

12.   The equity method tends to be most appropriate if an investment enables the investor to influence the operating or financial decisions of the investee.   The investor then has a degree of responsibility for the return on its investment, and it is appropriate to include in the results of operations of the investor its share of the earnings or losses of the investee.   Influence tends to be more effective as the investor's percent of ownership in the voting stock of the investee increases.   Investments of relatively small percentages of voting stock of an investee tend to be passive in nature and enable the investor to have little or no influence on the operations of the investee.

13.   Some hold the view that * * * the equity method is [not] appropriate accounting for investments in common stock where the investor holds less than majority ownership of the voting stock.   They would account for such investments at cost.   Under that view the investor is not entitled to recognize earnings on its investment until a right to claim the earnings arises, and that claim arises only to the extent dividends are declared.   The investor is considered to have no earnings on its investment unless it is in a position to control the distribution of earnings.   Likewise, an investment or an investor's operations are not affected by losses of an investee unless those losses indicate a loss in value of the investment that should be recognized.

OPINION

* * *

17.   The Board concludes that the equity method of accounting for an investment in common stock should also be followed by an investor whose investment in voting stock gives it the ability to exercise significant influence over operating and financial policies of an investee even though the investor holds 50% or less of the voting stock.   Ability to exercise that influence may be indicated in several ways, such as representation on the board of directors, participation in policy making

processes, material intercompany transactions, interchange of managerial personnel, or technological dependency. Another important consideration is the extent of ownership by an investor in relation to the concentration of other shareholdings, but substantial or majority ownership of the voting stock of an investee by another investor does not necessarily preclude the ability to exercise significant influence by the investor. The Board recognizes that determining the ability of an investor to exercise such influence is not always clear and applying judgment is necessary to assess the status of each investment. In order to achieve a reasonable degree of uniformity in application, the Board concludes that an investment (direct or indirect) of 20% or more of the voting stock of an investee should lead to a presumption that in the absence of evidence to the contrary an investor has the ability to exercise significant influence over an investee. Conversely, an investment of less than 20% of the voting stock of an investee should lead to a presumption that an investor does not have the ability to exercise significant influence unless such ability can be demonstrated. When the equity method is appropriate, it should be applied in consolidated financial statements and in parent-company financial statements prepared for issuance to stockholders as the financial statements of the primary reporting entity.

◆

FASB INTERPRETATION NO. 35—CRITERIA FOR APPLYING THE EQUITY METHOD OF ACCOUNTING FOR INVESTMENTS IN COMMON STOCK (May, 1981) *

An interpretation of APB Opinion No. 18.**

Introduction

1. The Board has been asked to clarify the provisions of APB Opinion No. 18, *The Equity Method of Accounting for Investments in Common Stock,* regarding application of that method to investments of 50 percent or less of the voting stock of an investee enterprise (other than a corporate joint venture).

Interpretation

2. Opinion 18 requires that the equity method of accounting be followed by an investor whose investment in voting stock gives it the ability to exercise significant influence over operating and financial policies of an investee. The presumptions in paragraph 17 of Opinion 18 are intended to provide a reasonable degree of uniformity in applying the equity method. The presumptions can be overcome by predominant evidence to the contrary.

3. Evidence that an investor owning 20 percent or more of the voting stock of an investee may be unable to exercise significant influence over the investee's operating and financial policies requires an evaluation of all the facts and circumstances relating to the investment. The presumption that the investor has the ability to exercise significant influence over the investee's operating and financial policies stands until overcome by predominant evidence to the contrary.

4. Examples of indications that an investor may be unable to exercise significant influence over the operating and financial policies of an investee include:

 a. Opposition by the investee, such as litigation or complaints to governmental regulatory authorities, challenges the investor's ability to exercise significant influence.

 b. The investor and investee sign an agreement under which the investor surrenders significant rights as a shareholder.

 c. Majority ownership of the investee is concentrated among a small group of shareholders who operate the investee without regard to the views of the investor.

 d. The investor needs or wants more financial information to apply the equity method than is available to the investee's other shareholders (for example, the investor wants quarterly financial information from an investee that publicly reports only annually), tries to obtain that information, and fails.

 e. The investor tries and fails to obtain representation on the investee's board of directors.

This list is illustrative and is not all-inclusive. None of the individual circumstances is necessarily conclusive that the investor is unable to exercise significant influence over the investee's operating and financial policies. However, if any of these or similar circumstances exists, an investor with ownership of 20 percent or more shall evaluate all facts and circumstances relating to the investment to reach a judgment about whether the presumption that the investor has the ability to exercise significant influence over the investee's operating and financial policies is overcome. It may be necessary to evaluate the facts and circumstances for a period of time before reaching a judgment.

*   *   *

7. The basic question raised is how to decide when use of the equity method is appropriate; in particular, how much weight should be given to the statement that " *   *   * applying judgment is necessary to assess the status of each investment" and how much weight to the presumptions based on percentage ownership? The Board has been advised that some investors view the presumptions as rigid rules and believe that achievement of 20 percent ownership requires use of the equity method to account for the investment regardless of circumstances. This Interpretation clarifies that the presumptions are to be applied using judgment and may be overcome by predominant evidence to the contrary.

8. A related question involves how an investor owning 20 percent or more of the voting stock of an investee should account for the

investment if the investee opposes the investor. That opposition might be in the form of the investee's filing a lawsuit against the investor or the investee's making allegations to appropriate governmental regulatory authorities. This Interpretation clarifies that opposition by the investee requires an assessment by the investor of all the facts and circumstances of the investment to determine whether they are sufficient to overcome the presumption.

9. A third question relates to the appropriateness of using the equity method if an investor and an investee have signed an agreement under which the investor agrees to limit its shareholding in the investee. (Because the investor usually agrees not to increase its current holdings, such agreements often are called "stand-still agreements.") Those agreements are commonly used to compromise disputes when an investee is fighting against a takeover attempt or an increase in an investor's percentage ownership. Depending on their provisions, the agreements may modify an investor's rights or may increase certain rights and restrict others compared with the situation of an investor without such an agreement. If the investor surrenders significant rights as a shareholder under the provisions of such an agreement, this Interpretation clarifies that the investor shall assess all the facts and circumstances of the investment to determine whether they are sufficient to overcome the presumption.

10. A proposed Interpretation. *Criteria for Applying the Equity Method of Accounting for Investments in Common Stock,* was released for comment on December 19, 1980. The Board received 45 letters of comment on the proposed Interpretation.

* * *

12. Some respondents suggested that the Interpretation would strengthen investees relative to investors in takeover disputes by making it more difficult for the investor to use the equity method to account for its investment. The Board disagrees with that suggestion for two reasons. First, the Board believes this Interpretation is a faithful interpretation of Opinion 18. The Board has not attempted to favor either investors or investees and does not believe that its role is to do so. The Board's role on this project is to faithfully interpret Opinion 18. Second, the Board notes that the actual cash returns on an investment and the income taxes that would be paid are unaffected by the method of accounting for the investment. Therefore, a decision not to proceed with an otherwise attractive investment simply because the equity method of accounting cannot be used would seem to be unlikely for the vast majority of companies. Conversely, an investment that is not otherwise attractive does not become so simply because the equity method will be used to account for that investment in the investor's financial statements.*

———————◆———————

* If this is correct, then why would the Financial Accounting Standards Board care which method was used? The relevance of the Efficient Capital Market Hypothesis in setting financial accounting standards is considered in Section E.2. of this Chapter, infra.

c. *The Potential for Abuse*

Before the adoption of APB No. 18, the equity method of accounting for investments was used primarily in situations in which the investor's interest was a majority or near majority of the investee's outstanding stock. Where the investment was less than a majority, the cost method was most commonly used.[14] The effect of the adoption of APB No. 18 was to greatly expand the availability of the equity method.

After APB No. 18 was adopted, it was generally perceived that an investor company which had acquired at least a 20% interest in the investee could use the equity method without futher inquiry as to whether, in the terms of APB No. 18, "the investor has the ability to exercise significant influence over an investee." [15] The reasoning that supported this practice was based on the Opinion's statement that the requisite ownership created a "presumption" of influence "in the absence of evidence to the contrary." Because it was hardly in the interest of an investor company seeking to use the equity method to discover such evidence, and because the Opinion was not interpreted to impose on the auditor an obligation to search it out, ownership alone was generally viewed as sufficient. Thus, while prior to APB No. 18 the equity method was essentially limited to investments in excess of 50%, APB No. 18 extended its availability to investments of between 20% and 50%.

The advantage of the equity method to an investor company that believes it is desirable to show higher earnings can be substantial. The following table contains examples of the substantial differences in earnings per share that would be reported by some public companies depending on whether the equity or cost method of accounting was used.

Investors Having 20–50% Long-Term Common Stock Investments [16]

	1971 Net Income*		1970 Net Income * †	
Investor	As Reported Which Includes Equity in Earnings of 20%–50% Owned Companies	Adjusted to Exclude Equity in Earnings of 20%–50% Owned Companies	As Reported Which Includes Equity in Earnings of 20%–50% Owned Companies	Adjusted to Exclude Equity in Earnings of 20%–50% Owned Companies
1. Hercules	$2.78	$2.67	$2.61	$2.51
2. Kaiser Industries	.14	.02	.94	.82
3. Marathon Oil	2.28	2.18	2.90	2.83
4. Penn Virginia Corp.	2.65	1.18	6.01	2.65
5. Phillips Petroleum	1.78	1.67	1.58	1.50
6. Sifco Industries	(.20)	(.55)	.91	.62
7. St. Regis Paper	1.34	1.26	2.56	2.50

* After extraordinary items.

† As required by APB *Opinion No. 18*, the investors retroactively restated their 1970 financial statements to reflect the change to the equity method of accounting for these investments.

Note: The preceding data was taken from the companies' 1971 annual reports.

[14] Barrett, *APB Opinion Number 18: A Move Toward Preferences of Users*, Fin. Analy.J. 47 (July-Aug., 1972).

[15] APB No. 18, ¶ 17.

[16] From Lynch, *Accounting for Investments by the Equity and Market Value Methods*, Fin.Analy.J. 62, 63 (Jan.-Feb., 1975).

Indeed, in part for precisely this reason, such "20% consolidations" recently have been described as "the newest fad" in the acquisition game. *Lawyer's Lament, Arbitrager's Delight,* Forbes 31–32, May 24, 1982.

APB No. 18's expansion of the availability of the equity method was the result of efforts by the business community to convince the Accounting Principles Board that it was appropriately used in broader circumstances. But why did the business community care? If the investor *actually could* "exercise significant influence" over the investee, it always was possible for an investor company to report higher earnings even under the cost method simply by causing the investee to pay a dividend. And if the investee company really needed the funds for internal use, the dividend could be reinvested after it was paid. In what ways would such an approach be less favorable than use of the equity method?

The mechanical character of APB No. 18's 20 percent test makes for easy work for planners. Suppose your client wanted to make a toehold acquisition in a high technology company that, because it was still in its early stages, operated at a loss. If the investment is held below 20%, is there any danger that the high tech company's losses would be included in your client's income statement? [17] What would you recommend after the high tech company became profitable?

The terms of the 20 percent test may have been somewhat tightened by the May, 1981, issuance of Interpretation No. 35 by the FASB. The impact of the new interpretation, however, is still unclear. While the Interpretation describes some circumstances—such as litigation by the investee against the investor—that would indicate the absence of the requisite influence, it also made clear that the presumption arising from 20% ownership remains sufficient in itself to justify use of the equity method "until overcome by predominant evidence to the contrary." Para. 3. Does the Interpretation impose any obligation on the investor or its auditor to investigate? The issue may have particular salience because, only one month after the FASB issued its Interpretation, the SEC filed suit against McLouth Steel Corp. charging that the company improperly used the equity method to account for its 19.87% interest in Jewell Coal & Coke Co.,[18] and, as a result, overstated its income in violation of the reporting requirements of the Securities Exchange Act of 1934. Although the complaint was settled by consent, and the reported facts do indicate substantial and overt hostility between the companies, the very filing of the complaint, described by the Wall Street Journal as the first of its kind,[19] may indicate that the new Interpretation will be taken seriously.

[17] How close to the line would you go?

[18] SEC v. McLouth Steel Corp., [1981 Transfer Binder] CCH Fed.Sec.L.Rptr. ¶ 98.032 (June 17, 1981).

[19] "Suit Filed by SEC, Believed to be the First of its Kind," Wall St.J., June 18, 1981, p. 13, col. 1.

3. Accounting for Majority Investments

S. DAVIDSON, C. STICKNEY & R. WEIL, FINANCIAL ACCOUNTING

461–67 (2d ed. 1979).*

MAJORITY INVESTMENTS

When a firm owns more than 50 percent of the voting stock of another company, the firm is called the *majority* investor, or *parent.* In most cases, the financial statements of the majority-owned *subsidiary* are combined, or *consolidated,* with those of the parent. In some instances, however, consolidated financial statements are not prepared. Instead, the investment is reported using the equity method. Whether consolidated statements are prepared or the equity method is used depends on the consolidation policy of the firm, which is discussed later in this section.

*   *   *

Purpose of Consolidated Statements

For a variety of reasons, then, a single economic entity may exist in the form of several legally separate companies. (The General Electric Company, for example, consists of about 150 separate legal companies.) Consolidated financial statements present the results of operations, financial position, and changes in financial position of an affiliated group of corporations under the control of a parent essentially as if the group of corporations were a single entity. The parent and each subsidiary corporation are legally separate entities, but they operate as one centrally controlled *economic entity.* Consolidated financial statements generally provide more useful information to the stockholders of the parent corporation than would separate financial statements of the parent and each subsidiary.

Consolidated financial statements also generally provide more useful information than does using the equity method. The parent, because of its voting interest, can effectively control the use of the subsidiary's assets. Consolidation of the individual assets and equities of both the parent and the subsidiary provides a more realistic picture of the operations and financial position of the single economic entity.

*   *   *

Consolidation Policy

Consolidated financial statements are generally prepared when all of the following three criteria are met:

1. The parent owns more than 50 percent of the voting stock of the subsidiary.

2. There are no important restrictions on the ability of the parent to exercise control of the subsidiary.

    3. The asset and equity structure of the subsidiary is not significantly different from that of the parent.

Ownership of more than 50 percent of the subsidiary's voting stock implies an ability to exert control over the activities of the subsidiary. For example, the parent can control the subsidiary's corporate policies and dividend declarations. There may be situations, however, where control of the subsidiary's activities cannot be carried out effectively, despite the ownership of a majority of the voting stock. For example, the subsidiary may be located in a foreign country that has severely restricted the withdrawal of funds from that country. Or the subsidiary may be in bankruptcy and under the control of a court-appointed group of trustees. In these cases, the financial statements of the subsidiary probably will not be consolidated with those of the parent. When the parent owns more than 50 percent of the shares and can exercise control, but consolidated statements are not prepared, then the equity method must be used.

If the asset and equity structure of the subsidiary is significantly different from that of the parent, the subsidiary's financial statements are frequently not consolidated with those of the parent and the equity method is used. For example, a consolidated statement might not be prepared if the parent is a manufacturing concern with heavy investments in property, plant, and equipment, whereas the subsidiary is a finance or insurance company with large holdings of cash, receivables, and marketable securities. The presentation of consolidated financial statements of corporations with significantly different asset and equity structures is sometimes thought to submerge potentially important information about the individual corporations. This is particularly true when the assets of the subsidiary are not, by law, fully available for use by the parent, such as when the subsidiary is a bank or an insurance company.

* * *

Understanding Consolidated Statements

The remainder of this section discusses the following [three] concepts essential for understanding published consolidated statements:

    1. The need for intercompany eliminations

    2. The meaning of consolidated income and retained earnings

    3. The nature of the minority interest

* * *

Need for Intercompany Eliminations. The items on consolidated statements are little more than the sum of the items on the financial statements of the corporations being consolidated. Consolidated statements are intended to reflect the results that would be achieved if the affiliated group of companies were a single company. The amounts resulting from a summation of the accounts of the companies being consolidated must therefore be adjusted to eliminate double counting and intercompany transactions.

For example, a parent may lend funds to its subsidiary. If the separate balance sheets were merely added together, those funds would be counted twice: once as the notes receivable on the parent's books and again as the cash or other assets on the subsidiary's books. Consolidated balance sheets eliminate intercompany transactions that would not be reported for a single, integrated enterprise. Thus, the note receivable of the parent and the note payable of the subsidiary are eliminated in preparing the consolidated balance sheet.

* * *

Similarly, certain intercompany transactions must be eliminated from the sum of income statement accounts so that the operating performance of the consolidated entity can be meaningfully presented. For example, if a manufacturing parent sells goods to a subsidiary which, in turn, sells the goods to the public, then the sum of individual income statements would double-count sales and costs of goods sold. Suppose that the parent sells to the subsidiary but that the subsidiary has not yet sold the goods to the public. The parent will have recorded profits on the sale, but from the standpoint of the overall economic entity, no profits for shareholders have actually been realized because the items are still in the inventory of the overall economic entity. Consequently, profits from the parent's sales to subsidiaries that have not been realized by subsequent sales to outsiders are eliminated from consolidated net income and balance sheet amounts. The consolidated income statement attempts to show sales, expenses, and net income figures that report the results of operations of the group of companies as though it were a single company.

Consolidated Income and Retained Earnings. The amount of consolidated net income for a period is the same as the amount that would be reported if the parent company used the equity method of accounting for the intercorporate investment. That is, consolidated net income is equal to

Parent Company's Net Income	+	Parent's Share of Subsidiary's Net Income	−	Profit (or Plus Loss) on Intercompany Transactions.

The principal difference between the consolidated income statement and the income statement where the subsidiary is accounted for under the equity method is the components of income presented. When a consolidated income statement is prepared, the individual revenues and expenses of the subsidiary (less intercompany adjustments) are combined with those of the parent. When the equity method is used for an unconsolidated subsidiary, the parent's share of the subsidiary's net income minus gain (or plus loss) on intercompany transactions is shown on a single line of the income statement with a title such as "Equity in Earnings (Loss) of Unconsolidated Subsidiary."

* * *

The amount shown on the consolidated balance sheet for retained earnings is likewise the amount that would be reported if the parent company used the equity method of accounting for the intercorporate investment. That is, consolidated retained earnings is equal to

Parent's	Parent's Share of the Change	Profit (or Plus Loss)
Retained +	in Subsidiary's Retained	− on Intercompany
Earnings	Earnings Since Acquisition	Transactions.

*   *   *

Minority Interest in Consolidated Subsidiary In many cases, the parent will not own 100 percent of the voting stock of a consolidated subsidiary. The owners of the remaining shares of voting stock are called *minority shareholders,* or the *minority interest.*[5] These shareholders continue to have a proportionate interest in the net assets (= total assets minus total liabilities) of the subsidiary as shown on the subsidiary's separate corporate records. They also have a proportionate interest in the earnings of the subsidiary.

An issue in the generally accepted accounting principles for consolidated statements is whether the statements should show only the parent's share of the assets and equities of the subsidiary or whether they should show all of the subsidiary's assets and equities along with the minority interests in them. The generally accepted accounting principle is to show all of the assets and equities of the subsidiary, since the parent, with its controlling voting interest, can effectively direct the use of all the assets and liabilities, not merely an amount equal to the parent's percentage of ownership. The consolidated balance sheet and income statement in these instances must, however, disclose the interest of the minority shareholders in the subsidiary that has been consolidated.

The amount of the minority interest shown on the balance sheet is generally the result of multiplying the common stockholders' equity of the subsidiary by the minority's percentage of ownership. For example, if the common shareholders' equity (or assets minus liabilities) of a consolidated subsidiary totals $500,000 and the minority owns 20 percent of the common stock, then the minority interest shown on the consolidated balance sheet is $100,000 (= .20 × $500,000).

The minority interest is typically presented among the equities on the consolidated balance sheet between the liabilities and shareholders' equity. *   *   *

The amount of the minority interest in the subsidiary's income shown on the consolidated income statement is generally the result of multiplying the *subsidiary's* net income by the minority's percentage of ownership. The consolidated income is allocated to show the portions applicable to the parent company and the portion of the subsidiary's income applicable to the minority interest. *   *   * Typically, the minority interest in the subsidiary's income is shown as a deduction in calculating consolidated net income.

[5] Do not confuse this minority interest in a consolidated subsidiary with a firm's own minority investments, discussed earlier. The minority *interest* belongs to others outside the parent and its economic entity. The parent's minority *investments* are merely those for which the parent owns less than 50 percent of the shares.

4. Summary of Accounting Treatment

S. DAVIDSON, C. STICKNEY & R. WEIL, FINANCIAL ACCOUNTING

491 (Figure 12.1) (1979).

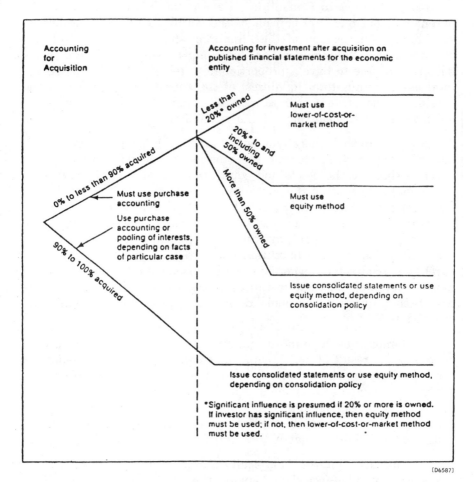

Accounting for Acquisition

Accounting for investment after acquisition on published financial statements for the economic entity

Less than 20%* owned — Must use lower-of-cost-or-market method

20%* to and including 50% owned

0% to less than 90% acquired — Must use purchase accounting

Use purchase accounting or pooling of interests, depending on facts of particular case

90% to 100% acquired

More than 50% owned — Must use equity method

Issue consolidated statements or use equity method, depending on consolidation policy

Issue consolidated statements or use equity method, depending on consolidation policy

*Significant influence is presumed if 20% or more is owned. If investor has significant influence, then equity method must be used; if not, then lower-of-cost-or-market method must be used.

[D6587]

For an excellent recent summary of the mechanics of accounting for acquisitions and an extensive bibliography, see Fiflis, *Accounting for Mergers, Acquisitions and Investments, in a Nutshell: The Interrelationships of, and Criteria for, Purchase or Pooling, the Equity Method, and Parent-Company-Only and Consolidated Statements,* 37 Bus.Law. 89 (1981).

B. The Theory: Gain to the Acquiring Company as a Result of Choice of Accounting Methods

The common explanation for the attention paid to how an acquisition is accounted for on the books of the acquiring corporation is that a higher reported earnings per share results in a higher market value for the acquiring company, even if the higher earnings are merely the creature of the accounting technique used and reflect no increase in actual cash flow. In this view, the ability to account for an acquisition using the pooling of interest method when the purchase method would result in higher depreciation charges and amortization of good will has real economic value to the acquiring company. What is commonly not discussed is the explanation for so mechanistic a linkage between earnings per share reported for financial accounting purposes and firm value. What is missing, of course, is not an explanation of why historical earnings are important in valuation, but why altering reported, but not real, earnings alters firm value. In the following, Professor Steiner offers a careful explanation of the linkage between choice of accounting method and firm value.

P. STEINER, MERGERS: MOTIVES, EFFECTS, POLICIES
103–19 (1975).*

The PE Ratio, the PE Game, and the Incentive to Merge

THE PRICE-EARNINGS RELATIONSHIP

* * *

[O]ne might expect a dollar's worth of present expected value of an annual earnings stream to command a value that is some well-defined multiple of the annual expected earnings, just as the present value of an annuity is some multiple of the annual payment. In a world of perfect knowledge of the future one might expect the price of every security to be the *same* multiple of the annual certainty-equivalent income stream. This multiple would be related to interest rates pertaining. It would be the same for all securities, for if it were not, profitable arbitrage would be undertaken until the various multiples were brought into equality.**

Unfortunately a company's future income stream is not known. Suppose instead that what is known are the earnings of the company in the years past, rather than the years ahead. We can still treat today's price as a multiple of present or past earnings. But now quite rationally the multiples (the price-earnings ratios) will not be the same for different companies because a dollar of past or current earnings may not be the same predictor of future earnings for different companies. Thus, in modern stock market discussions, it is common to regard variable future expectations about a company's earnings per share (and thus about its stock price per share) as embodied in an appropriate price-earnings (PE) ratio. Of course, one can add speculative considerations too. If for any reason one expects a particular company's stock to rise rapidly in the future, this justifies a higher price now, and thus a higher PE ratio.

* * *

All of the above is an elementary, and perhaps unnecessary, recital of why the PE ratio plays a role. The PE ratio is a perfectly reasonable summary concept for the whole congeries of things that lead to variable

** As an exercise to test your facility with the concepts covered in Part I, relate the description of securities pricing in this paragraph to the Capital Asset Pricing Model. [Ed.]

expectations of future events. The price of a company's stock at time t is by definition the product of its PE ratio at time t, and its earnings per share at time t.

Behavioral Assumptions Underlying the PE Theory of Incentives to Merge

The definitional identity just stated can be transformed into a *theory* of behavior that plays an important role in conglomerate acquisitions by the following assumptions:

1. The PE ratio of a particular company tends to become an established parameter and to change but slowly over time. Because of this, anything that increases earnings per share of the company tends to increase the price of its stock.

2. When a Company B acquires a Company S with a different historic PE ratio from its own, Company B's PE ratio becomes applicable to Company S's earnings per share.

3. The PE ratio tends to increase secularly if the rate of growth of earnings increases and if the profits per dollar of net assets increase.

These assumptions may make it possible and profitable to transfer by merger one company's PE ratio to another company's earnings, and thus create an incentive to merge.

A fourth assumption—that the relevant "earnings" to which the PE ratio applies are those as reported in the accounting statements of the firm—creates the role for accounting conventions and changes therein in affecting behavior.

The Pure PE Game

It may be intuitively obvious that otherwise unattractive mergers may be eagerly sought if a company with a high PE rating can by merger transfer this ratio to the earnings of a company with a lower one. Table 5–3 illustrates this possibility by an example that provides a useful benchmark for less obvious matters that follow. The example concerns two Companies B and S whose basic financial data is recorded in columns (1) and (2), respectively. Company B is assumed to have a price per share of $1 and earnings per share of .05; its PE ratio is thus 20. Company S's stock also sells for $1 per share, but it has earnings per share of .10 and a PE ratio of 10. A simple combination of these companies into $B + S$, column (3), would show earnings per share of .0667. One might expect its stock, absent any synergy, to have a price per share of $1, and a PE ratio of 15. In every way $B + S$ is the weighted average of Company B and Company S.

Now, however, assume Company B acquires Company S on a share for share exchange ($k = 1$) as shown in column (4). Earnings per share are .0667, as just above, but now these earnings are converted by the stock market into a price per share *using B's PE ratio of 20:1*. The price of C's stock is $1.33 per share instead of $1.0 and everyone is a winner! The same 3,000 shares of stock as in $(A + B)$ now command a third more on the market.[6]

[6] All of the above assumed $k = 1$, and thus avoided any problem of accounting for payments to S in excess of book value, a problem—indeed an opportunity—that will

But the advantages are not yet exhausted. Regarding C as the successor to B, B's earnings per share have risen from .050 before the merger to .0667 after it; moreover, its stock price has risen, and so have its earnings per dollar of net assets. Each of these changes is viewed as "favorable" by the market and may lead to an upward revision of B's PE ratio. If it rises to 25 (after all, investors may reason, this is a company showing good growth in profits and in stock prices), its price per share rises to $25 \times .0667 = \$1.67$. This rise is of a different kind from that of the previous paragraph. The earlier one (the rise in earnings per share of B due to the acquisition) is real enough and will continue as long as the two companies' earnings continue at the levels pertaining at the time of acquisition. In contrast, the rate of increase in earnings per share (that may lead to an inflation of the PE ratio) will not be maintained into the following years (absent a real gain somewhere) unless the company makes subsequent acquisitions of companies with positive earnings but relatively low PE's. Thus arises one source of the alleged inexorable search by so-called go-go firms for more and more merger partners: to maintain an upward rate of growth in earnings per share. This would work (by assumption) as long as the investing public continued to assign an appropriate PE ratio by the identity of the acquiring firm, not the source of the earnings.

* * *

Table 5–3

Example 1: The PE Game

	Company B (1)	Company S (2)	Company B + S simple combination k = 1 (3)	Company C (new B) B acquires S k = 1 (4)	Company C (new B) B acquires S k = 1.20 (5)
Net assets	$ 2,000	$ 1,000	$ 3,000	$ 3,000	$ 3,000
Net equity	$ 2,000	$ 1,000	$ 3,000	$ 3,000	$ 3,000
[Number of shares]	[2,000]	[1,000]	[3,000]	[3,000]	[3,200]
Earnings	$ 100	$ 100	$ 200	$ 200	$ 200
Earnings per share (e)	$ .05	$ .10	$ .0667	$ .0667	$ .0625
Price per share (p)	$ 1.00	$ 1.00	$ 1.00	$ 1.333*	$ 1.250*
PE ratio (PE)	20:1	$ 10:1	15:1	20:1	20:1
Market value	$ 2,000	$ 1,000	$ 3,000	$ 4,000	$ 4,000
Earnings/Net assets	.05	.10	.0667	.0667	.0667
Earnings/Equity	.05	.10	.0667	.0667	.0667

* $p_C = PE_\beta \cdot e_C$, where the subscripts refer to the company.

This example depended primarily on the willingness of investors to transfer an acquiring company's PE ratio to acquired earnings. To the incentives for merger so created, additional incentives existed in the opportunities to manipulate nominal earnings and the other determinants of PE ratios. Here was the role of imaginative accounting.

concern us below. Column (5) shows how the example works out if the exchange of stock occurred at a 20 percent premium to S's stockholders. Because there are more shares (3,200) the earnings per share rises only to .0625 and price per share (at a PE of 20:1) to $1.25 instead of to $1.33. The pie is divided somewhat differently. S's shareholders new get half (rather than one-third) of the gain from applying B's PE ratio to S's earnings.

Merger Accounting and Incentives to Merge

THE ROLE OF ACCOUNTING

To the economist, although not to the businessman, the first question requiring an answer is why accounting conventions matter.

* * *

The explanation * * * lies in the multiplicity and complexity of the measures of performance of huge corporations. Investors, potentially overwhelmed by a flood of measures of corporate performance, have come to rely upon accounting measures sanctioned by the APB and condoned by the Securities and Exchange Commission (SEC). This reliance creates the incentive and the opportunity to creative accountants to operate within the existing rules to achieve unintended ends. Such behavior in turn generates changes in the rules, but often with a sizable lag. Precisely such a period of discovered opportunities and lagged response occurred during the merger wave.

POOLING VERSUS PURCHASE ACCOUNTING

* * *

Pooling: market value above book value. In most acquisitions, the effective purchase price for assets is well above their *book* value, both because of the premium characteristically paid for stock and because in our economy average book values tend to be well below market values of assets. This is partly due to inflation and the use of original cost, and partly to various forms of accelerated depreciation in use. For present purposes the two sources have the same effect, and I will thus continue to assume the acquisition occurs without a premium being paid.[11]

Suppose, with no real changes, Company S in our example carries its assets (which are "worth" $1,000) at only $200 in its balance sheet. Table 5–5, column (4'), recomputes the pooled balance sheet. Comparison with column (4) (repeated from table 5–4) shows that this has no effect on earnings per share or price but does inflate the rate of earnings on assets and equity. This may result in a small advantage to merging companies' stockholders if it persuades the market to raise the PE ratio appropriate to the company.

The main advantage of pooling undervalued assets is that it creates the opportunity for "instant earnings" in any year that they are required. Suppose Company C now sells all the assets of Company S (worth $1,000, but carried at $200) to another party for $500. It foregoes thereby the $100 per year that those assets earn. *But on the books of Company C this transaction will appear to realize a gain of $300 not a loss of $500.*

[11] Thus we continue to assume $k = 1$, and stay with our example.

Table 5–5

Example 3: Pooling, Market Value Above Book Value

	Company B (from table 5–3) (1)	Company C (new B) B acquires S k = 1 (from table 5–3) (4)	Company S understated book values (2')	Company C B acquires S k = 1 (4')
Net assets	$ 2,000	$ 3,000	$ 200	$ 2,200
Net equity	$ 2,000	$ 3,000	$ 200	$ 2,200
[Number of shares]	[2,000]	[3,000]	[1,000]	[3,000]
Earnings	$ 100	$ 200	$ 100	$ 200
Earnings per share	$ .05	$ .0667	$ .10	$ .0667
Price per share	$ 1.00	$ 1.333	$ 1.00	$ 1.333
PE ratio	20:1	20:1	10:1	20:1
Market value	$ 2,000	$ 4,000	$ 1,000	$ 4,000
Earnings/Net assets	.05	.0667	.50	.091
Earnings/Equity	.05	.0667	.50	.091

The effect on Company C's earnings per share *in the year of the sale* may be spectacular as is illustrated in column (8) of table 5–6, and if the market continues to play the PE game the price of the stock can shoot up. Of course, the following year, things become less attractive: the company has lost the income stream the assets produced yet still has S's former shareholders among its owners, see column (9). But if another acquisition and another sale can be concluded, the effect on Company C's earnings per share may be counteracted, at least for another year. Once started on this track, the company must continue to acquire companies at an increasing rate if it is not to have its past conversion of future earnings into instant income catch up to it. The best analogy is to the chain letter.

Table 5–6

Example 4: Sale of Undervalued Assets to Create "Instant Income" Pooling Accounting

	Company C B acquires S k = 1 (from table 5–5) (4)	Company C after sale of S's assets for $500 (8)	Company C next year after sale (9)
Net assets	$ 2,200	$ 2,500*	$ 2,500
Net equity	$ 2,200	$ 2,500	$ 2,500
[Number of shares]	[3,000]	[3,000]	[3,000]
Earnings	$ 200	$ 400†	$ 100
Earnings per share	$ .0667	$ .1333	$ .0333
Price per share	$ 1.333	$ 2.667	$ .667
PE ratio	20:1	20:1	20:1
Market value	$ 4,000	$ 8,000	$ 2,000
Earnings/Net assets	.091	.16	.04
Earnings/Equity	.091	.16	.04

  * 2,200 + $500 receipts − $200 book value of assets sold.

  † $100 income from B's assets + $300 "gain on exchange." I here neglect capital gains taxes payable on this gain. Assume this is the net gain after such taxes.

◆

Although Professor Steiner focuses on the pooling versus purchase choice,[20] the equity versus cost choice fits the theoretical framework just as well. Perhaps even more easily than with pooling of interest, the equity method facilitates the transfer of earnings from low PE ratio companies to high PE ratio companies. Indeed, with the equity method all that is necessary is a stock market transaction; the investee's management need not even be involved. A company with a high PE ratio, by purchasing 20 percent of the stock of a low PE ratio company, can purchase 20 percent of the low PE ratio company's earnings at a price reflecting that lower PE ratio and then, in effect, sell those earnings back to the market, through its own shares, at its own higher PE ratio. Put simply, the idea is to buy earnings at wholesale, and sell them at retail. The same assumption is critical to the argument in both pooling and equity situations: that the acquisition not change the acquiring company's PE ratio.

C. Evaluation: Consistency With Analytic Tools and Empirical Evidence

The mechanistic relationship between reported earnings per share and firm value described by Professor Steiner depends critically on his fourth assumption—that the market considers *only* the financial ac-

[20] For a similar claim that price-earnings differentials resulting from choice of accounting method result in increased firm value, see Mead, *Instantaneous Merger Profit as a Conglomerate Merger Motive,* 7 Wes.Econ.J. 295 (1969).

counting data provided by the acquiring company in valuing the company's securities and, as a necessary but unstated corollary, that the market accepts that data at face value without discriminating among accounting data produced by different accounting methods. This assumption has obvious implications for the Efficient Capital Market Hypothesis considered in Chapter Five. For the assumption to be accurate, the information costs of recognizing that cosmetic changes in the acquiring company's accounting earnings do not change the company's cash flow, and of reconstructing the company's financial statements in a form that allows analysis of its real economic condition, would have to be quite high. If, alternatively, there are other sources of low cost information concerning the acquiring company, and if reconstruction of the company's performance is not costly, then the company's choice among accounting methods should not alter the value of the company's stock.

So stated, the proposition can be empirically tested by means of the cumulative abnormal return methodology considered in Chapter Six B. If Professor Steiner is right, then acquiring companies using the pooling of interest method of accounting for acquisitions should experience positive abnormal returns associated with their acquisitions. If, however, no positive abnormal returns appear, then the market is efficient with respect to cosmetic changes in accounting methods, and the ability to use the pooling of interest accounting method is an unjustifiable motivation for acquisitions. The following study reports the results of just such an empirical test.

POOLING vs. PURCHASE: THE EFFECTS OF ACCOUNTING FOR MERGERS ON STOCK PRICES *

Hai Hong, Robert S. Kaplan, and Gershon Mandelker.
53 Acctng.Rev. 31 (1978).

Considerable evidence has been assembled in recent work supporting the Efficient Capital Markets Hypothesis. The hypothesis has important implications for external accounting practices. Indeed, several recent studies have looked at the informational content of alternative accounting methods and their effects on stock prices. Accounting changes or manipulations not accompanied by real economic impacts seem to have no statistically significant effects on stock prices. Apparently, the presence of alternative and more timely sources of information on corporate performance enables investors to look beyond simple income numbers in valuing equity securities.

Accounting for business combinations has been an especially troublesome issue for accountants. Up until APB 16 was issued in October 1970, business combinations which were accomplished by means of an exchange of securities could have been accounted for either by the "purchase" method or the "pooling-of-interests" method. Such combinations are almost always nontaxable exchanges so that there is no difference in the cash flows associated with using one method or the other. Therefore, differences in reported earnings between the two methods, caused by amortizing goodwill under the purchase method, but not under pooling-of-interests, should not affect the valuation of the consolidated entity. Since the method of accounting for the combination is usually fully disclosed in the proxy statement, an efficient market should be able to respond to the real economic consequences of the combination and not be affected by the particular accounting method used.

Opposition to pooling has grown over the last 20 years, during which time it has been given names like "dirty pooling" and subjected to strong censure in the business literature. Lintner argues that "Dirty pooling suppression of asset costs at the time of merger to pad subsequent earnings, and other accounting devices which are likely to mislead many shareholders, clearly raise issues of the greatest practical importance. * * *" This argument suggests that stockholders of companies using pooling make abnormal gains from higher stock prices as a direct consequence of reporting relatively higher earnings. Purchase accounting, the argument continues, does not convey misleading information and hence does not tend to distort stock prices.

* * *

In this article, we will examine whether the use of the pooling of interests method does tend to increase the stock prices of acquiring companies. Our null hypothesis is that the market is efficient and thus able to distinguish between higher earnings caused by using pooling-of-interests from higher earnings caused by real economic events of the firm. If the use of pooling-of-interests in a merger were associated with an increased valuation of a firm, the market may be inefficient with respect to this accounting convention. * * *

In the empirical work reported below we shall investigate the pre-merger and post-merger stock prices of companies using pooling-of-interests accounting for mergers. We shall attempt to determine whether such firms tend to have abnormally high stock prices because of their so-called inflated earning reports.

Data and Sample

* * *

Sample Selection

Studies indicate that merger accounting was confused before Accounting Research Bulletin No. 43 was issued in 1953. Pooling-of-interests, as a well defined method of accounting for business combinations, became more widespread after 1954, and increased in popularity to become the predominant option in the latter half of the sixties. The period 1954–64 was chosen, therefore, as one in which purchase and pooling existed as distinct and practical alternative forms of accounting. Post-1964 mergers were not considered because securities returns data were available only up to June, 1968, in our CRSP file and also because the low incidence of purchase accounting in the late sixties would have led to a highly unbalanced sample in that time period.

To be admitted into the sample, a merger had to satisfy the following critieria:

1.   The merger must be significantly large relative to the acquiring firm. This criterion was adopted to avoid admitting the very large number of small and insignificant acquisitions whose inclusion in the sample would tend to dilute the impact, if any, of the merger events on average residuals. A relative size of three percent in net asset value was used as the rough cutoff point. This size was computed as the ratio of the number of shares issued in the acquisition to the number of shares outstanding in the acquiring firm just before the merger.

2.   There should be no other major mergers close in time to the one under consideration. This criterion was necessary to avoid confounding the effect of two or more mergers in the same time period. A major merger was considered to be one with an acquisition cost of more than one half of the value of the present acquisition. It should not occur within 18 months of this acquisition. Additionally, it was required that no other acquisition involving 25 percent of the value of the present one occurred within 12 months.

bs-23.   The acquiring firms must be listed on the NYSE and their returns data available for at least 24 months on each side of the merger date.

4.   The mergers must take place by exchange of shares. This means that each merger would have been a candidate for either pooling or purchase accounting given the great flexibility that accounting practice provided in the period under consideration. This criterion rules out cash acquisitions, which cannot be accounted for as poolings. It also virtually rules out taxable mergers.

*   *   *

Data and Sample Breakdown

Because details of mergers are difficult and tedious to collect, the entire set of mergers in the 1954–64 period was not used in the study. All eligible mergers involving acquisitions of NYSE firms were included, most of these being large acquisitions. In addition, random selections were taken of all remaining mergers by sampling volumes of NYSE listing applications. It is estimated that about 50 percent of all mergers in the period were thus considered.

The selection methods turned up 205 mergers for the study. Of these, 138 used pooling-of-interests, 62 used purchase accounting, and five had accounting treatments that were difficult to classify as either pooling or purchase. Of the 62 purchases, only 37 amortized positive goodwill; the rest either did not amortize, had negative goodwill, or involved an unknown amount and sign of goodwill. * * * Of the 138 pooling firms, 122 involved an acquisition price in excess of book value and the stock price reactions of these 122 firms received the most detailed attention. * * *

METHODOLOGY

The Market Model

In order to evaluate the performance of stocks around the merger dates, it is necessary to abstract from general market conditions which affect stock returns and isolate any specific effects that the merger event might have. The market model, developed by Sharpe and Fama among others, has been used in a number of similar studies of stock prices performance associated with accounting or financial events.

*   *   *

Shifts in Parameters σ_y and β_y

Since a merger may lead to important changes in the riskiness of a firm, it would seem reasonable to allow for different risk parameters in pre-merger and post-merger periods. Changes in β_y,* would come about by the addition of the acquired firm's assets to those of the surviving firm and also by a change in the debt-equity ratio of the acquiring firm which has issued new securities for its acquisition. Accordingly, one set of parameters is estimated for the pre-merger period and another for the post-merger period for each firm. In both periods, the parameters of the acquiring firm are estimated.

*   *   *

Selection of Critical Date

In this and similar studies, we look for abnormal behavior in months surrounding a critical event, such as the first earnings announcement when using a new accounting procedure. For this study, one might also identify the critical event as the merger itself. We will initially describe and present results with data centered about two earnings announcement dates: the month of the first annual earnings announcement after the merger and the month of the first earnings announcement, interim or annual, after the merger. If investors are to be "fooled" by the higher earnings reported because the pooling-of-interests method is used, the largest impact should show up in the earnings announcement immediately after the merger. Subsquently, we will also present the abnormal residuals centered on the month of the merger itself.

Define month 0 as the month of the critical event (e.g., post-merger earnings announcement); month 1 is then the month immediately following the event, and month -1 is the month immediately preceding it. *   *   *

Figures 1a and 1b display the CAR for these firms centered on the two earnings announcement dates corresponding to (i) the first earnings announcement, quarterly or annual, after the merger and (ii) the first annual earnings announcement date after the merger. The residuals in the estimation period, -60 to -13 and $+12$ to $+60$, are also shown to indicate the fluctuations in the CAR statistic which can be expected even in a period where the cumulative residual for each firm must sum to zero.

---

* β_y here refers to the beta of the acquiring company. [Ed.]

The results displayed in Figures 1a and 1b suggest that there is no abnormal price behavior associated with earnings announcements subsequent to a pooling-of-interests merger. While the level of cumulative abnormal returns appears high around the first earnings announcement in Figure 1a, this is caused by positive residuals ten to fifteen months prior to this event. Also, the variation in returns about the earnings announcement dates is indistinguishable from that in the four years prior to and four years subsequent to the merger. * * *

Figure 1a
Cumulative Abnormal Residuals for Poolings (122 Firms):
Centered on Earnings Announcement Dates
Month Relative to First Earnings Announcement
(Quarterly or Annual) after Merger

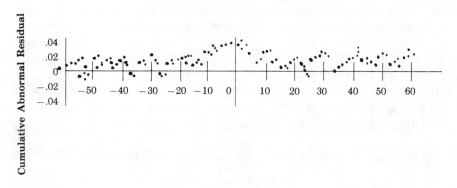

Figure 1b
Month Relative to First Annual Earnings Announcement after Merger

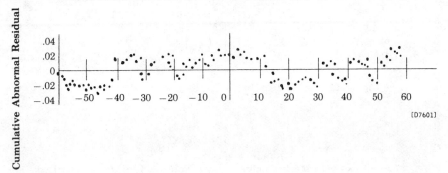

[D7601]

Merger Dates

The preceding analysis was replicated using the merger date as the critical date for centering the study of abnormal residuals. A merger is accompanied with analysis of proxy statements, tender offers, and pro forma financial statements. Thus, a merger accomplished under "favorable" accounting practices (i.e., pooling-of-interests) could be associated with unusual price behavior around the time of the merger. For purposes of comparison, we also present the results for our much smaller sample of firms who used purchase accounting for mergers with amortization of positive goodwill even though the conditions of the merger would have permitted the pooling method.

Plots of the cumulative abnormal residuals (see Figure 2a) for the pooling-of-interests firms are analogous to those displayed in Figures 1a and 1b with no abnormal price movement for the two years centered on the merger date. The purchase firms (see Figure 2b), however, show a strong positive price movement in the year prior to the merger date. The CAR increased by 8.8 percent during these 12 months and this increase was maintained for 8 subsequent months.

Statistical tests on these two samples * * * show the insignificant residuals for the pooling firms and the strong positive movement for the small sample of purchase firms. Except for a large positive residual ten months before the merger date, none of the monthly portfolio t-statistics is statistically significant. The large number of consecutive positive monthly statistics, from month -12 to -9 and from month -4 to 0, cause the cumulative t-statistic to exceed 2.0 in the period around the merger date. Apparently, firms who opt to use the more conservative purchase method have been doing well in the year prior to the merger. Perhaps a self-selection bias is operating, as has been suggested in previous studies * * * in that firms who choose the purchase method can "afford" to report the lower earnings caused by use of this method. The small sample of firms who used the purchase method in our sample, however, cautions as against drawing too strong an inference from this peculiar price behavior.

Other variations were also investigated. * * *

Figure 2a
Cumulative Abnormal Residuals 122 Poolings With Market Value > Book Value
Month Relative to Merger

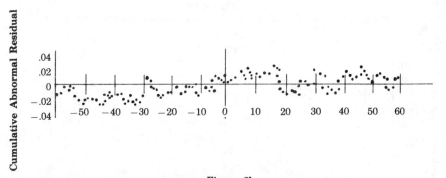

Figure 2b
37 Purchases with Market Value > Book Value and Goodwill Amortized:
Month Relative to Merger

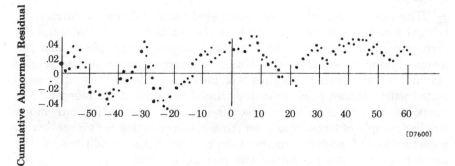

[D7600]

Finally, the importance of using different pre-merger and post-merger estimates of a firm's beta was highlighted by a CAR analysis when the parameters of the market model were estimated from observations running from months -40 to -13 and $+12$ to $+39$. The cumulative residuals and the portfolio t-statistics were much higher than those previously displayed. Thus, if we had not captured the nonstationarity in relative risk of merging firms by estimating separate pre- and post-merger betas, our t-statistics would have been biased upward toward significance.

DISCUSSION OF RESULTS

There is a clear lack of evidence to support the hypothesis that using the pooling-of-interests method raises the stock prices of acquiring firms around the time or in the year after the merger. Investors do not seem to have been fooled by this accounting convention into paying higher stock prices even though firms in our sample using pooling-of-interests accounting report higher earnings than if they had used the purchase method.

People who wish to continue to believe that "dirty pooling" raises the stock prices of acquiring firms may raise the following objections to our study. First, they could argue that the market is fooled by the pooling method but that the difference in earnings caused by pooling and the "proper" alternative of purchase accounting with a 40-year amortization of goodwill is too small to cause a change in stock prices that would be detected by our empirical procedures. This is certainly possible. But if the effect is so small that it is undetectable using what we consider to be fairly sophisticated and sensitive procedures, it would not be a very important effect, almost surely below the threshold of materiality.

* * *

Finally, one could argue that our procedure of excluding firms with multiple mergers within a two-year period excluded firms from whom the potential distortion was largest. Advocates of this position must then believe that the market is efficient with respect to one merger per year but somehow becomes inefficient when more than one merger per year occurs, an argument which we find less than convincing. A variant of this position would claim that the real excesses in the use of poolings in mergers occurred in the late 1960's with the boom in conglomerate mergers, and this period was excluded from our study. Again, supporters of this criticism must then argue that while the market appeared efficient with respect to merger accounting in the 1954–1964 time period, it somehow forgot how to adjust for pooling-of-interests accounting in the 1965-1970 time period. We must consider this event possible, since we have yet to look at the data in this time period, but quite unlikely in view of the findings in this and similar studies.

No single empirical study is ever completely convincing on settling a controversy. Problems in sample selection, financial and statistical models, and interpretation of results are inherent in all empirical work.

We believe, however, the effect of this study is to shift the burden of proof to those who claim that the stock price of acquiring firms is raised when the pooling-of-interests method is used in a merger. We have looked at a large sample of mergers and have been unable to find any evidence that the selection of an accounting method affects the valuation of the acquirng firm. In the absence of future studies that would demonstrate such an effect, we must believe that fully disclosed accounting policies are properly reflected in the stock prices of firms.

◆

Note: Methodological Problems and Alternatives

As stressed in Chapter Six, the interpretation of the data reported in CAR studies must be approached with caution: Calculating the relevant abnormal returns is a statistical exercise; understanding the meaning of the resulting numbers requires careful analysis and a good sense of the institutional setting in which the events under study took place. Examination of the Hong, Kaplan & Mandelker study suggests a possible problem concerning the relevant event date. The authors recognized that the announcement date of the first earnings report after the acquisition, on which they initially focused, may be too late to capture the effect they are looking for. Because the proxy statement delivered to shareholders (and which is therefore low cost information to the market) prior to approval of the transaction contains pro forma financial statements which detail how the transaction will be accounted for, the impact, if any, of the availability of pooling would occur far earlier than the first post-transaction earnings report. To meet this concern, the authors also measured the abnormal returns at an earlier date—that on which the transaction actually occurred. But is even this date early enough? The proxy statement containing the pro forma financial statements is mailed to shareholders some time before the shareholders' meeting at which the transaction is voted upon and, even then, there is often a delay between shareholder approval and the closing of the transaction. Can one determine from the presentation of the data whether the authors' conclusion would have changed had they considered the correct event date?

An alternative approach to studying the importance of the pooling versus purchase choice, and one that takes into account a different problem with selecting the relevant event date, would be to examine the impact of the adoption of APB No. 16 on companies with an announced acquisition program. If the ability to use the pooling of interest method did result in increased value, then APB No. 16's restriction on the use of pooling should have resulted in negative abnormal returns for acquisition minded companies. Here again, however, the question is whether the date of APB No. 16's adoption is early enough to capture any abnormal returns associated with restricting the use of pooling. The ultimate adoption of APB No. 16 was heralded by a number of events, including newspaper reports of internal APB drafts and the issuance of public exposure drafts even more restrictive than the opinion ultimately adopted. If the market is efficient, it would have anticipated the likely adoption of APB No. 16, and the impact of restricting the use of pooling of interest would have occurred at the time of these earlier events. From this perspective, abnormal returns would occur when the final opinion was actually adopted only if its ultimate terms differed from the market's expectation.

Schipper & Thompson, *The Impact of Merger-Related Regulations on the Shareholders of Acquiring Firms*, 21 J.Acctng.Res. 184 (1983), studied the events leading up to APB No. 16 in order to take into account the market's anticipation of the outcome of the APB's deliberations. The authors conclude, consistent with the Hong, Kaplan & Mandelker study, that "[e]vidence on the significance of * * * APB Opinions 16 and 17 is comparatively weak and suggest an overall insignificant impact for these regulations." Id. at 216.[21]

Note: Empirical Studies of APB No. 18

There has been no cumulative abnormal return study of the impact of APB No. 18 on stock prices. One study, however, did compare the valuation financial analysts placed on hypothetical companies where one group of analysts was given financial statements prepared using the cost method and a second group was given the identical statements except using the equity method. The results led the author to conclude that a switch from the cost to the equity method in response to the extended availability of the latter after the adoption of APB 18 "will probably have little, if any, direct effect upon the price of the firm's common stock." [22] The author noted, however, that valuations did differ when the cost method was used with insufficient footnote disclosure to allow reconstruction of the results if the equity method were used. Is this result inconsistent with the Efficient Capital Market Hypothesis? [23]

[21] Leftwich, *Evidence of the Impact of Mandatory Changes in Accounting Principles on Corporate Loan Agreements*, 3 J. Acctng & Econ. 3 (1981), conducted a similar study, but found negative abnormal returns associated with some events foretelling the ultimate adoption of APB No. 16. In evaluating their result, Schipper & Thompson stress that other regulatory activity that could be expected to make acquisitions less profitable—like the enactment of the Williams Act and the Tax Reform Act of 1969 (restricting debt financed acquisitions)—occurred at the same time, thereby causing a problem of confounding events. The Schipper & Thompson study attempted to control for this; the Leftwich study did not.

[22] Barrett, *APB Opinion Number 18: A Move Toward Preference of Users*, Fin. Analy. J. 47, 53 (July-Aug. 1972).

[23] While no cumulative abnormal return study of the impact of APB No. 18 has been done, Foster, *Valuation Parameters of Property-Liability Companies*, 32 J.Fin. 823 (1977), studied an analogous problem using a different econometric technique. Standard accounting practice for property-liability insurance companies was not to reflect unrealized gains and losses on their stock portfolios in their financial statements, even though these portfolios represented between 21.2 and 26.7 percent of the companies' total assets during the period studied. Despite the claim that investors and analysts ignored these unrealized gains and losses in valuing the companies (and the regulatory implication that disclosure was therefore unnecessary), Foster found that total earnings, including unrealized gains, was a much better predictor of stock price than only realized earnings. The implication is that, whatever the claim, the market does take into account unrealized gains and losses.

D. Toward a Theory of Choice of Accounting Method

The problem posed by accounting for acquisitions is hardly unique. There are a large number of circumstances where a company can choose among alternative accounting methods for reporting the same transaction, where the alternatives have vastly different impacts on the earnings, assets and liabilities reported in the company's financial statements, but where the choice of accounting method has no apparent impact on the company's real economic condition. Thus, it is important to know whether the result suggested by the Hong, Kaplan & Mandelker study generalizes: Does the market "see through" cosmetic accounting choices in valuing a company? Studies have shown, for example, that the market "sees through" the choice among different methods of depreciation for financial accounting purposes,[24] and the choice of whether to expense or capitalize research and development costs.[25] Indeed, even the number of surveys of empirical studies of market efficiency with respect to financial accounting information is substantial.[26]

But precisely because of the consistency with which the empirical studies support the proposition that the capital market is efficient with respect to choice of financial accounting methods, these results are, in a critical sense, very troubling: They do not seem to reflect the way people behave. Many major companies still seem to select among alternative accounting techniques based on which technique maximizes accounting earnings even if that choice has positive real costs. Consider, for example, the area of particular concern here: methods of accounting for acquisitions. The Hong, Kaplan & Mandelker study appeared in 1978; thus one might assume that the theory it refutes has by now been vanquished. Yet, that seems hardly the case, even for quite sophisticated observers. In May, 1982, the Head of both Arthur Anderson & Co.'s Corporate Reorganization Tax Speciality Team and its Chicago Merger and Acquisitions Assistance Program, made the following statement:

> [F]rom a practical standpoint, a major consideration in an acquisition is the impact the acquisition will have on the acquiring corporation's financial statements. This is due to the fact that the accounting rules are, in some measure, different from the tax rules dealing with corporate acquisitions. *Often, an acquiring corporation has foregone a tax basis step-up in the target corporation's*

---

[24] E.g., Beaver & Dukes, *Interperiod Tax Allocation and Delta-Depreciation Methods: Some Empirical Results*, 48 Acctng. Rev. 549 (1973); Cassidy, *Investor Evaluation of Accounting Information: Some Additional Empirical Evidence*, 14 J. Acctng. Res. 212 (1976).

[25] Dukes, *An Investigation of the Effects of Expensing Research and Development Costs on Security Prices*, in Proceedings of the Conference on Topical Research in Accounting (Schiff & Sorter eds. 1976).

[26] See, e.g., G. Foster, Financial Statement Analysis (1978); P. Griffin, *Useful-* *ness to Investors and Creditors of Information Provided by Financial Reporting: A Review of Empirical Accounting Research* (1981). One of the early researchers in this field recently wrote that, when "asked to do a paper surveying empirical research in accounting, I found it difficult to believe that the world need yet another survey on this topic." Kaplan, The Information Content of Financial Accounting Numbers: A Survey of Empirical Evidence, in *The Impact of Accounting Research on Practice and Disclosure* 134 (A. Abdel-Khalik & T. Keller eds. 1978).

assets where to do so would have had an adverse impact on its earnings for financial reporting purposes.

Statement of Earl C. Brown, Arthur Andersen & Co., on Proposed "Corporate Takeover Tax Act of 1982" (H.R. 6295) before the Subcommittee on Select Revenue Measures, Committee on Ways and Means, House of Representatives (May 24, 1982) (emphasis added.) Similarly, Arthur R. Wyatt, presently a member of the Financial Accounting Standards Board, and formerly a partner in a Big Eight accounting firm, reports that the abandonment of an economically sound acquisition transaction because it could not be accounted for as a pooling "isn't atypical." Wyatt, *Efficient Market Theory: Its Impact on Accounting,* 155 J. Acctng. 56, 60 (Feb. 1983).[27]

Why, then, do companies behave in this manner? Knowledge of the Efficient Capital Market Hypothesis is no longer limited to academics. Indeed, it is often the former MBA students of precisely the academics who conducted the relevant ECMH studies who seem to be ignoring the results. Since the impact of choice of accounting method on financial statements is thus by itself insufficient to explain this puzzling behavior, what factors *actually* determine the accounting methods selected by a company? And what is the tie between this choice and real economic results?

A growing recent literature in accounting research attempts to identify the link between the choice of accounting method and real economic results *given that markets are efficient.* The goal is to explain how even a cosmetic acounting change can have an impact on the cash flow of the firm or, perhaps, on that of the manager charged with choosing the accounting method to be used.

The following study is illustrative of this literature. It seeks to explain why companies switch from accelerated depreciation to straight line depreciation for financial accounting purposes.

EVIDENCE ON THE EFFECT OF BOND COVENANTS AND MANAGEMENT COMPENSATION CONTRACTS ON THE CHOICE OF ACCOUNTING TECHNIQUES

The Case of the Depreciation Switch-Back
Robert W. Holthausen
3 J. Acctng. & Econ. 73–109 (1981).

1. Introduction

The accounting literature at present has no fully developed theory which is capable of explaining how firms select accounting techniques. Recently, however, researchers have begun to examine management's incentives to influence the menu of accepted accounting techniques and

---

[27] Experienced business lawyers report the same result. For example, James Freund states that the use of earn-outs or contingent price arrangements in acquisitions, a particularly useful contractual technique that is considered in detail in Chapter Nineteen infra, declined sharply following the adoption of APB No. 16 because that opinion prohibits pooling if a transaction has an earn-out. J. Freund, *Anatomy of a Merger: Strategies and Techniques for Negotiating Corporate Acquisitions* 205 (1976).

to choose among available alternatives. [Some commentators] hypothesize that management considers the effects of reported accounting numbers on taxes, regulation, political costs, management compensation, information production costs and restrictions found in bond indenture provisions. These advances differ from most earlier attempts to explain the demand for alternative accounting techniques because the incentives of the parties involved in the process are explicitly considered and the efficiency of the capital markets in processing publicly available information is assumed. * * *

2. The effects of bond covenants and management compensation contracts on the choice of accounting techniques

Recent research in economics has modeled the firm as a set of contracts among individuals, which are factors of team production. These factors are all motivated to maximize their own welfare which is in part determined by the performance of the entire team or firm. However, because the compensation of these individuals is determined differentially, conflicts of interest arise. In this section, I review the potential conflicts between stockholders and bondholders and managers as well as the contractual agreements that have been hypothesized to reduce those conflicts.[4] The agreements which utilize accounting numbers are examined to yield predictions on the choice of accounting techniques by managers. Specific hypotheses are developed on the effects of a switch from accelerated to straight-line depreciation. These hypotheses are contrasted with two alternative hypotheses which have appeared in the literature, the no effects hypothesis and the mechanistic hypothesis.

* * *

2.1. *The stockholder-bondholder conflict of interests and predictions arising from bond indentures*

The potential conflict of interests between stockholders and bondholders has been investigated extensively in the finance literature. In summary, this literature identifies actions that can transfer wealth between bondholders and stockholders. For example, if the manager chooses a higher variance project than anticipated by the bondholders, wealth is transferred from the holders of risky debt to the stockholders. Wealth can also be transferred from the bondholders to the stockholders by reducing planned investments and paying out the saved outlays as a dividend.

Temporarily, it is assumed that managers follow a decision rule to maximize the value of the common shares. If the bondholders have rational expectations concerning the potential wealth transfers resulting from maximizing shareholder wealth, they price the bonds such that they are compensated for the managers' expected actions. Hence, they are indifferent to the specifications of the contract. If the gain

---

[4] Throughout this paper I assume that there are no conflicts of interest within groups. For example, I assume away conflicts between senior and junior debtholders and between managers facing different compensation packages and/or time horizons. This simplification does not change the basic tenor of the discussion.

from a realized wealth transfer that the stockholders receive is exactly equal to the bondholders' loss from that wealth transfer, i.e., a zero sum game, then the stockholders have no incentive to enter into costly contracts to limit the decisions the firm may take. However, if the game is a negative sum game, i.e., the bondholders' loss from a wealth transfer is larger in absolute value than the stockholders' gain, then the stockholders are not indifferent to the form of the contract since the bondholders charge for those expected losses in setting the price of the bonds.[6] In the latter case, the stockholders' wealth is affected by the contractual arrangement and they will seek to reduce the costs associated with the conflict of interests.

While there are many restrictions contained in the indenture agreements, only those which are based on accounting numbers are important for this study. Covenants which rely on accounting numbers commonly use minimum working capital and maximum leverage constraints. For example, the firm is not permitted to merge, issue new debt, or pay a dividend if leverage is about the specified maximum and or working capital is below the stated minimum. If the firm violates the required working capital and leverage constraints, the firm is in 'technical default' which gives the bondholders the discretion to accelerate the maturity of the debt or renegotiate the contract. In addition to using leverage and working capital to constrain dividend payments, the direct dividend constraint defines the maximum dividend which can be paid in any period as a positive function of cumulative earnings and proceeds from new stock issues and a negative function of cumulative dividends paid and funds used for share repurchase. All of these variables are cumulated from the year of issue of the bond. The maximum amount which can be paid as a dividend, is referred to as the inventory of payable funds.

The contractual definitions of accounting variables specified in the covenants use generally accepted accounting principles (GAAP) as a benchmark. Some covenants, particularly in private placements, then make adjustments to GAAP which are designed to reduce management discretion. Aside from these requirements, firms are not prohibited from changing accounting techniques. Thus, if alternative procedures for dealing with an accounting problem are generally accepted, and if the indenture does not specifically prohibit one or more of them, management is free to choose any of the generally accepted techniques.

Thus, the choice of an accounting method for financial reporting purposes generally affects the contractual constraints in bond covenants. Managers of firms which face these constraints on production, investment and financing decisions have incentives to relax those constraints if the value of the stock or stock options held by the manager can be increased by relaxing the restrictions. Since the empirical work to be performed in this paper concerns the switch from accelerated to straight-line depreciation for financial reporting pur-

---

[6] Examples of negative sum games would include switching to higher variance but lower present value projects than were expected to be taken. Another example would be dropping planned *positive* net present value projects to increase dividends.

poses only, the analysis that follows, while quite general, is framed within that depreciation choice.

The switch to straight-line (SL) from accelerated (ACC) decreases the book value of leverage because it increases both net tangible assets and stockholders' equity. The decreased leverage affects the firm's ability to issue new debt, pay dividends, merge, lease or be construed to be in default through the leverage restriction in bond indentures. The switch also increases the amount of dividends that can be paid as measured by the direct dividends constraint.

Consider a firm which is using ACC for book purposes and which is facing some bond covenant restrictions which are imposing costs given the firm's current opportunity sets. If switching to SL is less costly than the costs of renegotiating the covenants, repurchasing the debt, or operating within the constraints without alteration, then firms have an incentive to change their depreciation method (or any other accounting technique) to relax those constraints.

Ceteris paribus, the potential wealth transfers to the stockholders from the bondholders increase as the firm's leverage rises. Of course, bondholders are aware of this, and price the bonds accordingly. If the management wishes to avoid this reduction in the price the bondholders are willing to pay, they write more restrictive constraints. Kalay presents cross-sectional evidence consistent with the joint hypothesis that firms write more restrictive dividend constraints as leverage increases, and that the cost of deviations from the constraint increases with leverage. He finds that more highly levered firms are closer to their dividend constraint. Thus, ceteris paribus, the market value of the common stock increases more as a result of an accounting change for firms with higher leverage and for firms which are closer to their constraints. In addition, the greater the impact of the accounting change on the restrictiveness of the covenants, ceteris paribus, the greater the increase in the market value of the equity. This analysis suggests the following hypotheses:

> *Hypothesis 1. The common stock of firms changing to straight-line depreciation for financial reporting purposes only, experiences positive abnormal performance at the time of the announcement of the change, which is, ceteris paribus, an increasing function of the impact of the change in depreciation method on earnings.*

> *Hypothesis 2. The positive abnormal performance of the stockholders' claims at the time of the announcement of a switch to straight-line depreciation for book purposes only, is, ceteris paribus, an increasing function of the firm's leverage.*

> *Hypothesis 3. The positive abnormal performance of the common stock at the time of a firm's announcement of a switch to straight-line depreciation for book purposes only, is, certeris paribus, a decreasing function of the firm's inventory of payable funds.*

An alternative to relaxing bond covenant constraints by choice of accounting techniques is to renegotiate the bond covenants.[13] Since the

---

[13] Another alternative to changing accounting techniques is to repurchase or call the debt. However, all the debt would have to be retired since most indentures

owners of publicly placed debt are more diffuse than the holders of private placements, it is likely that renegotiation costs are much higher for public issues. Since the costs of renegotiation are higher for public debt relative to private placements, firms with more public debt outstanding (relative to firm size) should experience greater gains. This suggests the following:

> *Hypotheses 4. The positive abnormal performance of the common stock at the time of a firm's announcement of a switch to straight-line depreciation for book purposes only, is, ceteris paribus, greater for firms as the relative proportion of public debt leverage to private debt leverage increases.*[15]

2.2   The stockholder-manager conflict of interests and a prediction arising from management compensation contracts

In the previous discussion of the stockholder-bondholder conflict of interests, it is assumed that the manager's self-interest is best served by maximizing the market value of stockholders' equity. In general, however, the manager's incentives are determined by how his wealth is affected by his decisions. Until that function is specified there is no *a priori* argument to indicate whether the manager's interests are more closely aligned with one group or another.

Without full *ex post* settling up, contracts among the various parties will be devised in an attempt to bring the stockholders, bondholders and managers together in an efficient manner. The conflicts between stockholders and bondholders have been discussed previously. Conflicts also exist between managers and non-manager equity owners. [Studies] indicate that as the manager's percentage ownership of the residual claims of a firm decreases, increases in the value of those claims have less of an impact on the manager's wealth. Thus, the manager has less incentive to maximize the value of the residual or equity claims. To assure the stockholders that their interests will be protected, the manager could agree to a contract with the stockholders giving him the incentive to maximize the market value of the common equity. However, contracts of this type increase the costs of assuring the bondholders that their interests will be protected. In addition to balancing these conflicts, an efficient compensation package must consider tax effects and potential portfolio-underdiversification costs of the manager.

What is of interest for the topic at hand is not the optimal combination of contracts, but whether any of the components of the compensation package gives managers an incentive to change accounting techniques. One form of compensation observed is incentive plans which determine bonuses as a function of accounting earnings. These plans typically provide that a management compensation committee,

require that more than ⅔ of all *outstanding* bonds, approve any changes in covenants. Thus, this is probably a more expensive alternative to renegotiating or changing accounting techniques in most cases.

[15] While abnormal performance is positively related to public and private debt, Hypothesis 4 predicts that the effect of public debt is more positive.

which is ineligible to participate in the plans, is authorized by the stockholders to award a total bonus not to exceed an amount which is a positive function of accounting earnings and a negative function of capitalization. The bonuses often are constrained to a maximum amount determined as a percentage of dividends paid to stockholders, salaries paid to eligible managers, or a fixed dollar amount. Thus, earnings above some maximum have no impact on the manager's bonus. Furthermore, earnings often have to be above a minimum, a specified percentage of capitalization, before the manager receives any bonus.

The plans state that the accounting numbers used in the plans must agree with the equivalent numbers in the financial statements, and that the statements must be prepared in accordance with generally accepted accounting principles. The choice of accounting principles within the set of GAAP is not constrained which may be due to the costs of writing such a contract and the benefits of potentially renegotiating the compensation agreements with the managers through accounting technique changes at a relatively low cost. For example, assume a standard-setting body changes GAAP which adversely affects earnings. Without changing accounting techniques, the compensation committee might be unable to pay the manager his marginal product since they are constrained to a maximum bonus which is a function of accounting net income. A change in accounting techniques can allow the compensation committee to continue paying managers their marginal product without obtaining stockholder approval for a change in the bonus plans. Of course, the extent of this renegotiation is limited by the latitude that generally accepted accounting principles allow.

The manager's incentive to increase earnings by changing accounting techniques, which arises from these contracts, does not exist in all periods. If accounting earnings, both before and after the change, are below the minimum or above the maximum bounds of the compensation scheme, the change has no impact on compensation paid. In these cases, the manager has an incentive to decrease reported earnings and use the 'saved' earnings in future periods when they can affect his compensation.

* * *

A necessary condition to change accounting techniques in an attempt to increase bonus compensation is that the manager must expect that any increase in his wealth from the higher present value of bonus compensation is not offset by declines in the value of his portfolio of stock and stock options.[17]

Despite these arguments, which seem to cast doubt on the manager's incentive to switch accounting methods to impact his bonus compensation empirical evidence of a suggestive nature exists. Zmijewski

---

[17] In most cases, the bonus compensation effect will exceed any decline in the value of the portfolio. However, the net effect on the manager's wealth depends upon the relative percentage of the compensation pool the manager receives, his percentage holding of the firm's stock and options, and the other effects of an accounting change on the market value of the common stock such as information production costs.

and Hagerman * find evidence that managers choose income increasing techniques more often in firms with accounting based compensation plans than in those firms without them.   If managers can *appreciably* affect their bonus by changing to income increasing techniques, abnormal performance of the common stock should be negatively related to the existence of a management compensation plan which is based on accounting net income at the time of the announcement of an unanticipated change.   The following hypothesis concerning the switch to SL depreciation is suggested:

> *Hypothesis 5.   The abnormal performance of the common equity of firms switching to straight-line depreciation from accelerated depreciation is, ceteris paribus, negatively related to the existence of a management compensation plan which defines management bonuses as a function of accounting income.*[18]

Thus, Hypotheses 1 to 5 are derived from the form of bond indenture agreements and management compensation contracts which use accounting numbers to define the rights of the parties in the contracts.   In addition, the hypotheses are based on assumptions about the costs of renegotiation, proximity to the constraints, etc., and how the market's expectation of a change varies with these factors.   The hypotheses are an attempt to determine both the effects of and the rationale for accounting technique changes.   Two altenative hypotheses which appear in the literature are discussed next.

2.3   Two alternative hypotheses

Previous research on changes in accounting techniques provides two alternative hypotheses that have consistently appeared in the literature.   The two hypotheses are the Mechanistic Hypothesis and the No Effects Hypothesis.

The Mechanistic Hypothesis states that increases (decreases) in earnings necessarily lead to increases (decreases) in the prices of the outstanding claims of the firm regardless of the source of the earnings.   Thus, the Mechanistic Hypothesis implies that changes in accounting techniques which increase (decrease) earnings should be associated with increases (decreases) in the value of the common stock of the firm.   The assumption is that the market is not efficient in processing the information content of publicly available accounting information.   The formal statement of the Mechanistic Hypothesis for this study is:

> *Mechanistic Hypothesis.   The common stock of firms changing to straight-line depreciation for reporting purposes only, experience positive abnormal performance at the time of the announcement of*

---

* Zmijewski & Hagerman, *An Income Strategy Approach to the Postivie Theory of Accounting Standard Setting/Choice,* 3 J. Acctng. & Econ. 129 (1981).

[18] Realistically, the magnitude of the effect of management compensation plans on the market value of the common stock is likely to be small and thus, is likely to prove insignificant given the variability of common stock returns.   Again it must be assumed that the market's expectation of an accounting change because of the existence of an accounting based bonus plan does not vary sufficiently across firms to nullify the hypothesized effect of the switch on stock returns.

the change, which is, ceteris paribus, an increasing function of the impact of the change in depreciation methods on earnings.

* * *

Another alternative hypothesis is that implicitly assumed by * * * the No Effects Hypothesis. Under the No Effects Hypothesis, it is assumed that there are no real cash flow effects associated with changes in accounting techniques and that the market is efficient with respect to publicly available information. Thus, under the No Effects Hypothesis, changes in accounting techniques are either random or the result of misguided management. The No Effects Hypothesis serves as the Null Hypothesis for this paper.

No Effects (Null) Hypothesis. The common stock of firms changing to straight-line depreciation for financial reporting purposes only, experience no abnormal performance at the announcement of the change.

* * *

4. Summary and interpretation

The results presented in the paper can be summarized as follows:

(i) The average abnormal performance of switch-back firms is negative but insignificantly different from zero in the period immediately surrounding the announcement of the switch.

(ii) The abnormal performance of the switch-back firms varies significantly with the type of announcement (i.e., concurrent, not concurrent, etc.). It is not implied that the type of announcement itself is the cause of the differential performance, rather, it appears a self-selection is occurring, though no conjectures to explain that phenomenon are presented.

(iii) The abnormal performance of the switch-back firms * * * is positively related to the unexpected earnings and negatively related to leverage over the period day -3 to day $+2$. Furthermore, there is evidence which suggests that leverage and the firm's deviation from its leverage constraint are significantly negatively correlated. Thus, more highly levered firms are closer to their leverage constraints.

(iv) The abnormal performance of the firms is not systematically related to the existence of a management compensation plan, the impact of the depreciation change on reported earnings, the firm's deviation from its dividend constraint or the size of the firm.

(v) The firm's deviation from its dividend constraint does not appear to become smaller from seven years before to three years after the depreciation change for switch-back firms. * * *

In attempting to interpret the evidence presented, two questions should be addressed. First, what is the impact of the change to straight-line depreciation on the market value of the equity? For the entire portfolio, the effect of the change is insignificant, but more highly levered firms perform significantly worse than less levered firms. This evidence is not consistent with the hypotheses generated from the contracts which rely on accounting numbers, the Mechanistic Hypothesis or the No Effects Hypothesis.

The second question to address is why do managers change accounting techniques? This is an especially important question given that the results indicate the market value of the common stock of highly levered firms is adversely impacted. Since the change is voluntary, it is reasonable to assume that someone benefits. Perhaps the managers gain at the expense of the stockholders, but if this is true, the tests used in this paper are not powerful enough to measure the economic significance of the management's gain (i.e., the market value of the equity appears unrelated to the existence of a management compensation plan). Perhaps the market value of the common stock would have fallen more if the change in depreciation methods had not been made because of binding dividend or new debt issue constraints. If this is true, however, either the tests used to measure the deviation from the dividend constraint are not well enough specified to detect closeness to the constraint or the leverage constraint is more important for this sample of firms. What is lacking, is a theory of the optimal deviation from the constraint as a function of variables which are endogenous to the firm.

The evidence in this paper concerning abnormal performance may be weak for several reasons. * * * [R]esults which support the hypotheses may not be obtained because of variation in the market's assessed probability of a firm making an accounting change and failure to isolate the period in which market expectations are revised. Second, the effects of other events must be eliminated in order to measure the stock price impact of the accounting change. To the extent that firms changing accounting techniques are not a random selection of firms, the other events may be confounding the results, even though an attempt has been made to control for them by adjusting for the effects of earnings announcements and eliminating firms with other significant announcements. Third, the hypotheses developed may be based on incorrect assumptions about relative costs which lead to incorrect predictions about the determinants of cross-sectional variation in the value of the equity resulting from the effect of the accounting change on bond covenants and management compensation contracts. Fourth, the change in the value of the common stock from accounting changes may be too small relative to the variation in common stock returns to measure their significance using presently available techniques. Finally, the bond covenants and management compensation contracts which use accounting numbers, may not be related to the choice of accounting techniques. * * * The evidence in this paper is not conclusive enough to allow a determination of which of these factors contributes to the lack of more definitive results.

◆

Note. *Alternative Links Between Accounting Method and Economic Performance.* While the Holthausen study focuses on the terms of bond covenants and management compensation plans as a link between choice of accounting method and real economic performance, other studies have considered two additional potential links. The first is the existence of governmental regulation. In a variety of settings, a regulation is written in terms of financial accounting numbers. Examples include the capital adequacy tests and reserve requirements of federal and state banking authorities, and any form of rate setting in public utility regulation. In these settings, one would predict companies to choose accounting standards that most successfully exploit the particular regulatory structure. For example, public utilities would choose accounting methods that increase the value of the assets in its rate base and decrease the reported return on those assets. The second potential link is a concern over political visibility. In particular situations, high earnings might be politically undesirable. For example, companies in the oil industry might be embarrassed to report high earnings during an oil shortage, or companies in the steel industry might think it politically disadvantageous to report high earnings while lobbying for domestic protection from foreign competition.

The variety of studies that have explored this approach to explaining why companies choose particular financial acounting methods are comprehensively surveyed in Holthausen & Leftwich, *The Economic Consequences of Accounting Choice: Implications of Costly Contracting and Monitoring,* 5 J. Acctng. & Econ. 77 (1983).[28] On balance, the empirical results reported are considerably and disappointingly less compelling than the logic of the agency approach to accounting choice. The authors explain the problem as follows:

> Economic consequence theories are based on contracting and monitoring costs, and those costs place an upper limit on the wealth effect of any accounting choice. Our priors are that accounting choice is not a major determinant of firm values, relative to other decisions a manager makes, such as investment decisions. Likewise, we expect that accounting choice has only a small impact on managers' wealth through compensation plans, although the relative effect is probably larger than for firm values.

> If accounting choice has relatively small wealth effects, powerful tests are required to detect economic consequences. * * * [CAR] tests are the least likely to detect the economic consequences of most voluntary or mandatory accounting changes. [C]urrent techniques for measuring firm-specific stock price performance are probably not sufficiently powerful to detect hypothesized economic consequences, given that the magnitude of the economic impact of most accounting choices is unlikely to be large relative to the variability of the value of the common equity.

Id. at 108–09.

E. How Should Financial Accounting Standards Be Set?

The body of theory and empirical evidence examined in the previous sections has important implications for how financial accounting

[28] For a review of the more technical, non-empirical literature, see Balman, *Agency Research in Managerial Accounting: A Survey,* 1 J. Acctng.Lit. 154 (1982).

standards should be set. Recently, for example, the Financial Accounting Standards Board has moved toward a policy of eliminating the availability of alternative accounting methods for the same transaction in favor of a single mandatory standard.[29] The Efficient Capital Market Hypothesis suggests that, so long as there is sufficient footnote disclosure provided in the financial statements to allow their reconstruction to reflect alternative methods, the imposition of one or another mandatory standard should have no impact. In contrast, the costly contracting and monitoring approach exemplified by the Holthausen study suggests that the imposition of a particular mandatory standard may have a real impact because accounting information is used for purposes where mere form does affect substance. In sum, there is at least surface conflict over whether it is very important to set financial accounting standards at all. The traditional approach to standard setting—for example, the search for the Platonic ideal of a pooling transaction—assumes that the standard selected makes a difference. The ECMH implies that it does not. The costly contracting and monitoring approach of the most recent literature suggests that standard selection may matter after all, albeit for reasons very different from those underlying the traditional approach.

In the face of this apparent conflict, it is helpful to examine how financial accounting standards are actually set, and to evaluate, in light of the three conflicting approaches, how they should be set.

1. The Formal Structure
J. COX, FINANCIAL INFORMATION, ACCOUNTING AND THE LAW
6–12 (1980).

A. *Accounting Standard Setters*

1. The Private Sector—The AICPA and FASB [1]

A business' financial statements, the primary source of financial information, are prepared in accordance with an established body of assumptions and standards designed to fulfill the objective of disclosing relevant financial information. This body, called *generally accepted accounting principles* defines the accepted accounting practices of a particular time.[2] These principles, largely established by both private

---

[29] See, e.g., FASB Statement No. 8, *Accounting for the Translation of Foreign Currency Transactions and Foreign Currency Financial Statements* (1975).

[1] An expanded discussion of the history of the private sector's role in the establishment of accounting and auditing standards and the organizational structure of each professional body is contained in Chatov, Corporate Financial Reporting 133–169, 195–199 (1975); Sprouse and Vagts, The Accounting Principles Board And Differences And Inconsistencies In Accounting

Practice: An Interim Appraisal, 30 Law and Contemp.Prob. 706 (1965).

[2] A principle or practice of accounting is deemed part of the body of generally accepted accounting principles if there is substantial authoritative support for the principle or practice. Grady, Inventory of Generally Accepted Accounting Principles for Business Enterprises 52–53, (AICPA, Accounting Research Study No. 7, 1965) identifies the bases for such support:

"1. In the practices commonly found in business. This does not follow from

and public organizations, also arise from practices in businesses and opinions held by practicing and academic accountants.

The important professional organization for accountants is the American Institute of Certified Public Accountants (AICPA), whose membership primarily comprises accountants performing independent audits of their client's financial statements. In 1938, within the AICPA, the Committee on Accounting Procedures was created with the purpose of promulgating accounting principles. Prior to the Committee's establishment, accounting principles had been made infrequently and never through a systematic process.

The Committee on Accounting Procedures was the profession's first attempt to institutionalize and therefore regularize the consideration and adoption of accounting standards in the private sector. Over the next 20 years, it issued 51 Accounting Research Bulletins (ARB); the first 42 were restated and revised in ARB No. 43 in 1953.

The bulletins were in the form of *recommendations* of acceptable accounting practices for treating a range of unrelated accounting issues. Compliance with these positions, however, was not mandatory. In fact, the Committee, in recommending accounting methods for specific topics, did not list a number of methods deemed included in the generally accepted accounting principles. Accountants could opine that financial statements were in compliance with these principles as long as the method used had some acceptance in practice or theory. Thus, the authority of the Accounting Research Bulletins depended upon the independent accountants' and their clients' broad acceptance of the methods recommended.

Dissatisfaction with the development of the ARBs arose because the Committee did not conduct any research prior to releasing a bulletin but based its decisions on its members' notions of what was desirable. In 1959, as a result of this dissatisfaction, the Accounting

the mere fact that a practice exists, but from the fact that experience of the business has demonstrated that the practice produces dependable results for the guidance of management and for the information of investors and others.

"2. The requirements and views of stock exchanges as leaders in the financial community; similarly the views and opinions of commercial and investment bankers would be entitled to weight.

"3. The regulatory commissions' uniform systems of accounts and accounting rulings exercise a dominant influence on the accounting practices of the industries subject to their jurisdiction. * * *

"4. The regulations and accounting opinions of the Securities and Exchange Commission have the controlling authority over reports filed with the Commission. The Commission and its chief accountants have demonstrated a high degree of objectivity, restraint and expertness in dealing with accounting mat-

ters. The regulations and opinions issued to date are entitled to acceptance by their merit as well as on the basis of the statutory authority of the Commission.

"5. The affirmative opinions of practicing and academic certified public accountants constitute authoritative support for accounting principles or practices. These may be found in oral or written opinions, expert testimony, textbooks and articles.

"6. Published opinions by committees of the American Accounting Association and of the American Institute of CPAs."

To the last category must be added the Financial Accounting Standards Board, which as later material will make clear, is currently the leading body in the private sector concerned with the establishment of accounting principles and procedures.

Also, see APB Statement No. 4 paragraph 138 (1970).

Principles Board (APB) was created to replace the Committee on Accounting Procedures.

The APB initially had 18 members (later 21) selected mainly from the large accounting firms with a few from business, academia, or government, all of whom served in a part-time capacity. The APB had a small, albeit permanent, research staff to provide input on subjects which were under consideration. Small project advisory committees were formed from time to time for specific accounting problems, and, frequently, research reports, called Accounting Research Studies, prepared by leading academicians or practitioners, preceded APB actions. During its existence, the APB issued 31 opinions and 4 statements.

The APB opinions posed the same question as the pronouncements of its predecessor: Could financial statements prepared using an accounting method which differed substantially from that adopted by the APB be viewed as complying with generally accepted accounting principles? The answer, a qualified yes, was not provided by the AICPA until 1964. Without qualification, the APB opinions had substantial authoritative support and, therefore, fell within the realm of generally accepted accounting principles. The use of methods other than those embraced by the APB could, however, qualify as generally accepted accounting principles, provided they had substantial authoritative support, such as "practices commonly found in business," "requirements and views of stock exchanges," "the views of commercial and investment bankers," "regulatory commissions' uniform systems of accounts and accounting rules," "the regulations and accounting opinions of the Securities Exchange Commission," and finally, "affirmative opinions of practicing and academic * * * accountants."

Throughout its existence, the APB encountered a seemingly endless flow of criticism: it produced an insufficient amount of work, it failed to concern itself with broad statements on the objective of financial statements and the underlying principles of accounting, and its opinions fed the ever-present disquiet over the ability of the accounting profession to establish standards adverse to the interest of its clients. Also, there was the concern that the procedures and organization did not insure participation on the APB or its advisory committee by nonaccountants, such as security analysts and financial executives, whose concern for meaningful accounting standards was at least equal to that of the independent public accountants.

In response to such criticism, the AICPA, in the early 1970s, appointed a special committee, headed by Francis M. Wheat, a distinguished lawyer and former Commissioner of the SEC, to study and make recommendations for improving the process and to make the APB more responsive to the needs of those who rely on financial statements. The "Wheat" Committee's recommendations, rendered in its report in March 1972, presented the criticisms and concerns listed above which had arisen over the APB's 13-year life. It strongly recommended that accounting standards in the private sector be established by a body whose organizational structure assured (1) independence of standard setters from the business community, (2) inclusion of groups other than accountants not only in the collection of information necessary for the establishment of accounting standards, but also as a part of the deliberative body itself, and (3) greater efficiency by requiring its members to serve full-time and providing them with the services of a well-financed and highly qualified research and technical staff.[4]

In response to the "Wheat" Committee's recommendations, the APB was disbanded and the Financial Accounting Standards Board (FASB) came into existence in July 1973 as the leading body in the private sector for establishing accounting standards. Its organization is essentially that recommended by the Committee; it comprises seven members who are required to sever all ties with their former employers to assure their independence, with a maximum of only four members being certified public accountants drawn from private practice. The FASB receives extensive research and technical support from a substantial permanent staff which is frequently augmented by leading academicians who prepare studies for it in areas of concern. The FASB's procedures for indentifying pressing accounting issues, obtaining input necessary for their resolution, and considering the action to be taken are much more systematic than those of the APB.

ARMSTRONG, THE WORK AND WORKINGS OF THE FINANCIAL ACCOUNTING STANDARDS BOARD
29 Bus.Law. 145, 147–148 (Supp.1974).

* * * The standard setting process begins with the placing of a question on the Board's technical agenda. For advice in this regard, FASB looks to all segments of the economic community, and particularly to the 28-member Financial Accounting Standards Advisory Council which has been meeting quarterly starting with its first meeting on March 28, 1973. Decisions on adopting agenda items are made by the Board itself. After a topic has been placed on the agenda, a Board member is assigned to prepare with staff assistance, a preliminary definition of the problem and a bibliography of significant literature on the subject.

When the preliminary definition of the problem has been completed and reviewed by the FASB, a task force normally is appointed. Task forces include at least one member of the Board, who serves as Chairman, as well as members of the Advisory Council and other persons who are aware of the responsibilities of preparers and the needs of users of financial statements, or who possess an expertise or viewpoint particularly relevant to the project. The task force is responsible for refining the definition of the problem and its financial accounting and reporting issues, and for preparing a neutral and comprehensive discussion memorandum which outlines alternative solutions to the problem and the arguments and implications relative to each alternative solution. The task force also considers the nature and extent of additional research

---

[4] AICPA, Establishing Financial Accounting Standards, Report Of The Study Of Accounting Principles (1972).

that seems necessary, and recommends by whom it might be performed. Research generally is carried out by the Board's internal research staff, but some projects may be contracted to independent consultants.

Due process continues, when, upon completion of research and preparation of the discussion memorandum, the Board normally will seek the views of all interested parties by holding a public hearing. Both oral testimony and written position papers will be solicited. At least 60 days notice will usually precede a public hearing, to give those wishing to participate ample time to prepare their submissions—and the discussion memorandum will be made public at the time a public hearing is announced.

After the public hearing, the Board will begin its evaluation of the information at hand, and on the basis of this evaluation an exposure draft of a proposed Statement of financial accounting standards will be prepared. Affirmative vote by at least five of the seven members of the Board is required before the draft statement will be released for public comment. The public comment exposure period normally will be 60 days—after which the Board will review the exposure comments, and if new and persuasive information has been received, it may make revisions in the proposed Statement. When a final draft is completed, an affirmative vote by at least five of the seven members of the Board is required before a Statement of Financial Accounting Standards is issued.

To insure the FASB's financial independence from the accounting profession, the Financial Accounting Foundation (FAF) was established to raise funds from all sectors of the financial community. The nine trustees of the FAF include five public accountants, three representatives from the finance-corporate sector (financial analysts, business executives, bankers, etc.), and one accounting educator. Also, the FAF trustees appoint members to vacancies on the FASB.[5]

Today, Rule 203 of the AICPA Code of Professional Ethics governs the FASB's pronouncement, as well as the effectiveness of the earlier Accounting Research Bulletins and Opinions of the Accounting Principles Board.

> *Rule 203—Accounting Principles.* A member shall not express an opinion that financial statements are presented in conformity with generally accepted accounting principles if such statements contain any departure from an accounting principle promulgated by the body designated by [the AICPA] Council to establish such principles which has a material effect on the statements taken as a whole,

---

[5] Since the FASB's creation, the AICPA's principal role has been to express its views on accounting standards to the FASB. Occasionally it issues pronouncements on matters not already governed by the SEC or the FASB. Also, generally accepted auditing standards continue to be the exclusive domain of the AICPA.

In 1939, the Committee on Auditing Procedure (subsequently renamed the Audit-ing Standards Executive Committee) was formed. It has established standards and procedures for the conducting of audits by independent certified public accountants set forth in the AICPA's Statements on Auditing Standards, and has prepared a number of Industry Audit Guides which provide help in specific audit situations.

unless the member can demonstrate that due to unusual circumstances the financial statements would otherwise have been misleading. In such cases his report must describe the departure, the approximate effects thereof, if practicable, and the reasons why compliance with the principle would result in a misleading statement.

Rule 203, through its requirement that the auditor's opinions "demonstrate that due to unusual circumstances" departure from the accounting method prescribed in official bulletins is necessary, reduces the freedom of accountants and their clients to choose nonofficial accounting methods. Formerly, the accountant could approve use of a method that had "substantial authoritative support" although different from those pronounced by the professional body or the SEC. The AICPA's standards require that an accountant using accounting methods not promulgated by AICPA or FASB bodies be satisfied that unusual circumstances require such methods to avoid a misleading presentation.

2. The Public Sector—The SEC

After the Great Depression, Congress created the Securities Exchange Commission (SEC) as the agency having primary authority over the regulation of American securities markets. Among the many governmental regulatory agencies which influence business' accounting and reporting practices, the SEC's impact is the most pervasive. Its power is derived from provisions in the acts it enforces; the most important are the Securities Act of 1933 and the Securities Exchange Act of 1934.

The Securities Act requires the registration of a public offering of new securities and the filing of the related financial statements audited by independent public accountants. The SEC is empowered to establish the precise content and form of financial statements filed with it.[8] Implicit in this authority is the power to prescribe the accounting principles and practices to be used in registering securities.

The Securities Exchange Act also confers equal power upon the SEC to regulate the accounting principles and practices used in preparing periodic financial reports such as those required for companies whose shares are traded on national stock exchanges or whose total assets and number of shareholders exceed a certain level.[9] The most

[8] Section 19(a) of the Securities Exchange Act further confers authority upon the SEC to define accounting terms, the form in which financial information is to be set forth, the items and details to be reflected in financial statements, and the accounting methods to be used in connection with statements subject to the SEC's jurisdiction.

[9] The SEC has similar power over accounting principles and practices in other areas of its regulatory jurisdiction. See e.g., The Investment Company Act of 1940, §§ 30–31; the Public Utility Holding Company Act of 1935 §§ 14–15. The proposed

Federal Securities Code prepared by the American Law Institute confers broad power over accounting practices and principles in § 1805 of the Code.

"Sec. 1805. [*Accounting, records, and nonregistrant reports.*] (a) [*Rulemaking authority.*] For purposes of this Code and in addition to its authority under section 1804, the Commission, by rule, may (1) define accounting terms, (2) prescribe the form and content of financial statements and the accounting principles and standards used in their preparation, (3) require the examination of and reporting of financial statements by inde-

notable are Form 8–K, required for timely disclosure of material changes in the company arising from current events or transactions; Form 10–Q, filed quarterly and containing quarterly unaudited financial statements; and Form 10–K, an extensive description of the company's business, technical information, and annual fianncial statements certified by accountants. Furthermore, the Act gives the SEC power over financial reporting by broker-dealers and requires disclosure of proxy solicitations and takeover attempts involving large publicly-traded companies.

The SEC has deferred to the private sector as the primary standard setter but continues to guide the form and substance of disclosure of financial information in important ways. Examples include the issuance of Regulation S–X, an extensive, detailed description of the form and content of financial statements required to be filed; the issuance of its Accounting Series Releases (ASR's) dealing with accounting matters not specifically dealt with by any of the private sector's bulletins, opinions, or statements; and beginning in 1975, the issuance of Staff Accounting Bulletins, which do not have the official sanction of the SEC, but represent the accounting approach, interpretation, and practices of the staff in administering the disclosure requirements.[10] Occasionally, however, the SEC has prescribed in its ASRs a different accounting method than that established by the private sector.[11]

————————◆————————

2. Choice of Accounting Standards With Efficient Markets

WILLIAM H. BEAVER, WHAT SHOULD BE THE FASB'S OBJECTIVES?

136 J. Accountancy
49–56. (Aug. 6, 1973).*

Was the acrimony arising out of the investment tax credit much ado about nothing? Does it matter whether special gains and losses are reported in the ordinary income or in the extraordinary item section? When firms switch from accelerated to straight-line depreciation, what is the effect upon investors? Did the Accounting Principles Board allocate its resources in an appropriate manner? If its priorities needed reordering, where should the emphasis have been shifted? What objectives should be adopted for financial accounting standards? * * * [N]ow is an appropriate time to take stock of the current body

pendent public accountants, (4) establish standards of independence for public accountants insofar as they practice before it, and (5) prescribe the form and content of the independent public accountant's report."

[10] See ASR No. 180 (Nov. 4, 1975).

[11] For a more extensive discussion of the SEC powers over accounting and auditing

standards and practice, see Strother, *The Establishment of Generally Accepted Accounting Principles and Generally Accepted Auditing Standards,* 28 Vand.L.Rev. 201 (1975).

of knowledge [concerning market efficiency] and assess its implications for the setting of financial accounting standards. * * * The findings have a direct bearing on the questions raised at the outset and suggest that our traditional views of the role of policy-making bodies, such as the APB, SEC and FASB, may have to be substantially altered. * * * There are at least four major implications.

First. Many reporting issues are trivial and do not warrant an expenditure of FASB resources. The properties of such issues are twofold: (1) There is essentially no difference in cost to the firm of reporting either method. (2) There is essentially no cost to statement users in adjusting from one method to the other. In such cases, there is a simple solution. Report one method, with sufficient footnote disclosure to permit adjustment to the other, and let the market interpret implications of the data for security prices.

Unfortunately, too much of the resources of the APB and others has been devoted to issues that warrant this straightforward resolution. For example, the investment credit controversy belongs in this category, as do the issues regarding the definition of extraordinary items, interperiod tax allocation, earnings per share computations involving convertible securities, and accounting for marketable equity securities. By contrast, the FASB should shift its resources to those controversies where there is nontrivial additional cost to the firms or to investors in order to obtain certain types of information (for example, replacement cost accounting for depreciable assets). Whether such information should be a required part of reporting standards is a substantive issue.

Second. The role of financial statement data is essentially a preemptive one—that is, to prevent abnormal returns accruing to individuals by trading upon inside information. This purpose leads to the following disclosure policy: If there are no additional costs of disclosure to the firm, there is prima facie evidence that the item in question ought to be disclosed.

This relatively simple policy could greatly enhance the usefulness of financial statements. Many forms of information are currently being generated internally by the firm and could be reported with essentially no additional cost (e.g., the current market value of marketable equity securities). Such information, if not publicly reported, may constitute inside information. Merely because prices reflect publicly available information in no way implies that they also fully reflect inside information. One information cost that investors may be incurring currently is abnormal returns earned by those who have monopolistic access to inside information. Opponents of greater disclosure bear the burden of proof of showing that individuals can be prevented from earning excess returns with the undisclosed information or that the cost of disclosure exceeds the excess returns. Given the private incentives to trade on inside information, such a condition is very difficult to ensure.

* * *

Third. The FASB must reconsider the nature of its traditional concern for the naive investor. If the investor, no matter how naive, is in effect facing a fair game, can he still get harmed? If so, how? The naive investor can still get harmed, but not in the ways traditionally thought. For example, the potential harm is not likely to occur because firms use flow-through v. deferral for accounting for the investment credit. Rather, the harm is more likely to occur because firms are following policies of less than full disclosure and insiders are potentially earning monopoly returns from access to inside information. Harm is also likely to occur when investors assume speculative positions with excessive transactions costs, improper diversification and improper risk levels in the erroneous belief that they will be able to "beat the market" with published accounting information.

This implies that the FASB should actively discourage investors' beliefs that accounting data can be used to detect overvalued or undervalued securities. This also implies that the FASB must not attempt to reduce the complex events of multimillion dollar corporations to the level of understanding of the naive, or, perhaps more appropriately labeled, ignorant investor. We must stop acting as if all—or even most—individual investors are literally involved in the process of interpreting the impact of accounting information upon the security prices of firms.

An argument often advanced against fuller disclosure is that the increased disclosure will befuddle and confuse the naive investor. A specific manifestation of this argument is that earnings under market value rules are more volatile and hence may lead to more volatile security prices. For example, the insurance industry currently opposes the inclusion of such information on marketable securities in the income statement, even though market values are already reported on the balance sheet. Given that market values on the balance sheet are already part of public information, it is absurd to think that there is going to be any further effect on security prices because of the income statement disclosure. Yet considerable resources of the APB, the insurance industry and others have been wasted on an attempt to resolve this issue. In the more general case where there is no reporting of market values, the efficient market evidence implies that the market is not reacting naively to the currently reported numbers but, rather, is forming "unbiased" assessments of the market values and their effects on prices. Since the market is currently being forced to assess the effects of market values indirectly, they are probably estimating the values with error. Hence, if anything, reporting the actual numbers may eliminate the estimation errors which may be one source of volatility in security prices.

Moreover, one message comes through loud and clear from finance theory. The investor is concerned with assessing risk as well as expected return. In this context, one role of financial statement data is to aid the investor in assessing the risk of the security. By presenting less volatile numbers, we may be doing him a disservice by obscuring the underlying riskiness of his investment. Hence, it is impossible to argue that less volatile numbers per se are better than more volatile numbers. Taken together with the evidence in the efficient market, this suggests that the market can decide for itself how it wishes to interpret a given piece of information. The same sort of reasoning should be applied to the currently hot topic of reporting and attesting to forecasts. In an efficient market, a paternalistic attitude is unwarranted; furthermore, operationally, if it is used to rationalize lesser disclosure, it is much more likely to result in the protection of management than in the protection of investors, which is its ostensible purpose.

Fourth. Accountants must stop acting as if they are the only suppliers of information about the firm. Instead, the FASB should strive to minimize the total cost of providing information to investors. In an efficient market, security prices may be essentially the same under a variety of financial accounting standards, because, if an item is not reported in the financial statements, it may be provided by alternative sources. Under this view, which is consistent with the evidence cited earlier, the market uses a broad information set, and the accountant is one—and only one—supplier of information. One objective is to provide the information to investors by the most economical means. In order to accomplish this objective, several questions must be addressed: What are the alternative sources of information to financial statements? What are the costs of providing a given piece of information via the alternative source vis-à-vis the financial statements? Most importantly, do financial statement data have a comparative advantage in providing any portion of the total information used by the market, and, if so, what portion?

The nature of the costs has already been alluded to. One set of costs is the "cost" of abnormal returns being earned by insiders because of monopolistic access to information. A second set of costs is excessive information costs. They can occur in two situations:

1. When the accountant fails to report an item that must be conveyed to the investing public through some other, more expensive source.

2. When the FASB requires firms to report an item that has a "value" less than its cost or items that could have been reported through other, less expensive sources of information. A third set of costs is incurred when investors erroneously believe that they can "beat the market" using published financial statement information. This set includes excessive transaction costs stemming from churning their accounts, improper diversification because of disproportionately large investment in "underpriced" securities and the selection of improper risk levels.[11]

---

[11] The costs of holding erroneous beliefs regarding market efficiency extend beyond investors. For example, consider the recent decision by Chrysler to change inventory methods because of alleged inefficiencies in the capital markets (both debt and equity markets). Even though Chrysler had reported supplemental statements in its previous annual reports, this was judged to be inadequate to overcome the inability of the capital market to look behind the reported numbers. The initial effect of a switch in inventory methods for both book and tax purposes was an incremental tax bill of approximately $50 million spread over a 20-year period. The efficient market evidence suggests that such a decision was a serious misallocation of resources. In fact, if anything, Chrysler is in worse economic position now because it is paying higher tax bills. For a summary of facts, see "Chrysler Posts $7.6 Million Loss for the Year," *The Wall Street Journal*, February 10, 1971.

* * *

Erroneous interpretations

The implications of market efficiency for accounting are frequently misunderstood. There are at least two common misinterpretations.

The first belief is that, in an efficient market world, there are no reporting issues of substance because of the "all-knowing" efficient market. Taken to its extreme, this error takes the form of asserting that accounting data have no value and hence the certification process is of no value. The efficient market in no way leads to such implications. It may very well be that the publishing of financial statements data is precisely what makes the market as efficient as it is. As I was careful to point out earlier, merely because the market is efficient with respect to published data does not imply that market prices are also efficient with respect to nonpublished information. Disclosure is a substantive issue.

A second erroneous implication is, simply find out what method is most highly associated with security prices and report that method in the financial statements. As it stands, it is incorrect for several reasons. One major reason is that such a simplified decision rule fails to consider the costs of providing information. For example, a nonreported method may be less associated with security prices than the reported method because the cost of obtaining the nonreported numbers via alternative sources is too high. Yet such information may be provided via financial statements at substantially lower costs. In another context, suppose the nonreported method showed the higher association with security prices; does it follow that the nonreported method should be reported? No, not necessarily. Perhaps the market is obtaining the information at lower cost via the alternative sources.

Moreover, the choice among different accounting methods involves choosing among differing consequences, as reflected in the incidence of costs and security prices which affect individuals differently. Hence, some individuals may be better off under one method, while others may be better off under an alternative method. In this situation, how is the optimal method to be selected? The issue is one of social choice, which in general is an unresolvable problem because of the difficulty (impossibility) of making interpersonal welfare comparisons.

———◆———

Note. *Incorporating the Costly Contracting Approach into Setting Financial Acounting Standards.* While Beaver's recommendations take account of the implications of the Efficient Capital Market Hypothesis for how financial accounting standards should be set, they do not consider the implications of the costly contracting and monitoring approach. For example, the costly contracting and monitoring approach suggests a rational explanation for Chrysler switching from LIFO to FIFO for inventory accounting, despite Beaver's derision of the decision. If Chrysler was approaching (or was expected to approach) the limits of its bond covenants at that time, might not management conclude that the cost to the company from defaulting on its debt would be greater than the present value of $50 million in additional taxes paid over 20 years?

In any event, it remains to consider how the implications of the monitoring and costly contracting approach should be taken into account in setting financial accounting standards. And for this purpose, we need to take into account the role of self-help. Can the parties themselves deal with the problem of management manipulation of the terms of a bond contract? Leftwich, *Accounting Information in Private Markets: Evidence from Private Lending Agreements,* 58 Acctng. Rev. 23 (1983), examined a sample of lending agreements obtained from five major private lenders and the terms of the American Bar Foundation's *Commentaries on Indentures* (1971). He found that although the agreements generally specified that references to accounting information referred to within the agreement meant accounting information calculated in accordance with GAAP, there were a substantial number of contractually specified deviations from GAAP. For example, the loan agreements typically mitigated the impact of the accounting method used for acquisitions by prescribing rules that minimized the manipulative potential inherent in both pooling and purchase methods.

When the ability of private parties to contract out of GAAP is taken into account, the differences between the ECMH and the costly contracting and monitoring approach with respect to how financial accounting standards should be set begin to shrink. Beaver suggests choosing standards that facilitate reconstruction by users who have different preferences. Leftwich's analysis reinforces this suggestion by demonstrating that private parties will alter GAAP when necessary to achieve their own purposes and that the more easily financial statements prepared in accordance with GAAP can be reconstructed, the more effective will be the private contracting. Additionally, the Leftwich analysis suggests that GAAP should be set to reflect the needs of those who are not in a position to negotiate directly with the company. Negotiation of alterations would be left to the parties for whom this type of contracting is cheapest—those who will be negotiating with the company in any case.

From the perspective of this synthesis, both the ECMH and the costly contracting and monitoring approach counsel that the critical determinant of financial accounting standards should be reduction in information costs. First, standards should reflect the needs of those users not in a contractual relation with the company. Second, standards should minimize the costs of reconstructing financial statement information by those who need the information in a format different from that specified in the standards.[30]

---

[30] For a recent effort to evaluate the importance of financial accounting standards in light of both the ECMH and the costly contracting and monitoring approach, see Ronen, *The Dual Role of Accounting: A Financial Economic Perspective,* in Handbook of Financial Economics (J. Bicksler ed., 1979).

CHAPTER NINE. DIVERSIFICATION

This Chapter considers another financial explanation for how an acquisition can overcome the principle of value additivity. Chapter Eight examined an information based explanation for how an acquisition can increase the value of the constituent companies—that the method of presenting accounting information affects firm value. This Chapter examines an ownership based explanation for the same result: why two companies are expected to be worth more if commonly owned than if separately owned, despite the absence of any change in their real economic performance.

A. The Theory

HAIGHT, THE PORTFOLIO MERGER: FINDING THE COMPANY THAT CAN STABILIZE YOUR EARNINGS, 16 MERGERS & ACQUISITIONS
33–34 (Summer, 1981).

The pricing of an acquisition is a difficult task which often requires that buyers predict future performance in risky areas. In making this assessment, buyers must consider the candidate's strategic fit, the effect of both financial and operating leverage on their income stream, and the acquisition's impact on their overall earnings growth rate. However, there is another kind of acquisition benefit, one which is often overlooked: the "portfolio" effect.

Although as individual investors m&a * practitioners are likely to seek the benefits of portfolio diversification, few, if any, have incorporated the classic portfolio diversification model into their merger decisions by considering the earnings stability that the diversification-motivated merger can bring. To be sure, some acquirers value "diversification" in its pure sense—as when Penn Central bought amusement parks—but few have examined the benefits of diversification in its technical sense. By this I mean the portfolio or "mean-variance" approach to investment—read merger—evaluation. The technical portfolio model can allow the buyer to estimate earnings flow from potential acquisition, then select the flow which will achieve the greatest earnings stability. It can also be applied to divestiture decisions.

The basic balance sheet elements of the portfolio model are: earnings before depreciation, interest, and taxes (EBDIT), and adjusted gross assets (AGA). The "EBDIT/AGA" approach can help identify the acquisition which will bring the greatest—or, in the case of a spin-off candidate, the least—earnings stability. This will depend not only upon the degree of correlation between the two firms' sales, but also on the relative mix and correlation of *fixed* and *variable* costs in their respective operating cost structures. Firms in capital-intensive indus-

---

* I.e., mergers and acquisitions. [Ed.]

tries, for example, have a higher percentage of fixed (vs. variable) costs. In such cases, changes in sales will contribute to greater variability in return on real assets due to operating leverage. To determine the degree of diversification effect, the buyer should ask if the merged firms' operating cost structures are compatible in these ways.

Here's how to use the model for this purpose: select a *preinterest, pretax* cash flow measure of return for a profit measure *above* EBDIT. Because it does not consider post-tax, postinterest, and below break-even measures for earnings, this technique will not be sensitive to financial leverage, and therefore will not distort your operating earnings picture.

If you measure potential diversification benefits in terms of asset yields, you can see the extent to which an acquisition can stabilize your earnings.

To measure return on assets (ROA) in terms of its operational impact, you can set the ROA of the combined entities equal to their EBDIT divided by their combined AGA. This EBDIT/AGA approach adds back depreciation expense to operating income, and accumulated depreciation to net asset value. To apply this same principle to divestiture decisions, simply *subtract* contributions of the spin-off candidate from your calculations.

There are two reasons for adding back the depreciation amounts. First, without these adjustments, earnings measurement will be affected by the firm's depreciation method. Thus, the economic benefit of the combination may be clouded by the asset depreciation methods which will have little bearing on future performance.

Second, depreciation, which is usually a fixed cost, will increase the amount of leverage in the return measure. Remember, operating leverage increases with any increase in fixed costs.

If you are considering the purchase of a manufacturing or mining firm, you should recognize that a large portion of their fixed costs comes in the form of depreciation and/or depletion expenses. By eliminating the noncash portion of fixed costs in the return measure, you can increase the proportion of variable to total costs in your firm's operating cost structure. The larger the proportion of variable to total costs, the less pronounced will be changes in operating profits resulting from revenue fluctuation. As a result, the measures you take will be more representative of the operating environment.

To calculate what your return on real assets will be after a merger, average the premerger returns of both the acquiring and acquired firms. The weights to be applied to each firm's return should be a function of each one's contribution to the total assets at the time the merger is consummated. In addition, you should calculate the "coefficient of correlation" for the combined earnings of the two merged firms.

Every dealsmaker knows that there is a gray area in earnings estimates. You don't really know exactly what will happen to your earnings when you merge, only the range of likely results—plus or minus what the statisticians call the "standard deviation."

The postmerger standard deviation is a function of the standard deviation of each firm's premerger return and the degree to which these returns are correlated—technically, a "coefficient of correlation." *The lower the correlation between these two streams, the greater the stabilizing effect of the merger.*

One indicator is particularly useful for evaluating the impact an acquisition or divestiture will have on your firm's earnings stability. This indicator is the estimated standard deviation of postmerger returns and can be calculated relatively easily.

This calculation, along with the others the AGA/EBDIT approach suggests, can predict post-acquisition or divestiture earnings results for even the most complex transactions. For example, given only 1979 information, according to the model, the 1980 post-merger returns of Dart & Kraft should have been 15.8449 percent $\pm$ .77 percent. The actual 1980 combined results were 16.1659 percent, well within the forecasted amount. The coefficient of correlation was negative ($-$.82118), indicating that the two firms were a good fit for diversification purposes.

Remember, the portfolio approach does *not* apply to mergers where synergy, whether positive or negative, is expected to add or detract from the earnings picture. But despite the vogue of synergy, many firms do choose to make acquisitions or divestitures for the purpose of financial diversification. If you contemplate making such a deal, the EBDIT/AGA "portfolio" approach can help you predict the future firm's earnings stability.

◆

For an argument that the historical persistence of diversifying acquisitions demonstrates that there must be some economic rationale for them, see Leontiades, *Rationalizing the Unrelated Acquisition,* 24 Cal. Management Rev. 5 (Spring, 1982).

Note: Diversification at the Company Level

The acquisition strategy recommended by Haight can be better understood by returning to the concept of diversification discussed in Chapter Four. In the following exerpt, Professors Brudney and Chirelstein describe the advantages of holding a diversified portfolio in the context of two companies.

V. BRUDNEY & M. CHIRELSTEIN, CORPORATE FINANCE
1151–52 (2d ed. 1979)

[Imagine two companies:] Warco, which manufactures weapons, and of Peaceco, which builds low-income housing. Both stocks sell at the same price. Performance of Warco depends on the size of the defense budget, as indicated in the following table:

Event	Probability of Event	Warco Return
Large Defense Budget	$\frac{1}{3}$	12%
Medium-Size Defense Budget	$\frac{1}{3}$	8%
Small Defense Budget	$\frac{1}{3}$	4%

Performance of Peaceco depends on non-defense government expenditures, which are always inversely proportional to defense expenditures, e.g., a large defense budget means a small non-defense budget and low earnings for Peaceco. Peaceco's performance can be related directly to the size of the defense budget, as indicated in the following table:

Event	Probability of Event	Peaceco Return
Large Defense Budget	$\frac{1}{3}$	4%
Medium-Size Defense Budget	$\frac{1}{3}$	8%
Small Defense Budget	$\frac{1}{3}$	12%

If an investor decides on a portfolio divided equally between Warco and Peaceco, he can expect the following results:

Event	Prob.	Warco Return	Peaceco Return	Average Return
Large Defense Budget	$\frac{1}{3}$	12%	4%	8%
Medium-Size Defense Budget	$\frac{1}{3}$	8%	8%	8%
Small Defense Budget	$\frac{1}{3}$	4%	12%	8%

Because Warco and Peaceco *always* react in *exactly* opposite ways to the same event, the return on a portfolio composed equally of both securities does not vary *at all*. Accordingly, if we assume that the size of the defense budget is the only event of significance to either company, an equal investment in both stocks produces an absolutely certain 8% return. By contrast, an investment in either company by itself, while it produces the same *expected* rate of return (8%), also produces the risk that the actual rate may fall substantially short of the expected rate.

———◆———

The lesson of Chapter Four was that, as between two investments with equivalent expected returns, less risk, defined as the variability of returns, is preferable to more. Thus, an individual would prefer to hold a portfolio divided equally between Warco and Peaceco, rather than one composed entirely of either. While the expected return of such a portfolio is no higher than that of a portfolio composed of either security alone, the portfolio is riskless with respect to the size of the defense budget.

A diversification motive for corporate acquisitions simply elevates this concept from the level of the investor to the level of the firm. Suppose you are the President of Warco and are interested in increasing the value of your company's common stock and, hence, the wealth of its stockholders. Suppose further that Peaceco can be acquired at only a small premium over its market price (assumed equal to Warco's because their pre-acquisition risk and expected returns are identical).

The theory is that significantly decreasing the risk associated with Warco's returns while decreasing the returns only to the extent of the premium, should increase the value of Warco's stock. The combined company would have the same expected return as did Warco prior to the acquisition (reduced somewhat due to the premium paid) but, as the Brudney and Chirelstein excerpt shows, with substantially less risk. As a result, the theory predicts that the value of Warco's stock will increase simply because of the common ownership of the two companies, despite the absence of any change in the real economic performance of either Warco or Peaceco.

Haight thus presents an acquisition theory that views the corporation as a portfolio of businesses whose management consists of reducing firm specific risk (unsystematic risk) through diversification.

B.   EVALUATION: CONSISTENCY WITH ANALYTIC TOOLS AND EMPIRICAL EVIDENCE

LEVY & SARNAT, DIVERSIFICATION, PORTFOLIO ANALYSIS AND THE UNEASY CASE FOR CONGLOMERATE MERGERS
25 J. Fin. 795 (1970).

That horizontal and vertical mergers potentially can produce real economic gains is nowhere denied, but the economic case for a conglomerate merger is somewhat less clear. Much of the traditional analysis relating to the possible creation of economies of scale in production, research, distribution and management is not relevant for the pure conglomerate in which there are no discernible economic relationships between the parties to the merger. Recognizing the need for an alternative approach to conglomerate growth, [some authors] have analyzed the diversification inherent in a conglomerate acquisition as a special case of the general theory of diversification and portfolio selection.

Such an approach identifies the reduction in standard error engendered by the combination of statistically independent or negatively correlated income streams as a "conglomerate effect" produced by the merger of firms whose economic activities are unrelated, and the purely conglomerate type of merger, as one in which profits are not increased, "but only stabilized by bringing together centers with zero or negative correlations."

It would seem to follow that even in the absence of economies of scale and complimentaries (synergism), the stabilization of the profit stream, induced by the merger, should still produce a clear-cut economic gain. But despite the plausibility of this argument, it can be shown that in a perfect capital market an economic advantage cannot be achieved by a purely conglomerate merger.

I.

Let us assume such a merger between two completely unrelated companies. In the absence of synergistic effects, the postmerger return to shareholders in the new firm will be the weighted average of the returns of each of the individual firms making up the merger:

$$z = wx_1 + (1 - w)x_2 \qquad (1)$$

where:

z = a random variable denoting the postmerger return to shareholders of the new firm,

x_1 and x_2 = random variables denoting the return to shareholders of the two individual firms, in the absence of the merger.

w = the relative size of the first firm, and

$1 - w$ = the relative size of the second firm.

The expected return after the merger, (u_z), equals the weighted average of the expected returns (u_1 and u_2) of the individual firms making up the merger:

$$u_z = wu_1 + (1 - w)\,u_2$$

* * *

Since we are assuming the absence of perfect correlation between the returns of the individual firms, the total postmerger variance is lower than the simple sum of the individual variances.[3] And as we have also assumed that the expected return after the merger is a weighted average of the individual returns, the risk-return characteristics of the new shares represent an "efficient" combination, i.e., one for which total risk has been reduced with no change in the level of return. It would appear to follow that the shares of the new firm should sell at a premium *vis-a-vis* the weighted sum of the premerger prices of the individual firms. However, such a premium will not be forthcoming in a perfect capital market because the superior risk-return combination could have been achieved by investors, even in the absence of the merger, by combining the individual shares in a portfolio in the proportions w and l-w.

Thus, despite the stabilizing diversification effect, a conglomerate merger per se does not necessarily create opportunities for risk diversification over and beyond what was possible to individual (and institutional) investors prior to the merger. In a perfect capital market, the premerger equilibrium prices of the shares would reflect the possibility of all such combinations. Therefore, after the merger has been effected, no increase in the combined market value of the two firms is to be expected or, in fact, is even possible.

* * *

[T]he optimal proportion of investment after the merger is simply the sum of the proportions which were invested in the individual companies prior to the merger. Thus, the merger per se calls forth no market forces to change the equilibrium share prices which existed prior to the change and, therefore, we may conclude that the stabilizing

---

[3] Throughout this paper, the analysis is carried out within the framework of the [CAPM] i.e., reduction of the variance (or standard deviation) of returns serves as a measure of risk diversification, and optimal portfolio selection is a function solely of the mean and variance of the distribution of returns.

diversification effected by pure conglomerate merger cannot produce an economic gain in a perfect capital market.

This result, which follows from one of the fundamental characteristics of a perfect capital market, i.e., that the optimal proportion of investment in various securities and the variance of the optimal share portfolio are equal for all investors independent of their tastes, is illustrated in Figure 1.* AMC is the [frontier] of efficient combinations of the three companies (A, B, and C) assumed to comprise the market; the market opportunity line ra rising from the riskless rate of interest, r, reflects the assumption that lending or borrowing, at the rate r, can take place. The scope of line ra * * * uniquely determines the market value of a unit of risk, i.e., the measure of the tradeoff between expected return and risk, for *all* investors, independent of their tastes. As a result, the proportions of investment in each share included in portfolio M are optimal for every investor in the market. Since * * * a pure conglomerate merger does not alter the optimum proportions of investment in the various shares, point M represents both the premerger and postmerger equilibrium share portfolio in a perfect market.

Figure 1

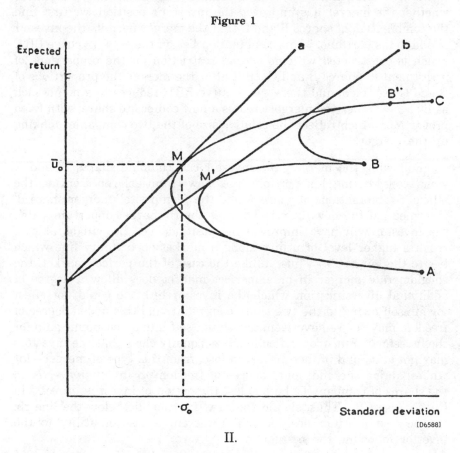

II.

Given the neutrality of a pure conglomerate merger in a perfect capital market, we now turn to the possible influence of market

---

* This diagram is similar to figure 3–5 in the Van Horne excerpt in Chapter Four B. Review that material now if you are having trouble here. [Ed.]

imperfections on the economic effects of such mergers. In practice investors do not include all security issues in their portfolios because of indivisibilities, differential transactions costs, cost of acquiring information, and the difficulties of keeping track of numerous investments. For simplicity we assume that for all, or some, of the above reasons, an investor restricts his portfolio to two shares only, A and B. The impact of such restrictions on optimal portfolios can again be seen in Figure 1.

All possible efficient combinations of A and B lie on the * * * curve AM'B, with M' on this curve representing the optimum portfolio, given the constraint that the investor restricts his portfolio to these two shares only. The new optimum share portfolio is tangent to the market opportunity line rb which lies below the ra line. Thus, all attainable positions under the two share constraint are inferior to the three share case and represent a reduction of utility to the investor.

Despite the two share constraint, the investor, following a merger of companies B and C, can invest in all of the shares of the market, i.e., in the new merger (B + C) and in company A. In order to determine whether the merger has improved the investor's position, we first find the combination of shares B and C that the merger permits the investor to add to his portfolio. This combination lies on the * * * curve BB'C which is constructed with no special restriction on the proportions of investment in shares B and C. But after the merger the proportions of B and C are fixed, and the * * * curve BB'C reduces to a point, such as B'; * * * i.e., the merger creates a new composite share, with fixed proportions which reflect the relative size of the two companies making up the merger.

Following the merger, the investor can combine shares B' and A when constructing his portfolio. A new [frontier] representing the efficient combinations of share A and the "composite" merger share B' is formed. If the new [frontier] crosses the rb market opportunity line the investor will have improved his position; i.e., he will be able to reach a higher level of utility along a market opportunity line which lies to the left of rb. Thus, unlike the case of the perfect market, the conglomerate merger in an imperfect market does allow a degree of additional diversification which the investor hitherto could not effect for himself owing to the two share constraint, and this added degree of freedom may, as we have seen, translate itself into an economic gain for the investor.[8] But upon reflection, it is equally clear that the investors may not gain, and in fact may even lose, from this type of merger—for while gaining the additional degree of freedom to invest *indirectly* in the shares of company C, he has lost the option of investing *directly* in the shares of B. Thus, should the new [frontier] lie below the line rb, the new equilibrium position will represent a loss of utility to the investor following the merger.

[8] By permitting a greater degree of diversification to the small investor, the conglomerate merger serves as a sort of substitute for a mutual fund or closed-end investment company. To the degree that the merger creates an increase in market value, this might be interpreted as the economic return on the more efficient diversification offered by this type of merger. * * *

MASON & GOUDZWAARD, PERFORMANCE OF CONGLOMERATE FIRMS: A PORTFOLIO APPROACH

31 J. Fin. 39 (1976).

I. INTRODUCTION

Several authors have recently attempted to evaluate the perform-ance of mergers. Most have dealt with highly diversified firms or those which have been heavily involved in conglomerate mergers and acquisi-tions. Methodological approaches have differed, as have the conclu-sions regarding the benefits (or lack thereof) accompanying mergers and acquisitions. Controversy continues particularly with respect to the benefits of the conglomerate merger. While we cannot expect to settle the controversy, our methodological approach is different and our results indicate that conglomeration may not provide positive economic benefits to either the firm or its shareholders. Our contribution to the understanding of the conglomerate phenomenon centers around our method of measuring relative performance, i.e., the use of simulated portfolios which mirror the asset structures of conglomerate firms. Our results indicate that randomly selected portfolios offered superior earnings performance and shareholder returns than did the conglomer-ates in our sample.

* * *

III. METHODOLOGY

Given knowledge of the composition of the asset base for each conglomerate, it was possible to construct matching portfolios for 1962 and 1967. The population of candidate firms to be included in a particular portfolio consisted of those listed in *Newsfront's Directory* of 25,000 U.S. Firms. Twenty-two portfolios were constructed—one for each conglomerate. To test the hypothesis that conglomerate firms should outperform a portfolio of the same asset content, the rules of construction were as follows:

1. Assign random numbers to each *Newsfront* firm participating in each SIC classification identified by the conglomerate as an area of participation. Firms in the population had to exist in both 1962 and 1967. From this group of firms select at random five firms in each of these SIC classifications and assign weights to each firm for 1962 and 1967.

2. Calculate the ratio of net earnings (before interest, taxes and dividends) to total assets for each firm in the portfolio.

3. Using the weights, arrive at an aggregate rate of return to the portfolio for both 1962 and 1967.

To test the hypothesis that stockholders in the conglomerate should fare better than those holding a portfolio, we used the 1962 and 1967 lists of firms developed above. We assumed that an investor in 1962 had the option of investing either in the conglomerate of his choice or a portfolio approximating the asset composition of the conglomerate. Furthermore he could adopt one of three portfolio strategies.

1. He could manage the portfolio himself and buy and sell stocks in order to maintain the portfolio in the exact composition of the conglomerate, i.e., when the conglomerate's composition changed he would sell off stock in those SIC classifications which shrank and buy stock in those SIC classifications which grew. He would also reinvest all dividends, pay brokerage fees and pay income and capital gains taxes at an average rate of 25%. Also he would confine his portfolio to the list of firms chosen above in the construction of the portfolios.

2. He could employ a mutual fund manager who would follow strategy one and in so doing pay any brokerage fees at standard rates and pay income and capital gain taxes at the rate of 25%. In addition the fund manager received an annual fee of 0.75% of average assets.

3. He could buy and hold i.e., not emulate the conglomerate but maintain the 1962 portfolio composition. Because the stock prices in his portfolio changed relative to one another over time and because he received dividends, there were some adjustments necessary between 1962–1967. The same rules of brokerage fees and taxation used in strategy one (1) were applied.

On November 15, 1962, the investor would buy in, and regardless of the strategy chosen (conglomerate, self-managed portfolio, mutual fund portfolio or buy and hold portfolio), the investor would sell his entire holding of stock plus reinvested dividends on November 15, 1967.

*   *   *

IV. RESULTS OF THE SIMULATION

We can look upon the conglomerates and their counterpart portfolios as two samples receiving different treatments. One receives the treatment of management control while the other does not.   *   *   *

Table 2

Empirical Results of Comparisons Among Conglomerate and Simulated Portfolios

	Direction of Difference
a) *Rate of Return to Total Assets*	
a.1) Conglomerates vs. Portfolios: 1962	No difference
a.2) Conglomerates vs. Portfolios: 1967	Portfolio superior
a.3) Conglomerates: 1962 vs. 1967	1962 superior
a.4) Portfolios: 1962 vs. 1967	No difference
b) *Rate of Return to Stockholders*	
b.1) Conglomerates vs. Self-managed portfolio	Portfolio superior
b.2) Conglomerates vs. Managed (Mutual Fund) portfolio	Portfolio superior
b.3) Conglomerates vs. Buy and hold portfolio	Portfolio superior

We had neither hypothesized nor expected the results reported in Table 2. We had expected the sample of conglomerate firms to either significantly outperform or at least perform as well as a set of randomly selected portfolios—simply because operating control should confer certain advantages to a diversified portfolio of assets. We find quite the opposite from the data at hand. The statistical tests indicate that the portfolios outperformed the conglomerates in terms of both rates of return on assets and accumulated stockholder wealth over the 1962 to 1967 period. There was no statistically significant difference in the rate of return for 1962, but in 1967 the portfolios outperformed the conglomerates. This is further verified by the deterioration in rate of return for the conglomerates between 1962 and 1967 while the earnings performance of our portfolios were not significantly different between the two years. In the case of stockholder wealth, portfolios demonstrated superior performance despite the fact that our hypothetical stockholder was forced to incur transactions costs, taxes and fees associated with buying and selling stocks.

*   *   *

Randomly-selected, stratified portfolios, not characterized by management control, outperformed a sample of conglomerate firms having centralized management.

As far as the stockholder was concerned, he would have been significantly better off between 1962 and 1967 to have opted for any of the random portfolio strategies rather than buy into conglomerates. This is not to say that the portfolios outperformed the conglomerates in every case (in 19 of 22 cases they did). A potential stockholder would have experienced better performance by buying a cross-section of portfolios rather than a cross-section of conglomerates. Despite having to pay transactions costs and management fees, a mutual fund of comparable composition to the conglomerates was, on average, modestly superior. One dollar invested in the conglomerate cross-section in 1962 and held along with reinvested dividends, until 1967 would have yielded a rate of return of 7.46% over the five year period. This is not inconsiderable. Yet the portfolio cross-sections yielded rates of return of 12.75%, 11.82%, and 13.99% depending on the strategy followed, i.e., self-managed, mutual fund and buy and hold respectively.*

———◆———

At this point, it is important to emphasize that the issue posed is not whether there is value in diversification. Rather, it is whether there is value in diversification *at the company level.* The response to the claim that acquisitions can overcome the principle of value additivity by reducing the variance of the companies' expected returns by diversification is that the shareholders of the acquiring company can diversify their own portfolios. So long as that is possible, the price of the acquiring company's stock will already reflect the value of diversifi-

---

* For a similar conclusion using different methodology, see Melcher & Rush, *The Performance of Conglomerate Firms: Re-* *cent Risk and Return Experience,* 28 J. Fin. 381 (1973). [Ed.]

cation.   Diversification by the company, rather than directly by its shareholders, thus cannot add value *unless* the company can diversify more cheaply than the shareholders.   This, however, is a tall order. An individual can diversify at no greater cost than the brokerage commission paid to purchase stock or the load factor and management charge paid when mutual fund shares are acquired (even the load factor is eliminated if a no-load fund is chosen).   The acquisition of another company, however, typically takes place at a substantial premium.   To choose an extreme example, if shareholders of U.S. Steel had thought it wise to diversify their portfolios by acquiring holdings in Marathon Oil, they could have done so at a substantially lower per share price than paid by U.S. Steel to acquire Marathon.[1]   If this is all that is involved, diversification at the company level may actually *reduce* the value of the acquiring company.

Another approach to justifying company level diversification is not that the company can diversify more cheaply, but that it can do so more effectively.   The argument would be that the company is better at selecting appropriate candidates for diversification, or monitoring their performance after acquisition, than individual shareholders.   Assuming a CAPM approach to security pricing, and in light of the evidence reported by Lorie and Hamilton in Chapter Five concerning the performance of mutual funds, is this justification convincing?

C.   Qualifications

If capital markets were perfect, and if agents were always costlessly loyal, there would be no qualifications of the conclusion reflected in the Levy & Sarnat and Mason & Goudzwaard articles: that pure conglomerate acquisitions cannot increase the values of the constituent firms.   Indeed, to the extent that the acquisition is costly to the acquiring company, because of transaction costs or a premium paid to the target company's shareholders, the effect of the transaction will be to reduce the value of the acquiring company.   But if markets or agents are imperfect, there may be motivations for diversification by acquisition that withstand analysis.

1.   The Closely Held Corporation

The essence of the Levy & Sarnat argument is that diversification at the company level is undesirable because it both can be replicated more cheaply, and tailored more carefully to individual preferences, if undertaken by the shareholders themselves.   What happens to this argument when the company is owned by a single individual or by a family that views itself as a single economic unit?   In this setting there is no longer anything but a formal distinction between diversification at the shareholder level and diversification at the company level and, in the absence of taxes, there is no reason to prefer one to another.   With

[1] Prior to the first offer made for Marathon, its stock traded for approximately $60 per share, at which price U.S. Steel shareholders could have acquired Marathon shares for purposes of diversifying their portfolios.   The price paid by U.S. Steel for Marathon shares, valued on the payment date and taking into account the two-step character of the transaction, was approximately $100 per share.

the addition of taxes, however, the analysis changes because there may be a penalty imposed—the dividend tax—on distributing to the shareholders the resources necessary for them to diversify. More careful consideration of this and other claims that the tax system serves as a motivation for acquisitions is deferred until Chapter Twelve.

If a close corporation is owned by more than a single individual, the problem of diversification becomes more complicated. Recall that the stock price of a publicly traded company is based on the risk-return characteristics of the company's anticipated income stream, without regard to the risk preferences or personal tastes of its shareholders. This proposition, commonly referred to as the "separation theorem," follows from the existence of an efficient public market. Shareholders may then individually arrange their portfolios to reflect their own tastes for risk diversification without regard to what investment decisions are made by the company. If a shareholder wishes to diversify, some of his holdings of one stock can be sold and other stocks bought. If the company's systematic risk is too high for a shareholder's tastes, the shareholder can sell some of its shares and either purchase shares of lower risk companies or even buy Treasury securities. If the company's systematic risk is too low for a shareholder's tastes, the shareholder can purchase additional shares using borrowed funds. In this situation, the personal tastes of shareholders for diversification and all other investment characteristics can be ignored by the company because shareholders can individually alter any corporate investment decision by making changes in their personal portfolio. It then follows that shareholders' only interest in decisions made at the company level is that the decisions maximize the market value of the company's stock and, hence, the resources available to shareholders to pursue their individual tastes.

The situation in a close corporation is drastically different, however, precisely because of the close corporation's principal characteristic. By definition, the shares of a close corporation are not publicly traded, a result that flows from the nature of the organization. The close corporation form is particularly suited to businesses where individuals must have substantial authority to make decisions and where those decisions are difficult for others to monitor. In this setting, the most effective way to encourage decision makers to perform well is to make them the owners, so that they bear the consequences of poor decisions.[2] A correspondence between decision makers and shareholders, however, makes the identity of each shareholder quite important to the others. As a result, contractual restrictions that prohibit a shareholder from transferring his shares without the approval of the other shareholders are commonplace in close corporations. But this restriction on transfer—which obviously makes a public market for the corporation's stock impossible—has important implications for the level at which diversification should take place.[3]

[2] See generally Alchian & Demsetz, *Production, Information Costs, and Economic Organization,* 62 Am.Econ.Rev. 777 (1972).

[3] The analysis applies with equal force to partnerships.

Because there is no market for the close corporation's stock, shareholders lack the ability to alter corporate investments decisions by rearranging their individual portfolios. If, for example, one shareholder wishes to further diversify, he or she cannot sell shares of the close corporation and use the proceeds to make other investments. Rather, the diversification must take place at the company level. The problem, however, is that other shareholders may have different individual preferences and, as a result, different ideas about what investment policy the corporation should pursue. Two conclusions flow from this reasoning. First, the investment decisions made by the close corporation will *not* necessarily be those that maximize the value of the firm. Because the personal tastes of the shareholders for diversification, risk or liquidity must be dealt with at the company level, the close corporation's investment decisions will be based on these considerations in addition to maximizing the value of the firm.[4] Second, the need to take shareholder preferences into account in making corporate investment decisions reinforces the incentives to maintain control over changes in shareholders; put simply, shareholders would be best off if all had homogeneous tastes.[5]

The fact that close corporations may not be pure profit maximizers would seem to put them at a competitive disadvantage in the product market vis-a-vis publicly traded corporations. However, the continued survival of this organizational form suggests the existence of offsetting advantages in other areas. E. Fama & M. Jensen, *Organizational Form and Investment Decisions,* 14 J.Fin.Econ. 101 (1985), on which the preceding discussion draws, suggest that close corporations survive in smaller businesses where central decision making is cheaper and more efficient than the diffuse decision making systems associated with larger companies. In their analysis, this savings outweighs the costs— like failure to profit maximize—that result from the absence of a public market for the corporation's shares.

2. Market Imperfections: Bankruptcy and Conflict Between Debt and Equity

SCOTT, ON THE THEORY OF CONGLOMERATE MERGERS
32 J.Fin. 1235 (1977).

I. INTRODUCTION

[I]f the securities markets are efficient, are there any purely financial benefits to merging? The answers to this question constitute the theory of conglomerate mergers and are the subject of this paper.

*   *   *

[4] See Gilson, *The Case Against Shark Repellant Amendments: Structural Limitations on the Enabling Concept,* 34 Stan. L.Rev. 775, 831–34 (1982).

[5] For an application of this analysis to the partnership selection policies of law firms see Gilson & Mnookin, *Sharing Among the Human Capitalists: An Economic Inquiry into the Corporate Law Firm and How Partners Split Profits,* 37 Stan.L. Rev. 313, 378 n. 110 (1985).

Assuming that corporate bankruptcy is possible, Lewellen has argued that if a merger reduces the probability that one of the firms would default on its debt, then the value of the debt will increase and the merger will be beneficial.[1] However, Higgins conjectured that if bankruptcy is costless then any increase in the value of the firms' debt will be exactly offset by a decrease in the value of the equity.[2]

On the other hand assuming bankruptcy is costly, Rubinstein[3] suggested that conglomerate mergers which reduce the probability of bankruptcy may be capable of benefiting both stockholders and bondholders. Higgins and Schall[4] considered the issue explicitly and argued that the effects of bankruptcy costs are ambiguous.

This paper deals with five unexplored or unresolved issues. First, what objective function should one consider when analyzing conglomerate mergers? For example, should an optimizing firm seek to maximize the value of its equity, or the total value of all of its outstanding securities? * * *

Second, the paper examines the effect on mergers of a class of corporate liabilities neglected by other studies. These are noncontractual obligations and include such things as damages awarded in law suits and sales taxes. Third, more can be said about the impact of bankruptcy costs on the profitability of mergers, especially when the cash flows of the merging firms are similar.

Fourth, under the assumption that bankruptcy is possible, Higgins and Schall have argued that the corporate income tax will have no effect on the profitability of conglomerate merger. The analysis presented below argues to the contrary that the corporate income tax provides a slight encouragement to merger. Finally, Lewellen has argued that conglomerate mergers are profitable because the debt capacity of the merged firm exceeds the sum of the debt capacities of the unmerged firms. Although Lewellen's assertion may be true in many cases, this paper * * * show[s] that it is not true in general.

* * *

III. Conglomerate Mergers of All Equity Firms

* * *

[A] conglomerate merger of all equity firms can never be profitable. Intuitively, this type of merger is unprofitable because the limited liability protection of a merged firm is weaker than that of two unmerged firms. In general the merged firm goes bankrupt less frequently than do the unmerged firms. In future states where the merged firm remains solvent while one of the unmerged firms would have gone bankrupt, cash flows from the solvent firm are used to pay the noncontractual creditors of the otherwise bankrupt firm. Had there been no merger the firm would have gone bankrupt, and the

---

[1] Lewellen, *A Pure Financial Rationale For the Conglomerate Merger*, 26 J.Fin. 521 (1971).

[2] See Higgins & Schall, *Corporate Bankruptcy and Conglomerate Merger*, 30 J.Fin. 93 (1975).

[3] Rubenstein, *A Mean-Variance Synthesis of Corporate Finance*, 28 J.Fin. 167 (1972).

[4] Supra note 2.

firm's noncontractual creditors would not have been paid, or at least would not have been paid in full. A merger simply transfers wealth from stockholders to noncontractual creditors. Under these circumstances, a firm seeking to maximize stockholder wealth will engage in conglomerate divestitures.

Notice that if there are no noncontractual creditors, [and if the transaction were costless], stockholders would be indifferent to conglomerate mergers.

IV. COVENANTS ON DEBT AND THE OBJECTIVE FUNCTION OF A FIRM WITH DEBT AND EQUITY OUTSTANDING

*   *   *

When the firm has both debt and equity outstanding, the problem is more complex. Within the neoclassical framework two possible, and possibly conflicting, objectives are usually discussed: the maximization of the market value of currently outstanding equity and the maximization of the market value of all of the firm's currently outstanding securities.

These objectives can conflict with each other because some policies which maximize equity value do not maximize total value and vice versa. It is well known that these conflicts can arise with respect to decisions involving investment and capital structure policy as well as merger policy. With respect to mergers, a conglomerate merger that leaves total market value unchanged can decrease the market value of equity. Thus stockholders might oppose a merger which all the firm's security holders, taken as a group, would find a matter of indifference.

In order to simplify the discussion, assume that firms only issue debt and equity * * * Furthermore, [assume that] firm decisions change only the market values of that firm's securities. This assumption rules out conflicts that occur when an investor owns equity in each of two firms, and a decision by one firm affects the value of the other.

Many theorists assume that firms maximize total market value, because all of the firm's security holders, taken as a group, are better off if that criterion is followed, i.e. total value maximization is Pareto optimal vis a vis all of the firm's security holders. Unfortunately, the problem is complicated because stockholders may decide to maximize the market value of equity. Since they have the legal power to make the firm's decisions, there is the possibility that stockholders may find it in their own best interest to follow a policy which is suboptimal from the point of view of all of the firm's security holders.

Fama and Miller [5] propose one possible solution to this dilemma. A stockholder controlled firm will maximize total value (1) if stockholders and bondholders are free to make side payments to each other, and (2) if both parties negotiate with each other on a rational basis. In this case, bondholders will find it both possible and profitable to bribe stockholders to insure the maximization of total value.

[5] E. Fama & M. Miller, *The Theory of Finance* Ch. 7 (1972).

A second possible solution to the dilemma follows from the fact that a stockholder controlled firm will maximize total value if the firm's stockholders happen to hold a sufficient amount of its debt. * * * In that framework an investor holds the same fraction of a firm's debt as he does of its equity. As a result, a conglomerate merger which leaves total firm values unaffected will be a matter of complete indifference, even if equity value falls.

Unfortunately a firm's stockholders are also its bondholders only in unusual circumstances, and while Fama-Miller type renegotiation clauses commonly exist in debt contracts, side payments are relatively rare because negotiations between stockholders and bondholders can be expensive. Thus one should expect to find additional mechanisms which mediate the potential conflict between stockholders and bond-holders, i.e. additional mechanisms that induce stockholder controlled firms to maximize total value.

As Haley and Schall point out, the maximization of shareholder wealth will always maximize total value as long as the market value of the firm's outstanding debt cannot be altered by management decisions. Thus equity maximization and total value maximization can be made consistent if some way can be found to insulate the market value of debt from changes in firm policies. The inclusion of two covenants in the debt contract is sufficient to obtain this result.

First, the debt must be "perfectly protected" in the sense that the protective covenants attached to it must effectively prohibit management from making any operating, financial, or investment decisions which would decrease the market value of the debt *unless* bondholders are exactly compensated for their losses. Given such a covenant, stockholders would not benefit from a merger which increased equity value solely because it made debt riskier, because they would have to compensate bondholders by exactly the amount of the increase in equity.

Second, as has been suggested by Higgins and Schall the debt contract must allow the firm to repurchase or call all of its outstanding debt by paying a price equal to the market price of the debt an instant before the call is announced. This type of perfect callability insures that stockholders will not avoid projects which increase total firm value but would, in the absence of perfect callability, decrease equity value.[7]

These two covenants effectively insulate bond values from changes in management policies (but not from changes in exogenous factors such as general interest rates), and thus change the incentive structure

---

[7] One might suppose that even without perfect callability a firm can simply repurchase debt at its premerger or predecision market value. In general this will not be the case. For example if a firm has to raise external capital to repurchase its debt, it may have to announce what it plans to do with the capital to be raised. The announcement of an impending repurchase (or even an unannounced attempt to repurchase) may be taken by the market as a signal that the debt is worth more than its current price. Thus its price would rise before a repurchase could be completed. * * * Note that the aspect of callability discussed here is in addition to its more frequently discussed function as a hedge against shifts in the rate of interest. [It has been] persuasively argued that in an efficient market this more familiar aspect of callability is a zero sum game.

faced by stockholders. If these covenants are included in all of the firm's debt then rational stockholders will seek policies that maximize total firm value. Furthermore, investors in a perfect capital market will value such a firm more highly than an identical firm which follows an objective inconsistent with total firm maximization. As a result since the total value of the firm is higher with covenants and since it is stockholders who ultimately receive any proceeds raised from a sale of debt, it is in stockholders' best interest to include these covenants in the debt they issue.

This rationale for the existence of protective covenants differs from that of Fama and Miller and of Haley and Schall who argue that bondholders demand covenants to protect themselves. On the contrary, given an efficient market, bondholders simply determine the price they are willing to pay for the bonds. The inclusion or omission of covenants in a particular firm's debt contract may change the price of the debt, but that price will fairly reflect the market's expectations and preferences for risk and rate of return. Covenants do not exist because investors demand them, but because it is in stockholders interest to design debt contracts that create [an] optimal incentive structure vis a vis the firm's security holders.

Finally, note that the value of claims to noncontractual creditors is not included in the total value of the firm's outstanding securities, and thus does not appear in the firm's objective function. The present value of these claims (e.g. sales taxes) is omitted because (1) as long as the firm does not default, these creditors have no ownership rights, and (2) unlike debt, these claims are not or cannot be protected from stockholder actions which decrease their value.

In summary it is in stockholder's interest to issue debt which can be renegotiated, or if renegotiation is costly to issue perfectly callable, perfectly protected debt. Given that, the maximization of the total value of a firm's outstanding securities is a necessary condition for shareholder wealth maximization. Thus the following sections will investigate the effects of conglomerate mergers on the total value of the firm's outstanding securities.

V. Mergers of Firms With Debt and Equity Outstanding

According to the argument in the previous section, a merger will be profitable if the total value of the merged firm exceeds the total value of the two unmerged firms.

* * * [A] conglomerate merger does not change cash flows in future states where both A and B would have remained solvent. Thus if bankruptcy is impossible, a conglomerate merger will not change total firm values. This familiar result indicates that in a [perfect] market, conglomerate mergers are profitable or unprofitable because of their effects on the present value of cash flows upon bankruptcy.

There are three separate ways that the possibility of bankruptcy affects merger profitability. The first effect flows from the provisions of the corporate income tax and is distinct from the well known encouragement given mergers by tax loss carry forwards. Carry forwards are not modeled in this paper, however the tax deductibility of debt payments is, and this deductibility also encourages mergers. * * * Intuitively, a merger reduces future tax payments if there are future states where one of the merging firms would have gone bankrupt while the other would have remained solvent. In these states a merger makes the losses of the bankrupt firm available to lower the taxes that would have been paid by the solvent one.

* * *

The second effect of bankruptcy results from the noncontractual obligations and can either decrease or increase the profitability of a conglomerate merger. * * * Other things equal, a merger tends to be unprofitable to the extent that there are future states in which the merged firm remains solvent while one of the unmerged firms would have gone bankrupt. In states such as these, security holders receive less because part of the cash flow of the otherwise solvent (unmerged) firm is used to pay the noncontractual creditors of the otherwise bankrupt (unmerged) firm. Conversely security holders are better off to the extent that there are future states where the merged firm goes bankrupt while one of the unmerged firms would have remained solvent. In such states, payments which would have been made by the solvent (unmerged) firm to noncontractual creditors are diverted to pay the bondholders of the otherwise bankrupt (unmerged) firm.

The costs of bankruptcy constitute the third and perhaps most important factor affecting the profitability of conglomerate mergers. * * *

[A] merger tends to be profitable to the extent that there are future states where, by means of a merger, one firm is able to save another from bankruptcy and its costs. * * * [A] merger is unprofitable to the extent that there are future states in which because of the merger one firm pulls an otherwise solvent firm into bankruptcy and its costs. Roughly speaking this implies that a merger between a large stable firm and a small, profitable, but unstable firm may tend to reduce the present value of future bankruptcy costs and thus increase value. Conversely, a merger between a small stable firm and a large volatile one may reduce value by increasing the present value of future bankruptcy costs.

Corporate strategists often argue that there are positive benefits to diversification, so that, other things equal, firms should avoid merging when the earnings streams of the two companies are highly correlated. However, most mergers involve firms in the same industry, where high correlations can be expected. Although most of these mergers are based on expectations of positive synergy, it is interesting to note that these mergers can provide financial benefits as well.

For example, assume a merger of two firms whose cash flows are positively related in the sense that if they were unmerged, they would have gone bankrupt in the same future states and remained solvent in the same future states. * * * [A] conglomerate merger of this type will either be profitable or leave total value unchanged.

This type of merger is profitable because of the economies of scale in bankruptcy costs. Quite simply, it is cheaper for one big firm to go bankrupt than for two little ones to do so. If there were no economies of scale, * * * the merger would leave total value unchanged.

———————◆———————

For a description of the way in which bond rating agencies take acquisitions into account in assigning ratings to corporate debt, see O'Neill & Weinberger, *Corporate Restructurings and Bond Ratings,* 17 Mergers & Acq. 36 (1982). The authors are, respectively, Group Vice President—Fixed Income Division, and Managing Vice President, Industrial Ratings, of Standard & Poor's Corporation.

Note that Scott's analysis suggests that one purely financial approach to overcoming the principle of value additivity is to undertake transactions that *increase* the risk of the combined firms rather than *decrease* it by diversification at the company level. The idea is that those creditors who are not protected by elaborate contractual covenants, like trade creditors, employees, and taxing authorities, can be made worse off and shareholders made better off by increasing the company's risk because all the gains from that increase go to the shareholders while any losses that result are shared by the unprotected creditors. For example, the interest rate on overdue tax payments is the same regardless of the company's risk of bankruptcy.

In evaluating the importance of this motivation for acquisitions, consider the following points.

1.   How much of an advantage is gained depends on the size of the company's debt to unprotected creditors. Moreover, whatever is obtained is offset by any premium paid target shareholders and by the transaction costs of the acquisition. The question is whether the magnitude of the net advantage gained will be large enough to explain very many acquisitions.

2.   The advantage gained is a function of how quickly the company's debt to unprotected creditors turns over. Once the outstanding debt to trade creditors is paid off, creditors can adjust the price of the goods or services sold to the company to reflect the higher risk resulting from the acquisition. Thus, the opportunity for profitable strategic behavior by the debtor is a function of the extent to which such credit is short-term. What are your guesses about the magnitude of the possible gain? Is there any class of unprotected creditors who would have difficulty in responding to an increase in their credit risk? For an argument that the middle-management employees of the target corporation are one such class, see Coffee, *Regulating the Market for Corporate Control: A Critical Assessment of the Tender Offer's Role in Corporate Governance,* 84 Colum.L.Rev. 1145, 1243–49 (1984).

3. The Problem of Agency: Diversification of Managers' Portfolios

Our analysis thus far leads to the conclusion that diversification at the company level cannot benefit an acquiring company's shareholders;

the principle of value additivity remains untrammeled. What happens, however, if we change the point of the inquiry? Although it is true that shareholders may not benefit from diversification at the company level, it is also true that shareholders do not make the decision to diversify at the company level. That decision is made by management. From this perspective, then, the question is whether diversification at the company level can make *management* better off, regardless of its impact on shareholders. And if diversifying acquisitions can benefit management, then we have found a rational motivation for some types of acquisitions, even if it is not one that results in value maximization for shareholders. This possibility—that management, when given the opportunity, will maximize their own interests at the expense of the shareholders'—should not be surprising. It represents the classic agency problem and, indeed, was explicitly raised in Chapter Seven's discussion of the application of option pricing theory to analysis of incentives.

In the following excerpt, Professors Amihud and Lev develop and empirically test the hypothesis that conglomerate mergers are motivated by managers' desire to diversify their own portfolios.

AMIHUD & LEV, RISK REDUCTION AS A MANAGERIAL MOTIVE FOR CONGLOMERATE MERGERS
12 Bell J.Econ. 605 (1981).

1. Introduction

■ Despite extensive research, the motives for conglomerate mergers are still largely unknown: What drives a substantial number of firms to engage in conglomerate mergers, given that *a priori* no real economic benefit (synergism) is expected from the combination of such functionally unrelated parties? The motive of risk reduction through diversification appeared at first to provide a natural explanation for the conglomerate merger phenomenon. However, it has been argued convincingly * * * that in perfect capital markets such risk reduction cannot be beneficial to stockholders, since they can achieve on their own the desired level of risk through portfolio diversification. Even when market imperfections, such as transaction costs, are admitted, the risk-reduction benefits of conglomerate mergers from the stockholders' point of view seem highly questionable, given the relatively low cost of portfolio diversification in the capital market. Moreover, the [option] pricing model * * * suggests that adoption of projects which reduce the variance of the firm's income distribution (i.e., diversification) may adversely affect equity holders by inducing a wealth transfer from stockholders to bondholders. How, then, can the widespread and persisting phenomenon of conglomerate mergers be explained?

It is argued below that the fast growing literature on "managerialism," and in particular the agency cost models, provide a possible explanation for the conglomerate merger phenomenon. In essence, such mergers may be viewed as a form of management perquisite intended to decrease the risk associated with managerial human capital. Accordingly, the consequences of such mergers may be regarded as an agency cost. The validity of this hypothesis is empirically examined below and found to be consistent with the data.

2. Conglomerate mergers and agency cost

■ Managers' income from employment constitutes, in general, a major portion of their total income. Employment income is closely related to the firm's performance through profit-sharing schemes, bonuses, and the value of stock options held by managers. Hence, the risk associated with managers' income is closely related to the firm's risk. Quite often, a firm's failure to achieve predetermined performance targets, or in the extreme case the occurrence of bankruptcy, will result in managers' losing their current employment and seriously hurting their future employment and earnings potential. Such "employment risk" cannot be effectively diversified by managers in their personal portfolios, since unlike many other sources of income such as stocks, human capital cannot be traded in competitive markets. Risk-averse managers can therefore be expected to diversify this employment risk by other means, such as engaging their firms in conglomerate mergers, which generally stabilize the firm's income stream and may even be used to avoid the disastrous effects bankruptcy has on managers. Thus, conglomerate mergers, while not of obvious benefit to investors, may benefit managers by reducing their employment risk, which is largely undiversifiable in capital or other markets.[3]

Managers' efforts to engage their firms in conglomerate mergers may be viewed as an agency problem. The parties to the agency relationship (managers vs. stockholders) can be assumed to be expected utility maximizers and therefore "there is good reason to believe that the agent [manager] will not always act in the best interests of the principal." * * *

Managers' benefits from risk reduction through conglomerate mergers and other means may thus be viewed as a form of perquisite appropriated from the firm. The welfare loss to the principal, due to the real cost of mergers and the possible wealth transfer from stockholders to bondholders (suggested by the options model), thus constitutes an agency cost.

* * *

Consider a fully equity-financed firm facing two alternative projects, X_1 and X_2, which are identical with respect to both expected

---

[3] Treynor and Black, "Corporate Investment Decisions" in *Modern Developments in Financial Management* (S.C. Myers, ed. 1976) 311.

There is some difference between the stockholders' and managers' points of view on the question of risk. If the corporation undertakes a risky new venture, the stockholders may not be very concerned, because they can balance this new risk against other risks that they hold in their portfolios. *The managers, however, do not have a portfolio of employers.* If the corporation does badly because the new venture fails, they do not have any risks except the others taken by the same corporation to balance against it. They are hurt by a failure more than the stockholders, who also hold stock in other corporations, are hurt. Thus the managers may be interested in an acquisition because it will give their company more stability; because it will balance the risks in their company against the somewhat independent risks of the acquired company. The managers' jobs and incomes will be more stable. But this reason for an acquisition need not concern stockholders.

return and *systematic* risk. However, the unsystematic risk associated with X_1 is smaller than that of X_2. (X_1 may be considered a pure conglomerate merger or any other activity which increases the diversification of the firm.) Under the assumption that assets are priced according to the capital asset pricing model, the value of the firm will be independent of the project adopted. However, the manager will prefer X_1, since its adoption will increase [the value of his human capital by decreasing the variance associated with its value.]

In this case, stockholders will be indifferent to the diversifying activities undertaken by the manager, and therefore no conflict arises.

Now let the expected return of X_1 be smaller than that of X_2. Thus, X_1 is equivalent to undertaking a costly merger for the sake of reducing unsystematic risk. This situation may produce a conflict between stockholders and the manager: The former will prefer X_2 over X_1, since $V_2 > V_1$ (where V_i is the value of the firm with project X_i), while the manager's choice is unclear, since he is faced with a tradeoff between risk and return. The manager may choose X_1 when the increase in [the value of his human capital] due to risk reduction outweighs the reduction in his * * * income due to the smaller expected return of project X_1. This is a classical agency problem.

Assume further that the firm is partially financed by debt. If the two projects have identical expected return and systematic risk (but differ in the unsystematic risk), there is again a possible conflict between stockholders and the manager. While (under the CAPM) the *total* value of the firm is independent of the project adopted, it has been shown * * * that the adoption of the project with the smaller unsystematic risk, X_1, will induce a wealth transfer from equity holders to existing bondholders.

* * *

3. The hypothesis

■ It has been suggested above that conglomerate mergers may be motivated by managers' own preferences. Testing the validity of this argument is obviously not an easy task, since all firms are run by managers. However, the discretion managers can exercise in following their own preferences differs across firms. In particular, this difference appears to be pronounced between *manager-controlled* and *owner-controlled* firms. In the former, where ownership is widely dispersed across stockholders, managers are relatively free to exercise their discretion and pursue their own preferences, while in the latter group of firms, where ownership is concentrated, the owners-stockholders are generally able to exert rather tight control on managers' decisions and to see to it that owners' interests are not compromised. Furthermore, the active role in management often taken by major stockholders of owner-controlled firms, and the consequent intimate knowledge of management's activities, reduce substantially the noise and monitoring costs associated with the evaluation of management's performance, relative to the noise and monitoring costs in management-controlled firms.

We can therefore expect more intensive risk-reduction activities in manager-controlled firms than in owner-controlled firms. This then constitutes a basis for testing the hypothesis that when allowed to pursue their own preferences, managers of management-controlled firms will engage in risk-reduction activities, such as conglomerate mergers, to a greater extent than managers of owner-controlled firms.

4.　Test procedures and results

[We examine] the hypothesis which associates conglomerate mergers with managerial risk-reduction motives [by using] the actual number of mergers performed by each firm as a measure of the propensity to diversify.　This test is aimed at finding whether the intensity of conglomerate mergers is associated with the type of control of firms.

*　　*　　*

■ **Test I: number of acquisitions and type of control.**　The hypothesis above suggests that the propensity of a firm to engage in conglomerate mergers will be related to the type of control structure in the firm. In the following test, the propensity to engage in merger is measured by the number of relatively large acquisitions made by a firm during a specified period.　Formally, the following cross sectional relationship is examined:

$$M_{ij} = \beta_o + \beta_1 D_{mi} + \beta_2 D_{wi} + \beta_3 S_i + u_i, \qquad (1)$$

where:

M_{ij} = the number of corporate acquisitions made by firm i within the ten-year period, 1961–1970.　The index j ($j = 1$, . . . , 5) denotes the type of acquisition according to the following well-known categorization:

$j = 1$: *horizontal mergers;* between companies producing one or more of the same, or closely related, products.

$j = 2$: *vertical mergers;* between companies having a buyer-seller relationship before the merger.

$j = 3$: *conglomerate mergers—product extension;* when products of the acquiring/acquired companies are functionally related in production or distribution, but do not compete with one another.

$j = 4$: *conglomerate mergers—market extension;* when the acquiring and acquired companies manufacture the same products, but sell them in different geographic markets.

$j = 5$: *pure conglomerate mergers;* between firms that are functionally unrelated.

D = a dummy variable, indicating the type of control exercised in firm i: D_m stands for management control, D_w for weak owner control, and D_s for strong owner control.　Therefore,

D_m D_w = O in case of *strong owner control;* where one party or a specific group owns at least 30% of the outstanding common stock of the corporation;

D_w = 1 for *weak owner control;* where a single party holds between 10% and 29.9% of the stock;

D_m = 1 for *management control;* where no single party holds 10% or more of the outstanding stock of the company.

S_i = the size of firm i, measured by total sales in 1961—the first year of the period examined.

Equation (1) can be estimated cross sectionally for each of the five types of acquisitions, thereby yielding five equations. The equation in (1) can also be estimated for a meaningfully aggregated group of acquisitions, such as all conglomerate mergers: $M_{i,3+4+5}$. In our estimation (later shown in Table 2) we report the results for horizontal mergers ($j = 1$), vertical mergers ($j = 2$), conglomerate mergers ($j = 3 + 4 + 5$), and for all types of mergers combined ($j = 1 + 2 + . . . + 5$). A total of four separate equations is estimated.

If our hypothesis is valid, we expect to find both β_1 and β_2 positive for conglomerate mergers, thus implying that the weaker the owner control (as we move from strong owner through weak owner to management control), the stronger the firm's propensity to engage in conglomerate acquisitions.[9] * * * In addition, we would expect $\beta_1 > \beta_2$, implying that the propensity of firms to engage in conglomerate mergers is monotonically increasing as we move from strong owner through weak owner to manager control.

Since the number of acquisitions might also be affected by firm size, we introduced an explicit size variable (S_i) into relationship (1) to focus on the net relationship between type of control and the number of acquisitions. Of course, size not only may affect the number of acquisitions, but also is affected by acquisitions. Hence, to distinguish between these two effects, we measured size at the *beginning* of the examined period, 1961.

The sample selection started from * * * classification of *Fortune*'s five hundred largest industrial U.S. firms by type of control. This classification pertains to the year 1965, which is the mid-point of the period examined.

Table 1

Average Number of Acquisitions Per Firm, 1961–1970

Type of Merger	Type of Control			
	Management	Weak Owner	Strong Owner	Average
HORIZONTAL (1)	.099	.061	.098	.091
VERTICAL (2)	.153	.182	.049	.146
CONGLOMERATE— PRODUCT EXTENSION (3)	.748 >	.576 >	.293	.650
CONGLOMERATE— MARKET EXTENSION (4)	.059 >	.030 >	.000	.045
PURE CONGLOMER-ATE (5)	.297 >	.167 >	.073	.239
ALL CONGLOMER-ATES (3 + 4 + 5)	1.104 >	.773 >	.360	.935
ALL TYPES	1.356 >	1.015 >	.512	1.172

[9] The magnitude of the β_1 and β_2 coefficients reflects the difference in the average number of mergers between the two types of control (compared with strong owner control) as well as the change in the probability of being engaged in a merger.

Standard and Poor's Compustat tape had the required data on sales, income, and income, and equity for the entire period examined for 309 of these 500 firms. These 309 firms constitute our sample. The sampled firms were then checked against the FTC *Statistical Report on Mergers and Acquisitions* (1976) to determine the number and type of acquisitions carried out during the period 1961–1970. Not all sampled firms had acquisitions during that period. Since the acquiring firms in the sample were the largest in the U.S., and since very small acquisitions cannot be expected to result from risk-reduction motives nor will their impact be detected by our statistical tools, we concentrated in this study on relatively large acquisitions for which the total asset size of the acquired firm was at least ten million dollars.

A general indication of the propensity of firms to merge is provided in Table 1, which presents the average number of acquisitions per firm by type of merger and control. For merger types 1 and 2 (horizontal and vertical), for which risk reduction does not appear to be the primary motive, there is no clear pattern for the average number of acquisitions as we move from "management control" to "strong owner control." On the other hand, for the conglomerate types of acquisitions, types 3 through 5, the pattern is clear and consistent with our hypothesis: The average number of acquisitions per firm decreases as we move from "management control" to "strong owner control".

*   *   *

Table 2

Estimates From Equation: $M_{ij} = \beta_0 + \beta_1 D_{mi} + \beta_2 D_{wi} + \beta_3 S_i + M_i$ **(Tobit Method) (t-Values in Parentheses)**

Coefficient	Type of Acquisition			All Types
	Horizontal (j = 1)	Vertical (j = 2)	Conglomerate (j = 3 + 4 + 5)	
β_0	−2.39 (4.89)	−4.16 (5.06)	−1.56 (3.20)	−1.06 (2.70)
β_1	.0004 (.0008)	1.29 (1.52)	1.93 (3.72) **	1.83 (3.63) **
β_2	−.45 (.69)	1.43 (1.54)	1.26 (2.16) *	1.15 (2.02) *
β_3	.00008 (.53)	.0003 (1.69) *	−.0001 (.75)	.000001 (.008)

* Significant at .05 Level (One-Tail).
** Significant at .01 Level (One-Tail).

Equation (1) was estimated separately for horizontal mergers ($j =$ 1), vertical mergers ($j = 2$), conglomerate mergers ($j = 3 + 4 + 5$), and all types of mergers combined ($j = 1 + 2 + \ldots + 5$). Our estimates, presented in Table 2, are consistent with our hypothesis. Consider first acquisition types 1 and 2 (horizontal and vertical), for which risk reduction does not appear to be a primary motive. The type-of-control coefficients, β_1 and β_2, are not significantly different from zero (at the 5% level), indicating that for these kinds of mergers, there appears to be no difference in the propensity to acquire between manager- and owner-controlled firms. On the other hand, the β_1 and

β_2, coefficients are statistically significant for conglomerate acquisitions. This indicates that for conglomerate mergers, where diversification is generally considered to be a primary motive, there is a significant difference between manager-controlled and strong owner-controlled firms. Further, the sizes of β_1 and β_2 for conglomerate mergers are consistent with our hypothesis, namely β_1 is larger than β_2. Finally, firm size does not appear to be associated with the number of acquisitions, since in most cases β_3 is insignificantly different from zero.

* * *

5. Concluding remarks

■ Risk reduction through conglomerate merger may be convincingly rejected on *a priori* grounds as a merger motive from the stockholders' point of view. However, this motive appears to be plausible for managers who are striving to decrease their "employment risk." The empirical findings presented above are consistent with this managerial motive. [M]anager-controlled firms were found to engage in more conglomerate acquisitions than owner-controlled firms. * * * It should be noted, however, that "type of control" is to some extent an endogenous factor, since to retain control, the owners of owner-controlled firms might be expected to make fewer acquisitions.

* * *

The above empirical findings should be considered along with available evidence on the earnings behavior of manager-controlled firms *vis-á-vis* those of owner-controlled firms. Both Boudreaux[1] and Holl[2] found that the earnings variability of manager-controlled firms is lower than that of owner-controlled firms. This evidence is consistent with ours. However, we extended the evidence on earnings variability to a specific means of risk reduction—conglomerate merger.

* * *

◆

Note: Evaluating the Managerialist Motivation for Acquisitions

Focusing on the interests of the parties who must decide to proceed with an acquisition, rather than on just the interests of shareholders, sheds light on the behavior of another party who plays an important role in an acquisition. It has become commonplace that a target company's major bank may play a central role in financing its customer's acquisition by another company.[6] Why would a bank participate in a transaction that might result in the loss of a major customer?

[1] Boudreaux, *"Managerialism and Risk-Return Performance," Southern Economic Journal* 366 (1973).

[2] Holl, *"Effect on Control Type on the Performance of the Firm in the U.K.,"* J.Ind.Econ. 257 (1975).

[6] The apparent conflict of interest in this situation spawned substantial litigation between target companies and their former banks. Despite an early trial court victory by a target company, appellate courts have consistently held that banks do not stand in a fiduciary relationship to their customers for this purpose. See generally Note, *Responsibilities of Banks in Financing Takeovers of Customers,* 48 U.Chi.L.Rev. 439 (1981); Note, *Bank Financing of Hostile Acquisitions of Corporate Loan Customers,* 21 Case W.Res.L.Rev. 132 (1980).

Recall from Chapter Seven that variability in the future value of the company affects shareholders and debt holders differently. Once the debt is priced—the interest rate and other terms set—an *increase* in the variability of the company's future income benefits the shareholders at the expense of those holding the company's debt, while a *decrease* in variability has the opposite result. Professors Amihud and Lev argue that managers have more interest in diversification at the company level than do shareholders, because diversification decreases the risk associated with, and hence increases the value of, the managers' human capital. Therefore, managerially controlled firms should engage in more diversifying acquisitions than those controlled by owners. Diversifying acquisitions may produce similar benefits for the target company's lenders. The assumption of the target company's debt to the bank by the more diversified combined company decreases the risk of the debt and, as a result, increases its value. Thus, the debt held by the target company's bank increases in value as a result of the target's acquisition in a diversifying acquisition even if the shareholders of neither company gain as a result of the transaction. Here the interests of two critical decision makers—management of the acquiring company and the target company's bank—coincide.

Returning to the Amihud & Lev analysis, there are a number of questions concerning their use of agency analysis to identify the incentives facing management of a management controlled company, and the incentives of owners of an owner controlled company. If these incentives are misspecified, then their data are subject to alternative explanations. Consider first the incentives facing managers of a company that they control. Does focusing on management's inability to diversify their human capital investment capture all of management's personal incentives with respect to making acquisitions? An additional consideration might be the extent to which their reputations as managers would be affected by self-serving decisions to make diversifying acquisitions. If such self-serving behavior reduced the value of their human capital, might it not offset the increase in the value of their human capital resulting from greater diversification?[7] Does the answer depend on who actually hires managers—owners or other managers? If the hiring is done by other managers who share the same values, is it possible that diversifying acquisitions will not result in a reduction in the value of the responsible managers' human capital?

To further complicate the bundle of incentives facing managers, what happens if we consider their position from an option perspective? If managers have substantial numbers of unexercised stock options, are they made better off by an increase or a decrease in the variability of the company's future value? See Chapter Seven C, supra. How might this analysis change your interpretation of the Amihud & Lev data? Is this a situation where options can be used to balance management's incentives so that they are closer to those of the shareholders?

[7] See Fama, *Agency Problems and the Theory of the Firm*, 88 J.Pol.Econ. 288 (1980) for a development of the concept that a market for managers constrains self-serving behavior by managers.

Similar questions can be raised with respect to whether Amihud & Lev fully capture the incentives facing the owners of the firms designated as owner-controlled. Their analysis necessarily assumes that owners can adequately diversify their portfolios outside the company. Otherwise, they would share management's incentive to diversify at the company level. Thus, their hypothesis that owner-controlled companies will make fewer diversifying (conglomerate) acquisitions is based on this assumption. But what if owners cannot diversify their portfolios through investments outside the company because their investment in the company represents too large a percentage of their total portfolio? In that event, an alternative hypothesis is possible. A non-diversified owner would have the same incentive to diversify at the company level as the owner of a close corporation which, in turn, would coincide with the incentives of management at least in direction if not in magnitude. From this perspective, the Amihud & Lev data also may shed light on what kinds of owners behave consistently with the Amihud & Lev hypothesis.

A final question concerning the Amihud & Lev study is definitional. The study is based on the theory that diversification cannot increase the value of a publicly held company because shareholders can accomplish this result for themselves. This theory does not, however, speak to whether acquisitions can increase firm value for reasons other than increased diversification. For example, in Chapter Eleven we will examine the idea that acquisitions may be motivated by synergy—the possibility that economies of scale, scope or organization may cause the two companies, once combined, to be worth more than the sum of their parts. Amihud & Lev include within the category of conglomerate mergers both product extension acquisitions, where the products of both companies are functionally related but do not compete, and market extension acquisitions, where the products of both companies are the same but are sold in different geographic markets. In both situations there may be significant opportunities for synergy. For example, product extension acquisitions may present an opportunity to share excess distribution capacity that could result in cost savings and increased value following the combination without regard to diversification. What would be the impact on the analysis and intepretation of the Amihud & Lev data if, as appears to be the case, it includes substantial numbers of transactions that have the potential for increasing firm value by means other than greater diversification?

Despite the difficulties identified with the Amihud & Lev study, it does provide empirical support for a position that predates the more recent agency literature but is, at least in its premise, entirely consistent with it. See, e.g., W. Baumol, *Business Behavior, Value and Growth,* (rev. ed. 1967); O. Williamson, *The Economics of Discretionary Behavior: Managerial Objectives in a Theory of the Firm* (1964); R. Marris, *The Economic Theory of "Managerial" Capitalism* (1964). This "managerial" literature posits that managers maximize their own self-interest to the extent possible and that this results, for a variety of reasons, in a preference for growth.[8] The diversification analysis made possible by the subsequent development of portfolio theory adds theoretical rigor to the managerialists' claims.

One approach to evaluating Amihud & Lev's hypothesis is to generalize it somewhat. Managers with undiversified portfolios want to reduce the risk associated with their company. To be sure, making diversifying acquisitions is one way of accomplishing the desired result, but acquisitions are hardly the only investment decision a company makes that affects its risk. For example, diversification can be accomplished by internal growth as well as by acquisition. If Amihud & Lev's hypothesis concerning management's incentives is correct, then their penchant for risk reduction should be reflected in nonacquisition related behavior as well. For a study that offers empirical evidence that management controlled firms more frequently try to smooth their income over periods and have lower systematic and unsystematic risk than owner controlled firms, see Amihud, Kamin & Ronen, *'Managerialism', 'Ownerism' and Risk,* 7 J.Banking & Fin. 189 (1983).[9]

Once the issue is cast in more general terms—managerial preference for risk reduction—it ceases to be an acquisitions question. Rather, we are directed toward examining the entire package of incentives confronted by management. How can we tailor those incentives—through compensation plans, stock options, etc.—so that managers have an incentive to maximize firm value? Acquisitions that benefit managers but not shareholders are only one of a number of symptoms of the disease of badly defined management compensation packages. For recent efforts to consider the more general problem, see, e.g., Beck & Zorn, *Managerial Incentives in a Stock Market Economy,* 37 J.Fin. 1151 (1982); Diamond & Verrecchia, *Optimal Managerial Contracts and Equilibrium Security Prices,* 37 J.Fin. 275 (1982); Miller & Scholes, *Executive Compensation, Taxes and Incentives,* in Financial Economics: Essays in Honor of Paul Cootner 179 (W.F. Sharpe & C.M. Cootner eds. 1982). See also Marshall, Yawitz & Greenberg, *Incentives for Diversification and the Structure of the Conglomerate Firm,* 51 So.Econ.J. 1 (1984) (profit streams of firms diversified at the company level provide a better basis for management incentive contracts). For a survey of the legal standards governing management compensation, see Vagts, *Challenges to Executive Compensation: For the Markets or the Courts,* 8 J.Corp.L. 231 (1983).

---

[8] For example, managers have been said to prefer growth because compensation is a function of firm size; because size itself provides protection against hostile takeovers; because the personal prestige of managers is a function of firm size; and because growth increases the opportunity for promotion within the firm. See Coffee, *Regulating the Market for Corporate Control: A Critical Assessment of the Tender* *Offer's Role in Corporate Governance,* 84 Colum.L.Rev. 1145, 1167–69 (1984).

[9] For an argument that the conflict of interest described by Amihud & Lev should lead to tightened legal standards governing the fiduciary duty of acquiring company management, see Note, *The Conflict Between Managers and Shareholders in Diversifying Acquisitions,* 88 Yale L.J. 1238 (1979).

CHAPTER TEN: DISPLACEMENT OF INEFFICIENT MANAGEMENT: THE MARKET FOR CORPORATE CONTROL

The motivations for acquisitions examined in the two previous chapters share one important characteristic: They are purely financial in character. The idea that firm value can be increased either by altering the information disclosed about the firm's economic performance (financial statement alchemy) or by reducing the total variability of the firm's earnings by acquisition (diversification) contemplates no alteration in the firm's real economic behavior; these approaches require neither an increase in post-acquisition output or efficiency, nor a decrease in post-acquisition costs. In contrast, the explanation for acquisitions considered in this Chapter is concerned entirely with a firm's productive, as opposed to financial, characteristics. It posits that some firms perform poorly because they are inefficiently managed; their acquisition allows the substitution of good management for bad and, hence, an increase in post-acquisition value.

A. The Theory

GILSON, A STRUCTURAL APPROACH TO CORPORATIONS: THE CASE AGAINST DEFENSIVE TACTICS IN TENDER OFFERS
33 Stan.L.Rev. 819, 933–44 (1981).*

A. *The Structure of the Corporation and the Theory of the Firm*

All corporate statutes define the corporate skeleton in essentially identical terms. Owners of freely transferable voting securities elect a board of directors which, in turn, selects executive officers who, with the help of lesser employees, manage the business of the corporation. The remainder of the corporate structure and the behavioral characteristics exhibited by the various participants depend heavily on matters not the subject of statutory concern. For the publicly held corporation, the markets in which the corporation participates—product, managerial, and capital—are the central determinants of that structure and behavior. To understand the role these markets play in the structure of public corporations, we must begin at what was the beginning of modern corporate analysis—the separation of ownership and management.

That the identity of the nominal owners of a public corporation—the shareholders—and those managing it diverged resulted inevitably from industry's capital needs in an expanding economy. The founder of a business, lacking the personal resources to exploit available opportunities, turned to outside sources of capital to finance expansion. As capital flowed into the corporation from nonmanagement sources, so did overall ownership of the corporation flow to the providers of capital. As Berle and Means stressed in their classic work, "[i]t is precisely this separation of control from ownership which makes possible tremendous aggregations of property." [56]

As the number of shareholders increased, separating the management function from the function of providing capital also became affirmatively desirable. Active managerial participation by shareholders faces enormous barriers. First, acquiring the information necessary to participate in corporate management is costly. Even if the corporation, as the least costly producer, distributed such information, the shareholder time necessary to understand and evaluate the information is still significant. Second, the cost of coordinating shareholder participation—of creating mechanisms to determine what decision the shareholder owners had made—is also great. Finally, successful management of a large corporation requires specialized skills which individual shareholders are unlikely to possess. It is therefore beneficial for those having capital but lacking managerial expertise to hire those with expertise at managing capital but lacking the capital to manage. As Professor Clark has recently commented, "the assertion of any individual shareholder that he knows better than the managers how to run the company borders on hubris."

The advantages of centralized, specialized management, however, are not without cost. Management monitors the performance of components of the enterprise in order to achieve efficient production.[60] But a mechanism is necessary to ensure that management carries out its monitoring function efficiently; the performance of management must also be monitored, and hiring yet another team of monitors merely recreates the problem one level removed.[61] What succeeds in short-

[56] A. Berle & G. Means, The Modern Corporation and Private Property 5 (1932); * * * My description of shareholders as the "owners" of the corporation does not suggest that the role described for them in the following pages flows, normatively, from their "ownership." It derives, rather, from the need for those holding the residual interest in corporate profits to have the means to displace management which performs poorly. As will be apparent, this position is based on matters other than a preconception of the rights associated with "ownership"; indeed, if the statute did not provide for shareholders we would have to invent them.

[60] Alchian & Demsetz, *Production, Information Costs and Economic Organization,* 62 Am.Econ.Rev. 777, 782 (1972).

[61] Alchian and Demsetz ask: "But who will monitor the monitor?" Id. at 782. The best description of the problem I have discovered is that in T. Geissel (Dr. Seuss), Did I Ever Tell You How Lucky You Are? 26–29 (1973) (emphasis in the original):

"Oh, the jobs people work at!
Out west, near Hawtch-Hawtch,

there's a Hawtch-Hawtcher Bee-Watcher.
His job is to watch * * *
is to keep both his eyes on the lazy town bee.
A bee that is watched will work harder, you see.
Well * * * he watched and he watched.
But, in spite of his watch,
that bee didn't work any harder. Not mawtch.
So then somebody said,
"Our old bee-watching man
just isn't bee-watching as hard as he can.
He ought to be watched by *another* Hawtch-Hawtcher.
the thing that we need
is a Bee-Watcher-Watcher."
WELL * * *

The Bee-Watcher-Watcher watched the Bee-Watcher.

He didn't watch well. So another Hawtch-Hawtcher

had to come in as a Watch-Watcher-Watcher.

and today all the Hawtchers who live in Hawtch-Hawtch

circuiting the process is a reward system that allows the monitor to retain the benefits of the successful discharge of its function; self-interest is substituted for supervision to encourage efficient monitoring.[62] This describes, of course, the close corporation, where the owners—the residual claimants who benefit from the increased profits resulting from efficient production—are also the management. In the public corporation, however, ownership and management are separated, and "the cost of * * * production is increased because the residual claim is not held entirely by the central monitor." [63]

The costs resulting from delegating the monitoring responsibility to professional management have been more precisely developed by Jensen and Meckling.[64] Management acts as agents of the shareholders. They can be expected, if otherwise unconstrained, to maximize their own welfare rather than the shareholders'. As a result, it is in the owners' interests to incur "monitoring" costs: expenditures like third-party audits, designed to make it more difficult for management to prefer itself at the expense of the shareholders. But even third-party monitoring cannot be fully effective,[65] and it will also be in the owners' interests to provide profit-sharing incentives designed to reduce the divergence of interests between management and shareholders.[66]

The sum of these costs—of efforts to prevent management from favoring itself and to positively motivate management to operate in the shareholders' interests—together with the loss in potential value of the enterprise resulting from the inability to entirely prevent divergence of management and shareholder interest, "are the costs of 'separation of ownership and control'" in the public corporation.[67]

are watching on Watch-Watcher-Watchering-Watch,
Watch-Watching the Watcher who's watching that bee.
Your're not a Hawtch-Hawtcher. You're lucky, you see."
I am grateful to Catherine Hillary Gilson and Rebecca Ann Gilson for calling this source to my attention. To be fair, Dr. Suess does ignore the likelihood that some monitoring will be at least partially effective. See note 72 infra.

[62] Alchian & Demsetz, supra note 60, at 783.

[63] Id. at 786.

[64] Jensen & Meckling, *Theory of the Firm: Managerial Behavior, Agency Costs and Ownership Structure*, 3 J.Fin.Econ. 305 (1976).

[65] The more specialized the management function becomes, the more difficult the problem becomes. "The more complicated the service or the product, the more difficult and costly it is to detect cheating, and the more likely it is that cheating will occur." Anderson, supra note 16, at 740. Moreover, securing the benefits of speciali-

zation requires that the provider of the service be given the discretion to use its expertise. Since the effect of monitoring is to reduce the discretion accorded the specialist, it also reduces the amount of benefits arising from the specialist's services. Id. at 744.

[66] Incentive plans are also never fully effective. It is difficult to design a plan which measures only the performance of a single manager undiluted by the efforts of others. Moreover, once the performance measures are specified, strategic behavior is possible which manipulates the system in a fashion which favors participants without achieving the productivity gains intended. See e.g., Rappaport, *Executive Incentives vs. Corporate Growth*, Harv.Bus. Rev., July-Aug. 1978, at 81; *Some Middle Managers Cut Corners to Achieve High Corporate Goals*, Wall St.J., Nov. 8, 1979, at 1, col. 6. * * *

[67] Jensen & Meckling, supra note 64, at 327; see Fama, *Agency Problems and the Theory of the Firm*, 88 J.Pol.Econ. 288, 296 (1980).

B. *Constraints on Management Discretion*

Understanding the roles of management and shareholders in the structure of the modern public corporation thus requires considering when and how that structure dissuades management from acting other than in the shareholders' best interest. For my purpose, the opportunities for management to favor itself at the expense of shareholders fall into two broad categories. First, management may be inefficient—if the managers worked harder, or were more careful, or were smarter, the shareholders' return might increase. This inefficiency affects shareholders by reducing production and therefore the amount of the corporation's income. Second, management may appropriate part of the corporation's income stream. For example, management may engage in transactions with the corporation which are unfair to the corporation, may provide itself luxurious office facilities or other perquisites, or in some other fashion may retain for itself more than a competitive return for managerial services. These two forms of managerial discretion are limited by several mechanisms, important aspects of which are market rather than legal.

Management's self-interest should constrain significant deviation from efficient operation.[69] The viability of the corporation, critical to both the shareholders' investment and management's continued employment, depends on the corporation's success in the market for the good or service it provides. Competition in the product market will penalize a company with inefficient management. Ultimately, the corporation will fail, so that management lose their jobs and the shareholders lose their capital.[71] The market for managerial talent also provides incentives for management efficiency. The corporation's performance is commonly treated as a measure of a manager's skills, and hence is a central determinant of the future value of the manager's services.[72] Finally, managerial inefficiency is constrained by the capi-

---

[69] The problem of inefficient production—of "shirking"—exists for all levels of supervisors, not merely senior management. But one would expect the self-interest of lower level managers to aid more senior management in policing this conduct. Lower level supervisors, interested in their own advancement, have an incentive to be sure that their supervisors are made aware of their successes and the failures of their competitors for promotion, thus reducing the cost of securing information. Fama, supra note 67, at 293. Lower level managers also monitor the performance of their supervisors: "Lower managers perceive that they can gain by stepping over shirking or less competent managers above them. Moreover, in the team or nexus of contracts view of the firm, each manager is concerned with the performance of managers above and below him since his marginal product is likely to be a positive function of theirs." Id.

[71] E.g., R. Posner, Economic Analysis of Law 302 (2d ed. 1977); R. Winter, Government and the Corporation. Indeed the cost of failure may be far greater for manage-

ment than for stockholders. The latter, it will be recalled, are presumed to hold a diversified portfolio of securities, the value of which should not be significantly affected by events—like business failure due to the inefficiency of management—affecting only a particular firm * * *. In contrast, the manager has invested his human capital in the firm through his employment decision, an investment which cannot easily be diversified * * *.

[72] The role of the managerial market as a mechanism for constraining managerial discretion to deviate from profit maximization is considered in detail in Fama, supra note 67. * * * As developed by Professor Fama, this mechanism operates both within the firm, powered by the ambition of lower managers, Fama, supra note 67, at 293, and through external forces such as the price of the corporation's stock as a measure of managerial talent, id. at 292. Ultimately, however, the extent of the constraint on top management depends on the extent to which top management can be policed. So long as these managers control their own tenure, the constraint imposed

tal market. A corporation's poor performance in its product market is reflected in the market price of the corporation's stock. Where poor performance is due to management inefficiency, the potential for gain exists through purchasing the corporation's shares at the depressed price and then installing efficient management.[73] Thus, inefficiency may be policed before it results in business failure even if management ignores earlier signals.

Where incentive mechanisms created by one part of the corporate structure—the various markets in which the corporation and its managers function—constrain managerial discretion to perform inefficiently, one would not expect a different part of that structure to provide redundant controls. As we have seen, the legal elements of the corporate structure are consistent with this conclusion. The typical corporate statute assigns management responsibility to the board of directors. The business judgment rule measures the discharge of that responsibility. The rule operates to bar courts from providing additional, and unnecessary, constraints on management discretion through judicial review of operating decisions.

The role of low-cost market mechanisms in restraining managerial discretion is more limited with respect to management's incentive to allocate to itself an excessive portion of the corporation's income. Incentives to succeed in the product market are less likely to constrain managerial self-dealing, since what is of concern is management's ability to allocate to itself income generated through *successful* operation of the corporation's business. Nor will the capital market provide a substantial constraint. Although a lower rate of return to shareholders may increase the corporation's cost of new equity capital by decreasing the value of the corporation's shares, this constraint operates only to the extent the corporation cannot finance its activities through retained earnings and debt. In any event, the cost is borne by existing shareholders through dilution of their interests.

The managerial services market is also less likely to constrain self-dealing than to constrain inefficiency. The buyers of managers for

---

by a potential reduction in the market value of their services if they were forced to change jobs is reduced: "Having gained control of the board, top management may decide that collusion and expropriation of security holder wealth are better than competition among themselves." Id. at 293. Independent directors might serve to limit the extent of such collusion: "In a state of advanced evolution of the external markets that buttress the corporate firm, the outside directors are in their turn disciplined by the market for their services which prices them according to their performance as referees." Id. at 294. And, one must acknowledge, displacement of top management by independent boards of directors does seem to be occurring with increasing frequency. See Bauer, *Why Big Business is Firing the Boss,* N.Y. Times, March 8, 1981, § 6 (Magazine), at 22. But the question remains as to what force prevents "collusion and expropriation" from circumventing market discipline on the outside directors. Fama falls back on the role of the capital markets as a mechanism which will allow the forcible displacement of unfaithful managers, something which the market for managers, even as he formulates it, will not accomplish. Fama, supra note 67, at 294–95.

[73] * * * The impact of capital market constaints is also felt through the product market. To the extent that the corporation's performance is reduced through inefficiency, providers of capital will require a greater return before making their capital available to the corporation. * * * This should result, for example, in higher borrowing costs for less efficient corporations, which should put them at a disadvantage in the product market compared to companies with more efficient management and lower capital costs.

public corporations are, realistically, other managers. There is no reason to believe that an efficient manager's penchant for high pay or perquisites will be negatively viewed.

Thus, except for the potential constraint imposed by the market for corporate control, the market component of the corporate structure is not likely to impose substantial limits on management's ability to self-deal. In contrast to its function with respect to managerial inefficiency, the legal component of the corporate structure has a significant role in constraining management's self-dealing.

Consistent with this conclusion, the courts (and some statutes) require that management demonstrate the fairness of its dealings with the corporation. But while a judicially enforced fairness standard may reduce management discretion to self-deal in many settings, there are important situations where the potential for management's favoring itself at the expense of shareholders cannot be limited by reference to fairness.[81] For example, where corporate income is diverted to acquiring new businesses rather than being distributed to the shareholders, the question of fairness, as measured by the price paid for the business, is beside the point. Judicially determining whether a particular acquisition was "fair," or whether the funds should instead have been returned to the shareholders by way of dividends, is impossible. * * * [T]he same problem exists when management's self-dealing takes the form of resisting changes in corporate control.

Thus far, the structure of the corporation—market constraints and a judicially enforced fiduciary duty—does not effectively limit management's ability to self-deal by protecting its control position. The market for corporate control is the remaining potential source of constraint.

C. The Market for Corporate Control

Owing to the groundbreaking work of Henry Manne,* it is now commonly acknowledged that the market for corporate control is an important mechanism by which management's discretion to favor itself at the expense of shareholders may be constrained. Indeed, where that favoritism is expressed in subtle ways, the market for corporate control may be the only potentially serious force for limiting management discretion. Thus, the fit of this constraint within the legal and market structure of the corporation is of central importance.

The theory of a corporate control market posits that a decrease in corporate profits, whether because of inefficient management or because efficient but self-dealing management has diverted too much income to itself, causes the price of the corporation's stock to decline to a level consistent with the corporation's reduced profitability. This creates an opportunity for entrepreneurial profit. If shares represent-

---

[81] What goals managers pursue when given the discretion has been the subject of a substantial literature, which has recently been surveyed in Marris & Mueller, *The Corporation, Competition, and the Invisible Hand,* 18 J.Econ.Lit. 32 (1980). For an early review, see Machlup, *Theories of the Firm: Marginalist, Behavioral, Manageri-*

al, 57 Am.Econ.Rev. 1 (1967). For my purpose, the existence of the discretion, rather than its use, is of principal interest.

* The original work was Manne, *"Mergers and the Market for Corporate Control,"* 73 J.Pol.Econ. 110 (1965). [Ed.]

ing control can be purchased at a price which, together with the associated transaction costs, is less than the shares' value following displacement of existing management, then everyone—other than the management to be displaced—benefits from the transaction. Selling shareholders receive more for their stock than its value under previous management; new management receives an entrepreneurial reward through the increased value of acquired shares; and society benefits from more efficiently used resources.

Two important conditions are necessary for this happy concurrence of results. First, the market price of the corporation's stock must accurately reflect incumbent management's inefficiency or greed. Second, there must be mechanisms available for displacing incumbent management. * * *

------◆------

B. Evaluation: Consistency With Analytic Tools and Empirical Evidence

An explanation for corporate acquisitions based on the role of the capital markets in facilitating the transfer of control over productive assets from inefficient to efficient managers is perfectly compatible with the financial theory discussed in Part I. Put in terms of the capital asset pricing model, superior management generates greater return for equivalent amounts of systematic risk, therefore supporting a higher value for the capital assets following the transfer of control.

This explanation yields a number of testable hypotheses. As stated in Ellert, *Mergers, Antitrust Law Enforcement and Stockholder Returns,* 31 J.Fin. 715, 723 (1976): "The capital market, through stock price adjustments, provides our only objective standard of managerial efficiency. Superior management capabilities, once recognized, will be reflected in stock price appreciation. If the function of the market for corporate control is to transfer assets from poorly managed firms to well managed ones, then it would not be surprising to observe positive abnormal returns for acquiring firms in periods preceding merger activity." Similarly, if corporate acquisitions are motivated by the opportunity to displace poorly performing management, we would expect target companies to perform poorly in periods prior to their acquisition, thereby causing a reduction in their stock price that signals the opportunity for profit by acquisition.

Both these hypotheses can be empirically tested by an event study using the CAR methodology described in Chapter Five. One would gather a sample of acquiring and acquired companies and compute their abnormal returns over specified periods prior to the announcement of the acquisition transaction. If the motive for acquisitions is to displace the target company's inefficient managers and replace them with the acquiring company's better managers, the CAR for acquiring firms should be positive, and that for acquired firms should be negative, in the pre-acquisition period. A number of recent studies have undertaken this analysis with more or less consistent results. These results are summarized in Table 10.

Table 10

Pre-Acquisition Performance of Target and Acquiring Companies
A. Pre-Acquisition Performance—Target Companies

Study	Sample	Period (month of announcement = 0)	CAR
Mandelker, Risk and Return: The Case of Merging Firms, 1 J.Fin.Econ. 303 (1974)	252 firms acquired between 11/41 and 8/62 (91% after 1/51)	-40 through -9 [1]	-3.0%
Ellert, Mergers, Antitrust Law Enforcement and Stockholder Returns, 31 J.Fin. 715 (1976)	311 NYSE firms acquired between 1950 and 1970	-100 through -8 [1]	-11.7%
Dodd & Ruback, Tender Offers and Stockholder Returns: An Empirical Analysis, 5 J.Fin.Econ. 351 (1977)	136 target firms subject to successful tender offers between 1958 and 1976 that appear on CRSP tapes.[2]	-60 through -8	2.1%*
Kummer & Hoffmeister, Valuation Consequences of Cash Tender Offers, 32 J.Fin. 505 (1978)	50 NYSE firms subject to successful cash tender offers between 1/56 and 6/74	-40 through -3	-5.3%*
Langetieg, An Application of a Three-Factor Performance Index to Measure Stockholder Gains from Merger, 6 J.Fin.Econ. 365 (1978)	149 NYSE firms which merged between 11/41 and 8/62	-72 through -19 [1] -18 through -7	-12.58% 0.2%
Asquith, Mergers and the Market for Acquisitions, unpublished paper, University of Chicago, January, 1979 [3]	305 NYSE firms acquired between 1946 and 1976	-47 through -3 -23 through -3	-14.0% -9.0%
Asquith & Kim, The Impact of Merger Bids on the Participating Firms' Security Holders, 37 J.Fin. 1209 (1982)	21 firms acquired in a conglomerate merger[4] between 1960 and 1978, whose book value exceeded 10% of that of the acquiring company	-12 through -3	-0.48%*
Asquith, Merger Bids, Uncertainty and Stockholder Returns, 11 J.Fin.Econ. 51 (1983)	211 NYSE firms subject to successful mergers between 1962 and 1976	-16 through -3	-13.8%
Malatesta, The Wealth Effect of Merger Activity and the Objective Functions of Merging Firms, 11 J.Fin.Econ. 155 (1983)	85 firms acquired between 1969 and 1974 with more than $10 million in assets	-60 through -25 -24 through -4 -60 through -4 -24 through -4	12.6% -8.5%* -$29.088 million [5] -25.561 million

Table 10

Pre-Acquisition Performance of Target and Acquiring Companies—Continued

B. Pre-Acquisition Performance—Acquiring Companies

Study	Sample	Period (month of announcement) = 0	CAR
Asquith (1979) (supra)	286 NYSE acquiring firms involved in mergers between 1946 and 1976	-24 through -1	11.0%
Asquith & Kim (supra)	27 acquiring firms making a conglomerate merger[4] between 1960 and 1978, where target firm's book value exceeded 10% of that of the acquiring firm	-12 through -3	4.21%*
Mandelker (supra)	241 NYSE firms making acquisitions between 11/41 and 8/62 (91% after 1/51)	-40 through -9[1]	3.1%
Ellert (supra)	772 NYSE firms making acquisitions of $10 million or more between 1950 and 1970	-100 through -8[1]	18.5%
Dodd & Ruback (supra)	124 acquiring firms making successful tender offers between 1958 and 1976 that appear on CRSP tapes	-60 through -8	3.23*
Kummer & Hoffmeister (supra)	Subsample of 17 successful acquiring firms (see above)	-40 through -1	17.0%
Langetieg (supra)	149 NYSE firms which merged between 11/41 and 8/62	-72 through -19 -18 through -7 -72 through -7	6.09% 4.97% 11.06%

Table 10

Pre-Acquisition Performance of Target and Acquiring Companies—Continued

B. Pre-Acquisition Performance—Acquiring Companies

Study	Sample	Period (month of announcement) = 0	CAR
Asquith (1983) (supra)	196 NYSE acquiring firms making successful mergers between 1962 and 1976	-16 through -3	13.4%
Malatesta (supra)	256 acquiring firms making successful mergers between 1969 and 1974 where target firm had more than $10 million in assets	-60 through -25 -24 through -4 -60 through -4 -24 through -4	3.9% -1.6%* -$83.529 million [5] -$24.593 million

*Not statistically significant.

[1] For this study, month 0 = the month in which the merger was consummated.

[2] The CRSP tapes maintained by the Center for Securities Price Research at the University of Chicago contain stock price data for exchange listed and over-the-counter stocks. See Introduction to Part I, supra.

[3] As reported in G. Benston, *Conglomerate Mergers: Causes, Consequences and Remedies* 41-42 (1980).

[4] As classified by the Federal Trade Commission.

[5] Cumulative abnormal dollar return computed by multiplying percentage abnormal returns by the dollar value of the firm's outstanding equity.

Note: Evaluating the Data

The general pattern displayed for target companies in Table 10 is one of negative abnormal returns in the pre-acquisition period except for the months immediately preceding announcement of the transaction, in which *positive* abnormal returns are earned.[1] This is consistent with a displacement of inefficient management motivation for acquisitions: Target companies do seem to perform poorly for substantial periods of time before their acquisition, thereby signalling the opportunity for gain by if more successful managers are installed.

The general pattern displayed for acquiring companies is also consistent with a displacement of inefficient management motivation for acquisitions. They earn positive abnormal returns in the pre-acquisition period, thus suggesting that they possess efficient management.

In evaluating these empirical results, however, a number of qualifications should be kept in mind. First, although they are consistent with a displacement of inefficient management motivation, they do not exclude alternative motivations. For example, synergy is also possible between firms with the abnormal return histories displayed in Table 10.

Second, there are methodological differences between the studies whose results are summarized in Figure 10, most notably Malatesta's use of abnormal dollar returns to overcome the relative nature of CAR measures, and the state of the art does not yet allow specifying the impact of the differences.[2]

Third, there are some pieces of the evidence that do not quite fit. Malatesta's finding that acquiring companies earned negative abnormal dollar returns (although the CAR was not significantly different from zero) is anomalous. And there are studies not summarized in Table 10 that, relying on financial accounting data, report results that are inconsistent with the proposition that acquiring companies are more efficient than target companies. For example, Levine & Aaronovitch, *The Financial Characteristics of Firms and Theories of Merger Activity,* 30 J.Indus.Econ. 149 (1981), reached this conclusion with respect to 154 target companies in large mergers in the United Kingdom in 1972.[3] Similarly, Lowenstein, *Pruning Deadwood in Hostile Takeovers: A Proposal for Legislation,* 83 Colum.L.Rev. 249 (1983), calculated that, of the 10 subjects of major hostile tender offers in 1981 who did not

---

[1] Positive abnormal returns in the immediate pre-acquisition period reflect the premium typically paid to target shareholders. Returns for this period and the period in which the acquisition is announced are set out in Chapter Eleven, Table 11, infra.

[2] For discussions of the methodological differences see, e.g., Halpern, *Corporate Acquisitions: A Theory of Special Cases? A Review of Event Studies Applied to Acquisitions,* 38 J.Fin. 297 (1983); Malatesta, *supra.* Jensen & Ruback, *The Market for*

Corporate Control: The Scientific Evidence, 11 J.Fin.Econ. 5 (1983), conclude that the overall results of the studies "appear robust with respect to the various estimation techniques used" although they acknowledge Malatesta "raises some interesting questions." Id. at 9 n. 1.

[3] In this study, efficiency was measured by rate of return, growth of capital employed, growth of rate of return and valuation ratio, all computed using financial accounting data.

survive as independent companies, five had a higher average return on equity than the ultimate acquiring company and eight had a higher average return on equity than the bidder that initiated the control contest. Id. at 289 n. 165. The problem with studies of this sort, however, is their reliance on financial accounting data. As discussed in Chapter Eight, management of poorly performing firms may have an incentive to choose accounting methods that maximize measures of efficiency. Moreover, accounting data does not measure a company's future value, only its current condition. Thus, a target company pursuing a short-run maximization strategy may display more attractive current financial accounting data than a company taking a long-run view. As a result, use of financial accounting data to measure efficiency may serve to minimize differences between efficient and inefficient companies.[4]

Finally, the results summarized in Table 10—suggesting that target firms are poor performers characterized by inept management—are inconsistent with recent views expressed by prominent practitioners in the mergers and acquisitions field. A financial consultant and former partner in the investment banking firm of Lazard Freres, speaking at an American Bar Association National Institute on Corporate Takeovers, stated that "if you look at the businesses which have been target companies in recent years, you'll find that, by and large, they're successful companies except in limited instances. One doesn't normally buy a company that has a history of losses." Troubh, *Characteristics of Target Companies,* 32 Bus.Law. 1301, 1302 (1977). Similarly, a practicing lawyer with a major corporate law firm has argued that "one would be hard pressed to argue that the companies involved in the most prominent hostile takeovers in 1976 and 1977 were managed by inefficient executives. * * * [W]hile meaningful data has not been collected and made generally available, the common belief is that the typical target companies today are successful participants in their particular fields and are managed by able personnel." Steinbrink, *Management's Response to the Takeover Attempt,* 28 Case W.Res.L.Rev. 882, 892 (1978).[5] And a survey of corporate directors conducted by Touche Ross & Co. in 1981 disclosed that 84% of the directors listed "excellent management" as a "major attraction" in selecting a target company for acquisition.[6]

In light of this conflict, more data would be helpful. Additional empirical evidence bearing, albeit indirectly, on the extent to which displacement of inefficient management is a motivation for acquisitions

[4] In light of the studies concerning the economic consequences of accounting choice described in Chapter Eight, how could a study be designed to test whether poorly performing firms selected accounting methods that maximized income more frequently than more successful firms?

[5] It is possible that the conflict Steinbrink notes is more apparent than real. In practicular, the existence of negative abnormal returns does *not* imply that the company has been unprofitable in a financial accounting sense. Rather, it simply states that the return to shareholders has been lower than that which would normally be associated with the company's level of systematic risk. The *absolute* return may nonetheless be positive.

[6] Touche Ross & Co., *The Effect of Mergers, Acquisitions and Tender Offers on American Business: A Touche Ross Survey of Corporate Directors' Opinions* 12 (1981), reported in Coffee, *supra,* at 1212.

can be drawn from the price behavior of the stock of a target company *after* an acquirer secures control. The data and the inferences which can be drawn from it are discussed in the following excerpt.

GILSON, A STRUCTURAL APPROACH TO TENDER OFFERS: THE CASE AGAINST DEFENSIVE TACTICS IN TENDER OFFERS

33 Stan.L.Rev. 819, 873–74 (1981).*

If the motivation of a successful tender offer is to increase the efficiency of the target firm, the value of the target firm should increase substantially following the acquisition, and this subsequent increase in target firm value should be the source of the acquirer's gain from the transaction.

The data do not appear consistent with this conclusion. While the price of target company stock increases following completion of the transaction relative to its pre-offer value, perhaps reflecting some gain from the displacement of inefficient management,[190] "this re-evaluation is significantly less than the premium paid target shareholders. * * * [A]cquiring firms did not profit from the purchase and subsequent appreciation in the target shares; they suffered an average capital loss of 13% on each target share they bought." [191] The source of gains to the acquirer seems inconsistent with the inefficiency assumption. * * * [192]

In what manner, then, do acquiring companies gain from the transaction? The data indicate that gains accrue from increases in the postoffer price of the *acquirer's* stock.[193] This is most consistently explained by synergistically motivated acquisitions—"corporate acquirers value target shares primarily for the attached rights to control of the target's resources." [194] If the acquirer can more than proportionately appropriate the synergistic benefit, the postoffer increase in the value of the acquirer's shares will not be matched in magnitude by the postoffer increase in the shares of the target—precisely the result described in the data, and one consistent with the numerous opportunities for the parent company to favor itself at the expense of the subsidiary in an affiliated group setting.[195]

The point may be clarified by referring to a familiar, albeit extreme, example. In Perlman v. Feldmann,[196] Korean War price con-

---

[190] Bradley, ["*Interim Tender Offers and the Market for Corporate Control*," 53 J.Bus. 345, 364 (1980)]; Jarrell & Bradley, ["*The Economic Effects of Federal and State Regulations of Cash Tender Offers*," 23 J.L. & Econ. 371, 392–93 (1980)].

[191] Bradley, supra, at 364.

[192] Id. at 350–51.

[193] Id. at 365–67; Jarrell & Bradley, supra, at 381–82.

[194] Jarrell & Bradley, supra, at 381–82.

[195] "The checks on unfair dealing by the parent are few. In theory, of course, the fairness of the parent's behavior is subject to the check of judicial review; but in practice such review is difficult even where the courts have the will to engage in it, and they often lack the will." M. Eisenberg, [*The Structure of the Corporation*] 309 (citations omitted).

[196] 219 F.2d 173 (2d Cir.1955).

trols prevented Newport Steel Company from exploiting the wartime steel shortage by charging a market-clearing price. If a steel consumer gained control of Newport Steel, it would gain the benefit of an assured source of supply in a short market, and so long as it paid Newport only the legally set price, it would appropriate all the synergistic gains from the transaction. The acquirer's gain would then come from the increase in the price of its stock resulting from the value of the "rights to control of the target's resources," [197] precisely the result described by the data.[198]

*   *   *

◆

Thus, some indirect empiricial evidence,[7] augmented by the anecdotal evidence offered by experienced practitioners in the acquisitions field, presents at least a surface conflict with the results summarized in Table 10. The studies examining the pre-acquisition performance of target companies show negative abnormal returns, while data bearing on post-acquisition performance at the very least allow the inference that expectations of gain from displacing inefficient management may go unmet.

Is there any way to reconcile the conflicting results? Some insight can be gained by looking more closely at the samples of acquisitions that were the basis of the studies summarized in Table 10. All turn out to include a substantial number of acquisitions from the pre–1975

[197] Jarrell & Bradley, supra, at 382.

[198] The data do not, however, rule out the possibility that the acquirer secures its return by displacing inefficient management but then disproportionately appropriates the gains from increased efficiency. While this result is possible, it seems to me less likely than the synergistic explanation. Appropriation of benefits in a parent-subsidiary relationship takes place through intercompany dealings, like transfer pricing in a vertically integrated affiliated group. The opportunities for such dealings increase with greater operational or financial relations between the parent and the subsidiary. The greater these relations, however, the more likely that there was a synergistic motivation for the transaction in the first place. Of course, even a completely diversified conglomerate can overcharge subsidiaries for central services, like accounting, employee benefit plans and the like, which do not require a special relationship between the characters of the companies, but at the same time the opportunity for misappropriation is of a significantly lower magnitude.

[7] McConnell & Nantell, *Corporate Combinations and Common Stock Returns: The Case of Joint Ventures*, 40 J.Fin. 519 (1985), provide additional indirect evidence that at least some acquisitions are motivated by

synergy rather than displacement of inefficient management. Reasoning that an acquisition is only one way of taking advantage of the opportunity for synergy between two companies, McConnell & Nantell examined the abnormal returns associated with the announcement of joint ventures. In these transactions, they argue, any gains must result from synergy because neither participant's management is displaced. Consistent with a synergistic motivation, joint ventures earn positive abnormal returns on the announcement of the venture similar to those earned by the parties to an acquisition. The inference that this result supports the more general proposition that synergy, as opposed to displacement of inefficient management, motivates acquisitions, however, is subject to two qualifications. First, does the data demonstrate any more than that synergy is possible? Why is not the data consistent with joint ventures motivated by synergy and acquisitions motivated by displacement of inefficient management? Second, is it clear that a joint venture cannot serve to displace management? Suppose that management of the joint venture is the responsibility of only one of the venturers. Could not the transaction be described as shifting control over one company's resources to management of another?

period when hostile takeovers by means of tender offers were far less common than in more recent years. In contrast, the Bradley data concerning post-acquisition prices is drawn more heavily from the period in which hostile takeovers became respectable and much more numerous.[8] As was stressed at the close of the first excerpt in this Chapter, the market for corporate control requires a mechanism by which inefficient management can be displaced involuntarily in order for it to discipline—to provide an efficiency incentive for—management of potential targets. In the absence of such a mechanism, the market for corporate control would be ineffective and poor performance would be more common. Once a displacement mechanism became available, however, management might be expected to respond to the newly operative incentive and improve their performance, thereby eliminating the potential for profit merely from their displacement. As a result, one would expect acquisitions that occurred after this shift to be motivated by something other than gains from displacing inefficient management. From this perspective, the principle impact of an effectively operating market for corporate control would be general deterrence, and in such an environment target companies as a group would be less likely to exhibit negative abnormal returns in the pre-acquisition period.[9]

In fact, history seems to be consistent with this explanation of the conflict. The event that energized the market for corporate control was the gain in respectability of the hostile tender offer—the principle means by which target management can be displaced without its consent—in the mid-1970's.[10] And there is some empirical support for the proposition that an effective market for corporate control operates through general deterrence. James, *An Analysis of the Effect of State Acquisition Laws on Managerial Efficiency: The Case of the Bank Holding Company Acquisitions*, 25 J.L. & Econ. 211 (1984), studied the deterrent effect on management of an operating market for corporate control by comparing two groups of banks, one from states whose banking laws severely restricted bank acquisitions, and one from states without restrictions. The idea was that the deterrent effect of an active market for corporate control would limit management inefficiency and that this could be measured by comparing the two groups of banks with respect to a measure of management expense preference.[11] "[C]onsistent with the hypothesis that the market for corporate control serves to enforce managerial efficiency," James found that "[s]alary expenses, occupancy expenses, and total employment are * * * higher certeris paribus for banks located in states prohibiting acquisi-

---

[8] Salter & Weinhold, supra Chapter One B., point out that although there were only one-half as many acquisitions in 1975–76 as in 1968, there were twice as many hostile acquisitions.

[9] A small number of acquisitions would still be motivated by the opportunity to displace those managements that remained inefficient, but these instances likely would be buried in any measurement of the pre-

acquisition CAR of a portfolio of target companies.

[10] The legitimization of the hostile tender offer is described in Salter & Weinhold, Chapter One B. supra.

[11] The measure was of expenditures on salary expense, employment and occupancy expense.

tions than for banks in states which do not restrict acquisitions." [12] Thus, one would expect fewer inefficient companies in an economy characterized by an effective market for corporate control and, as a result, a smaller percentage of acquisitions to be motiviated by displacement of inefficient management. This hypothesis should be amenable to testing. One could compare the pre-acquisition abnormal returns of targets acquired prior to 1975 with those of targets acquired after, say, 1980. [13]

In any event, there is ample reason to consider additional motivations for acquisitions. The Bradley data discussed above suggests synergy as a likely candidate. It is the subject of the next Chapter.

[12] Id. at 226. James was actually testing a somewhat different hypothesis. His concern was whether the market for corporate control acted as a constraint on management inefficiency beyond that imposed by the market for managers. If it did not, there should have been no difference in management expense preference between states where only the market for managers operated (states that prohibited bank acquisitions) and states where both markets operated (states that allowed bank acquisitions).

[13] The gap between 1975 and 1980 is designed so that the entire pre-acquisition period for the second group of targets occurred after the market for corporate control became effective.

Professor Scherer has pointed to data that may be inconsistent with the hypothesis of increased managerial efficiency resulting from an increase in the number of tender offers. He notes that the annual growth of output per work hour in the nonfarm business sector "declined from 2.6 percent over 1947–64 to 1.7 percent over 1964–74 to 1.4 percent over 1974–84." Testimony of F.M. Scherer before the Subcommittee on Telecommunications, Consumer Protection, and Finance, House Committee on Energy and Commerce 3 (March 12, 1985). He then asks "why industrial productivity growth in the 1950's and early 1960's was so strong *despite* the absence of appreciable takeover discipline"? Id. (emphasis in the original). Is the market for corporate control the principal tool in constraining managerial inefficiency? See Section A. of this Chapter, supra.

CHAPTER ELEVEN. SYNERGY AND STRATEGY

The concept of synergy is the flip side of value additivity. The latter asserts that two plus two equal four; synergy exists when the answer is five or more. Without more, however, synergy is less a theory than a tautology; it simply states the fact of success but offers no hint of what caused it. To be helpful in explaining the motivation for acquisitions, the concept of synergy must be expanded from an after-the-fact description of a result, to a predictive theory that offers guidance concerning how that result can be achieved. For this purpose, it is useful to divide the concept into two parts: financial synergy and operational synergy. The former concerns the potential value of reducing the variance of a company's earnings by diversifying at the company level, and was the subject of Chapter Nine. The latter concerns gains from alterations in the real productive activities of the two companies made possible by acquisition. From this perspective, displacement of inefficient management, while warranting its separate treatment in Chapter Ten because of its prominence in the legal and economic literature, is simply one variant of operating synergy. In this Chapter we first examine a range of factors that have the theoretical potential to create operational synergy in appropriate cases, and then review the available empirical evidence bearing on the extent to which this potential has been realized in practice.

A. The Theory

1. Strategic Planning

M. SALTER & W. WEINHOLD, DIVERSIFICATION THROUGH ACQUISITION
49–78 (1979).*

The STRATEGY MODEL * * * focuses on the process of defining how an enterprise should compete in its economic environment and how its performance can be measured. * * *

According to the strategy model, a company's special competences are defined in terms of a set of core skills—that is, what the company is good at. In one case, this might mean the manufacture of high-volume, low-value-added metal assemblies; in another, the mass distribution of frequently purchased consumer products. This set of core skills is not just what the company does well, but what it does particularly well. The model's test of consistency asks strategists and policymakers to look at the fit of these skills and resources with the profit and service opportunities in the company's environment.

* Reprinted with permission of The Free Press, a Division of Macmillan, Inc. from *Diversification Through Acquisition* by M. Salter and W. Weinhold. Copyright © 1979 by Malcolm S. Salter and Wolf A. Weinhold.

The goal of the strategy model is to facilitate a rational choice among the strategic options facing the company. By identifying the company's capabilities and limitations and the risks and opportunities facing it, the model leads management to seek alternate ways of exploiting these opportunities or accommodating those risks.

* * *

Implications for the Diversification Decision

The strategy model provides specific guidelines within which managers are to approach the diversifying acquisition. The key issue to be considered in the evaluation of an acquisition candidate is the fit it provides with the company's resources and the extent to which it furthers the attainment of corporate goals and objectives.

* * *

Put in different terms, users of the strategy model favor closely related diversification. The underlying theory is both simple and intuitively appealing: Really successful results in business require the development of a distinctive competence or competitive advantage and the ability to anticipate trends in markets and technology. The ability to maintain a distinctive competence and to anticipate is greatly enhanced by a knowledge of the industry and its environment. Thus, where diversification is related to a company's current industrial environment, the advantages of special competence and industry knowledge can create more opportunity for above-average results than unrelated diversification can.

It is not surprising that, seen in this light, questions relevant to the diversification decision posed by the model stress the notions of strategic fit and operating compatibility. These questions can be summarized as follows:

1. What opportunities and risks does the potential acquisition present?

2. What is the basis of competition in the acquisition candidate's industrial environment? What must he do well to succeed there?

3. Can we assist the acquisition candidate in any way? Do our resources and skills fit the needs of the acquisition candidate? Which of our resources are transferable?

4. Quite apart from assisting the acquisition candidate, do we understand the strategic logic, or key success factors, of this new business sufficiently well to make intelligent resource allocation decisions?

* * *

Given the model's emphasis on strategic fit, any analysis of diversification options involving acquisitions must include a careful assessment of whether or not the resource requirements of the two companies are sufficiently similar to warrant a combined or linked strategy of some sort. Where the resource requirements are similar for each company and where the diversifying company's strengths can be reinforced or extended and/or its weaknesses minimized or eliminated, the elements of strategic fit will be present and a diversifying acquisition will represent an attractive strategic option.

* * *

How, then, can an assessment of corporate resources be systematically pursued so that a company's conclusions about its strengths and weaknesses are sufficiently detailed and objective to serve as the basis for serious diversification planning? Such an assessment requires, first, that a company develop a profile of its principal resources and skills. These tend to cluster around three dimensions:

    1. *financial dimension,* including such resources as cash flow, debt capacity, and the ability to attract new capital;

    2. *operating dimension,* including tangible assets, such as office buildings, manufacturing plant and equipment, warehouses, inventories, and service and distribution facilities, and more intangible resources, such as high-quality products, low-cost production methods, and high brand loyalty; and

    3. *management and organization dimension,* including such resources as scientists, engineers, sales personnel, financial analysts, general managers, and bureaucratic traditions embodied in quality assurance systems, cash-management systems, and management-control systems.

Once such a profile has been developed, a company then should compare the strength of its resources with those factors critical to the company's success in its relevant product markets to see what characteristics make the company uniquely qualified to carry out its key tasks or inhibit the company's ability to fulfill its purpose. This steps in the analysis yields what is called a capability or competence profile. The final step in the process is to compare this capability profile with that of major competitors in order to identify those areas where the company may be able to build a competitive advantage in the marketplace.

The most difficult characteristics to categorize as strengths and weaknesses are nonfinancial in nature. An effective way of coping with this difficulty is to sketch a capability profile along the nonfinancial dimensions by functional area (R & D/engineering, manufacturing, marketing, control, and so on). This can proceed as outlined below for the marketing function of McCord Corporation.

McCord Corporation was one of the first companies to start supplying the automotive industry. As the automotive market grew to maturity, McCord become a major supplier of gaskets, radiators, and other automotive equipment. By 1963 the company was a well-established manufacturer selling most of its production in the original equipment (O/E) market. The consolidated 1963 sales of $45 million and profits of $1.8 million had some fluctuations but little real change over the previous five years.

In 1963 management attention was focused on growth and diversification through acquisition and internal development. The company was dependent on three major auto makers in the O/E market for over half its total corporate sales. Previous efforts of internally generated diversification and recent attempts at acquisition had borne no fruits. The question facing McCord was how could the company build on its strengths and compensate for or eliminate its weaknesses? This question needed to be answered in the context of the company's four principal objectives:

— to minimize the pressure of the cyclical O/E market
— to find more productive uses for the company's financial resources
— to grow at a more rapid pace
— to generate a greater level of public interest and confidence in the company.

* * *

What happened to McCord? A merger in 1964 with the Davidson Rubber Corporation, a manufacturer of padded trim products for the automotive industry, provided a certain degree of fit from a marketing, financial, and manufacturing point of view even though the company was not able to build a strong hedge against the market power of the "Big Three" automakers. As it turned out, many of each company's resource requirements were similar, and Davidson offered McCord a broader product line, a position in the emerging safety market, more modern plants, and a younger middle-level management experienced in the auto supply market. But in the final analysis, the extent to which Davidson fit McCord's strategic needs can only be judged in light of McCord's strengths and weaknesses in the automotive supply market and the overall attractiveness of that market or industry. As depicted in Figure 3–1, both business position (defined in terms of relative market share, relative product quality, price, marketing strength, new product activity, manufacturing scale, and overall experience) and industry or market attractiveness (defined in terms of market size and growth, number and size of competitors, position in the product of life cycle, rate of technological change, and industry profitability) can help define appropriate related diversification strategies for companies like McCord. Without going into all the details of McCord's situation in 1963–1964, we can show that while Davidson offered McCord some benefits of related-supplementary diversification, the company's real needs, based on an analysis of its strengths and weaknesses and industry attractiveness, lay more in the direction of related-complementary diversification. Let's look first at this argument in conceptual terms and then return to the McCord case.

Figure 3–1.

Framework for Selecting Appropriate Related Diversification Strategy

		Business Position		
		High	Medium	Low
Industry Attractiveness	High	No Diversification	Related-Complementary Diversification	Related-Complementary Diversification
	Medium	Related-Supplementary Diversification	No Diversification	Related-Complementary Diversification
	Low	Related-Supplementary Diversification	Related-Supplementary Diversification	No Diversification

The Related Diversification Grid

[R]elated-complementary diversification involves expanding a business by adding new functional activities and skills to its existing set without substantially changing its product-market orientation. Related-supplementary diversification involves expanding a business by entering new product markets requiring functional skills similar to those already possessed by the company. Figure 3–1 suggests the following guidelines regarding related-complementary and related-supplementary diversification:

1. *No diversification* First, where a company has a strong position in an attractive industry, diversification is usually unnecessary from an economic perspective. Second, where a company possesses few unique strengths but operates in an industry of average or medium attractiveness, it may make sense to work at developing existing skills and improving its business position before considering any diversification. Finally, a weak company in an unattractive industry is clearly in a desperate situation, unlikely to be able to afford diversification or to present itself as an attractive merger partner.

2. *Related-Complementary Diversification* Where a company participates in a highly attractive industry but possesses only average or even below-average skills, related-complementary diversification can help that company add functional skills critical to improving its overall business position. Even where a company finds itself as a weak competitor in an industry of average or medium attractiveness, some benefits can accrue from improving its competitive position through related-complementary diversification.

3. *Related-Supplementary diversification* Where a company has a strong business position but participates in a market of only

average attractiveness or low attractiveness, there is the obvious potential to increase rates of growth and profitability by committing existing functional skills and resources to new, more attractive markets. Where a company qualifies as only an average competitor in a specific industry or market, but where that market has become relatively unattractive, there are potential benefits of using existing skills and resources to enter more attractive, related product markets.

Using the related diversification grid requires a healthy dose of judgment since there is no simple, useful system for assessing relative business position or relative industry attractiveness. Nevertheless, the grid does suggest some crude propositions that can channel thinking along the lines of the strategy model. More specifically, the grid can help companies study their related diversification options in the light of corporate strengths and weaknesses as well as industry or market characteristics.

Returning to the case of the McCord Corporation, the company can be characterized as having "low to medium" business position in an industry of "medium" attractiveness. The automotive equipment industry has two major segments, the O/E market and the replacement market, commonly referred to as the aftermarket. McCord participated in both segments. As indicated above, the O/E market experienced severe cyclical swings, while overall growth was more or less on a part with that of the economy as a whole. This market was also dominated by a powerful oligopoly who posed a continuous threat of backward integration into McCord's lines. Any failure of McCord to meet preestablished product specifications, delivery schedules, or price expectations would cause a punitive shift of purchases away from McCord. The aftermarket, supplied by chains such as Sears and independent wholesale distributors who sold to service stations and the public, was more fragmented, less price-sensitive, and less cyclical. On balance, however, the automotive equipment industry was not a "growth" industry, nor was it characterized by above-average returns to automotive-equipment suppliers. In addition, while McCord was a competitive participant in the industry, the company was not a leader either in terms of market-share position, product quality, new-product activity, or manufacturing efficiency.

Viewed from the perspective of the related-diversification grid, McCord appeared to be in a position to benefit either from reinforcing its current strategic posture or, possibly, from pursuing related-complementary diversification. With respect to diversification, one can argue that the company could have improved its business position and performance by acquiring companies with the ability to place McCord in a stronger market-share position in the aftermarket or a stronger technological position in the O/E market. Had McCord been able to broaden its participation and increase its power in the automotive aftermarket or to develop a more proprietary position in the O/E market through more fruitful product development activities, the traditional core of McCord's business might have been strengthened. While the Davidson acquisition clearly offered McCord the opportunity to exploit a new technology and a new market segment, it is less clear that the attendant economic advantages were superior to those offered by a complementary diversifying acquisition.

* * *

THE PRODUCT/MARKET–PORTFOLIO MODEL

While the strategy model was developed to deal with overall corporate environment, the several variants of the product/market-portfolio model focus on the overall economic characteristics of a company's business or portfolio of businesses. One of the early expressions of the product/market-portfolio model was developed by the Boston Consulting Group (BCG) and emphasizes a matrix of relative market share and market growth. This framework has been used widely during the past decade as a way of analyzing the competitive position of a business and the business portfolios of multiproduct, multimarket companies.

* * *

Product/market-portfolio models focus on the strengths of a company's portfolio of products or businesses, such strengths being defined in terms of market position and market attractiveness. The key relationship stressed by the BCG variant is the relationship between the cash flow of a business and its market-share/market-growth characteristics. These characteristics are used as key indicators of a company's market position and the attractiveness of its market commitments. The model tells managers to look at the competitive situation and market growth within their business units and then construct a cluster of businesses through which high cash flow can be achieved.

The goal of the product/market-portfolio model is to maximize the total strength of the company. This goal can be best achieved, according to the model, by balancing the generation and use of cash within the company. * * *

Propositions of the Product/Market-Portfolio Model

[T]he product/market-portfolio model holds that in most competitive environments relative market share and market growth determine the cash-generation or cash-usage characteristics of businesses. The logic of this proposition can be explained as follows.

When companies pursue marketing and pricing strategies geared to increasing production volume faster than their competitors, cost advantages relative to competitors will normally follow. This relationship between the accumulated experience associated with increased production volume and declining costs is referred to by BCG as the "experience-curve" effect. The experience curve relationship, as described by BCG, states that unit costs decline by approximately 20 to 30 percent (in constant dollars) with each doubling of accumulated production. While similar to the well-known and documented learning-curve phenomenon, BCG has found this effect to extend to most elements of value added, including capital, labor, and overhead. The reasons for this empirically observed relationship are not known with certainty, but the underlying forces are believed to include (1) labor efficiency, (2) new processes and improved methods, (3) product redesign that conserves material, allows greater efficiency in manufacture, and takes advantage of less costly resources, (4) product standardization, and (5) scale effects. Each of these forces is related to growth in accumulated production experience and provides opportunities that alert managements can exploit. The experience-curve relationship is often shown in a graph of unit costs (or prices if a constant profit margin is assumed) versus total production, such as those shown for * * * Integrated Circuits in Figure 4–1.

Figure 4–1
The Experience Curve for Integrated Circuits

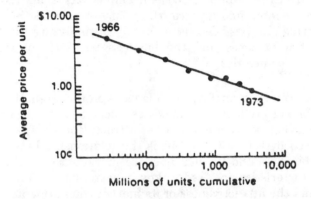

Source: Texas Instruments, Inc., First Quarter and Stockholders' Meeting Report, April 18, 1973.

Figure 4–2
Value of Market Share

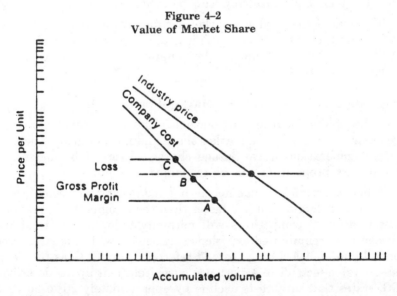

Source: Texas Instruments, Inc., First Quarter and Stockholders' Meeting Report, April 18, 1973.   [D6589]

As is the case with accumulated experience, market share can have enormous value. Indeed, according to the model, a company's accumulated experience can best be measured by relative market share. When competitors follow similar experience curves, the dominant producer in an industry will have the greatest accumulated experience and the lowest unit costs. Assuming a single industrywide price, he will therefore have the highest profit margins. This is seen in Figure 4–2, where three different companies in an industry have different cost positions based upon their cumulative volume. Company C, the smallest, loses money, while Company B is at best marginal. The value of market share to Company A is clearly seen. As the industry's dominant producer, it is able to generate a significantly larger cash flow than its competitors because of both its greater volume and a greater contribution per unit sold.

While cash generation is a function of accumulated experience, best summarized through relative market share, cash use or investment, according to the model, is a function of market growth. To maintain market share in a growing market requires the infusion of cash for both working capital and capacity expansion. Attempting to gain additional market share further increases the business unit's growth rate and thus compound the need of cash. * * *

Figure 4–3

Market-Share/Market-Growth Portfolio Chart

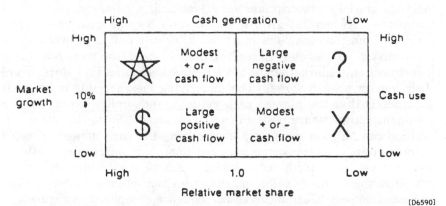

[D6590]

Based on the general proposition outlined above, the product market-portfolio model isolates businesses into four categories reflecting their cash-use and cash-generation characteristics. Market growth is separated into high or low by an arbitrary dividing line, usually 10 percent, and cash use is depicted as high or low accordingly. Market share is viewed in terms of relative share—that is, company sales in that business divided by the sales of the company's leading competitor. Since only one competitor can have a relative market share greater than 1.0, this figure is used to identify companies within an industry with high or low relative market shares and, therefore, high or low levels of relative cash generation. These four business categories are portrayed by BCG in a portfolio chart depicted in Figure 4–3.

Each quadrant in Figure 4–3 has its own pattern of cash generation and use, and BCG has given each its own name to reflect these characteristics.

— *Stars* in the upper left quadrant are the investment opportunities. With high cash use and cash generation (due to a favorable cost position in its industry), they are relatively self-sufficient.

— *Cash Cows* in the lower-left quadrant generate high cash flows yet use little in their low-growth market. These are net providers of cash.

— *Dogs* in the lower-right quadrant are cash traps in that additional cash investments cannot be recovered. Increasing market share in a stable market is futile because no one can afford to increase capacity any more than they can afford to run at much less than full capacity. Dogs are candidates for liquidation.

— *Question Marks* in the upper-right quadrant are the real risks. Left alone they will become dogs as market growth slows, and their profit margins contract relative to those of the industry's dominant competitors. To make stars of them requires a great deal of cash for investment in increased market share and, therefore, accumulated experience.

* * *

So far we have only described the static situation as viewed by the product/market-portfolio model. The dynamics of the product life cycle yield the model's prescriptions for developing a balanced portfolio of businesses. As market growth slows, stars become cash cows. The throwoff from the cash cows must be either distributed to investors or reinvested in new assets. According to this model, the most rewarding investment is in market share to turn question marks into stars before their market growth slows. The underlying logic for this investment sequence is that the highest cash returns (and profits) occur when a dominant market share position can be obtained. Since this dominant position can be most easily achieved during the early phases of rapid market growth, when competitive positions and purchasing patterns have not yet been firmly established, it can be worthwhile for aggressive investment in question marks (high-market-growth/low-market-share businesses). Such a successful sequence is depicted in Figure 4–4.

* * *

Figure 4–4

Successful Portfolio Dynamics [a]

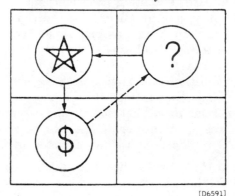

[D6591]

[a] The solid line connotes product movement over time. The dotted line connotes the optimal cash-flow pattern.

Implications for the Diversification Decision

The focus of the product/market-portfolio model is on the cash-flow characteristics of a business. A high-potential business is one with the opportunity to stake out a leadership position in a growing industry. If this business can maintain or expand its market share position before industry growth slows, it will subsequently be in the best position to "harvest" the investments it made during the market's period of growth. The product/market-portfolio model argues and empirical evidence supports the notion that higher market share leads to higher cash flow and return on investment. Evidence * * * indicates that, on the average, a 5 percent increase in ROI typically accompanies every 10 percent increase in market share. Experience also shows that the market-share investments with the highest incremental returns are those made during a business' growth phase. Since stars are relatively self-sufficient and already have dominant market share positions, such investments are best made for businesses that are question marks.

These observations on market-share investments and cash-flow returns reveal the benefits of constructing a portfolio of businesses through unrelated diversifying acquisitions. A company with a balanced portfolio of cash cows feeding question marks and stars is in a position both to reap the current benefits of its high market share and advantageous cost position and to develop sources of future cash flow. Sustained growth is thus ensured by investing surplus cash from mature businesses in less mature, high-potential businesses.

The benefits of a balanced product/market-portfolio suggest a set of criteria by which to evaluate a potential diversifying acquisition. The key criterion is the fit of the target company's cashflow characteristics with those of the existing portfolio. The degree of fit will be governed by the target company's competitive position, the expected growth of its market, the cost of retaining or improving its competitive position, and the cash-flow characteristics of the acquiring company's existing portfolio of businesses.

* * *

According to the logic of the model, changes in the business portfolio are intended to fill in financial weak spots or build upon financial strengths. For example, a company in a high-growth industry may feel that access to a secure (and inexpensive) cash-flow source would enable it to maintain its present growth and possibly improve its market share position. This situation is similar to that faced by Tyco Labs, a manufacturer of high-technology products, in the mid-1970s. To fund both its rapid growth and its research-and-development programs, Tyco acquired (at a price equivalent to only four times cash flow) the Grinnel Co. from ITT. Grinnel was a major competitor in the low-growth, low-capital-intensity business of fire protection. The cash flow from Grinnel was able to fuel Tyco's internal growth as well as its active acquisition program. Alternatively, a mature company generating substantial cash flows may see an opportunity to nourish emerging growth companies or to convert a so-called question mark into a star. This was the situation in which Philip Morris found itself in the late 1960s with its tobacco business. The question mark Philip Morris acquired was Miller High Life, at the time number five in the brewing industry. With an infusion of over $500 million in production facilities and Philip Morris's marketing talent, Miller's growth exploded. By 1978 Miller was second in the industry with strong prospects of becoming number one. * * *

Philip Morris's acquisition of Miller High Life provides an interesting insight into the product/market-portfolio model and its implications for the diversification decision. Philip Morris brought to Miller not only a large, surplus cash flow but also a formidable marketing talent that had established Philip Morris as the strongest competitor in the cigarette market. Prior to Philip Morris's entry, the brewing business was production oriented; brewmasters brewed beer and let the beer sell itself. Philip Morris's enormous cash flow enabled Miller to compete on this basis by building large, low-cost breweries; but Philip Morris's marketing skills also introduced a new competitive tactic into the industry. Miller High Life was both brewed and marketed. Caught between Miller's low-cost production and high marketing expenditures, the brewing industy underwent a major strategic and competitive transition in the mid-1970s.

While the notion of a balanced portfolio of cash flows appears to argue for broadly based or unrelated diversification, further reflection on the concepts underlying the model reveals even stronger arguments for related diversification. The logic behind related diversification rests on a company's ability to develop "overlapping experience curves" or the ability to transfer accumulated experience from one business to another. This, in fact, is a part of what happened at Miller as Philip Morris brought its marketing talent to bear. When distinct product markets have overlapping experience curves, exposure to each alters the markets' cost curves. Relevant cumulative volume no longer depends on the industry's narrowly defined experience curve, since a business's costs in one product market can reflect the experience gained in the other and vice versa. Thus, diversifying acquisitions that offer overlapping experience curves can be highly desirable.

◆

Professors Salter and Weinhold, of the Harvard Business School, examine two general approaches to business decisionmaking in the context of acquisitions. Both focus attention on essentially the same question: Can real productive, as opposed to purely financial, advantages be obtained from a particular acquisition?

The strategy model emphasizes that a "distinctive competence" or "competitive advantage" is necessary for business success and, in considering an acquisition, looks for a "fit" between the two companies. This "fit" refers to the ability of one of the companies to share its distinctive competence or competitive advantage with the other or, by the act of combination, to create a competence or competitive advantage where one had not previously existed.

The product/market-portfolio model also emphasizes distinctive competence or competitive advantage, but expresses the emphasis through the concept of a declining experience curve. From this perspective, greater competence is a function of cumulative production totals. That competence, because it results in lower costs than can be achieved by less experienced producers, creates a competitive advantage. These factors, in turn, can be summarized in terms of market share alone. Market share serves as a proxy both for cumulative experience—the greater the market share, the greater the cumulative experience—and for competitive advantage—the company with the greatest market share is further down the experience curve and, therefore, has a cost advantage.[1] In the acquisition context, the market-portfolio approach directs attention to the cash flow characteristics of a business. Existing businesses with high market shares in stable industries generate cash that can be used to acquire market share for businesses in industries with growing markets. Acquisitions present an opportunity to share the cash flow of a "cow" by acquiring a "question mark." Alternatively, acquisitions of businesses requiring similar or related skills allow the two companies to pool their experience and thereby secure a competitive advantage before having achieved a substantial market share.

While the potential for increased value as a result of cumulative experience curves is clear enough, what is so special about the opportunity for the acquiring company to share its cash flow? From the perspective of the acquiring company, the choice is among alternative investment opportunities. One alternative is to distribute the cash flow to the shareholders and let them invest it. Has the acquiring company any special competence in selecting the best "question marks" in which to invest or, perhaps, special access to these investments not available to its shareholders? From the perspective of the target company, the acquiring company is not the only source of funds available to finance the growth of its business. Why would a target company prefer to secure funds from an acquiring company as compared to other alternatives such as borrowing the funds from a bank or selling securities to the public? Is there any reason to believe that the acquiring company is able to charge less for financing than the price charged by the capital market? The answer, at least theoretically, must be one of special competence. The acquiring company may have cheaper and more accurate sources of information that allow it to better evaluate the risk presented by the target company than can competitive suppliers of capital. Also, because of its position within the

---

[1] Strategies based on the experience curve concept have been particularly common in the electronics industry where manufacturing costs are a critical competitive factor. The idea is to price a new product low, even at an initially unprofitable level, so as to acquire market share and descend the experience curve faster than your competitors. Because costs will decline as you descend the curve, the initially unprofitable price will become profitable for you, but not for your competitors who, because you acquired market share more quickly, have less accumulated experience and higher costs. Put differently, one acquires market share early at a loss, and makes a profit later when your market share gives you a competitive advantage. What happens, however, in an industry that is characterized by rapid technological change? There may be a danger that, by the time you reach the point on the experience curve that allows you to recoup your initial investment in market share, technological change will have made the product obsolete. In this setting, the key seems to be less estimating the slope of the experience curve than estimating its duration.

target company's industry, it may be better able to evaluate existing public information concerning the target. The idea of the acquiring company serving, in these and other respects, as an alternative to the capital market is considered specifically in Section A.2.d. of this Chapter.

The essential consistency between the strategy model and the product/market-portfolio model can be seen by examining the Philip Morris-Miller High Life acquisition discussed by Salter and Weinhold. From the product/market-portfolio perspective, Philip Morris's cigarette business—a cow—threw off the funds necessary to acquire Miller High Life—a question mark—and expand its market share in a growing industry. Further, its ability to acquire market share was enhanced because the two businesses shared a common required skill—marketing. Philip Morris could transfer its cumulative experience in marketing to Miller, thereby creating a competitive advantage even before acquiring market share. From the strategy perspective, Philip Morris had a special competence—marketing—that could be transferred to Miller and that would create a competitive advantage for Miller given the prior competitive environment in the beer industry. Because both approaches stress the need for an acquisition to result in the creation of a real productive advantage, their correspondence is hardly surprising.[2]

2. Sources of Synergy: Defining the Economic Boundaries of the Firm

The strategy and product/market-portfolio models are both really just ways of thinking carefully about the same problem: What would enable an acquisition to transcend the principle of value additivity? Both focus on *general* concepts, such as fit, special competence, or competitive advantage. In this section we consider a variety of *specific* factors—economies of scale, economies of vertical integration, economies of scope and economies of organization—that add precision to the more general formulation presented by the models.

For this purpose, the value additivity problem should be considered as an economic, as opposed to a strategic planning, problem.[3] Economists studying the theory of the firm seek to explain what functions will be undertaken within a firm and what functions will be accomplished through market transactions between the firm and outside suppliers. Thus, for example, Albert Chandler reports that early factories in the United States were not under common ownership, but were a symbiotic relationship between separately owned businesses, each of which occupied a different stage in the production of the product. The efficiency gains from a common production location were

---

[2] Philip Morris attempted to duplicate its success with Miller High Life by acquiring another beverage maker—Seven Up—in early 1978. Despite the importance of marketing in the soft-drink industry and the fact that Miller and Seven-Up were both recreational beverages, the Seven-Up acquisition has proved substantially less successful than the Miller acquisition. From the perspective of the strategy and product/market-portfolio models, what might account for the different results?

[3] For an interesting discussion of the economic basis of strategic analysis, see Teece, *Economic Analysis of Business Strategy,* 26 Calif.Mgmt.Rev. 87 (1984).

achieved by contract rather than by common ownership.[4] Considered from this perspective, the principle of value additivity states a presumptive boundary for the firm. Unless some form of synergy results, there can be no gain from expansion of the size of the firm through acquisition. The survey of potential sources of synergy in the remainder of this Chapter thus can be seen as an effort to define the economic boundary of the firm in three dimensions: horizontal, vertical and conglomerate.

a. *Economies of Scale: The Horizontal Dimension*

F. SCHERER, INDUSTRIAL MARKET STRUCTURE AND ECONOMIC PERFORMANCE
81–104 (2nd ed. 1980).

ECONOMIES OF SCALE

One condition that could lead to concentrated market structures is the existence of substantial scale economies, permitting relatively large producers to manufacture and market their products at lower average cost per unit than relatively small producers. Economies of scale are best analyzed in terms of three categories: product-specific economies, associated with the volume of any single product made and sold; plant-specific economies, associated with the total output (possibly encompassing many products) of an entire plant or plant complex; and multi-plant economies, associated with an individual firm's operation of multiple plants. Each deserves consideration.

Ball bearing manufacturing provides a good illustration of several product-specific economies. If only a few bearings are to be custom-made, the ring machining will be done on general-purpose lathes by a skilled operator who hand-positions the stock and tools and makes measurements for each cut. With this method, machining a single ring requires from five minutes to more than an hour, depending upon the part's size and complexity and the operator's skill. If a sizeable batch is to be produced, a more specialized automatic screw machine will be used instead. * * * [This machine will produce] at a rate of from 80 to 140 parts per hour. A substantial saving of machine running and operator attendance time per unit is achieved, but setting up the screw machine to perform these operations takes about eight hours. If only 100 bearing rings are to be made, setup time greatly exceeds total running time, and it may be cheaper to do the job on an ordinary lathe. As the number of parts made increases, setup time per unit of running time falls—e.g., to 88 percent of running time with 1,000 rings and 9 percent with 10,000 rings. The larger the batch, the lower the average cost (i.e., setup *plus* running time per unit) will be. * * * If very large quantities (i.e., a million per year) of a single bearing design can be sold, * * * even more specialized higher speed machines are used,

[4] A. Chandler, *The Visible Hand: The Management Revolution in American Business* Chapter 2 (1977).

and parts are transferred automatically to the next processing stage in a continuous straight-line flow. * * * With such an automated straight-line bearing production approach, unit costs may be 30 to 50 percent lower than with medium-volume batch methods. But in order to realize these savings, the production line must be kept running without change-over two shifts per day, and this requires a large and continuous volume.

* * *

Product-specific economies of scale also have an important dynamic dimension. When intricate labor operations must be performed, as in shoe stitching and aircraft or computer assembly, workers tend to gain proficiency in their jobs with experience—that is, they learn by doing. Output per hour of work rises, the number of errors tends to fall, and unit costs decline along a so-called learning curve with increases in the cumulative volume of a specific product manufactured. Studies of World War II aircraft production show that labor costs per unit fell by approximately 20 percent with each doubling of cumulative output.

* * *

At the plant-specific level, the most important economies of scale come from expanding the size of individual processing units. This is especially apparent in the process industries such as petroleum refining, iron ore reduction and steel conversion chemical transformation, cement making, and steam generation. The output of a processing unit tends within certain physical limits to be roughly proportional to the volume of the unit, other things being equal, while the amount of materials and fabrication effort (and hence investment cost) required to construct the unit is more apt to be proportional to the surface area of the unit's reaction chambers, storage tanks, connecting pipes, and the like. Since the area of a sphere or cylinder of constant proportions varies as the two-thirds power of volume, the cost of constructing process industry plant units can be expected to rise as the two-thirds power of their output capacity, at least up to the point where they become so large that extra structural reinforcement and special fabrication techniques are required. * * *

What checks the realization of scale economies? It is clear that economies of scale exist and that unit costs fall with increases in product volume, plant size, and firm size, at least within limits. Does this decline in costs continue indefinitely? There are many reasons for believing that it does not.

In nearly all production and distribution operations, the realization of scale economies appears to be subject to diminishing returns. With a large enough volume, setup costs dwindle to insignificance. Learning curves flatten out as very large cumulative output volumes are attained. Cement kilns experience unstable internal aerodynamics above 7 million barrels per year capacity. Other scaled-up process vessels and machines become unwieldy or require special structural reinforcement beyond some point, increasing unit costs rather than reducing them. * * * And so on.

* * *

Psychological surveys show that for reasons still imperfectly understood, workers express less satisfaction with their jobs, and especially with the challenge their jobs offer, in large plants than in small plants. To attract a work force in the face of such alienating job conditions, large plants must in effect buy off their workers with a wage premium—one that has apparently been growing over time.

* * * Second, especially in smaller cities and towns, increasing the size of a plant's work force may require expanding the geographic radius from which workers are drawn, which in turn implies higher worker commutation costs and higher offsetting wages. Third, materials flows lengthen and become more complex as plant scales increase, and handling costs rise commensurately, discouraging continued expansion at a given plant site. Fourth, the risks of fire, explosion, and wildcat strikes are at a maximum when all production is concentrated at a single plant site, and so firms enjoying sufficient sales volume generally prefer to expand at other locations once they have achieved the minimum optimal scale (and sometimes even before) at one site. Finally, it is much harder to manage a big plant than a small one, all else being equal. To keep their operations taut and under control, companies characteristically avoid expanding individual plants beyond the size required by equipment scale-up and work force specialization imperatives.

* * *

The measurement of cost-scale relationships. We have proposed viewing economies of scale in terms of the minimum optimal scale of production [MOS] * * * at which all attainable unit cost savings are realized. The crucial question remains: Is the MOS large or small in relation to the demand for an industry's output? Whether there is room for many firms in the market, each large enough to enjoy all scale economies, for only one firm (a *natural monopoly* situation), or for just a few (*natural oligopoly*) depends upon two key variables: the relevant technology, and the size of the market (i.e., the output that would be demanded at a price just sufficient to cover minimum unit cost).

* * *

The impact of technological change and market growth. How high concentration must be to secure production efficiency depends, as we have seen, upon the balance between technology and market size. Thus far our view of this balance has been static—i.e., a snapshot at one moment in time. But conditions change. In the early 1950s, Professor Bain found, an MOS flat-rolled steel products plant had a capacity of from 1.0 to 2.5 million tons per year. By 1965 the MOS capacity had increased to 4.0 million tons. * * * [S]cale-up advances in blast furnace and basic oxygen furnace technology raised the optimum further by 1975—most likely to a capacity of about 12 million tons per year.

Table 4.4

The Impact of Regionalization on MOS Plant Market Shares

Industry	Approx. No. of Regional Mkts. in Cont. U.S.	MOS Plant Share Per Ave. Regional Mkt.
Beer brewing	6	20.4
Paints	5	7.0
Petroleum refining	5	9.5
Glass bottles	9	13.5
Cement	24	40.8
Steel works	4	10.4
Storage batteries	6	11.4

Source: F.M. Schere, "Economies of Scale and Industrial Concentration," in Harvey J. Goldschmid, H. Michael Mann, and J. Fred Weston, eds., *Industrial Concentration: The New Learning* (Boston: Little, Brown, 1974), pp. 28–31; adapted in part from Leonard W. Weiss, "The Geographic Size of Markets in Manufacturing," *Review of Economics and Statistics* 54 (August 1972): 245–66. Reprinted with permission.

  * * * [A]t least up to the late 1970s, what one observed was an unbroken history of optimal scale increases.

This pattern has been repeated again and again during the 20th century. There has been a general movement toward larger minimum optimal plant sizes. Saul Sands analyzed 46 industries for which comparable data on physical output and the number of plants were available, and found that average physical output per plant increased between 1904 and 1947 by about 3 percent per annum. But while plants have been getting larger, so have the markets for their output. According to estimates by the National Bureau of Economic Research, physical output of all manufacturing industries increased by nearly 4 percent per year between 1904 and 1947. If Sands' sample were representative of all manufacturing industries, this comparison would suggest a *decline* in average plant size relative to market size.

  * * *

Economies of multi-plant operation. Our analysis up to this point has been concerned primarily with economies at the plant level or lower—that is, with plant-specific and product-specific economies. Although we have seen that concentration increases with the need to operate plants largely relative to the market, this is not the only, or perhaps even the main, cause of high concentration. That other influences are at work is shown by the fact that the leading firms in most industries operate multiple plants supplying a similar array of products. * * * Table 4.5 presents the distribution of 417 * * * industries according to the average number of industry-specific plants per Big Four seller (excluding warehouses, R & D laboratories, headquarters and sales offices, and the like). The leading four sellers operated a single plant each in only 22 industries.

Table 4.5

Extent of Multi-Plant Operation in 417 Manufacturing Industries

Plants per Big Four Member	Number of Industries	Percent of Industries
1.00 to 1.5 plants	78	18.7
1.75 to 2.5 plants	89	21.3
2.75 to 4.0 plants	87	20.9
4.25 to 7.0 plants	87	20.9
7.25 to 10 plants	28	6.7
10.25 to 20 plants	35	8.4
More than 20 plants	13	3.1
All industries	417	100.0

Source: U.S., Congress, Senate, Subcommittee on Antitrust and Monopoly report, *Concentration Ratios in Manufacturing Industry:* 1963, Part 2, 89th Cong., 1st sess., Table 27.

Evidently, the preeminent position of most leading firms can be attributed not merely to maintaining large plants, but to operating *many* of them. * * *

The crucial remaining question is, does this multi-plant operation by leading firms confer economies above and beyond those associated with operating a single plant of optimal scale? And, if so, how significant are they? Or to reverse the focus, how seriously disadvantaged are firms operating only a single MOS plant, compared to the largest multi-plant enterprises?

We shall organize our analysis into three main categories—economies of multi-plant production, investment, and physical distribution; economies of risk spreading and finance; and advantages of sales promotion on a multi-plant scale. As we shall see, these have varying performance implications, some entailing clear-cut efficiency gains, some redistributions of income, and some a blend of efficiency, redistributive, and monopolistic effects. * * *

To begin analyzing such economies, it is useful to divide firms operating multiple plants in an industry into three categories (recognizing of course that hybrid cases also exist). First is the case in which a market of considerable geographic expanse is served and outbound transportation costs are appreciable. Then the firm's least-cost strategy is likely to involve operating multiple geographically dispersed plants, each supplying for the most part only the customers nearest its location. The operating patterns of sizeable firms in the cement, beer, petroleum refining, and glass bottle industries provide relatively pure examples. Second is the case of firms with low shipping costs * * * but complex product lines. Then each plant of a multi-plant enterprise may specialize in some narrow segment of the product array—e.g., one plant in women's cemented-sole fashion shoes, another in women's casuals, a third in men's Goodyear welts, a fourth in work shoes, and so on. * * *

Now, if delivery costs are substantial, as they are for beer or cement or steel reinforcing rods, it is obviously more economical, if one is to serve the entire continental United States market, to have multiple dispersed plants than to ship everything from one giant centrally located installation. But this begs the fundamental question: Why does a firm have to serve the entire continental market? Are there any production, investment, and/or distribution cost differences between the case in which a single enterprise operates five optimal-sized, geographically dispersed plants and the one in which five independent geographically dispersed firms operate a single MOS plant each?

There may be. It can be shown that when demand is fixed at any any moment in time but grows over time and when scale economies can be realized by expanding capacity in large indivisible chunks, excess capacity carrying costs can be reduced, and the scale economy opportunities exploited more fully, by playing a kind of investment whipsaw game. First a large investment is made at location A, with other plants reducing their shipping radii to satisfy growing nearby demand more fully and letting plant A serve what would normally be their peripherally located customers. Later plant B expands and territories are readjusted to utilize its new capacity, and so on. Transportation costs are higher under this coordinated investment staging scheme than with autarkic expansion by each individual plant, jointly or independently owned, but investment carrying costs may be lower by a more than offsetting amount. However, such a scheme will not yield net savings if the individual plants can cover temporary capacity deficits by buying from recently expanded *nearby* competitors at prices approximating marginal cost and if they can sell excess supplies to such competitors, or if *local* supply and demand (no longer assumed fixed) can be equilibrated by market price adjustments before and after major expansions. The more smoothly local markets work in facilitating adjustment to capacity jumps, the smaller are the benefits from coodinated multi-plant, multi-region investment staging. In other words, such investment coordination economies are of a second-best character, realizable when and because local markets fail to balance demand and supply.

Economies may also result from the operation of multiple geographically dispersed plants as an integrated system. For instance, the demand for automobile batteries peaks during the winter months in the northern United States and during the summer in the South. A firm with plants in both areas might be able to maintain less peak-load capacity by shipping north in the winter and south in the summer.

* * *

The other main interesting mode of multiplant operation occurs when plants specialize in some narrow slice of a product array—e.g., small mass-produced ball bearings at one plant, other small ball bearings at a second, large ball bearings at a third, tapered bearings at a fourth, and so on. Plants with a narrow line of products are easier to manage. For a plant of given size, production run lengths will be greater, and hence product-specific economies will be realized more fully, the narrower the line manufactured is. The key interpretive questions are, can't the same degree of plant specialization be achieved by single-plant firms that choose to offer only a narrow line of products? And are the plants of multi-plant sellers in fact more narrowly specialized than those of single-plant firms?

In answer to the first question, it appears that at least in some industries, there are marketing advantages to being a broad-line supplier. This in turn argues for multi-plant operation unless one's product line can be rounded out through purchases from other competing manufacturers.

* * *

The second question in effect asks whether single-plant producers in multi-product industries incur only a marketing disadvantage by not offering a broad line, or whether they also tend to cram relatively more low-volume products into the production schedules of their only plant and therefore sacrifice product-specific economies as well. The evidence on this point is weak and mixed. There does appear to be a tendency in some industries for single-plant firms to experience shorter production runs than their multi-plant rivals. However, many exceptions exist, and the shorter runs of some relatively small firms may signify nothing more than specialization on low-volume items in which the larger companies have no interest—e.g., because their management structures may be too hierarchical to cope with the challenges of small-lot production. Also, multi-plant size and the attainment of product-specific economies do not appear to be closely correlated. Many large multi-plant firms are large because they produce commensurately more products than single-plant rivals, not because they produce a given array of products in higher volume. The overall picture is quite complex, and we must conclude that there is far too little hard evidence on this important dimension of multi-plant scale economies.

———————◆———————

Professor Scherer's discussion of economies of scale—decreasing unit production costs as volume of production increases—emphasizes the opportunity to improve performance by increasing the scale of tangible assets involved in production, such as plant size or number. The concept, however, need not be so limited. There may also be economies of scale in a non-tangible asset, such as management. For example, it might be that the best managers only can be attracted by large companies. If this were the case, then scale economies could be attained by increasing the size of the company under management in order to attract more talented executives. Considered from this perspective, a motivation for acquisitions based on displacement of the target company's inefficient management is also based on economies of scale. The assumption underlying the displacement theory is that the target's inefficient managers will be replaced by the acquiring company's efficient managers. But this would not be possible unless the acquiring company had unused managerial capacity, whether because senior management's time was not entirely occupied with the company's existing business, or because there were junior managers who had the ability to undertake more responsible positions, but for whom there were no opportunities within the acquiring company.

Consider again Philip Morris's acquisition of Miller High Life. Can the explanation for the success of that acquisition be described in terms of economies of scale?

b. Economies of Vertical Integration: The Vertical Dimension

M. PORTER, COMPETITIVE STRATEGY
300–13 (1980).*

Vertical integration is the combination of technologically distinct production, distribution, selling, and/or other economic processes within the confines of a single firm. As such, it represents a decision by the firm to utilize internal or administrative transactions rather than market transactions to accomplish its economic purposes. For example, a firm with its own sales force instead could have contracted, through the market, an independent selling organization to supply the selling services it requires. Similarly, the firm mining the raw materials it fabricates into end products could have contracted an independent mining organization to supply its needs.

In theory, all the functions we now expect a corporation to perform could be performed by a consortium of independent economic entities, each contracting with a central coordinator, which itself need be little more than desk and a single manager. In fact, segments of the book publishing and recording industries take approximately this form. Many publishers contract for editorial services, layout, graphics, printing, distribution, and selling, retaining for the firm little more than decisions about which books to publish, marketing, and finance. Some recording companies similarly contract with independent artists, producers, recording studios, disc-pressing facilities, and distribution and marketing organizations to create, manufacture, and sell each record.

In most situations, however, firms find it advantageous to perform a significant proportion of the administrative, productive, distributive, or marketing processes required to produce their products or services in-house rather than through contracts with a series of independent entities. They believe that it is cheaper, less risky, or easier to coordinate when these functions are performed internally.

Many vertical integration decisions are framed in terms of the "make or buy" decision, focusing on the financial calculations such a decision entails. That is, they are preoccupied with estimating the cost savings of integration and balancing them with the investment required. However, the vertical integration decision is much broader than this. The essence of the vertical integration decision is not the financial calculation itself but rather the numbers that serve as the raw material for the calculation. The decision must go beyond an

* Reprinted with the permission of The Free Press, a Division of Macmillan, Inc.   from *Competitive Strategy* by M. Porter. Copyright © 1980 by The Free Press

analysis of costs and investment requirements to consider the broader strategic issues of integration versus use of market transactions, as well as some perplexing administrative problems in managing a vertically integrated entity that can affect the success of the integrated firm. These are very hard to quantify. It is the magnitude and strategic significance of the benefits and costs of vertical integration, both in direct economic terms and indirectly through its affect on the organization, that are the essence of the decision.

*   *   *

BENEFITS AND COSTS OF VERTICAL INTEGRATION

Vertical integration has important generic benefits and costs which need to be considered in any decision but whose significance will depend on the particular industry. * * * For purposes of this discussion, the *upstream* firm is the selling firm and the *downstream* firm is the buying firm in the vertical chain.

VOLUME OF THROUGHPUT VERSUS EFFICIENT SCALE

The benefits of vertical integration depend, first of all, on the volume of products or services the firm purchases from or sells to the adjacent stage relative to the size of the efficient production facility in that stage. For ease in exposition let us take the case of a firm integrating backward. The volume of purchases of the firm contemplating backward integration must be large enough to support an in-house supplying unit large enough to reap all economies of scale in producing the input, or the firm faces a dilemma. Either it must accept a cost disadvantage in producing the input internally, or it must sell some of the production of the upstream unit in the open market. [But] selling extra output on the open market may be difficult because the firm might have to sell to its competitors. If the firm's needs *do not* exceed the scale of an efficient unit, the firm faces one of two costs of integrating, which must then be figured against the benefits. Either it builds an inefficiently small facility that meets only its needs, or it builds an efficient facility and must bear the possible risk of sales or purchases on the open market.

STRATEGIC BENEFITS OF INTEGRATION

ECONOMIES OF INTEGRATION

If the volume of throughput is sufficient to reap available economies of scale,[2] the most commonly cited benefit of vertical integration is the achievement of *economies,* or cost savings, in joint production, sales, purchasing, control, and other areas.

Economies of Combined Operations. By putting technologically distinct operations together, the firm can sometimes gain efficiencies. In manufacturing, for example, this move can reduce the number of

---

[2] Or the cost penalty is small enough to be offset by other benefits of integration to be discussed.

steps in the production process, reduce handling costs, reduce transportation costs, and utilize slack capacity which arises from indivisibilities in one stage (machine time, physical space, maintenance facilities, etc.).
* * *

Facilities can be located in close proximity to each other, as is the case with the many large sulfuric acid users (fertilizer companies, oil companies) who have established backward integration into sulfuric acid production. This step eliminates transportation costs, which are substantial for a hazardous and difficult to handle product like sulfuric acid.

Economies of Internal Control and Coordination. The costs of scheduling, coordinating operations, and responding to emergencies may be lower if the firm is integrated. Adjacent location of the integrated units facilitates coordination and control. There is also likely to be more trust placed on an insider to keep the needs of its sister unit in mind, and therefore, less slack built into the business to cope with unforeseen events. Steadier supply of raw materials or the ability to smooth deliveries may result in better control of production schedules, delivery schedules, and maintenance operations. This is because the revenue foregone by suppliers who fail to deliver may be much less than the cost of disruption, and hence their motivation to deliver punctually is hard to assure. * * * Such economies of control can reduce idle time, the need for inventory, and the need for personnel in the control function.

Economies of Information. Integrated operations may reduce the need for collecting some types of information about the market, or more likely, may reduce the overall cost of gaining information. The fixed costs of monitoring the market and predicting supply, demand, and prices can be spread over all parts of the integrated firm, whereas they would have to be borne by each entity in an unintegrated firm. For example, the integrated food processor can use sales projections for the final product in all segments of the vertical chain. Similarly, market information may well flow more freely through an organization than through a series of independent parties. Integration may thus allow the firm to obtain faster and more accurate information about the marketplace.

Economies of Avoiding the Market. By integrating, the firm can potentially save on some of the selling, price shopping, negotiating, and transactions costs of market transactions. Although there will usually be some negotiating in internal transactions, its cost should not be nearly as great as that of selling to or purchasing from outside parties. No sales force and no marketing or purchasing departments are needed. Moreover, advertising is unnecessary, as are other marketing costs.

Economies of Stable Relationships. Both upstream and downstream stages, knowing that their purchasing and selling relationship is stable, may be able to develop more efficient, specialized procedures for dealing with each other that would not be feasible with an independent supplier or customer—where both the buyer and the seller in the transaction face the competitive risk of being dropped or squeezed by the other party. Specialized procedures for dealing with customers or suppliers can include dedicated, specialized logistical systems, special packaging, unique arrangements for record keeping and control, and other potentially cost-saving ways of interacting.

It is also possible that stability of the relationship will allow the upstream unit to tune its product (in quality, specifications, etc.) to the exact requirements of the downstream unit, or for the downstream unit to adapt itself more fully to the characteristics of the upstream unit. To the extent that such adaptation would lock independent parties into each other, its occurrence without vertical integration may require payment of a risk premium, which raises costs.

*   *   *

STRATEGIC COSTS OF INTEGRATION

The costs of vertical integration basically involve entry cost, flexibility, balance, ability to manage the integrated firm, and the use of internal organizational incentives versus market incentives.

COST OF OVERCOMING MOBILITY BARRIERS

Vertical integration obviously requires the firm to overcome the mobility barriers to compete in the upstream or downstream business. Integration is, after all, a special case (though a common one) of the general strategic option of entry into a new business. Because of the internal buying and selling relationship implied by vertical integration, the integrating firm can often readily surmount some mobility barriers into the adjacent business, such as access to distribution channels and product differentiation. However, overcoming barriers caused by cost advantages from proprietary technology or favorable sources of raw materials can be a cost of vertical integration, as can overcoming other sources of mobility barriers, such as economies of scale and capital requirements. As a result, vertical integration occurs most frequently in industries like metal containers, aerosol packaging, and sulfuric acid, in which the technology is well known and the minimum efficient scale of a plant is not great.

INCREASED OPERATING LEVERAGE

Vertical integration increases the proportion of a firm's costs that are fixed. If the firm was purchasing an input on the spot market, for example, all the costs of that input would be variable. If the input is produced internally, the firm must bear any fixed costs involved in its production even if a downturn or some other cause reduces the demand for it. Since the sales of the upstream business are derived from the sales of the downstream business, factors that cause fluctuations in either business cause fluctuations in the whole chain. Fluctuations can be caused by the business cycle, by competitive or market developments, and so on. Thus integration increases the operating leverage of the firm, exposing it to greater cyclical swings in earnings. Vertical integration thereby *increases business risk* from this source, though the net effect of integration on risk depends on whether it decreases business risk in other dimensions, as has been discussed. * * *

A good example of the risk of operating leverage created by extensive vertical integration is the Curtis Publishing Company. Curtis built an immense vertical enterprise to supply its relatively few magazines, primarily the *Saturday Evening Post.* When the magazine ran into difficulty in the late 1960s, the impact on the financial performance of Curtis was disastrous.

* * *

FORECLOSURE OF ACCESS TO SUPPLIER OR CONSUMER RESEARCH AND/OR KNOW-HOW

By integrating, the firm may cut itself off from the flow of technology from its suppliers or customers. Integration usually means that a company must accept responsibility for developing its own technological capability rather than piggybacking on others. However, if it chooses not to integrate (whereas other firms do), suppliers are often willing to support the firm aggressively with research, engineering assistance, and the like.

Foreclosure of technology can be a significant risk when there are numerous independent suppliers or customers doing research or where suppliers or customers have large-scale research efforts or have particular know-how difficult to replicate. * * *

MAINTAINING BALANCE

The productive capacities of the upstream and downstream units in the firm must be held in balance or potential problems arise. The stage of the vertical chain with excess capacity (or excess demand) must sell some of its output (or purchase some of its inputs) on the open market or sacrifice market position. This step in such a circumstance may be difficult because the vertical relationship often compels the firm to sell or buy from its competitors. They may be reluctant to deal with the firm for fear of getting second priority or to avoid strengthening their competitor's position. If excess output can be readily sold on the open market or excess demand for inputs readily satisfied, on the other hand, the risks of imbalance are not great.

Vertical stages go out of balance for a variety of reasons. First, efficient increments to capacity are usually unequal for the two stages, creating temporary periods of imbalance even in a growing market. Technological change in one stage may require changes in methods that effectively increase its capacity relative to the other stage; or changes in product mix and quality may affect effective capacity in the vertical stages unequally. The risk of imbalance will depend on predictions about the likelihood of these factors.

DULLED INCENTIVES

Vertical integration means that buying and selling will occur through a captive relationship. The incentives for the upstream business to perform may be dulled because it sells in-house instead of competing for the business. Conversely, the business buying internally from another unit in the company may not bargain as hard as it would with outside vendors. Thus, dealing in-house can reduce incentives. A related point is that internal projects to expand capacity, or internal contracts to buy or sell, may get less stringent review than external contracts with customers or suppliers.

Whether or not these dulled incentives actually reduce perform-ance in the vertically integrated firm is a function of the managerial structure and procedures that govern the relationship between the administrative units in the vertical chain. One often reads policy statements concerning internal transactions that give managers the freedom to use outside sources or to sell outside if the inside unit is not competitive. The mere presence of such procedures is not enough, however. The use of an outside instead of an inside source often places the burden of proof on the unit manager and requires an explanation to top management; most managers may well try to avoid interacting with top management on such a basis. Also there is a sense of fairness and comradeship within an organization that may make strictly arms-length agreements difficult, especially if one unit or the other is earning very low returns or otherwise is in serious trouble. Yet this is where arms-length relationships are the most necessary.

The difficulty just discussed, leads to the "bad apple" problem. If the upstream or downstream unit is sick (strategically or otherwise), its problems may spill over to its healthy partner. One unit can be pressured or even voluntarily attempt to rescue the troubled unit by accepting higher-cost products, products of inferior quality, or lower prices on internal sales. This situation can damage the healthy unit strategically.

———————◆———————

One potential benefit from vertical integration that Professor Porter does not consider explicitly is of particular interest to lawyers. Recent economic scholarship concerning the theory of the firm has stressed that the firm is best understood as a nexus of contracts among all those—management, labor, suppliers of capital, suppliers of raw materials—whose skills or assets are necessary to produce the firm's product.[5] Put this way, the question of vertical integration can be phrased in terms of which skills, capital, and raw materials the firm will supply for itself by implicit contract, and which it will acquire in market transactions by explicit contract. Again, this helps define the boundary of the firm. Among the considerations bearing on the deci-sion is the cost of explicit contracting in market transactions. These costs include not only expenditures on preparing the written document, but also and perhaps more importantly, the costs of efforts to eliminate the potential for "opportunistic behavior" by either party, and the costs

[5] See, e.g., Fama, *Agency Problems and the Theory of the Firm,* 88 J.Pol.Econ. 288 (1980); Jensen & Meckling, *Theory of the* *Firm: Managerial Behavior, Agency Costs and Ownership Structure,* 3 J.Fin.Econ. 305 (1976).

of never entirely succeeding. The nature of opportunistic behavior, and the circumstances in which vertical integration, through acquisition or otherwise, may provide an effective response, are considered in the following excerpt from an important contribution to the literature.

KLEIN, CRAWFORD & ALCHIAN, VERTICAL INTEGRATION, APPROPRIABLE RENTS, AND THE COMPETITIVE CONTRACTING PROCESS *
21 J.L. & Econ. 297–306 (1978).

More than forty years have passed since Coase's fundamental insight that transaction, coordination, and contracting costs must be considered explicitly in explaining the extent of vertical integration.[1] Starting from the truism that profit-maximizing firms will undertake those activities that they find cheaper to administer internally than to purchase in the market, Coase forced economists to begin looking for previously neglected constraints on the trading process that might efficiently lead to an intrafirm rather than an interfirm transaction. This paper attempts to add to this literature by exploring one particular cost of using the market system—the possibility of postcontractual opportunistic behavior.

Opportunistic behavior has been identified and discussed in the modern analysis of the organization of economic activity. Williamson, for example, has referred to effects on the contracting process of "*ex post* small numbers opportunism,"[2] and Teece has elaborated:

> Even when all of the relevant contingencies can be specified in a contract, contracts are still open to serious risks since they are not always honored. The 1970's are replete with examples of the risks associated with relying on contracts . . . [O]pen displays of opportunism are not infrequent and very often litigation turns out to be costly and ineffectual.[3]

The particular circumstance we emphasize as likely to produce a serious threat of this type of reneging on contracts is the presence of appropriable specialized quasi rents. After a specific investment is made and such quasi rents are created, the possibility of opportunistic behavior is very real. Following Coase's framework, this problem can be solved in two possible ways: vertical integration or contracts. The crucial assumption underlying the analysis of this paper is that, as assets become more specific and more appropriable quasi rents are created (and therefore the possible gains from opportunistic behavior increases), the costs of contracting will generally increase more than the costs of vertical integration. Hence, *ceteris paribus*, we are more likely to observe vertical integration.

* Copyright © 1978. Reprinted by permission of The University of Chicago Press.

[1] R.H. Coase, *The Nature of the Firm*, 4 Economica 386 (1937), reprinted in *Readings in Price Theory* 331 (George J. Stigler & Kenneth E. Boulding eds. 1952).

[2] Oliver E. Williamson, *Markets and Hierarchies: Analysis and Antitrust Implications* 26–30 (1975).

[3] David J. Teece, *Vertical Integration and Divestiture in the U.S. Oil Industry* 31 (1976).

I. Appropriable Quasi Rents of Specialized Assets

Assume an asset is owned by one individual and rented to another individual. The quasi-rent value of the asset is the excess of its value over its salvage value, that is, its value in its next best *use* to another renter. The potentially appropriable specialized portion of the quasi rent is that portion, if any, in excess of its value to the second highest-valuing *user*. If this seems like a distinction without a difference, consider the following example.

Imagine a printing press owned and operated by party A. Publisher B buys printing services from party A by leasing his press at a contracted rate of $5,500 per day. The amortized fixed cost of the printing press is $4,000 per day and it has a current salvageable value if moved elsewhere of $1,000 (daily rental equivalent). Operating costs are $1,500 and are paid by the printing-press owner, who prints final printed pages for the publisher. Assume also that a second publisher C is willing to offer at most $3,500 for daily service. The current quasi rent on the installed machine is $3,000 (= $5,500 − $1,500 − $1,000), the revenue minus operating costs minus salvageable value. However, the daily quasi rent from publisher B relative to use of the machine for publisher C is only $2,000 (= $5,500 − $3,500). At $5,500 revenue daily from publisher B the press owner would break even on his investment. If the publisher were then able to cut his offer for the press from $5,500 down to almost $3,500, he would still have the press service available to him. He would be appropriating $2,000 of the quasi rent from the press owner. The $2,000 difference between his prior agreed-to daily rental of $5,500 and the next best revenue available to the press once the machine is purchased and installed is less than the quasi rent and therefore is potentially appropriable. If no second party were available at the present site, the entire quasi rent would be subject to threat of appropriation by an unscrupulous or opportunistic publisher.

Our primary interest concerns the means whereby this risk can be reduced or avoided. In particular, vertical integration is examined as a means of economizing on the costs of avoiding risks of appropriation of quasi rents in specialized assets by opportunistic individuals. This advantage of joint ownership of such specialized assets, namely, economizing on contracting costs necessary to insure nonopportunistic behavior, must of course be weighed against the costs of administering a broader range of assets within the firm.

An appropriable quasi rent is not a monopoly rent in the usual sense, that is, the increased value of an asset protected from market entry over the value it would have had in an open market. An appropriable quasi rent can occur with no market closure or restrictions placed on rival assets. Once installed, an asset may be so expensive to remove or so specialized to a particular user that if the price paid to the owner were somehow reduced the asset's services to that user would not be reduced. Thus, even if there were free and open competition for entry to the market, the specialization of the installed asset to a particular user (or more accurately the high costs of making it available to others) creates a quasi rent, but no "monopoly" rent. At the other extreme, an asset may be costlessly transferable to some other user at no reduction in value, while at the same time, entry of similar assets is restricted. In this case, monopoly rent would exist, but no quasi rent.

* * *

[W]e investigate a different reason for joint ownership of vertically related assets—the avoidance of postcontractual opportunistic behavior when specialized assets and appropriable quasi rents are present.
* * *

We maintain that if an asset has a substantial portion of quasi rent which is strongly dependent upon some other particular asset, both assets will tend to be owned by one party. For example, reconsider our printing press example. Knowing that the press would exist and be operated even if its owner got as little as $1,500, publisher B could seek excuses to renege on his initial contract to get the weekly rental down from $5,500 to close to $3,500 (the potential offer from publisher C, the next highest-valuing user at its present site). If publisher B could effectively announce he was not going to pay more than, say, $4,000 per week, the press owner would seem to be stuck. This unanticipated action would be opportunistic behavior (which by definition refers to unanticipated nonfulfillment of the contract) if the press owner had installed the press at a competitive rental price of $5,500 anticipating (possibly naively) good faith by the publisher. The publisher, for example, might plead that his newspaper business is depressed and he will be unable to continue unless rental terms are revised.

Alternatively, and maybe more realistically, because the press owner may have bargaining power due to the large losses that he can easily impose on the publisher (if he has no other source of press services quickly available), the press owner might suddenly seek to get a higher rental price than $5,500 to capture some newly perceived increase in the publisher's profits. He could do this by alleging breakdowns or unusually high maintenance costs. This type of opportunistic behavior is difficult to prove and therefore litigate.

As we shall see, the costs of contractually specifying all important elements of quality varies considerably by type of asset. For some assets it may be essentially impossible to effectively specify all elements of quality and therefore vertical integration is more likely. But even for those assets used in situations where all relevant quality dimensions can be unambiguously specified in a contract, the threat of production delay during litigation may be an effective bargaining device. A contract therefore may be clearly enforceable but still subject to post-contractual opportunistic behavior. For example, the threat by the press owner to break its contract by pulling out its press is credible even though illegal and possibly subject to injunctive action. This is because such an action, even in the very short run, can impose substantial costs on the newspaper publisher.[6]

---

[6] While newspaper publishers generally own their own presses, book publishers generally do not. One possible reason book publishers are less integrated may be

This more subtle form of opportunistic behavior is likely to result in a loss of efficiency and not just a wealth-distribution effect. For example, the publisher may decide, given this possibility, to hold or seek standby facilities otherwise not worthwhile. Even if transactors are risk neutral, the presence of possible opportunistic behavior will entail costs as real resources are devoted to the attempt to improve posttransaction bargaining positions in the event such opportunism occurs. In particular, less specific investments will be made to avoid being "locked in." In addition, the increased uncertainty of quality and quantity leads to larger optimum inventories and other increased real costs of production.

II. CONTRACTUAL SOLUTIONS

The primary alternative to vertical integration as a solution to the general problem of opportunistic behavior is some form of economically enforceable long-term contract. Clearly a short-term (for example, one transaction, nonrepeat sale) contract will not solve the problem. The relevant question then becomes when will vertical integration be observed as a solution and when will the use of the market-contracting process occur. * * *

Long-term contracts used as alternatives to vertical integration can be assumed to take two forms: (1) an explicitly stated contractual guarantee legally enforced by the government or some other outside institution, or (2) an implicit contractual guarantee enforced by the market mechanism of withdrawing future business if opportunistic behavior occurs. Explicit long-term contracts can, in principle, solve opportunistic problems, but, as suggested already, they are often very costly solutions. They entail costs of specifying possible contingencies and the policing and litigation costs of detecting violations and enforcing the contract in the courts.[14] Contractual provisions specifying compulsory arbitration or more directly imposing costs on the opportunistic party (for example, via bonding) are alternatives often employed to economize on litigation costs and to create flexibility without specifying every possible contingency and quality dimension of the transaction.

because a book is planned further ahead in time and can economically be released with less haste. Presses located in any area of the United States can be used. No press is specialized to one publisher, in part because speed in publication and distribution to readers are generally far less important for books than newspapers, and therefore appropriable quasi rents are not created.

[14] The recent Westinghouse case dealing with failure to fulfill uranium-supply contracts on grounds of "commercial impossibility" vividly illustrates these enforcement costs. Nearly three years after outright cancellation by Westinghouse of their contractual commitment, the law-suits have not been adjudicated and those firms that have settled with Westinghouse have accepted substantially less than the original contracts would have entitled them to. A recent article by Paul L. Joskow, *Commercial Impossibility, the Uranium Market, and the Westinghouse Case*, 6 J.Legal Stud. 119 (1977), analyzes the Westinghouse decision to renege on the contract as anticipated risk sharing and therefore, using our definition, would not be opportunistic behavior. However, the publicity surrounding this case and the judicial progress to date are likely to make explicit long-term contracts a less feasible alternative to vertical integration in the situations we are analyzing.

Since every contingency cannot be cheaply specified in a contract or even known and because legal redress is expensive, transactors will generally also rely on an implicit type of long-term contract that employs a market rather than legal enforcement mechanism, namely, the imposition of a capital loss by the withdrawal of expected future business. This goodwill market-enforcement mechanism undoubtedly is a major element of the contractual alternative to vertical integration.

* * *

One way in which this market mechanism of contract enforcement may operate is by offering to the potential cheater a future "premium," more precisely, a price sufficiently greater than average variable (that is, avoidable) cost to assure a quasi-rent stream that will exceed the potential gain from cheating. The present-discounted value of this future premium stream must be greater than any increase in wealth that could be obtained by the potential cheater if he, in fact, cheated and were terminated. The offer of such a long-term relationship with the potential cheater will eliminate systematic opportunistic behavior.

The larger the potential one-time "theft" by cheating (the longer and more costly to detect a violation, enforce the contract, switch suppliers, and so forth) and the shorter the expected continuing business relationship, the higher this premium will be in a nondeceiving equilibrium. This may therefore partially explain both the reliance by firms on long-term implicit contracts with particular suppliers and the existence of reciprocity agreements among firms. The premium can be paid in seemingly unrelated profitable reciprocal business. The threat of termination of this relationship mutually suppresses opportunistic behavior.

* * *

The firms collecting the premium payments necessary to assure fulfillment of contractual agreements in a costly information world may appear to be earning equilibrium "profits" although they are in a competitive market. That is, there may be many, possibly identical, firms available to supply the services of nonopportunistic performance of contractual obligations yet the premium will not be competed away if transactors cannot costlessly guarantee contractual performance. The assurance services, by definition, will not be supplied unless the premium is paid and the mere payment of this premium produces the required services.

Any profits are competed away in equilibrium by competitive expenditures on fixed (sunk) assets, such as initial specific investments (for example, a sign) with low or zero salvage value if the firm cheats, necessary to enter and obtain this preferred position of collecting the premium stream. These fixed (sunk) costs of supplying credibility of future performance are repaid or covered by future sales on which a premium is earned. In equilibrium, the premium stream is then merely a normal rate of return on the "reputation," or "brand-name" capital created by the firm by these initial expenditures. This brand-name capital, the value of which is highly specific to contract fulfillment by the firm, is analytically equivalent to a forfeitable collateral bond put up by the firm which is anticipated to face an opportunity to take advantage of appropriable quasi rents in specialized assets.

While these initial specific investments or collateral bonds are sometimes made as part of the normal (minimum-cost) production process and therefore at small additional cost, transaction costs and risk considerations do make them costly. We can generally say that the larger the appropriable specialized quasi rents (and therefore the larger the potential short-run gain from opportunistic behavior) and the larger the premium payments necessary to prevent contractual reneging, the more costly this implicit contractual solution will be. We can also expect the explicit contract costs to be positively related to the level of appropriable quasi rents since it will pay to use more resources (including legal services) to specify precisely more contingencies when potential opportunities for lucrative contractual reneging exist.

Although implicit and explicit contracting and policing costs are positively related to the extent of appropriable specialized quasi rents, it is reasonable to assume, on the other hand, that any internal coordination or other ownership costs are not systematically related to the extent of the appropriable specialized quasi rent of the physical asset owned. Hence we can reasonably expect the following general empirical regularity to be true: the lower the appropriable specialized quasi rents, the more likely that transactors will rely on a contractual relationship rather than common ownership. And conversely, integration by common or joint ownership is more likely, the higher the appropriable specialized quasi rents of the assets involved.

———————◆———————

c. *Economies of Scope: The Conglomerate Dimension*

The problem posed by economies of scale and vertical integration is to define the efficient boundary of the firm with respect to the production of a *single* product. The same type of problem is also posed, however, with respect to the range of *different* products produced by a single firm. Why do firms produce more than one product or participate in more than one industry? The first part of the answer is the concept of economies of scope: not the savings from increased production of the same product, as in economies of scale, but, rather, the savings from the joint production of a number of different products. Here the notion is that even where the particular products are different, the production processes may be sufficiently similar that scale economies of a sort, now called economies of scope because they concern a reduction in the costs of producing multiple products rather than a single product, can still be achieved with respect to the common inputs. Analysis of the availability of economies of scope in connection with the physical production process thus resembles Scherer's discussion of economies of scale and depends, in major respects, on technological evaluation of the production process.

The second part of the answer is less technological than transactional. As with vertical integration, access to the common input can be obtained and economies of scope achieved either through a market transaction whereby firms continue to produce only a single product but share the benefits of the economies of scope by sharing the common input by contract, or by acquiring ownership of the common input and producing both products within the same firm. When the shared input is tangible, whether the economy of scope is best achieved through the market by contract or within the firm by acquisition depends on the same type of analysis as presented by Klein, Crawford and Alchian with respect to the transaction cost determinants of vertical integration. When the shared input is intangible, like technological know-how and other forms of knowledge, analysis of the difficulties of gaining access to the shared input by market contract is quite different. This subject is considered by Professor Teece in the following discussion.

TEECE, ECONOMIES OF SCOPE AND THE SCOPE OF THE ENTERPRISE

1 J.Econ.Behav. & Org. 223, 223–30 (1980).

1. Introduction

Explaining the scope of activities pursued by the modern business enterprise is clearly central to our understanding of the organization of industry. Yet, as Ronald Coase points out, the received theory of industrial organization is unable to explain why General Motors is not a dominant factor in the coal business, or why A & P does not manufacture airplanes. Nor does the received theory explain why aircraft manufacturers are now producing missiles and space vehicles, why Union Oil is producing energy from geothermal sources, or why Exxon is looking for uranium. One reason for this neglect is suggested by [the] observation that microeconomic analysis views the enterprise as little more than a black box, and the distribution of economic activity between markets and firms is taken as datum. * * *

2. Economies of scope and diversification

Efforts have recently been made to formulate an efficiency-based theory of the multiproduct firm. These endeavors rest upon specifying cost functions which exhibit economies of scope. Economies of scope exist when for all outputs y_1 and y_2, the cost of joint production is less than the cost of producing each output separately * * *

[But] even if the technology displays scope economies the joint production of two goods by two firms need not be more costly than production of the two goods by one enterprise. This can be readily established by counterexample.[3] * * * Just as technological interde-

---

[3] Consider mixed farming. Orchardists must have space between fruit trees in order to facilitate adequate growth of the trees and the movement of farm machinery between the trees. This land can, however, be planted in grass, and sheep may graze to advantage in the intervening pasture. Economies of scope are clearly realized (land is the common input) but [r]ather than producing both fruit and sheep, the orchardist can lease the pasture to a sheep farmer. The scope economies in sheep farming and fruit production are realized, but the single product focus of the sheep farmer and the orchardist are preserved. Clearly, market contracts can be used to undo the organization implications [of] the cost function.

pendency between successive stages of a production process [alone] do not explain vertical integration nor do scope economices explain the multiproduct firm. * * *

A sensitive treatment of the organizational issues involved when the cost function displays economies of scope would indicate that *the origin of the scope economies must first be identified.* As a general matter, economies of scope arise from inputs that are shared, or utilized jointly without complete congestion. The shared factor may be imperfectly divisible, so that the manufacture of a subset of the goods leaves excess capacity in some stage of production, or some human or physical capital may be a public input which, when purchased for use in one production process, is then freely available to another. I submit that the facility with which the common input or its services can be traded across markets will determine whether economies of scope will require the enterprise to be multiproduct in its scope. Where such trading is difficult, and intrafirm governance is superior, then [a multiproduct firm will be efficient.] Only two classes of common inputs can be readily identified where [this] market failure appears to hold. The common inputs in question are knowhow and specialized and indivisible physical assets. Yet even here, market processes are often sustained. The remainder of this paper seeks to identify the circumstances under which markets for these inputs may break down and where intrafirm transfer is called for. * * *

3. Knowhow

A principal feature of the modern business enterprise is that it is an organizational entity possessing knowhow. To the extent that knowhow has generic attributes, it represents a shared input which can find a variety of end product applications. Knowhow may also display some of the characteristics of a public good in that it can sometimes be used in many different non-competing applications without its value in any one application being substantially impaired. Furthermore, the marginal cost of employing knowhow in a different endeavor is likely to be much less than its average cost of production and dissemination (transfer). Accordingly, although knowhow is not a pure public good,[5] the transfer of proprietary information to alternative activities is likely to generate scope economies if organizational modes can be discovered to conduct the transfer at low cost. In this regard, the relative efficiency properties of markets and internal organization need to be assessed. If reliance on market processes is surrounded by special difficulties—and hence costs—internal organization, and in particular multiproduct enterprise, may be preferred.

An examination of the properties of information markets readily leads to the identification of several difficulties. They can be summarized in terms of (1) recognition, (2) disclosure and (3) team organization. Thus consider a firm which has accumulated knowhow which can potentially find application in fields of industrial activity beyond its

---

[5] This is because the value of information often declines with its dissemination and it cannot be transferred at zero marginal cost.

existing markets. If there are other firms in the economy which can apply this knowhow with profit, then according to received microtheory, trading will ensue until Pareto Optimality conditions are satisfied. * * * However, one cannot in general expect this happy result in the market for proprietary knowhow. Not only are there high costs associated with obtaining the requisite information but there are also organizational and strategic impediments associated with using the market to effectuate transfer.

Consider, to begin with, the information requirements associated with using markets. In order to carry out a market transaction it is necessary to discover who it is that one wishes to deal with, to inform people that one wishes to deal and on what terms, to conduct negotiations leading up to the bargain, to draw up the contract, to undertake the inspection needed to make sure that the terms of the contract are being observed, and so on. Furthermore, the opportunity for trading must be identified. As Kirzner has explained:

'* * * for an exchange transaction to be completed it is not sufficient merely that the conditions for exchange which prospectively will be mutually beneficial be present; it is necessary also that each participant be aware of his opportunity to gain through exchange * * *. It is usually assumed * * * that where scope for (mutually beneficial) exchange is present, exchange will in fact occur * * *. In fact of course exchange may fail to occur because knowledge is imperfect, in spite of conditions for mutually profitable exchange.

The transactional difficulties identified by Kirzner are especially compelling when the commodity in question is proprietary information, be it of a technological or managerial kind. This is because the protection of the ownership of technological knowhow often requires suppressing information on exchange possibilities. By its very nature, industrial R & D requires disguising and concealing the activities and outcomes of the R & D establishment. * * * Except as production or marketing specialists within the firm perceive the transfer opportunity, transfer may fail by reason of non-recognition.

Even where the possessor of the technology recognizes the opportunity, market exchange may break down because of the problems of disclosing value to buyers in a way that is both convincing and does not destroy the basis for exchange. A very severe information impactedness* problem exists, on which account the less informed party (in this instance the buyer) must be wary of opportunistic representations by the seller. If, moreover, there is insufficient disclosure, including veracity checks thereon, to assure the buyer that the information possesses great value, the 'fundamental paradox' of information arises: 'its value for the purchaser is not known until he has the information, but then he has in effect acquired it without cost'.

---

* "Information impactedness" exists when all of the facts relating to a transaction are known to one party but cannot be costlessly discovered by the other. [Ed.]

Suppose that recognition is no problem, that buyers concede value, and are prepared to pay for information in the seller's possession. Occasionally that may suffice. The formula for a chemical compound or the blue prints for a special device may be all that is needed to effect the transfer. However, more is frequently needed. Knowhow has a strong learning-by-doing character, and it may be essential that human capital in an effective team configuration accompany the transfer. Sometimes this can be effected through a one-time contract (a knowhow agreement) to provide a "consulting team" to assist start-up. Although such contracts will be highly incomplete, and the failure to reach a comprehensive agreement may give rise to dissatisfaction during execution, this may be an unavoidable, which is to say irremediable, result. Plainly, diversification is an extreme response to the needs of a one-time exchange. In the absence of a superior organizational alternative, reliance on market mechanisms is thus likely to prevail.

Where a succession of proprietary exchanges seems desirable, reliance on repeated contracting is less clearly warranted. Unfettered two-way communication is needed not only to promote the recognition and disclosure of opportunities for information transfer but also to facilitate the execution of the actual transfer itself. The parties in these circumstances are joined in a small numbers trading relation and * * * contracting may be shot through with hazards for both parties.

The seller is exposed to hazards such as the possibility that the buyer will employ the knowhow in subtle ways not covered by the contract, or the buyer might "leap frog" the licensor's technology and become an unexpected competitive threat in third markets. The buyer is exposed to hazards such as the seller asserting that the technology has superior performance or cost reducing characteristics than is actually the case; or the seller might render promised transfer assistance in a perfunctory fashion. While bonding or the execution of performance guarantees can minimize these hazards, they need not be eliminated since costly haggling might ensue when measurement of the performance characteristics of the technology is open to some ambiguity. Furthermore, when a lateral transfer is contemplated and the technology has not therefore been previously commercialized by either party in the new application, the execution of performance guarantees is likely to be especially hazardous to the seller because of the uncertainties involved. In addition, if a new application of a generic technology is contemplated, recurrent exchange and continuous contact between buyer and seller will be needed. These requirements will be extremely difficult to specify ex ante. Hence, when the continuous exchange of proprietary knowhow between the transferor and transferee is needed, and where the end use application of the knowledge is idiosyncratic in the sense that it has not been accomplished previously by the transferor, it appears that something more than a classical market contracting structure is required. As Williamson notes "The nonstandardized nature of (these) transactions makes primary reliance on market governance hazardous, while their recurrent nature permits the cost of the specialized governance structure to be recovered." This can take the form of bilateral governance, where the autonomy of the parties is maintained; or unified structures, where the transaction is removed from the market and organized within the firm subject to an authority relation. Bilateral governance involves the use of what Williamson has labelled "obligational contracting".

Exchange is conducted between independent firms under obligational arrangements, where both parties realize the paramount importance of maintaining an amicable relationship as overriding any possible short-run gains either might be able to achieve. But as transactions become progressively more idiosyncratic, obligational contracting may also fail, and internal organization (intrafirm transfer) is the more efficient organizational mode. The intrafirm transfer of knowhow avoids the need for repeated negotiations and ameliorates the hazards of opportunism. Better disclosure, easier agreement, better governance, and therefore more effective execution of knowhow transfer are likely to result. Here lies an incentive for enterprise diversification.

The above arguments are quite general and extend to the transfer of many different kinds of proprietary knowhow. Besides technological knowhow, the transfer of managerial (including organizational) knowhow, and goodwill (including brand loyalty) represent types of assets for which market transfer mechanisms may falter, and for which the relative efficiency of intrafirm as against interfirm trading is indicated.

*   *   *

———————◆———————

The excerpt from Professor Teece's study focuses on the opportunities for the creation of economies of scope through the transfer of information and other intangible assets. For a review of efforts to consider economies of scope arising from shared tangible assets, see Bailey & Friedlander, *Market Structure and Multiproduct Industries*, 20 J.Econ.Lit. 1024 (1982).

For a more detailed examination of the problems associated with technology transfer by contract, see Teece, *Technology Transfer by Multinational Firms: The Resource Cost of Transferring Technological Know-How*, 87 Econ.J. 242 (1977).

d.   *Economies of Organization: The Pure Conglomerate Dimension*

None of the explanations for how acquisitions can overcome the principle of value additivity that we have considered thus far extends to a theory of how real economic gains can result from a pure conglomerate acquisition. Economies of scale, vertical integration and scope all posit either the potential for decreased costs through increased utilization of an input in the production of a single product (as with economies of scale) or in the production of different products (as with economies of scope), or the potential to reduce the costs of contracting for inputs necessary to the production process (as with economies of vertical integration). In contrast, the central characteristic of the pure conglomerate firm is that neither shared inputs nor a supplier relationship exist between its units. All that is shared in a conglomerate is a common organization and it is this shared factor that has provided the focus for a possible explanation for the conglomerate phenomenon. Oliver Williamson, whose work was critical to the view of vertical integration discussed by Klein, Crawford and Alchian, has focused on the role of organizational structure in determining the boundary of the firm and, hence, the potential for gain from acquisitions. In its focus on the role of management, this approach is similar to the displacement of inefficient management motivation considered in Chapter Ten. And in its implicit assumption that there is unused managerial capacity in the acquiring company, this approach has an element in common with the discussions of economies of scale and scope considered in this Chapter. The Williamson explanation differs from these, however, in its focus on financial management in contrast to operational management. While economies of scale, scope and vertical integration pose the issue of when to internalize the acquisition of inputs that would otherwise have been obtained through transactions in particular *factor* markets, Williamson's approach to the conglomerate is to consider when the firm should internalize the functions of the *capital* market. Thus, it has potential to shed light on the motives for conglomerate acquisitions.

WILLIAMSON, THE MODERN CORPORATION: ORIGINS, EVOLUTION, ATTRIBUTES
19 J.Econ.Lit. 1537, 1555–60 (1981).

The Multidivisional Structure

The most significant organizational innovation of the 20th century was the development in the 1920s of the multidivisional structure. Surprisingly, this development was little noted or widely appreciated as late as 1960. Leading management texts extolled the virtues of "basic departmentation" and "line and staff authority relationships," but the special importance of multidivisionalization went unremarked.

* * *

The leading figures in the creation of the multidivisional (or M-form) structure were Pierre S. du Pont and Alfred P. Sloan; the period was the early 1920s; the firms were Du Pont and General Motors; and the organizational strain of trying to cope with economic adversity under the old structure was the occasion to innovate in both. The structures of the two companies, however, were different.

Du Pont was operating under the centralized, functionally departmentalized or unitary (U-form) structure. General Motors, by contrast, had been operated more like a holding company by William Durant— whose genius in perceiving market opportunities in the automobile industry evidently did not extend to organization. Chandler summarizes the defects of the large U-form enterprise in the following way:

> The inherent weakness in the centralized, functionally departmentalized operating company * * * became critical only when the administrative load on the senior executives increased to such an extent that they were unable to handle their entrepreneurial

responsibilities efficiently. This situation arose when the operations of the enterprise became too complex and the problems of coordination, appraisal, and policy formulation too intricate for a small number of top officers to handle both long-run, entrepreneurial, and short-run, operational administrative activities.

The ability of the management to handle the volume and complexity of the demands placed upon it became strained and even collapsed. Unable meaningfully to identify with or contribute to the realization of global goals, managers in each of the functional parts attended to what they perceived to be operational subgoals instead. In the language of transaction cost economics, bounds on rationality* were reached as the U-form structure labored under a communication overload while the pursuit of subgoals by the functional parts (sales, engineering, production) was partly a manifestation of opportunism.

The M-form structure fashioned by du Pont and Sloan involved the creation of semi-autonomous operating divisions (mainly profit centers) organized along product, brand, or geographic lines. The operating affairs of each were managed separately. More than a change in decomposition rules were needed, however, for the M-form to be fully effective. Du Pont and Sloan also created a general office "consisting of a number of powerful general executives and large advisory and financial staffs" to monitor divisional performance, allocate resources among divisions, and engage in strategic planning. The reasons for the success of the M-form innovation are summarized by Chandler as follows:

> The basic reason for its success was simply that it clearly removed the executives responsible for the destiny of the entire enterprise from the more routine operational activities, and so gave them the time, information, and even psychological commitment for long-term planning and appraisal. * * *
>
> [The] new structure left the broad strategic decisions as to the allocation of existing resources and the acquisition of new ones in the hands of a top team of generalists. Relieved of operating duties and tactical decisions, a general executive was less likely to reflect the position of just one part of the whole

In contrast with the holding company—which is also a divisionalized form but has little general office capability and hence is little more than a corporate shell—the M-form organization adds (1) a strategic planning and resource allocation capability and (2) monitoring and control apparatus. As a consequence, cash flows are reallocated among divisions to favor high yield uses, and internal incentive and control instruments are exercised in a discriminating way. In short, the M-form corporation takes on many of the properties of (and is usefully regarded as) a miniature capital market, which is a much more ambi-

---

* "Bounded rationality" is the limit on human ability to solve complicated problems and in utilizing (receiving, storing, retrieving and transmitting) information. See O. Williamson, *Markets and Hierarchies* 21–24 (1975). The comparable popular term might be "informational overload." [Ed.]

tious concept of the corporation than the term holding company contemplates.

Although the structure was imitated very slowly at first, adoption by U.S. firms proceeded rapidly during the period 1945 to 1960. * * * The M-form structure represented a different solution to the coupling problem than the earlier unitary form structure. It effected decomposability along product or brand lines to which profit center standing could be assigned and it more clearly separated operating from strategic decision making.

* * *

As compared with the U-form organization of the same activities, the M-form organization of the large, complex corporation served both to economize on bounded rationality and attenuate opportunism. Specifically:

> Operating decisions were no longer forced to the top but were resolved at the divisional level, which relieved the communication load. Strategic decisions were reserved for the general office, which reduced partisan political input into the resource allocation process. And the internal auditing and control techniques which the general office had access to served to overcome information impactedness conditions and permit fine timing controls to be exercised over the operating parts.

The Conglomerate

Chandler's studies of organizational innovation do not include the conglomerate form of corporate enterprise. These are more recent developments, the appearance of which would not have been feasible but for the prior development of the M-form structure.

* * *

Although diversification as a corporate strategy certainly predates the 1960s, when general awareness of the conglomerate began to appear, the conglomerate is essentially a post World War II phenomenon. To be sure, General Electric's profit centers number in the hundreds and GE has been referred to as the world's most diversified firm. Until recently, however, General Electric's emphasis has been the manufacture and distribution of electrical appliances and machinery. Similarly, although General Motors was more than an automobile company, it took care to limit its portfolio. Thus Sloan remarked that "tetraethyl lead was clearly a misfit for GM. It was a chemical product, rather than a mechanical one. And it had to go to market as part of the gasoline and thus required a gasoline distribution system." Accordingly, although GM retained an investment position, the Ethyl Corporation became a free-standing entity rather than an operating division. Similarly, although Durant had acquired Frigidaire, and Frigidaire's market share of refrigerators exceeded 50 percent in the 1920s, the position was allowed to deteriorate as rivals developed market positions in other major appliances (radios, ranges, washers, etc.) while Frigidaire concentrated on refrigerators.

* * *

The conglomerate form of organization, whereby the corporation consciously took on a diversified character and nurtured its various parts, evidently required a conceptual break in the mind-set of Sloan and other prewar business leaders. This occurred gradually, more by evolution than by grand design and it involved a new group of organizational innovators—of which Royal Little was one. The natural growth of conglomerates, which would occur as the techniques for managing diverse assets were refined, was accelerated as antitrust enforcement against horizontal and vertical mergers became progressively more severe. Conglomerate acquisitions—in terms of numbers, assets acquired, and as a proportion of total acquisitions—grew rapidly with the result that "pure" conglomerate mergers, which in the period 1948–1953 constituted only 3 percent of the assets acquired by merger, had grown to 49 percent by 1973–1977.

* * *

I submit that some phenomena, of which changing internal organization is one, need to be addressed on their own terms. Adopting this view, the conglomerate is best understood as a logical outgrowth of the M-form mode for organizing complex economic affairs. Thus once the merits of the M-form structure for managing separable, albeit related, lines of business (e.g., a series of automobile or a series of chemical divisions) were recognized and digested, its extension to manage less closely related activities was natural. This is not to say that the management of product variety is without problems of its own. But the basic M-form logic, whereby strategic and operating decisions are distinguished and responsibilities are separated, carried over. The conglomerates in which M-form principles of organization are respected are usefully thought of as internal capital markets whereby cash flows from diverse sources are concentrated and directed to high yield uses.

The conglomerate is noteworthy, however, not merely because it permitted the M-form structure to take this diversification step. Equally interesting are the unanticipated systems consequences which developed as a byproduct. Thus once it was clear that the corporation could manage diverse assets in an effective way, the possibility of takeover by tender offer suggested itself. In principle, incumbent managements could always be displaced by waging a proxy contest. In fact, this is a very expensive and relatively ineffective way to achieve management change. Moreover, even if the dissident shareholders should succeed, there was still a problem of finding a successor management.

Viewed in contractual terms, the M-form conglomerate can be thought of as substituting an administrative interface between an operating division and the stockholders where a market interface had existed previously. Subject to the condition that the conglomerate does not diversify to excess, in the sense that it cannot competently evaluate and allocate funds among the diverse activities in which it is engaged, the substitution of internal organization can have beneficial effects in goal pursuit, monitoring, staffing, and resource allocation respects. The goal-pursuit advantage is that which accrues to M-form organizations in general: since the general management of an M-form conglomerate is disengaged from operating matters, a presumption that the general office favors profits over functional goals is warranted. Relatedly, the general office can be regarded as an agent of the stockholders whose purpose is to monitor the operations of the constituent parts. Monitoring benefits are realized in the degree to which internal monitors enjoy advantages over external monitors in access to information—which they arguably do. The differential ease with which the general office can change managers and reassign duties where performance failures or distortions are detected is responsible for the staffing advantage. Resource-allocation benefits are realized because cash flows no longer return automatically to their origins but instead revert to the center, thereafter to be allocated among competing uses in accordance with prospective yields.[36]

This has a bearing on the problem of separation of ownership from control, noted by Adolph Berle and Gardiner C. Means in 1932. Thus they inquired, "have we any justification for assuming that those in control of a modern corporation will also choose to operate it in the interests of the stockholders." The answer, then as now, is almost certainly no. ＊ ＊ ＊

There are important differences, however, between the U-form structure, which was the prevailing organization form at the time Berle and Means were writing, and the M-form structure, which in the U.S. was substantially in place by the 1960s. For one thing, as argued above, U-form managers identified more strongly with functional interests and hence were more given to subgoal pursuit. Secondly, and related, there was a confusion between strategic and operating goals in the U-form structure which the M-form served to rectify—with the result that the general office was more fully concerned with enterprise goals, of which profits is the leading element. Third, the market for corporate control, which remained ineffectual so long as the proxy contest was the only way to challenge incumbent managements, was activated as conglomerates recognized that tender offers could be used to effect corporate takeovers. As a consequence, managements that were otherwise secure and would have permitted managerial preferences to prevail were brought under scrutiny and induced to self-correct against egregious managerial distortions.

To be sure, managerial preferences (for salary and perquisites) and stockholder preferences for profits do not become perfectly consonant as a result of conglomerate organization and the associated activation of the capital market. The continuing tension between management and

---

[36] To be sure, this substitution of internal organization for the capital market is subject to tradeoffs and diminishing returns. Breadth—that is, access to the widest range of alternatives—is traded off for depth—that is, more intimate knowledge of a narrower range of possible investment outlets—where the general office may be presumed to have the advantage in the latter respect. The diminishing returns feature suggests that the net benefits of increased diversity eventually become negative. Were further diversification thereafter to be attempted, effective control would pass back into the hands of the operating divisions with problematic performance consequences.

stockholder interests is evident in the numerous efforts that incumbent managements have taken to protect target firms against takeover. Changes in internal organization have nevertheless relieved these concerns. A study of capitalist enterprises which makes no allowance for organization form changes and their capital market ramifications will naturally overlook the possibility that the corporate control dilemma posed by Berle and Means has since been alleviated more by *internal* than it has by regulatory or external organizational reforms.

---◆---

Note. *Empirical Analysis of M–Form Organization.* There have been efforts to test empirically the proposition that the move from "U-form" to "M-form" organization results in better economic performance. The studies do not use the CAR methodology discussed in Chapter Seven because of the difficulty in specifying the event date— how can you tell exactly when the shift to "M-Form" organization was announced or even when the reorganization was first anticipated—and because of doubts concerning the efficiency of the market both with respect to some of the time periods under consideration and with respect to its ability to evaluate the particular motivations for the reorganization. While the particular empirical techniques that have been used vary, the most recent study compared rate of return on assets and rate of return on shareholders' equity between competitive firms in two periods, using financial accounting data. The two periods consisted of a "before" period in which one firm had adopted "M-form" organization and the other had not, and an "after" period in which both firms had adopted "M-form" organization. The hypothesis that "M-form" organization leads to superior performance would be supported by either of two results: if the "M-form" firm was the superior performer in the "before" period, the differential should narrow in the "after" period; alternatively, if the "M-form" firm's performance was not superior in the "before" period, the differential should widen in the "after" period. The results were consistent with the "M-form" hypothesis. Teece, *Internal Organization and Economic Performance: An Empirical Analysis of the Profitability of Principal Firms,* 30 J.Indus. Econ. 173 (1981). For other efforts using different methodology, see Armour & Teece, *Organizational Structure & Economic Performance: A Test of the Multidivisional Hypothesis,* 9 Bell J. Econ. 196 (1978); Burton & Obel, *A Computer Simulation Test of the M-form Hypothesis,* 25 Admin.Sci.Q. 457 (1980); Cable & Steer, *Internal Organization and Profit: An Empirical Analysis of Large U.K. Companies,* 27 J.Indus. Econ. 13 (1980). Note, however, that these studies do *not* test the conglomerate hypothesis offered by Williamson in the previous excerpt.

B. Evaluation: Consistency With Analytic Tools and Empirical Evidence

The financial theory considered in Part I provides a frame of reference for evaluating claims that certain types of corporate acquisitions result in synergy. The value of each of the constituent corporations in an acquisition, and of the resulting combined entity, are reflected in their respective stock prices. The capital asset pricing model tells us that a stock's price is determined by its return (dividends plus appreciation) and its systematic risk (the variation in return attributable to variability in market return which cannot be reduced by diversification). This, in turn, suggests two possible means by which firm value can be increased through synergistic acquisitions. Return may be increased without an offsetting increase in systematic risk, or risk may be reduced without an offsetting reduction in return. Each of the sources of synergy considered in this Chapter can be evaluated as an effort to alter either risk or return.

The strategies for increasing return through acquisitions are most straightforward. Consider, for example, the impact of economies of scale discussed by Professor Scherer. If an acquiring company has a decreasing long-run average cost curve, an increase in unit sales may increase profits more than proportionately because of higher margins on the new sales. Thus, a combination that allows an acquiring company to expand production to a more efficient portion of its average cost curve can result in the desired synergy as the return on the combined corporation will exceed the pre-acquisition return on each of the parties to the acquisition.

While this example may seem self-evident, the result is, in fact, less clear than may appear. In our analytic model, a greater return is preferable to a lesser return *only* if the level of systematic risk is held constant. Even in the case of economies of scale, the assumption of constant risk may be troublesome and, in any event, requires examination. For example, different segments of industry demand may respond quite differently to alterations in general economic conditions—a critical element of systematic risk. An extreme example demonstrates the relevance of this fact. Assume that an acquiring company and a target company manufacture essentially the same products, but that the acquiring company is principally a defense contractor, the demand for whose product is relatively less responsive to overall economic conditions than that of the target company, whose market is largely civilian. If the same assembly lines can produce the products sold in both markets or if the product is essentially the same in both markets—as with the military and civilian versions of the same aircraft—the acquiring company may believe that expanding production to accommodate civilian demand will allow realization of economies of scale (or scope), resulting in an increase in return and, therefore, an increase in the value of the combined company over its constituent parts. The problem, however, is that the systematic risk of the combined company has also increased over that of the pre-transaction acquiring corporation alone. At a minimum, the new civilian demand is more responsive to changes in general economic conditions and this increased risk should require an increase in return simply to *maintain* value. What other sources of increased systematic risk might exist?

The lesson is that it may be easy to be taken in by the prospect of increased return without paying sufficient attention to whether or not the increase in return is commensurate with any increase in systematic risk. This is the point stressed in Brealey & Myers' discussion of capital budgeting procedures in light of the capital asset pricing model in Chapter Four. A focus on return alone, even in comparison to an acquiring company's existing return on equity, makes for misleading project choices. The attractiveness of increased return is entirely dependent on the level of systematic risk associated with the increase.

How does this analysis apply to the product/market-portfolio model described in this Chapter? The product/market-portfolio approach "says to invest in market share." [6] The reward from increased market share and movement down the experience curve should be increased return. Does the existence of a declining experience curve suggest anything about the impact of increased market share on systematic risk?

Each explanation for synergy thus requires analysis of the implications for *both* return and systematic risk. To be sure, an increase in value may occur; however, the analysis may be more difficult than at first appears. As an exercise, think through the explanations for synergy provided by economies of vertical integration, scope and organization in terms of risk and return. Which primarily focuses on risk and which on return? Does this perspective alter your evaluation of the likelihood of successfully achieving synergy?

A synergistic motivation for acquisitions does suggest an empirically testable hypothesis. If one or more of the potential sources of synergy are operative, the post-acquisition value of the combined firm should exceed the sum of the pre-acquisition values of the individual corporations. Put in terms of CAR methodology, the merger should result in positive net abnormal returns after taking into account both the acquiring and target companies.

Table 11 displays the CAR for target and acquiring companies during the period surrounding public disclosure of an acquisition transaction and during the period following the transaction as reported in various empirical studies. The data presented in Table 11 are consistent in their picture of the impact of an acquisition on the wealth of the target company's shareholders: They earn significant positive abnormal returns.[7] Jensen and Ruback, *The Market for Corporate Control:*

[6] M. Salter & W. Weinhold, *Diversification Through Acquisition* 122 (1980).

[7] It is interesting that all of the studies reported in Table 11 show that target companies earn significant positive CAR in the period immediately preceding public announcement of the acquisition transaction. This should be contrasted with the data reported in Table 10 showing that target companies earned negative abnormal returns over earlier pre-acquisition periods. Keown & Pinkerton, *Merger Activity and*

Insider Trading Activity: An Empirical Investigation, 36 J.Fin. 855 (1981), found that approximately half of the total abnormal returns earned by a target from its acquisition occurs prior to the announcement date, and "that 79, 60, and 64 *percent* of the acquired firms exhibited higher volume one, two, and three weeks prior to the announcement date than they had three months earlier with the weekly average volume over the three week period 247, 112, and 102 percent higher than it was

The Scientific Evidence, 11 J.Fin.Econ. 5 (1983), summarize the results of most of the studies reported in Table 11 [8] by computing the weighted average of the abnormal returns reported by them. Target companies subject to successful tender offers earn positive weighted average abnormal returns of 29.1% in the month or two surrounding announcement of the offer, and target companies subject to successful mergers earn weighted average abnormal returns of 15.9% over roughly the same period. Moreover, the averages mask no variation in the results: No study reports other than large positive abnormal returns for target companies.

three months earlier." Id. at 863. The authors conclude that their data "show what appears to be common knowledge on the street: impending merger announcements are poorly held secrets, and trading on this nonpublic information abounds." Id. at 866. Although the data is consistent with insider trading, it is also consistent with other explanations. For example, if incomplete information concerning the probability that the transaction will occur is gradually made public in the period prior to the formal public announcement of the transaction, then the data may reflect only the market's reflection of the partial information as it becomes available. For those transactions that did take place, review of a plot of abnormal returns with the benefit of hindsight will suggest insider trading. As well, it might not take very much real insider trading to trigger the derivatively-derived trading mechanisms discussed in Chapter Five. These mechanisms would also serve to reflect the inside information in price but without violating prohibitions on trading on inside information. Indeed, if insider trading in fact "abounds," then the puzzle is not that there are such large gains before public

announcement but, rather, why *all* gains do not occur in the pre-announcement period. The point is not to deny the existence of insider trading, but only to question whether there are not additional elements that share responsibility for the abnormal returns Keown & Pinkerton report. Finally, the volume increase reported in the pre-announcement period is also consistent with the operation of the derivatively-derived trading mechanisms as well as with the familiar practice of an acquiring company making market purchases of the target's shares prior to the public announcement of the acquisition. Purchase of target shares by the acquiring company prior to public announcement of the transaction also does not violate prohibitions against insider trading.

[8] Jensen & Ruback exclude the Mandelker, Ellert and Langeteig studies because these studies treat the event date as the month in which the merger was consummated, rather than the date it was publicly announced. Additionally, they do not include the Asquith & Kim and Dennis & McConnell studies.

Table 11

Offer Period and Post-Acquisition Performance of Target and Acquiring Companies

A. Target Companies

Study	Sample	Period (month of announcement = 0)	CAR
Mandelker, Risk and Return: The Case of Merging Firms, 1 J.Fin.Econ. 303 (1974)	252 firms acquired between 11/41 and 8/62 (91% after 1/51)	-7 months through -1 month [1,2]	13.6%
Ellert, Mergers, Antitrust Law Enforcement and Stockholder Returns, 31 J.Fin. 715 (1976)	311 NYSE firms acquired between 1950 and 1970	-7 months through -1 month [2] month 0	14.7% 1.4%
Dodd & Ruback, Tender Offers and Stockholder Returns: An Empirical Analysis, 5 J.Fin.Econ. 351 (1977)	136 firms subject to successful tender offers between 1958 and 1976 that appear on CRSP tapes	-7 months through -1 month month 0	7.36% 20.89%
Kummer & Hoffmeister, Valuation Consequences of Cash Tender Offers, 32 J.Fin. 505 (1978)	50 NYSE firms subject to successful cash tender offers between 1/56 and 6/74	-7 months through -1 month month 0	5.76% 16.85%
Langeteig, An Application of a Three-Factor Performance Index to Measure Stockholder Gains from Merger, 6 J.Fin.Econ. 365 (1978)	149 NYSE firms which merged between 1929 and 1969 (90% after 1950; 60% after 1960)	6 months through -1 month [1,2] + 1 month through + 6 months	10.63% -2.75%

Table 11

Offer Period and Post-Acquisition Performance of Target and Acquiring Companies—Continued

A. Target Companies

Study	Sample	Period (month of announcement = 0)	CAR
Osborne, Returns to Shareholders of Acquiring and Acquired Companies: The Case of Acquisitions of Technology-Based Firms in the Over-the-Counter Market, S.E.C. Capital Market Working Paper No. 3 (1980)	14 technology based firms traded over-the-counter acquired between 1972 and 1977	−40 days through −1 day (0 = day of announcement)[3] day 0	21.83% 6.17%
Dodd, Merger Proposals, Management Discretion and Stockholder 8 J.Fin.Econ. 105 (1980)	71 NYSE firms acquired by merger between 1/70 and 12/77	−40 days through −1 day (0 = day of announcement)[3] day 0	20.6% 3.41%
Bradley, Interfirm Tender Offers and the Market for Corporate Control, 53 J.Bus. 345 (1980)	161 NYSE or ASE firms subject to successful cash tender offers between 7/62 and 12/77	−20 days through +20 days (0 = day of announcement)[3]	32.18%[4]
Jarrell & Bradley, The Economic Effects of Federal and State Regulation of Cash Tender Offers, 23 J.L. & Econ. 371 (1980)	147 NYSE or ASE firms subject to successful cash tender offers between 7/62 and 12/77	−40 days through +5 days (0 = day of announcement)[3]	34.06%
Asquith & Kim, The Impact of Merger Bids on the Participating Firms' Security Holders, 37 J.Fin. 1209 (1982)	21 firms acquired in a conglomerate merger[5] between 1960 and 1978, whose book value exceeded 10% of that of the acquiring company	−7 months through −1 month month 0	5.81%* 17.66%

Table 11
Offer Period and Post-Acquisition Performance of Target and Acquiring Companies—Continued

A. Target Companies

Study	Sample	Period (month of announcement = 0)	CAR
Asquith, Merger Bids, Uncertainty and Stockholder Returns, 11 J.Fin.Econ. 51 (1983)	211 NYSE firms subject to successful mergers between 1962 and 1976	-100 days through 15 days (0 = days of announcement)[3] day 0 day 0 through outcome day[6]	3.5% 9.5% 9.3%
Eckbo, Horizontal Mergers, Collusion, and Stockholder Wealth, 11 J.Fin.Econ. 241 (1983)	57 firms acquired in horizontal mergers between 1963 and 1978 not challenged on antitrust grounds where book value of target firm was $10 million or more	-20 days through -1 day (0 = day of announcement)[3] day 0	10.95% 3.13%
Asquith, Bruner & Mullins, The Gains to Bidding Firms from Merger, 11 J.Fin.Econ. 121 (1983)	35 firms acquired in mergers between 1963 and 1979	-20 days through day 0 (0 = day of announcement)[3]	20.5%[4]
Malatesta, The Wealth Effect of Merger Activity and the Objective Function of Merging Firms, 11 J.Fin.Econ. 155 (1983)	85 firms acquired between 1969 and 1974 with more than $10 million in assets	-3 months through -1 month month 0 -3 months through -1 month month 0	5.7% 17.57% $8.353 million[7] $7.443 million
Dennis & McConnell, Corporate Mergers and Security Returns, Working Paper (March, 1985)	76 firms acquired between 1962 and 1980 with assets greater than $70 million or 5% of the book value of the acquirer's assets	-19 days through day 0[3] -19 days through day 0	16.6% $31.8 million[7]

Table 11

Offer Period and Post-Acquisition Performance of Target and Acquiring Companies—Continued

B. Acquiring Companies

Study	Sample	Period (month of announcement = 0)	CAR
Mandelker (supra)	241 NYSE firms making acquisitions between 11/41 and 8/62 (91% after 1/51)	-7 months through -1 month[2]	1.4%*
		month 0	0.18%*
		+1 month through +7 months	0.05%*
Ellert (supra)	772 NYSE firms making acquisitions of $10 million or more between 1950 and 1970	-7 months through -1 month	1.8%
		month 0	0.5%
Dodd & Ruback (supra)	124 firms making successful tender offers between 1958 and 1976 that appear on CRSP tapes	-7 months through -1 month	7.63%
		month 0	2.83%
		+1 month through +7 months	+1.82%
Kummer & Hoffmeister (supra)	17 NYSE firms making successful cash tender offers between 1/56 and 6/74	-7 months through -1 month	4.95%
		month 0	5.2%
		+1 month through +7 months	-1.6%
Langeteig (supra)	149 NYSE firms which merged between 1929 and 1969 (90% after 1950; 60% after 1960)	-6 months through -1 month[1]	-2.82%
		+1 month through +12 months	-6.59%

Table 11

Offer Period and Post-Acquisition Performance of Target and Acquiring Companies—Continued

B. Acquiring Companies

Study	Sample	Period (month of announcement = 0)	CAR
Osborne (supra)	11 firms traded over-the-counter which acquired technology-based firms traded over-the-counter between 1972 and 1977	-40 days through -1 day (0 = day of announcement)[3]	-.32%
		day 0	-2.68%
		+1 day through +14 days	-3.94%
Dodd (supra)	60 NYSE firms making acquisitions by merger between 1/70 and 12/77	-40 days through -1 day (0 = day of announcement)[3]	5.09%
		day 0	-0.2%
		+1 day through +40 days	1.18%
Bradley (supra)	88 NYSE or ASE firms making successful cash tender offers between 7/62 and 12/77	-20 days through +20 days (0 = day of announcement)[3]	4.36%[4]
Jarrell & Bradley (supra)	88 NYSE or ASE firms making successful cash tender offers between 7/62 and 12/77	-40 days through +20 days (0 = day of announcement)[3]	6.66%
		+20 days through +80 days	0.15%
Asquith & Kim (supra)	27 acquiring firms making a conglomerate merger[5] between 1960 and 1978, where target firm's book value exceeded 10% of that of the acquiring firm	-7 months through -3 months	+3.67%
		-2 months through -1 month	-6.02%*
		month 0	+1.0%*
		+1 month through +12 months	-0.18%

Table 11

Offer Period and Post-Acquisition Performance of Target and Acquiring Companies—Continued

B. Acquiring Companies

Study	Sample	Period (month of announcement = 0)	CAR
Asquith (1983) (supra)	196 NYSE acquiring firms making successful mergers between 1962 and 1976	−100 days through −5 days (0 = day of announcement)[3]	0
		day 0	1.1%*
		outcome day[6] through day +120	−1.9%*
		day +121 through day +240	−5.3%
Eckbo (supra)	102 acquiring firms making horizontal mergers between 1963 and 1978 not challenged on antitrust grounds where book value of target firm was $10 million or more	−20 days through −1 day (0 = day of announcement)[3]	1.31%*
		day 0	0.07%*
		day 0 through +10 days	0.21%*
Asquith, Bruner & Mullins (supra)	170 acquiring firms making successful mergers between 1962 and 1976	−20 days through day 0 (0 = day of announcement)[3]	3.48%[4]
Malatesta (supra)	256 acquiring firms making successful mergers between 1969 and 1974 where target firm had more than $10 million in assets	−3 months through −1 month	1.1%*
		month 0	0.9%*
		−3 months through −1 month	−$16.9 million[7]
		month 0	$2.567 million

Table 11

Offer Period and Post-Acquisition Performance of Target and Acquiring Companies—Continued

B. Acquiring Companies

Study	Sample	Period (month of announcement = 0)	CAR
Dennis & McConnell (supra)	90 acquiring firms making successful acquisitions between 1962 and 1980 where target had assets greater than $70 million or 5% of the book value of the acquirer's assets	-19 days through day 0 -19 days through day 0	1.70* $5.4 million*

* Not statistically significant.
1 Abnormal returns not computed for the month in which the merger was completed.
2 For this study, month 0 = the month in which the merger was consummated.
3 This study computed daily rather than monthly abnormal returns.
4 As reported in Jensen & Ruback, The Market for Corporate Control: The Scientific Evidence, 11 J.Fin.Econ. 5, 11–13 (1983) (Table 3).
5 As classified by the Federal Trade Commission.
6 The outcome day is that on which the merger is consummated. Between the announcement day and the outcome day is an "interim period" which varies in length with each merger.
7 Cumulative abnormal dollar return computed by multiplying percentage abnormal returns by the dollar value of the firm's outstanding equity.

The results for acquiring companies are both less favorable and more variable. Jensen and Ruback calculate that acquiring companies making successful tender offers earn positive weighted average abnormal returns of 3.8% over the same period, while those making successful acquisitions by merger seem to earn only normal returns, exhibiting neither positive nor negative abnormal returns.[9] Additionally, the data with respect to acquiring companies are less consistent than for target companies. While the weighted average abnormal return is positive, some studies report negative abnormal returns for acquiring companies.[10]

The data presented in Table 11 provides empirical support for the synergy hypothesis. Despite the fact that shareholders of target companies were paid large premiums,[11] the acquiring companies' shareholders seem to have earned on average either much smaller positive abnormal returns or, at the least, did not lose as a result of the transaction. Thus, the combined post-transaction value of the acquiring and target companies seem to exceed their pre-transaction value by an amount at least as large as the premium paid in the transaction— the principle of value additivity appears to have been overcome.

We can also learn something from the apparent distribution of the gains from the transaction between the acquiring and target companies. Target companies seem to capture the lion's share of the gains from the transaction—the weighted average positive CARs for target companies are at a minimum seven times greater than those for acquiring companies—suggesting that the possibility for synergy results from some unique resource possessed by the target company that is capable of producing gains when combined with any of a large number of potential acquirers. Competition among potential acquirers then results in the bulk of the gains going to the target company.[12]

Additional analysis of the data summarized in Table 11, however, especially with respect to the returns reported for acquiring firms, raises a number of questions concerning the accuracy of these inferences from the data. First, where the acquiring company is significant-

[9] The weighted averages were computed using sample sizes as weights and without adjustment for overlap among samples. It was not possible to test the weighted average returns for statistical significance. Jensen & Ruback, supra at 10 n. 4.

[10] Would not we expect acquiring company abnormal returns to be more variable than those of target companies? For the acquiring company, the transaction is based on its prediction about the value of combining the two companies. The quality of that prediction will vary among companies and will never be completely accurate even for quite capable companies. On those occasions when the market believes an acquiring company has made a mistake, negative abnormal returns will result. In contrast, so long as target companies receive a premium and the transaction was not anticipated, they cannot earn negative abnormal returns. Mistakes by the target company—taking a lower premium than might have been obtained—will not be reflected in negative abnormal returns over the entire transaction, although one might expect negative abnormal returns for the day on which the unfavorable offer was accepted.

[11] For example, Bradley, supra, reports that an average premium of 49% was paid in the tender offers comprising his sample, and Jarrell & Bradley, supra, report tender premiums of some 73% for offers subject to state regulation.

[12] See, e.g., Asquith (1983) supra at 52. Dennis & McConnell, in contrast, report that market adjusted dollar gains, as opposed to abnormal returns, are more evenly divided between the acquiring and target companies.

ly larger than the target company, as is generally the case, conclusions drawn from netting out the CAR of the acquiring and target companies may be problematical.   An extreme example illustrates the point. Suppose McDonald's Corporation acquired a single store from the franchise holder and paid a substantial premium despite the absence of any expectation of synergy.   One would expect the seller to earn positive abnormal returns as a result of the transaction because of the premium.   What would investigation of the abnormal returns of Mc-Donald's stock in this period show?   When the target is very much smaller than the acquiring company, the premium paid may well be simply too small to measurably alter the overall returns earned by McDonald's shareholders.   The same result would follow if the acquiring company gained as a result of the transaction.   Even large gains relative to the transaction would still be buried in the normal variation in the acquiring company's equity value.   Put differently, CAR is a relative, not an absolute number.   Large abnormal returns for the target shareholders may be no more than a drop in the acquiring company's income stream.

Evidence of this problem is presented by Asquith, Bruner & Mullins, supra, who divided their sample into two groups: one in which the equity value of the target company was 10% or more of that of the acquiring company; and one in which the equity value of the target company was less than 10% of that of the acquiring company.   Consistent with the preceding discussion, companies that acquired relatively large targets earned abnormal returns some 2.4 times greater than those that acquired smaller targets (4.1% and 1.7% respectively).[13]   A conclusion that synergy can overcome the principle of value additivity based on the data reported in Table 11 may then need to be qualified at least to the extent that acquiring companies greatly exceed target companies in size: Statistically insignificant abnormal losses by the acquiring company may exceed in absolute size very large percentage abnormal gains by the target.   The converse, however, is also true. Statistically insignificant abnormal gains by an acquiring company that is large relative to the target may substantially understate the value of the transaction to the acquiring company.[14]

The same qualification extends to inferences drawn from the apparent distribution of net gain between the acquiring and target companies based on the size of their respective abnormal returns.   If, for example, the acquiring company's equity value is 100 million dollars and the target company's equity value is 10 million dollars, abnormal returns of 1% for the acquiring company and 10% for the target

[13] Both figures are statistically significant. Dennis & McConnell did not find evidence of this fact in their study. Returns for subsamples which included an acquiring company only if the book value of the assets of the target company was at least 10 percent in one subsample, or at least 20 percent in a second, of the book value of the assets of the acquiring company, were similar to those for the sample as a whole.

[14] So, for example, the zero weighted average abnormal return for acquiring companies reported by Jensen & Ruback may mask large gains relative to the size of the transaction, if not relative to the size of the acquiring company.

company translate into an equal sharing of the gain from the transaction.[15]

The effort by Malatesta, supra, Dennis & McConnell, supra, and by Ruback in his analysis of the DuPont-Conoco merger in Chapter Six, to calculate dollar, in contrast to percentage, abnormal returns is an effort to overcome the relative size problem.[16] In particular, Malatesta calculated the abnormal returns to the combined equity value of the acquiring company and its specific merger partner in 30 mergers between January, 1969, and December, 1974. In the month before and the month of the public announcement, there were statistically significant positive abnormal dollar returns to the combined equity of 16.2 million dollars.[17] Dennis & McConnell reported similar results. In 108 acquisitions, there were positive abnormal dollar returns on the value of the combined firm of $76.7 million and on the value of the common stock alone of $59.3 million.

A second difficulty concerning measurement of the gain to acquiring companies involves the expectations problem discussed in Chapter Six. Many acquiring companies engage in a program of acquisitions. Once the market realizes this, any abnormal returns associated with anticipated acquisitions in general may be reflected at that time, leaving returns at the time of a particular transaction to reflect only the extent to which that acquisition altered the market's evaluation of the expected benefits from the company's overall acquisition program. As a result, returns around the time of a particular transaction would understate the value of acquisitions to the acquiring company. Schipper & Thompson, *Evidence on the Capitalized Value of Merger Activity for Acquiring Firms*, 11 J.Fin.Econ. 85 (1983), found evidence of abnormal returns in the year leading up to announcement of acquisition programs, but the substantial uncertainty concerning determination of the actual date on which the market learns of adoption of an acquisition program makes evaluation of their results difficult. Asquith, Bruner & Mullins, supra, approached the same problem somewhat differently. They examined abnormal returns associated with the first through fourth acquisitions made by a company. Their hypothesis was that if the market anticipated the value of an acquisition program,

[15] The acquiring company's abnormal return translates into an abnormal gain of one million dollars ($100,000,000 × 1%), just as does that of the target company ($10,000,000 × 10%). Dennis & McConnell, supra, report results consistent with this qualification. They found that market-adjusted dollar gains, in contrast to abnormal returns, were more evenly divided between the acquiring and target companies. McConnell & Vantell, *Corporate Combinations and Common Stock Returns: The Case of Joint Ventures*, 40 J.Fin. 519 (1985), report similar results in the case of joint venture formation. Although the smaller of the two firms forming the ventur (corresponding to the target company) earned abnormal returns in the announcement period of 1.10 percent while the larger firm (corresponding to the acquiring company) earned abnormal returns of only .63 percent, the dollar abnormal returns to the parties were more equally split: $4.54 million to the smaller firm and $6.65 million to the larger firm.

[16] It will not, however, overcome the difficulties created by the greater variance in equity value associated with the larger company.

[17] This illustrates the continued problem of the greater variance associated with a larger acquiring company. Taken alone, the average abnormal dollar returns to the acquiring companies, while of comparable magnitude to those of the target companies, were not statistically significant. Malatesta, supra at 170–71.

there would be higher abnormal returns associated with the first acquisitions than with the last. Their results were inconsistent with the hypothesis, showing instead constant positive abnormal returns associated with each acquisition.[18]

A final difficulty with interpreting the gains to acquiring companies reported by the studies summarized in Table 11 results from the fact that almost all of the studies lump together all types of acquisitions. Our theoretical analysis, however, suggests that different types of acquisitions hold different levels of promise for overcoming the principle of value additivity. For example, the discussion in Chapter Nine suggests that pure conglomerate acquisitions are unlikely to generate overall positive returns. Indeed, because of premiums paid to target shareholders, the expectation would be that shareholders of the acquiring company would earn negative returns. If this is correct, then the effect of including both conglomerate and non-conglomerate acquisitions in the same samples would be to understate the returns earned by shareholders of acquiring companies in non-conglomerate acquisitions.[19] This result, positive abnormal returns for acquiring company's shareholders in synergistically motivated transactions and negative abnormal returns in conglomerate acquisitions motivated by diversification is, of course, consistent with our analytic model. Nonetheless, it might well be obscured by the average results reported by the studies. It is interesting to note in this regard that the study by Asquith & Kim of conglomerate mergers and that by Eckbo of horizontal mergers report similar returns to acquiring companies. The problem with this comparison, however, is the same as was noted with respect to the Amihud & Lev study in Chapter Nine—conglomerate mergers are quite difficult to define *ex ante*. Before the fact, Phillip Morris' acquisition of Miller High Life was conglomerate; after the fact, Phillip Morris' ability to provide Miller High Life marketing expertise suggests synergy. Without more, synergistic and conglomerate mergers then reduce to descriptive labels for those acquisitions that succeeded and those that did not.

Summary. Taken as a whole, the body of existing empirical evidence yields the conclusion that, on average, corporate acquisitions result in a net increase in the combined value of the acquiring and target companies, and that synergy is the most likely explanation for how the principle of value additivity is overcome. That said, however, the various qualifications voiced in the preceding pages must also be

[18] Analysis of the same sample studied by Schipper & Thompson using a different methodology also found evidence of a positive announcement effect with a model that was also consistent with the constant announcement effect found by Asquith, Bruner & Mullins. Malatesta & Thompson, *Partially Anticipated Events: A Model of Stock Price Reactions with an Application to Corporate Acquisitions*, 14 J.Fin. Econ. 237 (1985).

[19] One study which is not included in Table 11, Haugen & Langetieg, *An Empirical Test for Synergism in Merger*, 30 J.Fin. 1003 (1975), attempted to avoid this problem by comparing the post-acquisition performance following 59 industrial mergers involving New York Stock Exchange listed firms with the performance of control companies chosen to most closely resemble the merging firms. The authors found that merger did not alter the distribution of returns associated with the merged companies; that is, no reduction in risk resulted. However, the authors acknowledged that they did not consider the possibility that the mergers might have increased returns. "A change of this type will go undetected by our analysis." Id. at 1013.

stressed.[20] The methodology on which the studies summarized in Table 11 are based continues to develop at a rapid pace but still has important shortcomings. As well, much remains to be learned about the organizational, institutional and regulatory settings in which acquisitions take place in order both to frame interesting hypotheses and to properly interpret the empirical data that we have.[21] Finally, there is a puzzling anomaly in the data. A number of studies [22] report that acquiring firms making successful acquisitions earn negative abnormal returns in the period following the transaction. It is quite difficult to explain the juxtaposition of positive abnormal returns in the period surrounding the transaction and negative abnormal returns thereafter. Moreover, the result seems inconsistent with market efficiency since it suggests a profitable trading strategy: Sell acquiring companies' stock short on the announcement date. At present, however, the data remains a puzzle. As Jensen & Ruback concluded, "[e]xplanation of these post-event negative abnormal returns is currently an unsettled issue." [23]

C. A Brief Review of Three Additional Motivations for Acquisitions

Three additional explanations for acquisitions should also be briefly considered. They share the common characteristic that, unlike synergy and displacement of inefficient management, they do not hold out the promise of societal gain from increased real productivity.

1. Corporate Raiders

Among the oldest explanations for acquisitions is one which has had a substantial judicial and legislative impact. Judicial opinions examining the legitimacy of target company action to defeat a disfavored acquisition take quite seriously the possibility that the acquiring company is a raider that seeks control over the target's assets in order to divert them to its own benefit at the expense of other shareholders.[24] Similarly, the tone of debate over the passage of the Williams Act, designed to constrain the conduct of acquiring companies in making tender offers, was set by Senator Williams' oft-cited reference, made

[20] Conn, *A Re-examination of Merger Studies that Use the Capital Asset Pricing Model Methodology,* 9 Cambridge J.Econ. 43 (1985), and Roll, *The Hubris Hypothesis of Corporate Takeovers,* Working Paper # 14–83, Graduate School of Management, U.C.L.A. (May, 1983), also provide critical surveys of the CAR evidence bearing on corporate acquisitions.

[21] It would be very useful to have a systematic account of the post-acquisition operating experience of acquiring companies. Like any effort at acquiring detailed "local knowledge," it is much more difficult and time-consuming than statistical research where the data is already available on the CRSP tapes. Professor Scherer reports an ongoing research project that may alleviate this deficiency. Testimony of F.M. Scherer before the Subcommittee on Telecommunications, Consumer Protection, and Finance, House Committee on Energy and Commerce (March 12, 1985).

[22] E.g., Asquith, Asquith & Kim, Langeteig, and Kummer & Hoffmeister.

[23] Jensen & Ruback, supra, at 22.

[24] See, e.g., Cheff v. Mathes, 41 Del.Ch. 494, 199 A.2d 548 (1964).

when introducing the legislation, to the fate of "proud old companies" at the hands of "white collar pirates." [25]

Stated in terms of a testable hypothesis, the corporate raider explanation predicts that, in tender offers for less than all of the target company's shares, the remaining target shareholders will suffer a loss, compared to pre-offer prices, on the target shares not bought by the acquiring firm. That loss would be the measure of the raider's plunder. In other words, the post-offer price of the shares of target company stock remaining outstanding after the transaction should fall below the pre-offer price to reflect the raiding of the target company's assets.

The empirical evidence is inconsistent with the corporate raider hypothesis. Bradley, *supra*, examined 98 target firms listed on the New York Stock Exchange or the American Stock Exchange which remained listed for at least 80 days following a successful partial tender offer. Rather than the price of the target stock dropping below its pre-offer level following the transaction, it remained 36% *above* its pre-offer level, a result inconsistent with a raiding motivation.

2. An Information Based Explanation for Acquisitions

In Section B of this Chapter, the empirical evidence summarized in Table 11—that corporate acquisitions result in positive abnormal returns for stockholders of both the acquiring and target companies—was treated as supporting a synergistic explanation for acquisitions. An alternative hypothesis, which is also consistent with this evidence, explains the increase in value of the target company by reference to new information. Bradley, Desai & Kim, supra at 184, describe this explanation in the alternative:

> There are two forms of this 'information hypothesis.' The first argues that the dissemination of the new information prompts the market to revalue previously 'undervalued' target shares. We might refer to this variant as the 'sitting on a gold mine' hypothesis. The second argues that the new information induces (allows) the current target management to implement a higher-valued operating strategy on its own. We might call this the 'kick in the pants' variant. In either event, the information hypothesis posits that the revaluation of the target shares is generated by actions of the market on the target managers in response to new information. That is, the positive revaluation does not require a successful acquisition of the target resources.

Empirical testing of the information, as opposed to the synergistic, explanation for acquisitions, turns on the valuation consequences of *unsuccessful* tender offers. If synergy is necessary for an increase in the value of the target company shares, then no abnormal gains should result from an unsuccessful tender offer. By definition, the synergistic benefits are available *only* if control over target company resources is

[25] 111 Congressional Record 28, 257–58 (1965).

shifted to another party. In contrast, if new information arising out of the tender offer causes the revaluation, the new higher value should remain even if the offer is unsuccessful.

Some empirical evidence is consistent with the information hypothesis. Studies by Bradley, supra, and Dodd & Ruback, supra, show that target companies that are the subject of unsuccessful tender offers retain a new, higher value. But this evidence is also consistent with a synergistic explanation; the continued increase in value may result from anticipation of another, more attractive offer.

Bradley, Desai & Kim test these alternative interpretations by dividing a sample of target companies that were the subject of unsuccessful tender offers into two groups: one composed of companies that were not later the subject of a successful bid and one composed of those that were. They found that those target companies that subsequently were taken over not only retained their gains, but showed further positive abnormal returns even after the unsuccessful offer. In the two years following the unsuccessful offer these firms showed a statistically significant positive abnormal return of 17.35%. In contrast, those target companies that were not the subject of a subsequent successful offer lost all of the increase in value that followed the unsuccessful offer. By two years after the unsuccessful offer, the 20.16% positive abnormal returns earned between one month before and one month after the unsuccessful offer was offset by negative abnormal returns of 27.47%. This result is consistent only with the synergy hypothesis. In the absence of a shift in control over a target company's resources by means of a later tender offer, all gains from the unsuccessful offer were dissipated within two years.

3. A Market Power Explanation for Acquisition

Not all sources of synergy are socially desirable. If the increase in value arising from an acquisition is the result of the creation of market power, then the gains to the combining firm come at the expense of efficient allocation. Stillman, *Examining Antitrust Policy Towards Horizontal Mergers*, 11 J.Fin.Econ. 225 (1983), and Eckbo, supra, test the hypothesis that acquisitions create market power by studying the returns to *competitors* of parties to horizontal acquisitions at the time of announcement of the acquisition and at the time the acquisition is challenged under the antitrust laws. Their hypothesis is that if market power is created by the acquisition, the result will be increased prices for the products sold by the combined firm and its competitors. Thus, the hypothesis predicts positive abnormal returns to the combining companies *and* to its competitors at the time of the acquisition, and, conversely, negative abnormal returns at the time the acquisition is challenged. Stillman finds positive abnormal returns for competitors associated with only one of the eleven acquisitions in his sample, a result inconsistent with the market power hypothesis. Eckbo's study of a much larger sample discloses positive abnormal returns for rivals of the combining companies on the announcement of the transaction, a result consistent with the market power hypothesis. He found, however, that competitors do not experience negative abnormal returns when the acquisition is challenged, a result inconsistent with the market power hypothesis and which leads Eckbo ultimately to reject it. Query, however, why the fact that competitors earn positive abnormal returns on the announcement date of the acquisition is not alone sufficient to lend support to the market power hypothesis regardless of what happens when the acquisition is challenged. The argument would be that if the gains to the parties to the acquisition resulted from anticipation of improved efficiency, then the acquisition would make their competitors worse off, and they should experience negative abnormal returns. How might an improvement in the combining companies' efficiency result in gains for their competitors? Eckbo argues that the method by which the combining companies achieve their efficiency gains is somehow disclosed to close competitors as a result of the transaction, who can then match their combining rivals' increased efficiency by adopting the same method. But why would this result in positive gains for these competitors on the announcement of the acquisition? If everyone can match the efficiency gains, then industry profits would increase only at the expense of other industries whose products exhibit some cross-elasticity of demand with those of the combining companies' industry. The market power hypothesis has not yet been vanquished.

CHAPTER TWELVE. TAX INCENTIVES FAVORING ACQUISITIONS

A common explanation for acquisitions is that the federal income tax system, both individual and corporate, creates incentives which favor them.[1] The idea is really that a particular form of synergy is possible: The acquisition results in a higher value than the sum of the pre-acquisition values of the constituent companies because one or another aspect of the tax system provides "better" treatment for acquisitions. Even at the outset, however, there is a need to state the argument with greater precision. The notion of an incentive implies that one activity is favored over another; the phrase "better tax treatment" states a conclusion derived from measuring the tax treatment of acquisitions against the tax treatment of something else. Both formulations assume a comparison between the tax treatment of two different activities and evaluation of the theory that tax considerations are a motivation for acquisitions requires as a first step an understanding of the activity with which acquisitions should be compared. Compared to what is the tax treatment of acquisitions more favorable?

That the tax system may create incentives or disincentives with respect to particular forms of business activity is hardly an unusual argument. Certain provisions of the Internal Revenue Code are really not "tax" provisions at all; rather they are explicitly intended to encourage or discourage particular types of activity. In this sense, provisions like the investment tax credit,[2] which provides for a direct reduction of taxes if certain types of capital assets are acquired, really operate as if they were a direct governmental expenditure, such as a subsidy, instead of a credit against taxes due.[3] Favorable tax treat-

---

[1] See, e.g., Federal Trade Commission, *Economic Report on Corporate Mergers* 142–58 (1969); Hellerstein, *Mergers, Taxes, and Realism*, 71 Harv.L.Rev. 254 (1957); Lintner, *Expectations, Mergers and Equilibrium in Purely Competitive Securities Markets*, 61 Am.Econ.Rev. 101, 107 (Papers & Proceedings, 1971); Bebchuck, *The Case for Facilitating Competing Tender Offers: A Reply and Extension*, 35 Stan.L.Rev. 23, 34 (1982); Weston & Chung, *Do Mergers Make Money? A Research Summary*, 18 Mergers & Acquisitions 40 (Fall, 1983); F.M. Scherer, Testimony before the Subcommittee on Telecommunications, Consumer Protection, and Finance, House Committee on Energy and Commerce 15 (March 12, 1984).

Congress has also evidenced this belief. It seems clearly the case that significant portions of the changes in the corporate income tax enacted by the Equity Tax and Fiscal Responsibility Act of 1982 (TEFRA) were motivated by the level of acquisition activity rather than concern over pure tax

policy. The original legislation that became part of TEFRA was introduced by Representative Stark as H.R. 6295, 97th Cong., 2d Sess. (1984), as the Corporate Takeover Tax Act of 1982. Professor Ginsburg describes the legislation as responding to the public impression "of a nation overwhelmed by a spreading rash of enormous corporate acquisitions motivated and financed in significant part by extraordinary tax avoidance." Ginsburg, *Taxing Corporate Acquisitions*, 38 Tax L.Rev. 171, 216 (1983).

[2] IRC §§ 38, 48.

[3] See, e.g., Surrey, *Tax Incentives as a Device for Implementing Government Policy: A Comparison with Direct Government Expenditures*, 83 Harv.L.Rev. 705 (1970); Surrey, *Federal Income Tax with Direct Governmental Assistance*, 84 Harv.L.Rev. 352 (1970); Bittker, *Accounting for Federal "Tax Subsidies" in the National Budget*, 22 Nat'l Tax J. 244 (1969).

ment for low-income housing [4] or rehabilitation of historic buildings [5] are other familiar examples. The argument that the tax system favors acquisitions, however, is more complicated. With respect to acquisitions, the point is not that the tax system favors a generic *type* of activity, like investment in capital assets, but that it favors a particular *means* of engaging in that activity. Thus, the argument that the tax system provides an incentive to acquisitions requires two steps. It is not enough to show that the tax system favors corporate growth; one must also demonstrate that it favors corporate growth by acquisition rather than by internal expansion.

Examining this argument requires some familiarity with the federal tax treatment of corporate acquisitions, a domain of enormous complexity. The following section provides a simple review of those aspects of the subject necessary for evaluation of the argument that the tax system favors acquisitions. This discussion must come, however, with the express disclaimer that the review is inadequate for any other purpose. Even the leading corporate tax treatise [6] provides no more than an overview of the area and a more detailed understanding requires recourse to the voluminous professional literature.

A. A Review of the Federal Income Tax Treatment of Corporate Acquisitions

Because our concern is with the incentives created by the federal income tax system with respect to a particular type of transaction, it is most helpful to structure our review around the principal tax concerns of the participants in the transaction: the acquiring company on the one hand, and the target shareholders on the other. From the perspective of the target shareholders, the principal concern is whether they will be required to recognize gain or loss when they exchange their shares in the target company for the consideration offered by the acquirer. From the perspective of the acquiring company, the principal concern is the extent to which the tax attributes of the target company will survive the transaction—most importantly, the tax basis to be used for depreciation of its assets, whether recapture of previous depreciation will be required, and the continued availability of the target's net operating loss. The outcomes with respect to these concerns depends, in the first instance, on the initial determination of whether the transaction satisfies one of the definitions of the term "reorganization" in Internal Revenue Code (hereinafter IRC) §368.

1. Reorganization Transactions

Implicit in the Internal Revenue Code provisions dealing with the consequences of the disposal of property is the concept that taxation is not appropriate until a gain or loss is "realized." The taxpayer must substantially alter the form in which wealth is held, for example by

---

[4] IRC § 167(k).

[5] IRC § 191. This section was repealed for taxable years ending after 1981 by P.L. 97–34, 95 Stat. 239.

[6] B. Bittker & J. Eustice, *Federal Income Taxation of Corporations and Shareholders* (4th ed. 1979).

selling stock for cash, before the tax system is triggered. A mere increase in the market value of the property held will not result in tax.[7] The problem of defining when realization has occurred, which can be difficult when only an individual is involved,[8] becomes quite complicated when the property held is corporate stock. What happens when the particular corporate entity in which the shareholder holds stock changes, but the assets of the business remain in corporate form and the shareholder continues to hold stock in the successor corporation? The concept of a tax-free reorganization contained in the Internal Revenue Code reflects the conclusion that, when specified conditions are met, changes in the identity or business of the corporation in which the shareholder holds stock will not be considered a realization, and recognition of gain or loss at either the corporate or shareholder level will be deferred until a later time.[9] Put in concrete terms, when the requirements of the Code are satisfied the corporation in which the shareholder holds stock may be acquired by another corporation, and a shareholder can receive consideration for his stock, without a tax becoming due at that time from anyone.

a. *Definitions*

IRC §368(1) defines the three basic types of acquisitive reorganizations. In general terms, an "A" reorganization (so termed because it is defined in §368(a)(1)(A)), is a statutory merger, a "B" reorganization is an exchange offer by which the acquiring company purchases sufficient stock of the target company from the target company's shareholders so that it owns at least 80% after the transaction, and a "C" reorganization is an asset acquisition by which the acquiring company purchases substantially all of the assets of the target company and thereafter the target company liquidates.[10] The concept underlying the definitions is that because all three represent functionally equivalent methods by

---

[7] See generally 2 B. Bittker, *Federal Taxation of Income, Estates and Gifts* ¶ 40.1 (1981).

[8] Id. at ¶ 40.2. For example, IRC § 1031 allows the non-recognition of gain or loss on the exchange of business or investment property for other property "of a like kind." While the section's application to a simple exchange of real estate is straightforward enough, it is clear that it also covers an exchange in which A exchanges property with B, even though B had purchased the property to be exchanged from C for cash in order to allow A the opportunity for non-recognition treatment. See, e.g., Biggs v. U.S. 69 T.C. 905 (1978).

[9] Regulation § 1.1002–1(c) states that "[t]he underlying assumption of the [non-recognition] provisions is that the new property is substantially a continuation of the old investment still unliquidated; and in the case of reorganizations, that the new enterprise, the new corporate structure, and the new property are substantially continuations of the old still unliquidated."

[10] Although the target company typically was liquidated, liquidation was not required until the Tax Reform Act of 1984 added §368(a)(2)(G) which requires that the target company in a "C" reorganization distribute the proceeds it receives in pursuance of the plan of reorganization.

The Code also allows, subject to greater or fewer restrictions, triangular and reverse triangular variations of the three standard reorganization formats in which the acquiring company makes use of a wholly owned subsidiary to affect the acquisition. See generally Ferguson & Ginsburg, *Triangular Reorganizations,* 28 Tax L.Rev. 159 (1973). The non-tax aspects of these forms of acquisition are considered in Chapter Thirteen infra; however, examination of the extreme complexity of their tax treatment is not necessary to evaluate the argument that the tax system provides a motivation for acquisitions.

452 MOTIVATIONS FOR ACQUISITIONS Pt. 2

which a corporate acquisition may be effected, all three should receive equivalent tax treatment. Even at the definitional level, however, this concept is imperfectly executed; the transactions are *not* defined in equivalent terms. Most importantly, the type of consideration that may be used in each of the three forms of the transaction are different. The definition of an "A" reorganization makes no reference to the type of consideration received by the target shareholders. Judicial gloss on the definition, by means of the "continuity of interest" doctrine, requires only that a substantial portion of the consideration be stock of the acquiring company.[11] And the Internal Revenue Service generally requires that stock constitute only 50 percent of the consideration in a merger before it will rule that the transaction will meet the "A" reorganization definition.[12] In contrast, the "B" reorganization definition limits much more severely the type of consideration that can be used in the transaction; *only* voting stock of the acquiring company can be given the target shareholders. The "C" reorganization fits somewhere between these extremes, allowing only voting stock as consideration but not treating the assumption of the target's liabilities by the acquiring company as consideration for this purpose. In an exception with mirage-like qualities, the "C" reorganization definition allows up to 20 percent non-stock consideration but includes the assumption of liabilities as non-stock consideration for purposes of determining the availability of the exception.[13]

Section 368, for all its detail, provides only definitions. While certain forms of transactions are described as "reorganizations," specification of the consequences of a transaction falling within that definition is left to other sections of the Code. Because our interest in the tax treatment of acquisitions is in the incentives created, it is most useful to consider the consequences of satisfying the reorganization definition in terms of their impact on the principal concerns of the parties to the transactions.

b. Treatment of Target Shareholders in a Reorganization

If target shareholders exchange their stock for stock of the acquiring company in a transaction which meets one of the definitions of a reorganization in §368(a)(1), the concept underlying the reorganization

[11] The continuity of interest doctrine, reflected in Reg. §1.368–1(b), is part of the effort to distinguish reorganizations, where there has been a change in form but not substance, from sales. The requirement that shareholders of the target company receive a significant portion of their consideration in the form of the stock of the acquiring company is intended to insure that they retain a continuing interest in the future of the combined corporation consistent with the concept that only the form, but not the substance, of their investment has changed.

[12] Rev.Proc. 77–37, § 3.02, 1977–2 C.B. 568. The courts have been more lenient than the Internal Revenue Service, having

approved transactions where as much as 62%, Nelson & Helvering, 296 U.S. 374 (1935), and 75%, Miller v. Commissioner, 84 F.2d 415 (6th Cir.1936), of the total consideration was cash.

[13] A "C" reorganization typically involves an assumption of the liabilities of the target company because the consideration for the transaction is voting stock and the target otherwise would have no means to discharge its obligations. Because liabilities assumed will typically represent in excess of 20% of the total consideration in the transaction, the exception offered in subsection C is of little practical significance.

provisions dictates that gain not be recognized because nothing has happened that changes the essential character of the shareholders' investment. This concept is made operative by §354 which provides (with qualifications) that gain or loss is not recognized when stock or securities of a party to a reorganization are exchanged solely for stock or securities in another corporation that is a party to the reorganization.[14] It is the fact that the exchange occurs without recognition of gain that accounts for the popular description of this form of transaction as "tax-free."

This description, however, is a misnomer in any other than transitory terms because the tax consequences of the exchange are merely deferred, not forgiven. Deferral is accomplished by §358 which provides that the stock or securities of the acquiring company received by a former target shareholder have a "carryover" basis, that is, the shareholder has the same basis in his or her new holdings as in the old. The carryover preserves the potential for gain or loss that was present in the holding of target stock or securities. If the market value of the acquiring company stock received exceeds the shareholders' basis in the target stock given up, the carryover basis retains this potential gain which then would be recognized upon the disposition of the acquiring company stock received. For example, suppose a target shareholder receives in a reorganization transaction $100 in value of acquiring company stock in exchange for target stock in which the shareholder has a $50 basis, and then sells the acquiring company's stock for $100 a week later. No gain or loss would be recognized on the original exchange pursuant to §354; however, the shareholder's basis in the acquiring company's stock would be $50, a carryover of the previous basis in the target company's stock, thereby preserving the potential for

---

[14] The use of the qualification "solely" in §354 serves a very different purpose than it does in the definitions in §368. In the latter it is jurisdictional in character, that is, if other than voting stock is used as consideration in a "B" or "C" transaction, it is not a reorganization. In §354 the term is used to deal with the situation where, in a transaction in which §368 does not limit the consideration to voting stock, the shareholder receives some cash or other nonqualifying consideration. There is no reason why gain should not be recognized as to this portion of the consideration. The "solely" qualification in §354 thus limits the nonrecognition rule so that recognition of gain occurs in this situation pursuant to the terms of §356.

A question remains, however, as to the character of the gain recognized on receipt of non-qualifying consideration in a qualifying transaction. For years after the Supreme Court's decision in Commissioner v. Bedford's Estate, 325 U.S. 283 (1945), the Internal Revenue Service took the position that any non-qualifying consideration received in a reorganization was automatical-

ly a dividend. This "automatic" dividend rule was ultimately rejected by the courts in favor of application of the dividend equivalency tests of §302(b). See, e.g., Wright v. U.S., 482 F.2d 600 (8th Cir.1973), and the Internal Revenue Service followed suit in Rev.Rul. 74–515, 1974–2 C.B. 118, and Rev.Rul. 74–516, 1974–2 C.B. 121. Controversy remains, however, concerning whether the test of dividend equivalency should be applied as if the non-qualifying consideration were received in a redemption occurring prior to the reorganization, which is the more restrictive position taken by the Internal Revenue Service, Rev. Rul. 75–83, 1975–1 C.B. 112, and the Fifth Circuit, Shimberg v. U.S., 577 F.2d 283 (5th Cir.1978), or as if the redemption took place after the reorganization, which is the position taken by the court in *Wright*. To understand the difference in result, apply both approaches to a reorganization in which a corporation wholly owned by a single shareholder is acquired in an "A" reorganization for consideration consisting of one-half stock in a widely held company and one-half cash.

gain that existed at the time of the exchange. When the sale of the acquiring company's stock occurs, the deferred gain is recognized.

From the perspective of the target shareholder, the tax deferral is desirable when the shareholder's basis in his or her target company stock is lower than the market value of the securities offered—i.e., when the shareholder would recognize a gain if the exchange were taxed—for two important reasons. The first is simply the time value of money. The effect of the deferral serves to reduce the real amount of tax paid. In the previous example, if the $50 tax were put off for two years, the present value of the tax, assuming a discount rate of 10 percent, is only $41.32.[15] The second advantage of the deferral caused by reorganization treatment is that it can reduce the cost of diversification. Recall the discussion of the closely held corporation in Chapter Nine C.1. Because of the absence of a public market for a closely held company's stock, diversification occurs at the company level. However, this results in an efficiency cost due to the resulting divergence from pure profit maximization as the only criterion for company investment decisions. An alternative to company level diversification would be to sell the company in exchange for the securities of a publicly traded company, thereby acquiring an investment for which there was an existing public market that allowed further diversification at the shareholder level. The desirability of this alternative, however, depends on the costs, tax and other, of accomplishing it. If it can be accomplished without tax cost, that is if the diversifying transaction is treated as a reorganization and tax is deferred, the result is more desirable than if the gain is immediately taxed and only the amount remaining after paying tax on the recognized gain is available for reinvestment.[16]

Where the target shareholder has a basis in his or her target stock higher than the value of the consideration offered by the acquiring corporation, the shareholder's incentives are reversed. Immediate recognition is most beneficial because the effect of reorganization treatment would be to defer receipt of the benefit—a tax loss that could be used to offset tax on other income. The present value of this benefit would be reduced by deferral in the same manner as deferral reduces the present value of the tax due in a transaction which results in a gain.

While it is important to understand that the preference of target shareholders for reorganization treatment will depend on whether or not the value of the offered consideration exceeds their basis in their target stock, it is also important to understand that the intensity of their preference is unlikely to be symmetrical. If target shareholders are better served by a reorganization, an individual shareholder cannot achieve deferral unless the overall acquisition transaction is structured

[15] If the shareholder dies before disposing of the stock in the acquiring company, the deferral becomes a forgiveness because § 1014 provides for a step-up in basis to market value at the time of death.

[16] The deferral also allows the shareholder to continue to earn a return on the amount that would have been paid as tax absent deferral, until the time of disposal of the acquiring company's stock results in recognition.

to meet the Code's requirements.[17] If, alternatively, target shareholders are better served by a nonreorganization transaction because the acquisition would result in a loss, this result can be achieved by each shareholder individually even if the overall transaction qualifies as a reorganization. A shareholder, in effect, can elect recognition simply by selling the securities of the acquiring company received in the transaction. Put differently, while the entire transaction must meet the reorganization requirements in order for any shareholder to defer gain, an individual shareholder can easily cause the results of his or her small part of the transaction to be recognized without regard to the preferences of other shareholders.[18]

From the target shareholders' perspective, the importance of whether the transaction qualifies as a reorganization also may be attenuated by the character of the target shareholders. The critical difference between reorganization and nonreorganization treatment is whether the target shareholder will have to treat the transaction as a recognition event, one that triggers tax consequences, for the shareholder. But if the shareholder is a pension fund or other non-taxable entity, the distinction in tax treatment is without a difference. This is a point of increasing importance as the percentage of the outstanding stock of publicly held companies owned by such entities increases.

c.   *Vehicles for Shareholder Choices*

The ability of target shareholders to individually select recognition treatment in a reorganization reduces the extent to which the tax treatment of the transaction has a bearing on the value of the transaction to shareholders. However, this is not the case where what the shareholder desires is non-recognition. This result requires the entire transaction to be treated as a reorganization, a determination made at an aggregate, rather than at an individual level.[19] But while simply structuring the transaction as a reorganization, leaving those shareholders who prefer recognition treatment (or cash) to so elect by individually disposing of the consideration they receive, should satisfy shareholder interest in flexibility, the acquiring company may have an independent interest in the manner in which the problem is resolved.

---

[17] One way in which deferral could be accomplished in what would otherwise be a nonreorganization transaction is to give the shareholder desiring deferral an installment note. See generally T. Ness & W. Indoe, *Tax Planning for Dispositions of Business Interests* ¶ 6.01[1][a] at 6–3 to 6–4 (1985). If the interest rate were set to yield, after tax, the after-tax rate of return on the acquiring company's stock, the result would be essentially the same as receiving stock in a reorganization transaction. The viability of this alternative will depend, at least in large part, on the risk associated with the acquiring company's stock and the cash flow consequences of the payout. The use of bonds or guaran-

tees securing the acquiring company's obligations under the installment note will not interfere with qualification under IRC § 453. Id. at ¶ 6.01[2][f]. Additionally, the installment sales alternative has significant transaction costs if used in a public acquisition.

[18] There are some transactions costs, such as brokerage fees, associated with electing recognition treatment in a reorganization transaction. Also, it should be apparent that the election is practically available only if there is a public market in the acquiring company securities received.

[19] Unless an installment sale is a feasible alternative.

Most importantly, the acquiring company may want to use cash as a significant portion of the consideration.

There are a variety of reasons why an acquiring company might prefer to use cash as consideration. Given the size of the premiums paid in recent acquisitions, use of cash may avoid the dilution in earnings per share that would result if stock were used. Suppose the acquiring company earned $3.00 per share in the year prior to the acquisition. Further suppose that acquisition of the target company, which has an identical number of shares outstanding, would add $3.00 per share to those earnings. If more than one share of the acquiring company's stock were issued for each share of the target company's stock, the net result of the acquisition would be to *reduce* the earnings per share of the acquiring company. In our example, if the premium necessary to acquire the target resulted in an exchange rate of two shares of the acquiring company for each target share, the post-acquisition earnings per share of the acquiring company would drop to $2.00 per share.[20] (Why should this phenomenon matter if markets were efficient? Is the concern really with earnings per share, an accounting phenomenon, or with whether the price paid by the acquiring company was too high?)

The acquiring company may also prefer to use cash to avoid regulatory delays. As will be considered in more detail in Chapter Sixteen, the applicable pattern of securities regulation differs in important ways, particularly with respect to the delay imposed, depending on whether stock or cash is used as consideration. If stock is used, its offer and sale must be registered under the Securities Act of 1933, a process that can entail substantial delay between the announcement that the acquirer intends to make the offer and the date the Securities and Exchange Commission declares the registration effective and the offer can proceed. During this delay a variety of events unfavorable to the acquiring company may occur, including defensive action by the target if the offer is unwelcome or, even if welcome, the appearance of a competitive bidder. The use of cash as consideration avoids this delay. Cash offers are governed by the Williams Act which, although also requiring substantial disclosure of information, does not impose an explicit delay before the offer can commence.[21]

Taking the needs of the target shareholders and those of the acquiring company together, there will then be situations where the goal is to devise an acquisition technique that: 1) allows shareholders the option of reorganization treatment; 2) allows the acquiring company the opportunity to use a substantial amount of cash as consideration; and 3) where speed is important, allows the acquiring company to

---

[20] The one-third drop in earnings per share results from the fact that earnings have only doubled while the number of outstanding shares has tripled.

[21] As will be discussed in Chapter Sixteen, a determined target company can use litigation under the Williams Act to cause substantial delay. A cash transaction may also reduce delay resulting from the Hart-Scott-Rodino Pre-Merger Notification Act under which the waiting period for cash offers can be shorter than for stock transactions. See Chapter Seventeen supra. Other motives for the use of cash as consideration are considered in 1 M. Lipton & E. Steinberger, *Takeovers and Freezeouts* § 1.84 (1978).

avoid the regulatory delays associated with the use of stock as consideration.

Where cash must be part of the consideration used but the transaction must still offer the opportunity for nonrecognition to the target shareholders who prefer that result, attention necessarily focuses on an "A" reorganization because the definitions of both "B" and "C" reorganizations limit the consideration that can be used solely to voting stock. The definition of an "A" reorganization, it will be recalled, makes no reference to the type of consideration used. Judicial gloss requires only that enough stock be used to satisfy the "continuity of interest" test, an amount which the Internal Revenue Service treats as 50 percent for purposes of issuing revenue rulings, and which the courts appear to treat as a significantly lower percentage.[22] The flexibility in type of consideration allowed in an "A" reorganization has given rise to an acquisition technique referred to as the *cash-option merger*. In this form of transaction the target is merged into the acquiring company [23] and the target shareholders are given the choice of receiving cash or stock in the acquiring company. To insure that a sufficient number of target shareholders choose stock to satisfy the continuity of interest doctrine, the terms of the merger typically limit the cash option to 45 to 49 percent of the target's stock with a provision for either proration or selection by lot if cash elections exceed the ceiling.[24]

Note, however, that the "one-step" cash election merger does not meet the acquiring company's need for speed; because the transaction still involves issuing the acquiring company's securities in addition to cash, registration under the Securities Act of 1933 would still be required before any part of the transaction could be completed. This problem of delay can be solved if the two aspects of the transaction—cash and stock—can be segregated. In the *two-step cash-option merger,* the first step is a cash tender offer for 45 to 49 percent of the target's stock which, because governed by the Williams Act rather than the Securities Act of 1933, can be made without the delay of registration. Once this has been accomplished, the ownership of a near majority of the target company's stock substantially reduces the threat of defensive tactics or competing bids, and the remaining shares can be acquired by a second step merger using stock as consideration.[25] For tax purposes, the two steps are treated as one under the familiar step transaction doctrine and "A" reorganization treatment is available.[26]

---

[22] See note 12 supra.

[23] The transaction can also be structured in triangular and reverse triangular variations.

[24] Note that if proration is used, there is a danger the cash portion of the consideration would be treated as a dividend under the Internal Revenue Service's interpretation of the application of the dividend equivalency rules of § 302(b) to reorganizations. See note 14 supra. Because corporate shareholders, as a result of the 85% dividend received deduction under § 243, pay only an effective tax rate of 6.9% on dividends but a much higher rate on capital gains, dividend treatment may be preferable for them.

[25] See generally Freund & Easton, *The Three-Piece Suitor: An Alternative Approach to Negotiated Corporate Acquisitions,* 34 Bus.Law 1680 (1979).

[26] King Enterprises, Inc. v. U.S., 189 Ct. Cl. 466, 418 F.2d 511 (1969); see generally Levin & Bowen, *Taxable and Tax-Free Two-Step Acquisitions and Minority Squeeze-Outs,* 33 Tax L.Rev. 425 (1978). Where the predominant form of consideration is to be cash, securing nonrecognition treatment for

d. Treatment of the Acquiring Company in a Reorganization

The concept underlying the reorganization provisions of the Internal Revenue Code—that only the form but not the substance of the shareholders' investment has changed—carries over to the treatment of the corporations which are parties to the reorganization. Just as the transaction is disregarded at the shareholder level through the nonrecognition principle, it is also disregarded at the corporate level. For our purposes two aspects of this corporate level nonrecognition are most important: (1) basis determination and (2) the survival of the tax attributes of the target company, particularly its net operating loss.

Basis Determination. In an "A" or "C" reorganization, the acquiring company succeeds directly to ownership of the target company's assets. The major question then focuses on the acquiring company's basis in these assets, both for depreciation purposes and for purposes of determining gain if any of the acquired assets are subsequently sold. Consistent with the notion that only a formal shift in ownership has occurred, §362(b) provides that the acquiring company retains the target company's basis in the assets acquired: a carryover basis. The tax incentives of the acquiring company then depend on whether the target's basis in its assets exceeds the consideration to be paid. If so, reorganization treatment is desirable so that the target's higher basis, and resulting higher depreciation, can be maintained. Alternatively, if the value of the consideration exceeds the target's basis, nonreorganization treatment, pursuant to which a cost basis would be assigned as with the purchase of any asset pursuant to §1012, would be preferable.

The analysis is somewhat different in a "B" reorganization, where the acquiring company has merely acquired the target company's stock, and title to the target's assets has not changed hands. In this situation the target retains its original basis in its assets unless a further step is taken: either the liquidation or merger of the target, now a controlled or wholly owned subsidiary, into the parent. If a liquidation follows as part of a pre-arranged plan, the step transaction doctrine is applied and the transaction is recharacterized as if the end result of both steps, the target's assets coming to rest inside the parent, had been accomplished in a single step. On that basis, the entire transaction is treated as a "C" reorganization.[27] Alternatively, if the mechanism by which the assets of the target acquired in a "B" reorganization become directly

the minority who will receive stock is more problematic. For a survey of a variety of approaches, including acquisitive incorporation transactions in which the target shareholders wishing non-recognition treatment initially exchange their stock in the target for shares in a newly formed subsidiary of the acquiring company which then becomes the acquisition vehicle, and a merger of the acquiror into the target followed by a redemption of the holdings of the target shareholders who prefer cash, see 1 M. Lipton & E. Steinberger, supra, at § 10.2.3.2; Milefsky, *The Hybrid Acquisition: A New*

Concept in Acquisition Planning, Mergers & Acquisitions, Fall 1980, at 23.

[27] See, e.g., Rev.Rul. 67–274, 1967–2 C.B. 141. Because the requirements of "B" and "C" reorganizations differ somewhat—for example, a "creeping B" reorganization, where the acquiring company has a previous position in the target's stock before making the acquisition, is acceptable while a "creeping C" reorganization is not—the shift in the rules against which the transaction will be tested as a result of the application of step transaction doctrine can serve to disqualify an otherwise qualifying

owned by the parent is a merger, under the step transaction doctrine both portions of the transaction are collapsed and treated as a single "A" reorganization.[28] In either event, the acquiring company takes a carryover basis.

Survival of Tax Attributes. Application of the Code's nonrecognition concept at the corporate level has implications for the manner in which the transaction should be treated that extend beyond determination of the acquiring company's basis in the target's assets. If the target company is to be regarded, in some metaphysical sense, as in substance continuing to exist within the formal bounds of the acquiring company, what happens to the other tax attributes of the target company? Do they disappear, as merely part of the formal structure of the target company that has been shed, like the shell of a hermit crab in pursuit of larger quarters; or do they become part of the target company's genetic heritage which follow its substance to the acquiring company?

The subject of the survival of the target company's tax attributes is the province of IRC §381. Twenty-three tax attributes of the target company—ranging from its historical earnings and profits, tax accounting methods, and investment tax credits to, most importantly, its net operating losses—are specified to carry over to the acquiring company, in each case subject to quite extensive statutory and regulatory detail.

The types of transactions which are governed by the survival rules of §381 are described in §381(b). The tax attributes of the target company carry over in "A" and "C" reorganizations as both transactions result in the acquiring company holding the assets of the target company directly. These tax attributes also carry over following the liquidation of a controlled subsidiary under §332 provided that the basis of the liquidated company in its assets also carries over to the surviving parent. Most commonly, the latter situation describes the second step typically taken at some point after a "B" reorganization (tender offer), when the liquidation serves to freeze out the remaining minority.[29] Of course, when a "B" reorganization is not followed by a second step freezeout, it remains as an existing entity and the problem of "survival" of tax attributes does not arise except with respect to the filing of consolidated returns [30] and the use of its net operating loss, to which we now turn.

Of principal relevance to our concern with motivations for acquisitions is the treatment of the target company's net operating loss carryover. One can easily imagine circumstances where a company has a net operating loss that, because it is too large to dissipate during

transaction. See B. Bittker & J. Eustice, supra at 14–148 to 14–152; Levin & Bowen, supra at 439–41.

[28] King Enterprises, supra; Levin & Bowen, supra at 444–46.

[29] Where the second step liquidation was anticipated, the entire transaction would be treated as a single step "C" reorganization. See text at note 27, supra.

[30] IRC § 1501 allows an affiliated group of corporations, affiliation being defined, in essence, as 80% common ownership, to file a single return that treats the group as a single taxable entity. The rules governing both eligibility to file a consolidated return and the method of computing consolidated taxable income are extraordinarily complex and tax even the clarifying power of Professor Bittker. See B. Bittker & J. Eustice, supra at Ch. 15.

the carry forward period, or because there is uncertainty concerning whether the company will ever return to profitability, or merely because the number of years necessary to use the carry forward inevitably reduces its value, would be of greater value to another company. If that loss can be transferred, it becomes an asset, and if, as has been the case over the greatest period of time, the asset can be transferred only by selling the entire company,[31] a potentially substantial motivation for acquisitions is provided. The following excerpt from the General Explanation of the Tax Reform Act of 1976, prepared by the Staff of the Joint Committee on Taxation, describes the terms on which net operating loss carryovers can be transferred by acquisition, both under pre-1976 law and as a result of the substantial changes effected by the Tax Reform Act of 1976. Both regimes remain of critical importance because the changes enacted in 1976 have yet to become effective, Congress having extended the effective date of these changes each time it approached.

STAFF OF THE JOINT COMMITTEE ON TAXATION

94th Cong., 2d Sess., General Explanation of the Tax Reform Act of 1976 at
190–204 (1976), 1976–3 Cum.Bull. (vol. 2) 202–216.

Special Limitations on Net Operating Loss Carryovers (Sec. 806(e) of the Act and Sec. 382 and 383 of the Code)

Prior Law

Prior law * (sec. 382(a)) provided that where new owners buy 50 percent or more of the stock of a loss corporation during a 2-year

---

[31] Operating losses also can be transferred if the deductions that will create the losses can be transferred. Leveraged leasing techniques have for some time allowed the transfer of depreciation deductions and investment tax credits by companies which needed the buildings or equipment but not the deductions or credits associated with their purchase and ownership. The availability of this technique, however, was limited prior to 1981 because the transfer of tax benefits required sufficient transfer of attributes of actual ownership of the physical assets so that the transaction involved not only tax, but investment risks as well. In the Economic Recovery Tax Act of 1981, Congress enacted safe harbor leasing provisions that effectively allowed the structuring of a sale and leaseback transaction that had no substance other than to effectively transfer the depreciation deductions and investment tax credits associated with the equipment under "lease"; no transfer of non-tax attributes of ownership was necessary. Thus, the lease amounted to a simple sale of tax benefits not usable by one company to another company that could use them. At least prospectively, such transactions would substantially reduce the problem of the sale of loss carryovers

through acquisitions because the ability to sell depreciation deductions would go a long way toward eliminating any future tax losses. The 1981 safe harbor lease provisions are explained and evaluated, and references to the professional literature provided, in Warren & Auerbach, *Transferability of Tax Incentives and the Fiction of Safe Harbor Leasing*, 95 Harv.L. Rev. 1752 (1982). The expansion of transferability of losses through safe harbor leasing proved of short duration, however. In the Tax Equity and Fiscal Responsibility Act of 1982, Congress repealed the safe harbor provisions after December 31, 1983, and reduced the benefits from safe harbor leasing until then. For leases entered into after 1983, the requirement that some nontax attributes of ownership also be transferred was reimposed. See, e.g., Warren & Auerbach, *Tax Policy and Equipment Leasing after TEFRA*, 96 Harv.L.Rev. 1579 (1983).

* The "prior law" referred to will remain current law until such time as Congress allows the amendments to §382 contained in the Tax Reform Act of 1976 to take effect. [Ed.]

period, its loss carryovers from prior years were allowed in full if the company continued to conduct its prior trade or business or substantially the same kind of business. It could add or begin a new business, however, and apply loss carryovers incurred by the former owners against profits from the new business (unless tax avoidance was the principal purpose for the acquisition). If the same business was not continued, however, loss carryovers were completely lost. In the case of a tax-free reorganization, loss carryovers were allowed on a declining scale (sec. 382(b)). If the former owners of the loss company received 20 percent or more of the fair market value of the stock of the acquiring company, the loss carryovers were allowed in full. For each percentage point less than 20 which the former owners received, the loss carryover was reduced by 5 percentage points. It was immaterial whether the business of the loss company was continued after the reorganization (sec. 382(b)).

The former "purchase" rule of section 382(a) applied where one or more of the 10 largest shareholders increased their stock ownership, within a 2-year period, by 50 percentage points or more in a transaction in which the purchasers took a cost basis in their stock (except where the stock was acquired from "related" persons within the constructive ownership relationships described in section 318 of the Code.) The constructive ownership rules of section 318 applied, with some modifications, in determining the ownership of stock for purposes of section 382(a).

*   *   *

Section 382(a) also became operative if a person's stock ownership increased by at least 50 percentage points by reason of a decrease in total outstanding stock, such as occurs in a redemption of stock owned by other shareholders (except redemptions under sec. 303 to pay death taxes).

Section 383 incorporates by reference the same limitations as are contained in section 382 for carryovers of investment credits, work incentive program credits, foreign tax credits, and capital losses.

The tax law also contains a general provision which authorizes the Treasury to disallow a net operating loss carryover where any persons acquire stock control of a corporation for the principal purpose of evading or avoiding Federal income tax by obtaining a benefit which such persons would not otherwise have obtained (sec. 269(a)(1)). A similar rule also applies to tax free acquisitions of one corporation's assets by an unrelated corporation where the acquiring company takes a carryover basis in such assets (sec. 269(a)(2)). For purposes of these rules, control means ownership of at least 50 percent of the total combined voting power of voting stock or at least 50 percent of the total value of all classes of stock.

Reasons for change

In general, the limitations contained in sections 382, 383, and 269 recognize that any rules which permit an operating loss (or other tax deductions or credits) to continue despite a substantial change in shareholders can be manipulated for tax avoidance purposes. For example, a free traffic in loss carryovers could result in large windfalls for buyers of stock or assets who could take advantage of the weak bargaining position of the existing owners of a loss business and acquire large carryovers for substantially less than their tax value.* Such buyers are effectively buying a tax shelter for their expected future profits, whereas if the same persons had used their capital to start a new business on their own, no such loss offsets would be available.

On the other hand, a going business may lose money for a variety of reasons, such as bad economic conditions, competition, location, or poor business judgments by its owners. In many cases the loss can be fairly well traced to an inability or unwillingness by the existing owners to see, or to make, needed changes. In situations such as these, the owners often seek out additional co-owners to help turn the business around with fresh ideas or better management.

In several ways the former loss limitations did not deal adequately with the genuine concerns which taxpayers and the Government have in both kinds of situations described above. Generally, old section 382(a) covered stock acquisitions and section 382(b) covered asset acquisitions. These rules were not coordinated, however. They also failed to cover some transactions where "trafficking" in loss carryovers could still occur, and there were several loopholes. For example, where enough stock of a loss corporation was purchased for cash, carryovers were lost if the corporation did not continue to carry on the same kind of business it had conducted previously. However, losses could still be carried over after a tax-free reorganization whether or not the same trade or business was continued. Conversely, after a purchase of stock, losses could be carried over in full if the former business was continued even though a new profitable business could be added to absorb the existing loss carryovers; but after a reorganization, the loss carryover could be reduced even if the old business were continued.

The former purchase rules required no continuity of interest by the former owners of a loss company, since a 100 percent change in stock ownership could preserve all the carryovers if at least the same kind of business was continued. By contrast, the reorganization rules required at least 20 percent continuity by former owners if carryovers were to survive in full. Where the purchase limitations applied, the loss carryovers were completely disallowed. Where the reorganization rules applied, loss carryovers were merely reduced in proportion to the change in stock ownership.

The rule that a loss company must continue the same business when new owners buy control of its stock presented special problems. Many critics of this test argued that it is uneconomic to compel new owners of a failing business to continue to operate that business if a new activity can be found in which to make profits. Besides running counter to normal business practice, this test was also difficult to apply in specific cases, i.e., it was difficult for taxpayers and for the courts to

---

* What does this example assume about
the level of competition in the market for
loss carryovers? [Ed.]

determine at what point a change in merchandise, location or size of the business, or a change in the use of its assets, should be treated as a change in the business. The tax law has also generally permitted the continuing owners of a loss business to abandon that business entirely but still apply loss carryovers from the discontinued activity against profits from a new business.

The reorganization limitations did not apply to a "B"-type reorganization (stock for stock). This meant that a profitable company could acquire the stock of a loss company in exchange for the profit company's stock, liquidate the loss company after a reasonable interval (or transfer profitable assets into the loss company), and use its loss carryovers without limit against the future income from profitable operations. Where a profitable company used a controlled subsidiary to acquire the assets of a loss company for stock in the profitable company, the reorganization rules could also be effectively avoided because the 20 percent continuity of interest rule for the loss company's shareholders was not applied by reference to the percentage interest which these shareholders received in the profitable company (sec. 382(b) (6)).

*   *   *

Explanation of provisions

The Act amends sections 382 and 383 to provide more nearly parallel rules for acquisitions of stock and tax-free reorganizations involving a loss company; to eliminate the test of business continuity and base the rules solely on changes in stock ownership; and to increase the amount and kind of continuity of ownership required under these rules.

The increased ownership standard applies to the continuing interest in the loss company held by its former owners where its stock is acquired by new owners or where the loss company is the acquiring company in a reorganization. And, as under prior law, where the loss company is acquired in a reorganization, the new standard applies to the interest received by the former loss company owners in the company which acquires the loss company. The Act also increases the types of reorganizations specifically covered by sec. 382; it covers in detail reorganizations in which stock is transferred for stock ("B" reorganizations) and triangular reorganizations.

For purposes of new section 382, the continuity required of the former shareholders of a loss company is now 40 percent. For each percentage point (or fraction thereof) less than 40 but not less than 20 which the loss shareholders retain (or receive), the allowable loss carryover is reduced by 3½ percentage points. For each percentage point (or fraction thereof) less than 20, the loss carryovers are reduced by 1½ percentage points.[1]

*   *   *

[1] This weighted scale reflects the fact that for many tax purposes, such as tax-free liquidations under sec. 332 and the filing of consolidated returns, an acquisition of 80 percent ownership is virtually equivalent to total ownership, so that increases in ownership up to 80 percent are usually more significant than any particular ownership level above 80 percent. [Footnotes renumbered. Ed.]

These tests mean, in effect, that carryovers can survive in full under the new rules only if a loss company's shareholders retain an interest in at least 40 percent of the continuing company's total current value *and* at least 40 percent of its future growth. This continuing interest must be retained directly in the loss company or retained indirectly through stock received in a company which acquires the loss company.

*   *   *

Purchases, etc. of stock. The Act changes section 382(a) to focus on changes in stock ownership alone. The continuation of business rule is eliminated along with the former all-or-nothing effect of section 382(a). It will no longer be necessary to make detailed factual inquiries into the different degrees or ways that an existing business may have been changed. As a result, when a sufficient increase in stock ownership by new owners occurs, net operating loss carryovers will be limited even if the new owners continue the same trade or business. On the other hand, where carryovers are allowable under the new rules, the company may change, contract or abandon an existing business without affecting its loss carryovers.

Section 382(a) continues to measure continuity by former owners indirectly by looking to the increase in new owners' percentage ownership of a loss company's stock. However, the Act raises the point at which a specified acquisition brings the limitations into play from 50 to more than 60 percentage points. If the increase in a buyer's stock ownership is greater than 60 percentage points, the company's net operating loss carryovers are reduced by a percentage of the carryovers equal to 3½ percentage points for each percentage point increase by the buyer above 60 and up to 80 points. If the buyer's increase is more than 80 percentage points, loss carryovers are also reduced by 1½ percentage points for each 1 percentage point increase over 80 and up to 100.

The shareholders taken into account under the new section 382(a) test to determine the increases in interest are those who hold the 15 largest percentages of the total fair market value of all the stock of the company on the last day of its taxable year. *   *   *

The new rules expand the list of transactions governed by section 382(a). In all cases, the increase in percentage points must be attributable to one or more of the following types of transactions:

1. A purchase of stock of a loss company from an existing shareholder or from the company itself. The term "purchase" is defined as a cost-basis acquisition.

2. A purchase of stock of a corporation which owns stock in a loss company; or a purchase of an interest in a partnership or trust which owns such stock.

3. An acquisition by contribution, merger or consolidation of an interest in a partnership which owns loss company stock, or an acquisition of such stock by a partnership by means of a contribution, merger or consolidation.

4.   An exchange to which section 351 applies, i.e., a transfer of property to a loss company after which the transferors own 80 percent or more of the company, or an acquisition by a corporation of loss company stock in an exchange in which section 351 applies to the transferor.

5.   A contribution to the capital of a loss company.

6.   A decrease in the total outstanding stock of a loss company (or in the stock of a corporation which owns such stock). This category thus includes, but is not limited to, a redemption from other shareholders (except a section 303 redemption). * * *

7.   Any combination of these transactions.

* * *

Exceptions are made for the following acquisitions:

1.   Stock acquired from a person if the stock is already attributed to the acquirer because of section 318's constructive ownership rules.

2.   Stock acquired by inheritance or by a decedent's estate from the decedent * * *; by gift; or by a trust from a grantor.

3.   Stock acquired by a creditor or security holder in exchange for relinquishing or extinguishing a claim against the loss company, unless the claim was acquired for the purpose of obtaining such stock.

4.   Stock acquired by persons who were full-time employees of the loss company at all times during the 36-month period ending on the last day of the company's taxable year (or at all times during its existence, if that period is shorter). This exception is not to apply, however, to an increase in the stock ownership of a person who is both an employee and has been a substantial shareholder of a loss company.

5.   Employer stock acquired by a qualified pension or profit-sharing trust or by an employee stock ownership plan * * *.

6.   Stock acquired in a tax-free recapitalization described in section 368(a)(1)(E).[2]

The Act brings under section 382(a) carryovers of operating losses from earlier taxable years to the taxable year at the end of which an over-60 percentage point increase in stock ownership has occurred, and also carryovers of an operating loss incurred in the latter year itself. However, the Act also adopts a "minimum ownership" rule (sec. 382(a) (3)), under which an operating loss incurred in the latter acquisition year can be carried over in full to later years if the persons who increased their ownership by over 60 percentage points owned at least 40 percent of the fair market value of the participating stock, and of all the stock, of the loss company during the entire last half of the acquisition year.

---

[2] This exception may not apply to a recapitalization and acquisition which together result in increased ownership by outside investors. The Service may examine such a recapitalization and, if appropriate in the situation, treat it as part of a step transaction which is subject to the rules of section 382 without regard to this exception. * * *

* * *

The Act contains a successive application rule (sec. 382(a)(6)), providing that if a loss carryover has been once reduced under section 382(a), and if the new owners do not increase their interest further during the following two years, the same carryover will not be reduced again under section 382(a) at the end of either later year. On the other hand, if the persons whose increase in ownership caused a reduction in carryovers (or other persons collaborating with them under a concerted plan) buy additional stock during the first or second succeeding years, a further reduction in the unused carryovers should be made, based on the total increase in ownership by the new owners during the three-year period. In order to deal with this situation, the Service is authorized to provide regulations dealing with the computation of the further reduction in carryovers.

Mergers and other tax-free reorganizations. Where a profit company acquires the stock or assets of a loss company (or vice versa) in a tax-free reorganization, section 382(b) measures continuity by the loss shareholders' collective percentage ownership of stock of the acquiring company as the result of the reorganization. As already indicated, the new continuity test for full survival of loss carryovers is 40 percent, with a reduction of 3½ percentage points in the allowable carryover for each percentage point of continuing stock ownership less than 40 and down to 20, plus a reduction of 1½ percentage points for each percentage point of continuing stock ownership less than 20.

As under prior law, section 382(b) continues to apply to statutory mergers or consolidations and to C, D and F reorganizations (sec. 368(a)(1)(C), (D), (F)), except spinoffs under section 355.[3] The Act also brings under these rules stock acquisitions solely for voting stock, as described in section 368(a)(1)(B). The rules of section 382(b) test the above reorganizations both where a loss company is the acquired or the acquiring (or surviving) company.

* * *

If a loss company acquires the stock of a profit company in a "B" reorganization, the general rules of section 382(b) will apply to produce the proper results (that is, continuity of ownership will be determined by reference to the stock owned by the loss company's shareholders in their own company after the exchange). However, if a profit company acquires the stock of a loss company, the Act contains special provisions requiring the continuity rules of section 382(b) to be applied by direct reference to the stock ownership of the loss company after the exchange. Exchanging shareholders will be treated as owning a percent-

---

[3] * * * As under prior law, a purchase of stock followed by a liquidation under conditions which give the buyer an asset basis determined under section 334(b)(2) does not allow carryovers to the buyer (sec. 381(a)(1)). A liquidation of a less than wholly-owned loss subsidiary by a controlling parent corporation, in the form of an "upstream" statutory merger, must also be tested under section 382(b). Even though the parent's tax treatment will ordinarily be governed by section 332, the transaction will ordinarily be tested (as under prior law) as a reorganization as to the subsidiary's minority shareholders. The availability of the loss carryovers to the parent will then depend on the tests of section 382(b). These tests will come into play because, for purposes of section 382(b)(1), the transaction in this example will be a reorganization "described in" section 368(a)(1)(A).

age of the loss company's stock acquired by the acquiring company equal to the percentage of the latter's stock which such shareholders received in the exchange. This percentage will then be combined with the percentage (if any) of the loss company's stock which its shareholders did not exchange. * * *

Under a special rule in prior law (former sec. 382(b)(6)), a profit company could arrange for a controlled subsidiary to acquire the assets of a loss company for stock of the parent company and a full carryover could be obtained if the fair market value of the loss company shareholders' stock in the parent equalled at least 20 percent of the fair market value of all the stock of the acquiring subsidiary. If the acquiring company were a newly created shell, this rule would almost always be satisfied, even though the loss company shareholders' stock in the parent may have been less than a 20-percent interest in the parent (and thus less than a 20-percent indirect interest in their former company).

The Act now requires that in this type of "triangular" reorganization, the continuity rules are to be applied by reference to the loss company shareholders' actual percentage ownership of participating stock and of all stock, respectively, of the parent company (sec. 382(b)(3) (B)).[4] In the case of a triangular B reorganization, where a subsidiary of a profit company acquires the stock of a loss company in exchange for stock of the profit company, a special rule requires, in effect, a two-step calculation converting the loss shareholders' percentage ownership in the parent of the acquiring company into an equivalent percentage ownership of the acquiring subsidiary and then, in turn, into an indirect percentage ownership of the loss company (sec. 382(b)(5)(C)).

* * *

The Libson Shops doctrine. In Libson Shops, Inc. v. Koehler, 353 U.S. 382, 77 S.Ct. 990, 1 L.Ed.2d 924, reh. denied 354 U.S. 943, 77 S.Ct. 1390, 1 L.Ed.2d 1542 (1957), the Supreme Court, in a case decided under the 1939 Code, adopted an approach to the loss carryover area under which loss carryovers would basically follow the specific business activities which gave rise to the losses. Some uncertainty existed after this decision as to whether the business continuity approach represents a separate, nonstatutory test for determining carryovers of net operating losses. As a result of the changes made by the Act, Congress intends that the so-called *Libson Shops* test should have no application to determining net operating loss carryovers after stock purchases or reorganizations to tax years governed by the new rules. However, Congress intends that no inference should be drawn concerning the applicability or nonapplicability of the *Libson Shops* case in determining net operating loss carryovers to tax years governed by prior law.[5]

---

[4] This new rule also applies to "forward" and "reverse" triangular reorganizations pursuant to section 368(a)(2)(D) and (E) of the Code. It applies to the situation existing immediately after the exchange and, at that point, the loss company's shareholders will own stock in a corporation which controls the loss company.

[5] Congress does not intend the changes in section 382 to affect the "continuity of business enterprise" requirement which the courts and the Service have long established as a condition for basic nonrecognition treatment of a corporate reorganization (see sec. 1.368–1(b) of the regulations).

The general tax avoidance test. Congress did not change the basic provisions of section 269 of the Code. Congress believes, however, that section 269 should not be applied to disallow net operating loss carryovers in situations where part or all of a loss carryover is permitted under the specific rules of section 382, unless a device or scheme to circumvent the purpose of the carryover restrictions appears to be present. Congress also concluded that this general disallowance provision should be retained for transactions not expressly within the fixed rules of section 382. Section 269 is retained, for example, to deal with "built-in-loss" transactions, other post-acquisition losses, acquisitions expressly excepted from section 382, and other exchanges or transfers which are apparent devices to exploit continuing gaps in the technical rules for tax avoidance purposes.

*   *   *

The statements above concerning the relationship between the new section 382 rules and section 269 of present law and the *Libson Shops* case are intended to operate initially with respect to the first taxable year to which carryovers are governed by the new rules of section 382.

◆

2. Nonreorganization Transactions

In some circumstances, the deferral associated with the treatment of an acquisition as a reorganization may be undesirable to the shareholders of the target because the transaction would otherwise result in a loss that they would prefer to recognize immediately. In other circumstances, reorganization treatment may be undesirable to the acquiring company because the consideration to be paid exceeds the target company's basis in its assets and the acquiring company prefers that the higher purchase price be reflected in a higher basis for the target company's depreciable assets. Given the structure of the Code, a preference for nonreorganization treatment is easily implemented; all that is required is to purchase the target company's stock or assets using even a small percentage of cash, thereby violating the solely for voting stock requirement of both the "B" and "C" reorganization definitions.[32]

Congress also does not intend to deprive the Service of other weapons to attack transactions in which the benefits of loss carryovers are improperly transferred in ways other than by transfers of stock, or transactions where section 382 is otherwise satisfied (in whole or part). For example, the new rules do not affect the principles of substance over form, step transaction, corporate entity, assignment of income, or the rules of Code sections 482 or 704(b) (relating to allocations). Nor do the new rules prevent the Service, in appropriate cases, from challenging situations where a loss company pays more than fair market value for stock or assets of another company.

[32] This is an example of a peculiar characteristic of Subchapter C of the IRC. The application of many of its provisions is, in fact, elective, but only transactionally, rather than formally. That is to say, the election is made by selecting the appropriate formal structure for the transaction from among substantive equivalents, rather than by checking a box on a tax return. It is such transactional elections that create tax "traps for the unwary." See Ginsburg, *Taxing Corporate Acquisitions*, 38 Tax L.Rev. 171, 196 (1983).

Once nonreorganization treatment is selected, the parties' major concerns, at least in a setting where the transaction will result in gain to the target shareholders, are clear. The target shareholders want to insure that they pay only a capital gain tax and that a corporate level tax is not imposed; from the acquiring company's perspective, the emphasis is on securing a step up in basis in the target's assets to reflect its presumably higher purchase price.

Prior to the revisions of subchapter C of the Code by the Tax Equity and Fiscal Responsibility Act of 1981 (TEFRA),[33] how these concerns were treated for tax purposes depended on whether the transaction was structured as a purchase by the acquiring company of the stock of the target company's shareholders or as a purchase of the target company's assets. In the former case, the acquiring company succeeded to the target company's assets by liquidating its newly acquired subsidiary, and in the latter case a liquidation of the target company was initiated by its shareholders in which the shareholders exchanged their target shares for the proceeds of the asset sale. It should be readily apparent that, when the dust settled, the substantive result was the same in either case. That is, the acquiring company owned the target company's assets, the target company's shareholders received the consideration paid for the assets, and the target company went out of existence. But while the pre-TEFRA structure of the Code was designed to cause the two forms of transaction, identical in substance, to be treated identically for tax purposes, it did not always work out quite that way, particularly with respect to the initial incidence of some of the tax burdens of the transaction. Because an understanding of the pre-TEFRA treatment of these transactions is critical to understanding both the changes made by TEFRA, and the argument that the federal income tax system favors acquisitions, an historical account of this era is a necessary first step. For ease of exposition, description of the tax treatment of these alternative transactional forms is best structured around the choice between a stock and an asset acquisition.[34]

a. Stock Acquisitions in the Pre-TEFRA Era

Given the tax concerns of the shareholders of the target company, a stock acquisition—a sale of each shareholder's stock directly to the acquiring company—was the most simple and desirable structure for the transaction. Provided only that the target stock was a capital asset in the hands of the shareholder and that the requisite holding period was met, the sale was taxed as a capital gain to the shareholders and, at least as a result of the initial transaction, no taxable event occurred at the corporate level.

The simplicity of the stock transaction from the perspective of the selling shareholders was offset by the complexity of the transaction from the perspective of the acquiring company. After the initial stock

---

[33] Pub.L. No. 97–248, 96 Stat. 324 (codified in various sections of 26 U.S.C.).

[34] For a more detailed treatment of these issues, see Frei, *Tax Problems in Corporate Acquisitions Other than Reorganization—* *From the Seller's Point of View,* 1974 Taxes 821; Morrison, *Tax Problems in Corporate Acquisitions—From the Buyer's Point of View,* 1974 Taxes 843.

sale the acquiring company had control of the target but, thus far, had not satisfied its principal tax concern in the transaction: a step up in the basis of the target company's assets to reflect the higher purchase price. So long as the target company remained a separate entity, there was no occasion to alter its basis in its assets. In order to secure the desired basis alteration, it was necessary to liquidate the target pursuant to Sections 332 and 334.

Section 332, which was unaffected by TEFRA, provides, in essence, that no gain or loss is recognized when an 80 percent or more owned subsidiary is liquidated into its parent in complete cancellation of the subsidiary's stock.[35] Thus, from the perspective of gain recognition, a purchase of stock followed by liquidation did not result in the imposition of a second tax at the stage at which the assets finally reached the acquiring company.

When the desired step-up in basis is considered, the result was somewhat more complicated. Under the general rule of §334(b)(1), also unaffected by TEFRA, the liquidation of a subsidiary under §332 results in a carryover of basis in the assets received in the liquidation. The application of this rule in the acquisition context, however, would have the unfortunate consequence of causing the acquiring company to take a different basis in the assets ultimately received depending on whether the transaction was structured as a purchase of assets, or as a purchase of stock followed by a liquidation. From the perspective of a planner, the result would be a costless basis election. If the purchase price were lower than the target company's basis in its assets, the transaction would be structured as a stock purchase followed by a liquidation in order to retain the target's higher basis. Alternatively, if the purchase price were higher than the target's basis, the transaction would be structured as an asset purchase in order to secure the higher cost basis. The courts responded to this problem by the creation of the *Kimball-Diamond* doctrine, an application of step transaction analysis to collapse a taxable stock purchase followed by a liquidation into an asset acquisition.[36]

The uncertainty of the application of the judicial doctrine resulted in the adoption by Congress in 1954 of §334(b)(2) in order to codify the principles emanating from *Kimball-Diamond*. Under its terms the parent in a subsidiary liquidation took a basis in the assets received equal to the amount it initially paid for the stock of the liquidated

---

[35] Technically, § 332 provides only that the parent does not recognize gain. Section 336 extends non-recognition to the subsidiary.

[36] Kimball-Diamond Milling Co. v. CIR, 14 T.C. 74, affirmed per curiam 187 F.2d 718 (5th Cir.1951), cert. denied 342 U.S. 827 (1951). In *Kimball-Diamond*, the taxpayer company's milling plant was destroyed, and the insurance proceeds used to purchase for $110,000 all of the outstanding stock of another corporation whose principal asset was a milling plant. The acquired company's basis in the plant was $134,000. Following the stock purchase the acquired company was liquidated and the acquiring company claimed a carryover basis. The Internal Revenue Service successfully argued that the acquiring company always intended to acquire the target company's assets rather than its stock. The step transaction doctrine was then applied to cause the entire transaction to be treated as a purchase of assets which resulted in a cost, rather than a carryover basis.

subsidiary [37]—in effect, a step up in basis when the purchase price in the acquisition exceeded the target company's basis in its assets—provided that specified requirements were met. Eighty percent of the subsidiary's stock must have been acquired in one or more purchases, defined in §334(b)(3) to exclude acquisitions of stock in which the acquirer took a carry over basis,[38] within a 12 month period. Additionally, the distribution of assets must have occurred pursuant to a plan of liquidation adopted within two years after the purchase.[39]

While the effect of §334(b)(2) was to eliminate the potential for different basis determinations for the acquiring company depending on whether the transaction was structured as a stock or asset acquisition, the resulting equivalence in transactional form was not complete. The problem was that the nonrecognition provisions of §332 did not block the application of the depreciation recapture rules of §§1245 and 1250, or the investment tax credit recapture provisions of §47.[40] When the basis allocated to assets subject to recapture exceeds the basis of the target company in them, tax at ordinary income tax rates is imposed, with the legal burden falling on the acquiring company.

b. Asset Acquisitions in the Pre-TEFRA Era

When the nonreorganization took the form of a purchase by the acquiring company of the assets of the target company, followed by a liquidation of the target company in which the target shareholders

[37] The determination of how the higher basis is allocated among the assets acquired can be quite complicated. See B. Bittker & J. Eustice, supra at 11–46 to 11–54.

[38] This requirement serves to exclude stock acquired in a "B" reorganization in order to preserve the Code's conceptual correspondence between basis adjustment and gain recognition: A step-up in basis should not be attainable if the stock was acquired in a transaction in which the sellers did not recognize gain.

[39] Following the enactment of §334(b)(2), there developed what amounted to a tax lawyer's theological question: Was Kimball-Diamond dead? Put more directly, was either the taxpayer or the Internal Revenue Service still free to argue that the subjective intent of the parties to the transaction demonstrated that it was the assets, rather than the stock of the target, that were "really" acquired and, thus, a cost rather than a carryover basis appropriate even though the transaction did not meet the specific terms of §334(b)(2)? The issue was critical from a planning perspective because the brightline rules of §334(b) (2) could be easily avoided. For example, if the purchase price of the target company's stock was to be less than its basis in its assets, could the transaction be structured so that the stock was acquired over one day more than twelve months in order to avoid

the application of §334(b)(2)? Although the Internal Revenue Service seemed to concede that the Kimball-Diamond doctrine survived the enactment of §334(b)(2), Rev.Rul. 74–35, 1974–1 C.B. 85, the courts generally held that the statute had occupied the field. Compare American Potash & Chem. Corp. v. U.S., 185 Ct.Cl. 161, 399 F.2d 194 (1968) with, e.g., Broadview Lumber Co. v. U.S., 561 F.2d 698 (7th Cir.1977) and International State Bank, 70 T.C. 183 (1978). The issue was finally resolved by Congress through its TEFRA amendments. In contrast to the ambiguity of the legislative history of §334(b)(2), the Conference Report accompanying TEFRA states explicitly that "[t]he bill is also intended to replace any nonstatutory treatment of a stock purchase as an asset purchase under the Kimball-Diamond doctrine." H.R.Rep. No. 760, 97th Cong.2d Sess., at 536 (Conference Report).

For an appreciation of the potential complexity of the pre-TEFRA tax planning considerations in this area see, e.g., Pugh, Combining Acquired and Acquiring Corporations and Their Subsidiaries Following a Purchase of Stock: Some Anomalies of Form and Substance, 35 Tax L.Rev. 359 (1980); Levin & Bowen, supra.

[40] Issues of income recognition may also arise under the tax benefit and assignment of income rules. See B. Bittker & J. Eustice, supra, at 11–61 to 63.

received in a liquidating distribution the consideration paid in exchange for their target shares, the burden of complexity shifted from the acquiring company to the target. From the perspective of the acquiring company, its major tax goal in the transaction was achieved in a straightforward manner. Under §1012, the purchaser of an asset takes a basis equal to the cost of the asset and, because the initial incidence of the recapture rules is on the party disposing of the asset, this problem then remained with the target company rather than, in effect, being transferred to the acquiring company with the target stock as in a stock acquisition.

The complexity of the asset acquisition structure from the shareholders' perspective resulted from the fact that in this transactional form they bore the problem of eliminating the target company in order to receive the consideration paid for the target's assets. The principal tax goal of the target shareholders, it will be recalled, was to receive the proceeds of the asset sale reduced by only a single tax imposed on the shareholders. The simplicity of the stock transaction was that this result was so easily obtained. When the transaction is structured as an asset acquisition, however, the specter of two taxes—one imposed on the target company when it sold its assets and one imposed on the target shareholders when they received the proceeds of that sale through liquidation—is raised. Thus, equivalency in the tax treatment of the target shareholders as between stock and asset acquisitions required that one level of tax, either at the corporate (i.e., sale of assets) level, or at the shareholder (i.e., liquidation) level, be eliminated.

Equivalency was sought to be obtained by providing the opportunity to avoid the corporate level tax on the sale of the target company's assets. Under §337, which remained unchanged by TEFRA, no gain or loss is recognized by the target company upon the sale of its assets, provided that the sale is pursuant to a plan of complete liquidation adopted before the sale and the proceeds are distributed to the shareholders within twelve months after adoption of the plan.

While §337 thus allowed the target shareholders to meet their goal that only a single tax be imposed on the transaction, albeit with the target shareholders now bearing the burden of actually liquidating the target company, the symmetry between the treatment of the target shareholders under the stock and asset forms of the transactions was still not complete. The initial incidence of the recapture rules fell on the party disposing of the assets, in both cases the target company and, like §332, §337 does not suspend operation of the recapture rules. The difference, however, was that in a stock acquisition the shares of the target company were owned by the acquiring company at the time the assets were disposed of by liquidation under §332, while in the asset acquisition the target company was still owned by the target shareholders at the time the assets were sold pursuant to §337. Thus, unless the problem was anticipated and the incidence of the recapture altered by negotiation, the acquiring company bore the cost of recapture if the transaction took the form of a stock purchase, while the target shareholders bore the cost if the transaction took the form of an asset acquisition.

c. *Changes in Form and Substance as a Result of the Tax Equity and Fiscal Responsibility Act of 1982*

Changes in the tax treatment of nonreorganization transactions as a result of TEFRA alter the form of analysis previously described but, with one simplifying exception, do not significantly alter the substance of any of the parties' positions. The limited role of these changes for our purpose is best understood in the context of the types of pre-TEFRA transactions that motivated Congressional action.[41]

Suppose an acquiring company intended to acquire a target company with a substantial net operating loss for consideration the value of which substantially exceeded the basis of the target company in its assets. Under pre-TEFRA law, the acquiring company might at first glance appear to be put to a choice. On the one hand, if the goal was to structure the transaction so that the net operating loss survived, two approaches were possible under §381(a): (1) the transaction could be cast in the form of a reorganization; or (2) the stock at the target company could be acquired in a nonreorganization transaction and the target company either retained as a subsidiary or liquidated under §§334(b)(1) and 332. In either case, however, survival of the net operating loss would come at the price of sacrificing a step-up in basis to reflect the higher purchase price. Section 358 provides for a carryover basis in reorganizations, and in a nonreorganization stock transaction there is no occasion to alter the target company's basis in its assets if it is not liquidated, or, if it is, §334(b)(a) provides for a carryover basis. On the other hand, if the transaction was to be structured to achieve the step-up in basis, nonreorganization treatment was required. However, this would come at the price of sacrificing the survival of the target company's tax attributes because a step-up in basis required either a taxable asset acquisition or a taxable stock acquisition followed by a §334(b)(2) liquidation. In either case the result was to eliminate the target company without survival of its tax attributes. Therefore, it fell to ingenious tax planners to devise methods by which the acquiring company could have its cake—the survival of the target company's tax attributes—and eat it too—the step-up in basis.

This result was achieved by two variations on a theme. In the first, the depreciable assets of the target company were purchased, resulting in a step-up in basis as to these under §1012. And while recapture income might be recognized by the target company, its net operating loss carryover remained available as an offset. Thereafter, the acquiring company purchased the stock of the target company, but did not liquidate it, thereby allowing the target company's tax attributes to survive. In the second variation, the target company transferred the depreciable assets to related corporations prior to the trans-

---

[41] That is not to say that the TEFRA changes are either simple, or do not further complicate the acquisition planner's task. For discussions of the impact of TEFRA on tax planning, see, e.g., in ascending order of detail, Bonovitz, *Taxable Dispositions of a Corporate Business Before* *and After TEFRA,* 60 Taxes 12 (1982), 61 Taxes 325 (1983) (Parts I & II); Ward, *The TEFRA Amendments to Subchapter C: Corporate Distributions and Acquisitions,* 8 J.Corp.Law 277 (1983); Ginsburg, *Taxing Corporate Acquisitions,* supra.

action. Thereafter, the acquiring company would purchase their stock and then liquidate them pursuant to §334(b)(2). The stock of the corporation which retained the net operating loss would be purchased separately but not liquidated. The overall result would be the same as in the first variation, that is, the achievement of both a step-up in basis *and* the survival of the target's tax attributes. In both cases, the result was contrary to the underlying structure of the Code. An acquisition that resulted in basis adjustments to the target's assets should not also result in survival of its tax attributes because the latter result was appropriate only when there had been no change in the target entity significant enough to warrant basis adjustments.[42]

Congress acted in TEFRA to eliminate the ability of the acquiring company to elect the best of both worlds. Section 334(b)(2) was repealed and replaced with a new §338, the structure of which is intended to force the acquiring company to choose between a step-up in basis and the survival of the target company's tax attributes. Under §338, an acquiring company which makes a "qualified stock purchase," defined as the term "purchase" was defined in §334(b)(3), may elect to have the transaction treated *as if* the target company had sold all of its assets to a new corporation in a transaction to which §337 applied. The target company's basis in its assets would thereafter be determined by reference to the acquiring company's basis in the stock of the target. Thus, the step-up in basis would be accomplished (and recapture triggered) without the necessity of a formal liquidation as was previously required, a desirable elimination of one of the formalities required for a step-up in basis under §334(b)(2) that frequently had significant non-tax consequences.[43] Because the post-acquisition target company is treated as a new corporation which had purchased the assets of the pre-acquisition company on the day following the acquisition date, the target's pre-acquisition tax attributes, including any net operating loss, are therefore eliminated. If the §338 election is not made, no step-up basis is possible because, in the absence of the application of §338, the basis of a parent in the assets received upon the liquidation of a subsidiary is a carryover as specified in §334(a). In that case, however, the target company's tax attributes survive pursuant to §381.

Avoidance of the inconsistent results possible under prior law was achieved by specifically providing for the situation where the acquiring company, in addition to purchasing the target company's stock, also either makes a separate acquisition of part of the target's assets, or acquires a corporation affiliated with the target company. In the case

---

[42] The same technique could be used to avoid recognition of substantial recapture income. In some circumstances the potential for recapture will be associated with only a few identifiable assets. If most of the increase in the value which results in the higher purchase price is associated with different assets, they can be spun off to a related corporation. The target company is then acquired in a transaction structured to result in a step-up in basis, while the corporation holding the assets with the potential for recapture is acquired in a stock transaction and then *not* liquidated, thereby avoiding recapture.

[43] A liquidation, or a transaction initially structured as an asset acquisition, has the potential for causing termination of, for example, franchise rights, leases, or government licenses, because of non-assignability clauses in the original grant. See Chapter Thirteen infra.

of a partial asset acquisition, §338(e)(1) generally treats the acquiring company *as if* it had made an election with respect to the stock acquisition. In the case of parallel acquisition of an affiliate of the target company, §338(f) assures that the acquiring company will treat the acquisition of each affiliated corporation consistently by treating the election decision made with respect to the first acquisition as binding with respect to all subsequent acquisitions of affiliated companies. In either case, the acquiring company would be forced to choose which tax goal it preferred and sacrifice the other.[44]

B. The Theory

Acquisitions are, of course, one form of investment available to a corporation and there can be little question that the structure of the corporate income tax is *not* neutral with respect to corporate investment policy. Indeed, even before the issue of the tax system's influence on a particular type of investment is reached, the impact of the tax system on whether the corporation will make any investments at all must be considered.

In a world without taxes, whether to pay a dividend depends on the investment opportunities available to the corporation and its shareholders. If more favorable opportunities are available to the shareholders than to the corporation, earnings will be distributed as dividends and invested by the shareholders. Shareholder wealth is affected only by differential opportunities, not by whether a dividend is paid or not, *i.e.,* by whether the investment is made by the corporation or the shareholders. This result follows from the proposition that the value of a corporation depends on the present value of its future income stream, not on whether that income stream is reinvested or is paid out as dividends. This can be seen by decomposing shareholder wealth into two parts: that invested in the corporation and the balance held

[44] TEFRA also eliminates a form of transaction which, although less commonplace, was also perceived as a substantial abuse. The prototype of the disfavored transaction was the acquisition by Mobil Oil Corporation of Esmark, Inc.'s wholly owned subsidiary TransOcean Oil, Inc. The problem facing the planners was that the purchase price of the subsidiary was greatly in excess of Esmark's basis in it, and a transaction that allowed Mobil the basis benefit of its purchase price also would result in the recognition of hundreds of millions of dollars of gain by Esmark. The solution was for Mobil to tender for 54% of Esmark's common stock following which Esmark redeemed the Esmark shares held by Mobil in exchange for all of the outstanding shares of TransOcean. Immediately after the exchange Mobil liquidated TransOcean in order to secure a step-up in basis under §334(b)(2). Esmark claimed nonrecognition of the appreciation in value of the TransOcean stock based on §311(d)(2)(b) which provided an exception to the general requirement that gain be recognized on the distribution of appreciated property, when a subsidiary's stock (here TransOcean) is used to redeem stock of the parent (here Esmark). The Esmark transaction and other variations on the theme are described in Axelrod, *Esmark's Tax-Free Disposition of a Subsidiary: Too Good to be True?* 9 J.Corp.Tax. 232 (1982); see generally Henderson, *Federal Tax Techniques for Asset Redeployment Transactions,* 37 Tax. L.Rev. 325 (1982); Rollin & Sherck, *Fragmenting a Business Enterprise to Improve the Tax Position of Corporations and Stockholders,* 59 Taxes 870 (1981).

In response, TEFRA amended both §311 and §346, the latter dealing with partial liquidations. The overall result of the amendments is to require recognition of gain by corporations distributing appreciated assets, such as Esmark, unless the recipient, such as Mobil, treats the distribution as a dividend.

outside the corporation. If corporate earnings result in a $100 increase in corporate value, total shareholder wealth increases by $100. If, thereafter, the corporation distributes the $100 as a dividend, total shareholder wealth is unchanged. While the value of the shareholders' investment in the corporation decreases by $100, the value of the shareholders' wealth held outside the corporation increases by $100, exactly offsetting the decline in the value of the corporation. Put differently, a dividend alone does no more than effect a transfer between two pockets in the same pair of pants; value is affected only if the funds can be more profitably used in the front pockets than in the back.[45]

The first part of the claim that the structure of the corporate income tax favors acquisitions argues that the theoretical irrelevancy of dividend policy is fundamentally undermined by the differential tax treatment of corporate earnings that are retained and reinvested by the corporation and those that are distributed as dividends and reinvested by shareholders. The latter pattern, it is argued, is taxed more heavily than the former, thereby creating a substantial incentive to keep the earnings in a particular pocket.[46]

The differential in tax treatment flows from the fact that corporate income is taxed once, under the corporate income tax, when earned by the corporation, and a second time, under the individual income tax, when distributed to the shareholders as a dividend. Table 12 shows a simple example that highlights the difference in the amount available for reinvestment after all taxes depending on whether earnings are reinvested directly by the corporation, or reinvested by the shareholders after a dividend. Assume a corporation earns $185 and, following imposition of a flat corporate tax of 46 percent,[47] has $100 left either to

---

[45] This argument originates with Miller & Modigliani, *Dividend Policy, Growth, and the Valuation of Shares,* 34 J.Bus. 411 (1961). Its common presentation, in contrast to that of the text, focuses on the alternatives available to the firm to finance a particular investment, demonstrating that, in a tax and transaction cost-free world, there is no difference in firm value depending on whether the investment is financed with retained earnings and dividends are not paid, with the proceeds of a stock issue following a payout of retained earnings as a dividend, or by borrowing following a dividend. Developed in this way, the argument focuses on the decrease in value of the corporation, measured by the price at which new shares could be sold, following a dividend payment that reduces the value of the shareholders' stock in an amount that just offsets the value of the dividend received. See, e.g., J. Van Horne, *Financial Management and Policy* 325–28 (5th ed. 1980); R. Brealey & S. Myers, *Principles of Corporate Finance* 329–33 (1981). The conclusion that dividend policy is irrelevant is not, however, without dispute, even in the ab-

sence of taxes. The arguments that dividend policy can make a difference in firm value focus, *inter alia,* on the role of dividends as a signalling phenomenon, a means of conveying information about management's expectations concerning future earnings, on shareholder preferences concerning uncertainty, and on a clientele effect based on the preferences of different classes of investors for current income. The substance of the arguments are summarized in J. Van Horne, supra, at 328–33, and R. Brealey & S. Myers, supra, at 334–38, and extensive sources collected in Brudney, *Dividends, Discretion, and Disclosure,* 66 Va.L.Rev. 85 (1980); and Fischel, *The Law and Economics of Dividend Policy,* 67 Va.L.Rev. 699 (1981).

[46] See generally A. Feld, *Tax Policy and Corporate Concentration* 55–80 (1982).

[47] The corporate tax rate is actually graduated with brackets of 15 percent for the first $25,000 of income, 18 percent for the second $25,000, 30 percent on the third $25,000, 40 percent on the fourth $25,000 and 46 percent on all income over $100,000. Section 66(a) of the Tax Reform

reinvest or distribute as a dividend. If the corporation reinvests, there is no further tax and the full $100 is reinvested. Alternatively, if a dividend is paid and the shareholder reinvests, the $100 dividend is subjected to individual income tax at a marginal rate of up to 50 percent.[48] Assuming the shareholder is subject to a 50 percent rate, the amount remaining for reinvestment is only $50. The result is a substantial tax incentive to retain earnings rather than distribute them to shareholders.

Table 12

Differential Impact of Tax System on Choice Between Retention and Distribution of Corporate Earnings

	Retention of Earnings	Payment of Dividend
Available Earnings	$185.00	$185.00
(less 46% corporate income tax)	(85.00)	(85.00)
Amount Available for Retention or Distribution	$100.00	$100.00
(less 50% individual income tax on dividend)	(0.00)	(50.00)
Amount Remaining for Reinvestment	$100.00	$ 50.00

The incentive in favor of retaining earnings [49] rather than paying dividends is, in turn, magnified by the impact of another manifestation of the dual tax on corporate income. While receipt of corporate dividends by individuals is taxed at ordinary income rates of up to 50 percent, capital gains, which are receipts from the sale of capital assets including corporate stock, realized by individuals are taxed at a maximum of 20 percent. Thus, even if shareholders wanted to withdraw their portions of retained earnings for individual reinvestment, they would be better off by selling their shares, thereby subjecting the portion of the proceeds representing retained earnings only to the lower capital gains rate. Moreover, because each shareholder can decide individually when to sell their stock, each maintains flexibility to tailor

Act of 1984, P.L. 98–369, eliminates the graduated rate benefits for large corporations by imposing a 51 percent tax on income between $1,000,000 and $1,400,000.

[48] The Economic Recovery Tax Act of 1981 reduced the maximum individual bracket from 70% to 50%.

[49] The effect of the disparity between effective tax rates on earnings reinvested by the corporation and those paid out as dividends is further increased when compounding is taken into account. The additional amount available for reinvestment if dividends are not paid and a second tax thereby avoided will itself earn a return on reinvestment, thus increasing the initial difference by the present value of the income stream earned from the amounts not paid as tax following a dividend distribu-

tion. The tax system attempts to minimize the incentive to retain earnings in order to avoid the dual tax by imposing an accumulated earnings tax of up to 38½ percent on amounts in excess of $250,000 accumulated "beyond the reasonable needs of the business * * *." See generally B. Bittker & J. Eustice, supra; §§ 8.01–8.09. How much of a constraint the accumulated earnings tax actually imposes is subject to doubt. References to the reasonable needs of the business is an invitation to planning. After all, the determination of an investment policy at the corporate level in turn goes a long way toward determining the business's reasonable needs and the fact is that, despite the tax's technical application to publicly held corporations, it is rarely, if ever, so applied.

the corporation's dividend/reinvestment policy to their own needs, in contrast to the collective decision required at the corporate level to declare a dividend.[50]

At this point it is necessary to step back and evaluate precisely how much bearing the argument that the tax system is biased in favor of earnings retention by corporations really has on the issue of whether the tax system provides an incentive for acquisitions. That evaluation suggests, with one interesting qualification, the absence, at least thus far, of any bias in favor of acquisitions. Recall that the incentive created by the double tax on dividends is to retain earnings, that is, to reinvest at the corporate rather than at the shareholder level.[51] But this incentive alone does not provide a motivation for acquisitions. A corporation that has decided to retain its earnings must then determine how to invest them, and acquisitions are merely one of a number of available investment vehicles. To demonstrate that the incentive to retain earnings also operates as a motive for acquisitions one also must show that the incentive causes acquisitions to be more attractive than competing investment opportunities. And the distinction may have significant policy consequences because, for some commentators, investment in new capacity may be socially more desirable than the purchase of existing capacity through an acquisition.[52]

[50] The corporate capital structure can be shaped to facilitate this strategy. For example, the Citizens Utilities Plan involved the issuance of two classes of stock, identical except that one class received cash dividends and the other stock dividends. Shareholders were free to exchange shares of one class of stock for shares of the other with the result that they could elect whether to receive their share of corporate earnings in cash or by increasing their percentage ownership of retained earnings. This and other more sophisticated efforts to achieve the same result were effectively stymied by the 1969 amendments to IRC §305 and the regulations promulgated under its authority.

[51] Even this incentive is not present if the stockholders are non-taxable entities like pension funds and it is substantially reduced if the stockholders are other corporations which have the benefit of the 85 percent dividends received deduction of §243. It is difficult to determine what the impact of these types of holdings on retention policy really is, but some speculation is possible. If the effect of legal restrictions on the investment decisions of low rate taxpayers—such as the prudent man standard applicable to pension funds under ERISA, and the variety of "legal lists" governing investments by other types of institutions, see generally Langbein & Posner, *Market Funds and Trust Investment Law*, 1976 Am.Bar Found. Research J. 1— is to concentrate their holdings in larger companies, leaving smaller companies with higher percentages of individual shareholders, one would expect higher dividend payouts in larger firms. This is consistent with evidence showing "a substantial and steep decline in [earnings] retention from small corporations to large." A. Feld, supra, at 60–61. There are, however, competing explanations for this phenomenon including greater relative growth by smaller companies and, because of market imperfections, less access on their part to other sources of financing.

It should also be noted that some scholars argue that there is really no tax incentive in favor of retention because individuals can alter their personal tax strategy— for example, by borrowing to purchase more stock (thus creating deductible interest and creating the potential for earnings withdrawal of gains from their increased leverage at capital gains rates)—so as to tailor the corporation's after-tax dividend policy to their own preferences. See Miller & Scholes, *Dividends and Taxes*, 6 J.Fin. Econ. 333 (1978).

In light of the extensive controversy over whether dividend policy affects firm value, and in the face of the fact that firms continue to pay dividends despite the double tax and despite the lengthy period over which the academic debate has raged, it is hardly surprising that Professors Brealey and Myers regard the dividend controversy as one of the "[t]en unsolved problems in finance." R. Brealey & S. Myers, supra at 739.

[52] Harold Williams, while Chairman of the Securities and Exchange Commission,

One argument comes to mind that, on first consideration, does suggest a bias in favor of acquisitions. Rather than focusing on the competing investment opportunities available to the corporation, consider instead whether the same investment opportunities are available to the shareholders as to the corporation. If acquisitions present an unusually attractive investment opportunity, compared to other types of investments, then transaction cost considerations may favor retention rather than distribution. Put simply, making an acquisition requires collective action. If retained earnings are distributed to the shareholders, then there also must be incurred the cost of having individual shareholders agree to pool their funds to make the acquisition, i.e., the costs of creating a joint venture for the purpose of the acquisition. The corporation, in contrast, has already incurred these costs and, the argument runs, is therefore a more cost effective vehicle for making the acquisition. Put this way, taxes and transaction costs combine to create an incentive for acquisitions at the corporate level, in preference to dividend distribution and shareholder level investment.

The difficulty with this argument, however, is that it depends entirely on the premise that acquisitions are an especially valuable investment opportunity. If that premise is correct, then retention is called for, even in the absence of tax incentives, because the investments available at the corporate level are more valuable than investments available at the shareholder level. But whether acquisitions are a more valuable opportunity depends on the evaluation of the motivations for acquisitions examined in Part II. The superiority of the corporate level acquisition and, hence, the extent to which retention of earnings favors acquisitions as compared to other investments, depends on the existence of special opportunities presented by an acquisition. This was the focus of Chapters Eight through Eleven, and tax policy favoring retention of earnings adds little to this inquiry.

A more sophisticated argument concerning the relationship between the tax treatment of dividends and acquisitions builds on the fact that interest paid on debt is deductible but dividends paid on stock are not, thereby effectively reducing the cost of debt, as opposed to equity, financed investment. This fact yields a bias in favor of acquisitions based on the dual claims that banks prefer low variance projects to high variance projects and that diversification, which reduces a firm's variance, is more easily achieved by acquisition than by internal expansion. As a result, tax subsidized debt financing will be more readily available for acquisitions than for internal diversification.[53]

argued that "[i]n the last five years, I would estimate that $100 billion of corporate cash resources—resources which could have been devoted to new production and employment opportunities—have been diverted to rearranging the ownership of existing corporate assets through tender offers alone. These are reserves that do not flow back as new capacity, improvements in productivity, new products or new jobs." *Tender Offers and the Corporate Director,* Address before the Seventh Annual Securities Regulation Institute in San Diego, Cal. Jan. 17, 1980, reprinted in [1979–1980 Transfer Binder] Fed.Sec.L.Rep. (CCH) ¶ 82,445, at 82,877. What do you suppose Chairman Williams thinks the target shareholders do with the funds they receive?

[53] Wiggins, *A Theoretical Analysis of Conglomerate Mergers,* in *The Conglomerate Corporation* 53, 63 (Blair & Lanzillotti eds. 1981). Note, however, that the argu-

The difficulty with this argument is specifying precisely why a bank would prefer low variance projects. Because a bank presumably charges an interest rate that reflects the risk associated with a proposed project (and with the borrower's general credit rating), the assumption should be that, in the absence of a demonstration of why the bank is systematically risk averse rather than risk neutral, the bank would be indifferent to the risk associated with the particular project. While this response might not hold when regulatory restrictions, like usury laws, prevent banks from charging interest rates that compensate for the risk associated with high variance projects and thereby restricting such projects to more expensive equity financing, the bias then results not from the tax system but from the offending regulatory regime.

There is one situation, however, when a bank would have a preference for financing low variance projects. If a bank already has loans outstanding to a borrower at an interest rate fixed in light of the risk associated with the borrower at the time the loans were made, it would have an opportunistic reason for financing projects thereafter which, by reducing the overall variance of the borrower's earnings, had the effect of reducing the risk of the bank's outstanding loans without a compensating reduction in interest rate. But this situation should be recognizable as simply the other side of the strategic conflict between debt and equity discussed in Chapter Seven. If either side can alter the risk of the company in its favor without a corresponding alteration in the interest rate, the effect is a transfer of wealth from one side to the other. It was pointed out in Chapter Seven that lenders protect themselves against opportunistic behavior by borrowers through contractual covenants that prohibit actions by the borrower that would increase the risk of the loan. There was no mention, however, of lenders' ability to behave opportunistically because a lender, unlike a borrower, cannot act unilaterally. The borrower's investment decisions are made by its management and, therefore, no variance reducing project would be undertaken unless the borrower was compensated. So long as the interests of the management and shareholders of the borrower coincide, the danger of lender opportunism—the condition necessary for the deductibility of interest payments to favor acquisitions rather than internal expansion—does not exist.

The danger is real, however, when management and shareholders of the borrower have conflicting interests concerning the borrower's appropriate risk level. Here the problem is that, as pointed out in Chapter Nine C. 3, management may wish to reduce the variance associated with the firm's earnings as a means of reducing the risk associated with management's non-diversified investment of their human capital, even though this diversification is not beneficial to the shareholders. Management's opportunistic behavior then may coincide with a lender's desire to opportunistically reduce the risk associated with its outstanding loans to the borrower. In that event, both the decision maker of the borrower and the lender will favor a risk

ment requires that dividends actually be paid. Does the argument hold up, in light of the Miller-Modigliani approach, if no dividends are paid?

reducing investment even though the equity holders of the borrower are not compensated for the reduction. Again, however, the critical problem is not the distinction between the deductibility of interest and dividends, but the coincidence of opportunities for opportunistic behavior by both the lender and by the borrower's management.

The more interesting question concerning the impact of the structure of the tax system on motives for acquisition then is not the extent to which it creates an incentive for corporate growth—the retention of earnings issue—but whether it creates tax incentives favoring acquisitions over alternative investments. The deductibility of interest but not dividends does not create such an incentive; therefore, a broader inquiry is necessary. The following discussion by Professor Allan Feld undertakes that task.

A. FELD, TAX POLICY AND CORPORATE CONCENTRATION
81–100 (1982).*

Most combinations proceed from a mixture of motives, and both the acquiring corporation and the target corporation generally consider carefully the tax consequences of their decision. Tax considerations may consist of direct tax incentives to combine two corporations in order to reduce the total tax burden on the two separate enterprises. Major combinations sometimes involve these tax considerations. A more common set of tax considerations, however, deals with the method for shareholders to realize the benefits of corporate success. The tax law provides favorable treatment for gains realized by shifting investment from one corporation to a combined corporation.

This discussion uses the terms *acquisition* and *combination* to include both taxable and tax-deferred acquisitions and combinations, whatever their form. For convenience, it sometimes speaks of the two participating corporations as an acquiror (A) and a target (T) corporation.

Tax Benefits for the Form of the Combination

Acquisitions for Cash

Capital-gain and -loss taxation generally replaces ordinary income treatment on the sale or exchange of stock in a corporation. A capital-gain-ordinary-loss regimen applies to resale of many corporate business assets. One of the purposes asserted in support of the more favorable treatment of long-term capital gains is to prevent investors from being "locked in" to their investment by the desire to avoid ordinary tax treatment on the gain. In other words, capital-gain treatment seeks to facilitate sale or exchange of stock or appreciated assets.

This tax benefit has no particular effect on concentration when individual stockholders sell to other individuals in the ordinary course.

* Reprinted by permission of the publisher from *Tax Policy and Corporate Concentration* by Alan L. Feld, (Lexington, Mass.: Lexington Books, D.C. Heath and Company, Copyright 1982, D.C. Heath and Company).

But the bias toward sale instead of retention of stock is conducive to concentration when a corporation seeks to acquire stock of another corporation from the individual shareholders or the operating assets of a business directly from the corporation.

[We have previously considered] the way in which the preference in taxing capital gains over dividends to individuals encouraged corporate retention of earnings. [We] also noted that, although individuals generally prefer capital gains over dividends, the reverse applied to corporations. Under code section 243 a corporation may deduct 85 percent of any intercorporate dividend and may deduct the dividend in full when distributed by a member of the same affiliated group.

This difference in dividend tax treatment between individuals and corporations encourages individuals to sell their stock in a corporation with substantial retained earnings to a corporate purchaser. First the tax rules induce the target-corporation shareholders to balk at distributions of the corporate earnings lest they incur ordinary income tax on the dividends. They then sell their business and retained earnings and incur capital-gains tax. Were the purchaser an individual, however, he would confront the same dividend tax as the selling shareholders if he tried to reach T's accumulated earnings. But a corporation can buy the stock and distribute the target's retained earnings to itself at little or no tax cost.

For example, suppose individuals who own the stock of T corporation, with an adjusted basis of $1 million in their stock, sell their shares to A corporation for $10 million. Suppose further that T has $9 million in retained earnings. If T had distributed $9 million to its old shareholders, they would have netted $4.5 million, assuming a marginal individual tax rate of 50 percent. They also would have kept a business worth $1 million, for a total of $5.5 million in net worth. Instead, on the sale the T shareholders incur tax at an average capital-gain rate of 20 percent on their $9 million of gain. They net $8.2 million. A willingly pays the full $10-million price, for, unlike an individual purchaser, A incurs no tax when it causes T to distribute $9 million to it after the purchase.

Moreover, if A wishes, it can liquidate T after the purchase and obtain T's assets with a tax basis equal to A's purchase price even if T's basis was far below this market value. Unrealized appreciation in T's assets is wiped out and permanently escapes corporate tax, providing an additional advantage of sale over retention of the corporate investment. For example, if T owns mineral deposits that have advanced significantly in value, T or its shareholders would have incurred tax on the gain if T had continued in operation. On the sale to A, followed by a liquidation of T, A takes a current-value basis in the minerals and wipes out this potential tax.

Thus, under current law a corporate purchaser of T has two tax advantages over T's current individual shareholders: it can reach T's retained earnings without tax and it can erase potential tax liability in T's appreciated assets. The tax rules appear to push toward combining T with another corporation.

Reorganization Exchanges

* * *

In some cases a reorganization represents nothing more than a change in the corporate form of an enterprise; the code properly treats such a transaction as giving rise to no taxable event. But tax-deferred reorganizations also encompass transactions involving a substantial change in the subject matter of the investment, as when two ongoing businesses merge. Justification for the nonrecognition of gain or loss to the shareholder on such reorganization exchanges lies partly in the assertion that the exchanging shareholder has not altered his economic position sufficiently to warrant tax. The regulations describe nonrecognition for reorganization exchanges as applicable when the property acquired differs from the property given up, but the differences are "more formal than substantial." The new enterprise is a substantial continuation of the old "still unliquidated". This judgment, plausible when two corporations each operating a corner grocery store merge, is not self-evident for other exchanges that qualify as reorganizations, such as an exchange of a controlling stock interest in a local grocery store for a small percentage interest in a national supermarket chain.

* * *

The inconsistency in treatment between reorganization and nonreorganization exchanges creates a proconcentration advantage that would disappear if both were either taxable or nontaxable. The advantage lies in the way present tax rules render stock issued by publicly traded corporations a favored medium of exchange, one that other would-be acquirors of target companies cannot match.

The advantage comes from the joinder of tax deferral to liquidity. When the T shareholders exchange their T stock for A stock in a reorganization and A's stock is publicly traded, the exchange often will be more attractive to the T shareholders than a sale for cash at the same price. A sale for cash incurs capital-gain tax, whereas an exchange in a reorganization often can net the T shareholder something almost as liquid as cash but without tax. A selling shareholder, of course, may prefer cash to taking an investment risk in stock in the purchaser. But the offset of possible investment gain, coupled with deferral of tax, may make the stock more attractive than cash. The reorganization flexibility that allows cash-and-stock mergers can even resolve different shareholder evaluations of these risks: some T shareholders can elect to receive cash with current tax, whereas others can enjoy tax deferral by receiving stock. Even where no cash changes hands, investment risk in the acquiror can be reduced, often to the vanishing point, by tailoring the acquiror's stock received on the exchange so as to combine a preference in dividend and liquidation rights with equity growth, as in a preferred stock convertible into common. Finally, although the benefit of deferral inures to the T shareholders in the first instance, A can share in it through an adjustment in the price, paying less than other bidders for the stock of T.

To illustrate, suppose the T shareholders, with an adjusted basis of $1 million in their stock, would agree to sell T for $10 million cash. Assuming an average tax rate on net capital gain of 20 percent, the sale would net the T shareholders $8.2 million, after taxes of $1.8 million. Suppose now that A, a publicly held corporation, offers $9 million in A stock in a tax-deferred reorganization. The T shareholders may prefer this exchange with A, under which they receive $0.8 million more. A also is better off, paying $1 million less for T in stock than in cash.

This saving to the parties of $1.8 million on the exchange comes at some tax cost for the future, both to the shareholders of T and to A. The shareholders of T carry over their low adjusted basis in the T stock ($1 million in the illustration) to the new A stock they receive. This renders the $9 million in A stock less attractive than $9 million cash because the shareholders will incur tax on any sale or other taxable disposition of the stock. Reorganization treatment grants the shareholders deferral of the tax, not complete forgiveness; the exact tax benefit to them consists of the capital-gain tax deferred (20 percent of $8 million, or $1.6 million, on the exchange for A stock) less the discounted value of the tax when (and if) paid. In many cases, however, this discounted value will be quite low. A shareholder may dispose of the stock without tax if he gives it to charity or passes it on death, or he can obtain further deferral by giving the stock to family members. Even if he sells the stock, he can choose a year in which his marginal tax rate is low or he has offsetting losses, so as to minimize or eliminate gains tax. Thus the future tax cost of deferral to the T shareholders often is of little concern to them.

To A, the price of reorganization treatment comes in its tax basis in the assets of T.

A purchaser for cash takes as his basis the amount he paid; an acquiror in a reorganization takes the old basis in the assets. For most successful corporations, basis in the assets is less than their fair market value. Carryover basis in a reorganization thus often produces a lower basis and smaller deductions than a cost basis.

If the parties find the current deferral more attractive than these costs, they will go forward with the exchange. The tax reorganization rules then will render A's offer of $9 million in its stock more attractive to both sides than $10 million in cash. This result distorts the flow of investment capital in that the "market" in businesses now fails to direct the exchange to the highest bidder. From a concentration standpoint, the rules make the publicly held acquiror's offer more attractive than a similar offer from a closely held corporation either in cash or in its stock: cash produces taxability to the T shareholders, and stock of this rival lacks liquidity and cannot be converted readily into cash. Thus the tax advantage in giving stock rather than cash favors corporations over other bidders and widely held corporations over closely held ones.

* * *

Apart from the funneling of acquisitions to publicly held corporations, the concentration effects of reorganization are less clear. If the parties would have gone forward with a sale in any event, as the illustration assumes, then the tax reorganization rules do not "cause" the combination to occur. Of the many reorganizations that take place, however, there doubtless are a few that would not have occurred at the higher price mandated by a taxable transaction; how many and how significant they are we do not know. An acquisition that probably would take place in any event now can be accomplished more cheaply. Part of the net benefit of the tax-deferred form accrues to the acquiror; in this sense, the deferral enriches the acquiror by allowing it to pay less than it otherwise might.

The reorganization rules thus distort the purchase and sale of businesses by allowing publicly held corporations to offer a tax-deferred and liquid form of consideration not available to other bidders. This may influence both the choice of partners in a merger and the price the acquiror pays.

* * *

Direct Tax Incentives to Combine

"Wasting" Tax Benefits

The code limits a number of tax benefits by particular characteristics of the corporation, such as its income, the source of the income, or the corporation's tax liability. Often the corporation can apply the excess tax benefit in another tax year. Three examples concern net operating losses, the investment tax credit, and the foreign-tax credit.

Present Losses and Carrybacks. The code computes taxable income and income-tax liability by entity rather than by line of business. A corporation that incurs a loss in one endeavor reports it on its tax return in conjunction with profits earned in others. It thereby reduces or eliminates the tax otherwise payable on the profits.

A taxpayer may use losses to offset income between different time periods as well as between different lines of business. In order to overcome some of the arbitrariness inherent in an annual accounting system, the code provides for a net-operating-loss (NOL) deduction, under which the NOLs in one year may be carried back * * * and forward. * * * The carryback deduction deems the loss in the current year to offset the earlier profits and thereby produces an immediate refund of the earlier taxes paid. In effect, a corporation that had profits within the carryback period, even if otherwise unrelated to the current losses, can require the government to share the financial burdens of the current loss through the income tax.

These rules may favor established corporations over new ones. Consider corporation E, which has a history of profits, and corporation N, newly formed to compete in the same industry. In N's first year both E and N incur losses, perhaps occasioned by N's entry into the industry. E will carry its NOL back, offset earlier profits, receive a tax refund, and bear only part of the loss incurred. N will bear the losses in full. If N later has taxable income, it will be able to carry the NOL forward and reduce taxes in a future year. If so, E will have enjoyed an advantage over N in getting its tax benefit sooner for the same loss. If N does not later have taxable income, the tax benefit may be lost permanently, and E's advantage will be even greater. In either case, the existing tax treatment enables E to sustain a loss more easily than N.

* * *

Both the current deductibility of losses against unrelated profits and the loss-carryback rule for corporations thus favor the incumbent over the newcomer to an industry, particularly when there are start-up costs in excess of initial profits. Among corporate newcomers, they tend to favor corporations closely associated with a profit-making group over those that are not.

Loss Carryovers. The carryover of losses has provoked greater concern in administering the NOL rules. A history of losses can render a corporation more valuable if the losses can be brought into conjunction with profits before the carryover period expires. Both the profit-making acquiror and the loss-burdened target hope to profit if they combine: the profit-making corporation seeks to obtain the use of the tax benefits, and the target corporation or its shareholders realize something on the losses before they expire.

When a corporation applies current losses against current or past profits, it generally matches economic losses against income of the same investor group. In the case of carryovers, however, if the original investors of the loss corporation sell out to a new investor group, then the tax benefit of the prior losses will accrue in the first instance to the new investors and not to those who originally put up the investment that produced the loss. On sale of the corporation that suffered the losses, however, the sales price is likely to divide the benefits between the selling and acquiring investors. To illustrate, corporation A, which is highly profitable, would pay $2 million to acquire the business of corporation L. L has $1 million of NOL carryover; the carryover can net A $460,000 in taxes saved. In addition to the $2-million purchase price, A will be willing to pay the shareholders of L something less than $460,000—say, $100,000—to acquire and use L's losses.

Other Carryovers. Other tax benefits subject to specific limitations also may produce carryovers that present similar exchange opportunities. A corporation may claim the investment credit only up to a stated percentage of the tax liability. It carries any excess as a credit to other years—first back, then forward. The foreign-tax credit limiting fraction, determined by the proportion of the corporation's taxable income from foreign sources, similarly gives rise to "excess credits"— foreign taxes paid that do not offset U.S. tax. These excess credits may be carried back, then forward. These carryovers likewise present opportunities for one corporation to use tax attributes that the target corporation cannot effectively use by itself, to pay part of the purchase price for its business.

C. Evaluation: How Persuasive is the Argument?

The claim that the tax system creates an incentive in favor of acquisitions has an old and distinguished history. The Federal Trade Commission's Economic Report on Mergers in 1969 stressed the role of a non-neutral tax system in encouraging mergers,[54] and Professor Willard Mueller, Chief Economist of the FTC during the period that report was prepared, testified before the Senate Subcommittee on Antitrust and Monopoly that "[a]lthough the tax treatment accorded corporate mergers is only one of many factors propelling the current merger movement, it clearly exerts a significant and positive influence."[55] Professor Feld's analysis follows in this tradition. The difficulty with the traditional claim that the tax system favors acquisitions, however, is that it focuses on the preferences conferred by the tax system on acquisitions without a clear specification of the alternative transaction against whose treatment the asserted preferences are measured.[56] Compared to what is the tax treatment of acquisitions favorable? In the following the focus will be on examining the tax treatment of acquisitions compared to other investment alternatives available to both the acquiring company and to the shareholders of the target. Only in that way can the last step in the tax motivation argument be evaluated: that the tax system causes acquisitions to be preferred to alternative investment opportunities.

1. Incentives Arising From the Treatment of the Transaction

A major part of the tax incentive argument typically focuses on the advantages offered by an acquisition in comparison to the parties' position if no transaction occurred. Framing the analysis in this way, however, diverts attention from consideration of what alternative transactions were available and the comparative tax treatment of the alternatives.

a. Nonreorganization Transactions

We can start with nonreorganization transactions. Here the argument is that an acquiring company is at a substantial advantage vis-a-vis a target company with respect to the tax-free use of the target's retained earnings. Recalling our earlier survey of the tax treatment of nonreorganization transactions, an acquiring company can purchase the stock or assets of the target company, and thereby have use of all of its assets without paying a tax but, the argument goes, the individual shareholders of the target company would have to incur a dividend tax to have use of these assets individually.[57] The difficulty, however, is

---

[54] Federal Trade Commission, supra, at 142–58.

[55] Statement of Willard Mueller, Hearings before the Subcommittee on Antitrust and Monopoly of the Senate Committee on the Judiciary, 91st Cong., 2nd Sess., 4544, 4576 (Nov. 4, 1969).

[56] Professor Steiner stresses the same analytical point. P. Steiner, *Mergers: Motives, Effects, Policies* 75–79 (1975).

[57] An initial confusion in Feld's argument should be corrected. Feld contrasts the difficulty confronting the target company's shareholders in securing access to the target's retained earnings before acquisi-

that the comparison is, at the very least, much more difficult from either the perspective of the acquiring company or that of the shareholders of the target company.

Consider first the acquiring company's position with respect to the acquisition. It is making an investment decision and, presumably, has decided that it is desirable to acquire assets of the sort owned by the target company. The argument that the tax system favors acquisitions seems at this point to suggest that the acquiring company is made "better off" by the "non-neutral" tax treatment of acquisitions because it will have easier access to the target's assets than the target shareholders would have in the absence of the transaction. But from the acquiring company's perspective, the comparison is without meaning. In its decision process, the acquiring company evaluated not the tax treatment of the alternatives facing target company shareholders, but the tax treatment of its own alternatives—how the acquisition compares to other methods of securing similar assets. If, for example, the assets were to be acquired new from their manufacturer or from an individual, the acquiring company could also secure their use without the intervention of the tax system, precisely the same result, from its perspective, as if the assets were acquired from the target company. That the tax position of the target company shareholders may differ because of the acquisition is relevant to the acquiring company's decision *only* if it causes the price of the desired assets to be systematically lower when acquired in a corporate acquisition than when acquired from other sources. Two lines of argument suggest this result. Both are not only difficult, but unlikely to affect substantial amounts of activity even if there prove to be areas in which they are correct.

The first, and most straightforward, explanation for why assets might be purchased more cheaply by an acquisition than from other sources assumes a nonreorganization transaction and argues that there is a net tax savings as a result of the acquisition. That is, a subsidy is available from the Federal government only if the assets are purchased from a particular source, in a sense a vendor-specific cents-off coupon. The key to the argument is the differential tax rates applicable to corporate income and shareholder capital gain. If the consideration paid exceeds the target company's basis in its depreciable assets, the acquisition will result in a new, higher basis for the assets which, through depreciation, shelters acquiring company income that would otherwise be taxed at 46 percent. The price of the step-up in basis is

tion—the 50% dividend tax—with the ease of access to the proceeds of the sale of those retained earnings—a mere 20% capital gains tax. A. Feld, supra. The problem, however, is more than just a differential tax rate and the comparison is inopposite. Prior to the sale of the business, the company may have substantial retained earnings; however, it is correct to say that these are "available" for dividend distribution only in an accounting sense. Dividends are not paid with retained earnings, they are paid with cash. Unless the company's net worth prior to the sale is totally liquid, it is terribly misleading to suggest that it is capable of distribution. In other words, the sale of the business does more than alter the applicable tax rate on the distribution to shareholders; by reducing the company's assets to liquid form, it makes the distribution possible. Again, the problem is one of lack of precision in specifying precisely the appropriate alternative against which to measure the tax treatment of acquisitions.

only a 20 percent capital gain tax to the target shareholders on the appreciation in value. In this situation, so long as any portion of the differential accrues to the acquiring company, the net price of the assets should be lower if acquired from the target company than from other sources. For example, assume the target company has a basis of $100 in its assets and the target shareholders a basis of $100 in their shares. If the acquiring company purchases the target's assets at their appreciated market value of $200, the acquiring company gets additional basis worth $46 (it shelters $100 in income that would have been taxed at 46 percent) while the price of that benefit, the tax paid by the target shareholders on the sale, is only $20 (20 percent capital gain tax on the $100 gain).[58]

It should be apparent, however, that the example is far too simple. Most importantly, it ignores the fact that the increased depreciation can be used only over the useful life of the asset, rather than immediately. In the example, what is the impact on the tax differential if the benefits of the increased depreciation flow in equal amounts over 10 years? [59] It will be recalled from Chapter Two that this determination requires the calculation of the present value of a stream of payments of $4.60 a year for 10 years in order to compare the benefit from the additional depreciation with its price—the $20 tax payable by the target shareholders in the year of the transaction. If a discount rate of 10% is used, the present value of the increased depreciation is only approximately $28.27.[60] Taking the point a bit further, present value is principally a function of two factors: (1) the discount rate used; and (2) the useful life of the asset.[61] For example, if the discount rate is increased to 15%, the present value is reduced to $23.09. Alternatively, if the useful life of the asset is increased to 20 years, the present value of the increased depreciation at 10 percent is $19.58, and at 15 percent is $14.40. As an exercise, try to determine the range of these variables over which the balance of the tax effects is favorable using the sensitivity analysis technique described in Chapter Six.

The balance of tax advantage is further tipped if there is any recapture income. For present purposes it is irrelevant whether this tax, at ordinary income rates, is actually paid by the acquiring company following a stock acquisition and §338 election, or by the target company as a result of a sale of assets pursuant to §337. In either case the result is to reduce the differential between acquiring company benefit and target shareholder price on which the incentive argument is based. For example, if 20 percent of the gain is treated as recapture and taxed at an assumed ordinary income rate of 50 percent, then the

---

[58] See P. Steiner, supra, at 93, for a formal presentation of the argument. Note that this assumes that the increase in basis is allocated entirely to depreciable assets. If some portion must be allocated to nondepreciable assets such as land or goodwill, the value of the additional basis will be to that extent less than $46.

[59] This assumes that the assets in question have a ten year life and are depreciated on a straightline basis.

[60] This calculation can be checked by use of Table A–2 at the end of Chapter Two.

[61] It is also a function of the timing of the payments; i.e., the depreciation method used.

total shareholder tax is increased to $26. This factor can also be incorporated into the sensitivity analysis.[62]

The second line of argument suggesting that the price of the target's assets may be cheaper when secured from the target company through a nonreorganization acquisition than from competitive suppliers turns on the need of the target shareholders for liquidity. Here the problem is that the target shareholders may desire to reduce all or a portion of their holdings to cash. While a dividend could be paid, achieving liquidity in this way is quite costly, as it is subject to individual income tax rates of up to 50 percent. In contrast, the argument goes, liquidity can be achieved through the sale of the target company subject only to lower capital gains rates. This analysis is consistent with some formulations of capital asset pricing theory in which target shareholders value factors in addition to risk and return. If one of these additional factors, such as liquidity, is included as part of the consideration, the price charged for the asset by target shareholders would be lower than if the factor were not present.[63]

But whether target shareholders would be willing, in effect, to pay a price for liquidity depends on whether that benefit can be secured in other, less costly, ways. Are there other methods by which target shareholders can achieve liquidity at capital gains rates other than by selling the company?

For shareholders in publicly held corporations, the alternative is obvious. Each shareholder can simply sell on the market that portion of his or her holdings necessary to satisfy the need for liquidity. The tax cost of achieving liquidity in this way is identical to that of achieving liquidity by selling the target company: Both alternatives result in only a capital gains tax. Moreover, the price the target shareholder receives for his stock should be somewhat better in a market transaction because the separation theorem teaches that where a market exists for the corporation's stock, its shareholders' need for liquidity should not enter the pricing process because the shareholders can meet that need through adjustment of their individual portfolios.[64]

Focus on the separation theorem, however, identifies one area where the argument that shareholders will pay a price for liquidity

[62] The following example takes into account all of the factors discussed in the text. Assume, as in the text, a $100 target shareholder gain, 20 percent of which is subject to recapture; a $100 increase in basis, 80 percent of which is allocated to depreciable assets; a capital gains rate of 20 percent and a shareholder ordinary income rate of 50 percent; a useful life of the acquired depreciable assets of 10 years with straightline depreciation; and a discount rate of 10 percent. On these assumptions, the tradeoff is as follows:

(a) Benefit to Acquiring Company		(b) Cost to Target Company Shareholders	
Increase in Basis	$80.00	Capital Gain Tax on 80% of Gain	$16.00
Annual Depreciation Charge	$ 8.00	Ordinary Income Tax on 20% of Gain	$10.00
After-tax Value	$ 3.68		
Present Value	$21.61	Total Tax	$26.00

[63] See Chapter Four C.2., supra.   [64] See Chapter Four B.

and, therefore, will sell the company's assets more cheaply than alternative sources, may hold. Recall the discussion of the closely held corporation in Chapter Nine C. It was there pointed out that, because of the absence of a public market for such a corporation's stock, diversification often takes place at the company rather than shareholder level, with a resulting decrease in efficiency and in the value of the firm, because a factor other than profit maximization is taken into account in making the corporation's investment decisions. Here the argument is that the absence of a public market makes it impossible for shareholders to satisfy their need for liquidity independently so that this consideration also must be taken into account at the corporate level with the resulting decrease in firm value. Selling the company meets the shareholders' liquidity needs but at the cost of a lower price. For shareholders in closely held corporations there may be no alternative to accepting the lower price.[65]

While we thus can identify an area where a bias in favor of the purchase of assets by acquisition rather than from competing sources may be present, the question remains of how much acquisition activity the bias actually explains. This, of course, is an empirical question; however, it can be noted that the impact of the bias [66] is limited only to closely held corporations and could hardly account for the magnitude of the overall acquisition phenomenon.[67]

b. Reorganization Transactions

The argument that the tax system favors nonreorganization transactions does not rule out making similar arguments with respect to reorganization transactions.

[65] If liquidity needs could be met only by selling the company, the incentive to screen potential shareholders to insure similarity in tastes described in Chapter Nine C.1. is substantially reinforced. What other ways are available to shareholders of closely held corporations to meet their liquidity needs? Does it matter whether all shareholders are active in the operation of the business?

There are, however, at least two other possibilities. First, if selling the company is desirable only because a public market is not available, then we also need to consider the alternative of creating a public market, i.e., going public. What costs are relevant to this alternative? Second, the shareholders can achieve liquidity without incurring any taxes by borrowing against their stock. How would you evaluate the costs of this alternative?

[66] Where the search for bias is extended to include the impact of the estate tax on closely held businesses, the causal relation between taxes and acquisitions becomes more real. While the need for liquidity does not itself favor sale by acquisition over sale by public offering, where it is tax liability that creates the liquidity need in the first place, a causal relationship exists as long as acquisitions can be expected to be the means of meeting the liquidity need some of the time. Clearly the need to pay estate taxes on the value of a closely held business creates a liquidity need and it has been argued that the estate tax is a principal cause of the increasing concentration in the daily newspaper industry. See "Economic Incentives to Merge," Testimony by J. Dertouzos & K. Thorpe, The Rand Corporation, on Proposed Corporate Takeover Tax Act of 1982 (H.R. 6295) before the Subcommittee on Select Revenue Measures, Committee on Ways and Means, House of Representatives (May 24, 1982) (describing results of study conducted for the Small Business Administration).

[67] Some of the same problems may be present, however, when a publicly held corporation has a dominant shareholder. In that case, the market may not be available to dispose of a very large block of stock without significant information effects. See Scholes, *The Market for Securities: Substitution versus Price Pressure and the Effects of Information on Share Prices*, 45 J.Bus. 179 (1972).

The most familiar claim for the existence of tax incentives favoring acquisitions focuses on the availability of a deferral of gain for target shareholders when the transaction is structured as a reorganization.[68] Again, however, the common presentation of the argument is flawed because of an incorrect specification of the alternatives against which the tax treatment of reorganization transactions is implicitly compared.

From the acquiring company's perspective, the relevant comparison remains the price of the target company's assets from alternative sources. From this perspective, however, the effect of the tax system may create a bias against acquiring the assets in a reorganization transaction. In order for the deferral to be valuable to the target company shareholders, we must assume that they would otherwise report a gain on the transaction, i.e., that their stock has appreciated in value. It is a quite small step then to assume that the value of the target company's assets has also increased over original costs. Thus, even without considering the impact of depreciation taken by the target company, it is a fair assumption that in precisely those situations where the deferral offered by reorganization is desirable to the target shareholders, it will result in the acquiring company taking a lower basis in—and lower depreciation from—the acquired assets than their market value and, hence, the basis that would result if the assets were acquired from alternative sources.[69] And this difference is exacerbated by the asymmetrical terms of the trade-off. While the benefit to target shareholders is only a deferral, the increased basis foregone by the acquiring company is not merely deferred, but lost forever. Moreover, the direction of the ordinary income/capital gain rate differential has been reversed from that encountered in the nonreorganization situation. Here the taxes deferred are only at the 20 percent capital gains rate while the benefits lost would have been at the 46 percent corporate income rate. In short, the tax system may make an acquisition treated as a reorganization a *less* attractive way of acquiring assets when considered solely from the perspective of the acquiring company. If the overall tax treatment of this type of transaction creates an incentive favoring acquisitions, it must be because the deferral offered the target shareholders is so valuable that they can compensate the acquiring company for its extra tax burden and still be better off. Consideration of this possibility requires focusing on the target shareholders.

Evaluation of the incentives created by the tax treatment of the target shareholders in a reorganization transaction depends, as it did for the acquiring company, on how alternative methods of achieving the shareholders' objectives are treated. The problem, once again, is that the alternatives typically considered are the wrong ones. To be sure, deferral is a benefit if the alternative is immediate recognition. But so narrow a view of the available alternatives is possible only if one treats

---

[68] The Federal Trade Commission once stated that the "[t]ax exemption of corporate reorganizations has the most pervasive impact of all tax provisions favoring mergers." Federal Trade Commission, Economic Report on Corporate Mergers, supra at 143.

[69] The problem is mitigated to the extent that the assets acquired would not be depreciable and to the extent recapture would otherwise be triggered.

the shareholders' goal as a sale of the company, and that conclusion requires more careful consideration.

The central issue is why the shareholders want to sell the target company in the first place.   And at this stage of the inquiry the favorable tax treatment of the sale transaction is hardly the answer. After all, the target shareholders can also achieve nonrecognition of the appreciation in value of their investment by *not selling* the company, and at substantially lower transaction costs.

The most common goal said to be achieved by sale of the company is the increased potential for target shareholders to diversify their portfolios without the imposition of a tax.   But if this is the goal, the relevant comparison for purposes of determining the tax incentives for acquisitions is not how the sale transaction might otherwise be taxed, but the tax treatment of alternative means by which target shareholders can increase their diversification.   Viewed in this way, the argument becomes problematic.

Most obviously, the argument becomes troublesome if the target company is itself publicly held.   In that case, target company stock is already priced as if target shareholders' portfolios were fully diversified.   There is no barrier to diversification at the shareholder level as might be the case if the target were closely held and, as a result, there is no obvious reason why target shareholders as a group predictably would be in need of further diversification.[70]

Even if the target company is privately held and diversification therefore is presumably unavailable at the shareholder level, it may be accomplished without tax cost by means other than the sale of the target to a more diversified acquirer.   Most directly, the target can diversify at the company level.   As has already been discussed, this alternative imposes some limits on the character of acceptable shareholders so as to assure uniformity in taste for diversification, and some efficiency costs because a factor in addition to profit-maximization is being taken into account in making the company's investment decisions.   But achieving diversification by sale of the company through a reorganization transaction also has its limits.   Most importantly, the reorganization transaction still leaves the shareholder with an investment in a single company.   Further diversification would require disposal of the acquiring company shares received, and that would result in recognition.   The real benefit may be that as a result of the acquisition the target shareholder gains access to a previously unavailable public market and the target company then may be worth more because its investment decisions can be based only on efficiency concerns.   This benefit, however, simply suggests that the assets of the target company may be worth less to a company without access to a public market, a form of synergy argument, and that the availability of a nonrecognition transaction sale may facilitate this result.   Even here, however, one must explain why access to a public market is most

[70] It is possible to imagine that changes in relative values of the shareholders' portfolios might require some shifting in investments in order to restore the desired weighting; however, this factor seems an unlikely candidate to explain major shifts in corporate ownership.

efficiently secured through the target company's acquisition rather than through an obvious alternative that has the same tax consequences as an acquisition—a public offering of the target company's stock. If the answer is anything other than the tax system, such as the transaction or information costs of going public, the incentive in favor of acquisitions no longer arises from the tax system.

Other explanations for why shareholders might wish to sell the target company are also not directly tied to the transaction being treated as a reorganization. Sale may seem desirable because the target company is underpriced in error, not because it is closely-held, and the company's intrinsic value is realized by, and can be obtained from, only the acquiring company. In this setting the question is then why only the acquiring company has been able to discover the target company's true value, and why similar analysis cannot be provided the market in general so as to correct the mispricing. Like a reorganization transaction, this disclosure approach corrects the mispricing without imposing a current tax cost; it does not, however, require selling the company. Something more is necessary, perhaps a theory of why the market might be inefficient in this setting, before a bias in favor of an acquisition is created. While there may be settings in which doubt as to market efficiency is appropriate, once again the setting where there is no public market for the target company's stock comes to mind, substantial doubt would still remain as to the amount of activity actually being influenced.

A final explanation for why the target shareholders might want to sell the company is because the combination with the acquiring company creates synergy. That is, apart from the tax treatment of the transaction, the two companies will be worth more together than separately. In this situation, there is no alternative to an acquisition as a means of realizing the potential gains, but it is hardly true that the availability of reorganization treatment motivates the transaction. There may be situations in which the availability of the deferral resulting from reorganization treatment, in contrast to immediate recognition, makes a difference at the margin, but efforts at defining the marginal transaction suggest, again, that substantial amounts of activity may not be involved. For example, identifying what balance of factors would put a synergistically motivated transaction at the point where the availability of deferral would push it over the edge, would require balancing the tax on the target shareholders' gain if immediately recognizable, taking into account the number of target shareholders who are institutions not subject to tax, against the present value of the tax that would be recognized by the target shareholder on disposal of the consideration, in light of the cost to the acquiring company in foregone basis. Put differently, how much is the deferral really worth?

In summary, the availability of reorganization treatment may create some tax incentive in favor of acquisitions as a means of achieving acquiring company and target shareholder goals, but the circumstances in which the incentive is operative seems to be largely limited to the sale of closely held corporations. Neutrality in tax treatment remains an important issue with respect to other areas, but the case that the income tax treatment of corporate acquisitions explains significant amounts of acquisition activity remains to be made.

2. Incentives Arising Out of the Transfer of Tax Attributes

The final argument that the tax system creates incentives that favor acquisitions over other means of accomplishing financially similar goals is based on the potential for survival of some of the target company's tax attributes in an acquisition, most importantly, the target company's net operating loss carryover ("NOL"). Two steps are necessary to establish the point. The first, which should be clear from our earlier overview of the tax treatment of acquisitions, is that the NOL must be transferable only—or at least on much more favorable terms— by means of an acquisition than by alternative methods. But this step is not in itself sufficient to establish the incentive since an alternative remains which does not require transfer—the target company could use its NOL itself. To show that the transferability of the target's NOL by acquisition creates an incentive to engage in the transaction, it must also be shown that the asset, the NOL, is worth more to the acquiring company than to the target. In the absence of that discrepancy in value, there is no *tax* incentive for the acquisition.

The key to demonstrating the potential for a differential in valuation of the carryover is the recognition that the NOL has value only if there is income in future periods that the NOL can be used to offset. Suppose a potential target company has fallen on hard times and, over a number of unsuccessful years, has accumulated an NOL of $50,000. Suppose as well that, for precisely the same reasons that caused the losses, there is only a 50/50 chance that the company will return to profitability so that the NOL could be used. Ignoring for the moment the problem of *when* the target company would become profitable, the value of the NOL to the target company is equal to the amount of the NOL, multiplied by the tax rate, multiplied by the likelihood that income to shelter would actually be earned or:

$$\$50,000 \times 46\% \times .5 = \$11,500.$$

In contrast, if the acquiring company, because of the earnings history of its businesses, is certain of at least $50,000 in earnings to shelter, the last term of the calculation becomes 1 and the value of the NOL increases to $23,000.

The discrepancy in valuation grows even larger if timing considerations are taken into account. Suppose that the target company believes that it will break even for the next two years and that the probability of earning $50,000 applies only to the third year, while the acquiring company is certain of having earnings available to offset immediately. In this situation, the value of the NOL to the target company also must be reduced to present value to take into account the fact that it will not receive the value of the NOL for three years. If a discount rate of 10 percent is used, the calculation of the value of the NOL to the target then becomes:

$$\$50,000 \times 46\% \times .5 \times .75131 = \$8,640.[71]$$

Thus, there is no question but that the tax system, by its treatment of the transfer of NOL in acquisitions, does create the potential for gain from an acquisition that could not otherwise be achieved.[72] Nonetheless, it should be noted that the strength of this argument depends critically on precisely how the target's NOL can be used after the acquisition. Suppose that the tax treatment were changed so that the target company's NOL still survived the acquisition, but could only be used to offset the future earnings of the target company's business.[73] In that situation, the value of the NOL to the acquiring company is no different than to the target company, because the probability of income against which to offset is not different, *unless* one assumes that the acquiring company's management is more skillful and, hence, the target company's likelihood of earnings goes up as a result of their tenure. This, however, is simply a displacement of inefficient management argument that is invariant to the tax system. That is, the asset

---

[71] The discount figure is taken from Table A–1 at the end of Chapter Two. Because the acquiring company could make use of the NOL immediately, no discount is applied to its valuation. This, of course, is a simplification because it ignores the timing of tax payments *within* the first post-acquisition year.

[72] One should be quite careful about the policy implication one draws from this conclusion. While the immediate reaction is to consider restricting the transferability of NOL's by means of acquisition to make them *less* valuable to the *acquiring* company, more careful consideration suggests that a desirable reform may be to make them *more* valuable to the *target* company. The effect of limiting the value of a net operating loss to the offset of future in-

Corporation A

(.5) ($20,000) (1–.46) = $5,400
(.3) (0) (1–.46) = 0
(.2) (–20,000) (1–.46) = –2,160
$3,240

In these tables, the figure (1–.46) represents an assumed corporate tax rate of 46 percent so that the expected value figures are reduced by the amount of the tax. Where the outcome is a loss, however, the ability to use that loss to shelter other income from tax reduces the actual loss by the amount of the tax savings of 46 percent. Thus, the value of the loss to Company A is reduced by the amount of the tax rate which is accomplished in the table by multiplying the loss by (1–.46). It is this fact, that Corporation A's loss is reduced by 46 percent while Corporation B's loss is not reduced at all, that results in the dif-

come creates an obvious tax incentive in favor of diversification at the company rather than the shareholder level, and in favor of existing as opposed to new firms. Campisano & Romano, *Recouping Losses: The Case for Full Loss Offsets,* 76 Nw.U.L. Rev. 709, 719–22 (1981), demonstrate this effect by considering the value of a risky project to two bidders, Corporation A which has a certainty of future earnings, and Corporation B which has been formed for the purpose of engaging in this project and whose only revenue would come from the project. If the project has a 50 percent chance of a $20,000 profit, a 20 percent chance of losing $20,000 and a 30 percent chance of breaking even, the after-tax expected value of the project to the two companies is as follows:

Corporation B

(.5) ($20,000) (1–.46) = $5,400
(.3) (0) (1–.46) = 0
(.2) (–4,000) (1) = –4,000
$1,400

ference in their respective valuations of the project.

This disparity leads Campisano & Romano to favor not limiting the transfer of an NOL but, rather, providing a refundable credit for an NOL that would eliminate the disparity in value necessary to make transferability an issue at all.

[73] This would be the case in a taxable stock acquisition where no §338 election was filed, whether or not the acquiring company sought to file returns on a consolidated basis. See Reg. §1.1502–21(c). This result will change if the amendments to

is worth more to the acquiring company than to the target not because
the tax system allows transferability, but because the acquiring company's more skillful management allows the asset to be more efficiently
used.

The question remains as to the amount of behavior affected. In
Chapter Ten we reviewed the empirical and anecdotal evidence concerning the characteristics of acquiring and target companies. There
was no indication that target companies were not profitable, although
there was evidence that they were less profitable than acquiring companies, and the anecdotal evidence indicated that the most desirable
target companies were not losers. This suggests that the ability to
transfer the target company's NOL by acquisition is not a substantial
motivation for acquisition, a conclusion consistent with the fact that
neither Chrysler Corporation nor International Harvester were discussed as likely takeover candidates. A moment's consideration explains why this might be the case. Early Congressional efforts to limit
trafficking in NOL resulted in restrictions which require that, in stock
purchases, the target's business be continued following the acquisition
in order for the NOL to survive. This meant that an acquiring
company had to purchase not only a shell corporation which retained a
tax history, but also had to purchase and continue to operate the very
assets that had resulted in the NOL, and that might well continue to
incur a loss. If this risk is also taken into account, then the calculation
of the value of the NOL to the acquiring company in our previous
example must be altered. If there were a 50/50 chance that the target
company would lose an additional $30,000 after acquisition, then the
calculation becomes:

$$(\$50,000 \times 46\% \times 1) - (30,000 \times 46\% \times .5) = \$16,100$$

The second term of the calculation reflects the probability and after tax
cost of the additional loss to the acquiring company. And while the
possibility of additional losses must be taken into account in determining the value of the NOL to the target company, which also has to
operate the company in order to utilize the NOL, this analysis may be
somewhat different. If the target company is already at a stage where
its shareholders would receive nothing upon liquidation, then their loss
is bounded by zero, and their analysis of future prospects begins to
resemble that of an option.

A final argument concerning the incentives for acquisitions created
by the existence of an NOL turns the analysis around somewhat. Up
to this point we have focused on the acquisition of a target company
with an NOL by a profitable company. What happens to the analysis if
we consider instead the opposite situation. Suppose we have an *acquiring* company with a large NOL, like the reorganized Penn Central
Corporation,[74] that seeks to obtain profitable activities in order to
utilize this tax asset.[75] An initial reaction is that this argument is no

§382 contained in the Tax Reform Act of
1976 ever become effective.

[74] See Terry v. Penn Central Corporation, Chapter Thirteen infra.

[75] As a general principle, the Internal
Revenue Code does not prevent a loss corporation from utilizing its losses through
the acquisition of a profitable business, although this principle will be qualified

different from the others we have canvassed. Profitable activities can be obtained both by acquisition and by internal expansion; a tax incentive in favor of acquisition must favor *that method* of obtaining the profitable activity, not merely obtaining profitable activities generally. More careful consideration, however, suggests that this is a situation where an incentive in favor of acquisitions over internal expansion in fact exists.

The key to the argument is a point that we have already considered in another context: that the value of the tax loss depends on how soon it can be used. If an acquisition will generate immediate earnings, while internal expansion will generate earnings only after, for example, a three year development period, simple present value concepts will cause the value of the acquiring company's NOL to be greater if the acquisition is made because it then can be used more quickly. Even if the investment alternatives are identical in all other respects, that is, the delay in reaching profitability by internal expansion is exactly offset by an increase in anticipated profits, the greater value of the NOL if the acquisition is made results in the sought after incentive. To be sure, the argument depends on the empirical assertion that acquisitions can result in more immediate profits than internal expansion, but that hardly seems counter-intuitive.

We are left again, however, with the question of how much behavior this incentive really explains. And again, although empirical evidence is lacking, one cannot avoid the feeling that there is less there than meets the eye.

3. Summary

Taking the variety of arguments considered as a whole, there seems to be strong evidence that the extent to which tax incentives provide a motivation for acquisitions has been substantially overstated. Although there are situations where particular acquisitions may be explained by tax factors, and also situations where there appears to be a systematic tax bias in favor of acquisitions as opposed to alternative methods of achieving a substantive goal—as with close corporations and methods of exploiting an NOL by a loss company—they do not seem to explain a large portion of the overall acquisition phenomenon.[76]

somewhat if and when the amendments to §382 contained in the Tax Reform Act of 1976 go into effect. See B. Bittker & J. Eustice, supra, at ¶ 16.03.

[76] For an extension of the arguments considered here, especially the development of alternative methods by which a corporation may increase the value of its NOL without an acquisition, see R. Gilson, M. Scholes & M. Wolfson, *Taxation and the Dynamics of Corporate Control: The Uncertain Case for Tax Motivated Acquisitions*, Stanford Law School Law and Economics Working Paper No. 24 (January, 1986).

PART III.   CORPORATE LAW PLANNING CONSIDERATIONS

The examination in Part II of possible explanations for why companies make acquisitions did not for the most part require drawing distinctions between different methods by which corporate acquisitions can be carried out. Our attention centered on the preconditions for and subsequent impact of the transaction; the mechanics of the acquisition itself were treated essentially as a black box. The focus of Part III, dealing with corporate law planning considerations, and Part IV, dealing with non-corporate law concerns, is on understanding what determines the size and shape of the box. These matters loom particularly large for business lawyers if only because determining the box's architectural specifications is traditionally considered a business lawyer's major role.

Of course, were there but a single technique by which an acquisition could be accomplished, the inquiry would be trivial. Only the existence of a choice creates the opportunity to *plan*—to select among future alternatives in order to maximize predetermined goals. But choice alone is insufficient to justify expenditures for planning. As should be clear from Parts I and II, one would not expect the desirability of an acquisition to turn on the mechanical form chosen to accomplish it *unless* collateral consequences attach to the selection of the form. The planner's task then is to choose the form which imposes the fewest undesirable collateral consequences but that otherwise leaves unaltered the substance of the transaction. And it is precisely because the substance of a commercial transaction can be cast in a myriad of forms without altering its economic reality, that most regulatory systems—whose jurisdictional boundaries and actual requirements are commonly expressed in terms of transactional form rather than substantive effect—act as an invitation to the business lawyer to maximize the client's interests by selecting a transactional form that minimizes regulatory intrusion.[1] As was stressed in Chapter One A, the inevitable result is a regulatory eternal triangle. Efforts by the objects of regulation to structure transactions so that their form falls outside the literal terms of the regulation, and responsive efforts by regulators to cast a wider net,[2] are mediated by courts which, applying such tools as

[1] Cf. Deutsch, *The Mysteries of Corporate Law: A Response to Brudney and Chirlstein*, 88 Yale L.J. 235, 237 (1978) (correspondence) ("[T]he clearer and more uniform a rule is, the more likely it is to be regarded as a formality that can justifiably be manipulated so long as compliance with its explicit formulation is maintained!").

[2] A good example of the length to which regulators occasionally go is IRC §338(i), added by the Tax Reform and Fiscal Responsibility Act of 1984, which is intended to back up §338's effort to prevent selectiv-

ity with respect to basis step up and recapture recognition in nonreorganization acquisitions:

> The Secretary [of Treasury] shall prescribe such regulations as may be necessary to ensure that the purposes of this section to require consistency of treatment of stock and asset purchases with respect to a target corporation and its target affiliates (whether by treating all of them as stock purchases and all of them as asset purchases) may not be circumvented through the use of any

form versus substance [3] and step transaction [4] doctrine in tax law and the de facto merger doctrine in acquisitions,[5] must determine whether to credit the form in which the planner has cast the transaction, or to vindicate the public policy reflected in the regulation by expanding its reach beyond its language.[6]

This is the public ordering aspect of private transactions [7] in which the business lawyer's role is to cast a transaction in the form that minimizes the cost to the client of the variety of complex and conflicting regulatory systems that may touch on the transaction. In this Part we begin a survey of the regulatory influences on the structure of corporate acquisitions by examining the corporate law considerations bearing on transaction structure and conduct. Chapter Thirteen considers the mechanics of alternative acquisition techniques, the collateral consequences associated with each, and the character of courts' responses to planning efforts to minimize undesirable collateral consequences without altering the substance of the transaction. Chapter Fourteen then moves on to the special corporate law concerns of the target company and Chapter Fifteen to the corporate law concerns of the acquiring company. Both serve to flesh out the contours of the planning choice among alternative acquisition techniques by demonstrating the consequences of the choice. Part IV then expands the inquiry to encompass non-corporate law planning considerations.

provision of law or regulations (including the consolidated return regulations).

[3] See, e.g., Isenberg, *Musings on Form and Substance in Taxation,* 49 U.Chi.L. Rev. 859 (1982); Chirlstein, *Learned Hand's Contribution to the Law of Tax Avoidance,* 77 Yale L.J. 440 (1968).

[4] See, e.g., Paul & Zimet, *Step Transactions,* in Selected Studies in Federal Taxation 200 (2d Ser.1938).

[5] See Chapter Thirteen E.

[6] For an excellent effort at linking substantive policy to the decision whether to disregard the form in which planners have cast a transaction, see Chirlstein & Lopata, *Recent Developments in the Step Transaction Doctrine,* 60 Taxes 970 (1982).

[7] See Chapter One A for differentiation of the public and private ordering aspects of private transactions.

CHAPTER THIRTEEN. THE MECHANICS OF ALTERNATIVE ACQUISITION TECHNIQUES

In this Chapter we examine the menu of alternative acquisition techniques from which the transaction planner may choose and the mechanics—of voting rights, appraisal rights and the like—associated with each. What shapes the planner's problem is that each of the alternatives has different requirements and different burdens despite the fact that, absent those differences in process, the outcome of all the alternatives is essentially the same. The result of this tension between form and substance has been a continuing debate concerning when the planner's selection of the form of the transaction will be disregarded in favor of a recharacterization which triggers requirements the court thinks somehow more appropriate.

In the acquisition area, the terms of this debate have centered on the idea of equivalence. Once past the initial barrier of statutory language, the theory is that like transactions should be treated alike. The task is then to identify those characteristics that identify whether transactions which differ in form are equivalent in substance. In the materials that follow, the alternative techniques provided by typical statutes, and their corporate law collateral consequences are described. The judicial and scholarly debate concerning equivalency is next considered and an effort made to apply the analysis developed in Parts I and II to determining both the bases on which equivalence might be determined, and the limits of the concept itself.

A. Merger

1. The Statute

Delaware General Corporation Law

§ 251. Merger or consolidation of domestic corporations

(a) Any two or more corporations existing under the laws of this State may merge into a single corporation, which may be any one of the constituent corporations or may consolidate into a new corporation formed by the consolidation, pursuant to an agreement of merger or consolidation, as the case may be, complying and approved in accordance with this section.

(b) The board of directors of each corporation which desires to merge or consolidate shall adopt a resolution approving an agreement of merger or consolidation. The agreement shall state: (1) the terms and conditions of the merger or consolidation; (2) the mode of carrying the same into effect; (3) such amendments or changes in the certificate of incorporation of the surviving corporation as are desired to be effected by the merger or consolidation, or, if no such amendments or changes are desired, a statement that the certificate of incorporation of

501

one of the constituent corporations shall be the certificate of incorporation of the surviving or resulting corporation; (4) the manner of converting the shares of each of the constituent corporations into shares or other securities of the corporation surviving or resulting from the merger or consolidation, and, if any shares of any of the constituent corporations are not to be converted solely into shares or other securities of the surviving or resulting corporation, the cash, property, rights or securities of any other corporation which the holders of such shares are to receive in exchange for, or upon conversion of such shares and the surrender of the certificates evidencing them, which cash, property, rights or securities of any other corporation may be in addition to or in lieu of shares or other securities of the surviving or resulting corporation; and (5) such other details or provisions as are deemed desirable, including, without limiting the generality of the foregoing, a provision for the payment of cash in lieu of the issuance or recognition of fractional shares, interests or rights, or for any other arrangement with respect thereto. * * *

(c) The agreement required by subsection (b) shall be submitted to the stockholders of each constituent corporation at an annual or special meeting thereof for the purpose of acting on the agreement. Due notice of the time, place and purpose of the meeting shall be mailed to each holder of stock, whether voting or nonvoting, of the corporation at his address as it appears on the records of the corporation, at least 20 days prior to the date of the meeting. At the meeting the agreement shall be considered and a vote taken for its adoption or rejection. If a majority of the outstanding stock of the corporation entitled to vote thereon shall be voted for the adoption of the agreement, that fact shall be certified on the agreement by the secretary or assistant secretary of the corporation. If the agreement shall be so adopted and certified by each constituent corporation it shall then * * * [be] filed, and shall become effective. * * *

(d) Any agreement of merger or consolidation may contain a provision that at any time prior to the filing of the agreement with the Secretary of State, the agreement may be terminated by the board of directors of any constituent corporation notwithstanding approval of the agreement by the stockholders of all or any of the constituent corporations.

* * *

(f) Notwithstanding the requirements of subsection (c), unless required by its certificate of incorporation, no vote of stockholders of a constituent corporation surviving a merger shall be necessary to authorize a merger if (1) the agreement of merger does not amend in any respect the certificate of incorporation of such constituent corporation, (2) each share of stock of such constituent corporation outstanding immediately prior to the effective date of the merger is to be an identical outstanding or treasury share of the surviving corporation after the effective date of the merger, and (3) either no shares of common stock of the surviving corporation and no shares, securities or obligations convertible into such stock are to be issued or delivered under the plan of merger, or the authorized unissued shares or the treasury shares of common stock of the surviving corporation to be issued or delivered under the plan of merger plus those initially issuable upon conversion of any other shares, securities or obligations to be issued or delivered under such plan do not exceed 20 percent of the shares of common stock of such constituent corporation outstanding immediately prior to the effective date of the merger. * * *

§ 259. Status, rights, liabilities, etc., of constituent and surviving or resulting corporations following merger or consolidation

(a) When any merger or consolidation shall have become effective under this chapter, for all purposes of the laws of this State the separate existence of all the constituent corporations, or of all such constituent corporations except the one into which the other or others of such constituent corporations have been merged, as the case may be, shall cease and the constituent corporations shall become a new corporation, or be merged into one of such corporations, as the case may be, possessing all the rights, privileges, powers and franchises as well of a public as of a private nature, and being subject to all the restrictions, disabilities and duties of each of such corporations so merged or consolidated; and all and singular, the rights, privileges, powers and franchises of each of said corporations, and all property, real, personal and mixed, and all debts due to any of said constituent corporations on whatever account, as well for stock subscriptions as all other things in action or belonging to each of such corporations shall be vested in the corporation surviving or resulting from such merger or consolidation; and all property, rights, privileges, powers and franchises, and all and every other interest shall be thereafter as effectually the property of the surviving or resulting corporation as they were of the several and respective constituent corporations, and the title to any real estate vested by deed or otherwise, under the laws of this State, in any of such constituent corporations, shall not revert or be in any way impaired by reason of this chapter; but all rights of creditors and all liens upon any property of any of said constituent corporations shall be preserved unimpaired, and all debts, liabilities and duties of the respective constituent corporations shall thenceforth attach to said surviving or resulting corporation, and may be enforced against it to the same extent as if said debts, liabilities and duties had been incurred or contracted by it.

* * *

§ 261. Effect of merger upon pending actions

Any action or proceeding, whether civil, criminal or administrative, pending by or against any corporation which is a party to a merger or consolidation shall be prosecuted as if such merger or consolidation had not taken place, or the corporation surviving or resulting from such merger or consolidation may be substituted in such action or proceeding.

§ 262.　Appraisal rights

(a) Appraisal rights under this section shall be available only for the shares of any stockholder who has complied with the provisions of subsection (b) of this section and has neither voted in favor of the merger nor consented thereto in writing. * * * When used in this section, the word "stockholder" means a holder of record of stock in a stock corporation and also a member of record of a non-stock corporation; the words "stock" and "share" mean and include what is ordinarily meant by those words and also membership or membership interest of a member of a non-stock corporation.

(b) Appraisal rights under this section shall be determined as follows:

(1) If a proposed merger or consolidation for which appraisal rights are provided under this section is to be submitted for approval at a meeting of stockholders, the corporation, not less than 20 days prior to the meeting, shall notify each of its stockholders entitled to such appraisal rights that appraisal rights are available for any or all of the shares of the constituent corporations, and shall include in such notice a copy of this section. Each stockholder electing to demand the appraisal of his shares under this section shall deliver to the corporation, before the taking of the vote on the merger or consolidation, a written demand for appraisal of his shares. Such demand will be sufficient if it reasonably informs the corporation of the identity of the stockholder and that the stockholder intends thereby to demand the appraisal of his shares; provided, however, that such demand must be in addition to and separate from any proxy or vote against the merger. Within 10 days after the effective date of such merger or consolidation, the surviving corporation shall notify each stockholder of each constituent corporation who has complied with the provisions of this subsection and has not voted in favor of or consented to the merger or consolidation of the date that the merger or consolidation has become effective.
* * *

(k) Unless otherwise provided in the certificate of incorporation of the corporation issuing such shares, no appraisal rights under this section shall be available for the shares of any class or series of stock which, at the record date fixed to determine the stockholders entitled to receive notice of and to vote at the meeting of stockholders to act upon the agreement of merger or consolidation, were either (1) listed on a national securities exchange or (2) held of record by more than 2,000 stockholders. No appraisal rights shall be available for any shares of stock of the constituent corporation surviving a merger if the merger did not require for its approval the vote of the stockholders of the surviving corporation as provided in subsection (f) of section 251 of this Title.

(l) Notwithstanding the provisions of subsection (k) of this section, appraisal rights under this section shall be available for the shares of any class or series of stock of a constituent corporation if the holders thereof are required by the terms of an agreement of merger or consolidation pursuant to section 251 or section 252 of this Title to accept for such stock anything except (1) shares of stock of the corporation surviving or resulting from such merger or consolidation; (2) shares of stock of any other corporation which at the effective date of the merger or consolidation will be either listed on a national securities exchange or held of record by more than 2,000 stockholders; (3) cash in lieu of fractional shares of the corporations described in clauses (1) and (2); or (4) any combination of the [consideration described in clauses (1), (2), or (3)].

$$\diamond$$

2.   Variations in Who Votes, How Many Votes Are Needed, How the Votes Are Counted, and Who Gets to Complain

The Delaware statute is typical of the merger provisions of all jurisdictions in the character of the transaction contemplated. Following approval by the boards of directors and shareholders of the affected corporations, the actual combination—the act of "merger"—occurs instantaneously upon the filing of a document with the designated state official.[1] At one moment two corporations exist; at the next, the acquiring corporation has enveloped the target, like an amoeba engulfing its prey, and has succeeded to all of its properties, rights and other attributes. The technique has significant advantages in reducing the transaction costs associated with the mechanical aspects of accomplishing an acquisition. If all of a target company's assets and liabilities had to be separately transferred to or assumed by the acquiring company, each (or at least each class) would require a separate document of transfer or assumption and, for example, multiple filings for different recording systems (e.g., U.C.C., real property records, the F.A.A. Aircraft Records Branch) would be necessary. The effect of statutory provisions like Delaware §259 is to substitute a single document, the merger agreement, for the flood of paper that would otherwise be required to effect the transaction.

Despite the similarity of the transaction contemplated by the statutory provisions in each state, there is substantial variation among jurisdictions as to the precise steps necessary to authorize the statutory transfer. Of principal interest are differences in the percentage vote necessary to authorize the transaction, which corporate constituents are allowed to vote, how the votes are counted, and who gets to complain.

How many votes are needed? As late as 1886 the leading corporate law treatise stated unequivocally that business combinations required the *unanimous* consent of shareholders. 2V. Morawetz, *A Treatise on the Law of Private Corporations* 908–09 (2d ed. 1886).[2] But by the close of the first third of the 20th century, allowing such a fundamental

---

[1] See Del.Gen.Corp. Code §259(a) *supra*; see generally B. Fox & E. Fox, *Corporate Acquisitions and Mergers* §24.02 (1981) (exhaustive survey of jurisdictions).

[2] The history of the shift from unanimous consent to approval by a specified percentage of shareholders is traced in detail in Carney, *Fundamental Corporate*

change by less than unanimous vote had become the norm.[3] The precise percentage required still varies substantially among jurisdictions. Prior to the 1960's, the great majority of states required a two-thirds vote. This pattern was broken in 1962 when the Model Business Corporation Act reduced the required percentage approval to a majority. 2 ABA–ALI Model Bus. Corp. Act Ann.2d. §73, ¶ 2. Many of the major commercial jurisdictions then followed suit, Delaware reducing the vote requirement in its statute from two-thirds to a majority in 1967. E. Folk, *The Delaware General Corporation Law* 318 (1972). See Cal.Corp. Code §§152, 1201; Mich.Comp. Laws Ann. §§ 450, 1703; Pa. Stat.Ann. §902, and N.J.Stat.Ann. §14A:10–3. New York, however, still maintains a two-thirds requirement. New York Bus. Corp. Act §903.[4]

The balance of interests reflected in the reduction of the percentage approval required to authorize a merger to a majority was described by the American Bar Association's Committee on Corporate Laws, the group responsible for ongoing revision of the Model Act, as follows:

> Because of the fundamental change in corporate existence that may result from a merger or consolidation, it was thought that sound reasons exist for requiring more than a mere majority of voting shares for the imposition of such an alteration on the minority. The extent to which the margin may be increased above that point involves a balancing with the need to prevent a small minority from arbitrarily blocking the wishes of a substantial majority. Accordingly, the Model Act originally adopted two-thirds as a point for attaining reasonable balance. However, in 1969 an amendment reduced the required vote from two-thirds to a majority in recognition of the generally prevailing view that * * * a minority should not be permitted to block the wishes of the majority.[5]

2 ABA–ALI Model Bus.Corp. Act Ann.2d §73 ¶ 2 (1971). The concept underlying the balance struck in the Model Act seems fairly straightforward. Stated generally, the idea is that the percentage chosen should be one that facilitates a transaction that, although perhaps not beneficial to *all* shareholders, represents an overall *net* gain (taking all shareholder gains and losses into account). A majority requirement satisfies this concern based on the simple assumption that if more shareholders favor a transaction than oppose it, the gains to those

Changes, Minority Shareholders, and Business Purposes, 1980 Am.B. Foundation Res. J. 69.

[3] Id. at 94.

[4] A compilation of the voting requirements of different jurisdictions can be found in B. Fox & E. Fox, supra, at §24.02. See also Schulman & Schneck, *Shareholders' Voting and Appraisal Rights in Corporate Acquisition Transactions*, 38 Bus.Law. 1529 (1983).

In recent years a number of states have amended their corporate statutes to require a higher percentage approval when the acquiring company already holds a substantial percentage of the target's stock. Because these provisions were uniformly enacted as a response to judicial invalidation of state efforts at strengthening target management's hand in a hostile takeover, they will be considered in Chapter Sixteen B. concerning state securities law regulation of tender offers.

[5] Note that the drafters had already lost sight of the direction of historical change. It seems quite clear that the movement was from unanimity down rather than from a majority up.

favoring it will exceed the losses to those opposing it and, therefore, the transaction will result in a net gain.

This shift from unanimity to a majority requirement, motivated by a desire to prevent a minority from blocking otherwise beneficial transactions, has a parallel in economic theory. Stated more generally, the problem is to specify a test which, if satisfied, would guarantee that we would be better off as a result of taking a particular action rather than not taking it. Two formulations of such a standard are relevant here. One, Pareto Optimality, states that we can be certain an action will improve our collective well-being if no one is made worse off by it, but at least one person's position is improved. An alternative, Kaldor-Hicks Efficiency, asserts that an action is beneficial, even if some individuals are made worse off, so long as those who are made better off gain enough that they could (although they are not required to) compensate the losers and still end up ahead.[6]

The shift from unanimity to majority rule for approval of corporate combinations can be seen as a shift from a rule requiring Pareto Optimality to one requiring only Kaldor-Hicks Efficiency. If unanimity is required, we can be relatively certain that anyone whom the transaction would make worse off would object, thereby assuring that any transaction which received unanimous approval was Pareto Optimal. A majority rule, in contrast, requires only that the winners outnumber the losers, thereby, at least on the surface, satisfying the Kaldor-Hicks criteria. The move to a majority rule is thus justified as one which allows transactions which increase the overall welfare even though a minority is injured as a result.[7]

While he does not disagree with a move from a Pareto to a Kaldor-Hicks measure of efficiency, Professor Carney, in the previously mentioned article, in effect takes issue with the assertion that a majority requirement for corporate combinations really assures that the Kaldor-Hicks standard is satisfied.

CARNEY, FUNDAMENTAL CORPORATE CHANGES, MINORITY SHAREHOLDERS, AND BUSINESS PURPOSES

1980 Am.B.Found. Research J. 110–18.

The long and painful development of the law of fundamental corporate changes * * * has been designed to assure majority rule and to provide methods for bringing the minority along or at least making certain that they do not frustrate the desires of the majority. To conclude that these transactions, accomplished over the objections of

[6] The distinctions between Pareto Optimality and Kaldor-Hicks Efficiency are discussed in an accessible fashion in Coleman, *Efficiency, Utility and Wealth Maximization,* 8 Hofstra L.Rev. 509 (1980).

[7] This formulation assumes that shareholders are acting in good faith. If, however, some shareholders act strategically, that is, hold out their vote unless they receive more than a proportionate share of the benefit, then a reduction in the percentage necessary for action also reduces the costs of the decision-making process itself. See generally J. Buchanan & G. Tullock, *The Calculus of Consent* 43–62 (1965).

some minority stockholders, have all of the benefits of freely bargained exchanges involves an unwarranted leap.

What is true of individual welfare may not be true of group welfare where exchanges are between groups rather than individuals. * * *

When a group makes a collective decision binding all its members to engage in an exchange, and does so by majority rule, it is possible that large losses to the minority may exceed, in the aggregate, the gains to the majority.

* * *

Any test that attempts to weigh costs and benefits in a fundamental corporate change or to assure that some benefits of substance do exist faces a difficult if not impossible task. To determine whether a fundamental change is "efficient" in the sense of enhancing aggregate welfare, we must determine aggregate shareholder gains and losses. In voluntary transactions, where control is transferred entirely through stock purchases, we can be certain that both sides agree that there are gains involved. In a successful tender offer for control, we can be certain that there are gains to the new controlling shareholder or that gains are anticipated after completion of the squeeze-out merger. In a competitive market, these gains should produce a competitive rate of return for the acquiring corporation. If it were possible to draw an accurate supply curve for the selling shareholders * * * it would be possible to measure the gains of this group by determining the difference between the tender offer price, which is normally at a premium over the market, and the supply curve. Some approximation of this is possible, since we do know the terminal points on the segment of the supply curve represented by the shares tendered.[183] The premium paid to this group of shareholders represents the identifiable benefit to this group over the marginal benefit that otherwise would have persuaded them to sell their shares.

Against these gains to the majority who have tendered we must balance the losses suffered by the minority who declined to tender at the

---

[183] If, for example, the acquiring corporation begins owning no shares of the target, the point of zero supply or at least of a minimal supply (in the short run) is represented by the current market price: (It is possible that a gradual process might lead to an accumulation of a significant number of shares through market transactions carefully disguised, but this is a longer run view of the supply curve.) The other end of the segment of the supply curve we can chart is represented by the percentage of shares tendered in response to the invitation for tenders at what is presumably a premium over the market price that prevailed prior to the tender offer regardless of whether the acquiring corporation accepts all of them. If not all are accepted at that price, a surplus exists. Diagrammed below are two supply curves, illustrating the premium paid, represented by the difference between the supply curve and the tender offer price. In the second example (fig. 1b) where not all shares are taken, we know something about the supply curve beyond the number of shares purchased. Thus, in fig. 1a, we know the share of the curve SS up to the tender offer price but not beyond: the rest is merely an extension of the earlier segment. We do not, of course, know the precise slope of the curve between these points. In fig. 1b, we know the general shape of the curve SS up to the tender offer price, even though the acquiring corporation did not take all of the shares tendered, but took only 51 percent of the total shares. This suggests either a miscalculation of the supply curve by the acquiring corporation or intervening events that caused a greater tender than required by the acquiring corporation. The latter could be the endorsement of the offer by target management, adverse business developments for the target in the interim, or a failure of target management to mount an effective defense against the tender offer.

offering price. In many cases they may be squeezed out at the tender offer price.[184] Since no market transactions are involved, any measure of the magnitude of their losses, based on the supply curve, is purely speculative. These shareholders suffer a loss when their shares are taken at a price they did not freely consent to. We can only speculate about the slope of the supply curve beyond the point of the last voluntary transaction and thus cannot measure the magnitude of the difference between the price demanded by these shareholders in the aggregate and the price received, which would determine the amount of the losses to be balanced against the gains to other participants in the exchange, both sellers and buyers. Supply curves can be determined only by revealed behavior of market participants. To the extent that the curve involves persons unwilling to sell at current market prices, descriptions of such curves are speculation, albeit more or less informed.

In a situation where a minority's shares are acquired in involuntary transactions, such as those involved in squeeze-outs, whether aggregate gains exceed aggregate losses depends on (1) whether the slope of the supply curve is relatively less elastic beyond the point of the last voluntary sale than over the balance of its length and (2) the relative length of each section.[185] Put another way, if the last dissenters exhibit

Fig. 1 (note 183)

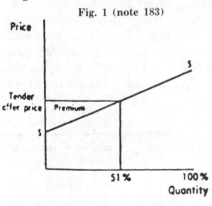

a

[185] This can be illustrated in two ways. First, we must look at the slope of the supply curve. To the extent it slopes more steeply upward as we reach higher quantities of stock, the potential losses to dissenters will be greater. In fig. 1a below, constant elasticity of supply at all levels, illustrated arbitrarily here by a constant slope of the supply curve, indicates that a 51 percent approval of a squeeze-out merger will result in benefits only slightly exceeding costs. Put another way, the premium to voluntary sellers slightly exceeds the losses to forced sellers. In fig. 1b, the supply curve slopes more steeply at higher quantities and illustrates that the losses to forced sellers will be greater at the same price, and losses will exceed gains to sellers.

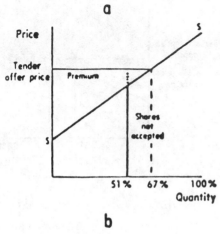

b

[D6592]

Fig. 1 (note 185)

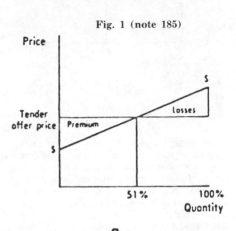

a

a high degree of inelasticity in their behavior, and if they hold a relatively large number of shares (say 49 percent), their losses may exceed the gains of a great many willing sellers who are relatively indifferent about whether to hold this particular stock.

    * * * [Thus,] the only certain guarantee of efficient mergers [191] is unanimous consent of the shareholders, but this has been rejected as impractical or impossible. The higher the percentage vote required, the more certain we are that aggregate shareholder gains are likely to exceed losses. The English Company Act's requirement of approval by holders of 90 percent of the shares within a limited time provides far greater assurance than our own system that only efficient acquisitions will proceed.

    ◆

    The problem that Professor Carney describes is one that students of the branch of microeconomics known as "public choice" have long recognized as inherent in any voting system that requires less than unanimous approval but does not account for different intensities among voters. Carney sets that problem in an acquisition context by questioning the relative slope of the supply curve for a target's shares above the acquisition price. The problem is that if 49% of the voters feel more strongly about an issue than the remaining 51%, there will be a net loss in welfare as a result of the transaction if a majority rule applies. See generally Mueller, *Public Choice: A Survey*, 14 J.Econ.Lit. 395 (1976), J. Buchanan & G. Tullock, *The Calculus of Consent* 131–46 (1962).

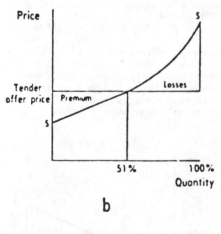

b

[D7301]

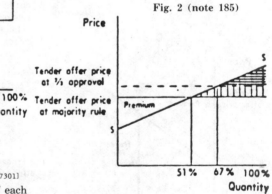

curred under a rule of two-thirds consent to fundamental changes, while the larger lightly shaded area represents the losses under a rule of simple majority approval.

    * * *

Fig. 2 (note 185)

[D7302]

    The second factor is the length of each segment of the supply curve, which reflects the percentage voting requirement of state law for fundamental changes. Thus a rule of simple majority approval for fundamental changes increases the number of shares whose holders may suffer losses, which is illustrated by fig. 2 below.

    The heavily cross-hatched area represents the smaller losses that would be in-

    * * *

[191] It should be emphasized that an efficient merger is one in which there is gain for the aggregate of all shareholders, when the gain and loss of each shareholder is measured individually.

One approach to this problem would be to allow vote buying or selling, thereby allowing those who feel strongly about the result to acquire enough votes to match their intensity. If capital markets were perfect, the existence of a market for the corporation's shares might serve this purpose and eliminate Professor Carney's concern. Then a minority who valued the corporation's shares at a price sufficiently greater than the majority that a transaction favored by the majority would result in a net overall loss would simply purchase the shares held by the majority (or a sufficient number to block the transaction under the applicable decision rule). See Fama, *The Effect of a Firm's Investment and Financing Decisions on the Welfare of its Security Holders*, 68 Amer.Econ.Rev. 272, 282–83 (1978). The difficulty, however, is that transaction costs and problems associated with collective action by the minority, such as free riding, make it quite unlikely that this corrective action would occur with sufficient frequency to ease Professor Carney's concern. The question is then whether any other forces operate to minimize the problem.

Some guidance on this point can be derived from the financial theory considered in Part I. The capital asset pricing model states that all shareholders will value the target's stock based only on the systematic risk associated with its return. Individual circumstances will not enter into the determination of stock price, the separation theorem relegating such concerns to a determination of the content of the individual's portfolio. See Chapter Four B supra. If that is correct, i.e., that the shareholders view a corporation's stock as only a fungible stream of income with a particular risk, then under the assumptions on which the CAPM is based there is no reason to expect that different shareholders will value the target's stock differently. Therefore, the problem posed by Professor Carney will not exist. In other words, the supply curve will be horizontal. Cast in terms of public choice, the implication is that all voters hold their views with equal intensity, in which event public choice theorists have demonstrated that a majority decisional rule is efficient in Kaldor-Hicks terms. Mueller, supra, at 402–03.

The persuasiveness of this response to Professor Carney diminishes, however, when it is recalled that one of the assumptions on which the CAPM is based is that there are homogeneous expectations, i.e., that all stockholders have the same beliefs about the future risk and return characteristics of the corporation. See Chapter Four C supra. What if shareholders have *different* expectations about the future? How does this alter analysis of a majority requirement in mergers?

The answer seems to depend on whether a shareholder can expect his or her beliefs about the future to be systematically more accurate than those of other shareholders. Only in that event does a greater than majority rule, which reduces below 50% the likelihood that a shareholder will be in the minority, seem desirable. Put differently, only if a shareholder's views are systematically more accurate than the majority's will a greater than majority rule make the shareholder better off. See Gilson, *The Case Against Shark Repellant Amendments:*

Structural Limitations on the Enabling Concept, 34 Stan.L.Rev. 775, 822–31 (1982); Mueller, supra, at 402. At this point, data concerning the Efficient Capital Market Hypothesis become relevant. The semi-strong form of the ECMH suggests that none of us can expect to outperform the majority over time; hence, we should all prefer a majority voting requirement.

Are there circumstances where capital market theory fails to justify the efficiency of a majority vote requirement? For example, what happens to reliance on the separation theorem to eliminate the problem of different intensities if there is a single dominant shareholder? See Gilson, *The Case Against Shark Repellant Amendments,* supra, at 833–34.[8] What kind of a voting rule might then be appropriate? Similarly, what happens to our justification if the market is not strong-form efficient and some shareholders have inside information?

Who gets to vote? Whatever the percentage approval required by the particular statute, the question of who gets to vote on the issue remains. Do shares that are nonvoting for other matters, as is commonly the case with preferred stock, nonetheless get to vote on a merger? The major commercial jurisdictions do not allow preferred or other nonvoting shares to vote on a merger, although there are notable exceptions. E.g., Cal.Corp. Code §§152, 1201, Conn.Gen.Stat. §33–366(b). Other states do provide the right to vote if the effect of the transaction is to change the rights, preferences or privileges of preferred shares in a way that would require their approval if attempted by means other than a merger. For example, if the effect of a merger will be to reduce the priorities of the preferred stock because of differences between the terms of the stock to be received and that held before the merger, the preferred stockholders will be allowed to vote. ABA–ALI Model Bus.Corp. Act Ann.2d §73(b); Wis.Stat.Ann. §180.64(2).

The assumption underlying this approach is that so long as the terms of the preferred are not altered, the transaction will not affect holders of preferred and, therefore, they do not need voting rights to protect themselves. But while this assures that the preferred's position will not be nominally altered, might they nonetheless be adversely affected? The value of the preferred depends not only on its return—presumably the preferred dividend rate is protected by the statute from alteration without consent—but also on the systematic risk associated with those returns. If the effect of the merger is to cause the preferred stockholders to receive identical stock, but in a corporation having

---

[8] This formulation raises the problem of under what circumstances a shareholder would prefer to have the firm deviate from profit-maximization. Among other circumstances, if some shareholders' welfare is affected in their nonshareholder capacities, because the firm's decisions alter consumer prices or because some shareholders are subject to externalities produced by the firm, there will not be unanimity concerning the firm's investment decisions even with homogeneous expectations, because different shareholders will be affected dif-

ferently. See Milne, *The Firm's Objective Function as a Collective Choice Problem,* 37 Public Choice 473 (1981). For more detailed development of the circumstances formally necessary for unanimity, see DeAngelo, *Competition and Unanimity,* 71 Am.Econ.Rev. 18 (1981); Grossman & Stiglitz, *Stockholder Unanimity in Making Production and Financial Decisions,* 94 Q.J. Econ. 543 (1980); Baron, *Investment Policy, Optimality, and the Mean-Variance Model,* 34 J.Fin. 207 (1979) (review article).

greater systematic risk, then the value of what they have received is lower than that which they have given up, a danger not protected against by the typical corporate statute.

The problem may be seen more clearly when posed in terms of the strategic considerations bearing on how to divide the price to be paid for the target company between common and preferred stockholders. If the amount that the acquiring company will pay for the entire company is fixed, then it is to the advantage of the common to negotiate the terms of the transaction so that the value of the preferred is reduced, and, to that extent, the value of the common is increased. If this transfer of value from the preferred to the common is accomplished by increasing the systematic risk associated with the preferred, under typical statutes the *nominally* equivalent terms of the consideration given the preferred vest exclusive voting power in the common. Ironically, this gives the sole approval right to precisely those who have an incentive to favor themselves at the expense of the preferred. Cf. Dalton v. American Investment Co., 490 A.2d 574 (Del.Ch.1985) (transaction structured to avoid sharing premium with preferred shareholders).

This problem is identical to that facing debenture holders of the target company who also have no statutory right to vote on the transaction.[9] To protect themselves against the risk that the common stockholders will structure the transaction to their own advantage, debt holders typically secure a contractual right to prior approval of an acquisition—in substance a contractual class vote. See Smith & Warner, *On Financial Contracting: An Analysis of Bond Covenants,* 7 J.Fin. Econ. 117 (1979). Similarly, in the majority of states where preferred stockholders do not have a statutory right to vote on a merger, the preferred stock contract typically grants a class vote in an acquisition. See Buxbaum, *Preferred Stock—Law and Draftsmanship,* 42 Calif.L. Rev. 243 (1954).

A comparatively recent statutory trend extends to common shareholders the approach of eliminating the requirement of a shareholder vote when the transaction does not alter the shareholders' position. California is the leading commercial jurisdiction to adopt this extension, Cal.Corp. Code §1201(b) and (d), combining to eliminate the need for a vote of acquiring company shareholders in a merger if the rights, preferences and privileges of the shareholders are not changed and if those shareholders own immediately after the transaction shares of the acquiring company representing more than five-sixths of the voting power of the acquiring company.[10] The California pattern was followed in the recently proposed revision of the Model Business Corporation Act, except that the trigger for eliminating voting rights is that the

[9] No state affirmatively grants debt holders the right to vote, and only a few states even allow such a provision as an option. See, e.g., Cal.Corp. Code §204(a)(7).

[10] The California statute was patterned after the New York Stock Exchange requirement of a shareholder vote as a prerequisite to listing shares issued in an acquisition if the issued shares represent an increase in outstanding shares of approximately 18.5 percent or more. New York Stock Exchange, Company Manual A–283–284 (1978).

acquiring company not issue in the merger shares amounting to more than twenty percent of the number of shares outstanding before the merger.[11]

How the votes are counted. Once otherwise nonvoting shares are given the right to vote on a proposed merger, a question arises as to how to count their votes. Are their votes simply added to the total of common stockholder votes in determining whether the statutory percentage is met or, as the preceding discussion assumed, are they given a class vote? That is, in addition to approval by the common, must the statutory percentage of preferred stockholders also approve the transaction? Typically, if non-voting shares are allowed to vote on a merger transaction, the vote contemplated is a class vote, although in New York, for example, preferred stockholders are both given a class vote and have their votes counted along with the common in determining whether the overall statutory percentage is required.

The discussion in the preceding paragraph focused on the number that appears in the numerator in determining whether the statutory percentage for approval is satisfied. Another question concerning the manner in which the votes are counted is how to determine the proper denominator. In a majority approval jurisdiction, for example, is the required number of shares 51% of the shares represented and voting at the meeting, or the almost certainly higher number, 51% of all outstanding shares eligible to vote whether actually voting or not? This distinction is drawn in the California Corporations Code where some actions, like mergers, require the "approval of the outstanding shares," defined in §152 as a "majority of the outstanding shares entitled to vote," while others, such as election of directors, require only "approval of the shareholders," defined in §153 as a "majority of the shares represented and voting at a duly held meeting." Typically, the higher number is required for mergers, see Delaware General Corporations Law §251(c), supra, although Tennessee, for example, allows approval either by a majority of shares eligible to vote or by two-thirds of the shares represented at the meeting. Tenn.Code Ann. §48–907.

Who gets to complain? Except where voting rights are eliminated for all acquiring company shareholders (as in California or New Jersey when fewer than a specified number of shares are issued in the merger), or for all target company shareholders (as in a short form merger, see Chapter Fifteen, infra), appraisal rights are typically limited to those having voting rights. If one's interests are sufficiently affected to require a vote, then it seems to be assumed that those on the losing end of the vote may require appraisal rights. Conversely, if voting is unnecessary to protect a particular class of stockholders, then so are appraisal rights. The wisdom of this assumption, which extends beyond mergers to other acquisition techniques, is also considered in Chapter Fifteen.

[11] Model Business Corporations Act § 11.03(g) (Exposure Draft 1983). See also N.J.Stat.Ann. §§14A:10–3, 14A:11–1 (West Supp. 1982–83); Ohio Rev.Code Ann. §§1701.78(D)(3), 1701.83(A), (B), (D) (1978); R.I.Gen. Laws §§7–1.1–67, 7–1.1–73 (1969 & Supp. 1982).

B. Sale of Substantially All Assets

1. The Statutes

Delaware General Corporation Law

§ 271. Sale, lease or exchange of assets; consideration; procedure

(a) Every corporation may at any meeting of its board of directors sell, lease, or exchange all or substantially all of its property and assets, including its good will and its corporate franchises, upon such terms and conditions and for such consideration, which may consist in whole or in part of money or other property, including shares of stock in, and/or other securities of, any other corporation or corporations, as its board of directors deems expedient and for the best interests of the corporation, when and as authorized by a resolution adopted by a majority of the outstanding stock of the corporation entitled to vote thereon at a meeting thereof duly called upon at least 20 days notice. The notice of the meeting shall state that such a resolution will be considered.

Model Business Corporation Act

§ 79. Sale of Assets Other Than in Regular Course of Business

A sale, lease, exchange, or other disposition of all, or substantially all, the property and assets, with or without the good will, of a corporation, if not in the usual and regular course of its business, may be made upon such terms and conditions and for such consideration, which may consist in whole or in part of cash or other property, including shares, obligations or other securities of any other corporation, domestic or foreign, as may be authorized in the following manner:

(a) The board of directors shall adopt a resolution recommending such sale, lease, exchange, or other disposition and directing the submission thereof to a vote at a meeting of shareholders, which may be either an annual or a special meeting.

(b) Written notice shall be given to each shareholder of record, whether or not entitled to vote at such meeting, not less than twenty days before such meeting, in the manner provided in this Act for the giving of notice of meetings of shareholders, and, whether the meeting be an annual or a special meeting, shall state that the purpose, or one of the purposes is to consider the proposed sale, lease, exchange, or other disposition.

(c) At such meeting the shareholders may authorize such sale, lease, exchange, or other disposition and may fix, or may authorize the board of directors to fix, any or all of the terms and conditions thereof and the consideration to be received by the corporation therefor. Such authorization shall require the affirmative vote of the holders of a majority of the shares of the corporation entitled to vote thereon, unless any class of shares is entitled to vote thereon as a class, in which event such authorization shall require the affirmative vote of the holders of a majority of the shares of each class of shares entitled to vote as a class thereon and of the total shares entitled to vote thereon.

(d) After such authorization by a vote of shareholders, the board of directors nevertheless, in its discretion, may abandon such sale, lease, exchange, or other disposition of assets, subject to the rights of third parties under any contracts relating thereto, without further action or approval by shareholders.

§ 80. Right of Shareholders to Dissent and Obtain Payment for Shares

(a) Any shareholder of a corporation shall have the right to dissent from, and to obtain payment for his shares in the event of, any of the following corporate actions:

* * *

(2) Any sale or exchange of all or substantially all of the property and assets of the corporation not made in the usual or regular course of its business, including a sale in dissolution, but not including a sale pursuant to an order of a court having jurisdiction in the premises or a sale for cash on terms requiring that all or substantially all of the net proceeds of sale be distributed to the shareholders in accordance with their respective interests within one year after the date of sale;

* * *

2. What Is "Substantially All"?

GIMBEL v. SIGNAL COMPANIES, INC.

Court of Chancery of Delaware, 1974.
316 A.2d 599.

QUILLEN, Chancellor:

This action was commenced on December 24, 1973 by plaintiff, a stockholder of the Signal Companies, Inc. ("Signal"). The complaint seeks, among other things, injunctive relief to prevent the consummation of the pending sale by Signal to Burmah Oil Incorporated ("Burmah") of all of the outstanding capital stock of Signal Oil and Gas Company ("Signal Oil"), a wholly-owned subsidiary of Signal. The effective sale price exceeds 480 million dollars.[1] The sale was approved at a special meeting of the Board of Directors of Signal held on December 21, 1973.

* * * It should be noted that the plaintiff is part of an investment group which has some 2,400,000 shares representing 12% of the outstanding stock of signal.

* * *

Count 1 of the complaint asserts that * * * the proposed sale requires authorization by the majority of the outstanding stock of Signal pursuant to 8 Del.C. § 271(a).

---

[1] The purchase price consists of 420 million dollars cash to be paid by Burmah at the closing, the cancellation of approximately 60 million dollars in indebtedness of Signal to Signal Oil, and the transfer by Signal Oil to Signal of a 4¾% net profits interest in the unexplored portion of Block 211/18 in the North Sea.

* * *

A sale of less than all or substantially all assets is not covered by negative implication from the statute.[3]

It is important to note in the first instance that the statute does not speak of a requirement of shareholder approval simply because an independent, important branch of a corporate business is being sold. The plaintiff cites several non-Delaware cases for the proposition that shareholder approval of such a sale is required. But that is not the language of our statute. Similarly, it is not our law that shareholder approval is required upon every "major" restructuring of the corporation. Again, it is not necessary to go beyond the statute. The statute requires shareholder approval upon the sale of "all or substantially all" of the corporation's assets. That is the sole test to be applied. While it is true that test does not lend itself to a strict mathematical standard to be applied in every case, the qualitative factor can be defined to some degree notwithstanding the limited Delaware authority. But the definition must begin with and ultimately necessarily relate to our statutory language.

In interpreting the statute the plaintiff relies on Philadelphia National Bank v. B.S.F. Co., 41 Del.Ch. 509, 199 A.2d 557 (Ch.1964), rev'd on other grounds, 42 Del.Ch. 106, 204 A.2d 746 (Supr.Ct.1964). In that case, B.S.F. Company owned stock in two corporations. It sold its stock in one of the corporations, and retained the stock in the other corporation. The Court found that the stock sold was the principal asset B.S.F. Company had available for sale and that the value of the stock retained was declining. The Court rejected the defendant's contention that the stock sold represented only 47.4% of consolidated assets, and looked to the actual value of the stock sold. On this basis, the Court held that the stock constituted at least 75% of the total assets and the sale of the stock was a sale of substantially all assets.

But two things must be noted about the *Philadelphia National Bank* case. First, even though shareholder approval was obtained under § 271, the case did not arise under § 271 but under an Indenture limiting the activities of B.S.F. for creditor financial security purposes. On appeal, Chief Justice Wolcott was careful to state the following:

> "We are of the opinion that this question is not necessarily to be answered by references to the general law concerning the sale of assets by a corporation. The question before us is the narrow one of what particular language of a contract means and is to be answered in terms of what the parties were intending to guard against or to insure."

42 Del.Ch. at 111–112, 204 A.2d at 750.

[3] * * *

The predecessor statute was evidently originally enacted in 1916 in response to Chancellor Curtis' statement of the common law rule in Butler v. New Keystone Copper Co., 10 Del.Ch. 371, 377, 93 A. 380, 383 (Ch. 1915):

"The general rule as to commercial corporations seems to be settled that neither the directors nor the stockholders of a prosperous, going concern have the power to sell all, or substantially all, the property of the company if the holder of a single share dissent."

Secondly, the *Philadelphia National Bank* case dealt with the sale of the company's only substantial income producing asset.

The key language in the Court of Chancery opinion in *Philadelphia National Bank* is the suggestion that "the critical factor in determining the character of a sale of assets is generally considered not the amount of property sold but whether the sale is in fact an unusual transaction or one made in the regular course of business of the seller." (41 Del.Ch. at 515, 199 A.2d at 561). Professor Folk suggests from the opinion that "the statute would be inapplicable if the assets sale is 'one made in furtherance of express corporate objects in the ordinary and regular course of the business'" (referring to language in 41 Del.Ch. at 516, 199 A.2d at 561).

But any "ordinary and regular course of the business" test in this context obviously is not intended to limit the directors to customary daily business activities. Indeed, a question concerning the statute would not arise unless the transaction was somewhat out of the ordinary. While it is true that a transaction in the ordinary course of business does not require shareholder approval, the converse is not true. Every transaction out of normal routine does not necessarily require shareholder approval. The unusual nature of the transaction must strike at the heart of the corporate existence and purpose.

* * * It is in this sense that the "unusual transaction" judgment is to be made and the statute's applicability determined. If the sale is of assets quantitatively vital to the operation of the corporation and is out of the ordinary and substantially affects the existence and purpose of the corporation, then it is beyond the power of the Board of Directors. With these guidelines, I turn to Signal and the transaction in this case.

Signal or its predecessor was incorporated in the oil business in 1922. But, beginning in 1952, Signal diversified its interests. In 1952, Signal acquired a substantial stock interest in American President lines. From 1957 to 1962 Signal was the sole owner of Laura Scudders, a nationwide snack food business. In 1964, Signal acquired Garrett Corporation which is engaged in the aircraft, aerospace, and uranium enrichment business. In 1967, Signal acquired Mack Trucks, Inc., which is engaged in the manufacture and sale of trucks and related equipment. Also in 1968, the oil and gas business was transferred to a separate division and later in 1970 to the Signal Oil subsidiary. Since 1967, Signal has made acquisition of or formed substantial companies none of which are involved or related with the oil and gas industry. * * * As indicated previously, the oil and gas production development of Signal's business is now carried on by Signal Oil, the sale of the stock of which is an issue in this lawsuit.

According to figures published in Signal's last annual report (1972) and the latest quarterly report (September 30, 1973) and certain other internal financial information, the following tables can be constructed.

SIGNAL'S REVENUES (in millions)

	9 Mos. Ended September 30, 1973	December 31, 1972	1971
Truck manufacturing	$655.9	$712.7	$552.5
Aerospace and industrial	407.1	478.2	448.0
Oil and gas	185.8	267.2	314.1
Other	16.4	14.4	14.0

SIGNAL'S PRE–TAX EARNINGS (in millions)

	9 Mos. Ended September 30, 1973	December 31, 1972	1971
Truck manufacturing	$ 55.8	$ 65.5	$ 36.4
Aerospace and industrial	20.7	21.5	19.5
Oil and gas	10.1	12.8	9.9

SIGNAL'S ASSETS (in millions)

	9 Mos. Ended September 30, 1973	December 31, 1972	1971
Truck manufacturing	$581.4	$506.5	$450.4
Aerospace and industrial	365.2	351.1	331.5
Oil and gas	376.2	368.3	369.9
Other	113.1	102.0	121.6

SIGNAL'S NET WORTH (in millions)

	9 Mos. Ended September 30, 1973	December 31, 1972	1971
Truck manufacturing	$295.0	$269.7	$234.6
Aerospace and industrial	163.5	152.2	139.6
Oil and gas	280.5	273.2	254.4
Other	(55.7)	(42.1)	(2.0)

Based on the company's figures, Signal Oil represents only about 26% of the total assets of Signal. While Signal Oil represents 41% of Signal's total net worth, it produces only about 15% of Signal's revenues and earnings. Moreover, the additional tables shown in Signal's brief * * * are also interesting in demonstrating the low rate of return which has been realized recently from the oil and gas operation.

PRE–TAX DOLLAR RETURN ON VALUE OF ASSETS

9 Mos. Ended

	September 30, 1973	1972	1971
Truck manufacturing	12.8%	12.9%	8.1%
Aerospace and industrial	7.5	6.1	5.9
Oil and gas	3.6	3.5	2.7

PRE–TAX DOLLAR RETURN ON NET WORTH

9 Mos. Ended

	September 30, 1973	1972	1971
Truck manufacturing	25.1%	24.2%	15.5%
Aerospace and industrial	16.8	14.1	14.0
Oil and gas	4.8	4.7	3.9

While it is true, based on the experience of the Signal-Burmah transaction and the record in this lawsuit, that Signal Oil is more valuable than shown by the company's books, even if, as plaintiff suggests in his brief, the $761,000,000 value attached to Signal Oil's properties by the plaintiff's expert Paul V. Keyser, Jr., were substituted as the asset figure, the oil and gas properties would still constitute less than half the value of Signal's total assets. Thus, from a straight quantative approach, I agree with Signal's position that the sale to Burmah does not constitute a sale of "all or substantially all" of Signal's assets.

In addition, if the character of the transaction is examined, the plaintiff's position is also weak. While it is true that Signal's original purpose was oil and gas and while oil and gas is still listed first in the certificate of incorporation, the simple fact is that Signal is now a conglomerate engaged in the aircraft and aerospace business, the manufacture and sale of trucks and related equipment, and other businesses besides oil and gas. The very nature of its business, as it now in fact exists, contemplates the acquisition and disposal of independent branches of its corporate business. Indeed, given the operations since 1952, it can be said that such acquisitions and dispositions have become part of the ordinary course of business. The facts that the oil and gas business was historically first and that authorization for such operations are listed first in the certificate do not prohibit disposal of such interest.

* * *

It is perhaps true, as plaintiff has argued, that the advent of multi-business corporations has in one sense emasculated § 271 since one business may be sold without shareholder approval when other substantial businesses are retained. But it is one thing for a corporation to evolve over a period of years into a multi-business corporation, the operations of which include the purchase and sale of whole businesses, and another for a single business corporation by a one transaction revolution to sell the entire means of operating its business in exchange for money or a separate business. In the former situation, the processes of corporate democracy customarily have had the opportunity to restrain or otherwise control over a period of years. Thus, there is a chance for some shareholder participation. The Signal development illustrates the difference. For example, when Signal, itself formerly called Signal Oil and Gas Company, changed its name in 1968, it was for the announced "need for a new name appropriate to the broadly diversified activities of Signal's multi-industry complex." * * *

The situation is also dramatically illustrated financially in this very case. Independent of the contract with Burmah, the affidavit of Signal's Board Chairman shows that over $200,000,000 of Signal Oil's refining and marketing assets have been sold in the past five years. This activity, prior to the sale at issue here, in itself constitutes a major restructuring of the corporate structure.

I conclude that measured quantatively and qualitatively, the sale of the stock of Signal Oil by Signal to Burmah does not constitute a sale of "all or substantially all" of Signal's assets.

* * *

KATZ v. BREGMAN
Court of Chancery of Delaware, 1981.
431 A.2d 1274.

MARVEL, Chancellor:

The complaint herein seeks the entry of an order preliminarily enjoining the proposed sale of the Canadian assets of Plant Industries, Inc. to Vulcan Industrial Packaging, Ltd., the plaintiff Hyman Katz allegedly being the owner of approximately 170,000 shares of common stock of the defendant Plant Industries, Inc. * * *

The complaint alleges that during the last six months of 1980 the board of directors of Plant Industries, Inc., under the guidance of the individual defendant Robert B. Bregman, the present chief executive officer of such corporation, embarked on a course of action which resulted in the disposal of several unprofitable subsidiaries of the corporate defendant located in the United States, namely Louisiana Foliage Inc., a horticultural business, Sunaid Food Products, Inc., a Florida packaging business, and Plant Industries (Texas), Inc., a business concerned with the manufacture of woven synthetic cloth. As a result of these sales Plant Industries, Inc. by the end of 1980 had disposed of a significant part of its unprofitable assets.

* * * Mr. Bregman thereupon proceeded on a course of action designed to dispose of a subsidiary of the corporate defendant known as Plant National (Quebec) Ltd., a business which constitutes Plant Industries, Inc.'s entire business operation in Canada and has allegedly constituted Plant's only income producing facility during the past four years. The professed principal purpose of such proposed sale is to raise needed cash and thus improve Plant's balance sheets. And while interest in purchasing the corporate defendant's Canadian plant was thereafter evinced not only by Vulcan Industrial Packaging, Ltd. but also by Universal Drum Reconditioning Co., which latter corporation originally undertook to match or approximate and recently to top

Vulcan's bid, a formal contract was entered into between Plant Industries, Inc. and Vulcan on April 2, 1981 for the purchase and sale of Plant National (Quebec) despite the constantly increasing bids for the same property being made by Universal. One reason advanced by Plant's management for declining to negotiate with Universal is that a firm undertaking having been entered into with Vulcan that the board of directors of Plant may not legally or ethically negotiate with Universal.

* * *

In seeking injunctive relief, * * * plaintiff relies on * * * 8 Del.C. § 271 to the effect that a decision of a Delaware corporation to sell "all or substantially all of its property and assets * * *" requires not only the approval of such corporation's board of directors but also a resolution adopted by a majority of the oustanding stockholders of the corporation * * *.

Turning to the possible application of 8 Del.C. § 271 to the proposed sale of substantial corporate assets of National to Vulcan, it is stated in Gimbel v. Signal Companies, Inc., as follows:

> "If the sale is of assets quantitatively vital to the operation of the corporation and is out of the ordinary and substantially affects the existence and purpose of the corporation then it is beyond the power of the Board of Directors."

According to Plant's 1980 10K form, it appears that at the end of 1980, Plant's Canadian operations represented 51% of Plant's remaining assets. Defendants also concede that National represents 44.9% of Plant's sales' revenues and 52.4% of its pre-tax net operating income. Furthermore, such report by Plant discloses, in rough figures, that while National made a profit in 1978 of $2,900,000, the profit from the United States businesses in that year was only $770,000. In 1979, the Canadian business profit was $3,500,000 while the loss of the United States businesses was $344,000. Furthermore, in 1980, while the Canadian business profit was $5,300,000, the corporate loss in the United States was $4,500,000. And while these figures may be somewhat distorted by the allocation of overhead expenses and taxes, they are significant. In any event, defendants concede that "* * * National accounted for 34.9% of Plant's pretax income in 1976, 36.9% in 1977, 42% in 1978, 51% in 1979 and 52.4% in 1980."

While in the case of Philadelphia National Bank v. B.S.F. Co., the question of whether or not there had been a proposed sale of substantially all corporate assets was tested by provisions of an indenture agreement covering subordinated debentures, the result was the same as if the provisions of 8 Del.C. § 271 had been applicable, the trial Court stating:

> "While no pertinent Pennsylvania case is cited, the critical factor in determining the character of a sale of assets is generally considered not the amount of property sold but whether the sale is in fact an unusual transaction or one made in the regular course of business of the seller * * *".

In the case at bar, I am first of all satisfied that historically the principal business of Plant Industries, Inc. has not been to buy and sell industrial facilities but rather to manufacture steel drums for use in bulk shipping as well as for the storage of petroleum products, chemicals, food, paint, adhesives and cleaning agents, a business which has been profitably performed by National of Quebec. Furthermore, the proposal, after the sale of National, to embark on the manufacture of plastic drums represents a radical departure from Plant's historically successful line of business, namely steel drums. I therefore conclude that the proposed sale of Plant's Canadian operations, which constitute over 51% of Plant's total assets and in which are generated approximately 45% of Plant's 1980 net sales, would, if consummated, constitute a sale of substantially all of Plant's assets. By way of contrast, the proposed sale of Signal Oil in Gimbel v. Signal Companies, Inc., supra, represented only about 26% of the total assets of Signal Companies, Inc. And while Signal Oil represented 41% of Signal Companies, Inc. total net worth, it generated only about 15% of Signal Companies, Inc. revenue and earnings.

I conclude that because the proposed sale of Plant National (Quebec) Ltd. would, if consummated, constitute a sale of substantially all of the assets of Plant Industries, Inc., as presently constituted, that an injunction should issue preventing the consummation of such sale at least until it has been approved by a majority of the outstanding stockholders of Plant Industries, Inc., entitled to vote at a meeting duly called on at least twenty days' notice.

* * *

♦

Note: Qualitative Gloss on a Quantitative Statute

The problem posed by the construction of statutes like Del. § 271 and Model Act § 79 has both quantitative and qualitative dimensions. Consider first the purely quantitative side. Assuming the statutory phrase "substantially all" is to be given its commonplace meaning—that a specified large percentage, say 75%, 85% or 90% of the company's assets must be sold to trigger the requirement of a shareholder vote—how is the percentage to be calculated? At the most obvious level, is book value the measure, which certainly makes the calculation process easier, or must market value be taken into consideration? Certainly it must have been market value which management had in mind when it determined that the transaction was attractive. At the same time, however, it must be recognized that the computational problems associated with a market value determination are potentially substantial. While the arms-length sales price for the assets may make determination of the numerator, the market value of the assets being sold, straightforward, how is the denominator, the market value of the remaining assets (and liabilities), to be determined? The task essentially involves the reconstruction of the target company's entire balance sheet without the application of the historical cost convention, a problem similar to that presented by efforts to alter financial accounting standards to take into account inflation and changing prices. For a sense of the extreme complexity of the issues presented and the range of possible solutions, see Siegel, *Accounting and Inflation: An Analysis and A Proposal,* 29 U.C.L.A.L.Rev. 271 (1981). Which figures were used in Gimbel v. Signal Companies, Inc., and Katz v. Bregman? In this regard, how do you evaluate the following advice offered by three experienced practitioners:

> [A] guideline derived from the Delaware cases on the subject, which gives some useful information, is that if the sale involves more than 75 percent of the balance sheet assets, at market value, then a court probably would consider the sale to be of substantially all the assets, but if the sale involves less than 26% of the assets, courts probably would not consider the sale to be of substantially all of the assets, notwithstanding qualitative significance. In between these quantitative limits a careful analysis of the qualitative significance of the sale to the corporation must be made.

Herzel, Sherck & Colling, *Sales and Acquisitions of Divisions,* 5 Corp.L. Rev. 3, 25 (1982).

That advice raises the second problem of construction, which, as the quoted passage suggests, covers all the interesting cases. Whatever percentage is chosen to correspond to the statutory phrase "substantially all," and however asset values are measured in determining whether the chosen percentage has been met, the much more difficult problem posed by the statute remains. Is there a qualitative aspect to the inquiry? [12] Suppose that a company sold substantially all of its operating assets but retained sufficient liquid assets so that a strictly quantitative measure was not met. See Stiles v. Aluminum Products Co., 338 Ill.App. 48, 86 N.E.2d 887 (1949) (retention of liquid assets amounting to approximately 35% of total assets); Campbell v. Vose, 515 F.2d 256 (10th Cir. 1975) (retention of liquid assets amounting to approximately 66% of total assets).

Is the question any harder when a multidivision company sells a division? To be sure, Gimbel v. Signal Companies, Inc., speaks to the sale of one division among many in a situation where the company has become a conglomerate. What of the sale of one of two divisions? While 50% is certainly not "substantially all" in commonplace quantitative terms, Professor Melvin Eisenberg has argued, in effect, that this language reflects not a legislative determination of the primacy of the quantitative measure, but merely the historical fact that, at the time this type of statutory provision was first enacted, single-purpose corporations were the rule. M. Eisenberg, *The Structure of the Corporation* 259 n. 15 (1976). But if the quantitative aspect of the statute is the result of historical coincidence, what is the statute's real concern? The task then becomes one of identifying the non-quantitative circum-

---

[12] In Gimbel v. Signal Companies, Inc., the court stressed that the definition of "all or substantially all" must "begin with and ultimately relate to our statutory language." How does the court in Katz v. Bregman deal with the fact that the assets sold represented only fifty-one percent of the company's assets? Isn't there a major linguistic difference between "substantially all" and "a majority"?

stances which make shareholder approval a necessary protection. And posing the question in this way pushes the issue back yet another step: Against what must shareholders be protected? At what problem is the statute really directed?

Professor Eisenberg has recently approached this issue by trying to identify the appropriate allocation of responsibilities between shareholders and the board of directors. If the function of the board of directors is to "manage the business" of the corporation, as the typical corporations statute provides,[13] then dispositions of significant corporate businesses "should be shareholder matters: they work a significant change in the structure of the enterprise; they involve investment rather than purely business skills—an evaluation of whether the business in question is worth the offering price; they occur relatively infrequently in the life of the corporation; and they are likely to take a relatively long time to consummate in any event." M. Eisenberg, supra at 260.

The thrust of Professor Eisenberg's distinction is that a corporate divestiture is an investment rather than a business decision and, thus, appropriately a shareholder rather than purely a director determination. The dichotomy suggested—business decisions for directors, investment decisions for shareholders—has an appealing logic and simplicity. Shareholders, after all, are by definition investors; directors, in contrast, are selected by shareholders to supervise the running of the business. Nevertheless, the explanation seems flawed in two critical aspects. Most importantly, the assumption that one can meaningfully distinguish between business skills and investment skills, or business decisions and investment decisions, in an acquisition context simply seems wrong. To be sure, selling a business is like selling stock in that it involves a determination of the value of what is sold. But the sale of an entire business also involves, for example, determination of the synergy to be lost, the cost of restructuring existing businesses, and the tax treatment of the sale at the corporate level, all of which seem much more like business decisions than investment decisions. In any event, they are matters which we hardly believe shareholders are *better* at evaluating than managers. This is not to say, at least as yet, that shareholders should not vote on them, but only that one cannot base a determination to allow them to vote on the premise that these decisions are inherently ones belonging to shareholders because of their special competence.

The second difficulty with Professor Eisenberg's business skills/ investment skills dichotomy is that the statute itself belies the construction. While the entire quotation applies with equal force to *acquisitions* of a significant corporate business, the typical corporate statute does not require shareholder approval of the cash acquisition of a substantial business even if approval would be required for disposition of the same business thereafter.

Ultimately the problem with Professor Eisenberg's construction is that it never offers an explanation of the function that the sharehold-

---

[13] E.g., Del.Code Ann. tit. 8, § 141; N.Y.Bus.Corp.Law § 701; Cal.Corp.Code Model Business Corporation Act Ann. § 35; § 300.

ers' vote is intended to serve. As a result, it no more provides a way of determining which transactions, although not meeting a purely quantitative measure of "substantially all," still should have shareholder approval than does the simple fiat of the court in Katz v. Bregman.[14] Considered in this way, it should not be surprising that construction of the phrase "substantially all" in the sale of assets section raises precisely the same problem as the de facto merger doctrine raises with respect to a broader range of transactions. That is, by what principle can we identify those transactions whose substantive characteristics should require a shareholder vote even though their formal terms, because too small a percentage of all assets are to be sold or because not cast in the form of a statutory merger, fall outside the language of the statute. Consideration of potential solutions to the broader problem must await discussion of the de facto merger doctrine in Section E of this Chapter.

3. Note: Variations on Who Votes, How Many Votes Are Needed, How the Votes Are Counted, and Who Gets to Complain

The advantage of a statutory merger is its reduction in transaction costs. By the filing of a single document, all assets of the target are transferred to the acquiring company, which simultaneously assumes all of the target company's liabilities, and the target company itself blinks out of existence at the same time and without further ado. While the same result can be accomplished by means of an asset acquisition, each step must be separately accomplished. Documents of transfer must be prepared for all assets; written assumptions must cover all liabilities; and, following these transfers, the target company typically must be formally dissolved pursuant to the dissolution procedures specified in the corporate statute, and its remaining assets—the consideration received in the transaction and any assets not sold in the transaction—distributed to its shareholders.

Thus far a statutory merger seems vastly more desirable than an asset acquisition. Why go through the multiple steps required in an asset acquisition when a statutory merger accomplishes the same result with so much less effort? When the desired results of the transactions are the same, the merger is preferable; however, the attractiveness of an asset acquisition becomes more apparent when the desired result is *not* the same as a merger.

---

[14] The court in Katz v. Bregman seems to conclude that the shift in the company's business from manufacturing steel drums to manufacturing plastic drums was what made the sale "quantitatively vital" as required by Gimbel v. Signal Companies, Inc. Is the notion that the drum business differs so significantly depending on the material from which the drum is manufactured, or was it that, because the company was moving out of its only profitable business into a related, but untried one, the decision was a very risky one? If the latter is the critical element, then what happens to the quantitative side of the test? After all, it is not difficult to imagine that business changes as significant as that in Katz v. Bregman could be implemented by borrowing funds and retrofitting existing manufacturing machinery, thereby requiring the sale of a much smaller percentage of assets. Is the sale still "quantitatively vital"? If so, is there a trade-off between the riskiness of the business decision and the percentage of assets that must be sold?

The ease with which assets are transferred, liabilities assumed, and the target company eliminated in a statutory merger comes at the price of flexibility. Only if it is desired that *all* assets be transferred, *all* liabilities assumed, *and* the target company dissolved, does a statutory merger provide the intended result. An asset acquisition, in contrast, provides the flexibility to alter each of these aspects, albeit at the cost of increased transaction costs. If the acquisition of less than all of the assets is desirable, or if certain liabilities, like contingent or as yet unasserted claims, are not to be assumed, or if, perhaps for tax reasons, it is desirable to keep the target in existence, an asset acquisition may be preferable.[15] Indeed, it is precisely this flexibility—to transfer assets *not* subject to liabilities—that results in asset acquisitions being scrutinized under such doctrines as successor liability in tort or labor law. See Chapter Eighteen, infra.

As with mergers, there is substantial variation among the states with respect to the statutory procedure for authorizing asset aquisitions. Additionally, the statutory requirements for asset acquisitions typically vary in significant respects from those for mergers.

How many votes are needed? As a general rule, the shareholder vote required to approve the sale of substantially all of a company's assets is the same as required for approval of a statutory merger, although Delaware required only a majority vote for an asset sale even prior to the 1967 amendment which reduced the approval required for mergers from two-thirds to a majority. As with mergers, such transactions at common law required unanimous consent. See Carney, supra; Gimbel v. Signal Companies, Inc., supra, at n. 3.

Who gets to vote and how the votes are counted. The issues raised by participation by nonvoting shares and the need for class voting in asset acquisitions are virtually identical to those raised in the context of a statutory merger. A distinction drawn by the California Corporations Code, however, is worth noting. While class voting for all shares, voting and nonvoting, is generally required, Cal.Corp.Code § 1201, the requirement of a class vote and the enfranchising of otherwise nonvoting shares is eliminated when the consideration to be received is cash or debt securities which are adequately secured and which have a maturity date of five years or less. Cal.Corp.Code §§ 181, 1001.[16] Why should the form of consideration alter the need for protection against a decision made solely by the common? To be sure, because they receive cash or short-term debt, the nonvoting shareholders are not forced to become shareholders in a different enterprise as would be the case if the consideration in the transaction were stock in the acquiring corporation, but the danger of a transfer of wealth from nonvoting share-

---

[15] That is not to say that pre-merger planning may not allow similar results to be achieved even though the final step will be a statutory merger. For example, if certain assets are not to be acquired, they can be transferred to another corporation in anticipation of the merger. See generally Handler, *Variations on a Theme: The Disposition of Unwanted Assets,* 35 Tax L.Rev. 389 (1980). Note, however, that not all flexibility can be recovered and, in any event, the machinations necessary quickly begin to erode the transaction cost advantage of the merger technique.

[16] The referenced sections of the California Corporations Code are reproduced in Section E.3. of this Chapter, infra.

holders to common shareholders remains, particularly since, as discussed infra, appraisal rights are also eliminated. Moreover, if the concern is only with nonvoting shareholders being locked in, rather than with their being ripped off, could not the exception be extended to stock consideration so long as a public market for it existed?

Despite the substantial similarities in approach, statutory treatment of an asset acquisition raises one critical question about the relevant electorate not posed by the treatment of mergers. In most jurisdictions, shareholder approval of an asset acquisition is required only for the selling corporation. Unlike in a merger, there is no involvement of the acquiring corporation's shareholders.[17] This distinction prompts much of the controversy over the de facto merger doctrine considered in Section E of this Chapter.

Who gets to object? As with mergers, the typical statutory pattern allows dissenter's rights in asset acquisitions only to those who have the right to vote on the transaction. The result, however, is quite different than in mergers; because shareholders of the acquiring company have no vote, they also lose the appraisal rights they would have had in the merger. Additionally, there are some significant differences in the way asset acquisitions are treated. Most important, the Delaware General Corporation Law does not grant appraisal rights even to shareholders of the target company in an asset acquisition, another distinction between mergers and sales of assets which has fueled controversy over the de facto merger doctrine.[18] The Model Act also restricts appraisal rights in asset acquisitions. Section 80(a)(2) eliminates appraisal rights—but not voting rights—in connection with a sale of assets where the consideration is cash and the net proceeds are required to be distributed within one year, and some states provide similar exceptions.[19] The California Corporations Code goes somewhat further in this direction by eliminating appraisal rights where the consideration is either cash *or* adequately secured debt securities with maturities of five years or less, and imposes no requirement that the proceeds be distributed. The elimination of appraisal rights seems even more puzzling than the elimination of voting rights because appraisal rights directly concern whether the amount received is fair.

C. Triangular Transactions

NOTE, THREE–PARTY MERGERS: THE FOURTH FORM OF CORPORATE ACQUISITION
57 Va.L.Rev. 1242 (1971).

* * *

A straight three-party merger involves a parent corporation, the acquirer; its subsidiary, which may be a shell formed for the purpose of

---

[17] Cal.Corp.Code § 1200(a) and New York Stock Exchange Company Manual A–284 are the principal exceptions and are discussed in Section E.3. of this Chapter, infra.

[18] A few other states follow Delaware's example. See D.C.Code Ann. §§ 29–373, –

375 (1981); Hawaii Rev.Stat. §§ 461–33, 417–19 (1976 & Supp.1982); Kan.Stat.Ann. 17–6712, –6801 (1981); Nev.Rev.Stat. 78.505, .565 (1979).

[19] See, e.g., Ariz.Rev.Stat.Ann. § 10–080.A.2 (1977); N.Y.Bus.Corp.Law § 910(a) (1)(B) (McKinney Supp.1983).

completing the acquisition, and capitalized solely with the stock of the parent; and a target corporation, the corporation to be acquired. Using the stock of the parent as consideration the basic merger is consummated between the subsidiary and the target, with the subsidiary surviving.

The 1967 revision of the Delaware Corporation Law greatly facilitated the use of the three-party merger. An amendment to section 251(b) permitted a party to a merger to use the stock or securities of a corporation not a party to the merger as consideration. Other states have followed suit. * * * The effect of these revisions is to allow a subsidiary to participate in a statutory merger using the stock of its parent as consideration.

* * *

TRADITIONAL FORMS OF ACQUISITION V. THREE-PARTY MERGERS

Two-party Merger v. Three-party Merger

For purposes of avoiding recognition of taxable gain, the statutory merger, or A reorganization, is the most advantageous form of corporate acquisition. As long as continuity of interest requirements are satisfied, the [Internal Revenue] Code places few limits on the types of consideration that may be used in a tax free merger. In contrast, the Code places severe restrictions on the types of consideration that the parties may give in stock or asset acquisitions. Only in A reorganizations (statutory mergers) can the parties give appreciable amounts of [nonvoting stock] in consideration for the acquisition.

Beyond tax considerations, there are other advantages of the merger form. In a merger, the surviving corporation obtains one hundred percent control of the acquired corporation. There is no problem with continuing minority interest. The directors of the survivor are thus given greater flexibility in their actions vis-a-vis the acquired corporation.

The transfer of assets by operation of law is perhaps the most advantageous aspect of the merger form, but the concurrent transfer of liabilities can be very dangerous, especially if the acquired company has unknown or contingent liabilities. In traditional two-party mergers, there is no way for the acquiring, or surviving corporation to avoid assuming these liabilities. Therefore, before the advent of the three-party merger, when the acquiring corporation felt behooved to protect itself from potential liability, it had to abandon the merger form and resort to stock or asset acquisitions which were treated more harshly by the Internal Revenue Code.

If, however, a statutory merger can be consummated between a wholly owned subsidiary of an acquirer-parent and a target, the acquirer-parent can gain control of the target without incurring separate liability for its debts. Thus, by utilizing the three-party merger technique, the acquirer can avoid a major disadvantage of the traditional merger form, while maintaining the favorable tax treatment accorded mergers.

A more important problem with the traditional merger form is that statutes normally require that proposed mergers be approved by vote of the [acquiring company's] shareholders, and that those who oppose the plan be given appraisal rights. The necessity of submitting a plan to shareholders for approval is always inconvenient, but rarely fatal to an acquisition. The prospect of having to buy out shareholders who oppose the acquisition, on the other hand, can cause the entire transaction to be aborted. Especially when the merging corporations are illiquid, the opposition of even a small minority of one party's shareholders may have a profound effect. In order to avoid this unpleasant aspect of the traditional merger form, parties were often forced into stock acquisitions * * * or asset acquisitions * * *.* Now, by using the three-party merger technique, the impact of voting and appraisal requirements can be substantially mitigated in a merger, thus obviating the need to resort to stock or asset acquisitions. In a three-party merger, the shareholders of the acquirer-parent are denied voting and appraisal rights, since the parent-acquirer is the only shareholder of the merging subsidiary capable of voting and dissenting. The parent-acquirer's shareholders have no voice in the merger transaction.

Of course, the shareholders of the acquired corporation still have to approve the merger and may demand appraisal rights if they dissent. But the use of the three-party form will effectively deny voting and appraisal rights to the shareholders of one of the substantive parties to the acquisition.

* * *

A final possible disadvantage of the traditional merger form is that the acquired corporation must disappear. Only one of the two corporations can continue to exist. The amalgamation of corporate entities may foster such unpleasant results as demands for new labor contracts, lowered management and employee morale, and impaired customer relations. By utilizing the three-party merger technique, these problems may be avoided, since the subsidiary may be kept in existence. Moreover, as will be seen below, when it is desirable to maintain the corporate existence of the target corporation, a reverse three-party merger may be used. Of course, the parties might have chosen another acquisition form, the stock acquisition (B reorganization) to achieve the desired result—continued separate existence of the acquiring and acquired corporations—but the tax limitations on the type of consideration which can be used in a stock acquisition would impair management's flexibility in working out the plan. The three-party merger is thus the superior acquisition form.

Stock Acquisition v. Reverse Three-party Merger

* * * Several of the disadvantages of the merger form can be avoided by the use of the stock acquisition * * * technique. For example, no shareholder vote is required when the acquiring corporation goes directly to the shareholders of the target corporation to buy their stock. [T]hose shareholders will effectively have voting rights

---

* Recall that no vote of the acquiring company's shareholders is necessary to au- thorize the acquisition of either the stock or assets of a target company. [Ed.]

[through deciding whether to sell their stock]. But the shareholders of neither corporation will have appraisal rights. Another advantage of the stock acquisition technique is that the target corporation may remain in existence. A final advantage is that the acquiring corporation generally will not assume the liabilities of the acquired corporation.

But the stock acquisition technique is not without substantial disadvantages, the foremost of which are the inflexible consideration requirements imposed by the Internal Revenue Code, if tax free status is to be maintained. To qualify for non-recognition treatment as a B reorganization, the acquirer must receive an 80 percent or more controlling stock interest in the acquired corporation. Consideration is limited to voting stock, and extreme care must be taken to avoid boot in any form; otherwise, the reorganization may be disqualified. The strict requirements of the B reorganization contrast sharply with the flexibility available in A reorganizations. Thus, where tax considerations prevail, the stock acquisition runs a poor second to mergers.

Another important disadvantage of the stock acquisition technique is that complete control is nearly impossible to obtain, since at least a few of the acquired corporation's shareholders are likely not to sell out. At best, it may take an unjustified premium to induce the recalcitrant minority to sell. When there is a minority interest in a subsidiary, the parent must deal at arm's length with the subsidiary in intercorporate matters. Here again, the merger form is superior, since no minority remains after a merger.

By reversing the three-party merger technique, all the disadvantages of the stock acquisition technique may be avoided, and most of the advantages may be maintained. In a reverse three-party merger, the subsidiary merely merges into the target. Subsidiary stock held by the parent is converted into target stock, and the parent stock which was funneled through the subsidiary is distributed to the target's shareholders in exchange for their target stock.

After completion of the reverse three-party merger, the parent has complete control of the target. The effect of the transaction is a forced 100 percent stock acquisition, a forced B reorganization. The parent will not be hobbled by fiduciary duty to the subsidiary, since there is no minority interest to affront.

* * *

Asset Acquisition v. Three-party Merger

If substantially all of the assets of the selling corporation are exchanged for voting stock of the acquirer, the acquisition will qualify for tax-deferred treatment as a C reorganization. The consideration that may be exchanged for assets in a C reorganization, however, is limited to voting stock and small amounts of cash and other consideration. While an asset acquisition may be used to achieve a merger result, the more stringent requirements of a C reorganization do not allow the federal tax flexibility permitted by the A reorganization merger or consolidation.

Under state law, a sale of substantially all the assets of a corporation normally requires approval by the seller's shareholders. Several states do not provide appraisal rights for the shareholders of the selling corporation, and voting or appraisal rights for shareholders of an acquiring corporation are rare. The principal disadvantage of the asset acquisition is its cumbersome form. Deeds, contract assignments, and other similar instruments must be executed. If any rights and privileges are nonassignable, the acquisition cannot be completed without consent, and amalgamation via the asset acquisition route may be impossible. Thus, in many situations the transfer of assets by operation of law in a merger may be a practical necessity if the acquisition is to be completed. In these situations the three-party merger technique is the obvious choice, since it avoids many of the problems of the traditional merger.

◆

D. Compulsory Share Exchange

The most recently devised acquisition technique is the compulsory share exchange, added to the Model Business Corporation Act in 1976.[20] Although the Model Act's lead has been followed in a number of jurisdictions,[21] this technique has not been adopted by any major commercial jurisdiction.[22] Professors Schulman and Schenk describe the technique as a simplified alternative to the reverse triangular merger:

> Under this form of acquisition, all shareholders (or shareholders of a particular class of shares) of the acquired company must transfer their shares to the acquiring corporation for the consideration set forth in the plan of exchange. Thus, assuming that the exchange involves all classes of target shares, the target remains alive as a wholly owned subsidiary of the acquiror—precisely the result obtained by a reverse triangular merger. Although the Act requires approval of the plan by the boards of both corporations and grants voting and dissenters' rights to the shareholders of the target, it provides no rights for the acquiror's shareholders.[23]

[20] Model Business Corp.Act.Ann. § 72A (1982). See Committee on Corporate Laws, *Final Changes in the Model Business Corporation Act Revising Sections 63, 74, 76, 77, 80 and Adding a New Section—72–A,* 31 Bus.Law. 1747 (1976).

[21] Schulman & Schenk, supra, at 1532 n. 13, report that the compulsory share exchange has been included in the corporate statutes of the following jurisdictions: Colo.Rev.Stat. 7–7–102.5 (Supp.1982); Idaho Code § 30–1–72A (1980); Md.Corps & Ass'ns Code Ann. § 3–105 (Supp.1982); Mont.Code Ann. 35–1–801(3) (1981); Neb. Rev.Stat. § 21–2071.01 (Cum.Supp.1982); N.H.Rev.Stat.Ann. 293–A: 73 (Supp.1981); Or.Rev.Stat. 57.462 (1981); S.C.Code Ann. § 33–17–25 (Law.Co-op.Supp.1982); Va.

Code § 13.1–69.1 (Supp.1982); Wash.Rev. Code Ann. 23A.20.025 (West Supp.1982); Wyo.Stat.Ann. § 17–1–402.1 (Supp.1982).

[22] Although California Corporations Code § 181 defines an "exchange reorganization," unlike the Model Act technique shareholders of the target company are not bound and the definition serves only to grant shareholders of the *acquiring* company voting and appraisal rights if the number of shares issued in the transaction exceeds one-sixth of the company's outstanding shares prior to the transaction. Cal.Corp.Code §§ 1200, 1201.

[23] Schulman & Schenk, supra, at 1532–33.

One possible explanation for the apparent lack of success of an innovative effort to develop a new acquisition technique illustrates a serious problem confronting drafters of corporation statutes. While the drafters control only the corporation statute, the planners' choice among available acquisition techniques depends on a balance of all regulatory regimes bearing on the transaction. For tax purposes, within which of the definitions of reorganization in IRC § 368(a) would a compulsory share exchange fall? While it seems closest to a B reorganization, it does seem more like a merger in that it is compulsory with respect to the target company shareholders rather than voluntary as in the typical B reorganization. To be sure, there would seem to be little risk that the transaction would be found to fall outside all of the reorganization definitions, but even a very small amount of uncertainty must be balanced against the gains from a less complicated alternative to a reverse triangular merger. How large a saving in transaction costs does the compulsory share exchange really offer? If the savings are not large, and if new techniques carry with them some uncertainty, success-ful reform—successful in the sense that planners choose to use the technique—may be very difficult to accomplish.

E. The De Facto Merger Doctrine

Viewing the choice among alternative acquisition techniques from the perspective of the corporate planner, the assertion of something akin to what has come to be called the de facto merger doctrine was inevitable. A statutory merger provides the most protection to both shareholders and creditors. From the shareholders' point of view, it requires a vote by the shareholders of the acquiring and target compa-nies and grants appraisal rights to both. From the point of view of the creditors of the target company, all of the liabilities of the target company, including those which are unknown, or have not yet accrued, at the time of the transaction, are assumed by the acquiring company as a matter of law. It was predictable that in particular circumstances such protection would be viewed as undesirable by those planning an acquisition transaction, and that if alternative techniques—such as a sale of assets or triangular merger—were available which both avoided them and did not alter the substance of the transaction, an alternative would be chosen. It was equally predictable that in precisely those circumstances when the planners thought it advantageous to eliminate the protection given shareholders and creditors under a statutory merger, those denied the protection would complain. The assertion by creditors that the acquiring company should be deemed to have as-sumed their claims, as would have occurred in a statutory merger but did not under the arguably functionally equivalent technique actually chosen by the planners, is considered in Chapter Eighteen, infra. The claim by shareholders that they are entitled to the very statutory protections which the planners sought to avoid by their selection of the acquisition technique is the traditional province of the de facto merger doctrine and is the subject of our attention here. Invariably the claim reflects an effort made by those disadvantaged by a transaction to recast it in a form, usually a statutory merger, which would have afforded them greater protection, even though the transaction as carried out did not formally fall within the statutory definition of the more protective alternative form.

1. Recharacterization of Statutory Alternatives

a. *Sale of Substantially All Assets*

FARRIS v. GLEN ALDEN CORP.

Supreme Court of Pennsylvania, 1958.
393 Pa. 427, 143 A.2d 25.

COHEN, Justice.

We are required to determine on this appeal whether, as a result of a "Reorganization Agreement" executed by the officers of Glen Alden Corporation and List Industries Corporation, and approved by the shareholders of the former company, the rights and remedies of a dissenting shareholder accrue to the plaintiff.

Glen Alden is a Pennsylvania corporation engaged principally in the mining of anthracite coal and lately in the manufacture of air conditioning units and fire-fighting equipment. In recent years the company's operating revenue has declined substantially, and in fact, its coal operations have resulted in tax loss carryovers of approximately $14,000,000. In October 1957, List, a Delaware holding company owning interests in motion picture theaters, textile companies and real estate, and to a lesser extent, in oil and gas operations, warehouses and aluminum piston manufacturing, purchased through a wholly owned subsidiary 38.5% of Glen Alden's outstanding stock.[1] This acquisition enabled List to place three of its directors on the Glen Alden board.

On March 20, 1958, the two corporations entered into a "reorganization agreement," subject to stockholder approval, which contemplated the following actions:

1. Glen Alden is to acquire all of the assets of List, excepting a small amount of cash reserved for the payment of List's expenses in connection with the transaction. These assets include over $8,000,000 in cash held chiefly in the treasuries of List's wholly owned subsidiaries.

2. In consideration of the transfer, Glen Alden is to issue 3,621,703 shares of stock to List. List in turn is to distribute the stock to its shareholders at a ratio of five shares of Glen Alden stock for each six shares of List stock. In order to accomplish the necessary distribution, Glen Alden is to increase the authorized number of its shares of capital stock from 2,500,000 shares to 7,500,000 shares without according preemptive rights to the present shareholders upon the issuance of any such shares.

3. Further, Glen Alden is to assume all of List's liabilities including a $5,000,000 note incurred by List in order to purchase Glen Alden

---

[1] Of the purchase price of $8,719,109, $5,000,000 was borrowed.

stock in 1957, outstanding stock options, incentive stock options plans, and pension obligations.

4. Glen Alden is to change its corporate name from Glen Alden Corporation to List Alden Corporation.

5. The present directors of both corporations are to become directors of List Alden.

6. List is to be dissolved and List Alden is to then carry on the operations of both former corporations.

Two days after the agreement was executed notice of the annual meeting of Glen Alden to be held on April 11, 1958, was mailed to the shareholders together with a proxy statement analyzing the reorganization agreement and recommending its approval as well as approval of certain amendments to Glen Alden's articles of incorporation and bylaws necessary to implement the agreement. At this meeting the holders of a majority of the outstanding shares, (not including those owned by List), voted in favor of a resolution approving the reorganization agreement.

On the day of the shareholders' meeting, plaintiff, a shareholder of Glen Alden, filed a complaint in equity against the corporation and its officers seeking to enjoin them temporarily until final hearing, and perpetually thereafter, from executing and carrying out the agreement.[2]

The gravamen of the complaint was that the notice of the annual shareholders' meeting did not conform to the requirements of the Business Corporation Law, 15 P.S. § 2852–1 et seq., in three respects: (1) It did not give notice to the shareholders that the true intent and purpose of the meeting was to effect a merger or consolidation of Glen Alden and List; (2) It failed to give notice to the shareholders of their right to dissent to the plan of merger or consolidation and claim fair value for their shares, and (3) It did not contain copies of the text of certain sections of the Business Corporation Law as required.[3]

By reason of these omissions, plaintiff contended that the approval of the reorganization agreement by the shareholders at the annual meeting was invalid and unless the carrying out of the plan were enjoined, he would suffer irreparable loss by being deprived of substantial property rights.

The defendants answered admitting the material allegations of fact in the complaint but denying that they gave rise to a cause of action because the transaction complained of was a purchase of corporate assets as to which shareholders had no rights of dissent or appraisal.

[2] The plaintiff also sought to enjoin the shareholders of Glen Alden from approving the reorganization agreement and from adopting amendments to Glen Alden's articles of incorporation, certificate of incorporation and bylaws in implementation of the agreement. However, apparently because of the shortness of time, this prayer was refused by the court.

[3] The proxy statement included the following declaration: "Appraisal Rights.

"In the opinion of counsel, the shareholders of neither Glen Alden nor List Industries will have any rights of appraisal or similar rights of dissenters with respect to any matter to be acted upon at their respective meetings."

For these reasons the defendants then moved for judgment on the pleadings.[5]

The court below concluded that the reorganization agreement entered into between the two corporations was a plan for a *de facto* merger, and that therefore the failure of the notice of the annual meeting to conform to the pertinent requirements of the merger provisions of the Business Corporation Law rendered the notice defective and all proceedings in furtherance of the agreement void. * * *

This appeal followed.

When use of the corporate form of business organization first became widespread, it was relatively easy for courts to define a "merger" or a "sale of assets" and to label a particular transaction as one or the other. * * * But prompted by the desire to avoid the impact of adverse, and to obtain the benefits of favorable, government regulations, particularly federal tax laws, new accounting and legal techniques were developed by lawyers and accountants which interwove the elements characteristic of each, thereby creating hybrid forms of corporate amalgamation. Thus, it is no longer helpful to consider an individual transaction in the abstract and solely by reference to the various elements therein determine whether it is a "merger" or a "sale". Instead, to determine properly the nature of a corporate transaction, we must refer not only to all the provisions of the agreement, but also to the consequences of the transaction and to the purposes of the provisions of the corporation law said to be applicable. We shall apply this principle to the instant case.

Section 908, subd. A of the Pennsylvania Business Corporation Law provides: "If any shareholder of a domestic corporation which becomes a party to a plan of merger or consolidation shall object to such plan of merger or consolidation * * * such shareholder shall be entitled to * * * [the fair value of his shares upon surrender of the share certificate or certificates representing his shares]."

This provision had its origin in the early decision of this Court in Lauman v. Lebanon Valley R.R. Co., 1858, 30 Pa. 42. There a shareholder who objected to the consolidation of his company with another was held to have a right in the absence of statute to treat the consolidation as a dissolution of his company and to receive the value of his shares upon their surrender.

The rationale of the Lauman case, and of the present section of the Business Corporation Law based thereon, is that when a corporation combines with another so as to lose its essential nature and alter the original fundamental relationships of the shareholders among themselves and to the corporation, a shareholder who does not wish to continue his membership therein may treat his membership in the

---

[5] Counsel for the defendants concedes that if the corporation is required to pay the dissenting shareholders the appraised fair value of their shares, the resultant drain of cash would prevent Glen Alden from carrying out the agreement. On the other hand, plaintiff contends that if the shareholders had been told of their rights as dissenters, rather than specifically advised that they had no such rights, the resolution approving the reorganization agreement would have been defeated.

original corporation as terminated and have the value of his shares paid to him. * * *

Does the combination outlined in the present "reorganization" agreement so fundamentally change the corporate character of Glen Alden and the interest of the plaintiff as a shareholder therein, that to refuse him the rights and remedies of a dissenting shareholder would in reality force him to give up his stock in one corporation and against his will accept shares in another? If so, the combination is a merger within the meaning of section 908, subd. A of the corporation law.

* * *

If the reorganization agreement were consummated plaintiff would find that the "List Alden" resulting from the amalgamation would be quite a different corporation than the "Glen Alden" in which he is now a shareholder. Instead of continuing primarily as a coal mining company, Glen Alden would be transformed, after amendment of its articles of incorporation, into a diversified holding company whose interests would range from motion picture theaters to textile companies, Plaintiff would find himself a member of a company with assets of $169,000,000 and a long-term debt of $38,000,000 in lieu of a company one-half that size and with but one-seventh the long-term debt.

While the administration of the operations and properties of Glen Alden as well as List would be in the hands of management common to both companies, since all executives of List would be retained in List Alden, the control of Glen Alden would pass to the directors of List; for List would hold eleven of the seventeen directorships on the new board of directors.

As an aftermath of the transaction plaintiff's proportionate interest in Glen Alden would have been reduced to only two-fifths of what it presently is because of the issuance of an additional 3,621,703 shares to List which would not be subject to pre-emptive rights. In fact, ownership of Glen Alden would pass to the stockholders of List who would hold 76.5% of the outstanding shares as compared with but 23.5% retained by the present Glen Alden shareholders.

Perhaps the most important consequence to the plaintiff, if he were denied the right to have his shares redeemed at their fair value, would be the serious financial loss suffered upon consummation of the agreement. While the present book value of his stock is $38 a share after combination it would be worth only $21 a share. In contrast, the shareholders of List who presently hold stock with a total book value of $33,000,000 or $7.50 a share, would receive stock with a book value of $76,000,000 or $21 a share.

Under these circumstances it may well be said that if the proposed combination is allowed to take place without right of dissent, plaintiff would have his stock in Glen Alden taken away from him and the stock of a new company thrust upon him in its place. He would be projected against his will into a new enterprise under terms not of his own choosing. It was to protect dissident shareholders against just such a result that this Court one hundred years ago in the Lauman case, and the legislature thereafter in section 908, subd. A, granted the right of dissent. And it is to accord that protection to the plaintiff that we conclude that the combination proposed in the case at hand is a merger within the intendment of section 908, subd. A.

Nevertheless, defendants contend that the 1957 amendments to sections 311 and 908 of the corporation law preclude us from reaching this result and require the entry of judgment in their favor. Subsection F of section 311 dealing with the voluntary transfer of corporate assets provides: "The shareholders of a business corporation which acquires by sale, lease or exchange all or substantially all of the property of another corporation by the issuance of stock, securities or otherwise shall not be entitled to the rights and remedies of dissenting shareholders * * *."

And the amendment to section 908 reads as follows: "The right of dissenting shareholders * * * shall not apply to the purchase by a corporation of assets whether or not the consideration therefor be money or property, real or personal, including shares or bonds or other evidences of indebtedness of such corporation. The shareholders of such corporation shall have no right to dissent from any such purchase."

Defendants view these amendments as abridging the right of shareholders to dissent to a transaction between two corporations which involves a transfer of assets for a consideration even though the transfer has all the legal incidents of a merger. They claim that only if the merger is accomplished in accordance with the prescribed statutory procedure does the right of dissent accrue. In support of this position they cite to us the comment on the amendments by the Committee on Corporation Law of the Pennsylvania Bar Association, the committee which originally drafted these provisions. The comment states that the provisions were intended to overrule cases which granted shareholders the right to dissent to a sale of assets when accompanied by the legal incidents of a merger. See 61 Ann.Rep.Pa.Bar Ass'n 277, 284 (1957).[7] Whatever may have been the intent of the *committee,* there is no evidence to indicate that the *legislature* intended the 1957 amendments to have the effect contended for. But furthermore, the language of these two provisions does not support the opinion of the committee and

[7] "The amendment to Section 311 expressly provides that a sale, lease or exchange of substantially all corporate assets in connection with its liquidation or dissolution is subject to the provisions of Article XI of the Act, and that no consent or authorization of shareholders other than what is required by Article XI is necessary. The recent decision in Marks v. Autocar Co., D.C.E.D.Pa., Civil Action No. 16075 [153 F.Supp. 768] is to the contrary. This amendment, together with the proposed amendment to Section 1104 expressly permitting the directors in liquidating the corporation to sell only such assets as may be required to pay its debts and distribute any assets remaining among shareholders (Sec- tion 1108, [subd.] B now so provides in the case of receivers) have the effect of overruling Marks v. Autocar Co., * * * which permits a shareholder dissenting from such a sale to obtain the fair value of his shares. The Marks case relies substantially on Bloch v. Baldwin Locomotive Works, 75 [Pa.] Dist. & Co.R. 24, also believed to be an undesirable decision. That case permitted a holder of stock in a corporation which *purchased* for stock all the assets of another corporation to obtain the fair value of his shares. That case is also in effect overruled by the new Sections 311 [subd.] F and 908 [subd.] C." 61 Ann.Rep.Pa. Bar Ass'n, 277, 284 (1957).

is inapt to achieve any such purpose. The amendments of 1957 do not provide that a transaction between two corporations which has the effect of a merger but which includes a transfer of assets for consideration is to be exempt from the protective provisions of sections 908, subd. A and 515. They provide only that the shareholders of a corporation which acquires the property or purchases the assets of another corporation, *without more*, are not entitled to the right to dissent from the transaction. So, as in the present case, when as part of a transaction between two corporations, one corporation dissolves, its liabilities are assumed by the survivor, its executives and directors take over the management and control of the survivor, and, as consideration for the transfer, its stockholders acquire a majority of the shares of stock of the survivor, then the transaction is no longer simply a purchase of assets or acquisition of property to which sections 311, subd. F and 908, subd. C apply, but a merger governed by section 908, subd. A of the corporation law. To divest shareholders of their right of dissent under such circumstances would require express language which is absent from the 1957 amendments.

Even were we to assume that the combination provided for in the reorganization agreement is a "sale of assets" to which section 908, subd. A does not apply, it would avail the defendants nothing; we will not blind our eyes to the realities of the transaction. Despite the designation of the parties and the form employed, Glen Alden does not in fact acquire List, rather, List acquires Glen Alden, and under section 311, subd. D [8] the right of dissent would remain with the shareholders of Glen Alden.

We hold that the combination contemplated by the reorganization agreement, although consummated by contract rather than in accordance with the statutory procedure, is a merger within the protective purview of sections 908, subd. A and 515 of the corporation law. The shareholders of Glen Alden should have been notified accordingly and advised of their statutory rights of dissent and appraisal. The failure of the corporate officers to take these steps renders the stockholder approval of the agreement at the 1958 shareholders' meeting invalid. The lower court did not err in enjoining the officers and directors of Glen Alden from carrying out this agreement.[9]

Decree affirmed at appellants' cost.

---

[8] "If any shareholder of a business corporation which sells, leases or exchanges all or substantially all of its property and assets otherwise than (1) in the usual and regular course of its business, (2) for the purpose of relocating its business, or (3) in connection with its dissolution and liquidation, shall object to such sale, lease or exchange and comply with the provisions of section 515 of this act, such shareholder shall be entitled to the rights and remedies of dissenting shareholders as therein provided."

[9] Because of our disposition of this appeal, it is unnecessary for us to consider * * * whether amended sections 908, subd. C and 311, subd. F of the corporation law may constitutionally be applied to the present transaction to divest the plaintiff of his dissenter's rights.

HARITON v. ARCO ELECTRONICS, INC.

Court of Chancery of Delaware, 1963.
41 Del.Ch. 74, 188 A.2d 123.

SOUTHERLAND, Chief Justice.

This case involves a sale of assets under § 271 of the corporation law, 8 Del.C. It presents for decision the question presented, but not decided, in Heilbrunn v. Sun Chemical Corporation, Del., 150 A.2d 755.* It may be stated as follows:

A sale of assets is effected under § 271 in consideration of shares of stock of the purchasing corporation. The agreement of sale embodies also a plan to dissolve the selling corporation and distribute the shares so received to the stockholders of the seller, so as to accomplish the same result as would be accomplished by a merger of the seller into the purchaser. Is the sale legal?

The facts are these:

The defendant Arco and Loral Electronics Corporation, a New York corporation, are both engaged, in somewhat different forms, in the electronic equipment business. In the summer of 1961 they negotiated for an amalgamation of the companies. As of October 27, 1961, they entered into a "Reorganization Agreement and Plan." The provisions of this Plan pertinent here are in substance as follows:

1. Arco agrees to sell all its assets to Loral in consideration (inter alia) of the issuance to it of 283,000 shares of Loral.

2. Arco agrees to call a stockholders meeting for the purpose of approving the Plan and the voluntary dissolution.

3. Arco agrees to distribute to its stockholders all the Loral shares received by it as a part of the complete liquidation of Arco.

At the Arco meeting all the stockholders voting (about 80%) approved the Plan. It was thereafter consummated.

Plaintiff, a stockholder who did not vote at the meeting, sued to enjoin the consummation of the Plan on the grounds (1) that it was illegal, and (2) that it was unfair. The second ground was abandoned. Affidavits and documentary evidence were filed, and defendant moved for summary judgment and dismissal of the complaint. The Vice Chancellor granted the motion and plaintiff appeals.

The question before us we have stated above. Plaintiff's argument that the sale is illegal runs as follows:

---

* In *Heilbrunn* a shareholder of the *acquiring* company, Sun Chemical, objected to the loss of appraisal rights resulting from casting the transaction as a sale of assets rather than a merger. The Court did not reach the de facto merger claim because it "fail[ed] to see how any injury has been inflicted upon the [shareholders of the acquiring company.] Their corpora- tion has simply acquired property and paid for it in shares of stock. The business of Sun will go on as before, with additional assets. The Sun stockholder is not forced to accept stock in another corporation. Nor has the reorganization changed the essential nature of the purchasing corpora- tion." [Ed.]

The several steps taken here accomplish the same result as a merger of Arco into Loral.** In a "true" sale of assets, the stockholder of the seller retains the right to elect whether the selling company shall continue as a holding company. Moreover, the stockholder of the selling company is forced to accept an investment in a new enterprise without the right of appraisal granted under the merger statute. § 271 cannot therefore be legally combined with a dissolution proceeding under § 275 and a consequent distribution of the purchaser's stock. Such a proceeding is a misuse of the power granted under § 271, and a *de facto* merger results.

* * *

Plaintiff's contention that this sale has achieved the same result as a merger is plainly correct. The same contention was made to us in Heilbrunn v. Sun Chemical Corporation, Del., 150 A.2d 755. Accepting it as correct, we noted that this result is made possible by the overlapping scope of the merger statute and section 271 * * *

We also adverted to the increased use, in connection with corporate reorganization plans, of § 271 instead of the merger statute. Further, we observed that no Delaware case has held such procedure to be improper, and that two cases appear to assume its legality. Finch v. Warrior Cement Corporation, 16 Del.Ch. 44, 141 A. 54, and Argenbright v. Phoenix Finance Co., 21 Del.Ch. 288, 187 A. 124. But we were not required in the Heilbrunn case to decide the point.

We now hold that the reorganization here accomplished through § 271 and a mandatory plan of dissolution and distribution is legal. This is so because the sale-of-assets statute and the merger statute are independent of each other. They are, so to speak, of equal dignity, and the framers of a reorganization plan may resort to either type of corporate mechanics to achieve the desired end. This is not an anomalous result in our corporation law. As the Vice Chancellor pointed out, the elimination of accrued dividends, though forbidden under a charter amendment (Keller v. Wilson & Co., 21 Del.Ch. 391, 190 A. 115) may be accomplished by a merger. Federal United Corporation v. Havender, 24 Del.Ch. 318, 11 A.2d 331.

In Langfelder v. Universal Laboratories, D.C., 68 F.Supp. 209, Judge Leahy commented upon "the general theory of the Delaware Corporation Law that action taken pursuant to the authority of the various sections of that law constitute acts of independent legal significance and their validity is not dependent on other sections of the Act." 68 F.Supp. 211, footnote.

* * *

Plaintiff concedes, as we read his brief, that if the several steps taken in this case had been taken separately they would have been legal. That is, he concedes that a sale of assets, followed by a separate proceeding to dissolve and distribute, would be legal, even though the same result would follow. This concession exposes the weakness of his

** The plan also specified that Loral would assume all of Arco's liabilities and required Arco's prompt liquidation following the closing of the transaction. See the Vice Chancellor's opinion, 40 Del.Ch. 326, 182 A.2d 22 (1962). [Ed.]

contention. To attempt to make any such distinction between sales under § 271 would be to create uncertainty in the law and invite litigation.

We are in accord with the Vice Chancellor's ruling, and the judgment below is affirmed.

———————◆———————

The Delaware Supreme Court's approach to the corporate statute in *Hariton* seems strikingly at odds with the approach taken in Gimbel v. Signal Companies, Inc., and Katz v. Bregman, supra. Although *Hariton* dealt with an effort to turn a sale of assets into a merger, while *Signal Companies* and *Katz* dealt with whether there had been a sale of substantially all the target company's assets, in a critical respect all three cases presented precisely the same issue. Could a transaction whose formal terms fell outside the literal language of the statute be recharacterized in light of its alleged substance to fall within the statute? In *Hariton,* the court read the language of the statute as a Fundamentalist reads the Bible; each passage was "of equal dignity" even though, as in Genesis for example, different passages describe exactly the same events quite differently. In contrast, the court in *Signal Companies* and *Katz* treated the statutory language with far less reverence. Why did the court in either case go beyond the language of the statute? A *Hariton* -like approach would simply have concluded that the sale of somewhere between 26% and 50% of total assets in *Signal Companies,* and 51% of total assets in *Katz,* did not constitute the sale of "all or substantially all" of the target company's assets. The puzzle is then to explain why a form of statutory interpretation that looks to substance rather than form is appropriate in determining whether shareholders require the protection associated with the sale of assets provisions rather than no protection at all, but not in determining whether shareholders require the protection associated with the merger provisions rather than the lesser protection associated with the sale of asset provisions.

b. Triangular Transactions

TERRY v. PENN CENTRAL CORPORATION
United States Court of Appeals, Third Circuit, 1981.
668 F.2d 188.

ADAMS, Circuit Judge.

The Penn Central Corporation ("Penn Central"), an appellee in this case, has sought to acquire Colt Industries Inc. ("Colt"), also an appellee, by merging Colt with PCC Holdings, Inc. ("Holdings"), a wholly-owned subsidiary of Penn Central. Howard L. Terry and W.H. Hunt, the appellants, are shareholders of Penn Central who objected to the transaction. In a diversity action before the United States District Court for the Eastern District of Pennsylvania, appellants sought injunctive and declaratory relief to enforce voting and dissenters' rights to which appellants asserted they were entitled. Appellants further sought to enjoin Holdings from proceeding with the proposed merger, and in particular moved to enjoin a vote on the transaction, scheduled for October 29, 1981, by the shareholders of Penn Central. In an opinion issued on October 22, 1981, Judge Pollak denied appellants' requests. Appellants thereupon filed an appeal in this Court. * * *

The shareholders of Penn Central voted, as scheduled, on October 29. * * *

After argument on appeal, the shareholders disapproved of the merger in that vote, and the corporations thereafter publicly announced their abandonment of this particular meger. Penn Central, however, has not abandoned its proposed series of acquisitions, of which the Colt acquisition was merely one instance.

I.

Penn Central is the successor to the Penn Central Transportation Corporation, which underwent a reorganization under the bankruptcy laws that was completed in 1978. No longer involved in the railroading business, Penn Central, since 1978, has had the advantage, for tax purposes, of a large loss carry-forward. In order to put that loss carry-forward to its best use, Penn Central has embarked on a program of acquiring corporations whose profits could be sheltered. To this end Penn Central created Holdings, a wholly-owned subsidiary which was to acquire the businesses that Penn Central desired. The first acquisition under the plan was Marathon Manufacturing Company ("Marathon"), in 1979. In the Marathon acquisition, a class of preferred Penn Central stock was created, and 30 million shares of "First Series Preference Stock" was issued to the owners of Marathon stock. Appellants were shareholders of Marathon who thereby acquired shares of this First Series Preference Stock. Terry was promptly elected to the Penn Central board of directors.

In 1981, Penn Central decided upon a second acquisition: Colt. The management and directors of Colt and Penn Central agreed upon a merger of Colt into Holdings, compensated for by issuance of a second series of Penn Central preference stock to Colt shareholders. Terry opposed the merger at the directors' meeting, and now seeks to preclude the consummation of the transaction.

* * * [A]ppellants argue that under Pennsylvania's corporate law, they are entitled to dissent and appraisal rights if the merger is adopted over their opposition. * * * The district court held that [the claim was incorrect] as a matter of law. * * *

Because Colt and Penn Central have now announced their abandonment of the proposed merger, the request for injunctive relief considered by the district court is now conceded by all parties to be moot. However, the appellants' request for declaratory relief, which the appellants now contend is moot as well, involves legal questions that go to Penn Central's plan of acquisitions, rather than to the Colt transaction alone, and these questions appear likely to recur in future disputes between the parties here. It is clear from the record that the Colt merger was one in a series of similar acquisitions by Penn Central.

The appellants, one of whom has now objected to each of the last two proposed mergers by Penn Central, will continue to have a lively interest in challenging any future acquisitions structured in roughly the same manner as the transaction before us now. The declaratory relief requested here thus arises from a genuine and continuing controversy, and involves adverse parties who have diligently presented their cases to this Court. The continuing threat of legal action creates some present injury, and not merely a speculative future injury, to Penn Central: without a judgment on the merits of this appeal, Penn Central's present ability to negotiate other acquisitions will be severely impaired by the desire of companies to avoid the legal complications faced by Penn Central and Colt. In a case such as this, a voluntary termination by the parties of the specific activity challenged in the lawsuit—in this case, the proposed treatment of the dissenting preferred shareholders in the Colt-PCC plan—does not render the case moot because there is "a reasonable likelihood that the parties or those in privity with them will be involved in a suit on the same issues in the future." American Bible Society v. Blount, 446 F.2d 588, 595 (3d Cir. 1971); Marshall v. Whittaker Corp., 610 F.2d 1141, 1147 (3d Cir.1979).

* * *

III.

Terry and Hunt contend that under Pennsylvania law they are entitled to dissent and appraisal rights if a merger is approved by the Penn Central shareholders.

* * *

Briefly, appellants' argument is that the proposed merger between Holdings and Colt constitutes a *de facto* merger between Colt and Penn Central, and that the Penn Central shareholders are therefore entitled to the protections for dissenting shareholders that Pennsylvania corporate law provides for shareholders of parties to a merger. Although this reasoning, with its emphasis on the substance of the transaction rather than its formal trappings, may be attractive as a matter of policy, it contravenes the language used by the Pennsylvania legislature in setting out the rights of shareholders.

Section 908 of the Pennsylvania Business Corporation Law (PBCL) provides that shareholders of corporations that are parties to a plan of merger are entitled to dissent and appraisal rights, but adds that for any acquisition other than such a merger, the only rights are those provided for in Section 311 of the PBCL. Section 311, in turn, provides for dissent and appraisal rights only when an acquisition has been accomplished by "the issuance of voting shares of such corporation to be outstanding immediately after the acquisition sufficient to elect a majority of the directors of the corporation." In this case the shares of Penn Central stock to be issued in the Colt transaction do not exceed the number of shares already existing, and thus the transaction is not covered by Section 311. Any statutory dissent and appraisal rights for Penn Central shareholders are therefore contingent upon Penn Central's status as a party to the merger within the meaning of Section 908. And as the district court points out, the PBCL describes the parties to a merger as those entities that are *actually* combined into a single corporation. Section 907 states that:

> Upon the merger or consolidation becoming effective, the several corporations parties to the plan of merger or consolidation shall be a single corporation which, in the case of a merger, shall be that corporation designated in the plan of merger as the surviving corporation. * * *

At the end of the proposed merger plan here, both Holdings and Penn Central would survive as separate entities, and it would therefore appear that Penn Central is not a party within the meaning of Section 907. We can discern no reason to infer that the legislature intended the word "party" to have different meanings in Sections 907 and 908, and accordingly conclude that Penn Central is not a party to the merger.

Appellants argue that Penn Central is nevertheless brought into the amalgamation by the *de facto* merger doctrine as set out in Pennsylvania law in Farris v. Glen Alden Corp., 393 Pa. 427, 143 A.2d 25 (1958). *Farris* was the penultimate step in a *pas de deux* involving the Pennsylvania courts and the Pennsylvania legislature regarding the proper treatment for transactions that reached the same practical result as a merger but avoided the legal form of merger and the concomitant legal obligations. In the 1950s the Pennsylvania courts advanced the doctrine that a transaction having the effect of an amalgamation would be treated as a *de facto* merger. See, e.g., Bloch v. The Baldwin Locomotive Works, 75 Pa.D. & C. 24 (1950). The legislature responded with efforts to constrict the *de facto* merger doctrine. *Farris,* addressing those efforts, held that the doctrine still covered a reorganization agreement that had the effect of merging a large corporation into a smaller corporation. In a 1959 response to *Farris,* the legislature made explicit its objection to earlier cases that found certain transactions to be *de facto* mergers. The legislature enacted a law, modifying *inter alia* Sections 311 and 908, entitled in part:

> An Act * * * changing the law as to * * * the acquisition or transfer of corporate assets, the rights of dissenting shareholders, * * * abolishing the doctrine of de facto mergers or consolidation and reversing the rules laid down in Bloch v. Baldwin Locomotive Works, 75 D & C 24, and Marks v. The Autocar Co., 153 F.Supp. 786, * * *.

Act of November 10, 1959 (P.L. 1406, No. 502).*

Following this explicit statement, the *de facto* merger doctrine has rarely been invoked by the Pennsylvania courts. Only once has the Pennsylvania Supreme Court made reference to it, in In re Jones & Laughlin Steel Corp., 488 Pa. 524, 412 A.2d 1099 (1980). Even there, the Court's reference was oblique. It merely cited *Farris* for the proposition that shareholders have the right to enjoin "proposed unfair or fraudulent corporate actions." 488 Pa. at 533, 412 A.2d at 1104. This Court, sitting in diversity in Knapp v. North American Rockwell

---

* This Act added the language in § 311 concerning issuance of shares sufficient to   elect a majority of directors quoted in the text, supra. [Ed.]

Corp., 506 F.2d 361 (3d Cir.1974), cert. denied, 421 U.S. 965 (1975), invoked the *de facto* merger doctrine to hold that a transaction structured as a sale of assets could nevertheless be deemed a merger for purposes of requiring the merging corporation to assume the acquired corporation's liability for damages to a worker who was injured by a faulty piece of equipment manufactured by the acquired company. Perhaps the broadest application of the doctrine was made in In re Penn Central Securities Litigation, 367 F.Supp. 1158 (E.D.Pa.1973), in which the district court held that the doctrine provided the plaintiffs in that case with standing for a 10b–5 lawsuit alleging *fraud* and also gave rise to dissent and appraisal rights in a triangular merger situation.

None of these cases persuades us that a Pennsylvania court would apply the *de facto* merger doctrine to the situation before us. Although *Jones & Laughlin Steel* suggests that dissent and appraisal rights might be available if fraud or fraudulent unfairness were shown, we are not faced with such a situation. No allegation of fraud has been advanced, and the only allegation of fundamental unfairness is that the appellants will, if the merger is consummated, be forced into what they consider a poor investment on the part of Penn Central without the opportunity to receive an appraised value for their stock. Even if appellants' evaluation of the merits of the proposed merger is accurate, poor business judgment on the part of management would not be enough to constitute unfairness cognizable by a court. And the denial of appraisal rights to dissenters cannot constitute fundamental unfairness, or the *de facto* merger doctrine would apply in every instance in which dissenters' rights were sought and the 1959 amendments by the legislature would be rendered nugatory.[7]

The two federal cases invoking the doctrine, *Knapp* and *Penn Central Securities,* are not persuasive as to the applicability of the *de facto* merger to the present situation. *Knapp* was not concerned with the rights of shareholders as the Pennsylvania legislature was in 1959. Although *Penn Central Securities* did hold, in part, that the triangular merger in that case constituted a *de facto* merger, it is clear from the briefs submitted to the district court in that case that the court was not made aware of the post-*Farris* 1959 amendments or the legislative statement of intent to limit the *de facto* merger doctrine.

In the absence of any explicit guidance to the contrary by the Pennsylvania courts, we conclude that the language of the legislature in 1959 precludes a decision that the transaction in this case constitutes a *de facto* merger sufficient to entitle Penn Central shareholders to dissent and appraisal rights. We therefore hold that appellant does not possess such rights if a transaction such as the one involved here is consummated.

----

[7] A different result might be reached if here, as in *Farris,* the acquiring corporation were significantly smaller than the acquired corporation such that the acquisition greatly transformed the nature of the successor corporation. But in this situation we do not have such a case; after the merger Penn Central would remain a major, diversified corporation, and would continue on the course of acquiring other corporations.

2. Recharacterization of Nonstatutory Alternatives

Up to this point, we have focused on the judicial response to efforts by planners to eliminate some of the rights granted shareholders under a statutory merger—which is the most restrictive statutory technique— by choosing among alternative acquisition techniques also authorized by the corporate statute. What happens, however, when planners accomplish what is claimed to be the functional equivalent of a statutory technique by an alternative which, rather than providing *fewer* protections than other statutory techniques, is not, at least in form, covered by the statute at all and, therefore, provides *no* protection?

A sense of the opportunity for creative planning this approach provides can be obtained by recalling the perspective on the corporation offered by the Klein, Crawford & Alchian, Teece and Williamson articles in Chapter Eleven. In this view, any function necessary to the corporation's business can be accomplished either within the corporation or through a market transaction by means of contract. For example, a corporation engaged in manufacturing a consumer product needs a means by which that product can be sold to the public. This can be accomplished either by contract with a third party, a distribution agreement is a common approach, or by having the company vertically integrate by engaging in retailing itself. One means by which this integration can be achieved, of course, is by acquisition. And the availability of a contractual alternative to acquisition is not limited to vertical integration. Where horizontal expansion is sought, either to acquire additional capacity or to allow the pursuit of a cooperative rather than a competitive strategy, a joint venture (contractual) approach is a functional alternative to acquisition.[24]

The question then becomes what factors influence a corporation to choose between an acquisition and a contractual solution: What determines the economic boundary of the firm? While more general answers to this question were considered in Chapter Eleven, in particular cases one factor may be the cost of protections for shareholders and others imposed by the corporate statute on the acquisition alternative. Is the de facto approach still available if the need for a shareholder vote or appraisal rights increases the costs of an acquisition and, thus, causes the planner to choose a contractual alternative rather than merely a less restrictive statutory alternative?

PRATT v. BALLMAN–CUMMINGS FURNITURE CO.

Supreme Court of Arkansas, 1973.
254 Ark. 570, 495 S.W.2d 509.

BROWN, Justice.

The appellants are minority stockholders of Ballman-Cummings Furniture Company of Ft. Smith. They claim that by a vote of the majority stockholders of Baldwin-Cummings, the corporation, under the

---

[24] See McConnell & Nantell, *Corporate Combinations and Common Stock Returns:*   *The Case of Joint Ventures,* 40 J.Fin. 519 (1985).

pretext of forming a partnership with Ft. Smith Chair Company, Inc., accomplished a de facto merger or consolidation of the two corporations. If the arrangement is in fact a partnership it is authorized by Ark.Stat.Ann. § 64–104 (B.6) (Repl.1966); if the arrangement constitutes a merger then the appellants, protesting minority stockholders, are entitled to be paid by the succeeding corporation, the fair value of their stock. Ark.Stat.Ann. § 64–707 (Repl.1966).

* * *

The Ayers family of Ft. Smith, by virtue of its stock holdings, is in control of both corporations and the corporations have interlocking directors.

The partnership agreement was executed in November 1967. It provided that the partnership would consist of two partners, naming the two corporations. The name of the partnership was designated Ayers Furniture Industries. Each partner would contribute $1500 to the initial capital of the partnership. It was agreed that each corporation would sell its merchandise to the partnership. The partnership would be responsible for all merchandising functions in connection with the promotion and sale of furniture. It would also handle billing and collection of accounts receivable. The partnership would also assume the responsibility for the delivery of furniture to customers. (It was explained by witness John Ayers, ownership of the furniture by the partnership made it possible to load furniture produced by both factories in a single trailer which otherwise was not permitted by ICC regulations.) It was also explained by the same witness that the partnership would eliminate the duplication of expenses of billing and collections. It was also provided that the partners would designate one individual as a general manager of the partnership who would be fully authorized to conduct the business and affairs of the partnership.

It would be most difficult to say that the partnership arrangement, as exemplified by the agreement which we have briefly described, constituted in and of itself a merger of the two corporations.

* * *

On the other hand, there are well recognized in the law, de facto mergers—an association under the guise of a partnership whereby one of the corporations loses its identity as such and is actually controlled by the management of the partnership. When a particular corporate combination "is in legal effect a merger or a consolidation, even though the transaction may be otherwise labeled by the parties, the courts treat the transaction as a de facto merger or consolidation so as to confer upon dissenting stockholders the right to receive cash payment for their shares". 15 Fletcher Cyclopedia Corporations § 7165.5.

Mr. John Ayers is the chief officer of Ballman-Cummings, of Ft. Smith Chair, and of the partnership. It is the position of appellants, while asserting that they do not accuse Mr. Ayers of fraud, that under his executive direction, Ballman-Cummings has lost its long standing identity in the market place. That development, so they say, has resulted in consistent annual losses by the corporation of thousands of dollars, while the profits of Ft. Smith Chair remained stable. The evidence shows that Ballman-Cummings is in the process of liquidation.

* * *

According to appellants the events which brought about the alleged destruction of Ballman-Cummings are summarized in their brief and their argument, and absent any other explanation, are persuasive:

> Not only is the separate identity of the merging corporations as marketing entities replaced by the image of a separate and new entity, but Article 2, Section 5 (Articles of Partnership) provides: "The partners shall designate one individual as a General Manager of the partnership who will be fully authorized to conduct the business and affairs of the partnership".

> Furthermore, the management, sales and bookkeeping functions of the two corporations were entirely merged together, with a single officer, not the one elected by the directors of each corporation, in charge of each function. John Ayers became the General Manager of both corporations and the partnership, or more properly of both corporations in the partnership. Prior to the merger each corporation had a sales manager, after the merger Gene Rapley who had been sales manager for Ballman-Cummings became sales manager for the combined operations, while Tom Condren who had been sales manager for Chair Company became the designer for the combined operations. The controller for one corporation, Mr. Layman, was placed in charge of the accounting processes for the combined operations, while the controller for the other corporation, Mr. Thompson, took over the credit collection and customer service activities of the combined operation. Dale Keller, who had been purchasing agent for Ballman-Cummings, became purchasing agent for the combined operations, while Mr. Keller who had been with Chair Company became the chief assistant in the purchasing department.

Whether there is a correlation between the shifting of the described responsibilities and the resultant folding of Ballman-Cummings is not the question; the question is whether a prima facie case was made. We think it was. We might add that no solid reason was given by Mr. Ayers for Ballman-Cummings' collapse. There was only a general statement that it was due to economic reasons. Mr. Ayers said he had no explanation why the loss of Ballman-Cummings rose so severely except "apparently loss cycles that we had been experiencing, the problems we had been experiencing in production were pyramiding on us during that year". Appellees are also burdened by the fact that the partnership was proposed on the basis that it would increase profits, which of course it did not do.

[The Court concluded that the facts established a prima facie case for the application of de facto merger doctrine.]

Reversed and remanded.

GOOD v. LACKAWANNA LEATHER CO.

Supreme Court of New Jersey, 1967.
96 N.J.Super. 439, 233 A.2d 201.

MINTZ, J.S.C.

Plaintiffs Donald A. Good and Marjean M. Good are minority stockholders of defendants Good Bros. Leather Co. (hereinafter referred to as Good Bros.) and Lackawanna Leather Co. (hereinafter referred to as Lackawanna). They seek an appraisal of the value of their shares in accordance with N.J.S.A. 14:12–6 and 7 and N.J.S.A. 14:3–5. Alternatively, they seek an appraisal of their shares in both corporations in accordance with alleged common law rights. Plaintiffs specifically charge that Lackawanna and Good Bros. have been merged without the stockholder approval of either corporation required by N.J.S.A. 14:12–3, despite a rejection of the proposed merger by the majority of the stockholders of Good Bros.   *   *   *

Defendant corporations have enjoyed a close relationship over the years. The predecessor to both corporations was a partnership between Herman B. Good and his brother Robert C. Good formed in 1896. This partnership engaged in various phases of the leather processing business. In 1903 the partners arranged for the incorporation of Lackawanna, which corporation chrome-tanned leather for the automobile trade. The plant was located in Hackettstown, N.J., where it still exists. In 1914 Herman and Robert Good organized Good Bros., Inc., which established a plant in Newark. Herman B. Good was president and general manager. Robert's son, Donald S. Good, entered the employ of Lackawanna in about 1920, and upon the death of his father in 1944 became president of the company. Donald's son, Donald A. Good, is one of the plaintiffs in the within cause of action. Carl F. Good, one of the defendants, is the son of the late Herman B. Good.

Since 1957 Carl F. Good, Ross L. Dimm, Jr., Gerard K. Lind and Dale McKnight have been the majority shareholders and have controlled the boards of directors of both Good Bros. and Lackawanna. Carl F. Good is the president of Good Bros. and the chairman of the board of Lackawanna. Ross L. Dimm, Jr. is the president of Lackawanna and vice-president of Good Bros.

Almost since its inception Lackawanna has engaged in the business of finishing and selling fine leather for use by furniture and automobile manufacturers. It worked closely with Good Bros. purchasing much of its russet leather from it. Lackawanna was Good Bros.' principal customer for russet-tanned top grains. However, in 1956 Lackawanna acquired additional facilities in Hackettstown where it could accomplish the russet-tanning [1] of top grains cheaper than it would cost it to purchase the russet leather from Good Bros. Thus when in 1956

---

[1] Russet-tanning is the first tanning operation taken to start the hides on their way toward a finished product. Beaming is the operation of soaking, defurring and defleshing green salted hides after they are received from the slaughter house. Splitting is the longitudinal splitting of the hides into component parts; the top section is the top grain and the lower section is referred to as the split. Splitting of the whole hide is part of the beam house operation.

Lackawanna was able to russet-tan its own hides, Good Bros. went out of this phase of hide processing. The only tanning operations in which it thereafter engaged was on the splits, which it conducted for a period of approximately three years.

In 1956 Donald S. Good, who was then president of Lackawanna, offered to buy the majority interest in that company. The offer was rejected by the majority stockholders. He thereupon resigned, as did the executive vice-president and several other key employees. They immediately went to work for the Good-McCree Leather Company, a competitor, in Hackettstown, of which plaintiff Donald A. Good was president. In the fall of 1956, as a consequence of these resignations, Carl F. Good was elected president of Lackawanna, Ross L. Dimm, Jr. executive vice-president and Dale McKnight vice-president in charge of sales. Lackawanna was in poor condition. Its building, machinery and equipment had received little maintenance. The credit of the company was limited. Its customer relations were impaired and it had no inventory.

In the 1950s "lime splitting," a technological advance in the industry, was adopted in various tanneries. Theretofore, tanneries were unable to produce all the russet leather which they required. They looked to beam house processors, such as Good Bros., to supplement their needs for russet leather. With the advent of lime splitting they were able, with their current facilities, to produce all the russet leather needed. Thus, this new process seriously affected Good Bros. business. Lackawanna, however, did not become a fully integrated plant. Sewage problems at its Hackettstown plant would not permit the beam house operation. Hence, Good Bros. remained a source of supply of beamed hides.

In the light of this situation the boards of directors of Lackawanna and Good Bros. considered merger proposals. In December 1957 a memorandum proposing the merger of Good Bros. and Lackawanna was circulated among the directors, assigning the following reasons for the merger:

> "The largest and most important leather finishing companies now have their own tanning departments which can supply all of their needs and, therefore, Good is dependent upon Lackawanna for the disposal of a major portion of its products. Obviously it would not be wise for Lackawanna to be dependent upon its competitors for its supply of partially processed hides. Under present conditions, probably neither Good nor Lackawanna could successfully operate independently of the other. Obviously, it is important for both companies and for the stockholders of both companies that the company producing the finished product and offering it in the competitive market be in the strongest position possible to meet its competition."

The merger memorandum recommended that about one-third of the machinery and tools of Good Bros. be disposed of at salvage value, the Newark property of Good Bros. be sold, and the beaming operations of the merged companies be moved to a new location. The memorandum also called for the exchange and distribution of 1.85 shares of Lackawanna for each share of Good Bros. It further indicated that if dissents were filed, the proposed merger would not be effectuated because the appraisal rights attaching to the shares of the dissenters would cause a cash drain upon the affected companies which they could ill afford.

A formal merger agreement was approved by the boards of directors of both Good Bros. and Lackawanna. On April 26, 1958 said merger agreement was submitted to the stockholders of Lackawanna, at which time a resolution adopting the agreement of merger was passed by the two-thirds vote of the stockholders, as required by N.J.S.A. 14:12–3. However, the shares held or controlled by plaintiffs, comprising approximately 20% of the outstanding shares, were voted against the merger, thereby entitling them to receive the appraisal value of their stock.

On May 24, 1958 Carl F. Good, as president of both corporations, advised the stockholders as follows:

"This is to advise you that the proposed merger of Good Bros. Leather Co. into The Lackawanna Leather Company dated as of March 31, 1958, will not be consummated. The holders of 1345½ shares of stock of The Lackawanna Leather Company and the holders of 75 shares of stock of Good Bros. Leather Co. have given the respective corporations written notice of their dissent. Consequently if the merger were consummated the surviving corporation would be obliged to purchase the share of these dissenting stockholders at the appraised market value of such shares. * * * Accordingly, at the adjourned meeting of the stockholders of Good Bros. Leather * * * a vote on the merger will be taken, but the shares owned by members of the Board of Directors and their families will be voted to reject the proposed merger."

On June 7, 1958, the proposed merger was rejected by a majority of the stockholders of Good Bros. Plaintiffs allege, however, that defendants achieved the very objectives sought by the statutory merger plan notwithstanding the rejection, and thus actually accomplished a *de facto* merger as of about December 31, 1960. Plaintiffs also contend that by the end of 1961 Good Bros. sold substantially all of its assets without the stockholder authorization required by N.J.S.A. 14:3–5. It is asserted that the subsequent course of conduct on the part of the respective corporations confirms and establishes the *de facto* merger and alleged unauthorized sale of all the assets of Good Bros.

Plaintiffs point to the marked change and curtailment in the nature of Good Bros. operations after 1959. Good Bros. faltering business is evidenced by the fact that at the end of 1959 it had but one remaining customer, namely, Lackawanna for whom it beamed hides. The sales pattern also manifests a business decline. In 1958 its gross sales amounted to $1,291,524. Although in 1959 its gross sales increased to $2,192,395, this substantial increase was in some measure attributable to the sale in December of its entire hide inventory to Lackawanna, and a temporary increase in demand and price for its beamed products. However, in 1960 sales totalled only $260,544. In 1961 sales totalled $267,360, and in 1964 $306,893.

On December 1, 1960 Good Bros. sold its land, buildings and improvements in Newark to the Remis Trust Fund. At the same time it entered into a contract with H. Remis & Co. to perform such beaming operations as Good Bros. should require for a period of five years. Good Bros. tried to sell its beaming equipment to Remis but Remis would not purchase it. For the following five years Good Bros. was able to do the beaming required by Lackawanna and to make a profit by charging Lackawanna a competitive price which was in excess of the price under its subcontract with Remis. In addition to the beaming for Good Bros., Remis did some beaming for its own account for which it paid Good Bros. for the use of the latter's machinery.

In 1961 all personnel at the Newark plant were transferred to the Remis payroll except for a supervisor and Carl F. Good. Remis performed the beaming of hides owned by Lackawanna under its subcontract with Good Bros. This arrangement continued until August 1, 1966. As a consequence of the change in the Good Bros. operation after 1959, there was little need for the fixed assets, which accordingly were sold, scrapped or abandoned. There was a gradual disposal of the operating assets, such as inventories which were sold to Lackawanna, and accounts receivable which were converted into cash or its equivalent.

In the 1960s the net worth of Good Bros. averaged about $400,000. By 1964, when 94% of its assets were reduced to cash or its equivalent, the only equipment included in the net worth figure was the beaming machinery being used by Remis, having a book value of $25,900.

As early as June 1, 1960, and perhaps prior thereto, the officers and directors of Good Bros. made known to its stockholders its plan, if possible, to sell its Newark property and relocate its beaming and pickling operations in another area. The testimony indicates that substantial freight as well as other charges could be eliminated by the relocation of the beam house in close proximity to the raw hide market.

During the period 1960–1966 the risk of purchasing hides in a highly volatile and fluctuating market was borne by Lackawanna. During this period, green hides when purchased by Good Bros., were billed to Lackawanna at cost. Good Bros. from time to time loaned funds to Lackawanna to finance the purchase of hides by Lackawanna which were beamed by Good Bros. under its subcontract with Remis. On such borrowings Good Bros. was paid interest at current bank rates. Resolutions were adopted from time to time by Lackawanna and Good Bros. authorizing the loans. The first such resolution was adopted by the directors of Lackawanna on December 23, 1959. This resolution authorized the corporation to borrow approximately $100,000 from Good Bros. at current interest rates. The funds were to be used to purchase green hides and to pay for the processing of the hides by Good Bros. in Newark.

Good Bros. likewise on December 23, 1959 adopted a resolution authorizing said corporation to loan up to $100,000 to Lackawanna at current interest rates to enable Lackawanna to purchase the hide inventory required for its business. Subsequently, this loan authorization was increased to $200,000. On September 12, 1961, at a special meeting of the board of directors of Lackawanna, its officers were authorized to borrow an additional $50,000 in excess of the $200,000 then permitted from Good Bros. as a temporary measure until October 2, 1961. Apparently on that date Lackawanna was unable to repay the $50,000 to Good Bros. There is a journal entry under date of October 2, 1961 for the purchase of green hides by Good from Lackawanna in the amount of $49,715.66 and a charge to interest income on the Good Bros. books in the sum of $284.34. A credit in favor of Lackawanna was entered on the notes receivable account for $50,000, thereby reducing the loan account to $200,000. Good Bros. subsequently resold the green hides to Lackawanna for $50,123. In other words, as an accommodation to Lackawanna, Good Bros. temporarily carried the green hides on its books as an asset. It also appears that God [sic] Bros. occasionally purchased hides for its own account which were later resold to Lackawanna at cost.

In 1965 the directors of Good Bros. and Lackawanna were apprised of an available location in Omaha, Nebraska, on which to erect a tannery. Apparently it was agreed between the corporations that Good Bros. purchase the site and erect a building thereon in which beaming operations would be conducted by a corporation to be formed, in which Good Bros. and Lackawanna would be the stockholders. Accordingly, Good Bros. purchased the property and erected a building thereon. The two corporations organized Lackawanna of Omaha, a Delaware corporation, two-thirds of the stock being subscribed to by Lackawanna and one-third by Good Bros. The invested capital of Good Bros. in Lackawanna of Omaha was $10,000. Good Bros. erected a building on the property which it, in turn, leased to Lackawanna of Omaha. The land and building cost Good Bros. approximately $200,000. The lease with Lackawanna of Omaha was for a period of 20 years, with Good Bros. receiving as rent a 12% return upon its investment. The beam house equipment was apparently installed by Lackawanna of Omaha. In August 1966 Lackawanna of Omaha commenced beaming hides under contracts for Lackawanna. At about this time Good Bros. disposed of its machinery then used for beaming in the Newark plant.

It is anticipated that the new beam house operations in Omaha will prove mutually beneficial to Good Bros. and Lackawanna. As already observed, Lackawanna cannot operate a beam house at its Hackettstown plant because of sewage problems. It now has an assured and advantageously located source of beamed hides in Omaha. Good Bros. has an advantageous real estate investment under lease to Lackawanna of Omaha. It will also participate, by virtue of its one-third interest in Lackawanna of Omaha, in the profits that are expected to be earned by it in the beaming operation. And as already observed, Good Bros. is relieved from the risk of dealing in the volatile green hides market.

I

It is plaintiffs' theory that the close working relationship existing between Good Bros. and Lackawanna is tantamount to a merger of the two companies. Plaintiffs assert that Good Bros. assets are fully at the disposal of Lackawanna and that Good Bros. is, in effect, a private bank to be utilized in accordance with the whims of the directors of Lackawanna. It is argued that although Good Bros. was not liquidated, it had no active business or tanning function to perform after December 31, 1960, and that by December 31, 1964, 94% of its plant and equipment was converted into money or investment securities.

Plaintiffs allege that the gross sales appearing on Good Bros. records for the year 1961 and thereafter are really not gross sales at all. For example, the gross sales for 1964 reflect sales in hide processing and sales of green hides. Actually, the only hide processing Good Bros. performed was for Lackawanna through its arrangement with Remis. The sales of green hides were billed to Lackawanna at cost. It is thus contended that all the objectives of the proposed merger stated in the merger resolutions were in fact accomplished.

Initially, it may be noted that this is not a stockholder's derivative action. There is no charge of mismanagement or fraud to the detriment of either corporation. There is no charge that Good Bros. has been unfairly treated. True, the net worth of Good Bros. has not increased since 1959. However, this was in good measure due to loss of business because of changes in the industry and the obsolescence of its operation. The fact remains that since 1959 dividends have been paid annually to the stockholders of Good Bros.

A merger is defined in the leading New Jersey case dealing with the doctrine of *de facto* merger as the absorption by one corporation of one or more usually smaller corporations, which latter corporations lose their identity by becoming part of the larger enterprise. Applestein v. United Board & Carton Corp., 60 N.J.Super. 333, 342, 159 A.2d 146 (Ch. Div.1960), affirmed 33 N.J. 22, 161 A.2d 474 (1960). The court in *Applestein* made the following findings, which it held spelled out a *de facto* merger of the two companies:

> "Thus, every factor present in a corporate merger is found in this corporate plan, except, perhaps, a formal designation of the transaction as a 'merger.' There is proposed: (1) a transfer of all the shares and all the assets of Interstate to United; (2) an assumption by United of Interstate's liabilities; (3) a 'pooling of interests' of the two corporations; (4) the absorption of Interstate by United, and the dissolution of Interstate; (5) a joinder of officers and directors from both corporations on an enlarged board of directors; (6) the present executive and operating personnel of Interstate will be retained in the employ of United; and (7) the shareholders of the absorbed corporation, Interstate, as represented by the sole stockholder, Epstein, will surrender his 1,250 shares in Interstate for 160,000 newly issued shares in United, the amalgamated enterprise."

Although every element found by the court in *Applestein* may not be essential in determining the existence of a *de facto* merger, there are certain key elements existing therein which are not present in the case at bar. Significantly, there has been no exchange or transfer of shares between Good Bros. and Lackawanna. A consolidation or merger always involves a transfer of the assets and business of one corporation to another in exchange for its securities. Ballantine on Corporations, § 280, p. 664. The leading cases discussing the applicability of the *de facto* merger doctrine all concern situations where there is a transfer of assets by one corporation in exchange for shares of the purchasing corporation. Applestein v. United Board & Carton Corp., supra; * * * Hariton v. Arco Electronics, Inc., 40 Del.Ch. 326, 182 A.2d 22 (Ch.Del.1962), affirmed 188 A.2d 123 (Del.Sup.Ct.1963); Farris v. Glen Alden Corp., 393 Pa. 427, 143 A.2d 25 (Sup.Ct.1958). The issue common to all of the cited cases was whether the sale of assets in exchange for the shares of the purchasing corporation actually comprised a *de facto* merger of the corporations, thus making available dissenters' rights under the respective merger statutes. A concomitant of all the cases was that the corporation disposing of its assets terminated all business functions and virtually went out of existence.

This is not the factual pattern presented in the case at bar. There has not been a transfer of assets by Good Bros. to Lackawanna in exchange for shares as called for in the rejected merger agreement. Good Bros. has not ceased its corporate functions in furtherance of its charter. It earned interest on its loans to Lackawanna, and made an annual profit on the hide processing performed for Lackawanna through Remis. Good Bros. is very much alive and is enjoying profitable operations. It owns a building and land in Omaha from which it expects a 12% return on its investment. It also owns a one-third interest in Lackawanna of Omaha, Inc., a beaming operation, which corporation leases the aforementioned Omaha land and building. Good Bros. thus indirectly maintains its interest in the hopefully profitable phase of the hide processing industry. Lackawanna and Good Bros. always maintained and continue to maintain separate boards of directors and officers who hold regular meetings. Each corporation has its own accountant and files its separate tax returns. Each maintains its own bank accounts and investments.

Also lacking in the instant case, and of key importance, is the fact that Good Bros. has not assumed any of the liabilities of Lackawanna. True, Good Bros. has loaned working capital to Lackawanna, but in no instance has Good Bros. guaranteed the debts of Lackawanna. It has no liability to the creditors of Lackawanna and has not directed that the borrowed funds be utilized in any particular manner. Furthermore, Lackawanna has repaid its entire obligation to Good Bros., and the loan account was closed as of September 30, 1966.

Thus, it may be seen that virtually all of the elements which comprised a *de facto* merger in *Applestein* and the other cited decisions are lacking. There does exist a close working relationship between the two companies and there is an interlocking of directors and officers.

However, the presence of these factors do not *per se* constitute a merger. The definition of merger in *Applestein* has not been satisfied. There has been no absorption of one corporation of the other, with the absorbed corporation losing its identity. This finding is illustrated by the fact that if appraisal rights were to be granted, it would be impossible to decide which corporation, Good Bros. or Lackawanna, would be responsible for paying the value of the shares. N.J.S.A. 14:12–7, incorporating N.J.S.A. 14:12–6, provides for court-appointed appraisers to value the shares of the dissenters. N.J.S.A. 14:12–6 specifically provides that the "*consolidated* corporation shall pay to such stockholder the value of his stock * * *" (emphasis supplied). The existence of two functioning corporate entities, each owning respective assets and carrying on distinct business functions, makes the statute impossible to apply. There is no consolidated corporation that may be called upon to pay the dissenters the value of their shares.

Although many of the economic objectives sought to be accomplished under the proposed and rejected statutory merger in fact have been achieved, this without more does not constitute a *de facto* merger.

———◆———

If the facts in Pratt v. Ballman-Cummings Furniture Company and Good v. Lackawanna Leather Company are viewed most favorably to the planners of the transactions in each, their strategy is entirely understandable. The potential for synergy seemed to exist—in *Ballman-Cummings* because of ICC regulations concerning the availability of truck load shipping rates,[25] and in *Lackawanna* because of gains from vertical integration—if the operations of the two companies could be combined. The cost of doing so by one of the statutory techniques was to provide appraisal rights to minority shareholders who, apparently, had no other way to liquidate their investment. Not wanting the loss of capital that would have resulted from appraisal and, perhaps, because of the unavoidable uncertainty associated with judicial valuation, the planners in each case devised an extra-statutory technique to accomplish their ends. Is either the Delaware "equal dignity" approach or the Pennsylvania approach to statutory interpretation helpful in identifying where the line ought to be drawn?

3. The Concept of Equivalency

It takes no great insight to conclude that what is troubling about the differing statutory treatment of alternative acquisition techniques is the sense that functionally equivalent transactions are treated differently. The motive for applying the de facto merger doctrine is then to prevent the elevation of form over substance and its goal is to cause functionally equivalent transactions to be treated alike. It would

[25] Even though the two furniture companies were controlled by the same families and had interlocking directorates, ICC regulations apparently respected the formality of their separate existence. As a result, the lower shipping rates available when one company hired an entire truck were not available if the two companies shared a truck. This suggests a motivation for merger not directly considered in Part II: regulatory failure.

follow that a measure of the quality of the judicial response to the planner's ingenuity would be the extent to which planners were thereafter indifferent to transactional form.

But the ease with which this goal can be achieved and, perhaps, the wisdom of its pursuit, turn on our ability to clearly delineate the basis on which two forms of acquisitions can be said to be functionally equivalent. The difficulty of this inquiry is considered by Bayless Manning in an excerpt from a well known evaluation of the desirability of one of the consequences of the application of the de facto merger doctrine, the availability of appraisal rights. This is followed by a recent effort by Professor Melvin Eisenberg, the current Chief Reporter of the American Law Institute project on corporate governance and a major influence on the relevant portions of the California Corporations Code, to describe how the lines of equivalency should be drawn.

MANNING, THE SHAREHOLDER'S APPRAISAL REMEDY: AN ESSAY FOR FRANK COKER
72 Yale L.J. 223, 239–44 (1962).*

TRIGGERING TRANSACTIONS

* * *

When, under what circumstances, should * * * shareholders be given a statutory appraisal remedy so they can jump clear of the corporate enterprise if they do not like its course? One possible reply would be: "Under all circumstances."

* * *

In earlier pages, the point was made that the appraisal statutes, where applicable, pose a difficulty for the corporation because of the drain on the company's liquidity and because of procedural difficulties. Every extension of the appraisal remedy increases the burdens on the going enterprise. Indiscriminate extension of the remedy is pernicious. The remedy should apply only where the risks to the shareholder are great. And the remedy should not be made applicable to a class of transactions unless the benefits to the minority shareholders outweigh the consequent burden imposed upon the enterprise.

We must be selective. To help us to be selective it is useful to consider and compare a series of candidates. Following and on succeeding pages are three lists of events that may occur in the normal life course of an incorporated enterprise. The reader is asked to read over the lists with some deliberation. The question is: Should objecting shareholders be given the appraisal remedy in some, all, or none of the listed transactions or events—and why?

List I

— A rise in the United States balance of payments deficit

* Reprinted by permission of The Yale Law Journal Company and Fred B. Roth-   man & Company from *The Yale Law Journal*, Vol. 72, pp. 223, 239–244.

— An Antitrust suit brought by the Justice Department against the company

— A Presidential heart attack [35]

— Introduction of a promising new product by a competitor

— A declining stock market

— Nationalization of some of the company's foreign assets

— Large scale disarmament

In each of the cases in List I the shareholder may suddenly find his investment in the company threatened with extinction. He would be delighted to have the appraisal option open to him. But despite his desires in the matter and despite the economic fate about to overtake him, the appraisal statutes are, as every lawyer knows, not available to him. It is said that risks of the kind just listed are "assumed" by the investor. This answer is no more satisfactory here than it ever is, for the question is: Why are these risks imposed upon the investor while others are not?

All the events listed above have one feature in common. They are all, in a manner of speaking, external to the corporate enterprise—that is, they are events that were not, in a direct sense, brought about any any of the constituencies of the corporation. One may say, and it is usually said, that the "reason" these transactions are not triggering transactions under the appraisal statutes is that they are not transactions brought about by the will of the majority and objected to by the minority. This statement may be accepted as descriptively accurate. But it is hardly a satisfactory "explanation," for it leaves open the question: Why are we interested in protecting the investor against internal risks only? Let us leave that one with the answer that we are interested in internal risks because we are, and move on.

Here then is a second list of events out of a corporate biography. To meet the criterion just set, each of these transactions is internal to the constituent structure of the corporation, and not imposed by outside forces:

List II

— Mass resignation by the management

— An involuntary petition in bankruptcy for the corporation

— A demand by the relevant union for higher wages, accompanied by strike threat

— The refusal by a majority of the debenture holders to approve an indenture amendment considered by the shareholders to be vital to the continued successful operation of the enterprise

— A buyers' strike

---

[35] On the day following President Eisenhower's first heart attack the aggregate market value of all securities listed on the New York Stock Exchange dropped fourteen billion dollars. N.Y.Times, Sept. 28, 1955, p. 1, col. 6.

— A refusal by important suppliers to continue to supply the company

Each of these events is fraught with danger to the shareholder's investment. And each is precipitated by a group that is in some sense "internal" to the enterprise, is in some degree committed to its fortunes, and is in a position to affect those fortunes directly. Yet the appraisal statutes do nothing to protect the shareholder against the decisions of his fellow constituents in any of these instances. Creditors, workers, officers, customers, suppliers—all may whip things about as they will, and the shareholder will have to hold on to his seat and ride it out. When these people rock his world, the dissenter may not order it stopped for him to get off. He is never given that option unless the transaction was brought on by his fellow shareholders, or, very occasionally, by the directors. No one else counts.

The significance of this evident fact is seldom observed. To limit statutory concern to shareholders' and directors' acts is wholly arbitrary. The dissenters' investment can be as much threatened by acts of bondholders as by acts of shareholders, as much by wage paid workers and salary paid officers as by fee paid directors. It is circular and meaningless to say that the remedy is available in transaction X but not in transaction Y, "because" shareholders decide transaction X while transaction Y is brought on by non-shareholders.

To limit our concern to acts of shareholders makes it now apparent that we are not dealing with an economic problem or with economic solutions. The economic risk to the shareholder does not turn on the question of who was responsible for the event giving rise to the risk; and when the statutes undertake to differentiate among those effectively causing the event, they do not make the differentiation in economic categories, but in lawyer's categories. We may say of an operating business enterprise that a variety of economic constituencies play important parts, and we can to some extent isolate and describe these. In statements of this kind we are seeking to make operational statements about economic phenomena. But when we say that we are interested only in those events that are brought about immediately by "shareholders" and "directors" we are no longer in the world of the economist or political scientist—we have reconfirmed our disinterest in economics and climbed onto a level of unadulterated legal categories. * * * We have fled the brassy realm of practical effects and entered upon the golden realm of lawyers' abstraction where the din of the market place can scarcely be heard.

Just *why* we should have proceeded in this way is not at all clear. But accepting as given that no shareholder will be accorded the appraisal remedy except in events or transactions brought about by other shareholders or directors, we should now look at a third list of transactions, all of which meet this condition. This list is somewhat more detailed and, for ease of comparison, the events have been arranged into crude groupings. Which, if any, of the following events should give what shareholders a statutory out?

List III

— The shareholders vote out the board. Ninety-eight per cent of the shareholders mark their proxies "da" on a resolution of confidence in the management currently languishing in jail under Sherman Act convictions. A majority interest in the corporation's stock or other securities changes hands.

— In 1962, the company shifts from the manufacture of buggy whips to the manufacture of seat belts. The company shifts from the manufacture of seat belts to the manufacture of buggy whips. The company plunges into, or pulls out of, European operations. The company buys 100,000 shares of New Haven Railroad stock. The company files a voluntary petition in bankruptcy.

— The shareholders amend the purpose clause in the charter. They amend the charter to: change the corporate name; change the home office; change the number of directors; scrap cumulative voting; change the par value of a class of stock.

— The company pays a large dividend. The company refuses to pay any dividends. The company makes a large distribution of assets to junior security holders. The company makes periodic distributions of cash or of other assets, looking forward to a distribution of all assets. The corporation donates a million dollars to charity.

— The corporation dissolves.

— The company enters into a long term labor contract under which all foreseeable profits will go to the union. The company enters into a long term labor contract under which, by prevailing standards, the workers are grossly underpaid. The company enters into long term executive employment contracts calling for astronomical salaries and lavish perquisites.

— The company issues senior stock. It issues * * * junior stock. It issues stock for cash. It issues stock for securities or other noncash assets. It issues stock for cash or assets at less than the "market." It grants stock options to a management group at less than "market." It grants stock options to others at less than "market."

— Corporation *A* merges with Corporation *B*, the latter "surviving." Corporation *A* merges with Corporation *B*, the former "surviving." Corporation *A* consolidates with Corporation *B*, Corporation *C* resulting. Corporation *A* acquires all the stock of Corporation *B*. Corporation *B*, a 100 per cent subsidiary of Corporation *A*, is eliminated by merger with Corporation *A*, by dissolving and handing over its assets as a liquidating distribution, by distributing its assets without dissolving, by buying up and cancelling all the *B* securities held by *A*.

— Corporation *A* buys $1 million of assets from Corporation *B*. *A* sells $1 million in assets to *B*. *A* sells all its assets to *B* for $1

million. *A* buys *B's* blast furnace for cash; *B* buys *A's* cash for
a blast furnace. *A* sells real estate to *B* with a lease back to *A*.
A buys real estate from *B* with a lease back to *B*. *A* buys
assets, paying for them by issuing its securities—equity and
debt. *A* translates its fixed assets into cash or securities in one
transaction. *A* translates its fixed assets into cash or securities in a series of transactions.

— Corporation *A* buys all the assets of Corporation *B* for *A*
   securities, and after X months, *B* distributes the *A* securities to
   its shareholders; sells the *A* securities on the market and
   distributes the cash to the *B* shareholders; dissolves and distributes the *A* securities; dissolves and sells the *A* securities.

— The corporation lists or delists on the New York Stock Exchange.

If a man from Mars were to read over this list of events, how would
he assess their significance to the objecting shareholder and pick out
those transactions so direful as to call for the extraordinary measures
of the appraisal remedy? Only the most highly sophisticated Mar-
tian—or the most unsophisticated—would be able to guess what our
statutes have done.

M. EISENBERG, THE STRUCTURE OF THE CORPORATION
224–35, 250–51 (1976).

§ 14.1 Stock-For-Assets Combinations Under the Traditional Cor-porate Statutes—A Problem in Statutory Ambiguity

The Delaware position, although a minority view, has generally
received the commentators' approbation.[1] Thus, the *Farris* result has
been described as a "blaze of Platonism," because it is based upon
finding "a 'true and real merger' that exists beyond, and is merely
reflected in, the merger statutes," [2] whereas the Delaware cases are
praised for "requiring only adherence to form," thereby affording an
objective test and avoiding "the inherent complexities of a judicial test
which seeks a 'real' merger beyond the form of the transaction." [3] Is
this analysis just?

Let us begin with the typical stock-for-assets combination, in which
the survivor assumes all of the transferor's rights and obligations, and
the transferor dissolves pursuant to the underlying agreement. The
first question to be determined in such a case, obviously, is whether the
transaction constitutes a "merger" or a "sale" within the meaning of
the statute. The Delaware court has dealt with this question by
invoking its equal-dignity theory—that the validity of "action taken
under one section of [the Delaware corporation] law * * * is not

---

[1] See, e.g., Folk, *De Facto Mergers in Del-aware: Hariton v. Arco Electronics, Inc.*, 49 Va.L.Rev. 1261 (1963); Manning, *The Shareholder's Appraisal Remedy: An Es-say for Frank Coker*, 72 Yale L.J. 223, 257 (1959) * * *

[2] Manning, *The Shareholder's Appraisal Remedy*, supra note 1, at 257. See also Folk, *De Facto Mergers in Delaware*, supra note 1, at 1277.

[3] Folk, *De Facto Mergers in Delaware*, supra note 1, at 1277.

dependent upon, nor to be tested by the requirements of other unrelated sections." Applied to combination cases, this theory apparently means that the validity of action taken under sale-of-substantially-all-assets provisions is not to be tested by the requirements of the merger provisions. But such an answer is virtually irrelevant to the question it purports to address. The question in these cases is whether a given combination *is* a sale. It is in no way responsive to that question for the court to say, as Delaware says, that *if* a combination is a sale, it need not meet the requirements laid down for mergers. In applying its so-called equal-dignity theory to cases like *Hariton,* all the Delaware court has done is assume its own conclusion.

What led Delaware into this logical dead end? Pretty clearly, two implicit assumptions: (1) that the terms "merger" and "sale," as used in the corporate statutes, are unambiguous; and (2) that the combinations before the court were sales, and not mergers, within the meaning of those unambiguous terms. The first assumption, at least, is also reflected in the work of those commentators who have criticized cases like *Farris* for platonically finding "a 'true and real merger' that exists beyond, and is merely reflected in, the merger statutes." To a certain extent this assumption is implicit even in *Farris,* * * * since the combinations in those cases were held to be mergers de facto rather than mergers within the meaning of the statutes.

A close examination of the statutes, however, reveals that the terms "merger" and "sale," rather than being unambiguous, are marked by nothing so much as by ambiguity. Take for example the New York statute, which is typical in this regard. Mergers between domestic corporations (other than short-form, parent-subsidiary mergers) are governed by Sections 901–904, 906, and 910.[4] Section 901(a)(1) provides that "[t]wo or more domestic corporations * * * may [m]erge into a single corporation which shall be one of the constituent corporations." Section 901(b)(1) provides that "[w]henever used in this article * * * '[m]erger' means a procedure of the character described in subparagraph (a)(1)." Section 902 provides that to consummate a merger, the board of each constituent shall first adopt a plan of merger setting forth the name of each constituent, its capitalization, and the terms of the proposed merger, including the manner of converting the shares of each constituent into shares or other securities of the survivor, or the cash or other consideration to be paid, a statement of any amendments to the survivor's certificate, and such other provisions as the board considers necessary or desirable. Section 903 provides that the plan shall then be submitted to the shareholders of the constituents for their approval. Section 904 provides for the filing of a certificate of merger. Section 906 provides that upon the filing of such a certificate, the surviving corporation shall succeed to the assets, rights, and liabilities of each constituent. Section 910 provides for appraisal rights.

And that is all. The statute (and to repeat, the New York statute is typical in this regard) lays down the procedures to *effect* a merger,

[4] N.Y.Bus.Corp.Law §§ 901–904, 906, 910 (McKinney 1963 & Supp.1974).

and it lays down the operative *results* of a merger, but it nowhere defines a merger. We know that if a merger is effected, two corporations become one. We know little more—at least from the statute. Why not? Probably because the legislature thought that a merger was a well-understood business transaction, no more in need of definition than a mare. In other words, a merger is *precisely* something that "exists beyond, and is merely reflected in, the merger statutes." A merger is a real-live-flesh-and-blood thing that businessmen do and legislators regulate. The platonist is one who thinks that mergers are created by Caesar rather than Crassus.

But then what is the business transaction which the legislature contemplated? In common usage, as evidenced by *Webster's*, "merger" means the "absorption by a corporation of one or more others. * * *"[6] Similarly, *Black's Law Dictionary* defines a corporate merger as "the union of two or more corporations by the transfer of property of all to one of them, which continues in existence, the others being swallowed up or merged therein."[7] Economic and financial usage tends to subsume under the term "merger" any business combination involving the issuance of stock.

All this, and the statutory scheme itself, points in one direction: the prototypical transaction contemplated by the legislature when it used the term "merger" is a combination of two corporations, effected through the issuance of consideration—normally stock—by one in exchange for shares of the other, and resulting in a fusion of the constituents and the consequent disappearance of the transferor as a going enterprise. In fact, once it is understood that the statutes do not define a merger, it is difficult to see how the term can be construed so as not to include such combinations. The only alternative would be to construe the statutes to cover only combinations which the board *labels* a merger. But such a construction seems impermissible. First, it would render almost meaningless the legislative prescription that a merger requires shareholder approval and gives rise to appraisal rights. This prescription is intended to protect shareholders. Unless the legislature clearly so indicates, therefore, it cannot be presumed to intend that management could nullify these rights through the mere expedient of labeling. * * *

Thus at least some stock-for-assets combinations seem to constitute mergers within the meaning of the corporate statutes—not "de facto," but de jure. But this still leaves a second question: Are such transactions also sales? Based on common usage, a strong argument can be made that they are not. For example, suppose *A* and *B* organize a partnership, *AB*, and each contributes to the partnership a going business. Generally speaking, neither lawyers nor laymen would say that *A* has "sold" his business (or that *AB* has "purchased" it). The reason *A* 's transfer would not normally be called a "sale" is that the term "sale usually refers to a transaction in which a transferor *disposes* of his interest in the thing transferred, whereas in the hypothetical *A*

---

[6] *Webster's New International Dictionary*   [7] *Black's Law Dictionary* 1140 (4th rev. *of the English Language* 1414 (3d ed. 1961).   ed. 1968) * * *

retains an interest in the transferred business. Now suppose that *AB* is not a partnership, but a corporation? Again, generally speaking neither lawyers nor laymen would call *A*'s transfer of his business to *AB* in exchange for *AB* stock a "sale" by *A* (or a "purchase" by *AB*), and for the same reason. *   *   *

But then suppose *A* transfers his business to *AB* in exchange for *AB* stock when *AB* is an existing corporation, wholly owned by *B*? Here too the transaction would not normally be described as a "sale" of his business by *A* (or a "purchase" by *AB*), again for the same reason: *A*'s continuity of interest in the transferred business. But this last transaction is, of course, a stock-for-assets combination.

It therefore appears that many stock-for-assets transactions could be deemed *either* mergers or sales under the corporate statutes. Which characterization should be applied must then depend on which would best reconcile the overlapping merger and sale provisions, and best effectuate the apparent statutory purpose. For reasons already reviewed, the label given the transaction cannot be dispositive. However, there are several other techniques, consistent with the statutory schemes, which may be employed to segregate sales and mergers. Thus, a distinction could be drawn between those stock-for-assets transactions which do not involve any other indicia of a merger—"without more," to use the language of *Farris*—and those which are accompanied by some such indicia; for example, a requirement that the transferor dissolve and an assumption by the survivor of the transferor's liabilities.[16] Alternatively, those transactions in which the survivor issues principally common or other voting stock could be distinguished from those in which it issues principally nonvoting securities—treating the former as a merger and the latter as a sale.

*   *   *

Still a third possibility would be to draw a distinction on the basis of the relative size of the two constituents. Reverting to the hypothetical transfer of a business by *A* to the existing corporation *AB*, if *AB*'s business is so much larger than *A*'s that *A* receives only a negligible interest in *AB*—for example, if *A*'s business consists of several small supermarkets and *AB* is a national chain of supermarkets—both laymen and lawyers probably would say that *A* had "sold" his business. This is so because while *A* retains a continuity of interest in his former assets, his stake in those assets and in *AB* as a whole is so small that for all practical purposes *A* has parted with substantially all of that interest. What constitutes a substantial stake? Although the corporate cases have not addressed themselves to this question, the courts are nevertheless not without guidelines; as will be shown below, several statutes and the rules of the American and New York stock exchanges have recognized 15–20 percent as a cutoff for closely related

[16] Such an approach has been criticized on the ground that an assumption of the transferor's liabilities merely constitutes additional consideration for the assets received, while dissolution of the transferor is "frequently, if not usually" an incident of a stock-for-assets transaction. 59 Colum.L.Rev. 366, 370 (1959). But if such requirements are "frequently, if not usually" an incident of stock-for-assets transactions, that may simply indicate that such transactions are "frequently, if not usually" mergers within the meaning of the statutes.

purposes. Under this line of analysis, if the transferor's shareholders receive less than a 15–20 percent stake in the reconstituted enterprise the transaction would be deemed a sale within the meaning of the statute; if more, a merger.

§ 14.2 A Modern Statutory Treatment of Stock-For-Assets Combinations (Including Classical Mergers)

If we put aside the problems raised by the traditional statutes, and consider instead the optimal legislative treatment of stock-for-assets combinations and classical mergers, three things seem clear: (1) A classical merger (that is, a merger so denominated) is simply a special case of a stock-for-assets transaction; (2) Shareholder rights in such transactions should depend on the real impact of the transaction (which may of course include significant changes in legal rights), not on how the transaction is labeled; and (3) The impact of such a transaction on shareholders of a transferor may differ from the impact on shareholders of a survivor, so that the rights of each body of shareholders must be considered separately.

A. The Transferor's Shareholders

On the transferor's side, the issues are relatively straight-forward. If one corporation transfers substantially all of its assets to a second in exchange for stock in the latter (or indeed for any consideration other than cash), from the perspective of the transferor's shareholders the result is a radical reconstitution of the enterprise—so radical that it should not only require approval by the transferor's shareholders, but give rise to appraisal rights for those of the transferor's shareholders who do not choose to participate; and this is true whether the transaction is denominated a merger, or not.

B. The Survivor's Shareholders

On the survivor's side, the picture is somewhat more complex. If a stock-for-assets combination has a significant economic or legal impact on the survivor's shareholders it should certainly require approval by those shareholders, and give rise to appraisal rights on their part, for much the same reasons that apply to shareholders of the transferor. But if the amount of stock issued by the survivor is not significant in terms of its previously outstanding stock, and no significant change is made in the control structure of the legal entity in which the survivor's corporate enterprise is enveloped, the combination is unlikely to have a significant economic impact on the survivor's shareholders. Such a transaction, therefore, should neither require approval of the survivor's shareholders nor give such shareholders appraisal rights; and this is true even if the combination is denominated a merger.

*   *   *

[Such an approach is] taken by the New York * * * Stock Exchange, which require[s] shareholder approval as a condition to listing new stock issued by listed companies to effect business combinations, "[w]here the present or potential issuance [to the transferor] of common stock or securities convertible into common stock could result in an increase in outstanding common shares approximating 20% or more * * *." [32] [Professor Eisenberg goes on to point out that the New York Stock Exchange provision also covers the acquisition of assets other than by means of a business combination and recommends that approach as well.]

A. Cash-For-Assets Combinations

1. The transferor's shareholders. Under the traditional statutes, a sale of substantially all assets for cash requires the approval of the transferor's shareholders. This is as it should be: such a transaction constitutes a radical reconstruction of the enterprise from the transferor's perspective. There is, however, an important difference between a stock-for-assets and a cash-for assets transaction. Where the transfer is for stock, the result is not only a radically restructured but a continuing enterprise; but where the transfer is for cash and the transferor is immediately liquidated (as is typically the case), the transferor's shareholders are not being brought along in a continuing enterprise, and appraisal rights may therefore be unnecessary, except perhaps as a check on the fairness of price in a self-dealing situation.

2. The survivor's shareholders. A cash-for-assets transaction looks much different from the perspective of the survivor's shareholders. An initial question from this perspective is whether such transactions are mergers within the meaning of the traditional statutes. At one time it would have been fairly clear they were not, since a classical merger involved the issuance of stock by the survivor. Today, however, it is common for merger provisions to contemplate the issuance of cash,[34] and it seems likely that, properly or improperly, these provisions will be interpreted to permit the issuance solely of cash. Under such an interpretation, a cash-for-assets transaction could be viewed as a merger within the meaning of the traditional statutes. On the other hand, such transactions could also be viewed as purchases, and which view should be taken may properly depend on underlying policy considerations. Unlike stock-for-assets combinations, an acquisition of substantially all of a transferor's assets by a survivor for cash may involve neither an increase in the size of the survivor's assets (but instead only a reshuffling of liquid into fixed assets), nor a reallocation of ownership interests. From the survivor's perspective cash-for-assets combinations will therefore frequently be difficult to distinguish from internal expansion; that is, they will frequently not rise to the level of a structural change. Therefore, such transactions should not normally require approval by the survivor's shareholders nor give rise to appraisal rights for such shareholders.

◆

Unlike most academics who must passively wait for others to implement their recommendations, Professor Eisenberg had the opportunity to take up that burden himself as a participant in the revision process that led up to the California Corporations Code that became effective January 1, 1977. The following are the principal provisions of the California Corporations Code bearing on acquisitions.

CALIFORNIA CORPORATIONS CODE—SECTIONS BEARING ON ACQUISITIONS

Chapter 1. General Provisions and Definitions

§ 152. Approved by (or Approval of) the Outstanding Shares

"Approved by (or approval of) the outstanding shares" means approved by the affirmative vote of a majority of the outstanding shares entitled to vote. Such approval shall include the affirmative vote of a majority of the outstanding shares of each class or series entitled, by any provision of the articles or of this division, to vote as a class or series on the subject matter being voted upon and shall also include the affirmative vote of such greater proportion (including all) of the outstanding shares of any class or series if such greater proportion is required by the articles or this division.

§ 153. Approved by (or Approval of) the Shareholders

"Approved by (or approval of) the shareholders" means approved or ratified by the affirmative vote of a majority of the shares represented and voting at a duly held meeting at which a quorum is present (which shares voting affirmatively also constitute at least a majority of the required quorum) or by the written consent of shareholders (Section 603) or by the affirmative vote or written consent of such greater proportion (including all) of the shares of any class or series as may be provided in the articles or in this division for all or any specified shareholder action.

§ 160. Control

(a) Except as provided in subdivision (b), "control" means the possession, direct or indirect, of the power to direct or cause the direction of the management and policies of a corporation.

(b) "Control" in Sections 181, 1001 and 1200 means the ownership directly or indirectly of shares possessing more than 50 percent of the voting power.

§ 161. Constituent Corporation

"Constituent corporation" means a corporation which is merged with one or more other corporations and includes the surviving corporation.

§ 175. Parent

Except as used in Sections 1001, 1101 and 1200, a "parent" of a specified corporation is an affiliate controlling such corporation directly or indirectly through one or more intermediaries. In Sections 1001 and

1101, "parent" means a person in control of a corporation as defined in subdivision (b) of Section 160.

§ 181. Reorganization

"Reorganization" means:

(a) A merger pursuant to Chapter 11 (commencing with Section 1100) other than a short-form merger (a "merger reorganization");

(b) The acquisition by one corporation in exchange in whole or in part for its equity securities (or the equity securities of a corporation which is in control of the acquiring corporation) of shares of another corporation if, immediately after the acquisition, the acquiring corporation has control of such other corporation (an "exchange reorganization"); or

(c) The acquisition by one corporation in exchange in whole or in part for its equity securities (or the equity securities of a corporation which is in control of the acquiring corporation) or for its debt securities (or debt securities of a corporation which is in control of the acquiring corporation) which are not adequately secured and which have a maturity date in excess of five years after the consummation of the reorganization, or both, of all or substantially all of the assets of another corporation (a "sale-of-assets reorganization").

§ 190. Surviving Corporation

"Surviving corporation" means a corporation into which one or more other corporations are merged.

§ 1001. Sale, Lease, Exchange, etc.; of Property or Assets; Approval; Abandonment; Terms, Conditions and Consideration

(a) A corporation may sell, lease, convey, exchange, transfer or otherwise dispose of all or substantially all of its assets when the principal terms are

(1) Approved by the board, and

(2) Unless the transaction is in the usual and regular course of its business, approved by the outstanding shares (Section 152), either before or after approval by the board and before or after the transaction.

A transaction constituting a reorganization (Section 181) is subject to the provisions of Chapter 12 (commencing with Section 1200) and not this section (other than subdivision (d) hereof).

* * *

(d) If the buyer in a sale of assets pursuant to subdivision (a) of this section or subdivision (g) of Section 2001 is in control of or under common control with the seller, the principal terms of the sale must be approved by at least 90 percent of the voting power unless the sale is to a domestic or foreign corporation in consideration of the nonredeemable common shares of the purchasing corporation or its parent.

* * *

Chapter 12.   Reorganizations

§ 1200.   Approval by Board

A reorganization (Section 181) shall be approved by the board of:

(a) Each constituent corporation in a merger reorganization;

(b) The acquiring corporation in an exchange reorganization;

(c) The acquiring corporation and the corporation whose property and assets are acquired in a sale-of-assets reorganization; and

(d) The corporation in control of any constituent or acquiring corporation under subdivision (a), (b) or (c) and whose equity securities are issued or transferred in the reorganization (a "parent party").

§ 1201.   Approval of Shareholders; Abandonment by Board; Actions to Attack Validity of Party Directly or Indirectly Controlled by Other Party

(a) The principal terms of a reorganization shall be approved by the outstanding shares (Section 152) of each class of each corporation the approval of whose board is required under Section 1200, except as provided in subdivision (b) and except that (unless otherwise provided in the articles) no approval of any class of outstanding preferred shares of the surviving or acquiring corporation or parent party shall be required if the rights, preferences, privileges and restrictions granted to or imposed upon such class of shares remain unchanged (subject to the provisions of subdivision (c)). For the purpose of this subdivision, two classes of common shares differing only as to voting rights shall be considered as a single class of shares.

(b) No approval of the outstanding shares (Section 152) is required by subdivision (a) in the case of any corporation if such corporation, or its shareholders immediately before the reorganization, or both, shall own (immediately after the reorganization) equity securities, other than any warrant or right to subscribe to or purchase such equity securities, of the surviving or acquiring corporation or a parent party (subdivision (d) of Section 1200) possessing more than five-sixths of the voting power of the surviving or acquiring corporation or parent party. In making the determination of ownership by the shareholders of a corporation, immediately after the reorganization, of equity securities pursuant to the preceding sentence, equity securities which they owned immediately before the reorganization as shareholders of another party to the transaction shall be disregarded. For the purpose of this section only, the voting power of a corporation shall be calculated by assuming the conversion of all equity securities convertible (immediately or at some future time) into shares entitled to vote but not assuming the exercise of any warrant or right to subscribe to or purchase such shares.

(c) Notwithstanding the provisions of subdivision (b), a reorganization shall be approved by the outstanding shares (Section 152) of the surviving corporation in a merger reorganization if any amendment is made to its articles which would otherwise require such approval.

(d) Notwithstanding the provisions of subdivision (b), a reorganization shall be approved by the outstanding shares (Section 152) of any class of a corporation which is a party to a merger or sale-of-assets reorganization if holders of shares of that class receive shares of the surviving or acquiring corporation or parent party having different rights, preferences, privileges or restrictions than those surrendered. Shares in a foreign corporation received in exchange for shares in a domestic corporation have different rights, preferences, privileges and restrictions within the meaning of the preceding sentence.

(e) Notwithstanding the provisions of subdivisions (a) and (b), a reorganization shall be approved by the affirmative vote of at least two-thirds of each class of the outstanding shares of any close corporation if the reorganization would result in their receiving shares of a corporation which is not a close corporation; provided, however, that the articles may provide for a lesser vote, but not less than a majority of the outstanding shares of each class.

(f) Any approval required by this section may be given before or after the approval by the board. Notwithstanding approval required by this section, the board may abandon the proposed reorganization without further action by the shareholders, subject to the contractual rights, if any, of third parties.

§ 1300. Reorganization or Short-form Merger; Dissenting Shares; Corporate Purchase at Fair Market Value; Definitions

(a) If the approval of the outstanding shares (Section 152) of a corporation is required for a reorganization under subdivisions (a) and (b) or subdivision (e) of Section 1201, each shareholder of such corporation and each shareholder of a disappearing corporation in a short-form merger may, by complying with this chapter, require the corporation in which the shareholder holds shares to purchase for cash at their fair market value the shares owned by the shareholder which are dissenting shares as defined in subdivision (b). The fair market value shall be determined as of the day before the first announcement of the terms of the proposed reorganization or short-form merger, excluding any appreciation or depreciation in consequence of the proposed action, but adjusted for any stock split, reverse stock split or share dividend which becomes effective thereafter.

(b) As used in this chapter, "dissenting shares" means shares which come within all of the following descriptions:

(1) Which were not immediately prior to the reorganization or short-form merger either (i) listed on any national securities exchange certified by the Commissioner of Corporations under subdivision (*o*) of Section 25100 or (ii) listed on the list of OTC margin stocks issued by the Board of Governors of the Federal Reserve System, and the notice of meeting of shareholders to act upon the reorganization summarizes the provisions of this section and Sections 1301, 1302, 1303 and 1304; provided, however, that this provision does not apply to any shares with respect to which there

exists any restriction on transfer imposed by the corporation or by any law or regulation; and provided, further, that this provision does not apply to any class of shares described in clause (i) or (ii) if demands for payment are filed with respect to 5 percent or more of the outstanding shares of that class.

(2) Which were outstanding on the date for the determination of shareholders entitled to vote on the reorganization and (i) were not voted in favor of the reorganization or, (ii) if described in clause (i) or (ii) of paragraph (1) (without regard to the provisos in that paragraph), were voted against the reorganization, or which were held of record on the effective date of a short-form merger; provided, however, that clause (i) rather than clause (ii) of this paragraph applies in any case where the approval required by Section 1201 is sought by written consent rather than at a meeting.

(3) Which the dissenting shareholder has demanded that the corporation purchase at their fair market value, in accordance with Section 1301.

(4) Which the dissenting shareholder has submitted for endorsement, in accordance with Section 1302.

(c) As used in this chapter, "dissenting shareholder" means the recordholder of dissenting shares and includes a transferee of record.

--------♦--------

The present California Corporations Code represents the most thorough response to Professor Eisenberg's call for a modern statutory approach focusing on the impact upon shareholders rather than the boundaries of assertedly ambiguous statutory terms. As described by a prominent practitioner, its distinctive structure—defining the term "reorganization" to include each common acquisition technique, and then specifying the statutory requirements for "reorganization" generally rather than for each technique—was intended "to create a statutory framework under which both the form of the transaction and the entity chosen to be the acquiring or surviving corporation are determined by considerations other than avoidance of stockholders' voting and appraisal rights." Small, *Corporate Combinations Under the New California General Corporation Law*, 23 U.C.L.A.L.Rev. 1190, 1191 (1976). As an exercise, work through how the transactions described in *Farris* and *Penn Central* would have been treated under the California statute. Also note, as was pointed out earlier, that the California statute, following Professor Eisenberg's recommendation, treats shareholders of corporations selling substantially all of their assets for cash or cash equivalents differently than if the consideration was securities of the purchaser; appraisal rights are not available in the former situation.[26] Although it is true that the distinction may reflect the fact that shareholders receiving cash are not forced to become shareholders in a different corporation, which is an argument believed to originally

---

[26] This is accomplished by excluding such transactions from the definition of a reorganization in § 181(c). Under § 1300, appraisal rights are available only in a reorganization.

explain the development of appraisal rights, (see M. Eisenberg, supra, at 75 and sources there cited), the point then should also extend to shareholders of target corporation in a cash merger. How does the California statute treat the latter transaction? Also keep in mind that the California statute does not require the approval of, or grant appraisal rights to, the shareholders of the acquiring company in an asset acquisition if the consideration is cash or cash equivalents. In this regard, the statute is consistent in that no vote of the acquiring company shareholders is required in a stock transaction if they retain five-sixths of the voting power of the surviving corporation.

California is not the only state which has updated its corporate statute to acknowledge the equivalence of alternative statutory techniques. See, e.g., Ohio Rev.Code Ann. tit. 17, §§ 1701.01(Q), 1701.83(A), 1701.84(D); N.J.Stat.Ann. 14A:10–3, 14A:10–12; Pa.Stat.Ann. tit. 15, § 1311(F).

Note: The Scope of the Inquiry

The goal of the de facto merger doctrine is to cause functionally equivalent transactions to be treated alike. The problem, however, is in specifying the touchstone against which functional equivalence should be measured. In its most straightforward application the doctrine asserts that statutory acquisition techniques which are functionally equivalent to mergers should provide shareholders of the constituent corporations the same protections as are provided in mergers. This seems clearly to be Professor Eisenberg's approach in concluding that the statutory terms "merger" and "sale" are ambiguous and then resolving that ambiguity by reference to functional equivalence. Certainly recommendations for a modern statutory approach, triggering equivalent protections in connection with any of the statutory transactional forms, reflects the notion that the protections given shareholders in mergers should be the measure.

But why limit the inquiry concerning the existence of equivalence to statutory alternatives? If all transactions which are functionally equivalent to mergers should offer shareholders the same protections, then the de facto merger doctrine should also apply to efforts by planners to achieve the results of a merger by nonstatutory techniques. This problem may be seen more clearly with an example. Recall that Professor Eisenberg recommends that a modern statute should require approval by the acquiring company's shareholders where the consideration used is stock, but not when the consideration is cash. This is accomplished in the new California Corporations Code for cash asset acquisitions by excluding them from the definition of "reorganizations," in Section 181 and thereby from the requirements of Sections 1200 and 1300 dealing with shareholder approval and appraisal rights. The same result is accomplished for cash mergers by Section 1201(b) which eliminates voting and appraisal rights if a constituent corporation "or its shareholders immediately before the reorganization, or both, shall own (immediately after the reorganization) equity securities * * * possessing more than five-sixths of the voting power" of the acquiring corporation. Because no shares are issued in a cash merger, shareholders of the acquiring company obviously meet the five-sixths requirement. But what happens when the planner goes to work? Can approval of the shareholders of the acquiring company be avoided by making a public offering of new stock, representing one-sixth of the company's voting power, and then, after more or less time has passed, using the cash proceeds from that offering to acquire substantially all of the assets of another corporation or to effect a cash merger? Similarly, should transactions be aggregated for the purposes of the five-sixths calculation? Suppose an acquiring company contemplates a series of transactions as in Terry v. Penn Central Corporation, no one of which will involve issuance of shares representing one-sixth of the company's voting power, but which fairly can be expected to exceed that figure in the aggregate?

The issue posed is how broadly the de facto merger doctrine extends. Even if the claimed ambiguity concerning the words "merger" and "sale" in traditional statutes is eliminated,[27] what of a transaction which, in the absence of a de facto analysis clearly falls outside of the statute entirely? The issue is particularly important with respect to statutes like that of California whose legislative history indicates that its approach was selected "for the purpose of codifying the 'de facto merger' doctrine." *Report of the Assembly Select Committee on the Revision of the Corporations Code* 93 (1975). Does the doctrine survive the enactment of such a statute or will the response to efforts to apply it to non-statutory alternatives meet an analysis of the sort found in Terry v. Penn Central Corporation?

That the problem at which the de facto merger doctrine was directed was not eliminated in California by enactment of a modern statutory approach was demonstrated by Woods v. Natomas Co., No. 811–238 (Cal.Super.Ct., Aug. 1, 1983). That case involved Diamond Shamrock's acquisition of Natomas Company by merging Natomas with a Diamond-Shamrock subsidiary created for that purpose,[28] and the

---

[27] How persuasive is Professor Eisenberg's argument that the statutory terms "merger" and "sale" are, in fact, ambiguous? His point is essentially that the typical statute does not define either word in terms of their result, but only in terms of the mechanism by which a common result is accomplished. This distinction is then rejected as merely involving "labels" and a construction giving substance to it is therefore deemed "impermissible." But the type of distinction drawn by the statute can be described in a more favorable light. What the statute actually does is define two different processes, both of which reach the same result but by quite different means. Viewed in this way, it is not unusual to distinguish between different means to a common result. It is, for example, hardly persuasive to argue that natural childbirth and caesarian section are really the same thing because their results, a child, are indistinguishable; the difference in the processes is itself significant. Similarly, the difference in the processes by which the same result is achieved in a merger and in a sale of assets is also very important. The planner is given the option of trading efficiency for flexibility and the result of that decision with respect to such things as contingent liabilities and union contracts can be critical. The question of whether the *unambiguous* differences in processes justify the difference in shareholder voting and appraisal rights of course still remains; however, that question must be considered directly rather than avoided by treating the differences as if they did not exist.

[28] The facts have been simplified for ease of presentation. In the actual transaction, a new holding company was created and both Natomas and the pre-transaction Diamond Shamrock were merged with the holding company's newly formed subsidia-

issue posed was whether Natomas' preferred shareholders were entitled to a class vote on the transaction under Cal.Corp.Code § 1201(a). If the transaction had been structured as a typical triangular merger, in which Natomas was merged into the newly formed Diamond Shamrock subsidiary, there would have been no doubt that the transaction would have required the approval of the Natomas preferred shareholders voting as a class. However, the transaction planners were clever indeed. Section 1201(a) eliminates the requirement of a class vote for the preferred shareholders of the "surviving corporation," as defined in Section 190, so long as the rights, preferences, privileges and restrictions of the preferred shares are not altered in the transaction. The planners' solution, then, was to structure the transaction not as a forward triangular merger in which Natomas would be merged into the new subsidiary (and a class vote would have been required), but as a *reverse* triangular merger in which the new subsidiary would be merged into Natomas. By reversing the transaction, Natomas became the "surviving corporation" and § 1201(a) then operated to eliminate the preferred shareholders' class vote.

Not surprisingly, the preferred shareholders made a de facto merger type argument. Regardless of the literal language of the statute, the effect of either a forward or a reverse triangular merger on the Natomas preferred shareholders was the same—they would become minority shareholders in a Diamond Shamrock subsidiary for which there was no public market. If a class vote is necessary to protect preferred shareholders in a forward triangular merger, nothing but form is changed by casting the transaction as a reverse triangular merger. The court disagreed. Despite a statute designed explicitly to cause shareholder protection in acquisitions to depend on substance, the court credited the form in which the planners cast the transaction, and the preferred shareholders were denied their class vote.

In short, the problem to which the de facto merger doctrine responds has proven difficult to eliminate by statute even when the drafters were trying and, in all events, the problem is more complicated than simply determining which acquisition transactions, statutory or not, are the functional equivalent of a merger. The choice of merger as a touchstone may be only a contextual shorthand for a set of circumstances that presents special risks and thus requires special protections in the form of voting and appraisal rights for shareholders. Should not then the de facto doctrine also extend to those events which are functionally equivalent to mergers not because they are acquisition transactions but, more fundamentally, because they pose the same special risks as mergers?

This seems to be Manning's point in creating his three different lists of events, that no meaningful distinction separates the three categories of events from the perspective of their impact on shareholders. The implication is that appraisal rights are appropriate in all of the situations described or in none. If we are unwilling to extend

ry. The analysis in the text is not affected
by this complication.

appraisal rights to all equivalent events, they should be eliminated where they do exist. Put in the context of the de facto merger doctrine, the question becomes not how far the equivalence argument carries in extending protection, but how far it forces us to roll back the protection that already exists.

The challenge that Manning articulates—to either distinguish among his lists in a manner that intelligently identifies when additional protection is appropriate or, as it seems he expects, admit our inability to do so and accept the implications of our failure—is, in fact, more easily met than he believed.

A sensible approach to drawing the distinctions of whose existence Manning seems so skeptical begins with evaluating his lists in terms of whether the events they contain represent systematic or unsystematic (diversifiable) risk. Consider first List I, containing occurrences like a rise in the United States balance of payments deficit or a Presidential heart attack. Manning asks with respect to these: "Why are these risks imposed upon the investor [without additional protections] while others are not?" The question, however, is not difficult and the answer is not, as Manning puts it, "because [they] are."

Examination of the risks described in List I discloses that they are essentially all systematic in character.[29] They are assumed by the shareholder because under the capital asset pricing model it is *only* for bearing these risks that the shareholders receive more than a risk-free return. Since the shareholders receive a return that is strictly proportionate to how susceptible the security is to systematic risk, the shareholder is paid to assume *precisely* the kinds of risk exemplified in List I and additional protections are thus hardly necessary.

Does this analysis then suggest that special protections should be provided in connection with events of the sort comprising Manning's List II, resignations of executives or labor strife, because shareholders are *not* paid to assume these? Here again financial theory provides an answer, also in the negative. List II risks are entirely unsystematic which, portfolio theory teaches us, can be entirely diversified away by the shareholder. The shareholders are not paid to assume unsystematic risks because they do not bear them; *a fortiori*, they do not need protection from them.

The problem, however, cannot be made to disappear entirely. Financial theory does identify one kind of risk that can be imposed on shareholders and for which they may not be otherwise compensated. This point focuses attention on the kinds of events described in Manning's List III. The price of a company's stock depends on the responsiveness of its return to systematic risk, its beta. From the shareholder's perspective, a corporation's stock represents only a future income stream with a particular sensitivity to systematic risk. As a result, the only important change is one that alters that sensitivity.[30] The com-

---

[29] The filing of an antitrust suit against the company, as well as a competitor's new product and expropriation of some of the company's property, are exceptions. From this perspective they belong in List II.

[30] See Scholes, *The Market for Securities: Substitution versus Price Pressure and the Effects of Information in Share Prices*, 45 J.Bus. 179 (1972).

mon linkage between the events comprising List III is the ability of those events, by altering the asset makeup or leverage of the company, or the businesses in which the company is engaged, to alter the company's beta in a fashion that the shareholders could not have anticipated. Thus, putting feasibility aside for the moment, could we completely respond to Manning's challenge by ignoring the risks on Lists I and II and selecting as candidates for additional protection those voluntary events on List III that alter the beta of the company's stock by more than, say, 25 percent? This approach is, in fact, similar to that taken under current law, although our theoretical statement of the kinds of transactions which require additional protection is very different in formulation than the present statutory alternatives backstopped by a poorly delineated de facto merger doctrine.

Coming back to the effort to develop a satisfactory solution, the suggested theoretical criterion for additional protection is, to be sure, hopelessly unworkable; measurement of beta is hardly an exact science and there is also a question concerning the stability of betas over time.[31] But it does suggest an approach that is feasible, draws definable distinctions between different types of transactions, and provides an answer to the question with which we began: How broadly should the inquiry concerning functional equivalence, the de facto merger doctrine, extend?

What is necessary is a means that can realistically distinguish transactions that are likely to present real risks of change in the systematic risk of the company without reliance on what are, as yet, statistical techniques that cannot bear up to the strain. The effort to develop one begins with recognition that it is not all changes in beta which present a risk to shareholders. As the discussion of capital budgeting in Chapter Four D. indicated, a project with a different risk than that of the company as a whole still will be desirable so long as the project's return is commensurate with the different level of risk. From this perspective, there is no difference in terms of the relevant impact on shareholders between the acquisition of assets and their disposition; both have the capacity of affecting the shareholders of the transacting corporation in the same way. And although Manning put it differently, it was, after all, the fact that the typical statutory and doctrinal approach draws precisely this distinction between acquiring and target companies without attempting a justification, that provides the basis of Manning's criticism. The justification for the particular distinction and a framework for a workable solution appears when it is recognized that statutory language and judicial doctrine are not the only sources of shareholder protection.

The Gilson excerpt in Chapter Ten presented the corporate structure as an interplay of statutory, judicial and market elements that mesh to provide a coherent check on the discretion necessarily associated with specialized management. Both Manning's difficulty in distinguishing between acquisitions and nonacquisitions, and the inherent

---

[31] For the difficulties in measuring beta see, e.g., J. Van Horne, *Financial Management and Policy*, 196–200 (5th ed. 1980). The stability of betas over time is discussed in R. Brealey & S. Myers, *Principles of Corporate Finance* 162–66 (1981).

strain in Eisenberg's effort to distinguish between business decisions and investment decisions based on whether the corporation is a buyer or a seller, seem to result from too narrow a view of the corporate structure. Just because one form of transaction receives statutory protection does not mean that the other is unprotected; it may only be protected in a different manner.

The first step in putting the problem in a structural perspective is to recognize that in most situations management provides the best (and cheapest) protection for shareholders against an uncompensated alteration in the company's beta. Put most simply, a transaction that results in an uncompensated alteration in beta is just a bad deal. Normally, however, we do not require that shareholders approve *all* transactions to protect themselves against a bad deal; instead we rely on the business judgment of management for that purpose. Under ordinary circumstances management has precisely the same orientation as the shareholders in evaluating prospective transactions, that is, to maximize risk-adjusted return. And we recognize our inability to devise any better judicial or statutory protective device by insulating management from after-the-fact challenge of their efforts by the virtually absolute barrier created by the business judgment rule. The shareholders are thus saved the cost of judicial intervention and, because the risk of management bad judgment can be diversified, suffer little harm when it occurs. In order for a category of transactions to be a candidate for additional protection, there must be a danger of management self-dealing. In this situation management can no longer be relied upon to protect shareholders and, because all managers can be expected to favor themselves if given the opportunity, the risk *cannot* be diversified away. It is for precisely this reason that the traditional business judgment rule does not apply to self-dealing transactions, and it is for precisely this reason that it makes sense to distinguish between the treatment of acquiring company shareholders and target company shareholders in an acquisition transaction.

Consider first the acquiring company. In an acquisition setting its management is subject to a variety of constraints limiting their freedom to make both bad judgments and self-interested ones. If the acquisition is a poor one for either reason, then all of the constraints on managerial inefficiency and self-dealing discussed in Chapter Ten—the product market, the capital market, the market for managers, and the market for corporate control—remain operative to penalize the offending management and, thus, create a substantial *ex ante* incentive for management to avoid uncompensated alterations in beta. The critical point is that this may well *not* be the case for target company management. And recognition of why these market contraints may not operate with respect to target company management provides an explanation for the general statutory pattern of requiring a shareholder vote only for the target company [32] and, in turn, suggests a workable principle for determining when the de facto merger doctrine should apply to nonstatutory transactions.

[32] See Schulman & Schenk, supra, at 1533.

The expectation of acquiring company management that after the acquisition they will continue to operate the company and remain subject to the discipline of the various markets in which they and the company operate serves to constrain management's self-interest in evaluating the acquisition. In contrast, when the company is instead the object of the acquisition, the constraint imposed by anticipation of post-transaction market penalties on self-dealing management is severely reduced by what economists call "final period problems."

Simply put, in a situation where parties expect to have repeated transactions, the recognition that a party who cheats in one transaction will be penalized by the other party in subsequent transactions reduces the incentive to cheat. Where, however, a transaction is the last (or only) in a series, the final period, the incentive to cheat reappears because, by definition, the penalty for doing so has disappeared.[33]   In the context of an acquisition nothing stops target management from selling out the shareholders in return for side payments from the acquiring company because target management, by definition, will no longer be subject to the constraints of the product, capital and control markets after the acquisition. Perhaps more importantly, if the remaining professional careers of target management are getting short, the size of the side payment may more than compensate them for any *ex post* penalty imposed by the market for managers.

In a structural approach to corporate law, it is precisely when market constraints on managerial misbehavior fail that there is a role for legal constraints. The typical corporate structure reflects this in the historical distinction between the protections given the shareholders of acquiring and target companies. It is only the latter who are subject to last period problems and therefore cannot rely on their management for protection, and require, instead, the barrier of a shareholder vote as a protection against management. It is, of course, recognition of this problem that prompts the statutory and judicial concern for the situation in which the form of the transaction is cast as a minnow swallowing a whale in order to circumvent statutory protection against final period problems given target shareholders. And it is precisely the principle derived from understanding the problem—transactions which present final period problems require additional mechanisms for shareholder protection—which should govern determination of the breadth of application of the de facto merger doctrine.[34]   In this

---

[33] Analysis of the differences in the incentives of parties to a transaction depending on whether the transaction is the last (or only) one contemplated also has been used, for example, to determine the optimum compensation arrangements for law enforcers, Becker & Stigler, *Law Enforcement, Malfeasance, and Compensation of Enforcers,* 3 J.Leg.Stud. 1 (1974); to understand the incentives for performing contractual obligations even if performance is purely voluntary, Telser, *A Theory of Self-enforcing Agreements,* 53 J.Bus. 27 (1980); and to evalute market mechanisms developed to deal with final period problems,

Klein, *The Role of Market Forces in Assuring Contractual Performance,* 89 J.Pol. Econ. 615 (1981).

[34] From this perspective, the typical de facto merger analysis with respect to acquiring company shareholders is turned on its head. The issue is no longer whether acquiring shareholders should receive the same protections with respect to other acquisition techniques as they do in mergers, but why the protections should be provided in mergers in the first place. If, as appears, the only answer is historical, then the use of protections accorded in mergers

regard, it is interesting that Professor Fischel's treatment of the economic function of appraisal rights, Fischel, *The Appraisal Remedy in Corporate Law,* 1983 Am.B.Found.Research J. 875, as a means of protecting minority shareholders against opportunism, a danger created by the anticipation of a final period, is directly consistent with this analysis of the de facto merger doctrine. See also Kanda & Levmore, *The Appraisal Remedy and the Goals of Corporate Law,* 32 U.C.L.A.L. Rev. 429 (1985) (a "discovery" goal, in order to constrain management self-dealing, best explains the need for an appraisal remedy).

Statutory literalism—the province of the Delaware equal dignity approach and the apparent explanation for an otherwise inexplicable result in Woods v. Natomas Co.—should prove no barrier to resolving the problem in this fashion. Professor Eisenberg has recognized that "American corporate statutes * * * are 'in no sense a code of company law. * * *'"[35] Extrastatutory principles, like the de facto merger doctrine, are required to flesh out the statutory skeleton and their shape is discernible only through an understanding of the entire corporate structure in its statutory, judicial and market elements.

At this point we can come back to an issue that we raised earlier in Section B.2. of this Chapter, but deferred. If determination of whether a sale of substantially all of the assets of a target company includes a qualitative as well as a quantitative element, for what quality are we to look? The answer again should be the final period principle. In the context of an asset sale, the appropriate inquiry concerns whether the assets of the target company remaining after the transaction will be operated in a manner so that target management can expect to remain subject to market constraints.[36]

That leaves for consideration the final form of acquisition, the tender offer, which raises quite different problems in explaining both its typical statutory treatment and the application of the non-statutory de facto merger doctrine to it.

F. Tender Offers: Limits on the Equivalency Concept

While the state and federal securities law treatment of tender offers can be quite complex, see Chapter Sixteen infra, their corporate law treatment is very simple indeed. The essence of a tender offer is that the proposal for business combination is made directly to the shareholders without the necessity of prior approval by the board of directors of the target company. Moreover, because the offer is addressed to the shareholders in their individual capacities, no action by shareholders as a group is necessary either. At this formal level, corporate law treats the technique as if a separate, unrelated offer has

as a touchstone is clearly misplaced. The issue is the presence of particular risks, not the form of the transaction.

[35] M. Eisenberg, supra, at 86 (quoting, in part, L. Gower, *The Principles of Modern Company Law* 8 (2nd ed. 1957)).

[36] In some circumstances, like the sale by Brunswick Corp. of its most profitable, but by no means only, subsidiary, in order to thwart a takeover bid by Whittaker Corporation, even the final period principle provides insufficient protection. This type of problem must be handled through the consideration of defensive tactics generally which will be undertaken in Chapter Fourteen, infra.

been made to purchase the stock of each target shareholder without acknowledging that the effect of aggregating these individual purchases is the transfer of control of the target company, i.e., a corporate acquisition.[37]

Viewed in this fashion, the tender offer poses the most difficult challenge for traditional analysis, both in understanding why its statutory treatment differs so greatly from that of mergers and sales of assets and why, despite that difference, the de facto merger doctrine has not been applied to it. Not only are the shareholder voting and appraisal rights associated with mergers eliminated, but so is the formal role of the target company's board of directors, a role that is required not only in mergers, but in any other acquisition technique, statutory or non-statutory. Moreover, the final period principle that governs the application of the de facto merger doctrine should also be operative in the context of tender offers. While the absence of a requirement of management approval may ease the problem somewhat, the importance of a favorable recommendation by management leaves substantial room for its existence.

The question then is what explains this disparity in statutory shareholder protection, and, perhaps even more puzzling, what explains the failure to apply the de facto merger doctrine to a statutory disparity in shareholder protection substantially more significant than that between merger and sale of assets in *Farris?* And to complete the statement of the puzzle, what accounts for the fact that even a firm proponent of functional equivalence like Professor Eisenberg concludes that less protection is appropriate for tender offers:

> Under traditional statutes * * * the nontransferring shareholders would have neither voting nor appraisal rights. Nor would voting rights seem desirable in such cases. For one thing, by its very mechanics the transaction requires shareholder approval of sorts, because the combination cannot take place unless a sufficient number of the transferor's shareholders agree to exchange their shares. * * * More important, it would be unwise to give the shareholders as a body a right to vote on whether some shareholders can sell their stock, and it would seem virtually impossible to develop a mechanism pitched to that objective without placing an inordinate restriction on the normally free alienability of shares.

M. Eisenberg, supra, at 239. Clearly something distinguishes tender offers from other acquisition techniques. The following develops a structural basis for the distinction.

Note: The Structural Role of Tender Offers

The argument that a particular acquisition technique is really like a merger and, thus, that shareholders should have the same protections

---

[37] In recent years, a number of states have amended their corporate statutes to require a vote of target shareholders, or approval of the target company's board of directors, before a tender offer can be made. Because these provisions were uniformly enacted as a response to judicial invalidation of state antitakeover statutes, they will be considered in Chapter Sixteen B., infra, dealing with state securities law regulation of tender offers.

as accorded in a merger, has a flip side in connection with tender offers. Not only do target shareholders get no statutory protection when the acquisition transaction takes the form of a tender offer, but the statutory role accorded target management in this acquisition form is critically different from that accorded them in mergers and sales of assets. While both mergers and sales of assets *require* approval by the target company's board of directors, the corporate statute makes no express provision for any management role in tender offers. Not surprisingly, management has claimed a role in tender offers similar to that accorded them in mergers and sales of assets and the argument advanced by them is strikingly similar to that on which the de facto merger doctrine is traditionally based. In the following excerpt, limits on target management's functional equivalence argument are developed by reference to the fit of particular acquisition techniques in the overall corporate structure.

GILSON, A STRUCTURAL APPROACH TO CORPORATIONS: THE CASE AGAINST DEFENSIVE TACTICS IN TENDER OFFERS

33 Stan.L.Rev. 819, 846–51 (1981).*

Corporate statutes properly place the ultimate responsibility for evaluating proposals for merger or sale of assets with management. These complicated transactions require substantial time investments for shareholders to understand them.[101] Assuming loyal management, a rational shareholder would not invest time considering a merger or sale of assets unless management, through application of its specialized skills, had already approved it. The problem is ensuring, within reasonable limits, that management's determination—for example, to reject an offer—is motivated by the shareholders', rather than management's, best interests. * * * The solution is the check and balance of the tender offer. If management, in rejecting merger or sale of assets proposals, gives priority to its own interests rather than those of the shareholders, the spurned suitor can make a tender offer to the

[101] Where the transaction involves the issuance of the offeror's securities, the offer must be registered with the Securities and Exchange Commission pursuant to the Securities Act of 1933 unless an exemption from registration is available. See generally R. Jennings & H. Marsh, *Securities Regulation: Cases and Materials* 464–95 (4th ed. 1977). Until recently, such a transaction would be registered on Form S–14, 17 C.F.R. § 239.23 (1980), which has been described as generating "some of the longest and most complex disclosure documents presented to investors," with an average length of 110 pages, and some ex-

ceeding 200 pages. House Comm. on Interstate and Foreign Commerce, 95th Cong., 1st Sess., Report of the Advisory Comm. on Corporate Disclosure to the Securities and Exchange Commission 440 (Comm. Print 1977) [hereinafter cited as Report on Corporate Disclosure]. The SEC has recently adopted Form S–15, 45 Fed. Reg. 63,647 (1980) (to be codified in 17 C.F.R. § 239.29), intended to be an abbreviated alternative to Form S–14, for use in a limited range of acquisition transactions. See generally Eppler, *Short Form Registration in Business Combination Transactions—Form S–15,* in Practising Law Institute, Acquisitions and Mergers: Tactics and Techniques 87 (1980).

shareholders.[103] Should management become too recalcitrant, an alternative is available.

This system of check and balance, of management control of some mechanisms by which control may be shifted but with unfettered access to shareholders through another, is precisely the structure reflected in the typical corporation statute. While control of the merger and sale of asset mechanisms is firmly ensconced in management, the tender offer mechanism generally is not even mentioned in the statute, let alone placed within management's control.[104] *   *   *

The most common argument supporting managerial discretion to block a tender offer asserts that a tender offer is functionally no different from any other acquisition technique.[105] If management has effectively complete discretion over whether shareholders will be given the opportunity to vote on a merger or sale of assets, then it should have a comparable role with respect to tender offers. Certainly, the argument continues, the mere form chosen for substantively equivalent transactions should not determine management's role.[106]

[103] Where management favors itself by accepting an offer—perhaps because of favorable side payments in the form of employment contracts or stock options— the statute provides an explicit *   *   * check through the statutory requirement of shareholder approval. * * * The constraint of shareholder approval, however, is buttressed by the operation of the market for corporate control. Between the public announcement of board of director approval of the transaction and the date of the shareholder meeting, competing offers—via tender offers—may be made if the transaction negotiated by management was too favorable to the offeror or to management. [Thus, protection against final period problems in tender offers, as in mergers or sales of assets, comes from shareholder action, although in tender offers the shareholders do not act by a statutory process. Note that the availability of shareholder action in response to a tender offer made in competition with an acquisition approved by target management adds a level of market protection to the statutory protection against final period problems existing with respect to mergers and sales of assets. Ed.]

[104] Where the tender offer is explicitly mentioned, it is in an effort to provide a statutory solution to the de facto merger problem. For example, Cal.Corp.Code § 181 (West 1977) defines three types of reorganizations, including an "exchange reorganization" which amounts to an acquisition by means of a tender offer where the consideration is the offeror's stock. Section 1201 requires a vote of the shareholders of the offeror if, following the transaction, these shareholders will own shares of the offeror representing less than five-sixths of the voting power. No role at all is created for the target board. See generally Small, *Corporate Combinations Under the New California General Corporation Law,* 23 U.C.L.A.L.Rev. 1190 (1976).

That the statute does not assign management a role in traditional tender offers is underscored by the addition in 1976 of Model Business Corporation Act § 72A. ABA–ALI Model Bus.Corp.Act Ann. 2d § 72A (Supp.1977). This section creates a mechanism by which an exchange offer can be made binding on target shareholders if both the board of directors and the shareholders approve the transaction by the same procedures required for mergers and sales of assets. While management is given a role where the transaction is made binding, the statute expressly preserves the option of a traditional tender offer, and in that setting no role is accorded target management. * * *

[105] See, e.g., * * * Lipton, *Takeover Bids in the Target's Boardroom,* 35 Bus. Law. 101, 104, 116 (1979); Pearlmutter, *Shareholders vs. The Corporation,* N.Y. Times, Mar. 9, 1980, § 3, at 18, col. 3 (Mr. Pearlmutter is a general partner of Lazard Freres & Co., a major investment banking firm); Steinbrink, *Management's Response to The Takeover Attempt,* 28 Case W.Res.L. Rev. 882, 892 (1978). When the transaction is friendly—i.e., target management has approved the acquisition—a tender offer *is* the equivalent of the alternative acquisition techniques and the choice among them is made on the basis of criteria other than the need to avoid a management veto.

[106] Some commentators have taken the point a good deal further by pointing to the statutory award of the duty to manage the corporation to the board of directors, and then arguing that a tender offer presents a

The argument extrapolates the typical statutory terms dealing with mergers and asset sales to a form of transaction—the tender offer—rarely mentioned in the typical statute. A nonstructural response is that a technical construction of the statute—contrasting the pivotal role assigned management with respect to mergers and asset sales with the absence of any statutory role with respect to tender offers—favors a more limited tender offer role for management. The statutory silence regarding tender offers may simply reflect a legislative assumption that free alienation of property is the norm, so that management's affirmative role in mergers and asset sales needs to be stated, while its nonrole in tender offers need not. And while functional equivalence advocates argue that the earlier statutes were silent because they were adopted prior to the time when hostile tender offers became popular acquisition techniques, even a vigorous proponent of management discretion acknowledges that "continuation of [the statutory silence] in recently adopted statutes is disquieting." [110]

One need not, however, limit response to the language of the statute. Under a structural view, functional equivalence among acquisition techniques is important, but this view favors a nonequivalent, much more limited, role for management in tender offers. The management monopoly of the market for corporate control which would result from extending management autonomy to tender offers eliminates the discipline imposed on management by that same market. Restricting management's role in a tender offer does not deny the value of management's expertise in evaluating and negotiating complex corporate transactions, but rather validates the unfettered discretion given management with respect to mergers and sales of assets.

For this purpose, the crucial distinction is not between different acquisition techniques, but between negotiated and hostile transactions. In a negotiated transaction, the acquisition terms result from bargaining between the offeror and target management, and shareholders benefit from management's skill and experience. The problem, however, is that target management may elect not to negotiate, or not to negotiate in good faith. Management's interest in remaining in office creates a conflict which the traditional standards of care and loyalty

policy decision no different from others— like plant investment—which no one disputes should be made solely by management. E.g., Pearlmutter, supra note 105, at 18, col. 3 ("is a takeover bid of such a different nature from other important business decisions, such as hiring a new chief executive officer or approving a large capital expenditure program, that the shareholders should decide the issue themselves?"); see Lipton, supra note 105, at 120.

The broader position proves too much. The basic equivalence argument asserts that a tender offer is the same as a merger or sale of assets. But in those decisions, the typical corporation statute clearly gives the shareholders a role different from that given with respect to other "important" policy decisions: Actions which involve direct sales of the corporation, like mergers and sales of assets, require shareholder approval, while the supposedly analogous policy decisions do not. See M. Eisenberg, at 213–51; Carney, *Fundamental Corporate Changes, Minority Shareholders, and Business Purposes*, 1980 Am. B. Foundation Res. J. 69. Therefore, the analogy between takeover bids and other policy decisions, given the equivalence argument, should also apply to mergers and sales of assets, which is inconsistent with the structure of the statute.

[110] Steinbrink, supra note 105, at 890 (citations omitted).

are incapable of policing. In this setting, the tender offer provides a self-executing check on management's discharge of its responsibility as holder of primary control over the acquisition process. "If negotiations break down, it is still possible for the acquiring company or someone else to go forward with a tender offer. The existence of this safety valve against the directors' conflict of interest is an important justification for giving the directors unfettered discretion in the process of negotiating acquisitions." [111]

Moreover, offerors should not prefer to use a tender offer to side-step target management and thereby deprive target shareholders of management's guidance and bargaining. The negotiation process typically involves transferring to the offeror substantial amounts of non-public information concerning the target.[112] This information reduces uncertainty about the future return on the acquisition and hence

---

[111] Herzel, Schmidt & Davis, "*Why Corporate Directors Have a Right to Resist a Tender Offer*," 61 Chi.B.Rec. 152, 159 (1979).

[112] While substantial consideration will have been given to the selection of an acquisition candidate prior to the point at which actual negotiations begin, it is commonly recognized that the negotiation process itself generates large amounts of information concerning the target which is available through no other source. * * * Consider, for example, the process of negotiating the representations and warranties contained in a typical acquisition agreement. The target will be asked to warrant, *inter alia,* the accuracy of financial statements and the absence of significant change since the date of the most recent audited statement; the absence of any liabilities for taxes or other matters not disclosed in the agreement including, most importantly, the absence of contingent liabilities; the condition of various assets believed to be of importance to the operation of the target's business; the existence of litigation against the target, whether actual or threatened; and the extent to which various elements of the target's work force are unionized or with respect to which organization efforts are underway. * * * Freund, a prominent practitioner in the acquisition area, stresses the information-producing role of such contractual provisions and the negotiation process generally: "There are no known statistics on the subject, but I'm willing to bet my briefcase that lawyers spend more time negotiating 'Representations of the Seller' than any other single article in the typical acquisition agreement. * * *

"From the purchaser's viewpoint, representations serve [several] distinct, although overlapping, purposes. First, they are useful as a device to obtain the maximum degree of disclosure about the acquired business prior to the purchaser undertaking a binding commitment to make the acquisition. In other words, representations constitute a systematic smoke-out of the data about the seller which the buyer feels is important. * * *

" * * * This focusing aspect of representations can often alert the purchaser to questionable areas for more detailed investigation, and may even provide ammunition for use in renegotiating the price or other terms of the deal.

"The second general purpose of representations, from the purchaser's viewpoint, is to set the stage for the purchaser to walk away from the deal if the facts develop that make it unwise to consummate the acquisition. Although in most cases the purchaser has been able to make a preliminary investigation prior to signing the agreement and has relied on certain data supplied to him by the seller, purchaser's *definitive* investigation—the opening up of all seller's doors and drawers—usually takes place *after* the agreement has been signed."

J. Freund, *Anatomy of a Merger: Strategies and Techniques for Negotiating Corporate Acquisitions* 229–31 (1975) (emphasis in the original).

A similar point was made recently by the investment banker for St. Joe Minerals Corp. in explaining Seagram Co.'s loss to Fluor Corp., the white knight, in the contest for St. Joe: "Seagram 'underbid' for St. Joe because the Montreal-based distiller apparently had access only to public information on St. Joe's asset value and earning power. 'Seagram was fighting from the outside. It's like a guy fighting blind against a guy with clear vision.' " *Seagrams Ends $2.13 Billion Bid for St. Joe,* Wall St. J., Apr. 8, 1981, at 3, col. 1.

increases the value of the investment to the offeror.[113] Even though target management may drive a hard bargain on behalf of the shareholders, the offeror has an incentive to negotiate, because resort to a hostile tender offer eliminates access to valuable information.[114]

◆

How would a structural approach limit the argument that a tender offer is the functional equivalent of a merger not from the perspective of target management but, rather, from the perspective of a shareholder of the target? This, of course, is not quite the traditional de facto merger argument where target management will have already approved the transaction and it is protection against their self-interest that is sought. In the tender offer context, might not a shareholder still want protection against a transaction which, whatever management's role and even though imposed by a majority through a sale of their stock, is involuntary with respect to the shareholder who does not approve the transaction?

In this regard, it is helpful to consider what rule a shareholder would choose to govern the application of the de facto merger doctrine to tender offers if the choice had to be made before the shareholder knew whether he would favor or oppose a particular transaction. This is an approach suggested by Professors Easterbrook and Fischel in two important articles: *The Proper Role of a Target's Management in Responding to a Tender Offer,* 94 Harv.L.Rev. 1161 (1981); *Corporate Control Transactions,* 91 Yale L.J. 737 (1982). Given the role of tender offers in the corporate structure, a rule that encouraged them would benefit all stockholders of potential target companies by increasing the market constraints on managerial discretion and, presumably, increasing shareholder return as a result. To be balanced against this benefit is the chance that a tender offer will occur concerning which the shareholder will find himself in the minority which opposes it and who, in that event, would benefit from more restrictive rules. In evaluating the costs associated with the latter situation, the shareholder must

[113] Assuming the offeror is risk-averse, the additional information can increase the value of the acquisition even if it does not affect the expected return on the investment. See W. Sharpe, Portfolio Theory and Capital Markets 20–33 (1970); Modigliani & Pogue, *An Introduction to Risk and Return,* 30 Fin. Analysts J. 68 (1974). Moreover, because the information disclosed may eliminate some risks which the offeror had considered in determining an initial offering price, such as particular contingent liabilities, or may disclose assets, such as favorable lease renewal terms, of which the offeror had not known, the expected return on the transaction may increase as well.

[114] Existing empirical data provide indirect support for the information value of the negotiation process. Dodd, [*Merger Proposals, Management Discretion and*

Stockholder Wealth, 8 J.Fin.Econ. 105 (1980)] compared the market response to the cancellation of previously announced nonhostile acquisitions when the cancellation was due to target management veto and when the cancellation was due to the offeror backing away from the transaction. When management vetoed the deal, the market price of the target shares, although it dropped from the offer price, remained some 10% above the pre-announcement price. Id., at 131. When the transaction was terminated by the offeror, the market value of the target shares dropped, on average, to their pre-announcement price. Id. This suggests that the market interprets offeror termination as signalling the discovery of negative information concerning the target *during* the negotiating process.

consider whether his view of a prospective transaction can be expected to be better than that of the majority, an analysis which should be similar to that undertaken in Section A.2. of this Chapter with respect to how high a vote should be required to approve a merger. The shareholder must also estimate the costs associated with being a minority shareholder in an enterprise controlled by someone else. This estimate, and the legal rules bearing on the manner of estimation, is taken up in connection with the problem of freeze-outs and freeze-ins in Chapter Fifteen. Because the application of the de facto merger doctrine to tender offers also focuses on the position of the minority shareholder after a successful transaction, evaluation of it is deferred until Chapter Fifteen.

CHAPTER FOURTEEN. CORPORATE LAW CONCERNS OF THE TARGET COMPANY

A. The Willing Subject: The Plight of the Large Shareholder and Limitations on Sale of Control

Despite the publicity surrounding bitterly contested transactions in which target companies seek to ward off efforts by acquirers to thrust upon target shareholders substantial premiums over market value, most acquisition transactions still involve willing subjects eager to be acquired at a premium. This seeming convergence of interest between a target company and its shareholders, however, is not exact, nor does it entirely eliminate the possibility of litigation. There may still be conflict over which target shareholders will be allowed to benefit from the transaction, and in what proportions. In its traditional setting, this problem is posed by an acquisition transaction in which the controlling shareholders sell their shares to the acquirer at a premium and provision is made for the minority shareholders to participate only at a lower price, or not at all. The question is then whether the minority shareholders are entitled to share in the "control" premium, and the dilemma is highlighted by the fact that the form of the transaction could have been structured, without altering the substantive position of the *acquirer,* as a pro rata purchase with all shareholders participating equally. If the transaction were structured in this way, however, the controlling shareholders would get less—in total and per share. That, of course, is the rub.

The problem posed for the controlling shareholder may be, in some circumstances, more complicated. What if the controlling shareholder is itself a corporation? Does the controlling shareholder then have a responsibility to its *own* shareholders to keep all of the premium, or to its *fellow* shareholders to share it?

These issues, considered in this section, have generated more controversy in relation to their substantive importance than virtually any other issue in corporate law. Nonetheless, only recently have efforts been made to give substance to the competing claims of "fairness" that have dominated the discussion. The material, which follows focuses on efforts to identify whose interests are affected, and in what way, by competing solutions.

1. The Traditional Problem

PERLMAN v. FELDMANN
United States Court of Appeals, Second Circuit, 1954.
219 F.2d 173.

Before CLARK, Chief Judge, and SWAN and FRANK, Circuit Judges.

CLARK, Chief Judge.

This is a derivative action brought by minority stockholders of Newport Steel Corporation to compel accounting for, and restitution of, allegedly illegal gains which accrued to defendants as a result of the sale in August, 1950, of their controlling interest in the corporation. The principal defendant, C. Russell Feldmann, who represented and acted for the others, members of his family,[1] was at that time not only the dominant stockholder, but also the chairman of the board of directors and the president of the corporation. Newport, an Indiana corporation, operated mills for the production of steel sheets for sale to manufacturers of steel products, first at Newport, Kentucky, and later also at other places in Kentucky and Ohio. The buyers, a syndicate organized as Wilport Company, a Delaware corporation, consisted of end-users of steel who were interested in securing a source of supply in a market becoming ever tighter in the Korean War. Plaintiffs contend that the consideration paid for the stock included compensation for the sale of a corporate asset, a power held in trust for the corporation by Feldmann as its fiduciary. This power was the ability to control the allocation of the corporate product in a time of short supply, through control of the board of directors; and it was effectively transferred in this sale by having Feldman procure the resignation of his own board and the election of Wilport's nominees immediately upon consummation of the sale.

* * * Jurisdiction below was based upon the diverse citizenship of the parties. Plaintiffs argue here, as they did in the court below, that in the situation here disclosed the vendors must account to the nonparticipating minority stockholders for that share of their profit which is attributable to the sale of the corporate power. Judge Hincks denied the validity of the premise, holding that the rights involved in the sale were only those normally incident to the possession of a controlling block of shares, with which a dominant stockholder, in the absence of fraud or foreseeable looting, was entitled to deal according to his own best interests. * * * Plaintiffs appeal from these rulings of law which resulted in the dismissal of their complaint.

The essential facts found by the trial judge are not in dispute. Newport was a relative newcomer in the steel industry with predominantly old installations which were in the process of being supplemented by more modern facilities. Except in times of extreme shortage Newport was not in a position to compete profitably with other steel mills for customers not in its immediate geographical area. Wilport, the purchasing syndicate, consisted of geographically remote end-users of steel who were interested in buying more steel from Newport than they had been able to obtain during recent periods of tight supply. The price of $20 per share was found by Judge Hincks to be a fair one for a

---

[1] The stock was not held personally by Feldmann in his own name, but was held by the members of his family and by personal corporations. The aggregate of stock thus had amounted to 33% of the outstanding Newport stock and gave working control to the holder. The actual sale included 55,552 additional shares held by friends and associates of Feldmann, so that a total of 37% of the Newport stock was transferred.

control block of stock, although the over-the-counter market price had not exceeded $12 and the book value per share was $17.03. But this finding was limited by Judge Hincks' statement that "[w]hat value the block would have had if shorn of its appurtenant power to control distribution of the corporate product, the evidence does not show." It was also conditioned by his earlier ruling that the burden was on plaintiffs to prove a lesser value for the stock.

Both as director and as dominant stockholder, Feldmann stood in a fiduciary relationship to the corporation and to the minority stockholders as beneficiaries thereof. Pepper v. Litton, 308 U.S. 295, 60 S.Ct. 238, 84 L.Ed. 281; Southern Pac. Co. v. Bogert, 250 U.S. 483, 39 S.Ct. 533, 63 L.Ed. 1099. His fiduciary obligation must in the first instance be measured by the law of Indiana, the state of incorporation of Newport. * * * Although there is no Indiana case directly in point, the most closely analogous one emphasizes the close scrutiny to which Indiana subjects the conduct of fiduciaries when personal benefit may stand in the way of fulfillment of trust obligations. In Schemmel v. Hill, 91 Ind.App. 373, 169 N.E. 678, 682, 683, McMahan, J., said: "Directors of a business corporation act in a strictly fiduciary capacity. Their office is a trust.

When a director deals with his corporation, his acts will be closely scrutinized. Directors of a corporation are its agents, and they are governed by the rules of law applicable to other agents, and, as between themselves and their principal, the rules relating to honesty and fair dealing in the management of the affairs of their principal are applicable. They must not, in any degree, allow their official conduct to be swayed by their private interest, which must yield to official duty. In a transaction between a director and his corporation, where he acts for himself and his principal at the same time in a matter connected with the relation between them, it is presumed, where he is thus potential on both sides of the contract, that self-interest will overcome his fidelity to his principal, to his own benefit and to his principal's hurt." And the judge added: "Absolute and most scrupulous good faith is the very essence of a director's obligation to his corporation. The first principal duty arising from his official relation is to act in all things of trust wholly for the benefit of his corporation."

In Indiana, then, as elsewhere, the responsibility of the fiduciary is not limited to a proper regard for the tangible balance sheet assets of the corporation, but includes the dedication of his uncorrupted business judgment for the sole benefit of the corporation, in any dealings which may adversely affect it. * * *

Although the Indiana case is particularly relevant to Feldmann as a director, the same rule should apply to his fiduciary duties as majority stockholder, for in that capacity he chooses and controls the directors, and thus is held to have assumed their liability. Pepper v. Litton, supra, 308 U.S. 295, 60 S.Ct. 238. This, therefore, is the standard to which Feldmann was by law required to conform in his activities here under scrutiny.

It is true, as defendants have been at pains to point out, that this is not the ordinary case of breach of fiduciary duty. We have here no fraud, no misuse of confidential information, no outright looting of a helpless corporation. But on the other hand, we do not find compliance with that high standard which we have just stated and which we and other courts have come to expect and demand of corporate fiduciaries. In the often-quoted words of Judge Cardozo: "Many forms of conduct permissible in a workaday world for those acting at arm's length, are forbidden to those bound by fiduciary ties. A trustee is held to something stricter than the morals of the market place. Not honesty alone, but the punctilio of an honor the most sensitive, is then the standard of behavior. As to this there has developed a tradition that is unbending and inveterate. Uncompromising rigidity has been the attitude of courts of equity when petitioned to undermine the rule of undivided loyalty by the 'disintegrating erosion' of particular exceptions." Meinhard v. Salmon, supra, 249 N.Y. 458, 464, 164 N.E. 545, 546, 62 A.L.R. 1. The actions of defendants in siphoning off for personal gain corporate advantages to be derived from a favorable market situation do not betoken the necessary undivided loyalty owed by the fiduciary to his principal.

The corporate opportunities of whose misappropriation the minority stockholders complain need not have been an absolute certainty in order to support this action against Feldmann. If there was possibility of corporate gain, they are entitled to recover. In Young v. Higbee Co., 324 U.S. 204, 65 S.Ct. 594, two stockholders appealing the confirmation of a plan of bankruptcy reorganization were held liable for profits received for the sale of their stock pending determination of the validity of the appeal. They were held accountable for the excess of the price of their stock over its normal price, even though there was no indication that the appeal could have succeeded on substantive grounds. And in Irving Trust Co. v. Deutsch, 2 Cir., 73 F.2d 121, 124, an accounting was required of corporate directors who bought stock for themselves for corporate use, even though there was an affirmative showing that the corporation did not have the finances itself to acquire the stock. Judge Swan speaking for the court pointed out that "The defendants' argument, contrary to Wing v. Dillingham [5 Cir., 239 F. 54], that the equitable rule that fiduciaries should not be permitted to assume a position in which their individual interests might be in conflict with those of the corporation can have no application where the corporation is unable to undertake the venture, is not convincing. If directors are permitted to justify their conduct on such a theory, there will be a temptation to refrain from exerting their strongest efforts on behalf of the corporation since, if it does not meet the obligations, an opportunity of profit will be open to them personally."

This rationale is equally appropriate to a consideration of the benefits which Newport might have derived from the steel shortage. In the past Newport had used and profited by its market leverage by operation of what the industry had come to call the "Feldmann Plan." This consisted of securing interest-free advances from prospective purchasers of steel in return for firm commitments to them from future production. The funds thus acquired were used to finance improvements in existing plants and to acquire new installations. In the summer of 1950 Newport had been negotiating for cold-rolling facilities which it needed for a more fully integrated operation and a more marketable product, and Feldmann plan funds might well have been used toward this end.

Further, as plaintiffs alternatively suggest, Newport might have used the period of short supply to build up patronage in the geographical area in which it could compete profitably even when steel was more abundant. Either of these opportunities was Newport's, to be used to its advantage only. Only if defendants had been able to negate completely any possibility of gain by Newport could they have prevailed. It is true that a trial court finding states: "Whether or not, in August, 1950, Newport's position was such that it could have entered into 'Feldmann Plan' type transactions to procure funds and financing for the further expansion and integration of its steel facilities and whether such expansion would have been desirable for Newport, the evidence does not show." This, however, cannot avail the defendants, who—contrary to the ruling below—had the burden of proof on this issue, since fiduciaries always have the burden of proof in establishing the fairness of their dealings with trust property.   *   *   *

Defendants seek to categorize the corporate opportunities which might have accrued to Newport as too unethical to warrant further consideration. It is true that reputable steel producers were not participating in the gray market brought about by the Korean War and were refraining from advancing their prices, although to do so would not have been illegal. But Feldmann plan transactions were not considered within this self-imposed interdiction; the trial court found that around the time of the Feldmann sale Jones & Laughlin Steel Corporation, Republic Steel Company, and Pittsburgh Steel Corporation were all participating in such arrangements. In any event, it ill becomes the defendants to disparage as unethical the market advantages from which they themselves reaped rich benefits.

We do not mean to suggest that a majority stockholder cannot dispose of his controlling block of stock to outsiders without having to account to his corporation for profits or even never do this with impunity when the buyer is an interested customer, actual or potential, for the corporation's product. But when the sale necessarily results in a sacrifice of this element of corporate good will and consequent unusual profit to the fiduciary who has caused the sacrifice, he should account for his gains. So in a time of market shortage, where a call on a corporation's product commands an unusually large premium, in one form or another, we think it sound law that a fiduciary may not appropriate to himself the value of this premium. Such personal gain at the expense of his co-venturers seems particularly reprehensible when made by the trusted president and director of his company. In this case the violation of duty seems to be all the clearer because of this triple role in which Feldmann appears, though we are unwilling to say, and are not to be understood as saying, that we should accept a lesser obligation for any one of his roles alone.

Hence to the extent that the price received by Feldmann and his co-defendants included such a bonus, he is accountable to the minority stockholders who sue here. Restatement, Restitution §§ 190, 197 (1937); Seagrave Corp. v. Mount, supra, 6 Cir., 212 F.2d 389. And plaintiffs, as they contend, are entitled to a recovery in their own right, instead of in right of the corporation (as in the usual derivative actions), since neither Wilport nor their successors in interest should share in any judgment which may be rendered. * * *

Defendants cannot well object to this form of recovery, since the only alternative, recovery for the corporation as a whole, would subject them to a greater total liability.

The case will therefore be remanded to the district court for a determination of the question expressly left open below, namely, the value of defendants' stock without the appurtenant control over the corporation's output of steel. We reiterate that on this issue, as on all others relating to a breach of fiduciary duty, the burden of proof must rest on the defendants. Judgment should go to these plaintiffs and those whom they represent for any premium value so shown to the extent of their respective stock interests.

The judgment is therefore reversed and the action remanded for further proceedings pursuant to this opinion.

SWAN, Circuit Judge (dissenting).

With the general principles enunciated in the majority opinion as to the duties of fiduciaries I am, of course, in thorough accord. But, as Mr. Justice Frankfurter stated in Securities and Exchange Comm. v. Chenery Corp., 318 U.S. 80, 85, 63 S.Ct. 454, 458, 87 L.Ed. 626, "to say that a man is a fiduciary only begins analysis; it gives direction to further inquiry. To whom is he a fiduciary? What obligations does he owe as a fiduciary? In what respect has he failed to discharge these obligations?" My brothers' opinion does not specify precisely what fiduciary duty Feldmann is held to have violated or whether it was a duty imposed upon him as a dominant stockholder or as a director of Newport. Without such specification I think that both the legal profession and the business world will find the decision confusing and will be unable to foretell the extent of its impact upon customary practices in the sale of stock.

The power to control the management of a corporation, that is, to elect directors to manage its affairs, is an inseparable incident to the ownership of a majority of its stock, or sometimes, as in the present instance, to the ownership of enough shares, less than a majority, to control an election. Concededly a majority or dominant shareholder is ordinarily privileged to sell his stock at the best price obtainable from the purchaser. In so doing he acts on his own behalf, not as an agent of the corporation. If he knows or has reason to believe that the purchaser intends to exercise to the detriment of the corporation the power of management acquired by the purchase, such knowledge or reasonable suspicion will terminate the dominant shareholder's privilege to sell and will create a duty not to transfer the power of management to such purchaser. The duty seems to me to resemble the obligation which everyone is under not to assist another to commit a tort rather than the obligation of a fiduciary. But whatever the nature of the duty, a violation of it will subject the violator to liability for damages sustained by the corporation. Judge Hincks found that Feldmann had no reason to think that Wilport would use the power of management it would acquire by the purchase to injure Newport, and that there was no proof that it ever was so used. Feldmann did know, it is true, that the reason Wilport wanted the stock was to put in a board of directors who would be likely to permit Wilport's members to purchase more of Newport's steel than they might otherwise be able to get. But there is nothing illegal in a dominant shareholder purchasing from his own corporation at the same prices it offers to other customers. That is what the members of Wilport did, and there is no proof that Newport suffered any detriment therefrom.

My brothers say that "the consideration paid for the stock included compensation for the sale of a corporate asset", which they describe as "the ability to control the allocation of the corporate product in a time of short supply, through control of the board of directors; and it was effectively transferred in this sale by having Feldmann procure the resignation of his own board and the election of Wilport's nominees immediately upon consummation of the sale." The implications of this are not clear to me. If it means that when market conditions are such as to induce users of a corporation's product to wish to buy a controlling block of stock in order to be able to purchase part of the corporation's output at the same mill list prices as are offered to other customers, the dominant stockholder is under a fiduciary duty not to sell his stock, I cannot agree. For reasons already stated, in my opinion Feldmann was not proved to be under any fiduciary duty as a stockholder not to sell the stock he controlled.

Feldmann was also a director of Newport. Perhaps the quoted statement means that as a director he violated his fiduciary duty in voting to elect Wilport's nominees to fill the vacancies created by the resignations of the former directors of Newport. As a director Feldmann was under a fiduciary duty to use an honest judgment in acting on the corporation's behalf. A director is privileged to resign, but so long as he remains a director he must be faithful to his fiduciary duties and must not make a personal gain from performing them. Consequently, if the price paid for Feldmann's stock included a payment for voting to elect the new directors, he must account to the corporation for such payment, even though he honestly believed that the men he voted to elect were well qualified to serve as directors. He can not take pay for performing his fiduciary duty. There is no suggestion that he did do so, unless the price paid for his stock was more than its value. So it seems to me that decision must turn on whether finding 120 and conclusion 5 of the district judge are supportable on the evidence. They are set out in the margin.[1]

[1] "120. The 398,927 shares of Newport stock sold to Wilport as of August 31, 1950, had a fair value as a control block of $20 per share. What value the block would

Judge Hincks went into the matter of valuation of the stock with his customary care and thoroughness. He made no error of law in applying the principles relating to valuation of stock. Concededly a controlling block of stock has greater sale value than a small lot. While the spread between $10 per share for small lots and $20 per share for the controlling block seems rather extraordinarily wide, the $20 valuation was supported by the expert testimony of Dr. Badger, whom the district judge said he could not find to be wrong. I see no justification for upsetting the valuation as clearly erroneous. Nor can I agree with my brothers that the $20 valuation "was limited" by the last sentence in finding 120. The controlling block could not by any possibility be shorn of its appurtenant power to elect directors and through them to control distribution of the corporate product. It is this "appurtenant power" which gives a controlling block its value as such block. What evidence could be adduced to show the value of the block "if shorn" of such appurtenant power, I cannot conceive, for it cannot be shorn of it.

The opinion also asserts that the burden of proving a lesser value than $20 per share was not upon the plaintiffs but the burden was upon the defendants to prove that the stock was worth that value. Assuming that this might be true as to the defendants who were directors of Newport, they did show it, unless finding 120 be set aside. Furthermore, not all the defendants were directors; upon what theory the plaintiffs should be relieved from the burden of proof as to defendants who were not directors, the opinion does not explain.

The final conclusion of my brothers is that the plaintiffs are entitled to recover in their own right instead of in the right of the corporation. This appears to be completely inconsistent with the theory advanced at the outset of the opinion, namely, that the price of the stock "included compensation for the sale of a corporate asset." If a corporate asset was sold, surely the corporation should recover the compensation received for it by the defendants. Moreover, if the plaintiffs were suing in their own right, Newport was not a proper party. * * *

I would affirm the judgment on appeal.

ANDREWS, THE STOCKHOLDER'S RIGHT TO EQUAL OPPORTUNITY IN THE SALE OF SHARES

78 Harv.L.Rev. 505, 505–29 (1965).*

The right violated [in *Feldmann*] * * * is simply the right of all stockholders to have an equal opportunity to participate ratably in a

---

have had if shorn of its appurtenant power to control distribution of the corporate product, the evidence does not show."

"5. Even if Feldmann's conduct in cooperating to accomplish a transfer of control to Wilport immediately upon the sale constituted a breach of a fiduciary duty to Newport, no part of the moneys received by the defendants in connection with the sale constituted profits for which they were accountable to Newport."

sale of stock pursuant to an offer to purchase controlling shares at a favorable price.   *   *   *

The rule to be considered [to prevent that violation] can be stated thus: whenever a controlling stockholder sells his shares, every other holder of shares (of the same class) is entitled to have an equal opportunity to sell his shares, or a prorata part of them, on substantially the same terms.   Or in terms of the correlative duty: before a controlling stockholder may sell his shares to an outsider he must assure his fellow stockholders an equal opportunity to sell their shares, or as high a proportion of theirs as he ultimately sells of his own. *   *   *

Now let us look briefly at what the rule means.   First, it neither compels nor prohibits a sale of stock at any particular price; it leaves a controlling stockholder wholly free to decide for himself the price above which he will sell and below which he will hold his shares.   The rule only says that in executing his decision to sell, a controlling stockholder cannot sell pursuant to a purchase offer more favorable than any available to other stockholders.   Second, the rule does not compel a prospective purchaser to make an open offer for all shares on the same terms.   He can offer to purchase shares on the condition that he gets a certain proportion of the total.   Or he can even make an offer to purchase 51 per cent of the shares, no more and no less.   The only requirement is that his offer, whatever it may be, be made equally or proportionately available to all stockholders.

*   *   *

The asserted right would prevent just what happened in *Feldmann*: a private sale by a controlling stockholder at a price not available to other stockholders.   But there are two modes of compliance with the rule: either the purchaser can extend his offer to all stockholders, or the seller can offer participation in the sale to his fellow stockholders. A sale is prevented from taking place only when the purchaser is unwilling to buy more than a specified percentage of the shares, and the seller will sell only if he can sell out completely.   Indeed, even under these circumstances it is an overstatement to say the rule would prevent a sale taking place, since the minority stockholders may consent to the sale.   They may even sell to the purchaser at a lower price than what he pays the controlling stockholder, provided they are adequately informed of what is going on.   Thus the rule only operates to prevent a sale when (1) the purchaser is unwilling to purchase more shares, (2) the seller insists on disposing of all his shares, and (3) the minority stockholders are unwilling to stay in the enterprise under the purchaser's control.

*   *   *

2.   *Economic Analysis.*—The rule of equal opportunity prevents a purchaser, in a certain sense, from paying a premium for controlling shares.   One way to evaluate the rule, therefore, is to examine the implications of the premium.   Does the premium reflect factors that ought properly to enter into an evaluation of the controlling shares? Can the effects of different factors in producing a premium be separated from one another?

The assertion that a premium shows controlling shares to be worth more than noncontrolling shares has an important kernel of truth in it. But it needs to be analyzed in terms of the various reasons a purchaser might rationally have for paying a premium, in order to separate that kernel of truth from a considerable amount of chaff.

(a).—We can begin with cases already discussed. Why were the purchasers in the looting cases, and in *Feldmann*, willing to pay a premium? In the looting cases the answer is simple—the premium represents payment for the opportunity to get into a position where the purchaser can steal from the corporation. The courts have recognized this motive, and have relied heavily on the premium paid to reach the conclusion that the sellers had adequate notice of the purchaser's intentions. * * *

Why was Wilport willing to pay a premium for Feldmann's stock? Again the answer is fairly obvious—because it was willing to pay something extra in order to acquire power to control Newport's sales of steel. And again the court recognized this perfectly clearly when it spoke of the corporate product commanding a premium in the form of a premium price for stock. * * *

But different as it is from the corporation's standpoint, for the purchaser the significance of the premium is much the same in *Feldmann* as in the looting cases. In both situations the purchaser is paying a premium for an opportunity to profit from his investment in some other way than through dividends and appreciation in the value of his stock. In both situations the purchaser plans to use his position of control to create additional relationships between himself and the corporation, for his own profit and benefit, and the premium represents payment for that additional expectation of return on his investment. * * *

The *Feldmann* case is unique in that it involved a reasonably precise market price for the corporate product, but under rather artificial circumstances. Members of the purchasing syndicate were willing to play the game, paying the established price for Newport's product. But in this case the one clear thing was that the price established did not reflect the full amount the purchasers were willing to pay for a sure supply of steel. It might be impossible to say exactly what the purchasers would have paid, in an unrestrained market situation, for contracts that would have assured their requirements of steel, but clearly it would have been more than the prevailing market price. It was this premium for steel, forced by the peculiar circumstances of the case to take the form of a premium price for stock, for which the court required Feldmann to account.

As compared with other cases where the value to the purchaser of entering into extra-stockholder relations is not accurately gauged by some objective market figure—all of the cases, for instance, where the purchaser makes himself a paid executive employee of the acquired corporation—*Feldmann* is only unique for the rather graphic way it displays the relationship between what the corporation gets for its product (or pays for executive services) and what the controlling stockholder gets for his shares. In principle the case of a premium paid by a purchaser for the opportunity of making himself an executive employee, or of making a profit out of any other extra-stockholder relationship, is no different from that of a purchaser like Wilport who pays a premium in order to make himself a favored customer.

(b).—The most important reason a purchaser might pay a premium for controlling shares, and one that has to be met squarely, is that an investment in controlling shares is a more promising, or at least a safer, investment than one in noncontrolling shares for the simple reason that it will enable the investor to implement what he believes to be the best policies in the management of his investment. * * *

This is the strongest part of any argument against a broad reading of *Feldmann*. It is the kernel of truth in the assertion that a premium paid for controlling shares only shows that controlling shares are inherently worth more than minority shares. It refutes any literal interpretation of the corporate asset theory by showing that control under some circumstances necessarily gives an element of value to some shares that it does not give to others.

*   *   *

The rule of equal opportunity does not, however, prevent a purchaser from offering more per share if he acquires control, than if he does not. The rule tends to operate automatically to distinguish between a premium paid for the opportunity of entering into extra-stockholder relations, and one that reflects a change in investment appraisal resulting from a shift in control. This is one of the greatest advantages of the rule of equal opportunity over any corporate asset theory of control, and it needs to be set out and explored in some detail.

*   *   *

The argument can be made first in relatively abstract terms. Assume that the only factors that would cause a particular purchaser to pay more for some shares than for others are the two so far discussed: (a) that he wants to enter into some advantageous extra-stockholder relationship with the corporation, which he can only achieve by gaining control; and (b) that he views the corporate stock as a better (safer or more profitable or both) investment if he is in control than if he is not. Assume further that the purchaser can be made to state the top price he would pay for any particular portion of the company's outstanding shares.

On these assumptions, if in a particular case the purchaser is only actuated by the second factor—by a difference in investment appraisal associated with his acquisition of control—then the only differential that will appear in his schedule of prices will be a differential between what he will pay per share if he does not achieve control, and what he will pay per share if he does achieve control. There will be no difference between his price per share for a bare controlling block, and his price per share for any larger amount. The return on his investment will be proportionate to the number of shares he owns; therefore he will be willing to pay in proportion to the number of shares he acquires; and his marginal price for supercontrol shares will be equal to what he would pay per share for a controlling block. For this purchaser, in this case, the rule of equal opportunity imposes no burden. The rule permits him to condition an offer to purchase at a particular price, on his achieving control. If he purchases a controlling block the rule only requires him to offer the same price per share for more shares, something he should be willing to do in any event.

On the other hand, if a purchaser is willing to pay more per share for a barely controlling block of shares than for a larger block—still making the assumptions stated above—this would show that he is actuated in part at least by the first factor, by the intention or expectation of enjoying some profit or advantage from entering into some extra-stockholder relationship with his newly acquired corporation. The measure of his investment appraisal with himself in control is the marginal price per share he would pay for shares in excess of those required to achieve control. If he is willing to pay more than that marginal price, for any number of shares, he must be paying for something other than the investment value of the shares. On the assumptions stated above, it must be an intention to derive a profit from some sort of extra-stockholder relationship. And that explanation fits the fact because the profit to be derived from an extra-stockholder relationship will be no greater on account of the purchase of supercontrol shares; therefore if a purchaser were motivated by an intention to derive that sort of profit, one would expect him to offer more per share for a controlling block than for supercontrol shares.

* * *

EASTERBROOK & FISCHEL, CORPORATE CONTROL TRANSACTIONS
91 Yale L.J. 698–718 (1982).*

Transactions in corporate control often produce gains for the corporation. Substitution of one set of managers for another, for example, often produces gains because assets increase in value under better management, and would-be managers offer payments to shareholders to compete for the right to manage the firm's pool of assets. * * *

[D]evices for allocating corporate control pose a common problem because they sometimes involve an unequal division of the gains from the transaction. Shares in a control bloc, for example, may be sold at a price greater than that paid for the remaining shares; * * * one might argue that the gains should be distributed more widely. Such "sharing" arguments are popular among academic lawyers, and courts are beginning to apply these arguments to some corporate control transactions. We argue, in contrast, that those who produce a gain should be allowed to keep it, subject to the constraint that other parties to the transaction be at least as well off as before the transaction. Any attempt to require sharing simply reduces the likelihood that there will be gains to share.

* Reprinted by permission of The Yale Law Journal Company and Fred B. Roth- man & Company from *The Yale Law Journal*, Vol. 91, pp. 698–718.

II. Equal Treatment, Fiduciary Duty, and Shareholders' Welfare

Many scholars, and a few courts, conclude that one aspect of fiduciary duty is the equal treatment of investors. Their argument takes the following form: fiduciary principles require fair conduct; equal treatment is fair conduct; hence, fiduciary principles require equal treatment. The conclusion does not follow. The argument depends upon an equivalence between equality and fair treatment, which we have questioned elsewhere. To say that fiduciary principles require equal (or even fair) treatment is to beg the central question—whether investors would contract for equal or even roughly equal treatment.

Our analysis of this question requires that a distinction be drawn between rules that maximize value *ex ante* and actions that maximize the returns of certain investors *ex post*. A simple example illustrates the point. A corporation may choose to invest its capital in one of two ventures. Venture 1 will pay $100, and the returns can be divided equally among the firm's investors. Thus, if there are 10 investors in the firm, the expected value to each investor is $10. Venture 2 will pay $150, in contrast, but only if the extra returns are given wholly to five of the ten investors. Thus, five "lucky" investors will receive $20 apiece, and the unlucky ones $10. Because each investor has a 50 percent chance of being lucky, each would think Venture 2 to be worth $15. The directors of the firm should choose Venture 2 over Venture 1 because it has the higher value and because none of the investors is worse off under Venture 2.

Now consider Venture 3, in which $200 in gains are to be divided among only five of the ten investors with nothing for the rest. If investors are risk neutral, fiduciaries should choose Venture 3 over Venture 2 (despite the fact that some investors end up worse off under Venture 3), because the expected value to each investor is $20 under Venture 3 and only $15 under Venture 2.

In sum, if the terms under which the directors obtain control of the firm call for them to maximize the wealth of the investors, their duty is to select the highest-paying venture and, following that, to abide by the rules of distribution. If unequal distribution is necessary to make the stakes higher, then duty requires inequality. The *ex post* inequality under Ventures 2 and 3 is no more "unfair" than the *ex post* inequality of a lottery, in which all players invest a certain amount but only a few collect. The equal treatment of the investors going into Ventures 2 and 3, and the gains they receive from taking chances, make the *ex post* inequality both fair and desirable.

We hope that our analysis of Ventures 2 and 3 above are uncontroversial. If corporate control transactions sufficiently resemble Ventures 2 and 3, this analysis supplies a guide for analyzing the fiduciary duties of corporate managers. A class of control transactions resembles Ventures 2 and 3 if: (1) control changes and financial restructurings produce gains for investors to enjoy; (2) the existence or amount of the gain depends upon unequal distribution; and (3) shareholders would prefer the unequal distribution to a more equal distribution of smaller gains from an alternative transaction (or no transaction). We address these issues in the remainder of Part II and conclude by advancing a fiduciary principle under which managers always are free to engage in transactions resembling Venture 2. For practical reasons, however, our principle prohibits transactions resembling Venture 3.

A. *The Potential Gains from Control Transactions*

It should be clear that managers do not always maximize the wealth of investors. * * * Managers may not work as hard as they would if they could claim a higher share of the proceeds—they may consume excessive perquisites, and they may select inferior projects for the firm without bearing the consequences of their action. Corporate control transactions can reduce agency costs * * *

The sale of a control bloc of stock, for example, allows the buyer to install his own management team, producing the same gains available from a tender offer for a majority of shares but at lower cost to the buyer. Because such a buyer believes he can manage the assets of a firm more profitably, he is willing to pay a premium over the market price to acquire control. The premium will be some percentage of the anticipated increase in value once the transfer of control is effectuated. If there were no anticipated increase in value, it would be irrational for the buyer to pay the premium. There is a strong presumption, therefore, that free transferability of corporate control, like any other type of voluntary exchange, moves assets to higher valued uses.

Of course, some control transactions do not produce gains * * * At least for publicly-traded firms, the market offers information that distinguishes value-increasing control transactions from others in which looting or mismanagement may be in store. The information is contained in the price of a firm's shares. If the control change is associated with an increase in price, the investors apparently do not fear looting or other harm to the firm. If a syndicate acquires a control bloc of shares, and the price of the remaining shares *rises,* relative to the market as a whole, then the shareholders are betting on the basis of available information that the new controller will be better for their interests than the old.

B. *The Gains May Depend on Unequal Division*

In many cases the apportionment of the gain makes little difference to the success of the transaction. If the gain from taking over a corporation exceeds the cost incurred by the acquiror, he would be indifferent to who receives the premium that is necessary to obtain control. But a sharing requirement * * * may make an otherwise profitable transaction unattractive to the prospective seller of control. To illustrate, suppose that the owner of a control bloc of shares finds that his perquisites or the other amenities of his position are worth $10. A prospective acquiror of control concludes that, by eliminating these perquisites and other amenities, he could produce a gain of $15. The shareholders in the company benefit if the acquiror pays a premium of $11 to the owner of the controlling bloc, ousts the current managers, and makes the contemplated improvements. The net gains of $4 inure to each investor according to his holdings, and although the acquiror obtains the largest portion because he holds the largest bloc, no one is left out. If the owner of the control bloc must share the $11 premium with all of the existing shareholders, however, the deal collapses. The owner will not part with his bloc for less than a $10 premium. A sharing requirement would make the deal unprofitable to him, and the other investors would lose the prospective gain from the installation of better managers.

C. *Investors Prefer the Fiduciary Principle That Maximizes Aggregate Gains*

Do investors prefer a larger pie even if not everyone may have a larger slice in every case? We argue here that they do, for two reasons. First, their expected wealth is greatest under this interpretation of the fiduciary principle, and second, they may deal with any risk by holding diversified portfolios of investments.

Clearly, if control transactions produce gains, and if the gains depend on unequal allocation, then the expected wealth of the shareholders in the aggregate is maximized by a rule allowing unequal allocation. *All* share prices *ex ante* will be highest when the probability of a value-increasing transaction in the future is the greatest. Shareholders can realize this value at any time by selling their shares, or they can hold the shares and take the chance of gaining still more as a result of the unequal allocation of gains *ex post.*

This argument may seem to disregard the fact that many investors are risk averse—they prefer a sure $10, say, to a one in ten chance of receiving $100. On the surface, therefore, it seems that investors might benefit from equal or fair division of gains notwithstanding the loss of some gains as a result. This argument, however, ignores the lessons of modern portfolio theory. By investing in many firms simultaneously, risk averse investors can reduce the risk of losses without extinguishing profitable-but-risky transactions.

The risks involved in corporate control transactions are diversifiable. * * * Indeed, there is a strongly negative correlation among the risks. An investor with a reasonably diversified portfolio would be on the winning side of some transactions and the losing side of others. For example, if shareholders of one corporation obtain little of the gain from a given merger, the shareholders of the other corporation obtain more. An investor holding a diversified portfolio with stock in both corporations is concerned with the total gain from the transaction, not with how the gain is allocated. Indeed, the investor with shares of both would see any expense in allocating the gain as pure loss. To the extent an unequal allocation raises the number and amount of gain transactions, therefore, investors with diversified portfolios would prefer to allow the unequal allocation to continue.

We have shown that the *ex post* inequality under Ventures 2 and 3, like the *ex post* inequality in a lottery, is not "unfair" if, *ex ante*, all investors have an equal chance to win and can eliminate risk through diversification. We now consider a potential objection to this reasoning. One might argue that this *ex ante* equality is absent in corporate control transactions because insiders systematically benefit at the expense of outsiders. Small shareholders, the argument runs, consistently will be frozen out, deprived of control premiums, and otherwise disadvantaged by insiders.

The argument loses its plausibility on close examination. One need not be wealthy to be on the "winning side" of a control transaction, and neither wealth nor status as an insider ensures being a winner. If corporation A purchases from corporation B a control bloc of shares in corporation C, a small (or outside) shareholder might participate in the gains by holding shares in any of the three firms.

There is no need for the small shareholder to identify these situations in advance. By holding a diversified portfolio containing the securities of many firms, the small shareholder can ensure that he will participate in the gains produced. All shareholders therefore have a chance of receiving the gains produced by corporate control transactions—if not an equal chance, at least enough of a chance to allow diversification of the risk. There remain cases in which it is impossible for an investor to share in gains or diversify away the risk by holding stock in both firms. This would be true, for example, where one of the firms is privately held. The shareholder can minimize this non-diversifiable risk, however, by not investing in firms that are controlled by an individual or a privately-held firm.

D. *Market Value as a Benchmark Under the Fiduciary Principle*

In the circumstances we have discussed, shareholders unanimously prefer legal rules under which the amount of gains is maximized, regardless of how the gains are distributed. The ideal transaction is one like Venture 2 above, in which the gains are unequally distributed but all shareholders are at least as well off as they were before the transaction. Shareholders may also benefit from transactions in which the distribution of gains leaves some shareholders worse off than before the transaction—as in Venture 3—but there are probably few such transactions. We cannot imagine why gains would depend on making some investors worse off, and we have not encountered any example of such a transaction. In a world of costly information, investors will view Venture 2 transactions very differently from Venture 3 transactions, which would raise all-but-insuperable difficulties in determining whether the transaction produced gain. One can imagine instances, of which looting is a good example, in which the person acquiring control pays a premium to some investor(s) in order to obtain control and obliterate the remaining claims, recouping the premium without putting resources to a more productive use. A requirement that all investors receive at least the market value of their positions prior to the transactions would be a useful rule-of-thumb for separating beneficial deals from potentially harmful ones. If every investor receives at least what he had before, and some receive a premium, the transaction *must* produce gains.

The requirement that everyone receive at least the value of his investment under existing conditions serves much the same function as the rule against theft. A thief *might* be able to put stolen resources to a better use than his victim, but if so then he can pay for those resources. Thus, a requirement of payment increases the likelihood that transactions are value-increasing. Moreover, the proscription of theft also reduces the incentive of property owners to take elaborate precautions against theft. For example, investors might resort to costly monitoring devices to reduce the chance of confiscation of their shares. When all transactions are consensual, these precautions become unnecessary. By prohibiting confiscation, therefore, the fiduciary principle reduces wasteful expenditures while simultaneously reducing the number of socially inefficient corporate control transactions.

III. The Fiduciary Principle in Operation

*   *   *

A. *Sales of Control Blocs*

Sales of controlling blocs of shares provide a good example of transactions in which the movement of control is beneficial. The sale of control may lead to new offers, new plans, and new working arrangements with other firms that reduce agency costs and create other gains from new business relationships. The premium price received by the seller of the control bloc amounts to an unequal distribution of the gains. For the reasons we have discussed, however, this unequal distribution reduces the costs to purchasers of control, thereby increasing the number of beneficial control transfers, and increasing the incentive for inefficient controllers to relinquish their positions.

Numerous academic commentators, however, argue for some form of sharing requirement. * * * This proposal would entitle the minority shareholders to sell their shares on the same terms as the controlling shareholder.

Both of these proposed treatments of the control premium would stifle transfers of control. If * * * minority shareholders may sell on the same terms as the controlling shareholder, bidders may have to purchase more shares than necessary, possibly causing the transaction to become unprofitable. Minority shareholders would suffer under either rule, as the likelihood of improvements in the quality of management declined.

The mountain of academic commentary calling for some type of sharing requirement has not been influential, and the legal treatment of control sales is largely along the lines of wealth maximization. Sales at a premium are lawful, and the controlling shareholder generally has no duty to spread the bounty. The rhetoric of the cases, however, is not uniform. In particular, the famous case of *Perlman v. Feldmann* suggests that the gains may have to be shared in some circumstances.

In *Perlman* the president and chairman (Feldmann) of the board of Newport Steel, a producer of steel sheets, sold his controlling bloc of shares for $20 per share at a time when the market price was less than $12 per share. The purchasers, a syndicate organized as Wilport Company, consisted of end-users of steel from across the country who were interested in a secure source of supply during a period of shortage attributable to the Korean War.

Because of the war, steel producers were prohibited from raising the price of steel. The "Feldmann Plan", adopted by Newport and some other steel producers, effectively raised the price of steel to the market-clearing price. Under the plan, prospective purchasers provided Newport and other steel producers with interest-free advances in exchange for commitments for future production. Newport had used those advances to replace equipment in order to expand and compete more effectively with other steel producers.

The Second Circuit held in *Perlman* that the seller of the control bloc had a duty to share the control premium with other shareholders. The court's holding that Feldmann could not accept the premium paid by Wilport without violating his fiduciary duty was based on a belief that the steel shortage allowed Newport to finance needed expansion via the "Plan", and that the premium represented an attempt by Wilport to divert a corporate opportunity—to secure for itself the benefits resulting from the shortage. * * *

There are several problems with this treatment. Foremost is its assumption that the gain resulting from the "Plan" was not reflected in the price of Newport's stock. Newport stock was widely traded, and the existence of the Feldmann Plan was known to investors. The going price of Newport shares prior to the transaction therefore reflected the full value of Newport, including the value of advances under the Feldmann Plan. The Wilport syndicate paid some two-thirds more than the going price and thus could not profit from the deal unless (a) the sale of control resulted in an increase in the value of Newport, or (b) Wilport's control of Newport was the equivalent of looting. To see the implications of the latter possibility, consider the following simplified representation of the transaction. Newport has only 100 shares, and Wilport pays $20 for each of 37 shares. The market price of shares is $12, and hence the premium over the market price is $8 × 37 = $296. Wilport must extract more than $296 from Newport in order to gain from the deal; the extraction comes at the expense of the other 63 shares, which must drop approximately $4.75 each, to $7.25.

Hence, the court's proposition that Wilport extracted a corporate opportunity from Newport—the functional equivalent of looting—has testable implications. Unless the price of Newport's outstanding shares plummeted, the Wilport syndicate could not be extracting enough to profit. In fact, however, the value of Newport's shares rose substantially after the transaction. Part of this increase may have been attributable to the rising market for steel companies at the time, but even holding this factor constant, Newport's shares appreciated in price.[43]

[43] Charles Cope has computed changes in the price of Newport shares using the market model, well developed in the finance literature, under which the rate of return on a firm's shares is a function of the market rate of return, the volatility of the firm's price in the past, a constant, and a residual component that represents the consequences of unanticipated events. Increases in this residual reflect good news for the firm. Cope found a significant positive residual for Newport in the month of the sale to Wilport. See Cope, Is the Control Premium Really a Corporate Asset? (April 1981) (unpublished paper on file with *Yale Law Journal*).

The data refute the court's proposition that Wilport appropriated a corporate opportunity of Newport.

It seems, then, that the source of the premium in *Perlman* is the same as the source of the gains for the shares Wilport did not buy: Wilport installed a better group of managers and, in addition, furnished Newport with a more stable market for its products. The gains from these changes must have exceeded any loss from abolition of the Feldmann Plan.

———————◆———————

In light of the discussion of the cumulative abnormal returns technique in Chapter Six B, how persuasive is Easterbrook and Fischel's use of the data concerning returns on Newport stock? Although Newport may have had a positive CAR in the month of the sale of its control, is the *fact* of the CAR sufficient to establish that the sale of control was its *cause?* Recall that the statistical technique measures only the difference between Newport's actual returns and its expected returns, the latter estimated by use of its historical beta. The technique itself establishes nothing about the *cause* of a differential between actual and expected returns. That analysis requires review of what was happening at the time and the possibility always exists that the measured effect is the net result of multiple events, each of which somewhat offsets the effect of the others. For example, an expectation that price controls might be lifted would result in a positive CAR for Newport and this might camouflage negative performance resulting from the sale of control. The problem of confounding events is exacerbated by the use of monthly data which hinders efforts at separating the effect on price of the sale of control from the effect of other events.

How might this ambiguity be resolved? Suppose that we calculated the CAR for the month of the Newport sale for a portfolio of all steel companies. How would the result of this calculation bear on Easterbrook and Fischel's assumption about the causal relationship between the Newport sale and their data?

Before considering the competing claims of Andrews and Easterbrook & Fischel concerning whether a sharing rule really would benefit minority shareholders, it would be helpful to know more about what the premium paid for control really represents. The following excerpt is an effort to explain the existence of control premiums and to offer some empirical observations concerning their size and the characteristics of the groups offering them. In evaluating the authors' hypotheses and empirical results, keep in mind that their sample contains only

The raw price data are no less telling. The $12 price to which the Perlman court referred was the highest price at which shares changed hands before the sale of control. The average monthly bid prices for Newport stock during 1950 were:

July: 6¾

August: 8½

September: 10⅞

October: 12½

November: 12⅜

December: 12

The sale to the Wilport syndicate took place on August 31, 1950. This pattern of prices certainly does not suggest that the 63% interest excluded from the premium perceived any damage to Newport.

close corporations. Does that limit the applicability of the results to public corporations that are the subject of the debate between Andrews and Easterbrook & Fischel?

MEEKER & JOY, PRICE PREMIUMS FOR CONTROLLING SHARES OF CLOSELY HELD BANK STOCK
53 J.Bus. 297 (1980).*

* * *

The purpose of this paper is to theoretically and empirically examine the relationship between controlling and minority share prices in closely held banks. Shares are defined as controlling shares when they give an individual, a group of individuals, or a bank holding company ownership in excess of 50% of a bank's outstanding common stock. We refer to differences between minority and controlling share prices as "price premiums" on controlling shares.

* * *

We propose that, in equilibrium, controlling interest transactions in closely held banks would command price premiums relative to minority interest transactions. For this to occur, three conditions must be met: (1) control must provide special benefits not available to minority shareholders; (2) control group members must, individually, be able to exploit those benefits of control; and (3) control shares must be effectively isolated from minority shares in the market. Correspondingly, we discuss the benefits of control, controlling ownership structure, and equilibrium pricing.

Benefits of Control

* * *

Controlling shareholders in banks have several means of obtaining benefits that are not generally available to minority shareholders. First, they can hire themselves into managerial positions at rates above their value as hired resources. Second, they can direct the use of bank resources to benefit themselves, friends, and business associates. Third, they can adjust the payment of dividends to meet their own investment and consumption needs. Fourth, controlling stockholders can often obtain financing of their stock ownership from correspondent banks and, in some instances, use bank resources to obtain more favorable loan terms. Fifth, there may be quasi-financial benefits in the form of expense accounts, overdraft privileges,[3] plush offices, a company provided automobile, company paid trips to conferences, and so forth. Sixth, controlling shareholders can be expected to be better informed about their bank's current condition and future prospects than minority shareholders. This serves to reduce uncertainty, which is also an important investment parameter. Another potential benefit of controlling ownership is the access to information from and about

---

[3] This advantage existed during our study period but, as a result of the Financial Institutions Regulatory and Interest Rate Control Act of 1978 (Public Law 95–630), is severely restricted in the current banking environment.

bank customers. To the extent this information can be utilized on personal account, it too is a benefit of control.

Differentially allocating bank resources to benefit controlling shareholders raises the possibility of stockholder conflicts and, in some instances, conflicts with bank regulatory agencies. While law concerning fiduciary responsibilities of management would act as a restraint on such practices, it would not eliminate them. It is often difficult for minority shareholders to obtain financial information about the operations of small banks. Second, legal issues about applications of bank resources are not clear-cut. For example, the legitimacy of the banking activities of Bert Lance is yet to be decided at this writing. Given the cost of filing stockholder lawsuits and the uncertainty of their outcome, it is likely that many self-serving differential allocations of a bank's resources, even if known to minority shareholders, would go unchallenged unless they were of sufficient magnitude and of a nature that violated banking laws or threatened the soundness of the bank and attracted regulatory attention.

Controlling Ownership Structure

Data presented below indicate that many control positions are "shared" by groups of investors. This raises questions about the ability of individuals within these groups to exploit the benefits of control. In particular, the nature of many control rewards is such that an equitable division of rewards among control group members may be difficult. Furthermore, the costs of operating a group and making group decisions are a disadvantage not present in single-owner control. Both of these factors contribute to the crucial stability problem with groups.

Control group stability is a necessary condition for the existence of controlling share price premiums. Otherwise, a group of minority shareholders could entice some of the current control group shareholders to join a new control group or to sell their shares. The control-seeking coalition could justify paying up to an amount offsetting its increased benefits from becoming controlling shareholders. In a market characterized by rational expectations, such possibilities would tend, in equilibrium, to eliminate differences between controlling and minority share prices. Two factors would contribute to the elimination of the control share price premiums: buyer uncertainty about being able to realize the premiums when the shares were sold and competition among suppliers of shares. * * *

In practice, there are many ways to achieve group stability. A common one in smaller firms is family ownership of controlling shares. Friendship and business associate ties are the binding fabric of many groups. More legally binding, and not infrequently used, are formal agreements restricting the rights of control coalition members to sell their shares. Buy-sell agreements, for example, force the potential seller to set a price at which he would be willing to either buy other coalition members' shares or sell his own shares. First right of refusal agreements require that all proposed sales of shares by controlling coalition members to noncoalition members be offered first to other control coalition members at the agreed upon price with the noncoalition buyers. In addition, a variety of covenants restricting stock sales by controlling shareholders may be used. Collectively, these factors help bind selling groups together and provide group stability.

An important consideration in assessing coalition stability is coalition size. Larger groups are more likely to be unstable than smaller groups for several reasons. First, they are more difficult to bind together: they are better targets for prospective control coalitions. Second, in larger controlling groups, it is more difficult for individual group members to partake of many of the controlling ownership rewards or for the rewards to be shared equitably. * * * Third, group formation and operation costs will increase with group size. Large groups would be more likely to necessitate complex and costly legal arrangements among members to achieve group stability. Ongoing "operating" costs would be greater for larger groups than for smaller groups.

All of these considerations suggest that controlling shares in small banks would be worth more to smaller coalitions. That is, smaller groups of buyers would be willing to pay more for shares and smaller groups of sellers would demand more. Two factors, however, may complicate the testing of this hypothesis—wealth and portfolio constraints. Wealth constraints may make some investments impossible for single individuals and relatively small coalitions. Larger group sizes may also be desirable for portfolio reasons. To the extent that investment in a control position in (even) a small bank causes investor portfolios to be too heavily weighted in a single asset or a single type of assets, ownership through a coalition may be advantageous.

Equilibrium Pricing

While the differential benefits of control imply that control-seeking coalitions would be willing to pay more for control shares than minority shares, and that existing controlling owners would have an incentive to demand more for their shares, they do not guarantee price premiums for controlling shares. Competition for controlling shares and among suppliers of controlling shares will determine equilibrium share prices. In that regard, we discuss equilibrium pricing considerations for three important and distinct types of control share transactions.

First are transactions involving the acquisition of absolute control from sellers having absolute control. These types of transactions are the focus of our empirical work. In these cases, * * * both potential buyers and current owners have incentives to pay and demand, respectively, price premiums for controlling bank shares. The buyers expect to reap control benefits, and the sellers are currently receiving those benefits. If control groups are stable, there is no possibility of *within-*bank share supply competition to furnish control to prospective buyers, so potential buyers must deal with the existing controlling owner(s) or seek control of another bank. Across banks, however, there is still little likelihood that buyers would be able to acquire absolute control of a bank from a single seller or stable coalition with no price premium.

Competition from other buyers as well as the demands of the seller would prevent it. The only possibilities for acquiring absolute control at a lower cost would be if control groups were unstable, or if it were possible to assemble an absolute control block of shares in a bank where absolute control was not held by a clearly definable entity. The latter possibility is an important second type of control transaction: the acquisition of absolute control from dispersed minority shareholders.

In acquiring absolute control from dispersed minority interests, supply competition exists, by definition, within banks as well as across banks. Within a bank, absolute control shares can be acquired from many possible combinations of share purchases from minority shareholders. Providing none of the minority shareholders is receiving control benefits, they have no incentive from their current share ownership to demand higher than minority share prices for their shares. While competition among the minority shareholders to supply shares at any higher prices would tend to keep share prices at the minority share price level, competition among potential buyers would act to raise share prices. Given that control has a positive differential value relative to minority share ownership, there would be an incentive for existing minority shareholders to form a control coalition. For this to occur, the value of the control position would have to exceed the previously discussed costs associated with the formation and mainte- nance of a control coalition. Thus, outside buyer competition as well as inside competition to form a control coalition would cause share prices to be bid above minority share price levels. Since there is a risk in this type of control acquisition of having a control-gaining attempt thwarted by another competing group, the premiums paid in such acquisitions should be lower by an amount necessary to offset the risk involved. We do not empirically test this proposition in this paper.

The third type of control share transaction involves the acquisition of a "working" control interest, whereby the controlling owner controls less than 50% of the bank's outstanding shares but a substantial enough block of shares to effectively control bank policies. As long as such a position carried greater benefits than a minority position, there would be an incentive for prospective working control shareholders to bid prices up for those shares. Similarly, as long as suppliers of large blocks of minority shares could clearly sell a working control position from which they were receiving control benefits, they would demand price premiums for their shares. The market would reflect working control share price premiums as long as the benefits of working control exceeded the costs of forming and maintaining control coalitions. Since working control involves a less secure control position than absolute control, the premiums for working control would be less than the premiums for absolute control. We do not, however, empirically test this proposition here.

* * *

IV. Data Sources and Demographics

Price data for this study were taken from two primary sources. These data were divided into two separate "sets" for statistical testing purposes. The rationale for this division will become apparent as we proceed.

Data Set A: Independent Control and Minority Observations

Data on controlling share ownership were taken from reports filed by banks in compliance with Public Law 88–593 passed by Congress on September 12, 1964. This law, recently superseded by the Change in Bank Control Act of 1978, required the reporting of a number of details concerning bank stock transactions that had the potential to produce changes in bank management or policies. However, it did not require acquisitions of bank stock by groups or individuals to be reported if the individuals or groups held less than 10% of the subject bank's outstanding common stock subsequent to the transaction.

The control share data source included virtually all such transactions reported in compliance with Public Law 88–593 in the Tenth Federal Reserve District since the law was enacted through 1975.
* * *

We defined a control change transaction to be one where the trade involved more than 50% of the bank's shares.

In total, there were 563 control observations in data set A for 1964–75. * * *

Our minority share price data were drawn from Federal Deposit Insurance Corporation (FDIC) examination reports on banks in Kansas, Missouri, Colorado, Nebraska, and Oklahoma. While no circumstances surrounding the transactions were known, there was little reason to believe that most of the transactions were not arm's length. To limit the possibilities of a transaction being part of a control change in a bank, we eliminated transactions where the block of shares traded exceeded 5% of the bank's outstanding common shares. The resultant data consisted of 584 transactions spanning 1970–75.

Data Set B: Matched Control-Minority Observations

Observations in this data collection also come from the Public Law 88–593 source. Data set B consists of transactions where there was a clearly identified control change sale and at least one associated concurrent or subsequent minority sale. Within this set are 37 matched pairs of prices that relate to 37 control transactions and 46 minority transactions occurring in 1965–75.[7] Observations were excluded for reasons similar to those described in data set A. While data set B contains relatively few observations, its "matching" nature affords very strong inference possibilities.
* * *

V. Statement of Hypotheses

The central contention of this paper is that controlling shares should bring price premiums relative to minority shares. An empirical

[7] There are more minority than control transactions in data set B because in some situations there were multiple minority transactions associated with a single control change trade. In such instances we averaged the multiple minority prices so that there would be one matched minority-control price pair for each control observation. This was done to facilitate the statistical analysis performed later.

finding of no significant premiums would imply one or more of the following: that the purported benefits of control do not exist or are not attainable, that ownership structures are unstable, or that within bank share supply competition eliminates control premiums. Conversely, a finding of significant price premiums would indicate that control benefits exist and are attainable, that ownership structures are generally stable, and that controlling and minority shares can be effectively isolated in the market.

Table 4

Distribution of Purchase Amounts for Controlling and Minority Share Transactions

Transaction Amount	Data Set A (%)		Data Set B (%)	
	Control Transactions	Minority Transactions	Control Transactions	Minority Transactions
Less than $10,000	0	8	0	16
$10,000–$50,000	2	22	0	38
$50,000–$250,000	32	34	41	32
$250,000–$1 million	44	28	41	14
Over $1 million	22	8	18	0
Total	100	100	100	100

We present tests of two specific hypotheses: H_1—prices for control shares exceed prices of minority shares; H_2—control premiums vary inversely with the size of the ownership coalition. H_1 is a direct test of the control premium contention. H_2 is a test of an important implication of the control premium contention. We will refer to these as the "control premium" and "coalition-size" hypotheses, respectively.

VI. Empirical Testing

We first present evidence on the control premium hypothesis. This is done for both data sets, A and B. Then we present evidence on the coalition-size hypothesis.

Price Premium Analysis of Data Set A

Since we are comparing prices of different banks in this set, it is necessary to standardize the price measures. Scaling by book value has been commonly used * * * and, as shown below, has a relevant interpretation in reference to minority share prices. Consequently, the price variable is price divided by the previous year's book value (P/B).
* * *

Table 5 shows sample sizes, means and standard deviations (σ) of P/B, and price premiums for data set A samples, for several different time intervals. * * *

Table 5

P/B Ratios for Data Set A

Time	Control n	Control P/B	Control σ	Minority n	Minority P/B	Minority σ	Test of Difference between Means (Control—Minority) t-Score	Price Premiums (P/B Control / P/B Minority)
1964–66	102	1.48	.38	...	...	...	...	...
1967–69	159	1.56	.47	...	...	...	...	...
1970–72	149	1.65	.51	205	1.03	.38	12.9*	1.60
1973–75	153	1.88	.46	379	1.02	.46	19.5*	1.84
1964–69	261	1.53	.43	...	...	...	...	...
1970–75	302	1.77	.50	584	1.03	.43	23.1*	1.72

* Significant at the .001 level or better.

Table 5 also shows the results of testing the control premium hypothesis * * * * Results in both 3-year subperiods and in the 6-year period 1970–75 indicated a highly significant premium for control shares that averaged 72%.

These results are subject to several criticisms. First, we have not held other things constant in making the price comparisons, so it is possible that other factors influence the test results. There are also problems associated with the data, apart from possible transcription and transmission errors. As shown below, it is quite common for controlling shares of stock to be acquired from several individuals, and when the number of shares acquired exceed what is necessary to just gain control, it may not be evident if it were necessary to acquire those *additional* shares for control or if they were acquired subsequent to control. In the latter case, presumably they could have been acquired at a lower price. However, the reports may simply indicate a total amount paid for all shares. To the extent that such "aggregated" cases are present in sufficient numbers, it is possible that average control share prices shown in table 5 are biased downward.

With respect to minority shares, since we had no means of determining if transactions were arm's length, there may be a negative bias imparted to average minority prices reported in table 5. This could cause us to overstate the significance level associated with H_1, as well as the average control premiums implied in table 5. However, our minority prices do not appear to be low in comparison to similar data from other studies.

Price Premium Analysis of Data Set B

In this analysis, direct price comparisons are made between prices of controlling and minority shares of stock that are traded at approximately the same time and in the same bank.[10] This avoids the ceteris paribus problem in the previous analysis. Table 6 shows price premium ratios (control price ÷ minority price) for data set B.

[10] The "equal price offer" guideline enforced by the Board of Governors of the Federal Reserve System until 1973 for ac- quisitions of bank shares by bank holding companies did not directly affect the data in data set B. * * * *

Table 6

Summary of Price Premium Ratio Distributions for
Data Set B: 1965–75

Price Premiums*	
P_c/P_m†	Frequency
1.0	2
1.0–1.5	15
1.5–2.0	16
Over 2.0	4
Total	37

Note.—In terms of data set B, hypothesis H_1 is: H_1: $\overline{P_c/P_m} > 1$, where P_c = control prices and P_m = minority prices. Average P_c/P_m = 1.52; σ = .37.

* Where more than one companion minority transaction was present and where prices for these transactions were different, a weighted average minority share price was computed.

† Price premium = control price/minority price = P_c/P_m.

Average P/B ratios for control and minority shares were 1.64 and 1.08, respectively. Therefore, the average control price premium was 1.52, which was significantly greater than one, as evidenced by a t-score of 8.52. Thus, controlling shares commended a significant (52%) premium over minority prices for data set B. These results are consistent with but lower than those from data set A. The different results are likely attributable to the different time periods covered. As can be seen in table 5, P/B values for control shares increased consistently from 1964 through 1975.

To put the data set B premiums into more meaningful perspective, it may be useful to consider their dollar magnitude, where dollar magnitude is defined as the difference between the per share control price and the per share minority price multiplied times the number of control shares traded. These premium magnitudes ranged from zero to $1,240,000; the mean and median amounts were $215,000 and $102,000, respectively.

One of the major criticisms of the analysis of data set B relative to that of data set A is the small sample size, which brings into question the representativeness of the sample. However, tables 1–3 indicate no startling disparities between the characteristics of the two data sets. Moreover, data used in this section's analysis have the exemplary feature that all controlling and minority observations are perfectly matched with respect to bank characteristics and the time dimension.

* * *

Control Prices and Buyer/Seller Coalitions

The coalition size hypothesis, H_2, asserts that other things equal, control should be worth more to smaller groups than larger ones. In equilibrium, we would expect to see virtually all control positions taken by individual owners. Wealth and portfolio constraints, however, would act to mitigate this. If the group size hypothesis is correct *and* wealth and portfolio constraints are important, we would expect to see most control positions taken by relatively small coalitions, including many single-owner cases.

Figure 1 shows the number of buyers and sellers in control coalitions for a subset of our data. Observations in figure 1 were taken from both data sets A and B and were for cases involving noncorporate purchasers who did not own shares prior to the trade.[11] Transactions involving corporations were not used because the number of buyers and sellers is somewhat ambiguous, and we used only "new" purchasers, because "old" purchasers may already be members of existing coalitions.

The data in figure 1 show that the vast majority of the observations involved either small groups or single buyers and sellers. These data are consistent with H_2, that control is more valuable to relatively smaller groups, as they indicate that relatively smaller groups are more successful in acquiring control. Since control is not exclusive to single owners, wealth and portfolio constraints apparently are important.

Fig. 1

Number of Buyers and Sellers in Control Group

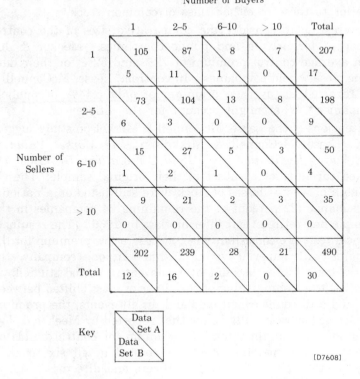

[D7608]

* * *

[11] In many of the transactions we were unable to clearly identify the numbers of people involved.

There has been an interesting recent effort to establish the existence and amounts of control premia in public corporations. Reasoning that control ultimately is a function of voting rights, Lease, McConnell and Mikkelson, *The Market Value of Control in Publicly-Traded Corporations,* 11 J.Fin.Econ. 439 (1983), examined a sample of 30 public companies that had two classes of common stock outstanding that were identical in all respects except voting rights; in each company, one class of common stock had either exclusive or superior voting rights. Their hypothesis—that the class of common stock conferring voting control would trade at a premium relative to the non-control class—was consistent with the data except for one intriguing anomaly. For the 26 companies with two classes of common stock but no class of voting preferred stock outstanding, the control class of common stock traded at an average premium of 5.44% compared to the non-control class, and at some premium for 729 of the 828 monthly observations. For the four firms that also had a class of voting preferred oustanding, the result was reversed. The class of common stock with superior voting rights traded at an average *discount* of 1.25% compared to the class of common stock with inferior voting rights. Note, however, that in three of the four companies in this group, the preferred stock had voting rights superior to those of either class of common stock.

It is interesting to consider the comparative sizes of the control premia recorded for private and public companies. Meeker & Joy reported an average control premium of 72% and 52% for their data sets covering closely held companies. In contrast, Lease, McConnell & Mikkelson reported an average premium of only 5.44% in publicly traded companies. What might account for the difference?

Two extensions of the Lease, McConnell & Mikkelson study suggest an answer. Lease, McConnell & Mikkelson, *The Market Value of Differential Voting Rights in Closely Held Corporations,* 57 J.Bus. 443 (1984), looked carefully at a subset of their original sample: The six companies both of whose classes of stock were still listed on a national securities exchange (22 percent of the remaining 24 companies in the original sample had retired their inferior class by 1966). The results of their empirical tests are consistent with, at best, a low premium for the class of shares with superior voting rights. In one company, the superior class traded at a discount over the entire period studied; in four companies, the trading value of the superior class shifted between a premium and a discount over time; and, in all events, the premium observed remained substantially below that reported by Meeker & Joy. One explanation for the apparent low premium for control builds on the fact that "[t]he ownership of voting control of all six firms is concentrated in the hands of principal officers and directors." Id. at 466. That leads the authors to suggest that "the observed market prices of the superior share classes typically represent the marginal valuation of [non-controlling] investors." Id. On that basis, any observable premium must result from expectations of a premium takeover bid discounted by, among other factors, the likelihood that the premium offered would be high enough to persuade the controlling shareholders—management—to accept it. Id. In contrast, Meeker & Joy measured the value of controlling shares in actual transfers of control. From this perspective, Meeker & Joy measured the value of controlling shares, while both classes of stock studied by Lease, McConnell & Mikkelson represented noncontrolling shares.

This explanation finds empirical support in DeAngelo & DeAngelo, *Managerial Ownership of Voting Rights: A Study of Public Corporations with Dual Classes of Stock,* 14 J.Fin.Econ. 33 (1985). Like Lease, McConnell & Mikkelson, they found that management commonly controlled the companies with dual classes of stock.[1] DeAngelo & DeAngelo, however, took the issue one step further by examining the price paid in acquisitions of companies with dual classes of stock. In 4 of 30 such acquisitions, the controlling class of stock received an explicit price premium for control [2] ranging from 83.3% to 200% of the premium received by the inferior class of stock. These figures, which measure the value of controlling shares, are much more in line with those reported by Meeker & Joy.

Note: The Scope of the Theoretical Debate

Although Andrews and Easterbrook & Fischel disagree as to the most desirable rule, they do not seem to disagree as to the standard by which the rules should be judged. Both rules—"equal opportunity" and "unequal division"—are argued to be most beneficial to shareholders in general, an *ex ante* determination. Further, both sides agree that control changes are potentially beneficial to all concerned. The disagreement is over whether unequal division—Feldmann keeping the entire premium—is necessary to secure those benefits. The resolution of the issue then depends on the reason why a premium is paid at all.

Consider first a situation where the buyer is willing to pay a premium only because efficiency gains in the operation of the target company would result from replacing the current control holder, and where the current control holder derives no benefit from control not shared proportionately by other shareholders.[3] In this admittedly unrealistic setting, it seems that an equal opportunity rule would be selected by shareholders. As Andrews points out, the division of the premium would not affect the *purchaser's* incentives to make the acquisition. And to complete the argument, unequal division would not be necessary to convince the *holder* of control to sell. Although a control holder would like the right to take advantage of control by keeping the premium to himself, he would still sell even if unequal division were prohibited because, by definition, he has been offered a price higher than the market value of his shares. In this situation, then, an equal opportunity rule would not reduce the number of

---

[1] Twenty-seven of the 45 sample firms were majority controlled by management. Id. at 51.

[2] In 12 of the 30 acquisitions both classes of shares received identical payment, and in 14 the controlling class received a complex form of preference although an equal per share nominal price. Id. at 57.

[3] For example, where the control holder provides goods or services to the company, only the market price is received.

beneficial control transactions and, even considered *ex ante,* shareholders would choose such a rule in preference to one that allowed a controlling shareholder to exploit his strategic advantage.

Note, however, that even the conclusion in this strikingly artificial situation is not without qualification. What if the very existence of a control group has a positive benefit so that, all other things being equal, minority shareholders would prefer that there be a controlling shareholder? This hypothetical is in fact substantially less artificial than that which just supported the choice of an equal opportunity rule. As was stressed in the Gilson excerpt in Chapter Ten, and by Easterbrook & Fischel, the separation of ownership and control imposes substantial agency and monitoring costs on shareholders. The creation of a control group reduces these costs by reducing the separation. The relation between the reduction in agency costs by forming a control group and a choice of a rule governing the division of a premium can be examined by considering the incentives associated with the formation of such a control group.

Assume a corporation characterized by a dispersal of share ownership such that, individually, no shareholder has "control." Further assume that a group of shareholders, whose holdings together would comprise control, are considering forming a coalition to exercise that control. If they do so, they would bear the costs of creating and maintaining the coalition,[4] but would share the resulting reduction in agency costs proportionately with shareholders who were not members of the coalition. But where a control coalition cannot capture all the benefits arising from their investment in creating control, it is predictable that fewer such coalitions, beneficial to all, would be created. To solve the incentive problem, minority shareholders then would be willing to cede to the control coalition a disproportionate amount of the gains resulting from the formation of the coalition by means of the sort described by Joy & Meeker: excess salaries, favorable transactions with the corporation, and so on. Thus, minority shareholders would prefer a rule which left some room for self-dealing by a control coalition, but which limited the amount "stolen" by the holders of control below the per-share gain from the reduction in agency costs accruing to the minority shareholders. Where within this range the "price" of monitoring would be pegged is indeterminant. It would depend, in part, on the level of competition in the market for monitors (including substitutes for owner monitoring such as independent auditors) and, in part, on the skill at strategic bargaining possessed by each side.

If this analysis is correct, an equal opportunity rule for sale of control would be untenable. Once it is conceded that minority shareholders would allow a disproportionate return to members of the control coalition, then it follows that the control shares are, in fact, worth more than the minority shares. Controlling shareholders would require a higher price to sell their shares than would the holders of minority shares, and an equal opportunity rule would result in fewer control transactions.

---

[4] Some of these costs are discussed in the Joy & Meeker excerpt, supra.

The illustration can be taken a step further. Assume that, following the creation of the coalition, a third party wishes to acquire the corporation because of the potential for synergy. What rule would the minority choose in this setting? Surely an equal opportunity rule would not be chosen; the holders of control, already having been given a disproportionate share of the corporation's income because it was to the minority shareholders' advantage to encourage the formation of a control coalition, would not sell their shares except at a premium which reflected the capitalized value of that disproportionate share. Thus, in order to induce the control coalition to enter into a transaction that would be beneficial to the minority, the coalition must be allowed to keep at least that part of the premium which reflects the sum of (i) the value of their disproportionate share of income; plus (ii) their proportionate part of that part of the synergistic gain anticipated to result from the transaction that will accrue to the target.

At this point, a proponent of an equal opportunity rule might object that a standard of the sort suggested would be impossible in application. How could one so carefully limit the unequal division of the premium? The response, reflected in Easterbrook & Fischel's emphasis on market price, is that there is an obvious limit to the extent to which the minority would allow unequal division: The minority must get some of the premium from the synergistic aspect of the transaction. This limit, moreover, can be easily expressed. As long as the minority shares increase in price following the transaction, they have received some portion of the synergistic benefit in the transaction. On this basis, as Easterbrook & Fischel argue, minority shareholders would prefer a rule allowing precisely the transaction which occurred in Perlman v. Feldmann because there were positive abnormal returns associated with Newport stock following the transaction.

This conclusion, however, is somewhat harder to reach than Easterbrook & Fischel acknowledge. Their formulation specifies the minimum amount necessary to induce minority shareholders to participate in the transaction. One can specify just as easily, however, the minimum amount necessary to induce members of the control coalition to participate. They also must receive some portion of the synergy created by the transaction, but as long as they receive more than the pre-transaction value of their shares (reflecting the value of their disproportionate income stream) this condition will be satisfied. These two formulations then leave the issue of how to divide the bulk of the surplus from the transaction—the amount of the synergistic gain in excess of the minimum amount necessary to induce both the minority and the control coalition to participate—unresolved. At this point, however, there is no obvious efficiency consideration that dictates how the remaining surplus should be shared. The issue is to that extent only distributional and issues of "fairness," however difficult to articulate, are unavoidable.

There nonetheless may be a practical reason for favoring the unequal division rule Easterbrook & Fischel advocate. Although efficiency considerations would not dictate how the bulk of the surplus should be divided if both formulations could be specified with equal precision, if one formulation is subject to a greater risk of error than the other, a basis for choice may exist. If there is, because of ambiguity in the rule chosen, uncertainty concerning whether the control coalition will gain from a proposed transaction, the result will be that some transactions that should take place, and would take place if the control coalition could be assured its full share, will not take place because of the danger that the control coalition will turn out to be under-compensated. From this perspective, the Easterbrook & Fischel formulation may have an advantage. Because there is a market for minority shares, it will be easy to determine whether minority shares receive a portion of the synergistic gains. In contrast, because, as the Lease, McConnell & Mikkelson studies suggest, there is no market price for control shares, there is no easy or precise way to determine whether the control coalition receives more than the value of their disproportionate income stream. As a practical matter, then, there may be some efficiency benefit to a rule of unequal division.

Even at this point, however, an ardent proponent of an equal opportunity rule might not be stymied. Such an egalitarian could respond to the proposed market value limit by pointing out that, despite its precision in dividing the gain, its integrity ultimately depends on the integrity of the rule that limits the disproportionate share of the company's ongoing income taken by the control coalition to an amount below the savings in agency costs resulting from the coalition's existence. This response has merit to it. If the rule governing unequal sharing of *income*, in contrast to *premium*, were not so limited, then shareholders would choose to allow no disproportionate sharing of income which, in turn, would eliminate any justification for unequal division of a control premium.

Note, then, where the dispute is left. What is important, ultimately, is less the rule concerning equal opportunity to share in a premium, than the rule governing the conduct of a controlling shareholder in the ongoing operation of the business. If the rule restricting the size of the disproportionate share of ongoing income allowed the controlling shareholder is taken as given, then Easterbrook & Fischel may be correct: Minority shareholders might well choose to allow unequal division of a control premium limited only by a requirement that minority shareholders earn positive abnormal returns as a result of the transaction. This, in turn, suggests that focusing so much academic attention on the equal opportunity aspect of Perlman v. Feldmann may be to allow the tail to wag the dog. Some of this energy might instead be devoted to formulating more effective fiduciary rules governing the manner in which controlling shareholders operate the company on an ongoing basis, an area which has received neither substantial judicial nor academic attention. In any event, it should be clear that the *worst* result from the perspective of the minority shareholder would be a rule that both leaves the controlling shareholder free to divert too much of the corporation's income stream on an ongoing basis *and,* by requiring equal division of any premium, discourages the occurrence of transfers of control which do benefit the minority.

Note: The Results—Judicial and Other

While the academic literature concerning the desirability of an equal opportunity rule for minority shareholders has been both voluminous and conflicting,[5] the case law after Perlman v. Feldmann has been remarkably consistent. In general, it rejects any obligation on the part of a controlling shareholder either to share a premium received with other shareholders, or to require that the purchaser allow other shareholders to participate, whether at the same price or at all.[6] Three exceptions to the general rule are worth noting.

Be on the Lookout for Looters. A number of cases assert the principle that a seller of control may be liable to minority shareholders when, following the sale, the purchaser loots or otherwise injures the corporation. E.g., Insuranshares Corp. v. Northern Fiscal Corp., 35 F.Supp. 22 (E.D.Pa.1940); DeBaun v. First Western Bank & Trust Co., 46 Cal.App.3d 686, 120 Cal.Rptr. 354 (2d Dist.1975); Clagett v. Hutchinson, 583 F.2d 1259 (4th Cir.1978); McDaniel v. Painter, 418 F.2d 545 (10th Cir.1969). The efficacy of such a rule turns on the question of who is the cheapest cost avoider. Looting is undesirable and should be deterred in the manner which uses up the least resources subject, in all events, to the limit that the resources used to deter not exceed the benefits of reduced looting. One of the costs of deterrence is the number of otherwise desirable transactions which do not take place because of the potential liability of sellers. For this purpose, how clearly the rule specifies the seller's obligation is central. For example, must a seller investigate a buyer even in the absence of circumstances which would arouse suspicion? Compare Clagett v. Hutchinson, supra (circumstances must put seller on notice of possibility of fraud; sale at a premium is not alone enough), with Northway, Inc. v. TSC Industries, Inc., 512 F.2d 324, 342 (7th Cir.1975), reversed on other grounds, 426 U.S. 438 (1976) (court "unable to read *Insuranshares* as holding that absent suspicious circumstances there is no duty to investigate prior to the transfer of a controlling interest"). How the rule is drawn— whether there is a an absolute duty to investigate, the specificity of the statement of the circumstances which should lead a seller to forego the transaction—bears substantially on the kind of transactions which will be deterred and, as a result, on the costs of imposing the rule in the first place:

> [O]ther things being equal, the more specific the prohibition, the less likely it is to deter socially desirable behavior not intended to be prohibited. Uncertainty concerning whether particular conduct

---

[5] Hazen, *Transfers of Corporate Control and Duties of Controlling Shareholders— Common Law, Tender Offers, Investment Companies—And a Proposal for Reform,* 125 U.Pa.L.Rev. 1023, 1024–25 n. 1 (1977), and Brown, *Fiduciary Problems of the Large Stockholder (other than the Acquiring Corporation) in a Target Corporation,* in Fiduciary Problems in Acquisitions and Takeovers 523, 549–51 (PLI 1981), provide extensive bibliographies of the controversy.

[6] E.g., Clagett v. Hutchinson, 583 F.2d 1259 (4th Cir.1978); McDaniel v. Painter, 418 F.2d 545 (10th Cir.1969); Ritchie v. McGrath, 1 Kan.App.2d 481, 571 P.2d 17 (1977); Yerke v. Barman, 376 N.E.2d 1211 (Ind.Ct.App.1978); Zetlin v. Hanson Holdings, Inc., 48 N.Y.2d 684, 421 N.Y.S.2d 877, 397 N.E.2d 387 (1979).

is prohibited deters that conduct; precision, by reducing the uncertainty, reduces the unintended deterrence. The move toward specificity, however, is not costless. The more specific the prohibition, the more likely it is that undesirable conduct, which was intended to be prohibited and which would have been covered by a more general prohibition, will not be barred.

Gilson, *A Structural Approach to Corporations: The Case Against Defense Tactics in Tender Offers,* 33 Stan.L.Rev. 819, 883 (1981) (citations omitted). See Erlich & Posner, *An Economic Analysis of Legal Rulemaking,* 3 J. Legal Stud. 257 (1974). The balance chosen, which will differ depending on the circumstances, can go a long way toward insuring that desirable transactions are not deterred while the few egregious situations remain covered. For an effort to tailor a corporate law rule in light of these considerations, see Gilson, supra, at 882–87.

Corporate Opportunity. What if the purchaser first approaches the controlling shareholder in the shareholder's capacity as an officer or director, and proposes to acquire the target corporation in a transaction in which all shareholders can participate? May the controlling shareholder divert the transaction so that only his shares are purchased at a higher price? Compare Brown v. Halbert, 271 Cal.App.2d 252, 76 Cal. Rptr. 781 (1969) (liability found), with Tyron v. Smith, 191 Or. 172, 229 P.2d 251 (1951) (no liability). *Brown* has gathered little following. See, e.g., Treadway Companies, Inc. v. Care Corp., 638 F.2d 357, 375–77 (2d Cir.1980). Even if desirable, would a rule that allowed a controlling shareholder to sell his stock at a premium, but did not allow the same shareholder to divert a transaction originally proffered to all shareholders, be workable? Suppose a well counseled controlling shareholder responded to the broader offer by stating only that, in his capacity as an officer and director, he would transmit the offer to the board. Further suppose that, thereafter, the shareholder, in his individual capacity, advised the board and the offerer that he would vote against (or not participate in) the proposed transaction, and would sell his shares only at a price that, implicitly, would result in him receiving a disproportionate share of the premium. On the one hand, even Brown v. Halbert, the post-*Perlman* case going furthest toward imposing an equal opportunity rule, can be read to allow a controlling shareholder to sell his shares at a premium so long as he "act[s] affirmatively and openly with full disclosure". 271 C.A.2d at 256. On the other hand, how can the rule have any impact if it can be avoided so easily by altering the form, but not the substance, of the controlling shareholder's response?

Tender Offer Rules. While the rules applicable to tender offers under the Williams Act will be considered in detail in Chapter Sixteen, it should be noted here that, under particular circumstances, federal law may have moved a long way in precisely the direction that state courts have steadfastly refused to proceed. If a transaction is a "tender offer" within the meaning of the Williams Act, a question which itself has engendered substantial controversy, Sections 14(d)(6) and (7) of the

Securities Exchange Act of 1934 require that all shareholders be permitted to participate proportionately in the transaction and that all receive the highest price offered to any shareholder. These requirements are backed up by Rule 10b–13 which bars the purchase by the offeror of any shares other than "pursuant to such tender offer." The upshot is that when federal jurisdictional standards are met, the freedom given a controlling shareholder under state law to keep the premium to himself is beside the point; federal law effectively imposes the equal opportunity rule for which some academics long have campaigned. See Schwartz, Editor's Headnote to Block & Schwarzfeld, *Curbing the Unregulated Tender Offer,* 6 Sec.Reg.L.J. 133 (1978).

This federal equal opportunity rule still has limited applicability. Most important, it applies only in a "tender offer." Although the definition of a tender offer is taken up in Chapter Sixteen, for now it is sufficient to note that a negotiated transaction with one or a small number of shareholders would not fall within the definition. This would leave the transactions like Feldmann's untouched by the Williams Act.

Expansion of the scope of federal regulation in this area has recently been proposed. The Securities and Exchange Commission's Advisory Committee on Tender Offers was established in early 1983 "to examine the tender offer process and other techniques for acquiring control of public issuers and to recommend to the Commission legislative and/or regulatory changes . . . considered necessary or appropriate." Report of Recommendations to the Securities and Exchange Commission ("Advisory Committee Report") 1 (July 8, 1983). The Advisory Committee's Recommendation 14 proposed expanding extensively the federal equal opportunity rule:

> No person may acquire voting securities of an issuer, if, immediately following such acquisition, such person would own more than 20% of the voting power of the outstanding voting securities of the issuer unless such purchase were made (i) from the issuer, or (ii) pursuant to a tender offer. The Commission should retain broad exemptive power with respect to this provision.

How would the Advisory Committee's recommendation have affected the transaction in Perlman v. Feldmann? The SEC's current views on this subject are considered in Chapter Sixteen A.1.c. infra.

Not all reform efforts, however, express a preference for an equal opportunity rule. The Commentary to Section 5.11 of the American Law Institute, Principles of Corporate Governance: Analysis and Recommendations (Tent. Draft No. 3, 1984), states that the black letter "rejects the rule proposed by some commentators, but not supported by judicial decisions, that a controlling shareholder must share with other shareholders any premium from sale of a controlling block of shares or provide an opportunity for all shareholders to sell their shares on the same terms." Id. at 162–63.

2.   The Special Problem of the Portfolio Company: The Liquidation of Kaiser Industries*

The choice of an equal opportunity or unequal division rule also involves the interests of shareholders of companies other than that whose control is being sold. This point is exemplified by the liquidation of Kaiser Industries Corporation. Although it directly operated a number of active businesses, Kaiser Industries' principal assets, which placed it among the 250 largest industrial companies in America, consisted of controlling interests in three publicly traded affiliates— 56.3% of Kaiser Steel Corporation, 37.4% of Kaiser Aluminum & Chemical Corporation, and 37.1% of Kaiser Cement & Gypsum Corporation—with an aggregate market value of some $418 million. The problem confronting Kaiser Industries shareholders was that its stock traded at a substantial discount from the per share market value of its holdings in the affiliates. This discount was as much as 32% in the two years preceding announcement of a proposal to liquidate the company, a proposal that was motivated in large part by the desire to eliminate that discount.

The method chosen for liquidation contemplated the pro rata distribution of Kaiser Industries' holdings in its affiliates directly to its shareholders. This method would dissipate, at least on the surface, the acknowledged control held by Kaiser Industries and thus eliminate the possibility that a control premium—as in Perlman v. Feldmann—could be achieved by selling the holdings in the affiliates as separate blocks. Minority shareholders of Kaiser Industries responded by filing suit claiming that the proxy statement soliciting approval of the plan was materially misleading because it failed to disclose that the company's holdings in its affiliates could have been sold to a single buyer so as to capture a control premium.[7] The court had little difficulty disposing of the claim. It held that uncertainty over "whether any 'control premium' would be dissipated by the requirement, emerging in California and other jurisdictions, that minority shareholders [of the affiliate] be invited to share in it,"[8] as well as uncertainty over whether a sale of the affiliates' stock would qualify for the same favorable federal tax treatment as the distribution plan, rendered the nondisclosure "immaterial as a matter of law."[9]

Although the court gave little indication of how seriously it took the potential conflict of interest facing the directors of Kaiser Industries in discharging their responsibilities both as directors to Kaiser Industries shareholders, and as controlling shareholders to minority shareholders of the affiliates, the case nonetheless poses some interesting questions. Why did the shares of Kaiser Industries trade at a substantial discount from the market value of its holdings in the affiliates in the first place? This phenomenon has frequently been observed in connection with closed-end investment companies, and has

---

* I am grateful to Louis Cohen for calling this problem to my attention and, more importantly, for the benefit of his thoughts.

[7] Umbriac v. Kaiser, 467 F.Supp. 548 (D.Nev.1979).

[8] Id. at 551.

[9] Id.

been sufficiently difficult to explain that a leading commentator was led to conclude: "The pricing of closed-end funds shares does * * * seem to provide an illustration of a market imperfection in capital-asset pricing." Malkiel, *The Valuation of Closed-End Investment Company Shares*, 22 J.Fin. 847 (1977).

Whatever may be the general explanation for such a discount, might not our earlier analysis of the sources of control premiums provide a clue in the Kaiser Industries situation? If controlling shareholders of Kaiser Industries were diverting more than their pro rata share of the value of Kaiser Industries' holdings, then would it not be more beneficial to hold an interest directly in the affiliate, rather than indirectly through an interest in Kaiser Industries? [10] Because the resulting discount could only be eliminated by liquidation—by dissipating the control that allowed diversion—and because the decision to liquidate was in the hands of precisely those whose diversion caused the discount, the market would have little reason to expect that liquidation would ever occur, and the discount would remain.[11] But if this is correct, why would those controlling Kaiser Industries propose a liquidation that would dissipate control, an "asset" which appeared to have a capitalized value to them of at least the difference between the market value of Kaiser Industries stock and the higher market value of the affiliates' stock each Kaiser share represented (and perhaps more if Kaiser Industries' other assets were taken into account)?

In this regard, consider whether control of the affiliates was, in fact, dissipated by the liquidation. At the time of the transaction, the Henry J. Kaiser Family Foundation owned 30.6% of the outstanding stock of Kaiser Industries which would result in it receiving, in distribution from the liquidation, 17.23% of the outstanding stock of Kaiser Steel (it already owned 17.2%), 11.44% of the outstanding stock of Kaiser Aluminum (it already owned 11.4%), and 11.35% of the outstanding stock of Kaiser Cement (it already owned 11.3%). What hypothesis does this suggest about the post-distribution performance of the affiliates' stock, and how might that hypothesis be tested?

B. The Unwilling Subject: Defensive Tactics by Target Companies

Although most corporate acquisitions are negotiated transactions willingly entered into by the parties, an increasing number of acquisitions take place despite the fact that target management has rejected an overture from the acquiring company and, often, has done its best to prevent the transaction from ever taking place. Other acquisitions, although initiated by target company management, are nonetheless hardly voluntary. In these, target management would have preferred

[10] If the interest were held directly, controlling shareholders would get only one bite at the apple rather than two.

[11] The discount disappeared following management's announcement of the liquidation plan. This and other information concerning the liquidation plan was drawn from the Proxy Statement of Kaiser Industries Corporation (March 21, 1977) distributed in connection with a special stockholders' meeting called to vote on the liquidation plan. It was this proxy statement that was the subject of the litigation discussed in the text.

that the company remain independent and, if it were not for an unfriendly offer from an undesirable suitor, would never have initiated the transaction at all. Once an unfriendly offer was made, however, target management at least wanted to choose by whom the company would be acquired.

In all events, there is no doubt that the number of hostile offers—tender offers made directly to the shareholders because the target company's board of directors rejected or would have rejected a friendly proposal—has risen substantially. Professors Salter and Weinhold give a sense of the growth in the number of unfriendly offers, reporting that "[t]hough there were only half as many acquisitions in 1975/76 as in 1968, there were almost twice as many hostile tender offers." [12] Thus, for management which hopes to keep their company independent, the problem posed by the prospect of an unwelcome offer is how such an offer can be defeated or, better yet, prevented from ever taking place.

For our purposes, the subject of defensive tactics—actions taken by a target company that are intended to reduce the likelihood that an unfriendly offer will be made or, if made, will be successful—can be divided into three parts. First, of what does the defensive arsenal consist? What methods have been devised to insulate a company from unwelcome overtures? Second, and more important, how effective are these tactics at actually defeating or deterring hostile offers? The answer to this question helps put the final part of the inquiry in context. What are—and what should be—the legal standards governing the use of defensive tactics by target companies?

1. The Defensive Arsenal

An inquiry into the range of techniques that can be used to resist an unwanted offer is typically triggered in one of two ways. In the first, no hostile offer has actually been made, but the chief executive officer, aware of the increased frequency with which uninvited offers occur, discovers that his company displays some of the characteristics of a potential target—for example, smug management unresponsive to shareholder needs, surplus liquid assets that might help an offeror to pay for the acquisition, little debt, and the right concentration of shareholdings.[13] He then wants to know what can be done ahead of time to prepare the company if a hostile offer is made, or preferably, to prevent that event from ever occurring. In the second, things have gone further. With little or no warning the chief executive officer receives a "bear hug" letter like the following:

[12] M. Salter & W. Weinhold, supra, Chapter One B.

[13] *See* generally E. Aranow & H. Einhorn, *Tender Offers for Corporate Control* 1–9 (1973); Troubh, *Characteristics of Target Companies*, 32 Bus.Lwyr. 1301 (1977). Note that there is often disagreement over what characteristics are important. For example, Aranow & Einhorn, supra at 6, specify corporations with concentrated share ownership, while Troubh, supra at 1301, looks for "wide-spread stock ownership." The possibility that different types of companies are potential targets in different periods is discussed in Chapter Eleven B. supra.

200 EAST RANDOLPH DRIVE, CHICAGO, ILLINOIS

MAREMONT
CORPORATION

July 29, 1977

Board of Directors
Pemcor, Inc.
2121 South Mannhaim Road
Westchester, Illinois 60153

Att: Mr. Edward F. Anixter

Gentlemen:

As you know, Maremont Corporation has agreed to purchase 225,886 shares of common stock ("Shares") of Pemcor, Inc. (approximately 11.5% of the outstanding Shares) for $2,936,518 in cash. As you also know, you and I have been attempting to arrange to meet on several occasions in the past week (the most recent being today) to discuss Maremont's investment in Pemcor. I now understand that you will not be in a position to let me know whether a meeting is appropriate until the latter part of next week.

In view of this, Maremont believes that it is important for Pemcor directors to be aware of its interest in, and present intention with respect to, Pemcor. Accordingly, you are hereby advised as follows:

Maremont presently intends to offer to purchase any and all of the remaining outstanding Shares at $16.75 per Share net to the seller in cash. This represents a premium of 168.0% over the price for Pemcor shares a year ago, 109.4% over the price six months ago, 30.1% over the price one month ago and 10.7% over the closing price yesterday. Furthermore, this price is higher than the stock has sold for at any time in the last 15 years.

We are preparing a form of offer which we will submit to you shortly and we will be willing to consider any disclosures or suggestions that you may wish to make with respect thereto. We request that you cooperate in permitting your stockholders to have an opportunity to determine for themselves whether or not to accept the offer either by recommending its acceptance or by agreeing to take steps, which may include making available to Maremont a current list of your stockholders, to assure full and fair disclosure to your stockholders. In this connection, it would be acceptable to us if your agreement to facilitate the offer is conditioned on our making satisfactory modifications to reflect any material matters which you or your associates may feel, in good faith, are required for full and fair disclosure to your stockholders.

We have no plans to change the manner of Pemcor's operations or corporate structure or the composition of its management. We would expect to seek appropriate representation on your Board of Directors. Appropriate arrangements would be made to protect your stock option and other employee benefit plans.

*   *   *

I hope that you will give this proposal, which has been approved by our Board of Directors, your prompt and favorable consideration. As you can appreciate, with a proposal of this kind, time is of the essence. Accordingly, I request that you respond to my office by 3:00 p.m. August 2, 1977.

Very truly yours,

MAREMONT CORPORATION

Richard B. Black
President and Chief Executive
Officer [14]

◆

An inquiry prompted by realization that one's company might in the future become the subject of a hostile offer invites consideration of actions that can be taken before an offer occurs and that might deter the offer from ever being made. An inquiry prompted by the actual receipt of an offer looks to actions that will cause the offer to be withdrawn by the acquirer or rejected by target company shareholders. There are, to be sure, substantial questions concerning the desirability from the target shareholders' perspective of actions that prevent them from having the opportunity to decide whether to accept an acquisition offer. Consideration of these questions, however, is deferred until Section B.3. of this Chapter; for now we are still at the stage of assessing the available options.

a. Pre-Offer Planning

(1) Early Warning Systems

E. ARANOW & H. EINHORN, TENDER OFFERS FOR CORPORATE CONTROL
223–27 (1973).*

PROCEDURES TO ALERT MANAGEMENT TO A POTENTIAL TAKEOVER ATTEMPT

Where a company obtains knowledge of a proposed tender offer in advance of the actual bid, it gains valuable time in which to prepare an effective defense. Toward this end, there are a number of steps that a potential target may be able to take to reduce the risks of a surprise takeover attempt.

A daily review of trading in the company's stock is an essential part of an early warning system and will enable the target to pinpoint any unusual trading activity. The "Fitch sheets," which provide a daily breakdown of each transaction in sequence for every security traded on the New York, American and National stock exchanges, serve as a valuable tool in analyzing trading activity. Regional exchange trading should also be reviewed regularly to determine if there

---

[14] This letter was reproduced with permission from A. Fleischer, *Tender Offers, Defenses, Responses and Planning* Ex. 31A at 529 (1st ed. 1981).

* © 1973, Columbia University Press. By permission.

are any unusual price or volume movements. Although information regarding individual trades on over-the-counter transactions is not available to the public, the newly automated NASDAQ quotation system will shortly make available volume figures on selected issues traded over-the-counter. In addition, close contact with the company's exchange specialist and/or OTC market makers [15] is advisable.

Stockholders' lists and transfer sheets should also be continuously reviewed to determine if there is any concentrated accumulation pattern in any individual or nominee names. An analysis of stock ownership by class of investor may also prove useful, particularly where there is some evidence of accumulation by institutional investors.[16] * * *

A company which has developed a reputation for fair dealing and frankness with the professional investment community, financial institutions and the press, may often find these sources to be of assistance in locating and identifying a budding takeover attempt. In addition, a company which develops a reputation of willingness to listen to and entertain legitimate acquisition offers may thereby reduce the odds of a surprise takeover attempt.

* * *

DEFENSIVE MEASURES PRIOR TO THE TENDER OFFER

If the potential target company hopes to offer any meaningful resistance to a takeover attempt, it is essential that it mobilize its defenses in advance of the actual offer. The inability to respond with a show of strength during the crucial first days of an offer may result in the loss of certain tactical advantages. It may also create the impression of ineptness or unpreparedness, with resulting loss of investor confidence in management.

Accordingly, consideration must be given to what can be done to insure that the target is prepared to respond effectively as soon as the offer is announced. Perhaps the best method of preparation is the fire-drill approach, whereby management assumes that a tender offer, the terms of which are unknown, will take place sometime within the next several weeks. Such an approach will necessarily require management to review its decision-making procedure as well as insure that the company has the ability to translate decision-making into effective action. In this regard it is recommended that the corporation obtain the advice and guidance of experienced experts at the earliest possible stage. The preparedness measures described below are truly a full-time occupation. It is highly recommended that these measures be delegated to qualified experts.

[15] Those firms active in the third market, i.e., trading in NYSE-listed securities over-the-counter, should not be overlooked in reviewing trading activity. The SEC's "Statistical Bulletin" provides quarterly third market volume figures for individual securities. See also SEC 36th Annual Report (1970), at 81–82.

[16] "Vickers Guide to Investment Company Portfolios" (Vickers Associates, Inc., Huntington, L.I., N.Y., publishers), and the "International Securities Locator" (Scheinman Ciaramella International Ltd., N.Y., N.Y., publishers) may serve as valuable reference sources in identifying the most recently reported holdings of institutional investors.

General policy discussions, establishing the realistic parameters as to the type of offer, if any, that would be acceptable to the board of directors, would be a useful starting point in planning a defense. If the offer does not meet the board's guidelines, consideration must be given to the tactics—legal, financial, and psychological—that the company will employ to defend against the bid. If acquisitions, private placements, or stock splits are a possibility, there should be sufficient authorized but unissued shares available. If the potential target chooses to consider the repurchase of its own shares as a defensive tactic, it must make certain that sufficient funds are on hand or that adequate financing is available. Drafts of sample letters to shareholders as well as advertisements and press releases should be prepared and available well in advance of the actual bid.

Mechanically, management must first insure that the board can be quickly convened. If there is a requirement in the charter or by-laws providing for a lengthy notice period in calling a board meeting, consideration should be given to reducing the notice period in order to prevent one or more directors from delaying action by refusing to give a waiver. In addition, telephone numbers of all board members, officers, and key operating and administrative personnel should be kept current and accessible. Emergency duplicating and printing facilities should be available on a stand-by basis. An extra set of pre-addressed shareholders envelopes should be maintained to eliminate any additional delays.

To insure that the offeror is not afforded any unintended advantage, the company should strictly limit access to its shareholders' lists. Items such as mailing plates or pre-addressed envelopes, which can form the basis for a shareholders' list, should also be carefully guarded. A review of the security procedures of the company's dividend disbursing and transfer agents is advisable to insure that appropriate steps are being taken to eliminate unauthorized access to shareholders' lists.

◆

If all a professional adviser can present to a concerned chief executive officer is the ability to know in advance that an offer was coming, the adviser should expect little in the way of gratitude.[15] The real issue in the pre-offer stage is whether the offeror can be deterred, that is, somehow convinced never to make the offer at all.

---

[15] Some commentators have suggested that certain types of pre-offer preparation may actually be counter-productive. Although not counseling unpreparedness, they point out that disclosure during litigation that a plan of resistance had been developed even before *any* offer was made might suggest that the decision to resist a *particular* offer was less thoughtful than claimed. See, e.g., 1 A. Fleischer, *Tender Offers: Defenses, Responses, and Planning* 5–6 (2nd ed. 1983).

(2) Deterrence: Shark Repellent Amendments

GILSON, THE CASE AGAINST SHARK REPELLENT AMENDMENTS: STRUCTURAL LIMITATIONS ON THE ENABLING CONCEPT

34 Stan.L.Rev. 775–90 (1982).*

The tactical history of the tender offer movement resembles an unrestrained arms race. Faced with offeror assaults in the form of Saturday night specials, various types of bear-hugs, godfather offers, and block purchases,[2] target management responded with equally intriguing defensive tactics: the black book, reverse bear-hug, sandbag, show stopper, white knight, and, drawing directly on military jargon, the scorched earth.[3] But however varied the labels given particular

* Copyright 1982 by the Board of Trustees of the Leland Stanford Junior University.

[2] A *Saturday night special* is an offer made without prior consultation with the target and left open for only the minimum offering period. The technique is intended to minimize the target's response time and to maximize the pressure on target shareholders. A conflict exists as to the origin of the term. *Compare* Troubh, *Purchased Affection: A Primer on Cash Tender Offers*, Harv.Bus.Rev., July-Aug. 1976, at 79, 86 (term arose out of General Cable Corporation's attempt to acquire Microdot, Inc.), with Gurwin, *The Scorched Earth Policy*, The Institutional Investor, June 1979, at 33, 34 (term attributed to public relations man Richard Cheney as an effort to convey the impression that an offer by Colt Industries was "cheap and that it went off quickly" (quoting Cheney)).

There are at least three variants of the *bear-hug*. In a classic bear-hug, the target is notified of the offeror's intention to make a tender offer at a specified price but without a concurrent public announcement. The strong bear-hug contemplates a simultaneous public announcement of the offer and attempts to negotiate for the target's cooperation. The super strong bear-hug adds to this the threat that opposition or delay by the target will result in a decrease in the offering price. E.g., A. Fleischer, *Tender Offers: Defenses, Responses, and Planning* 57–59 (1981); Greenhill, *Structuring an Offer*, 32 Bus.Law. 1305, 1308 (1977).

A *godfather offer* is a "cash offer so rich that * * * the directors do not believe * * * they can reasonably refuse it." A. Fleischer, *supra*, at 103 n. 291.

A *block purchase* is the preoffer accumulation of a significant position in the target's stock, meant both to exert leverage over the target and to prevent others from joining the bidding. E.g., Freund & Easton, *The Three-Piece Suitor: An Alternative Approach to Negotiated Corporate Acquisitions*, 34 Bus.Law. 1679, 1683 (1979). A preoffer accumulation of target stock also allows an unsuccessful offeror to recover at least some of the costs incurred in connection with the offer if a competing bidder is ultimately successful. See Gilson, *A Structural Approach to Corporations: The Case Against Defensive Tactics in Tender Offers*, 33 Stan.L.Rev. 819, 871–72 (1981).

[3] A *black book* is an outline of the actions to be taken if a tender offer should occur. E.g., P. Davey, *Defenses Against Unnegotiated Cash Tender Offers* 2 (1977).

In a *reverse bear-hug*, a target responds to an offer by expressing a willingness to negotiate a friendly acquisition but at a price far in excess of that proposed by the offeror. A. Fleischer, *supra* note 2, at 63–64.

A *sandbag* is intended to delay the making of a tender offer following a bear-hug. The target agrees to negotiate, but draws out the negotiations as long as possible. Reuben & Elden, *How to be a Target Company*, 23 N.Y.L. Sch.L.Rev. 423, 441 (1978).

A *show stopper* is a lawsuit by the target seeking a permanent injunction barring the offer. The most common claim is that the acquisition of the target will violate the antitrust laws. E.g., Pargas, Inc. v. Empire Gas Corp., 423 F.Supp. 199 (D.Md.), aff'd per curiam, 546 F.2d 25 (4th Cir.1976).
* * *

A *white knight* is a third party to whom the target turns for a friendly acquisition as an alternative to the tender offer.
* * *

A *scorched earth* defense seeks to convince the offeror that the target's defense will be so vigorous as to reduce its value to the offeror. Gurwin, *supra* note 2. One

defensive strategies, they share the common characteristic of being responsive: They are available only after an offer is made and the battle for the target's independence joined. From the target's perspective, what was missing from the defensive arsenal was a deterrent—a tactic that would convince a potential offeror not even to attempt the attack, thereby not only saving the target the substantial costs associated with tender offer conflicts but, more importantly, eliminating the not insubstantial risk that all defenses would fail and the offer prove successful.[5]

Shark repellant amendments are intended to fill this gap in a prospective target's defenses. The idea is to amend the target's articles of incorporation to make it a less desirable or more difficult acquisition, and thereby to encourage the "shark" to seek a more appetizing or more easily digested alternative.[6]

* * *

I. A SURVEY OF THE PHENOMENON

Shark repellant amendments and the theories behind their asserted deterrent effect fall into three general categories. A first group of amendments is directed at impeding a successful offeror from taking control of the target's board of directors by protecting the incumbency of existing management. A second group is directed at making more difficult a second-step freezeout merger which eliminates any nontendering shareholders. The third group is intended to deprive the offeror of control over the total cost of the acquisition by specifying the price to be paid nontendering shareholders in a freezeout transaction or, at the extreme, by allowing nontendering shareholders to require the offeror to purchase their shares at a formula price even if the offeror does not initiate a freezeout transaction. All three categories of amendment will usually share a further provision—the requirement of

example of this approach was Houghton Mifflin's success in causing its authors to advise an offeror that they would sever their relationships with the target if the offer was successful. Id. at 37.

[5] Recent statistics indicate that only a minority of target corporations remain independent following a tender offer. A study of 69 tender offers made between 1976 and 1979 found that only 13 targets (19%) were able to maintain their independence. Fleischer, *Business Judgment Rule Protects Takeover Targets,* Legal Times Wash., Apr. 14, 1980, at 15, col. 1 (reporting Goldman Sachs study). Data covering the period from 1956 through June 30, 1979, show a postoffer independence rate of only 20%. Austin, *Tender Offer Update: 1978-1979,* Mergers & Acquisitions, Summer 1980, at 13, 16 (table 4).

[6] The literature concerning shark repellent amendments is extensive. E.g., E. Aranow & H. Einhorn, *Tender Offers for Corporate Control* 223 (1973); E. Aranow,

H. Einhorn & G. Berlstein, *Developments in Tender Offers for Corporate Control* 194–96 (1977); P. Davey, supra note 3, at 13–14; A. Fleischer, supra note 2, at 6; Black & Smith, *Antitakeover Charter Provisions: Defending Self-Help for Takeover Targets,* 36 Wash. & Lee L.Rev. 699 (1979); Cohen, *Takeover Bids: How Target Companies Fight Back,* Fin. Analysts J., Jan.–Feb. 1970, at 26; Hochman & Folger, *Deflecting Takeovers: Charter and By-law Techniques,* 34 Bus.Law. 537 (1979); Mullaney, *Guarding Against Takeovers—Defensive Charter Provisions,* 25 Bus.Law. 1441 (1970); Rose & Collins, *Porcupine Proposals,* 12 Rev.Sec.Reg. 977 (1979); Schmults & Kelly, *Cash Take-over Bids—Defense Tactics,* 23 Bus.Law. 115 (1967); Smith, *Fair Price and Redemption Rights: New Dimensions in Defense Charter Provisions,* 4 Del.J.Corp.L. 1 (1978); Yoran, *Advance Defensive Tactics Against Takeover Bids,* 21 Am.J.Comp.L. 531 (1973).

a supermajority shareholder vote for further amendment or repeal.
* * *

A. *The Three Categories of Shark Repellent Amendments*

1. *Impeding transfer of control of the board of directors*

Under a typical corporation statute, an offeror, having successfully tendered for a majority of a target's shares, will encounter little delay in replacing the target's board of directors. Most corporations elect their board of directors annually, without cumulative voting. A new majority shareholder who is unwilling to wait until the next annual meeting of shareholders to install his designees may remove the incumbent directors without cause and select their replacements, either by written consent or at a special shareholders' meeting called pursuant to the majority holder's request.

Shark repellant amendments in theory can delay this process substantially. The initial step is to classify the board into, for example, three classes of which only one is elected annually.[24] The effect, of course, is to require up to two annual meetings for a successful offeror to select a majority of the board through the normal election process.

But classification alone will not prevent a majority shareholder from removing and replacing incumbent directors or, if the particular state statute bars removal of directors without cause or bars such removal where the board is classified, from "packing" the board of directors by amending the charter or bylaws so that directors elected by the offeror to fill new vacancies will constitute a majority. Therefore, a complete set of amendments to protect the tenure and majority of pre-offer board members must go beyond classification and reserve to the board the sole right to determine the number of directors and to fill any vacancies created by resignation or increase in the number of directors. Amendments may also limit the mechanics of "flanking" action—the call of special meetings of shareholders and shareholders' ability to act by written consent—as well as restrict removal of directors to instances of "cause" narrowly defined.

Even a full complement of these amendments, however, can only delay the transfer of control. If the offeror is content to wait the period necessary to secure control of the target's board of directors, the protective amendments will achieve little, save for distinguishing the target from other corporations that may not have adopted similar measures. However, delay in the shift in control of the target's board of directors may be a significant deterrent to making an offer.

2. *Barriers to second-step transactions*

Often a tender offer represents only the first step in a plan for the complete acquisition of the target. The second step is commonly a

---

[24] While the corporate laws of some states allow creation of more than three classes, e.g., Fla.Stat.Ann. § 607.114(4) (West 1977) (not more than four); N.Y.Bus. Corp.Law § 704(a) (McKinney 1963) (two, three, or four), both Delaware, Del.Code Ann. tit. 8, § 141(d) (Supp.1980), and the New York Stock Exchange, New York Stock Exchange Company Manual § A–15, at A–280 (Aug. 1, 1977), limit the number of classes to three.

merger in which any remaining minority shareholders are frozen out of the new subsidiary. The second group of shark repellent amendments is intended to make this second-step transaction more difficult.

All corporate statutes require that shareholders approve a statutory merger, and most allow the articles of incorporation to impose a greater-than-majority vote requirement with respect to particular transactions. The typical defensive amendment package can therefore impose a barrier to second-step transactions through a supermajority shareholder vote requirement—generally from two-thirds to as high as 95%—for a freezeout merger or comparable transaction with a "related person"—an intricately defined term which will always include a successful tender offeror. The percentage required for approval is often chosen to approximate the average number of shares represented at the past few annual meetings,[40] in effect requiring an offeror to procure a virtually unanimous vote. Since the combined shareholdings of incumbent directors, officers, and their affiliates often approach or exceed the number of shares necesary to block the requisite supermajority,[41] these provisions may present a significant barrier to a second-step transaction by a successful tender offeror.

Anti-freezeout amendments, however, usually do not impede all transactions falling within their complex definitions. Having broadly defined the covered "transactions" in order to avoid circumvention, the amendments usually include exceptions to the supermajority requirement to permit transactions *favored* by management, such as a friendly takeover or other transaction not motivated by an impending tender offer. These exceptions allow transactions that are approved by a supermajority of "continuing" directors—those who were in office at the time the related party initially acquired any substantial interest in the corporation. The purpose of that formulation, of course, is to prevent recourse to the exception by a board of directors "packed" or otherwise controlled by the "related person."

3. *Fair price and compulsory redemption provisions*

Fair price amendments are a variation on the supermajority theme. They provide another exception to a supermajority vote requirement for a second-step transaction where the price to be paid minority shareholders exceeds a specified amount which may be greater than the price paid in the initial tender offer.[49]

[40] See, e.g., Proxy Statement of J.M. Smucker Co. (July 25, 1977), reprinted in A. Fleischer, supra note 2, at 425, 427 (extract) (supermajority requirement represents "the average percentage of shares represented at the last five annual meetings").

[41] See, e.g., Proxy Statement of Baldor Electric Co. (Mar. 30, 1979), reprinted in A. Fleischer, supra note 2, at 400–21 to –25 (proposing 80% requirement; officers and directors as a group owned 37.6%); Proxy Statement of Farm House Foods Corp. 3 (Sept. 8, 1980) ("The anti-takeover provisions will also enable the present principal shareholders [management] of the Company, if they act as a group, to veto any proposed merger, tender offer or other attempt to gain control of the Company."); Proxy Statement of Thomas Indus., Inc. 6 (Mar. 24, 1980) ("If the proposed amendment is adopted, the Board of Directors believes that under present circumstances it could prevent any proposed merger or similar transaction which, in its judgment, should be rejected.")

[49] A typical formulation waives the supermajority requirement if the price to be paid is equal to or greater than the highest of: (1) the highest price paid by the

In an important sense, fair price provisions are inconsistent with the approach reflected in the standard supermajority provision. Rather than strengthening the barriers to second-step transactions, a fair price exception instead provides a way to effect the second-step transaction, albeit at a share price that may be higher than that paid in the initial tender offer.[50] Further, it can be said that a fair price provision, rather than reflecting management self-interest, recognizes the potential danger to minority shareholders in second-step transactions by tying the application of the supermajority requirement to "fairness" to minority shareholders.

The position of minority shareholders following a tender offer is also emphasized in right of redemption provisions, the newest and, so far, least popular variety of shark repellant amendment. This amendment, seemingly borrowed in concept from section 209(2) of the English Companies Act, allows any minority shareholder, following a successful offer for more than a specified percentage of the target's outstanding shares, to require the target company to purchase the remaining shares at a formula price that equals or may even exceed the price paid in the tender offer.

While a right of redemption provision focuses on the position of the minority shareholder who does not tender, it may be a more substantial deterrent to an offeror than a fair price provision in certain circumstances. If a potential offeror contemplates an offer for less than 100% of a target's stock, a right of redemption provision may remove control over the size of an offeror's total investment from its hands. Because shareholders may in effect force a second-step transaction by exercising their right to require redemption, they, and not the offeror, have the last word on the number of shares ultimately acquired and, if the provision's pricing formula could yield a price higher than the offer, on the price to be paid. Indeed, a fair price provision may even deter an offeror who is willing and financially able to tender for all the outstanding shares. If the pricing formula assures holdouts a price no lower than the tender offer and provides the potential of a higher price, target shareholders will be given an incentive *not* to tender in the original offer.[54]

offeror for any shares acquired during the offer; (2) a price which reflects the same percentage premium (based on the price of the target's stock at the time the second-step transaction was announced) as the initial offer (based on the price of the target stock at the commencement of the initial offer); and (3) an amount determined by multiplying the *target's* average earnings per share over the previous four years by the *offeror's* price-earnings ratio over that time.

[50] It has been suggested that a premium be added to the fair price determined under the formula—for example, 50% "of the highest consolidated balance of domestic and foreign cash, cash equivalents and marketable securities" held by the target during a specified period—as an asset bo-

nus. Smith, supra note 6, at 17. Additionally, the formula itself is capable of yielding a price in excess of the initial tender price.

[54] This phenomenon is described with respect to a fair price provision in Hochman & Folger, supra note 6, at 555:

Chicago Pneumatic Corporation recently had occasion to make use of its fair price provision after learning that 5 per cent or more of its shares had been purchased by another company. It announced to brokers that, under its fair price provision, shareholders who chose not to sell to a raider might profit handsomely from a higher price if a raider gains control and then attempts to squeeze out remaining shareholders.

B. *Lock-up Amendments*

While not themselves shark repellants, lock-up amendments are probably the most important * * * of the amendments a potential target commonly adopts to deter unwanted tender offers. Consider a potential offeror's evaluation of a target draped with the full panoply of protective amendments. While a 95% vote may be required for a second-step transaction, unless the target's charter also has been amended to require a supermajority to further amend the charter itself, a successful offeror can eliminate the supermajority provision by the vote for charter amendment specified in the statute—typically a simple majority. The carefully plotted defensive measures would then be left, like the Maginot Line, with their guns pointing in the wrong direction. To avoid this result, virtually all shark repellant amendments also require a supermajority vote for repeal or further amendment.

Lock-up amendments are thus the key to whatever potential for deterrence any of the shark repellant amendments may possess.

* * *

---◆---

(3) Deterrence: "Poison Pill" Preferred Stock

A recent innovation in the field of pre-offer defensive tactics— "poison pill" preferred stock—is related in concept to shark repellant amendments, especially fair price and right of redemption amendments. The operation of this technique is described in a memorandum prepared by Wachtel, Lipton, Rosen & Katz, the law firm that devised it.

According to Robert Metz of the New York Times, "the announcement—calculated to guarantee full disclosure to existing stockholders—evidently had the desired effect. Brokers from all over the nation called Chicago Pneumatic's headquarters in New York City and asked for copies of the charter."
(quoting Metz, *Brokers Heed Stock Warning*, N.Y. Times, May 30, 1978, at D–5, col. 1). The effect might be even more pronounced in a right of redemption context since the offeror would no longer have the option not to squeeze out the minority.

Although not shark repellent amendments in that they are not intended to pose a deterrent to an offeror, social justice amendments, pioneered by Control Data, see Proxy Statement of Control Data Corp., reprinted in A. Fleischer, supra note 2, at 448–11 (extract), and more recently adopted by McDonald's, see Proxy Statement of McDonald's Corp., reprinted in A. Fleischer, supra note 2, at 448–13 (extract), warrant comment. These amendments, purportedly offered "in the spirit of social responsibility and justice," Proxy Statement of Control Data Corp., supra, at 448– 11, direct the board of directors, in their evaluation of an acquisition offer, to "give due consideration to all relevant factors, including without limitation the social and economic effects on the employees, customers, suppliers and other constituents of the Corporation and its subsidiaries and on the communities in which the Corporation and its subsidiaries operate or are located." Id. at 448–12.

Social justice amendments do not provide a deterrent to a potential offeror, but rather attempt to protect management from subsequent shareholder claims based on management's rejection of an offer. Indeed, the McDonald's Corporation proxy statement proposing such an amendment was explicit in stating that the provision was not intended "to create any rights on behalf of franchisees, employees, suppliers, customers or any other persons." Proxy Statement of McDonald's Corp., supra, at 448–13. While an offeror might conceivably be deterred by the potential increase in discretion the board of directors may gain from a social justice provision, the likelihood of deterrence seems remote at best.

* * *

[Memorandum]

While the ["Poison Pill" Preferred Stock] Plan can be put into effect after a tender offer has been made, it is most effective if it is done before there is even a threat of takeover. It is something that every corporation should consider now, before it becomes a target.

The Plan is simple. The corporation distributes to its common stockholders a dividend in the form of a convertible preferred stock. The preferred is convertible into the same (or larger) number of shares of common as are outstanding so that the distribution is the equivalent of a 2 for 1 (or greater) stock split with the result that half (or more) of the outstanding equity is represented by the preferred. In other words, a corporation with 10,000,000 shares of common distributes, as a dividend to the holders of its common, a new issue of preferred that is convertible into an additional 10,000,000 shares of common. This is accomplished by creating a class of 400,000 shares of preferred with each share of preferred being convertible into 25 shares of common. One share of the preferred is distributed for each 25 shares of common. The corporation now has outstanding 10,000,000 shares of common and 400,000 shares of preferred with the preferred being convertible into 10,000,000 shares of common. A holder of 100 shares of common has those 100 shares plus 4 shares of preferred which are convertible into 100 shares of common. After the distribution the common and preferred would trade separately. Each would be listed. The distribution of the preferred to the holders of the common is tax-free.

Since the distribution of the preferred is the equivalent of a 2 for 1 stock split, the cash dividend on the common is reduced by 50% and the cash dividend on each share of the preferred is set at slightly more than 25 times the halved common stock dividend. Thus each holder of common has the same cash dividend he had before the distribution plus a little bit more. Since the dividend on the preferred will be set so as to increase with any increase in the dividend on the common, the preferred dividend will always be a little bit more than the common and there will therefore be a disincentive for the holders of preferred to convert into common.

The preferred will be noncallable for 10, 15 or more years— whatever period is set by the corporation, keeping in mind that too short a period might raise tax questions. Also, when the preferred becomes callable, the protection of the Plan disappears. Therefore, we recommend at least 10 to 15 years as the noncallable period.

For those companies that do not have sufficient authorized common stock and blank check preferred stock, it would be necessary to have a shareholder vote to authorize the requisite stock. Those companies that have sufficient authorized stock can implement the Plan through action by their board of directors alone.

The preferred does not contain any blocking votes, shark repellents or other provisions inhibiting a tender offer or merger. The preferred votes with the common as one class with each share of preferred having a number of votes equal to the number of shares of common into which it is convertible.

The preferred would contain the normal boilerplate provisions protecting the conversion rights in the event of a merger or other business combination, including a "flip-over" provision which is the essence of the Plan.

In the event of a tender offer followed by a freezeout merger the conversion rights would flip-over to the common stock of the raider and the preferred would be convertible into the common stock of the raider. This conversion into the common stock of the raider would be accomplished pursuant to a conversion exchange ratio that results in the holder of the preferred receiving shares of common stock of the raider having a market value at the time of the conversion equal to not less than the cash tender offer price for the target.

In addition, if the cash tender offer results in the raider acquiring 50% (this percentage could be set anywhere between say 20% and 50%) of the target's common, the preferred is thereafter redeemable by the stockholder, at any time, at a redemption price equal to the cash tender offer price. Thus, even if there is no second-step merger, the holder of the preferred is assured of the tender offer price in cash as a floor and has upside potential if there is a second-step merger and the market price of the raider's common goes up. The holder of the preferred has no market risk if the raider's common goes down; he always gets a sufficient number of shares of the raider to at least equal the tender offer price. Since the tender offer sets a floor cash value for the preferred and it continues to have valuable conversion features, after a tender offer is announced it should sell in the market at a premium over the tender offer price for the common and therefore there is little incentive for a holder of the preferred to tender unless there is a separate tender for the preferred at a price that reflects the extra premium. The conversion exchange ratio formula is expressed as the greater of the tender offer price or the highest market price of the target's common prior to the date of conversion divided by the lower of the raider's market price on the date of the second-step merger or on the date of conversion. Thus, the raider runs the risk of a decline in the market price of its common.

If the preferred dividend is the equivalent of a 2 for 1, 3 for 1 or 4 for 1 split, then 50%, $66^2/3\%$ or 75% of the target's common equity is protected against being frozen out and is assured of the tender offer premium. This gives the shareholders of the target a real alternative to tendering in that with respect to the bulk of their holdings it protects them against being locked into a minority position and subjected to a future freezeout at a price less than the tender price. Since the preferred dividend is fixed, it also protects them against the raider reducing or eliminating dividends on the target's common, if the raider decides to attempt only partial ownership and does not effectuate a second-step merger.

The target which has implemented the Plan presents a difficult problem to a raider contemplating a hostile tender offer. A raider must think twice about the economics of being faced with the issuance of a significant number of shares of its own common stock, valued for conversion exchange purposes at the lower of current market at the time of the second-step merger or at the time of conversion. The raider is faced with a conversion exchange ratio that results in increased dilution as the market price of its common goes down, which dilution may further depress the market price of the raider's common stock.

One way for the raider to deal with the Plan is to tender for the target's preferred and common and to set a high (80% or greater) minimum condition in the tender offer so as to be faced with a relatively small number of shares of preferred in the second-step merger. Of course, this helps achieve the objectives of the Plan— elimination of partial and front-end loaded tender offers, assurance that all shareholders will have a reasonable opportunity to receive the full cash bid for their shares, and reduction of bootstrap bids by raiders who must use their own securities and the target's assets to finance the takeover. In addition, high minimums inhibit arbitrage by casting doubt on whether the tender offer will succeed. Further, since the preferred is fully protected against loss of the tender offer premium and being locked into a minority position and being squeezed by reduction or elimination of dividends, there is much less incentive to tender for a holder of preferred who does not hold common.

Similar results may be achievable through charter amendments * * *.

◆

A principal goal of the poison pill preferred stock plan is to protect target company shareholders from a transaction in which, after the acquiring company secures control, the remaining shareholders will be frozen out at a low price. See, e.g., Finkelstein, *Antitakeover Protection Against Two-Tier and Partial Tender Offers: The Validity of Fair Price, Mandatory Bid, and Flip-Over Provisions under Delaware Law*, 11 Sec. Reg.L.J. 291 (1984); Note *Protecting Shareholders Against Partial and Two-Tiered Takeovers: The "Poison Pill" Preferred*, 97 Harv.L.Rev. 1964 (1984). This is, in fact, precisely the same goal sought to be achieved by fair price and right of redemption shark repellant amendments. Indeed, the right of redemption and the related pricing formula are central to the poison pill concept. What does the poison pill technique offer that shark repellant amendments do not?

One critical difference between the two approaches is the character of the approvals necessary to implement them. Shark repellant amendments, like virtually all amendments of a corporation's charter, must be approved by the vote of a majority of the shareholders. This requirement has taken on greater prominence of late as institutional holders increasingly have announced that they will vote against shark repellant amendments as a matter of policy.[16] In contrast, so long as

---

[16] For example, in a survey of the voting behavior of 92 institutional investors during the 1980 and 1981 proxy seasons, 19 of the 31 banks (including 12 of the 20 largest commercial banks), and 10 of 16 insurance companies and investment firms (including 7 of the 10 largest life insurance companies) routinely opposed supermajority amendments. J. Heard, *Voting Policies of Institutional Investors on Corporate Governance Issues* 14–16, 26–28 (1981).

the corporate charter authorizes the procedure, statutes like Delaware General Corporation Law § 151(a) allow the issuance of preferred stock "which * * * may have such voting powers * * * and such designations, preferences, * * * or other special rights * * * as shall be stated * * * in the resolution * * * providing for the issue of such stock adopted by the board of directors. * * *" Del.Code Ann. tit. 8, § 151(A) (1983). This "blank-check" authorization means that the board of directors can issue "poison pill" preferred stock without shareholder approval.

Other permutations of the poison pill approach are possible. For example, a distribution of exploding warrants, which authorize the purchase of new common stock at a price which is substantially reduced if a triggering event—such as a hostile tender offer—occurs, has also been used. See Gearhart Indus., Inc. v. Smith Intn'l, Inc., 741 F.2d 707 (5th Cir.1984).

(4) Deterrence: The Marshall Field & Company Approach

It is a familiar tactic in the post-offer period for the target company to make an acquisition that, in turn, creates antitrust problems in connection with the offeror's acquisition of the target. See Section B. 1.b.(4) of this Chapter. When the identity of the offeror is known, as it will be in the post-offer period, this kind of defensive acquisition is relatively easy to plan. Counsel for the target company can evaluate the effectiveness of potential defensive acquisitions in light of definitions of product market, concentration and other elements of a cause of action under Section 7 of the Clayton Act, 15 U.S.C. § 18 (1976), just as counsel for the offerer considered the same elements in evaluating the legality of the hostile acquisition of the target company. During the pre-offer period, however, the potential target typically does not know the identity of the hypothetical acquiring company. Indeed, given continued popularity of diversifying acquisitions, the potential target may not even know what industry an offeror might be in. This uncertainty makes selection of an effective defensive acquisition in the pre-offer period quite difficult.

In some cases, however, a potential target believes it can predict from where the offeror will come. In that event, a defensive acquisition strategy is possible. Perhaps the best example of this approach was the acquisition activity of Marshall Field & Company, a Chicago based department store chain, that had learned from experience that its offerors were likely to come from the retailing industry. Marshall Field's acquisition strategy was described in some detail by the Seventh Circuit in a case involving the claim that the strategy's implementation violated Field's management's fiduciary duty:

> On several occasions in the late 1960's and continuing to the mid-1970's, Field's management was approached by would-be merger or takeover suitors. In 1969 Field's sought the help of Joseph H. Flom, an attorney with expertise in such matters, in determining how best to respond to the overtures of interested parties. Flom

advised the board that the interest of the shareholders was the paramount concern, and that management should listen to such proposals, evaluate whether the proposal was serious, and whether the proposal raised questions of antitrust violations. He also advised Field's directors and management to invest the company's reserves and use its borrowing power to acquire other stores, if such acquisitions were in accord with the sound business judgment of the board, and in the best interest of the company and its shareholders. He counseled that such acquisitions were a legal way of coping with unfriendly takeover attempts.

Flom's advice was followed during this period in conjunction with a series of tentative approaches to Field's by or on behalf of potential acquirors. Thus, when in 1969 a third party interested in acting as a "catalyst" for a Field's-Associated Dry Goods merger approached the board, it considered the matter and rejected further exploration. While this offer was under consideration, Field's acquired Halle Brothers, a retailer with stores in communities in which Associated already had stores.

In 1975, investment bankers representing Federated Department Stores, then the nation's largest department store chain, approached Field's about a possible merger. Again, the Field's board considered the matter, but in light of advice of counsel that it would raise antitrust problems and damage the chances of a proposed Field's acquisition of the Wanamaker Company, the board determined not to pursue the contact.

Panter v. Marshall Field & Co., 646 F.2d 271, 278 (7th Cir.1981), cert. denied, 454 U.S. 1092 (1981).

Marshall Field continued this strategy, albeit on a post-offer basis, in response to an offer from Carter Hawley Hale, the operators of the Neiman-Marcus chain. Field's opened a Field's store in Houston, a major Neiman-Marcus market, and acquired five Liberty House stores in the Pacific Northwest. Id. at 280–81. Following defeat of the Carter Hawley Hale offer, Marshall Field continued the strategy on a pre-offer basis again with the acquisition of John Breuner & Co., a large California furniture chain, 11 department stores in Oregon and Washington, and 23 J.B. Ivey department stores in Florida and the Carolinas. *Marshall Field's Too Successful Strategy*, Fortune 82, 84 (March 22, 1982).

Assuming that this strategy would be effective in deterring potential offers, what impact would you expect it to have on the price of Field's stock?

b. After the Offer

The variety of possible defensive tactics after a hostile offer has been made is substantial and has spawned a voluminous literature. The material which follows describes the most important categories of tactics and provides a context in which to develop a general approach both to determining when a familiar tactic has the potential to be effective and to designing new defensive tactics that hold the promise of being effective. For more exhaustive surveys of the extensive range of tactics which have at one time or another been suggested, see, e.g., E. Aranow, H. Einhorn & G. Berlstine, *Developments in Tender Offers for Corporate Control* (1977); P. Davey, *Defenses Against Unnegotiated Cash Tender Offers* (1977); A. Fleischer, *Tender Offers, Defenses, Responses, and Planning* (2nd ed. 1983); M. Lipton & E. Steinberger, *Takeovers and Freezeouts* (1979).

(1) Litigation

The single most common response to an unwanted offer is litigation. If one thinks about that response for a moment, it really has two components. First, litigation is a means by which a substantive claim is vindicated. It is merely a transaction cost necessarily incurred to vindicate the claim and has no value independent of the substantive claim being pursued. From this perspective, if the litigation ultimately is not successful in vindicating the claim, it will have been a waste of time and money. Second, litigation is a means of inflicting additional costs on someone else's transaction, where the goal sought is not vindication of a substantive claim, but merely the creation of an impediment to someone else's activities. In the latter case, the creation of transaction costs is not a necessary, albeit undesirable, byproduct of the exercise, but its very point. In considering the following excerpt by a senior partner in one of the prominent law firms specializing in takeovers, think about which function is being discussed at which point.

WACHTELL, SPECIAL TENDER OFFER LITIGATION TACTICS
32 Bus.Law. 1433 (1977).*

Takeover litigation is a unique area. * * *

You are operating at what is essentially an interface of big case litigation, in the very highly sophisticated and specialized areas of securities law, financing law, margin requirements and antitrust law. It is not the place to have on-the-job training.

You are operating in a pressure atmosphere where you have constant surprise. You have very little turnaround time. The company goes running for counsel: help us. You have to commence litigation immediately. You have to get out your deposition notices. You have to get out your discovery notices. You have to make your motions for expedited discovery. You have to set up your teams for taking what could be two or three sets of simultaneous depositions, often in different cities. You have to be prepared to flow all the information you're getting from depositions and documents into affidavits and briefs almost simultaneously with the taking of the depositions and the review of the documents. You have to be scheduling your applications for temporary restraining orders, stays, preliminary injunctions and the like. You are essentially compressing into a span of four, five or six days what would normally be months and months, if not years, of typical big case litigation, including analysis of antitrust ramifications, industry studies, competitive lines of product and the like. It is unique.

* * *

[T]he tender is made. Now, it used to be thought that at this point counsel for the tendering company really didn't have very much to do except to sit back and wait for the inevitable lawsuit to be brought for an injunction against the offer. But in recent times a nuance has been added to the litigating tactics in tender offer cases. This sometimes is referred to as the preemptive lawsuit and sometimes as the "one-two punch."

First, a surprise tender offer is made for a target company. Then, before the target company has caught its breath from that body blow, the company making the tender sues the target. Well, the question is: why bother? What's to be gained? Why has this become a tactic?

* * *

There are a couple of sound reasons why in certain cases this may be a very good litigating tactic. The first has to do with choice of forum. If the target is left to its own devices, it is going to choose to bring the suit for an injunction in what it would deem to be a favorable forum. Often this will be its own home District where it can invoke perhaps a general feeling against outside predators coming in and preying on local industry. In certain instances, this could be a real problem. It can very largely color what is going to happen in the litigation.

By having the bidder bring the initial lawsuit against the target, the bidder can essentially choose a forum of its own liking and then, by invoking the mystique that anything the target now wants to do really lies under the compulsory counterclaim rule, can effectively preclude the target from litigating in any jurisdiction other than the jurisdiction of the bidder's choice.

* * *

A second advantage which can be gained by the bidder's actually commencing the litigation is a very real psychological one, both in the general marketplace of the tender offer and in the courthouse as well. What is being done here is: the target company essentially is coming in and is saying to the world at large, including the arbitrageurs, "we are not afraid of litigation here. We welcome it. We are going to court. These fellows are the wrongdoers. We have nothing to fear here." And by seizing this initiative and by staking out a position of plaintiff before the court, one almost makes that inevitable counterclaim, when it comes, anticlimatic both in the courthouse and in the marketplace. So there is a tactical advantage to be gained as well as a forum advantage.

Now, having said that, someone might ask the question, "what do you sue them for?"

I mean, here's this company that's peacefully minding its own business with this weak management that we've all heard about. It gets hit by a "Saturday night special." What conceivable cause of action can now exist for the bidder to sue the target?

Well, actually, it really isn't hard at all because of what oftentimes happens in this kind of situation: a surprise tender is made. The executives of the target company hurriedly caucus. Panic reigns supreme. Someone comes up with a bright idea: "Hey, we had better get out a press release and we had better get it out fast and we ought to say that the price which is being offered is inadequate and besides our lawyers tell us that there are some very serious antitrust problems here."

And so they do. And you now have your lawsuit. The first cause of action will recite that management is engaged in illegal opposition and solicitation in opposition to a lawful tender offer in violation of the Williams Act without having filed the requisite Schedule 14D setting forth that they are opposing; and the second cause of action will set forth that they are engaged in making false and misleading statements in violation of the antifraud provisions of section 14(e), because when they said that the offer was inadequate, they failed to point out that the offer was 20 percent in excess of any price that the stock has traded for in the last five years, and they also failed to point out that six months ago they themselves bought some of the stock cheaper. So how could the present offer be inadequate?[2] That's a material omission. And besides, when they say it violates the antitrust laws, that really isn't true, so that's a material misstatement. You now have your lawsuit. There's usually three or four other causes of action. You could throw in, for good measure, allegations such as manipulating the market and engaging in a conspiracy to entrench themselves in their management positions in violation of the interests of everybody in sight. You're in. You're home. You're in court.

*   *   *

Let's turn now to the job of unhappy counsel for the target company. He brings a lawsuit. We all agree about that. And he brings it fast. Now, one of the questions you might ask is: Why? What's the purpose of the lawsuit—except that it's obviously something that always gets done and it's axiomatic that he bring it.

Well, of course, one purpose is to seek to obtain an injunction to bar the offer from going forward. However, in many of these cases a close observer can detect that there are other consequences of the lawsuit than merely the attempt to obtain an injunction, and it behooves counsel for the target company to be aware of the ramifications and consequences of his lawsuit in the marketplace outside of the courthouse because there are very real consequences in a tender offer context.

For example, one of the consequences of lawsuits in takeover situations is to chill the arbitrage. It was pointed out * * * that if the arbitraguers go into the market and buy heavily in the stock, they in essence are going to be the owners of that company. They have a

[2] See, e.g., Emhart Corp. v. USM Corp., 403 F.Supp. 660 (D.Mass.1975).

very short-term interest in their investment which means a 99 percent chance that that company is going to get owned by *someone* in the end—be it the original bidder or someone else—but it is not in all likelihood going to remain independent.

So, one might be very interested, if one is representing the target company, in chilling the arbitrage, and chilling it fast, which means that a complaint has to get out very quickly. There's no point saying: "Well, gee, I have ten days to get a preliminary injunction. I can afford to go into court on the eighth day," because by the eighth day the battle is going to be all over.

So, it is important to get in very fast and it is important to get in with a complaint that is not only a sound legal document, but which also sounds terribly legal. Then when the arbitrageurs' counsel read it, they are going to be impressed. The arbitrageurs are going to be weighing the likelihood of the success of the offer. If they read the complaint and if the legal theories are spelled out in a way that is impressive, understandable and "good sounding," the arbitrageurs' counsel are going to say to the arbitrageurs, "I would be careful on this one. It sounds like these fellows might have a chance of getting an injunction." And that heavy arbitrage buying may well not develop.

Another thing that sometimes happens as a result of a lawsuit is that there can be delay. The offer can be ordered to be extended by the court and, of course, the investment bankers can scurry around looking for some other marriage partner which might be more preferable to the target than the original bidder. And that is a possible consequence of the lawsuit that very much has to be kept in mind.

Another function or consequence of the lawsuit, and one that should not be underestimated, is a very simple moral-building psychological one. A "Saturday night special" has a traumatic effect upon the executives of a target company, particularly if they have not done their homework in advance and are not prepared. It can be shattering and demoralizing, and they can for all practical purposes virtually stop functioning.

A lawsuit becomes a focal point for rallying the troops. Everyone can feel good—"we're doing something. We're hitting back. Boy, we really have got something there to protect us." And people will then start to function again in a real way to see what actually can be done to defend against this tender, which defense may not be in the courthouse at all.

Now, by the same token, you can't let your clients overrate the likelihood of success in that lawsuit or they may just blindly assume that they have this Maginot Line of the lawsuit and that they really don't have to do anything else. That would be extremely foolhardy.

Of course, ultimately one may even get an injunction in one of these lawsuits. Now, I've heard a lot about the antitrust laws as a basis for injunctive relief in these suits and I must say I do not share the general feeling I detected—and maybe I'm overstating it—that the antitrust laws are a sound defense in these tender offer cases. The leading case on the subject, which is the *Missouri Portland/Cargill* case in this Circuit,[3] basically told the District Courts: never grant a preliminary injunction on antitrust grounds because such a preliminary injunction, where you're going to have a three-year trial, is the equivalent of a permanent injunction. And the only case that I'm aware of since then where a preliminary injunction has issued—maybe there are others—on an antitrust ground is *Pargas/Empire Gas*,[4] where there were other grounds as well and where it was essentially a very specialized case. Everyone throws up the antitrust defense, but the likelihood of getting relief on it is really not very good except in a terribly aggravated kind of case.[*]

Securities disclosure grounds are obvious: the offer omits this or that material fact—but the trouble with that is the courts increasingly have taken the position of permitting amendment and it is rare now that a court will say that the defect is not curable. Sometimes, however, you can come up with a disclosure problem which is more than merely a disclosure problem, and which really shows that there's something wrong. For example, if you can come up with something that's terribly wrong with the financing or if you can come up with a margin violation or something of that nature, then the injunction may actually bar the offer in pragmatic terms forever.

In any event, getting a preliminary injunction has a major psychological effect. It throws the bidder off stride. It scares the arbitrageurs and it is a very great victory in litigation of this nature.

Now, as I say, speed is essential in getting out a complaint, and the question is, what kinds of things do you do? How do you know what you're going to sue for? What kinds of defenses can you throw up against the tender offer?

Well, what you have to do is to make a very fast canvass of every possible theory you can think of where the offer may be lacking. Look for pragmatic pressure points. Zero in on the financing. Read the offer through a microscope. Is there anything queasy about the financing? Does it sound peculiar? Is it close to the line on margin? Does it look conditional? Does it sound as if there's an "if" there? Is there any other language in the offer—be it with respect to financing, plans, intent or whatever—that sounds unusual? Is there any peculiar choice of language which may indicate that someone was doing a clever drafting job to conceal an iceberg, of which the peculiar choice of language in the offer may be the tip, and which may be the signal that there's something there to look at.

What are some of the obvious causes of action, the ones that get thrown up every day in cases of this nature? "They fail to make adequate disclosure of their plans. In other words, they really intend

---

[3] Missouri Portland Cement Co. v. Cargill, Inc., 498 F.2d 851 (2d Cir.1974), cert. denied 419 U.S. 883 (1974).

[4] Pargas, Inc. v. Empire Gas Corp., 423 F.Supp. 199 (D.Md.1976).

[*] Antitrust suits have been rather more successful of late. Both Grumman Corp. and Marathon Oil Co. successfully raised antitrust defenses against hostile offers by LTV Corp. and Mobil Corp., respectively. See Grumman Corp. v. LTV Corp., 665 F.2d 10 (2d Cir.1981); Marathon Oil Co. v. Mobil Corp., 669 F.2d 378 (6th Cir.1981), cert. denied 455 U.S. 982 (1982). [Ed.]

to have a two-step merger." That's one thing to look for. Is the financing such or are the finances of the bidder such that in pragmatic terms it is inevitable that it's going to have to use the assets of the target in order to handle the debt service and repayment that it's taking on? Is it inevitable that this has to be the first step of a two-step transaction and it has not adequately disclosed the second step—or possible complications of the second step—such as if it acquires less then 50 percent by tender, maybe it then will have an investment security. Maybe you can stake out an argument that the bidder will be an investment company under the Investment Company Act. That would be an impediment to the second step.

"They fail to disclose material information regarding the value of the target." That can come into play sometimes where there have been preliminary discussions between the parties and you can utilize the theory that a lot of information about value has been disclosed to the bidder and it has failed to disclose it in its offer.

Antitrust. The question comes up. Why bother to put antitrust in if it can't win anyway? Also, there's another possible complication with antitrust: when the bidder raises its price $3 a share, your management may decide to give the offer a blessing, and there you are on record about this terrible, horrible offer that's violating section 7 of the Clayton Act and which should not conceivably be permitted to go ahead. Or the investment bankers may come up with another company for a marriage where the antitrust problems on their face may be far more serious than those you've already damned in your complaint attacking the first offer. These are pragmatic considerations. Nonetheless, you usually come up with the point of view: "I'll argue the antitrust defense today and I'll worry about the complications tomorrow. I need every argument I can get." Besides, there's a lot of discovery you can do with people on antitrust grounds. You can ask them a great many questions; you can get numerous executives and can ask for a great many documents.

* * *

Now, from the target company's lawyer's point of view, speed is of essence in the litigation. Keep in mind that no matter how many counterclaims may be thrown up against you and no matter how many theories the other fellow may come up with, don't be diverted. You are the one who needs relief. He doesn't. So, keep your eye on the ball. You want to get into court. You want to set up the timetable in such a way that if you're going to get relief from the court, you're going to get that relief before the offer is over and the game is finished. This which means that if you want to have any prayer whatsoever of getting an injunction, you have to have *evidence,* and the way you're going to get evidence means you have to fire out immediate notices of deposition and immediate document demands. And immediately, I mean within hours (24 hours at the outside), you have to file your complaint. You have to be in court with the notices of deposition, the demands for document production and your motion for expedited discovery: "What was said at the Board meeting? What documents were given to the bankers? What documents were given to the investment bankers?

How was the $50,000,000 loan justified to the bank in order to get this loan commitment? What did you say you were going to do with the company when you got it?" These are the areas where gold is to be mined, but you have to be in there doing it by asking the right questions and demanding the right documents.

You have to press very hard on this question of document discovery and depositions, which means you need great availability of experienced man-power in order to mount one of these litigations. You cannot afford to take a leisurely course of depositions. You want to be taking the depositions of the principal executive officer of the tendering company. You want to be taking the deposition of the financial officer. You want to be taking depositions of anyone in the acquisition program. You want to be taking depositions of the banks that they went to. You want to be taking depositions of the investment bankers—in certain extraordinary situations where that might really be crucial— and all of this has to be done not *seriatim,* but rather on two or three tracks simultaneously. And in the meantime they're going to be taking the depositions of your people. You also have depositions on the antitrust grounds which mean you may well be taking all the operating officials of the bidder in order to develop the requisite facts for an antitrust defense.

The manpower that must be brought into play—and sometimes in many different cities because you can't necessarily haul people around—really becomes extraordinary. At the same time, you need a team which will be collating all the information as it's developed on depositions, reviewing the documents, pulling it all in, writing affidavits and briefs, going to court, seeking scheduling orders and asking the court when it's going to hear the temporary restraining order and preliminary injunction applications. And that is a whole subject in and of itself, which is: when do you seek to ask the court for a temporary restraining order? Do you do it early? Do you do it late? The considerations can vary from case to case.

Also, there are numerous practical matters to be kept in mind. You need local counsel in many jurisdictions. That's already been referred to, but also keep your eye on some mundane mechanics which can easily be lost sight of given the pressures. You need court reporters for all of those depositions. They have to be lined up for daily copy. You may need airline reservations to get all your people to the right places. You need hotel reservations. You must make arrangements to type all the papers and get them across country, perhaps to a court in a different jurisdiction. There are very practical considerations, all of which have to mesh at the same time.

◆

Note: Purely Tactical Litigation

Do issues of professional responsibility arise when litigation is pursued for purposes of delay, psychological advantage or to influence the behavior of non-litigants such as arbitrageurs? The relevant portions of the American Bar Association's Model Rules of Professional Responsibility as orginally proposed provided as follows:

RULE 3.1 MERITORIOUS CLAIMS AND CONTENTIONS

A lawyer shall not bring or defend a proceeding, or assert or controvert an issue therein, unless there is a basis for doing so that is not frivolous, which includes a good faith argument for an extension, modification or reversal of existing law. A lawyer for the defendant in a criminal proceeding, or the respondent in a proceeding that could result in incarceration, may nevertheless so defend the proceeding as to require that every element of the case be established.

Comment

The advocate has a duty to use legal procedure for the fullest benefit of the client's cause, but also a duty not to abuse legal procedure. The law, both procedural and substantive, establishes the limits within which an advocate may proceed. However, the law is not always clear and never is static. Accordingly, in determining the proper scope of advocacy, account must be taken of the law's ambiguities and potential for change.

The filing of an action or defense or similar action taken for a client is not frivolous merely because the facts have not first been fully substantiated or because the lawyer expects to develop vital evidence only by discovery. Such action is not frivolous even though the lawyer believes that the client's position ultimately will not prevail. The action is frivolous, however, if the client desires to have the action taken primarily for the purpose of harassing or maliciously injuring a person or if the lawyer is unable either to make a good faith argument on the merits of the action taken or to support the action taken by a good faith argument for an extension, modification or reversal of existing law.

Model Code Comparison

DR 7–102(A)(1) provided that a lawyer may not "[f]ile a suit, assert a position, conduct a defense, delay a trial, or take other action on behalf of his client when he knows or when it is obvious that such action would serve merely to harass or maliciously injure another." Rule 3.1 is to the same general effect as DR 7–102(A)(1), with three qualifications. First, the test of improper conduct is changed from "merely to harass or maliciously injure another" to the requirement that there be a basis for the litigation measure involved that is "not frivolous." This includes the concept stated in DR 7–102(A)(2) that a lawyer may advance a claim or defense unwarranted by existing law if "it can be supported by good faith argument for an extension, modification, or reversal of existing law." Second, the test in Rule 3.1 is an objective test, whereas DR 7–102(A)(1) applied only if the lawyer "knows or when it is obvious" that the litigation is frivolous. Third, Rule 3.1 has an exception that in a criminal case, or a case in which incarceration of the client may result (for example, certain juvenile proceedings), the lawyer may put the prosecution to its proof even if there is no nonfrivolous basis for defense.

RULE 3.2 EXPEDITING LITIGATION

A lawyer shall make reasonable efforts to expedite litigation consistent with the interests of the client.

Comment

Dilatory practices bring the administration of justice into disrepute. Delay should not be indulged merely for the convenience of the advocates, or for the purpose of frustrating an opposing party's attempt to obtain rightful redress or repose. It is not a justification that similar conduct is often tolerated by the bench and bar. The question is whether a competent lawyer acting in good faith would regard the course of action as having some substantial purpose other than delay. Realizing financial or other benefit from otherwise improper delay in litigation is not a legitimate interest of the client.

Model Code Comparison

DR 7–101(A)(1) stated that a lawyer does not violate the duty to represent a client zealously "by being punctual in fulfilling all professional commitments." DR 7–102(A)(1) provided that a lawyer "shall not * * * file a suit, assert a position, conduct a defense [or] delay a trial * * * when he knows or when it is obvious that such action would serve merely to harass or maliciously injure another."

---◆---

Note particularly the comment to Rule 3.2 which states that "[r]ealizing financial or other benefit from otherwise improper delay in litigation is not a legitimate interest of the client."

The discrepancy between the reality described by Wachtell and the standards set forth by the Model Rules of Professional Responsibility is substantial. A possible explanation for the discrepancy is that standards like those of the Model Rules and their predecessors [17] have never been enforced by the bar; the principal enforcement agent has been a lawyer's conscience. Moreover, self-enforcement is particularly likely to be unsuccessful when those who are asked to exercise self-restraint must sell their services in a competitive market. Imagine that a client asks her lawyer to file a lawsuit against a hostile offeror merely to buy the time necessary for the client to find a more desirable purchaser. The benefit from the lawyer exercising self-restraint by refusing to initiate litigation in violation of the Model Rules of Professional Con-

---

[17] See, e.g., American Bar Association, Model Rules of Professional Responsibility, Disciplinary Rule 7–102(A)(1) (1978); State Bar of California, Rules of Professional Conduct, Rule 2–110(1) (1977).

duct accrues to the profession as a whole and, in the end, to society in general. The lawyer, however, bears all the costs. Analysis of this situation in terms of the free rider problem suggests that there may be little self-enforcement in a competitive market. For a discussion of the increasing competitiveness of the market for legal services, including, in particular, lawyer shopping by corporate clients, see Gilson & Mnookin, *Sharing Among the Human Capitalists: An Economic Inquiry into the Corporate Law Firm and How Partners Split Profits*, 37 Stan.L. Rev. 313 (1985).

For discussion of the problems posed by the use of litigation as a strategic technique see, e.g., Patterson, *A Preliminary Rationalization of the Law of Legal Ethics*, 57 N.Car.L.Rev. 522 (1979); Schuchman, *"Relations Between Lawyers," in Ethics and Advocacy* (American Trial Lawyers Foundation ed. 1978).

Problems of Injury and Standing. A number of the areas Wachtell suggests as fruitful sources of claims against the offerer raise questions about whether the target company has suffered any injury as a result of the offer and, therefore, about whether the target has standing to raise the claims. A claim that the acquisition would violate Section 7 of the Clayton Act is the best example of the problem.

In Brunswick Corp. v. Pueblo Bowl-O-Mat, Inc., 429 U.S. 477 (1977), the Supreme Court held that a competitor of an acquired company could not recover damages under § 7 of the Clayton Act for loss of business as a result of increased competition from the combined company. The Court stressed that § 7 was intended to prevent a lessening of competition, while the plaintiff's injury resulted from too much competition. Damages are recoverable, the Court held, only when the injury results from the anti-competitive effect "which makes the defendant's act illegal." 429 U.S. at 488.

What damage does a target company suffer as a result of being acquired in a transaction that might violate the Clayton Act? Even if the motivation for the acquisition is to earn monopoly profits, as proscribed by § 7, by substantially lessening competition, the premium offered to target shareholders demonstrates that the target company only *gains* (by sharing in the monopoly profits) from the transaction; no injury at all is suffered. One then would suppose that the target lacks standing to assert a damage claim.[18]

Is there anything different about injunctive relief? The courts of appeal have split on the issue. Compare Missouri Portland Cement Co. v. Cargill, Inc., 498 F.2d 851 (2d Cir.1974), cert. denied 419 U.S. 883 (1974), with Grumman Corp. v. LTV Corp., 665 F.2d 10 (2d Cir.1981)

---

[18] Even if the target could demonstrate injury—that a takeover would cause talented employees to quit, or interfere with ongoing projects, or result in disclosure of trade secrets, are among the types of injuries commonly asserted—the question would still arise as to whether these were the types of injury the antitrust laws were intended to prevent. In *Brunswick*, the court limited recovery under the Clayton Act to injuries which reflect "the anticompetitive effect either of the violation or of anti-competitive acts made possible by the violation." 429 U.S. at 489. See, e.g., Central National Bank v. Rainbolt, 720 F.2d 1183 (10th Cir.1983) (prospective loss of job by chairman of target is not an antitrust injury because it does not result from decreased competition).

and Marathon Oil Corp. v. Mobil Corp., 669 F.2d 378 (6th Cir.1981), cert. denied 455 U.S. 982 (1982).

For a careful analysis of the standing problem, on which this discussion relies, see Easterbrook & Fischel, *Antitrust Suits by Targets of Tender Offers,* 80 Mich.L.Rev. 1155 (1982). In a related vein, Sidak, *Antitrust Preliminary Injunctions in Hostile Tender Offers,* 30 Kan.L. Rev. 492 (1982), examines the common legal formulations of standards for the issuance of preliminary injunctions from the perspective of the costs of granting, as well as denying, antitrust preliminary injunctions in tender offer settings.

The same type of analysis is appropriate with respect to areas other than antitrust, especially the Williams Act. How is the target company, as opposed to its shareholders, injured by nondisclosure by the offerer? Standing under various sections of the Williams Act is considered in Chapter Sixteen A.1.b.(1), infra.

(2) Stock Repurchases

NATHAN & SOBEL, CORPORATE STOCK REPURCHASES IN THE CONTEXT OF UNSOLICITED TAKEOVER BIDS
35 Bus. Lwyr. 1545 (1981).*

* * *

STRATEGIC, LEGAL AND RELATED IMPLICATIONS OF DEFENSIVE STOCK ACQUISITION PROGRAMS

A. Introduction

In contrast to the "preventive" use of a stock acquisition program as a general means of reducing an issuer's vulnerability to unsolicited acquisition bids, the "defensive" stock acquisition program is a response to a particular imminent or already pending takeover bid. The defensive stock repurchase program may serve several, often complementary, purposes:

(a) To increase the percentage of the issuer's stock held by a control group that has decided not to tender to a point which will, or it is hoped will, defeat the "hostile" tender offer;

(b) To thwart the pending acquisition proposal by raising the bidding price beyond the level the bidder is willing or able to pay or, at the least, to cause the bidder to raise its price;

(c) To deny the bidder access to a significant block of stock held by a dissident or "weak" shareholder; and/or

(d) To "settle" out with a potential bidder by buying its stock at a profit to the bidder.

B. The Stock Acquisition Program as a Means of Enhancing the Strength of an Existing Control Position or Raising the Bidder's Price

1. BUSINESS ANALYSIS

Where a strong control block already exists, this tactical move has the [objective of increasing the percentage ownership of the control group by buying in the public's stock. Where supermajority provisions exist, the ability to block a transaction may arise at less than majority ownership.] In the absence of such an existing control block, the strategy is simply one of pricing the acquisition out of the third party bidder's reach or, at the least, increasing the third party's bidding price.

Because the stock must be purchased quickly if either variant of this strategy is to succeed, the stock acquisition program almost certainly has to be accomplished through an issuer cash tender offer under SEC rule 13e–4.[26] The only other possibly viable alternative from a timing point of view would be through negotiated block purchases. However, the success of a negotiated purchase program would depend upon the ability of the issuer and its financial advisors to locate large blocks of stock the holders of which can be persuaded to sell. The negotiated purchase technique, moreover, might leave the issuer vulnerable to a claim that it has engaged in an illegal "unconventional" tender offer not in compliance with rule 13e–4, particularly if the blocks are purchased at a premium over current market and the total amount of the stock involved represents a substantial percentage of the issuer's outstanding capitalization.* There is also the practical problem of making sure the potential sellers are fully apprised of the pending bid, if it has not yet been publicly announced (as well as any other material non-public information concerning the issuer), and persuading the sellers to give up the potential profits of any bidding war.

Assuming the issuer chooses the cash tender offer route, a number of tactical questions would be presented. The first is whether the issuer should try to strike first by announcing its cash offer before the bidder announces its offer. There is always something to be said for seizing the initiative in a takeover contest. For example, an issuer self-tender at a substantial premium over market may well confuse the bidder, disrupt its planning and timing and cause it to reassess the desirability of the acquisition.

However, it must be recognized that more often than not the bidder will have more pricing flexibility and frequently more pricing capability than the issuer. Many issuers are subject to financial covenants

---

[26] SEC rule 13e–4 under the Securities and Exchange Act of 1934 (the "1934 Act") and related Schedule 13e–4, SEC, Sec.Ex. Act Rel. No. 16112 (Aug. 16, 1979), regulating issuer tender offers, became effective on September 21, 1979. The rule applies to all tender offers by an issuer for its own equity securities if the issuer has a class of equity securities registered pursuant to Section 12 of the 1934 Act, is required to file periodic reports under § 15(d) of the 1934 Act, or is a closed-end investment company registered under the Investment Company Act of 1940. [The Williams Act Rules concerning issuer tender offers are considered in Chapter Sixteen A.l.c. infra. Ed.]

* What types of transactions are "tender offers" within the meaning of the Williams Act is considered in Chapter Sixteen, infra. [Ed.]

that depend upon maintaining certain debt/equity ratios, and, more fundamentally, even the most strongly capitalized issuer can only buy back so much of its stock within the limits of sound financial planning. * * * Finally, if the issuer's purpose is to increase the ultimate tender offer price and/or to give at least some of its shareholders the opportunity to sell at a better price than the bidder is offering, it can more certainly achieve that goal by responding to a third party bid than by initiating the bidding itself. The question ultimately reduces to one of bidding strategy. If the analysis is that the issuer has more limited resources and less flexibility to participate in several rounds of competing bids, saving its first bid for use as a response is probably a better tactic.

A second and more fundamental question is whether an issuer tender offer that, by definition, will be only for a portion (usually a minority) of its outstanding stock makes sense in competition with an any and all third party tender offer. The answer is probably yes, as long as there is a sufficiently large group of insider shareholders so that, in combination with a successful partial tender offer by the issuer, the control group would own at least a veto block against major corporate actions (such as a merger or sale of the issuer's assets) and ideally a majority of the issuer's outstanding stock. An issuer tender offer under these circumstances should force the bidder to the choice of raising its price sufficiently to defeat the issuer's tender offer or abandoning the hostile tender offer.

An example of this strategy is illustrated by MITE Corp. v. Dixon. In *MITE*, MITE Corporation made a tender offer to purchase any and all of Chicago Rivet & Machine Company's outstanding shares for cash at $28 per share. Chicago Rivet's board of directors determined that MITE's offer was inadequate, and, in response to that offer, announced a tender offer to purchase, with corporate funds, 350,000 (approximately 40 percent) of Chicago Rivet's outstanding shares at $30 per share. Chicago Rivet's offer stated that all of the officers and directors and certain other shareholders who owned, in the aggregate, approximately 285,000 shares of Chicago Rivet did not intend to tender their shares in response to MITE's tender offer. Chicago Rivet had 866,264 shares outstanding; hence, if its offer were successful, the officers, directors, and other key shareholders holding 285,000 shares would be in effective control. MITE raised its offering price in response to Chicago Rivet's offer, but for various reasons later withdrew its bid for Chicago Rivet.

On the other hand, absent a strong and loyal control block, the issuer's self-tender, standing alone, almost certainly would not defeat a hostile bid. As is the case for all preventive and defensive stock acquisition programs, the issuer is working for the bidder to the extent it reduces its outstanding capitalization and lowering the number of shares the bidder must acquire in order to achieve control. Absent some other goal, such as causing the bidder to raise its price, self-tender by an issuer as a defensive technique has no rational purpose. Indeed, there is a real question whether an issuer self-tender standing alone (that is to say, without an inside control group whose position will be enhanced) will be able to achieve even the goal of causing the bidder to raise its price. The "hostile" bidder may conclude that its original price is high enough to attract a majority of the issuer's outstanding stock, notwithstanding the higher partial offer by the issuer. The question, then, would be whether the issuer tender offer is worth the time, expense and litigating risk it would almost certainly entail.

The issuer's tactical position in this context should be enhanced if the "hostile" bid is for less than all of the issuer's stock. Now both the issuer and the "hostile" bidder would be asking the public to assume a prorationing risk. This presumably would cool the ardor of the arbitrageurs and might lead a number of other shareholders to forego the opportunity of tendering to both parties. Even if this does not occur, the issuer would not face the pricing disadvantage inherent in matching its partial bid against an any and all third party bid—that is, the pricing differential necessary to overcome the prorationing risk inherent in the issuer's partial offer.

In sum, although not without its attractions in some situations, the fact that so few issuers have adopted a strategy of self-tender as a response to a hostile bid strongly suggests that the device is of limited utility and rarely will be ultimately successful. For example, in the MITE-Chicago Rivet situation, MITE was able to defuse this defense merely by raising its tender offer price from $28 to $31.

* * *

D. The Stock Acquisition Program as a Means of "Settling" Out with a Potential Bidder

1. BUSINESS ANALYSIS

This strategy presents a scenario that has been played out with some regularity in recent years. An issuer becomes aware that another company, usually with a reputation as an aggressive acquiror, has accumulated a threateningly large block of its stock. Sometimes the issuer's awareness comes through the filing of a Schedule 13D or a Hart-Scott-Rodino Notification and Report Form. Not infrequently, however, the acquiring company overtly or covertly makes this fact known to the issuer before any such reports are due. In an ensuing conversation, the issuer will usually reject any overture for an acquisition and take a determinedly "hostile" stance. The acquiror then suggests, or signals in a more subtle way, that it would be amenable to selling the block to the issuer at what often turns out to be a very handsome profit. The issuer accepts, usually not without trepidation, and the repurchase is consummated.

This chain of events, of course, has its variations. Sometimes, the issuer extracts a promise from the acquiror not to engage in a "hostile" tender offer against the issurer, or a similar form of "standstill" arrangement. Sometimes, the issuer tries various forms of leverage on the acquiror such as suggesting that a combination of the two companies does indeed make some sense, but, from a financial point of view, the issuer should be the acquiring company and to this end it has just happened to prepare a Schedule 14D–1 and Hart-Scott-Rodino filing for the issuer's tender offer for the acquiror.

Variations notwithstanding, an observer is left with the strong impression that often the acquiror wanted the result. By playing the role of a tough acquisition minded company, the acquiror acheives something close to a "no lose" situation. If the issuer "rolls over" and "plays dead", the acquiror gets a friendly acquisition without a great risk of a bidding war; if the issuer fights by promoting a bidding war, the acquiror can always sell out to the white knight, usually at a large profit; if the issuer is willing to discuss a stock repurchase, again the acquiror can win financially. In effect, the acquiror is counting on the fact that if it can assemble its block at a relatively low price and then stimulate the dynamics of the acquisition game, it is almost certainly going to come out with a favorable transaction.

◆

Note: Open Market Repurchases, Pension Plan Purchases and Greenmail

Repurchases on the Open Market. Nathan & Sobel do not consider open market purchases as a means by which an issuer can repurchase substantial amounts of its own stock, presumably because of the belief that such an effort would be treated as a tender offer under the Williams Act. As will be considered in Chapter Sixteen A.1.c. infra, once the Williams Act is triggered, the rules governing the mechanics of tender offers make it impossible to carry out a statutory tender offer through open market purchases. At least for now, however, the belief that large open market purchases by an issuer would be treated as a tender offer has been proven wrong. In response to a hostile offer by the Limited, Inc., Carter Hawley Hale (CHH) announced a repurchase plan that would have increased the holdings in CHH of a friendly party to approximately 33 percent. The repurchase was carried out in the following manner:

> On April 16, 1984, after the NYSE had closed, at approximately 4:00 p.m., E.S.T., CHH began to repurchase its shares on the PSE. In a one-hour period, CHH purchased approximately 244,000 shares of its common stock at an average price of $25.25 per share. On April 17, CHH purchased approximately 6.5 million shares of its common stock in a two-hour period at an average price of $25.88 per share. CHH's purchases on that date amounted to approximately 18 percent of the shares of its stock then outstanding. During the next four trading days, CHH continued to purchase its shares. CHH announced on April 22 that its Board had increased the number of shares authorized for purchase from 15 million to 18.5 million. At the end of the seven (trading) day period from April 16 through April 24, CHH had purchased approximately 17.9 million shares, over 50% of the shares of CHH common stock outstanding before CHH began its repurchase program.

SEC v. Carter Hawley Hale Stores, Inc., 587 F.Supp. 1248, 1251 (C.D.Ca. 1984), affirmed 760 F.2d 945 (9th Cir.1985). After the repurchase program was completed, the SEC filed a complaint claiming that the program was in fact a tender offer and, therefore, violated the Williams Act. While the substance of the court's decision will be considered in Chapter Sixteen, infra, for now it is sufficient to note that the court rejected the SEC's contention, holding that the program was not a tender offer. If this decision is followed, open market purchases may prove to be the preferred technique for issuer repurchase.

Purchase by the Target Company's Pension Plan. One problem with an issuer repurchase is that it can serve to reduce the cost of the takeover for the acquiring company. Unless the reduction in the number of shares outstanding inflates the shares controlled by friendly hands into a blocking position, the repurchase simply "bootstraps" the acquiring company's offer by using target resources to fund a portion of the payment to outside shareholders.[19] One way this might be avoided would be to have the repurchases made by a friendly third party who could be counted on not to tender the shares to the acquiring company. An obvious candidate is the target's pension plan. Not only will it have the funds to make the purchases, but it will also have the inclination; the plan's trustees often will be officers of the target.

Two problems with this tactic stand out sharply, one concerning the pension plan's ability to make the purchase, and the second concerning the plan's freedom not to tender. Under sections 404 and 406 of the Employee Retirement Income Security Act of 1974 (ERISA),[20] the trustees are held to high fiduciary standards for the benefit of plan participants, especially with respect to transactions which benefit "parties in interest." ERISA section 406(a).[21] If the purchases are made after announcement of an offer, so that the price paid by the plan is higher than the pre-offer price, the plan will take a substantial loss on its investment if the offer is defeated and the price of target company stock then drops back to its pre-offer level. In Donovan v. Bierwirth, 538 F.Supp. 463 (E.D.N.Y.1981), modified, 680 F.2d 363 (2d Cir.1982), the trustees of the Grumman Corporation pension plan were held to have violated their fiduciary duty under ERISA when just these events transpired in connection with Grumman's successful defense against a hostile tender offer by LTV Corporation.[22]

Plan trustees are put in a similar position in deciding whether to tender shares they already own. In light of the empirical evidence that target company shareholders gain substantially from tender offers surveyed in Chapter Eleven, could a decision not to tender meet the ERISA requirement that a trustee meet the "prudent man" rule for investment decisions? Would the answer be different if the trustee were a bank instead of a target company official? What if the trustee

---

[19] This problem is considered in greater detail in Section B.2.b. of this Chapter, infra.

[20] 29 U.S.C. §§ 1104, 1106.

[21] 29 U.S.C. § 1106(a).

[22] The court stopped short, however, of adopting the Department of Labor's position that a corporate insider acting as a plan trustee during a hostile tender offer was a per se violation of ERISA § 406(b).

allowed each beneficiary to decide whether the shares allocated to his or her account should be tendered?

See generally Fein, Shumate & McClintock, *Officers and Directors as ERISA Fiduciaries,* in Officers' and Directors' Liability 503 (D. Goldwasser ed. 1985); Brecker, Lazarus & Gray, *The Function of Employee Retirement Plans as Impediments to Takeovers,* 38 Bus.Law. 503 (1983); Note, *The Duties of Employee Benefit Plan Trustees under ERISA in Hostile Tender Offers,* 82 Colum.L.Rev. 1692 (1982).

Greenmail. Perhaps more than any other defensive tactic, "greenmail"—the practice of a target company repurchasing at a premium the shares held by a potential offerer in order to eliminate the threat of an offer—has engaged the public's attention and approbation. The SEC's Advisory Committee on Tender Offers has recommended prohibiting the practice, and the Chairman of the SEC has stated that the SEC agrees with the Advisory Committee's recommendation.[23] Additionally, legislation has been introduced in both the House of Representatives[24] and the Senate[25] that would preclude an issuer from purchasing at a price above market the shares of any person who has held more than 3% of the issuer's stock for less than two years, unless the shareholders have approved the transaction or the issuer makes an offer of comparable value to other shareholders. It is worth recalling that although the furor over the technique is of recent origin, its use is not. See, e.g., Cheff v. Mathes, 41 Del.Ch. 494, 199 A.2d 548 (1964). However, the frequency with which the tactic is used, and the magnitude of the payments made, have changed substantially. The Office of the Chief Economist of the Securities and Exchange Commission has reported that between January, 1979, and March, 1984, $5.5 billion was paid in greenmail, representing a premium over market price of over $1 billion. Office of the Chief Economist, *The Impact of Targeted Share Repurchases (Greenmail) on Stock Prices* 1 (September 11, 1984).

(3) Scorched Earth

GURWIN, THE SCORCHED EARTH POLICY

The Institutional Investor
(June 1979).

"We must organize a merciless fight. The enemy must not lay hands on a single means of transport, on a single loaf of bread, on a single liter of fuel. Collective farmers must drive their livestock away and remove their grain. What cannot be removed must be destroyed. Bridges and roads must be dynamited. Forests and depots must be burned down. Intolerable conditions must be created for the enemy."

—Joseph Stalin, proclaiming the Soviets' "scorched earth" defense against the Nazis, July 3, 1941

[23] Statement of John S.R. Shad, Chairman of the Securities and Exchange Commission, before Hearings of the House Subcommittee on Telecommunications, Consumer Protection, and Finance, March 28, 1984, reprinted in CCH Fed.Sec.L.Rep. ¶ 83,511 (Current Vol.).

[24] H.R. 5693, 98th Cong., 2d Sess.

[25] S.2851, 98th Cong., 2d Sess.

The second-floor conference room in the McGraw-Hill Building was packed with reporters one day earlier this year when chairman Harold McGraw Jr. entered and walked up to the podium. It was the afternoon that McGraw was to announce his board's response to a proposed takeover by American Express, and while just about everyone expected McGraw-Hill to oppose the offer, no one was quite prepared for what happened next. Perspiring from the hot television lights, and speaking in a voice trembling with emotion, McGraw read a letter he was sending to the Amex board.

In it, he denounced the offer as—among other things—"illegal," "unconscionable," "improper," "reckless," "impulsive" and even "immature." And that was just a preview of what was to come. Two days later, the scathing words were reprinted as part of a two-page newspaper ad of scorching rebuttal, in an apparent effort to rally to the McGraw-Hill cause such groups as employees, authors and customers. In the weeks that followed, McGraw-Hill went on raising embarrassing questions—embarrassing for Amex whether or not they were true— such as whether the company had complied with the Arab boycott of Israel and whether it was entitled to its special exemption from the 1970 Bank Holding Company Act. Moreover, in a personal attack on the integrity of Amex's top management, it portrayed Amex president Roger Morley as a "Trojan horse," who had used his position on McGraw-Hill's board to help plot Amex's "conspiratorial" raid.

On March 1, American Express, having decided it had had enough, let its final $40-per-share offer expire. But McGraw-Hill's victory stunned the Street—not only because it is so rare to defeat a cash tender offer at such a huge premium, but because McGraw-Hill won without having to turn to a "white knight" to bail it out. For its part, American Express cited McGraw-Hill's highly successful "scorched earth" defense as its reason for withdrawing; even though it felt its offer was a just one, the company simply could not stand the heat.

Much more important than McGraw-Hill's dramatic victory, in fact, were the tactics employed. Investment bankers and corporate officers now openly wonder whether it all signals a significant and far-reaching change in the rules of the takeover game. Will other target companies now be tempted to use similar "scorched earth" defenses, making the takeover battles of today as dirty as the most virulent of the proxy fights of the 1950s? And if they do, will would-be raiders who might be vulnerable to such mud-slinging attacks be deterred from even considering hostile bids? In short, will the corporate world's equivalent of street demonstrations become a decisive factor in the outcome—and even the instigation—of unfriendly takeovers?

First, a definition is in order here. "Scorched earth," in its purest sense, is what Joseph Stalin said: If you're going to lose something to the enemy, you might as well destroy it so he has nothing to gain. No one, of course, has accused Harold McGraw of plotting to burn down the McGraw-Hill Building, but his defense team did work hard to convince Amex that the company would be decimated by critical employee defections if the takeover bid went through. For example, when *Business Week* editor-in-chief Lewis Young wrote a memo to his staff expressing his concern that Amex might not respect the editorial independence of the magazine, McGraw-Hill's defense team made sure that copies of the memo were made available to the press. Such acts added to Amex's fears that McGraw-Hill might really become a "shell" after a long and acrimonious takeover. And even though many observers felt that was hardly likely, the fact is one of Amex's lawyers acknowledged to *Institutional Investor* that his client thought it might be. It decided that "McGraw-Hill was a 'people' company," the lawyer said, "And if passions were going to be so inflamed by its management, there wasn't going to be anything left when they took it over."

Yet in today's takeover parlance, "scorched earth" has also come to focus on the last part of Stalin's definition—creating "intolerable conditions" for the enemy. In the business world this means broad-based attacks on the raider's reputation—with the mud-slinging campaign targeted not merely at the traditional narrow audience of shareholders, but just about everywhere else, including the press, the courts, government authorities, employees, customers, suppliers and the public at large. Although, for example, McGraw-Hill's stand has been compared with Mead Corp's defense last year against Occidental Petroleum, it was really quite different. While they contained elements of "scorched earth," Mead's attacks on Oxy were aimed largely at convincing Mead shareholders that the securities Oxy was planning to swap for their stock would be a "bad investment." Mead's intensive PR campaign, in other words, was addressed primarily to Mead shareholders.

McGraw-Hill's defense, on the other hand, took this to a new level by placing the emphasis on constituents other than its shareholders. This was made clear by the fact that when Harold McGraw's letter to Amex was reprinted as the newspaper ad, a caption said it was being run in response to "concerns voiced by many of the constituents served by McGraw-Hill—authors, journalists, business people around the world, employees and shareholders of McGraw-Hill, Inc. * * *" It is significant that "shareholders" were listed last. What's more, the letter said nothing about the economics of the offer—normally the heart of any takeover defense (though McGraw-Hill did attack the price later).

While this broad campaign certainly worked for McGraw-Hill, and has been used to a lesser degree in other successful defenses of the past, the question remains: Will its well-publicized success in thwarting Amex encourage increasing numbers of target companies to try the same thing? Takeover experts interviewed by *Institutional Investor* say much of the future success of "scorched earth" tactics will depend on such factors as the nature of the businesses of both the raider and the target, as well as the personalities of the raider's top management and board. "As a practical matter, whether you're successful or not has a lot to do with whom you're being raided by," says Stephen Friedman of Goldman Sachs, who has acted for the defense in a number of unfriendly takeovers * * *

Seeking skeletons

Some raiders, for example, will be highly susceptible to attacks simply because they have a lot of skeletons in their corporate closets— which was exactly why Occidental was so vulnerable to Mead's attacks. During the four-month battle, Mead probed deeply into Oxy's past, dredging up damaging material on, for example, Oxy's questionable foreign payments and pollution by its Hooker Chemical subsidiary. Similarly, when Victor Posner's Sharon Steel went after Foremost-McKesson three years ago, * * * Foremost's accountants dug into Sharon's financial statements, which ultimately forced Sharon to restate its earnings and effectively aborted the raid. As one investment banker puts it: "Sometimes you have a bigger target to shoot at. Going after Posner is like having a turkey to shoot at with a twenty-millimeter cannon."

Still other raiders, such as American Express, will be vulnerable simply because the nature of their business makes them sensitive to attacks on their reputation, whether they are justified or not. "The most maddening thing," said Amex chairman James Robinson III, "is the way [Harold McGraw] has taken off on our integrity. Integrity is fundamental to every business we're in. It's the kind of business where you make promises to pay and you keep those promises." Amex was so stung by those attacks that it actually sued McGraw-Hill for libel, a step believed to be the first in a takeover battle.

Actually, in deals involving a sizable raider and target company, there are often countless potential issues that the target could use as ammunition. Says Goldman Sachs' Friedman: "If you're looking at a $100 million company that makes only monkey wrenches and has only domestic sales, fewer things pop out. But when you're dealing with a giant, multinational, multi-business company, there are more areas to probe. There's more of a chance of antitrust and other regulatory problems, of questionable foreign payments by the raider, more of a chance that things will come out in depositions."

Quitters, or not?

Another crucial element as takeover candidates ponder how to fight back will be their assessment of the strength of the personalities on the raiding side. Though, as one investment banker puts it, "nobody likes to pick up the newspaper and see his name and personal reputation abused," some raiders can stand that kind of abuse more than others. In an effort to gauge how a raider will respond to various defense tactics, First Boston's Joseph Perella says that he will often put together a "psychological profile" of a raiding company's CEO, based on such factors as "how the company has reacted whenever they've been charged with something by the federal government or various local authorities. Have they counterattacked swiftly? Or have they acted like a pushover? How tenacious have they been in past takeovers? And in this battle, how badly do they want to be in the [target's] business?" Perella notes that when he worked on Seven-Up's defense team, he felt that raider Philip Morris "was committed to owning that company, they had the money and they weren't quitters. Finally, they were willing to make the highest bid."

It will also be important, bankers say, for the target company to carefully analyze the raider's board. As one investment banker puts it, "There are a lot of responsible and established businessmen on boards of directors who don't like to see their names in the paper and their motives and practices questioned. They don't need those kinds of problems." The board of Amex, for example, "reads like a 'Who's Who'," in the words of one Amex adviser, who points to such luminaries as former Fed chairman William McChesney Martin Jr. and former UN ambassador William Scranton. "They just weren't about to sit there and have this garbage thrown at them."

Another example: when Dictaphone was fighting off Canada's Northern Electric (now Northern Telecom), Dictaphone's advisers sensed that Northern's board might not have the stomach for a bloody fight—and made sure that the directors were served with subpoenas. Recalls one member of the Dictaphone team: "They're very gentlemanly up in Canada; they're not used to being served at garden parties."

First Boston's Perella agrees that some raiders can be worn down through the legal process. "A key part of the litigation strategy," he says, "is wearing down the [raider's] CEO by putting him on the witness stand. Here's a guy who's the head of a company, used to flying around in the corporate jet. He isn't used to being grilled by these tough lawyers. Finally, he says, 'Who needs this'?"

On the other hand, takeover experts note that some raiders seem virtually immune to such tactics. "There are some CEOs who, if you do a very vicious PR campaign, will dig in their heels to win," says J. Tomilson Hill of Smith Barney, Harris Upham. Sticks and stones may break the bones of United Technologies chairman Harry Gray, but he is often cited as the classic example of the raider who figures names will never hurt him. Gray—who was portrayed as Count Dracula in a financial writers' skit last year—seems impervious to ferocious defenses. In a recent bid for Carrier Corp., for example, he waited patiently for the courts to sink Carrier's raft of legal challenges, then proceeded with the tender offer.

Hanging tough

If personal attacks do become more common, the kind of psychological analysis practiced by First Boston's Perella is also likely to become more common. Guy Wyser-Pratte of Bache Halsey Stuart Shields predicts that he and his fellow arbitrageurs are likely to "put much more effort into gauging the endurance, fortitude and tenacity of buyers, which means that more emphasis will be given to personalities. We'll ask if these guys are a bunch of pushovers or whether they're going to hang tough."

Not all takeover candidates can wage a massive counterattack of McGraw-Hill's variety, of course. One important reason, again, is the size of the target company. "Larger companies have the wherewithal to mount these kinds of defenses," notes Goldman Sachs' Friedman,

"and they're also more prone to fight. Big companies do not roll over."
So-called "people-intensive" companies also have an advantage, since
they're able to use the threat of employee walkouts because of a
potential change in management. Indeed, in defending itself against
the Northern Electric, Dictaphone exploited the "hatchet man" reputation of Northern chairman John Lobb. Public relations man Richard
Cheney, * * * an adviser to Dictaphone, recalls: "I called up a client
of mine in Pittsburgh who used to work for Lobb and I asked his
secretary if she had anything on him. She said: 'You mean John Slob?
I've got a whole file on him'." The secretary air-expressed the file to
Cheney, who found that it was stuffed with juicy clippings describing
"massive employee purges" and "executive bloodbaths" at companies
Lobb had run. Cheney then helped Dictaphone president E. Lawrence
Tabat draft a letter to his employees, in which he quoted extensively
from the clippings, then asked for the employees' support in thwarting
the raid.

The fear of employee discontent was apparently also a factor in
persuading Occidental to withdraw its bid for Mead. After the deal
was aborted, Oxy president Joseph Baird observed that Mead's fierce
opposition reflected resistance by a large proportion of Mead management, which led Oxy to conclude that even if it had prevailed "we
would have had a hell of a time managing that company."

The picket line

But appeals to employees won't always work. Copperweld, which
probably did more than any other target company to rouse its employees' ire, still lost its independence. The Pittsburgh-based company, in
its fight against a 1975 offer by Rothschild-controlled Société Imetal,
exploited employees' fears that their job security would be jeopardized
by the "foreign takeover," which prompted the United Steelworkers
Union to join the defense effort. A press release from union president
I.W. Abel was reprinted by Copperweld as a full-page newspaper ad,
and Copperweld secretly paid for trips to New York and Washington by
Copperweld employees, where they picketed Imetal's investment bankers, Kuhn Loeb and New Court Securities, and the French embassy.
Their hand-made placards carried such slogans as "Frenchie Go Home"
and "Stomp a Frog Today." The same xenophobic approach was used—
though a bit less crudely—in Copperweld's letters to its shareholders.
In one letter, chairman Phillip Smith used the word "foreign" five
times, as in "foreign-based company," "foreign owners of Imetal" and
even "foreign offer." Needless to say, he reminded his shareholders
that Copperweld was "an American company."

Similar protests by writers for *New York* magazine failed to deter a
bid by Australian publisher Rupert Murdoch. Though several of the
magazine's top writers theatened to walk out—and followed through on
their threat—Murdoch went ahead with the acquisition.

If history is any indication it's probable that some target companies
can even count on appeals to customers and suppliers in a "scorched
earth" defense. In 1975 takeover lawyer Joseph Flom devised the now

legendary "Jewish dentist defense" for Sterndent, a dental supply house. Flom seized on the fact that a minority owner of the offerer was the Kuwait Investment Co.—a leader in the attempted boycott of "Jewish" Euromarket underwriters—while many of the dentists and precious metal dealers who were Sterndent's customers and suppliers were of the Jewish faith. Though Sterndent's advisers emphasize that the attacks were aimed at KIC—and not at Arabs in general—much of the press nonetheless portrayed it as an "Arab takeover." In fact, a headline in a dental industry publication screamed "The Arabs Are Coming! The Arabs Are Coming!"

Suppliers, in this case, authors, were instrumental in thwarting last year's bid by Western Pacific for the Houghton Mifflin publishing company. Such prominent authors as Arthur Schlesinger Jr., John Kenneth Galbraith and Archibald MacLeish wrote letters indicating that they would review their relationships with the Boston publisher if it were acquired. Even more persuasive, however, were protests from the relatively anonymous writers for Houghton Mifflin's highly profitable textbook division. One adviser to the publisher says that when Western Pacific chairman Howard (Micky) Newman got the first few letters from authors, "he thought it was a big laugh, and called it a 'put-up job.' When he began getting more letters, he began to realize, 'I'm going to buy this company and I ain't going to have nothing'." After Newman withdrew his bid, Houghton Mifflin president Howard Miller observed airily: "I couldn't conceive of anyone paying money for a publishing company whose authors would walk out. How reasonable would it be to force the issue?"

The effectiveness of a public relations-oriented campaign will also depend on solid research and skillful execution. As J. William Robinson of Georgeson & Co., the investor relations firm, puts it: "You can't run a PR campaign unless you have information—you've got to have solid facts." And the digging up of those facts has already been raised to an art. In addition to the legal process—the key information-gathering tool—information also comes in from tipsters such as Cheney's secretarial source in the Northern Electric-Dictaphone battle. Often these are disgruntled former employees of the raiding company's CEO. In Uarco's recent defense against Daylin, the defense team was tipped off that Daylin chairman Sanford Sigoloff had been accused of expense account improprieties while working at another company. And, from time to time, detective firms have been retained to dig into the raider's background, though this technique is more often used in proxy fights.

Moreover, in nearly every defense effort analyzed in this article, the target's advisers spent countless hours digging through old clippings and court records searching for damaging nuggets on the raider. An adviser to Kennecott Copper, which was a target of a proxy fight waged by Curtiss-Wright last year, recalls that, "We went through every reference thing in our libraries, we got magazine articles going back years, we looked for every scrap of information. Everybody involved was searching for everything they could get their hands on."

Among the tidbits uncovered—and prominently mentioned in ads and letters to shareholders—was a 1949 decision by a federal court that Curtiss-Wright's chairman had improperly disclosed confidential information on a corporation to his brother-in-law.

Once the dirt is gathered, the raided company must decide whom to show it to and how. Indeed, the effectiveness of "scorched earth" tactics, say bankers, will largely depend on how carefully practitioners zero in on their targets. The importance of precise aim is illustrated by two broad-based defense campaigns, one conducted by Microdot against General Cable in 1975 and the other by Chemical Bank against Leasco six years earlier. In the Microdot defense, CEO Rudolph Eberstadt Jr. went on a rampage against *all* hostile takeovers, seeking the support of the entire business community. He ran ads with the headline "American Business—Are You Next?" and sent personal letters asking for help from the CEOs of the Fortune 1,000 companies. Though Eberstadt's quixotic campaign attracted considerable attention, he wound up selling to a white knight at only a slight premium over General Cable's offer.

Chemical Bank, on the other hand, probably sealed Leasco's fate with one phone call to Continental Illinois, Leasco's lead bank. When the chairman of the Chicago bank informed Leasco chairman Saul Steinberg that he thought the deal would be "bad for banking," Steinberg got the message. Referring to the importance of a deftly executed attack, one investment banker says, "Some people do with a bludgeon what should be done with a scalpel."

Thinking four times

A lesson from all this for would-be raiders is not to get into a fight if you can't stand a bitter counterattack. Which means that in the future a corporation's executives will have to indulge in some considerable soul-searching before they launch a hostile takeover bid. "If a big company plans to raid another big company," says Goldman Sachs' Friedman, "they've got to be very conscious of the fact that their past operations are going to be put under a spotlight, and it may be a very painful experience." Adds Salomon Brothers' J. Ira Harris: "Anyone who has any susceptibility at all should think twice or three times or four times before doing an unfriendly deal."

So, bankers say, if a company is determined to go ahead with a hostile offer, it should do everything possible to free itself from apparent conflicts of interest, so as not to give additional ammunition to its adversary. For example, Brascan Ltd.'s use of F.W. Woolworth's lead bank to finance its raid on the retailer became a key issue in Woolworth's defense. Similarly, Amex president Morley's seat on the McGraw-Hill board was deemed by a number of observers—with some justification—as a conflict of interest. As Georgeson's Robinson advises: "If you stay out of conflict-of-interest situations with banks, with dealer-managers, etc., you'll avoid 80 percent of the problems."

In point of fact, there already are indications that some corporations have developed a healthy respect for the effectiveness of "scorched earth" tactics—and have backed off from even trying unfriendly take-overs. A number of investment bankers, for instance, attribute the paucity of raids by foreign companies to fears of damaging publicity. And First Boston's Perella says that many U.S. companies "have probably opted not to do a raid because they knew that skeletons would come out of the closet." More recently, Occidental Petroleum, while still recovering from the wounds inflicted by Mead Corp., said it will only go the friendly route from now on. It's a painful lesson, but by no means an entirely new one. Indeed, after his unsuccessful raid on B.F. Goodrich a decade ago, Northwest Industries chairman Ben Heineman said he would only do friendly deals in the future. That's not surprising. According to one account of the battle, Goodrich portrayed Heineman as "something akin to a marauding barbarian intent upon ravaging the women of Akron and pillaging the town."

The dramatic success of "scorched earth" tactics to date—both in scaring off unfriendly raiders and deterring would-be raiders—certainly seems to suggest that it will be widely imitated by other target companies in the future. But as might be expected, takeover experts are divided over whether this really will happen. Arthur Long, president of D.F. King, the investor relations firm, says flatly: "No way." Most corporations, says Long, are smart enough to realize that "scorched earth" is a double-edged sword, and that a sufficiently angered raider might sling back some mud of his own. "Personal attacks can boomerang," says Long. Others point out that almost any corporate board that mounts an all-out, no-holds-barred defense knows it risks a spate of shareholder lawsuits.

Still, as the premiums being offered to target companies' shareholders grow larger, it becomes exceedingly hard to rely on the traditional argument that a tender offer is "grossly inadequate" and "not in the shareholders' best interests." At times, flinging mud at the raider may be the only defense available. "One of the few ways to remain independent," concludes Goldman Sachs' Friedman, "is to be lucky enough to be hit by someone with a chink in his armor."

---

(4) Defensive Acquisitions

The approach taken by Marshall Field & Company on a pre-offer basis can also be attempted after an offer is made. Because the identity of the offeror is known at this stage, it is much easier to devise a defensive acquisition that will raise serious antitrust barriers. Additionally, knowledge of the identity of the offeror may also allow defensive acquisitions that raise other regulatory barriers.

A. FLEISCHER, TENDER OFFERS: DEFENSES, RESPONSES, AND PLANNING
51–61 (1983).

THE CREATION OF REGULATORY PROBLEMS

[T]argets may seek to deter or prevent takeover attempts by developing or acquiring business operations which are subject to governmental regulation of changes in their ownership or control.[127] Examples include radio and television stations, insurance companies, merchant fleet vessels, domestic air carriers, atomic energy facilities, defense facilities, public utilities, and business operations in states with takeover statutes or in certain foreign jurisdictions, such as Canada.

Particularly where the prospective bidder is a foreign national or a corporation with a substantial percentage of its stock held by foreigners, the target may be able to take advantage of statutory restrictions on foreign investment based on security considerations or the "national interest."[129] In fact, recent bids for American companies by foreign corporations have been met with what has become known as the "political defense." Politicians, primarily from the areas in which the target conducts its activities, actively oppose the acquisition, initiating legislative hearings on the implications of the takeover or even introducing legislation aimed at blocking the takeover.[130] To date these activities have not barred or caused the termination of any bid.

In rare instances, applicable regulations may directly prohibit a prospective bidder from taking over the target.[131] More commonly, they will require approval by an agency or licensing authority. In these instances, the impact on the prospective bidder generally depends upon (i) its prospects of obtaining approval from the agency; (ii) the time when approval must be obtained; (iii) its ability to avoid the regulatory problem; and (iv) the impact of added costs and delay on its

[127] It should be noted that the recent attitude of certain federal agencies, such as the Civil Aeronautics Board, the Federal Communications Commission, the Federal Reserve Board, and the Nuclear Regulatory Commission, has been not to permit the use of the regulatory statutes administered by them as anti-takeover devices. See § I notes 138 and 142 infra.

[129] These restrictions are concentrated in industries which are likely to be integral to any American defense efforts, such as navigation, see, e.g., 46 U.S.C. §§ 802, 808, 883 (1976 & Supp. V 1981); civilian air commerce, see, e.g., 49 U.S.C. §§ 1371, 1378 1301(3) & (16) (1976 & Supp. V 1981); communications, see, e.g., 47 U.S.C. § 310 (1976); natural resource development, see, e.g., 30 U.S.C. § 181 (1976 & Supp. V 1981); power generation, see, e.g., 16 U.S.C. § 797(e) (1976); and, of course, the defense industry itself, see, e.g., Department of Defense ("DOD") Industrial Security Manual

for Safeguarding Classified Information §§ 21c, 72a, DOD Industrial Security Regulation §§ 2–201a, 2–205. In addition, a number of states restrict foreign ownership of real property and certain interests in natural resources.

[130] Congressional committees may review major acquisitions by non-U.S. persons. For example, hearings were held in connection with Canadian Pacific Enterprises Ltd.'s proposed acquisition of Hobart Corp., Seagram's bid for Conoco and the Kuwaiti acquisition of Santa Fe International.

[131] For example, U.S. maritime laws provide that no more than 25% of the stock of certain American shipping companies may be owned or controlled by aliens. 46 U.S.C. § 883 (1976 & Supp. V 1981). See Exhibit 38, N.Y.S.E. Memorandum on Alien Ownership (Feb. 8, 1977). See also Rubin, *Arbitrage*, Corporate Finance Council 25 (Apr. 1, 1976).

willingness to proceed.[132]   Approval may be necessary at various stages: before an offer is made, before any purchases are made, before control is acquired,[133] or after control is acquired.[134]

Acquisitions by tender offer require compliance with the federal tender offer rules, which require an offer to be held open for twenty business days (or approximately thirty calendar days).   Given this delay, the additional cost and time required to obtain approval from other regulatory authorities may be insignificant.   Consequently, the need for regulatory approval may not discourage a prospective bidder if it expects to be able to obtain the approval or if the "tainted" operations are not material and approval is essentially not required prior to consummation of the bid.   Nevertheless, where regulatory approval must be obtained before the bid can proceed or purchases made, the prospective bidder faces the possibility of protracted delays, in hearings or otherwise,[136] and, where the bidder is uncertain as to the outcome of an application, even the possibility that approval will not be given.

Either by statute [137] or by agency determination,[138] agency approval may not be required until after consummation of the offer.   In such

---

[132] * * *

The regulated business may also create opportunities for other defensive measures by the target.   For example, § 151(b) of the Delaware Corporation Law permits a corporation in a regulated or licensed industry to redeem its own shares "to the extent necessary to prevent the loss of such license, franchise or membership or to reinstate it."

[133] See, e.g., N.Y. Ins. Law § 67 et seq. (McKinney's Supp.1982).   Section 69–f(1) states: "No person * * * shall acquire control of any domestic insurer, whether by purchase of its securities or otherwise, except (1) after 20 days' written notice to the insurer, or such shorter period as the superintendent may permit, of its intention to acquire control, and (2) with the prior written approval of the superintendent."

Statutes such as this may pose serious obstacles even to bidders seeking to acquire a relatively small percentage of an insurance company's stock.   Most of the statutes include a presumption that 10% ownership constitutes control, and allow for a finding of control even if less than 10% has been acquired.   Compare American Gen. Corp. v. NLT Corp., 1982 Fed.Sec.L.Rep. (CCH) ¶ 98,808, at 94,139 (S.D.Tex.) (purchase of up to 9.9% neither met control presumption nor constituted "control in fact") with In re Application of Sun Life Ins. Co. (Md. Comm'n Ins. Mar. 21, 1979) (purchase of 9% violated statute based on finding of fact that Sun Life's 9% holding conferred actual control of the issuer).

[134] See, e.g., Canadian Foreign Investment Review Act, Eliz. 2, chap. 46 (1973).

[136] For example, under the Model Insurance Holding Company System Regulatory Act, which has been adopted in major part by 45 states, the approval proceeding could be expected to last at least 60 days since the Model Act provides for a 30-day pre-hearing notice period and 30-days for the administrator to adjudicate.   This time span would be lengthened by the duration of any hearing to be held as well as any adjournments in the proceeding. * * * Other regulatory schemes with a potential for long delays include the Interstate Commerce Commission approval of motor carrier acquisitions, and the Federal Reserve Board approval of bank or bank holding company acquisitions.

[137] See, e.g., Canadian Foreign Investment Review Act, Eliz. 2, chap. 46 (1973).

[138] The Nuclear Regulatory Commission (NRC) decided that it "would not be appropriate" to delay United Technologies' bid for Babcock & Wilcox shares even though the target company held several nuclear licenses.   The NRC said that any approval could be obtained after the acquisition, which was "purely speculative."   Response letter of the NRC to Babcock's request for emergency action (May 9, 1977).   Babcock sought judicial review of the NRC's failure to act, but was denied an expedited hearing in the D.C. Circuit Court of Appeals.   The district court in which Babcock sued to enjoin the offer ruled that, under the Atomic Energy Act, only the U.S. Attorney General has standing to sue for violations of the Act.   Babcock & Wilcox Co. v. United Tech. Corp., 435 F.Supp. 1249, 1288 (N.D. Ohio 1977).   As Nathan and Kapp commented in *Recent Developments Under the Williams Act in Takeovers and Acquisi-*

cases, the bidder may proceed with the offer, but must disclose the approvals which must be obtained and any potential monetary loss to the target company resulting from the loss of the regulated business.

*   *   *

On the other hand, a bidder may be able to avoid potential problems created by target ownership of a regulated business. It appears that, with respect to certain industries, the bidder can agree not to exercise control over the business [141] or to place control in the hands of an independent trust pending regulatory approval or divestiture. The bidder may also commence its transactions with consummation conditioned on receipt of the regulatory approval. If the regulated business does not constitute a significant part of the target's operations or is not of interest to the bidder, the bidder can commit itself to divestiture of that business to avoid regulatory problems.

*   *   *

———◆———

(5) Miscellaneous Techniques

In addition to the mainstream of tactics already described, a number of other approaches merit mention.

—*Control Clauses.* It has been suggested that an offerer may be deterred if the target company's loan agreements or other material contracts allow, or are amended to allow, the lender or other party to accelerate the loan or terminate the contract in the event of a change of control. See Kamen, *Special Problems of Institutional Lenders,* 32 Bus.Law. 1423 (1977). The option analysis in Chapter Seven makes it easy to understand why a creditor would like the opportunity to accelerate or terminate. It serves as a check on opportunistic behavior by preventing the company from increasing the risk associated with the loan or contract by transferring control to a more risky party. Additionally, it allows the creditor to accelerate the loan or terminate the contract when the transfer of control coincides with an unrelated event, like an increase in interest rates or a decrease in the market price of

tions, 9 Ann.Inst.Sec.Reg. 263, 294–95 (P.L.I. Course Handbook No. 257, 1977):

> The federal courts and the regulatory agency in the B & W case seemingly evidenced a reluctance to allow the target to use the regulatory provisions of the Atomic Energy Act as a weapon in defending against a takeover bid. If other regulatory agencies were to adopt a similar "hands-off" approach to takeover contests, this line of defensive strategy would be greatly weakened.

[141] In the bid by MCA Corporation for the Coca-Cola Bottling Company of Los Angeles (which owned a radio station) the offering material stated:

> If at any time during the Offer or thereafter it becomes apparent that transfer

of control of CCLA [the target] to the Purchaser has taken place, the Purchaser will submit a timely application to the FCC for approval thereof * * *. The Purchaser will not, without prior FCC approval, transfer control of the FM station or in any way exercise any right or power of control over CCLA Communications, Inc. or its capital stock, including without limitation, any right or power to change or interfere with the board of directors or the present management of CCLA Communications, Inc.

Offer to Purchase § 6F, at 14 (Oct. 11, 1977). This procedure was not cleared by the FCC and may not be effective when FCC-regulated activities are significant.

the goods to be delivered under the contract, that causes it to be to that party's advantage to accelerate or terminate regardless of a change in control. Although this explains why a creditor would want a control clause, it does not explain why a target company would be willing to agree to one. The advantage to the creditor, at least with respect to amending existing loans and contracts, comes at the expense of the target unless the terms of the loan or contract are otherwise adjusted to compensate the target for the reduction in risk. If the only benefit to the target is the ability to defend against an unwanted takeover by making the target less valuable, the technique is only another manifestation of the "scorched earth" tactic.

—*Golden Parachutes.* A tactic of growing popularity involves the target company awarding very favorable employment contracts to its senior management which become effective only in the event of a change in control. Once effective, the employee is commonly given the unilateral right to terminate employment and receive a substantial lump sum payment or, if the right is not entirely unilateral, to do so if the employee's situation—e.g., duties, benefits, employment location, etc.—are changed.[26] In a recent instance, Conoco, Inc., awarded new employment contracts to senior management following expression of interest by suitors such as Seagrams, Cities Services Co., and Texaco, Inc. The contract given the Chairman of the Board, for example, granted him the right to quit and receive a $5 million lump sum payment if Conoco were taken over. See generally Cooper, *The Spread of Golden Parachutes,* Institutional Investor 65 (Aug. 1982) (collecting examples).

Categorizing golden parachutes as a defensive tactic is subject to debate. First, unless large numbers of employees are covered, it is unlikely that the total payments called for will be large enough to affect the acquiring company's decision in a major transaction.[27] Second, golden parachutes are commonly justified not as a defensive tactic, but as a means of *eliminating* the conflict of interest between target management and target shareholders with respect to a takeover. One way this can be described is by reference to portfolio diversification. In this analysis, target management starts with a one asset portfolio—its investment of firm specific human capital in the target[28]—which is subject to the risk of a hostile takeover. Without more, target manage-

---

[26] See, e.g., Profusek, *Executive Employment Contracts in the Takeover Context,* 6 Corp.L.Rev. 99 (1983); Riber, *On Golden Parachutes—Ripcords or Ripoffs? Some Comments on Special Termination Agreements,* 3 Pace L.Rev. 15 (1982); Note, *Golden Parachutes and the Business Judgment Rule: Toward a Proper Standard of Review,* 94 Yale L.J. 909 (1985).

[27] Some golden parachute arrangements, however, do reach a magnitude that would affect an acquiring company's decision. A recent analysis of a sample of 90 firms that had adopted golden parachute programs disclosed that the maximum payout under the contracts averaged only 1.73% of the market value of the company's equity and only 12.13% of annual earnings. Although the averages are low, they mask a large variation within the sample. The payout under one plan was approximately 11.23% of the market value of the company's equity. Similarly, the payout as a percentage of annual earnings was as high as 65% and this excluded companies that had losses. Lambert & Larker, *Golden Parachutes, Executive Decision-Making, and Shareholder Wealth* (Working Paper, J.L. Kellogg Graduate School of Management, Northwestern University, March, 1984).

[28] See, e.g., DeAngelo & DeAngelo, supra at 35.

ment will try to reduce that risk (and protect the value of its human capital investment) by resisting takeovers. Awarding management golden parachutes adds a second asset to management's portfolio: the expectation of a large termination payment which can be realized only if a takeover actually occurs. The result, it is argued, is a portfolio the value of which is invariant to the risk of a takeover. As a result, management will consider a proposed offer solely from the perspective of what is best for shareholders because management's personal positions are protected either way.

Aligning the interests of managers and shareholders may not be quite that easy. Indeed, the result may be only to bias decision making in the opposite direction. If the payout under the golden parachute is greater than the amount by which the present value of a manager's future earnings with the target (including the psychic value of control) exceeds the present value of the manager's future earnings in alternative employment, the manager will have a financial incentive *to cause* the target to be taken over and accept the next most remunerative position, even if that result is *not* in the shareholders' best interests. The perverse incentive to facilitate a takeover may be even stronger for older executives whose future earnings will be smaller because of their shorter remaining worklife, but whose lump sum payment under a golden parachute award is likely higher due to greater seniority and current earnings. In this setting something akin to a final period problem is created.[29]

If the terms of the golden parachute are negotiated at arm's length—for example, as part of the negotiations to attract the executive to the company in the first place—we may feel confident that the executive's portfolio has not been overbalanced. But what if the golden parachute is awarded unilaterally, only after a hostile offer has been made?[30] Is there any way out of the final period problem at that point? What legal rule concerning the validity of golden parachutes does this analysis suggest?

What of the argument that employees have a justifiable interest in the identity of the people for whom they work? A manager may be willing to work for people he knows and trusts without an employment contract, but may want protection if the identity of those for whom he works changes. If this is the case, however, it is difficult to explain why the employee should have the right to pull the ripcord on his parachute—to unilaterally terminate his employment and thereby secure the payout. Wouldn't this justification seem more credible if the employee could pull the ripcord only if there was a material involuntary change in the conditions of his employment?

As a practical matter, much of the controversy concerning golden parachutes may have been put to rest, although hardly resolved, by

[29] For example, William Agee, Chief Executive Officer of Bendix, was given a $4 million parachute only after it was clear that Bendix would not succeed in its acquisition of Martin Marietta and, instead, would be acquired by Allied Corporation.

Cochran & Wartick, *Golden Parachutes: A Closer Look*, 26 Cal.Mngmt.Rev. 111 (1984).

[30] How could you structure a golden parachute contract to eliminate the perverse incentive associated with golden parachutes?

provisions of Section 67 of the Deficit Reduction Act of 1984 [31] which limit, following a change in control, the amount the target company can deduct as salary expense to three times a manager's average annual gross income from the company over the previous five years. Additionally, the manager would be subject to a twenty percent excise tax on amounts in excess of the limit.

—*Placing Securities in Friendly Hands.* Where the acquiring company intends a complete acquisition, the target may create some deterrence by issuing a substantial block of the target's stock to a friendly party. This tactic should be distinguished, however, from a similar issuance intended to facilitate the acquisition of the target by another company whom the target prefers to the offerer. The latter tactic, commonly called a "lock-up," is simply part of an effort to seek out a more attractive competing bid and is not intended to keep the target company independent. As such, it is more accurately a negotiated surrender rather than a defensive tactic.[32] In the purely defensive setting, the friendly party is typically prevented from becoming less friendly once it is a target shareholder through the use of a "standstill" agreement which (i) limits future purchases on the part of the friendly purchaser, (ii) prohibits the purchaser from attempting to exercise control or otherwise influence the conduct of the target's business, (iii) grants the target a right of first refusal should the purchaser determine to sell the shares, and (iv) requires the purchaser to vote its stock as target management directs or, in some cases, in the same proportion as all shares are voted. In return, the purchaser is commonly given board representation and registration rights. See, e.g., Bartlett & Andrews, *The Standstill Agreement: Legal and Business Considerations Underlying a Corporate Peace Treaty,* 62 B.U.L.Rev. 143 (1982); Bailkin, *The Use of Standstill Agreements in Corporate Transactions,* in Thirteenth Annual Institute on Securities Regulation 91 (P.L.I.1981); Note, *The Standstill Agreement: A Case of Illegal Vote Selling and a Breach of Fiduciary Duty,* 93 Yale L.J. 1093 (1984).

Whether standstill agreements should be categorized as a defensive tactic depends in large measure on when the stock acquisition to which the standstill agreement relates is made and the purpose of the acquisition. At one extreme is a standstill agreement that accompanies a stock purchase by a party with whom the target expects to have important future dealings.[33] In this situation, the investment is not made in anticipation of an acquisition and the restrictions might be justified as an effort to prevent the target from inadvertently facilitating a later acquisition at a price lower than could have been negotiated in the absence of the pre-existing purchase. This use of a standstill agreement does not seem to operate as a defensive tactic.

At the other extreme, standstill agreements are also entered into *after* a purchaser has unilaterally acquired its shareholdings in the

[31] P.L. 98–369, 988 Stat. 494 (codified at IRC §§ 280, 4999).

[32] Problems associated with lock-ups and avoiding competing bids are considered in Chapter Fifteen A.

[33] Because of the difficulties involved in technology transfers, see Chapter Eleven A.2.c. supra, such purchases may be particularly useful when the future dealings contemplate such transfers.

target, and seem clearly designed to neutralize a party whom target management perceives might launch a hostile takeover. This use of standstill agreements does seem to operate as a defensive tactic since it serves to eliminate an important potential bidder for the target.[34]

—*Dividend Payments.* Where the target company believes that its liquid assets explain a large part of its attractiveness, dissipation of those assets by dividend payment may discourage suitors. Alternatively, increased dividends are sometimes thought to result in a higher stock price, thereby increasing the cost of acquisition. Note, however, that the second argument requires specifying the link between the dividend increase and the increase in stock price. If all that happens is the transfer of assets out of the target company in a one-time transaction, would not the stock price go *down* after the dividend? What would the market have to believe about the dividend to support a higher stock price?

—*The "Pac-Man" Defense.* In a number of recent hostile takeover battles, including Cities Service-Mesa Petroleum and Martin Marietta-Bendix, the target company resorted to a tactic playfully styled the "Pac-Man strategy" by participants. As described by a merger specialist at a major investment banking firm, "[t]hat's where my client eats yours before yours eats mine." [35] In the Martin Marietta-Bendix transaction, for example, Martin Marietta responded to Bendix's tender offer for all outstanding Martin Marietta stock by making a tender offer for all outstanding Bendix stock. Despite the public controversy surrounding the transaction and the dire predictions of what might happen if both offers were successful so that the ownership of the two parties became a loop—Bendix owned a majority of Martin Marietta which owned a majority of Bendix which owned a majority of Martin Marietta and so on—neither of the parties was willing to admit defeat and both offers went forward. The original Bendix offer drew over 70 percent of Martin Marietta's outstanding stock and the Martin Marietta counter offer drew 75 percent of Bendix's outstanding stock.[36]

This looped ownership raised a number of unusual issues of corporate law. For example:

[34] A broadly drafted confidentiality agreement, intended to protect the target company against the would-be acquiring company's later use of proprietary information of the target disclosed during friendly negotiations that failed, may serve the same function as a standstill agreement. In General Portland, Inc. v. LaFarge Coppee S.A., [1981 Transfer Binder] Fed.Sec.L.Rep. (CCH) ¶ 99,148 (N.D.Tex. 1981), the would-be acquirer agreed, as a condition to friendly negotiations, that it would not purchase target shares without consent so long as it was "in possession of confidential information." When the friendly negotiations failed and the acquirer threatened a hostile tender offer, the tender offer was enjoined on the ground that the acquirer was prohibited from acting by the confidentiality agreement "so long as information furnished by [the target] to [the acquirer] remains competitively sensitive and confidential."

[35] Metz & Inman, *Martin Marietta Spurns Bendix Offer as 'Inadequate,' Countering with $75–a–Share Bid for Control of Suitor,* Wall St.J., Aug. 31, 1982, p. 3, c. 1.

[36] The tangled histories of the Martin Marietta-Bendix battle and other transactions in which the Pac-Man technique was used are traced in Kramer, *Other Current Developments in Acquisition Techniques* in 1 *Fourteenth Annual Institute on Securities Regulation* 821 (PLI, 1982).

(1) Where a statute like Del. Gen. Corp. Act § 160(c) prohibits a corporation that owns a majority of the stock in another corporation from voting that stock, who then could exercise control over either Martin Marietta or Bendix?

(2) How should the rules governing the mechanics of noticing and holding shareholders meeting be applied when their application—which corporation's shareholders can meet first to remove the original directors—may determine the outcome of the battle?

(3) To whom do the directors of each corporation owe their fiduciary duty? If the answer is that the duty is owed to the majority shareholder, is another loop created? [37]

In the end, none of these issues were resolved in the Martin Marietta-Bendix transaction because the legal conflict was cut short by the acquisition of Bendix by Allied Corporation in a transaction in which Allied purchased all of Bendix's stock (paying for Martin Marietta's block with part of Bendix's block of Martin Marietta stock) and retained a 39 percent in Marietta stock subject to a standstill agreement. Thus, when the smoke cleared, the two participants in the reciprocal control battle ended up in a very different position from where they started. Rather than making an acquisition, Bendix was itself acquired. Martin Marietta remained independent, but with a new 39% shareholder and with a vast amount of new debt that was incurred to finance the original acquisition of Bendix stock.

Beyond the arcane legal issues, the economics of the conflicting tender offers pose an interesting situation from the perspective of the shareholders of Martin Marietta and Bendix. Although it was clear that the managements of the two companies viewed the offers as competing, considering the interests of the shareholders of both companies as a group suggests a different analysis. If we consider the two corporations as one, hardly unreasonable in light of the dual acquisition efforts, the entire transaction can be recharacterized as a massive recapitalization. The combined corporation simply borrowed substantial sums from banks (the financing secured by both companies in order to fund their respective tender offers) which was then used to repurchase at a substantial premium more than 70 percent of the combined company's outstanding shares (through the tender offers). The net result, then, was simply a large shift in the combined company's capital structure from equity to debt. What belief about the future income of the combined company would be necessary to justify paying a substantial premium for the privilege of substituting high interest debt financing for existing equity?

A final question about this most peculiar transaction concerns identification of the winners and the losers. The empirical results described in Chapter Eleven indicate that target shareholders gain substantially from acquisitions, but that acquiring company shareholders earn, at best, returns in the normal range. In the Martin Marietta-

[37] For a discussion of these issues, see DeMott, *Pac-Man Tender Offers*, 1983 Duke L.J. 116.

Bendix transaction, who would have been, in effect, the target company shareholders and who the acquiring company shareholders (assuming Allied never appeared)? If this phenomenon can be generalized by the statement that the losers will be the providers of capital to the surviving entity, who would have played that role in Martin Marietta-Bendix?

2. The Effectiveness of the Arsenal

a. Pre-Offer Planning

(1) Early Warning Systems

There is little question that some kinds of preparedness are helpful simply because the sooner one learns of an offer, the more time will be available to respond. There is, however, an increasingly widely held view that a "black book"—a specification of the steps to be taken in the event of a hostile offer, forms of letters to be sent to shareholders, draft press releases and advertisements—is not only ineffective, but affirmatively undesirable. In particular, the following two points are made: (i) that disclosure in litigation of a plan to oppose an offer even before one was made and without regard to its terms will create a "credibility gap" concerning management's intentions while the offer was in progress; (ii) and that the book will create a false sense of security. 1 M. Lipton & E. Steinberger, *Takeovers and Freezeouts* 263 (1978); A. Fleischer, supra at 2–3.

(2) Deterrence: Shark Repellent Amendments

GILSON, THE CASE AGAINST SHARK REPELLENT AMENDMENTS: STRUCTURAL LIMITATIONS ON THE ENABLING CONCEPT
34 Stan.L.Rev. 775, 792–804 (1982).*

Efficacy of the Deterrent

Despite the logic underlying the expectation that shark repellent amendments will deter potential offerors, and despite the chorus of voices urging their adoption, some prominent practitioners have asserted that such provisions do not fulfill their promise.[67] An examination of the three categories of amendments I have considered suggests that there is substantial basis for questioning the extent of their deterrence. While there are circumstances where shark repellent amendments will have some effect, it seems clear that their potential for deterrence has been substantially exaggerated.

1. *Impeding transfer of control of the board of directors*

The deterrent effect of an incumbency amendment is premised on the belief that immediate control of the target's board of directors is so

---

* Copyright 1982 by the Board of Trustees of the Leland Stanford Junior University.

[67] Indeed, Joseph Flom has characterized the approach as a "total waste of time."

Transcript, Tenth Annual Institute on Securities Regulation 443 (1978). And Martin Lipton has concluded that shark repellent amendments' "efficacy is open to debate."

important to the offeror that the prospect of substantial delay in achieving it will make a particular acquisition less attractive. Still, the extent of any deterrence ultimately depends on how effective the delaying mechanism is. Amendments seeking to delay transfer of board control necessarily assume that the incumbent directors will choose to remain in office and exercise the authority given them by the shark repellent amendments to control board size and name successor directors in a manner inconsistent with the desires of the successful offeror. This central assumption about the behavior of incumbent directors is open to serious question. It depends, in the final analysis, on the potential offeror believing that even after the offer is successful, members of the incumbent board will act in a fashion inconsistent with their own self-interest.

Consider the position of a target company's incumbent directors following a successful tender offer. A new majority shareholder now exists who wishes to control the target's board. The incumbent board will consist of some combination of owner-managers, professional managers, and, increasingly, independent directors. Analysis suggests that none of the incumbents in these three categories has an incentive to continue the defense by delaying the inevitable shift in board control. An independent director should certainly recognize the potential for time-consuming and expensive litigation brought by a successful offeror intent on securing board control. Free of the ties that may encumber other categories of directors, an independent director has no reason to fight a fall-back action in the face of both inevitable defeat and the ideology of majority rule.

Professional management would also have little reason to go down with the ship. Their behavior during and after a tender offer can be expected to have a significant impact both on the likelihood of continued employment with the target following a shift in control of the board and on employment prospects with other firms. While loyalty and a commitment to a tenacious takeover defense could make a manager an attractive employee to other potential targets, one must wonder whether this extends to activity occurring after the defense has failed. Moreover, professional managers remain in a position to sell their future services to the offeror, just as shareholders sell their shares, and thereby secure a portion of the benefits of the transaction. Because any payment for resignation from the board would be difficult if not impossible to distinguish from a legitimate payment for future services, the rational reaction by professional management would be surrender, albeit at a price.[75] In this sense, the potential for delay may

[75] It might be possible, however, in effect to prepay existing management to act in what would otherwise be an irrational manner. If, for example, target management were given employment contracts guaranteeing, in the event of a successful takeover, either their continued employment at a substantial salary or the right to quit and receive a substantial lump-sum payment, an offeror might have reason to believe that the fight would continue to the bitter end. The target would, of course, encounter a problem of moral hazard; at some point the lump-sum payment following takeover becomes more attractive than continued control. A classic example of this phenomenon is the recent award of what have been styled "golden parachutes." * * *

operate more as a means to allocate the pie between target management and target shareholders than as a way to discourage an offeror.

The only directors who might have an interest in holding out "to the last man" are owner-managers—substantial shareholders and often founders of the concern—who likely draw substantial nonmonetary benefits from their controlling positions in an independent concern, and who simply do not look forward to evaluation of the quality of their performance by a different owner. Even here, however, one must doubt the wisdom and, hence, the likelihood of recourse to the mechanisms provided by incumbency amendments. While there is an incentive to successfully defend the target's independence, there is no reason to continue the fight—to the individual's financial disadvantage—when it has already been lost. Thus, while a target bristling with hostility before the offer may deter even if the individual quills are not alarming,[76] once the offer succeeds one would expect rational owners to secure whatever compensation they can for their cooperation.[77]

In sum, the logic underlying the asserted deterrent effect of charter amendments designed to impede transfer of control of the board of directors is substantially flawed because it is based on the expectation that incumbent directors will act irrationally.

2. Barriers to second-step transactions

Effectiveness in preventing freezeout mergers. Because its effectiveness does not depend on the behavior of individuals whose self-interest is inconsistent with the desired result, an amendment preventing second-step transactions has more promise as a deterrent than one directed at maintaining the incumbent board of directors. If a supermajority requirement for a second-step transaction is waivable only by "continuing directors"—effectively the preoffer board—the resignation or replacement of the incumbent board will not render the amendment ineffective. In that event the supermajority requirement may not be waivable at all.

Because the goal of an offeror to whom a second-step transaction is important is, by definition, to acquire all of the target's stock, the initial impact of a supermajority amendment—to cause the offeror to increase the number of shares sought by tender to an amount in excess of the supermajority required—is not itself a serious burden. The potential for deterrence arises, however, from the possible increase in the total cost of the transaction even if the offeror had intended to pay the same price in the second-step transaction. If the supply curve for the target's stock is upward-sloping, the need to acquire a greater number of shares will result in an increased price not only for the marginal shares acquired due to the supermajority requirement, but, because the Williams Act requires the same price to be paid for all shares tendered,[80] for the original shares as well.[81]

---

[76] The information content, in contrast to the operative effect, of shark repellent amendments is considered in notes 100–09 infra and accompanying text.

[77] The common phenomenon of target management turning to a white knight fol-

lowing an initial offer, and the fact that a company that is a raider in one transaction may be a white knight in the next, suggest the accuracy of this prediction.

[80] See Securities Act Release No. 6159, Securities Exchange Act Release No.

The alteration in offeror strategy required by a supermajority provision may also increase the cost of the total transaction through its impact on the type of consideration used and the amount of financing necessary for the complete acquisition of the target. It is not uncommon for an offeror to make an initial cash tender offer for a bare majority of the target's outstanding shares, expecting that its securities will be the consideration in the second-step transaction. This approach reduces the cash cost of the acquisition to the offeror and benefits the target shareholders by providing them the option of a tax-free exchange. Increasing the number of shares that must be acquired in the initial offer to satisfy the supermajority requirement raises the cash cost of the acquisition and, necessarily, the cost of the financing necessary to complete it. It may also reduce the opportunity to offer target shareholders the choice between a taxable and tax-free exchange, a benefit which presumably must be replaced if the transaction is to remain equally attractive to shareholders.

The deterrent potential of supermajority amendments obviously increases where target management itself owns or controls enough shares to block the supermajority vote even if the offeror tenders for all the outstanding shares. However, as with the efficacy of shark repellent amendments protecting the incumbent board of directors, the deterrent effect of management power to block a second-step transaction depends not only on the existence of the power, but also on the offeror's evaluation of management's will to use it in the face of a successful tender offer for a controlling, but not supermajority, interest. From this perspective, it must be kept in mind that target management pays a substantial price by exercising its power to block the second-step transaction. While such an action prevents the offeror from securing the potential benefits from eliminating minority shareholders, members of management will then remain minority shareholders with sharply reduced opportunities to liquidate their investment. Thus, the deterrent effect of the provision again depends, in part, on the offeror's willingness to believe that management will act in a financially irrational manner. Indeed, if one assumes that management's investment in the shares used to block the supermajority vote represents a significant portion of each manager's assets—a not unreasonable assumption with respect to professional management—the behavior necessary for the provision to operate as an effective deterrent is even more irrational than for incumbency amendments.

16,385 * * * (interpreting Exchange Act § 14(d)(7), 15 U.S.C. § 78n(d)(7) (1976), to require the same price be paid for all shares).

[81] The notion of an upward-sloping supply curve for the target's stock is not inconsistent with existing empirical evidence suggesting that because shares of stock represent only a right to a future income stream with a particular risk-return relationship, as to which a multitude of substitutes exist, more or less of a security can be purchased without a resulting change in price. Scholes, *The Market for Securities: Substitution versus Price Pressure and the Effects of Information on Share Prices*, 45 J.Bus. 179 (1972). Professor Scholes points out that particular purchases or sales may reflect new information concerning the issuer which warrants alteration in the price of its shares relative to substitutes. A tender offer may be the most extreme example since the offer to purchase reflects information that, for at least one buyer, there are no substitutes for the security, thus allowing a much greater role for price as opposed to substitution effects.

Importance of second-step transactions. Evaluation of the deterrence created by supermajority requirements thus far has assumed that the availability of second-step transactions is critical to the offeror. To the extent this assumption overstates the importance of these transactions to the offeror, the potential deterrence of even a perfectly effective amendment [85] is reduced. In fact, on examination the reasons commonly offered for the desirability of a second-step transaction, although real, hardly seem compelling. The constraints on a parent's discretion in allocating synergistic benefits between itself and its subsidiary with public shareholders do not appear to be substantial. The administrative costs associated with public shareholders, while nontrivial, are hardly large enough to affect a transaction of significant size. Finally, the available empirical evidence strongly suggests that the offeror's return comes from the right "to control * * * the target's resources," [89] not from a postoffer increase in the value of the target's shares. This, of course, would counsel against a second-step transaction, because once the offeror achieves control, its rate of return on the investment may well *decrease* with the purchase of additional shares.

Nonetheless, from a different perspective of the tender offer process, the ability to effect a second-step transaction may retain its importance. That an offer is made reflects the offeror's view that after completion of the transaction the value of the shares acquired will exceed the price to be paid. A rational shareholder might then decide not to tender, but to "free-ride" on the offer. Thus, one might argue that the ability to freeze out these free-riders at a price not reflecting the offeror's anticipated profits is crucial to the offer's success. [92]

But a second-step transaction is not the only way to prevent target shareholders from free-riding on the offeror's profits. Whether an offeror's anticipated profit results from synergy or the displacement of inefficient management, current case law presents little barrier to the

---

[85] One can imagine a form of shark repellent that could be effective at blocking a second-step transaction. A very high vote requirement together with a requirement for approval by a majority of nontendering shareholders, * * * and with no exceptions other than approval by the target board prior to the offeror's acquisition of a significant percentage of target shares * * * might make a second-step transaction impossible even if target management conceded after the success of the initial offer.

[89] Jarrell & Bradley, *The Economic Effects of Federal and State Regulations of Cash Tender Offers*, 23 J.L. & Econ. 371, 381–82 (1980).

[92] Grossman & Hart, *Takeover Bids, the Free-Rider Problem, and the Theory of the Corporation*, 11 Bell J.Econ. 42 (1980) argue that no takeover will occur unless the value of the shares after the offer exceeds the price paid by the offeror plus transaction costs. But this excess

represents a profit shareholders could have made if they had not tendered their shares to the raider. In particular, suppose each shareholder is so small that his tender decision will not affect the outcome of the raid. Then, if a shareholder thinks that the raid will succeed and that the raider will improve the firm, he will not tender his shares, but will instead retain them, because he anticipates a profit from their price appreciation.

Id. at 43. The authors argue that no takeovers will succeed in the absence of mechanisms to discourage free-riders. The ability to eliminate minority shareholders at a price that does not reflect the inceased value resulting from the transaction is the most obvious means to do this. Grossman and Hart argue that the incentive to make a tender offer at a premium is reduced if the ability to freeze out minority shareholders at an unfavorable price is constrained. Id. at 44–47.

offeror's retaining a disproportionate amount of the profit.[93] Anticipation of such behavior by the offeror should dissuade target shareholders from free-riding in expectation of an increase in the price of their shares following a successful tender. Empirical investigation is consistent with this analysis, suggesting that the market price of a target's stock following a successful offer drops below the offer price,[94] and that the offeror's gain results from an increase in the value of its own stock, an increase in which the minority cannot share by free-riding.

In sum, shark repellent amendments creating a barrier to second-step transactions have more promise as a deterrent than incumbency amendments. The significance of this barrier is attenuated by the reality facing target management when an offeror secures majority, but not supermajority, control, and by doubts about the overall importance of the second-step transaction to the offeror. Still, to the extent that a second-step transaction is desirable, these provisions retain the potential, because of Williams Act requirements, for disproportionately increasing the cost of the offer by increasing the number of shares an offeror must acquire to accomplish it.

3. *Fair price and compulsory redemption provisions*

Fair price amendments act as a backstop to supermajority barriers to second-step transactions. Although they can help the overall package of amendments to appear more balanced by providing a means to avoid the supermajority requirement, the formulas contained in these amendments may increase the price required to be paid in the second-step transaction, perhaps to a level above the initial tender price, so that the option is illusory. Because fair price amendments focus only on second-step transactions, their effectiveness as a deterrent, like that of supermajority requirements generally, depends on the belief that target management will choose to enforce the requirements, on the size of the resulting increase in total acquisition cost, and ultimately on the overall importance of a second-step transaction to the offeror.

Right of redemption provisions, in contrast, promise greater deterrence than either supermajority or fair price amendments. Like fair price amendments, right of redemption provisions make the entire acquisition more expensive by increasing the price of the second-step

[93] The opportunities for a parent company to favor itself at the expense of the subsidiary are legion, and "[t]he checks on unfair dealing by the parent are few. In theory, of course, the fairness of the parent's behavior is subject to the check of judicial review; but in practice such review is difficult even where the courts have the will to engage in it, and they often lack the will." M. Eisenberg, *The Structure of the Corporation* 309 (citations omitted); see Brudney, *Efficient Markets and Fair Values in Parent Subsidiary Mergers,* 4 J.Corp.L. 63, 69–71 (1978).

[94] The data concerning the size of the premium paid in a tender offer, and the extent of the postoffer increase in the price of the target's stock, are consistent with

the offeror according itself, presumably through inter-company transactions and charges, a disproportionate share of the benefits resulting from the acquisition. If the offeror gained only through the increased value of the target's stock following the acquisition, the postoffer value of target stock would have to exceed the price paid by the offeror. Minority shareholders would then share equally with the offeror in the gains resulting from the transaction. In fact, postoffer prices average some 13% below the tender price, Bradley, *Interfirm Tender Offers and the Market for Corporate Control,* 53 J.Bus. 345, 364 (1980), strongly suggesting that offerors gain from the acquisition in ways which exclude the participation of minority shareholders.

transaction. But they go a step further by removing the offeror's alternative of *not* proceeding with a second-step transaction if its cost appears too great or its benefits too small. Right of redemption provisions thereby institutionalize the free-rider problem that I argued was not significant with respect to second-step transactions alone. If shareholders understand that a successful tender offer will give them the *right* to demand a higher price for their shares—a fact target management might be expected to disseminate with enthusiasm—there is no avoiding the incentive to hold out in the hope that other shareholders will tender and the offer will succeed.[98]

Thus, of the categories of share repellent amendments, right of redemption provisions, the type least frequently adopted, present the greatest potential for deterring an offeror.

4. *Shark repellent amendments as "corporate signals"*

I have demonstrated that the direct deterrent effect of the most common shark repellent amendments has been greatly exaggerated. But even where shark repellent amendments are not effective on their own terms, there is an argument that they may nonetheless serve to steer offerors away. The idea is that their deterrence derives not from the actual effect of the amendments, but from what the amendments suggest about the target's future actions. This view of shark repellent amendments is based upon developments in "signaling theory," which posits that the information value of certain corporate behavior is not in the action taken, but in what that action "signals" about attributes of the corporation not otherwise discernible at that time.[100] Thus, for example, it is argued that investors may respond favorably to a more highly leveraged financial structure, despite the accepted theory that firm value is determined by the present value of future income streams regardless of the firm's debt-equity ratio, if investors perceive that increased leverage reflects that management has favorable nonpublic information about the firm's future.

---

[98] The classic example is that of a closed-end, mutual fund. Although the only assets held by the fund are the securities of other companies, so that net asset value and liquidation value are virtually identical, the securities of many of them, for significant periods of time, have traded at a price below net asset value. See generally Boudreaux, *Discounts and Premiums on Close-End Mutual Funds: A Study in Valuation*, 28 J.Fin. 515 (1973); Malkiel, *The Valuation of Closed-End Investment-Company Shares*, 32 J.Fin. 847 (1977); Mendelson, *Closed-End Fund Discounts Revisited*, 2 Fin. Rev. 48 (1978). Thus, one acquiring control of the fund at market price and liquidating it would profit by the amount of the pre-existing discount from net asset value. But a shareholder who believed that the offer would be successful would refuse to sell for a premium less than the full discount since, on liquidation, the shareholder would receive the full benefit.

[100] For the application of signaling theory in a variety of contexts, see e.g., A. Spence, Market Signaling: Informational Transfer in Hiring and Related Screening Processes (1974); Akerlof, *The Market for "Lemons": Quality Uncertainty and the Market Mechanism*, 84 Q.J.Econ. 438 (1970); Gonedes, *Corporate Signaling, External Accounting, and Capital Market Equilibrium: Evidence on Dividends, Income, and Extraordinary Items*, 16 J. Acct. Research 26 (1978); Grossman & Hart, *Disclosure Laws and Takeover Bids*, 35 J. Fin. 323 (1980); Ross, *Disclosure Regulation in Financial Markets: Implications of Modern Finance Theory and Signaling Theory*, in Issues in Financial Regulation 177 (F. Edwards ed. 1979); Ross, *The Determination of Financial Structure: The Incentive Signalling Approach*, 8 Bell J. Econ. 23 (1977) [hereinafter cited as Ross, *Determination of Financial Structure*].

* * *

In the context of defensive tactics, the signaling argument is that even though everyone knows that shark repellent amendments will not themselves deter an otherwise interested offeror, they do represent a way in which management can communicate to the universe of potential offerors before an offer is made, and therefore at a time when the communication can still affect the potential offeror's behavior. The message is simply that the company intends to defend itself vigorously against any offer. While the shark repellent amendments themselves may not be effective, their adoption tells the potential offeror that other action, which cannot be taken until an offer is made—such as a scorched earth defense—will be undertaken.

This application of signaling theory is questionable. For a signal to be effective—to "reflect information about the unobservable attributes of firms' decisions" [104] —it must be clear what attribute is being disclosed. No clear message appears to be sent by adoption of shark repellent amendments. While some commentators state that shark repellent amendments have an *"in terrorem* effect: * * * a signal to a would-be raider that it might better look elsewhere if it wishes to avoid a spirited struggle," others suggest that their adoption is a sign of weakness, and testify to a "growing feeling that * * * these charter provisions are counter-productive in that they call attention to the company as a prospective target." A further conditon to a signal's effectiveness is that it must "facilitate distinguishing between firms whose decisions have different unobservable characteristics." [107] The difficulty with shark repellent amendments is their popularity; as more and more firms adopt them, they no longer distinguish between firms that will react passively and those that will react aggressively, and so the value of the signal diminishes.

* * *

◆

Note: Empirical Results

Two recent studies have attempted to empirically determine the deterrent effect of shark repellent amendments using the cumulative abnormal returns methodology considered in Chapter Six. DeAngelo & Rice, *Antitakeover Charter Amendments and Stockholder Wealth*, 11 J.Fin.Econ. 329 (1983), and Linn & McConnell, *An Empirical Investigation of the Impact of 'Antitakeover' Amendments on Common Stock Prices*, 11 J.Fin.Econ. 361 (1983), examined samples of companies that had adopted shark repellent amendments to test competing explanations for why the amendments were proposed. One explanation—the managerial entrenchment hypothesis—posits that shark repellent amendments are efforts by management to protect their positions. Because this is achieved by reducing the likelihood of future tender offers at a premium, and because managers are thereby shielded from the discipline of the capital market on their performance, their increased security comes at the expense of shareholders. If this hypothe-

[104] Gonedes, supra note 100, at 27. [107] Gonedes, supra note 100, at 30.

sis is correct, one would expect *negative* CARs as a result of the amendments because they serve to reduce the expected value of the company. The alternative explanation—the stockholder interests hypothesis—claims that shark repellent amendments benefit shareholders because they facilitate effective bargaining by target management with the acquiring company over the division of synergistic gains and do little to reduce overall market discipline on managerial performance because the operation of the managerial labor market provides sufficient discipline itself. If this hypothesis is correct, one would expect *positive* CARs as a result of the amendments because the resulting increase in expected premium would outweigh any decrease in the likelihood of future offers.

The empirical results reported by the two studies differ somewhat. DeAngelo & Rice found small, but statistically insignificant, negative abnormal returns associated with shark repellent amendments. Nonetheless, the authors tentatively, and somewhat reluctantly, treat the data as supportive of the managerial entrenchment hypothesis: "If forced to choose between the managerial entrenchment and stockholder interest hypothesis, we conclude that the preponderance of observed negative returns at the time of amendment proposal can be viewed as weak preliminary support for the managerial entrenchment hypothesis." Id. at 40. Linn & McConnell, in contrast, reach a different, albeit also tentative, conclusion. Like DeAngelo & Rice, they found that the CAR for their sample was not significantly different from zero around the *date* (i) when the companies' boards of directors approved the shark repellent amendments, (ii) when the proxy statements concerning the amendments were mailed to shareholders, and (iii) of the stockholder meetings concerning the amendments. Looking at the *periods* between the proxy mailing date and the shareholders' meeting date, and over the 90 days following the shareholders' meeting, however, they found small but statistically significant, positive abnormal returns. On this basis Linn & McConnell concluded that: "Although the results are not unambiguous, the overall impression yielded by the analysis is that the introduction and adoption of antitakeover amendments is associated with an increase in common stock prices * * *. From the perspective of individual firms, the implication is that antitakeover amendments are proposed by managers who seek to enhance shareholder wealth * * *."[38]

One important problem in evaluating these results should be noted. What if the proposal of shark repellant amendments also transmits to the market private information previously held only by company management? From this perspective, management's proposal of shark repellent amendments signals that management believes that there is a significant risk of a hostile tender offer. If this causes the market to increase its assessment of the likelihood of a premium tender offer, then the result would be a positive CAR. This possibility may make the empirical results reported by both articles not somewhat, but entirely ambiguous: Any abnormal return reported can be explained by

[38] Linn & McConnell, supra at 397.

a number of different combinations of the signalling effect and either the managerial entrenchment hypothesis or the stockholder interests hypothesis.[39]

Even if the data reported are taken at face value, the predominant result—no abnormal returns—seems more consistent with the no-effects hypothesis offered by Gilson in the previous excerpt: that because shark repellent amendments are unlikely to be effective, their proposal and adoption should not result in positive or negative abnormal returns. This, in fact, is the predominant empirical result reported.[40] But although both studies recognize that the data support such a hypothesis, it is dismissed without discussion.[41]

What may account for this dismissal is the fact that, at least on first consideration, the no-effects hypothesis seems to posit irrationality: Why would anyone adopt amendments that will have no effect? If, however, there is an explanation of why the two groups who must act in order to adopt shark repellent amendments—target management who must propose them, and target shareholders who must approve them—rationally might do so even though little can be expected to result from their adoption, the no-effects hypothesis may be the most persuasive account of the empirical results.

Gilson explicitly discusses the question of why rational shareholders might approve shark repellent amendments in the excerpt. He argues that approving shark repellent amendments is the rational response by shareholders precisely *because* they are ineffective. Gilson, supra, at 822–27. Why bother to oppose management's proposal of the amendments when they will make so little difference? The more interesting question, however, is why target management proposes antitakeover amendments given that they also must know the amendments are likely to be ineffective. And the problem becomes even more

[39] For example, a positive abnormal return might reflect the combination of a negative abnormal return resulting from the adoption of the shark repellent amendment (the managerial entrenchment hypothesis) that is more than outweighed by a positive signalling effect.

[40] Of course, the possibility that shark repellant amendments may have a signalling effect confounds this interpretation of the empirical results as well.

A recent study by the Office of the Chief Economist of the Securities and Exchange Commission of the effects of shark repellant amendments, *Shark Repellants and Stock Prices: The Effects of Antitakeover Amendments Since 1980* (July 24, 1985), lends further empirical support to the no-effects hypothesis. The study examined 649 antitakeover amendments adopted between January, 1979, and May, 1985, broken down in a variety of ways, including by type—487 firms proposed fair price amendments, 104 proposed supermajority amendments, and 58 firms proposed classified board amendments or authorized blank preferred. No statistically significant abnormal returns were found except for firms adopting supermajority amendments that allowed the target board of directors to waive the supermajority requirement. This group of firms experienced statistically significant *negative* abnormal returns of 4.86 percent. Interestingly, the firms in this group had large blocks of stock, averaging 19.2 percent but as high as 23.8 percent for non-exchange listed firms, held by insiders. Because most supermajority amendments specify 80 percent as the necessary supermajority, id. at 31, the combination of the amendment and the size of the insiders' holdings gave the insiders an absolute veto over a second-step transaction. Gilson identified this situation as one where the potential deterrent effect of supermajority amendments is likely to be greatest if a second-step transaction is important to the acquirer. This issue is explored in Chapter Fifteen B. infra.

[41] DeAngelo & Rice, supra at 355; Linn & McConnell, supra at 396.

intriguing when viewed in the agency perspective of the managerial entrenchment hypothesis: Can the proposal of ineffective charter amendments be explained consistently with an agency model which posits that management acts to further its own self-interest?

One explanation comes from understanding the incentives facing both target management and the professionals who have been retained to assist management—the lawyers and the investment bankers—at a time when target management fears a takeover. It is hardly surprising that the lawyers and investment bankers propose adoption of antitakeover amendments, and the literature of both professions is replete with their advocates. The professionals have been hired for the explicit purpose of providing protection to management. At a time when the value of their services is difficult to evaluate, at least the *appearance* of activity may be critical from the professional's perspective even if only as a signal from the professional to management that the defensive effort has begun.

Although this explains why professional advisers recommend the adoption of antitakeover amendments, the question of why target management goes to the expense of causing their adoption still remains. Here it is helpful to consider the incentives facing target management at the time their advisers recommend that the amendments be proposed. It is apparent that management perceives its company as a potential takeover candidate; indeed, a control contest was a matter of public record in some 40% of the DeAngelo & Rice sample.[42] In that setting, it is hardly surprising that management feels the need to do something and, given that professional advisers recommend antitakeover amendments, what, after all, is their cost? From the managers' perspective, the amendments' adoption is essentially costless because the expenses are paid by the company. As a result, even if there is only a very small chance that the antitakeover amendments will be effective—a probability sufficiently low that its potential would not appear through the cumulative abnormal returns technique—it would still pay rational managers to cause their adoption. Whatever gain there is goes to the managers; whatever cost is borne by the shareholders.

In short, the no effect hypothesis is both consistent with analysis of the incentives of all parties to the adoption process and it is far more consistent with the empirical data than either of the two competing hypotheses.

(3) Deterrence: "Poison Pill" Preferred Stock

Because of the recent origin of the "poison pill" preferred stock concept, there is little systematic empirical evidence bearing on its effectiveness. As noted earlier, however, the poison pill concept is quite similar to that of fair price and right of redemption shark repellant amendments. The question, then, is to what extent the

---

[42] DeAngelo & Rice, supra, at 346–47.

empirical results reported with respect to the ineffectiveness of shark repellant amendments extend to poison pill preferred stock.

Caution is in order before making this extension. Recall that the Gilson excerpt acknowledges that right of redemption shark repellant amendments "present the greatest potential for deterring an offerer." Moreover, the empirical evidence we have considered is not inconsistent with that conclusion. Gilson notes that right of redemption amendments are "the newest and, so far, least popular variety of shark repellant amendment." As a result, the DeAngelo & Rice sample apparently included no instance where a right of redemption provision was adopted [43] and less than 2.4 percent of the Linn & McConnell sample involved right of redemption provisions.[44] The upshot is that the results of the two studies may drastically understate the effectiveness of right of redemption amendments and, by implication, the effectiveness of the poison pill preferred stock concept.

The only abnormal return study of poison pill defenses to date is consistent with this analysis. Malatesta and Walking, *The Impact of "Poison Pill" Securities on Stockholder Wealth* (Working Paper, 1985), calculated the abnormal returns surrounding the date on which the Wall Street Journal reported the adoption of a poison pill defense by all firms (a total of 14) which did so between December, 1982, and February, 1985. They found statistically significant negative abnormal returns of 1.861 percent. The authors also attempted to control for the problem of a confounding information effect of the announcement—i.e., the very adoption of the defensive tactic may reveal management's private information about an increased likelihood of a tender offer that offsets the effect of the defensive tactic—that was discussed in the preceding Section in connection with shark repellant amendments. First, the two firms that announced poison pill defenses simultaneously with the announcement of a tender offer for their stock were excluded from the sample. This caused the negative abnormal returns to increase to 2.752 percent. Second, a subsample of seven firms which either already were the subject of tender offers at the time of the poison pill announcement, or had recently been the subject of a tender offer, was created. The logic underlying the subsample is that for these seven firms the likelihood of a tender offer was a certainty (or virtually so) with the result that the confounding information effect of the poison pill announcement is eliminated. For this subsample, the negative abnormal returns increased to 3.357 percent.

There is, however, already evidence that poor planning can make the technique ineffective. In response to takeover efforts by Sir James Goldsmith, Crown Zellerbach Corp. adopted a poison pill defense that, when an acquirer's holdings reached 20 percent, gave all shareholders the right to buy $200 of stock in the surviving company for $100 if Crown Zellerbach were merged or liquidated. The poison pill had no

---

[43] DeAngelo & Rice, supra, at 348 (Table 3).

[44] Linn & McConnell, supra, at 374 (Table 4). In fact, the actual percentage may be substantially smaller than 2.4 percent because that figure includes the more popular fair price amendments as well as right of redemption amendments. Linn & McConnell treat the two as a single category for purposes of empirical analysis.

effect, however, if the acquirer did not eliminate minority shareholders. Apparently content to freeze minority shareholders in, rather than freeze them out,[45] Goldsmith called Crown Zellerbach's bluff. He first triggered the poison pill by acquiring more than 20 percent, thereby, according to a leading takeover lawyer, making the company "almost unmarketable to other potential bidders." [46] Goldsmith then increased his holdings to a majority and Zellerbach management capitulated.[47]

(4) The Marshall Field & Company Approach

The deterrent technique used by Marshall Field was to make the company a less likely takeover candidate by making acquisitions which posed antitrust problems for the most likely suitors. Even assuming the acquisitions themselves offer competitive returns, what would be the impact on the company's stock as a result of the decreased likelihood of a takeover? The problem is exacerbated if the acquisitions offer less than a competitive return, a fact asserted with respect to the acquisitions actually made by Marshall Field. See *Marshall Field's Too Successful Strategy,* Fortune 82 (March 22, 1982).

This suggests that some defensive tactics have the capacity to backfire If a defensive acquisition makes the target *generally* less attractive, that should be reflected in a lower price for the company's stock. This decrease, in turn, may have the ironic effect of making the target a *more* desirable takeover candidate, especially if the defensive acquisition can be divested and the damage mitigated. Two recent situations illustrate this phenomenon.

Following the sale of its Peabody Coal Company subsidiary because of a Federal Trade Commission order, Kennecott Copper Company found itself with some $800 million in cash and $400 million in 30 year notes—an amount of liquid assets which was thought to make it an attractive target. The next year, in an acquisition widely believed to be defensive, Kennecott paid $567 million in cash to acquire the Carborundum Company. Thereafter, Curtiss-Wright Corp. accumulated Kennecott stock and waged an unsuccessful proxy fight for control of Kennecott on the platform that Carborundum should be sold and the proceeds distributed to the shareholders.[48] To forestall another proxy contest, Kennecott announced a tender offer for Curtiss-Wright which responded by tendering for its own shares.[49] The complicated settlement eventually reached involved some $280 million [50] and the final chapter in the story was the announcement, some months later, that Kennecott

---

[45] The freeze-in alternative is discussed in Chapter Fifteen B.6., infra.

[46] *"Goldsmith's Move on Crown Zellerbach Prompts 'Poison Pill' Potency Questions,"* Wall St. J., May 16, 1985, p. 7, col. 1.

[47] *"Goldsmith Wins Fight for Crown Zellerbach Corp.,"* Wall St. J., July 26, 1985, p. 3, col. 1.

[48] Kennecott Copper Corp. v. Curtiss-Wright Corp., 584 F.2d 1195 (2d Cir.1978)

(detailing the history of the control contest).

[49] See *Kennecott's Battle with Curtiss-Wright Involves Ambitions, Strategies and Money,* Wall St. J., Jan. 5, 1980, at 6, col. 3.

[50] *Kennecott and Curtiss-Wright End Corporate Battle by Agreeing to a 10-Year Truce Involving $289 Million,* Wall St. J., Jan. 29, 1981, at 3, col. 1.

was to be acquired by Standard Oil Co. (Sohio) in a transaction reportedly motivated by the damage to Kennecott from the long conflict that began with the Carborundum acquisition.[51]

The second situation which illustrates the potential for defensive acquisitions to backfire involves Marshall Field itself. The technique successfully defeated Carter Hawley Hale's $42 per share tender offer when Field's stock was trading at approximately $30 per share immediately prior to the offer. The defensive acquisitions proved unsuccessful in business terms, *Marshall Field's Too Successful Strategy,* supra, and the market price had dropped to as low as $15 per share when Carl Icahn began purchasing Field's stock. By the time Icahn's position became public, Field's management had began looking for a White Knight, and ultimately approved an offer by Batus at $30 per share.

b. *After the Offer*

Note: What Makes a Defensive Tactic Effective

Despite the widespread publicity associated with successful defenses against hostile takeover attempts—witness the extensive newspaper coverage of Mead Corp.'s victory over Occidental Petroleum, McGraw-Hill's defeat of American Express, or Martin Marietta's deflection of Bendix—the overall record compiled by target companies is hardly cause for optimism in the board room of a potential target. Available statistics indicate that only a minority of target companies remain independent following a tender offer. A study of 69 tender offers made between 1976 and 1979 found that only 13 targets (19%) were able to maintain their independence.[52] Data covering the period from 1956 through June 30, 1979, show a post-offer independence rate of only 20%.[53] Thus, at least at the outset, the puzzle is less how to select among the vast number of tactics that have been recommended by the commentators,[54] than how to understand what makes a tactic

---

[51] *Kennecott Holders Approve Takeover of Firm by Sohio,* Wall St. J., May 6, 1981, at 20, col. 4.

[52] Fleischer, *Business Judgment Rule Protects Takeover Targets,* Legal Times Wash., Apr. 14, 1980, at 15, col. 1 (reporting a Goldman Sachs study).

[53] Austin, *Tender Offer Update; 1978–1979,* Mergers & Acquisitions, Summer 1980, at 13, 16 (table 4).

[54] An enormous literature has grown up concerning defensive tactics, largely produced by practitioners; indeed, the three leading treatises in the field are all the work of lawyers practicing in New York City. See E. Aranow & H. Einhorn, *Tender Offers for Corporate Control* (1973); E. Aranow, H. Einhorn & G. Berlstein, *Developments in Tender Offers for Corporate Control* (1978); A. Fleischer, *Tender Offers: Defenses, Responses, and Planning* (1983); M. Lipton & E. Steinberger, *Takeovers and Freezeouts* (1978).

The extensive practitioner literature in this field, as well as that in corporate tax, poses an interesting puzzle in itself: Why are practicing lawyers so willing, in effect, to give away their human capital by writing articles and books that can be purchased by their competitors? The practice may be best explained as an effective way to advertise the authors' professional services in a market where the consumers of their services—largely corporations with their own legal departments, or practicing lawyers who refer this type of work to specialists—are quite sophisticated and use such publications as an important source of information bearing on their choice of counsel. If this is correct, we would expect that the frequency of publication by practitioners in a field would be a function of the sophistication of the purchasers of their services. Tax and acquisitions lawyers, for example, would write; divorce and personal injury lawyers, in general, would not. For a development of this approach to un-effective. Because there seem to be so few successful defenses, the best search strategy is first to identify what attributes are necessary to make a defensive tactic effective. Armed with that knowledge, we can then try to choose from among the many weapons in the arsenal one that is loaded with something other than blanks.

Approaching the problem from this perspective necessitates shifting our attention from the target company's choice of tactics to the acquiring company's decision to proceed with the offer. An effective defensive tactic is, by definition, one that persuades the acquirer to change its mind. The key, then, is to somehow change the balance of factors bearing on the acquiring company's decision from one favoring proceeding with the transaction to one favoring retreat. And this, in turn, requires understanding why the offer was made in the first place.

We canvassed a variety of potential motivations for an acquisition in Part II [55]; however, for present purposes a much more general formulation will suffice. Consider the following: A tender offer is made when the value to the acquiring company of the shares acquired exceeds the price paid plus transaction costs. Put in terms of a formula, a necessary condition for a hostile offer is that $V > P + TC$, where V = post transaction value to the acquiring company, P = price paid, and TC = transaction cost.[56] The benefit of this approach is clearly not its ability to predict when takeover bids will be made. Part II demonstrated the complexity of that subject and, in any event, the formula offers no explanation for *why* post-transaction value may be greater than the cost of the acquisition. Rather, its benefit is to provide a systematic way of thinking about what might make a defensive tactic effective. Unless the tactic in question can change the value of one of the components of the formula in the appropriate direction— reduce V, or increase P or TC—it should have no effect on the acquiring company's decision to proceed with the offer.

This approach to devising effective defensive tactics can best be understood by examining each component of the formula and the types of defensive tactics each suggests.

Post-transaction Value. What kinds of defensive tactics have the potential for decreasing the post-transaction value of the target company to the acquiring company? Suppose the target knew that the acquiring company was relying upon a particular opportunity for synergy in its forecast of post-transaction value. If the target could demonstrate that the acquiring company would not be able to capitalize on that opportunity after the transaction, the acquiring company's forecast of post-transaction value would decrease. If the decrease was sufficient to entirely eliminate the inequality necessary to induce the

derstanding the sometimes subtle methods of competition in the market for legal services, see Gilson & Mnookin, supra at 364 n. 88.

[55] Chapters Eight through Twelve, supra.

[56] This is the condition commonly considered necessary to induce a takeover bid. See, e.g., Grossman & Hart, *Takeover Bids,*

the Free-Rider Problem, and the Theory of the Corporation, 11 Bell J. Econ. 42 (1980); Kummer & Hoffmeister, *Valuation Consequences of Cash Tender Offers,* 33 J.Fin. 505 (1978); Smiley, *Tender Offers, Transactions Costs and the Theory of the Firm,* 58 Rev. Econ. & Statistics 22 (1976).

acquiring company to proceed with the transaction, the defensive tactic should then be successful.

A rather extreme defensive strategy of this sort was successfully used by Brunswick Corporation in fending off an unwanted takeover by Whittaker Corporation. Determining that the principle motivation for the Whittaker offer was to acquire Brunswick's Sherwood Medical Industries subsidiary, Brunswick simply sold Sherwood to another company. See Whittaker Corp. v. Edgar, 535 F.Supp. 933 (N.D.Ill.), affirmed mem. (7th Cir.1982). Although the tactic was successful, it was not without cost to Brunswick. In the Brunswick Annual Report to Shareholders for the year immediately preceding that in which the Whittaker offer occurred, the Chairman of Brunswick's Board of Directors described the company's business plan as using its recreational business "as a source of cash flow to fund the growth of our medical [Sherwood Medical Industries] and technical operations." Thus, in order to remain independent, Brunswick was forced to sell, in terms of Chapter Eleven's product/market portfolio analysis, its "star." [57]

A less extreme version of this approach is usually credited to McGraw-Hill, and was described in the "scorched earth" excerpt earlier in this Chapter. There the idea was that McGraw-Hill was unusually dependent on its employees for profitability. In the publishing business, one commentator remarked, the assets go home very night at 5:00 P.M. Apparently with this in mind, McGraw-Hill unleashed a public relations campaign intended to demonstrate that American Express was unfit to operate the McGraw-Hill business by claiming that editorial responsibility would be eliminated, and that the integrity of McGraw-Hill publications would be compromised for the benefit of American Express.[58] The target of the campaign was less McGraw-Hill shareholders than McGraw-Hill employees, and its object was to persuade American Express that, if it persisted with the offer, the number of employees who would quit as a result would substantially reduce McGraw-Hill's post-transaction value.

In evaluating tactics intended to reduce the target's post-transaction value, a particular difficulty, bordering on a paradox, must be kept in mind. In order for the tactic really to be effective, the reduction in post-transaction value must be permanent. The acquiring company would have no reason to adjust downward the post-transaction value component of its decison calculus as a result of a defensive tactic if the tactic could be reversed, and the original post-transaction value restored, once the acquiring company obtained control of the target. To be effective, the decline in value must therefore be irreversible. The problem with an irreversible tactic, however, is that unless its effect is specific to the acquiring company, the value of the target company will

---

[57] For detailed histories of the Brunswick-Whittaker battle, see Fleischer & Raymond, *Developments in Defensive Tactics to Tender Offers: A Study of the Whittaker-Brunswick Bid,* 5 J.Comp.Bus. & Cap. Mkt.L. 97 (1983); Thackray, *The Battle of Brunswick,* Institutional Investor 73 (June, 1982).

[58] For example, one of the McGraw-Hill businesses rated the credit worthiness of municipal bonds while American Express was a major investor in such bonds (employing the "float" generated by its traveler's checks operations).

remain reduced even if the acquiring company is successfully deterred. In this regard, was the defensive tactic used by Brunswick or by McGraw-Hill more successful?

Transaction Costs. Put simply, a defensive tactic that increases the acquiring company's transaction costs causes the acquiring company to expend more money, thereby decreasing the potential for gain from the transaction. Litigation by the target company, a tactic we will come back to in more detail shortly, is a good example. It was reported that the total costs associated with Occidental Petroleum's unsuccessful offer for Mead Corp. were in excess of $15 million. Similarly, the professional fees alone—for lawyers, accountants, investment bankers, proxy solicitors and public relations representatives—incurred by the three parties in the battle between McDermott, Inc. and Wheelabrator-Frye, Inc. for Pullman, Inc., amounted to $17 million.[59] Putting a value on the time acquiring company management is forced to spend on the litigation—having their depositions taken, conferring with their own lawyers, distracting them from daily operations—would substantially increase the totals.

It should be noted, however, that litigation, as with most defensive efforts to interpose third party regulators like courts and administrative agencies as a barrier to the takeover, is likely to cost the target company at least as much as the acquiring company. This suggests that the cost-benefit analysis undertaken by the target company in its decision whether to pursue the tactic must be somewhat skewed. If the tactic proves unsuccessful there is no cost to the target; in that event, the takeover succeeds and the acquiring company ends up paying the bill.[60] Only if the tactic is successful is the cost borne by the target company and the question then is whether the benefits of remaining independent are worth the costs. Here the question gets sticky, however, because the answer may be quite different depending on *whose* costs and benefits are considered. If management is allowed to take into account only its own costs and benefits, the analysis and the resulting decisions will be predictably biased: Management gets the benefits of remaining independent while shareholders bear the cost. Thus, whether target management must include shareholders' concern in its decision-making is critical to what decision will be made. This issue, which depends heavily on the legal standards governing target management conduct in hostile takeovers, is considered in detail later in Section B.3. of this Chapter.

In thinking about how to impose additional transaction costs on the acquiring company, it is important to recognize that the impact of some of the most significant, and therefore potentially most destructive, transaction costs are not necessarily easy to quantify in dollar terms.

[59] *Outside Professionals Play an Increasing Role in Corporate Takeovers,* Wall St.J., Dec. 2, 1980, at 1, col. 6.

[60] If the acquiring company really was willing to spend more to acquire the target, the additional amounts paid as transaction costs could have gone to target shareholders. Although from the acquiring company's perspective the two types of costs—P and TC— are fungible, from the target shareholders' perspective there is a critical difference in that increases in P go to the shareholders while increases in TC go to the lawyers and investment bankers.

For example, it is widely believed that a court decision—requiring Anderson Clayton to make detailed disclosure concerning questionable foreign payments before it would be allowed to proceed with its offer for Gerber Products Company—was the reason the offer was withdrawn. See Berman v. Gerber Products Co., 454 F.Supp. 1310 (W.D.Mich.1978). If disclosure would interfere with the conduct of Anderson Clayton's foreign business, or open it to prosecution in foreign jurisdictions for the disclosed activities, the transaction costs of the takeover would be substantially increased.[61] Similarly, embarrassment, particularly of acquiring company management, can also be a significant transaction cost. The continued disclosure of unfavorable information about Armand Hammer, the Chairman of Occidental Petroleum, is often credited with that company's decision to withdraw its offer for Mead Petroleum.[62]

Price. The effect of a tactic that increases the market price of the target company's shares relative to the tender offer price is to reduce the premium offered target shareholders. This will decrease the attractiveness of the transaction to target shareholders and might require an increase in the offered price for the takeover to succeed. An increased price, of course, would unfavorably alter the acquiring company's offering calculus.

Commentators have made a number of suggestions as to how target companies might act to increase their stock price.[63] One is for the target company to repurchase its own stock. On closer inspection, however, the tactic seems to have a substantial possibility of backfiring. Although a reduction in the number of outstanding shares by repurchase should increase the price of the remaining shares, the total cost of the acquisition should not change because the number of shares outstanding has decreased. Indeed, if the acquiring company has a preexisting investment in the target company, the tactic likely *reduces* the total cost of the transaction. Assume that a target company has one million shares outstanding which trade at $10 per share, and that the acquiring company already owns 100,000 shares and would like to acquire 400,000 more (a 50 percent position). If the additional shares could be purchased at the $10 market price, the total cost to raise the acquiring company's position to 50 percent would be $400,000. Now assume that target management decides to raise its share price to discourage the offer and, to accomplish this, repurchases half its out-

---

[61] Put differently, the post-transaction value of Anderson Clayton's existing business would be reduced.

[62] It will be recalled that precisely this point was made in the excerpt on the "scorched earth" defense in section B. 1.b.(3) of this Chapter. With respect to the success of McGraw-Hill's defense against the American Express offer, the following analysis was offered:

"There are a lot of responsible and established businessmen on boards of directors who don't like to see their names in the paper and their motives and prac-

tices questioned. They don't need those kinds of problems." The board of directors of Amex, for example, "reads like a 'Who's Who'," in the words of one Amex adviser, who points to such luminaries as former Fed chairman William McChesney Martin, Jr., and former UN Ambassador William Scranton. "They just weren't about to sit there and have this garbage thrown at them."

[63] If there were easy ways to increase the price of the target's stock, why would a hostile offer be required before they were implemented?

standing stock. In that event, the market price of the remaining shares presumably would double. The total cost of the acquisition, however, would *fall*. As a result of the repurchase, the number of shares the acquiring company must purchase to secure the desired 50 percent has been reduced from 400,000 to 150,000 (assuming the acquiring company did not sell any of its pre-existing holdings). Although the per share price of these shares has doubled, the number of shares that must be purchased has been reduced by more than one-half, resulting in a decrease in the total cost of acquiring control from $400,000 to $300,000. The target company has simply helped finance its own acquisition.[64]

Other ideas for increasing the price of target shares typically include an increase in dividends, or a stock split. What impact would you expect either tactic to have? [65]

Evaluation of Litigation as a Defensive Tactic. Evaluation of the effectiveness of defensive tactics based on their impact on the acquiring company's decision calculus can be illustrated by applying the approach to the single most common defensive tactic—litigation. As the Wachtell excerpt in section 1.b.(1) of this Chapter describes, the target company's first post-offer defensive tactic is almost always to commence litigation against the acquiring company. It should be clear from Wachtell's discussion, however, that the point of the litigation is usually not to achieve a "showstopper"—an injunction against the transaction on, for example, antitrust grounds, that would prevent the acquisition from ever taking place. Rather, Wachtell is refreshingly straightfoward in acknowledging that lawsuits are filed by target companies for a number of reasons other than their likelihood of achieving both success on the merits and a remedy that would prevent the transaction. We considered in section B.1.b. of this Chapter the ethical issues bearing on this use of litigation; now the issue is whether, ethical or not, the tactic is effective.

The first explanation Wachtell offers for why litigation might be useful, even if it could not block the offer, is that the litigation can chill arbitrage in the target's stock.[66] Wachtell argues that once the arbi-

---

[64] As pointed out by Nathan & Sobel in section B.1.b.(2) of this Chapter, a defensive repurchase may be effective when management already owns a sufficient number of shares that, after the repurchase, they can themselves prevent the hostile offer's success. In the example in the text, if management held 250,001 shares at the outset and did not sell any of their shares in repurchase, they would own one share more than 50% of the outstanding shares after the offer, just enough to prevent the offer from ever being made.

[65] Would it make a difference if the market believed that the new dividend level would be maintained in the future?

[66] The critical role of the arbitrage community in determining the success of a tender offer is described as follows:

The activities of arbitrageurs have a major impact on the success of tender offers, and offers are structured with a view toward the reactions of the arbitrageurs. Arbitrageurs are market professionals who purchase the shares of the target in the market in order to tender to the offeror, thereby narrowing the spread between the pre-offer market price and the offer price and providing market liquidity at or near the offer price for those who do not wish to wait for, or take the risk of, the consummation of the tender offer. An arbitrageur will set the price he is willing to pay on the basis of this assessment of the probability that the offer will be consummated and, in the case of a partial offer, of the number of shares that will be tendered and accepted. In an any-and-

trage community has taken a substantial position in a target's stock, it ultimately will be taken over by someone. A lawsuit that is perceived as having some potential to prevent the offer will discourage purchase by arbitrageurs (or at least reduce the price they are willing to pay) and, hence, reduce the offer's likelihood of success. For this to be effective, however, one would have to believe one of three things about arbitrageurs, all of which seem problematical.

First, one might believe that the arbitrage community is not very smart. The idea is that although the target company knows its litigation is unlikely to prevent the offer, the arbitrage community does not and, therefore, will overestimate the likelihood that the litigation will be successful. The problem, however, is that arbitrageurs themselves hire high quality lawyers to evaluate the potential success of the litigation, and it is difficult to explain why counsel for an arbitrageur would systematically overestimate the likelihood of the litigation's success.[67]

Second, one might believe that the litigation serves as a signal. The argument is similar to that made with respect to shark repellent amendments in section B.2.a.(2) of this Chapter: Litigation will convince the arbitrage community that the target is a fighter. Although the litigation itself will not be effective, it informs the world that the target intends to take effective defensive action in the future. Viewed in this way, the effectiveness of litigation as a tactic depends on the believability of the signal. This, in turn, depends on the availability of other, more effective, tactics. If, in fact, there are few effective tactics, the signalling explanation begins to sound like the "not very smart" explanation.

Finally, and most persuasively, one might believe that litigation results in delay and that delay has a particularly significant impact on arbitrageurs. If because of litigation an arbitrageur must purchase and hold the target's shares longer than otherwise would be the case, the result is to decrease the arbitrageur's return on investment (by increasing both the holding period and the amount of interest accruing on funds borrowed to make the investment). The result should be to reduce the price the arbitrageur would be willing to pay and the number of shares ultimately purchased. Moreover, the longer the period necessary to complete the offer, the greater the opportunity for

all offer, where significant litigation is unlikely, an arbitrageur may pay as much as the offer price plus a portion of the soliciting dealer fee. If the arbitrageurs believe that the offer may fail or that due to proration they will not have 100% of their tendered shares purchased, they will take such risks into account in setting their purchase price, and such price will be substantially below the tender offer price. If the arbitrageurs believe that the original offer will be topped or that management of the target will be friendly and negotiate an increased price in consideration of management endorsement of the take-

over, the arbitrageurs will pay more than the original offer price.

1 M. Lipton & E. Steinberger, *Takeovers and Freezeouts* 19–20 (1978). For a thorough discussion of the mechanics of risk arbitrage, see Wyser-Pratte, *Risk Arbitrage,* N.Y.U.C.J. Devine Inst.Fin.Bull., May 1971, at 1.

[67] Although arbitrageurs initially might lack some information necessary for careful evaluation of the merits of the litigation, it clearly would be in the interests of the acquiring company to provide that information.

exogenous events to occur—e.g., a Middle Eastern war, an oil embargo, a significant change in interest rates—which, wholly apart from the target's tactics, might cause the acquiring company to withdraw the offer. But while the importance of delay on the success of an offer goes beyond its effect on the arbitrage community, and will be considered separately shortly, it should be noted here that one result of delay will be viewed quite differently by the arbitrage community than by the acquiring company. The acquiring company may object to delay for no other reason than that it expands the target company's opportunity to find a white knight to outbid the acquiring company's initial offer.[68] The arbitrageur, however, will be delighted at the potential for a higher bid. Thus, an arbitrageur may not object to some delay, depending on its perception of the purpose of the delay and the likely result.

In the end, Wachtell's most persuasive argument is that litigation can cause delay and that delay can defeat hostile offers both by its effect on arbitrageurs and by its effect on the acquiring company more generally. Evaluation of the latter point requires more careful consideration of precisely how delay increases the acquiring company's costs. As previously mentioned, the most obvious impact of delay on acquisition costs is to provide the target an opportunity to find a white knight willing to pay a higher price. The effect on the acquiring company's calculus is obvious. If its offer is to succeed, it must increase the price. But while the acquiring company's costs are increased, it is misleading, at least for present purposes, to characterize this aspect of delay as defensive. The final result, whether it is the first bidder or white knight that ultimately offers the most, is that the target is taken over by someone. In this sense, delay which allows the target to do no more than secure a white knight provides not a defense, but only the opportunity to secure a negotiated surrender.

Delay can, however, reduce the likelihood of any offer. The question is only the significance of the reduction. Consider the effect of delay on transaction costs. If, for example, a cash offer will be financed by bank loans, lenders charge a standby fee as the price of the commitment to have funds available to allow the acquiring company to complete the purchase. Thus, the longer the transaction takes to complete, the higher the commitment fee paid. A comparable problem is presented even when the acquiring company is financing the offer with its own funds. If the funds must be invested in short-term instruments pending completion of the transaction, then there is presumably an opportunity cost in delaying the long term investment of the funds in the business. In either event, the issue is the magnitude of the transaction costs imposed. It has been reported that the typical standby fee runs approximately $1/10$ of one percent per month. While the absolute size of the fee might seem high in a large transaction, one must be skeptical whether so small an increase in overall costs would

---

[68] The desirability of competitive bidding from the perspective of public policy is considered in section B.4.e. of this Chapter, infra. How the acquiring company can structure its offer to reduce the likelihood of a competitive bid is considered in Chapter Fifteen A, infra.

substantially alter the acquiring company's evaluation of the transaction.

Finally, as was considered in the discussion of the impact of delay on the arbitrage community, the more time that must pass before an offer is completed increases the likelihood, even though small, that something will happen that will make the acquiring company go away of its own accord. Again, however, the overall likelihood of this occurring seems small.

Overview. The lesson to be learned from this discussion is that there are *not* generally available, easily implemented, off-the-rack defensive tactics that have the promise of success. In order for a defensive tactic to have a significant chance of working, it must be carefully created with a view to the particular motivation of the acquiring company in making the offer. And it must be recognized that there is a substantial danger that any tactic capable of significantly influencing the offerer's decision calculus also will have a substantial, if not identical, impact on the target. In sum, the statistics concerning the success of defensive tactics described at the outset of this Note are surprising only in two unanticipated respects: first, that the number of successful defenses is as high as 20 percent; and second, that defensive tactics remain so common despite their low probability of success. Evaluation of the latter point requires an understanding of the legal standards governing management conduct in hostile takeovers. If, for example, the costs of defense were borne by target shareholders, but the benefits of a successful defense reaped only by target management, the frequency to which defensive tactics were resorted might not be surprising even though the effort is not often successful.

3. Legal Standards Governing Use of Defensive Tactics

Target management faces an unavoidable conflict of interest in responding to an unsolicited takeover proposal. On the one hand, the shareholders will receive a substantial premium over market price if the offer goes forward. On the other hand, target management might well lose their positions if the offer is successful and, in all events, certainly would lose their autonomy. The problem, then, is how to minimize that conflict of interest. Two general approaches come to mind. The first is to eliminate the conflict by giving target management the same interests as shareholders. This could be accomplished by incentive compensation plans that reward management only when shareholders gain. Most straightforwardly, it is accomplished when management are substantial shareholders. In either case, the result is that management gains and loses when shareholders gain and lose. Put in the context of takeovers, this approach predicts that target management's incentive to undertake defensive tactics is inversely related to the amount of target company stock they own.[69] This

[69] See Baron, *Tender Offers and Management Resistance,* 38 J.Fin. 331 (1983).

prediction finds empirical support in a recent study of 95 cash tender offers made between 1972 and 1977. Walking & Long, *Agency Theory, Managerial Welfare and Takeover Bid Resistance,* 15 Rand J. Econ. 54 (1984), found that the greater the impact of an offer on the wealth of target management (through ownership of target company stock and options to purchase target company stock), the less likely it was that target management would resist the offer.

The second approach, and the object of our attention here, is to cause managers to internalize the costs of defensive tactics imposed on shareholders by means of a threat to impose legal liability. Here the idea is simply that management will take the cost to shareholders (including opportunity costs) from resisting an offer into account in making its decision if, because of liability rules, management will be forced to bear those costs. See Kraakman, *Corporate Liability Strategies and the Costs of Legal Controls,* 93 Yale L.J. 857 (1984). The legal rules defining the circumstances when management will be liable to shareholders for resisting a takeover offer (or when resistance will be enjoined) thus provide an opportunity to help eliminate management's conflict of interest by realigning the interests of target management so that they are compatible with those of target shareholders. In this section we will examine the traditional legal rules governing the behavior of target management when confronted by a hostile takeover and the extent to which they accomplish this realignment.

a. *The Traditional Approach: Policy Conflict/Primary Purpose*

CHEFF v. MATHES
Court of Chancery of Delaware, 1964.
41 Del.Ch. 494, 199 A.2d 548.

CAREY, Justice. This is an appeal from the decision of the Vice-Chancellor in a derivative suit holding certain directors of Holland Furnace Company liable for loss allegedly resulting from improper use of corporate funds to purchase shares of the company. * * *

Holland Furnace Company, a corporation of the State of Delaware, manufactures warm air furnaces, air conditioning equipment, and other home heating equipment. At the time of the relevant transactions, the board of directors was composed of the seven individual defendants. Mr. Cheff had been Holland's Chief Executive Officer since 1933, received an annual salary of $77,400, and personally owned 6,000 shares of the company. He was also a director. Mrs. Cheff, the wife of Mr. Cheff, was a daughter of the founder of Holland and had served as a director since 1922. She personally owned 5,804 shares of Holland and owned 47.9 percent of Hazelbank United Interest, Inc. Hazelbank is an investment vehicle for Mrs. Cheff and members of the Cheff-Landwehr family group, which owned 164,950 shares of the 883,585 outstanding shares of Holland. As a director, Mrs. Cheff received a compensation of $200.00 for each monthly board meeting, whether or not she attended the meeting.

The third director, Edgar P. Landwehr, is the nephew of Mrs. Cheff and personally owned 24,010 shares of Holland and 8.6 percent of the outstanding shares of Hazelbank. He received no compensation from Holland other than the monthly director's fee.

Robert H. Trenkamp is an attorney who first represented Holland in 1946. In May 1953, he became a director of Holland and acted as general counsel for the company. During the period in question, he received no retainer from the company, but did receive substantial sums for legal services rendered the company. Apart from the above-described payments, he received no compensation from Holland other than the monthly director's fee. He owned 200 shares of Holland Furnace stock. Although he owned no shares of Hazelbank, at the time relevant to this controversy, he was serving as a director and counsel of Hazelbank.

John D. Ames was then a partner in the Chicago investment firm of Bacon, Whipple & Co. and joined the board at the request of Mr. Cheff. During the periods in question, his stock ownership varied between ownership of no shares to ownership of 300 shares. He was considered by the other members of the Holland board to be the financial advisor to the board. He received no compensation from Holland other than the normal director's fee.

Mr. Ralph G. Boalt was the Vice President of J.R. Watkins Company, a manufacturer and distributor of cosmetics. In 1953, at the request of Mr. Cheff, he became a member of the board of directors. Apart from the normal director's fee, he received no compensation from Holland for his services.

Mr. George Spatta was the President of Clark Equipment Company, a large manufacturer of earth moving equipment. In 1951, at the request of Mr. Cheff, he joined the board of directors of Holland. Apart from the normal director's fee, he received no compensation from the company.

The board of directors of Hazelbank included the five principal shareholders: Mrs. Cheff; Leona Kolb, who was Mrs. Cheff's daughter; Mr. Landwehr; Mrs. Bowles, who was Mr. Landwehr's sister; Mrs. Putnam, who was also Mr. Landwehr's sister; Mr. Trenkamp; and Mr. William DeLong, an accountant.

Prior to the events in question, Holland employed approximately 8500 persons and maintained 400 branch sales offices located in 43 states. The volume of sales had declined from over $41,000,000 in 1948 to less than $32,000,000 in 1956. Defendants contend that the decline in earnings is attributable to the artificial post-war demand generated in the 1946–1948 period. In order to stabilize the condition of the company, the sales department apparently was reorganized and certain unprofitable branch offices were closed. By 1957 this reorganization had been completed and the management was convinced that the changes were manifesting beneficial results. The practice of the company was to directly employ the retail salesman, and the management considered that practice—unique in the furnace business—to be a vital factor in the company's success.

During the first five months of 1957, the monthly trading volume of Holland's stock on the New York Stock Exchange ranged between 10,300 shares to 24,200 shares. In the last week of June 1957, however, the trading increased to 37,800 shares, with a corresponding increase in the market price. In June of 1957, Mr. Cheff met with Mr. Arnold H. Maremont, who was President of Maremont Automotive Products, Inc. and Chairman of the boards of Motor Products Corporation and Allied Paper Corporation. Mr. Cheff testified, on deposition, that Maremont generally inquired about the feasibility of merger between Motor Products and Holland. Mr. Cheff testified that, in view of the difference in sales practices between the two companies, he informed Mr. Maremont that a merger did not seem feasible. In reply, Mr. Maremont stated that, in the light of Mr. Cheff's decision, he had no further interest in Holland nor did he wish to buy any of the stock of Holland.

None of the members of the board apparently connected the interest of Mr. Maremont with the increased activity of Holland stock. However, Mr. Trenkamp and Mr. Staal, the Treasurer of Holland, unsuccessfully made an informal investigation in order to ascertain the identity of the purchaser or purchasers. The mystery was resolved, however, when Maremont called Ames in July of 1957 to inform the latter that Maremont then owned 55,000 shares of Holland stock. At this juncture, no requests for change in corporate policy were made, and Maremont made no demand to be made a member of the board of Holland.

Ames reported the above information to the board at its July 30, 1957 meeting. Because of the position now occupied by Maremont, the board elected to investigate the financial and business history of Maremont and corporations controlled by him. Apart from the documentary evidence produced by this investigation, which will be considered infra, Staal testified, on deposition, that "leading bank officials" had indicated that Maremont "had been a participant, or had attempted to be, in the liquidation of a number of companies." Staal specifically mentioned only one individual giving such advice, the Vice President of the First National Bank of Chicago. Mr. Cheff testified, at trial, of Maremont's alleged participation in liquidation activities. Mr. Cheff testified that: "Throughout the whole of the Kalamazoo-Battle Creek area, and Detroit too, where I spent considerable time, he is well known and not highly regarded by any stretch." This information was communicated to the board.

On August 23, 1957, at the request of Maremont, a meeting was held between Mr. Maremont and Cheff. At this meeting, Cheff was informed that Motor Products then owned approximately 100,000 shares of Holland stock. Maremont then made a demand that he be named to the board of directors, but Cheff refused to consider it. Since considerable controversy has been generated by Maremont's alleged threat to liquidate the company or substantially alter the sales force of Holland, we believe it desirable to set forth the testimony of Cheff on this point: "Now we have 8500 men, direct employees, so the problem is entirely different. He indicated immediately that he had no interest in that type of distribution, that he didn't think it was modern, that he felt furnaces could be sold as he sold mufflers, through half a dozen salesmen in a wholesale way."

Testimony was introduced by the defendants tending to show that substantial unrest was present among the employees of Holland as a result of the threat of Maremont to seek control of Holland. Thus, Mr. Cheff testified that the field organization was considering leaving in large numbers because of a fear of the consequences of a Maremont acquisition; he further testified that approximately "25 of our key men" were lost as the result of the unrest engendered by the Maremont proposal. Staal, corroborating Cheff's version, stated that a number of branch managers approached him for reassurances that Maremont was not going to be allowed to successfully gain control. Moreover, at approximately this time, the company was furnished with a Dun and Bradstreet report, which indicated the practice of Maremont to achieve quick profits by sales or liquidations of companies acquired by him. The defendants were also supplied with an income statement of Motor Products, Inc., showing a loss of $336,121.00 for the period in 1957.

On August 30, 1957, the board was informed by Cheff of Maremont's demand to be placed upon the board and of Maremont's belief that the retail sales organization of Holland was obsolete. The board was also informed of the results of the investigation by Cheff and Staal. Predicated upon this information, the board authorized the purchase of company stock on the market with corporate funds, ostensibly for use in a stock option plan.

Subsequent to this meeting, substantial numbers of shares were purchased and, in addition, Mrs. Cheff made alternate personal purchase of Holland stock. As a result of purchases by Maremont, Holland and Mrs. Cheff, the market price rose. On September 13, 1957, Maremont wrote to each of the directors of Holland and requested a broad engineering survey to be made for the benefit of all stockholders. During September, Motor Products released its annual report, which indicated that the investment in Holland was a "special situation" as opposed to the normal policy of placing the funds of Motor Products into "an active company". On September 4th, Maremont proposed to sell his current holdings of Holland to the corporation for $14.00 a share. However, because of delay in responding to this offer, Maremont withdrew the offer. At this time, Mrs. Cheff was obviously quite concerned over the prospect of a Maremont acquisition, and had stated her willingness to expend her personal resources to prevent it.

On September 30, 1957, Motor Products Corporation, by letter to Mrs. Bowles, made a buy-sell offer to Hazelbank. At the Hazelbank meeting of October 3, 1957, Mrs Bowles presented the letter to the board. The board took no action, but referred the proposal to its finance committee. Although Mrs. Bowles and Mrs. Putnam were opposed to any acquisition of Holland stock by Hazelbank, Mr. Landwehr conceded that a majority of the board were in favor of the purchase. Despite this fact, the finance committee elected to refer the offer to the Holland board on the grounds that it was the primary concern of Holland.

Thereafter, Mr. Trenkamp arranged for a meeting with Maremont, which occurred on October 14–15, 1957, in Chicago. Prior to this meeting, Trenkamp was aware of the intentions of Hazelbank and Mrs. Cheff to purchase all or portions of the stock then owned by Motor Products if Holland did not so act. As a result of the meeting, there was a tentative agreement on the part of Motor Products to sell its 155,000 shares at $14.40 per share. On October 23, 1957, at a special meeting of the Holland board, the purchase was considered. All directors, except Spatta,[1] were present. The dangers allegedly posed by Maremont were again reviewed by the board. Trenkamp and Mrs. Cheff agreed that the latter informed the board that either she or Hazelbank would purchase part or all of the block of Holland stock owned by Motor Products if the Holland board did not so act. The board was also informed that in order for the corporation to finance the purchase, substantial sums would have to be borrowed from commercial lending institutions. A resolution authorizing the purchase of 155,000 shares from Motor Products was adopted by the board. The price paid was in excess of the market price prevailing at the time, and the book value of the stock was approximately $20.00 as compared to approximately $14.00 for the net quick asset value. The transaction was subsequently consummated. The stock option plan mentioned in the minutes has never been implemented. In 1959, Holland stock reached a high of $15.25 a share.

On February 6, 1958, plaintiffs, owners of 60 shares of Holland stock, filed a derivative suit in the court below naming all of the individual directors of Holland, Holland itself and Motor Products Corporation as defendants. The complaint alleged that all of the purchases of stock by Holland in 1957 were for the purpose of insuring the perpetuation of control by the incumbent directors. The complaint requested that the transaction between Motor Products and Holland be rescinded and, secondly, that the individual defendants account to Holland for the alleged damages. Since Motor Products was never served with process, the initial remedy became inapplicable. Ames was never served nor did he enter an appearance.

After trial, the Vice Chancellor found the following facts: (a) Holland directly sells to retail consumers by means of numerous branch offices. There were no intermediate dealers. (b) Immediately prior to the complained-of transactions, the sales and earnings of Holland had declined and its marketing practices were under investigation by the Federal Trade Commission. (c) Mr. Cheff and Trenkamp had received substantial sums as Chief Executive and attorney of the company, respectively. (d) Maremont, on August 23rd, 1957, demanded a place on the board. (e) At the October 14th meeting between Trenkamp, Staal and Maremont, Trenkamp and Staal were authorized to speak for Hazelbank and Mrs. Cheff as well as Holland. Only Mr. Cheff, Mrs. Cheff, Mr. Landwehr, and Mr. Trenkamp clearly understood, prior to

---

[1] Spatta agreed by telephone.

the October 23rd meeting, that either Hazelbank or Mrs. Cheff would have utilized their funds to purchase the Holland stock if Holland had not acted. (g) There was no real threat posed by Maremont and no substantial evidence of intention by Maremont to liquidate Holland. (h) Any employee unrest could have been caused by factors other than Maremont's intrusion and "only one important employee was shown to have left, and his motive for leaving is not clear." (i) The Court rejected the stock option plan as a meaningful rationale for the purchase from Maremont or the prior open market purchases.

The Court then found that the actual purpose behind the purchase was the desire to perpetuate control, but because of its finding that only the four above-named directors knew of the "alternative", the remaining directors were exonerated. No appeal was taken by plaintiffs from that decision.

An examination of the record indicates that a substantial portion of the evidence presented to the Vice Chancellor consisted of deposition testimony and documentary evidence. The only individuals who testified personally (aside from a financial expert) were Mr. Cheff, Trenkamp and Staal. Depositions of the other directors were introduced, but no deposition was taken from Maremont. The standard of review governing this court in such cases was established in Blish v. Thompson Automatic Arms Corp., 30 Del.Ch. 538, 64 A.2d 581, wherein we stated:

> " * * * regardless of the state of the evidence below, if there be sufficient oral testimony in the record to support the findings of fact below, such findings should not be disturbed by this Court." (30 Del.Ch. at page 604, 64 A.2d at page 604).

Under the provisions of 8 Del.C. § 160, a corporation is granted statutory power to purchase and sell shares of its own stock. Such a right, as embodied in the statute, has long been recognized in this State. The charge here is not one of violation of statute, but the allegation is that the true motives behind such purchases were improperly centered upon perpetuation of control. In an analogous field, courts have sustained the use of proxy funds to inform stockholders of management's views upon the policy questions inherent in an election to a board of directors, but have not sanctioned the use of corporate funds to advance the selfish desires of directors to perpetuate themselves in office. See Hall v. Trans-Lux Daylight Picture Screen Corp., 20 Del.Ch. 78, 171 A. 226. Similarly, if the actions of the board were motivated by a sincere belief that the buying out of the dissident stockholder was necessary to maintain what the board believed to be proper business practices, the board will not be held liable for such decision, even though hindsight indicates the decision was not the wisest course. See Kors v. Carey, Del.Ch., 158 A.2d 136. On the other hand, if the board has acted solely or primarily because of the desire to perpetuate themselves in office, the use of corporate funds for such purposes is improper. See Bennett v. Propp, Del., 187 A.2d 405, and Yasik v. Wachtel, 25 Del.Ch. 247, 17 A.2d 309.

Our first problem is the allocation of the burden of proof to show the presence or lack of good faith on the part of the board in authorizing the purchase of shares. Initially, the decision of the board of directors in authorizing a purchase was presumed to be in good faith and could be overturned only by a conclusive showing by plaintiffs of fraud or other misconduct. * * *

In Kors, cited supra, the court merely indicated that the directors are presumed to act in good faith and the burden of proof to show to the contrary falls upon the plaintiff. However, in Bennett v. Propp, supra, we stated:

"We must bear in mind the inherent danger in the purchase of shares with corporate funds to remove a threat to corporate policy when a threat to control is involved. The directors are of necessity confronted with a conflict of interest, and an objective decision is difficult. * * * Hence, in our opinion, the burden should be on the directors to justify such a purchase as one primarily in the corporate interest." (187 A.2d 409, at page 409).

The case of Martin v. American Potash and Chemical Corp., 33 Del. Ch. 234, 92 A.2d 295, 35 A.L.R.2d 1140, relied upon by defendants to support their contention that the burden of proof should be on plaintiffs, is inapposite. As noted in Bennett, Martin was concerned with a statutory reduction of capital, which has the additional safeguards of notice to stockholders and shareholder approval.

To say that the burden of proof is upon the defendants is not to indicate, however, that the directors have the same "self-dealing interest" as is present, for example, when a director sells property to the corporation. The only clear pecuniary interest shown on the record was held by Mr. Cheff, as an executive of the corporation, and Trenkamp, as its attorney. The mere fact that some of the other directors were substantial shareholders does not create a personal pecuniary interest in the decisions made by the board of directors, since all shareholders would presumably share the benefit flowing to the substantial shareholder. See Smith v. Good Music Station, Inc., 36 Del. Ch. 262, 129 A.2d 242. Accordingly, these directors other than Trenkamp and Cheff, while called upon to justify their actions, will not be held to the same standard of proof required of those directors having personal and pecuniary interest in the transaction.

As noted above, the Vice Chancellor found that the stock option plan, mentioned in the minutes as a justification for the purchases, was not a motivating reason for the purchases. This finding we accept, since there is evidence to support it; in fact, Trenkamp admitted that the stock option plan was not the motivating reason. The minutes of October 23, 1957 dealing with the purchase from Maremont do not, in fact, mention the option plan as a reason for the purchase. While the minutes of the October 1, 1957 meeting only indicated the stock option plan as the motivating reason, the defendants are not bound by such statements and may supplement the minutes by oral testimony to show that the motivating reason was genuine fear of an acquisition by Maremont. See Bennett v. Propp, cited supra.

Plaintiffs urge that the sale price was unfair in view of the fact that the price was in excess of that prevailing on the open market. However, as conceded by all parties, a substantial block of stock will normally sell at a higher price than that prevailing on the open market, the increment being attributable to a "control premium". Plaintiffs argue that it is inappropriate to require the defendant corporation to pay a control premium, since control is meaningless to an acquisition by a corporation of its own shares. However, it is elementary that a holder of a substantial number of shares would expect to receive the control premium, as part of his selling price, and if the corporation desired to obtain the stock, it is unreasonable to expect that the corporation could avoid paying what any other purchaser would be required to pay for the stock. In any event, the financial expert produced by defendant at trial indicated that the price paid was fair and there was no rebuttal. Ames, the financial man on the board, was strongly of the opinion that the purchase was a good deal for the corporation. The Vice Chancellor made no finding as to the fairness of the price other than to indicate the obvious fact that the market price was increasing as a result of open market purchases by Maremont, Mrs. Cheff and Holland.

The question then presented is whether or not defendants satisfied the burden of proof of showing reasonable grounds to believe a danger to corporate policy and effectiveness existed by the presence of the Maremont stock ownership. It is important to remember that the directors satisfy their burden by showing good faith and reasonable investigation; the directors will not be penalized for an honest mistake of judgment, if the judgment appeared reasonable at the time the decision was made.

In holding that employee unrest could as well be attributed to a condition of Holland's business affairs as to the possibility of Maremont's intrusion, the Vice Chancellor must have had in mind one or both of two matters: (1) the pending proceedings before the Federal Trade Commission concerning certain sales practices of Holland; (2) the decrease in sales and profits during the preceding several years. Any other possible reason would be pure speculation. In the first place, the adverse decision of the F.T.C. was not announced until *after* the complained-of transaction. Secondly, the evidence clearly shows that the downward trend of sales and profits had reversed itself, presumably because of the reorganization which had then been completed. Thirdly, everyone who testified on the point said that the unrest was due to the possible threat presented by Maremont's purchases of stock. There was, in fact, no *testimony* whatever of any connection between the unrest and either the F.T.C. proceedings or the business picture.

The Vice Chancellor found that there was no substantial evidence of a liquidation posed by Maremont. This holding overlooks an important contention. The fear of the defendants, according to their testimony, was not limited to the possibility of liquidation; it included the alternate possibility of a material change in Holland's sales policies, which the board considered vital to its future success. The *unrebutted* testimony before the court indicated:

> (1) Maremont had deceived Cheff as to his original intentions, since his open market purchases were contemporaneous with his disclaimer of interest in Holland; (2) Maremont had given Cheff some reason to believe that he intended to eliminate the retail sales force of Holland; (3) Maremont demanded a place on the board; (4) Maremont substantially increased his purchases after having been refused a place on the board; (5) the directors had good reason to believe that unrest among key employees had been engendered by the Maremont threat; (6) the board had received advice from Dun and Bradstreet indicating the past liquidation or quick sale activities of Motor Products; (7) the board had received professional advice from the firm of Merrill Lynch, Fenner & Beane, who recommended that the purchase from Motor Products be carried out; (8) the board had received competent advice that the corporation was over-capitalized; (9) Staal and Cheff had made informal personal investigations from contacts in the business and financial community and had reported to the board of the alleged poor reputation of Maremont. The board was within its rights in relying upon that investigation, since 8 Del.C. § 141(f) allows the directors to reasonably rely upon a report provided by corporate officers.

Accordingly, we are of the opinion that the evidence presented in the court below leads inevitably to the conclusion that the board of directors, based upon direct investigation, receipt of professional advice, and personal observations of the contradictory action of Maremont and his explanation of corporate purpose, believed, with justification, that there was a reasonable threat to the continued existence of Holland, or at least existence in its present form, by the plan of Maremont to continue building up his stock holdings. We find no evidence in the record sufficient to justify a contrary conclusion. The opinion of the Vice Chancellor that employee unrest may have been engendered by other factors or that the board had no grounds to suspect Maremont is not supported in any manner by the evidence.

As noted above, the Vice-Chancellor found that the purpose of the acquisition was the improper desire to maintain control, but, at the same time, he exonerated those individual directors whom he believed to be unaware of the possibility of using non-corporate funds to accomplish this purpose. Such a decision is inconsistent with his finding that the motive was improper, within the rule enunciated in Bennett. If the actions were in fact improper because of a desire to maintain control, then the presence or absence of a non-corporate alternative is irrelevant, as corporate funds may not be used to advance an improper purpose even if there is no non-corporate alternative available. Conversely, if the actions were proper because of a decision by the board made in good faith that the corporate interest was served thereby, they are not rendered improper by the fact that some individual directors were willing to advance personal funds if the corporation did not. It is conceivable that the Vice Chancellor considered this feature of the case to be of significance because of his apparent belief that any excess corporate funds should have been used to finance a subsidiary corporation. That action would not have solved the problem of Holland's over-capitalization. In any event, this question was a matter of business judgment, which furnishes no justification for holding the directors personally responsible in this case.

Accordingly, the judgment of the court below is reversed and remanded with instruction to enter judgment for the defendants.

_____◆_____

What is wrong with Maremont's "achiev[ing] quick profits by sales or liquidations of companies acquired by him?" If Holland shareholders were bought out at a premium, they would not suffer as a result of the liquidation. Indeed, even if minority shareholders took part in the liquidation, Maremont could not profit from liquidation without the minority shareholders participating on an equal basis. Who, in particular, would lose if Maremont acquired Holland and liquidated?

_____◆_____

PANTER v. MARSHALL FIELD & CO.
United States Court of Appeals, Seventh Circuit, 1981.
646 F.2d 271, cert. denied 454 U.S. 1092 (1981).

Before PELL and CUDAHY, Circuit Judges, and DUMBAULD, Senior District Judge.*

PELL, Circuit Judge.

The nineteen named plaintiffs in these consolidated cases appeal from a judgment of the district court which granted the defendants' motion for a directed verdict at the close of the plaintiffs' presentation of evidence to the jury. Panter v. Marshall Field & Co., 486 F.Supp. 1168 (N.D.Ill.1980). The plaintiffs, shareholders of Marshall Field & Company (Field's) sought to prove that the defendants, the company and its directors, had wrongfully deprived the plaintiffs of an opportunity to dispose of their shares at a substantial premium over market when the defendants successfully fended off a takeover attempt by Carter Hawley Hale (CHH), a national retail chain.

* * *

Field's is a Delaware corporation with its principal office in Chicago, Illinois. The company has been engaged in the operation of retail department stores since 1852, and on December 12, 1977, it was the eighth largest department store chain in the United States, with thirty-one stores. Fifteen of the stores were located in the Chicago area: * * * Other divisions included the Frederick & Nelson division in the state of Washington; the Halle Division of Halle Brothers Company

_____

* Edward Dumbauld, Senior Judge of the
United States District Court for Western
Pennsylvania, is sitting by designation.

in Ohio and Pennsylvania; and the Crescent Division of Halle with stores in Spokane, Washington.

[Of] the ten directors of Marshall Field & Company during the period from December 12, 1977 to February 22, 1978, seven of the directors were not affiliated with Field's management; the remaining three were officers of Field's.

CHH is a California corporation engaged in the operation of retail department, specialty, and book stores. It was not a party here, although its efforts to acquire Field's gave rise to this litigation. CHH's Neiman-Marcus division operates retail stores in Texas and the southeastern United States. As of December 12, 1977, it had one store in Northbrook Court in north suburban Chicago. CHH also had acquired land on North Michigan Avenue, one block south of Field's Water Tower Place Store, and had expressed its intent to put a Neiman-Marcus Store there, although those plans were in abeyance during the relevant time period. CHH had also been attempting for some time to enter the Oakbrook Shopping Center in west suburban Chicago where Field's already had a store. * * *

B. *The Pre-1977 Events*

On several occasions in the late 1960's and continuing to the mid-1970's, Field's management was approached by would-be merger or takeover suitors. In 1969 Field's sought the help of Joseph H. Flom, an attorney with expertise in such matters, in determining how best to respond to the overtures of interested parties. Flom advised the board that the interest of the shareholders was the paramount concern, and that management should listen to such proposals, evaluate whether the proposal was serious, and whether the proposal raised questions of antitrust violations. He also advised Field's directors and management to invest the company's reserves and use its borrowing power to acquire other stores, if such acquisitions were in accord with the sound business judgment of the board, and in the best interest of the company and its shareholders. He counseled that such acquisitions were a legal way of coping with unfriendly takeover attempts.**

* * *

In 1977 the Field's board decided to hire Angelo Arena, then head of CHH's Neiman-Marcus division, to commence employment with the company in 1977, work with its current president, Joseph Burnham, for two or three years, and then assume the presidency of Field's on Burnham's retirement. However, when Burnham died unexpectedly in October of 1977, the Field's board determined, in an emergency meeting held three days after Burnham's death, to elect Arena to the presidency immediately and ask him to come to Chicago earlier than originally planned. In the three day interval CHH made informal contacts with intermediaries and expressed an interest in merging with Field's. The board was informed of those contacts at the October 13 meeting and resolved at that time not to consider the merger.

** Field's pattern of defensive acquisitions was described in section B.1.c. of this Chapter, supra. [Ed.]

CHH continued to press its attentions however, and on November 16, Arena asked Field's antitrust counsel, the Chicago law firm of Kirkland & Ellis, to investigate the antitrust aspects of such a merger. Field's board met the next day, and authorized Arena and George Rinder, another director and Field's executive, to meet with representatives of CHH. That meeting took place the next day. The CHH team expressed their reasons why a merger would be good for both companies, and noted that a foreign firm was likely to make a $60.00 tender offer for Field's at any time. Field's representatives conveyed the board's position that internal expansion would be best for Field's, and expressed concern about antitrust problems of such a merger. CHH responded that their counsel had opined that there was no antitrust deterrent to the merger. Field's representatives agreed to report the discussions to the Field's board.

On December 2, Hammond Chaffetz of the Kirkland firm advised Field's management that in the opinion of Kirkland & Ellis the proposed combination would be illegal under the antitrust laws in light of (a) the existing competition between Field's stores and the Northbrook Neiman-Marcus store; (b) the potential competition between Field's Chicago stores and the Chicago Stores Neiman-Marcus was planning to open; and (c) the existing competition between Field's stores (second in book sales in Chicago) and the stores operated by CHH's Walden division. Chaffetz' opinion was conveyed to Field's directors.*

On December 10, Philip Hawley, the president and chief executive officer of CHH, called Arena and told him that unless Field's directors agreed to begin merger negotiations by the following Monday, December 12, he would make a public exchange proposal. He told Arena that CHH would propose beginning negotiations with an offer that for each share of Field's common stock CHH would exchange a number of its shares roughly equivalent to $36.00. Arena refused to enter such negotiations. Field's shares were trading on the market at around $22.00 per share on the Friday before Hawley delivered his ultimatum.

Arena construed Hawley's call as the beginning of an unfriendly takeover attempt by CHH. He contacted Flom, and arranged a meeting of key Field's directors, counsel, and investment bankers for the next day. At the meeting Arena reported the Kirkland & Ellis opinion. It was agreed to poll the absent directors for authorization to file a suit seeking resolution of the antitrust issues posed by the merger proposal. The group also determined to inform the New York Stock Exchange, and to call an emergency meeting of the Field's board for December 13.

On Monday, December 12, 1977, the CHH letter was received. Arena contacted all Field's directors but one by telephone, and they authorized the filing of the antitrust suit.

The special meeting of the board took place the next day with all members present. Also at the meeting were Field's attorneys and

---

* After successfully fending off CHH, Field's ultimately agreed to be acquired by Batus to avoid being taken over by a less attractive suitor. In evaluating Field's commitment to obeying the antitrust laws, keep in mind that Batus owns the Saks Fifth Avenue department store chain which has stores in some of the same shopping centers as Field's. [Ed.]

investment bankers. The lawyers particularly Chaffetz, opined on the lack of legality of the merger, and the investment bankers evaluated the financial aspects of the merger. Field's management then made a report and projected that the company's future performance would be generally favorable. Many of the directors agreed with the investment bankers that a share of common stock would bring more than $36.00 in a sale of control of the company. After consideration of the above factors the directors voted unanimously to reject the proposal because in their judgment the merger as proposed would be "illegal, inadequate, and not in the best interests of Marshall Field & Company, its stockholders and the communities which it serves."

The directors also authorized issuance of a press release conveying their decision. On December 14, Field's issued the press release, which indicated that Field's directors and management had faith in the momentum of the company, and that "it would be in the best interests of our stockholders, customers and employees for us to take advantage of this momentum and continue to implement our growth plans as an independent company." Field's shares traded in the market in a range of $28.00 to $32.00 that day, and continued in approximately that range until January 31, 1978.

* * *

On January 19, 1978, Field's directors had their regular meeting. Two expansion proposals were on the agenda: one that the company expand into the Galleria, a Houston shopping mall where a planned Bonwit Teller store had failed to materialize, creating an attractive opening; the other that the company acquire a group of five Liberty House stores in the Pacific Northwest. The Galleria already contained a CHH Neiman-Marcus store. The board resolved to pursue both expansion programs. Field's executives and directors had long considered expansion into these two areas, and the company's interest in such expansion was well known to investment analysts in the department store field.

On February 1, CHH announced its intention to make an exchange offer of $42.00 in a combination of cash and CHH stock for each share of Field's stock tendered. The offer was conditioned on the fulfillment or non-occurrence of some twenty conditions. Appropriate documents for announcement of a tender offer were filed with the SEC. The market price of Field's stock rose to $34.00 per share, and stayed in the $30.00 to $34.00 range until February 22, 1978.

A special meeting of the Field's board was convened the next day to consider the new offer. The legal implications of the CHH filing were explained to the board by counsel, and Chaffetz brought the group up to date on the antitrust suit. There was no discussion of the adequacy of the offer in light of the board's determination that the proposed combination would clearly be illegal. The board also determined to go ahead with the Galleria plan, and approved the signing of a letter of agreement to enter the mall.

After the meeting Field's issued another press release reaffirming its opposition to the proposed merger. It concluded with a statement by Arena that "I assumed my position with Marshall Field & Company with the understanding that I would devote myself to making Marshall Field & Company a truly national retail business organization. We * * * are determined not to be deterred from this course. Our recently announced agreement to acquire five Liberty House Stores in Tacoma, Washington and Portland, Oregon was one step in our program."

On February 8, another Field's press release announced that Field's had concluded negotiations for a department store to be opened in the Galleria. On February 22, CHH announced that it was withdrawing its proposed tender offer before it became effective, because "the expansion program announced by Marshall Field since February 1st has created sufficient doubt about Marshall Field's earning potential to make the offer no longer in the best interests of Carter Hawley Hale's shareholders." None of the events that conditioned CHH's tender offer had occurred since February 1. Following the announcement, the market price of Field's shares dropped to $19.00, lower than it had been on December 9, the last trading day prior to CHH's first proposed offer.

* * *

IV. THE STATE LAW CLAIMS

The plaintiffs here have also sought to establish that the defendants committed two violations of state law. First, they contend, the defendants breached their fiduciary duty as directors to the corporation and its shareholders by adopting a secret policy to resist acquisition regardless of benefit to the shareholders or the corporation; by failing to disclose the existence of such a policy; by making defensive acquisitions; and by filing an antitrust suit against CHH. * * *

A. *The Business Judgment Rule*

Under applicable Delaware corporate law, claims such as those made by the plaintiffs are analyzed under the "business judgment" rule. The trial court described this rule as establishing that

> [d]irectors of corporations discharge their fiduciary duties when in good faith they exercise business judgment in making decisions regarding the corporation. When they act in good faith, they enjoy a presumption of sound business judgment, reposed in them as directors, which courts will not disturb if any rational business purpose can be attributed to their decisions. In the absence of fraud, bad faith, gross overreaching or abuse of discretion, courts will not interfere with the exercise of business judgment by corporate directors.

486 F.Supp. at 1194 (citations omitted). We find this an apt summary of appropriate Delaware law. * * * In the recent case of Johnson v. Trueblood, 629 F.2d 287 (3d Cir.1980), the U.S. Court of Appeals for the Third Circuit had occasion to analyze the purpose of the Delaware business judgment rule in the context of a takeover attempt. The plaintiffs contended that an allegation of a purpose to retain control

was enough to shift the burden to incumbent directors to show the rational business purpose of the disputed transaction. In rejecting that contention Chief Judge Seitz, formerly a Delaware Chancellor, stated:

> First, the purpose of the business judgment rule belies the plaintiffs' contention. It is frequently said that directors are fiduciaries. Although this statement is true in some senses, it is also obvious that if directors were held to the same standard as ordinary fiduciaries the corporation could not conduct business. For example, an ordinary fiduciary may not have the slightest conflict of interest in any transaction he undertakes on behalf of the trust. Yet by the very nature of corporate life a director has a certain amount of self-interest in everything he does. The very fact that the director wants to enhance corporate profits is in part attributable to his desire to keep shareholders satisfied so that they will not oust him.

> The business judgment rule seeks to alleviate this problem by validating certain situations that otherwise would involve a conflict of interest for the ordinary fiduciary. The rule achieves this purpose by postulating that if actions are arguably taken for the benefit of the corporation, then the directors are presumed to have been exercising their sound business judgment rather than responding to any personal motivations.

> Faced with the presumption raised by the rule, the question is what sort of showing the plaintiff must make to survive a motion for directed verdict. Because the rule presumes that business judgment was exercised, *the plaintiff must make a showing from which a factfinder might infer that impermissible motives predominated in the making of the decision in question.*

> The plaintiffs' theory that "a" motive to control is sufficient to rebut the rule is inconsistent with this purpose. Because the rule is designed to validate certain transactions despite conflicts of interest, the plaintiffs' rule would negate that purpose, at least in many cases. As already noted, control is always arguably "a" motive in any action taken by a director. Hence plaintiffs could always make this showing and thereby undercut the purpose of the rule.

Id. at 292–93 (emphasis added).

* * *

We also note that a majority of the directors of Field's were "independent": they derived no income from Field's other than normal directors' fees and the equivalent of an employee discount on merchandise. The presumption of good faith the business judgment rule affords is heightened when the majority of the board consists of independent outside directors. See, e.g., Warshaw v. Calhoun, 221 A.2d 487, 493 (Del.1966); Puma v. Marriott, 283 A.2d 693, 695 (Del.Ch.1971).

* * *

However, rather than proceeding under the business judgment rule, the plaintiffs here seek to apply a different test in the takover context, and propose that the burden be placed upon the directors to establish the compelling business purpose of any transaction which would have the effect of consolidating or retaining the directors' control. In light of the overwhelming weight of authority to the contrary, we refuse to apply such a novel rule to this case. Crouse-Hinds Co. v. InterNorth, Inc., 634 F.2d 690, 701–03 (2d Cir.1980); Treadway Cos. v. Care Corp., 638 F.2d 357, 381 (2d Cir.1980); Johnson v. Trueblood, supra; Gimbel v. Signal Cos., 316 A.2d 59, 601, 609 (Del.1974); Sinclair Oil Corp. v. Levien, 280 A.2d 717, 720 (Del.1971); Warshaw v. Calhoun, 221 A.2d 487 (Del.1966); GM Sub Corp., supra; Kaplan v. Goldsamt, 380 A.2d 556, 568 (Del.Ch.1977). To the extent that dicta in Klaus v. Hi-Shear Corp., 528 F.2d 225 (9th Cir.1975), suggest a different result under the corporation law of California, we decline to follow that rule.[7]

* * *

B. *The Breach of Fiduciary Duty*

1. The Policy of Independence

The plaintiffs contend that they have presented sufficient evidence to go to the jury on the existence of the secret policy, both circumstantially, from the history of prior rebuffs, and directly, from the testimony of two Field's directors.

On the resistance to prior approaches, we have established above that evaluation and response to such approaches is within the scope of the directors' duties. The plaintiffs have presented no evidence of self-dealing, fraud, overreaching or other bad conduct sufficient to give rise to any reasonable inference that impermissible motives predominated in the board's consideration of the approaches. The desire to build value within the company, and the belief that such value might be diminished by a given offer is a rational business purpose. The record reveals that appropriate consideration was given to each individual approach made to Marshall Field & Company. The plaintiffs have

[7] We are not persuaded by the dissent's attempts to distinguish the line of cases culminating in *Crouse-Hinds*. We believe the *Crouse-Hinds* court, in reversing an interpretation of *Treadway* similar to that espoused by the dissent, foreclosed that construction of the business judgment rule. It found that allegations of intent to retain control were insufficient as a matter of law even to raise a sufficiently serious question to make a fair ground for litigation. As the *Trueblood* court concluded, "at a minimum, the Delaware cases require that the plaintiff must show some sort of bad faith on the part of the defendant * * *. We do not think that a showing of 'a' motive to retain control, without more, constitutes bad faith in this context unless we are to ignore the realities of corporate life." 629 F.2d at 293. Because our examination of the board's conduct does not reveal such bad faith, we do not believe an evaluation of the fairness or wisdom of the board's conduct is called for as long as it can be attributed to any rational business purpose.

Nor are we persuaded by the dissent's reliance on Klaus v. Hi-Shear, 528 F.2d 225 (9th Cir.1975), and Royal Indus., Inc. v. Monogram Indus., Inc. [1976–77 Transfer Binder] Fed.Sec.L.Rep. (CCH) ¶ 95,863 (C.D. Cal.1976), both of which apply California corporate law. We note as a general matter that California law seems to impose a higher standard of fiduciary care than does the law of Delaware, which is applicable here. Compare, e.g., Sinclair Oil Corp. v. Levien, 280 A.2d 717 (Del.1971) (absent proof of self-dealing, fraud, or "gross and palpable over-reaching," courts will not examine the intrinsic fairness of the majority's control of the corporation even if it is to the detriment of the minority) with Jones v. H.F. Ahmanson & Co., 1 Cal.3d 93, 81 Cal.Rptr. 592, 600, 460 P.2d 464 (1969) (majority has a fiduciary duty to minority, and transactions involving control will be examined under "a comprehensive rule of 'inherent fairness from the viewpoint of the corporation and those interested therein.'"). See 59 Cal.L.Rev. 167, 180 (1971); 7 Pac.L.Rev. 613, 617–19 (1976).

failed to introduce evidence supporting a reasonable inference that any of the rejections of these approaches were made in bad faith. Therefore the presumption of good faith afforded by the business judgment rule applies, and the plaintiffs cannot survive the motion for directed verdict.

Having failed to establish the presence of an improper motive in any one of the defendants' responses to acquisition approaches, the plaintiffs seek to establish from the series of rejections the illogical inference that this reflects an invidious policy of independence regardless of benefit to the shareholders. All that the plaintiffs' evidence in this regard establishes is that Field's directors evaluated the merits of each approach made, and determined to implement their decisions as to each of the approaches by following the advice of counsel on how to respond to unwanted acquisition approaches.

The mere fact that two of the ten directors felt that the word "independence" reflected the board policy of trying to build value within the company rather than putting it up for sale, does not reveal an impermissible motive to reject all acquisition attempts regardless of merit. Furthermore, there is testimony by both directors who used the word "independent" that neither meant by it resistance at all costs, or against the best interests of the shareholders. We therefore affirm the district court's holding that the plaintiffs failed to raise a jury question on the issue of the alleged policy of independence.

*   *   *

2. The Defensive Acquisitions

The plaintiffs also contend that the "defensive" acquisitions of the five Liberty House stores and the Galleria were imprudent, and designed to make Field's less attractive as an acquisition, as well as to exacerbate any antitrust problems created by the CHH merger. It is precisely this sort of Monday-morning-quarterbacking that the business judgment rule was intended to prevent. Again, the plaintiffs have brought forth no evidence of bad faith, overreaching, self-dealing or any other fraud necessary to shift the burden of justifying the transactions to the defendants. On the contrary, there was uncontroverted evidence that such expansion was reasonable and natural. Thus even if the desire to fend off CHH was among the motives of the board in entering the transactions, because the plaintiffs have failed to establish that such a motive was the sole or primary purpose, as has been required by Delaware law since the leading case of Cheff v. Mathes, 41 Del.Ch. 494, 199 A.2d 548 (1964), the mere allegation, or even some proof, that a given transaction was made on "unfavorable" terms does not meet the fairly stringent burden the business judgment rules imposes on plaintiffs.

3. The Antitrust Suit

The plaintiffs also contend that the bringing of the antitrust suit against CHH was a breach of the directors' ficuciary duty. Because it is the duty of the directors to file an antitrust suit when in their business judgment a proposed combination would be illegal or otherwise detrimental to the corporation, see Chemetron Corp. v. Crane Co., 1977–2 Trade Cas. ¶ 61,717 at 72,933 (N.D.Ill.1977); Gulf & Western Industries, Inc. v. Great A & P Tea Co., 476 F.2d 687, 698 (2d Cir.1973), their decision to file an antitrust suit is also within the scope of the business judgment rule. There was substantial evidence before the court that the defendants were fairly and reasonably exercising their business judgment to protect the corporation against the perceived damage an illegal merger could cause, see Copperweld Corp. v. Imetal, 403 F.Supp. 579, 607 (W.D.Pa.1975) ("No doubt that [divestiture] would have a debilitating effect on the acquired company * * *.").*

Not only were the directors acting in good faith reliance on the advice of experienced and knowledgeable antitrust counsel, which in itself satisfies the requirements of the business judgment rule, * * * but one member of the board was an experienced antitrust lawyer with a background of experience to evaluate the soundness of the legal claims. See Abramson v. Nytronics, Inc., 312 F.Supp. 519, 531–32 (S.D. N.Y.1970) ("Boards of directors are deliberately chosen from the ranks of businessmen, bankers, and lawyers because of their expertise in evaluating the merits of precisely this sort of proposal."). The plaintiffs have introduced no evidence that the suit was brought in bad faith, but merely cite it as an example of the defendants' desire to perpetuate their control. However, because the bringing of the suit clearly served the rational business purpose of protecting Field's from the damage forced divestiture would cause, it is protected by the business judgment rule. Field's decision to resolve the antitrust question through litigation in federal court rather than some other method or in some other forum is a matter for the discretion of the directors when it is exercised within the scope of the rule.

Because we find insufficient evidence on which a jury could base a rational verdict that the defendants breached any fiduciary duty, neither can any claim of concealment of bad faith activity give rise to a jury question. We therefore affirm the district court's ruling on the state law claims of breach of fiduciary duty.

* * *

CUDAHY, Circuit Judge, concurring in part and dissenting in part:

Unfortunately, the majority here has moved one giant step closer to shredding whatever constraints still remain upon the ability of corporate directors to place self-interest before shareholder interest in resisting a hostile tender offer for control of the corporation. There is abundant evidence in this case to go to the jury on the state claims for breach of fiduciary duty. I emphatically disagree that the business judgment rule should clothe directors, battling blindly to fend off a threat to their control, with an almost irrebuttable presumption of sound business judgment, prevailing over everything but the elusive hobgoblins of fraud, bad faith or abuse of discretion. * * *

---

* What effect would divestiture have on the former shareholders of the acquired company? Would former Field's shareholders have to return the consideration they received from CHH if, after the acquisition, a court required CHH to divest Field's? [Ed.]

I.

Addressing first the state law claims of breach of fiduciary duty by the Board, the majority has adopted an approach which would virtually immunize a target company's board of directors against liability to shareholders, provided a sufficiently prestigious (and expensive) array of legal and financial talent were retained to furnish *post hoc* rationales for fixed and immutable policies of resistance to takeover. Relying on several recent decisions interpreting the Delaware business judgment rule, the majority fails to make the important distinction

> between the activity of a corporation in managing a business enterprise and its function as a vehicle for collecting and using capital and distributing profits and losses. The former involves corporate functioning in competitive business affairs in which judicial interference may be undesirable. *The latter involves only the corporation-shareholder relationship, in which the courts may more justifiably intervene to insist on equitable behavior.*

Note, *Protection for Shareholder Interests in Recapitalizations of Publicly Held Companies,* 58 Colum.L.Rev. 1030, 1066 (1958) (emphasis supplied).

The theoretical justification for the "hands off" precept of the business judgment rule is that courts should be reluctant to review the acts of directors in situations where the expertise of the directors is likely to be greater than that of the courts. But, where the directors are afflicted with a conflict of interest, relative expertise is no longer crucial. Instead, the great danger becomes the channeling of the directors' expertise along the lines of their personal advantage—sometimes at the expense of the corporation and its stockholders.[1] Here courts have no rational choice but to subject challenged conduct of directors and questioned corporate transactions to their own disinterested scrutiny. Of course, the self-protective bias of interested directors may be entirely devoid of corrupt motivation, but it may nonetheless constitute a serious threat to stockholder welfare.

* * *

Under the business judgment rule, once a plaintiff demonstrates that a director had an interest in the transaction at issue, the burden of proof shifts to the director to prove that the transaction was fair and reasonable to the corporation. Treadway Companies v. Care Corp., 638 F.2d 357 at 382 (2d Cir.1980). Accord, Crouse-Hinds Co. v. InterNorth, Inc., 634 F.2d 690 (2d Cir.1980). There was more than sufficient evidence in the instant case to permit the jury to shift the burden of proof to Field's directors and to consider the reasonableness of the

---

[1] Hostile tender offers unavoidably create a conflict of interest. * * * Nearly all directors and managers are interested in maintaining their compensation and perquisites. * * * [A] hostile tender offer unavoidably involves forces tending to shape decisions that are not necessarily for the benefit of all shareholders. As a result a * * * business judgment approach in hostile tender offer cases is inappropriate.

Gelfond and Sebastian, *Reevaluating the Duties of Target Management in the Hostile Tender Offer,* 60 B.U.L.Rev. 403, 435–37 (1980) (hereinafter "Gelfond and Sebastian").

transactions. The majority here, however, affirms a directed verdict which determines that the evidence was insufficient *as a matter of law* to establish that Field's directors were interested in this transaction. A brief examination of the majority's "overwhelming weight of authority" demonstrates that even these cases do not support its notion of the quantum of evidence necessary to create a jury question in this case.

In Crouse-Hinds Co. v. InterNorth, 634 F.2d 690 (2d Cir.1980), the tender offeror (InterNorth) arrived on the scene *after* a merger of the target (Crouse-Hinds) with a third party (Belden) had been announced. The tender offeror sought to enjoin preliminarily an exchange of stock in furtherance of the merger on the grounds that the exchange was designed merely to perpetuate the target management in office. Even though the target directors were allegedly "interested" in the merger because they would remain in control of the new corporation after its consummation, the court declined to shift the burden of proof to the directors for essentially two reasons.[6] First, at the time the merger was negotiated, the tender offeror had indicated no interest in the target and, hence, the directors could not have been motivated by a desire to retain control. Second, the tender offer was conditioned on abandonment of the merger and the target company directors' attribution of the exchange of stock to the facilitation of the merger was entirely credible.

Crouse-Hinds is distinguishable from the instant case. * * * [T]he Crouse-Hinds/Belden merger, which provided the basis for the self-interest charges, was negotiated *prior* to the tender offer. There was sufficient evidence (independent of any judgment made after the takeover attempt had been announced) to demonstrate that the combination was in the best interest of the stockholders. Thus, any activity to facilitate the merger after the tender offer could legitimately be ascribed to a valid business purpose.

---

[6] The court affirmed the "normal requirement that a complaining shareholder present evidence of the director's interest in order to shift the burden of proof," but rejected the logic of the district court's conclusion that "if the directors are to remain on the board after the merger, perpetuation of their control must be presumed to be their motivation." *Crouse-Hinds,* 634 F.2d at 702. To the extent that this language may have been intended to prevent a shift in the burden of proof upon a showing that the directors of a target corporation had an interest in maintaining their control of the corporation, I reject the holding as inconsistent with apposite case law, corporate reality and sound public policy. I do not believe, however, that the Second Circuit intended to establish a rule which would preclude an examination of fairness in the instant case. The facts in *Crouse-Hinds* are complicated and special, and the Second Circuit summed up its holding by saying: "In short, when the tender offeror has presented the target company with an *obvious reason* to oppose the tender offer, the offeror cannot, on the theory that the target's management opposes the offer for some other, *unstated,* improper purpose, obtain an injunction against the opposition without presenting strong evidence to support its theory." Id. at 704 (emphasis supplied). In the instant case, CHH did not present Field's with an "obvious reason" to oppose the tender offer nor are there alternative reasons "unstated" by plaintiffs here. Further, the *Crouse-Hinds* opinion recites a number of reasons why the InterNorth tender offer might have been inadequate on the merits, including the fact that the offering price was only $40 per share against a closing price the day before the announcement of $38 per share. Id. at 694 n. 5. When examined from these perspectives, the Second Circuit's digression into the principles of logic does not negate the interpretation of the business judgment rule advocated here.

In the present case, however, the challenged board activity occurred *after* CHH made known its acquisitive intentions. The responses of Field's Board could not be justified, as they were in *Crouse-Hinds,* on documented negotiations and decisions made prior to the tender offer. When reviewed against a background of cast-in-concrete hostility to merger offers, the hasty acquisition of five Liberty House stores in the Pacific Northwest (two of which were acknowledged "dogs"), the $17 million commitment for a Field's store in the Galleria complex in Houston, Texas (the site of a CHH Neiman-Marcus store) and the institution of a major antitrust action within hours of a merger proposal (ostensibly on the mere oral opinion of company counsel) represent some of the facts from which a jury might reasonably conclude that the directors improperly sought to perpetuate their control of the corporation.

* * *

The recent decision in Treadway Companies v. Care Corp., 638 F.2d 357 (2d Cir.1980), is similarly inappropriate authority for the majority's result. In *Treadway,* the tender offeror (Care) challenged the issuance and sale of a substantial number of shares of the target company (Treadway) to a third company (Fair Lanes) on the ground that Treadway's directors improperly approved the sale to perpetuate their control over the corporation.

* * *

On appeal, the Second Circuit examined the business judgment rule and explained:

> In nearly all of the cases treating stock transactions intended to affect control, the directors who approved the transaction have had a real and obvious interest in it: *their interest in retaining or strengthening their control of the corporation. It is this interest which causes the burden of proof to be shifted to the directors, to demonstrate the propriety of the transactions.* (Citations omitted) * * * [Thus,] in attacking a transaction that was intended to affect control, *plaintiff* * * * *bears the initial burden of proving that the directors had an interest in the transaction,* or acted in bad faith or for some improper purpose.

Treadway, 638 F.2d at 382 (emphasis supplied). Although the court ultimately found that the Treadway Board had not acted to maintain control, the case does not, for several reasons, require a similar result in favor of Field's directors.

First, the *Treadway* court premised its finding on Care's failure to show that all or even a majority of the directors had a personal interest in having the merger consummated.

* * *

In the present case, the directors had a personal interest in defeating the takeover attempt—"their interest in retaining or strengthening control of the corporation." See *Treadway,* 638 F.2d at 382. Therefore, under the business judgment rule's burden-shifting doctrine the Board should be required to demonstrate that these transactions were fair and reasonable to the corporation. As in *Treadway,* the haste with which the Board acted in making acquisitions and filing a major lawsuit, the absence of shareholder scrutiny of any of the Board's actions and the apparent lack of a good faith effort to determine whether the takeover was really in the shareholder's best interest are troublesome.

* * *

The majority also relies on Johnson v. Trueblood, 629 F.2d 287 (3d Cir.1980) and quotes from Chief Justice Seitz's opinion essentially to establish that self-interest must be the sole or primary motive underlying a director's challenged action rather than merely "a" motive when control is implicated. The issue arose in *Trueblood*, however, in the context of *how a jury was to be charged*, not whether the evidence should go to a jury at all. The *Trueblood* court concluded (and the majority here agrees) that to survive a motion for a directed verdict, the "plaintiff must make a showing from which a factfinder might infer that impermissible motives predominated in the making of the decision in question." Id. at 292–93. Regardless whether "a" self-interested motive is sufficient or whether a "primary" self-interested motive is requisite, there is sufficient evidence in the instant case to satisfy either standard. Nothing in *Trueblood* supports the view that the district court properly foreclosed jury consideration of the claims of Field's shareholders.

Beyond this, however, I believe that Judge Rosenn's dissent in *Trueblood* states the proper interpretation of the business judgment rule in control cases: "Once a plaintiff has shown that the desire to retain control was 'a' motive in the particular business decision under challenge, the burden is then on the defendant to move forward with the evidence justifying the transaction as primarily in the corporation's best interest." *Trueblood,* 629 F.2d at 301. This statement of the rule is compatible with both the Delaware case law [9] and the realities of corporate governance, and is by no means a minority position. In Klaus v. Hi-Shear Corp., 528 F.2d 225 (9th Cir.1975), the logic of which the defendants ignore and the majority chooses to reject, the Court of Appeals for the Ninth Circuit approved the application of a rigorous rule which required directors of a target company, as fiduciaries, to demonstrate a "compelling business purpose" for their actions. Id. at 233–34. The *Klaus* standard is entirely consistent with the standard which the Second Circuit clearly spelled out in *Treadway* and left intact in *Crouse-Hinds.* See note 6, supra. See also Podesta v. Calumet Indus. Inc., [1978 Transfer Binder] Fed.Sec.L.Rep. (CCH) ¶ 96,433 (N.D.

[9] Nothing in Bennett [v. Propp, 41 Del. Ch. 14, 187 A.2d 405 (1962)] or Cheff [v. Mathes, 41 Del.Ch. 494, 199 A.2d 548 (1964)] suggests that the plaintiff must first prove that the sole or primary purpose of the transaction was the directors' desire to retain control over the corporation. Rather, the unequivocal thrust of *Bennett* is that once the record demonstrates that control is implicated in the transaction, a conflict of interest is *ipso facto* created. Once a conflict of interest is present, the burden of proof is shifted logically and pragmatically on the defendants 'to justify [the transaction] as one primarily in the corporate interest.' *Bennett,* supra, 187 A.2d at 409.

* * * Recent Delaware cases reveal a growing trend to impose obligations on management to justify control-related transactions. Cf. Singer v. Magnavox, 380 A.2d 969 (Del.1977) * * * Sinclair Oil v. Levien, 280 A.2d 717, 720 (Del. 1971) * * * Petty v. Penntech Papers, Inc., 347 A.2d 140, 143 (Del.Ch.1975).

Trueblood, 629 F.2d at 300–01 (Rosenn, J., dissenting).

Ill.1978); Royal Indus., Inc. v. Monogram Indus., [1976–77 Transfer Binder] Fed.Sec.L.Rep. (CCH) ¶ 95,863 (C.D.Cal.1976).

Thus, the majority here has no basis for asserting that in "control" cases an interpretation of the business judgment rule which shifts the burden of proof to interested directors and requires them to establish a valid business purpose for their actions is a "novel" rule contrary to the "overwhelming weight of authority." In none of the cases cited by the majority was the factfinder (whether judge or jury) precluded from evaluating the merits of the fiduciary duty claims. In the instant case, on the other hand, similar claims are buffered against jury examination by the *cordon sanitaire* of a distorted business judgment rule.

II.

The basic error of the majority in the instant case is in holding as a matter of law that there was insufficient evidence to go to the jury on the state claims of breach of fiduciary duty. In reviewing a directed verdict, this court must evaluate the evidence in a light most favorable to the appellant and determine "whether it is of sufficient probative value that members of the jury might fairly and impartially differ as to the inferences to be reasonably drawn therefrom." There was abundant evidence from which a jury in this case could have concluded that Field's directors breached their fiduciary duties to the shareholders: 1) by pursuing a fixed, nondebatable and undisclosed policy of massive resistance to merger with, or acquisition by, a series of the nation's foremost retailers; 2) by making hasty and apparently imprudent defensive acquisitions to reduce Field's attractiveness as a takeover candidate and to force the withdrawal of the CHH offer; and 3) by hastily filing a major antitrust suit to further impair persistent acquisitive efforts of CHH.

Reviewing first the evidence on the existence of a policy of independence in a light most favorable to appellants, it is difficult to understand the basis for the majority's conclusion that jurors could not fairly and impartially differ as to the inferences to be drawn from the facts presented. Marshall Field's Board of Directors had long been aware of the fact that the company's "accumulated worth, strong balance sheet, large cash reserves and borrowing potential" made Field's vulnerable to an involuntary merger or takeover. Panter v. Marshall Field & Co., 486 F.Supp. 1168 (N.D.Ill.1980). In December 1969, at approximately the same time that Associated Dry Goods expressed an interest in acquiring Field's, the Board retained Joseph Flom of the New York law firm of Skadden, Arps, Slate, Meagher & Flom for advice on defeating takeover bids. Id. at 1175–76. Flom recommended the application of his "pyramid theory" which is based on the principle that the best way to remain independent is to acquire other enterprises.[11] In this way, Field's would either become too large to be acquired or would have so

---

[11] Flom testified that he advised every Field's Chief Executive from 1970 to 1977 that acquisitions were the best means to prevent takeover. *Panter*, 486 F.Supp. at 1176.

much overlap that acquisition of Field's by another major retailer would inevitably create antitrust problems.

While the majority notes that Flom advised the Board to be interested and listen carefully to proposals from other retailers, the majority apparently overlooks the curious coincidence that Field's made a major acquisition and/or raised antitrust problems to fight off virtually every serious merger or takeover attempt after the company hired Flom. In response to the interest of Associated, a predominantly Ohio and Pennsylvania operation, Field's conveniently acquired the Cleveland and Erie retail operations of Halle Brothers. *Panter*, 486 F.Supp. at 1177. These stores have however, been less than profitable for Field's in the decade since they were acquired. *See* Plaintiffs' Exhibits 370, 372.

Similarly, after a merger proposal from Federated Department Stores in 1975, Field's actively employed Flom's antitrust approach to prevent a takeover.

No major acquisition was necessary in this instance because Federated's Chicago Division of I. Magnin and the Chicago, Seattle, and Milwaukee-based Boston Stores (which Federated offered to divest) created sufficient antitrust leverage for Field's to stave off the unwelcome opportunity. Again, in 1976, Field's was under siege by Dayton-Hudson, but sought to acquire overlapping stores in Portland, Oregon and Tacoma, Washington from Liberty House.[13] Although Field's Board vociferously contends that its fascination with the Pacific Northwest was part of a long-range plan to sustain growth and profitability, the Board's interest in the Liberty House stores coincidentally subsided as Dayton-Hudson's interest in Field's waned. See *Panter*, 486 F.Supp. at 1177. Finally, it should surprise no one that Field's initial response to the CHH proposal was to raise antitrust questions and hastily seek to acquire retail operations which were adjacent to CHH operations.

The majority accepts the defendants' claim that the Board's responses were tailored to a "desire to build value within the company and the belief that such value might be diminished by a given offer." [14] But one man's desire to "build value" may be another man's desire to "keep control at all costs," and a jury must decide which characterization is most consistent with the facts. A properly charged jury could have fairly concluded that Field's carefully weighed each merger or takeover offer to determine stockholder interest, but they could have just as fairly concluded that Field's carefully built its defenses against each offer without regard to stockholder interest. A directed verdict on these claims is therefore indefensible.

[13] When asked to examine the antitrust aspects of a Dayton-Hudson/Marshall Field's combination, William Blair & Co., Field's investment banker, could find no competitive overlap between the two retailers.

"diminished by a given offer." For the most part, Field's managed to squelch these offers before their impact on value could be fully appreciated by its stockholders.

[14] There seems to be a striking paucity of evidence on how value might have been

The plaintiffs also presented extensive evidence to substantiate their claims that Field's Board gave the CHH merger proposal no bona fide consideration and instead engaged in classic anti-takeover maneuvers. Throughout the busy Christmas season, the Board hastily solicited and apparently imprudently consummated several defensive acquisitions to reduce the company's attractiveness as a takeover candidate, create additional antitrust problems and ultimately force the withdrawal of the CHH offer. The documentary and testimonial evidence presented at trial provided a sufficient basis from which a jury could conclude that Field's Board in this respect breached its fiduciary duty.

The Board first learned of the CHH interest at a meeting following the death of Field's then chief executive, Joseph Burnham, in October 1977. *Panter*, 486 F.Supp. at 1178. A resolution passed at that meeting announced the Board's swift and uncompromising response: "The proposed business combination *should not be considered* because the best interests of the company's shareholders would be served by * * * continuing as an independent entity." Id. (emphasis added). When CHH presented a formal merger proposal to the Board on December 12, 1977, the directors received a limited review of the financial aspects of the merger,[15] heard conflicting reports on Marshall Field's future earnings,[16] and rejected the CHH proposal as "illegal, inadequate and not in the best interest of Marshall Field & Co., its stockholders and the community which it serves." Id. at 1181.

Less than two weeks later (and only four days before Christmas), a committee of Field's officers and investment bankers reviewed a list of candidates available for immediate acquisition by Field's. Record at 553. Within ten days of this meeting, committee members met with the principal stockholders of Dillard's, a southwestern retailer in direct competition with CHH's Neiman-Marcus division, to see if a deal could be struck.[17] Correspondence from one of Field's investment bankers established that the Board sought a speedy transaction which would not require shareholder approval.[18] Because there was no time for a full

---

[15] Field's investment bankers were never asked to evaluate the adequacy or the fairness of the CHH proposal or determine the range for an acceptable offer. The record only shows that Mr. Flom asked whether "it [was] reasonable to assume that if the Marshall Field Board chose to sell the company now, it could expect to attain a higher price than that proposed by CHH? The response was yes; [but] no price was specified." Plaintiffs' Exhibit 122.

[16] The investment bankers' "best professional judgment" was that Field's future earnings would rise 15% in 1978 and 12% each year thereafter.

However, Field's President Angelo Arena, who had been on the job less than two months, presented a hastily prepared "five-year plan" which projected an earnings per share increase of 23% for 1978 and approximately 20% for each year thereafter. The plan also showed that Field's management expected the 1977 earnings (year ending January 31, 1978) would be down some 7% from the prior year, but anticipated a five year increase of up to 193% in Field's per share earnings despite the fact that in the prior five years, Field's per share earnings had declined by 20%. The Board rejected the bankers' estimates in favor of Arena's five-year plan.

[17] The December 21, 1977 Acquisition Status Report indicates that less than two weeks prior to the meeting with Dillard's shareholders, Field's officers did not even know whether Dillard's was a standard retailer or a discount operation.

[18] The January 4, 1978, letter from a representative of William Blair & Co. to Field's Executive Vice-President stated:

The most important benefits to Marshall Field & Co. from an all cash transaction are as follows:

scale financial analysis, the banker relied on "the intuitive judgment [of a Field's officer] as to the business potential" of the acquisition. Plaintiffs' Exhibit 137. The deal ultimately fell through, however, when Dillard's was purchased by Dutch interests.

Shortly after the demise of the Dillard's deal, Field's Board considered a proposal to acquire five Liberty House stores in the Pacific Northwest.[19] In the absence of any historical operating data, and despite reports from Field's Vice-President of Corporate Development that the estimated earnings potential of these stores was marginal,[21] the Board unanimously approved a $24 million agreement to purchase these operations. Record at 603. The acquisition was publicly announced the following day.

* * *

The majority reviewed this sequence of events and concluded that there was "uncontroverted evidence that such expansion was reasonable and natural."

There was more than sufficient evidence here, however, for a jury to conclude that it was not "reasonable and natural" for the directors of a major retailer to make expansion commitments totalling more than $40 million dollars during and shortly after a busy Christmas season in which their "top priority" was to help a new chief executive officer become familiar with Field's operation.[28] Particularly when considered with the evidence of a long-standing and uncompromising policy of

The speed of consummation, since the approach will not require the filing of a registration statement and since it would be a friendly offer endorsed by Dillard management, it would not run afoul of anti-takeover laws *nor would there be a need for a stockholders meeting* by either company.

* * *

* * * The principal disadvantages of [a tax-free transaction] are the *time required to effect the total transaction* (registration and stockholders meetings) and the *risk of certain Field's stockholders throwing up roadblocks* to the transaction. * * *

[19] Defendants claim that the acquisition of these Liberty House stores was the fruit of a long-standing desire to expand its Seattle-based Frederick and Nelson division. They point to 1975 and 1976 visits to these locations as proof of their good intentions. They conveniently ignore two important facts, however: 1) in 1975 and 1976 when these visits were made, Field's was fighting off takeover attempts by Federated and Dayton-Hudson respectively; and 2) a December 1, 1977, letter from John Nannes of Skadden, Arps to Jospeh DeCoeur of Kirkland & Ellis suggests a Liberty House acquisition would bolster Field's potential competition theory:

Dear Joe:

The Wall Street Journal reported in November 25, 1977 (page 14, column 6), that Carter Hawley Hale acquired a Liberty House department store in San Jose California from Amfac, Inc. I understand that there are a number of Liberty House department stores in the Pacific Northwest and this may well bolster our potential competition theory.

This letter was written *before* CHH ever made a formal merger proposal which Field's Board could consider.

[21] The figures prepared by Field's Vice-President of Corporate Development were rejected by Field's management and replaced with more optimistic estimates dated January 19, 1978, the day of the Board meeting at which the Liberty House acquisition was approved.

[28] At one point during the trial, Director William Blair testified that the Board's "top priority" was to help Arena in the transition period following Burnham's death "because without capable management at the top of the company as our Christmas season was starting, we would have been in trouble and the stockholders would have suffered."

independence, I am astonished that the business judgment rule under any guise could keep this case from the jury.

* * *

One may, of course, argue that what the directors did here was merely to make the normal reflexive response of incumbent management to efforts by outsiders to take over control of a corporation. In fact, applicable federal and state takeover legislation suggests that incumbent management—protective of its own powers and perquisites—may almost automatically attempt to defeat hostile tender offers, whatever their merits. These assumptions may reflect a realistic view of human and corporate nature, and perhaps the law should simply excuse directors for thinking of themselves first and stockholders second in the event of a threatened takeover. In that regard I do not perceive the actions of Field's directors here as necessarily more egregious than many others in like circumstances. But under the legal norms which now must guide us (and no matter who has the burden of proof), there is no good reason to take this unfortunately too typical, but nonetheless important and substantial, case from the jury.

◆

Note.   The Judicial Mainstream

At this writing, Panter v. Marshall Field & Co. is a representative statement of the law concerning the obligations of target management when faced with a tender offer.[70] Courts treat the issue as one of business judgment. In order to validate their actions, management must show only that the defensive tactics adopted served a corporate purpose in addition to defeating the offer, or if not, that there was a basis for opposing the acquisition in addition to a desire to remain in office. Plaintiffs are, in effect, left with the burden of showing that self-preservation was the only motive for management's actions.

In evaluating the impact of this legal rule, however, it is necessary to take a step beyond merely extracting the doctrinal core from a line of cases. The real significance of the rule is how it affects the behavior of target management. How does management understand the standards to which their conduct must conform? Here lawyers play a critical role. Management typically does not itself read judicial opinions; when faced with a hostile offer at a premium, management's first step is to ask counsel what they can do. Moreover, counsel's advice likely will be of particular importance to independent directors who have much less to lose as a result of a takeover than does target management, but who stand to share equally in any liability imposed as a result of opposing the offer. Thus, understanding how the law *really* constrains behavior—what standards the actors, as opposed to the courts, believe govern their conduct—requires examination not only of

---

[70] See, e.g., Treadway Companies, Inc. v. Care Corp., 638 F.2d 357 (2d Cir.1980) (New Jersey law); Crouse-Hinds Co. v. InterNorth, Inc., 634 F.2d 690 (2d Cir.1980) (New York law); Johnson v. Trueblood, 629 F.2d 287 (3d Cir.1980), cert. denied 450 U.S. 999 (1981) (Delaware law).

judicial pronouncements, but also of how those pronouncements are translated by counsel to clients. What do the lawyers tell clients the rules are?

As one source of guidance as to what management is told the law is, there follows an opinion of counsel rendered by a prominent law firm to the Board of Directors of McGraw-Hill, Inc., in the course of the American Express tender offer. From the perspective of counsel, does the letter fairly represent the state of the law described by the court in Panter v. Marshall Field & Co.?[71] From the perspective of an independent director of McGraw-Hill, does the letter satisfy you that there is no possibility of director liability if McGraw-Hill chooses to follow a scorched earth campaign?

WACHTELL, LIPTON, ROSEN & KATZ

299 Park Avenue, New York, N.Y. 10017

(212) 371–0200

January 30, 1979

To the Board of Directors of
McGraw-Hill, Inc.
McGraw-Hill, Inc.
1221 Avenue of the Americas
New York, New York

Gentlemen:

We have been asked to render our opinion as to whether the directors of McGraw-Hill, Inc. are compelled to accept the proposal of American Express Company made by letter dated January 29, 1979 with respect to the making of a cash tender offer of $40 per share for the shares of common stock of McGraw-Hill, Inc. on the conditions set forth in such letter. Our opinion is that the directors are not required to accept such proposal.

It may be helpful to the Board to have us set forth the bases upon which we reach that conclusion. We note at the outset that the same general principles of law apply to this question as would apply to all other questions of the propriety of directors conduct: to wit, that absent fraud or self-dealing, the controlling test is simply that directors use their reasonable business judgment. No unique rule of law governs a takeover proposal, i.e., the fact that a third person, such as American Express, chooses unilaterally to make an offer for a company—including an offer at a premium over quoted market price for normal trading in the shares—does not mean that the directors are thereby placed under an obligation to sell the company (or facilitate a sale) at such time to that third person (or to another). The Board is entitled to take into account the interests of those shareholders who would *not* wish to terminate their investment in the enterprise as well as those who may. The directors are entitled in the exercise of their reasonable business

---

[71] Because the letter obviously predates *Panter,* the exercise is also a test of the statement in the text that *Panter* is representative of the general state of the law.

judgment to take into account all relevant economic factors: whether given the totality of circumstances—for example, the state of affairs of the business, its growth prospects, the state of the economy, present-day interest rates, and the like—this would be the optimum point in time to sell the company. The directors are entitled to take into account whether the interests of shareholders would not be better served— should an ultimate sale or business combination of the company be desired—by a decision to sell at a future date of the company's own selection: at a time and in a manner best calculated to realize the maximum value for the shareholders. The directors are also entitled to consider whether a particular proposal—as, for example, the all cash proposal being made by American Express in its January 29 letter—is best geared to meet the varying tax desiderata of a variety of shareholders (as opposed to the type of offer that can normally be obtained in negotiations of a company's own choosing).

Moreover, quite apart from economic considerations, if there exist serious questions of legality with respect to a proposed offer, this would in and of itself provide reason for rejection (and, indeed, active resistance) by a Board of Directors. In addition, if acceptance of a particular proposal would appear likely to subject the company to lengthy and complex litigation—involving inevitable disruption of the corporate business and diversion of executive time and effort—with great uncertainty as to whether the proposed transaction would ever ultimately be successfully consummated, the directors are entitled to take such factors into account, including the impact on the company business, its employees, shareholders, reputation and the like if—after a long person of uncertainty and government litigation—the proposed transaction should *not* be permitted to be consummated.

With respect to the present American Express proposal, we note a number of factors which the Board of Directors may deem appropriate to take into account in the exercise of its business judgment:

1. The very limited discovery that has been had to date— before American Express withdrew its previous formal proposed tender offer and simultaneously refused to go forward with further discovery—has served to confirm the existence of the serious questions of antitrust illegality that were noted for the Board at its meeting of January 12, 1979 and have been detailed in the counterclaims asserted on behalf of McGraw-Hill against American Express in the Federal Court litigation. Thus, even if the Board of Directors of McGraw-Hill should acquiesce in the new American Express proposal and itself refrain from pursuing any litigation with respect to an American Express takeover, there exists in our opinion a very strong likelihood of the institution of major litigation to bar such takeover by the Federal Trade Commission with prospects for lengthy delay of the transaction and ultimate prohibition.

2. There also exist serious questions—upon which discovery had yet to be had—as to whether American Express is presently an illegal bank holding company (and would thereby be prohibited

from going forward with the acquisition). Moreover, even if American Express at present technically transacts business within a narrow exemption to the Bank Holding Company Act, there exists question as to whether such exemption may be permitted to continue by the Congress or whether other congressional action may be taken to preclude an acquisition of the nature proposed by American Express. In this regard it may be noted that Congressman Henry S. Reuss, Chairman of the House of Representatives Committee on Banking, Finance and Urban Affairs has already called for inquiry by the Subcommittee on Financial Institutions Supervision, Regulation and Insurance, as well as the Federal Reserve Board and the Controller of the Currency, into the propriety of an acquisition of McGraw-Hill by American Express. The fundamental concerns voiced by Congressman Reuss would be as germane to the new American Express proposal as to the old.

3. Investigation conducted to date has given rise to very serious questions as to whether American Express in connection with its business operations in the Middle East has not been (and is not continuing to be) guilty of illegal compliance with the Arab boycott of Israel and certain Israeli-associated business entities. It may be noted in this regard that—notwithstanding express and repeated demand—American Express in the pending litigation involving its formal tender offer failed to produce the documentary materials in its possession which would have disclosed whether such illegal boycott compliance has indeed been taking place and then withdrew its formal offer (and refused to go forward with further litigation discovery) only minutes before the commencement of the initial deposition of an American Express representative at which this question (among others) would have been subject to probe. It would appear likely that this entire question could be the subject of intense scrutiny in connection with application by American Express to the Federal Communications Commission relating to the McGraw-Hill television facilities, with once again substantial possibility for lengthy delay and ultimate refusal of the American Express application (or withdrawal by American Express in the face of the ultimate necessity to make full disclosure of its Middle East conduct).

The above considerations are merely illustrative and are not meant to exhaust all of the legal problems and delays that would inhere to the American Express proposed offer. The Board may also deem it appropriate to take into account the impact upon McGraw-Hill and its shareholders—including the potentiality for damage to the credibility, integrity and business operations of McGraw-Hill—if McGraw-Hill (having heretofore cogently raised these very considerations both in judicial proceedings and proceedings before government agencies) were now with apparent hypocrisy to reverse field and acquiesce in the revised American Express proposal—and that offer, after a lengthy period of delay and uncertainty, were ultimately *not* to reach consummation.

In the exercise of its business judgment, the Board of Directors is also entitled to take into consideration the opinion of Morgan Stanley & Co. as to such matters as the adequacy of the price being proposed by American Express for a sale of the company, the optimum timing of a sale or other business combination of the company should such be deemed desirable; whether, should such sale or business combination be decided upon in the future, the same price (or a higher price) can be anticipated to be obtainable from other entities (which may not share the disabilities of American Express); and the fact that the American Express proposal is in terms of a cash offer only (with consequent tax disadvantages to many long-term McGraw-Hill shareholders).

In conclusion, it is our opinion that, should the Board of Directors determine in the exercise of its business judgment to reject the American Express proposal, such rejection would not violate the fiduciary duty of the Board of Directors to McGraw-Hill and its shareholders and there would be no liability of the Board of Directors and its members to McGraw-Hill or its shareholders.

> Very truly yours,
> Watchell, Lipton, Rosen & Katz

Note: What Can be Learned From the Losers?

While the discretion given directors by the business judgment rule approach is substantial, it is not entirely without limits; in a small number of cases some defensive tactics initiated by target management in the face of a hostile offer have been enjoined. The real significance of these limits can be seen by examining the few recent cases where a court has held that management violated their fiduciary duty by engaging in defensive tactics.

Podesta v. Calumet Industries, Inc., [1977–78 Transfer Binder] (CCH) ¶ 96,433 (N.D.Ill.1978), involved efforts by management to diffuse a proxy contest initiated for the purpose of replacing the company's chief executive officer and chairman of the board. These individuals also owned 27% of the company's outstanding stock. Two transactions were of particular concern. In the first, the company repurchased from a bank a warrant covering 18,500 shares of its stock. It then sold the warrant to a customer, joint venturer and supplier of the company, who immediately exercised. This put another 4% of the company's stock in hands friendly to management. In the second transaction, the company created an Employee Stock Ownership Trust and issued to it 50,000 shares of the company's stock, of which 22.3% would be voted by the company's directors and the remainder by the employees themselves. The result of the two transactions was to increase the number of shares owned or controlled by management from 27% to 37%.

The evidence concerning the circumstances in which both transactions occurred strongly suggested that they were motivated by the prospect of the proxy fight. The warrant transaction was only one of a number of plans to place new shares in friendly hands, including the CEO's daughter, and was structured to avoid the need for a shareholder vote to approve issuance of so many shares. The ESOP transaction also had a curious genesis. Despite the fact that establishment of an ESOP had never before been considered, it was arranged with such haste that there was no financing, and was specifically structured so that the shares issued could be voted in the contested election. Moreover, no effort had been made to establish the existence of a policy dispute between the insurgents and management. The court ultimately concluded that preservation of management's control was the primary purpose of the transaction, and prevented the shares held by the customer and by the ESOP from voting.

In Royal Industries, Inc. v. Monogram Industries, Inc., [1976–77 Transfer Binder] Fed.Sec.L.Rep. (CCH) ¶ 95,863 (C.D.Cal.1976), the court enjoined a defensive acquisition of a competitor of the acquiring company. The record disclosed that, on the day after the offer was announced, target management had never heard of the company which they agreed to purchase two days later, that no significant investigation had been made of the company being acquired, and that the acquisition terms were quite unfavorable to the target.

Norlin Corp. v. Rooney, Pace, Inc., 744 F.2d 255 (2d Cir.1984), is the most prominent in this line of cases. The battle commenced when Piezo Electric Products, Inc., in conjunction with its investment banker Rooney, Pace, acquired 32 percent of Norlin's common stock through separate transactions culminating on January 12, 1984. The following day, Norlin followed the advice given by Herbert Wachtell in the excerpt in section B.1.b. of this Chapter and filed suit claiming that Piezo's acquisition violated various statutes, and asking that Piezo be required to divest its Norlin stock. Motions for expedited discovery and for a temporary restraining order were also filed.

Norlin may have anticipated the court's response to its motions because, on January 20th, the same day the court denied Norlin's motions, Norlin transferred 28,395 shares of its own stock to a subsidiary, purportedly in exchange for the cancellation of a debt owed the subsidiary by Norlin. Five days later Norlin issued two additional large blocks of securities: 800,000 shares were issued to the same subsidiary in exchange for a promissory note, and 185,000 shares were issued to a newly formed ESOP, also in exchange for a promissory note. The result of the two transactions was to increase the shares controlled by Norlin's management to 49 percent.[72]

In keeping with prior cases, and consistently with the substance of the opinion of counsel just examined, Norlin argued that, because it had determined that a takeover by Piezo was not in the company's best interest, the business judgment rule shielded any actions taken to defeat it. The court disagreed with this analysis, but for reasons that are at very best unclear. In response to Norlin's claims that a Piezo

---

[72] The issuance of this amount of stock required shareholder approval under the rules of the New York Stock Exchange. Norlin did not seek shareholder approval and its stock was delisted as a result.

takeover might jeopardize Norlin's net operating loss carryforward, the court stated that "this would only help to justify the board's determination that an anticipated takeover attempt should be opposed as not in the corporation's best interest. It has no relevance to our evaluation whether the actions taken by the board in response to that decision were fair and reasonable." 744 F.2d at 267.[73]

It is hard to know what to make of this reasoning. If management had concluded that a takeover of Norlin by Piezo was not in Norlin's best interests, then why would a federal court, bound by Erie Railroad v. Tompkins[74] to apply state law, inquire into the fairness of the particular actions taken? To whom must the actions be fair? The business judgment rule, of course, is designed to prevent a fairness review of management's actions and that rule is hardly given latitude if the court's analysis of the fairness of the actions serves to make the business judgment rule inoperative. In terms of traditional state law doctrine, the analysis is simply backwards.[75]

What differentiates these cases from *Panter v. Marshall Field?* Is it relevant that the cases in which management lost involved smaller companies which operated without the assistance of special counsel and without the ongoing advice of investment bankers? The overall tone of the court's opinion in *Norlin* strongly suggests that it did not really believe that target management thought the acquisition would be detrimental to the company (although the court did not so hold). The court was obviously troubled in *Norlin* and in other cases by the haste with which the action was taken. Along the same line, Arthur Fleischer argues "that the courts frequently found that incumbent management justified their actions by what appeared to be incomplete or inaccurate records."[76] How would you have advised management in *Calumet Industries* or *Monogram Industries?* Would better planning and better records have altered the results? Finally, are there substantive differences between the activities engaged in by Marshall Field, particularly as described by the dissent, and those undertaken by target

---

[73] Note 13 of the court's opinion sheds some light on the court's confusion. In response to precedent supporting precisely Norlin's position, the court states: "This is, as we have explained, a correct statement of law absent a showing of board self-interest. In this case such a showing has been made * * *." 744 F.2d at 267 n. 13. The difficulty, however, is that the only showing of self-interest was that the transactions were not fair and reasonable. But under the traditional approach that should be beside the point if management has decided that the offer was not in the company's best interests. The court made no findings with respect to the actual motivation of Norlin's management, perhaps because the large majority of the board of directors were independent.

[74] 304 U.S. 64 (1938).

[75] For other cases in which courts enjoined defensive conduct by target management see Concec Corp. v. Luckenheimer Co., 43 Del.Ch. 353, 230 A.2d 769 (1972); Consolidated Amusement v. Rugoff, Fed.Sec.L.Rep. (CCH) ¶ 96,584 (S.D.N.Y. 1978); Applied Digital Data Systems, Inc. v. Milgo Elec. Corp., 425 F.Supp. 1145 (S.D. N.Y.1977). In Minstar Acquiring Corp. v. AMF Inc., [Current Volume] Fed.Sec.L. Rep. (CCH) ¶ 92,066 (S.D.N.Y.1985), the court relied on *Norlin* in holding that the fact that increased employee severance and incentive pay plans adopted by the target after the offer was made became effective only on a change in control "properly raises a strong inference that AMF's board acted only to entrench itself." Id. at ¶ 91,322. As in *Norlin*, the problem is that the inference raised is only that the adoption was defensive; it does not shed light on the motive for the defense.

[76] A. Fleischer, *supra*, at 194.

management in the cases in which management lost? The answers to these questions, in turn, may suggest something about the function counsel plays in this setting. Is one of counsel's functions, and perhaps one of the investment bankers' functions as well, to provide protective coloring?

b. *The Legal Status of Particular Defensive Tactics*

(1) **The Legality of Shark Repellent Amendments**

Because shark repellent amendments have as their purpose deterrence, they are typically adopted before an actual offer surfaces [77] and, thus, lack the immediacy of the conflict of interest that has animated judicial evaluations of other defensive tactics. Moreover, unlike other defensive tactics about which the corporate statute is entirely silent, the crucial characteristic of shark repellent amendments—a supermajority vote requirement [78]—seems to be expressly authorized by typical corporate statutes. It is hardly surprising then that the case law governing their legality is both more limited in volume and quite different in approach.

GILSON, THE CASE AGAINST SHARK REPELLENT AMENDMENTS: STRUCTURAL LIMITATIONS ON THE ENABLING CONCEPT
34 Stan.L.Rev. 775, 804–14 (1982).[*]

TRADITIONAL APPROACHES TO SHARK REPELLENT AMENDMENTS: ATTACK AND DEFENSE

Unlike other defensive tactics, most shark repellent amendments have the advantage of clarity of intent: Their only purpose is to reallocate decisionmaking power over tender offers in favor of management. A typical proxy statement disclosure states that the proposed shark repellent amendments "are designed to discourage any attempt to obtain control of [the target] in a transaction which is not approved by [the] Board of Directors." [112] The unavoidable consequence of this reallocation is to make incumbent managers more secure in their positions: "[S]uch amendments may result in the incumbent officers and directors * * * retaining their positions even though stockholders holding a majority of shares desire a change." [113] Management's role in the adoption of shark repellent amendments—whether by investing corporate resources in their development, by using proxy ma-

---

[77] The Martin Marietta-Bendix transaction is a recent exception.

[78] Recall that only a supermajority lockup provision gives shark repellant amendments any promise of effectiveness.

[*] Copyright © 1982 by the Board of Trustees of the Leland Stanford Junior University.

[112] Proxy Statement of PSA, Inc. Similar statements appear in the proxy statements of many companies proposing shark repellent amendments. See, e.g., Proxy Statement of Baldor Electric Co.; Proxy Statement of Ozark Airlines 4 (Apr. 16, 1979); Proxy Statement of Sterling Precision Corp. 14–15, 16 (Aug. 23, 1979).

[113] Proxy Statement of PSA, Inc.; see Proxy Statement of Sterling Precision Corp.

chinery to solicit their approval, or simply by recommending their adoption—therefore raises the question of whether management has acted in its own interest at the expense of the shareholders. In traditional terms, the obvious attack on management's activities would be framed in terms of a violation of fiduciary duty.

The obvious response is also traditional. The corporate statutes of most states expressly authorize the most common forms of shark repellent amendments. In modern "enabling act" statutes,[114] phrases such as "unless otherwise provided in the articles of incorporation" qualify almost all prescriptive provisions,[115] and all major statutes expressly authorize supermajority voting requirements.[116] Subject only to compliance with the required formalities concerning amending the articles of incorporation, it would be argued, the validity of shark repellant amendments is unassailable.

Textual Analysis of the Validity of Shark Repellent Amendments

Just as the duty of loyalty provides the traditional focus for an attack on the validity of shark repellent amendments, a textual analysis of the language of the corporate statute provides the traditional focus for their defense. This mode of analysis is straightforward and familiar: It argues that the language of the statute contemplates the challenged provision and that further inquiry is therefore unnecessary.

* * *

I have found only three cases that directly confront the validity of shark repellant amendments or their equivalents. Of these, Seibert v. Gulton Industries, Inc.[129] presents a useful example of the technical approach to the claim that shark repellent amendments are invalid.[131]

---

[114] An "enabling act" is one that explicitly allows those forming a corporation the freedom to structure their arrangement as they choose, "put[ting] the arrangements for the allocation of risk, control, profit, and residual ownership on a free contract basis," Latty, supra note 17, at 601, and provides "relatively unhampered procedures * * * to meet changing conditions by effecting changes in the corporate purposes and security structures," Katz, The Philosophy of Midcentury Corporation Statutes, 23 Law & Contemp.Prob. 177, 179 (1958).

[115] E.g., Cal.Corp.Code §§ 602(a), 603(a), 1201(a) (West 1977 & Supp.1981); Del.Code Ann. tit. 8, §§ 212(a), 215, 223(a), (d) (1974).

[116] Cal.Corp.Code § 204(a)(5) (West Supp. 1981); Del.Code Ann. tit. 8, § 102(b)(4) (1974); N.Y.Bus.Corp.Law § 616(a)(2) (McKinney 1963); ABA–ALI Model Bus.Corp. Act.Ann.2d § 145 (1971).

[129] Civ. Action No. 5631 (Del.Ch. June 21, 1979), summarily aff'd, 414 A.2d 822 (Del.1980).

[131] The third case, Seibert v. Milton Bradley Co., 405 N.E.2d 131 (Mass.1980), is a virtual replay of Seibert v. Gulton Industries, Inc., except that the latter raises the issue under the Delaware General Corporation Law while the former is concerned with the Massachusetts Business Corporation Law. The overall importance of Delaware corporate law as well as the greater familiarity of most lawyers with its provisions is the basis for my choice of Gulton for consideration in the text. [The second case is Providence & Worcester Co. v. Baker, 378 A.2d 121 (Del.1977) Ed.]

While these three cases stand alone in their direct consideration of the validity of shark repellent amendments, other cases have touched on the matter indirectly. In Joseph E. Seagram & Sons, Ltd. v. Conoco, Inc., 519 F.Supp. 506 (D.Del.1981), Seagrams challenged the validity of amendments to Conoco's bylaws which limited alien ownership by voiding stock transfer to an alien if that transfer would result in exceeding an applicable "Alien Permitted Percentage." The court elected not to reach the issue of the reasonability of the amendment, instead construing Del. Code Ann. tit. 8, § 202 (Supp.1980), to bar the application of a transfer restriction to

In *Gulton*, the plaintiff challenged the most common type of shark repellent amendment: a supermajority provision requiring an 80% shareholder vote for "a merger or consolidation or similar takeover" with anyone owning more than 5% of the company's shares unless the board of directors had approved the transaction before the acquisition of the 5% interest. Although the supermajority requirement had been adopted by a vote of only 54% of the shareholders, it was protected by a simultaneously adopted lock-up provision requiring an 80% vote for repeal or amendment.[134] The plaintiff's attack on the supermajority provision focused on the role it assigned the board of directors. Conceding that the articles of incorporation could have required a supermajority vote for the covered transactions under all circumstances,[135] she claimed that the Delaware General Corporation Law did not allow the percentage vote required to differ depending upon whether the board of directors had approved the transaction at the required time.

The court's analysis was pristinely technical. Section 102(b)(4) of the Delaware statute permits a corporation's certificate of incorporation to require a shareholder vote higher than the usual bare majority provided by the statute for "any corporate action."[136] Completing the syllogism, the court concluded that Gulton's supermajority provision did no more than require a different shareholder vote for a different "corporate action," precisely as authorized under section 102(b)(4). The percentage approval required was, in the court's words, "dependent

---

any shares outstanding prior to its adoption that had not voted in favor of the restriction. This construction had the effect of prohibiting the application of the bylaw amendment to any outstanding shares, since only the board of directors had approved it, and, due to difficulties of tracing share ownership, eliminated the value of such an amendment in a large public corporation even if approved by a majority of the shareholders. See Young v. Valhi, Inc., 382 A.2d 1372 (Del.Ch.1978) (striking down an attempt by a successful offeror who was unable to obtain a supermajority for a second-step transaction to circumvent that requirement through a subsidiary merger, thereby implying that the supermajority requirement was viewed as unobjectionable); see also Elgin Nat'l Indus., Inc. v. Chemetron Corp., 299 F.Supp. 367 (D.Del.1969) (challenge to adequacy of proxy disclosure concerning shark repellent proposals); McKee & Co. v. First Nat'l Bank of San Diego, 265 F.Supp. 1 (S.D.Cal.1967) (upholding validity of bylaw adopted during contest for control requiring, inter alia, that nominees for directors have been residents of San Diego County for one year and not be an attorney or otherwise connected with other banks); Telvest, Inc. v. Olson, Civ. Action No. 5798 (Del.Ch. Mar. 8, 1979) (available Mar. 9, 1982, on LEXIS. Del library, Chncry file) (directors alone cannot authorize class of preferred stock having 80% class vote requirement on mergers; shareholder vote required).

* * *

[134] The Gulton Industries Proxy Statement 8 (May 23, 1977) described the lock-up provision as follows:

> At present, only the vote of a majority of the outstanding shares of the Company entitled to vote is necessary to authorize corporate transactions requiring stockholder approval or amendment of the Certificate of Incorporation. Under the proposed amendment * * *, the holders of 21% of the outstanding shares of the Company would be able to prevent certain transactions or amendments to the Certificate of Incorporation even if the holders of 79% of the outstanding shares were in favor of such action.

[135] *Gulton*, slip op. at 3. I am unwilling to make this concession. See notes 142–52 infra and accompanying text.

[136] Del.Code.Ann. tit. 8, § 102(b)(4) (1974). Id. § 251 contains the majority requirement for mergers and § 271 for sales of assets. Section 242(a) authorizes amendment of the certificate of incorporation "in any and as many respects as may be desired, so long as [the] certificate of incorporation as amended would contain only such provisions as it would be lawful and proper to insert in an original certificate of incorporation."

upon the matter subject to the vote, i.e., a business combination with a 5 per cent shareholder approved by the board of directors or a combination with a 5 per cent shareholder opposed by the board." [137]   The supermajority amendment thus was expressly authorized by the language of the statute; finding no "public policy against the so-called 'shifting numbers' where corporate voting rights are concerned," [138] the court upheld the charter provision.

Simply as a matter of textual analysis, the court's construction of the statute is hardly persuasive. The argument reduces to an assertion that the amendment's shifting vote requirement satisfies the language of section 102(b)(4) because a merger which the board *has not* approved is a different "action" from one which it *has* approved. Regardless of one's position on the wisdom of such an amendment, the word "action" as it appears in the statute does not resolve the matter. A dictionary definition of the word refers to "a thing done"; [139] nothing in the text of the statute forecloses a construction that identifies the "thing" for which approval is sought as the merger, and rejects the exercise in subcategorization that distinguishes between types of mergers based on when approval of the board of directors is obtained. [140] But more important, examination of the corporate statute alone is not responsive to the question posed by shark repellent amendments—the appropriate allocation of roles between directors and shareholders in a battle for control.

It is necessary, however, to take analysis of the indeterminacy of the statutory language a step further. Some supermajority amendments do not provide for differing approval percentages based on director action. [142] With respect to these amendments, the statutory language is not ambiguous: Section 102(b)(4) expressly authorizes a greater-than-majority voting requirement. Indeed, the *Gulton* court pointed out that the plaintiff conceded "it would be permissible * * * to require an 80 per cent vote for approval of [any] merger * * *. This would simply be calling for 'the vote of a larger portion of the stock.' " [143] But the statute's apparent clarity is illusory. The history

---

[137] *Gulton*, slip op. at 7. In fact, the court's formulation of the alternatives is incorrect. Under the form of exception contained in the Gulton Industries provision, the determining factor was not whether the board of directors approved the transaction, since the board must approve any merger, but whether the board had approved the transaction before or after the shareholder had acquired 5% of the outstanding stock.

[138] Id. at 8–9.

[139] Webster's Third New International Dictionary 21 (unabr.1976).

[140] The court's treatment of this issue in Seibert v. Milton Bradley Co., 405 N.E.2d 131 (Mass.1980), was similarly linguistic. Responding to plaintiff's argument that the statutory authorization for a supermajority voting requirement did not allow differing votes depending on director approval, the court stated:

> This argument is unpersuasive. According to § 8(a), the by-law controls "whenever" it requires a greater proportion of shareholders to vote for a particular proposal than the statute specifies. The plaintiff has ignored the word "whenever." The by-law specifies precisely "when" a 75% shareholder vote rather than a statutory majority will be required. With the words "whenever" and "greater proportion" given their ordinary meaning, * * * the by-law fully complies with § 8(a).

Id. at 134 (citations omitted).

[142] In these a supermajority vote is required regardless of the board of director's approval and regardless of its composition.

[143] *Gulton*, slip op. at 3.

of statutory provisions that authorize supermajority requirements demonstrates that it is impossible to resolve the validity of shark repellent amendments without considering the decisionmaking roles of management and shareholders inherent in the structure of the corporation.

The origin of statutory provisions authorizing supermajority voting requirements lies in the recognition that:

> the enabling-act type of statute, which became standard by the 1930's, tacitly assumed that the corporation would be one with a substantial number of shareholders.
>
> * * *
>
> The more difficult problems which the standard form of incorporation posed for the close-held firm concerned control. A minority investor in a close-held corporation was peculiarly vulnerable vis-à-vis the majority. * * * Thus individuals investing in a close-held firm had reason to write into its organization requirements of unanimity or specially high requirements for a quorum or a deciding vote on critical matters, along with stipulations against dilution of their relative voting power. * * * The standard incorporation acts were not responsive to these interests.[144]

The legislative response took the form of statutes like Delaware section 102(b)(4) and its predecessors and section 143 of the Model Business Corporation Act and its predecessor, which authorized higher shareholder approval requirements than those specified in the statute.

While these statutory provisions are not on their face limited to close corporations, the legislative history is quite clear in pointing to the relationship between the needs of the close corporation and statutory authorization of supermajority voting requirements. For example, the drafting committee responsible for Model Act section 143 expressly states their belief that the "provisions authorized by section 143 are peculiarly for use by a close corporation." [147] Indeed, the numerous bibliographic references provided by the drafting committee deal *exclusively* with problems related to control in the close corporation.[148] Similarly, leading treatises commenting on the corporation laws of major commercial states identify the plight of the close corporation as the motivation for statutory validation of supermajority provisions. With respect to section 204(a)(5) of the recently adopted California Corporations Code, Ballantine and Sterling state:

> This * * * reason, the protection of minority shareholders (especially in a close corporation) from adverse or oppressive actions by other shareholders, is the principal reason for permitting a corporation to include a super-majority vote requirement in its articles of incorporation.[150]

[144] J. Hurst, The Legitimacy of the Business Corporation in the United States 1780–1970, at 76–78 (1970); see, e.g., Hornstein, *Judicial Tolerance of the Incorporated Partnership*, 18 Law & Contemp. Prob. 435, 443 (1953); Manne, *Our Two Corporation Systems: Law and Economics*, 53 Va. L.Rev. 259, 277 (1967).

[147] ABA–ALI Model Bus. Corp. Act Ann. 2d § 143, ¶ 2 (comment to § 143) (1971).

[148] Id. ¶ 5.

[150] 1 H. Ballentine & G. Sterling, California Corporation Laws § 61.03 (4th ed. 1979); accord, Report of the Assembly Select Committee on the Revision of the Cor-

A similar conclusion emerges regarding the New York statute:

> BCL § 616 is one of the more important statutes designed to meet the needs of close corporations. In such corporations, sometimes referred to as "incorporated partnerships," minority shareholders often desire protection against ordinary majority rule. Super-statutory quorum and vote requirements are one of the most common means of obtaining such protection, since they provide the minority with the means by which it can veto majority action.[151]

And Professor Folk, the official reporter and adviser to the Delaware Committee on the Revision of the General Corporation Law, commenting with respect to Delaware section 102(b)(4) itself, states that "it is evident that high vote requirements are chiefly of interest to the small corporation." [152]

My point is not that the statutory text, with or without its legislative history, makes supermajority provisions available only to close corporations.[153] It is merely that the text alone cannot justify the *Gulton* court's construction authorizing use of shark repellent amendments in public corporations to deter tender offers. An adequate inquiry requires consideration of the appropriate roles to be assigned to management and shareholders in the context of a change in control, something that the text of provisions like section 102(b)(4) simply does not address.

◆

The author's criticism of *Gulton* notwithstanding, *Gulton* remains the most detailed statement by the Delaware courts concerning the validity of shark repellent amendments. Note, however, that the Delaware Supreme Court has remained curiously silent on the subject. *Gulton* was summarily affirmed without opinion and, when the opportunity to consider the validity of shark repellent amendments was again presented, this time in the context of the Bendix-Martin Marietta contest, the Supreme Court stated explicitly that it "expresse[d] no opinion as to (1) the legality of the proposed anti-takeover amendments * * *." Martin Marietta Corp. v. The Bendix Corp., No. 298, 1982 (Sept. 21, 1982).

porations Code 38 (1975) [hereinafter cited as Select Committee Report].

[151] 3 I. Kantrowitz & S. Slutsky, White on New York Corporations § 616.03, at 6–379 (13th ed. 1981) (footnotes omitted); see Hornstein, *Analysis of Business Corporation Law*, in N.Y.Bus.Corp.Law app. 1, at 441, 454 (1963) ("The sections which 'accommodate' a statute primarily designed for public issue corporations to the needs of a close corporation are the following: Section 616 continues statutory authorization for the super-statutory shareholders' quorum and vote * * *.").

[152] E. Folk, The New Delaware Corporation Law 8 (1967).

[153] The same legislative history that establishes the prominence of close corporation concerns also seems to contemplate a limited application of the provisons to public corporations. See Select Committee Report, supra note 150, at 38 (in addition to close corporation use, "a higher percentage requirement may be useful in non-close corporations particularly where special protection is desired for a certain class of shares"); accord, ABA–ALI Model Bus. Corp. Act Ann.2d § 143, ¶ 2 (1971) ("[T]here may be reasons to increase the statutory percentages in case of publicly held corporations, particularly where special protection is desired for a particular class of shares."). * * *

(2) Developments in the Legality of Greenmail: Interpreting the Empirical Evidence and the Rise of Reverse Greenmail

In the rapidly changing world of corporate acquisitions, the shape of the debate over greenmail had a reassuring stability. On the one hand, the courts have remained true to *Cheff;* overall, greenmail is safe if a careful record is created. On the other hand, the commentators have uniformly condemned greenmail as the most blatant expression of management's conflict of interest. From this perspective, management protects its own position and the cost—the actual premium paid and the post-greenmail decline in the value of the target company's stock as a result both of the actual premium paid and of the diminished likelihood of a premium takeover because of the elimination of one potential offerer—is borne by the shareholders. The initial round of empirical studies supported the critics' position. The first two studies found that target companies who repurchase the shares of potential offerers experience statistically significant *negative* abnormal returns of 2.37 percent in one study [79] and 2.85 percent in the other [80] in the three days surrounding announcement of the repurchase. The third study found statistically significant negative abnormal returns of 5.2 percent over the ten days surrounding repurchase.[81] In contrast, studies of the impact of general stock repurchase programs on a company's stock show substantial *positive* abnormal returns.[82] That the control issue puts target management in a position where its interests and those of the shareholders conflict is apparent; that management succumbs to the conflict when it engages in greenmail seemed supported by the empirical data.

This stable pattern was upset by two later studies which call into question the conclusion that greenmail harms target shareholders. Holderness & Sheehan, *Raiders or Saviors? The Evidence on Six Controversial Investors,*[83] and Mikkelson & Ruback, *Corporate Investments in Common Stock,*[84] both measured the abnormal returns associated with the greenmail process not just on the days surrounding announcement of the greenmail payment, but over the entire period from the date an investor announces that it has made a significant purchase of target company stock through the date the target company

[79] Dann & DeAngelo, *Standstill Agreements, Privately Negotiated Stock Purchases, and the Market for Corporate Control,* 11 J.Fin.Econ. 275, 294 (1983).

[80] Bradley & Wakefield, *The Wealth Effect of Target Share Repurchases,* 11 J.Fin. Econ. 301, 308 (1983). The negative abnormal return increased to 5.51% when the sample was limited to repurchases that terminated a control contest. *Id.* at 311.

[81] Office of the Chief Economist, *The Impact of Targeted Share Repurchases (Greenmail) on Stock Prices* (Sept. 11, 1984) (Table 1). As did Bradley & Wakefield, supra, this study also reported that negative re-

turns increased, to 6.8%, when the sample was limited to control contests.

[82] See, e.g., Masulis, *Stock Repurchase by Tender Offer: An Analysis of the Causes of Common Stock Price Changes,* 35 J.Fin. 305 (1981); Vermaelen, *Common Stock Repurchases and Market Signalling: An Empirical Study,* 9 J.Fin.Econ. 139 (1981).

[83] Managerial Economics Research Center Working Paper No. 84–06, University of Rochester (April, 1985).

[84] Sloan School of Management Working Paper No. 1633–85, Massachusetts Institute of Technology (Feb., 1985).

repurchases the stock.   Both studies confirm the results of earlier studies in one respect: Target companies earn negative abnormal returns when they announce the payment of greenmail.   A surprising result appears, however, when one examines the net returns over the entire period from announcement of the investor's acquisition of target company stock to announcement of the repurchase.

Event	Holderness & Sheehan Abnormal Returns	Mikkelson & Ruback Abnormal Returns
Initial Stock Purchase	+ 4.1%*	+ 4.64%*
Intermediate Period	− 0.4%	− 1.40%
Greenmail Announcement	− 1.3%*	− 2.29%*
Net Return Over Period	+ 3.2%*	+ 1.69%*

   * Statistically significant.

These results seem to show that the negative abnormal returns associated with the payment of greenmail are more than offset by the positive abnormal returns associated with announcement of the initial investment.[85]   From this perspective, greenmail is good for target shareholders, and making its payment more difficult by altering the rule of Cheff v. Mathes is unjustified.

The insight of these studies was to extend the period over which the effects of greenmail was measured.   The problem may be that they did not take their insight far enough.   Bradley, Desai & Kim, *The Rationale Behind Interfirm Tender Offers: Information or Synergy?*, 11 J.Fin.Econ. 183 (1983), examined a similar puzzle: Target companies that successfully resisted takeovers did experience negative abnormal returns on the resolution of the takeover, but nonetheless ended up with a positive abnormal return of 20.16 percent as a result of the experience.   They found, however, that when the performance of these companies was tracked over the succeeding two years, companies that were not the subjects of successful takeovers experienced negative abnormal returns that more than offset the earlier gains.   The implication of the data is that the target gain that remains after an unsuccessful takeover reflects the market's anticipation of a future offer.   Unless that offer appears, the gains disappear.

The greenmail situation is strikingly similar.   Terminating a takeover by greenmail is just one means of successful resistance; indeed, one would expect that there would be an overlap among the samples used by the Bradley, Desai & Kim and the greenmail studies.   This suggests that the gains reported by Holderness & Sheehan and Mikkelson & Ruback will dissipate unless a new acquirer appears.

What does this mean for the desirability of restricting greenmail?   If geenmail only benefits shareholders if it leads to a takeover, what is lost by restricting it?   Those investors who were not exploiting the conflict of interest between target management and shareholders would

[85] There is contrary evidence as well. The Chief Economist's study, supra, measures abnormal returns over the period from 20 days prior to the initial stock purchase to five days after the greenmail announcement.   Net abnormal returns over the entire period were −3.7 percent for the entire sample and −6.0 percent for a subsample limited to control contests.

still gain from the subsequent takeover; the only losers would be the exploiters—expecting greenmail but not a third party takeover—who, by definition, only injure shareholders.[86] Is this argument affected if in some cases where investments are made in good faith, and which would have been terminated by greenmail absent a prohibition, investors suffer a loss because, in the end, no takeover ever results?

In contrast to developments in the empirical evidence concerning greenmail, the most interesting development in the legal standards governing greenmail grew out of a new tactic that might be called "reverse greenmail." In response to a front-end loaded, two-tier tender offer by Mesa Petroleum, Unocal Corporation refused to pay Mesa a premium not offered other shareholders. Instead, it paid its other shareholders a premium it denied Mesa. This was accomplished by means of a self-tender for approximately 40 percent of its common stock at a price in excess of the Mesa offer, but in which Mesa was not allowed to participate. Mesa sued to block the self-tender.

The issue of the validity of Mesa's exclusion can be presented in two ways. From Mesa's perspective, the issue was whether Unocal could discriminate between otherwise equivalent shareholders; the tactic was no different than paying a dividend to only some of the shareholders of the same class of stock. From Unocal's perspective, the issue was simply another manifestation of the legality of greenmail in particular, and of target management's discretion to engage in defensive tactics in general. Although the Court of Chancery saw it Mesa's way, the Delaware Supreme Court treated the issue as one of defensive tactics. Relying on *Cheff* as authorizing selective stock repurchases as a defensive tactic if the policy conflict/primary purpose test were met, the court treated reverse-greenmail as presenting the identical issue. Unocal v. Mesa Petroleum, 493 A.2d 946 (Del.1985).

In contrast, the Securities and Exchange Commission saw the issue Mesa's way. After the Delaware Supreme Court's decision, the Commission proposed an amendment to Rule 13e–4, governing issuer tender offers, which prohibits a tender offer that is not open to all shareholders of the class of shares sought.[87] Which institution has it right? Why is the Commission concerned about this particular defensive tactic? The Commission's commitment to the idea of equality of treatment among shareholders in tender offers is discussed in Chapter Sixteen A.1.c., infra. Assuming greenmail is allowed, are target shareholders better or worse off if reverse-greenmail is allowed?

(3) The Legality of the Poison Pill

The courts have reached conflicting results concerning the legality of poison pill defenses. A number of courts including, most important-

---

[86] In Heckman v. Steinberg, 168 Cal.App. 3d 119, 214 Cal.Rptr. 177 (1985), the court affirmed the grant of a preliminary injunction that imposed a constructive trust on the greenmail payment made by Walt Disney Productions to a group headed by Saul Steinberg on the grounds that the group aided and abetted the breach of fiduciary duty by the Disney directors in paying the greenmail.

[87] See Exch. Release No. 34–22199 (July 1, 1985).

ly, the Delaware Supreme Court in Moran v. Household International, Inc.,[88] have upheld poison preferred pill and exploding warrant and rights plans.[89]   Other courts have held poison pill defenses invalid.[90] One common thread, however, runs through all of the cases: There is a complete lack of agreement on the basis by which such plans should be evaluated.   The Chancery Court in *Moran,* 490 A.2d 1059 (1985), commenced its analysis by recognizing that a poison pill plan is unique among defensive tactics in its impact on the internal structure of the corporation.   As a result, the business judgment rule was of questionable relevance.

> Where * * * the takeover defensive tactic is itself calculated to alter the structure of the corporation, apart from the question of motive, and results in a fundamental transfer of power from one constituency (shareholders) to another (the directors) the business judgment rule will not foreclose inquiry into the directors' action.

> Because the [poison pill] plan permits the Household Board to act as the prime negotiator of partial tender offers through the power of redemption, the resulting allocation of authority affects the structural relationship between the Board and the shareholders.[91]

Having said that, however, the court went on to state that the measure of the plan's validity is whether it was "motivated primarily by a desire to maintain control," [92] citing *Cheff.*   But if the traditional primary purpose test is the standard, does the structural nature of the tactic make any difference in the end?

The Delaware Supreme Court answered this question in the negative.   Reasoning that the poison pill was not uniquely effective in light of Sir James Goldsmith's success in gaining control of Crown Zellerbach despite its use of a similar defensive tactic, see Section B.2.a.(3). of this Chapter, supra, the court concluded that the poison pill "results in no more of a structural change than any other defensive mechanism adopted by a board of directors."   Slip opinion at 14.   As a result, the legal standard is the same as applies to any other mechanism: "[T]he Household Directors receive the benefit of the business judgment rule in their adoption of the [poison pill] Plan."   Slip opinion at 20.   From the perspective of the Delaware courts, then, the legality of poison pill plans does not seem to depend on their effectiveness, an important point because the defects in the Crown Zellerbach plan that made Goldsmith's success possible are easy enough to remedy.[92a]

---

[88] No. 37 (Nov. 19, 1985).

[89] Gearhart Industries, Inc., v. Texas American/Fort Worth, 741 F.2d 707 (5th Cir.1984) (applying Texas law); Horwitz v. Southwest Forest Industries, 604 F.Supp. 1130 (D.Nev.1985).

[90] Minstar Acquiring Corp. v. AMF, Inc., [Current Volume] Fed.Sec.L.Rep. (CCH) ¶ 92,066 (S.D.N.Y.1985) (applying New Jersey law); Asarco, Inc. v. MRH Homes A Court, [Current Volume] Fed.Sec.L.Rep. ¶ 92,220 (D.N.J.1985) (applying New Jersey

law); Unilever Acquisition Corp. v. Richardson-Vicks, Inc., No. 85 (Civ. 7239) (S.D. N.Y. 9/27/85).

[91] Slip opinion at 36.

[92] Id.

[92a] Recall that the Crown Zellerbach poison pill was not operative until an acquirer held in excess of 20 percent of Crown Zellerbach's stock *and* attempted to freeze out the minority.   Nothing would prevent a variant which was operative sim-

The cases invalidating poison pill plans offer little more clarity in analysis. Both interpret the particular plans before then as discriminating between holders of the same class of stock and interpret the New Jersey Corporate Statute, in contrast to the Delaware General Corporation Law, as barring intra-class discrimination. As with the technical approach to the legality of shark repellant amendments reviewed earlier in the section, little guidance is provided about how defensive tactics should be approached; poison pill plans are perceived as different and worse than other tactics, but the reasons for the distinction remain obscure.

What is needed is an analytical framework into which defensive tactics can be placed so that the relevance, if any, of differences among tactics can be evaluated. The following sections attempt that task.

c. *Criticism of the Traditional Approach*

GILSON, A STRUCTURAL APPROACH TO CORPORATIONS: THE CASE AGAINST DEFENSIVE TACTICS IN TENDER OFFERS
33 Stan.L.Rev. 819, 821–31 (1981).*

I. THE TRADITIONAL APPROACH TO MANAGEMENT'S ROLE IN TAKEOVERS: APPLYING THE FIDUCIARY PRINCIPLE IN CONTROL SETTINGS

In traditional terms, the question posed by management's implementing defensive tactics in response to a tender offer is whether management has acted in its own self-interest at the expense of the shareholders. Cast in doctrinal terms, the attack on such activities would be framed in terms of management's violating its fiduciary duty. Examining the development and content of traditional fiduciary analysis, however, demonstrates that it is incapable of resolving the problem posed by defensive tactics. Under prevailing legal standards, the common measure of fiduciary obligation is virtually without content where the conflict of interest triggering its application concerns maintaining control.

The scope of management's fiduciary responsibility and the measure of its discharge are traditionally described by the content of and interplay between two statements of obligation—the duty of care and the duty of loyalty—and the corresponding standards by which courts measure discharge of those obligations—the business judgment rule and the fairness test. The statements of obligation are in themselves unremarkable. The duty of care states that management owes the corporation reasonable diligence described by a traditional negligence formula: "A director shall perform his duties * * * with such care as an ordinarily prudent person in a like position would use under similar

ply on the acquisition of a 20 percent interest.

circumstances." [6] The duty of loyalty requires only that the director's dealings with the corporation be consistent with the "fiduciary" position held. In both cases, the standards by which the discharge of these obligations is measured are of real significance.

A. *Duty of Care: The Business Judgment Rule*

The substance of the duty of care is contained in the measure of its discharge, the business judgment rule: "Absent bad faith or some other corrupt motive, directors are normally not liable to the corporation for mistakes of judgment, whether those mistakes are classified as mistakes of fact or mistakes of law." [8] In practice, however, the rule functions less as a standard of management conduct than as a statement of judicial restraint: "[T]he liability aspect of the rule may well have been incidental to its principal function. The rule is more likely to have survived because it functioned as a quasi-jurisdictional barrier to prevent courts * * * from exercising regulatory powers over the activities of corporate managers." [9] Put this way, the business judgment rule does not express the measure by which a court determines whether management has discharged its duty of care; rather, its application reflects a conclusion that the management action in question will not be reviewed at all.

The courts' abdication of regulatory authority through the business judgment rule may well be the most significant common law contribution to corporate governance. Although critics have complained that the "[d]irectors' duty of due care has almost been interpreted out of existence," [11] a broader judicial role is difficult to justify. First, courts are ill-suited to review the wisdom of complex business judgments; [12] it is, for example, almost impossible to distinguish between acts of corporate social responsibility and acts of long-term profit maximization. Second, even if such a review were possible, it seems virtually certain that the game would not be worth playing.

By definition, the issue of managerial performance arises only after a decision has turned out badly, and a court could accomplish little at this stage. The impact of the court's decision on future management does not justify judicial review. A general directive to be wise rather than foolish is of little help. More specific remarks concerning the wisdom of the competing alternatives and the manner in which they might better have been evaluated, even if correct, are unlikely to prove

---

[6] ABA–ALI Model Bus.Corp.Act Ann.2d § 35 (Supp.1977). * * *

[8] Cramer v. General Tel. & Elec. Corp., 582 F.2d 259, 274 (3d Cir.1978), cert. denied, 439 U.S. 1129 (1979).

[9] Manne, *Our Two Corporation Systems: Law and Economics,* 53 Va.L.Rev. 259, 271 (1967).

[11] Weiss, *Disclosure and Corporate Accountability,* 34 Bus.Law. 575, 587 (1979); see Cary, *Federalism and Corporate Law: Reflections Upon Delaware,* 83 Yale L.J. 663 (1974).

[12] On occasion this point is acknowledged by a court asked to consider applying the business judgment rule. E.g., Auerbach v. Bennett, 47 N.Y.2d 619, 630, 393 N.E.2d 994, 1000, 419 N.Y.S.2d 920, 926 (1979) ("It appears to us that the business judgment doctrine, at least in part, is grounded in the prudent recognition that courts are ill equipped and infrequently called on to evaluate what are and must be essentially business judgments.").

a source of guidance for future managers. And, in any event, litigation is an unjustifiably expensive way to develop a case study to aid in future business decisions.

Finally, judicial review, and the resulting potential for personal liability, cannot be justified as a necessary incentive for managers to behave responsibly. It is now widely recognized that a variety of markets—product, employment, capital, and corporate control—constrain inefficient management performance without the enormous transaction costs associated with litigation.[16] In short, the business judgment rule's wisdom—its declination to provide judicial regulation when other forces more cheaply accomplish the same end—is precisely what generates its most persistent criticism. It also, however, identifies the limits of its application.

B. *Duty of Loyalty: The Policy Conflict/Primary Purpose Test*

While the business judgment rule acts as a jurisdictional barrier to review of most managerial decisions, the common law also recognizes that regulation of management conduct is appropriate where management has a conflict of interest. Drawing on trust law doctrine by analogy, the duty of loyalty originally prohibited transactions between a corporation and its management.[17] This restriction, however, was bent over time to reflect commercial necessity. Prohibition gave way to an overriding emphasis on the substantive fairness of the transaction. In contrast to judicial restraint under the business judgment rule, courts adopted an active regulatory posture with respect to transactions posing conflicts of interest: A court would "review such a contract and subject it to rigid and careful scrutiny, and would invalidate the contract if it was found to be unfair to the corporation." [19] To be sure, fairness did not offer talismanic precision. A "fair" price is no more than one set somewhere between the lowest price a seller will accept and the highest price a buyer will pay. But the concept does offer an objective measure; recourse to comparable market transactions is possible and appraisals, although inexact, are available. This allows the structuring of beneficial transactions with some certainty of their consequences and without enormous regulatory costs. In short, the fairness standard is a thoroughly respectable rule of law as applied to the area of its original application.

The fairness standard, however, has been an inadequate measure of management's discharge of its duty of loyalty in the area of particular concern here—its application in the context of change of control. Indeed, it was never tried. There is little question that management is subject to a conflict of interest when confronted with a proposal for the corporation's acquisition. As Harold Marsh has commented, "It is impossible to command the directors in this situation to avoid any

[16] Among recent works by lawyers, see, e.g., R. Posner, Economic Analysis of Law 300–13 (2d ed. 1977); R. Winter, Government and the Corporation 5–46 (1978); Anderson, *Conflicts of Interest: Efficiency, Fairness and Corporate Structure*, 25 U.C. L.A.L.Rev. 738, 784–87 (1978); Werner, *Management, Stock Market and Corporate Reform: Berle and Means Reconsidered*, 77 Colum.L.Rev. 388, 389 (1977).

[17] See generally Marsh, *Are Directors Trustees?*, 22 Bus.Law. 35 (1966).

[19] Marsh, supra note 17, at 43.

conflict of interest, since it has been unavoidably thrust upon them." Because corporate statutes commonly require the approval of the target's board of directors before a proposed merger or sale of assets can even be put to the shareholders, most acquisitions cannot be undertaken without management consent. As a result, management can reject offers beneficial to shareholders to retain the emoluments, both pecuniary and nonpecuniary, that flow from a position of high authority in a public corporation. Alternatively, control over access to shareholders gives management the power to "sell" that access to an offeror for such things as favorable employment contracts and attractive treatment of existing fringe benefits like stock options. Thus, it is impossible to identify at the outset any path management might take which would eliminate the inherent conflict of interest; any action, whether rejection or approval, reflects the potential for diversion of benefit to management and away from shareholders.

A potential acquisition thus seems the paradigmatic setting for judicial regulation of management conduct. While the absence of judicial review was sensible in nonconflict settings because other constraints protected shareholders, the conflict of interest inherent in a potential change in control called for "rigid and careful scrutiny" of the fairness of management conduct. But while doctrinal logic demanded such a review, it did not occur. Faced with the problem of attempting to police management behavior in this setting, the courts abdicated, albeit, I will suggest, in an inventive manner.

The difficulty in policing management conduct in connection with changes of control, and the devices by which the courts chose to avoid the task, can best be seen by considering two common defensive tactics. In the first, a third party acquires a significant minority of shares and seeks either to acquire the remainder of the target's shares or to make substantial changes in the target's operations. Target management opposes either course and, after more or less conflict, the target corporation resolves the issue by repurchasing the dissident's shares at a price higher than market. In the second, an offeror announces its intent to tender for control and target management takes action—like placing a significant amount of the target's common stock in hands sympathetic to management's desire to remain independent—which prevents the change in control from occurring.

In the first setting, where the management action taken—repurchase of the outsider's stock—has as its announced purpose preventing a shift in control of the corporation, the conflict of interest is apparent. Reviewing management's action under the fairness standard, however, presents substantial difficulties. Inquiry could be made concerning whether the price paid by the company was fair, but in that sense, the transaction was arm's length; management had no interest in paying more for the shares than was necessary to convince the holder to sell. Moreover, that the price was "fair" only demonstrates the irrelevancy of the inquiry. Management's conflict of interest was not in the price paid, but in the decision to acquire the shares at all. Applying a fairness standard to this decision, however, requires a court to determine whether it was "fair" for control to remain with management rather than shift to the offeror. And this inquiry must necessarily focus on whether the shareholders would be better off with existing management or by selling their shares. But this is an investment decision, made continually by shareholders in deciding whether to sell their shares, and raises the same issue of judicial competence which justifies a restrictive judicial role with respect to the duty of care.

In the second setting, where the management action taken—a sale of target shares to a friendly party—has the effect of blocking a potential change in control, a court could also evaluate, whether the price received for the shares was fair. As in the first setting, however, inquiry into the fairness of the price is beside the point; management's conflict of interest goes not to the commercial reasonableness of the defensive action's terms, but to the decision to block a change in control. As in the first setting, a fairness review of the relevant conflict forces the court to consider precisely the factors which the business judgment rule excludes from consideration.

The manner in which the courts sidestepped this dilemma is a marvel of doctrinal development. The first setting is recognizable as *Cheff v. Mathes*, where the Delaware Supreme Court avoided the problem by shifting the focus of the inquiry. If the court was ill-equipped to review the fairness of management's belief that it was the better repository for future control of the corporation, it was at least competent to engage in an inquiry with which it *was* familiar, a review of motive:

> [T]he allegation is that the true motives behind such purchases were improperly centered upon perpetuation of control. * * * [I]f the actions of the board were motivated by a sincere belief that the buying out of the dissident stockholder was necessary to maintain what the board believed to be proper business practices, the board will not be held liable for such decision. * * * On the other hand, if the board has acted solely or primarily because of the desire to perpetuate themselves in office, the use of corporate funds for such purposes is improper.[30]

Recognizing that inventive counsel could always discover a conflict over policy between management and an insurgent, the court required an additional showing: that the board's determination that a policy conflict existed was based on "reasonable investigation." [31]

While the *Cheff* decision has been extensively criticized, note how neatly the court avoided the fairness dilemma. A conflict of interest existed which, in the court's view and, I think, in fact, was not subject to a traditional fairness review. An analysis of management's motives then served as a surrogate for a fairness review to validate the transaction: Where management's investigation demonstrates that a policy difference was the motivation for the transaction, then the conflict of interest has been exorcised. Absent a conflict of interest, the business judgment rule is the appropriate standard of review, precisely the standard applied by the court in *Cheff*:

---

[30] 41 Del.Ch. at 504, 199 A.2d at 554.   [31] Id. at 506, 199 A.2d at 555.

[T]he directors satisfy their burden by showing good faith and reasonable investigation; the directors will not be penalized for an honest mistake of judgment, if the judgment appeared reasonable at the time the decision was made.[33]

Since management can almost always find a conflict over policy between itself and an insurgent, the motive analysis collapses into the business judgment standard. And while this approach neither solved nor addressed management's conflict of interest, it did eliminate substantive review of questions which the court was institutionally incompetent to resolve.

The second setting arose in Northwest Industries, Inc. v. B.F. Goodrich Co.[35] Goodrich was a participant with Gulf Oil in a joint venture which both had concluded would be more valuable if owned entirely by either. Despite extensive negotiations, the parties could not agree upon a price at which Goodrich would acquire Gulf's interest, and so the matter stood for some four years. Then, ten days after the announcement of a tender offer for Goodrich by Northwest, negotiations reopened and, in a single day, without further study, Goodrich management agreed to acquire Gulf's interest in exchange for 700,000 shares of authorized but unissued Goodrich common stock.[36] The Goodrich board approved the transaction the following day on the basis of "a hastily prepared two page memorandum and a one page statistical analysis of the transaction." [37] Northwest sued to block the transaction, claiming that the stock issuance was a mechanism to defeat the Northwest tender.[38]

While the price paid for the joint venture could be reviewed in traditional fairness terms,[39] the court also had to deal with the claim that the transaction should not have taken place at any price. And this inquiry was particularly difficult because the court had to acknowledge that it was the Northwest tender offer which triggered the transaction.[40] Nonetheless, the court avoided reviewing the "fairness" of Goodrich's resistance by analyzing motive instead. While acknowledging that one of Goodrich's motives was to defeat the offer, the court expressly rejected the contention that " 'where a board of directors has as one of its motives manipulation for control the transaction is invalid, regardless of fairness, and regardless of whether a legitimate corporate

---

[33] 41 Del.Ch. at 506, 199 A.2d at 555.

[35] 301 F.Supp. 706 (N.D.Ill.1969).

[36] The court noted that "[w]hile Gulf's officers had updated their 1965 studies of Chemicals [the joint venture], the only Goodrich documents were a brief, handwritten memorandum of possible valuations of Gulf's one-half interest and a sheet of paper containing longhand calculations." Id. at 709 n. 3.

[37] Id. at 709.

[38] Although the court's opinion considers only the Gulf transaction, it was not the only defensive tactic undertaken by Goodrich. The Goodrich defense included liti-

gation claiming violation by Northwest of the federal securities laws, political pressure, an additional defensive acquisition designed to create an antitrust barrier, and the proposal of shark repellant amendments. See O. Williamson, Corporate Control and Business Behavior 100–02 (1970).

[39] 301 F.Supp. at 710. Among Northwest's claims was an assertion that the price paid by Goodrich for the Gulf joint venture interest was too high.

[40] Id. at 712 ("Northwest's tender offer announcement galvanized Goodrich and Gulf to complete the purchase at this time.").

purpose is also being served.' " [41] Only if "Goodrich officials' desire to remain in office was the sole or the primary motive for their decisions" [42] would resistance breach the duty of loyalty. Where dual motives are present—maintaining control *and* furthering a legitimate corporate interest—the conflict of interest is eliminated and the appropriate standard, as in *Cheff,* is the business judgment rule: "Goodrich's officers and directors appear to have been exercising their honest business judgment, so that their decision is conclusive." [43]

Despite the doctrinal ingenuity by which the policy conflict/primary purpose test avoids the impossible task of substantive judicial review of the merits of conflicting claimants for corporate control, the central problem still remains: Blocking a change in control may reflect management's self-interest regardless of policy differences with a rival for control, and regardless of whether the defensive tactic chosen also serves an unrelated corporate purpose. This approach converts the issue from one of duty of loyalty to one of duty of care, with the consequent "incongruity of applying a standard designed to vindicate the exercise of business judgment in non-conflict-of-interest situations as a measure of compliance with the duty of loyalty, which arises only in conflict-of-interest situations." So long as the policy conflict/primary purpose test is applied, management's conflict of interest cannot be and, I have argued, was not intended to be, confronted.

The courts were led to this impasse because they concentrated narrowly on the appropriateness of management conduct in the case at hand, an inquiry which, unless limited, would necessarily involve the court in an exercise resembling fundamental security analysis, rather than approaching the problem through a broader examination of the appropriate allocation of responsibility between management and shareholders with respect to change in control.

d. An Alternative Approach: Prohibition

GILSON, A STRUCTURAL APPROACH TO CORPORATIONS
Supra, at 845–48, 875–81*

The General Principle: Shareholders Must Make the Decision

The argument thus far presented is that other elements of the structure of the corporation, having statutory, judicial and market components, serve to constrain the managerial discretion unavoidably resulting from the modern corporation's need for specialized managerial skills and capital. The tender offer is the critical mechanism through which the corporate structure imposes constraints on certain forms of managerial self-dealing. It is in this context that a structural approach to corporate law considers the validity of defensive tactics.

---

[41] Id. (quoting Cummings v. United Artists Theatre Circuit, Inc., 237 Md. 1, 21, 204 A.2d 795, 805 (1964)).

[42] Id.

[43] Id.

The result of management adopting successful defensive tactics is to make impossible a tender offer which management has not blessed. For example, the postoffer acquisition by the target of a business which creates an antitrust barrier to the offer causes access to shareholders through a tender offer to be conditioned in the same manner that the corporate statute conditions access to shareholders in a merger of sale of assets. Absent approval of incumbent management, a tender offer, like a merger or sale of assets, is impossible.

This result, however, is flatly inconsistent with the structure of the corporation. The market for corporate control is crucial to the corporate structure because neither other markets nor a fiduciary "fairness" standard effectively constrains some forms of management self-dealing. Moreover, the control market allows a final constraint on management inefficiency short of business failure. In turn, the tender offer is crucial because no other displacement mechanism is available without management cooperation. If management can use defensive tactics to obtain a degree of control over tender offers similar to that given it over mergers and sales of assets, then the corporate structure is fundamentally altered in a fashion which allows management effective monopoly power over corporate control. Rather than displacement occurring when the gains from displacement (the benefits of synergy or the elimination of inefficiency or self-dealing) exceed the price to be paid (including transaction costs), transfer of control will occur only when the benefits to incumbent management from the transaction exceed the capitalized value to management of its existing discretion. In short, defensive tactics, if successful, circumvent the mechanism by which the corporate structure constrains managerial discretion and, therefore, are improper.

The structural argument establishing the invalidity of defensive tactics, generally based on the interplay between statute, courts, and markets, is perfectly consistent with a construction of the statutory terms dealing directly with displacement mechanisms. Not surprisingly, this construction is based on analysis of the relationships created by the statute itself; coming full circle, this is precisely the form of argument by which the courts initially developed the fiduciary duty concept.

Corporate statutes properly place the ultimate responsibility for evaluating proposals for merger or sale of assets with management. These complicated transactions require substantial time investments for shareholders to understand them.[101] Assuming loyal management, a rational shareholder would not invest time considering a merger or

---

[101] Where the transaction involves the issuance of the offeror's securities, the offer must be registered with the Securities and Exchange Commission pursuant to the Securities Act of 1933 unless an exemption from registration is available. See generally R. Jennings & H. Marsh, Securities Regulation: Cases and Materials 464–95 (4th ed. 1977). Until recently, such a transaction would be registered on Form S–14, 17 C.F.R. § 239.23 (1980), which has been described as generating "some of the longest and most complex disclosure documents presented to investors," with an average length of 110 pages, and some exceeding 200 pages. House Comm. on Interstate and Foreign Commerce, 95th Cong., 1st Sess., Report of the Advisory Comm. on Corporate Disclosure to the Securities and Exchange Commission 440 (Comm. Print 1977) [hereinafter cited as Report on Corporate Disclosure]. * * *

sale of assets unless management, through application of its specialized skills, had already approved it. The problem is ensuring, within reasonable limits, that management's determination—for example, to reject an offer—is motivated by the shareholders', rather than management's, best interests. And it was precisely the difficulty of making such a determination which forced courts to sidestep the problem by applying the business judgment rule to management's fiduciary role in changes of control. The solution is the check and balance of the tender offer. If management, in rejecting merger or sale of assets proposals, gives priority to its own interests rather than those of the shareholders, the spurned suitor can make a tender offer to the shareholders.[103] Should management become too recalcitrant, an alternative is available.

This system of check and balance, of management control of some mechanisms by which control may be shifted but with unfettered access to shareholders through another, is precisely the structure reflected in the typical corporation statute. While control of the merger and sale of asset mechanisms is firmly ensconced in management, the tender offer mechanism generally is not even mentioned in the statute, let alone placed within management's control.[104] Thus, to reiterate my basic point from a somewhat different perspective, all components of the structure of the modern corporation—market, judicial, and statutory— combine to establish a critical role for the tender offer: as the principal displacement mechanism by which the capital market may police the performance of management and thereby justify the central role accorded management in other displacement mechanisms. Defensive tactics, because they alter the allocation of tender offer responsibility

---

[103] Where management favors itself by accepting an offer—perhaps because of favorable side payments in the form of employment contracts or stock options— the statute provides an explicit, if in practice illusory, check through the statutory requirement of shareholder approval. The constraint of shareholder approval, however, is buttressed by the operation of the market for corporate control. Between the public announcement of board of director approval of the transaction and the date of the shareholder meeting, competing offers—via tender offers—may be made if the transaction negotiated by management was too favorable to the offeror or to management.

[104] Where the tender offer is explicitly mentioned, it is in an effort to provide a statutory solution to the de facto merger problem. For example, Cal.Corp.Code § 181 (West 1977) defines three types of reorganizations, including an "exchange reorganization" which amounts to an acquisition by means of a tender offer where the consideration is the offeror's stock. Section 1201 require a vote of the shareholders of the offeror if, following the

transaction, these shareholders will own shares of the offeror representing less than five-sixths of the voting power. No role at all is created for the target board. See generally Small, *Corporate Combinations Under the New California General Corporation Law*, 23 U.C.L.A.L.Rev. 1190 (1976).

That the statute does not assign management a role in traditional tender offers is underscored by the addition in 1976 of Model Business Corporation Act § 72A. ABA–ALI Model Bus. Corp. Act Ann.2d § 72A (Supp.1977). This section creates a mechanism by which an exchange offer can be made binding on target shareholders if both the board of directors and the shareholders approve the transaction by the same procedures required for mergers and sales of assets. While management is given a role where the transaction is made binding, the statute expressly preserves the option of a traditional tender offer, and in that setting no role is accorded target management. Only a few jurisdictions have followed the Model Act in adopting such a provision. See W. Cary & M. Eisenberg, Cases and Materials on Corporations, 1501 (5th ed. 1980).

between management and shareholders contemplated by this structure, are inappropriate.

*   *   *

REDUCING THE STRUCTURAL PRINCIPLE TO A RULE

In an important sense, my argument has come full circle. There has never been significant judicial debate over the principle that self-perpetuating action by target management is invalid. The difficulty, I have argued, has been the courts' inability to distinguish defensive tactics from neutral corporate action, particularly where dual effects are present. The traditional solution—an inquiry into motive—fails not in principle, but in implementation, in reducing the principle to a form which meaningfully separates management conduct into valid and invalid categories. This task still remains.

The effort, however, can now begin from a substantially different position. Unlike courts confronting the matter originally, we now understand the tender offer's role in the corporate structure and the relationship between management and shareholders dictated by that role. We have seen that the tender offer is centrally important to the structure of the corporation because it is the key displacement mechanism through which the market for corporate control constrains management behavior and because it is a critical safety valve against management's misuse of its controlling role in all other displacement mechanisms. Its success depends on independent shareholder action; shareholders tendering their shares transfer control to better management, and it is the potential for such shareholder action which constrains self-interested behavior by management in connection with mergers and asset sales. A structural approach to allocating responsibility between management and shareholders with respect to tender offers thus yields a straightforward principle: Shareholders must make tender offer decisions.

Before formulating a rule implementing that principle, it is worth pausing to identify the benefits which derive from a structural approach. The major pitfalls facing courts in reviewing management action under traditional standards are no longer present. It is simply no longer relevant to inquire whether management action was in the best interests of the shareholders, a question which, if confronted rather than avoided through the subterfuge of motive, requires judicial review of the alternative futures presented by the contestants for control. The structural principle focuses on how management action affects the role assigned to shareholders, a factual inquiry which ought not to pose special difficulties to courts. This question is one which the court is institutionally competent to answer.

*   *   *

We can now formulate a rule which reflects the structurally defined roles for management and shareholders by describing the effect to be avoided—interfering with shareholder decision—rather than specifying the particular techniques likely to have that effect. Recognizing that the desired generality lessens the demand upon the drafter, the following is a workable solution:

> During the period commencing with the date on which target management has reason to believe that a tender offer may be made for part or all of a target company's equity securities, and ending at such time thereafter that the offeror shall have had a reasonable period in which to present the offer to target shareholders, no action shall be taken by the target company which could interfere with the success of the offer or result in the shareholders of the target company being denied the opportunity to tender their shares, *except* that the target company (1) may disclose to the public or its shareholders information bearing on the value or the attractiveness of the offer, and (2) may seek out alternative transactions which it believes may be more favorable to target shareholders.

Limiting target management conduct by focusing on its effect on shareholder decision highlights the most important manner in which the rule differs from the traditional inquiry. The central difficulty with the policy conflict/primary purpose test is that it assigns management an important discretionary role in the tender offer process. So long as management "genuinely" concludes that an offeror's policy differs from its own, or otherwise determines that an offer is "not in the best interest of the corporation or its shareholders," traditional doctrine validates defensive action. Subject only to the effectiveness of the defensive tactic selected, target management is, in effect, authorized to act instead of the shareholders. So understood, the common criticism of traditional doctrine—that the tests are indeterminate because it is impossible to differentiate situations where there *really* are policy differences, or where management *really* believes it is acting in the best interests of the corporation or shareholders, from situations where such assertions are only a ploy—is beside the point. Under a structural approach the issue is not the wisdom or good faith of particular action, but simply whether, and what kind of, action has been taken. In other words, the approach has the flavor of *ultra vires*—certain actions are simply outside management's authority.

This distinction, between identifying appropriate areas of management actvity and identifying whether particular activity was correct or was taken for proper reasons, also distinguishes the proposed rule from other reform efforts. With few exceptions, proposed reforms, although manipulating the measure or burden of proof, have retained traditional fiduciary analysis as a framework. Thus, critics have suggested that the burden of proof be shifted to management and that management be required to show a "compelling business purpose" for the questioned action,[216] or that the result of the action was "fair," [217] or that manage-

---

[216] This standard was adopted in Klaus v. Hi-Shear Corp., 528 F.2d 225 (9th Cir. 1975), in which a number of defensive tactics were invalidated. Applying California law, Judge Choy rejected the policy conflict/primary purpose approach, id. at 233, and, relying on the California Supreme Court's opinion in Jones v. H.F. Ahmanson & Co., 1 Cal.3d 93, 460 P.2d 464, 81 Cal. Rptr. 592 (1969), suggested "a balancing of the good to the corporation against the

[217] See note 217 on page 751.

ment had objective reasons to believe that defeating the offer would result in shareholders receiving "their highest investment return." [218] Alternatively, recognizing the difficulty in separating pure from tainted motives, it has been suggested that procedural, rather than substantive, standards be used to validate management action. For example, Chairman Williams has urged that defensive action by target management be permitted if authorized by independent directors after reasonable investigation.[219]

The problem with all of these approaches is the underlying premise that target management under some circumstances can preempt shareholder decision in a tender offer. And the mistake of ever allowing target management to displace shareholder decision is exacerbated because neither a "higher" standard nor relying on the decisionmakers' independence provides any guidance in determining the bounds of management's preemptive role. The notion of "compelling business purpose" directs courts to undertake balancing, but does not elucidate what factors ought to weigh in the balance and how much weight should be accorded each. Nor is the failure to delineate target management's role remedied by relying on independent directors. Without substantive guidance as to the appropriate scope of their activity and that of the shareholders, independent directors are left free to define their role themselves. Although presumably less tainted by self-interest, a decision by independent directors to defeat an offer for nonpersonal reasons, such as a sense of responsibility to the town in which the company's major facilities are located, provides only a bootstrap justification for the directors having that discretion in the first place. The rule I propose suffers neither from indeterminacy nor from lack of a normative foundation.

◆

Note: The Definition of a Defensive Tactic

Gilson's proposed rule never explicitly defines a defensive tactic; the implicit definition is that any action that interferes with shareholders' opportunity to tender their shares is defensive. In some cases,

disproportionate advantage to the majority shareholders and incumbent management." 528 F.2d at 234. * * *

[217] Where a decision to adopt a defensive tactic has not been made through a procedurally acceptable mechanism, Gelfond & Sebastian, *Reevaluating the Duties of Target Management in a Hostile Tender Offer,* 60 B.U.L.Rev. 403, 470–72 (1980), recommend a fairness standard be developed by the courts on a case-by-case basis.

[218] Note, *Corporate Directors' Liability for Resisting a Tender Offer: Proposed Substantive and Procedural Modifications of Existing State and Fiduciary Standards,* 32 Vand.L.Rev. 575, 603–04 (1979) (directors must show that "they reasonably believed,

as a result of objective investigation, that defeating the tender offer would yield target shareholders their highest investment return").

[219] H. Williams, Tender Offers and the Corporate Director, Address Before the Seventh Annual Securities Regulation Institute, in San Diego, CA Jan. 17, 1980, reprinted in [1979–1980 Transfer Binder] Fed.Sec.L.Rep. (CCH) ¶ 82,445, at 82,880–82 (use of a special committee of independent directors); cf. Gelfond & Sebastian, *supra* note 217, at 467–70 (adoption of defensive tactics by independent directors with professional financial assistance allows application of the business judgment rule).

however, the issue may not be quite that easy. Suppose a target company sells one of its divisions following an unfriendly takeover offer. If the unfriendly offer is for 100 percent of the target company's stock, it seems clear that the transaction interferes with the shareholders' opportunity to tender. If the offer is only partial—one for less than all of the target's outstanding stock—the characterization of the transaction as a defensive tactic may be less clear.

Suppose, for example, that the bidder has offered $30 million for 40% of a target's outstanding stock. In response, target management proposes to sell a division representing 40% of the company's sales and earnings for $30 million, following which the proceeds would be distributed to the shareholders in a partial liquidation (thus generating the same tax consequences as the tender offer).

Although each transaction leaves the shareholders in a somewhat different position, the difference seems to be one of degree, not of kind. If the original offer were completed, the shareholders would have a 60% interest in the company, down from 100%, but would also have $30 million cash in hand. If management's alternative transaction were completed, the shareholders would have 100% of a corporation now only 60% of its original size but, again, with $30 million cash in hand. Which transaction is preferable depends, it seems, on your judgment concerning the relative value of different parts of the business. Both, however, are partial offers in a sense.

What distinguishes management's alternative transaction from the initial offer, and what justifies characterizing that alternative as a defensive tactic, is the fact that it gives shareholders no decision-making role. Unlike the initial offer, which shareholders approve by tendering their shares, the alternative transaction requires only target management's approval; shareholders have no role at all. If defensive tactics are those that interfere with the shareholders' opportunity to make a decision, then the alternative transaction, although similar in ultimate effect to the initial offer, is a defensive tactic because it serves to eliminate the shareholders' decision-making role. That analysis, however, does not end the matter. The lesson of Chapter Thirteen was that any regulatory restrictions on business transactions that are expressed in formal terms invite a restructuring of the transaction that meets the formal terms of the regulation without, however, altering the transaction's substance. Such a restructuring seems perfectly feasible here. Suppose the alternative transaction is altered so that it contemplates two steps. First, the third party to whom the division is to be sold makes a $30 million tender offer for 40% of the target's shares. Second, the target company redeems the target shares now owned by the third party with payment being the transfer of the division. The financial result, of course, is precisely the same as the original fomulation of the transaction: The shareholders end up owning 100% of a smaller company and have $30 million cash in hand.

Is this formulation of the alternative transaction less troublesome? If the touchstone of a defensive tactic is its interference with the shareholders' right to make a decision, then, perhaps, the second formulation of the transaction is acceptable. In this form, the shareholders do have a choice: If they believe the division is worth more than $30 million, then the preferred alternative would be to tender to the initial bidder. Thus, the shareholders, in effect, vote on the sale of the division. Characterized in this way the sale of the division is not a defensive tactic, but the type of alternative transaction that Gilson's rule exempts from its prohibition.

———————◆———————

e. *Evaluation of the Rebuttal*

GILSON, A STRUCTURAL APPROACH TO CORPORATIONS

Supra, at 848–65.*

RESPONSES TO ARGUMENTS FOR MANAGEMENT DISCRETION TO BLOCK A TENDER OFFER

There has been no shortage of defenders of a management role far broader than that assigned by my structural approach. The arguments offered by management's champions all seek to justify allowing management to *prevent* shareholders, *under particular circumstances*, from displacing management by tendering their shares. The common thread joining the arguments is the unlimited discretion accorded management to identify the circumstances.

A. *Functional Equivalence to Other Acquisition Techniques* **

*   *   *

B. *The Irrelevance of Inefficiency*

A second argument offered in support of management discretion to block tender offers simply denies that current tender offer practice operates to discipline inefficient or self-dealing management:

> [One] would be hard-pressed to argue that the companies involved in the most prominent hostile takeovers in 1976 and 1977 were managed by inefficient executives. * * * [W]hile meaningful data has not been collected and made generally available, the common belief is that the typical target companies today are successful participants in their particular fields and are managed by able personnel.[115]

** This argument—that management should have the same responsibility when an acquisition is structured as a tender offer as when structured as a merger or sale of assets—is addressed in Chapter Thirteen F., supra. [Ed.]

[115] Steinbrink, *Management's Response to the Takeover Attempt*, 28 Case W.Res.L. Rev. 882, 886–87 (1978).

See Troubh, *Characteristics of Target Companies*, 32 Bus.Law 1301, 1302 (1977); H. Williams, Tender Offers and the Corporate Director, Address before the Seventh Annual Securities Regulation Institute, in San Diego, Cal. Jan. 17, 1980, reprinted in [1979–1980 Transfer Binder] Fed.Sec.L. Rep. (CCH) ¶ 82,445, at 82,876.

There is by now a fair amount of empirical research measuring the performance of target companies and their securities in various periods prior to their becoming the subject of a tender offer. These studies generally conclude that the stock of target companies significantly underperforms the market during the pre-tender period.***

*   *   *

It is unnecessary, however, to rest the entire response on empirical measures of inefficiency. A target company may have greater value to the acquirer than as an independent entity for reasons quite distinct from target management's lack of skills. For example, a company with underutilized production capacity that acquires a competitor may reduce costs by spreading overhead over a larger volume in a manner not available to either company alone. Synergy—the idea that operational or financial economies of scale may result in a value for the combined entities greater than the sum of their indepenent values—explains some acquisitions in a fashion which expands the concept of inefficiency beyond that acknowledged by the proponents of managerial discretion. Target management may be inefficient because they lack the skills or inclination to effectively manage their company; target management may also be "inefficient" because the company they manage lacks the business opportunities or financial strength necessary to improve its return on invested capital. Companies inefficient in this sense may, for a significant period of time, nonetheless remain "successful participants in their particular fields."

Moreover, even where the proposed transaction may seem to yield no social gains, the absence of target company inefficiency does not justify target management discretion to block a tender offer. For example, some argue that acquisitions motivated purely by a desire for diversification are unlikely to benefit the shareholders of the acquiring corporation.†

Yet the potential inefficiency of the transaction—in contrast to the inefficiency of the target company—does not justify allowing target management to block shareholder access to tender offers. The argument against such mergers is not that *target* shareholders are injured by the transaction, but that shareholders of the *acquiring* corporation are injured because of the benefit given target shareholders. For the target shareholders the operative concept remains the Fundamental Theorem of Exchange: that "voluntary trade is mutually beneficial." As for protecting shareholders of the offeror, the market also restricts the ability of acquiring company management to manage inefficiently.[124] Target management is an unlikely substitute for market discipline as a means of constraining offeror management.

I do not argue that there is no cause for concern over the pace of acquisitions, principally by means of tender offers, in recent years.

*** The data is summarized in Chapter Nine B., supra. [Ed.]

† See Chapter Nine B., supra. [Ed.]

[124] There is increasing evidence that market disfavor of wide diversification is causing conglomerates to shed previously acquired businesses. See, e.g., H. Salter & W. Weinhold, Diversification through Acquisition 17 (1979) ("In 1976 divestitures involved over half of all acquisitions versus approximately 10 percent in the 1960's.").

Harold Williams has recently argued that the acquisition phenomenon diverts investment resources from more socially productive uses.[125] However, it seems highly unlikely that self-interested resistance to acquisitions by target management will increase net "productive" investment by eliminating one alternative use for corporate funds. The market for capital investment is highly competitive; a preference by some firms at certain times for investment in acquisitions rather than internal expansion likely results from real economic forces rather than the degree of discretion accorded target management. Indeed, Williams also points to regulation and prompt competitive response to new products as factors which "encourage the search for takeover targets rather than for capital spending, product development and innovation opportunities." [127] Such major macroeconomic problems are unlikely to be cured by increased discretion on the part of target management. Efforts to correct misincentives for capital investment created by governmental regulation are far more likely to be effective if directed at the problem's source.

C. Which Shareholders Benefit?

Yet another justification for an expansive role for target management in tender offers admits that shareholders profit from a tender offer, but focuses on the unsavory character of those tendering their shares. The interests of these shareholders—negatively characterized as speculators or arbitrageurs—in a quick profit are unfavorably compared to the other shareholders' interests in the long-term future of the

[125] H. Williams, supra, note 115, at 82,877 ("In the last five years, I would estimate that $100 billion of corporate cash resources—resources which could have been devoted to new production and employment opportunities—have been diverted to rearranging the ownership of existing corporate assets through tender offers alone. These are reserves that do not flow back as new capacity, improvements in productivity, new products or new jobs."). Chairman Williams does not address the question of what happens to the resources returned to target shareholders in cash tender offers. Unless the amounts paid are consumed or invested directly in productive assets by shareholders, the sums must be reinvested in financial assets, either directly or through financial intermediaries. See generally, J. Van Horne, Financial Market Rates and Flows 1–40 (1978). Thus, Williams' argument cannot be that the funds given to target shareholders are taken out of the financial system by, for example, being stuffed in a mattress. Rather, the argument must be that the new investments do not finance direct investment in real assets. This recharacterization of Williams' position does not alter the response which follows in the text, but merely shifts the inquiry to why the former target shareholders are presented with investment opportunities which favor other than real asset production.

An additional problem with Williams' position is that it views all takeover as having the same unfavorable results. Even if one ignores eventual reinvestment by target shareholders, recent empirical research indicates that takeovers of smaller high-technology firms are conducive to new production and employment opportunities because "capital formation by [smaller technology-based firms] is enhanced by the possibility that stockholders will eventually be able to sell their stock at a tender offer premium." R. Masulis, Acquisition of Technology-Based Firms by Tender Offer: An Economic and Financial Analysis 25 (SEC Capital Market Working Paper No. 1, 1980). Also, it has been argued that research and development by smaller firms followed by takeover by larger companies when new products reach the production and marketing stage is an efficient way to organize the innovation process. O. Williamson, Market and Hierarchies: Analysis and Antitrust Implications 198–207 (1975).

[127] H. Williams, supra, note 115, at 82,876.

corporation. The resulting conclusion, that short-run trading profits are worthy of less consideration by target management than, I suppose, long-term trading profits, is then offered to support management efforts preventing these less worthy interests from prevailing.[129]

Recognizing the actual role of arbitrageurs and speculators in the tender offer process, however, belies the distinction between short-term speculation and long-term investment. The success of an offer depends on a variety of factors. Arbitrageurs offer to purchase the target's stock at a price equal to the tender offer price discounted by the arbitrageur's evaluation of the risk that the offer will be unsuccessful and that the acquired shares will then be sold in the market at a lower price. Thus, it is not surprising that arbitrageurs favor a tender offer. In effect, they stand as surrogates, albeit less risk-averse, for long-term investors who have *already demonstrated,* by selling their shares to the arbitrageurs, that they perceived their "long-term" interests were outweighed by the size of the premium. In other words, the "short-term perspective" of the arbitrageurs is a red herring; their desire to sell merely reflects, by proxy, the desires of the selling shareholders.

D. *Management Knows Best*

A more recent addition to the promanagement portfolio of arguments by Martin Lipton makes no claim about the overall efficiency of tender offers, but asserts that interests of target shareholders in a higher return on their investment are best served by allowing management discretion to block a tender offer. Lipton examined 36 unsolicited tender offers that were defeated by targets between the end of 1973 and June 1979 and concluded that "the shares of more than 50% of the targets are either today at a higher market price than the rejected offer price or were acquired after the tender offer was defeated at a price higher than the offer price." [132] On that basis, Lipton argues that shareholders are best served by giving primacy to target management's judgment.

Lipton's analysis is subject to substantial methodological criticism. He takes no account, for example, of general price movements during the relevant period,[133] nor is there an effort to discount future values to present values to allow more accurate comparison. And the methodologically more careful empirical studies * * * are flatly inconsistent with Lipton's conclusions. These studies suggest that following an unsuccessful offer, target company shareholders earn no more than a market return, and that a non-trivial portion of the bid premium is

---

[129] *"It would not be unfair to pose the policy issue as: Whether the long-term interests of the nation's corporate system and economy should be jeopardized in order to benefit speculators interested not in the vitality and continued existence of the business enterprise in which they have bought shares, but only in a quick profit on the sale of those shares?'* Lipton, supra note 105, at 104 (emphasis in the original).

[132] Id. at 106.

[133] To the extent that the performance of the stocks in the Lipton sample reflects movement in the general price levels of stocks, the same gains would have been available to investors if the tender offer had been accepted through investing it in other stocks, but without giving up the premium offered on the tender.

lost.[135]   Indeed, Lipton's data refute his own conclusion.   On initial examination, share values of 19 of the 36 target companies considered increased in price, and 17 decreased, relative to the defeated offer, measured as of the earlier of August 10, 1979, or the date on which the target company was acquired by a different offeror.   Of the 19 companies whose share prices exceeded the rejected tender offer, two should be discounted since they appear to have involved transactions in which a white knight made a competitive bid at approximately the same time and in response to the defeated offer.[136]   Further, of the 17 remaining target companies whose shares increased in value beyond the price of the defeated offer, four show increases at a compounded annual rate of less than 3%, hardly a tribute to management's investment acumen. Finally, and fully recognizing that my statistical efforts are also misleading,[138] the subsequent share values of the 36 companies reflect an average compounded annual rate of return to target company shareholders, on the money they would have received if the tender offer had been successful, of −5.48%.[139]   In short, the available data, including Lipton's own, support the "popular belief on Wall Street" that shareholders are disadvantaged by defeat of a tender offer.*

In an important respect, however, Lipton's data are less important than the argument based upon them.   Capital market theory tells us that the market—the shareholders and others acting en masse—is the best unbiased estimate of the value of a corporation's stock.   If target management prevents shareholders from responding to an offer, that valuation process is bypassed.   The promanagement argument, however, suggests that management should be allowed to block tender offers, and so "short-circuit" the valuation process, because they are "better" market analysts.   But this argument fails for the same reason as the functional equivalence argument: Even if management could "beat the market," there must be a mechanism to check management's own interest in the transaction.   And if management's superior investment analysis is based on inside information, the only plausible explanation

[135] These studies present a consistent pattern.   The value of target shares increases substantially around the announcement date of a tender offer to reflect the offered premium.   Following defeat of the offer, the target shares drop in value but remain above the original pre-offer price. This pattern suggests, as the investigators describe, that the market views the offer as favorable new information bearing on the future value of the company and, therefore, supporting a higher post-rejection price. * * *

[136] The two targets involved were Latrobe Steel Co. and Unitek Corp.   While one might argue that securing a white knight at a higher price justifies management resistance, that position is not available to Lipton since he asserts the more extreme position that management should have the discretion to ignore this alternative as well.   Lipton, supra note 105, at 109.

[138] Among other problems presented by this shorthand form of data analysis, and which are not presented by the more sophisticated studies referred to in note 135 supra, is the bias toward negative returns resulting from the effect of compounding on more recently rejected offers.   Also, I did not weigh the various offers by their total value in computing the average, nor have I included dividends paid, if any, in the computation of annual return.

[139] This figure excludes the white knight transactions referred to in note 136 supra. If these transactions are included, the figure is −2.4%.

* Easterbrook & Jarrell, *Do Targets Gain from Defeating Tender Offers?*, 59 N.Y.U.L. Rev. 277 (1984), reach an identical conclusion using more extensive empirical analysis.   [Ed.]

for a claim of unusual ability, eliminating management discretion to block a tender offer does not deprive shareholders of the benefit of this skill. Management may still make public the reasons for its belief that the market undervalues the corporation.[142] *   *   *

F. *Corporate Social Responsibility*

There is a certain irony in the argument offered by some authorities that responsiveness to nonshareholder constituencies—employees, customers, suppliers, creditors, local communities, and the national economy—justifies management discretion in preventing takeovers. As Chairman Williams, himself no advocate of shareholder autonomy in tender offers, states, "[t]he corporate community cannot have it both ways. It cannot argue against added measures—legislative or otherwise—directed to improve corporate accountability by relying on the discipline of the marketplace as a vehicle to depose inadequate management, and then seek to neutralize that discipline by anti-takeover provisions." [155] Nonetheless, since commentators, corporate management, and occasionally courts assert the argument, it warrants consideration.

A first step is to define "corporate social responsibility." I will adopt David Engel's definition: "the obligations and inclinations * * * of corporations organized for profit, voluntarily to pursue social ends that conflict with the presumptive shareholder desire to maximize profit." Note that the definition excludes acts beneficial to nonshareholder constituencies which, although detrimental to profits in the short run, lead to long-run profit maximization.

Second, note that management which engages in acts of corporate social responsibility will rarely, if ever, be held liable for corporate waste. The distinction between corporate altruism and long-run profit maximization is blurred. Whether community aid efforts reflect the corporation's self-interest, however enlightened, or are merely charitable, involves precisely the type of decision review of which the courts appropriately have eschewed by applying the business judgment rule. So long as management is disingenuous when necessary, legal standards do not bar management from following a "socially responsible" course.

Thus, to the extent the tender offer process poses a question of corporate social responsibility, the question is not how to define it or whether it is a good thing. Rather, the question raised by asserting that issues of social responsibility justify target management's discretion to block a tender offer is more narrow and ideologically neutral: What checks are there on management's decision to engage in a particular *level* of nonprofitmaking, altruistic behavior? The issue is whether management—through defensive tactics—may secure immunity from the market consequences of its altruistic decisions comparable

---

[142] Management's possession of nonpublic information which would alter the maket's valuation of the target company's stock is not inconsistent with market efficiency in the semi-strong form

[155] H. Williams, *supra* note 115, at 82,881.

to the immunity from legal consequences provided by the business judgment rule.

To be sure, there is something quaint about a general assertion that matters of social responsibility require allowing target management to prevent tender offers; it has the decided flavor of Senator Williams' oft-cited reference, when introducing the Williams Act, to the fate of "proud old companies" at the hands of "white collar pirates." [161] But there is no reason to adopt the assumption that the management of all offerors are less socially responsible than those of all targets. Acts of social responsibility are no more than "a specialized class of suboptimization" [162] by target management which, as with other forms of management discretion which courts cannot effectively regulate, the structure of the corporation relies upon the tender offer process to control. If shareholders believe management is *too* responsible for their taste, they will tender their shares at the offered premium, some part of which reflects the potential gain if suboptimization—social responsibility—is reduced. Thus, to assert social responsibility as a basis for management discretion to block a tender offer is to argue not only that corporate social responsibility is a good thing, but that management should have the unrestrained discretion to determine *how much* corporate capital should be devoted to purposes *management* deems socially responsible. That position is quite difficult to support, and opposition need not be based on the proposition that corporate altruism results in inefficiency.

The decision as to what activities are socially responsible is a political rather than a corporate or economic one. Target management has no special expertise in such decisions, nor is there any reason to believe that the vision of a just society held by management will be shared by any larger body, whether shareholders or not. Rather, the issue turns on the appropriate institution to make this type of decision. The tender offer process constrains target management's social as well as business judgments; there is nothing about management's social judgments which renders them more sacrosanct than management's business judgments.

————————◆————————

Note: Three More Arguments on Behalf of Target Management Discretion

Three additional arguments advanced in favor of allowing target management to block unfriendly takeover offers warrant attention. Interestingly, the picture of target management painted by each is radically different, even though they support the identical outcome. In

---

[161] 111 Cong.Rec. 28,257–58 (1965). It is intriguing that the terms "raider" and "pirate," while often used, are rarely defined. Professor Cary has made one of the rare efforts: "As a Professor, I sometimes define a raider as somebody else's client." Cary, *Corporate Devices Used to Insulate* *Management From Attack,* 25 Bus.Law. 839, 842 (1970).

[162] Engel, *An Approach to Corporate Social Responsibility,* 32 Stan.L.Rev. 1, 8 (1979).

the first, management is portrayed as looking out for itself at the expense of shareholder interests, and discretion to block unfriendly offers is held out as a means to ameliorate that conflict. In the second and third arguments, management is instead portrayed as benevolently paternalistic, and discretion to block unfriendly offers is held out as necessary to prevent shareholders from making the wrong decision in the second, or to get a better price in the third. Despite this inconsistency, the arguments are not mutually inconsistent. If giving target management discretion to block an unfriendly offer reduces the conflict between management and shareholders, that discretion might then be exercised so as to protect shareholders from themselves, or from too low an offer.

Overcoming Target Management's Short-Term Bias. This argument, advanced most vigorously by Peter Drucker,[93] blames hostile takeovers for the claimed short-term outlook of American industry and our resulting competitive disadvantage in world markets. Because management is fearful of losing their jobs in a takeover, they ignore long-term planning and forward looking research and development in favor of short-term business strategies that will keep their company's stock price high and, as a result, discourage takeovers.[94] Drucker makes the point explicitly:

> Anyone working with management people knows that fear of the raider paralyzes our executives. Worse, it forces them into making decisions they know to be stupid and to damage the enterprise in their charge. A good many experienced business leaders I know hold takeover fear to be a main cause of the decline in America's competitive strength in the world economy. * * * It contributes to the obsession with the short term and the slighting of tomorrow in research, product development and marketing, and in quality of service—all to squeeze out a few more dollars in the next quarter's "bottom line." [95]

We would all be made better off, the argument goes, if managers could block hostile takeovers. They would then feel secure enough to engage in long-run profit maximization which, after all, is what we really want them to do.

The structure of this argument requires careful examination at two critical points. The first is the unstated assumption about market efficiency. In order for the price of the company's stock to go up when management shifts to a short-term from a long-term strategy, the stock market must undervalue long-term performance and overvalue short-term performance.[96] Whether the stock market is biased in favor of

---

[93] See, e.g., Drucker, *Taming the Corporate Takeover*, Wall St.J., Oct. 30, 1984, p. 30, col. 3; Drucker, *Curbing Unfriendly Offers*, Wall St.J., Jan. 5, 1983, p. 18, col. 4.

[94] Section B.2.b. of this Chapter, supra.

[95] Drucker, *Taming the Corporate Takeover*, supra. Takeovers cannot be the only cause. For example, two of the domestic industries that have declined most significantly in the world economy—automobiles

and steel—have hardly been the object of significant hostile takeover activity.

[96] In effect, the claim is that the market applies too high a discount rate to earnings in periods beyond the immediate future. The argument depends on inefficiency because, if a short-term strategy really were more beneficial to the company, one would assume that management would have

the short-term is an empirical question. But because of the enormous empirical literature which supports the proposition that the stock market is efficient, the burden of proof would seem to be on those claiming the anomalous result—that the market is inefficient in that it systematically undervalues long-term prospects. And it is important to be clear about how heavy that burden really is. What must be shown is not just that the stock market's predictions of the future are often wrong, but that they are *systematically* wrong in that too high a discount rate is applied to future earnings. Moreover, a proponent of the argument must also explain why the systematic bias persists in the face of how widely its existence has been trumpeted. Why have not investors taken advantage of the profit opportunity such a bias offers and, by so doing, eliminated its existence? If the explanation for a short-term bias is that managers are much more likely to have information about long-term prospects that the market does not have, would disclosure be a less drastic solution? [96a]

The second point at which the argument requires careful appraisal is the solution offered in response to the problem of managerial insecurity. As presented, the choice is between the lesser of two evils. If management is not given the discretion to block a hostile takeover, shareholders will bear the cost both of management's deviation from long-term profit maximization and the loss of access to premium takeovers. If management is given the discretion to block a hostile takeover, at least the incentive to deviate from profit maximization is eliminated. The difficulty with this approach is that it artificially limits the available solutions.

Once this limitation is removed, the problem can be restated more generally. Management understandably values job security; it is, in fact, a form of management compensation. So put, the task is to provide management with the desired security at the lowest possible cost. In these terms, both allowing management to adopt short-term strategies to prevent takeovers, and giving management outright power to prevent takeovers, seem very expensive means to this end. One way of thinking about how much it would cost to directly provide management the security they desire is to compare the size of severance payments called for under typical executive compensation agreements with the size of the premiums that shareholders would be forced to forego if management's job security were provided by allowing them to prevent hostile takeovers. Once the problem is properly identified as one of compensation, then concern over deviation from long-term profit maximization can be responded to by the design of direct incentive programs.

It should also be noted, however, that this analysis assumes that management's short-term strategy is not in the shareholders' best interests. Are there circumstances when a management group whose only interest was to maximize shareholder wealth might nonetheless

adopted it regardless of the potential of a hostile takeover.

[96a] For an interesting effort to specify the conditions under which it might be in the interest of managers to manage in the short-run, see Narayanan, *Managerial Incentives for Short-term Results*, 40 J.Fin. 1469 (1985).

favor the short term? What if there was a great deal of uncertainty concerning the future—for example, because of fears of renewed inflation or a change in tax rates. That might cause the company to apply a higher discount rate to long-term projects than short-term projects, much as long-term interest rates would be significantly higher than short-term rates under those circumstances. If managers are managing in the short run, how could we determine whether the explanation was a self-serving effort to protect their jobs, or a rational response to uncertain economic conditions?

Extracting Target Shareholders from the Prisoner's Dilemma. This argument suggests that target shareholders, if left to their own devices, will respond to a tender offer in a manner contrary to their best interests not because they lack wisdom, but because of the "special dynamics" [97] of the tender offer process. It is argued that, as in the game theorists' prisoner's dilemma, it may be in the best interests of an individual shareholder to tender in response to an offer, even if the shareholders as a group would be better off if no one tendered.[98] Management discretion to block an offer then rescues shareholders from the unfortunate result of pursuing their individual, as opposed to their collective, self-interest.

In game theory terms, the central characteristic of a prisoner's dilemma is an array of benefits and detriments associated with alternative courses of action such that the dominant individual strategy is not to cooperate even though, if the parties do not cooperate, pursuit of individual self-interest yields less than optimal results. Assume that a corporation is owned equally by two shareholders who believe their stock is worth $40 per share, but who, by definition, cannot agree to cooperate in deciding whether to tender. Further assume that a tender offer is made in which fifty percent of the outstanding stock will be purchased for $50 per share; that if both tender, the shares will be taken up pro rata; and that the remaining fifty percent of the outstanding stock will be purchased for $25 per share in a freezeout merger. The choices facing the shareholders are expressed in the following payoff matrix.

		SHAREHOLDER 2	
		Don't Tender	Tender
SHAREHOLDER 1	Don't Tender	$40, $40	$25, $50
	Tender	$50, $25	$37.50, $37.50

For the shareholders as a group, the best outcome occurs if neither shareholder tenders; all other courses of action result in their receiving an average price less than the $40 per share they believe the stock is

---

[97] Lipton, *Takeover Bids in the Target's Boardroom,* 35 Bus.Law. 101, 113 (1979).

[98] This analysis is most fully developed in Carney, *Shareholder Coordination Costs,*

Shark Repellent Amendments, and Takeout Mergers: The Case Against Fiduciary Duties, 1983 Am.B.Found.Res.J. 341.

worth. If, however, the shareholders must act independently, the best
outcome is unlikely to occur. Each shareholder will recognize that if
he, seeking the best group outcome, does not tender, and the other
shareholder, acting selfishly, does, the selfless shareholder will bear
substantial costs. In this situation, as represented in the northeast and
southwest quadrants of the matrix, the tendering shareholder receives
$50 per share for his stock while the nontendering shareholder receives
only $25 per share in the subsequent freezeout merger. The sensible
response is to tender, thus avoiding the risk of ending up with all of
one's shares being acquired at the lowest price. Because the decision
calculus is the same for both shareholders, both will tender and the
offer will be successful even though both shareholders would have been
better off had the offer failed.[99]

It is this result that target management discretion to block a
tender offer arguably will prevent. When management recognizes that
the shareholders are in a prisoner's dilemma, it can, by blocking the
offer, act in the way shareholders would have acted if they could have
cooperated in not tendering. To be sure, noncooperation is just an
assumption in the hypothetical. In the real world, however, noncooperation results from the large transaction costs associated with joint
shareholder action in a public corporation.[100] Thus, the potential for a
prisoner's dilemma does exist and, in this case, the proposed response
keys directly to the problem involved: By blocking the offer, management acts as a surrogate for the shareholders, choosing the alternative
shareholders would have chosen if cooperation was feasible.

In evaluating the force of this argument, a number of points should
be considered:

1. Does the solution extend beyond the problem? If in the hypothetical the offer was for one hundred percent of the outstanding stock
at $37.50 per share (the average per share price of both ends of the
hypothetical offer), do shareholders require management's assistance in
order to reject the offer? If the potential for a prisoner's dilemma
results only from the manner in which an offer is made, then the
argument for management discretion to block takeovers extends only to
offers whose structure creates the problem. What types of offers have
the potential to create a prisoner's dilemma, and how the coercion
associated with them can be directly attacked, is considered in Chapter
Fifteen A., infra.

2. What if the pre-offer market price in the hypothetical were $35
per share so that the shareholders gained, compared to the market
price if not to their own beliefs, as a result of the offer? If the market
price is a measure of the "real" value of the company, then a prisoner's
dilemma can exist only if the gain from the premium offered in the
first step of the transaction is less than the penalty imposed in the
second step on those who did not tender in the first step. Because the
average value of the tender offer in the hypothetical exceeds the

[99] This discussion is adapted from Gilson,   *Tender Offers,* 33 Stan.L.Rev. 819, 859–62
A Structural Approach to Corporations: (1981).
The Case Against Defensive Tactics in
[100] Carney, supra, at 347–57.

assumed pre-offer market price, the transaction, taken as a whole, has a positive value for the shareholders. It might then be in the best interests of the shareholders, both individually and as a group, to tender. In this situation, what is the relevance of the fact that the average value of the tender offer, although above the market price, is below what the parties believe the stock is worth? Does the rule you choose with respect to management discretion to block an offer depend on the likelihood that the market will be systematically incorrect? On this issue, compare the discussion of optimal voting rules in Section A. 2. of Chapter Thirteen with Carney, supra at 353–57.

3. Even if shareholders require a champion to protect their interests in some circumstances, is target management a likely candidate for that role? Because management has an inevitable conflict of interest with respect to hostile takeover offers, how can we ever tell whether their opposition results from circumstances that give rise to a genuine prisoner's dilemma or, alternatively, from their own self-interest. If the circumstances that give rise to a genuine prisoner's dilemma cannot be identified with precision, then we may remain unwilling to give management the discretion to block an offer, even though a prisoner's dilemma may occasionally occur, because the cost of the solution— managerial discretion—may be greater than the cost of the problem. Alternatively, if the offending circumstances can be identified with precision, then the preferable approach might be to deal with those circumstances directly—for example, by prohibiting two-tier, front-end loaded offers [101]—rather than to rely on the benevolence of target management.

Defensive Tactics to Initiate Auctions. This argument builds on empirical evidence developed in Jarrell, *The Wealth Effects of Litigation by Targets: Do Interests Diverge in a Merger?*, 28 J.L. & Econ. 151 (1985), to the effect that a portfolio of target companies that vigorously resisted an offer by litigation earned higher returns than a portfolio of target companies that were passive. This suggests that target management completely loyal to shareholders should still resist an offer, a result possible only if they have the discretion to do so. On closer analysis, however, the data suggests a much more limited policy recommendation.

Two facts concerning the empirical evidence are critical. First, the source of the increased return to the litigious portfolio is that target companies that do litigate are much more likely to be the subject of an auction among competing bidders than target companies that are passive. The gains come from being taken over, not from remaining independent. This point is underscored by the second critical fact. A subsample of the litigious targets who actually defeat the initial offer not only do not earn increased returns, they do significantly worse than passive targets. Thus, if there were a way to prevent this subsample from defeating all offers, the returns to the litigious portfolio would increase even further.

---

[101] See Chapter Fifteen A., infra.

The policy recommendation these facts suggest is much more limited than giving target management blanket discretion to resist offers. Consistent with the analysis in section B.2.b. of this Chapter, Jarrell identifies the role of litigation as creating enough delay that competing bids can be secured. Id. at 155–56. The best rule then is one that would delay the initial offer to allow an auction to develop, but would not allow management of the subsample of firms to block— whether intentionally or inadvertently—all offers. Such a rule is quite easy to design. Simply couple a passivity rule which allows seeking competitive bids, as developed in section B.3.d. of this Chapter, with a mandatory delay before a tender offer can be completed. See Bebchuk, *The Case for Facilitating Competing Tender Offers: A Reply and Extension*, 35 Stan.L.Rev. 23 (1982).

One problem remains. As Jarrell notes,[102] increasing the returns to target companies through auctions benefits the shareholders of companies that actually are the subject of offers, but may injure shareholders of other companies if the result is to decrease the total number of offers. That problem is considered in the next section.

f.   The Remaining Debate: Is There Any Role for Target Management?

Professors Easterbrook and Fischel have also argued for a rule prohibiting defensive tactics by target management—in their terms a rule of "managerial passivity." Easterbrook & Fischel, *The Proper Role of a Target's Management in Responding to a Tender Offer*, 94 Harv.L. Rev. 1161 (1981). Their proposal differs from Gilson's in that it would also prohibit efforts by target management to secure competitive bids. Their argument for this position initially focused on the effect of competitive bidding on the incentives of offerors to bid in the first place.

EASTERBROOK & FISCHEL, THE PROPER ROLE OF A TARGET'S MANAGEMENT IN RESPONDING TO A TENDER OFFER
94 Harv.L.Rev. 1161, 1178–79 (1981).

Prospective offerers must do substantial research to identify underpriced corporations and to determine how their management can be improved. They may engage investment banking houses and investigate the affairs of many corporations before finding one whose management could be improved. The position of a tender offeror is particularly precarious because, at the time it makes a bid, its investment in information about the target is sunk. Perhaps the first bidder will invest $10 per share in finding out about many potential targets and then exploring the prospects of X in depth. [Suppose it discovers that X is worth $90 per share.] If it can acquire X for $50 per share, it reaps a profit as high as $30 per share ($90 minus $10 investigation costs, minus $50 tender price). The bidder's profit falls to nothing

[102] Jarrell, supra at 175.

when the tender offer price reaches $80 per share. Once the offeror announces its bid, however, other potential acquirers learn the target's identity. The bid itself, and the accompanying disclosures under federal and state law, may reveal much of what the offeror has learned. If the offeror does not supply other bidders with valuable information, the target's management may do so as part of a strategy to set up an auction. But any other bidder need not bear costs as high as those already incurred by the first bidder. The subsequent bidders take a free ride, making a profit even if the price rises to $80 per share. As a result, no firm wants to be the first bidder unless it has some advantage, such as speed, over subsequent bidders to compensate for the fact that only it had to incur monitoring costs. And, of course, if there is no first bidder there will be no later bidders and no tender premium.

Perhaps most important of all, requiring bidders to pay a high premium will lead to a decrease in the price of the target's shares. A bidder facing the prospect of paying a high premium is less likely to monitor other firms, and the decrease in searching for targets leads to a decrease in the number of bids. Then the price of X's stock is likely to decrease because, with the reduction in monitoring, agency costs rise.

For instance, assume that a bid of 20% over the market price will attract enough shares under the acquiescence paradigm to achieve success, but under the resistance paradigm the premium must be 50% or more. As before, firm X's shares would trade for $90 under the best practicable management. The shareholder choosing one of the paradigm rules to bind the managers would ask: How effective will outside monitoring be in inducing my managers to come as close to optimality as possible? The governing rule would influence managers' performance; if takeovers are more costly, there will be fewer diligent managers in any given firm. Agency costs will tend to increase to the point where further increases precipitate a takeover.

◆

Gilson responded by questioning whether the first offerer's search costs really were lost if a competitive bid was successful. He further argued that the more efficient resource allocation resulting from competitive bidding would offset any decrease in incidence of tender offers.

GILSON, A STRUCTURAL APPROACH TO CORPORATIONS
Supra, at 870–72.

While acknowledging that shareholders of a target company faced with an existing offer will benefit from management bargaining, a number of commentators argue that shareholders of all potential targets as a class, and the economy as a whole, are adversely affected by the potential for such conduct. The argument is that the threat of a tender offer constrains management's discretion to perform inefficiently or to self-deal. Thus, anything which reduces the incidence of tender offers reduces the power of the threat to constrain management and is detrimental to society.

The problem with competitive bidding in the face of an initial offer, it is argued, is that the initial offerer incurs sunk costs in identifying and evaluating the target company. These investment costs must be covered by expected profit on the takeover. A competing bidder does not incur these sunk information costs, since the target is already identified and target management will assist the competing bidder in evaluating the target's value. As a result, the transaction is profitable for the competing bidder at a higher price than for the initial bidder. This increases the risk associated with investment in takeover investigations and decreases the return associated with those investments. Not only do competitive bids increase the likelihood that a competitor will win, with the result that the sunk costs are entirely lost, but by increasing the price necessary for success, they reduce the potential profit associated with the investment. Therefore, the incentive to make initial offers, and hence the total number of offers, decrease.

I find the argument unpersuasive on a number of levels. First, the sunk cost argument seems to me significantly overstated. In any tender offer of substantial size the information costs associated with identifying and evaluating the target are a small proportion of the entire purchase price,[182] and the white knight must also incur costs in verifying and assessing the significance of information provided by target management. One cannot help but suspect that success in most major transactions does not turn on differences of this magnitude.

More importantly, I suspect that the sunk costs are investments with a positive expected return even if the offeror is ultimately outbid. Increasingly, a potential bidder takes a substantial block position in the stock of a target before announcing its intentions. If the initial offeror is outbid, it will simply tender its target shares to its competitor, or sell them in the market, at a per-share profit approximately equal to the premium it initially offered plus the amount by which its offer was exceeded. McDermott, Inc.'s gross profit of approximately $15.5 million on shares purchased during its losing contest with Wheelabrator-Frye, Inc. for Pullman, Inc. is illustrative of the phenomenon.[185]

This phenomenon reflects, of course, no more than that the risk of competitive bidding, like most financial risks, can be hedged. The sunk information costs are an investment in a risky asset whose return derives from successfully completing the acquisition and whose risk is that the bidder will lose the acquisition to a higher bidder. Purchase of

[182] For example, the acquiring company's investment banker, which often undertakes the burden of identifying potential targets, appears to earn fees of something less than 1% of the acquisition price representing, on a $50 per share transaction, less than 50 cents per share. *Outside Professionals Play an Increasing Role in Corporate Takeovers*, Wall St.J., Dec. 2, 1980, at 1, col. 6.

[185] McDermott held 513,000 Pullman shares acquired at an average price of $22, for which Wheelabrator-Frye bid $52. It also held another 60,000 shares acquired at

higher prices but below the Wheelabrator offer. Wall St.J., Sept. 26, 1980, at 7, col. 5. Thus, McDermott's gross profit on the transaction was in excess of $15.5 million. The total outside expenses incurred by all *three* parties to the transaction, including investment banker fees, were estimated at only $17 million, at least $6 million of which was paid by Pullman to *its* investment banker. Even more recently, Seagrams Co. earned $10,659,750 on an approximately one month investment of $13,980,000 as a result of its loss of St. Joseph Minerals Corp. to Fluor Corp.

target shares in the market prior to making the offer hedges that risk because the return on that asset varies inversely with the return on the investment in information. Indeed, if the initial offeror treats the returns associated with a successful acquisition as certain, the effect of the hedge is to allow the initial offeror to *guarantee* a risk-free rturn on its investment in information.[186] Thus, it is not at all clear that the potential for competition should reduce the frequency of initial bids.[187]

A second problem with the argument asserting the evils of soliciting competitive bids is that it ignores the efficiency-inducing effect of price competition. As a general principle, allocating resources among competing claimants by price is desirable because it places resources with the most efficient users. To assert that one should maximize the total number of tender offers without regard to the allocative benefits of price competition, one must assume that all offerors can make equally efficient use of target resources. This is unlikely. Indeed, one major explanation for the efficiency of mergers—synergy—assumes differing abilities to make use of target's assets. The theory ultimately turns upon the fit of the particular offeror, or the skills of the particular offeror's management, with the target company, and I see no basis for assuming these attributes are identical among competing bidders. Thus, even if competitive bidding reduces the overall number of offerors, the increase in efficiency from allocating target assets to their most efficient user must be balanced against the reduction in efficiency from fewer offers. While this balance cannot be easily identified, the greater the importance of synergy as an explanation for the acquiring company's gains, the more important the efficiency gain through price competition relative to the efficiency loss due to a lower frequency of tender offers.

[186] This assumes that there is no risk that the acquisition will fail for other reasons. To be sure, the greater the likelihood that the initial bidder will lose the acquisition to a competitive bidder, the greater the likelihood it will earn the presumably lower risk-free rate. Whether this reduction in return will result in a reduction in the number of initial offers is a function of the potential initial offeror's alternative investments. And even if a reduction in the frequency of initial offers does result, this cost must still be compared to the benefits of competitive bidding. This balance is considered next in the text.

[187] Indeed, one cannot escape the suspicion that this phenomenon may actually encourage initial offers. If the initial offer is viewed as so distasteful that, at the hint of a takeover threat, the target management will seek a white knight—as seems to be the case with offers made by companies controlled, for example, by Victor Posner— the announcement of an initial block position may make a higher competing bid virtually certain even if the "raider" had no intention of a takeover, but acquired the block hoping to precipitate a competing takeover by someone else. Hirshleifer & Riley, *The Analytics of Uncertainty and Information—An Expository Survey*, 16 J.Econ.Lit. 1375, 1404–06 (1979), identify the potential for realizing through such speculation the value of information produced, and note that the incentive is then to disseminate rather than protect the confidentiality of the information. They also note that the ability to speculate may even lead to "excessive devotion of resources" to the production of new information—in our setting to monitoring potential target companies. Id. at 1405. This would suggest that specialists in monitoring—a new form of information intermediary—would develop, whose interest would be in disclosing the information discovered after taking a speculative position in the potential target's stock, thereby eliminating the sunk cost problem assertedly facing initial bidders. Casual evidence of the extent to which market professionals now play the "takeover game" is consistent with this prediction. Gilson, supra, at 870–72.

The debate, expanded by Lucian Bebchuk, *The Case for Facilitating Competing Tender Offers,* 95 Harv.L.Rev. 1028 (1982), continued, with each side broadening the scope of their arguments.

EASTERBROOK & FISCHEL, AUCTIONS AND SUNK COSTS IN TENDER OFFERS
35 Stan.L.Rev. 1 (1982).*

I. SUNK INFORMATION COSTS

Bebchuk and Gilson argue that we overestimate both the first bidder's interest in protecting its sunk information costs and the effect of auctioneering on this interest. They point out that investment bankers bear much of the cost of searching for targets, and that their fees are only a small portion of a target's value. Moreover, they argue that a bidder may recoup its costs by buying some shares at low prices before announcing its bid and by tendering to the eventual winner if an auction develops. Thus, they conclude, the first bidder's costs of information would not *prevent* searching under a rule allowing auctions.

Bebchuk and Gilson demonstrate that even in an auction first bidders might profit if they prevail, and that first bidders could recoup some of their costs even if they do not win; but they do not show, or even claim, that the same amount of search will occur as under a rule of managerial passivity. Their point goes to the magnitude of the sunk cost effect in determining search. The more important point, though, is that *any* reduction in the return from search is undesirable.

The takeover case is an example of a general phenomenon: the difficulty of establishing property rights in information. This difficulty arises because using information often gives it away, allowing others to obtain its benefits without compensating its originator. Unless either a legal regimen or some system of self-help creates informal property rights, firms will produce too little information, just as farmers will grow too few apples unless there is a rule against theft. So, for example, when Exxon searches for oil, its ability to realize the value of its information depends on contracts backed up by (or implied in) legal rules that prevent its employees from selling geophysical data to rivals, and on its legal privilege to buy land through nominees who need not disclose what they know. If, after finding oil, Exxon had to announce its discovery and wait for an auction on the tract in question, it would undertake a suboptimal amount of searching. It would be cold comfort to Exxon that it could buy five percent of the oil-bearing land before it entered the contest for the other 95 percent on equal terms with its passive rivals.

Similar practices exist throughout the economy. Firms line up profitable opportunities, from parcels of land in Manhattan to fleets of ships, in secret, through nominees and ruses, in order to appropriate more of the value of their information and thus have correct incentives to search. Contract law does not require the disclosure of information gained through deliberate efforts. Markets produce myriad devices for capturing the value of knowledge, from corporate integration to sales of closed bags of diamonds to maximum price arrangements among rivals.

In contrast to these familiar practices, the securities laws require the disclosure of great quantities of information, in tender offers and elsewhere. This disclosure reduces the likelihood that firms will produce the optimal amounts of knowledge or engage in the optimal amounts of activities that depend on information. The market's response was the Saturday Night Special tender offer, which required tenders before an auction could develop. It enabled bidders to capture much of the value of their investment in information, but the Williams Act has made it unlawful. A rule of managerial passivity, although not allowing bidders to capture the full value of their information, at least allows them to obtain some.

The difficulty of appropriating the benefits of investments in information results in underinvestment, and this does not depend on the costs of information being large or small. When any part of the value of information is lost to its producer, there will be inefficiently little produced. And when bidders produce too little information, there is too little monitoring and investors' wealth falls.

Although we thus conclude that the size of the first bidder's sunk costs is important only to the magnitude, not to the existence, of the problem, we are also skeptical of any assertion that the magnitude is small. Bebchuk and Gilson scrutinize the fees charged by investment bankers for providing information, but the fees in contested offers do not exhaust the bidder's costs. Bidders invest their own time in searching for targets, and the opportunity costs of managers' time so committed includes the value to the bidders of other projects foregone. Because the search will cover many firms in addition to the one eventually selected for a bid, it may take a substantial amount of time. Bidders must assemble and hold capital at the ready for a possible acquisition, and the first bidder's time and capital is committed for the longest time. Even investment bankers must incur the cost of keeping information at the ready. They too will produce suboptimal information if they anticipate fewer first bids.

The first bidder also bears another special risk that must be counted as part of the cost of searching for targets: It must make the offer under considerable uncertainty, often without access to the internal documents of the target. Some first bids are bound to exceed the offers that would be justified by complete information, and these bids will not provoke auctions. To the contrary, the first bidder will win every time it bids mistakenly high. Yet when it errs on the other side, an auction would drive the price up. The first bidder's risk, then, is that it will be left with a prize collection of losers when it overbids, while competition will deny it any gains on other offers.

The size of these costs is, of course, an empirical matter, on which we have no data. But one need not believe the claims of several white knights—which have maintained that they needed lock-up options on 25% or more of the target's shares or assets to make even a *second* bid worthwhile—in order to conclude that the costs are substantial. The costs are probably sufficiently great that the first bidder's ability to cover some of them by purchasing shares in advance of offers would not come close to providing first bidders with optimal incentives to invest in information about targets.

Our point ultimately does not depend on the size of first bidders' costs; so long as information costs are positive, their inability to appropriate the full value of their information will lead them to produce too little. That will reduce the number of tender offers and the effectiveness of the process in monitoring managers. This is a simple application of marginal analysis. We cannot tell how much the reduction will be, but it will exist, and *any* reduction is too much unless there are offsetting gains, a subject to which we now turn.

* * *

III. SOCIAL WEALTH

* * *

Moving assets to their highest-valued uses

We come now to the most interesting of the arguments. Bebchuk and Gilson maintain that auctions ensure that the target's assets move to their highest-valuing users. They therefore recommend that offers remain open so that competing bidders may come forth with or without the target's assistance.

Now many goods are sold by auction, including paintings, antiques, and old houses. Presumably these auctions enable higher-valuing users to obtain these assets. But many other goods, including new issues of stock in corporations, are not sold at auction. If *A* wants to buy widgets and *B* is willing to sell, there is no legal requirement that the offer remain open for an extended period so that another purchaser who values widgets more than *A* can learn of the offer and arrive on the scene. If *C* values the widgets more than *A*, he can buy them from *A* later.

We suggested in our original article that one difference between paintings and widgets is that the market offers a ready price for widgets, a price on which *A* and *B* can rely without conducting an auction. The shares of corporations, we said, are sold in liquid markets and are not at all unique goods like paintings or old houses.

This is not a dispositive answer, for targets and bidders are not quite interchangeable. * * * [T]he initial bidder may not be able to put the target to a use as efficient as some other firm. Our approach implies that a series of trades among firms would occur until the target's assets ended up with their highest-valuing users; perhaps, along the way, different parts of the target's assets and operations would be sold to different firms. Bebchuk and Gilson, in contrast, are skeptical of the first buyer's willingness to resell; they fear that managers would not reduce the size of their empires or that high transaction costs would impede subsequent transfers.

Whether buyers would resell assets to higher-valuing users—and, if so, what the costs of a series of sales would be—are questions that cannot be answered at the level of theory. We suspect that the costs of a drawn-out auction exceed the costs of an acquisition without auction, followed by retransfers, but we cannot be sure. We also suspect that the value of many targets is highest if different bundles of their assets are transferred to different firms, and this means that a drawn-out auction would not avoid the need for subsequent retransfers. Firms routinely sell parts of their operations to other firms, and these transfers increase the value of investments in the selling and buying firms alike. There is thus little evidence to support the belief that managers systematically reject the opportunity to profit by selling plants and divisions.

The allocational benefits of auctions thus seem to be small if not negative. At the same time, auctions increase the risk borne by the first bidder and make tender offers more costly (and less likely). Moreover, it is all too easy for managers to conduct a defensive strategy under the guise of running an auction. Although Bebchuk and Gilson would permit "auctioneering" only if it is neutral between the first and subsequent bidders, it does not take much imagination to see that managers could give white knights decisive advantages by selectively releasing information or striking deals. Such disguised resistance is an additional source of loss from a rule of auctioneering.

*   *   *

V. SEPARATING INFORMATION AND IMPLEMENTATION

Gilson's latest article significantly extends his earlier analysis of auctioneering versus passivity. * * * His new argument is that any proper treatment of the subject must decompose the bidder's costs into those of information and those of implementation. When that is done, he maintains, it becomes clear that auctions sometimes increase the returns on investment in information.

We do not doubt that learning about firms and taking them over are separate tasks. Nor do we doubt that here, as elsewhere, a division of labor may be beneficial. Just as Exxon, for example, may elect to buy its geophysical data from a specialty exploration firm rather than to do the work internally, those firms interested in completing corporate takeovers may elect to buy information from investment bankers, who may specialize in generating it.

Firms specializing in generating information might find their returns highest when they have other firms engage in tender offer auctions. But this is by no means clear.[39] Investigating a firm and

[39] See Perrin v. United States, 444 U.S. 37, 40 (1979). Independent exploration firms in the petroleum industry generate information about the location of oil. After developing information, they do not usually invest in the tract, announce the results of their search, and stage an auction for the tract. Rather, they usually

acquiring it are complementary inputs into takeovers, just as film and processing are complementary inputs into finished pictures. The price of one of the complementary inputs goes up when the price of the other goes down.[40] Thus, for example, people buy more film for higher prices when processing becomes cheaper, and a reduction in the price of film also leads to an increase in the number of finished photos purchased. Similarly, when the price of acquisition rises under a rule of auctioneering, people will buy less of the complementary input, information, rather than more. Gilson appears to argue, however, that people would buy more information as the prices of the targets rise. This is implausible.

Gilson argues that a firm selling information can buy shares as a hedge and can thus make a greater return on investment than a firm generating its own information and using it to acquire the target. Gilson gives hypothetical examples to illustrate the point. The examples involve the takeover of a corporation with one million outstanding shares, each with a market price of $50. Search costs are $2.5 million, and, in the absence of competitive bidding, a successful tender offer could be made for $100 per share. Under new management the firm's total value would increase from $50 million to $120 million. In Gilson's first hypothetical, the firm acquiring the target also conducts the search. It spends $97.5 million ($2.5 million for search costs plus $5 million for the pre-disclosure acquisition of 10% of the target's stock plus $90 million for the 90% of the stock acquired in the tender offer) to make $120 million, a return of 23%. In the second hypothetical, an information-generating firm acquires the needed information, and, after buying 10% of the target's stock, passes the information on to another firm that will complete the takeover. The firm generating the information spends $7.5 million ($2.5 million for search costs plus $5 million for the pre-disclosure acquisition of stock) to make $10 million, a return of 33%.

Even if firms behave as Gilson predicts,[41] his examples may nevertheless be misleading. Gilson's information-generating firm would make even *more* than $10 million if it could prevent an auction from arising. Then it could sell the knowledge to a prospective bidder for some part of the more than $20 million that, in Gilson's example, the bidder stands to make. By selling the information in a way that allows

work directly for a company seeking the information, going to great lengths to preserve the confidentiality of their information and to hold down the price of mineral rights. There is no reason why we should expect corporate acquisitions to be different.

[40] See G. Stigler, The Theory of Price 31–33 (3d ed. 1966).

[41] Gilson assumes that the bidder will acquire at $100 per share all of the target's stock it did not purchase before the bid. But the bidder need not follow this rule. Having purchased 10% before announcing its bid, it could seek an additional 41% of the stock for $100 per share and follow up

with a merger at the original market price of $50. The bidder then pays $50 for 59% of the shares and $100 for 41%. The bidder's total investment is $73 million ($70.5 million for stock and $2.5 million for information); its gain is $120 million; and its rate of return on investment 64%.

We, like Gilson, have used returns on investment in a highly artificial manner. We do not say return over what period of time, and we do not adjust the returns to account for the risk that the anticipated gains will not materialize. The return numbers thus are useful only for the crudest kinds of comparisons.

the bidder to maximize its gains, the information-specialist maximizes its own gains.[42]

Gilson properly points out that it may be hard for firms without reputations to sell information. They would need to issue warranties about the value of the information, and few would have the assets to back up their warranties. But the market's response to the difficulty of verifying information goes beyond the reputation, signaling, and bonding approaches Gilson discusses: Another approach is vertical integration. To the extent vertical integration is the market's response to the information problem, we are driven back to our initial position that the integrated information-generator and acquirer will do too little monitoring under an auctions rule.

Gilson presumably intends his numerical example to show that firms may gain from specialization: Some will be better at information generation and some will be better at implementing takeovers. One may grant the proposition that the division of labor sometimes provides gains in such cases, but Gilson's example does not depend on such gains. In the example, both the information generator and the acquiring firm earn $2.5 million on information and $5 million from purchasing shares. Neither has a comparative advantage in identifying potential targets. The difference in the rate of return comes wholly from the method of finance. The acquiring firm spends an additional $90 million to make an additional $110 million, a 22% return that depresses the 33% return on information alone. Yet why would firms spend $90 million in this way? If the risks of generating information are identical to the risks of acquisition (as they must be for a rate of return comparison to make sense), then either firm would spend its $90 million to buy information and stock, an activity at which it would earn 33%. All firms would be information-generators until the process of arbitrage had obliterated the differences in risk-adjusted returns. Gilson's example thus does not illustrate equilibrium.

* * *

GILSON, SEEKING COMPETITIVE BIDS VERSUS PURE PASSIVITY IN TENDER OFFER DEFENSE
35 Stan.L.Rev. 51 (1982).*

I. Sunk Costs and Property Rights

As Professors Easterbrook and Fischel now put the matter, auctions are undesirable if they result in "*any* reduction in the return from

---

[42] If, for example, the information-specialist could arrange for an acquisition of the target's shares at the no-auction prices given in note 41, supra, the bidder would have a profit of $49.5 million if it did not need to pay for information. But by hypothesis the acquisition depends on the information generated by the specialist. Thus firms would pay as much as $49.5 million (less the risk-adjusted competitive rate of return on an acquisition) to have the information. If the payment is as little as $10 million, the information-specialist obtains a return of 400% on its investment.

search." [7] The reduced return leads to reduced investment in search: This reduces the number of tender offers and, ultimately, reduces the beneficial impact on agency costs which we all ascribe to tender offers. Later in this article, I will argue that any reduction in these benefits may be offset by the increased allocational efficiency resulting from competitive bidding. But for now, I want to focus on a broader claim that I suggested, but did not emphasize, in my earlier article:[8] Not only can a first bidder recoup sunk costs if he loses an auction, but it may well be that, for certain kinds of information producers, auctions actually *increase* the return on investment in search. If this is correct, the argument against competitive bidding becomes substantially more difficult.

To understand the potential that competitive bidding has for increasing the return on investment in search, it is necessary to decompose a first bidder's investment in a takeover and examine the return associated with each portion of that investment. One portion of a bidder's investment is search costs, incurred to identify a target whose value can be increased by displacing inefficient management or through some form of synergy. The second portion is the amount paid to secure control and implement the strategy necessary to take advantage of the identified opportunity.

For purposes of illustration, assume that a potential bidder has invested $2.5 million searching for a profitable acquisition and has discovered a target with one million shares outstanding whose stock is trading at $50 per share but would be worth $120 per share if new management could be installed, corporate policies modified, and some synergistic benefits gained. The potential bidder believes that, in the absence of competitive bidding, a successful tender offer could be made for $100 a share.

Consider two strategies to exploit the investment in information. In the first, the traditional approach, the same entity that invests in information also invests in implementation: The acquiring company purchases 10% of the target's stock at $50 per share prior to the need to make public disclosure and then follows with a successful tender offer at the assumed price. Its total investment in information and implementation is $97.5 million ($2.5 million for information costs, $5 million for the pre-disclosure acquisition, and $90 million for the 90% of the target's stock which is acquired in the tender offer).[9] Its return

---

[7] Easterbrook & Fischel, *Auctions and Sunk Costs,* supra.

[8] See Gilson, *A Structural Approach,* at 871–72 & nn. 186–87.

[9] I intend the amount representing investment in information to reflect all information costs, including management time involved in the search. The figure representing investment in implementation, however, reflects only the cost of purchasing the remaining shares. It does not include transaction costs associated with the tender offer, nor the cost of implementing the strategy designed to increase the tar-

get's value after the successful offer, an amount the management literature considers substantial. Implementation costs include capital investment in the target, see, e.g., M. Salter & W. Weinhold, Diversification Through Acquisition: Strategies for Creating Economic Value 208–13 (1979) (analyzing Rockwell International's purchase of Admiral Corporation), as well as management time needed to integrate the new business into the acquiring corporation, see id. at 193. To the extent that these costs are significant, the example in the text overstates the percentage return

on the entire investment is $120 million—the target's presumed post-acquisition value—for a capital gain of $22.5 million or a return of approximately 23%.

The second strategy seeks to capitalize only on the value of the information and leaves the implementation to others. In a first variant of this approach, the information producer also takes a 10% stock position but then, instead of making the tender offer itself, passes the information along to another company who successfully completes the offer at $100 a share. In this variant, the information producer makes a total investment of $7.5 million ($2.5 million for information and $5 million on its recently acquired stock), receives a total return of $10 million for a capital gain of $2.5 million or a return of 33⅓%, some 10% higher than if it had also undertaken implementation. In a second variant, instead of simply passing the information along to a favored bidder, the information producer makes it public, presumably causing competitve bidding. As the auction drives up the premium, both the return on the information producer's stock position and, thus, the return on the investment in information increases: As the price approaches $120 per share, the return approaches 60%. The effect is to further increase the disparity between the return from information production and the return garnered from both producing and implementing the information.

This analysis suggests that a successful acquisition requires two different sets of attributes: one involving information production skills and not very much capital, the other involving the operating skills required for implementing the takeover and substantially more capital. I see no reason to expect that both sets will always be present in a single entity. And if, as this analysis suggests, specialization does occur, information producers would prefer a rule allowing target management to facilitate competitive bidding, since competitive bidding would increase the return on their investment in information. Implementers, on the other hand, would prefer a rule of pure passivity since that rule, by making competitive bidding less likely, would reduce takeover prices and enable implementers to secure higher returns by capturing some of the value associated with information production.[10]

on implementation. Thus, the example understates the amount by which the return on investment in information exceeds the return on implementation.

[10] As Easterbrook and Fischel suggest, as between one who produces only information and one who implements as well, the comparative advantage in return and, correspondingly, the incentive to invest in search depends on the price at which the acquisition can be completed. Easterbrook & Fischel, *Auctions and Sunk Costs,* at 18–19. The higher the price paid, the greater the advantage to the pure information producer because the higher price raises the return on the information producer's 10% investment in the target's stock. A higher price also increases the price that the integrated acquirer would have to pay to ac-

quire the remaining 90% of the target stock, thereby reducing its return more than proportionately. Thus, if in my example the buyer could acquire the remaining 90% of the target's stock at an average price of less than $73 a share, the return to an integrated acquirer would exceed that to a pure information producer. If an integrated acquirer could systematically make acquisitions below this figure, designing a system to promote the interests of integrated acquirers would result in greater aggregate expenditures on search.

But three considerations suggest that it is doubtful that the integrated acquirer would be able to purchase the remaining stock at a sufficiently low price for it to have greater incentives to invest in search than would the pure information producer.

In short, implementers, not information producers, are made worse off by competitive bidding. But that should not result in less than the appropriate number of takeovers, since the implementers will always capture the entire value of their investment in implementation.[11]

First, the potential advantage to the integrated acquirer depends on the extent to which the very act of making the offer results in an increase in the price of the target stock. It is true that a specific security represents only a right to a future income stream with a particular risk-return relationship, for which there are many substitutes, and this means that increased demand for the security should not by itself result in a price increase. But the offer itself may convey sufficient new information concerning the target that the price will rise to reflect this new information rather than because of supply and demand characteristics.

That there is substantial information value associated with a bid is suggested by the fact that even *unsuccessful* tender offers result in substantial abnormal returns to target shareholders, in some cases exceeding the returns they would have earned had the offer been successful. See Bradley, *Interfirm Tender Offers and the Market for Corporate Control*, 53 J.Bus. 345 (1980); Dodd & Ruback, *Tender Offers and Stockholder Returns: An empirical analysis*, 5 J.Fin.Econ. 351 (1977). To the extent that pre-bid leaks of information are unavoidable, the price of the stock will rise to reflect this information value, reducing the return to the integrated acquirer regardless of the likelihood of an auction.

Second, because implementation involves risk, it would not be surprising if integrated acquirers earned a higher return (unadjusted for risk) than pure information producers. Although the return to an independent information producer depends only on the accuracy of the information, the return to an integrated acquirer depends both on the quality of the information produced and on the acquirer's ability to implement the post-offer strategy necessary to achieve the envisioned gains. Because of the additional risk associated with implementation, integrated acquirers may well require a higher return (unadjusted for risk) per unit of search than specialized information producers.

Finally, and most importantly, the numerical example in the text does not, as Easterbrook and Fischel point out, include gains from specialization. See Easterbrook & Fischel, *Auctions and Sunk Costs*, supra, at 20. Adding these to the analysis, however, increases the information producer's advantage over the integrated acquirer. Suppose that the principal advantage to specialization in information producing is

that the specialist can produce more accurate information, rather than that the information will be less costly. Although cost savings from specialization are also plausible, the more important point is that the information has a higher probability of being correct. Cf. C. Holloway, Decision Making Under Uncertainty: Models and Choices 348–50 (1979) (discussing value of increased certainty and use of experts to obtain it). In the context of the example, the information producer can more accurately predict whether there is an opportunity for increasing the target's value by takeover.

Now suppose that the integrated acquirer assigns a 50/50 likelihood that its information concerning the acquisition opportunity is correct. In that situation, the opportunity has a negative expected value of $12.5 million to the integrated acquirer: a 50% likelihood of a profit of $22.5 million if the information proves correct, and a 50% likelihood of a $47.5 million loss (cost of $97.5 million, post-acquisition value of $50 million) if the information proves incorrect and the target is in fact worth no more than its pre-offer value. Further suppose that the pure information producer can identify the existence of the acquisition opportunity with certainty. In that situation, given the uncertainty associated with its information, the price at which an integrated acquirer could purchase the remaining 90% of the target would have to drop to approximately $60 per share before the acquisition would even be a break-even proposition. But even at a price of $120 per share, it would have a positive expected value for an acquirer with the benefit of the specialized producer's information. The fact that specialized information producers can thus produce more valuable information results in greater returns on their investment in search and, as a result, more search.

[11] This example is intended to be illustrative rather than conclusive, though I believe that the numbers are reasonable. It is important to note, however, that the comparison in the text is between *rates* of return rather than *absolute* returns. In order for the comparison to be fair, the assumption must be true that capital not invested in the takeover, when only the investment in information is pursued, can be invested in the search for other targets with an expected return that is also higher than the return on implementation. Otherwise, an average return incorporating

Easterbrook and Fischel take issue with my argument at this point by correctly pointing out that another alternative is available to the specialized information producer: Rather than initiating an auction by giving the information away, the producer could, if no competitive bidding were allowed, sell the information to an implementer for a price reflecting some part of the $20 million gain that would otherwise have been available to the implementer upon completing the takeover for the $100 million no-auction price. Applying their point to my example, so long as the payment for the information exceeds $2 million, the information producer's gain from selling it without an auction exceeds the increased value that an auction would give the information producer's target shares.[13]

Evaluation of the sale alternative puts the issue in a somewhat different context. Assuming that a specialized information producer earns a higher return on its investment in information than an integrated acquirer, the question becomes how the information producer can best exploit its advantage—by selling the information to an implementer or by formenting competitive bidding. In both alternatives the problem confronting the information producer is verification; whichever is pursued, in order for the information producer to secure any return on its investment in search, it must convince potential acquirers that its information is of a quality that warrants investment of up to $120 million. An information producer's preference between the two

the available alternative investments would be a more accurate comparison. Put differently, it assumes that the competitive return from investment in information is higher than from investment in implementation.

[13] In the example, the information producer holds 100,000 shares of the target stock. Since the auction can only increase the acquisition price from $100 per share to $120 per share, the maximum benefit from the auction is $20 × 100,000 or $2,000,000.

It should be stressed, however, that the problem of leakage still remains. And just as leakage strengthens the position of the pure information producer as opposed to the integrated acquirer, it also reduces the ability of the purchaser of the information to secure all of the benefits of its purchase, thus diminishing, to the pure information producer, the attractiveness of the sale alternative, compared to the competitive bidding alternative. That there is substantial leakage in tender offers is suggested by the results of studies tracking abnormal returns to target companies in the period prior to public announcement of the transaction. For example, Keown and Pinkerton, in *Merger Announcements and Insider Trading Activity: An Empirical Investigation*, 36 J.Fin. 855 (1981), reported positive abnormal returns to target companies beginning 25 trading days prior to public announcement, representing approximate-

ly half the total abnormal returns resulting from the transaction. Substantial increases in trading volume accompanied these abnormal returns:

It was found that 79, 60, and 64 *percent* of the acquired firms exhibited higher volume one, two, and three weeks prior to the announcement date than they had three months earlier with the weekly average volume over this three week period 247, 112, and 102 percent higher than it was three months earlier. Such a pattern of volume is, of course, what one would expect to find prior to a public merger announcement if inside information had leaked out.

Id. at 863 (emphasis in original). A professional in a major solicitation firm explains the leakage phenomenon as follows:

You start with a handful of people, but when you get close to doing something the circle expands pretty quickly. * * * You have to bring in directors, two or three firms of lawyers, investment bankers, public relations people, and financial printers, and everybody's got a secretary. If the deal is a big one, you might need a syndicate of banks to finance it. Every time you let in another person, the chance of a leak increases geometrically.

Klein, *Merger Leaks Abound, Causing Many Stocks To Rise Before the Fact*, Wall St. J., July 12, 1978, at 1, col. 6.

alternatives, then, turns on a transaction cost analysis of available solutions to the verification problem.

Consider first the sale alternative.[14] Information producers can respond to the verification problem by strategies—characterizable either as bonding or signaling—designed to ensure the authenticity of the information to the buyer. For example, one would expect information producers who hope to sell information to make substantial investments in reputation, thereby both signaling that their product is of a quality to warrant repeat purchases and putting their investment in reputation at risk should the information prove to be inaccurate.[15] One might also expect the information producer to allow payment for the information to be conditioned on the success of the transaction and, in order to avoid creating a conflict of interest that could dilute the signal sent by investment in reputation, to voluntarily limit speculation in the identified target.[16]

The pattern described, of course, is that of the major investment banking houses.[17] Having already made the investment in reputation, the transaction costs associated with selling their information are comparatively small. Further, their expectation of a continuing rela-

---

[14] For a discussion of the substantial transaction costs associated with sales of information, see Barzel, *Some Fallacies in the Interpretation of Information Costs*, 20 J.L. & Econ. 291, 304 (1977) and Hirshleifer, *The Private and Social Value of Information and the Reward to Inventive Activity*, 61 Am.Econ.Rev. 561, 565, 572 (1971).

[15] One commentator, in discussing market responses to authentication problems, gives the example of the diamond trade. Since diamond buying takes place without inspection or appraisal by buyers,

> De Beers has had to establish such a reputation that prospective buyers can be confident that the ultimate value of the [diamonds] exceeds [their] price. * * * The incentive for De Beers to engage in this peculiar form of trade seems to be that buyers are now in a position to spend on the actual purchase of diamonds the amount they otherwise might have spent on collecting information.

Barzel, supra note 14, at 304. My analysis is consistent with the more general observation that in markets where product quality is difficult to determine ex ante but not ex post, repeat sales are anticipated, and consumers have easy access to ex post information, competition takes the form of investments in firm specific capital, like brand names and advertising, that act as barriers to entry. Klein & Leffler, *The Role of Market Forces in Assuring Contractual Performance*, 89 J.Pol.Econ. 615, 626–33 (1981); see also Barzel, *Measurement Cost and the Organization of Markets*, 25 J.L. & Econ. 27 (1982).

[16] Easterbrook and Fischel point out that problems of information verification also can be solved by vertical integration. Easterbrook & Fischel, *Auctions and Sunk Costs,* supra note 3, at 19. See generally O. Williamson, Markets and Hierarchies: Analysis and Antitrust Implications 82–105 (1975). They suggest that combining the information and implementation functions avoids any problems specialization might create. The viability of vertical integration, however, involves more than economizing on transaction costs. It is also critical that the firm have an internal or external market for the function to be integrated that is sufficient to exhaust scale economies. See M. Porter, Competitive Strategy 300–28 (1980). Indeed, Williamson begins his discussion of vertical integration by assuming that each stage of production "exhausts scale economies." O. Williamson, supra, at 82. While I am not aware of any study of efficient scale in the merger and acquisition business, the success of the investment banking community in this area suggests that it is too large for vertical integration to be a readily available option for most acquiring companies.

[17] This analysis also explains the seemingly very high fees charged by the merger and acquisition departments of investment banking firms. While the fees might seem high in relation to the actual hours expended in the implementation stage—actually formulating the terms of the offer and accomplishing the transaction—they may not seem so high when considered as payment for information of assured quality.

tionship with the information buyer through provision of fungible investment banking services following the acquisition serves to make a portion of the banker's total fee for the information contingent not only on the successful acquisition of the target, but also on the ultimate accuracy of the information concerning the opportunity: If the information proves inaccurate, the buyer will terminate the continuing services, and fees, of the investment banker.[18] It is thus hardly surprising that investment bankers follow a sale alternative.[19]

But the sale alternative is not the only strategy open to information producers. Indeed, for producers without either a preexisting investment in reputation or the capital and time to adopt the verification techniques used by investment bankers, this strategy may not even be available. For them, disclosure of their information in order to promote competitive bidding may be the only verification mechanism available and, therefore, the only way to appropriate the return on their investment in information. First, the bidding process itself acts as a verification technique. Second, it can also be used to cause the producer's information to be verified by the best possible source: the target. An information producer might adopt the strategy of announcing, together with its information and its stock position, that it intended to cause the target to be acquired by someone. This would create an incentive for target management to select the ultimate acquirer—to seek a white knight. In this case, verification of the producer's information is provided by the target through its attempts to prove to those potential acquirers that it approaches the existence of the very opportunity the information producer has disclosed.

Institutional arrangements reflect this pattern as well. For example, Carl Icahn does not sell his information; he profits by reselling target stock to implementers. And his position on the benefits of auctions is also clear. When Marshall Field gave Batus lock-up options intended to prevent competitive bidding, Icahn attemped to invalidate them.

In short, the impact of auctions on incentives to produce information is at the very least mixed. Some producers will benefit from auctions, others will not, and the balance will depend on transaction costs and other factors associated with actual practices—about which we know far too little. But it is clear that theory alone, unadorned by evaluation of transaction costs, does not preordain either the direction or the magnitude of the impact.[22]

[18] * * * It is important to note that this is a very expensive verification technique because it is available only to a diversified information producer who, like an investment bank, can offer post-acquisition services to the buyer.

[19] * * * That investment bankers actually view themselves as information sellers is suggested by a recent *Wall Street Journal* advertisement placed by a major banker—Blyth Eastman Paine Webber. The advertisement stressed that in many instances Blyth "not only negotiated the acquisition, but initiated it as well—that is, we established the company's value, developed the strategy, and suggested the eventual buyer or seller. In fact, we initiated more mergers and acquisitions last year than any other investment banker, and are initiating and completing such transactions at an even higher rate this year." Wall St. J., Oct. 7, 1982, at 49.

[22] Specialization in information production—both as between implementers and information producers and as between different types of producers—should also

Another consideration also suggests that competitive bidding has a more complicated impact on incentives for search and takeover than Easterbrook and Fischel acknowledge. An initial bid does signal some of the first bidder's information; but competing bids also disclose information. Frequently a white knight overbids because the target has given it information, not available to the first bidder, that demonstrates that the target is worth more than the initial bid. Now consider the strategy that a potential first bidder should adopt when it discovers information which discloses, subject to some uncertainty, that a target is worth twice its market price. If the information is correct, the first bidder would be willing to pay a significant premium; but the initial bid will not fully reflect this premium. If the information is incorrect, the target is worth no more than the present market value, and this uncertainty will be reflected in the initial bid. In this setting the white knight's bid reduces the first bidder's uncertainty and, hence, should cause the first bidder to be willing to pay more for the target than it would have in the absence of a second bid. Thus, while a second bid increases the takeover price and therefore reduces the first bidder's *absolute* return, it may not reduce its *risk-adjusted* return. One could well imagine a strategy of bidding well under the expected value of the target with the intention not of seeking a bargain, but rather of withdrawing the offer in the absence of a second bid.

If either or both of these points are correct, Easterbrook and Fischel's argument that competitive bidding necessarily reduces the return on investment in information becomes much more difficult. Even if competitive bidding reduces the return in some cases, it may increase it in others, leaving the overall effect indeterminate. And even if there were a net reduction in the return on investment in search, it would be considerably smaller than Easterbrook and Fischel expect. Thus, the issue of which rule—competitive bidding or pure passivity—leads to greater allocational efficiency becomes more important. Indeed, if competitive bidding does result in a net increase in the total investment in search by all types of information producers, those favoring a rule of pure passivity would have to show that a series of sales would be a *more* efficient allocational mechanism than an auction, a position Easterbrook and Fischel seem prepared to advance.

have a beneficial impact on the amount of search, wholly apart from either the comparative returns on search and implementation or the comparative returns on the sale and competitive bidding alternatives. If a return on search can be earned only by those with the capital to implement, or with the capital also to invest in reputation and other verification techniques necessary to sell the information produced, substantial entry barriers to the search industry are created. Specialization and the allowance of competitive bidding remove these barriers and will lead to increased investment in search so long as the return on search that is obtainable by taking a speculative position is attractive in comparison to the return available on other available investments. This would be true even if the return on search is less than the return to implementers, or than the return to information producers with the capital investment necessary for sale. Thus, competitive bidding may increase the overall investment in search because the resulting increase in return to the potentially more numerous specialized information producers draws new entrants into the search industry. This influx will outweigh the reduction in search by non-specialized producers or investment bankers that is caused by decreases in their total return.

II. Allocational Efficiency

There is agreement that tender offers serve an allocational role, and that competitive pricing generally facilitates the shifting of assets to their most productive users. What separates Easterbrook and Fischel's position from mine is their claim that a series of independent sales can cause assets to be shifted to their most productive users as efficiently as competitive bidding in connection with a single sale. I disagree. * * *

Some considered speculation may suggest why competitive bidding is likely to be more efficient than a series of sales. Let me start with two important elements of transaction costs in the acquisition setting: information costs necessary to identify the opportunity; and mechanical costs—for example, lawyers', accountants', and investment bankers' fees—necessary to effect the transaction and cope with regulatory or other barriers (including defensive tactics by the target). I suspect that information costs are greater in a series of sales, simply because the wheel must be reinvented each time. In fact, the cost of reinvention may actually rise: While public information about the business is readily available from regulatory filings and shareholder reports at the time of the initial transfer, by the time of a succeeding transfer this information may be buried in a mass of less useful data covering the combined company.

With respect to mechanical costs, I see no reason to think that they will be materially higher in an auction setting; indeed, there are economies of scale in getting it all over at once. The clearest example is the saving in management time. After each sale in a series of sales substantial investments of management time would be needed to integrate the acquired business, a task which the management literature takes quite seriously.[28]

Finally, let me consider a third category of transaction costs—agency costs. Easterbrook and Fischel, arguing that a series of sales would result in allocational efficiency, state that "[t]here is * * * little evidence to support the belief that managers systematically reject the opportunity to profit by selling plants and divisions," any more than managers systematically reject the opportunity to profit by selling new products.[29] While there may be no hard evidence, there is good theory * * * suggesting that managers may overinvest in both new products and new divisions. Managers, when given the opportunity, will maximize their own welfare at the expense of shareholders. If managers personally gain from maximizing the size of their enterprise, they may well choose to forgo the opportunity to sell a division even at a price reflecting capitalization of a higher income than the division yields under their direction.[30]

[28] Easterbrook and Fischel, in *Auctions and Sunk Costs,* supra note 3, at 6, recognize the value of management time, and counsel against overlooking it in computing sunk information costs, but ignore it as a cost in this context.

[29] Easterbrook & Fischel, *Auctions and Sunk Costs,* supra, at 14–15.

[30] There is some evidence of this phenomenon. Reduction of risk by diversification at the company level does not increase the value of the company because share-

If allocational efficiency is to be achievable through a series of sales, this behavior must be constrained; agency theory demonstrates that to reject managerialism requires *imposing* limits on managers rather than relying on managerial altruism. If managers selfishly choose to forgo the profitable sale of a division, then resort to a tender offer—which we all acknowledge plays a central role in constraining management—is necessary. But the problem with achieving allocational efficiency by a series of sales is that tender offers face greater barriers when what is sought is a division, rather than an independent company of equivalent size. If management actively or passively resists the second sale in the series, the offer will not only be a hostile one, it will be a larger transaction than the original because the second round covers the combined corporation. This reduces the number of potential bidders, and hence reduces the likelihood that the assets will end up being used as efficiently as they would have been had they been initially acquired in an auction. While the problem may be ameliorated by the ability to resell unwanted assets after the transaction, a post-transaction sell-off would necessarily involve increased uncertainty, causing the problem to remain.[31]

Moreover, if any defensive tactics are pursued, moving assets to their most efficient users becomes far more expensive if done through a series of sales; costs that are incurred only once in the auction model must be repeatedly incurred in the series of transactions model. Because no prohibition is perfect, even if defensive tactics are prohibited, as Easterbrook, Fischel, and I all advise, they will nonetheless still exist to some extent.

◆

For a careful discussion of additional arguments suggesting that auctions increase social wealth, see Bebchuk, *The Case for Facilitating Competing Tender Offers: A Reply and an Extension*, 35 Stan.L.Rev. 23 (1982). The opposite position is presented by Amihud, *The Case Against a Mandatory Delay Period in Tender Offers*, New York University Graduate School of Business Administration Working Paper (Aug., 1985) and by Schwartz, *Imperfect Information and the Tender Offer*

holders can diversify their own portfolios more cheaply. Diversification at the company level, however, is of substantial value to managers; because of their human capital investment and the impact of incentive compensation plans, they would find it difficult to adequately diversify at the individual level. Because managers are affected differently than shareholders by different kinds of acquisitions, the more control managers have, the more frequent will be those transactions which favor them. The available date, while sketchy, is consistent with this prediction, suggesting that management-controlled firms, far more frequently than shareholder-controlled firms, make conglomerate, as opposed to horizon-

tal or vertical, acquisitions. Amihud & Lev, *Risk Reduction as a Managerial Motive for Conglomerate Mergers*, 12 Bell J.Econ. 605 (1981).

[31] That is not to say that sell-offs of divisions will not occur. Indeed, approximately half the acquisitions in recent years were not of previously independent companies, but of businesses being divested by someone else. See M. Salter & W. Weinhold, supra note 9, at 17. Rather, there will be a reduction in allocative efficiency at the margin, a problem which Easterbrook and Fischel recognize in the sunk cost context. *See* Easterbrook & Fischel, *Auctions and Sunk Costs*, supra, at 7.

Auction, University of Southern California Law Center Working Paper (June, 1985).

C. The Willing Subject: Directors' Responsibilities in Accepting an Offer

What standard governs review of target directors' decision to *accept* an acquirer's proposal of a friendly transaction? Under the structural approach developed in this Chapter, the answer is self-evident: the business judgment rule in its *jurisdictional* guise. If the directors have sold out too cheaply, shareholders are protected both by their opportunity to vote against the transaction and by the operation of the market for corporate control—low prices evoke competitive bids from other parties. After the fact judicial review adds little to these protections, and at substantial cost. As a result, target directors' decision to accept an arms-length offer [103] has been and should be essentially nonreviewable.

So matters stood when the Delaware Supreme Court decided the following case.

SMITH v. VAN GORKOM
Supreme Court of Delaware, 1985.
488 A.2d 858.

Before HERRMANN, C.J., and McNEILLY, HORSEY, MOORE and CHRISTIE, JJ., constituting the Court en banc.

HORSEY, Justice (for the majority):

This appeal from the Court of Chancery involves a class action brought by shareholders of the defendant Trans Union Corporation ("Trans Union" or "the Company"), originally seeking rescission of a cash-out merger of Trans Union into the defendant New T Company ("New T"), a wholly-owned subsidiary of the defendant, Marmon Group, Inc. ("Marmon"). Alternate relief in the form of damages is sought against the defendant members of the Board of Directors of Trans Union, New T, and Jay A. Pritzker and Robert A. Pritzker, owners of Marmon.[1]

Following trial, the former Chancellor granted judgment for the defendant directors by unreported letter opinion. Judgment was based on two findings: (1) that the Board of Directors had acted in an informed manner so as to be entitled to protection of the business judgment rule in approving the cash-out merger; and (2) that the shareholder vote approving the merger should not be set aside because

---

[103] Where the transaction involves a conflict of interest—for example, because the acquirer is a major shareholder or a group that includes members of target management—different rules apply. See Chapter Fifteen B., infra.

[1] The plaintiff, Alden Smith, originally sought to enjoin the merger; but, following extensive discovery, the Trial Court denied the plaintiff's motion for preliminary injunction by unreported letter opinion dated February 3, 1981. On February 10, 1981, the proposed merger was approved by Trans Union's stockholders at a special meeting and the merger became effective on that date. * * *

the stockholders had been "fairly informed" by the Board of Directors before voting thereon. The plaintiffs appeal.

Speaking for the majority of the Court, we conclude that both rulings of the Court of Chancery are clearly erroneous. Therefore, we reverse and direct that judgment be entered in favor of the plaintiffs and against the defendant directors for the fair value of the plaintiffs' stockholdings in Trans Union, in accordance with Weinberger v. UOP, Inc., Del.Supr., 457 A.2d 701 (1983).

We hold: (1) that the Board's decision, reached September 20, 1980, to approve the proposed cash-out merger was not the product of an informed business judgment; (2) that the Board's subsequent efforts to amend the Merger Agreement and take other curative action were ineffectual, both legally and factually; and (3) that the Board did not deal with complete candor with the stockholders by failing to disclose all material facts, which they knew or should have known, before securing the stockholders' approval of the merger.

I.

The nature of this case requires a detailed factual statement. The following facts are essentially uncontradicted:

–A–

Trans Union was a publicly-traded, diversified holding company, the principal earnings of which were generated by its railcar leasing business. During the period here involved, the Company had a cash flow of hundreds of millions of dollars annually. However, the Company had difficulty in generating sufficient taxable income to offset increasingly large investment tax credits (ITCs). Accelerated depreciation deductions had decreased available taxable income against which to offset accumulating ITCs. The Company took these deductions, despite their effect on usable ITCs, because the rental price in the railcar leasing market had already impounded the purported tax savings.

* * *

Beginning in the late 1960's, and continuing through the 1970's, Trans Union pursued a program of acquiring small companies in order to increase available taxable income. In July 1980, Trans Union Management prepared the annual revision of the Company's Five Year Forecast. This report was presented to the Board of Directors at its July, 1980 meeting. The report projected an annual income growth of about 20%. The report also concluded that Trans Union would have about $195 million in spare cash between 1980 and 1985, "with the surplus growing rapidly from 1982 onward." The report referred to the ITC situation as a "nagging problem" and, given that problem, the leasing company "would still appear to be constrained to a tax breakeven." The report then listed four alternative uses of the projected 1982–1985 equity surplus: (1) stock repurchase; (2) dividend increases; (3) a major acquisition program; and (4) combinations of the

above.   The sale of Trans Union was not among the alternatives.*
*   *   *

–B–

On August 27, 1980, Van Gorkom met with Senior Management of Trans Union.

*   *   *

Various alternatives were suggested and discussed preliminarily, including the sale of Trans Union to a company with a large amount of taxable income.

Donald Romans, Chief Financial Officer of Trans Union, stated that his department had done a "very brief bit of work on the possibility of a leveraged buy-out."   This work had been prompted by a media article which Romans had seen regarding a leveraged buy-out by management.   The work consisted of a "preliminary study" of the cash which could be generated by the Company if it participated in a leveraged buy-out.   As Romans stated, this analysis "was very first and rough cut at seeing whether a cash flow would support what might be considered a high price for this type of transaction."

On September 5, at another Senior Management meeting which Van Gorkom attended, Romans again brought up the idea of a leveraged buy-out as a "possible strategic alternative" to the Company's acquisition program.   Romans and Bruce S. Chelberg, President and Chief Operating Officer of Trans Union, had been working on the matter in preparation for the meeting.   According to Romans: They did not "come up" with a price for the Company.   They merely "ran the numbers" at $50 a share and at $60 a share with the "rough form" of their cash figures at the time.   Their "figures indicated that $50 would be very easy to do but $60 would be very difficult to do under those figures."   This work did not purport to establish a fair price for either the Company or 100% of the stock.   It was intended to determine the cash flow needed to service the debt that would "probably" be incurred in a leveraged buy-out, based on "rough calculations" without "any benefit of experts to identify what the limits were to that, and so forth."   These computations were not considered extensive and no conclusion was reached.

At this meeting, Van Gorkom stated that he would be willing to take $55 per share for his own 75,000 shares.   He vetoed the suggestion of a leveraged buy-out by Management, however, as involving a potential conflict of interest for Management.   Van Gorkom, a certified public accountant and lawyer, had been an officer of Trans Union for 24 years, its Chief Executive Officer for more than 17 years, and Chairman of its Board for 2 years.   It is noteworthy in this connection that he was then approaching 65 years of age and mandatory retirement.

* What if Trans Union used its positive cash flow to purchase taxable bonds the interest on which would generate taxable earnings? See R. Gilson, M. Scholes & M. Wolfson, *Taxation and the Dynamics of* *Corporate Control: The Uncertain Case for Tax Motivated Acquisitions*, Stanford Law School Law and Economics Working Paper No. 24 (Jan. 1986). [Ed.]

For several days following the September 5 meeting, Van Gorkom pondered the idea of a sale. He had participated in many acquisitions as a manager and director of Trans Union and as a director of other companies. He was familiar with acquisition procedures, valuation methods, and negotiations; and he privately considered the pros and cons of whether Trans Union should seek a privately or publicly-held purchaser.

Van Gorkom decided to meet with Jay A. Pritzker, a well-known corporate takeover specialist and a social acquaintance. However, rather than approaching Pritzker simply to determine his interest in acquiring Trans Union, Van Gorkom assembled a proposed per share price for sale of the Company and a financing structure by which to accomplish the sale. Van Gorkom did so without consulting either his Board or any members of Senior Management except one: Carl Peterson, Trans Union's Controller. Telling Peterson that he wanted no other person on his staff to know what he was doing, but without telling him why, Van Gorkom directed Peterson to calculate the feasibility of a leveraged buy-out at an assumed price per share of $55. Apart from the Company's historic stock market price,[5] and Van Gorkom's long association with Trans Union, the record is devoid of any competent evidence that $55 represented the per share intrinsic value of the Company.

Having thus chosen the $55 figure, based solely on the availability of a leveraged buy-out, Van Gorkom multiplied the price per share by the number of shares outstanding to reach a total value of the Company of $690 million. Van Gorkom told Peterson to use this $690 million figure and to assume a $200 million equity contribution by the buyer. Based on these assumptions, Van Gorkom directed Peterson to determine whether the debt portion of the purchase price could be paid off in five years or less if financed by Trans Union's cash flow as projected in the Five Year Forecast, and by the sale of certain weaker divisions identified in a study done for Trans Union by the Boston Consulting Group ("BCG study"). Peterson reported that, of the purchase price, approximately $50–80 million would remain outstanding after five years. Van Gorkom was disappointed, but decided to meet with Pritzker nevertheless.

Van Gorkom arranged a meeting with Pritzker at the latter's home on Saturday, September 13, 1980. Van Gorkom prefaced his presentation by stating to Pritzker: "Now as far as you are concerned, I can, I think, show how you can pay a substantial premium over the present stock price and pay off most of the loan in the first five years. * * * If you could pay $55 for this Company, here is a way in which I think it can be financed."

Van Gorkom then reviewed with Pritzker his calculations based upon his proposed price of $55 per share. Although Pritzker mentioned

---

[5] The common stock of Trans Union was traded on the New York Stock Exchange. Over the five year period from 1975 through 1979, Trans Union's stock had traded within a range of a high of $39½ and a low of $24¼. Its high and low range for 1980 through September 19 (the last trading day before announcement of the merger) was $38¼–$29½.

$50 as a more attractive figure, no other price was mentioned. However, Van Gorkom stated that to be sure that $55 was the best price obtainable, Trans Union should be free to accept any better offer. Pritzker demurred, stating that his organization would serve as a "stalking horse" for an "auction contest" only if Trans Union would permit Pritzker to buy 1,750,000 shares of Trans Union stock at market price which Pritzker could then sell to any higher bidder. After further discussion on this point, Pritzker told Van Gorkom that he would give him a more definite reaction soon.

On Monday, September 15, Pritzker advised Van Gorkom that he was interested in the $55 cash-out merger proposal and requested more information on Trans Union. Van Gorkom agreed to meet privately with Pritzker, accompanied by Peterson, Chelberg, and Michael Carpenter, Trans Union's consultant from the Boston Consulting Group. The meetings took place on September 16 and 17. Van Gorkom was "astounded that events were moving with such amazing rapidity."

On Thursday, September 18, Van Gorkom met again with Pritzker. At that time, Van Gorkom knew that Pritzker intended to make a cash-out merger offer at Van Gorkom's proposed $55 per share. Pritzker instructed his attorney, a merger and acquisition specialist, to begin drafting merger documents. There was no further discussion of the $55 price. However, the number of shares of Trans Union's treasury stock to be offered to Pritzker was negotiated down to one million shares; the price was set at $38—75 cents above the per share price at the close of the market on September 19. At this point, Pritzker insisted that the Trans Union Board act on his merger proposal within the next three days, stating to Van Gorkom: "We have to have a decision by no later than Sunday [evening, September 21] before the opening of the English stock exchange on Monday morning." Pritzker's lawyer was then instructed to draft the merger documents, to be reviewed by Van Gorkom's lawyer, "sometimes with discussion and sometimes not, in the haste to get it finished."

On Friday, September 19, Van Gorkom, Chelberg, and Pritzker consulted with Trans Union's lead bank regarding the financing of Pritzker's purchase of Trans Union. The bank indicated that it could form a syndicate of banks that would finance the transaction. On the same day, Van Gorkom retained James Brennan, Esquire, to advise Trans Union on the legal aspects of the merger. Van Gorkom did not consult with William Browder, a Vice-President and director of Trans Union and former head of its legal department, or with William Moore, then the head of Trans Union's legal staff.

On Friday, September 19, Van Gorkom called a special meeting of the Trans Union Board for noon the following day. He also called a meeting of the Company's Senior Management to convene at 11:00 a.m., prior to the meeting of the Board. No one, except Chelberg and Peterson, was told the purpose of the meetings. Van Gorkom did not invite Trans Union's investment banker, Salomon Brothers or its Chicago-based partner, to attend.

Of those present at the Senior Management meeting on September 20, only Chelberg and Peterson had prior knowledge of Pritzker's offer. Van Gorkom disclosed the offer and described its terms, but he furnished no copies of the proposed Merger Agreement. Romans announced that his department had done a second study which showed that, for a leveraged buy-out, the price range for Trans Union stock was between $55 and $65 per share. Van Gorkom neither saw the study nor asked Romans to make it available for the Board meeting.

Senior Management's reaction to the Pritzker proposal was completely negative. No member of Management, except Chelberg and Peterson, supported the proposal. Romans objected to the price as being too low;[6] he was critical of the timing and suggested that consideration should be given to the adverse tax consequences of an all-cash deal for low-basis shareholders; and he took the position that the agreement to sell Pritzker one million newly-issued shares at market price would inhibit other offers, as would the prohibitions against soliciting bids and furnishing inside information to other bidders. Romans argued that the Pritzker proposal was a "lock up" and amounted to "an agreed merger as opposed to an offer." Nevertheless, Van Gorkom proceeded to the Board meeting as scheduled without further delay.

Ten directors served on the Trans Union Board, five inside * * * and five outside * * *. Of the outside directors, four were corporate chief executive officers and one was the former Dean of the University of Chicago Business School. None was an investment banker or trained financial analyst. All members of the Board were well informed about the Company and its operations as a going concern. They were familiar with the current financial condition of the Company, as well as operating and earnings projections reported in the recent Five Year Forecast. The Board generally received regular and detailed reports and was kept abreast of the accumulated investment tax credit and accelerated depreciation problem.

Van Gorkom began the Special Meeting of the Board with a twenty-minute oral presentation. Copies of the proposed Merger Agreement were delivered too late for study before or during the meeting.[7] He reviewed the Company's ITC and depreciation problems and the efforts theretofore made to solve them. He discussed his initial meeting with Pritzker and his motivation in arranging that meeting. Van Gorkom did not disclose to the Board, however, the methodology by which he alone had arrived at the $55 figure, or the fact that he first proposed the $55 price in his negotiations with Pritzker.

[6] Van Gorkom asked Romans to express his opinion as to the $55 price. Romans stated that he "thought the price was too low in relation to what he could derive for the company in a cash sale, particularly one which enabled us to realize the values of certain subsidiaries and independent entities."

[7] The record is not clear as to the terms of the Merger Agreement. The Agreement, as originally presented to the Board on September 20, was never produced by defendants despite demands by the plaintiffs. Nor is it clear that the directors were given an opportunity to study the Merger Agreement before voting on it. All that can be said is that Brennan had the Agreement before him during the meeting.

Van Gorkom outlined the terms of the Pritzker offer as follows: Pritzker would pay $55 in cash for all outstanding shares of Trans Union stock upon completion of which Trans Union would be merged into New T Company, a subsidiary wholly-owned by Pritzker and formed to implement the merger; for a period of 90 days, Trans Union could receive, but could not actively solicit, competing offers; the offer had to be acted on by the next evening, Sunday, September 21; Trans Union could only furnish to competing bidders published information, and not proprietary information; the offer was subject to Pritzker obtaining the necessary financing by October 10, 1980; if the financing contingency were met or waived by Pritzker, Trans Union was required to sell to Pritzker one million newly-issued shares of Trans Union at $38 per share.

Van Gorkom took the position that putting Trans Union "up for auction" through a 90-day market test would validate a decision by the Board that $55 was a fair price. He told the Board that the "free market will have an opportunity to judge whether $55 is a fair price." Van Gorkom framed the decision before the Board not as whether $55 per share was the highest price that could be obtained, but as whether the $55 price was a fair price that the stockholders should be given the opportunity to accept or reject.[8]

Attorney Brennan advised the members of the Board that they might be sued if they failed to accept the offer and that a fairness opinion was not required as a matter of law.

Romans attended the meeting as chief financial officer of the Company. He told the Board that he had not been involved in the negotiations with Pritzker and knew nothing about the merger proposal until the morning of the meeting; that his studies did not indicate either a fair price for the stock or a valuation of the Company; that he did not see his role as directly addressing the fairness issue; and that he and his people "were trying to search for ways to justify a price in connection with such a [leveraged buy-out] transaction, rather than to say what the shares are worth." Romans testified:

> I told the Board that the study ran the numbers at 50 and 60, and then the subsequent study at 55 and 65, and that was not the same thing as saying that I have a valuation of the company at X dollars. But it was a way—a first step towards reaching that conclusion.

Romans told the Board that, in his opinion, $55 was "in the range of a fair price," but "at the beginning of the range."

* * *

The Board meeting of September 20 lasted about two hours. Based solely upon Van Gorkom's oral presentation, Chelberg's supporting representations, Romans' oral statement Brennan's legal advice, and their knowledge of the market history of the Company's stock,[9] the

---

[8] In Van Gorkom's words: The "real decision" is whether to "let the stockholders decide it" which is "all you are being asked to decide today."

[9] The Trial Court stated the premium relationship of the $55 price to the market history of the Company's stock as follows:

directors approved the proposed Merger Agreement. However, the Board later claimed to have attached two conditions to its acceptance: (1) that Trans Union reserved the right to accept any better offer that was made during the market test period; and (2) that Trans Union could share its proprietary information with any other potential bidders. While the Board now claims to have reserved the right to accept any better offer received after the announcement of the Pritzker agreement (even though the minutes of the meeting do not reflect this), it is undisputed that the Board did not reserve the right to actively solicit alternate offers.

The Merger Agreement was executed by Van Gorkom during the evening of September 20 at a formal social event that he hosted for the opening of the Chicago Lyric Opera. Neither he nor any other director read the agreement prior to its signing and delivery to Pritzker.

* * *

On Monday, September 22, the Company issued a press release announcing that Trans Union had entered into a "definitive" Merger Agreement with an affiliate of the Marmon Group, Inc., a Pritzker holding company. Within 10 days of the public announcement, dissent among Senior Management over the merger had become widespread. Faced with threatened resignations of key officers, Van Gorkom met with Pritzker who agreed to several modifications of the Agreement. Pritzker was willing to do so provided that Van Gorkom could persuade the dissidents to remain on the Company payroll for at least six months after consummation of the merger.

Van Gorkom reconvened the Board on October 8 and secured the directors' approval of the proposed amendments—sight unseen. The Board also authorized the employment of Salomon Brothers, its investment banker, to solicit other offers for Trans Union during the proposed "market test" period.

The next day, October 9, Trans Union issued a press release announcing: (1) that Pritzker had obtained "the financing commitments necessary to consummate" the merger with Trans Union; (2) that Pritzker had acquired one million shares of Trans Union common stock at $38 per share; (3) that Trans Union was now permitted to actively seek other offers and had retained Salomon Brothers for that purpose; and (4) that if a more favorable offer were not received before February 1, 1981, Trans Union's shareholders would thereafter meet to vote on the Pritzker proposal.

It was not until the following day, October 10, that the actual amendments to the Merger Agreement were prepared by Pritzker and delivered to Van Gorkom for execution. As will be seen, the amendments were considerably at variance with Van Gorkom's representations of the amendments to the Board on October 8; and the amendments placed serious constraints on Trans Union's ability to negotiate a

* * * the merger price offered to the stockholders of Trans Union represented a premium of 62% over the average of the high and low prices at which Trans Union stock had traded in 1980, a premium of 48% over the last closing price, and a premium of 39% over the highest price at which the stock of Trans Union had traded any time during the prior six years.

better deal and withdraw from the Pritzker agreement. Nevertheless, Van Gorkom proceeded to execute what became the October 10 amendments to the Merger Agreement without conferring further with the Board members and apparently without comprehending the actual implications of the amendments.

* * *

Salomon Brothers' efforts over a three-month period from October 21 to January 21 produced only one serious suitor for Trans Union— General Electric Credit Corporation ("GE Credit"), a subsidiary of the General Electric Company. However, GE Credit was unwilling to make an offer for Trans Union unless Trans Union first rescinded its Merger Agreement with Pritzker. When Pritzker refused, GE Credit terminated further discussions with Trans Union in early January.

In the meantime, in early December, the investment firm of Kohlberg, Kravis, Roberts & Co. ("KKR"), the only other concern to make a firm offer for Trans Union, withdrew its offer under circumstances hereinafter detailed.

On December 19, this litigation was commenced and, within four weeks, the plaintiffs had deposed eight of the ten directors of Trans Union, including Van Gorkom, Chelberg and Romans, its Chief Financial Officer. On January 21, Management's Proxy Statement for the February 10 shareholder meeting was mailed to Trans Union's stockholders. On January 26, Trans Union's Board met and, after a lengthy meeting, voted to proceed with the Pritzker merger. The Board also approved for mailing, "on or about January 27," a Supplement to its Proxy Statement. The Supplement purportedly set forth all information relevant to the Pritzker Merger Agreement, which had not been divulged in the first Proxy Statement.

* * *

On February 10, the stockholders of Trans Union approved the Pritzker merger proposal. Of the outstanding shares, 69.9% were voted in favor of the merger; 7.25% were voted against the merger; and 22.85% were not voted.

II.

We turn to the issue of the application of the business judgment rule to the September 20 meeting of the Board.

The Court of Chancery concluded from the evidence that the Board of Directors' approval of the Pritzker merger proposal fell within the protection of the business judgment rule. The Court found that the Board had given sufficient time and attention to the transaction, since the directors had considered the Pritzker proposal on three different occasions, on September 20, and on October 8, 1980 and finally on January 26, 1981. On that basis, the Court reasoned that the Board had acquired, over the four-month period, sufficient information to reach an informed business judgment on the cash-out merger proposal. The Court ruled:

> * * * that given the market value of Trans Union's stock, the business acumen of the members of the board of Trans Union, the

substantial premium over market offered by the Pritzkers and the ultimate effect on the merger price provided by the prospect of other bids for the stock in question, that the board of directors of Trans Union did not act recklessly or improvidently in determining on a course of action which they believed to be in the best interest of the stockholders of Trans Union.

The Court of Chancery made but one finding; i.e., that the Board's conduct over the entire period from September 20 through January 26, 1981 was not reckless or improvident, but informed. This ultimate conclusion was premised upon three subordinate findings, one explicit and two implied. The Court's explicit finding was that Trans Union's Board was "free to turn down the Pritzker proposal" not only on September 20 but also on October 8, 1980 and on January 26, 1981. The Court's implied, subordinate findings were: (1) that no legally binding agreement was reached by the parties until January 26; and (2) that if a higher offer were to be forthcoming, the market test would have produced it, and Trans Union would have been contractually free to accept such higher offer. However, the Court offered no factual basis or legal support for any of these findings; and the record compels contrary conclusions.

This Court's standard of review of the findings of fact reached by the Trial Court following full evidentiary hearing is as stated in Levitt v. Bouvier, Del.Supr., 287 A.2d 671, 673 (1972):

> [In an appeal of this nature] this court has the authority to review the entire record and to make its own findings of fact in a proper case. In exercising our power of review, we have the duty to review the sufficiency of the evidence and to test the propriety of the findings below. We do not, however, ignore the findings made by the trial judge. If they are sufficiently supported by the record and are the product of an orderly and logical deductive process, in the exercise of judicial restraint we accept them, even though independently we might have reached opposite conclusions. It is only when the findings below are clearly wrong and the doing of justice requires their overturn that we are free to make contradictory findings of fact.

Applying that standard and governing principles of law to the record and the decision of the Trial Court, we conclude that the Court's ultimate finding that the Board's conduct was not "reckless or imprudent" is contrary to the record and not the product of a logical and deductive reasoning process.

The plaintiffs contend that the Court of Chancery erred as a matter of law by exonerating the defendant directors under the business judgment rule without first determining whether the rule's threshold condition of "due care and prudence" was satisfied: * * * The defendants * * * submit that their decision to accept $55 per share was informed because: (1) they were "highly qualified;" (2) they were "well-informed;" and (3) they deliberated over the "proposal" not once but three times. On essentially this evidence and under our standard of review, the defendants assert that affirmance is required. We must disagree.

Under Delaware law, the business judgment rule is the offspring of the fundamental principle, codified in 8 *Del.C.* § 141(a), that the business and affairs of a Delaware corporation are managed by or under its board of directors. * * * The business judgment rule exists to protect and promote the full and free exercise of the managerial power granted to Delaware directors. The rule itself "is a presumption that in making a business decision, the directors of a corporation acted on an informed basis, in good faith and in the honest belief that the action taken was in the best interests of the company." Aronson v. Lewis, Del.Supr., 473 A.2d 805, 812 (1984). Thus, the party attacking a board decision as uninformed must rebut the presumption that its business judgment was an informed one. Id.

The determination of whether a business judgment is an informed one turns on whether the directors have informed themselves "prior to making a business decision, of all material information reasonably available to them." Id.[12]

Under the business judgment rule there is no protection for directors who have made "an unintelligent or unadvised judgment." Mitchell v. Highland-Western Glass, Del.Ch., 167 A. 831, 833 (1933). A director's duty to inform himself in preparation for a decision derives from the fiduciary capacity in which he serves the corporation and its stockholders.

Since a director is vested with the responsibility for the management of the affairs of the corporation, he must execute that duty with the recognition that he acts on behalf of others. Such obligation does not tolerate faithlessness or self-dealing. But fulfillment of the fiduciary function requires more than the mere absence of bad faith or fraud. Representation of the financial interests of others imposes on a director an affirmative duty to protect those interests and to proceed with a critical eye in assessing information of the type and under the circumstances present here.

Thus, a director's duty to exercise an informed business judgment is in the nature of a duty of care, as distinguished from a duty of loyalty. Here, there were no allegations of fraud, bad faith, or self-dealing, or proof thereof. Hence, it is presumed that the directors reached their business judgment in good faith, and considerations of motive are irrelevant to the issue before us.

The standard of care applicable to a director's duty of care has also been recently restated by this Court. In *Aronson,* supra, we stated:

---

[12] See Kaplan v. Centex Corporation, Del.Ch., 284 A.2d 119, 124 (1971), where the Court stated:

Application of the [business judgment] rule of necessity depends upon a showing that informed directors did in fact make a business judgment authorizing the transaction under review. And, as the plaintiff argues, the difficulty here is that the evidence does not show that this was done. There were director-committee-officer references to the realignment but none of these singly or cumulatively showed that the director judgment was brought to bear with specificity on the transactions.

While the Delaware cases use a variety of terms to describe the applicable standard of care, our analysis satisfies us that under the business judgment rule director liability is predicated upon concepts of gross negligence. (footnote omitted)

473 A.2d at 812.

We again confirm that view. We think the concept of gross negligence is also the proper standard for determining whether a business judgment reached by a board of directors was an informed one.

In the specific context of a proposed merger of domestic corporations, a director has a duty under 8 *Del.C.* 251(b), along with his fellow directors, to act in an informed and deliberate manner in determining whether to approve an agreement of merger before submitting the proposal to the stockholders. Certainly in the merger context, a director may not abdicate that duty by leaving to the shareholders alone the decision to approve or disapprove the agreement. Only an agreement of merger satisfying the requirements of 8 *Del.C.* § 251(b) may be submitted to the shareholders under § 251(c).

It is against those standards that the conduct of the directors of Trans Union must be tested, as a matter of law and as a matter of fact, regarding their exercise of an informed business judgment in voting to approve the Pritzker merger proposal.

III.

The defendants argue that the determination of whether their decision to accept $55 per share for Trans Union represented an informed business judgment requires consideration, not only of that which they knew and learned on September 20, but also of that which they subsequently learned and did over the following four-month period before the shareholders met to vote on the proposal in February, 1981. The defendants thereby seek to reduce the significance of their action on September 20 and to widen the time frame for determining whether their decision to accept the Pritzker proposal was an informed one. Thus, the defendants contend that what the directors did and learned subsequent to September 20 and through January 26, 1981, was properly taken into account by the Trial Court in determining whether the Board's judgment was an informed one. We disagree with this *post hoc* approach.

The issue of whether the directors reached an informed decision to "sell" the Company on September 20, 1980 must be determined only upon the basis of the information then reasonably available to the directors and relevant to their decision to accept the Pritzker merger proposal. This is not to say that the directors were precluded from altering their original plan of action, had they done so in an informed manner. What we do say is that the question of whether the directors reached an informed business judgment in agreeing to sell the Company, pursuant to the terms of the September 20 Agreement presents, in reality, two questions: (A) whether the directors reached an informed business judgment on September 20, 1980; and (B) if they did not, whether the directors' actions taken subsequent to September 20 were adequate to cure any infirmity in their action taken on September 20. We first consider the directors' September 20 action in terms of their reaching an informed business judgment.

–A–

On the record before us, we must conclude that the Board of Directors did not reach an informed business judgment on September 20, 1980 in voting to "sell" the Company for $55 per share pursuant to the Pritzker cash-out merger proposal. Our reasons, in summary, are as follows:

The directors (1) did not adequately inform themselves as to Van Gorkom's role in forcing the "sale" of the Company and in establishing the per share purchase price; (2) were uninformed as to the intrinsic value of the Company; and (3) given these circumstances, at a minimum, were grossly negligent in approving the "sale" of the Company upon two hours' consideration, without prior notice, and without the exigency of a crisis or emergency.

As has been noted, the Board based its September 20 decision to approve the cash-out merger primarily on Van Gorkom's representations. None of the directors, other than Van Gorkom and Chelberg, had any prior knowledge that the purpose of the meeting was to propose a cash-out merger of Trans Union. No members of Senior Management were present, other than Chelberg, Romans and Peterson; and the latter two had only learned of the proposed sale an hour earlier. Both general counsel Moore and former general counsel Browder attended the meeting, but were equally uninformed as to the purpose of the meeting and the documents to be acted upon.

Without any documents before them concerning the proposed transaction, the members of the Board were required to rely entirely upon Van Gorkom's 20-minute oral presentation of the proposal. No written summary of the terms of the merger was presented; the directors were given no documentation to support the adequacy of $55 price per share for sale of the Company; and the Board had before it nothing more than Van Gorkom's statement of his understanding of the substance of an agreement which he admittedly had never read, nor which any member of the Board had ever seen.

Under 8 *Del.C.* § 141(e),[15] "directors are fully protected in relying in good faith on reports made by officers." Michelson v. Duncan, Del. Ch., 386 A.2d 1144, 1156 (1978); aff'd in part and rev'd in part on other grounds, Del.Supr., 407 A.2d 211 (1979). The term "report" has been liberally construed to include reports of informal personal investigations by corporate officers. However, there is no evidence that any "report," as defined under § 141(e), concerning the Pritzker proposal,

---

[15] Section 141(e) provides in pertinent part:

A member of the board of directors * * * shall, in the performance of his duties, be fully protected in relying in good faith upon the books of accounts or reports made to the corporation by any of its officers, or by an independent certified public accountant, or by an appraiser selected with reasonable care by the board of directors * * *, or in relying in good faith upon other records of the corporation.

was presented to the Board on September 20.[16] Van Gorkom's oral presentation of his understanding of the terms of the proposed Merger Agreement, which he had not seen, and Romans' brief oral statement of his preliminary study regarding the feasibility of a leveraged buy-out of Trans Union do not qualify as § 141(e) "reports" for these reasons: The former lacked substance because Van Gorkom was basically uninformed as to the essential provisions of the very document about which he was talking. Romans' statement was irrelevant to the issues before the Board since it did not purport to be a valuation study. At a minimum for a report to enjoy the status conferred by § 141(e), it must be pertinent to the subject matter upon which a board is called to act, and otherwise be entitled to good faith, not blind, reliance. Considering all of the surrounding circumstances—hastily calling the meeting without prior notice of its subject matter, the proposed sale of the Company without any prior consideration of the issue or necessity therefor, the urgent time constraints imposed by Pritzker, and the total absence of any documentation whatsoever—the directors were duty bound to make reasonable inquiry of Van Gorkom and Romans, and if they had done so, the inadequacy of that upon which they now claim to have relied would have been apparent.

The defendants rely on the following factors to sustain the Trial Court's finding that the Board's decision was an informed one: (1) the magnitude of the premium or spread between the $55 Pritzker offering price and Trans Union's current market price of $38 per share; (2) the amendment of the Agreement as submitted on September 20 to permit the Board to accept any better offer during the "market test" period; (3) the collective experience and expertise of the Board's "inside" and "outside" directors; and (4) their reliance on Brennan's legal advice that the directors might be sued if they rejected the Pritzker proposal. We discuss each of these grounds *seriatim:*

(1)

A substantial premium may provide one reason to recommend a merger, but in the absence of other sound valuation information, the fact of a premium alone does not provide an adequate basis upon which to assess the fairness of an offering price. Here, the judgment reached as to the adequacy of the premium was based on a comparison between the historically depressed Trans Union market price and the amount of the Pritzker offer. Using market price as a basis for concluding that the premium adequately reflected the true value of the Company was a clearly faulty, indeed fallacious, premise, as the defendants' own evidence demonstrates.

---

[16] In support of the defendants' argument that their judgment as to the adequacy of $55 per share was an informed one, the directors rely on the BCG study and the Five Year Forecast. However, no one even referred to either of these studies at the September 20 meeting; and it is conceded that these materials do not represent valuation studies. Hence, these documents do not constitute evidence as to whether the directors reached an informed judgment on September 20 that $55 per share was a fair value for sale of the Company.

The record is clear that before September 20, Van Gorkom and other members of Trans Union's Board knew that the market had consistently undervalued the worth of Trans Union's stock, despite steady increases in the Company's operating income in the seven years preceding the merger. The Board related this occurrence in large part to Trans Union's inability to use its ITCs as previously noted. Van Gorkom testified that he did not believe the market price accurately reflected Trans Union's true worth; and several of the directors testified that, as a general rule, most chief executives think that the market undervalues their companies' stock. Yet, on September 20, Trans Union's Board apparently believed that the market stock price accurately reflected the value of the Company for the purpose of determining the adequacy of the premium for its sale.

In the Proxy Statement, however, the directors reversed their position. There, they stated that, although the earnings prospects for Trans Union were "excellent," they found no basis for believing that this would be reflected in future stock prices. With regard to past trading, the Board stated that the prices at which the Company's common stock had traded in recent years did not reflect the "inherent" value of the Company. But having referred to the "inherent" value of Trans Union, the directors ascribed no number to it. Moreover, nowhere did they disclose that they had no basis on which to fix "inherent" worth beyond an impressionistic reaction to the premium over market and an unsubstantiated belief that the value of the assets was "significantly greater" than book value. By their own admission they could not rely on the stock price as an accurate measure of value. Yet, also by their own admission, the Board members assumed that Trans Union's market price was adequate to serve as a basis upon which to assess the adequacy of the premium for purposes of the September 20 meeting.

The parties do not dispute that a publicly-traded stock price is solely a measure of the value of a minority position and, thus, market price represents only the value of a single share. Nevertheless, on September 20, the Board assessed the adequacy of the premium over market, offered by Pritzker, solely by comparing it with Trans Union's current and historical stock price.

Indeed, as of September 20, the Board had no other information on which to base a determination of the intrinsic value of Trans Union as a going concern. As of September 20, the Board had made no evaluation of the Company designed to value the entire enterprise, nor had the Board ever previously considered selling the Company or consenting to a buy-out merger. Thus, the adequacy of a premium is indeterminate unless it is assessed in terms of other competent and sound valuation information that reflects the value of the particular business.

Despite the foregoing facts and circumstances, there was no call by the Board, either on September 20 or thereafter, for any valuation study or documentation of the $55 price per share as a measure of the fair value of the Company in a cash-out context. It is undisputed that the major asset of Trans Union was its cash flow. Yet, at no time did the Board call for a valuation study taking into account that highly significant element of the Company's assets.

We do not imply that an outside valuation study is essential to support an informed business judgment; nor do we state that fairness opinions by independent investment bankers are required as a matter of law. Often insiders familiar with the business of a going concern are in a better position than are outsiders to gather relevant information; and under appropriate circumstances, such directors may be fully protected in relying in good faith upon the valuation reports of their management. See 8 *Del.C.* § 141(e).

Here, the record establishes that the Board did not request its Chief Financial Officer, Romans, to make any valuation study or review of the proposal to determine the adequacy of $55 per share for sale of the Company. On the record before us: The Board rested on Romans' elicited response that the $55 figure was within a "fair price range" within the context of a leveraged buy-out. No director sought any further information from Romans. No director asked him why he put $55 at the bottom of his range. No director asked Romans for any details as to his study, the reason why it had been undertaken or its depth. No director asked to see the study; and no director asked Romans whether Trans Union's finance department could do a fairness study within the remaining 36-hour [18] period available under the Pritzker offer.

Had the Board, or any member, made an inquiry of Romans, he presumably would have responded as he testified: that his calculations were rough and preliminary; and, that the study was not designed to determine the fair value of the Company, but rather to assess the feasibility of a leveraged buy-out financed by the Company's projected cash flow, making certain assumptions as to the purchaser's borrowing needs. Romans would have presumably also informed the Board of his view, and the widespread view of Senior Management, that the timing of the offer was wrong and the offer inadequate.

The record also establishes that the Board accepted without scrutiny Van Gorkom's representation as to the fairness of the $55 price per share for sale of the Company—a subject that the Board had never previously considered. The Board thereby failed to discover that Van Gorkom had suggested the $55 price to Pritzker and, most crucially, that Van Gorkom had arrived at the $55 figure based on calculations designed solely to determine the feasibility of a leveraged buy-out.[19] No

---

[18] Romans' department study was not made available to the Board until circulation of Trans Union's Supplementary Proxy Statement and the Board's meeting of January 26, 1981, on the eve of the shareholder meeting; and, as has been noted, the study has never been produced for inclusion in the record in this case.

[19] As of September 20 the directors did not know: that Van Gorkom had arrived at the $55 figure alone, and subjectively, as the figure to be used by Controller Peterson in creating a feasible structure for a leveraged buy-out by a prospective purchaser; that Van Gorkom had not sought advice, information or assistance from either inside or outside Trans Union directors as to the value of the Company as an entity or the fair price per share for 100% of its stock; that Van Gorkom had not consulted with the Company's investment bankers or other financial analysts; that

questions were raised either as to the tax implications of a cash-out merger or how the price for the one million share option granted Pritzker was calculated.

We do not say that the Board of Directors was not entitled to give some credence to Van Gorkom's representation that $55 was an adequate or fair price. Under § 141(e), the directors were entitled to rely upon their chairman's opinion of value and adequacy, provided that such opinion was reached on a sound basis. Here, the issue is whether the directors informed themselves as to all information that was reasonably available to them. Had they done so, they would have learned of the source and derivation of the $55 price and could not reasonably have relied thereupon in good faith.

None of the directors, Management or outside, were investment bankers or financial analysts. Yet the Board did not consider recessing the meeting until a later hour that day (or requesting an extension of Pritzker's Sunday evening deadline) to give it time to elicit more information as to the sufficiency of the offer, either from inside Management (in particular Romans) or from Trans Union's own investment banker, Salomon Brothers, whose Chicago specialist in merger and acquisitions was known to the Board and familiar with Trans Union's affairs.

Thus, the record compels the conclusion that on September 20 the Board lacked valuation information adequate to reach an informed business judgment as to the fairness of $55 per share for sale of the Company.

(2)

This brings us to the post-September 20 "market test" upon which the defendants ultimately rely to confirm the reasonableness of their September 20 decision to accept the Pritzker proposal. In this connection, the directors present a two-part argument: (a) that by making a "market test" of Pritzker's $55 per share offer a condition of their September 20 decision to accept his offer, they cannot be found to have acted impulsively or in an uninformed manner on September 20; and (b) that the adequacy of the $17 premium for sale of the Company was conclusively established over the following 90 to 120 days by the most reliable evidence available—the marketplace. Thus, the defendants impliedly contend that the "market test" eliminated the need for the Board to perform any other form of fairness test either on September 20, or thereafter.

Again, the facts of record do not support the defendants' argument. There is no evidence: (a) that the Merger Agreement was effectively amended to give the Board freedom to put Trans Union up for auction sale to the highest bidder; or (b) that a public auction was in fact permitted to occur. The minutes of the Board meeting make no

Van Gorkom had not consulted with or confided in any officer or director of the Company except Chelberg; and that Van Gorkom had deliberately chosen to ignore the advice and opinion of the members of his Senior Management group regarding the adequacy of the $55 price.

reference to any of this. Indeed, the record compels the conclusion that the directors had no rational basis for expecting that a market test was attainable, given the terms of the Agreement as executed during the evening of September 20. We rely upon the following facts which are essentially uncontradicted:

The Merger Agreement, specifically identified as that originally presented to the Board on September 20, has never been produced by the defendants, notwithstanding the plaintiffs' several demands for production before as well as during trial. No acceptable explanation of this failure to produce documents has been given to either the Trial Court or this Court. Significantly, neither the defendants nor their counsel have made the affirmative representation that this critical document has been produced. Thus, the Court is deprived of the best evidence on which to judge the merits of the defendants' position as to the care and attention which they gave to the terms of the Agreement on September 20.

Van Gorkom states that the Agreement as submitted incorporated the ingredients for a market test by authorizing Trans Union to receive competing offers over the next 90-day period. However, he concedes that the Agreement barred Trans Union from actively soliciting such offers and from furnishing to interested parties any information about the Company other than that already in the public domain. Whether the original Agreement of September 20 went so far as to authorize Trans Union to receive competitive proposals is arguable. The defendants' unexplained failure to produce and identify the original Merger Agreement permits the logical inference that the instrument would not support their assertions in this regard. Van Gorkom, conceding that he never read the Agreement, stated that he was relying upon his understanding that, under corporate law, directors always have an inherent right, as well as a fiduciary duty, to accept a better offer notwithstanding an existing contractual commitment by the Board.

The defendant directors assert that they "insisted" upon including two amendments to the Agreement, thereby permitting a market test: (1) to give Trans Union the right to accept a better offer; and (2) to reserve to Trans Union the right to distribute proprietary information on the Company to alternative bidders. Yet, the defendants concede that they did not seek to amend the Agreement to permit Trans Union to solicit competing offers.

Several of Trans Union's outside directors resolutely maintained that the Agreement as submitted was approved on the understanding that, "if we got a better deal, we had a right to take it." Director Johnson so testified; but he then added, "And if they didn't put that in the agreement, then the management did not carry out the conclusion of the Board. And I just don't know whether they did or not." The only clause in the Agreement as finally executed to which the defendants can point as "keeping the door open" is the following underlined statement found in subparagraph (a) of section 2.03 of the Merger Agreement as executed:

> The Board of Directors shall recommend to the stockholders of
> Trans Union that they approve and adopt the Merger Agreement
> ('the stockholders' approval') and to use its best efforts to obtain the
> requisite votes therefor. *GL acknowledges that Trans Union direc-*
> *tors may have a competing fiduciary obligation to the shareholders*
> *under certain circumstances.*

Clearly, this language on its face cannot be construed as incorporating
either of the two "conditions" described above: either the right to
accept a better offer or the right to distribute proprietary information
to third parties. The logical witness for the defendants to call to
confirm their construction of this clause of the Agreement would have
been Trans Union's outside attorney, James Brennan. The defendants'
failure, without explanation, to call this witness again permits the
logical inference that his testimony would not have been helpful to
them. The further fact that the directors adjourned, rather than
recessed, the meeting without incorporating in the Agreement these
important "conditions" further weakens the defendants' position. As
has been noted, nothing in the Board's Minutes supports these claims.
No reference to either of the so-called "conditions" or of Trans Union's
reserved right to test the market appears in any notes of the Board
meeting or in the Board Resolution accepting the Pritzker offer or in
the Minutes of the meeting itself. That evening, in the midst of a
formal party which he hosted for the opening of the Chicago Lyric
Opera, Van Gorkom executed the Merger Agreement without he or any
other member of the Board having read the instruments.

The defendants attempt to downplay the significance of the prohibition against Trans Union's actively soliciting competing offers by
arguing that the directors "understood that the entire financial community would know that Trans Union was for sale upon the announcement of the Pritzker offer, and anyone desiring to make a better offer
was free to do so." Yet, the press release issued on September 22, with
the authorization of the Board, stated that Trans Union had entered
into "definitive agreements" with the Pritzkers; and the press release
did not even disclose Trans Union's limited right to receive and accept
higher offers. Accompanying this press release was a further public
announcement that Pritzker had been granted an option to purchase at
any time one million shares of Trans Union's capital stock at 75 cents
above the then-current price per share.

Thus, notwithstanding what several of the outside directors later
claimed to have "thought" occurred at the meeting, the record compels
the conclusion that Trans Union's Board had no rational basis to
conclude on September 20 or in the days immediately following, that
the Board's acceptance of Pritzker's offer was conditioned on (1) a
"market test" of the offer; and (2) the Board's right to withdraw from
the Pritzker Agreement and accept any higher offer received before the
shareholder meeting.

(3)

The directors' unfounded reliance on both the premium and the
market test as the basis for accepting the Pritzker proposal undermines

the defendants' remaining contention that the Board's collective experience and sophistication was a sufficient basis for finding that it reached its September 20 decision with informed, reasonable deliberation.[21] Compare Gimbel v. Signal Companies, Inc., Del.Ch., 316 A.2d 599 (1974), aff'd per curiam, Del.Supr., 316 A.2d 619 (1974). There, the Court of Chancery preliminarily enjoined a board's sale of stock of its wholly-owned subsidiary for an alleged grossly inadequate price. It did so based on a finding that the business judgment rule had been pierced for failure of management to give its board "the opportunity to make a reasonable and reasoned decision." 316 A.2d at 615. The Court there reached this result notwithstanding the board's sophistication and experience; the company's need of immediate cash; and the board's need to act promptly due to the impact of an energy crisis on the value of the underlying assets being sold—all of its subsidiary's oil and gas interests. The Court found those factors denoting competence to be outweighed by evidence of gross negligence; that management in effect sprang the deal on the board by negotiating the asset sale without informing the board; that the buyer intended to "force a quick decision" by the board; that the board meeting was called on only one-and-a-half days' notice; that its outside directors were not notified of the meeting's purpose; that during a meeting spanning "a couple of hours" a sale of assets worth $480 million was approved; and that the Board failed to obtain a *current* appraisal of its oil and gas interests. The analogy of *Signal* to the case at bar is significant.

* * *

B. We now examine the Board's post-September 20 conduct for the purpose of determining first, whether it was informed and not grossly negligent; and second, if informed, whether it was sufficient to legally rectify and cure the Board's derelictions of September 20.[23]

(1)

First, as to the Board meeting of October 8: Its purpose arose in the aftermath of the September 20 meeting: (1) the September 22 press release announcing that Trans Union "had entered into definitive agreements to merge with an affiliate of Marmon Group, Inc.;" and (2) Senior Management's ensuing revolt.

Trans Union's press release stated:

FOR IMMEDIATE RELEASE:

CHICAGO, IL—Trans Union Corporation announced today that it had entered into definitive agreements to merge with an

---

[21] Trans Union's five "inside" directors had backgrounds in law and accounting, 116 years of collective employment by the Company and 68 years of combined experience on its Board. Trans Union's five "outside" directors included four chief executives of major corporations and an economist who was a former dean of a major school of business and chancellor of a university. The "outside" directors had 78 years of combined experience as chief executive officers of major corporations and 50 years of cumulative experience as directors of Trans Union. Thus, defendants argue that the Board was eminently qualified to reach an informed judgment on the proposed "sale" of Trans Union notwithstanding their lack of any advance notice of the proposal, the shortness of their deliberation, and their determination not to consult with their investment banker or to obtain a fairness opinion.

[23] As will be seen, we do not reach the second question.

affiliate of The Marmon Group, Inc. in a transaction whereby Trans Union stockholders would receive $55 per share in cash for each Trans Union share held. The Marmon Group, Inc. is controlled by the Pritzker family of Chicago.

The merger is subject to approval by the stockholders of Trans Union at a special meeting expected to be held sometime during December or early January.

Until October 10, 1980, the purchaser has the right to terminate the merger if financing that is satisfactory to the purchaser has not been obtained, but after that date there is no such right.

In a related transaction, Trans Union has agreed to sell to a designee of the purchaser one million newly-issued shares of Trans Union common stock at a cash price of $38 per share. Such shares will be issued only if the merger financing has been committed for no later than October 10, 1980, or if the purchaser elects to waive the merger financing condition. In addition, the New York Stock Exchange will be asked to approve the listing of the new shares pursuant to a listing application which Trans Union intends to file shortly.

Completing of the transaction is also subject to the preparation of a definitive proxy statement and making various filings and obtaining the approvals or consents of government agencies.

The press release made no reference to provisions allegedly reserving to the Board the rights to perform a "market test" and to withdraw from the Pritzker Agreement if Trans Union received a better offer before the shareholder meeting. The defendants also concede that Trans Union never made a subsequent public announcement stating that it had in fact reserved the right to accept alternate offers, the Agreement notwithstanding.

The public announcement of the Pritzker merger resulted in an "en masse" revolt of Trans Union's Senior Management. The head of Trans Union's tank car operations (its most profitable division) informed Van Gorkom that unless the merger were called off, fifteen key personnel would resign.

Instead of reconvening the Board, Van Gorkom again privately met with Pritzker, informed him of the developments, and sought his advice. Pritzker then made the following suggestions for overcoming Management's dissatisfaction: (1) that the Agreement be amended to permit Trans Union to solicit, as well as receive, higher offers; and (2) that the shareholder meeting be postponed from early January to February 10, 1981. In return, Pritzker asked Van Gorkom to obtain a commitment from Senior Management to remain at Trans Union for at least six months after the merger was consummated.

Van Gorkom then advised Senior Management that the Agreement would be amended to give Trans Union the right to solicit competing offers through January, 1981, if they would agree to remain with Trans Union. Senior Management was temporarily mollified; and Van

Gorkom then called a special meeting of Trans Union's Board for October 8.

Thus, the primary purpose of the October 8 Board meeting was to amend the Merger Agreement, in a manner agreeable to Pritzker, to permit Trans Union to conduct a "market test." [24] Van Gorkom understood that the proposed amendments were intended to give the Company an unfettered "right to openly solicit offers down through January 31." Van Gorkom presumably so represented the amendments to Trans Union's Board members on October 8. In a brief session, the directors approved Van Gorkom's oral presentation of the substance of the proposed amendments, the terms of which were not reduced to writing until October 10. But rather than waiting to review the amendments, the Board again approved them sight unseen and adjourned, giving Van Gorkom authority to execute the papers when he received them.[25]

Thus, the Court of Chancery's finding that the October 8 Board meeting was convened to *reconsider* the Pritzker "proposal" is clearly erroneous. Further, the consequence of the Board's faulty conduct on October 8, in approving amendments to the Agreement which had not even been drafted, will become apparent when the actual amendments to the Agreement are hereafter examined.

The next day, October 9, and before the Agreement was amended, Pritzker moved swiftly to off-set the proposed market test amendment. First, Pritzker informed Trans Union that he had completed arrangements for financing its acquisition and that the parties were thereby mutually bound to a firm purchase and sale arrangement. Second, Pritzker announced the exercise of his option to purchase one million shares of Trans Union's treasury stock at $38 per share—75 cents above the current market price. Trans Union's Management responded the same day by issuing a press release announcing: (1) that all financing arrangements for Pritzer's acquisition of Trans Union had been completed; and (2) Pritzker's purchase of one million shares of Trans Union's treasury stock at $38 per share.

The next day, October 10, Pritzker delivered to Trans Union the proposed amendments to the September 20 Merger Agreement. Van

---

[24] As previously noted, the Board mistakenly thought that it had amended the September 20 draft agreement to include a market test.

A secondary purpose of the October meeting was to obtain the Board's approval for Trans Union to employ its investment advisor, Salomon Brothers, for the limited purpose of assisting Management in the solicitation of other offers. Neither Management nor the Board then or thereafter requested Salomon Brothers to submit its opinion as to the fairness of Pritzker's $55 cash-out merger proposal or to value Trans Union as an entity.

There is no evidence of record that the October 8 meeting had any other purpose;

and we also note that the Minutes of the October 8 Board meeting, including any notice of the meeting, are not part of the voluminous records of this case.

[25] We do not suggest that a board must read *in haec verba* every contract or legal document which it approves, but if it is to successfully absolve itself from charges of the type made here, there must be some credible contemporary evidence demonstrating that the directors knew what they were doing, and ensured that their purported action was given effect. That is the consistent failure which cast this Board upon its unredeemable course.

Gorkom promptly proceeded to countersign all the instruments on behalf of Trans Union without reviewing the instruments to determine if they were consistent with the authority previously granted him by the Board. The amending documents were apparently not approved by Trans Union's Board until a much later date, December 2. The record does not affirmatively establish that Trans Union's directors ever read the October 10 amendments.[26]

The October 10 amendments to the Merger Agreement did authorize Trans Union to solicit competing offers, but the amendments had more far-reaching effects. The most significant change was in the definition of the third-party "offer" available to Trans Union as a possible basis for withdrawal from its Merger Agreement with Pritzker. Under the October 10 amendments, a better *offer* was no longer sufficient to permit Trans Union's withdrawal. Trans Union was now permitted to terminate the Pritzker Agreement and abandon the merger only if, prior to February 10, 1981, Trans Union had either consummated a merger (or sale of assets) with a third party or had entered into a "definitive" merger agreement more favorable than Pritzker's and for a greater consideration—subject only to stockholder approval. Further, the "extension" of the market test period to February 10, 1981 was circumscribed by other amendments which required Trans Union to file its preliminary proxy statement on the Pritzker merger proposal by December 5, 1980 and use its best efforts to mail the statement to its shareholders by January 5, 1981. Thus, the market test period was effectively reduced, not extended.

In our view, the record compels the conclusion that the directors' conduct on October 8 exhibited the same deficiencies as did their conduct on September 20. The Board permitted its Merger Agreement with Pritzker to be amended in a manner it had neither authorized nor intended. * * *

(2)

Next, as to the "curative" effects of the Board's post-September 20 conduct, we review in more detail the reaction of Van Gorkom to the KKR proposal and the results of the Board-sponsored "market test."

The KKR proposal was the first and only offer received subsequent to the Pritzker Merger Agreement. The offer resulted primarily from the efforts of Romans and other senior officers to propose an alternative to Pritzker's acquisition of Trans Union. In late September, Romans' group contacted KKR about the possibility of a leveraged buy-out by all members of Management, except Van Gorkom. By early October, Henry R. Kravis of KKR gave Romans written notice of KKR's "interest in making an offer to purchase 100%" of Trans Union's common stock.

---

[26] There is no evidence of record that Trans Union's directors ever raised any objections, procedural or substantive, to the October 10 amendments or that any of them, including Van Gorkom, understood the opposite result of their intended effect—until it was too late.

Thereafter, and until early December, Romans' group worked with KKR to develop a proposal. It did so with Van Gorkom's knowledge and apparently grudging consent. On December 2, Kravis and Romans hand-delivered to Van Gorkom a formal letter-offer to purchase all of Trans Union's assets and to assume all of its liabilities for an aggregate cash consideration equivalent to $60 per share. The offer was contingent upon completing equity and bank financing of $650 million, which Kravis represented as 80% complete. The KKR letter made reference to discussions with major banks regarding the loan portion of the buy-out cost and stated that KKR was "confident that commitments for the bank financing * * * can be obtained within two or three weeks." The purchasing group was to include certain named key members of Trans Union's Senior Management, excluding Van Gorkom, and a major Canadian company. Kravis stated that they were willing to enter into a "definitive agreement" under terms and conditions "substantially the same" as those contained in Trans Union's agreement with Pritzker. The offer was addressed to Trans Union's Board of Directors and a meeting with the Board, scheduled for that afternoon, was requested.

Van Gorkom's reaction to the KKR proposal was completely negative; he did not view the offer as being firm because of its financing condition. It was pointed out, to no avail, that Pritzker's offer had not only been similarly conditioned, but accepted on an expedited basis. Van Gorkom refused Kravis' request that Trans Union issue a press release announcing KKR's offer, on the ground that it might "chill" any other offer.[27] Romans and Kravis left with the understanding that their proposal would be presented to Trans Union's Board that afternoon.

Within a matter of hours and shortly before the scheduled Board meeting, Kravis withdrew his letter-offer. He gave as his reason a sudden decision by the Chief Officer of Trans Union's rail car leasing operation to withdraw from the KKR purchasing group. Van Gorkom had spoken to that officer about his participation in the KKR proposal immediately after his meeting with Romans and Kravis. However, Van Gorkom denied any responsibility for the officer's change of mind.

At the Board meeting later that afternoon, Van Gorkom did not inform the directors of the KKR proposal because he considered it "dead." Van Gorkom did not contact KKR again until January 20, when faced with the realities of this lawsuit, he then attempted to reopen negotiations. KKR declined due to the imminence of the February 10 stockholder meeting.

GE Credit Corporation's interest in Trans Union did not develop until November; and it made no written proposal until mid-January. Even then, its proposal was not in the form of an offer. Had there been time to do so, GE Credit was prepared to offer between $2 and $5 per share above the $55 per share price which Pritzker offered. But GE

---

[27] This was inconsistent with Van Gorkom's espousal of the September 22 press release following Trans Union's acceptance of Pritzker's proposal. Van Gorkom had then justified a press release as encouraging rather than chilling later offers.

Credit needed an additional 60 to 90 days; and it was unwilling to make a formal offer without a concession from Pritzker extending the February 10 "deadline" for Trans Union's stockholder meeting. As previously stated, Pritzker refused to grant such extension; and on January 21, GE Credit terminated further negotiations with Trans Union. Its stated reasons, among others, were its "unwillingness to become involved in a bidding contest with Pritzker in the absence of the willingness of [the Pritzker interests] to terminate the proposed $55 cash merger."

* * *

In the absence of any explicit finding by the Trial Court as to the reasonableness of Trans Union's directors' reliance on a market test and its feasibility, we may make our own findings based on the record. Our review of the record compels a finding that confirmation of the appropriateness of the Pritzker offer by an unfettered or free market test was virtually meaningless in the face of the terms and time limitations of Trans Union's Merger Agreement with Pritzker as amended October 10, 1980.

(3)

Finally, we turn to the Board's meeting of January 26, 1981. The defendant directors rely upon the action there taken to refute the contention that they did not reach an informed business judgment in approving the Pritzker merger. The defendants contend that the Trial Court correctly concluded that Trans Union's directors were, in effect, as "free to turn down the Pritzker proposal" on January 26, as they were on September 20.

* * *

The Board's January 26 meeting was the first meeting following the filing of the plaintiffs' suit in mid-December and the last meeting before the previously-noticed shareholder meeting of February 10. All ten members of the Board and three outside attorneys attended the meeting. At that meeting the following facts, among other aspects of the Merger Agreement, were discussed:

(a) The fact that prior to September 20, 1980, no Board member or member of Senior Management, except Chelberg and Peterson, knew that Van Gorkom has discussed a possible merger with Pritzker;

(b) The fact that the price of $55 per share had been suggested initially to Pritzker by Van Gorkom;

(c) The fact that the Board had not sought an independent fairness opinion;

(d) The fact that, at the September 20 Senior Management meeting, Romans and several members of Senior Management indicated both concern that the $55 per share price was inadequate and a belief that a higher price should and could be obtained;

(e) The fact that Romans had advised the Board at its meeting on September 20, that he and his department had prepared a study which indicated that the Company had a value in the range of $55 to $65 per share, and that he could not advise the Board that the $55 per share offer made by Pritzker was unfair.

The defendants characterize the Board's Minutes of the January 26 meeting as a "review" of the "entire sequence of events" from Van Gorkom's initiation of the negotiations on September 13 forward. The defendants also rely on the testimony of several of the Board members at trial as confirming the Minutes. On the basis of this evidence, the defendants argue that whatever information the Board lacked to make a deliberate and informed judgment on September 20, or on October 8, was fully divulged to the entire Board on January 26. Hence, the argument goes, the Board's vote on January 26 to again "approve" the Pritzker merger must be found to have been an informed and deliberate judgment.

On the basis of this evidence, the defendants assert: (1) that the Trial Court was legally correct in widening the time frame for determining whether the defendants' approval of the Pritzker merger represented an informed business judgment to include the entire four-month period during which the Board considered the matter from September 20 through January 26; and (2) that, given this extensive evidence of the Board's further review and deliberations on January 26, this Court must affirm the Trial Court's conclusion that the Board's action was not reckless or improvident.

We cannot agree. We find the Trial Court to have erred, both as a matter of fact and as a matter of law, in relying on the action on January 26 to bring the defendants' conduct within the protection of the business judgment rule.

Johnson's testimony and the Board Minutes of January 26 are remarkably consistent. Both clearly indicate recognition that the question of the alternative courses of action, available to the Board on January 26 with respect to the Pritzker merger, was a legal question, presenting to the Board (*after* its review of the full record developed through pre-trial discovery) *three* options: (1) to "continue to recommend" the Pritzker merger; (2) to "recommend that the stockholders vote against" the Pritzker merger; or (3) to take a noncommittal position on the merger and "simply leave the decision to [the] shareholders."

We must conclude from the foregoing that the Board was mistaken as a matter of law regarding its available courses of action on January 26, 1981. Options (2) and (3) were not viable or legally available to the Board under 8 *Del.C.* § 251(b). The Board could not remain committed to the Pritzker merger and yet recommend that its stockholders vote it down; nor could it take a neutral position and delegate to the stockholders the unadvised decision as to whether to accept or reject the merger. Under § 251(v), the Board had but two options: (1) to proceed with the merger and the stockholder meeting, with the Board's recommendation of approval; *or* (2) to rescind its agreement with Pritzker, withdraw its approval of the merger, and notify its stockholders that the proposed shareholder meeting was cancelled. There is no evidence that the Board gave any consideration to these, its only legally viable alternative courses of action.

But the second course of action would have clearly involved a substantial risk—that the Board would be faced with suit by Pritzker for breach of contract based on its September 20 agreement as amended October 10. As previously noted, under the terms of the October 10 amendment, the Board's only ground for release from its agreement with Pritzker was its entry into a more favorable definitive agreement to sell the Company to a third party. Thus, in reality, the Board was not "free to turn down the Pritzker proposal" as the Trial Court found. Indeed, short of negotiating a better agreement with a third party, the Board's only basis for release from the Pritzker Agreement without liability would have been to establish fundamental wrongdoing by Pritzker. Clearly, the Board was not "free" to withdraw from its agreement with Pritzker on January 26 by simply relying on its self-induced failure to have reached an informed business judgment at the time of its original agreement.

Therefore, the Trial Court's conclusion that the Board reached an informed business judgment on January 26 in determining whether to turn down the Pritzker "proposal" on that day cannot be sustained. The Court's conclusion is not supported by the record; it is contrary to the provisions of § 251(b) and basic principles of contract law; and it is not the product of a logical and deductive reasoning process.

* * *

Upon the basis of the foregoing, we hold that the defendants' post-September conduct did not cure the deficiencies of their September 20 conduct; and that, accordingly, the Trial Court erred in according to the defendants the benefits of the business judgment rule.

* * *

V.

The defendants ultimately rely on the stockholder vote of February 10 for exoneration. The defendants contend that the stockholders' "overwhelming" vote approving the Pritzker Merger Agreement had the legal effect of curing any failure of the Board to reach an informed business judgment in its approval of the merger.

The parties tacitly agree that a discovered failure of the Board to reach an informed business judgment in approving the merger constitutes a voidable, rather than a void, act. Hence, the merger can be sustained, notwithstanding the infirmity of the Board's action, if its approval by majority vote of the shareholders is found to have been based on an informed electorate.

The disagreement between the parties arises over: (1) the Board's burden of disclosing to the shareholders all relevant and material information; and (2) the sufficiency of the evidence as to whether the Board satisfied that burden.

On this issue the Trial Court summarily concluded "that the stockholders of Trans Union were fairly informed as to the pending merger. * * * " The Court provided no supportive reasoning nor did the Court make any reference to the evidence of record.

* * * In Lynch v. Vickers Energy Corp., supra, this Court held that corporate directors owe to their stockholders a fiduciary duty to disclose all facts germane to the transaction at issue in an atmosphere of complete candor. We defined "germane" in the tender offer context, as all "information such as a reasonable shareholder would consider important in deciding whether to sell or retain stock." Id. at 281.

Applying this standard to the record before us, we find that Trans Union's stockholders were not fully informed of all facts material to their vote on the Pritzker Merger and that the Trial Court's ruling to the contrary is clearly erroneous. We list the material deficiencies in the proxy materials:

(1) The fact that the Board had no reasonably adequate information indicative of the intrinsic value of the Company, other than a concededly depressed market price, was without question material to the shareholders voting on the merger.

Accordingly, the Board's lack of valuation information should have been disclosed. Instead, the directors cloaked the absence of such information in both the Proxy Statement and the Supplemental Proxy Statement. Through artful drafting, noticeably absent at the September 20 meeting, both documents create the impression that the Board knew the intrinsic worth of the Company. In particular, the Original Proxy Statement contained the following:

> [a]lthough the Board of Directors regards the intrinsic value of the Company's assets to be significantly greater than their book value * * *, systematic liquidation of such a large and complex entity as Trans Union is simply not regarded as a feasible method of realizing its inherent value. Therefore, a business combination such as the merger would seem to be the only practicable way in which the stockholders could realize the value of the Company.

The Proxy stated further that "[i]n the view of the Board of Directors * * *, the prices at which the Company's common stock has traded in recent years have not relected the inherent value of the company." What the Board failed to disclose to its stockholders was that the Board had not made any study of the intrinsic or inherent worth of the Company; nor had the Board even discussed the inherent value of the Company prior to approving the merger on September 20, or at either of the subsequent meetings on October 8 or January 26. Neither in its Original Proxy Statement nor in its Supplemental Proxy did the Board disclose that it had no information before it, beyond the premium-over-market and the price/earnings ratio, on which to determine the fair value of the Company as a whole.

(2) We find false and misleading the Board's characterization of the Romans report in the Supplemental Proxy Statement. The Supplemental Proxy stated:

> At the September 20, 1980 meeting of the Board of Directors of Trans Union, Mr. Romans indicated that while he could not say

that $55.00 per share was an unfair price, he had prepared a preliminary report which reflected that the value of the Company was in the range of $55.00 to $65.00 per share.

Nowhere does the Board disclose that Romans stated to the Board that his calculations were made in a "search for ways to justify a price in connection with" a leveraged buy-out transaction, "rather than to say what the shares are worth," and that he stated to the Board that his conclusion thus arrived at "was not the same thing as saying that I have a valuation of the Company at X dollars." Such information would have been material to a reasonable shareholder because it tended to invalidate the fairness of the merger price of $55. Furthermore, defendants again failed to disclose the absence of valuation information, but still made repeated reference to the "substantial premium."

(3) We find misleading the Board's references to the "substantial" premium offered. The Board gave us their primary reason in support of the merger the "substantial premium" shareholders would receive. But the Board did not disclose its failure to assess the premium offered in terms of other relevant valuation techniques, thereby rendering questionable its determination as to the substantiality of the premium over an admittedly depressed stock market price.

(4) We find the Board's recital in the Supplemental Proxy of certain events preceding the September 20 meeting to be incomplete and misleading. It is beyond dispute that a reasonable stockholder would have considered material the fact that Van Gorkom not only suggested the $55 price to Pritzker, but also that he chose the figure because it made feasible a leveraged buy-out. The directors disclosed that Van Gorkom suggested the $55 price to Pritzker. But the Board misled the shareholders when they described the basis of Van Gorkom's suggestion as follows:

> Such suggestion was based, at least in part, on Mr. Van Gorkom's belief that loans could be obtained from institutional lenders (together with about a $200 million equity contribution) which would justify the payment of such price, * * * Although by January 26, the directors knew the basis of the $55 figure, they did not disclose that Van Gorkom chose the $55 price because that figure would enable Pritzker to both finance the purchase of Trans Union through a leveraged buy-out and, within five years, substantially repay the loan out of the cash flow generated by the Company's operations.

* * *

VI.

To summarize: we hold that the directors of Trans Union breached their fiduciary duty to their stockholders (1) by their failure to inform themselves of all information reasonably available to them and relevant to their decision to recommend the Pritzker merger; and (2) by their failure to disclose all material information such as a reasonable stockholder would consider important in deciding whether to approve the Pritzker offer.

We hold, therefore, that the Trial Court committed reversible error in applying the business judgment rule in favor of the director defendants in this case.

On remand, the Court of Chancery shall conduct an evidentiary hearing to determine the fair value of the shares represented by the plaintiffs' class, based on the intrinsic value of Trans Union on September 20, 1980. Such valuation shall be made in accordance with Weinberger v. UOP, Inc., supra at 712–715. Thereafter, an award of damages may be entered to the extent that the fair value of Trans Union exceeds $55 per share.

*   *   *

REVERSED and REMANDED for proceedings consistent herewith.*

———◆———

The Delaware Supreme Court's decision in *Van Gorkom* was met by astonishment in the corporate bar. Professor Fischel, in a representative comment, described it as "one of the worst decisions in the history of corporate law * * *."[104] If the case is stated most simply, the vigorous reaction is understandable: Independent directors were held personally liable for a potentially enormous amount—the court's measure of damages was the amount by which "the fair value of transaction exceeds $55 per share" and the case was subsequently settled for approximately $23.5 million [105]—for approving a transaction reflecting a premium of some 60 percent over market. From a transactional perspective, the central issue is what, precisely, the Trans Union directors did wrong. If that can be identified, then business lawyers can help clients avoid liability in the future. The result of that inquiry, in turn, is central to evaluating the case from a doctrinal perspective. If the protective steps developed in response to *Van Gorkom* are improvements in transactional conduct, the case was correctly decided. If not, then we will still have the same question: What, precisely, did the Trans Union directors do wrong?

Although the court does not say so explicitly, the clear implication of the opinion is that Van Gorkom was looking out for Pritzker's interests rather than Trans Union's. As in most cases finding a violation of the business judgment rule, there are strong hints of breach of the duty of loyalty. Why would Van Gorkom have wanted the Pritzker deal so badly? After all, he owned 75,000 shares and would have benefitted along with other shareholders from any increase in price as a result of effectively shopping the company. The court does single out for comment the fact that Van Gorkom was approaching mandatory retirement; a $20 per share premium would have represented a $1.5 million additional retirement fund for him. Perhaps other

---

* Dissenting opinions of Justices McNeilly and Christie omitted. [Ed.]

[104] Fischel, *The Business Judgment Rule and the* Trans Union *Case,* 40 Bus.Law. 1437, 1455 (1985).

[105] Trans Union Corp.'s Ex-directors to Settle Suit for $23.5 Million, Wall St.J., Aug. 2, 1985, p. 10, col 5.

alternatives the board had considered, such as an acquisition program to use up Trans Unions' tax benefits, also might have raised the price of Trans Union stock. Compared to the Pritzker deal, however, all other alternatives involved substantially more risk. And if Van Gorkom had doubts that another offer could be obtained—after all, the company was not deluged by offers as a result of Salomon Brothers' efforts—then his impending retirement might have caused him to be more risk averse than the court would have preferred.

That Van Gorkom may have put his own interests above those of the shareholders (although the record apparently would not support that conclusion) would explain his liability. Why, however, include the other directors? The court treats the issue as one of the directors failing to inform themselves; it was not sufficient to rely on the judgment of the company's chief executive officer of 17 years. One could respond by reference to the price premium offered—the CEO is trustworthy and the price is good so why go any further—but the court also did not like the price.

If Van Gorkom's motives are the first mystery in the case, the court's treatment of value is the second. The court seemed to believe statements made by Trans Union management that its shares were undervalued because it could not use all of the tax benefits thrown off by its leasing activities. But that is only to say that Trans Union was accurately valued as it then existed, unable to fully utilize some of its assets. From this perspective, most American steel companies also are undervalued compared to what their value would be if only demand were sufficient to warrant using all of their production capacity. Nonetheless, the court concluded that market value was insufficient evidence of what the company was really worth.

So what should the directors have done? Professor Fischel has suggested that the principal transactional change after *Van Gorkom* "will be that no firm considering a fundamental corporate change will do so without obtaining a fairness letter * * * [from an investment banker]. * * * Firms will have no difficulty finding an 'expert' who is willing to state that a price at a significant premium over the market price in an arm's-length transaction is 'fair.' (I wish someone would pay me several hundred thousand dollars to state that $55 is greater than $35.)"[106] By this analysis, the big winners from *Van Gorkom* are the professional advisers, especially investment bankers. Lawyers, however, also should not fare too badly. It is notable how small a role Trans Union's lawyers seemed to play in the transaction; the emphasis in the court's opinion on the process of the board's decisionmaking may go a long way toward seeing that does not happen again.

What do target shareholders get out of *Van Gorkom?* Does the case add anything to the appraisal remedy that was always available to Trans Union shareholders who did not vote in favor of the merger? The measure of damages seems to be the same—"fair value." To be sure, the award in *Van Gorkom* was against the directors, while the award in an appraisal proceeding would have been against Trans

[106] Fischel, supra at 1453.

Union, but might not the liability better run against the company? Imposing the cost on Trans Union would have shifted it to Pritzker unless his obligation to close the transaction was conditioned on the number of dissenting shares. Even if Pritzker called off the transaction, the result would have been desirable from the court's perspective; a new offer could then have been solicited without the restraints imposed by Pritzker. Is anything gained by providing a substantively similar but procedurally quite different parallel remedy? This issue is considered in Chapter Fifteen B.3. *infra,* in the context of the exclusivity of the appraisal remedy.

Reference to appraisal suggests a different view of *Van Gorkom.* Perhaps it is really just a disclosure case; if the proxy statement had been complete, shareholders would have been able to exercise their appraisal rights intelligently. What kind of disclosure might have satisfied the court? What if the proxy statement had contained a boilerplate statement that only limited investigation of value beyond comparison of market price was possible within the limited time available, and that there was a potential difference between market value and intrinsic value?

In the end the *Van Gorkom* opinion reads like a half-finished mystery story: We never quite find out who did it, quite what they did, or the motive for the crime. The answers to these questions might do more to help illuminate the significance of the case—is it a sport on its facts or filled with meaning for the proper procedures to be followed by a target board of directors in approving a friendly transaction—then the extensive legal commentary the case is certain to generate.

CHAPTER FIFTEEN. CORPORATE LAW CONCERNS OF THE ACQUIRING COMPANY

We turn now to the corporate law concerns of the acquiring company. In particular, we will focus on two problems. The first bears on how to increase the likelihood that an offer, once made, will be successful. Can an acquiring company keep out, or at least substantially disadvantage, competitive bidders? The problem, in turn, has two distinct aspects. In a friendly transaction, what can be done with the cooperation of the target company to discourage competition? Alternatively, in an unfriendly transaction, what can be done without the target company's cooperation or, indeed, in the face of the target company's active efforts to find a white knight?

The second problem arises only after a tender offer has been successful. Even if the offer was for all of the target company's outstanding shares, studies suggest that some target shareholders, often as many as twenty or thirty percent, do not tender.[1] In the United States Steel offer for Marathon Oil, for example, ten percent of Marathon Oil shareholders did not tender their shares despite the announcement that a second-step transaction was contemplated in which non-tendering shareholders would receive approximately one-third less than the tender offer price.[2] The question, then, is under what circumstances the non-tendering minority shareholders can be eliminated from the target company even if they object: Can they be "frozen out"? A related question, though one that has received substantially less attention, concerns the status of non-tendering minority shareholders when the acquiring company does not undertake a second-step transaction: What standards govern the treatment of minority shareholders who are "frozen in"?

A. Discouraging Competitive Bidders

Section B.3.e. of Chapter Fourteen considered the problem of competitive bidding in terms of public policy: Does encouraging competing bids make shareholders of all potential target companies better or worse off? That discussion, however, does not resolve the issue for directors of a particular target company. Even the argument against seeking competitive bids recognizes that collective action would be necessary to enforce a determination that competitive bidding was undesirable. If a prohibition on seeking competitive bids was not rigorously enforced, free rider problems would erode any prohibition precisely because of the *ex ante/ex post* conflict. Although target shareholders as a *class* might be better off if no target company sought

---

[1] Bebchuk, *Towards Undistorted Choice and Equal Treatment in Corporate Takeovers*, 98 Harv.L.Rev. 1693, 1714 n. 58 (1985).

[2] See Radol v. Thomas, 534 F.Supp. 1302, 1305 (S.D.Ohio 1982).

a higher bid, the shareholders of a *particular* target are better off if a higher bid is attracted. Shareholders of that target both share in the gains to potential target shareholders as a class from the passivity of other companies and secure a private gain by seeking competitive bids when an offer is made for their company. In short, pure passivity cannot be a stable equilibrium in the absence of enforcement.

The disadvantages of competitive bidding to the initial offerer are simply the mirror image of the benefits to a target company from seeking competitive bids. This section considers the range of strategic approaches available to an offerer to reduce the likelihood of a competing bid that, at worst, will capture the prize and, in any event, will inevitably raise the price. We start with consideration of the problem in the context of friendly—negotiated—transactions where subsequent offers are uninvited and where the cooperation of the target can be expected in devising barriers to competition in the market for corporate control. We then consider the extent to which these or other strategies can be effective in the very different context of a hostile bid where the bidder's object is to discourage a white knight, who can be anticipated to have the target's cooperation, rather than to prevent a hostile overbid from interfering with a friendly transaction.

1. Friendly Transactions

In a friendly transaction, a potential acquirer and the target company have the occasion to cooperate in discouraging competing bids in two different situations. The first situation is that of a negotiated transaction, undertaken without pressure and where management of the target company believes its acquisition by the particular acquirer is desirable. In this situation, the acquiring company may want assurances that the transaction will succeed before beginning it and, precisely because target management favors the transaction, it is prepared to cooperate. The second situation where the target company and a potential acquirer have an incentive to cooperate is when a different acquirer has made an initial hostile bid which the target company disfavors. Here the target company is trying to persuade a would-be "white knight" to make a competitive bid and the favored acquirer is unwilling to proceed unless the target company will cooperate to assure that there will be no further bidding by the original hostile offerer or anyone else.

a. *Techniques*

FREUND & EASTON, THE THREE–PIECE SUITOR: AN ALTERNATIVE APPROACH TO NEGOTIATED CORPORATE ACQUISITIONS
34 Bus.Law. 1680, 1680–95 (1979).*

Aardvark Corp., a public company looking to be acquired, has a number of potential suitors. Your large corporate client is one of them.

*You are concerned, however, that the public announcement of an agree-
ment in principle on a merger will signal one or more other interested
companies to make a competing bid during the lengthy period prior to
the time the deal closes. You are also conscious of the risk that the
market price of Aardvark stock will run up toward the proposed premium while negotiations for the agreement in principle are underway.
Aardvark's two principal stockholders own 55 per cent of its outstanding
stock.*

* * *

[This situation] represents [an] instance where a fresh approach to
negotiated corporate acquisitions had been successfully utilized—[an]
instance in which, had the conventional format been followed, the
acquiring company might have lost out on the deal or wound up paying
a higher price. The new approach, which might be termed the multistep acquisition (and its architect, the three-piece suitor), begins with a
cash private purchase (generally from an insider) of a substantial block
of the target's stock; is followed by a cash tender offer to public
stockholders at the same price; and concludes with a cash merger of
the target and a subsidiary of the acquiring company at the same price.
When the dust clears, the acquiring company owns 100 per cent of the
target. In recent years, more and more deals involving public target
companies are being done this way. The purpose of this article is to
analyze this important and relatively new acquisition technique.

I. THE EMERGENCE OF THE MULTISTEP ACQUISITION

The Business Framework

In order to understand the increasing popularity of the multistep
acquisition, some brief business background is in order. In the old
black-and-white days, there used to exist a real dichotomy between
negotiated (or "friendly") acquisitions on the one hand, and hostile
takeovers on the other. In recent years, however, this dichotomy has
evolved into more of a continuum, with the absolutely friendly deal
(lacking even covert pressures) at one end of the spectrum; the absolutely unfriendly takeover (with no lines of communication open between the parties) at the other; and most deals falling somewhere
between the poles, not uncommonly possessing characteristics of each.

So, for example, a vulnerable target, lacking confidence in its
ability to thwart a potential acquiror's hostile approach, may turn from
discouraging the acquiror to negotiating a higher price for an uncon-
tested deal—or may seek a more tranquil haven with a willing third
party. A tart rebuff to the relatively friendly approach of an unwanted
suitor may lead to hostile maneuverings down the road. * * *

Just as the *substance* of acquisitions may vacillate on the friendly-
unfriendly scale, we are also witnessing the use of *methodologies*
formerly associated with unfriendly deals to accomplish friendly ones.
In the hostile situation, where the target's management and board
spurn an approach, the acquiror is forced to go over their heads to deal
directly with the target's stockholders by way of a tender offer—in
effect, to tempt them (with a substantial premium) to overrule manage-

ment. But, with the growing respectability of unfriendly acquisitions * * * the tender offer, having proved its effectiveness as a potent tool in accomplishing hostile takeovers, is now an accepted technique for use in friendly acquisitions, with little trace of the opprobrium formerly attending its deployment. Put another way, even in a transaction where matters can be dealt with at the corporate level—with the target's management and board fully involved and supportive—acquisition strategists are handling the initial stages at the stockholder level.

* * *

But the real impetus to the multistep acquisition has been the recognition that we are in the midst of an era of intense competition for desirable acquisition candidates—where auctions and bidding contests are very much the "in" thing.[15] Just as third parties invade hostile takeover territory—either invited in by the beleaguered target or simply attracted by the noise of the scuffle—uninvited acquirors are likely to barge in on friendly situations.[16]

Observe, e.g., Upforgrabs Inc. and Synergy Ltd., which have just agreed in principle that Synergy will acquire Upforgrabs. They announce their intentions. Pickemoff Corp., which has long had its eye on Upforgrabs (or whose interest is piqued by the announcement) decides to come in with a better offer than the one Synergy has made. Even if Pickemoff's intrusion is not warmly received, it must be dealt with by the Upforgrabs board. And Upforgrab's stockholders, whose concern may be less with management's feeling comfy in a new home than with the amount of money being paid for their shares, are likely to react favorably to the higher price. Synergy either has to quit or to fight (which presumably will entail upping its bid)—in the one case, losing the Upforgrabs deal; in the other, making it on less favorable terms.

So this is the context in which the multistep transaction has emerged as a highly practical alternative to the conventional one-step merger transaction for negotiated acquisitions of public companies— utilizing various tools of the acquisition trade formerly considered appropriate only in hostile or overreaching situations.

[15] Examples from recent years abound: United Technologies' bid for Babcock & Wilcox at $48 per share was "defeated" by J. Ray McDermott's final offer of $62.50 per share; Eaton's bid for Carborundum was topped by Kennecott's offer of $66.50 per share; and MCA's cash tender offer for Sea World at $22 per share was thwarted by Harcourt Brace's competing offer of $28.75 per share. See generally, *Take the Money and Run; Tender Offers Invariably Benefit Shareholders,* Barron's, Dec. 8, 1975, at 11, surveying a number of tender offers, which to the delight of the target company's stockholders, turned into bidding contests.

[16] Equitable General Corporation, for example, recently terminated a merger agreement with Great Southern Corporation to accept a higher offer from Gulf United Corporation. See Joint Proxy Statement of Gulf United Corporation and Equitable General Corporation, dated Nov. 24, 1978. Similarly, the Board of Directors of MBPXL Corporation recently cancelled a special meeting of its stockholders at which stockholders were to consider a proposed merger between MBPXL and ConAgra Inc. and recommended that MBPXL stockholders accept a tender offer being made at a higher price by Cargill, Incorporated. See Offer to Purchase Any and All Outstanding Shares of Common Stock of MBPXL Corporation by Cargill Holdings, Incorporated, a wholly owned subsidiary of Cargill, Incorporated, dated Dec. 7, 1978.

Synopsis of the Three Stages

[T]he "classic" multistep acquisition is accomplished in three consecutive stages, as follows:

1. The Block Purchase

The first step is a negotiated private purchase by the acquiring company (the "purchaser" or the "bidder"), usually for cash, of a substantial block of stock of the company being acquired (the "target") from a controlling stockholder or group if one exists, or from a large but noncontrolling holder (often institutional). The purchase agreement is generally quite short and simple.[19] Optimally, the parties provide for a simultaneous signing and closing; if delay is required,[20] it should be minimal with no substantial conditions to closing—just the passage of time. The principal collateral obligation contained in the agreement is the purchaser's undertaking to use its best efforts to make a cash offer to all other stockholders of the target, for any and all shares tendered, at the same price the blockholder is receiving. Upon signing of the agreement, a press release is issued—the first notice of the deal—announcing that the bidder has acquired (or, if the closing is not simultaneous, has signed a binding agreement to acquire) the block and has undertaken to make a tender offer on comparable terms to all other stockholders in the very near future.

2. The Tender Offer

The second step is the "friendly" tender offer itself, directed to all the stockholders of the target, for any and all of their shares, at the same price as was paid for the block. This should commence as soon as practicable after the signing and/or closing of the block purchase, subject to any delays required in order to obtain any necessary regulatory approvals. * * * Ideally, the target's board of directors should recommend acceptance of the offer to stockholders—or at least not oppose it and cooperate in its implementation (e.g., by furnishing a list of stockholders to facilitate mailing of the offer).

3. The Cash Merger

The third step is a merger transaction between the target and the bidder (or, more commonly, between the target and a subsidiary of the bidder), as a result of which the bidder ends up owning 100 per cent of the target. In this transaction, once the requisite stockholder vote is cast (with the presumption being that the bidder has acquired sufficient shares through the block purchase and tender to approve the merger), the target's remaining stockholders are involuntarily eliminated. In exchange for their shares, they receive a cash payment, which is generally equal to that received by the blockholder and tendering stockholders. In almost all cases, they have appraisal rights. Depend-

---

[19] An exception to this occurs where an employment contract is simultaneously negotiated. * * *

[20] In addition to any delay required in order to obtain necessary regulatory approvals, it may be necessary to defer the closing (or at least the closing of the pur-chase of a portion of the shares) in order to comply with the notification and waiting period requirements of the Hart-Scott-Rodino Antitrust Improvements Act of 1976, § 7A of the Clayton Act, 15 U.S.C. § 18a [hereinafter referred to as the "HSR Act"].

ing on the percentage of outstanding target shares owned by the bidder upon completion of the tender offer, a so-called short-form merger under applicable state corporate law may be utilized; [26] if not, regular statutory merger procedures apply, but with little suspense over the ultimate vote.

* * *

II. COMPARISON OF MULTISTEP ACQUISITION AND TRADITIONAL SINGLE–STEP MERGER

Review of Traditional Merger Phases

The variance in acquisition procedure and relative advantages and disadvantages of the three-piece suitor can best be examined if we turn for a moment to review the scenario for a traditional single-step merger.

The courtship begins with a period of preliminary negotiations between the parties—feeling each other out, trying to decide whether they can live together—with the principal emphasis on arriving at a mutually satisfactory price. If a meeting of the minds occurs, the parties are said to have reached an "agreement in principle" on the transaction. This might be oral, or it can be reduced to writing in a "letter of intent" or memorandum of understanding. This document reiterates the parties' mutual intent to merge at a stated (or formula) price, which is made expressly subject to the negotiation and execution of a definitive acquisition agreement, the approval of their respective boards of directors and at least the target's stockholders, and the obtaining of needed consents from major creditors and perhaps regulatory authorities. In other words, pending the signing and approval of the definitive agreement, the agreement in principle has no binding effect.

Nevertheless—and this is true whether it is written or oral—the agreement in principle is considered sufficient evidence of the parties' seriousness toward the transaction that a press release is invariably issued at this point, describing the basic terms of the deal. [41] As a result, the world is put on notice that the target is up for sale at a time when the parties are *not* contractually obligated to each other. There is nothing to stop any other company interested in acquiring the target from entering the fray. [42] Contrast this with the three-piece suitor's first public announcement, stating that it has *already* purchased (or at least entered into a firm agreement to purchase) the key block and that it is about to commence a tender offer for the balance of the target's shares.

---

[26] A short-form merger is a merger between a parent corporation and its subsidiary which does not require a vote of the subsidiary's minority stockholders where the parent owns at least a specified percentage (usually 90%) of the subsidiary's stock. Not all states permit short-form mergers.

[41] With respect to the legal obligation to make an announcement at this point, cf.

SEC v. Geon Industries, Inc., 531 F.2d 39 (2d Cir.1976); NYSE Company Manual § A–2 at A–18; ASE Manual § 402 at 101; (2d Cir.1976); SEC Securities Act Release No. 5092 (Oct. 15, 1970).

[42] This is true even where a definitive merger agreement has been signed. * * *

The period following agreement in principle in a conventional acquisition is one of three-fold activity: intense investigation of the target's affairs by the purchaser; [43] negotiation of the definitive merger agreement, with preparation of detailed schedules and lists concerning the target's structure and business; and preparation of a full-blown proxy statement containing detailed prospectus-style information about the deal, the target, and perhaps (if the purchaser will be issuing its securities) the purchaser, with full financial information including pro-forma statements. All this can easily take more than a month to complete. During the comparable period, a three-piece suitor is holding (or at least getting started on) its tender offer for any and all of the target's remaining shares. By the time the parties are ready to sign a binding agreement in a traditional acquisition, the three-piece suitor may well own a substantial majority of the target's shares—without any worries over preparing and clearing a detailed proxy statement at this stage.

Let's assume that all the information has been gathered and analyzed to everyone's satisfaction, the companies' respective boards of directors have met and approved the final form of the traditional merger agreement, and it is then signed by their designated officers. The agreement will invariably provide for a deferred closing, because prior to the deal being consummated some events have to occur which cannot even get underway until the agreement is signed—most notably, the proxy solicitation of the target's stockholders. Moreover, a number of other conditions have to be satisfied in order for the parties to be obligated to close; put another way, even with careful drafting, each party may have several "escape valves" were it to consider wriggling out of the agreement.

If the target is an attractive one, "grey knights"—dripping with cash or proffering attractive securities—can be expected to enter the picture. The obligations of the target's board of directors in the event a better offer materializes after an agreement of merger has been signed is the subject of some controversy [44] and a cautious target may want to provide specifically in the merger agreement that its board is free to accept—if not to solicit—a better offer.[45]

Even where the merger agreement itself contains no usable "out", the target's board is going to have to consider any higher third party proposals seriously—and would be hard-pressed to recommend the purchaser's lesser offer. And, as a practical matter, since approval by

[43] This is less likely to be *vice versa* if the deal is for cash; but if securities of the purchaser are to be issued, then the target has to investigate the purchaser also.

[44] See generally Ward, *The Legal Effect of Merger and Asset Sale Agreements Before Shareholder Approval,* 18 W.Res.L. Rev. 780 (1967).

[45] See, e.g., Agreement and Plan of Reorganization among Johns-Manville Corportion, JM Capital Corporation and Olinkraft, Inc., attached to Joint Proxy Statement of Johns-Manville Corporation and Olinkraft, Inc., dated Dec. 1, 1978, containing one version of the so-called "law firm out"—which provides that the target's board of directors will not approve or recommend to stockholders any business combination or similar transaction with a company other than the bidder unless in the opinion of the target's counsel the directors' fiduciary duties require them to do so.
* * *

the target's stockholders is always requisite, and since they can't be expected to vote for the negotiated deal if a better competing offer materializes,[46] the existence of a signed contract by no means assures the purchaser of ultimate success. Even if the third party were spurned by the target, it could go over the heads of the target's board directly to the stockholders—attempting to buy enough shares through a tender offer to defeat the merger. The chances are pretty good that, if the purchaser wants to preserve its deal, it will have to jack up the price to meet the competition. In contrast, by the time a three-piece suitor gets around to signing a merger agreement, it already owns sufficient shares to approve the transaction—and more than enough shares to discourage outside intervention by third party predators.

Once the traditional merger agreement has been signed, the proxy statement is filed with the SEC.[49] Processing by the staff can easily take a month before final clearance, at which time the material is mailed to stockholders with a solicitation period of another month before the meeting takes place.[50] Once the meeting has been held and the deal approved, it can close immediately—provided that all other conditions have been satisfied; and some, such as the receipt of tax rulings from the Internal Revenue Service, can take quite a while to come through.

If you add up the time—a month here, a month there—at best it will take three or four months from the time the deal is first announced until closing. In today's environment, that's a long time for the purchaser to own nothing except some tenuous contractual rights.

Advantages of the Multistep Technique

As must be obvious by now, the principal advantage of the multistep approach is to lessen the likelihood of a competing bid—to more effectively freeze out the competition. * * * In a multistep transaction, at the point when the world discovers what's up, the bidder already owns, or has locked up, a substantial chunk of the target's

---

[46] Information as to the higher competing offer would be required to be highlighted in the proxy statement for the negotiated transaction or a supplement thereto. See, e.g., U.S. Smelting, Refining and Mining Co. v. Clevite Corp., [1969–70 Transfer Binder] Fed.Sec.L.Rep. (CCH) ¶ 92,691 (N.D.Ohio 1968); Gerstle v. Gamble-Skogmo, Inc., 478 F.2d 1281, 1295 (2d Cir. 1973); cf. Scott v. Multi-Amp Corp., 386 F.Supp. 44 (D.N.J.1974).

[49] Actually, ther's no reason why the proxy materials cannot be filed prior to the time the agreement is executed, if the parties want to expedite the transaction. However, since much of the disclosure contained in the proxy staement consists of a description of the terms of the merger, it is advisable to wait before filing until a fully negotiated (albeit unsigned) agreement is produced.

[50] Most states require that notice of a meeting generally be given at least ten but not more than 50 or 60 days prior to the meeting. See, e.g., Del.Gen.Corp.Law § 222 (not less than ten nor more than 60 days); N.Y.Bus.Corp.Law § 605 (not less than ten nor more than 50 days). Some states have specific notice provisions applicable to mergers. See, e.g., Del.Gen.Corp. Law § 251(c) (at least 20 days' advance notice). Although the rules of the New York Stock Exchange do not specify a minimum advance notice requirement, the Exchange recommends that a minimum of 30 days be allowed between the record date and the meeting date. See NYSE Company Manual § A–8 at A–132. The rules of the American Stock Exchange require that at least ten days' written notice be given in advance of all stockholders' meetings, and the Exchange recommends that at least 20 days' advance notice be given. See ASE Company Guide § 703 at 181.

stock, and is about to launch its tender offer. Possession may not be nine-tenths of the law, but it is clear that any potential competitor is *not* starting from a point of equality—as it would be had the purchaser and target merely initialed a letter of intent, lacking contractual obligations, and with their mutual willingness to go forward subject to a variety of specified conditions.

Thus, in the first situation [noted at the outset of this article], since the announcement identified the bidder as now owning 55 percent of Aardvark Corp., no competition was allowed to develop—although there were later indications that, had the deal proceeded in traditional fashion, there may have been a competing bid at a higher price.

Secondly, the multistep method helps assure the bidder of success in consummating the deal. In a conventional merger, where either a majority or two-thirds vote of the target's outstanding shares is usually required to approve the transaction, the purchaser cannot be certain of achieving the requisite vote; after all, the purchaser itself is not voting, since it does not own any of the target's shares. The three-piece suitor, on the other hand, is likely to end up—through the block purchase and a successful tender offer—with the requisite stock ownership to authorize the final-step merger single-handedly, thereby lessening the risk that the deal will abort.

A third advantage of the multistep transaction relates to the stock market's significant role in acquisitions. It's quite typical today, no matter what form the deal takes, for bidders to pay significant premiums over the current market value of the target's stock. Where extended negotiations between the companies occur prior to an announcement—neither side wanting to make premature disclosure before reaching an agreement in principle [54]—rumors of an impending deal almost inevitably leak out. The rumors propel the stock price upward toward the bidder's anticipated premium. When the announcement finally comes, the merger price makes less of a splash than it would have prior to the market run-up.

Assume that the target's stock has been selling for around $10. The purchaser proposes to offer $15. Rumors inflate the market price to $12.50. Instead of a 50 per cent premium, the spread is only 20 per cent when the announcement is finally made. Stockholders, who have notoriously short memories, forget that the stock was selling at $10 only a few short days ago; the purchaser gets no credit for the run-up. The smaller premium makes it more likely that the target's board will become huffy about price (even to the point of trying to retrade the deal), more likely that other bidders will step up to the plate and, assuming the transaction is submitted to stockholders, less certain that they will vote in favor of the deal. More than once, this kind of involuntary market action has caused a purchaser to increase its initial price, in order to preserve the premium at a respectable level. So, one

[54] The New York Stock Exchange has expressed the view that once the negotiations have broadened in scope to include persons other than top management, and the risk of a leak or the misuse of inside information necessarily becomes greater, an announcement of the existence of negotiations should be made. See NYSE Company Manual § A–2 at A–19. * * *

of the real advantages of the multistep transaction is the reduced chances of a leak, since the target itself may not be directly involved in the early stages. With a little luck, the target's stock will still be selling at $10 when the announcement is made, and the bidder (and, indirectly, the target's management and board) will get credit for the entire five-point premium.

A fourth advantage of the multistep deal—which is perhaps more psychological than substantive, but definitely not to be discounted—is the sense of moving a lot faster than in traditional terms. With a conventional merger, nothing really definitive happens (such as shares or money actually changing hands) until three or four months pass. Contrast the three-piece suitor, who on the *first day* owns a substantial block of the target; a month or so later, it owns at least a majority (and maybe much more) with its first purchases under the tender offer. Corporate executives react favorably to the speed with which a multistep deal is implemented. Lawyers who suggest this format tend to be looked upon as expeditors—makers of deals rather than authors of complexities. This is particularly true if the businessman has been considering the deal in traditional terms; imagine the reaction when you tell him: "I can get you a controlling intestest in the target a lot faster, while minimizing the risks of being outbid or forced to raise the ante."

Disadvantages of the Multistep Technique

Nothing is perfect; there are also disadvantages inherent in multistep deals. For example, at the time the bidder buys the blockholder's stock, it cannot know for sure whether it will be able to successfully complete the balance of the transaction and achieve 100 percent ownership. Multistep deals are definitely not for the faint-hearted. If the tender offer is unsuccessful and the initial block is insufficient for working control, the bidder could be left with a substantial investment, purchased at a premium (which the market may not support), and yet not be in control of the target. If the size of the block isn't large enough to preempt a competing bid (and the bidder is not prepared to increase its price), the bidder could lose out to another suitor. (This is not necessarily a disaster, however, since the losing bidder can usually sell its block into the competing tender, presumably at a profit, thereby at least recouping its expenses—and generally without liability under section 16(b) of the Exchange Act even though the block exceeds 10 percent of the outstanding shares.) [58]

[58] Section 16(b) provides that any profits realized by, among others, a beneficial owner of more than 10% of a class of an issuer's registered equity securities from any purchase and sale or any sale and purchase of any of the issuer's equity securities within a period of less than six months are recoverable by or on behalf of the issuer. But since there can be no § 16(b) liability unless the person was a greater than 10% beneficial owner *prior* to *both* the purchase and the subsequent sale, there is no § 16(b) liability in respect of the initial purchase which makes the bidder a greater than 10% shareholder. See Foremost-McKesson, Inc. v. Provident Securities Co., 423 U.S. 232 (1976). Even if the purchaser has made additional purchases after becoming a greater than 10% stockholder and then sells its entire holdings within six months of its initial purchases, its liability will be limited to the profit realized on the purchases made after becoming a 10% stockholder. Cf. Reliance Elec. Co. v. Emerson Elec. Co., 404 U.S. 418 (1972).

Perhaps the most significant disadvantage of the three-step transaction is that the bidder has no chance to perform the extensive business and legal review that occurs in a traditional acquisition *before* the purchaser is bound. In the period between agreement in principle and execution of a definitive agreement, the one-step purchaser has its people swarming all over the target, collecting data on a great variety of matters. At the same time, the target is compiling reams of information about itself into formal schedules and lists which are usually attached to the contract and which—together with other business, financial and legal facts concerning the target— become the subject of elaborate representations and warranties. In the period between signing and closing the purchaser monitors the accuracy of these representations, which are deemed reiterated at the closing for purposes of a condition to the purchaser's obligation to close. All of this tends to insure that by the time the purchaser actually puts its money or securities on the line, it knows exactly what it's getting into; the risks based on ignorance of the facts are few and far between.

The three-piece suitor, however, is unlikely to have the same opportunities for investigation and verification, for extensive warranties and correlative conditions. As a matter of fact, the bidder would probably prefer not to know too much about the target's business at the time of the tender, since any significant nonpublic information in the bidder's possession (such as the target's favorable financial projections) would have to be disclosed in the bidder's offering materials. So, the bidder usually proceeds on the basis of the target's audited financial statements and other SEC filings, hoping that any shortfall will not be material, and forced into greater reliance on the honesty and candor of the selling blockholder.

Another disadvantage is that the multistep approach does not lend itself so well to noncash transactions—at least during the first two stages. Although securities could presumably be issued to the blockholder without a registration statement in reliance on section 4(2) of the Securities Act of 1933 or rule 146 thereunder, the blockholder may be unwilling to accept them because of the resale limitations under rule 144. If the second-step offer to the target's stockholders were to consist of the bidder's securities (rather than cash), a registration statement and prospectus would have to be filed and cleared with the SEC prior to commencing the offer, thereby causing considerable delay—which detracts from the preemptive nature of the multistep approach.

Unless a fixed maximum number of shares is built into the tender offer, exclusive use of cash at the first two stages will normally make it difficult, if not impossible, to structure the final-step merger as a tax-free reorganization—since the bidder will probably purchase so much of the target's stock for cash that the continuity of interest rules applicable to tax-free reorganizations will not be satisfied. A sizeable use of cash will also preclude accounting for the acquisition as a pooling of interests.

The multistep acquisition is more prone to litigation than a conventional transaction, particularly in connection with the final-step cash merger. In large part this is due to the recent flurry of "going private" cases, and the apparent resemblance of the final stage of the multistep transaction to freezeouts of minority stockholders (the bidder having sufficient votes to force only the target's remaining stockholders).*

———————————◆———————————

Note: Expanding the Concept: Lock-ups and Leg-ups

Both the problem and the solution identified by Freund & Easton can be generalized. Once the friendly offerer and the target have struck a deal, the problem of devising strategies for discouraging a competitive bid closely resembles the problem of devising effective defensive tactics: How do you alter the business opportunity confronting a potential competitive bidder (hostile offerer) so as to convince it that the transaction is no longer favorable? Thus, the same approach that we used to evaluate the efficacy of post-offer defensive tactics in Section B.2.b. of Chapter Fourteen also can be used to evaluate the efficacy of strategies intended to disadvantage competitive bidders. As with a hostile bidder, the competitive bidder's decision rule can be represented as $V > P + TC$ where V is the post-transaction value of the target to the competitive bidder, P is the price to be paid for the target, and TC are the transaction costs of effecting the acquisition. Any strategy intended to discourage a competitive bidder must either lower V and/or raise P and TC.

The range of strategies designed to discourage competitive bidding can be arrayed along a continuum of likely effectiveness. At the ineffective pole might be a single step transaction but with a contractual undertaking in the acquisition agreement committing target management to use its best efforts to cause the shareholders of the target to approve the transaction and, perhaps, also prohibiting target management from negotiating or providing non-public information to other parties. How does this approach effect the offer calculus?

Further along the continuum toward effectiveness is the general approach suggested by Freund & Easton, supra. Their solution is to acquire a large enough block of the target's shares, either by purchase from one or more substantial shareholders or through open-market purchases where there are no large holders, so that potential competitive bidders are effectively prevented from entering the fray because the contest is already over. Put in terms of our offer calculus, this strategy has the effective of raising P since the price necessary to make the acquisition is no longer that at which the target would have sold, but is now the presumably much higher price at which the acquiring company would sell its newly obtained position.

Other variations of this approach may be even more effective. As Freund & Easton point out, a block purchase may not be available in

* These issues are considered in Section
B. of this Chapter, infra. [Ed.]

the absence of some concentration of share holdings, and open market transactions may be difficult in the face of Federal regulation of tender offers. See Chapter Sixteen, infra. In any event, when the initial stock acquisition is of less than "real" control, there is also the risk that the transaction will not be successful and the "three piece suitor," now left with a minority position in a company controlled by someone else, will have lost his pants. Both difficulties—the absence of an available block and the risk of taking a block position before the ultimate success of the transaction can be assured—may be alleviated by casting the original transaction in the form of an acquisition of an option to purchase unissued shares from the target corporation. The downside risk is avoided because, if the acquisition ultimately turns out to be unworkable, the option simply is not exercised. The absence of large shareholders who will part with a block is avoided because the target company has an infinite number of unissued shares.[3]

The effect of this technique can be seen by considering the option granted United States Steel ("USS") by Marathon Oil Co. in order to induce USS to make a bid competing with an initial hostile bid by Mobil Oil.[4] At the time the USS option was granted, Mobil had offered to acquire 68% of Marathon's common stock for $85 per share in cash, with the remainder to be acquired in a second-step merger where the consideration would be Mobil debentures with a principal amount of $85 per share. The terms of the option gave USS the right to purchase ten million authorized but unissued Marathon shares (approximately 17% of Marathon's outstanding stock) for $90 per share at any time between the commencement of a USS tender offer for 51% of the Marathon shares at $125 per share in cash, and the effective date of a second-step merger in which the consideration would be USS debentures with a principal amount of $100 per share.[5] The impact of the option can be seen by considering the "leg up" the option would give USS in a subsequent bidding contest with Mobil. If Mobil were to increase its bid, it would have to purchase all shares at the increased bid price. In contrast, if USS were to increase its bid, it would still be able to purchase 17% of Marathon's stock at the lower option price, thereby insuring that it would always pay a lower total price than Mobil for the same number of shares. As stated in the opinion of the Sixth Circuit considering the validity of the option, the effect of the option was "that every dollar raise in the bid by USS would cost USS $30 million, while each such dollar raise would cost Mobil $47 million."[6]

---

[3] A problem exists if the target's articles of incorporation do not authorize a sufficient number of shares to accomplish the option, because there is unlikely to be enough time to amend the target's articles of incorporation.

[4] In the USS/Marathon transaction, the initial offer was hostile and the lock-up was intended to encourage a white knight to make a competing bid. The desired result was to cut off a responsive bid from the original hostile bidder. Analysis of the effectiveness of the technique is no different when the lock-up is given to encourage

an initial bid and discourage competing bids from third parties.

[5] The Stock Option Agreement between USS and Marathon is reproduced in Bialkin & Lampert, *Lock-Up Devices in Friendly and Hostile Acquisitions*, in 1 Fourteenth Annual Institute on Securities Regulation 669, 701 (PLI, 1982).

[6] Marathon Oil Company v. Mobil Corporation, 669 F.2d 366, 375 (6th Cir.1981). The legality of the options granted USS are considered later in this section and in Chapter Sixteen, infra.

A similar approach was used in the acquisition of Marshall Field & Company by BATUS at a time when a group controlled by Carl Icahn already owned 30% of Field's outstanding stock. See Section B.2.a. of Chapter Fourteen, supra. BATUS entered into a stock purchase agreement with Field committing BATUS to purchase and Field to sell two million shares of treasury stock at $25.50 per share. This was the same price as the original BATUS offer, although the tender offer price was increased to $30 per share shortly after the purchase agreement was announced. While cast in terms of a purchase agreement, the arrangement was in fact an option because BATUS could be relieved of its obligation to purchase the shares if it or a third party obtained 51% of Field's stock.[7] The effect of the arrangement was the same as that of the USS option.

Moving even further in the direction toward effectiveness is another form of option, this time covering target company assets instead of target company stock. Suppose you could identify that portion of the target's assets which were critical to its attractiveness to a competitive bidder—its "crown jewels" in takeover parlance. Giving the friendly bidder an option to purchase those assets exercisable only if the contest was lost to a competitive bid would have a substantial impact on the V element of the offer calculus of a competitive bidder. Again, the U.S. Steel/Marathon and Marshall Field/BATUS transactions illustrate how this technique works.

In the U.S. Steel/Marathon transaction, USS was granted an option to purchase for $2.8 billion Marathon's 48% interest in the oil and mineral rights in the Yates Field in West Texas, one of the most prolific domestic sources of oil ever discovered. The option was exercisable only if USS's offer was unsuccessful and a third party acquired control of Marathon.[8] In the court's terms, the effect of the option was that "a potential competing tender offeror could not acquire Yates Field upon a merger with Marathon." Marathon Oil Company v. Mobil Corporation, supra at 367. Stressing the importance of the Yates Field, the court pointed out that it had been referred to by Marathon as the company's "crown jewel," and that other companies had indicated that they would have no interest in Marathon in the absence of the Yates Field. Id.

In the Fields/BATUS transaction, the option covered Marshall Field's crown jewels: the assets of its Chicago division. See *Marshall Field's Too Successful Strategy,* Fortune 82 (March 22, 1982). BATUS obtained a right of first refusal to purchase the Chicago properties if they were sold at any time within a year of the termination of the Fields/BATUS transaction. If that option was exercised, payment could be made by transfer of Field's stock owned by BATUS (presumably acquired through its share option) which would be valued at the

---

[7] See Marshall Field & Company v. Icahn, 537 F.Supp. 413 (S.D.N.Y.1982). Why would BATUS wish to be relieved of its obligation under the purchase agreement if it obtained 51% of the stock under its tender offer?

[8] The Yates Field Option Agreement is reproduced in Bialkin & Lampert, supra at 709.

price paid by BATUS for the stock. Why would the provision specifying the value of the Field's shares be critical to BATUS?

Can the lock up approach be used in situations where the target does not have unique tangible assets? For example, could contingent employment contracts with key employees serve a similar purpose in high technology companies? Where business relationships were key, could creation of contingent joint ventures between the target and the friendly acquirer impact V in the desired fashion? To generalize, the key tasks in devising an effective lock-up are to identify what aspect of the target company is critical to a competitive bidder's estimate of the target company's value and to devise a means to transfer that asset or opportunity to the favored bidder on a contingent basis.

b. Legal Standards Governing the Use of Lock-Ups and Leg-Ups

In examining the courts' approach to the validity of lock-up and leg-up techniques, it is helpful to distinguish between two different settings based upon who is complaining. In one setting, the favored bidder is trying to enforce a commitment won from cooperative target management before a more desirable offer caused target management to switch sides. In a second setting, a shareholder of the target company or a competitive bidder objects to concessions granted the favored bidder. From the target shareholder's perspective, the complaint is that the concessions reduce the price the shareholder will ultimately receive by discouraging a competitive bid. From the competing bidder's perspective, the complaint is that the concessions block equal access to a desirable business opportunity and, hence, alter the structure of the market for corporate control. In both settings the complaining party seeks to narrow management's discretion; however, the goal of the favored bidder is to restrict competition, while the target shareholder or competitive bidder seeks to increase it.

(1) Enforcement by the Favored Bidder

Our discussion of the lock-up concept described techniques that varied substantially in their effectiveness. The least effective, it will be recalled, were contractual commitments by the target company to use its best efforts to secure shareholder approval of the transaction or to refrain from soliciting other bids. More effective were stock and asset lock-ups that committed to the original bidder much more than the target company's good faith. In determining what legal standards should apply to these two categories of lock-ups, the courts have taken sharply different paths.

GREAT WESTERN PRODUCERS CO-OPERATIVE v. GREAT WESTERN UNITED CORPORATION

Supreme Court of Colorado, 1980.
200 Colo. 180, 613 P.2d 873.

I.

Facts

* * *

Great Western United Corporation (United) is a holding company, the principal asset of which is a wholly-owned subsidiary, the Great Western Sugar Company (Sugar Company). In 1971 and 1972, as part of a recapitalization effort, United entered into negotiations for the sale of the stock of the Sugar Company to the Great Western Producers Co-Operative (Co-op), an organization comprised primarily of sugar beet producers. The Co-op had been formed in 1971 for the purpose of purchasing the Sugar Company from United.

* * *

[After an earlier agreement for the sale of Sugar Company to Co-op was not consummated,] on March 22, 1974, after further negotiations, United and the Co-op executed a second purchase agreement, pursuant to which United agreed to sell, and the Co-op agreed to buy, the outstanding stock of the Sugar Company. Immediately prior to the execution of the agreement, United's investment advisor had issued an opinion letter favoring the sale, and United's board of directors had unanimously determined that it was in United's best interests to sell the Sugar Company on the terms set forth in the purchase agreement.

Because the stock of the Sugar Company was United's major asset, it was necessary that United's security holders approve the sale to the Co-op.[2] Consummation of the purchase agreement was conditioned on that approval, and the agreement stated that:

> "United will use its best efforts to obtain the approval of its shareholders and debentureholders whose approval is solicited."

The purchase agreement was to be "deemed terminated and abandoned by mutual consent if not consummated on or before October 1, 1974," which was the closing date.

After the agreement was executed, United prepared proxy materials and submitted them to the federal Securities and Exchange Commission. At meetings in May and July 1974, United's board of directors voted unanimously in favor of the resolutions reaffirming the determination, first made in March 1974, that consummation of the purchase agreement would be in United's best interests.

---

[2] United is incorporated under the laws of the State of Delaware, and security holder approval of the purchase agreement is governed by Del.Code Ann. tit. 8, § 271(a). [See Chapter Thirteen B. Ed.]

During the summer and fall of 1974, the price of sugar and the projected and actual profits of the Sugar Company escalated, causing a corresponding increase in the value of the Sugar Company.

On August 15, 1974, United's board of directors reviewed the price and profit increases. For the first time, the members of the board were not unanimous in favoring the sale of the Sugar Company to the Co-op. Nonetheless, a majority voted to affirm the board's prior resolutions favoring the sale.

On August 24, 1974, the board of directors met to review the matters considered on August 15. A majority of the directors in attendance voted in favor of resolutions stating that the consideration to be received by United pursuant to the purchase agreement was fair and recommending that the security holders approve the sale.

On August 28, 1974, United distributed a proxy statement to its security holders, informing them that a majority of the board of directors believed the consideration stated in the purchase agreement to be fair and equitable and that a majority of the board recommended that the security holders approve the sale. The security holders were also informed that a minority of the directors disagreed because of the increases in sugar prices and operating profits. The August 28 proxy statement included a solicitation by United of proxies in favor of the purchase agreement.

Shortly after September 9, 1974, United's president learned that at least one-half of the members of the board of directors no longer favored the terms of the purchase agreement. Accordingly, United suspended proxy solicitation based on the information supplied to the security holders in the August 28 proxy statement.

A special meeting of the board of directors was held on September 14, 1974. At that meeting, the board voted to accept a revised, higher projection of sugar prices and operating revenues. On the basis of that vote, United's investment advisor withdrew its opinion favoring the terms of the purchase agreement. Two resolutions were adopted by a majority of the board of directors. The first recommended that the security holders disapprove the purchase agreement since the board no longer thought the consideration stated in the agreement to be fair. The second directed United's management to continue solicitation of proxies in favor of the purchase agreement "in view of the Corporation's obligations to the Co-Operative."

Meanwhile, on September 9 and 11, 1974, two shareholder derivative suits had been filed in the United States District Court for the Southern District of New York, alleging that the August 28 proxy statement violated both federal securities laws and the common law fiduciary duties of United's board of directors. On September 19, 1974, after learning of the September 14 change in the directors' recommendation to the security holders, the federal judge * * * entered a temporary restraining order enjoining United from using the proxies which it had received pursuant to the August 28 proxy statement. On September 20, 1974, the federal judge was further informed that United intended to continue proxy solicitation in favor of the purchase agreement, even though the revised proxy materials through which the favorable votes would be solicited would state that a majority of the board of directors had recommended that the security holders disapprove the purchase agreement. The judge enjoined the use of United's revised proxy materials, taking notice of the probability that United's security holders would erroneously assume that unmarked proxies would be voted consistently with the recommendation of the board of directors, i.e., against rather than for the purchase agreement.

Proxy solicitation in favor of the purchase agreement was never resumed. On September 20, 1974, United distributed a supplemental proxy statement advising the security holders that the board of directors recommended against the sale of the Sugar Company and that unmarked proxies would be voted consistently with that recommendation. On September 30, 1974, the security holders' meeting was held. Sufficient votes were not obtained to approve the purchase agreement.

* * *

United brought an action in the trial court, seeking a declaratory judgment that the purchase agreement had been terminated and abandoned by mutual consent of the parties. The Co-op counterclaimed, alleging a breach by United of its "best efforts" obligation under the purchase agreement.

* * *

Although this case involves a transaction of some complexity, the issue presented for review, as we perceive it, is well defined and narrow. That issue is whether the "best efforts" clause contained in the March 22, 1974, purchase agreement prevented or prohibited United's board of directors from reversing their original recommendation that United's security holders approve the sale of stock of the Sugar Company. The Co-op argues that such a limitation was placed on the directors and that the "best efforts" obligation was therefore breached on September 14, 1974, when the board of directors reversed its prior recommendation favoring the purchase agreement. We disagree.

* * *

In the absence of evidence justifying a contrary inference, it will be presumed that the parties to a contract intended to form a lawful and enforceable agreement. * * * On the basis of this rule, we conclude that United and the Co-op did not intend that the "best efforts" clause would impose on United's board of directors any obligation which would conflict with the directors' legal duties to the corporation's security holders. These duties include fidelity, good faith, and prudence with respect to the interests of security holders, as well as the duty to exercise independent judgment with respect to matters committed to the discretion of the board of directors and lying "at the heart of the management of the corporation." Chapin v. Benwood Foundation, Inc., 402 A.2d 1205, 1210 (Del.Ch.1979). * * * Pursuant to § 271(a) of the "General Corporation Law of the State of Delaware," United's directors were required to determine whether the terms, conditions, and consideration set forth in the 1974 purchase agreement were "expedient and for the best interests of the corporation." In our view, the determination required by § 271(a) lies "at the heart" of the directors' corporate management duties, and the directors may not lawfully agree to abrogate the continuing duty to exercise their independent judgment with respect to that determination.[6]

* * *

The "best efforts" obligation required that United and its board of directors make a reasonable, diligent, and good faith effort to accomplish a given objective, *viz.*, security holder approval of the purchase agreement. The obligation, however, must be viewed in the context of unanticipated events and the exigencies of continuing business development and cannot be construed to require that such events and exigencies be ignored or overcome at all costs. In short, the "best efforts" obligation was tempered by the directors' over-riding duties under §§ 141(a) and 271(a) of the General Corporation Law of the State of Delaware.

We therefore hold that the "best efforts" clause did not bind United's board of directors to recommend security holder approval of the purchase agreement when, subsequent to the execution of the agreement and the directors' initial determination under § 271(a), the directors inquired into changed circumstances and determined, pursuant to the exercise of their independent good faith judgment, that the terms of the purchase agreement were no longer in the security holders' best interests.

◆

Note: The Scope of the Tort of Intentional Inteference With Contractual Relations

In *Great Western*, the only issue posed was whether target management had breached its contractual obligation to the originally favored bidder to use its best efforts to cause the transaction to be approved. The form of the action becomes more complicated, however, when the event occasioning target management's change of heart is not a subsequent change in the target's business fortunes, as in *Great Western*, but a competitive bid which is more favorable to the target. In this situation, two potential defendants are available to the original bidder: The *target company*, whose management did not fulfill its contractual obligations to champion the original transaction, and the *competitive bidder* who really caused the problem by offering a higher price after the target company directors had approved the original transaction. Claims against the competitive bidder are typically cast in terms of the tort of intentional interference with contractual relations or competitive advantage.[9]

---

[6] Cf. Del.Code Ann. tit. 8, § 271(b), which authorizes a corporation's board of directors to abandon a proposed sale of all or substantially all of the corporation's assets after security holder approval for the sale has been secured. The abandonment authorized by § 271(b) is presumably predicated on a change in the directors' prior determination that the sale is "for the best interests of the corporation."

[9] For an analysis of this area of tort law, see, e.g., Perlman, *Interference with Contract and Other Economic Expectancies: A Clash of Tort and Contract Theory*, 49 U.Chi.L.Rev. 61 (1982).

Distinguishing between the two potential defendants in an action by the original bidder serves to highlight the different considerations that bear on selecting the standards that should apply to each. Consider first the position of the target company's management, confronted with a competitive offer more favorable than the offer which originally had been approved—the *Great Western* situation. In *Great Western*, the attractiveness of the original offer depended on one's expectations about the future price of sugar. Certainly if the business were a sole proprietorship, the owner would not be relieved of an obligation to sell the business simply because the buyer had more accurately predicted the future course of commodity prices. Similarly, a sole owner of a business would not be relieved of his obligations under a contract to sell the business simply because someone later offered a higher price. Is there anything about the agency relationship between management and shareholders that dictates releasing management from an agreement fairly made in light of the information then available?

The structural approach pursued in Chapters Thirteen and Fourteen sheds light on this question. A proposed acquisition presents target management with an unavoidable conflict of interest. Side payments may encourage approval of a transaction at too low a price; a desire to retain control may encourage rejecting a transaction despite a very favorable price. This conflict is controlled not by eliminating target management's role, but by adding a role for target shareholders. Thus, management is charged with making the best deal it can and the shareholders then express their independent evaluation of that deal either through the statutory vote required to approve a merger or sale of assets, or through their response to a competing bid made directly to them by means of a tender offer.

This analysis suggests that the enforceability of target management's contractual commitments—for example, not to negotiate with a competitive bidder—is a quite different issue from whether a competitive bidder interferes with the original bidder's contractual relations by doing no more than making a competitive tender offer. Opportunity for target shareholders to consider a competitive bid is central to the mechanisms that serve as a check on target management's discretion to enter into a negotiated transaction. In contrast, releasing target management from its contractual commitments provides no additional check.

This distinction was explicitly drawn by the court in Belden Corp. v. InterNorth, Inc., 90 Ill.App.3d 547, 45 Ill.Dec. 765, 413 N.E.2d 98 (1980). There Crouse-Hinds, Inc. ("Crouse") had agreed to acquire Belden Corporation through a merger. Pending the closing of the merger, InterNorth made a tender offer directly to Crouse shareholders that threatened to defeat the merger. Belden then sued InterNorth claiming that the InterNorth tender offer intefered with its contractual relations—the merger which Crouse's management had approved. The court responded by distinguishing between the contractual obligation of a target company's directors to recommend a transaction and the freedom of a target company's shareholders to reject that recommendation in the face of a more attractive competing offer:

> [The merger agreement] gives Belden [the original offeror] an unequivocal right to receive the performance of Crouse's management, i.e., Belden is entitled to have the merger presented and recommended to Crouse's shareholders. Belden and its shareholders do *not*, however, have an unequivocal right to the benefits of the merger, since the power to approve the merger lies with the Crouse shareholders, and the contract imposes no duty on the shareholders to ratify the merger agreement. Belden therefore has an enforceable expectation with regard to the performance of Crouse's management, but has a mere expectancy with respect to consummation of the merger.
>
> These two levels of expectation require that InterNorth's interference with the merger agreement be evaluated by * * * differing standards * * * * If InterNorth is to be held liable for inducing a breach of contract, Belden must show that the contract was in fact breached, or, alternatively, that a breach is imminent * * * * Belden has not alleged that Crouse's management has breached any contractual duty [to recommend the transaction].[10]

Under this analysis, a target company's management is bound by its contractual obligations, but a competing bidder is free to offer target shareholders an alternative.[11]

Although target shareholders then have the opportunity to consider a competing offer under the *Belden* approach, the freedom given target management may be substantially narrower than under the approach in *Great Western*. What is the result under each approach if target management concludes that, as in *Great Western*, changed business conditions have made the previously agreed transaction unfavora-

---

[10] 413 N.E.2d at 102.

[11] This issue was touched on in dicta in Smith v. Van Gorkom, 488 A.2d 858 (Del.S. Ct.1985), which appears in Chapter Fourteen C., supra. In reviewing directors' alternatives with respect to submitting to the shareholders a merger agreement previously approved by the board of directors, the court stated:

> Under § 251(b), the Board had but two options: (1) to proceed with the merger and stockholder meeting, with the Board's recommendation of approval; or (2) to rescind its agreement with Pritzker, withdraw its proposal of merger, and notify its stockholders that the proposed shareholder meeting was canceled.
>
> But the second course of action would have clearly involved a substantial risk—that the Board would be faced with suit by Pritzker for breach of contract * * *. As previously noted, under the terms of the October 10 agreement, the Board's only ground for release from its agreement with Pritzker was its entry

into a more favorable definitive agreement to sell the Company to a third party.

Id. at 888. The reference to a breach of contract action if option (2) were followed seems to be consisent with the *Belden* approach: The board can bind itself based on the facts available at that time. Ambiguity is added, however, by the comment, immediately preceding the quotation above, that "[t]he Board could not remain committed to the Pritzker merger and yet recommend that its stockholders vote it down; nor could it take a neutral position and delegate to the stockholders the unadvised decision as to whether to accept or reject the merger." Id. The implication of this comment is that the Trans Union board could not follow the *Belden* approach by recommending the merger to its stockholders, as contractually committed, even if it believed that a competing offer was more favorable. Thus, whether Delaware will follow the *Belden* or *Great Western* approach remains unclear.

ble and not only refuses to recommend the original transaction to the shareholders, but affirmatively seeks out and negotiates with competitive bidders?

This is the situation presented in Jewel Companies, Inc., v. Pay Less Drug Stores Northwest, Inc., 741 F.2d 1555 (9th Cir.1984). Jewel and Pay Less Drug Stores ("Pay Less") entered into a merger agreement which contemplated the acquisition of Pay Less by Jewel and, *inter alia,* obligated Pay Less' board of directors to "use its best efforts" to see that the merger was completed and not to enter into any contract not in the ordinary course of business.

The announcement of the merger agreement's execution had precisely the effect Freund & Easton predicted at the outset of this section. Pay Less Drug Stores Northwest, Inc. ("Northwest") made a competing tender offer at a higher price and, when Northwest raised the price offered, Pay Less' board of directors unanimously recommended that Pay Less shareholders accept the offer. The board also entered into (i) an indemnity agreement whereby Northwest would indemnify Pay Less and its directors for any breach of the merger agreement with Jewel, and (ii) a new merger agreement with Northwest. Jewel responded by filing an action against Northwest alleging tortious interference with contractual relations.

The court rejected Northwest's claim that "the marketplace is the proper forum to resolve competing tender offers," [12] instead remanding the case to the trial court to determine whether the terms of the merger agreement with Jewel prohibited Pay Less from entering into a competing merger agreement with Northwest. If so, the trial court was directed "to determine whether * * * the actions of defendant Northwest constituted tortious interference with that contract." [13]

For our purposes, the meaning of the court's decision turns entirely on which "actions" of Northwest might constitute tortious interference. If only the signing by Northwest of its own merger agreement with Pay Less is at issue, the decision preserves the structural distinction drawn in *Belden* between the role of target directors and that of target shareholders.[14] If, alternatively, Northwest's mere making of a competing offer might constitute tortious interference, then the court has misunderstood the role of competing tender offers in the corporate structure. It is the very potential for such an offer—acting as a check on target management's incentive to favor itself in negotiating the terms of a friendly transaction—that justifies granting target management the discretion to bind itself in the first place.

[12] 741 F.2d at 1567.

[13] Id. at 1569.

[14] Support for this interpretation is found in footnote 13 of the court's opinion: "We do not decide whether upon the unsolicited receipt of a more favorable offer after signing a merger agreement the board still must recommend to its shareholders that they approve the initial proposal." Id. at 1564 n. 13. There is at least an implication that the mere making of a competing offer would not constitute tortious interference.

See Conagra, Inc. v. Cargill, Inc., 222 Neb. 136, 382 N.W.2d 576 (1986) (following *Great Western*).

(2) **Attack by the Competitive Bidder or Target Shareholder**

When target company management desires to assure that a friendly transaction will be successful, we have seen that analysis of the potential effectiveness of lock-up techniques is identical to analysis of the effectiveness of defensive tactics. When a would-be competitive bidder (or a target shareholder) complains that a lock-up technique prevents a higher offer from being made to the target shareholders, the objection is analogous to a target shareholder's objection to defensive tactics that block any offer. Thus, it should not be surprising that judicial analysis of this objection to lock-up techniques parallels the traditional analysis of objections to defensive tactics that we examined in Chapter Fourteen B.3.a.

In Crouse-Hinds Co. v. InterNorth, Inc.,[15] InterNorth made an unsolicited competitive tender offer for Crouse-Hinds which threatened to defeat a previously negotiated merger between Crouse-Hinds and Belden Corporation. In an effort to prevent InterNorth's tender offer from interfering with the friendly combination, Crouse-Hinds and Belden modified the original merger agreement to provide for an initial exchange of Crouse-Hinds stock for a number of Belden shares representing 49% of Belden's outstanding shares, following which the merger would occur at the same exchange rate. InterNorth then challenged the first-step share exchange, asserting that the terms of the new transaction were designed merely to perpetuate Crouse-Hinds' management in office.

CROUSE–HINDS COMPANY v. INTERNORTH, INC.

United States Court of Appeals, Second Circuit, 1980.
634 F.2d 690.

* * *

The standard in this Circuit for the granting of a preliminary injunction requires the moving party to show

"(a) irreparable harm and (b) either (1) likelihood of success on the merits or (2) sufficiently serious questions going to the merits to make them a fair ground for litigation and a balance of hardships tipping decidedly toward the party requesting the preliminary relief."

Putting aside questions of injury and hardship, which we need not reach here, it is clear that under this test a party is not entitled to injunctive relief if he does not show either a likelihood of success on the merits of his claim or such substantial questions going to the merits as to make them fair ground for litigation. Our review of the record convinces us that InterNorth made neither showing, and that the granting of injunctive relief was an abuse of the district court's discretion.

[15] 634 F.2d 690 (2d Cir.1980). Both this case and Belden v. InterNorth, Inc., supra, arose out of the same transaction.

The InterNorth claim that the district court found presented substantial questions for litigation is the contention that the Exchange Offer has no valid business purpose and is designed merely to perpetuate Crouse-Hinds's management in office. The starting point for analysis of an attack by a shareholder on a transaction of the corporation is the business judgment rule. The New York Court of Appeals has recently stated the rule as follows:

> [The business judgment rule] bars judicial inquiry into actions of corporate directors taken in good faith and in the exercise of honest judgment in the lawful and legitimate furtherance of corporate purposes. "Questions of policy of management, expediency of contracts or action, adequacy of consideration, lawful appropriation of corporate funds to advance corporate interests, are left solely to their honest and unselfish decision, for their powers therein are without limitation and free from restraint, and the exercise of them for the common and general interests of the corporation may not be questioned, although the results show that what they did was unwise or inexpedient." (Pollitz v. Wabash R.R. Co., 207 N.Y. 113, 124, 100 N.E. 721.)

* * *

> It appears to us that the business judgment doctrine, at least in part, is grounded in the prudent recognition that courts are ill equipped and infrequently called on to evaluate what are and must be essentially business judgments. The authority and responsibilities vested in corporate directors both by statute and decisional law proceed on the assumption that inescapably there can be no available objective standard by which the correctness of every corporate decision may be measured, by the courts or otherwise. Even if that were not the case, by definition the responsibility for business judgments must rest with the corporate directors; their individual capabilities and experience peculiarly qualify them for the discharge of that responsibility. Thus, absent evidence of bad faith or fraud (of which there is none here) the courts must and properly should respect their determinations.

Auerbach v. Bennett, 47 N.Y.2d 619, 629–31, 419 N.Y.S.2d 920, 926–27, 393 N.E.2d 994 (1979). In Treadway Companies v. Care Corp.,* this Court summarized the workings of the business judgment rule as follows:

> Under the business judgment rule, directors are presumed to have acted properly and in good faith, and are called to account for their actions only when they are shown to have engaged in self-dealing or fraud, or to have acted in bad faith. Once a plaintiff demonstrates that a director had an interest in the transaction at issue, the burden shifts to the director to prove that the transaction was fair and reasonable to the corporation. Daloisio v. Peninsula Land Co., supra, 127 A.2d at 893; Geddes v. Anaconda Copper Co.,

---

* Treadway Companies v. Care Corporation, 638 F.2d 357 (2d Cir.1980). In that case the court was reviewing the validity of a merger with a white knight in the face of claims similar to those made by InterNorth in the instant case. [Ed.]

254 U.S. 590, 599, 41 S.Ct. 209, 212, 65 L.Ed. 425 (1921). Only if the director carries this burden will the transaction be upheld. *The initial burden of proving the director's interest or bad faith, however, always rests with the plaintiff.*

At 382 (emphasis added).

We find no basis in the present case for the district court's conclusion that InterNorth carried its burden of demonstrating self-interest or bad faith on the part of the Crouse-Hinds directors. As his starting point, the district judge gave extended consideration to the decision in *Treadway,* in which we found that because the Treadway directors, other than the chairman, were not to remain in office after the merger, perpetuation of their control could hardly have been their motivation for actions in furtherance of the merger. (See id. at 383.) Unfortunately, the district judge inferred from this that a quite different proposition must also be true—i.e., that if the directors *are* to remain on the board after the merger, perpetuation of their control *must be presumed* to be their motivation. This inference has no basis in either law or logic. *Treadway* did not disturb the normal requirement that a complaining shareholder present evidence of the directors' interest in order to shift the burden of proof to them.[21]

Such evidence as was offered by InterNorth to support the contention that the Exchange Agreement was intended solely to perpetuate the Crouse-Hinds directors' control must be viewed in the context of the two most striking aspects of this controversy. First, the Crouse-Hinds directors had negotiated the proposed merger with Belden in the belief that the merger was in the best interests of Crouse-Hinds. They had no indication at that time that InterNorth had any interest in Crouse-Hinds. Their good faith and lack of "interest" in entering into the merger agreement are unchallenged. (Indeed, their bona fides could not be attacked by InterNorth, because it was not a Crouse-Hinds shareholder when the proposed merger agreement was entered into.) * * * And the merger agreement required the Crouse-Hinds board to recommend approval by the shareholders.[22] Second, the InterNorth Tender Offer was expressly conditioned on the rejection or abandonment of the agreed-upon merger. There can be no genuine question that the Exchange Offer would increase the likelihood of consummation of the merger, since the Exchange Agreement requires Crouse-Hinds to

---

[21] In *Treadway,* for example, the conclusion that Treadway's chairman was "interested," was not based simply on the fact that he would remain in office following the merger. Rather, we noted that

[t]here was ample evidence to support a finding that Lieblich acted improperly, and determined, for his own selfish reasons and without giving the matter fair consideration, to oppose a Care takeover at all costs.[50]

[50] Most notable was the fact that Lieblich's view of the dollar value of the Fair Lanes merger proposal was apparently not affected

in any way by his learning that, contrary to his prior assumption, certain Fair Lanes assets were to be excluded from the deal.

At __.

[22] We know of no support for the district court's view that the Crouse-Hinds directors were required to "reconsider" the merger agreement that had been entered into and that they were contractually bound to recommend to shareholders. See Casey v. Woodruff, 49 N.Y.S.2d 625, 646 (Sup.Ct.N.Y.Co.1944). [*Great Western* was decided some three months before the court's decision here. Ed.]

vote all Belden shares acquired pursuant to the Exchange Offer in favor of the merger. In these circumstances, Crouse-Hinds's directors' attribution of the Exchange Offer to the facilitation of the merger they had negotiated is patently credible, at least in the absence of substantial evidence that their motives lie elsewhere.

The record support here for the contention and conclusion that the motivation for the Exchange Agreement was retention of control is unusually sparse, if not non-existent. No live testimony whatever was offered below, even though subjective issues such as motivation are particularly inappropriate for decision on the basis of a documentary presentation. * * * No depositions were taken by InterNorth of Crouse-Hinds officials on the subject of motivation.

* * *

What InterNorth relies on is (a) [Crouse-Hinds' Chief Executive Officer's] statement, upon hearing about the Tender Offer and the "Belden Condition," that Crouse-Hinds would resist the Tender Offer,[23] and (b) the statements in the Exchange Offer prospectus as to the goal of the Exchange Offer.[24] * * * What the prospectus said is that the Exchange Offer seeks (1) to facilitate the merger with Belden and (2) to discourage the InterNorth Tender Offer. But it must be recognized that InterNorth's imposition of the "Belden Condition" had made these purposes merely opposite sides of the same coin.

Thus, none of the proffered statements is sufficient to show director "interest" of the sort that is needed under the business judgment rule to shift the burden of proof to the directors. In short, when the tender offeror has presented the target company with an obvious reason to oppose the tender offer, the offeror cannot, on the theory that the target's management opposes the offer for some other, unstated, improper purpose, obtain an injunction against the opposition without presenting strong evidence to support its theory. We find no such evidence here.

The same court reached the same result when the issue was presented in a somewhat different context. In Buffalo Forge Co. v. Ogden Corp., 717 F.2d 757 (2d Cir.1983), cert. denied 464 U.S. 1018

[23] There is no statement in the Tender Offer that InterNorth would install a new Crouse-Hinds management; indeed, the Tender Offer states InterNorth has no such plans. InterNorth argues that if all its plans proceed to their intended conclusion, Crouse-Hinds will be a subsidiary company, with its board having to report to InterNorth, and that the Crouse-Hinds board would not be happy running a mere subsidiary company. This is far too meager a basis for a shifting of the burden of proof or the granting of a preliminary injunction.

[24] The fact that the initial decision to oppose the Tender Offer was made in four days does not prove that either that decision or the subsequent Exchange Agreement stemmed from a control motivation. Such decisions are required to be made promptly, * * * and are normally made quickly; and the district court recognized that this decision was not made without Crouse-Hinds's having consulted its expert advisers in an effort to be objective. [Note that Belden's investment banker would not issue a fairness opinion with respect to the exchange offer because InterNorth's opposition threatened the second-step merger. 634 F.2d at 696. Ed.]

(1983),[16] Ampco-Pittsburgh Corp. ("Ampco") made a hostile tender offer of $25 per share for all of the outstanding shares of Buffalo Forge Co. In response, Buffalo Forge encouraged Ogden Corporation by means of a two-part lock-up to enter into a white knight merger agreement at a price of $32.75 per share. First, Ogden was allowed to purchase immediately 425,000 Buffalo Forge treasury shares at $32.75 per share. Second, Ogden was given a one year option to purchase an additional 143,000 shares at the same price. Surprisingly, Ampco was not deterred by the lock-up. Bidding escalated and, when Ampco offered $37.50 per share, Ogden withdrew.

Ogden's withdrawal did not, however, end the conflict. When Ogden sought to take advantage of its lock-up despite having lost the bidding war, Ampco refused to let Ogden exercise its option, and refused to accept the tender of, or pay dividends on, the Buffalo Forge shares Ogden already had purchased. Ampco also sought rescission of both the purchase of the treasury shares and the grant of the option on the grounds that both were a breach of fiduciary duty by the Buffalo Forge board of directors and constituted waste.

The Court of Appeals had little difficulty rejecting Ampco's claim. Following *Crouse-Hinds,* it treated the decision to enter into the lock-ups as governed by the business judgment rule.

Despite the broad language of *Crouse-Hinds,* application of the business judgment rule no longer guarantees that a lock-up will be upheld. In a pair of cases after *Crouse-Hinds*—Hanson Trust PLC v. ML SCM Acquisition Inc., 781 F.2d 264 (2d Cir.1986), and MacAndrews & Forbes Holdings, Inc. v. Revlon, Inc., 501 A.2d 1239 (1985), aff'd, 506 A.2d 173 (Del.1986)—the Second Circuit and the Delaware Supreme Court invalidated lock-ups. Despite the lock-ups' authorization by independent directors seemingly acting in good faith, and despite both courts' assertion that the directors' decisions to enter into the lock-ups were subject to the business judgment rule, in both cases the courts reviewed in detail the substance of the directors' decisions and in both cases held that in adopting the lock-ups the directors had violated their duty of care.

The invalidation of lock-ups in *Hanson Trust* and *MacAndrews & Forbes* following detailed review of the substance of the directors' decisions, when combined with their validation in the *Crouse-Hinds* line of cases following a refusal to go beyond the directors' good faith and independence, demonstrates the difficulty with using business judgment analysis in this area. For example, what characteristics mark a lock-up as so unwise as to violate the directors' duty of care? A major focus in both *Hanson Trust* and *MacAndrews & Forbes* was how close the price for the businesses covered by asset lock-ups were to what the businesses would have sold for in independent transactions. It seems inconsistent, however, to compare the option price under an asset lock-up, the only justification for which is to induce a higher bid for the

---

[16] The facts are set forth in detail in the district court's opinion, 555 F.Supp. 892 (W.D.N.Y.1983).

entire business, to the price that could be secured in a separate transaction. Indeed, from this perspective, the lower the option price, and therefore the more effective the option at discouraging competitive bids, the more valuable it is to shareholders. This inconsistency led the court in *Hanson Trust* to draw a distinction between "good" lock-ups, "that induce a bidder to compete for control of a corporation," slip opinion at 21, and "bad" lock-ups, "that effectively preclude bidders from competing with the optionee bidder." Id. The distinction, however, is tenuous at best. The very characteristic of a lock-up which induces a bidder to compete is that it precludes potential competitive bidders. Thus, traditional business judgment analysis of lock-ups results in no review, while more rigorous review seems to take the form of a judicial search for a unicorn, an attractive beast to be sure, but one whose combination of attributes exists only in mythology.

A more consistent approach to evaluation of lock-ups is discussed in Section A.1.(c), infra.

(3) Attacking Lock-Ups Under Federal Law

The hostility of state corporate law to challenges to the validity of lock-up techniques has not entirely shielded them from attack. In the past when state corporate law has been perceived as unreceptive to claims of fiduciary breach, the federal courts, through resort to federal securities law, have provided a more receptive forum. As early as J.I. Case v. Borak, 377 U.S. 426 (1964), Justice Clark relied on the possibility that state law would not provide a cause of action for deceptive proxy statements as a justification for creating an implied federal cause of action for damages and equitable relief arising out of violations of Section 14(a) of the Securities Exchange Act of 1934.[17] Similarly, dissatisfaction with state law remedies seemed to fuel the more recent efforts of the Second Circuit to expand the coverage of Rule 10b–5 to include breach of fiduciary duty even in the absence of misrepresentation or non-disclosure. See Green v. Santa Fe Industries, Inc., 533 F.2d 1283 (2d Cir.1976), reversed 430 U.S. 462 (1977). Thus, it is hardly surprising that efforts to attack the validity of lock-up techniques also looked to federal law, specifically the prohibition in Section 14(e) of the Securities Exchange Act of 1934 of "any fraudulent, deceptive, or manipulative acts or practices, in connection with any tender offer. * * *" See e.g., Buffalo Forge Co. v. Ogden Corp., 717 F.2d 757 (2d Cir.1983) cert. denied 464 U.S. 1018 (1983); Mobil Corp. v. Marathon Oil Co., 669 F.2d 366 (6th Cir.1981); Marshall Field & Company v. Icahn, 537 F.Supp. 413 (S.D.N.Y.1982).

At the same time, however, the Supreme Court's reversal of the Second Circuit's opinion in *Santa Fe* has been viewed as imposing a limit on the expansion of federal coverage of matters traditionally the province of state corporate law. The resolution of these competing

[17] 377 U.S. at 435–36 ("Moreover, if federal jurisdiction were limited to the granting of declaratory relief, victims of deceptive proxy statements would be obliged to go into state courts for remedial relief. And if the law of the State happened to attach no responsibility to the use of misleading proxy statements, the whole purpose of the section might be frustrated.").

tensions—concerns over federalism in conflict with dissatisfaction over the performance of state law in areas at least tinged with federal interests—is considered in detail in Chapter Sixteen A.1.d. infra. Thus, examination of the federal limitations on the use of lock-up techniques is also best deferred until then.

c. Evaluation of the Legal Standards

Evaluation of the current legal rule that lock-up techniques are protected by the business judgment rule turns on the results of two inquiries: (1) is it desirable to encourage competitive bidding; and (2) regardless of whether competitive bidding is desirable in the abstract, are lock-ups consistent with the structure of the corporation, that is, with the overall allocation of roles between management and shareholders.

(1) The Desirability of Competitive Bidding

Here we re-enter the debate carried on between Easterbrook and Fischel on the one hand and Gilson on the other in Section B.3.e. of Chapter Fourteen. If the benefits of encouraging initial offers outweigh those resulting from price competition, then lock-up techniques should be encouraged.[18] A truly effective lock-up eliminates competing offers and therefore should encourage initial offers. Alternatively, if the benefits of price competition come out on top, lock-up techniques are of doubtful value because their very purpose is to eliminate competitive bidding.

Whichever way one comes out on this debate, analysis of the desirability of lock-up techniques becomes a great deal more complicated when we take into account the fact that lock-ups typically are negotiated by target company management without the necessity of shareholder approval. How desirable are lock-ups if the initial bids that they encourage favor target management at the expense of the shareholders?

(2) A Structural Approach to the Validity of Lock-ups

An important problem with the use of lock-up techniques is that they conflict with the acquisition role traditionally accorded target shareholders in the corporate structure. Recall from Chapter Fourteen B.2. that, regardless of what position target management takes with respect to a proposed acquisition, it may be motivated by a conflict of interest. Management's rejection of an offer may reflect a desire to maintain their position. Alternatively, management's acceptance of an offer may reflect personal benefits promised management by the acquiring company. Shareholder participation is used as a check against both forms of self-interest. If target management rejects an offer, the offerer may go directly to the shareholders by means of a tender offer. The shareholders then have the opportunity to evaluate the offer for

---

[18] This assumes, of course, that price competition does, in fact, discourage initial offers, a point on which the debaters disagree.

themselves. Indeed, it was in order to protect the existence of precisely this check that the Gilson excerpt in Chapter Fourteen B.3.c. proposed to limit management's discretion to discourage tender offers through defensive tactics. If, instead, management approves an offer, both the requirement that shareholders vote to approve a merger or sale of assets, and the possibility that a competing tender offer could be made during the period in which shareholder approval is sought,[19] acts as a check on management's approval of a transaction too favorable to themselves. The problem is that a lock-up, particularly one entered into to secure an initial offer, eliminates both checks—shareholder voting and the potential of a competitive bid—on target management accepting too low an offer.

Consider first the impact of a lock-up on the check on target management provided by shareholder voting. If the favored bidder is given an effective lock-up, target shareholders have little alternative but to approve the transaction. Because the lock-up will be enforceable even if shareholders reject the transaction, the real choice offered shareholders of a target company whose management has given a favored bidder a lock-up excludes the option of keeping the company just as it is. The only choices are to sell their shares on the terms proposed, or keep their shares but in a company that, because of a stock lock-up, may have a new controlling shareholder, or, because of a crown jewels option, may be without important assets. As a result, target shareholder approval of the acquisition transaction itself, but not of the lock-up, is hardly a serious check on target management favoring itself by accepting a transaction more attractive to management than to shareholders. If the lock-up is properly designed, its approval is the only meaningful decision bearing on the acquisition.

The check provided by the potential of a competitive bid is similarly disarmed; the lock-up's explicit purpose is to prevent a competing bid by a third party. The overall result of an effective lock-up is thus to create the *only* form of acquisition transaction that target management can approve without a realistic requirement of shareholder approval.[20]

This analysis suggests a prohibition on the use of lock-ups and leg-ups without shareholder approval. Only then is the statutory requirement that shareholders approve an acquisition more than an optional formality, which planners can avoid at their discretion by altering the form in which the acquisition is cast. Although this analysis has not been explicitly rejected by the courts, it is the case that they have not been sensitive to protecting target shareholders' voting rights. When the issue of voting rights, as opposed to fiduciary duty, has been raised, the courts have approached the issue as if the lock-up was an independent transaction, even though the lock-up would not have been given if acquisition of the entire company had not been contemplated.[21] From

---

[19] As occurred in Crouse-Hinds Co. v. InterNorth, Inc.; Jewel Companies v. Pay Less Drug Stores Northwest, Inc.; and Buffalo Forge Co. v. Ogden Corp., *supra*.

[20] What form does target shareholder approval take when the favored transaction is structured as a tender offer?

[21] See, e.g., Buffalo Forge Co. v. Ogden Corp., 555 F.Supp. 892, 905 (W.D.N.Y.

this perspective, as long as, for example, a crown jewels lock-up could be effected without shareholder approval if considered independently (because the lock-up would not itself amount to a sale of substantially all the target company's assets), merely combining that transaction with one that did require shareholder approval (for example, a merger) would not create a right of shareholder approval that otherwise would not have existed.

Evaluating the validity of a lock-up on the assumption that it is an independent transaction misstates the issue in two critical respects. First, the issue is not the effect of combining independent transactions. Rather, it is how seriously to take the planner's formal separation of a single transaction into two. Consider, for example, a negotiated merger. Here there is no question that at least target shareholders must approve the transaction. As a result of the merger, all of the assets of the target company will pass to the acquiring company when the certificate of merger (or the equivalent) is appropriately filed. What of significance is changed by adding a second agreement which transfers separately assets that, absent the second agreement, would have passed to the acquiring company by virtue of the merger? Unless we adopt the principle that form should control substance, it is difficult to take seriously the argument that the rights of shareholders can be fundamentally changed by so simple a device as dividing one agreement into two. Indeed, the crediting of form over substance in evaluating the validity of a lock-up is an even more extreme position than the Delaware courts have taken with respect to the de facto merger doctrine. As we saw in Chapter Thirteen E.1.a., the Delaware equal dignity approach respects the planner's choice of form in casting an acquisition as a sale of substantially all assets in preference to the more protective merger. But in determining whether a transaction is subject even to the more limited protections afforded shareholders in sales of assets, the courts in Gimbel v. Signal Companies and Katz v. Bregman both acknowledged that the substance of the transaction, not a formal percentage test, controlled the issue of whether "substantially all" of the company's assets were being sold. And in states in which—unlike Delaware—the de facto merger doctrine has not been rejected, it is difficult to understand why a planner's effort to avoid a shareholders' vote by separation of one transaction into two should be given more credence than a planner's selection of which constitutent company in a merger is technically the survivor.

1983), affirmed 717 F.2d 757 (2d Cir.1983), cert. denied 464 U.S. 1018 (1983):

Contrary to Ampco's argument that the sale of the stock and the grant of the option constituted an unlawful attempt to circumvent the requirement that two-thirds of Buffalo Forge's shareholders approve a merger between Buffalo Forge and Ogden, the court finds that the Merger Agreement was not, in itself, a plan of merger which required shareholder approval but was a contract to create a merger plan. The merger agreement contemplated preparation of a "plan of merger," which was thereafter to be submitted to the shareholders for a vote (see New York Business Corporation Law §§ 902, 903(a)), but neither the merger agreement nor the related transactions to which it referred (such as the treasury stock sale) were a "plan of merger" which, by law, must be submitted for shareholder approval, and New York law does not require shareholder approval of a sale of treasury shares.

The second respect in which treating a lock-up as an independent transaction misstates the issue is in equating management's function in approving the sale of less than substantially all the company's assets in a truly independent transaction, with management's function in approving a lock-up transaction covering the same assets in connection with a sale of the entire company. We are prepared to rely solely on management's business judgment when it sells less than substantially all of the company's assets in part because we are confident that management indeed has made a business judgment that the transaction would be beneficial. Moreover, as was argued in Chapter Thirteen E.3., such a transaction does not present final period problems; management remains subject to market discipline with respect to its judgment on the transaction. In contrast, in the lock-up situation management has *not* made a business judgment that the lock-up transaction, standing alone, is in the shareholders' best interests. In fact, management has made exactly the opposite business judgment—that the transaction is in the shareholders' best interests only when coupled with a sale of the entire company. But that is precisely the business judgment that the statute provides cannot bind the shareholders without their approval because final period problems clearly are present. The very setting in which the lock-up takes place thus demonstrates that the considered management judgment on which shareholders rely in an independent transaction where less than substantially all of the company's assets are sold is not present in a lock-up transaction. The lock-up is simply an entirely different animal.[22]

Suppose a target company agreed to reimburse a potential acquirer for its reasonable expenses in investigating and negotiating a friendly transaction in order to induce the acquirer to make an offer. Is this a lock-up, which should require shareholder approval, or is it a commitment by managment of the sort that should be governed by Belden v. InterNorth?

2. Hostile Transactions

Discouraging competing bids becomes more difficult in a hostile transaction. Not only will the target company be uncooperative, but it likely also will be actively seeking a higher bid or a more compatible acquirer—a white knight in takeover parlance. As a result, the disfavored bidder is limited to unilateral action, and the only significant element of the transaction that is under its sole control is the structure

---

[22] Although the structural role of lock-ups has been touched on by the courts, there is little indication that its significance has been understood. In Norlin Corp. v. Rooney, Pace Inc., 744 F.2d 255 (2nd Cir.1985), the Second Circuit stated that in battles for corporate control, the court's "most important duty is to protect the fundamental structure of corporate governance. While the day-to-day affairs of a company are to be managed by its officers under the supervision of its directors, decisions affecting a corporation's ul-timate destiny are for the shareholders to make in accordance with democratic procedures." Id. at 258. *Norlin,* however, did not involve a lock-up. In the first post-*Norlin* case in which a competitive bidder challenged a lock-up, the Second Circuit invalidated the lock-up, but on the basis of scrutiny of the directors' business judgment, rather than in recognition of the structural role of lock-ups. Hanson Trust PLC v. ML SCM Acquisition Inc., 781 F.2d 264 (2d Cir.1986).

of its bid. The problem is to identify what elements of a bid most effectively reduce the likelihood that a competing bid could be successful and, therefore, most effectively reduce the likelihood that one will be made.

From the hostile bidder's perspective, the most critical strategic element—in contrast to substantive matters such as the price offered and the number of shares sought—is speed. A competitive bid takes time to develop. However willing the target company may be to entertain an alternative transaction, a white knight must first be found, some investigation of the target by that company will still be necessary, some negotiation with the target (even if only over the terms of a lock-up) must still take place, and financing for the transaction must still be arranged. If the hostile bidder can structure its offer so that target shareholders must decide to tender *before* a competitive bid can be arranged, a substantial advantage will be secured. This is not to say that, in evaluating the hostile bid, target shareholders will not take into account the possibility that a more favorable bid may be forthcoming if the hostile bid is rejected. Indeed, in such a situation target company management likely will have disclosed that it is actively soliciting an alternative transaction. But for target shareholders, the difference between the *certainty* of a competitive bid and only the *possibility* of one is substantial.

Suppose a hostile bid has been made at a price of $25 per share when the target company's stock is trading at $15 per share. All other things equal, if a competing bid over $25 per share is made before the target shareholders must respond to the initial hostile bid, the competing bid will succeed. More is simply more. But the nature of the target shareholders' decision changes markedly if they have to respond to the initial hostile bid before they know with certainty whether and on what terms a competitive bid will be made. If the target shareholders believe there is only a 50 percent probability that a competitive bid ultimately will be made, at what price would they have to believe the uncertain competitive bid would be made, if in fact it was made, to be more attractive than the certain hostile offer?

If for ease of exposition we ignore complications like the time value of money over the presumably longer period before payment would be made pursuant to the anticipated competing bid and whether target shareholders are risk averse, the expected value of not tendering in the hostile offer can be expressed as

Expected Value of Not Tendering $= (\text{Prob}_{NB} \cdot P_{NB}) + (\text{Prob}_{CB} \cdot P_{CB})$

where

Prob_{NB} = the probability that no competitive bid will be made.
P_{NB} = the original market price of target company stock.[23]
Prob_{CB} = the probability that a competitive bid will be made.
P_{CB} = the expected price of the competitive bid.

[23] The assumption is that the value of the target's stock will drop back to its pre-offer price if the hostile offer is defeated and no competitive offer arises. This is consistent with existing empirical studies that find unsuccessful offers result in no

Since we are interested in knowing the price at which a competitive bid would have to be made for the expected value of not tendering to exceed the $25 value of the hostile bid, we can set the expected value at $26 and solve the equation for P_{CB}:

$$\$26 = (\text{Prob}_{NB} \cdot P_{NB}) + (\text{Prob}_{CB} \cdot P_{CB})$$
$$\$26 = (.5 \times \$15) + (.5 \times P_{CB})$$
$$\$26 = \$7.50 + .5\ P_{CB}$$
$$\$18.50 = .5\ P_{CB}$$
$$\$37 = P_{CB}$$

Thus, in our example, target shareholders would have to believe that a competitive bid, *if made,* would be at a price of at least $37 per share before they would be better off by rejecting the hostile bid on the 50 percent probability that a competitive bid would be made. Sensitivity analysis [24] can be used to understand the impact on the calculation of changes in the probability assigned to the competitive bid.

Individual target shareholders need not, however, undertake the difficult and time-consuming process of gathering the information and developing the skills necessary to make such detailed predictions concerning the likelihood and price of a potential competitive bid. Sophisticated investors, such as arbitrageurs and institutions, would make these forecasts which would then be reflected in the price of the target's stock by means of the professionally informed trading mechanism discussed in Chapter Five.[25] All an unsophisticated shareholder has to know is whether the market price of the target's shares is higher than the hostile bid.[26]

The upshot is that speed is the hostile bidder's greatest ally. In the absence of any regulation, the hostile bidder would structure its offer so that it was open for only the minimum length of time necessary to secure the required number of target shares. Not surprisingly, this was precisely the type of offer typically made when, prior to the passage of the Williams Act, there was no regulation of the terms of the offerer's bid. After the passage of the Williams Act, however, the problem of structuring the hostile bidder's offer so as to minimize the likelihood of a competitive bid became more complicated.

permanent revaluation of the target company. See Chapter Eleven C.2. supra. For ease of exposition, the hypothetical assumes that this happens quite quickly, although this assumption is not consistent with the data.

[24] See Chapter Six A., supra.

[25] Examples of circumstances where the market's anticipation of a competitive bid was reflected in the price of the target company's stock prior to its being made are commonplace. For example, on March 11, 1981, Seagram's made a $45 per share tender offer for St. Joe Minerals, which had traded at $28 a share immediately prior to announcement of the Seagram bid. The day after the Seagram's bid, the price of St. Joe stock rose to $49, which was attributed to arbitrageurs' belief that a competitive bid would be forthcoming. N.Y.Times, Mar. 12, 1981, at D1, col. 6; id., Mar. 13, 1981, at D3, col. 5.

[26] The hostile bidder's advantage is even greater if sophisticated investors are risk averse, a quite likely condition in light of the fact that most arbitrageurs operate with borrowed funds, a condition which serves to increase the risk of the transaction. In this event, the expected price of the uncertain competitive bid would have to exceed the minimum price described in the text by an amount that reflected the "market" level of risk aversion.

The Williams Act, which will be the subject of our attention in Chapter Sixteen, imposes significant restrictions on a hostile bidder's freedom to structure its offer in a manner designed to minimize the likelihood of a competitive bid. In addition to requiring that the hostile bidder make significant disclosure concerning its offer, the Williams Act also tries to reduce the pressure on target shareholders to make up their minds, the idea being that the information required to be disclosed is of little value if shareholders do not have the time to evaluate it. This regulatory goal is currently reflected in restrictions on three important elements of a bid's structure. First, SEC Rule 14e–1(a) requires that an offer remain open a minimum of 20 business days. Second, in the case of an offer for less than all of a target company's outstanding shares, Rule 14d–8 requires that when more shares are tendered than will be purchased, they must be taken up pro rata rather than, for example, on a first-come, first-served basis. Third, Rule 14d–7(a)(1) allows shareholders to withdraw their tenders during the first 15 business days of the offer. All time periods are extended by 10 business days if a competing bid is made. These restrictions serve not merely to give target shareholders an opportunity to evaluate the information concerning the offer disclosed by the hostile bidder; this function is discharged quite quickly in an efficient market and the evaluation reflected in the price of the target's stock. More important, the restrictions also serve to give the target company the time to seek out a competing bid, and, as a result, serve to make formulating a bidding strategy a quite complex task.

Lederman, *Tender Offer Bidding Strategy,* 17 Rev.Sec.Reg. 917 (1984), provides an example that illustrates the problem.[27] Assume that on June 1st an acquiring company ("Acquirer") makes a two-step, front-end loaded offer for a target company ("Target") whose shares, prior to the offer, were trading at $15 per share. Further assume that Target's management holds 15% of Target's shares, and that Acquirer has purchased 5% of Target's shares in market transactions before the offer. The offer's first step seeks 1,500,000 of the Target's 3,000,000 outstanding shares (50%) at $30 per share. The second step will be a freeze out merger in which the remaining target shareholders will receive securities valued at $20 per share. The average price of both steps of the offer is thus $25 per share. The importance of the two-tier structure of Acquirer's offer for our purposes becomes apparent when we consider its impact on a potential white knight.

Assume, not unrealistically, that it takes 15 calendar days for Target to locate a company ("White Knight") willing to make a competitive bid and an additional 5 days to work out the details of the bid. So, on June 20th, White Knight bids $27 per share for all of Target's outstanding stock. The competitive bid exceeds the average price of Acquirer's two-tier bid by $2 per share and, it seems, should win. However, despite the fact that it is only the SEC rules restricting the structure of Acquirer's bid that allow the time for a competitive bid to be made at all, the actual operation of these rules leaves open the

[27] Some of the numbers in the Lederman example have been altered here.

possibility that Acquirer may still prevail even in the face of White Knight's higher bid.

Under the rules, Acquirer can purchase shares under its hostile offer six days before White Knight can purchase shares under its competing offer.[28] This creates an interesting situation if arbitrageurs and other sophisticated investors have come to hold a substantial percentage of Target's shares.

For sophisticated investors, the critical issue in evaluating the competing bids is not the average price under Acquirer's two-step offer, which is computed on the assumption that all shares are tendered in the first-step and taken up pro rata, but the price they can actually expect to receive in the first-step based on the particular facts of the transaction. In our hypothetical, it can be assumed that Target management's 15%, Acquirer's 5%, and—because of ignorance or inertia— at least 10% of the remaining outstanding shares, will not be tendered in the first-step offer. The impact of the fact that each of these categories of shares will not be tendered on the price paid to those who do tender and, as a result, on the *real* average price of the transaction, is shown in the following table.

(1) Number of Shares Tendered in First-Step Transaction	(2) Shares not Tendered	(3) Pro-rata Percentage	(4) Per Share Value of First-Step Transaction ($30 × (3))	(5) Per Share Value of Second-Step Transaction ($20 × 1–(3))	(6) Real Average Per Share Price (4 + 5)
3,000,000	0	50%	$15.00	$10.00	$25.00
2,850,000	150,000 (Acquirer's Shares)	52.63%	$15.79	$9.47	$25.26
2,400,000	600,000 (Acquirer's and Management's Shares)	62.5%	$18.75	$7.50	$26.25
2,100,000	900,000 (Acquirer's and Management's Shares plus 10% non-tendering)	71.43%	$21.43	$5.71	$27.14

If sophisticated investors believe that only 2,100,000 shares will be tendered in the first-step transaction—that is, in addition to Acquirer and Target Management, holders of 10% of Target's outstanding shares also will not tender—then the relevant price to be compared with White Knight's competitive bid changes. For this purpose, the value of

---

[28] The effect of White Knight's offer was to extend Acquirer's withdrawal date (and the expiration and proration dates) until July 5th, which allows Acquirer to begin purchasing shares under its offer on July 6th. White Knight, however, cannot begin to purchase shares under its offer until its withdrawal period—15 business days— ends on July 12th. Note that because the proration period for a partial offer extends for the entire period of the offer, a minimum of 20 days, an offer for all shares normally has a time advantage over a partial offer. Purchasing can commence under an offer for all outstanding shares as soon as the withdrawal period ends, a minimum of 5 days before the proration period ends in a partial offer.

Acquirer's offer is not $25 per share, but $27.14 per share. The result is that Acquirer's offer will succeed even though it yields less in total than White Knight's offer.

How could White Knight overcome Acquirer's advantage? The easiest approach would be to structure its competitive bid on a two-tier basis as well. If White Knight offered $34 per share for half of Target's shares in the first round, and $20 per share for the remainder in the second round, the relevant comparison for sophisticated investors would then be between the real values of both first steps. For White Knight's competitive bid, that value would be $28.23, assuming that Target management does tender in the first-step and that, consistent with our analysis of Acquirer's bid, Acquirer and the holders of an additional 10% of Target's stock do not tender their shares. Moreover, White Knight's first-step transaction could be made even more attractive to sophisticated investors if Target management agreed to sell its shares to White Knight directly at $27 per share, the hypothetical average value of the offer. This would have the result of reducing the number of shares tendered in the first-step by an additional 450,000 and increasing the real average value to $30 per share.

At this point it is useful to examine the two critical elements of the front-end loaded, two-tier structure that makes it effective in a competitive bidding situation. First, in the case of an initial bid, it increases the time pressure by increasing the risk associated with waiting for a competitive offer to develop. If both ends of the offer were at the same price, waiting to see if a competitive bid developed would be virtually costless;[29] if a competitive bid was not forthcoming, the shareholder would still receive the same price as if he had tendered in the first round. Second, the technique operates to allow the bidder to favor sophisticated investors over unsophisticated investors. In our examples, the front-end loaded, two-tier structure did not change the total value of the offer. Rather, it merely transferred a portion of the first-step premium from those who did not tender, presumably through ignorance or lack of time, to sophisticated investors who did tender.

The coercive impact of front-end loaded, two-tier offers discussed in Chapter Fourteen B.3.d., and the extent to which such offers operate to affect competitive bidding, have given rise to various proposals that they be discouraged or even prohibited. Most recently, the SEC's Advisory Committee on Tender Offers recommended that the minimum offering period for tender offers for less than all of a target company's outstanding shares be approximately two weeks longer than an offer for all of a target company's outstanding shares.[30] This proposal would

[29] There would be a cost associated with waiting to be paid until the second-step transaction occurs if a competitive bid were not forthcoming.

[30] Advisory Committee on Tender Offers, Report of Recommendations, Recommendation No. 16, [1984 Transfer Binder] Fed. Sec.L.Rep. (CCH) ¶ 83,637 (July 8, 1983). Proposed legislation introduced at about the same time sought to double to 40 days the minimum period for all tender offers. H.R. 5693 (92nd Cong. 2nd Sess.) § 204(a)(4). Despite the recommendations of its Advisory Committee, the Securities and Exchange Commission opposed this aspect of the legislation. Memorandum of the Securities and Exchange Commission Regarding H.R. 5693, reprinted in [1984 Transfer Binder] Fed.Sec.L.Rep. (CCH) ¶ 83,659.

reduce the coercion problem by facilitating competitive bidding—if an initial offer were unfavorable, sufficient time would exist for a competitive bid to develop before a decision would have to be made on the first-step of the initial offer so that the coercive impact of an initial front-end loaded, two-tier offer would be limited. Additional time would also reduce the value of such bids in discouraging competitive bidding. The speed of an initial hostile offer would be reduced and much of the disadvantage suffered by unsophisticated shareholders would be eliminated by increasing the time in which they could tender their shares in a front-end loaded, two-tier offer. Because so much of the advantage of a two-tier offer would be eliminated, the proposal likely would substantially reduce their incidence.

Some empirical evidence exists with respect to the impact of two-tier bids on the incidence of competitive bidding. As part of the SEC's study of the Advisory Committee's recommendations, the Office of the Chief Economist studied 148 tender offers occurring in 1981, 1982 and 1983, including 91 any-or-all offers, 32 two-tier offers and 25 partial offers. The study found that the average premium in any-or-all offers was 63.4%, in two-tier offers was 55.1%,[31] and in partial offers was 31.3%.[32]

Analysis of the data provides little help in resolving the overall impact of two-tier offers on the competitive bidding process. If we consider only the average premiums for the entire three year period, the data are consistent with the proposition that two-tier offers discourage competitive bidding. If two-tier offers discourage competitive bidding, premiums should be lower in these offers than in any-or-all offers. In fact, average premiums over the entire three year period are lower in two-tier offers than in any-or-all offers (55.1% and 63.4% respectively). However, whether this difference counsels in favor of the Advisory Committee's recommendation to lengthen the minimum offering period for two-tier offers is unclear.[33] In December, 1982, the SEC amended Rule 14d–8 to require pro rata purchases of shares tendered in a partial offer for the entire period the offer is open—a minimum of 20 days. Prior to that date, the pro rata period was only 10 days,[34] thereby increasing the effectiveness of a two-tier offer in discouraging competitive bidding.[35] Thus, one would expect the lengthening of the proration period for partial offers made after December, 1982, to reduce the discrepancy between the premium size for any-or-all bids on the one hand, and two-tier and partial bids on the other. Analysis of only 1983

---

[31] The average for the sample was computed using the average of the two-tiers of each offer in the sample.

[32] The computation of the average premium for partial offers was somewhat complicated. Consistent with the discussion of partial offers in Chapter Fourteen B.3.d., partial offers were treated as if they were a two-tier offer where the value of the second-step transaction was the post-transaction value of the target's remaining outstanding stock. The average for the sample was then computed in the same way as that for explicitly two-tier offers.

[33] One might accept the empirical result and still not favor the recommendation if one believed that raising the price of tender offers by encouraging competitive bidding would result in fewer offers. See Chapter Fourteen C.

[34] As specified in § 14(d)(6) of the Securities Exchange Act.

[35] See Lederman & Vlahakis, *Pricing and Proration in Tender Offers,* 14 Rev.Sec. Reg. 813–19 (1981).

data—offers taking place after the SEC lengthened the minimum offering period—is consistent with this hypothesis. For only 1983 offers, two-tier offer premiums averaged 66.4%, any-or-all offer premiums averaged 49.6% and partial offer premiums averaged 49.4%. Thus, it may be that the problem of concern to the Advisory Committee has already been solved.

B. The Problem of Minority Shareholders

Even after a successful tender offer, an acquiring company inevitably will be left as the owner of a subsidiary with at least some minority shareholders. Whether because of sloth, lack of sophistication, or considered decision, some target company shareholders will not tender their shares.[36] And because a tender offer is technically not a single transaction at all, but a series of individual transactions between the acquiring company and each target shareholder who tenders his shares, non-tendering shareholders are not bound by the action of the majority as would non-voting shareholders in a merger or sale of assets. The acquiring company's second major corporate law concern is how the remaining target company shareholders must be treated. Can they be eliminated from further participation in the target company even if they object? Alternatively, if they are not eliminated from further participation in the target company, what standards govern their treatment by the acquiring company as the new majority shareholder?

We start by considering why an acquiring company would want to freeze out minority shareholders following a successful tender offer in the first place: What is gained by eliminating minority shareholders that is worth the substantial premium that is typically paid? Next we examine the mechanical techniques by which freezeouts can be effected and the development of state and federal standards governing their use. We then consider a related transaction: A management or leveraged buyout, in which a company's management acquires the company through acquiring the stock, typically comprising more than a majority, held by public shareholders. With this perspective, we turn finally to the other side of the freezeout problem: The situation of minority shareholders in a target company who, because the acquiring company *declines* to freeze them out, are effectively "frozen in."

1. How Serious is the Acquiring Company's Problem?

It seems quite clear that acquiring companies, or at least those counseling acquiring companies, regard the flexibility to eliminate minority shareholders as crucial to their acquisition planning. Two experienced practitioners put the matter flatly: "The ability to squeeze out minority shareholders and thus obtain 100 percent of the equity of a corporation is a basic condition of the current market for corporations." [37] The starting point for analysis is to understand why this

---

[36] See Bebchuk, supra.

[37] Herzel & Colling, *Squeeze-Out Mergers in Delaware—The Delaware Supreme Court*

Decision in Weinberger v. UOP, Inc., 7 Corp.L.Rev. 195, 196 (1984).

ability is thought to be central. From a planning perspective, the need for the inquiry is apparent. The decision to freeze out a minority should be made by carefully comparing the costs and benefits of the minority's continued participation with the costs and benefits of freezing them out. From a policy perspective, the inquiry is equally important. If the interests of the acquiring company and the remaining target shareholders ultimately must be balanced, it is necessary to understand what each side has at stake.

a. *Discouraging Free-riders*

One explanation for why it is important to acquirers to be able to freeze out minority shareholders focuses not on the post-acquisition consequences of minority shareholders' continued participation, but on the possibility that the tender offer will be less likely to succeed in the first place if target shareholders have the option of remaining shareholders in the target company following the offer. The idea is that when a tender offer is made, target shareholders will infer that the acquiring company must believe that the target company is worth more than the tender offer price or else it would not have made the offer. If this is correct, then target shareholders may respond strategically by not tendering, instead "free-riding" on the acquiring company's discovery of the target company's real value. If every target shareholder believes that his decision not to tender will not alter an offer's likelihood of success, no one will tender, no offer will succeed and, in anticipation of this behavior, the market for corporate control will grind to a halt. Thus, the argument runs, the ability to freeze out non-tendering shareholders is necessary to discourage free-riding. See Grossman & Hart, *Takeover Bids, the Free Rider Problem, and the Theory of the Corporation,* 11 Bell J.Econ. 42 (1980).

The problem with the argument is that it focuses on only one method of discouraging free-riding. There are, however, alternatives. If an acquiring company can allocate to itself a disproportionate share of the gains from post-acquisition transactions with its new subsidiary, there may be substantial barriers to free-riding even if minority shareholders cannot be frozen out. No matter how carefully the duty of loyalty is drawn, the costs of monitoring the numerous transactions between a parent company and a subsidiary with minority shareholders assures the parent the opportunity, at least to some extent, to structure transactions so as to favor itself. This irreducible friction serves to mitigate any free-rider problem because it makes it unattractive to become a minority shareholder in a subsidiary. To the extent the duty of loyalty is less than carefully drawn, a subject of inquiry in Section B. 1.d. of this Chapter, the incentive to free-ride is further reduced.

The available empirical evidence supports the idea that post-acquisition "self-dealing" by the acquiring company serves to discourage free-riding by target company shareholders. Michael Bradley examined the post-offer performance of target companies' stock following successful partial tender offers. For free-riding to be profitable, the value of the remaining target company stock would have to rise above the tender offer price. In fact, the post-offer price fell by 13 percent, leading

Bradley to conclude that acquiring companies profit not by an increase in the value of the *target* company stock acquired, which would be shared by the remaining target shareholders, but through an increase in the value of the *acquiring* company's stock as a result of the ability to control target company resources.[38] The remaining shareholders, however, cannot share in this gain, so free-riding is impossible.

b. Access to Target Assets

It is not uncommon for an acquiring company to be dependent on access to target company assets in order to pay off the debt incurred to finance the acquisition. If minority shareholders are not eliminated, the argument goes, then whether what is sought is the target company's existing cash, or the proceeds of post-acquisition sales of target company assets, the price of the acquiring company's access to those resources is the distribution of a proportionate amount to any remaining minority shareholders. That minority shareholders must participate proportionately in any distribution of target company assets does not, however, establish the desirability of freezing out the minority in order to eliminate that obligation. The missing step in the argument is to compare the cost of freezing out the minority with the cost of alternative methods of gaining access to target company assets.

This balance does not necessarily favor a freezout. Suppose an acquiring company has purchased through a tender offer 90 percent of the stock in a target company with a net book value of $500 million, including $50 million in cash. Further suppose that the acquiring company needs the target company's cash in order to repay its acquisition financing. One way of accomplishing this is to cause the target company to pay a $50 million dividend. This method would yield the acquiring company either $41.895 million or $45 million depending on whether it would be allowed to deduct 85% or 100% of the dividend in computing its taxable income:

	85% Dividend Deduction[39]	100% Dividend Deduction[40]
Gross Dividend	$50,000,000	$50,000,000
less: 10% to minority shareholders	(5,000,000)	(5,000,000)
less: Acquiring company tax on dividend receipt	(3,105,000)	0
Net amount received by acquiring company	$41,895,000	$45,000,000

---

[38] Bradley, *Interfirm Tender Offers and the Market for Corporate Control*, 35 J.Bus. 345, 364, 365–68 (1980); *see* Jarrell & Bradley, *The Economic Effects of Federal and State Regulations of Cash Tender Offers*, 23 J. L. & Econ. 371, 381–82 (1980).

[39] Under IRC § 243(a)(1), corporations are allowed to deduct 85 percent of the dividends received from other domestic corporations that are subject to federal income tax. Assuming a 46 percent maximum corporate tax rate, the effective tax rate for the acquiring corporation is 6.9 percent, the rate used for the calculation in the text.

[40] A corporation can achieve a 100 percent dividend deduction under IRC § 243(a)(3) with respect to dividends from affiliated corporations if all members of the affiliated group (under IRC § 243(a)(5), a parent-subsidiary group eligible to file a consolidated return) consent to divide a

Estimating the cost of securing access to the target company's cash through a freezeout is more difficult because of the need to specify what price minority shareholders would be paid for their shares. We can, however, at least identify the factors to which the calculation is sensitive. In order for the acquiring company to have after-tax access to as much cash by means of a freezeout as it would have if it merely caused the target company to pay out a dividend, the freezeout price would have to be less than book value if the 100 percent dividend received deduction applied,[41] or less than 106.2 percent of book value if the 85 percent dividend received deduction applied.[42]

Two objections can be raised to this analysis. The first recognizes that the acquiring company is left in an apparently quite different position depending on which method of securing access to the target company's assets is chosen: If a dividend is paid, the acquiring company still only owns 90 percent of the company while if the minority is frozen out, the acquiring company then owns the entire company. The validity of this objection depends on what price is paid in the freezeout. Because a dividend reduces the value of the company, it can be seen as a down payment on the purchase of the minority shares. As a result, the objection is only valid if the purchase price that would be paid in the freezeout is lower than the implicit price reflected in the decrease in the market value of minority stock following the dividend. Put differently, 90 percent of a larger number may be more than 100 percent of a smaller number.

There is reason to believe that the freezeout price may be higher than the implicit price of allowing the minority to remain. Here the comparison is between the constraints on the acquiring company's ability to set a low price in the freezeout and the contraints on its ability to reduce the value of the minority's continuing interest through favoring itself in the ongoing conduct of the business. The availability of a judicial appraisal proceeding in a freezeout, as discussed in Section B.2. of this Chapter, may well be more restrictive than judicial limits on self-dealing by the parent company in an affiliated group both because of lenient legal rules, and because it is expensive for minority shareholders to monitor effectively how much self-dealing actually takes place.[43]

single surtax exemption and accumulated earnings credit. A corporation can also achieve a 100 percent dividend deduction if the affiliated group of which it is part has elected to file a consolidated return under IRC § 1501.

[41] The book value of the remaining ten percent would be $50 million, leaving the acquiring company with complete ownership of a subsidiary with a book value of $450 million following the freezeout. After the dividend, the acquiring company would have $45 million in cash from the dividend plus 90 percent of the remaining book value of $450 million, a total of $450 million. Note, however, that the freezeout would use up the target company's cash, thereby necessitating a refinancing, rather than a pay off, of the acquisition debt.

[42] If the 85 percent dividend received deduction applied, the acquiring company would have $41.895 million in cash from the dividend after tax plus 90 percent of the remaining book value of $450 million, a total of $446.895 million. If the freezeout price of the minority shares were 106.2 percent of the book value, the total price would be $53.1 million, leaving the acquiring company with complete ownership of a subsidiary with a book value of $446.9 million.

[43] The legal rules governing the treatment of minority shareholders in an affiliated group are discussed in Section B.1.d. of this Chapter, infra.

The second objection to the claim that it may be more favorable to an acquiring company to gain access to the target company's assets by means of a dividend than by means of a freezeout is legal rather than financial: Would not the payment of a dividend solely because of the needs of the acquiring company violate the fiduciary duty owed minority shareholders by a majority shareholder? The Delaware Supreme Court considered precisely this point in the following case.

SINCLAIR OIL CORPORATION v. LEVIEN

Supreme Court of Delaware, 1971.
280 A.2d 717.

WOLCOTT, C.J., CAREY, J., and CHRISTIE, Judge, sitting.

WOLCOTT, Chief Justice.

This is an appeal by the defendant, Sinclair Oil Corporation (hereafter Sinclair), from an order of the Court of Chancery, 261 A.2d 911 in a derivative action requiring Sinclair to account for damages sustained by its subsidiary, Sinclair Venezuelan Oil Company (hereafter Sinven), organized by Sinclair for the purpose of operating in Venezuela, as a result of dividends paid by Sinven, the denial to Sinven of industrial development, and a breach of contract between Sinclair's wholly-owned subsidiary, Sinclair International Oil Company, and Sinven.*

Sinclair, operating primarily as a holding company, is in the business of exploring for oil and of producing and marketing crude oil and oil products. At all times relevant to this litigation, it owned about 97% of Sinven's stock. The plaintiff owns about 3000 of 120,000 publicly held shares of Sinven. Sinven, incorporated in 1922, has been engaged in petroleum operations primarily in Venezuela and since 1959 has operated exclusively in Venezuela.

Sinclair nominates all members of Sinven's board of directors. The Chancellor found as a fact that the directors were not independent of Sinclair. Almost without exception, they were officers, directors, or employees of corporations in the Sinclair complex. By reason of Sinclair's domination, it is clear that Sinclair owed Sinven a fiduciary duty. Getty Oil Company v. Skelly Oil Co., 267 A.2d 883 (Del.Supr. 1970); Cottrell v. Pawcatuck Co., 35 Del.Ch. 309, 116 A.2d 787 (1955). Sinclair concedes this.

The Chancellor held that because of Sinclair's fiduciary duty and its control over Sinven, its relationship with Sinven must meet the test of intrinsic fairness. The standard of intrinsic fairness involves both a high degree of fairness and a shift in the burden of proof. Under this standard the burden is on Sinclair to prove, subject to careful judicial scrutiny, that its transactions with Sinven were objectively fair. Guth v. Loft, Inc., 23 Del.Ch. 255, 5 A.2d 503 (1939); Sterling v. Mayflower Hotel Corp., 33 Del.Ch. 293, 93 A.2d 107, 38 A.L.R.2d 425 (Del.Supr. 1952); Getty Oil Co. v. Skelly Oil Co., supra.

---

* The portion of the opinion concerning the denial of development and the breach   of contract appears in Section B.1.d. of this Chapter, infra. [Ed.]

Sinclair argues that the transactions between it and Sinven should be tested, not by the test of intrinsic fairness with the accompanying shift of the burden of proof, but by the business judgment rule under which a court will not interfere with the judgment of a board of directors unless there is a showing of gross and palpable overreaching. Meyerson v. El Paso Natural Gas Co., 246 A.2d 789 (Del.Ch.1967). A board of directors enjoys a presumption of sound business judgment, and its decisions will not be disturbed if they can be attributed to any rational business purpose. A court under such circumstances will not substitute its own notions of what is or is not sound business judgment.

We think, however, that Sinclair's argument in this respect is misconceived. When the situation involves a parent and a subsidary, with the parent controlling the transaction and fixing the terms, the test of intrinsic fairness, with its resulting shifting of the burden of proof, is applied. Sterling v. Mayflower Hotel Corp., supra; David J. Greene & Co. v. Dunhill International, Inc., 249 A.2d 427 (Del.Ch.1968); Bastian v. Bourns, Inc., 256 A.2d 680 (Del.Ch.1969) aff'd. Per Curiam (unreported) (Del.Supr.1970). The basic situation for the application of the rule is the one in which the parent has received a benefit to the exclusion and at the expense of the subsidiary.

Recently, this court dealt with the question of fairness in parent-subsidiary dealings in Getty Oil Co. v. Skelly Oil Co., supra. In that case, both parent and subsidiary were in the business of refining and marketing crude oil and crude oil products. The Oil Import Board ruled that the subsidiary, because it was controlled by the parent, was no longer entitled to a separate allocation of imported crude oil. The subsidiary then contended that it had a right to share the quota of crude oil allotted to the parent. We ruled that the business judgment standard should be applied to determine this contention. Although the subsidiary suffered a loss through the administration of the oil import quotas, the parent gained nothing. The parent's quota was derived solely from its own past use. The past use of the subsidiary did not cause an increase in the parent's quota. Nor did the parent usurp a quota of the subsidiary. Since the parent received nothing from the subsidiary to the exclusion of the minority stockholders of the subsidiary, there was no self-dealing. Therefore, the business judgment standard was properly applied.

A parent does indeed owe a fiduciary duty to its subsidiary when there are parent-subsidiary dealings. However, this alone will not evoke the intrinsic fairness standard. This standard will be applied only when the fiduciary duty is accompanied by self-dealing—the situation when a parent is on both sides of a transaction with its subsidiary. Self-dealing occurs when the parent, by virtue of its domination of the subsidiary, causes the subsidiary to act in such a way that the parent receives something from the subsidiary to the exclusion of, and detriment to, the minority stockholders of the subsidiary.

We turn now to the facts. The plaintiff argues that, from 1960 through 1966, Sinclair caused Sinven to pay out such excessive dividends that the industrial development of Sinven was effectively prevented, and it became in reality a corporation in dissolution.

From 1960 through 1966, Sinven paid out $108,000,000 in dividends ($38,000,000 in excess of Sinven's earnings during the same period). The Chancellor held that Sinclair caused these dividends to be paid during a period when it had a need for large amounts of cash. Although the dividends paid exceeded earnings, the plaintiff concedes that the payments were made in compliance with 8 Del.C. § 170, authorizing payment of dividends out of surplus or net profits. However, the plaintiff attacks these dividends on the ground that they resulted from an improper motive—Sinclair's need for cash. The Chancellor, applying the intrinsic fairness standard, held that Sinclair did not sustain its burden of proving that these dividends were intrinsically fair to the minority stockholders of Sinven.

Since it is admitted that the dividends were paid in strict compliance with 8 Del.C. § 170, the alleged excessiveness of the payments alone would not state a cause of action. Nevertheless, compliance with the applicable statute may not, under all circumstances, justify all dividend payments. If a plaintiff can meet his burden of proving that a dividend cannot be grounded on any reasonable business objective, then the courts can and will interfere with the board's decision to pay the dividend.

Sinclair contends that it is improper to apply the intrinsic fairness standard to dividend payments even when the board which voted for the dividends is completely dominated. In support of this contention, Sinclair relies heavily on American District Telegraph Co. [ADT] v. Grinnell Corp., (N.Y.Sup.Ct.1969) aff'd. 33 A.D.2d 769, 306 N.Y.S.2d 209 (1969). Plaintiffs were minority stockholders of ADT, a subsidiary of Grinnell. The plaintiffs alleged that Grinnell, realizing that it would soon have to sell its ADT stock because of a pending anti-trust action, caused ADT to pay excessive dividends. Because the dividend payments conformed with applicable statutory law, and the plaintiffs could not prove an abuse of discretion, the court ruled that the complaint did not state a cause of action. * * *

We do not accept the argument that the intrinsic fairness test can never be applied to a dividend declaration by a dominated board, although a dividend declaration by a dominated board will not inevitably demand the application of the intrinsic fairness standard. Moskowitz v. Bantrell, 41 Del.Ch. 177, 190 A.2d 749 (Del.Supr.1963). If such a dividend is in essence self-dealing by the parent, then the intrinsic fairness standard is the proper standard. For example, suppose a parent dominates a subsidiary and its board of directors. The subsidiary has outstanding two classes of stock, X and Y. Class X is owned by the parent and Class Y is owned by minority stockholders of the subsidiary. If the subsidiary, at the direction of the parent, declares a dividend on its Class X stock only, this might well be self-dealing by the parent. It would be receiving something from the subsidiary to the exclusion of and detrimental to its minority stockholders. This self-dealing, coupled with the parent's fiduciary duty, would make intrinsic fairness the proper standard by which to evaluate the dividend payments.

Consequently it must be determined whether the dividend payments by Sinven were, in essence, self-dealing by Sinclair. The dividends resulted in great sums of money being transferred from Sinven to Sinclair. However, a proportionate share of this money was received by the minority shareholders of Sinven. Sinclair received nothing from Sinven to the exclusion of its minority stockholders. As such, these dividends were not self-dealing. We hold therefore that the Chancellor erred in applying the intrinsic fairness test as to these dividend payments. The business judgment standard should have been applied.

We conclude that the facts demonstrate that the dividend payments complied with the business judgment standard and with 8 Del.C. § 170. The motives for causing the declaration of dividends are immaterial unless the plaintiff can show that the dividend payments resulted from improper motives and amounted to waste. The plaintiff contends only that the dividend payments drained Sinven of cash to such an extent that it was prevented from expanding.

———◆———

c. *Eliminating the Costs of Public Ownership*

One reason for wanting to eliminate minority shareholders is simply that they cost too much. Issuers subject to reporting under Section 13 of the Securities Exchange Act of 1934 are required to file with the Securities Exchange Commission, *inter alia,* a Form 10–K Annual Report, Form 10–Q Quarterly Reports, and Form 8–K Current Reports. Additionally, those issuers registered under Section 12 of the Act, essentially all companies whose securities are listed on a national securities exchange and all companies having total assets in excess of $3 million and a class of equity securities held of record by 500 or more persons, are also subject to the proxy solicitation rules of Section 14.[44] Additional costs arise from the need to maintain transfer agents, stock exchange listings and the like. Of course, all of these obligations disappear with the elimination of minority shareholders.[45]

At least in absolute amounts, these costs appear to be non-trivial. Practitioners estimate that the out-of-pocket costs associated with public ownership of a company range generally from $30,000 to $100,000,[46] and from $75,000 to $200,000 for a company of a size that meets American Stock Exchange listing requirements.[47] Based on these

[44] There are also reporting requirements imposed by some state corporation laws. See, e.g., Cal.Corp.Code Section 1501 (mailing of annual balance sheet and income statement and, for corporations with more than 100 shareholders, information concerning transactions with directors and officers).

[45] Under Sections 12(g)(4) and 15(d), all reporting and other obligations under Sections 13 and 14 of the Securities Exchange Act are lifted when the number of shareholders drops below 300.

[46] Schneider, Manko & Kant, *Going Public: Practice, Procedure and Consequences,* 27 Vill.L.Rev. 1 (1981).

[47] Borden, *Going Private—Old Tort, New Tort, or No Tort?,* 49 N.Y.U.L.Rev. 987, 1007 (1977).

figures, the present value of eliminating these costs, assuming capitalization as a perpetuity at 10 percent, ranges from $300,000 to $2,000,000. Particularly when the target company is small, an acquiring company would find the opportunity to save amounts of this magnitude very attractive.

The larger the size of the target company, however, the less likely that these cost savings alone would be sufficient to justify paying the premium necessary to eliminate the target company's remaining minority shareholders. This can be seen by comparing the per share value of the savings with the per share premium that would be required in a freezeout. Because the costs of public ownership do not rise proportionately with the size of the company, we would expect that as the size of the target company increases, the likelihood that the cost of the premium will exceed the savings also increases.

A final qualification concerning the claim that it is important to be able to freeze out minority shareholders in order to save the costs of public ownership is that it ignores the possibility that there also may be gains from public ownership. This idea finds some support in the increased frequency with which public ownership of a minority interest in a previously wholly-owned subsidiary is intentionally created either by a public offering or by spinning off some portion of the subsidiary's shares to the parent company's shareholders. The explanation for this seeming retrogression is that the market will value the subsidiary more highly when it has a public minority than when it is a wholly owned subsidiary.[48] What assumptions about information costs would be necessary for this strategy to be consistent with the Efficient Capital Market Hypothesis?

d. *Capturing the Gains From Synergy*

In an important sense, it is really not very surprising that the desirability of preventing free-riding, or of having access to the target company's assets, or of avoiding the costs of a regulatory regime, do not seem to explain why acquiring companies believe that freezing out minority shareholders is so central to their acquisition strategies. One lesson of Part II was that the most persuasive explanation for how an acquiring company actually might make money through an acquisition is synergy—that combining the acquiring and target companies results in a post-acquisition value in excess of the sum of their pre-acquisition independent values. Most explanations for synergy, however, require

---

[48] Hite & Owers, *Security Price Reactions Around Corporate Spin-Off Announcements,* 12 J.Fin.Econ. 409 (1983), Miles & Rosenfeld, *An Emprical Analysis of the Effects of Spin-Off Announcements on Shareholder Wealth,* 38 J.Fin. 1597 (1983), and Schipper & Smith, *Effects of Recontracting on Shareholder Wealth: The Case of Voluntary Spin-Offs,* 12 J.Fin. 437 (1983), all report positive abnormal returns to the parent company shareholders of about three percent in the two day period ending on the date of the Wall Street Journal announcement of the spinoff. Schipper & Smith, *A Comparison of Equity Carve-Outs and Equity Offerings: Share Price Effects and Corporate Restructuring,* ___ J.Fin.Econ. ___ (forthcoming), report positive abnormal returns of 1.8 percent over the five day period around announcement of a public offering of a portion of the stock of a previously wholly owned subsidiary. The studies all note that spin-offs and carve-outs are principally phenomena of the last few years.

that there be central control of the combined businesses in order to maximize overall value. But what if maximizing overall value causes the resulting gains to be shared unequally, that is, minority shareholders of one member of the affiliated group may not do as well as shareholders of the parent? For example, opportunities for new activities must be allocated among companies in the affiliated group. Can they be allocated to the most appropriate member of the group or must all members who have minority shareholders be allowed to participate? [49] Similarly, where synergy is intended to result from the merger of the constituent companies' administrative and support systems, there may be problems with allocating the costs and benefits in a way in which the minority shareholders of different affiliates participate equally. If equality is required by law but cannot be achieved—either because inequality is necessary to achieving the synergy itself or because it is too expensive to create systems that measure and enforce equality—then the ability to freeze out minority shareholders actually may be critical to an acquisition's success.

Under this analysis, how important it is to be able to freeze out minority shareholders is a function of the stringency of the legal standard governing review of the acquiring company's post-transaction conduct of the target company's business. As with the legal standard governing acquiring company access to target company assets, Sinclair Oil Corporation v. Levien, supra, which also involved claims both of unequal allocation of opportunities for new activities and of unequal allocation of the benefits of transactions between members of the affiliated group, is the classic statement of the governing law.

SINCLAIR OIL CORPORATION v. LEVIEN
Supreme Court of Delaware, 1971.
280 A.2d 717.

* * *

The plaintiff proved no business opportunities which came to Sinven independently and which Sinclair either took to itself or denied to Sinven. As a matter of fact, with two minor exceptions which resulted in losses, all of Sinven's operations have been conducted in Venezuela, and Sinclair had a policy of exploiting its oil properties located in different countries by subsidiaries located in the particular countries.

From 1960 to 1966 Sinclair purchased or developed oil fields in Alaska, Canada, Paraguay, and other places around the world. The plaintiff contends that these were all opportunities which could have been taken by Sinven. The Chancellor concluded that Sinclair had not proved that its denial of expansion opportunities to Sinven was intrinsically fair. He based this conclusion on the following findings of fact. Sinclair made no real effort to expand Sinven. The excessive dividends paid by Sinven resulted in so great a cash drain as to effectively deny to Sinven any ability to expand. During this same period Sinclair active-

---

[49] Would a sharing requirement be consistent with WIlliamson's idea of achieving synergy by internalizing the allocative functions of the capital market? See Chapter Eleven A.2.d., supra.

ly pursued a company-wide policy of developing through its subsidiaries new sources of revenue, but Sinven was not permitted to participate and was confined in its activities to Venezuela.

However, the plaintiff could point to no opportunities which came to Sinven. Therefore, Sinclair usurped no business opportunity belonging to Sinven. Since Sinclair received nothing from Sinven to the exclusion of and detriment to Sinven's minority stockholders, there was no self-dealing. Therefore, business judgment is the proper standard by which to evaluate Sinclair's expansion policies.

Since there is no proof of self-dealing on the part of Sinclair, it follows that the expansion policy of Sinclair and the methods used to achieve the desired result must, as far as Sinclair's treatment of Sinven is concerned, be tested by the standards of the business judgment rule. Accordingly, Sinclair's decision, absent fraud or gross overreaching, to achieve expansion through the medium of its subsidiaries, other than Sinven, must be upheld.

Even if Sinclair was wrong in developing these opportunities as it did, the question arises, with which subsidiaries should these opportunities have been shared? No evidence indicates a unique need or ability of Sinven to develop these opportunities. The decision of which subsidiaries would be used to implement Sinclair's expansion policy was one of business judgment with which a court will not interfere absent a showing of gross and palpable overreaching. Meyerson v. El Paso Natural Gas Co., 246 A.2d 789 (Del.Ch.1967). No such showing has been made here.

Next, Sinclair argues that the Chancellor committed error when he held it liable to Sinven for breach of contract.

In 1961 Sinclair created Sinclair International Oil Company (hereafter International), a wholly owned subsidiary used for the purpose of coordinating all of Sinclair's foreign operations. All crude purchases by Sinclair were made thereafter through International.

On September 28, 1961, Sinclair caused Sinven to contract with International whereby Sinven agreed to sell all of its crude oil and refined products to International at specified prices. The contract provided for minimum and maximum quantities and prices. The plaintiff contends that Sinclair caused this contract to be breached in two respects. Although the contract called for payment on receipt, International's payments lagged as much as 30 days after receipt. Also, the contract required International to purchase at least a fixed minimum amount of crude and refined products from Sinven. International did not comply with this requirement.

Clearly, Sinclair's act of contracting with its dominated subsidiary was self-dealing. Under the contract Sinclair received the products produced by Sinven, and of course the minority shareholders of Sinven were not able to share in the receipt of these products. If the contract was breached, then Sinclair received these products to the detriment of Sinven's minority shareholders. We agree with the Chancellor's finding that the contract was breached by Sinclair, both as to the time of payments and the amounts purchased.

Although a parent need not bind itself by a contract with its dominated subsidiary, Sinclair chose to operate in this manner. As Sinclair has received the benefits of this contract, so must it comply with the contractual duties.

Under the intrinsic fairness standard, Sinclair must prove that its causing Sinven not to enforce the contract was intrinsically fair to the minority shareholders of Sinven. Sinclair has failed to meet this burden. Late payments were clearly breaches for which Sinven should have sought and received adequate damages. As to the quantities purchased, Sinclair argues that it purchased all the products produced by Sinven. This, however, does not satisfy the standard of intrinsic fairness. Sinclair has failed to prove that Sinven could not possibly have produced or someway have obtained the contract minimums. As such, Sinclair must account on this claim.

Finally, Sinclair argues that the Chancellor committed error in refusing to allow it a credit or setoff of all benefits provided by it to Sinven with respect to all the alleged damages. The Chancellor held that setoff should be allowed on specific transactions, e.g., benefits to Sinven under the contract with International, but denied an over all setoff against all damages claimed. We agree with the Chancellor, although the point may well be moot in view of our holding that Sinclair is not required to account for the alleged excessiveness of the dividend payments.

We will therefore reverse that part of the Chancellor's order that requires Sinclair to account to Sinven for damages sustained as a result of dividends paid between 1960 and 1966, and by reason of the denial to Sinven of expansion during that period. We will affirm the remaining portion of that order and remand the cause for further proceedings.

———————◆———————

Understanding what the *Sinclair* standard means is especially important because, in the end, the acquiring company's strategic decision depends on how stringent the standard is perceived to be. If the standard is thought to interfere with maximizing the post-transaction value of the combined companies, then the ability to freeze out the minority is important because it results in an increased post-transaction value. If the standard is thought to be sufficiently lenient that it does not interfere with maximizing post-transaction value, then the ability to freeze out the minority may not be very important after all. Finally, if the standard is thought to be so lenient that it allows the acquiring company to "exploit" the minority through favorable post-transaction dealings between the acquiring company and the target company, then the ability to freeze out the minority shareholders simply may be beside the point because no acquiring company would ever do so. That is, if the freezeout price would be the minority shareholders' pro rata share of future cash flows while, if the minority shareholders were not frozen out, they would receive less than their pro rata share, the acquiring company has little incentive to be rid of them.

This is an area where lawyers play a central role. The business decision—to freeze out or not to freeze out—depends on an analysis of judicial decisions. As a result, the client's perception of the importance of the ability to freeze out minority shareholders depends, in the end, on the substance and accuracy of the legal advice the client receives. The problem, however, is that there seems to be a conflict between the conventional wisdom concerning the rigor of the legal standard governing the acquiring company's post-transaction dealings with the target company, and the conventional wisdom that the ability to freeze out minority shareholders is critical to an acquisition's success.

The academic evaluation of the limitations imposed by the *Sinclair* standard is unambiguous.[50] Professor Eisenberg states this view clearly: "The checks on unfair dealing by the parent are few. In theory, of course, the fairness of the parent's behavior is subject to the check of judicial review; but in practice such review is difficult even where the courts have the will to engage in it, and they often lack the will."[51] On this basis, one would predict a low incidence of freezeout mergers; why freeze them when you can fleece them instead. This prediction, however, seems to be inconsistent with observed reality. As was stressed at the outset of this section, practitioners clearly think it desirable to freeze out any minority shareholders remaining after a successful acquisition and it seems their advice is followed: Second-step transactions are, if not the rule, then at least a familiar phenomenon.

One explanation for this conflict may be an important difference in orientation between the academics and the practitioners. Although the academic literature may accurately describe the forest, the fact is that there remains some significant variation among the trees. Not only do the courts of some states reach quite different conclusions than do those of Delaware,[52] but even the Delaware courts occasionally reach surprising results.[53] From the practitioner's perspective, it may make little

---

[50] That is not to say, however, that evaluation of the desirability of the standard is as consistent as evaluation of its content. Compare Cary, *Federalism and Corporate Law: Reflections Upon Delaware,* 83 Yale L.J. 663 (1974), *with* Easterbrook & Fischel, *Corporate Control Transactions,* 91 Yale L.J. 737 (1982).

[51] M. Eisenberg, *The Structure of the Corporation* 309 (1976).

[52] Suppose the target company has a large net operating loss carryover for federal income tax purposes that could be used to offset the acquiring company's taxable income if the acquiring company causes the target company to join in the filing of a consolidated federal income tax return (which generally is allowable if the acquiring company owns 80 percent or more of the target company's stock). Must some portion of the savings resulting from filing the consolidated return be allocated

to the target company so that minority shareholders benefit from the use of the target's "tax asset"? Delaware does not require an allocation. Meyerson v. El Paso Natural Gas Co., 246 A.2d 789 (Del Ch. 1967). California, in contrast, does require an allocation. Smith v. Tele-Communication, Inc., 134 Cal.App.3d 338, 184 Cal. Rptr. 571 (1982).

[53] For example, in TransWorld Airlines v. Summa Corp., 374 A.2d 5 (Del.Ch.1977), TransWorld Airlines (TWA) claimed that its 78 percent majority shareholder, Hughes Tool Company, had delayed TWA's acquisition of first generation commercial jet aircraft by controlling negotiations over the kind and number of aircraft acquired and the manner in which the acquisition would be financed. The Court held that "by preventing TWA from making its own arrangements for the acquisition of jet planes, the defendants retained the capa-

difference that the forest is accurately described if an aberrant tree nonetheless falls on his client. And if the lawyer also has an independent reason to be more risk averse than his client, we may have an explanation for why, despite the accurate academic characterization of how lenient the *Sinclair* standard really is, practitioners still advise clients that it is critical to be able to freeze out any remaining target shareholders.

If a client has perfect information, there would be little reason for a lawyer to be more risk averse than the client with respect to the freezeout decision. Assuming the academic characterization of the *Sinclair* standard is correct, the lawyer simply would advise the client both of the limited reach of the restrictions on how post-acquisition transactions with the target company can be structured, and of the lawyer's estimate of the likelihood of an aberrant judicial result if such post-acquisition transactions were ever challenged. If on that basis the client then chose not to effect a freezeout and the aberrant result in fact occurred, the lawyer would not need to fear an unhappy client. A client with perfect knowledge would know that the unfavorable result was not the fault of the lawyer—the client would realize that the lawyer accurately predicted the probability distribution of the outcomes associated with not freezing out the remaining target shareholders, but that the actual outcome just ended up at the unfavorable tail of the distribution.

If a client does not have perfect information, however, the lawyer's level of risk aversion may turn out to differ quite substantially from that of his client. As a result, the lawyer may give quite different advice then he would to a better informed client.

Two important aspects of the lawyer-client relationship change as a result of the client's imperfect information. First, the uninformed client lacks the ability to recognize the quality of legal services, whether *ex ante,* in choosing a lawyer, or *ex post,* in evaluating the quality of the services actually rendered by a lawyer. This results in the second alteration in the lawyer-client relationship: The lawyer then has an incentive to invest in developing a reputation for quality as a means of attracting clients.[54] These two factors interact in a manner that suggests a significant difference in level of risk aversion between the client and the lawyer with respect to decisions like whether to freeze out minority shareholders.

In the context of the freezeout decision, the client's inability to evaluate the quality of the lawyer's services even after they have been

---

bility of arranging the terms of such acquisitions so as to benefit themselves. * * * Thus, it is clear on the present record that the minority shareholders of TWA received nothing in exchange for the strictures imposed by defendants on plaintiff's operations and that such stockholders may have suffered injury as a result of the loss of TWA's freedom to compete." 374 A.2d at 10. This behavior was found to violate the *Sinclair* standard. In contrast, the Court held that the fact that the major-

ity shareholder profited by leasing jet aircraft it had acquired to competitors of TWA until permanent financing had been arranged for their acquisition by TWA, did not violate the *Sinclair* standard. Id.

[54] Gilson & Mnookin, *Sharing Among the Human Capitalists: An Economic Inquiry into the Corporate Law Firm and How Partners Split Profits,* 37 Stan.L.Rev. 313, 363 (1985).

rendered means that the client cannot determine whether the occurrence of an aberrant judicial result with respect to the validity of post-acquisition transactions reflects only the random bad luck of ending up on the unfavorable tail of a distribution the lawyer accurately described, or whether the lawyer misdescribed the distribution of possible outcomes in the first place. And in this circumstance, it is not at all surprising that a client may end up equating the quality of the lawyer's services with how favorable the outcome was to the client.[55] The result is that the lawyer bears the risk of the court's decision; he will be blamed for a bad result even if he was right.

Because the lawyer's investment in reputation is essentially an investment in human capital that cannot easily be diversified,[56] one of the few ways the lawyer can protect himself against the risk *he* bears when the *client* chooses a risky strategy—one with both favorable and unfavorable outcomes—is to shy away from recommending risk strategies to a client in favor of strategies whose outcome is certain. This is not necessarily in the client's best interest, however, because the lawyer is better off with certainty *even if the risky alternative has a higher expected value for the client.*

Clients, of course, do not have perfect knowledge. Thus, clients may well select a lawyer based on the lawyer's reputation for quality rather than on direct investigation of the lawyer's skills, and may well equate the quality of the services rendered with the desirability of the result actually achieved. If this is correct, then we would predict that risk averse lawyers would give their clients more conservative advice— in our setting, by recommending that minority shareholders be frozen out—even though there is a more attractive, but risky alternative available, that of exploiting minority shareholders through transactions favorable to the acquiring company.[57]

2. The Mechanics of Freezeouts

The most common technique for freezing out remaining target shareholders is a merger.[58] It will be recalled from Chapter Thirteen

[55] Id. at 360 n. 78.

[56] Id. at 324–29.

[57] What would happen if clients became better informed? One way this could happen is for the client's choice of a lawyer to be made by another lawyer, such as the client's general counsel. If, as seems to be the case, the influence and quality of general counsel increase, id. at 381–83, would this fact change the prediction of what advice outside counsel will give?

[58] For this purpose, the choice of merger form—straight, triangular, or reverse triangular—would be dictated by the concerns discussed in Chapter Thirteen C.

In the past freezeouts also took the form of 1) dissolution freezeouts in which the plan of dissolution provides for the distribution of the company's productive assets to the majority shareholder and only cash or notes to the minority shareholders; 2) sale of assets freezeouts in which the majority shareholder purchases for cash or notes the productive assets of the company leaving the minority shareholders with an interest only in the proceeds of the sale; and 3) reverse stock split freezeouts in which the outstanding shares of the company are consolidated pursuant to a plan that sets a ratio such that no minority shareholder own as much as one full share of stock, and also provides for the compulsory exchange of fractional shares for cash. With respect to dissolution and sale of assets freezeouts, see W. Cary & M. Eisenberg, *Cases and Materials on Corporations* 1517–30 (5th Ed.1980). With respect to reverse stock split freezeouts, see Comment, *Reverse Stock Splits: The Fiduciary's Obligations Under State Law,* 63 Calif. L.Rev. 1226 (1975).

A. that the vote of shareholders owning the requisite number of shares to approve a merger, typically a majority, binds those shareholders who either vote against the merger or who do not vote at all. At least as far as the text of the corporation statute is concerned, these shareholders must either accept the consideration offered or exercise their appraisal rights. Moreover, where the acquiring company's initial offer has been sufficiently successful, even the shareholder vote may be dispensed with. The corporation statutes of most leading commercial states allow a majority shareholder with a high enough ownership—Delaware and California, for example, require 90 percent [59]—to approve a merger without a vote of the target company shareholders, although target shareholders may still exercise appraisal rights following notification of the transaction.[60]

The critical aspect of the freezeout transaction is not, however, whether a vote of the target company shareholders is required. So long as there is no supermajority requirement to approve the transaction, the shareholder vote may be an inconvenience, but will not be a barrier; the acquiring company typically will have the votes necessary to approve the transaction itself. Rather, it is the type of consideration that can be used in the merger that is central to the freezeout concept. In particular, the very notion of a freezeout requires that the minority shareholders be paid off in cash. Target shareholders who receive shares of the acquiring company are not truly gone and, what may be worse, the issuance of the shares carries with it the potential to dilute the earnings of the acquiring company.

Authorization of the use of cash as consideration in mergers is of comparatively recent origin. In 1925, Florida became the first state to authorize "the distribution of *cash,* notes on bonds, in while or in part, in lieu of stock to stockholders of the constituent corporations of any of them." [61] Other states quickly followed suit, although some disagreement remains as to whether these early statutes really were intended to authorize freezeout transactions.[62] In any event, later action by the state legislatures definitively resolved the issue. In 1949, New York extended the reach of a public utility short-form merger statute that expressly authorized the use of cash to cover all corporations, and in 1961 authorized the use of cash in long-form mergers. Delaware authorized the use of cash in short-form mergers in 1957 and in long-form mergers in 1967, and the Model Act followed suit in 1968 and 1969, respectively.[63]

---

[59] Del.Gen.Corp.Law § 263; Cal.Corp. Code § 1110(b).

[60] See generally Note, *The Short Merger Statute,* 32 U.Chi.L.Rev. 596 (1965).

[61] Act of June 1, 1925, ch. 10096, § 36, 1925 Fla. Laws 134 (emphasis added), quoted in Weiss, *The Law of Take Out Mergers: A Historical Perspective,* 56 N.Y.U.L.Rev. 624, 632 (1981). The discussion of the de-velopment of the use of cash as consideration in a merger draws heavily on Professor Weiss' excellent article.

[62] Compare Weiss, supra, at 637–41, with Borden, *Going Private—Old Tort, New Tort or No Tort?,* 49 N.Y.U.L.Rev. 987, 1026–27 (1974).

[63] Weiss, supra at 648.

3. State Law Limitations on the Ability to Freeze Out Minority Shareholders

The history of state law limitations on the ability of an acquiring company to freeze out minority shareholders is one of the most interesting—and eventful—stories in modern corporate law. It reflects, among other influences, the impact of political forces on judicial opinions, the opening shots of an ongoing debate over the appropriate role of the federal and state governments in setting corporate law standards, and the practical circumstances governing whether minority shareholders have any meaningful way to challenge their treatment in a freezeout transaction. The stage on which this historical drama took place was, not surprisingly, the Delaware courts. Interestingly, its plot has a circular quality. In some critical respects, the denouement—the result of years of legal turmoil and thousands of pages of judicial opinions and legal commentary—may be to have returned the characters to where they began, albeit having covered a good deal of ground in the interim.

The first act of the drama began with the statutory changes authorizing cash mergers described in the previous section. The action continued with their broad judicial construction. In Coyne v. Park & Tilford Distillers Corp.[64] and Stauffer v. Standard Brands, Inc.,[65] the Delaware courts explicitly rejected minority shareholders' objections to the use of short-form cash mergers to freeze them out. In *Stauffer,* the court set the terms of the later debate by rejecting the claim that oppressive treatment by the majority would be grounds for challenging the merger; where "the real relief sought is the recovery of the monetary value of plaintiff's shares * * * the statutory appraisal provisions [provide] an adequate remedy." 187 A.2d at 80. While acknowledging the "ever-present power of equity to deal with illegality or fraud," id., the court severely limited the reach of those terms:

> Indeed it is difficult to imagine a case under the short-form merger statute in which there could be such actual fraud as would entitle a minority to set aside the merger. This is so because the very purpose of the statute is to provide the parent corporation a means of eliminating the minority shareholder's interest in the enterprise.

Id. The *Stauffer* holding was extended to long-form mergers in David J. Breene & Co. v. Schenley Industries, Inc.[66] Thus, the terms of the doctrinal debate, and at least its interim resolution, were quite clearly set. The issue was the exclusivity of the appraisal remedy—could minority shareholders who objected to a freezeout challenge the merger itself rather than merely contesting the adequacy of the price paid them by invoking appraisal. The resolution was virtual exclusivity.

The drama's second act was ushered in by a shift in the tactics of plaintiffs seeking to challenge freezeout mergers and the concomitant growth of a political threat to the dominance of state law, particularly Delaware law, in this area. Plaintiffs' tactical shift followed what was by then a familiar pattern in corporate litigation: When state courts

[64] 38 Del.Ch. 514, 154 A.2d 893 (1959).   [66] 281 A.2d 30 (Del.Ch.1971).
[65] 41 Del.Ch. 7, 187 A.2d 78 (1962).

were unreceptive to claims of fiduciary breach, the federal courts, through resort to federal securities law, were sought as a more receptive forum. This effort reached its high point in the decision by the United States Court of Appeals for the Second Circuit in Green v. Santa Fe Industries, Inc.[67] The Court there held that an allegation that a majority shareholder breached its fiduciary duty by effecting a freeze-out of the minority "without any justifiable business purpose"[68] stated a claim under Rule 10b–5, even though plaintiffs had elected not to pursue the appraisal remedy that was available under Delaware law, and even though there was full and accurate disclosure concerning the merger to the minority shareholders.

At the same time as federal law was making litigation inroads into areas previously the exclusive domain of state law, political activity developed in response to the same perceived problem—insufficient protection of shareholders, especially minority shareholders, under state law. This activity sought the same end as the litigation efforts— "federalizing" areas of state corporate law—but through Congressional, rather than judicial action. The legislative proposals generally contemplated some form of federal chartering of, or specification of minimum standards for, publicly held corporations, the terms of which would preempt more lenient state law. Again, Delaware law figured most prominently in the political debate. In an influential article, Professor William Cary accused the Delaware legislature and judiciary of pandering to corporate management by leading a "race to the bottom" in fiduciary standards.[69] In addition to castigating the substance of Delaware corporate law, Cary despaired of any likelihood of state judicial reform. Tracing the links between the Delaware legislature, judiciary and corporate bar, Cary concluded that "major participation in state politics and in the leading firms inevitably would align the Delaware judiciary solidly with Delaware legislative policy."[70] This led Cary to propose a "Federal Corporate Uniformity Act" that would override state law on critical fiduciary issues.[71] His proposal did not stand alone.[72]

Act III began with the United States Supreme Court's reversal of the Second Circuit's decision in *Santa Fe*. From Delaware's prespective, the Supreme Court's opinion contained both good and bad news. The good news was that the Supreme Court slowed the expansion of federal securities law into state corporate law by construing Rule 10b–5 to require deception—misrepresentation or nondisclosure—for a violation. Significantly, that construction was based in part on a recognition of the historic dominance of state law in setting corporate fiduciary standards. The Court stated that "[a]bsent a clear indication of con-

[67] 533 F.2d 1283 (2d Cir.1976), reversed 430 U.S. 462 (1977).

[68] Id. at 1291.

[69] Cary, *Federalism and Corporate Law: Reflections Upon Delaware*, 83 Yale L.J. 663 (1974).

[70] Id. at 692.

[71] Id. at 700–03.

[72] See, e.g., R. Nader, *The Case for Federal Chartering*, in Corporate Power in America 67 (1973); Schwartz, *Federal Chartering of Corporations: An Introduction*, 61 Geo.L.J. 71 (1972); Schwartz, *The Case for Federal Chartering*, 31 Bus.Law. 1125 (1976).

gressional intent, we are reluctant to federalize the substantial portion of the law of corporations that deals with transactions in securities, particularly where established state policies of corporate regulation would be overridden."[73] The bad news was that the opinion could also be read as giving support to the political effort to displace state law by the adoption of federal chartering or minimum standards legislation. Citing Professor Cary's article, the Court also noted that "[t]here may well be a need for uniform federal fiduciary standards to govern mergers such as that challenged in this complaint * * *."[74]

Against this background, the Delaware Supreme Court decided Singer v. Magnavox Co., which had been argued and was under submission at the time the *Sante Fe* opinion was issued.[75]

SINGER v. MAGNAVOX CO.
Supreme Court of Delaware, 1977.
380 A.2d 969.

Before HERMANN, C.J., DUFFY and McNEILLY, JJ.

DUFFY, Justice (for the majority):

In this action attacking a statutory corporate merger, plaintiffs appeal from an order of the Court of Chancery granting defendants' motion to dismiss the complaint for failure to state a claim upon which relief can be granted. Del.Ch., 367 A.2d 1349 (1976).

I

The litigation centers on a merger in July 1975 of The Magnavox Company (Magnavox) with T.M.C. Development Corporation (T.M.C.). Plaintiffs owned common stock of Magnavox at the time of the merger and they bring this class action for all persons who held such shares on the day before the merger. Defendants are: Magnavox, North American Philips Corporation (North American), North American Philips Development Corporation (Development), and individual members of Magnavox management who held their positions in July 1975. All corporations involved are chartered in Delaware. T.M.C. is a wholly-owned subsidiary of Development, which in turn is owned entirely by North American. Apparently, Development's only function was to assist North American in the acquisition of Magnavox.

II

The salient facts appear in the complaint and in a stipulation of the parties.[1] These develop the followig scenario:

[73] 430 U.S. at 479.

[74] Id. at 479–80.

[75] For other suggestions that the Delaware Supreme Court's decision in *Singer* was influenced by political considerations, see, e.g., Herzl & Colling, *Squeeze-Out Mergers in Delaware—The Delaware Supreme Court Decision in Weinberger v.*

UOP, Inc., 7 Corp.L.Ref. 195 (1984); Thompson, *Squeeze–Out Mergers and the "New" Appraisal Remedy,* 62 Wash.U.L.Q. 415, 420 (1984); Brudney & Chirlstein, *A Restatement of Corporate Freezeouts,* 87 Yale L.J. 1354, 1354 n. 2 (1978).

[1] For the purpose of the motion to dismiss, the facts are taken as true. * * *

On August 21, 1974, North American incorporated Development for the purpose of making a tender offer for the Magnavox common shares. Prior to that time, North American and Magnavox were independent, unaffiliated corporations. On August 28, Development offered to buy all Magnavox shares at a price of $8 per share.

The tender offer included a statement informing Magnavox shareholders of Development's intention to acquire the entire equity interest in Magnavox, and advising them of the possible effects thereof, including: (1) delisting of present or future Magnavox shares by the New York Stock Exchange; (2) creation of an unfavorable market for the shares; (3) loss of information rights granted under Rules of the Exchange and under Federal securities law; and (4) depending on the number of shares acquired, the employment of other means of acquisition, particularly: " *   *   * through open market purchases, through a tender or exchange offer, or by any other means deemed advisable by it or whether to propose a merger, a sale or exchange of assets, liquidation or some other transactions *   *   *."

The directors of Magnavox voted to oppose the offer on the grounds of price inadequacy, among other things, and so notified their shareholders by letter issued on August 30. The letter stated, in part, that the "Company was shocked at the inadequacy of the offer of $8 per share in relationship to a book value in excess of $11.00 *   *   *."

In September 1974, the respective managements of Magnavox, North American and Development compromised their differences over the terms of the tender offer. They agreed to terms which included an increase in the offer price to $9 per share and, at the request of North American and Development, two-year employment contracts for sixteen officers of Magnavox (including some of the individual defendants) at existing salary levels. As part of the agreement, Magnavox withdrew its opposition to the tender offer. As modified, the offer was thus not opposed by Magnavox and, in response thereto, Development acquired approximately 84.1% of Magnavox's outstanding common stock.

With Development firmly in control of Magnavox, the managements of those two companies, and of North American, then set about acquiring all equity interest in Magnavox through a merger. In May 1975, Development caused the creation of T.M.C. for that purpose.

The directors of Magnavox unanimously agreed to the merger with T.M.C. and scheduled a special stockholders meeting for July 24, 1975, to vote on the plan. At the time of this action, four of the nine Magnavox directors were also directors of North American, and three others each had an employment contract, referred to above, with Magnavox and an option to purchase five thousand of North American's common shares, effective on the date of merger. In June 1975, the shareholders of Magnavox were given notice of the meeting with a proxy statement advising on the book value ($10.16) and merger price ($9.00) of the shares, and they were told that approval of the merger was assured since Development's holding alone was large enough to provide the requisite statutory majority. The proxy statement also advised the shareholders of their respective options to accept the merger price or to seek an appraisal under 8 Del.C. § 262.

Magnavox had some 75,000 stockholders. All materials disseminated in connection with the tender offer and the merger had a point of origin outside of Delaware. About 225 tender offer documents were mailed into this State and some 75 proxy statements were mailed to Delaware stockholders (and about 150 payment checks were distributed within the State).

The meeting was held in Delaware as scheduled, the proxies were voted here, stockholder approval was given, and the merger was accomplished.

* * *

Thereafter, plaintiffs filed a complaint in the Court of Chancery alleging that: (1) the merger was fraudulent in that it did not serve any business purpose other than the forced removal of public minority shareholders from an equity position in Magnavox at a grossly inadequate price to enable North American, through Development, to obtain sole ownership of Magnavox; (2) in approving the merger, at a cash price per share to the minority which they knew to be grossly inadequate, defendants breached their fiduciary duties to the minority shareholders * * * * Plaintiffs seek an order nullifying the merger and compensatory damages.

Defendants moved to dismiss the complaint on the ground that it fails to state a claim upon which relief may be granted, arguing that: (1) their actions are expressly authorized by 8 Del.C. § 251, and they fully complied therewith; (2) the exclusive remedy for dissatisfaction with the merger is an appraisal under 8 Del.C. § 262 * * *.

The Court of Chancery granted the motion to dismiss, ruling that: (1) the merger was not fraudulent merely because it was accomplished without any business purpose other than to eliminate the Magnavox minority shareholders; (2) in any event, plaintiffs' remedy for dissatisfaction with the merger is to seek an appraisal * * *.

III

We turn, first, to what we regard as the principal consideration in this appeal; namely, the obligation owed by majority shareholders in control of the corporate process to minority shareholders, in the context of a merger under 8 Del.C. § 251,* of two related Delaware corporations. It is, in other words, another round in the development of the law governing a parent corporation and minority shareholders in its subsidiary.

A.

To state the obvious, under § 251 two (or more) Delaware corporations "may merge into a single corporation." Generally speaking, whether such a transaction is good or bad, enlightened or ill-advised,

---

* Section 251 is reproduced in Chapter Thirteen A., supra. [Ed.]

selfish or generous—these considerations are beside the point. Section 251 authorizes a merger and any judicial consideration of that kind of togetherness must begin from that premise.

Section 251 also specifies in detail the procedures to be followed in accomplishing a merger. Briefly, these include approvals by the directors of each corporation and by "majority [vote] of the outstanding stock of" each corporation, followed by the execution and filing of formal documents. The consideration given to the shareholders of a constituent corporation in exchange for their stock may take the form of "cash, property, rights or securities of any other corporation." § 251(b)(4). A shareholder who objects to the merger and is dissatisfied with the value of the consideration given for his shares may seek an appraisal under 8 Del.C. § 262.[4]

[4] 8 Del.C. § 262 provides in part, as follows:

"(a) Appraisal rights under this section shall be available only for the shares of any stockholder who has complied with subsection (b) of this section and has neither voted in favor of the merger nor consented thereto in writing pursuant to § 228 of this title. When used in this section, the word 'stockholder' means a holder of record of stock in a stock corporation and also a member of record of a nonstock corporation; the words 'stock' and 'share' mean and include what is ordinarily meant by those words and also membership or membership interest of a member of a nonstock corporation.

(b) Appraisal rights under this section shall be determined as follows:

(1) If a proposed merger or consolidation for which appraisal rights are provided under this section is to be submitted for approval at a meeting of stockholders, the corporation, not less than 20 days prior to the meeting, shall notify each of its stockholders entitled to such appraisal rights that appraisal rights are available for any or all of the shares of the constituent corporations, and shall include in such notice a copy of this section. Each stockholder electing to demand the appraisal of his shares under this section shall deliver to the corporation, before the taking of the vote on the merger or consolidation, a written demand for appraisal of his shares. Such demand will be sufficient if it reasonably informs the corporation of the identity of the stockholder and that the stockholder intends thereby to demand the appraisal of his shares; provided, however, that such demand must be in addition to and separate from any proxy or vote against the merger. Within 10 days after the effective date of such merger or consolidation, the surviving corporation shall notify each stockholder of each constituent corporation who has complied with this subsection and has not voted in favor of or consented to the merger or consolidation of the date that the merger or consolidation has become effective; or

(2) If the merger or consolidation was approved pursuant to § 228 or § 253 of this title, the surviving corporation, either before the effective date of the merger or within 10 days thereafter, shall notify each of the stockholders entitled to appraisal rights of the effective date of the merger or consolidation and that appraisal rights are available for any or all of the shares of the constituent corporations. A copy of this section shall be included in the notice. The notice shall be sent by certified or registered mail, return receipt requested, addressed to the stockholder at his address as it appears on the records of the corporation. Any stockholder entitled to appraisal rights may, within 20 days after the date of mailing of the notice, demand in writing from the surviving corporation the appraisal of his shares. Such demand will be sufficient if it reasonably informs the corporation of the identity of the stockholder and that the stockholder intends thereby to demand the appraisal of his shares.

* * *

(f) After the determination of the stockholders entitled to an appraisal, the Court shall appraise the shares, determining their fair value exclusive of any element of value arising from the accomplishment or expectation of the merger. Upon application by any stockholder entitled to participate in the appraisal proceeding or by the corporation, the Court may, in its discretion, permit discovery or other pretrial proceedings and may proceed to trial upon the appraisal prior to the final determination of those other

B.

In this appeal it is uncontroverted that defendants complied with the stated requirements of § 251. Thus there is both statutory authorization for the Magnavox merger and compliance with the procedural requirements. But, contrary to defendants' contention, it does not necessarily follow that the merger is legally unassailable. We say this because, (a) plaintiffs invoke the fiduciary duty rule which allegedly binds defendants; and (b) Delaware case law clearly teaches that even complete compliance with the mandate of a statute does not, in every case, make the action valid in law.

The last stated proposition is derived from such cases as Schnell v. Chris-Craft Industries, Inc., Del.Supr., 285 A.2d 437, 439 (1971) (which involved advancement of the date of an annual meeting, accomplished in compliance with the relevant statute) wherein this Court said that " * * * inequitable action does not become permissible simply because it is legally possible; " and from Guth v. Loft, Inc., Del.Supr., 23 Del.Ch. 255, 5 A.2d 503, 511 (1939), in which the Court, responding to an argument for a narrow examination of issues, said that "[t]he question [at issue] is not one to be decided on narrow or technical grounds, but upon broad considerations of corporate duty and loyalty." We apply this approach and reject any contention that statutory compliance insulates the merger from judicial review.

C.

From this premise we must now analyze the encounter between the exercise of a statutory right and the performance of the alleged fiduciary duty. As we have noted, § 251, by its terms, makes permissible that which the North American side of this dispute caused to be done: the

stockholders who have complied with this section. Any stockholder whose name appears on the list filed by the corporation pursuant to subsection (d) of this section and who has submitted his certificates of stock to the Register in Chancery, if such is required, may participate fully in all proceedings until the Court shall determine that he is not entitled to appraisal rights under this section.

(g) The Court shall direct the payment of the appraised value of the shares, together with interest, if any, by the surviving or resulting corporation to the stockholders entitled thereto upon the surrender to the corporation of the certificates representing such stock.

* * *

(h) The costs of the proceeding may be determined by the Court and taxed upon the parties as the Court deems equitable in the circumstances. Upon the application of any party in interest, the Court shall determine the amount of interest, if any, to be paid upon the value of the

stock of the stockholders entitled thereto. In making its determination with respect to interest, the Court may consider all relevant factors, including the rate of interest which the corporation has paid for money it has borrowed, if any, during the pendency of the proceeding. Upon application of a stockholder, the Court may order all or a portion of the expenses incurred by any stockholder in connection with the appraisal proceeding, including, without limitation, reasonable attorney's fees and the fees and expenses of experts, to be charged pro rata against the value of all of the shares entitled to an appraisal."

Counsel have pointed out to us that subparagraph (h), in its present form, became effective July 1, 1976 and now authorizes the Court to charge expenses (including attorney fees and the expense of employing experts) "against the value of all of the shares entitled to an appraisal." Realistically, that may broaden the scope of the value inquiry in an appraisal proceeding but it is not significant here.

merger of T.M.C. into Magnavox. We must ascertain, however, what restraint, if any, the duty to minority stockholders placed on the exercise of that right.

Plaintiffs contend that the Magnavox merger was fraudulent because it was made without any ascertainable corporate business purpose and was designed solely to freeze out the minority stockholders. After a review of the cases, the Trial Court concluded that to the extent the complaint charges that the merger was fraudulent because it did not serve a business purpose of Magnavox, it fails to state a claim upon which relief may be granted. Our analysis leads to a different result, not on the basis of fraud but on application of the law governing corporate fiduciaries.

The statute is silent on the question of whether a merger may be accomplished only for a valid business purpose, but two recent unreported decisions seem to suggest that such a showing is required under Delaware law. See Pennsylvania Mutual Fund, Inc. v. Todhunter International, Inc., Del.Ch.C.A. 4845 (August 5, 1975), and Tanzer v. International General Industries, Inc., Del.Ch.C.A. 4945 (December 23, 1975).[5] Neither decision was by this Court and the issue is one of first impression here.

Any inquiry into the business purpose of a merger immediately leads to such questions as: "Whose purpose?" or "Whose business?" Is it that of the corporations whose shares are (or were) held by the minority? If so, it may well be that the business purpose of that company (*qua* company) is advanced by the merger, but that could be an academic result if the complainants (as here) are no longer shareholders because they have been cashed-out. On the other hand, if the corporation in which the complainants held shares "vanishes" in the merger, inquiry as to purpose may be unrealistic if not academic. And if the business purpose of the parent (or dominant) corporation should be examined (as defendants argue), minority shareholders of the subsidiary (or controlled corporation) may have undue difficulty in raising and maintaining the issue.

---

[5] In *Todhunter*, the Court granted an order temporarily restraining the accomplishment of a merger which plaintiff alleged "constitute[d] an unlawful freeze-out of * * * [its] interest as a stockholder * * *." The Chancellor commented:

"* * * I have some doubt as to whether or not the merger under attack has a valid business purpose. In other words, this is probably or possibly not a case in which a dissenting stockholder is merely entitled to an appraisal because of his unwillingness to continue in a changed business. Here there is to be no change in the business but merely an elimination of unwanted minority stockholders.

I feel therefore that there is some possibility on further argument and development of the case of a showing of illegality of this plan by reason of it being a possible manipulation of corporate control for private purposes with no proper business purpose in mind."

Tanzer, on the other hand, involved a request for a preliminary injunction preventing the merger of two related corporations. The need for a finding of business purpose is implied in the following statement by the Court:

"The question presented is whether the merger should be enjoined because the purpose is to serve the interest of the parent. It should be noted in this regard that IGI has a legitimate and present and compelling business reason to be the sole owner of Kliklok. IGI is not freezing out the minority just for the purpose of freezing out the minority."

The point of this discussion is not that an exploration of the business purpose for a merger is without merit. It may well be necessary to examine that purpose in many mergers under judicial review. But as a threshold consideration in this opinion, it is not helpful in sorting out rights of the parties. It seems to us, rather, that the approach to the purpose issue should be made by first examining the competing claims between the majority and minority stockholders of Magnavox. That is what is really up for decision here, and so we look to the standards governing that relationship.

D.

It is a settled rule of law in Delaware that Development, as the majority stockholder of Magnavox, owed to the minority stockholders of that corporation, a fiduciary obligation in dealing with the latter's property. Sterling v. Mayflower Hotel Corp., Del.Supr., 33 Del.Ch. 293, 93 A.2d 107, 109–10 (1952). In that leading "interested merger" case, this Court recognized as established law in this State that the dominant corporation, as a majority stockholder standing on both sides of a merger transaction, has "the burden of establishing its entire fairness" to the minority stockholders, sufficiently to "pass the test of careful scrutiny by the courts." See 93 A.2d at 109, 110. See also Bastian v. Bourns, Inc., Del.Ch., 256 A.3d 680, 681 (1969), aff'd Del.Supr., 278 A.2d 467 (1970); and David J. Greene & Co. v. Dunhill International, Inc., Del.Ch., 249 A.2d 427, 430 (1968). The fiduciary obligation is the cornerstone of plaintiffs' rights in this controversy and the corollary, of course, is that it is likewise the measure of the duty owed by defendants.

Delaware courts have long announced and enforced high standards which govern the internal affairs of corporations chartered here, particularly when fiduciary relations are under scrutiny. It is settled Delaware law, for example, that corporate officers and directors, Guth v. Loft, Inc., supra, and controlling shareholders, Sterling v. Mayflower Hotel Corp., supra; Bennett v. Breuil Petroleum Corp., 34 Del.Ch. 6, 99 A.2d 236 (1953), owe their corporation and its minority shareholders a fiduciary obligation of honesty, loyalty, good faith and fairness. Other cases applying that equitable doctrine include Schnell v. Chris-Craft Industries, Inc., supra; Kaplan v. Fenton, Del.Supr., 278 A.2d 834 (1971); Dolese Bros. Co. v. Brown, Del.Supr., 39 Del.Ch. 1, 157 A.2d 784 (1960); Johnston v. Greene, Del.Supr., 35 Del.Ch. 479, 121 A.2d 919 (1956); Italo-Petroleum Corporation of America v. Hannigan, Del.Supr., 1 Terry 534, 14 A.2d 401 (1940); Condec Corporation v. Lunkenheimer Company, 43 Del.Ch. 353, 230 A.2d 769 (1967); Craig v. Graphic Arts Studio, Inc., 39 Del.Ch. 477, 166 A.2d 444 (1960); Brophy v. Cities Service Co., 31 Del.Ch. 241, 70 A.2d 5 (1949).

The classic definition of the duty was stated by Chief Justice Layton in *Guth,* where he wrote:

> " * * * While technically not trustees, * * * [corporate directors] stand in a fiduciary relation to the corporation and its stockholders. A public policy, existing through the years, and

derived from a profound knowledge of human characteristics and motives, has established a rule that demands of a corporate officer or director, peremptorily and inexorably, the most scrupulous observance of his duty, not only affirmatively to protect the interests of the corporation committed to his charge, but also to refrain from doing anything that would work injury to the corporation, or to deprive it of profit or advantage which his skill and ability might properly bring to it, or to enable it to make in the reasonable and lawful exercise of its powers. The rule that requires an undivided and unselfish loyalty to the corporation demands that there shall be no conflict between duty and self-interest. The occasions for the determination of honesty, good faith and loyal conduct are many and varied, and no hard and fast rule can be formulated. The standard of loyalty is measured by no fixed scale."

5 A.2d at 510. While that comment was about directors, the spirit of the definition is equally applicable to a majority stockholder in any context in which the law imposes a fiduciary duty on that stockholder for the benefit of minority stockholders. We so hold.

* * *

Defendants concede that they owe plaintiffs a fiduciary duty but contend that, in the context of the present transaction they have met that obligation by offering fair value for the Magnavox shares. And, say defendants, plaintiffs' exclusive remedy for dissatisfaction with the merger is to seek an appraisal under § 262. We disagree. In our view, defendants cannot meet their fiduciary obligations to plaintiffs simply by relegating them to a statutory appraisal proceeding.[7]

At the core of defendants' contention is the premise that a shareholder's right is exclusively in the *value* of his investment, not its *form*. And, they argue, that right is protected by a § 262 appraisal which, by definition, results in fair value for the shares. This argument assumes that the right to take is coextensive with the power to take and that a dissenting stockholder has no legally protected right in his shares, his certificate or his company beyond a right to be paid fair value[8] when the majority is ready to do this. Simply stated, such an argument does not square with the duty stated so eloquently and so forcefully by Chief Justice Layton in *Guth*.

We agree that, because the power to merge is conferred by statute, every stockholder in a Delaware corporation accepts his shares with notice thereof. See Federal United Corporation v. Havender, Del.Supr., 24 Del.Ch. 318, 11 A.2d 331, 338 (1940). Indeed, some Delaware

[7] See Vorenberg, *Exclusiveness of the Dissenting Stockholder's Appraisal Right,* 77 Harv.L.R. 1189 (1964).

[8] That argument was rejected in Jutkowitz v. Bourns, Cal.Super.Ct. C.A. 000268 (Nov. 19, 1975), wherein the Court correctly summarized some of the values besides money which may be at stake in a "going-private" merger:

"Money may well satisfy some or most minority shareholders, but others may have differing investment goals, tax problems, a belief in the ability of * * * management to make them rich, or even a sentimental attachment to the stock which leads them to have a different judgment as to the desirability of selling out."

Cf. Bryan v. Brock & Blevins Co., Inc., 5 Cir., 490 F.2d 563 (1974); Berkowitz v. Power/Mate Corporation, 135 N.J.Super. 36, 342 A.2d 566 (1975).

decisions have noted that to "the extent authorized by statute, ∗ ∗ ∗ [mergers] are 'encouraged and favored.' " *Folk* supra at 332. Beyond question, the common law right of a single stockholder to simply veto a merger is gone. Id. at 331. But it by no means follows that those in control of a corporation may invoke the statutory power conferred by § 251, a power which this Court in *Havender,* supra, said was "somewhat analogous to the right of eminent domain," 11 A.2d at 338, when their purpose is simply to get rid of a minority.[9] On the contrary, as we shall ultimately conclude here, just as a minority shareholder may not thwart a merger without cause, neither may a majority cause a merger to be made for the sole purpose of eliminating a minority on a cash-out basis.

E.

Plaintiffs allege that defendants violated their respective fiduciary duties by participating in the tender offer and other acts which led to the merger and which were designed to enable Development and North American to, among other things:

> "[C]onsummate a merger which did not serve any valid corporate purpose or compelling business need of Magnavox and whose sole purpose was to enable Development and North American to obtain sole ownership of the business and assets of Magnavox at a price determined by defendants which was grossly inadequate and unfair and which was designed to give Development and North American a disproportionate amount of the gain said defendants anticipated would be recognized from consummation of the merger."

Defendants contend, and the Court of Chancery agreed, that the "business purpose" rule does not have a place in Delaware's merger law. In support of this contention defendants cite: Stauffer v. Standard Brands, Incorporated, Del.Supr., 187 A.2d 78 (1962); Federal United Corporation v. Havender, supra; David J. Greene & Co. v. Schenley Industries, Inc., Del.Ch., 281 A.2d 30 (1971); Bruce v. E.L. Bruce Company, 40 Del.Ch. 80, 174 A.2d 29 (1961); and MacCrone v. American Capital Corporation, D.Del., 51 F.Supp. 462 (1943).

Each of these cases involved an effort to enjoin or attack a merger and each was unsuccessful. To this extent they support defendants' side of the controversy. But none of these decisions involved a merger in which the minority was totally expelled *via* a straight "cash-for-stock" conversion in which the only purpose of the merger was, as alleged here, to eliminate the minority.

[9] The Trial Judge, in blunt and descriptive language, addressed the "going private" problem in these words:

"Admittedly there seems something fundamentally inequitable about such a stark progression of events and perhaps a use of the Delaware statutes should not be permitted which would allow those with controlling interests who originally sought public participation to later kick out public investors for the sole reason that they have outlived their utility to those in control and are made easy pickings by existing market conditions."

367 A.2d at 1358. For a more detailed discussion of "going private," see: *Going Private,* 84 Yale L.J. 903 (1975).

In *Stauffer,* a § 253 case, the Court carefully examined plaintiffs' charges of majority oppression and concluded that the complaint alleged "nothing but a difference of opinion as to [the] value" of the converted shares. 187 A.2d at 80. Viewing the case in this light, the Court ruled that a statutory appraisal was plaintiffs' exclusive medium of relief. We do not read the decision as approving a merger accomplished solely to freeze-out the minority without a valid business purpose.

Without question, *Havender* is an important opinion under our merger law, but we do not regard it as precedent here because the Merger Statute in effect at the time it was written did not authorize a pure cash-for-shares conversion. Moreover, *Havender* stands for the proposition that a merger must be "fair and equitable in the circumstances of the case" in order to withstand the veto of a dissenting shareholder. See 11 A.2d at 338.

Likewise, neither *Schenley* nor *Bruce* involved a "cash-out merger," the *sole* purpose of which was to eliminate minority stockholders. Accordingly, those cases are inapposite. Any statement therein which seems to be in conflict with what is said herein must be deemed overruled.

We hold the law to be that a Delaware Court will not be indifferent to the purpose of a merger when a freeze-out of minority stockholders on a cash-out basis is alleged to be its sole purpose. In such a situation, if it is alleged that the purpose is improper because of the fiduciary obligation owed to the minority, the Court is duty-bound to closely examine that allegation even when all of the relevant statutory formalities have been satisfied.

Consistent with this conclusion is Bennett v. Breuil Petroleum Corp., supra, wherein plaintiff alleged that the dominant shareholder caused the issuance of new shares to impair his interest and to force him out of the corporation upon management's terms. At the outset the Court said:

> "As a starting point it must be conceded that action by majority stockholders having as its primary purpose the 'freezing out' of a minority interest is actionable without regard to the fairness of the price."

99 A.2d at 239. Thereafter, the Chancellor denied defendants' motions for dismissal and summary judgment, ruling:

> "It seems to me that plaintiff has set forth a legally recognized claim and the pleadings and affidavits have raised a *substantial factual dispute as to the legal propriety of the motives of the corporate defendant and its controlling stockholder* which can only be resolved by a hearing." (Emphasis added.)

Id.

And in Condec Corporation v. Lunkenheimer Company, supra, the Court applied a similar approach in an action for cancellation of stock alleged to be issued for the purpose of retaining corporate control, stating that "shares may not be issued for an improper purpose such as a take-over of voting control from others." 230 A.2d at 775. See Yasik v. Wachtel, 25 Del.Ch. 247, 17 A.2d 309 (1941). Quoting from the above language in *Bennett,* the Court reaffirmed that the "corporate machinery may not be manipulated so as to injure minority stockholders," 230 A.2d at 775, and ordered the shares cancelled.

Similarly, in Schnell v. Chris-Craft Industries, Inc., supra, this Court examined the purpose for advancement of the date of an annual meeting when it was allegedly done to perpetuate management in office. In ordering that the advanced date be nullified, Chief Justice (then Justice) Herrmann answered management's claim that strict statutory compliance insulated its action from attack by saying "that inequitable action does not become permissible simply because it is legally possible." 285 A.2d at 439.[10]

Read as a whole, those opinions illustrate two principles of law which we approve: First, it is within the responsibility of an equity court to scrutinize a corporate act when it is alleged that its purpose violates the fiduciary duty owed to minority stockholders; and second, those who control the corporate machinery owe a fiduciary duty to the minority in the exercise thereof over corporate powers and property, and the use of such power to perpetuate control is a violation of that duty.

By analogy, if not *a fortiori,* use of corporate power solely to *eliminate* the minority is a violation of that duty. Accordingly, while we agree with the conclusion of the Court of Chancery that this merger was not fraudulent merely because it was accomplished without any purpose other than elimination of the minority stockholders, we conclude that, for that reason, it was violative of the fiduciary duty owed by the majority to the minority stockholders.

We hold, therefore, that a § 251 merger, made for the sole purpose of freezing out minority stockholders, is an abuse of the corporate process; and the complaint, which so alleges in this suit, states a cause of action for violation of a fiduciary duty for which the Court may grant such relief as it deems appropriate under the circumstances.

This is not to say, however, that merely because the Court finds that a cash-out merger was not made for the sole purpose of freezing out minority stockholders, all relief must be denied to the minority stockholders in a § 251 merger.[11] On the contrary, the fiduciary obligation of the majority to the minority stockholders remains and proof of a purpose, other than such freeze-out, without more, will not necessarily discharge it. In such case the Court will scrutinize the circumstances for compliance with the *Sterling* rule of "entire fairness"

[10] Other cases following the *Bennett-Condec-Schnell* approach include Baron v. Allied Artists Pictures Corporation, Del.Ch. 337 A.2d 653 (1975); Petty v. Penntech Papers, Inc., Del.Ch., 347 A.2d 140 (1975); and, most recently, *Todhunter,* supra.

[11] Plaintiffs contend that a "business purpose" is proper in a merger only when it serves the interests of the subsidiary corporation; defendants contend, on the other hand, that if any such purpose is relevant, it is only that of the parent corporation. Since resolution of that question is not necessary to the disposition of this appeal, and since it was not central in the briefing and argument, we leave it to another day.

and, if it finds a violation thereof, will grant such relief as equity may require. Any statement in *Stauffer* inconsistent herewith is held inapplicable to a § 251 merger.

* * *

Accordingly, as to this facet of the appeal, we reverse.

━━━━◆━━━━

It is fair to read *Singer* as having imposed greater limits on an acquiring company's ability to freeze out minority shareholders. Although Sterling v. Mayflower Hotel Corp., upon which the Court relied so heavily in *Singer*, had never been explicitly overruled, "[m]ost observers, however, believed that the *Stauffer* line of cases rendered the *Sterling* rule inapplicable to cash mergers, in which appraisal rights were available to dissenters." [76] The problem, however, was that it was impossible to tell from the *Singer* opinion just how significant the new limitations really were.

Singer's first limitation was that a merger could not be for the "sole purpose of freezing out minority shareholders." [77] But what additional purpose would be sufficient? On the one hand, if the additional purpose had to be that of the *target* company, so that the minority shareholders somehow were served by the transaction, then freezeout transactions might be impossible. On the other hand, if the additional purpose could serve the business interests of only the *acquiring* company, the limitation was a mirage. Presumably an acquiring company would always have a business purpose for—an explanation for why it would gain from—freezing out the minority. If there was no benefit to the acquiring company—the freezeout really was for the "sole purpose of freezing out minority shareholders"—why would it bother?

Even if a freezeout merger satisfied the business purpose requirement, *Singer* also required that the merger comply with "the *Sterling* rule of 'entire fairness.'" [78] But what would constitute "entire fairness"? If it was merely that the price paid had to be "fair," and plaintiffs in *Singer* did allege the price to be "grossly inadequate," then scrutiny for "entire fairness" might not be any different than the appraisal proceeding that had been available to those who objected to a merger prior to *Singer*.

Finally, *Singer* only briefly considered the remedy that would be available should the merger fail either the business purpose or the entire fairness requirements. The Court stated that in such event, it would "grant relief as equity may require." [79] But if all equity required was a fair price, then how would the relief differ from that which would be forthcoming in an appraisal proceeding? If, alternatively, the measure of damages was something other than would be forthcoming in an appraisal proceeding, what measure would be appropriate? And, of course, if the measure of damages was different from the fair price

[76] Weiss, *The Law of Take Out Mergers: A Historical Perspective,* 56 N.Y.U.L.Rev. 624, 655 (1981).

[77] 380 A.2d at 980.

[78] Id.

[79] Id. at 980.

determined by appraisal standards, then, in turn, "entire fairness" had to mean something more than just the fairness of the price.

These issues were addressed in a number of cases over the five years following *Singer*. The character of the business purpose necessary to support a freezeout merger was explored in Tanzer v. International General Industries,[80] decided less than a month following *Singer*. In *Tanzer*, International General Industries, Inc. ("IGI"), the owner of 81 percent of the stock of Kliklok Corporation, accomplished the freeze-out of the Kliklok minority by means of a long-form triangular cash merger. Minority shareholders then challenged the merger, arguing that "a freeze-out merger imposed on a subsidiary corporation by a parent, and designed solely for the purpose of benefiting the parent, is impermissible under Delaware law." 379 A.2d at 1123. The Court joined the issue directly:

> As we observed at the outset, *Singer* determines that a cash-out of minority stockholders, when that is the sole purpose of a merger, is a violation of a fiduciary duty owed to them by a majority stockholder. In one sense, that may be said to be what is involved in the Kliklok merger because the minority were cashed out and it is not contended by defendants that Kliklok benefited from the merger. However, the real issue for decision centers around IGI's right to cause a merger "for a valid business reason" of its own, independent of any corporate interest of Kliklok. In short, the question is whether the parent may cause a merger to be made solely for its own benefit, or whether that is a violation of fiduciary duty and actionable under Delaware corporation law.

Id. The Court's conclusion was straightforward. So long as the freeze-out served a *bona fide* purpose of the parent, the *Singer* business purpose test was met. The Court stressed, however, as it had in *Singer*, that the *Sterling* test still had to be met, and remanded the case "for judicial scrutiny for 'entire fairness' as to all aspects of the transaction." Id. at 1125. As in *Singer*, no clue was provided as to what "entire fairness" might consist of.[81]

Thus, after *Tanzer*, the *Singer* business purpose test seemed hardly burdensome; to be sure, a record concerning the parent's *bona fide* purpose would have to be created, but this would impose no more than

---

80 379 A.2d 1121 (Del.1977).

81 Roland International Corp. v. Najjar, 407 A.2d 1039 (Del.1979), extended the *Singer* analysis to short-form mergers. For these transactions, where the statute dispenses with even the requirement that the target shareholders approve the freezeout, it could be argued that the very purpose of the statute was to allow the minority to be eliminated. Thus, for short-form mergers, further inquiry into "business purpose" should be unnecessary. The Delaware Supreme Court declined to draw this distinction between long-form and short-form mergers. It also declined to distinguish between types of freezeouts based on the

circumstances of the particular transaction. Some commentators had argued persuasively that a second-step freezeout merger which followed a first-step tender offer should not be subject to the *Singer* test because it was really part of a single arms-length transaction that, by tendering in the first-step, target shareholders had already approved. On this analysis, there was no fiduciary duty and no self-dealing problem. See Brudney & Chirlstein, *A Restatement of Corporate Freezeouts*, 87 Yale L.J. 1354 (1978). The court held that *Singer* "applies to all majority shareholders, no matter how, nor how recently such majority was obtained." 407 A.2d at 1034 n. 4.

a mechanical barrier to counsel planning the transaction. If *Singer* was to have any impact, it would have to come from the content of the entire fairness test and from the character of the remedy that would be forthcoming if the test was failed.

It is helpful to look first at the remedy question, and for this purpose to break that question into two parts: The procedure by which the remedy, whatever it is, is obtained, and the actual substance of the remedy. Consider first the procedure. Suppose that even if a violation of *Singer* were found, the remedy would be to award minority shareholders the "fair value" of their shares determined in the same way as "fair value" would be determined in an appraisal proceeding. In this situation one could argue that *Singer* was simply beside the point. Minority shareholders end up in the same place with or without *Singer:* The value of their stock is appraised. The argument, however, ignores the reality of the litigation process.

Under Delaware Section 262, a shareholder who wishes to invoke his appraisal rights must so notify the corporation prior to the vote on the freezeout transaction (Section 262(b)(1)) and must not vote in favor of it (abstention is sufficient). (Section 262(a)). Then, within 120 days after the merger, the shareholder must find a lawyer and commence an appraisal proceeding by petitioning the Court of Chancery (Section 262(e)). In the absence of a contingency fee, the shareholder must advance the costs and expenses, including expert witness fees, necessary to pursue the appraisal proceeding. Indeed, even a contingency fee would not entirely solve the problem of the expense of the proceeding. Unless the shareholder held a substantial number of shares, the potential reward would be too small to warrant the necessary investment of time and money by the lawyer. A solution would be to facilitate the lawyer's representation of a number of shareholders; however, it is not so easy to aggregate plaintiffs in an appraisal proceeding. Because under the corporate statute each shareholder must individually perfect his appraisal rights, the universe of potential clients is not determined until after the shareholder meeting. As a result, shareholders who do not have a large enough investment to warrant hiring a lawyer may well have eliminated themselves as potential plaintiffs by voting in favor of the transaction.

The situation is not much better with respect to those shareholders who, by luck or design, remain eligible to exercise their appraisal rights. There is no procedural analogue to a class action that would allow a single lawyer to represent all eligible shareholders with respect to what are entirely common issues of law and fact—the value of the shares—and thereby both reduce the costs of the proceedings for shareholders and their counsel, and allow the aggregation of minority shareholders claims necessary to make a contingency fee an attractive investment for a lawyer.[82]

[82] Delaware Section 262(h) does provide the potential for something of a class action with respect to those shareholders who do individually perfect their appraisal rights. The court is authorized to "order all or a portion of the expenses incurred by any stockholder in connection with the appraisal proceeding, including, without limitation, reasonable attorney's fees and the expenses of experts, to be charged pro rata

Under these circumstances, the best strategy for an acquiring company intent on freezing out the minority may be to "low-ball"—to set the freezeout price *below* what it believes a court would determine to be fair value in an appraisal proceeding. Because of the procedural expense and difficulty of appraisal, and especially because the absence of a class action mechanism makes it impossible for lawyers to act, in effect, as surrogates for minority shareholders with respect to whether to invest in an appraisal proceeding, most shareholders will not dissent. As a result, many of the minority shares can be purchased for less than what would be the "appraisal" price. Thus, to the extent it can be anticipated that some shareholders will not seek appraisal, the acquiring company has an incentive to set the freezeout price too low.

The analysis changes radically if, instead of an appraisal proceeding, there has been a violation of *Singer*. Even though we have assumed that the substance of the remedy for such a violation will be the same as in an appraisal proceeding, the procedure is radically different. Most important, the suit can be brought as a class action. Minority shareholders need take no affirmative action in order to participate, nor need they expend any resources to pursue the action. All the responsibility—both for initiating the action and for its expenses—is borne by the self-designated lawyer for the class who is compensated, one way or the other, out of the amount recovered. The lawyer then stands, in effect, as an independent investor who balances his estimate of the potential recovery to all shareholders against the cost of the proceeding and the uncertainty associated with its outcome. While the presence of transaction costs may still create some incentive for the acquiring company to "low-ball",[83] it is hardly of the magnitude of that created by the mechanics of the appraisal proceeding.

Thus, even if the substance of the *Singer* remedy did not differ one whit from that which would be forthcoming in an appraisal proceeding, the availability of the class action mechanism to enforce a violation of *Singer* meant that substantially more shareholders could benefit from it. Whatever else it might have done, *Singer* operated, in effect, to provide for class action appraisal.

against the value of all shares entitled to appraisal." If such an order could be obtained at the pre-trial stage, it at least would allow the designation of lead counsel and the avoidance of duplication of expense associated with a class action procedure.

[83] The advantages of a class action proceeding should not mask the conflict of interest problems that arise between the plaintiff's lawyer and the plaintiff class, especially with respect to settlement. Suppose the corporation has made a settlement offer of $25 per share and that the plaintiff's lawyer believes that if the matter goes to trial there is a 50 percent chance of receiving $40 per share and a 50 percent chance of receiving $15 per share. The plaintiff class might choose to go to trial because the expected value of the post-trial award, $27.50, exceeds the settlement offer. For the lawyer, however, the decision is more complex. To be sure, the lawyer, through the contingency arrangement, would share in the additional award; however, he would have to try the case in order to receive the additional fee, while the settlement could be achieved with no additional work. Thus, for the lawyer, the question is whether, at the margin, the additional fee is worth the time necessary to try the case. For an excellent discussion of such conflicts, *see* Coffee, *The Unfaithful Champion: The Plaintiff as Monitor in Shareholder Litigation*, Working Paper No. 11, Center for Law and Economic Studies, Columbia University Law School (Jan. 1985).

The question that then remains is what valuation standard would be applied in such a class action appraisal. Some indication of the answer was provided in *Lynch v. Vickers Energy Corp.*[84] That case involved not a freezeout merger, but a tender offer by the existing majority shareholder. The minority shareholders who had accepted the offer subsequently sued, claiming that the majority shareholder had violated its fiduciary duty to the minority by not disclosing to them with "complete candor" all of the facts bearing on the tender offer. In particular, it was alleged that the majority shareholder withheld the fact that the company's net asset value had been estimated at an amount substantially in excess of that offered to the minority in the tender offer, and that management of the company had been authorized to make open market purchases of the company's stock at prices up to 25% higher than the tender offer price. Following the Delaware Supreme Court's decision in an earlier appeal that the nondisclosures had violated the majority shareholder's fiduciary duty, on remand the trial court held that the appropriate remedy was "a proceeding analogous to an appraisal hearing such as is provided in merger cases is appropriate here." [85] The appeal from the trial court's determination of the appropriate remedy thus presented the Delaware Supreme Court with the opportunity to resolve an issue analogous to that left open by *Singer:* If minority shareholders are eliminated from the corporation as a result of a breach of the majority shareholder's fiduciary duty, whether by a freezeout merger or by a misleading tender offer, was an appraisal standard the appropriate measure of relief?

The Delaware Supreme Court rejected the appraisal standard. The court noted that because appraisal requires plaintiff's shares to be valued at the time of the transaction, it "has a built-in limitation, namely, gain to the corporation resulting from a statutory merger is not a factor in determining the value of the shares." [86] To avoid this limitation, the Court instead developed an alternative to the appraisal standard: The "monetary equivalent of rescission." [87] The value of plaintiff's stock would be determined not at the time of the transaction, as would be the case in appraisal, but at the time of judgment. This had the effect of giving the plaintiffs their share of the gain from the merger, which they would not have received in an appraisal.

At this point, the end of Act III of the drama, we knew the following with certainty. First, the appraisal remedy was not exclusive in freezeout mergers; minority shareholders could enjoin the merger if it was for the sole purpose of freezing them out, or if it was not entirely fair. A credible reason why the freezeout benefitted the acquiring company would satisfy the business purpose test, but there was still no clear statement of what would satisfy the entire fairness test. Second, there was substantial reason to believe that if either the business purpose test or the entire fairness test was violated, the remedy would not be limited to an appraisal standard; post-transaction gains would be taken into account. Finally, it was clear that, regardless of the

[84] 429 A.2d 497 (1981).

[85] 402 A.2d 5, 11 (Del.Ch.1979).

[86] 429 A.2d at 501.

[87] Id.

measure of the remedy, minority shareholders were better off with a pre-transaction *Singer* action than they would have been with a post-transaction appraisal hearing because of the differences between the two procedures; the *Singer* action could be brought as a class action.

It was at this point that the Delaware Supreme Court opened the final act of the drama with its decision in Weinberger v. UOP, Inc.[88]

WEINBERGER v. UOP, INC.
Supreme Court of Delaware, 1983.
457 A.2d 701.

Before HERRMANN, C.J., McNEILLY, QUILLEN, HORSEY and MOORE, JJ., constituting the Court en Banc.

MOORE, Justice:

This post-trial appeal was reheard en banc from a decision of the Court of Chancery. It was brought by the class action plaintiff below, a former shareholder of UOP, Inc., who challenged the elimination of UOP's minority shareholders by a cash-out merger between UOP and its majority owner, The Signal Companies, Inc.[2] Originally, the defendants in this action were Signal, UOP, certain officers and directors of those companies, and UOP's investment banker, Lehman Brothers Kuhn Loeb, Inc.[3] The present Chancellor held that the terms of the merger were fair to the plaintiff and the other minority shareholders of UOP. Accordingly, he entered judgment in favor of the defendants.

Numerous points were raised by the parties, but we address only the following questions presented by the trial court's opinion:

1) The plaintiff's duty to plead sufficient facts demonstrating the unfairness of the challenged merger;

2) The burden of proof upon the parties where the merger has been approved by the purportedly informed vote of a majority of the minority shareholders;

3) The fairness of the merger in terms of adequacy of the defendants' disclosures to the minority shareholders;

4) The fairness of the merger in terms of adequacy of the price paid for the minority shares and the remedy appropriate to that issue; and

5) The continued force and effect of Singer v. Magnavox Co., Del.Supr., 380 A.2d 969, 980 (1977), and its progeny.

In ruling for the defendants, the Chancellor re-stated his earlier conclusion that the plaintiff in a suit challenging a cash-out merger must allege specific acts of fraud, misrepresentation, or other items of misconduct to demonstrate the unfairness of the merger terms to the minority.[4] We approve this rule and affirm it.

---

[88] 457 A.2d 701 (Del.1983).

[2] For the opinion of the trial court see Weinberger v. UOP, Inc., Del.Ch., 426 A.2d 1333 (1981).

[3] Shortly before the last oral argument, the plaintiff dismissed Lehman Brothers

from the action. Thus, we do not deal with the issues raised by the plaintiff's claims against this defendant.

[4] In a pre-trial ruling the Chancellor ordered the complaint dismissed for failure

The Chancellor also held that even though the ultimate burden of proof is on the majority shareholder to show by a preponderance of the evidence that the transaction is fair, it is first the burden of the plaintiff attacking the merger to demonstrate some basis for invoking the fairness obligation. We agree with that principle. However, where corporate action has been approved by an informed vote of a majority of the minority shareholders, we conclude that the burden entirely shifts to the plaintiff to show that the transaction was unfair to the minority. See, e.g., Michelson v. Duncan, Del.Supr., 407 A.2d 211, 224 (1979). But in all this, the burden clearly remains on those relying on the vote to show that they completely disclosed all material facts relevant to the transaction.

Here, the record does not support a conclusion that the minority stockholder vote was an informed one. Material information, necessary to acquaint those shareholders with the bargaining positions of Signal and UOP, was withheld under circumstances amounting to a breach of fiduciary duty. We therefore conclude that this merger does not meet the test of fairness, at least as we address that concept, and no burden thus shifted to the plaintiff by reason of the minority shareholder vote. Accordingly, we reverse and remand for further proceedings consistent herewith.

In considering the nature of the remedy available under our law to minority shareholders in a cash-out merger, we believe that it is, and hereafter should be, an appraisal under 8 Del.C. § 262 as hereinafter construed. We therefore overrule Lynch v. Vickers Energy Corp., Del. Supr., 429 A.2d 497 (1981) (*Lynch II*) to the extent that it purports to limit a stockholder's monetary relief to a specific damage formula. See *Lynch II*, 429 A.2d at 507–08 (McNeilly & Quillen, JJ., dissenting). But to give full effect to section 262 within the framework of the General Corporation Law we adopt a more liberal, less rigid and stylized, approach to the valuation process than has heretofore been permitted by our courts. While the present state of these proceedings does not admit the plaintiff to the appraisal remedy per se, the practical effect of the remedy we do grant him will be co-extensive with the liberalized valuation and appraisal methods we herein approve for cases coming after this decision.

Our treatment of these matters has necessarily led us to a reconsideration of the business purpose rule announced in the trilogy of Singer v. Magnavox Co., supra; Tanzer v. International General Industries, Inc., Del.Supr., 379 A.2d 1121 (1977); and Roland International Corp. v. Najjar, Del.Supr., 407 A.2d 1032 (1979). For the reasons hereafter set forth we consider that the business purpose requirement of these cases is no longer the law of Delaware.

I.

The facts found by the trial court, pertinent to the issues before us, are supported by the record, and we draw from them as set out in the Chancellor's opinion.[5]

---

to state a cause of action. See Weinberger v. UOP, Inc., Del.Ch., 409 A.2d 1262 (1979).

[5.] Weinberger v. UOP, Inc., Del.Ch., 426 A.2d 1333, 1335–40 (1981).

Signal is a diversified, technically based company operating through various subsidiaries. Its stock is publicly traded on the New York, Philadelphia and Pacific Stock Exchanges. UOP, formerly known as Universal Oil Products Company, was a diversified industrial company engaged in various lines of business, including petroleum and petro-chemical services and related products, construction, fabricated metal products, transportation equipment products, chemicals and plastics, and other products and services including land development, lumber products, and waste disposal. Its stock was publicly held and listed on the New York Stock Exchange.

In 1974 Signal sold one of its wholly-owned subsidiaries for $420,000,000 in cash. See Gimbel v. Signal Companies, Inc., Del.Ch., 316 A.2d 599, aff'd, Del.Supr., 316 A.2d 619 (1974). While looking to invest this cash surplus, Signal became interested in UOP as a possible acquisition. Friendly negotiations ensued, and Signal proposed to acquire a controlling interest in UOP at a price of $19 per share. UOP's representatives sought $25 per share. In the arm's length bargaining that followed, an understanding was reached whereby Signal agreed to purchase from UOP 1,500,000 shares of UOP's authorized but unissued stock at $21 per share.

This purchase was contingent upon Signal making a successful cash tender offer for 4,300,000 publicly held shares of UOP, also at a price of $21 per share. This combined method of acquisition permitted Signal to acquire 5,800,000 shares of stock, representing 50.5% of UOP's outstanding shares. The UOP board of directors advised the company's shareholders that it had no objection to Signal's tender offer at that price. Immediately before the announcement of the tender offer, UOP's common stock had been trading on the New York Stock Exchange at a fraction under $14 per share.

The negotiations between Signal and UOP occurred during April 1975, and the resulting tender offer was greatly oversubscribed. However, Signal limited its total purchase of the tendered shares so that, when coupled with the stock bought from UOP, it had achieved its goal of becoming a 50.5% shareholder of UOP.

Although UOP's board consisted of thirteen directors, Signal nominated and elected only six. Of these, five were either directors or employees of Signal. The sixth, a partner in the banking firm of Lazard Freres & Co., had been one of Signal's representatives in the negotiations and bargaining with UOP concerning the tender offer and purchase price of the UOP shares.

However, the president and chief executive officer of UOP retired during 1975, and Signal caused him to be replaced by James V. Crawford, a long-time employee and senior executive vice president of one of Signal's wholly-owned subsidiaries. Crawford succeeded his predecessor on UOP's board of directors and also was made a director of Signal.

By the end of 1977 Signal basically was unsuccessful in finding other suitable investment candidates for its excess cash, and by February 1978 considered that it had no other realistic acquisitions available to it on a friendly basis. Once again its attention turned to UOP.

The trial court found that at the instigation of certain Signal management personnel, including William W. Walkup, its board chairman, and Forrest N. Shumway, its president, a feasibility study was made concerning the possible acquisition of the balance of UOP's outstanding shares. This study was performed by two Signal officers, Charles S. Arledge, vice president (director of planning), and Andrew J. Chitiea, senior vice president (chief financial officer). Messrs. Walkup, Shumway, Arledge and Chitiea were all directors of UOP in addition to their membership on the Signal board.

Arledge and Chitiea concluded that it would be a good investment for Signal to acquire the remaining 49.5% of UOP shares at any price up to $24 each. Their report was discussed between Walkup and Shumway who, along with Arledge, Chitiea and Brewster L. Arms, internal counsel for Signal, constituted Signal's senior management. In particular, they talked about the proper price to be paid if the acquisition was pursued, purportedly keeping in mind that as UOP's majority shareholder, Signal owed a fiduciary responsibility to both its own stockholders as well as to UOP's minority. It was ultimately agreed that a meeting of Signal's executive committee would be called to propose that Signal acquire the remaining outstanding stock of UOP through a cash-out merger in the range of $20 to $21 per share.

The executive committee meeting was set for February 28, 1978. As a courtesy, UOP's president, Crawford, was invited to attend, although he was not a member of Signal's executive committee. On his arrival, and prior to the meeting, Crawford was asked to meet privately with Walkup and Shumway. He was then told of Signal's plan to acquire full ownership of UOP and was asked for his reaction to the proposed price range of $20 to $21 per share. Crawford said he thought such a price would be "generous", and that it was certainly one which should be submitted to UOP's minority shareholders for their ultimate consideration. He stated, however, that Signal's 100% ownership could cause internal problems at UOP. He believed that employees would have to be given some assurance of their future place in a fully-owned Signal subsidiary. Otherwise, he feared the departure of essential personnel. Also, many of UOP's key employees had stock option incentive programs which would be wiped out by a merger. Crawford therefore urged that some adjustment would have to be made, such as providing a comparable incentive in Signal's shares, if after the merger he was to maintain his quality of personnel and efficiency at UOP.

Thus, Crawford voiced no objection to the $20 to $21 price range, nor did he suggest that Signal should consider paying more than $21 per share for the minority interests. Later, at the executive committee meeting the same factors were discussed, with Crawford repeating the position he earlier took with Walkup and Shumway. Also considered was the 1975 tender offer and the fact that it had been greatly oversubscribed at $21 per share. For many reasons, Signal's management concluded that the acquisition of UOP's minority shares provided the solution to a number of its business problems.

Thus, it was the consensus that a price of $20 to $21 per share would be fair to both Signal and the minority shareholders of UOP. Signal's executive committee authorized its management "to negotiate" with UOP "for a cash acquisition of the minority ownership in UOP, Inc., with the intention of presenting a proposal to [Signal's] board of directors * * * on March 6, 1978". Immediately after this February 28, 1978 meeting, Signal issued a press release stating:

> The Signal Companies, Inc. and UOP, Inc. are conducting negotiations for the acquisition for cash by Signal of the 49.5 per cent of UOP which it does not presently own, announced Forrest N. Shumway, president and chief executive officer of Signal, and James V. Crawford, UOP president.
>
> Price and other terms of the proposed transaction have not yet been finalized and would be subject to approval of the boards of directors of Signal and UOP, scheduled to meet early next week, the stockholders of UOP and certain federal agencies.

The announcement also referred to the fact that the closing price of UOP's common stock on that day was $14.50 per share.

Two days later, on March 2, 1978, Signal issued a second press release stating that its management would recommend a price in the range of $20 to $21 per share for UOP's 49.5% minority interest. This announcement referred to Signal's earlier statement that "negotiations" were being conducted for the acquisition of the minority shares.

Between Tuesday, February 28, 1978 and Monday, March 6, 1978, a total of four business days, Crawford spoke by telephone with all of UOP's non-Signal, i.e., outside, directors. Also during that period, Crawford retained Lehman Brothers to render a fairness opinion as to the price offered the minority for its stock. He gave two reasons for this choice. First, the time schedule between the announcement and the board meetings was short (by then only three business days) and since Lehman Brothers had been acting as UOP's investment banker for many years, Crawford felt that it would be in the best position to respond on such brief notice. Second, James W. Glanville, a long-time director of UOP and a partner in Lehman Brothers, had acted as a financial advisor to UOP for many years. Crawford believed that Glanville's familiarity with UOP, as a member of its board, would also be of assistance in enabling Lehman Brothers to render a fairness opinion within the existing time constraints.

Crawford telephoned Glanville, who gave his assurance that Lehman Brothers had no conflicts that would prevent it from accepting the task. Glanville's immediate personal reaction was that a price of $20 to $21 would certainly be fair, since it represented almost a 50% premium over UOP's market price. Glanville sought a $250,000 fee for Lehman Brothers' services, but Crawford thought this too much. After further discussions Glanville finally agreed that Lehman Brothers would render its fairness opinion for $150,000.

During this period Crawford also had several telephone contacts with Signal officials. In only one of them, however, was the price of the shares discussed. In a conversation with Walkup, Crawford advised that as a result of his communications with UOP's non-Signal directors, it was his feeling that the price would have to be the top of the proposed range, or $21 per share, if the approval of UOP's outside directors was to be obtained. But again, he did not seek any price higher than $21.

Glanville assembled a three-man Lehman Brothers team to do the work on the fairness opinion. These persons examined relevant documents and information concerning UOP, including its annual reports and its Securities and Exchange Commission filings from 1973 through 1976, as well as its audited financial statements for 1977, its interim reports to shareholders, and its recent and historical market prices and trading volumes. In addition, on Friday, March 3, 1978, two members of the Lehman Brothers team flew to UOP's headquarters in Des Plaines, Illinois, to perform a "due diligence" visit, during the course of which they interviewed Crawford as well as UOP's general counsel, its chief financial officer, and other key executives and personnel.

As a result, the Lehman Brothers team concluded that "the price of either $20 or $21 would be a fair price for the remaining shares of UOP". They telephoned this impression to Glanville, who was spending the weekend in Vermont.

On Monday morning, March 6, 1978, Glanville and the senior member of the Lehman Brothers team flew to Des Plaines to attend the scheduled UOP directors meeting. Glanville looked over the assembled information during the flight. The two had with them the draft of a "fairness opinion letter" in which the price had been left blank. Either during or immediately prior to the directors' meeting, the two-page "fairness opinion letter" was typed in final form and the price of $21 per share was inserted.

On March 6, 1978, both the Signal and UOP boards were convened to consider the proposed merger. Telephone communications were maintained between the two meetings. Walkup, Signal's board chairman, and also a UOP director, attended UOP's meeting with Crawford in order to present Signal's position and answer any questions that UOP's non-Signal directors might have. Arledge and Chitiea, along with Signal's other designees on UOP's board, participated by conference telephone. All of UOP'S outside directors attended the meeting either in person or by conference telephone.

First, Signal's board unanimously adopted a resolution authorizing Signal to propose to UOP a cash merger of $21 per share as outlined in a certain merger agreement and other supporting documents. This proposal required that the merger be approved by a majority of UOP's outstanding minority shares voting at the stockholders meeting at which the merger would be considered, and that the minority shares voting in favor of the merger, when coupled with Signal's 50.5% interest would have to comprise at least two-thirds of all UOP shares. Otherwise the proposed merger would be deemed disapproved.

UOP's board then considered the proposal. Copies of the agreement were delivered to the directors in attendance, and other copies had been forwarded earlier to the directors participating by telephone. They also had before them UOP financial data for 1974–1977, UOP's most recent financial statements, market price information, and budget projections for 1978. In addition they had Lehman Brothers' hurriedly prepared fairness opinion letter finding the price of $21 to be fair. Glanville, the Lehman Brothers partner, and UOP director, commented on the information that had gone into preparation of the letter.

Signal also suggests that the Arledge-Chitiea feasibility study, indicating that a price of up to $24 per share would be a "good investment" for Signal, was discussed at the UOP directors' meeting. The Chancellor made no such finding, and our independent review of the record, detailed infra, satisfies us by a preponderance of the evidence that there was no discussion of this document at UOP's board meeting. Furthermore it is clear beyond peradventure that nothing in that report was ever disclosed to UOP's minority shareholders prior to their approval of the merger.

After consideration of Signal's proposal, Walkup and Crawford left the meeting to permit a free and uninhibited exchange between UOP's non-Signal directors. Upon their return a resolution to accept Signal's offer was then proposed and adopted. While Signal's men on UOP's board participated in various aspects of the meeting, they abstained from voting. However, the minutes show that each of them "if voting would have voted yes".

On March 7, 1978, UOP sent a letter to its shareholders advising them of the action taken by UOP's board with respect to Signal's offer. This document pointed out, among other things, that on February 28, 1978 "both companies had announced negotiations were being conducted".

Despite the swift board action of the two companies, the merger was not submitted to UOP's shareholders until their annual meeting on May 26, 1978. In the notice of that meeting and proxy statement sent to shareholders in May, UOP's management and board urged that the merger be approved. The proxy statement also advised:

> The price was determined after *discussions* between James V. Crawford, a director of Signal and Chief Executive Officer of UOP, and officers of Signal which took place during meetings on February 28, 1978, and in the course of several subsequent telephone conversations. (Emphasis added.)

In the original draft of the proxy statement the word "negotiations" had been used rather than "discussions". However, when the Securities and Exchange Commission sought details of the "negotiations" as part of its review of these materials, the term was deleted and the word "discussions" was substituted. The proxy statement indicated that the vote of UOP's board in approving the merger had been unanimous. It also advised the shareholders that Lehman Brothers had given its opinion that the merger price of $21 per share was fair to

UOP's minority. However, it did not disclose the hurried method by which this conclusion was reached.

As of the record date of UOP's annual meeting, there were 11,488,302 shares of UOP common stock outstanding, 5,688,302 of which were owned by the minority. At the meeting only 56%, or 3,208,652, of the minority shares were voted. Of these, 2,958,812, or 51.9% of the total minority, voted for the merger, and 254,840 voted against it. When Signal's stock was added to the minority shares voting in favor, a total of 76.2% of UOP's outstanding shares approved the merger while only 2.2% opposed it.

By its terms the merger became effective on May 26, 1978, and each share of UOP's stock held by the minority was automatically converted into a right to receive $21 cash.

II.

A.

A primary issue mandating reversal is the preparation by two UOP directors, Arledge and Chitiea, of their feasibility study for the exclusive use and benefit of Signal. This document was of obvious significance to both Signal and UOP. Using UOP data, it described the advantages of Signal of ousting the minority at a price range of $21–$24 per share. Mr. Arledge, one of the authors, outlined the benefits to Signal: [6]

Purpose Of The Merger

1) Provides an outstanding investment opportunity for Signal—(Better than any recent acquisition we have seen.)

2) Increases Signal's earnings.

3) Facilitates the flow of resources between Signal and its subsidiaries—(Big factor—works both ways.)

4) Provides cost savings potential for Signal and UOP.

5) Improves the percentage of Signal's 'operating earnings' as opposed to 'holding company earnings'.

6) Simplifies the understanding of Signal.

7) Facilitates technological exchange among Signal's subsidiaries.

8) Eliminates potential conflicts of interest.

Having written those words, solely for the use of Signal, it is clear from the record that neither Arledge nor Chitiea shared this report with their fellow directors of UOP. We are satisfied that no one else did either. This conduct hardly meets the fiduciary standards applicable to such a transaction. While Mr. Walkup, Signal's chairman of the board and a UOP director, attended the March 6, 1978 UOP board meeting and testified at trial that he had discussed the Arledge-Chitiea report with the UOP directors at this meeting, the record does not

[6] The parentheses indicate certain hand-written comments of Mr. Arledge.

support this assertion. Perhaps it is the result of some confusion on Mr. Walkup's part. In any event Mr. Shumway, Signal's president, testified that he made sure the Signal outside directors had this report prior to the March 6, 1978 Signal board meeting, but he did not testify that the Arledge-Chitiea report was also sent to UOP's outside directors.

Mr. Crawford, UOP's president, could not recall that any documents, other than a draft of the merger agreement, were sent to UOP's directors before the March 6, 1978 UOP meeting. Mr. Chitiea, an author of the report, testified that it was made available to Signal's directors, but to his knowledge it was not circulated to the outside directors of UOP. He specifically testified that he "didn't share" that information with the outside directors of UOP with whom he served.

None of UOP's outside directors who testified stated that they had seen this document. The minutes of the UOP board meeting do not identify the Arledge-Chitiea report as having been delivered to UOP's outside directors. This is particularly significant since the minutes describe in considerable detail the materials that actually were distributed. While these minutes recite Mr. Walkup's presentation of the Signal offer, they do not mention the Arledge-Chitiea report or any disclosure that Signal considered a price of up to $24 to be a good investment. If Mr. Walkup had in fact provided such important information to UOP's outside directors, it is logical to assume that these carefully drafted minutes would disclose it. The post-trial briefs of Signal and UOP contain a thorough description of the documents purportedly available to their boards at the March 6, 1978, meetings. Although the Arledge-Chitiea report is specifically identified as being available to the Signal directors, there is no mention of it being among the documents submitted to the UOP board. Even when queried at a prior oral argument before this Court, counsel for Signal did not claim that the Arledge-Chitiea report had been disclosed to UOP's outside directors. Instead, he chose to belittle its contents. This was the same approach taken before us at the last oral argument.

Actually, it appears that a three-page summary of figures was given to all UOP directors. Its first page is identical to one page of the Arledge-Chitiea report, but this dealt with nothing more than a justification of the $21 price. Significantly, the contents of this three-page summary are what the minutes reflect Mr. Walkup told the UOP board. However, nothing contained in either the minutes or this three-page summary reflects Signal's study regarding the $24 price.

The Arledge-Chitiea report speaks for itself in supporting the Chancellor's finding that a price of up to $24 was a "good investment" for Signal. It shows that a return on the investment at $21 would be 15.7% versus 15.5% at $24 per share. This was a difference of only two-tenths of one percent, while it meant over $17,000,000 to the minority. Under such circumstances, paying UOP's minority shareholders $24 would have had relatively little long-term effect on Signal, and the Chancellor's findings concerning the benefit to Signal, even at a price of $24, were obviously correct. Levitt v. Bouvier, Del.Supr., 287 A.2d 671, 673 (1972).

Certainly, this was a matter of material significance to UOP and its shareholders. Since the study was prepared by two UOP directors, using UOP information for the exclusive benefit of Signal, and nothing whatever was done to disclose it to the outside UOP directors or the minority shareholders, a question of breach of fiduciary duty arises. This problem occurs because there were common Signal-UOP directors participating, at least to some extent, in the UOP board's decision-making processes without full disclosure of the conflicts they faced.[7]

B.

In assessing this situation, the Court of Chancery was required to:

examine what information defendants had and to measure it against what they gave to the minority stockholders, in a context in which 'complete candor' is required. In other words, the limited function of the Court was to determine whether defendants had disclosed all information in their possession germane to the transaction in issue. And by 'germane' we mean, for present purposes, information such as a reasonable shareholder would consider important in deciding whether to sell or retain stock.

* * *

* * * Completeness, not adequacy, is both the norm and the mandate under present circumstances.

Lynch v. Vickers Energy Corp., Del.Supr., 383 A.2d 278, 281 (1977) (*Lynch I*). This is merely stating in another way the long-existing principle of Delaware law that these Signal designated directors on UOP's board still owed UOP and its shareholders an uncompromising duty of loyalty. The classic language of Guth v. Loft, Inc., Del.Supr., 5 A.2d 503, 510 (1939), requires no embellishment:

A public policy, existing through the years, and derived from a profound knowledge of human characteristics and motives, has established a rule that demands of a corporate officer or director, peremptorily and inexorably, the most scrupulous observance of his duty, not only affirmatively to protect the interests of the corporation committed to his charge, but also to refrain from doing anything that would work injury to the corporation, or to deprive it of profit or advantage which his skill and ability might properly bring to it, or to enable it to make in the reasonable and lawful

---

[7] Although perfection is not possible, or expected, the result here could have been entirely different if UOP had appointed an independent negotiating committee of its outside directors to deal with Signal at arm's length. See e.g., Harriman v. E.I. duPont de Nemours & Co., 411 F.Supp. 133 (D.Del.1975). Since fairness in this context can be equated to conduct by a theoretical, wholly independent, board of directors acting upon the matter before them, it is unfortunate that this course apparently was neither considered nor pursued. Johnston v. Greene, Del.Supr., 121 A.2d 919, 925 (1956). Particularly in a parent-subsidiary context, a showing that the action taken was as though each of the contending parties had in fact exerted its bargaining power against the other at arm's length is strong evidence that the transaction meets the test of fairness. Getty Oil Co. v. Skelly Oil Co., Del.Supr., 267 A.2d 883, 886 (1970); Puma v. Marriott, Del.Ch., 283 A.2d 693, 696 (1971).

exercise of its powers. The rule that requires an undivided and unselfish loyalty to the corporation demands that there shall be no conflict between duty and self-interest.

Given the absence of any attempt to structure this transaction on an arm's length basis, Signal cannot escape the effects of the conflicts it faced, particularly when its designees on UOP's board did not totally abstain from participation in the matter. There is no "safe harbor" for such divided loyalties in Delaware. When directors of a Delaware corporation are on both sides of a transaction, they are required to demonstrate their utmost good faith and the most scrupulous inherent fairness of the bargain. Gottlieb v. Heyden Chemical Corp., Del.Supr., 91 A.2d 57, 57–58 (1952). The requirement of fairness is unflinching in its demand that where one stands on both sides of a transaction, he has the burden of establishing its entire fairness, sufficient to pass the test of careful scrutiny by the courts. Sterling v. Mayflower Hotel Corp., Del.Supr., 93 A.2d 107, 110 (1952); Bastian v. Bourns, Inc., Del.Ch., 256 A.2d 680, 681 (1969), aff'd, Del.Supr., 278 A.2d 467 (1970); David J. Greene & Co. v. Dunhill International Inc., Del.Ch., 249 A.2d 427, 431 (1968).

There is no dilution of this obligation where one holds dual or multiple directorships, as in a parent-subsidiary context. Levien v. Sinclair Oil Corp., Del.Ch., 261 A.2d 911, 915 (1969). Thus, individuals who act in a dual capacity as directors of two corporations, one of whom is parent and the other subsidiary, owe the same duty of good management to both corporations, and in the absence of an independent negotiating structure (see note 7, supra), or the directors' total abstention from any participation in the matter, this duty is to be exercised in light of what is best for both companies. Warshaw v. Calhoun, Del. Supr., 221 A.2d 487, 492 (1966). The record demonstrates that Signal has not met this obligation.

C.

The concept of fairness has two basic aspects: fair dealing and fair price. The former embraces questions of when the transaction was timed, how it was initiated, structured, negotiated, disclosed to the directors, and how the approvals of the directors and the stockholders were obtained. The latter aspect of fairness relates to the economic and financial considerations of the proposed merger, including all relevant factors: assets, market value, earnings, future prospects, and any other elements that affect the intrinsic or inherent value of a company's stock. Moore, *The "Interested" Director or Officer Transaction*, 4 Del.J.Corp.L. 674, 676 (1979); Nathan & Shapiro, *Legal Standard of Fairness of Merger Terms Under Delaware Law*, 2 Del.J.Corp.L. 44, 46–47 (1977). See Tri-Continental Corp. v. Battye, Del.Supr., 74 A.2d 71, 72 (1950); 8 Del.C. § 262(h). However, the test for fairness is not a bifurcated one as between fair dealing and price. All aspects of the issue must be examined as a whole since the question is one of entire fairness. However, in a non-fraudulent transaction we recognize that price may be the preponderant consideration outweighing other features of the merger. Here, we address the two basic aspects of fairness separately because we find reversible error as to both.

D.

Part of fair dealing is the obvious duty of candor required by *Lynch I,* supra. Moreover, one possessing superior knowledge may not mislead any stockholder by use of corporate information to which the latter is not privy. Lank v. Steiner, Del.Supr., 224 A.2d 242, 244 (1966). Delaware has long imposed this duty even upon persons who are not corporate officers or directors, but who nonetheless are privy to matters of interest or significance to their company. Brophy v. Cities Service Co., Del.Ch., 70 A.2d 5, 7 (1949). With the well-established Delaware law on the subject, and the Court of Chancery's findings of fact here, it is inevitable that the obvious conflicts posed by Arledge and Chitiea's preparation of their "feasibility study", derived from UOP information, for the sole use and benefit of Signal, cannot pass muster.

The Arledge-Chitiea report is but one aspect of the element of fair dealing. How did this merger evolve? It is clear that it was entirely initiated by Signal. The serious time constraints under which the principals acted were all set by Signal. It had not found a suitable outlet for its excess cash and considered UOP a desirable investment, particularly since it was now in a position to acquire the whole company for itself. For whatever reasons, and they were only Signal's, the entire transaction was presented to and approved by UOP's board within four business days. Standing alone, this is not necessarily indicative of any lack of fairness by a majority shareholder. It was what occurred, or more properly, what did not occur, during this brief period that makes the time constraints imposed by Signal relevant to the issue of fairness.

The structure of the transaction, again, was Signal's doing. So far as negotiations were concerned, it is clear that they were modest at best. Crawford, Signal's man at UOP, never really talked price with Signal, except to accede to its management's statements on the subject, and to convey to Signal the UOP outside directors' view that as between the $20–$21 range under consideration, it would have to be $21. The latter is not a surprising outcome, but hardly arm's length negotiations. Only the protection of benefits for UOP's key employees and the issue of Lehman Brothers' fee approached any concept of bargaining.

As we have noted, the matter of disclosure to the UOP directors was wholly flawed by the conflicts of interest raised by the Arledge-Chitiea report. All of those conflicts were resolved by Signal in its own favor without divulging any aspect of them to UOP.

This cannot but undermine a conclusion that this merger meets any reasonable test of fairness. The outside UOP directors lacked one material piece of information generated by two of their colleagues, but shared only with Signal. True, the UOP board had the Lehman Brothers' fairness opinion, but that firm has been blamed by the plaintiff for the hurried task it performed, when more properly the responsibility for this lies with Signal. There was no disclosure of the circumstances surrounding the rather cursory preparation of the Lehman Brothers' fairness opinion. Instead, the impression was given UOP's minority that a careful study had been made, when in fact speed was the hallmark, and Mr. Glanville, Lehman's partner in charge of the matter, and also a UOP director, having spent the weekend in Vermont, brought a draft of the "fairness opinion letter" to the UOP directors' meeting on March 6, 1978 with the price left blank. We can only conclude from the record that the rush imposed on Lehman Brothers by Signal's timetable contributed to the difficulties under which this investment banking firm attempted to perform its responsibilities. Yet, none of this was disclosed to UOP's minority.

Finally, the minority stockholders were denied the critical information that Signal considered a price of $24 to be a good investment. Since this would have meant over $17,000,000 more to the minority, we cannot conclude that the shareholder vote was an informed one. Under the circumstances, an approval by a majority of the minority was meaningless. *Lynch I,* 383 A.2d at 279, 281; Cahall v. Lofland, Del.Ch., 114 A. 224 (1921).

Given these particulars and the Delaware law on the subject, the record does not establish that this transaction satisfies any reasonable concept of fair dealing, and the Chancellor's findings in that regard must be reversed.

E.

Turning to the matter of price, plaintiff also challenges its fairness. His evidence was that on the date the merger was approved the stock was worth at least $26 per share. In support, he offered the testimony of a chartered investment analyst who used two basic approaches to valuation: a comparative analysis of the premium paid over market in ten other tender offer-merger combinations, and a discounted cash flow analysis.

In this breach of fiduciary duty case, the Chancellor perceived that the approach to valuation was the same as that in an appraisal proceeding. Consistent with precedent, he rejected plaintiff's method of proof and accepted defendants' evidence of value as being in accord with practice under prior case law. This means that the so-called "Delaware block" or weighted average method was employed wherein the elements of value, i.e., assets, market price, earnings, etc., were assigned a particular weight and the resulting amounts added to determine the value per share. This procedure has been in use for decades. See In re General Realty & Utilities Corp., Del.Ch., 52 A.2d 6, 14–15 (1947). However, to the extent it excludes other generally accepted techniques used in the financial community and the courts, it is now clearly outmoded. It is time we recognize this in appraisal and other stock valuation proceedings and bring our law current on the subject.

While the Chancellor rejected plaintiff's discounted cash flow method of valuing UOP's stock, as not corresponding with "either logic or the existing law" (426 A.2d at 1360), it is significant that this was essentially the focus, i.e., earnings potential of UOP, of Messrs. Arledge and Chitiea in their evaluation of the merger. Accordingly, the standard "Delaware block" or weighted average method of valuation, formerly employed in appraisal and other stock valuation cases, shall no longer exclusively control such proceedings. We believe that a more liberal approach must include proof of value by any techniques or methods which are generally considered acceptable in the financial community and otherwise admissible in court, subject only to our interpretation of 8 Del.C. § 262(h), infra. See also D.R.E. 702–05. This will obviate the very structured and mechanistic procedure that has heretofore governed such matters. See Jacques Coe & Co. v. Minneapolis-Moline Co., Del.Ch., 75 A.2d 244, 247 (1950); Tri-Continental Corp. v. Battye, Del.Ch., 66 A.2d 910, 917–18 (1949); In re General Realty and Utilities Corp., supra.

Fair price obviously requires consideration of all relevant factors involving the value of a company. This has long been the law of Delaware as stated in *Tri-Continental Corp.*, 74 A.2d at 72:

> The basic concept of value under the appraisal statute is that the stockholder is entitled to be paid for that which has been taken from him, viz., his proportionate interest in a going concern. By value of the stockholder's proportionate interest in the corporate enterprise is meant the true or intrinsic value of his stock which has been taken by the merger. In determining what figure represents this true or intrinsic value, the appraiser and the courts must take into consideration all factors and elements which reasonably might enter into the fixing of value. Thus, market value, asset value, dividends, earning prospects, the nature of the enterprise and any other facts which were known or which could be ascertained as of the date of merger and which throw any light on *future prospects* of the merged corporation are not only pertinent to an inquiry as to the value of the dissenting stockholders' interest, but *must be considered* by the agency fixing the value. (Emphasis added.)

This is not only in accord with the realities of present day affairs, but it is thoroughly consonant with the purpose and intent of our statutory law. Under 8 Del.C. § 262(h), the Court of Chancery:

> shall appraise the shares, determining their *fair* value exclusive of any element of value arising from the accomplishment or expectation of the merger, together with a fair rate of interest, if any, to be paid upon the amount determined to be the *fair* value. In determining such *fair* value, the Court shall take into account *all relevant factors* * * * (Emphasis added)

See also Bell v. Kirby Lumber Corp., Del.Supr., 413 A.2d 137, 150–51 (1980) (Quillen, J., concurring).

It is significant that section 262 now mandates the determination of "fair" value based upon "all relevant factors". Only the speculative elements of value that may arise from the "accomplishment or expectation" of the merger are excluded. We take this to be a very narrow exception to the appraisal process, designed to eliminate use of *pro forma* data and projections of a speculative variety relating to the completion of a merger. But elements of future value, including the nature of the enterprise, which are known or susceptible of proof as of the date of the merger and not the product of speculation, may be considered. When the trial court deems it appropriate, fair value also includes any damages, resulting from the taking, which the stockholders sustain as a class. If that was not the case, then the obligation to consider "all relevant factors" in the valuation process would be eroded. We are supported in this view not only by *Tri-Continental Corp.*, 74 A.2d at 72, but also by the evolutionary amendments to section 262.

Prior to an amendment in 1976, the earlier relevant provision of section 262 stated:

> (f) The appraiser shall determine the value of the stock of the stockholders * * * The Court shall by its decree determine the value of the stock of the stockholders entitled to payment therefor * * *

The first references to "fair" value occurred in a 1976 amendment to section 262(f), which provided:

> (f) * * * the Court shall appraise the shares, determining their fair value exclusively of any element of value arising from the accomplishment or expectation of the merger * * *.

It was not until the 1981 amendment to section 262 that the reference to "fair value" was repeatedly emphasized and the statutory mandate that the Court "take into account all relevant factors" appeared [section 262(h)]. Clearly, there is a legislative intent to fully compensate shareholders for whatever their loss may be, subject only to the narrow limitation that one can not take speculative effects of the merger into account.

Although the Chancellor received the plaintiff's evidence, his opinion indicates that the use of it was precluded because of past Delaware practice. While we do not suggest a monetary result one way or the other, we do think the plaintiff's evidence should be part of the factual mix and weighed as such. Until the $21 price is measured on remand by the valuation standards mandated by Delaware law, there can be no finding at the present stage of these proceedings that the price is fair. Given the lack of any candid disclosure of the material facts surrounding establishment of the $21 price, the majority of the minority vote, approving the merger, is meaningless.

The plaintiff has not sought an appraisal, but rescissory damages of the type contemplated by Lynch v. Vickers Energy Corp., Del.Supr., 429 A.2d 497, 505–06 (1981) (*Lynch II*). In view of the approach to valuation that we announce today, we see no basis in our law for *Lynch II*'s exclusive monetary formula for relief. On remand the plaintiff will be permitted to test the fairness of the $21 price by the standards we herein establish, in conformity with the principle applicable to an appraisal—that fair value be determined by taking "into account all relevant factors" [see 8 Del.C. § 262(h), supra]. In our view this includes the elements of rescissory damages if the Chancellor considers them susceptible of proof and a remedy appropriate to all the issues of fairness before him. To the extent that *Lynch II*, 429 A.2d at 505–06, purports to limit the Chancellor's discretion to a single remedial formula for monetary damages in a cash-out merger, it is overruled.

While a plaintiff's monetary remedy ordinarily should be confined to the more liberalized appraisal proceeding herein established, we do not intend any limitation on the historic powers of the Chancellor to grant such other relief as the facts of a particular case may dictate. The appraisal remedy we approve may not be adequate in certain cases, particularly where fraud, misrepresentation, self-dealing, deliberate waste of corporate assets, or gross and palpable overreaching are involved. Cole v. National Cash Credit Association, Del.Ch., 156 A. 183, 187 (1931). Under such circumstances, the Chancellor's powers are complete to fashion any form of equitable and monetary relief as may be appropriate, including rescissory damages. Since it is apparent that this long completed transaction is too involved to undo, and in view of the Chancellor's discretion, the award, if any, should be in the form of monetary damages based upon entire fairness standards, i.e., fair dealing and fair price.

Obviously, there are other litigants, like the plaintiff, who abjured an appraisal and whose rights to challenge the element of fair value must be preserved.[8] Accordingly, the quasi-appraisal remedy we grant the plaintiff here will apply only to: (1) this case; (2) any case now pending on appeal to this Court; (3) any case now pending in the Court of Chancery which has not yet been appealed but which may be eligible for direct appeal to this Court; (4) any case challenging a cash-out merger, the effective date of which is on or before February 1, 1983; and (5) any proposed merger to be presented at a shareholders' meeting, the notification of which is mailed to the stockholders on or before February 23, 1983. Thereafter, the provisions of 8 Del.C. § 262, as herein construed, respecting the scope of an appraisal and the means for perfecting the same, shall govern the financial remedy available to minority shareholders in a cash-out merger. Thus, we return to the well established principles of Stauffer v. Standard Brands, Inc., Del. Supr., 187 A.2d 78 (1962) and David J. Greene & Co. v. Schenley Industries, Inc., Del.Ch., 281 A.2d 30 (1971), mandating a stockholder's recourse to the basic remedy of an appraisal.

III.

Finally, we address the matter of business purpose. The defendants contend that the purpose of this merger was not a proper subject of inquiry by the trial court. The plaintiff says that no valid purpose existed—the entire transaction was a mere subterfuge designed to eliminate the minority. The Chancellor ruled otherwise, but in so doing he clearly circumscribed the thrust and effect of Singer. Weinberger v. UOP, 426 A.2d at 1342–43, 1348–50. This has led to the

---

[8] Under 8 Del.C. § 262(a), (d) & (e), a stockholder is required to act within certain time periods to perfect the right to an appraisal.

thoroughly sound observation that the business purpose test "may be
* * * virtually interpreted out of existence, as it was in *Weinberger* ".[9]

The requirement of a business purpose is new to our law of mergers
and was a departure from prior case law. See Stauffer v. Standard
Brands, Inc., supra; David J. Greene & Co. v. Schenley Industries, Inc.,
supra.

In view of the fairness test which has long been applicable to
parent-subsidiary mergers, Sterling v. Mayflower Hotel Corp., Del.
Supr., 93 A.2d 107, 109–10 (1952), the expanded appraisal remedy now
available to shareholders, and the broad discretion of the Chancellor to
fashion such relief as the facts of a given case may dictate, we do not
believe that any additional meaningful protection is afforded minority
shareholders by the business purpose requirement of the trilogy of
Singer, Tanzer, [10] *Najjar,* [11] and their progeny. Accordingly, such requirement shall no longer be of any force or effect.

The judgment of the Court of Chancery, finding both the circumstances of the merger and the price paid the minority shareholders to
be fair, is reversed. The matter is remanded for further proceedings
consistent herewith. Upon remand the plaintiff's post-trial motion to
enlarge the class should be granted.

* * *

Reversed and Remanded.

Where, then, do matters stand after *Weinberger?* Again, it is
helpful to focus on the business purpose test of *Singer,* the content of
the entire fairness test, and the remedy for violation, including both the
procedure by which relief is obtained and the substantive standard
governing its measure.

Business Purpose. *Weinberger* is quite clear with respect to this
aspect of *Singer.* The requirement that the acquiring company demonstrate a business purpose for the transaction "shall no longer be of any
force or effect." 457 A.2d at 715. This result, however, may have been
one of the great anticlimaxes in corporate law history. Following
Tanzer, "the Delaware chancellors reduced the business purpose test to
a minor irritant requiring only a little imagination, proper planning,
and rhetoric on the part of lawyers in formulating a business reason for
the merger." [89] *Weinberger* merely announced a death that had occurred some time before. The continuing legacy of *Singer,* and the real
significance of *Weinberger,* thus depend upon the substance of the
entire fairness test, and the manner of obtaining, and the substantive
measure of, relief for its violation.

---

[9] Weiss, *The Law of Take Out Mergers: A Historical Perspective,* 56 N.Y.U.L.Rev. 624, 671, n. 300 (1981).

[10] *Tanzer v. International General Indus- tries, Inc.,* Del.Supr., 379 A.2d 1121, 1124– 25 (1977).

[11] Roland International Corp. v. Najjar, Del.Supr., 407 A.2d 1032, 1036 (1979).

[89] Herzel & Colling, *Squeeze-Out Mergers in Delaware —The Delaware Supreme Court Decision in Weinberger v. UOP, Inc.,* 7 Corp.L.Rev. 195, 203 (1984).

Entire Fairness. The court in *Weinberger* emphasized that fairness had "two basic aspects: fair dealing and fair price." 457 A.2d at 701. The former aspect, it was stressed, included how the transaction "was initiated, structured, negotiated, disclosed to the directors, and how the approvals of the directors and the stockholders were obtained." Id. In this regard, the court endorsed the use of procedural techniques—like approval of the transaction by a majority of the minority shareholders and the appointment of an independent negotiating committee—designed to sanitize approval of the transaction from the majority shareholder's controlling influence. Where such techniques are used, the burden of proof with respect to unfairness "entirely shifts to the plaintiff. * * * " Id. at 703. But whether this aspect of the entire fairness standard makes any difference from a planning perspective depends on what the remedy is for its violation; if the absence of "fair dealing" gives shareholders only the right to a "fair price," then is the court's discussion of the benefits of procedural safeguards like an independent negotiating committee anything more than precatory? Put somewhat differently, if shareholders will have the same remedy whether or not these procedures are adopted, why would the acquiring company adopt them?[90] The answer requires more careful attention to *Weinberger*'s remedial aspects.

Remedy. In *Singer,* the court properly cast the doctrinal issue in terms of the exclusivity of the appraisal remedy: Under what circumstances can minority shareholders challenge a freezeout merger other than by initiating an appraisal proceeding? The issue is critical not only because, after *Lynch,* there was a distinct possibility that the measure of damages in a non-appraisal action would be more favorable to plaintiffs than in an appraisal proceeding, but because a non-appraisal action could be brought on behalf of the entire class of minority shareholders. *Weinberger* made important changes in both aspects of the exclusivity issue.

At a minimum, *Weinberger* does seem to go a long way toward eliminating any preference for a non-appraisal proceeding based on the measure of damages. The court specified a single measure of value—"fair value based upon all relevant factors" and determined in light of "generally accepted techniques used in the financial community"—that would be generally applicable both in an appraisal proceeding and in an action claiming violation of the entire fairness standard. This measure reflected two major changes in Delaware law. First, the court rejected the traditional Delaware "block" method of valuation that

---

[90] The procedures are not costless since they give the minority veto power over the transaction. Moreover, once veto power is given, the character of the required disclosure likely will also change, thereby increasing the possibility of a disclosure problem. See Berger & Allingham, *A New Light on Cash-Out Mergers: Weinberger Eclipses Singer,* 39 Bus.Law. 1, 23 (1983).

It is also possible that the similarity in the statement of the measure of value may mask a substantial difference in how seri-

ously the court takes its review task. In Rosenblatt v. Getty Oil Co., 493 A.2d 929 (Del.1985), the Delaware Supreme Court's first post-*Weinberger* effort, it seems clear that the court's belief in the arm's length nature of the negotiations—the fair dealing component—colored its view of the issue of fair price. Indeed, the court approved the fairness of a price set on the basis of the Delaware block method, precisely the method overruled in *Weinberger.*

determined value by three different methods—market value, asset value, and earnings value—and then took an average of the three following an *ad hoc* weighting of each.[91] Second, the court took substantial liberty with the statutory language to allow valuation to take into account, and therefore to allow minority shareholders to share in, synergistic gains from the transaction. Recall that in *Lynch* the court crafted a monetary rescission remedy precisely because an appraisal remedy, as adopted by the Chancery Court, would have excluded the minority shareholders from participation in any synergistic gains; under the then terms of Section 262, fair value was to exclude "any element of value arising from the expectation or accomplishment of the merger or consolidation." In *Weinberger,* the court construed that "language to be a very narrow exception to the appraisal process, designed to eliminate use of *pro forma* data and projections of the speculative variety relating to the completion of a merger. But elements of future value, including the nature of the enterprise, which are known or susceptible as proof as of the date of the merger and not the product of speculation, may be considered." 457 A.2d at 713.[92] Thus, having adopted the critical aspect of the *Lynch* measure of damages for both appraisal and a non-appraisal proceedings, the court overruled *Lynch,* so as to maintain a single measure of damages. It thereby eliminated at least this pre-*Weinberger* basis for preferring one type of proceeding to the other.[93]

Whether or not an appraisal proceeding is the exclusive remedy available to a minority shareholder, however, remains critical despite the identity of the subtantive measure of damages. As was emphasized earlier in this section, a non-appraisal claim can be brought as a class action thereby assuring that the total damages awarded will be higher than in an appraisal proceeding; even though the per share measure of damages now will be the same in both, the class action simply will cover a much larger number of shares. *Weinberger* does seem generally to hold that the principal remedy for those claiming a violation of the entire fairness standard is an appraisal proceeding; indeed, the court seems to hold that future plaintiffs in the same position as those in

[91] The Delaware block method of valuation is criticized in, e.g., Fischel, *The Appraisal Remedy in Corporate Law,* 1983 Am.B.F.Res.J. 875, 890–93; and Schaeffer, *The Fallacy of Weighting Asset and Earnings Value in the Appraisal of Corporate Stock,* 55 S.Cal.L.Rev. 1031 (1982).

[92] Professor Fischel describes this portion of the court's opinion as "[i]n apparent disregard of the plain language of the appraisal statute. * * *" Fischel, supra at 895.

[93] That is not to say, however, that *Weinberger* resolved all issues bearing on the measure of damages. Rather, it simply eliminates any difference between types of proceeding. One important issue that does remain open is the weight to be given to the price that a third party would have paid for the company—third party sale value—even though the majority shareholder had no intention or obligation to sell. Fischel, supra, argues that such a standard is undesirable because, by reducing the returns to those who create wealth, in this case by reducing the returns to the acquiring company by increasing the appraisal price, everyone is made worse off. *See also* Chazen, *Fairness from a Financial Point of View in Acquisitions of Public Companies: Is "Third-Party Sale Value" the Appropriate Standard?,* 36 Bus.Law. 1439 (1981). How different is this issue from that raised by Perlman v. Feldmann? Does the discussion of the scope of the theoretical debate between equal opportunity and unequal division advocates in Chapter Fourteen A.1. shed light on the issue?

Weinberger will be limited "to the basic remedy of an appraisal." 457 A.2d at 715. That is not, however, to say that the appraisal remedy is *exclusive.* The court is at pains to stress that it does "not intend any limitation on the historic powers of the Chancellor to grant such relief as the facts of a particular case may dictate. The appraisal remedy we approve may not be adequate in certain cases, particularly where fraud, misrepresentation, self-dealing, deliberate waste of corporate assets, or gross and palpable overreaching are involved." Id. at 714. Under these circumstances both injunctive relief and, presumably, a non-appraisal damage proceeding would remain available.

The critical question that remains, then, is what facts will fall within *Weinberger's* litany of exceptions to exclusivity.[94] Certainly *Weinberger* itself provides little guidance concerning this issue. In the following discussion, the Reporters of the American Law Institute's Corporate Governance Project advance their views on when appraisal should be exclusive.

THE AMERICAN LAW INSTITUTE

PRINCIPLES OF CORPORATE GOVERNANCE: ANALYSIS AND RECOMMENDATIONS

REPORTERS' STUDY NO. 1

TRANSACTIONS IN CONTROL *
pp. 3 to 15.
February 22, 1985.

I. *Simple Arm's-Length Combinations*

By "simple arm's-length combinations" we mean combinations in which the directors, senior executives, or dominating shareholders of an

---

[94] For example, in which of the exceptions to exclusivity does Smith v. Van Gorkom, 488 A.2d 858 (Del.1985), which appears in Chapter Fourteen C., supra, fall? Does violation of the business judgment rule amount to "deliberate waste of corporate assets"?

However the issue of the breadth of the exceptions to exclusivity is resolved, difficult procedural problems will remain. Suppose that non-disclosure in the proxy solicitation, because it may cause shareholders mistakenly not to seek appraisal, is sufficient to allow a non-appraisal remedy. Must a shareholder, in effect, elect a remedy so that if a nondisclosure action is filed and lost, the appraisal remedy has also been lost? Conversely, what happens if discovery in an appraisal proceeding uncovers evidence of non-disclosure? May the appraisal proceeding be transformed into a class action proceeding also covering those who did not dissent? Could a plaintiff try to hedge the election of remedies risk by pursuing parallel and simultaneous

appraisal and non-appraisal actions? These issues are considered in Prickett & Harrahan, *Weinberger v. UOP, Inc.: Delaware's Effort to Preserve a Level Playing Field for Cash Out Mergers,* 8 Del.J.Corp.L. 59 (1983), the authors of which were counsel to plaintiffs in *Weinberger.* Presumably all these problems could be resolved by simply authorizing a class action appraisal proceeding, thereby eliminating the only reason to prefer a non-appraisal proceeding. This would give minority shareholders, in effect, a put option—take the merger price or the appraisal price, whichever turned out higher. What impact would this have on the planning of acquiring companies?

* The Reporters' Study bears the following legend: "This Study is being circulated for discussion and comment. As of the date of its publication the views expressed in the Study have not been considered by the Council or the members of the American Law Institute and therefore do not represent the position of the Institute on

acquired corporation do not have an interest in the acquiring corporation, and which do not occur in the context of a contested tender offer. Much of the present study of corporate law relating to corporate combinations focuses on freezeouts and contested tender offers. However, simple arm's-length combinations also raise important issues bearing on the extent to which such a transaction should be subject to judicial review.

A. *Exclusivity of Appraisal Rights*

In the case of combinations that give rise to appraisal rights, the major issue concerning judicial review is whether the appraisal right is exclusive. Present corporate law does not afford a uniform answer to this question. In most states the applicable statutes do not expressly address the issue and various bases for judicial review have been recognized by the courts. Among these states, Delaware is particularly important. In Weinberger v. UOP, Inc., 457 A.2d 701 (Del.1983), the Delaware Supreme Court indicated that it may be inappropriate to make the appraisal remedy exclusive "in certain cases, particularly where, fraud, misrepresentation, self-dealing, deliberate waste of corporate assets, or gross and palpable overreaching are involved," and that under such circumstances the Chancellor is empowered to fashion any form of equitable and monetary relief that may be appropriate. Id. at 714.

The state statutes that do provide for exclusivity are somewhat diverse in the exceptions they specify. Colorado, Georgia, Idaho, Massachusetts, Michigan, Minnesota, Montana, Nebraska, New Hampshire, New Jersey, New Mexico, New York, Oregon, and Texas make the appraisal remedy exclusive except in the case of fraud or illegality. Minnesota and Pennsylvania make the appraisal remedy exclusive except in the case of fraud. Connecticut and Florida make the appraisal remedy exclusive without an exception for either fraud or illegality. California makes the appraisal remedy exclusive except in a transaction with a controlled corporation in which the shareholder does not elect to pursue the appraisal remedy.

Section 13.02(b) of the recently revised Model Business Corporation Act provides that "[a] shareholder entitled to dissent and obtain payment for his shares under this chapter may not challenge the corporate action creating his entitlement unless the action is unlawful or fraudulent with respect to the shareholder or the corporation." The Comment to Section 13.02(b) states:

2. *Exclusivity of dissenters' rights*

Section 13.02(b) basically adopts the New York formula as to exclusivity of the dissenters' remedy of this chapter. The remedy is the exclusive remedy unless the transaction is "unlawful" or "fraudulent." The theory underlying this section is as follows: when a majority of shareholders has approved a corporate change, the corporation should be permitted to proceed even if a minority considers the change unwise or disadvantageous, and persuades a court that this is correct. Since dissenting shareholders can obtain the fair value of their shares, they are protected from pecuniary loss. Thus in general terms an exclusivity principle is justified. But the prospect that shareholders may be 'paid off' does not justify the corporation in proceeding unlawfully or fraudulently. If the corporation attempts an action in violation of the corporation law on voting, in violation of clauses in articles of incorporation prohibiting it, by deception of shareholders, or in violation of a fiduciary duty—to take some common examples—the court's freedom to intervene should be unaffected by the presence or absence of dissenters' rights under this chapter. Because of the infinite variety of situations in which unlawfulness and fraud may appear, this section makes no attempt to specify particular illustrations. Rather, it is designed to recognize and preserve the principles that have developed in the case law of New York and other states with regard to the effect of dissenters' rights on other remedies of dissident shareholders. See generally Vorenberg, "Exclusiveness of the Dissenting Stockholders' Appraisal Right," 77 Harv.L.Rev. 1189 (1964).

Section 623(k) of the New York Business Corporation Law, upon which Section 13.02(b) of the Model Act is based, provides that appraisal is the exclusive remedy unless the shareholder seeks relief on the ground that corporate action is "unlawful or fraudulent as to him." In Walter J. Schloss Associates v. Arkwin Industries, 61 N.Y.2d 700, 472 N.Y.S.2d 605, 460 N.E.2d 1090 (1984), the Court of Appeals adopted the opinion of a dissenting Justice in the Appellate Division, who construed Section 623(k) as providing an exclusive appraisal remedy unless the shareholder both alleges grounds for a cause of action over which equity would exercise jurisdiction (e.g., fraud or breach of fiduciary duty) and makes a primary request for equitable relief. Accordingly, it appears that in an appropriate case the New York appraisal statute will not be exclusive if a shareholder alleges breach of fiduciary duty and seeks equitable relief to block the transaction.

Many of the key terms in these statutes and cases—such as "illegality," "fraud," and "fiduciary duty"—are ambiguous as to their scope. In our view, in the case of a simple arm's-length combination, if shareholders have an appropriate appraisal remedy, a parallel injunctive proceeding has little additional to offer. Because it is then shareholder approval of the combination that serves to relegate shareholders to an appraisal remedy, the exceptions to exclusivity should focus on the quality of the process by which shareholder approval was obtained.

We therefore plan to take an approach to the exclusivity of the appraisal remedy which is somewhat different from that taken in the Model Act. Essentially, we contemplate the following approach:

  1. Rather than aggregating all combinations for purposes of the exclusivity issue, we plan to single out for special treatment simple arm's-length combinations, which by their nature do not involve the duty of loyalty.

2. In the case of such combinations, if an appraisal remedy with the characteristics described in Section I–B below is granted, it should be exclusive, subject only to the exceptions described below.

3. Rather than providing a general exception for "fraud," which might be construed to include waste, we plan to focus on whether full disclosure of material facts *   *   * has been made to the shareholders when soliciting their approval of the transaction. *   *   *

4. Rather than providing a general exception for "illegality," which also might be construed to include waste, we plan to focus on whether the transaction was approved in accordance with applicable provisions of law and with the corporation's certificate and by-laws.

B. *Existence of an Appropriate Appraisal Remedy*

As noted, the approach we plan to take in the case of simple arm's-length transactions is contingent upon the availability of an appropriate appraisal remedy. *   *   *

Our present view is that [an appropriate appraisal remedy] should include the following characteristics:

1. The appraisal rights should be relatively simple for shareholders to exercise, and, in the event of judicial proceedings to determine fair value, should enable numerous small shareholders to have their claims resolved in one proceeding with the ability to avoid duplication of counsel fees. Compare Model Act §§ 13.30, 13.31(c).

2. Interest should be payable to dissenting shareholders from the time the relevant transaction is consummated until the time payment is made, and should be computed at the market rate. (See Model Act § 13.01(4); cf. New York B.C.L. § 623(h)(6).)

3. When the transaction is consummated, the corporation should offer to pay dissenting shareholders the amount it estimates to be the fair value of the shares. (See Model Act § 13.25.)

4. If the amount so paid is not a substantial portion of the amount ultimately determined by the court to constitute fair value, the corporation should pay the costs and expenses of the appraisal proceeding, including the shareholders' attorneys' and expert fees. (Cf. Cal.Corp.Code § 1305(e).)

Our consideration of what procedures should be followed in valuing dissenting shares is not as far advanced, but we are tentatively of the view that valuation should be determined through the use of techniques that are generally considered acceptable in the financial community (see Weinberger v. UOP, Inc., 457 A.2d 701 (Del.1983); New York B.C.L. § 623(h)(4)), and that in the case of freezeout transactions (see Section II, below), appreciation or depreciation in anticipation of the transaction itself should be considered as an element of value. (Cf. Model Act § 13.01(3) and Official Comment (3).)

We also intend to include in commentary the factors that should be taken into account in determining fair value, and to make clear that courts should not be bound to follow the three-element test of market value, book value, and capitalized past earnings traditionally used by the courts in appraisal proceedings.

Finally, we intend to follow the pattern adopted by § 13.02 of the Model Business Corporation Act (Rev. ed. 1984) by providing an appraisal remedy even if the shares of the corporation are widely traded. We are not persuaded that the presence of an active trading market affords an adequate alternative to an appraisal remedy. Since the market price of the shares will be affected both by the public announcement of the proposed transaction and (in many cases) by the leakage of information concerning the transaction before public announcement, availability of a trading market to dispose of one's shares is not the practical equivalent of an appraisal proceeding that expressly disregards the effect of the transactions.

* * *

II. *Freezeout by a Majority Shareholder* * * *

Majority shareholders may seek to eliminate other shareholders from an enterprise in a variety of ways. A majority shareholder may arrange a cash merger with or a sale of assets to a corporation owned or controlled by the majority shareholder. If the majority shareholder is itself a corporation, it may arrange a cash-out combination with itself, and if it holds a large percentage of the subsidiary's shares in any states this may be accomplished by means of a short-form merger.

* * *

The case law applicable to such transactions is not altogether clear or consistent. A number of cases have questioned the power of a majority shareholder to exclude minority shareholders from an enterprise, at least in the absence of a valid business purpose. See, e.g., Dower v. Mosser Industries, Inc., 648 F.2d 183 (3d Cir.1981); Bryan v. Brock & Blevins Co., 490 F.2d 563 (5th Cir.1974), cert. denied 419 U.S. 844 (1974); Lebold v. Inland Steel Co., 125 F.2d 369 (7th Cir.1941), cert. denied 316 U.S. 675 (1942), modified 136 F.2d 876 (7th Cir.1943); Perl v. I.U. Int'l Corp., 61 Haw. 622, 607 P.2d 1036 (1980); Singer v. Magnavox Co., 380 A.2d 969 (Del.1977); Tanzer v. Int'l Gen. Indus., 379 A.2d 1121 (Del.1977); Alpert v. 28 Williams St. Corp., ___ N.Y. ___, ___ N.E.2d ___ (N.Y. Court of Appeals Slip Opinion No. 507, 11/29/84). Others, most recently Weinberger v. UOP, Inc., 457 A.2d 701 (Del.1983), have held that minority shareholders can be eliminated even in the absence of a valid business purpose. (See also, e.g., Matteson v. Ziebarth, 40 Wn.2d 286, 242 P.2d 1025 (1952); Yanow v. Teal Indus. Inc., 178 Conn. 263, 422 A.2d 311 (1979).) However, the standards in Delaware as to the scope of judicial review of such transactions are continuing to evolve. Furthermore, it is not clear whether other courts will follow the lead of Delaware in this regard. See, in this connection, Alpert v. 28 Williams St. Corp., supra, Umstead v. Durham Hosiery Mills, 578 F.Supp. 342, 345 (M.D.N.C.1984), and the Official Comment to Section 11.01 of the revised Model Business Corporation Act, which states that mergers authorized by that Act "may in some circumstances constitute a breach of duty to minority common shareholders where the effect of the transaction is to eliminate them from further equity participation in the enterprise."

* * *

A. *Freezeout by a Majority Shareholder*

1. In our view, if a publicly traded corporation is majority-owned by a corporate parent or other sole shareholder, a cash-out combination in which minority shareholders are compelled to sell, following full disclosure, at a fair price determined pursuant to an appraisal remedy that has the characteristics set forth in Section I–B, should be permissible for three reasons. First, such a combination is likely to promote efficiency by eliminating the need for safeguards in intercorporate dealings that may be difficult to apply in specific cases. Second, such a transaction would probably not violate the minority shareholders' fair expectations because, so long as fair consideration is paid, alternative investments of a similar character remain available. In addition, where the majority shareholder is a corporation, the concept of freezeout at a fair price is supported by analogy to the short-form merger statutes.

Accordingly, the appraisal remedy should be the exclusive remedy of a minority shareholder in the case of a freezeout by a majority shareholder, if, as in the case of a simple arm's-length combination, there has been full disclosure of material facts and compliance with correct voting procedures, and if an appraisal remedy with the characteristics described in Section I–B is granted.** Full disclosure of material facts would require a statement to the shareholders as to whether the board is of the view that the consideration offered for the shares of minority shareholders represents fair value. * * *

2. If an appraisal remedy with the characteristics described in Section I–B is not provided, but the transaction has been approved by disinterested minority shareholders, a minority shareholder should be entitled to attack the transaction only on the grounds of failure to follow correct voting procedures, lack of full disclosure or waste.

3. If there is neither such an appraisal remedy nor approval by disinterested minority shareholders, a minority shareholder should also be entitled to attack the transaction on the basis of fairness. The burden would be on the majority shareholder to show that the price was fair.

◆

Not surprisingly, *Weinberger* triggered an outpouring of law review commentary. Among the more helpful are Berger & Allingham, *A*

** The Reporters intend to eliminate any requirement that the transaction have a valid "business purpose," thereby following the view of the Delaware Supreme Court in Weinberger v. UOP, Inc., 457 A.2d 701 (Del.1983), rather than the earlier view expressed by that Court in Singer v. Magnavox Co., 380 A.2d 969 (Del.1977).

New Light on Cash-Out Mergers: Weinberger Eclipses Singer, 39 Bus. Law 1 (1983); Burgman & Cox, *Reappraising the Role of the Shareholders in Modern Public Corporation: Weinberger's Procedural Approach to Fairness in Freezeouts,* 1984 Wis.L.Rev. 593; Herzel & Colling, *Squeeze-Out Mergers in Delaware—The Delaware Supreme Court Decision in Weinberger v. UOP, Inc.,* 7 Corp.L.Rev. 195 (1984); Prickett & Harrahan, *Weinberger v. UOP, Inc.: Delaware's Effort to Preserve a Level Playing Field for Cash Out Mergers,* 8 Del.J.Corp.L. 59 (1983); Steinberg & Lindahl, *The New Law of Squeeze-Out Mergers,* 62 Wash.U.L.Q. 351 (1984); Weiss, *The Law of Takeout Mergers: Weinberger v. UOP, Inc. Ushers in Phase Six,* 4 Cardozo L.Rev. 245 (1983); Note, *Approval of Take-out Mergers by Minority Shareholders: From Substantive to Procedural Fairness,* 93 Yale L.J. (1984).

4. Variations on a Theme: Management Buyouts and Going Private

To this point our attention has been focused on one type of transaction by which minority shareholders are frozen out: The acquiring company's prompt elimination of the remaining minority shareholders following a successful tender offer. Minority shareholders may also be frozen out in two other types of transactions: Going private transactions and management buyouts. Both differ sufficiently from a post-acquisition freezeout to warrant separate attention.

Going private transactions, in which existing management of a publicly held company, rather than an acquirer, determines to freeze out public shareholders, first appeared in the mid 1970s. Professor Lowenstein nicely describes their origin: "[M]ost of these transactions involved small firms which had gone public in the hot new issuer market of the late 1960s and early 1970s. By 1974 the stock market had declined considerably, and while the founders or managers of these new issue companies still owned controlling interests, the benefits of being a public company had paled. A number of them turned to their public shareholders and announced that, by one device or another, their shares would be bought back."[95]

In more recent years, the going private transaction has given way to management buyouts, a different form of transaction by which existing management assumes an increased ownership role and public shareholders are eliminated. This form of transaction typically involves the acquisition of a public company by a newly formed entity in which the public company's management has a substantial, but commonly minority, equity interest,[96] with the remainder of the equity held by institutional investors or investment banking firms.[97] The

[95] Lowenstein, *Management Buyouts,* 85 Colum.L.Rev. 730 (1985).

[96] In a sample of 28 such transactions between 1979 and 1984, management's equity interest increased from a pre-transaction average of 6.5 percent in the publicly held company to a post-transaction average of 24.3 percent in the newly formed entity. Lowenstein, supra at 737 (Table 1).

[97] A number of investment banking firms, such as Forstmann Little & Co. and Kohlberg, Kravis, Roberts & Co., specialize in such transactions.

consideration used in such transactions is typically cash [98] or noncon-
vertible debt, thereby resulting in the elimination of public shareholders from future participation in the enterprise. Management buyouts
thus occupy a middleground between going private transactions and
arm's length third party acquisitions. As in a going private transaction, management is on both sides of the deal, purporting to represent
public shareholders in setting the terms by which management will
participate in purchasing the interests of public shareholders. As in a
third party acquisition, outsiders have placed a value on the company
higher than its market price, thereby reflecting a disinterested view
that there is the potential for gain from the transaction. Moreover,
because in a management buyout the acquiring entity is typically
closely held, there is little risk that the decision to make the acquisition
reflects acquiring company management indulging its managerialist
interests at the expense of acquiring company shareholders. It should
be kept in mind, however, that the acquiring entity in management
buyouts usually is not an operating company and has no pre-existing
business which can be combined with the target company to yield
economies of scale or scope.

   The size of going private transactions and management buyouts,
and their relative frequency, have also changed over time. In the
period 1973 through 1980, the companies subject to both types of
transactions were relatively small, averaging only approximately $6
million in total market value in going private transactions, where no
third parties joined with management to effect the transaction, and
only approximately $15.3 million in management buyouts with third
party participation.[99] By the early 1980's, the size of companies subject
to management buyouts had risen significantly. Professor Lowenstein
describes a sample of 28 buyouts between 1979 and 1984 all of which
involved payments to shareholders in excess of $100 million and in-
cludes one transaction of some $2.5 billion.[100] Moreover, Lowenstein
reports that management buyouts had largely replaced the original
going private transaction,[101] an observation confirmed even in the 1973
through 1980 period. Of the 81 transactions studied in the entire
period, 49 occurred between 1974 and 1978 and, of these, 35 were going
private transactions and 14 were management buyouts. In 1979 and
1980, this relationship had reversed. Of 28 transactions, 16 were
management buyouts and 12 were going private transactions.[102]

   Legal commentary concerning these forms of transactions has had
two common themes. First, the transactions have been seen as inherently unfair because management's role in them reflects an inherent
conflict of interest. Second, the transactions have been characterized
as lacking an efficiency justification because all that changes is owner-

[98] Typically the cash is borrowed which
accounts for the alternative term for the
transaction: a leveraged buyout.

[99] DeAngelo, DeAngelo & Rice, *Going
Private: Minority Freezeouts and Stockholder Wealth*, 27 J.L. & Econ. 367, 382–84
(1984).

[100] Lowenstein, supra, at 736–37.

[101] Id. at 735. The absolute dollar volume of transactions also appears to have
risen considerably, going from less than $1
billion in 1980 to over $10 billion in the
first six months of 1984. Id.

[102] DeAngelo, DeAngelo & Rice, supra at
381 (Table 1).

ship; as the material in Part II indicated, purely financial explanations for how an acquisition can transcend the principle of value additivity are not yet very persuasive. Both types of criticism have combined to lead some commentators simply to recommend that the transactions be prohibited.[103] The Reporters of the American Law Institute's Corporate Governance Project have recommended a more limited reform.

THE AMERICAN LAW INSTITUTE

PRINCIPLES OF CORPORATE GOVERNANCE: ANALYSIS AND RECOMMENDATIONS

REPORTERS' STUDY NO. 1

TRANSACTIONS IN CONTROL*

pp. 15 to 18.
February 22, 1985.

Insider Buy-Outs

In the case of an insider buy-out when there is not a majority shareholder,** the considerations that may justify permitting a freeze-out when there is a majority shareholder are not present. The most significant efficiency gain from a freezeout—facilitation of transactions between members of an affiliated group—is by definition absent. More-over, shareholder expectations are likely to differ markedly from those existing when there is a majority shareholder, because shareholders anticipate that senior executivies and directors normally will act on the shareholders' behalf in a combination—an expectation that is less appropriate with respect to a majority shareholder. This difference in expectations mirrors the historic distinction in corporate law between the fiduciary obligations of directors and officers, who must always look first to the interest of shareholders, and the obligations of a majority shareholder, who is allowed to favor itself in certain circumstances. Finally, the analogy to short-form mergers does not apply. According-ly, in our view the following principles should apply to a buy-out accomplished through a cash-out combination with a corporation in which the directors or senior executives have a material interest:

[103] See, e.g., Brudney & Chrilstein, *A Restatement of Corporate Freezeouts*, 87 Yale L.J. 1354, 1367 (1978). Other commenta-tors, notably Easterbook & Fischel, *Corporate Control Transactions*, 94 Yale L.J. 698 (1982), have argued that these transactions produce gains and should not be impeded. Recall that the Delaware Supreme Court in Roland International Corp. v. Najjar, 407 A.2d 1039 (Del.1979), declined to draw a distinction between post-acquisition freezeouts, which Brudney & Chirlstein would allow, and going private and man-agement buyouts, which they would pro-hibit. 407 A.2d at 1034 n. 4.

* The Reporters' Study bears the follow-ing legend: "This Study is being circulated for discussion and comment. As of the date of its publication the views expressed in the Study have not been considered by the Council or the members of the Ameri-can Law Institute and therefore do not represent the position of the Institute on any of the issues with which the Study deals."

** As used in the Reporters' Study, the term "insider buyout" encompasses both going private transactions and manage-ment buyouts. [Ed.]

1. To ensure fairness of price, prior to consummating such a transaction the directors or senior executives should: (i) after having furnished adequate public notice of the proposed transaction, give responsible parties who express an interest in bidding in competition the opportunity to review the same information concerning the corporation that has been made available to the investment bankers who are representing the corporation, to the purchasing group that includes the directors or senior executives, and to any lenders who are providing financing for the buyout; and (ii) provide a reasonable period of time for such parties to acquaint themselves with this information. The corporation should be entitled to condition the opportunity to review such information on the execution of an agreement to keep the information confidential. This procedure allows the market to police the fairness of the price.

2. If the procedures described in paragraph 1 are complied with, and the transaction is negotiated in an arm's-length manner with disinterested directors who have their own counsel and investment-banking advisers, and is approved by disinterested shareholders after full disclosure of material facts, an objecting shareholder should have the burden of proving waste or failure to follow correct voting procedures.

Shareholders should be entitled to prove waste of corporate assets even though an appraisal remedy is provided that has the characteristics set forth in Section I–B above.*

3. If the corporation follows the procedures described in paragraphs 1 and 2 above, the transaction will be afforded a safe harbor against attack except as set forth in paragraph 2.

4. If the procedures described in paragraphs 1 and 2 have not been followed, the transaction can be attacked on the ground of fairness, and the directors and senior executives have the burden of establishing fairness. To discharge this burden, they must show that fair procedures were followed, disclosure of the material facts known to the directors or senior executives who are acquiring the business, concerning the transaction and their conflict of interest, was made to the shareholders who are asked to approve the transaction, and that the price to be paid is fair. * * * Failure to follow the procedures described in paragraph 1 should ordinarily demonstrate that fair procedures were not followed.

———◆———

The American Law Institute Reporters' Study proposes stricter standards for buyouts than for freezeouts. Which transaction is more like an arm's length transaction: Where the buyer already owns a majority of the company (as in a freezeout) or where the buyer is a third party, albeit with the cooperation and participation of target management (as in a buyout)? In this connection, note that the

* The relevant portion of Section I–B of the Reporters' Study is reproduced in Section 3 of this Chapter, supra.

principal difference between the Reporters' treatment of freezeouts and buyouts is the use of the market—by facilitating an auction—to police the fairness of the price in a buyout. Because a controlling shareholder already exists in a freezeout setting, recourse to the market is not possible.

———————◆———————

There is something of a puzzle concerning claims of unfairness and inefficiency in connection with going private transactions and management buyouts. The fact is that public shareholders do quite well in them. DeAngelo, DeAngelo & Rice report that, on average, public shareholders of the companies in their sample earned abnormal returns of 30.4 percent over the period from 40 days prior to the announcement of the transaction through the day of the announcement.[104] Moreover, as stressed earlier, there is no reason to think that either management in a going private transaction, or the outside investors in a management buyout, expect to lose money in the transaction. Where, then, can the gains come from? DeAngelo, DeAngelo & Rice survey a range of possible sources.

DeANGELO, DeANGELO & RICE, GOING PRIVATE: MINORITY FREEZEOUTS AND STOCKHOLDER WEALTH

27 J.L. & Econ. 367, 371–74 (1984).

III.   THE GAINS FROM GOING PRIVATE

Going private potentially generates real resource gains through reductions in registration, listing, and other stockholder servicing costs and through the introduction of an ownership structure that improves incentives for corporate decision makers. The savings in stockholder servicing costs alone can be significant. For example, in its 1976 proxy statement, Barbara Lynn Stores, Inc., estimated the annual cost of public ownership to be $100,000, which implies a total cost saving of $1,000,000 when capitalized in perpetuity at a conservative 10 percent. This cost saving is substantial when measured against the $1,383,017 market value of the company's publicly held stock immediately prior to announcement of its going-private proposal. More generally, Schneider, Manko, and Kant advise firms considering going public to expect recurring direct costs of public ownership in the range of $30,000 to $100,000 per year (not including management time).[12] Borden claims that the annual expenditures of public ownership are "$75,000 to $200,000 annually for an average public company of Amex size and considerably more if special problems should arise" (again excluding

---

[104] DeAngelo, DeAngelo & Rice, supra, at 388–89. Although Lowenstein did not calculate abnormal returns, he reports that the mean of all winning bids in his sample of 28 management buyouts reflected a 56% premium over the market price of the company's stock thirty days before announcement of the initial buyout offer. Lowenstein, supra at 738.

[12] Carl W. Schneider, Joseph M. Mank, & Robert S. Kant, *Going Public: Practice, Procedure and Consequences*, 27 Vill.L.Rev. 1 (1981).

management time and indirect costs such as additional audit fees).[13] These figures also indicate a substantial (capitalized) cost saving when compared with $2,838,000, the median value of the public stock interest for our sample of pure going-private proposals.

The magnitude of real resource gains from a more efficient (private) ownership structure are more difficult to estimate. Nevertheless, such benefits can be realized, for example, when managment's increased equity ownership percentage reduces their incentive to shirk. Management's equity ownership percentage necessarily increases in a pure going-private transaction where, by definition, management acquires 100 percent stock ownership in the private firm. Management's residual claim interest can also increase via leveraged buyout through increased stock ownership and, indirectly, through employment agreements that tie managerial income more closely to firm profitability.

As a general rule, productive gains from organizational structure change will be realized when (ex post) managerial rewards are more closely linked to (ex ante) discretionary effort. As [has been] argued, some profitable investment projects require a disproportionate effort by management and will therefore be undertaken only if management can capture a corresponding (disproportionate) share of the gains. In these cases, productive efficiency is enhanced by managerial compensation arrangements that deviate from strictly proportionate sharing of investment returns among all (public and management) stockholders. However, under public stock ownership, such compensation schemes are subject to legal challenge by outside stockholders as "overly generous" to management. This threat of litigation is reduced under private ownership, which should enable managerial reward to be tied more closely to managerial performance, so that fewer profitable projects are forgone.

A stronger link between managerial performance and reward also can be achieved through a leveraged buyout. These transactions introduce third-party investors who take a substantial equity position in the private firm and who therefore have a greater incentive to monitor management (and allocate rewards appropriately) then do dispersed stockholders in a public firm. These third-party participants apparently also have a comparative advantage in monitoring management, as evidenced by the observation that certain investor groups specialize in these transactions. Thus, a potential benefit from going private via leveraged buyout is superior managerial performance brought about because leveraged buyout specialists are better monitors of managerial decisions than are dispersed public stockholders.

A complementary monitoring effect is that going private through a leveraged buyout can reduce the marginal agency costs of debt financ-

[13] Borden, *Going Private: Old Tort, New Tort, or No Tort?*, 49 N.Y.U.L.Rev. 987, 1007 (1974). Borden's figures may overstate the annual costs of public ownership for companies seeking to go private, since these firms are likely to have a smaller than average public stock interest. On the other hand, if stockholder servicing expenditures contain a significant fixed-cost component, the burden on smaller firms may not differ materially from that on larger firms. The nature of this cost function is ultimately an empirical issue.

ing because third-party equity investors have long-term relationships with institutional lenders. Consequently, the new equity owners have reduced incentives to transfer wealth from lenders, which, of course, encourages additional borrowing and thus provides the indirect benefit of a greater corporate tax shield. Our data provide some support for this hypothesized leverage effect. Specifically, pro forma financial statements (that is, forecasted private ownership statements) were available for five leveraged buyout proposals. For these firms, the median debt-to-assets ratio increased radically from a pre-offer .11 to a forecasted value under private ownership of .86. (For thirteen pure going-private transactions for which we could obtain the relevant data, the median debt-to-assets ratio increased slightly from .26 to a forecasted .30.)

Our discussion has focused on the benefits of private ownership or, more precisely, the costs of public ownership that are avoided by going private. There are, of course, benefits to public ownership, such as access to capital at terms that reflect the beneficial effects of diversification. Clearly, different firms will select either public or private ownership depending on the organizational structure costs particular to their circumstances. However, there is no reason to expect that a firm currently operating with a given (public or private) ownership structure will always find the current structure to be most efficient. And, more to the point, some publicly held firms will find it cost effective to go private, for example, because they experience a reduction in profitable growth opportunities which, in turn, decreases the demand for access to the public capital markets.

◆

Lowenstein, in contrast, is skeptical that these sources are sufficient to explain the magnitude of the gains that his study suggests are earned by all participants in these transactions.[105] His candidate for the source of the gains is familiar from Chapter Twelve: Taxes. In particular, Lowenstein argues that the ability to write up the basis of the assets acquired in a taxable transaction creates a tax shelter of increased depreciation and amortization that results in a higher after tax cash flow than before the transaction.[106]

How do all of these arguments compare to those considered in Part II?

◆

The practical literature on management buyouts is growing. See, e.g., Practicing Law Institute, *Leveraged Acquisitions: Private and Public* (1984) (collection of articles); Banner, Finley, Volk & Dauman, *Leveraged Buyouts, Going Private Transactions and Employee Buyouts in the Context of Takeovers,* in 1 Hostile Battles for Corporate Control

---

[105] For example, how persuasive is the claim by DeAngelo, DeAngelo & Rice that management compensation is seriously "subject to legal challenge by outside stock-

holders as 'overly generous to management'?"

[106] Lowenstein, supra at 759–64.

1984, 325 (Practicing Law Institute, 1984) (case studies); Daitz, Kaufman, Lang, Ley & Messineo, *Leveraged Buy-Outs,* in Acquisitions and Mergers 1984: Tactics and Techniques 277 (Practicing Law Institute, 1984).

5. Federal Law Limitations on the Ability to Freeze Out Minority Shareholders

The litigation effort to use federal securities law to supplement state law limits on freezing out minority shareholders, discussed in Section B.3. of this Chapter, had an administrative law counterpart. Even before the decision of the Second Circuit in Green v. Santa Fe Industries [107] holding that a freezeout of minority shareholders without a business purpose violated Rule 10b–5, the Securities and Exchange Commission had begun to respond to criticism of freezeout transactions as unfair and to criticism of state law as unresponsive. In 1975, it issued for comment proposed Rule 13e–3 which would have authorized the Commission to block freezeout transactions it determined were "unfair." [108] In 1977, it proposed a similar prohibition,[109] even after the decision of the United States Supreme Court in *Santa Fe* held that Rule 10b–5 was limited to misrepresentations and nondisclosures and did not extend to simple breaches of fiduciary duty.

Rule 13e–3 as finally adopted in August, 1979 [110] did not contain a direct prohibition of "unfair" freezeouts. Responding to comments that it lacked the authority to regulate the substance of these transactions, the Commission limited the Rule to specify the required disclosure in connection with a freezeout transaction. At least part of the disclosure required, however, clearly seems to have a substantive intent. Item 8 of Schedule 13e–3—the disclosure schedule adopted with Rule 13e–3— requires the issuer to state whether it reasonably believes the transaction is fair or unfair to public shareholders. As Jennings and Marsh have put it, "The Commission obviously thought that no one would say to the minority shareholders, 'I believe that this transaction is unfair to you'; and that the shareholders could bring an action under the rule if the issuer said, 'I believe this transaction to be fair,' and, in fact, it is not, on the theory that the issuer didn't really believe it." [111]

The coverage and content of Rule 13e–3 is described in the Release which reported its adoption.

GOING PRIVATE TRANSACTIONS BY PUBLIC COMPANIES OR THEIR AFFILIATES
Sec.Exch.Act Rel. No. 16075.
August 2, 1979.

Most of the commentators were opposed to the requirement in the 1977 proposals that a Rule 13e–3 transaction must be both substantive-

---

[107] 533 F.2d 1283 (2d Cir.1976), reversed 430 U.S. 462 (1977).

[108] Sec.Exch.Act Rel. No. 11231 (Feb. 6, 1975).

[109] Sec.Exch.Act Rel. No. 14185 (Nov. 17, 1977).

[110] Sec.Exch.Act Rel. No. 16075 (Aug. 2, 1979).

[111] R. Jennings & H. Marsh, Securities Regulation 957 (5th Ed.1982).

ly and procedurally fair to unaffiliated security holders. A number of these commentators expressed the view that the Commission does not have the authority to adopt such a requirement. They also maintained that, in the absence of an explicit legislative mandate to regulate the fairness of going private transactions, the Commission should, as a matter of policy, refrain from doing so because substantive regulation of corporate affairs is, in their view, a subject for state and not federal cognizance. It was noted in this regard that recent decisions by state courts indicate that state law provides protection to unaffiliated security holders if control persons act unfairly when taking a company private. The imposition of a federal fairness requirement was also criticized because it would, in their view, result in the staff making decisions concerning the fairness of a proposed transaction in connection with its review of registration statements, preliminary proxy materials and tender offer documents relating to going private transactions. These commentators believe that the staff would not have the resources and expertise to handle such a role.

The Commission believes that the question of regulation of the fairness of going private transactions should be deferred until there is an opportunity to determine the efficacy of the provisions of Rule 13e–3. Further developments in the remedies provided by state law for unfairness in going private transactions will also be important in this regard. In the interim, the Commission believes that the protection of investors will be enhanced substantially by the more meaningful disclosure, particularly with respect to the fairness of going private transactions, and the other protections afforded by Rule 13e–3.

Several commentators criticized the application of the 1977 proposals to transactions which in their view do not involve the potential for abuse and overreaching associated with the normal going private transaction. Thus, they were of the view that the following types of transactions, among others, should not be covered: (i) mergers following an any and all tender offer by a bidder who, as a result of the tender offer, becomes an affiliate if the same price were being paid in each transaction; (ii) exchange offers to holders of non-redeemable preferred stock or convertible debentures; (iii) transactions structured to create a holding company or reincorporate the entity in a new jurisdiction; and (iv) mergers with and exchange offers by affiliates in which unaffiliated security holders would receive common stock of the surviving entity. In response to these comments, exceptions for such transactions are now provided by paragraphs (g)(1) and (g)(2) of Rule 13e–3, assuming that the other conditions of those provisions are satisfied.

(a) Overview of Application of Rule 13e–3

*   *   *

A Rule 13e–3 transaction is defined to mean any transaction or series of transactions involving one or more of the transactions specified in paragraph (a)(4)(i) which has either a reasonable likelihood or purpose of producing, directly or indirectly, any of the effects specified in paragraph (a)(4)(ii). The specified transactions are: (a) a purchase of any equity security by the issuer of such security or by an affiliate of such issuer; (b) a tender offer or request or invitation for tenders of any equity security made by the issuer of such class of securities or by an affiliate of such issuer; or (c) a solicitation or distribution subject to Regulation 14A or Regulation 14C in connection with certain corporate events. The corporate events include a merger, consolidation, reclassification, recapitalization, reorganization or similar corporate transaction by an issuer or between an issuer (or its subsidiaries) and its affiliates; a sale by the issuer of substantially all of its assets to its affiliate; or a reverse stock split of any class of equity securities of the issuer involving the purchase of fractional interests.

As proposed, the effects selected to trigger the application of Rule 13e–3 were entirely in the disjunctive. As noted by the commentators, this produced the unintended result of applying Rule 13e–3 to specified transactions which had the reasonable likelihood or purpose of causing, for example, a class of equity securities of the issuer to be subject to delisting from an exchange, even though the securities would have continued to be authorized to be quoted on an inter-dealer quotation system of a registered national securities association. As revised, Rule 13e–3 is triggered by a specified transaction which has either the reasonable likelihood or purpose of causing either (i) the termination of reporting obligations under the Exchange Act, by virtue of the class of securities being held of record by less than 300 persons, or (ii) the securities to be neither listed on any exchange nor authorized to be quoted on an interdealer quotation system of any registered national securities association. Accordingly, in the above illustration, delisting of a class of equity securities from an exchange would not trigger the application of Rule 13e–3 if the securities were nevertheless authorized to be quoted on an inter-dealer quotation system of a registered national securities association.

The tests of "a reasonable likelihood" or "a purpose" that the transaction or series of transactions will produce a specified effect operate as alternative standards. The tests are designed to operate independently; the presence of either will trigger the application of Rule 13e–3. In a given situation, however, both tests may be met. The tests would apply equally to issuers and affiliates of issuers. In resolving close questions as to the application of the tests, issuers and affiliates are encouraged to resolve such questions in favor of compliance with the more limited burdens imposed by the revised requirements of the rule.

Both tests were criticized by the commentators on the ground that they are overly subjective. However, a more objective standard would lend itself to circumvention through skillful planning. The Commission believes, moreover, that it is reasonable for the protection of investors to require the person who is engaging in a transaction which may have a specified effect to determine whether either or both of these tests are satisfied. In order to be effective, the disclosure required by Rule 13e–3 must be received by security holders before consummation of the transaction or the earliest transaction in a series of transactions having a specified effect. These tests ensure that this objective will be accomplished.

The special position occupied by the persons subject to Rule 13e–2 should enable them to make the necessary determination before the transaction without substantial difficulty. Thus, the issuer and affiliates, through their control of the issuer, have access to all of the information which is necessary to determine whether the reasonable likelihood test, which focuses on the circumstances of the issuer, is met. The "purpose test," on the other hand, focuses on the reasons for the transaction. The issuer or affiliate is obviously in a position to know whether a reason for the transaction is to produce a specified effect.

In addition, objectivity is provided by the effects selected for identifying a "going private transaction." These specific standards provide certainty and avoid, where practicable, having the application of the rule turn upon subjective evaluations of the purposes and intentions of persons proposing to enter into a transaction. Each of these effects has the result of depriving a security holder of the benefits of public ownership. The effects are selected because of this result and not because the Commission's regulatory jurisdiction with respect to such securities will be terminated.

Questions have been raised as to whether multi-step sale of assets transactions of the type described in Security Exchange Act Release No. 34–15572 fall within the definition of a Rule 13e–3 transaction. Typically, transactions of this type involve a cash sale of substantially all of the assets of a public company ("seller") to another company ("purchaser"), often a private company not otherwise engaged in a trade or business, with the management of the business continuing to be conducted by the managers of the seller. In some cases, the sale of assets, if approved, may be followed closely by a tender offer by the seller to repurchase its shares for cash out of the proceeds received from the sale. Another variation of such transaction involves a second sale of the seller's assets (which, after the sale, consist solely of cash) to a tax exempt bond fund. The seller is then dissolved and its shareholders receive shares of the tax exempt fund.

A multi-step sale of asset transactions of the type described above which involves an issuer tender offer or purchases by the issuer would normally constitute a Rule 13e–3 transaction. A Rule 13e–3 transaction is defined to include a series of transactions involving one or more of the transactions described in paragraph (a)(4)(i) which has either a reasonable likelihood or purpose of producing, directly or indirectly, any of the effects described in paragraph (a)(4)(ii). While a sale of assets to a non-affiliate is not a transaction specified in paragraph (a)(4)(i), a tender offer or purchases by the issuer is such a transaction. Thus, the combination of these transactions constitutes a series of transactions involving a transaction specified in paragraph (a)(4)(i). A tender offer or purchases by the issuer in these circumstances will generally have a purpose or a reasonable likelihood of producing the effects described in paragraph (a)(4)(ii). Accordingly, the requisite elements of a Rule 13e–3 transaction are usually present.

Even though a multi-step sale of assets transaction of this type is structured without a tender offer or purchases by the issuer, it will nevertheless constitute a Rule 13e–3 transaction if the purchaser is an affiliate of the seller. An Affiliate of the issuer is defined in Rule 13e–3(a)(1) to include a person that controls, is controlled by or is under common control with such issuer. Accordingly, if a person or group of persons owns a controlling equity interest in both the purchaser and the seller, the sale of assets would be made to an affiliate of the issuer and would be clearly covered by Rule 13e–3, assuming there is a solicitation or distribution subject to Regulation 14A or 14C, respectively. The determination of whether a person is in control of an issuer, of course, depends on all the facts and circumstances and is not limited to control obtained through ownership of equity securities. Thus, affiliates of the seller often become affiliates [6] of the purchaser through means other than equity ownership as part of the overall sales transaction and thereby are in control of the seller's business both before and after the transaction. In such cases the sale, in substance and effect, is being made to an affiliate of the issuer and would constitute a Rule 13e–3 transaction if a solicitation subject to Regulation 14A or distribution subject to Regulation 14C is involved.

If the requirements of a Rule 13e–3 transaction are present, the application of the rule would be triggered unless an exception is available. Accordingly, the second factor to be considered is the availability of the exceptions set forth in paragraph (g). The exceptions included in the 1977 proposals, *viz.* transactions by a holding company registered under the Public Utility Holding Company Act of 1935, certain solicitations by an issuer with respect to a plan of reorganization under Chapter X of the Bankruptcy Act, and redemptions, calls or purchases pursuant to the instruments creating or governing the class of equity securities involved, have been adopted essentially as proposed. Two new exceptions have also been added.

First, Rule 13e–3(g)(1) excepts second-step, clean-up transactions which occur within one year of a tender offer by or on behalf of a bidder who, as a result of such tender offer, became an affiliate, provided that the equal consideration, disclosure and other requirements of the rule are met. The Commission believes that if a transaction is structured to meet the conditions of that rule it may safely be viewed as a unitary transaction which is not within the purview of the purposes of Rule 13e–3.

Second, Rule 13e–3(g)(2) provides an exception for transactions, including recapitalizations, in which, *inter alia,* security holders are offered only an equity security which is either common stock or has essentially the same attributes as the equity security which is the subject of the Rule 13e–3 transaction. The Commission believes that such transactions are also outside the purpose of Rule 13e–3 since all holders of that class of security are on an equal footing and are permitted to maintain an equivalent or enhanced equity interest.

[6] For the purpose of these transactions, the Commission would not view a person as an affiliate of the purchaser solely because such person enters into or agrees to enter into a reasonable and customary employment agreement or is elected or there is an agreement to elect such person as an executive officer or director of the purchaser.

The third factor to be considered in the application of Rule 13e–3 is the status under the Exchange Act of the issuer or the class of equity securities of the issuer. If the class of equity securities, which is subject to the Rule 13e–3 transaction, is registered pursuant to Section 12 of the Exchange Act (a "Section 12 issuer"), Rule 13e–3(b) would apply. Rule 13e–3(b) is divided into two subparagraphs, the first of which defines fraudulent, deceptive or manipulative acts or practices in connection with a Rule 13e–3 transaction and the second of which prescribes means reasonably designed to prevent such acts and practices. Thus, a Section 12 issuer or an affiliate of such issuer proposing to engage in a Rule 13e–3 transaction would be required to comply with the anti-fraud provisions of proposed Rule 13e–3(b). Compliance with these provisions would be in addition to compliance by a Section 12 issuer or affiliate of such issuer with the filing, disclosure and dissemination requirements of paragraphs (d), (e) and (f) of Rule 13e–3, respectively.

If the issuer of the class of securities which is subject to the Rule 13e–3 transaction is required to file periodic reports pursuant to Section 15(d) of the Exchange Act (a "Section 15(d) issuer"), Rule 13e–3(c) would apply. Under paragraph (c), a Section 15(d) issuer or an affiliate of such an issuer proposing to engage in a Rule 13e–3 transaction would be required to comply with the filing, disclosure and dissemination requirements of paragraphs (d), (e) and (f) of Rule 13e–3, respectively.

Since the provisions of Rule 13e–3 are not exclusive, the transaction would also be subject to other applicable provisions of the Federal securities laws. For example, if an affiliate of a Section 12 issuer made a tender offer for a class of equity securities of such an issuer which would be deemed to be a Rule 13e–3 transaction, the affiliate would also be subject to the other requirements of the Federal securities laws including, but not limited to, Sections 10(b), 14(d) and 14(e) of the Exchange Act and the rules promulgated thereunder. Similarly, if an affiliate of a Section 15(d) issuer made a tender offer for a class of equity securities of such an issuer which would be deemed to be a Rule 13e–3 transaction, the affiliate would also be subject to the other requirements of the Federal securities laws, including, but not limited to Sections 10(b) and 14(e) of the Exchange Act, the rules promulgated thereunder, and Rule 13e–4.

(b) Filing Requirements

Under Rule 13e–3(d)(1), the issuer or affiliate engaging in a Rule 13e–3 transaction would be required to file a Rule 13e–3 Transaction Statement on Schedule 13E–3, including all exhibits thereto, with the Commission. The time for such an initial filing is set forth in General Instruction A to Schedule 13E–3. This instruction recognizes the variety of methods employed in such transactions. Consequently, the initial filing requirement for the proposed Schedule would depend on the type of Rule 13e–3 transaction involved. If the transaction involves the filing with the Commission of soliciting materials or an information statement pursuant to Regulations 14A or 14C, respectively, the Schedule 13E–3 would be filed concurrently with the filing of "Preliminary

Copies" of such soliciting materials or information statement. If the transaction involves the filing of a registration statement under the Securities Act, the Schedule would be filed concurrently therewith. If the transaction involves a tender offer, the Schedule would be filed as soon as practicable on the date the tender offer is first published, sent or given to security holders of the class of equity securities which is the subject of the Rule 13e–3 transaction. In cases where the transaction does not involve a solicitation, an information statement, the registration of securities or a tender offer, as described above, the Schedule would be required to be filed with the Commission at least 30 days prior to the date of any purchase by the issuer or affiliate of any securities of the class of securities subject to the Rule 13e–3 transaction. If the Rule 13e–3 transaction involves a series of transactions, the issuer or affiliate would file a Rule 13e–3 Transaction Statement on Schedule 13e–3 at the specified time for the first transaction in such series and would promptly amend the schedule with respect to each subsequent transaction.

* * *

A final amendment on Schedule 13E–3 disclosing the results of the Rule 13e–3 transaction would be required to be filed under Rule 13e–3(d)(3) promptly but not later than ten days after the termination of the transaction. If the Rule 13e–3 transaction is a tender offer governed by Rule 13e–4, the final amendment would be filed no later than ten business days after the termination of such tender offer.

* * *

(c) Disclosure Requirements

Rule 13e–3(e) establishes the information required to be included in the disclosure document furnished to holders of the class of equity securities which is the subject of the transaction. This disclosure provision consists of two elements: (1) the information required by Items 1 through 6 and 10 through 16 of Schedule 13E–3 * * * and Items 7, 8 and 9 of the Schedule and (2) and other information required to be disclosed pursuant to any other applicable rule or regulation under the Federal securities laws. * * *

(d) Dissemination Requirements

Rule 13e–3(f) prescribes the methods of dissemination of the information required to be disclosed to the security holders of the class of equity securities which is the subject of the Rule 13e–3 transaction. The method of dissemination applicable to a Rule 13e–3 transaction depends on the type of transaction involved.

If the Rule 13e–3 transaction is a purchase as described in Rule 13e–3(a)(4)(i)(A) or a vote, consent or authorization or distribution of information statements, as described in proposed Rule 13e–3(a)(4)(i)(C) Rule 13e–3(f)(1) would apply. While the disclosure would be disseminated in accordance with the provisions of applicable Federal or state law, in no event would such dissemination occur later than 20 days prior to: any such purchase; any such vote; consent or authorization; or with respect to the distribution of information statements, the meeting date, or if corporate action is to be taken by means of the written authorization or consent of security holders, the earliest date on which corporate action may be taken. Thus, Rule 13e–3(f)(1)(i)(A) would provide for a 20 day waiting period during which a Rule 13e–3 transaction could not be effected. Moreover, Rule 13e–3(f)(1)(i)(B) requires that the disclosure be disseminated to persons who are record holders as of the date not more than 20 days prior to the date of dissemination. For example, if the vote on a Rule 13e–3 transaction will occur on August 30, the disclosure would be disseminated no later than August 10. If August 10 is the date of dissemination, the disclosure would be transmitted to persons who are listed as record holders as of date not earlier than July 21.

* * *

(e) Schedule 13E–3

Schedule 13E–3 establishes specific disclosure requirements for Rule 13e–3 transactions.

* * *

The most significant change in the items of the Schedule is with respect to disclosure of the fairness of the transaction. Item 8 requires the issuer or affiliate to state whether it reasonably believes the Rule 13e–3 transaction is fair or unfair to unaffiliated security holders. The issuer or affiliate is also required to provide a detailed discussion of the material factors upon which that belief is based. This discussion is required to address the extent to which the following factors were taken into account: (1) whether the transaction is structured so that approval of at least a majority of unaffiliated security holders is required; (2) whether the consideration offered to unaffiliated security holders constitutes fair value; (3) whether the majority of non-employee directors has retained an unaffiliated representative to act solely on behalf of unaffiliated security holders for the purposes of negotiating the terms of the transaction and/or preparing a report concerning the fairness of the transaction; (4) whether the Rule 13e–3 transaction was approved by a majority of the directors of the issuer who are not employees of the issuer; and (5) whether a report, opinion or appraisal of the type described in Item 9 of the Schedule * was obtained. In order to minimize meaningless, boilerplate responses an instruction specifies that conclusory statements are not considered sufficient disclosure in responding to this requirement.

These factors are based to a large extent on the considerations set forth in the Note to proposed Rule 13e–3(b) which rule would have required that the transaction be fair to unaffiliated security holders. The commentators were concerned that the factors chosen would conflict with the standards under state law for determining fairness. Since a substantive fairness requirement is not being adopted at this time, this concern is now inapplicable. Moreover, Instruction 1 to Item 8(b) of Schedule 13E–3 indicates that the factors which are important in determining the fairness of a transaction to unaffiliated security holders, and the weight which should be given to them in a particular

---

* Item 9 covers any "report, opinion or appraisal relating to the consideration or the fairness of the consideration to be offered * * *." [Ed.]

context, will vary. The context in which this determination is made, of course, includes the applicable state law. Accordingly, accommodation with those requirements is assured.

In any event, the Commission believes that increased discussion of factors bearing upon fairness to unaffiliated security holders is necessary in view of the potential for abuse which exists in a Rule 13e–3 transaction. The absence of arms-length negotiations which is characteristic of going private transactions requires that unaffiliated security holders be furnished with detailed information so that they can determine whether their rights have been adequately protected.

-------◆-------

6. The Parallel Problem: The Plight of the Frozen In Minority

Section B.1. of this Chapter examined the claim that the ability to freeze out minority shareholders of a target company following a successful tender offer was critical to the acquiring company's decision to make the offer in the first place. Part of the evaluation consisted of evaluating the acquiring company's alternative to freezing out minority shareholders: freezing them in. The idea was that if a majority shareholder has substantial freedom to take a disproportionate part of the target company's future earnings, then an acquiring company's best strategy might well be simply to allow the remaining target shareholders to continue as an exploited minority. A fair reading of *Sinclair* suggested, consistent with the weight of the academic opinion, that an acquiring company does have substantial freedom to favor itself in its dealings with its controlled, but not wholly owned, subsidiaries. Indeed, in light of the substantial premiums typically paid to minority shareholders in freezeouts, the puzzle is to explain the fixation of American law with the plight of the shareholder who is frozen out, and its almost total disregard of the parallel plight of the shareholder who is "frozen in." Consider, for example, the December, 1985, addition of Section 912 to the New York Business Corporations Law. The new section essentially prohibits second-step transactions for a period of five years from the date the acquiring company first acquires 20 percent of the target company's stock, unless the entire acquisition was approved by the target's board of directors prior to the time the acquiring company's holdings reached 20 percent. Here the New York legislature has frozen in the minority for five years. Given the analysis in Section B.1. of this Chapter, how would this protect minority shareholders? Could it plausibly act as deterrent to the acquisition in the first place?

Actually, the puzzle is even more complicated. The result of the effort to protect frozen out shareholders, as expressed in *Weinberger,* may combine with the law's relative indifference to frozen in shareholders, as expressed in *Sinclair,* to give the acquiring company a valuable strategic option. *Weinberger* allows an acquiring company to freeze out the minority, with a liberalized appraisal standard to be sure, but without alteration of the procedural mechanisms of appraisal necessary to eliminate the acquiring company's incentive to "low-ball" in setting the freeze out price. The leniency of the standards of *Sinclair,* in turn, provides the freeze in alternative to freezing out the minority shareholders. Finally, there is yet a third alternative—freeze the minority shareholders in for now, but freeze them out later at the time acquiring company management thinks an appraisal proceeding will be most favorable to it. Given the availability of choices, an acquiring company could be expected in each case to choose the alternative most favorable to it. The strategic exercise of this choice by acquiring companies would provide an alternative explanation to that discussed in Section A. of this Chapter for why the recent study by the SEC's Office of the Chief Economist showed that the value of minority shares was higher when a second-step transaction was contemplated, even at a lower price, than when the transaction was only a partial offer. As Lucian Bebchuk has pointed out, "those instances where the acquirer currently elects not to effect an immediate takeout are exactly the instances where the acquirer expects that, through diverting earnings or a distant takeout or both, it will succeed to leave minority shareholders with even less than it would have to pay them in an immediate takeout." [112]

There are a number of ways by which the acquiring company's opportunity to behave strategically might be constrained. First, as *Weinberger* attempted, the attractiveness of an initial freezeout could be diminished by making the appraisal process more attractive to minority shareholders. Second, as *Sinclair* does not, the opportunity to exploit frozen in shareholders could be diminished by more stringent rules governing the conduct of the target company's business by the acquiring company. Third, as Brudney & Chirlstein have recommended, the opportunity to take advantage of both alternatives could be eliminated by prohibiting delayed freezeouts.[113] All of these approaches, however, present substantial difficulties.

Consider first the approach of improving the appraisal proceeding. Assuming that gains resulting from the transaction should be shared with target shareholders,[114] there are significant problems with designing procedural rules for appraisal that both could overcome the transaction costs and collective action problems associated with appraisal through the use of something like a class action, but still do not, in effect, give the shareholders the option to both accept the offer and challenge it at the same time.

The difficulties associated with designing and implementing more stringent rules governing the conduct of the target company's business by the acquiring company are even more significant. Not only must we

---

[112] Bebchuk, *Towards an Undistorted Choice and Equal Treatment in Corporate Takeovers* 75 (Discussion Paper No. 5, Harvard Law School Program in Law and Economics, October, 1984).

[113] Brudney & Chirlstein, *A Restatement of Corporate Freezeouts,* 87 Yale L.J. 1354 (1978).

[114] The issue is controversial. See Easterbrook & Fischel, *Corporate Control Transactions,* 91 Yale L.J. 737 (1982); Fischel, *The Appraisal Remedy in Corporate Law,* 1983 Am.B.F.Res.J. 875.

specify the standard of conduct we expect in a setting where no brightline rule is possible, but we must also find someone who has the skills and inclination actually to monitor the acquiring company's behavior. Given the myriad ways in which the parent company in an affiliated group can favor itself at the expense of minority shareholders in the affiliates, the investment in monitoring would have to be substantial to achieve significant improvement.

Finally, it is not clear that, without more, prohibiting delayed freezeouts would accomplish very much. An acquiring company would still have the opportunity after a successful tender offer to choose, at the outset, whether to freeze out or freeze in minority shareholders. Although the opportunity to take advantage of both alternatives would have been eliminated, the opportunity for strategic behavior by the acquiring company would still remain. It still would be able to choose between a freezeout and a freezein based on what was best for it.

In light of the difficulties in devising a system in which an acquiring company could not take advantage of minority shareholders through its choice of whether to freeze them out, or freeze them in, or both, a second best alternative commands attention. Instead of trying to ameliorate the problems associated with an acquiring company's strategic choice of how to treat minority shareholders, simply eliminate the choice. Some sense of how such a system might operate can be drawn from the British experience with an approach that essentially eliminates the acquiring company's option to freeze in minority shareholders—the prohibition of partial offers.

Takeover regulation in the United Kingdom is bifurcated between governmental regulation and industry self-regulation. The Prevention of Fraud (Investments) Act of 1958 [115] and the Licensed Dealers (Conduct of Business) Rules,[116] together with the Memorandum of Guidance of the Federation of Stock Exchanges [117] regulate the formal mechanism by which an offer can be made and the scope of the disclosure that must be made in connection with it. Standards governing the substance of takeover activity, however, are set forth in The City Code on Take-overs and Mergers which was written and is administered by an industry group, the Panel on Take-Overs and Mergers.[118]

[115] 6 & 7 Eliz. 2, c. 45.

[116] Stat.Inst. 1960, no. 1216, reprinted in M. Weinberg, *Take-Overs and Mergers* 441 app. (3d ed. 1971). These rules are promulgated by the Department of Trade pursuant to Section 7 of the Prevention of Fraud (Investment) Act.

[117] *Federation of Stock Exchanges in Great Britain & Ireland, Admission of Securities to Quotation: Memorandum of Guidance* (1964), reprinted in M. Weinberg, supra at 424 app.

[118] See generally A. Johnston, *The City Take-Over Code* (1980); DeMott, *Current Issues in Tender Offer Regulation: Lessons from the British*, 58 N.Y.U.L.Rev. 945 (1983). The Code was originally published

in 1968 and was the product of a committee organized by the Bank of England and made up of representatives of the merchant banks, the stock exchanges and pension fund organizations. A. Johnston, supra at 37–8. This exercise in self-regulation was openly recognized as a means to head off governmental regulation, as the introduction to the April, 1969, edition of the Code openly acknowledged: "It is generally accepted that the choice before the City in the conduct of Take-Overs and Mergers is either a system of voluntary self-discipline based on the Code and administered by the City's own representatives or regulation by law enforced by officials appointed by Government." M. Weinberg, supra at 437 app.

The Code itself consists of fourteen general principles that specify basic standards of conduct which are then implemented by 39 rules that add procedural and substantive content to the principles. General Principle 13, together with Rules 34 and 27, represent the British approach to limiting an acquiring company's options with respect to the treatment of minority shareholders.

General Principle 13

ACQUISITION OF CONTROL

Where control of a company is acquired by a person, or persons acting in concert, a general offer to all other shareholders is normally required; a similar obligation may arise when control is consolidated. *   *   *

General Principle 13 is given specific form by Rule 34 which requires that any person (or group of persons acting in concert) who accumulates in one or more transactions thirty percent or more of a target company's stock must offer to purchase all remaining target shares at the highest price paid for target shares by the acquiring person within the previous twelve months. Thus, once control is acquired—whether by tender offer or otherwise—the obligation to make an offer for all of the stock is triggered and minority shareholders are given a way out. The alternative of freezing in minority shareholders is thereby limited.

Rule 27, in turn, requires the Panel's consent before an acquiring company can make a partial offer for target company stock. The Rule states that consent for an offer for more than fifty but less than one hundred percent of the target company's stock will be granted only if a majority of the shares not held by the acquiring company approve the offer, and that consent for an offer for between thirty and fifty percent of the target's stock will be granted only if both the board of directors of the target company and a majority of the shares of the target company not held by the acquiring company approve the offer.

This regulatory pattern significantly limits the ability of an acquiring company to exploit a remaining minority. First, Rule 27 means that shareholders cannot be made into a minority without majority consent.[119] Second, Rule 34 means that minority shareholders cannot be frozen in because a mandatory offer would be forthcoming even after an approved partial offer. Finally, even those who choose to remain minority shareholders by declining a mandatory Rule 34 offer may eventually get a second bite at the apple under Section 209(2) of the 1948 Companies Act[120] which grants the remaining shareholders in a target, following the acquisition of ninety percent of the shares not

Self-discipline is also the principle method by which compliance with the Code is achieved. Although the Code does provide a mechanism by which complaints can be made, with decisions subject to an appeals process, the Panel has no independent authority to impose sanctions beyond public criticism. A. Johnston, supra at 56–57; M. Weinberg, supra at 122, 126–29.

[119] The use of majority approval here highlights the difference in the American and British approaches. Recall that *Weinberger* recommended its use as a condition to freezing out the minority; Rule 27 uses it as a condition to creating a minority in the first place.

[120] Companies Act, 1948, 11 & 12 Geo. 6, ch. 38, sec. 209(2) (amended 1976).

previously held by the acquirer, the right to require that the acquirer purchase their shares.

The British approach to eliminating the opportunity for acquiring companies to exploit minority shareholders is not, however, without cost. By essentially prohibiting partial bids through the interaction of Rules 34 and 27, the benefits of acquisitions by acquirers without the capital to make complete acquisitions are foregone.[121] If capital markets are complete, however, might not these rules be avoided by means that do not raise the risk of minority shareholder exploitation? Suppose a company that had sufficient funds only for a partial acquisition borrowed the funds necessary for a complete acquisition with the commitment that it would sell off a portion of the target company's equity—an "equity carve-out"[122]—immediately following the acquisition. The proceeds from that sale would then be used to pay off the acquisition indebtedness. While the carve-out would itself create a minority, presumably purchasers would have chosen that condition and paid a price that reflected the risks inherent in their position. What assumptions about transaction costs in the capital market are necessary for this strategy to be available?

[121] DeMott, supra at 986, and sources there cited.

[122] See Schipper and Smith, *A Comparison of Equity Carve-Outs and Equity Offerings: Share Price Effects and Corporate Restructuring,* — J.Fin.Econ. — (forthcoming).

PART IV. NON–CORPORATE LAW PLANNING CONSIDERATIONS

In this Part we continue study of the public ordering aspect of private transactions: The task of structuring a transaction to minimize the cost of the variety of regulatory systems that may touch on it. Part III began this survey by examining the influences of corporate law considerations on the structure of corporate acquisitions. Our focus here, in contrast, is on the influence of non-corporate law regulatory regimes on transactional structure. Chapter Sixteen considers the securities law aspects of corporate acquisitions with major emphasis on the Williams Act, the principal body of federal regulation bearing on tender offers. Chapter Seventeen then moves to the Hart-Scott-Rodino Antitrust Improvements Act of 1976, which imposes a regime of pre-transaction notification whose burden differs significantly depending on the form in which a transaction is cast. Finally, Chapter Eighteen focuses on a more general problem: The successor liability of the acquiring company. Here the concern is whether the form in which the transaction is cast does—or should—affect the acquiring company's ability to select which of the target company's liabilities and contractual obligations it assumes.

CHAPTER SIXTEEN. SECURITIES LAW ASPECTS OF CORPORATE ACQUISITIONS

Virtually any acquisition of a target company large enough—or, more accurately, small enough—to have a class of securities registered under the Securities Exchange Act of 1934,[1] will be subject to one or more aspects of Federal securities laws. If the acquisition is structured as a cash tender offer, the Williams Act will be applicable; if the acquisition is structured as a merger or sale of assets in which a portion of the consideration to be received by the target company or its shareholders will be securities of the acquiring company, the Securities Act of 1933 will be applicable; and if the acquisition is structured as an exchange offer—a tender offer in which the consideration is the acquiring company's securities—both the Williams Act and the Securities Act of 1933 will be applicable. Additionally, an increasing number of states have adopted special legislation regulating acquisition transactions, especially tender offers. Thus, the influence of securities law on corporate acquisitions is pervasive.

We begin in this Chapter with examination of Federal securities law regulation of corporate acquisitions. Our principal focus will be on that that aspect of Federal regulation most directly concerned with corporate acquisitions: The Williams Act. Because our concern is with transaction planning, we will then compare Federal regulation of alternative transaction forms—mergers and sales of assets—under the Securities Act of 1933. We next examine a more recent subject of interest: State regulation of corporate acquisitions. In recent years, an increasing number of states have begun to regulate acquisition transactions—especially tender offers—in ways radically different from traditional state corporation statutes. These efforts raise important issues of public policy toward acquisitions generally and, more specifically, important issues of Federalism.

A. Federal Securities Law Regulation of Acquisitions

1. Federal Regulation of Tender Offers: The Williams Act

Prior to July 29, 1967, cash tender offers were essentially unregulated. This was of little moment for most of the country's business history because, as Salter & Weinhold describe in Chapter One, there were very few such transactions. Things began to change in the early

---

[1] Under Section 12(g) of the Exchange Act, a company with total (*not* net) assets exceeding $1 million must register any class of equity securities held of record by more than 500 persons. These limits were raised in 1982 by the SEC's adoption of Rule 12g-1 which increased the total asset registration trigger to $3 million—an amount which, in the SEC's view, simply represented the $1 million statutory figure restated in 1982 dollars to adjust for inflation. Exchange Act Release No. 12375, System of Classification for Purposes of Exempting Smaller Issuers from Certain Reporting and Other Requirements (April 15, 1982), reprinted in 3 Fed.Sec.L.Rep. (CCH) ¶ 83,204, at 85,030–31.

1960's. Although in 1960 there were only eight cash tender offers for exchange listed companies, by 1966 the number had increased to 107.[2] Moreover, the technique was increasingly being used to displace target management who had no desire to give up the reins. Thus, concerned observers saw two challenges to the existing regulatory regime. First, those interested in the coherence of federal regulation of tender offers saw a critical gap in coverage. Tender offers in which the consideration was the offerer's securities were subject to the disclosure and anti-fraud rules of the Securities Act of 1933; tender offers in which the consideration was cash were not. Thus, transaction planners could avoid existing disclosure rules by selecting the "right" consideration. This "gap" in the coverage of the Federal securities law led to efforts, supported by the Securities and Exchange Commission, to fill it by legislation. Second, those whose interest was somewhat less academic noted that incumbent management were subject to challenge in a new and more threatening way. This "gap" in the ability of target management to protect themselves also fueled legislative efforts at gap-filling. In October, 1965, Senator Harrison Williams introduced legislation which he saw as responding directly to target management's problem:

> In recent years we have seen proud old companies reduced to corporate shells after white-collar pirates have seized control with funds from sources which are unknown in many cases, then sold or traded away the best assets, later to split up most of the loot among themselves.[3]

Senator Williams' initial legislative effort failed. However, a second effort in 1967 proved successful; the Williams Act, in the form of various amendments to the Securities Exchange Act of 1934, was enacted on July 29, 1968.[4] The Act was amended in 1970 to extend the Commission's rule-making authority and to expand the types of offers covered.[5]

The regulatory structure established by the Williams Act has four principal components. The first, expressed in Exchange Act Section 13(d), is an early warning system designed to alert target management and the market of any concentration in shareholdings that might foretell a future change in control by any method. The second, expressed in Exchange Act Section 14(d)(1) and the regulations adopted thereunder, requires extensive disclosure concerning any tender offer and the offerer's plans for the target company if the offer is successful, to assist target shareholders in deciding whether to tender their shares. The third, expressed in Exchange Act Sections 14(d)(4)–(7), regulates the substantive terms of a tender offer—including the length of time an offer must be left open, the right of a shareholder to withdraw previously tendered shares, the manner in which tendered shares must be purchased if more shares are tendered than the offerer is committed to purchase, and the effect of the offerer changing the terms of the offer

---

[2] 111 Cong.Rec. 24662–64 (Aug. 30, 1967).

[3] 111 Cong.Rec. 28,257 (Oct. 22, 1965).

[4] Act of July 29, 1968, Pub.L. No. 90–439, 82 Stat. 454.

[5] Most important, the 1970 Amendments reduced the percentage ownership that triggered a reporting obligation under Section 13(d) from 10 percent to 5 percent. See Section A.1.a. of this Chapter, infra.

during its pendency.[6] The fourth, expressed in Exchange Act Section 14(e), prohibits misrepresentation, nondisclosure or "any fraudulent, deceptive, or manipulative acts or practices" in connection with a tender offer.

We begin our review of the regulatory structure created by the Williams Act with the first three components. Then, having developed an understanding of the consequences of a transaction being subject to the Williams Act, we turn to the Act's jurisdictional limits: What is a "tender offer" for purposes of the Williams Act? Finally, we consider the scope of the anti-fraud rule in Section 14(e), and the elements of a cause of action under that section.

a. *Disclosure and Remedies Under Section 13(d)*

(1) **Introduction: The Statute and Regulations**

[Read Securities Exchange Act Section 13(d) and Regulation 13D–G in Appendix A.]

Although Section 13(d) was added to the Williams Act as something of an afterthought, it is the first part of federal securities law regulation of tender offers that an acquirer encounters. Indeed, because the purpose of the section is to provide information about any concentration of shareholdings, even an investor seeking just a significant passive investment—one *really* made only for investment and not for the purpose of acquiring control—will have to deal with its requirements.[7]

---

[6] The Williams Act also added Exchange Act Section 14(f) which requires disclosure equivalent to that called for by the proxy rules if, in connection with a transaction covered by Section 13(d) or 14(d), there is an arrangement or understanding pursuant to which any persons would be elected as directors of the target company other than at a meeting of shareholders if those persons would constitute a majority of the board of directors.

[7] The Commission has made special provision for one group of passive investors: institutional investment managers. Under Rule 13d–1(b) a person who would otherwise be required to file a Schedule 13D can instead file the much less burdensome Schedule 13G if (i) the securities were acquired in the ordinary course of business "and not with the propose nor with the effect of changing or influencing the control of the issuer, nor as a participant in any transaction having such purpose or effect * * *"; and (ii) the person is a registered broker or dealer, a bank, an insurance company, a registered investment company, a registered investment adviser, an employee benefit or pension fund subject to the Employee Retirement Security Act of 1974, or an endowment fund. If the person's eligibility under Rule 13d–1(b) terminates, a Schedule 13D must be filed

within ten days and, for ten days after filing, the person cannot vote its shares or acquire more. *Query:* Is a bank that finances a tender offer a "participant" in the transaction for purposes of determining the eligibility of its trust department to file Schedule 13G?

Section 13(g) itself, pursuant to which Schedule 13G was promulgated by the Commission, provides simply that anyone who is the beneficial owner of more than 5 percent of a class of securities must file more limited information than that listed in Section 13(d)(1). Although its terms at first glance seem similar to those of Section 13(d)(1), note that it picks up those persons who are exempt from filing under Section 13(d)(1) because Rule 13d–6 excludes from the definition of acquisition any transaction or series of transactions which involve less than 2 percent of any class of equity securities within the previous twelve months. This allows a shareholder who proceeds slowly—at a rate of no more than 2 percent a year—to accumulate a substantial amount of stock without having to file under the Williams Act. Section 13(g) was added by Section 203 of the Domestic and Foreign Investment Improved Disclosure Act of 1977, 91 Stat. 1499, to fill this gap.

Nonetheless, the disclosure obligation imposed by Section 13(d) has particular significance for a would-be acquirer.

From the perspective of an acquiring company, maintaining the secrecy of its acquisition plans, especially the identity of the target, is critically important. In Chapter Fifteen A.2. the need for secrecy was stressed with respect to limiting the target company's opportunity to seek a competitive bid. Here the concern is the acquiring company's ability to purchase the target company's stock at the then market price, before disclosure of the acquiring company's plans causes the price of target company stock to increase significantly. Empirical evidence indicates that the stock of target companies experiences an average abnormal return of 7.74% when an acquiring company files a Schedule 13D disclosing that it is only *considering* making an acquisition.[8] Thus, it is important to understand the operation of Section 13(d) because it serves to set the boundaries on the ability of an acquiring company to secretly purchase target company stock at the lower, pre-announcement price.

The elements of the operative portion of the section, set forth in Section 13(d)(1), can be stated simply. A Schedule 13D must be filed within ten days by

(1) any *person* who,

(2) after *acquiring*

(3) any *equity security* registered under Section 12 of the Exchange Act,

(4) becomes the *beneficial owner*

(5) of more than 5% of such security.

The surface simplicity of the Section's operation masks very substantial ambiguity; none of its central terms, italicized above, really mean what they say. Thus, some examination of these ambiguities and how the courts and the SEC have dealt with them is necessary in order to understand the Section's operation. But how much effort we should invest in that task, and how much care an acquiring company might invest in compliance, is at least in part a function of what happens if an acquiring company runs afoul of the Section's terms. After all, in the absence of an effective penalty, the opportunity to purchase target company stock at lower prices may sing a siren's song. Thus, it is useful to defer more detailed consideration of Section 13(d)(1)'s operation until after we examine the potential for noncompliance.

Section 13(f), a final aspect of the Williams Act dealing with passive investors, was added in 1975. Any institutional investment manager which holds at least $100 million in exchange listed or NASDAQ quoted securities at the end of the year must file Form 13F describing the number of shares and market value of each security held, and the managers' discretion with respect to the security, including its voting.

[8] Mikkelson & Ruback, *Corporate Investments in Common Stock* 16 (Massachusetts Institute of Technology, Sloan School of Management Working Paper # 1633–85 (Feb.1985) (Table 4)).

(2) Standing and Remedies

MAIWURM & TOBIN, CREATING WAVES IN THE MARKET PLACE AND UNCERTAINTY IN THE REGULATORY FRAMEWORK

38 Bus.Law. 419, 445–52 (1983).*

ENFORCEMENT OF THE ACCUMULATOR'S DISCLOSURE

The confrontation between the beachhead accumulator ** and the target usually comes to a head in litigation initiated by the target. The litigation may be triggered by a proxy contest, a tender offer, or even the accumulation of the beachhead itself. The target has a number of possible claims in such litigation, including allegations of disclosure violations, claims under federal and state legislation regulating take-overs, and charges that the accumulator has unlawfully manipulated the market for the target's securities. The first wave of litigation normally involves allegations of inadequate compliance with section 13(d).

* * *

Limitations on Section 13(d) Implied Rights of Action and Standing

A target must overcome several procedural hurdles before it can pursue an action against a beachhead accumulator under section 13(d). First, because section 13(d) does not provide an express reme-dy, an implied right of action must be found to permit a target to pursue a section 13(d) claim. A number of cases have specifically upheld the existence of such a right,[130] while several district courts, including the Northern District of Illinois,[131] the Northern District of

** A "beachhead accumulator" is one who acquires a significant block of target company stock—a beachhead—in anticipa-tion of an effort to acquire control. [Ed.]

[130] See, e.g., Federal Paper Bd. Co., Inc. v. Steinberg, No. 80–115 (D.N.J. Feb. 20, 1981) (holding, in a case brought by a tar-get in which the Cort v. Ash criteria were applied, that "[p]articularly in light of the context and circumstances under which Section 13(d) was enacted, it is fair to con-clude that Congress intended to create a private right of action," slip op. at 9); Spencer Co., Inc. v. Agency Rent-A-Car, Inc., [1981–1982 Transfer Binder] Fed.Sec. L.Rep. (CCH) ¶ 98,301 (D.Mass.1981) (dis-trict court refused to accept defendant's restrictive approach to implied private rights of action and, instead, relied on standing cases set forth below); Kaufman & Broad, Inc. v. Belzberg, 522 F.Supp. 35

(S.D.N.Y.1981) (court refused to accept the restrictive view of Touche Ross & Co. v. Redington, 442 U.S. 560 (1979) [hereinafter cited as Touche Ross], and Transamerica Mortgage Advisors, Inc. v. Lewis, 444 U.S. 560 (1979) discussed infra at note 141 [hereinafter cited as TAMA] and instead relied on GAF Corp. v. Milstein, 453 F.2d 709 (2d Cir.1971), cert. denied, 406 U.S. 910 (1972), which is essentially a standing case). * * *

[131] American Bakeries Co. v. Pro-Met Trading Co., [1981 Transfer Binder] Fed. Sec.L.Rep. (CCH) ¶ 97,925 (N.D.Ill.1981) (holding, in light of Gateway Indus., Inc. v. Agency Rent-A-Car, Inc., 495 F.Supp. 92 (N.D.Ill.1980), that an issuer had no im-plied private right of action for injunctive relief under § 13(d) since the intended ben-eficiaries of its disclosure requirements were target shareholders, not the target itself). * * * [In Indiana National Corp. v. Rich, 712 F.2d 1180 (7th Cir.1983), the court held, contrary to these district courts, that an issuer does have an implied

Alabama,[132] and the Northern and Southern Districts of Ohio,[133] have denied its existence. The trend of the most recent decisions,[134] supported strongly by the United States Supreme Court in Merrill Lynch, Pierce, Fenner & Smith, Inc. v. Curran,[135] has been to uphold the existence of an implied right.

The *Curran* decision is worthy of special note. In that case, the Supreme Court addressed the question whether a right of action should still be implied in favor of all commodities futures traders—buyers and sellers—under five separate provisions of the Commodities Exchange Act (the CEA) after congressional amendment of that Act. In support of its finding that a right of action should be implied, the Court analogized the implication of a remedy under the CEA to its implication of a private right of action under the 1934 Act, and particularly rule 10b–5, citing its early decisions in Blue Chip Stamps v. Manor Drug Stores [138] and J.I. Case Co. v. Borak.[139] The Court gave only lip service to the more recent Cort v. Ash,[140] Touche Ross & Co. v. Redington,[141] and Transamerica Mortgage Advisors, Inc. v. Lewis (*TAMA*) [142]—cases which would seem to require a contrary result— stating: "The routine recognition of a private remedy under the CEA prior to our decision in Cort v. Ash was comparable to the routine acceptance of an analogous remedy under the Securities Exchange Act of 1934." One can reason by analogy that if implied rights under the CEA survived Cort v. Ash, such rights under the 1934 Act survived as well when the Williams Act was enacted to amend the 1934 Act.

In a strong dissent, Justice Powell, writing for four members of the Court, noted and condemned the incongruity between the *Curran* decision and the Court's decision in the *Cort* and *TAMA* cases, but

---

right of action for injunctive relief under § 13(d). Ed.]

[132] First Ala. Bancshares v. Lowder, [1981 Transfer Binder] Fed.Sec.L.Rep. ¶ 98,015 (N.D.Ala.1981); Liberty National Insurance Holding Co. v. Charter Co. (The), [Current] Fed.Sec.L.Rep. (CCH) ¶ 98,797 (N.D.Ala.1982).

[133] SZRL Realty Inv. v. U.S. Realty Inv., No. C81–327 (N.D.Ohio May 7, 1981); Leff v. CIP Corp., [Current] Fed.Sec.L.Rep. (CCH) ¶ 98,662 (S.D.Ohio 1981).

[134] See cases cited in note 130 supra.

[135] 456 U.S. 353 (1982).

[138] 421 U.S. 723 (1975).

[139] 377 U.S. 426 (1964).

[140] 422 U.S. 66 (1975). The Supreme Court relied heavily on its decision in Cannon v. University of Chicago, 441 U.S. 677 (1979), which implied a private right of action under Title IX of the Education Amendments of 1972 to the Civil Rights Act of 1964 on the basis of an analysis of the four factors cited as determinative in Cort v. Ash: (1) plaintiff was a member of the class for whose special benefit the statute was enacted; (2) legislative history in-

dicated a congressional intent to create a private right; (3) implication of a private right of action would assist in achieving the statutory purpose; and (4) the federal courts have traditionally protected citizens against invidious discrimination. In the *Curran* decision, however, the Court focused almost exclusively on the factor of congressional intent.

[141] 442 U.S. 560 (1979). In *Touche Ross* and *TAMA*, infra note 142, the Supreme Court appeared to reject its earlier emphasis in cases like J.I. Case Co. v. Borak, 377 U.S. 426 (1964), on "the desirability of implying private rights of action in order to provide remedies thought to effectuate the purposes of a given statute," *TAMA*, infra note 142, at 15, in favor of a more restrictive view. In *Touche Ross*, the Court refused to recognize a private cause of action for damages under § 17(a) of the 1934 Act, 15 U.S.C. § 78q(a) (1976), and, in *TAMA*, the Court rejected a similar claim under anti-fraud provisions of the Investment Advisors Act of 1940, 15 U.S.C. §§ 80b–1 et seq. (1976).

[142] 444 U.S. 11 (1979).

Curran remains the most recent Supreme Court pronouncement on the issue.

The courts have often merged their analyses of the implied rights issue with the separate question whether a target corporation should have standing to maintain a cause of action under section 13(d).[145] The majority rule answers this question in the affirmative with respect to the target's ability to seek injunctive and other equitable relief for violations of section 13(d), usually on the ground that a target is in the best position to recognize section 13(d) violations and to protect the interests of its shareholders or that the potential benefit to target shareholders would further the purpose of the Williams Act. No federal appeals court has denied standing to a target. Some district courts, however, have taken the opposite view and have denied targets standing to allege Williams Act violations. For example, in *First Alabama Bancshares v. Lowder,*[150] the Northern District of Alabama reasoned that a target has no standing to sue either for damages or for injunctive relief because the sole purpose of the Williams Act is to protect investors confronted by a tender offer. * * *

Relief Under Section 13(d)

Assuming that an implied right of action and standing to sue can be established, a target can bring an action challenging the adequacy of the beachhead holder's schedule 13D disclosures or alleging a failure to file a schedule 13D or a required amendment thereto. False and misleading statements as to the acquiring party's financial position or the source of funds for an offer, its formation of an offering "group," and its intentions and purposes have all been successfully alleged by targets. Frequently, when a tender offer follows on the heels of a schedule 13D filing, the target will allege that the bidder made a material omission in its 13D filing by not stating an intent to acquire a particular percentage interest in the target or to acquire control of, or make a tender offer for, the target.

The results of this type of litigation have varied with the specific facts of each case, but the most common remedy for a section 13(d) violation has been an order requiring amended disclosure and prohibiting further purchases until corrective disclosure, in the form of an amendment to the defective schedule 13D, is made.

If the most recent filing is accurate, i.e., amended vis-a-vis the prior filing complained of, the courts generally will not enjoin further purchases or grant other extraordinary relief. If material disclosure defects are found at the time of the hearing or trial, the courts have sometimes restrained further stock purchases until curative amendments are filed. If equitable relief is granted, however, the courts

---

[145] The standing question is not "*whether* the statute created an implied private remedy," but rather "*who* may invoke that remedy." Piper v. Chris-Craft Indus., Inc., 430 U.S. 1, 55 n. 4 (1977) (Stevens, J., dissenting) (emphasis in original). See also Merrill Lynch, Pierce, Fenner & Smith, Inc. v. Curran, supra note 135, (standing question does not require the four-part Cort v. Ash analysis).

[150] *First Alabama Bancshares,* supra note 132.

rarely extend injunctions beyond the time needed to file a properly amended statement.[161] In the most extreme such case, the court upheld a thirty-day cooling-off period, during which the reporting person's right to acquire the stock in question was suspended in order to "give the market an opportunity to 'settle'." [162]

Courts have generally been reluctant to issue orders requiring divestiture by the acquiring party or suspension of voting rights or solicitation of proxies with respect to shares purchased while section 13(d) was not complied with, reasoning that such extraordinary relief is warranted only upon a showing of irreparable harm. Thus, section 13(d) has been of little use to targets in ultimately forestalling a tender offer. However, several recent district court decisions indicate that a more expansive view of the range of remedies available in section 13(d) cases may be in the offing.

The Recent Expansion of Section 13(d) Remedies

In framing its request for relief under section 13(d), a target may seek an order enjoining further purchases and the making of a tender offer, rescission rights for shareholders who sold their target securities during the accumulation, divestiture of shares acquired unlawfully, and suspension of the right to solicit proxies and vote such shares. One or more of such remedies have been granted to targets in appropriate circumstances, primarily in the early years of the Williams Act,[166] and the recent trend appears to favor expanding the scope of equitable relief under section 13(d) in ways that could be effective against beachhead accumulators.

General Steel Industries, Inc. v. Walco National Corp.[167] awarded a target almost all of the above-mentioned remedies. The plaintiff General Steel Industries (GSI) moved for a preliminary injunction enjoining Walco's tender offer for 750,000 shares of GSI common stock. The district court granted the motion and enjoined Walco from doing anything to advance its tender offer or influence GSI until corrective disclosures were approved by the court. Furthermore, Walco was ordered to rescind the purchases or otherwise divest itself of the shares acquired by it while its "false and misleading" schedule 13D was effective. The order was eventually vacated pursuant to a court-approved settlement between the parties.

---

[161] The rationale is that revisions are quickly digested by the marketplace.

* * *

[162] Kirsch Co. v. Bliss Loughlin Indus., Inc., 495 F.Supp. 488, 507 (W.D.Mich.1980).

* * *

[166] Bath Indus., Inc. v. Blot, 427 F.2d 97 (7th Cir.1970) (injunction against calling special shareholders' meeting); Graphic Sciences, Inc. v. International Mogul Mines, Ltd., 397 F.Supp. 112 (D.D.C.1974) (injunction against further acquisitions, soliciting proxies, and proceeding with tender offer); Water & Wall Assoc., Inc. v. American Consumer Indus., Inc., [1973 Transfer Binder] Fed.Sec.L.Rep. (CCH) ¶ 93,943 (D.N.J.1973) (injunction against voting shares and certifying election if defendants were successful); Committee for New Management of Butler Aviation v. Widmark, 335 F.Supp. 146 (E.D.N.Y.1971) (injunction against voting in proxy context shares acquired after 13D should have been filed). See also Ozark Airlines, Inc. v. Cox, 326 F.Supp. 1113 (E.D.Mo.1971) at 119–20 (court "would have considered" disenfranchisement if there had been no 13(d) filing before litigation commenced).

[167] [1981–82 Transfer Binder] Fed.Sec.L. Rep. (CCH) ¶ 98,402 (E.D.Mo.1981).

More recently, the Northern District of Ohio went beyond the result in *Walco* and granted broad remedial relief to a target company where the acquiring party purchased an 8.8% beachhead, filed a schedule 13D that stated an investment purpose, made no further purchases for a number of months, announced a tender offer, and then filed a 13D amendment stating its intent was to obtain control.[169] In contrast to *Walco,* where the far-reaching relief described above was applied to those shares purchased *after* an allegedly misleading schedule 13D was filed, the district court in Hanna Mining Co. v. Norcen Energy Resources Ltd. issued an expansive preliminary injunction affecting shares that had been acquired *prior* to the filing of a schedule 13D. Specifically, the court enjoined the beachhead holder from acquiring additional shares, publicly announcing or commencing a tender offer, exercising influence, directly or indirectly, on target management, selling or disposing of any shares already acquired, or engaging in any step to further its plan to obtain control. As in *Walco,* the SEC filed an amicus curiae brief in the appellate court generally supporting the power of federal district courts to fashion remedies beyond amended disclosure for violations of section 13(d).[171]

These decisions and others like them [172] may enhance the effectiveness of section 13(d) as a defensive weapon, particularly where a postviolation purchase or an intentional violation can be shown. The SEC amicus briefs dealing with section 13(d) ✳ ✳ ✳ may foreshadow new regulatory or legislative proposals involving section 13(d).✳

------◆------

(3) The Triggers to Disclosure

Person and Beneficial Owner. The first step in construing the terms governing Section 13(d)'s operation is specifying whose acquisitions and stock ownership are to be counted in determining whether

[169] Hanna Mining Co. v. Norcen Energy Resources, Ltd., No. C82–959 (N.D.Ohio, June 11, 1982).

[171] The thrust of the SEC's brief in Hanna Mining Co. and Walco was summarized in SEC Litigation Release No. 9533, [1981–82 Transfer Binder] Fed.Sec.L.Rep. (CCH) ¶ 98,387 at 92,344:

The Commission urged in its brief that the district court's equitable jurisdiction to remedy Section 13(d) violations includes the authority to enter any relief appropriate under the circumstances. The Commission expressed the view that equitable remedies in addition to corrective disclosures, such as rescission and divestiture, may be necessary or appropriate to remedy violations of the Williams Act, particularly in cases where the defendant deliberately violated Section 13(d) and the illegal conduct has permitted the defendant to obtain a sufficient number of shares to inhibit

competing tender offers or merger proposals. In such cases, absent rescission or divestiture or other remedy removing the wrongfully obtained blocking position, shareholders could be irreparably harmed and the defendant would be permitted to benefit from its wrongful conduct.

[172] See Spencer Cos., Inc. v. Agency Rent-A-Car, Inc., supra note 130 (defendant enjoined from voting or exercising any rights with respect to shares purchased while materially misleading schedule 13D's were in effect and from accepting tenders made prior to supplying amended disclosure).

✳ The authors may be somewhat optimistic. In Liberty National Insurance Holding Co. v. Charter Co., [1984 Transfer Binder] Fed.Sec.L.Rep. (CCH) ¶ 91,539 (11th Cir. 1984), the court held that an issuer did not have an implied right of action under § 13(d) to force a bidder to divest issuer stock alledgedly acquired illegally. [Ed.]

the obligation to file a Schedule 13D has been triggered. Two statutory terms are implicated in this inquiry: "Person" and "beneficial owner."

With respect to the term "person," Section 13(d)(3) provides that a group formed "for the purpose of acquiring, holding, or disposing of securities of an issuer" will be treated as a single person in determining whether a filing obligation has been triggered. The need for such a provision is obvious; in its absence, a planner could avoid Section 13(d)(1)'s 5 percent trigger at will simply by splitting stock acquisitions among a number of individuals who had agreed to act in concert. However, it would be very difficult to draw a brightline rule that would determine whether a group exists. If the group concept were limited to combinations held together by formal agreement, it could be avoided by individuals whose existing relationship—as family members or co-venturers in other projects—provided the means to enforce informal obligations undertaken in connection with a new project. Thus, it was predictable that determining whether a group existed would depend on examination of the detailed facts and circumstances of each case,[9] and that, much as with respect to the existence of a conspiracy under the Sherman Act, circumstantial evidence alone would support a finding that a group exists.

This, however, does not end the matter of line drawing. Even informal agreements to act in concert do not spring to life full blown; preliminary discussion necessarily proceeds the formation of a group and Section 13(d)(1) can hardly require a filing with respect to a group that has not yet been formed. As the court stated in Pantry Pride, Inc. v. Rooney, 598 F.Supp. 891, 900 (S.D.N.Y.1984): "Section 13(d) allows individuals broad freedom to discuss the possibilities of future agreements without filing under securities laws." The resulting conflict—between the need for a general standard to prevent avoidance and the need to avoid imposing a filing obligation too early in the process of negotiating the formation of the group—may help explain the courts' reluctance, as discussed in Section A.1.a.(2). of this Chapter and exemplified by the Supreme Court in Rondeau v. Mosinee Paper Co.,[10] to impose meaningful sanctions for violations of Section 13(d)(1). Given the inherent uncertainty in distinguishing between, on the one hand, the informal formation of a group and, on the other, nonbinding discussions preliminary to forming a group, it would be difficult to justify a significant penalty if the penalty's application depended upon the inevitably somewhat random resolution of that uncertainty. Yet this can be precisely the case in some Section 13(d) settings; where a group is involved, the filing obligation often accrues 10 days after the group is formed even though the date from which one begins the count is unclear.[11]

[9] See, e.g., Jacobs v. Pabst Brewing Co., 549 F.Supp. 1050 (D.Del.1982); Financial General Bankshares, Inc. v. Lance, 80 F.R.D. 22 (D.D.C.1978); Jewelcor, Inc. v. Pearlman, 397 F.Supp. 221 (S.D.N.Y.1975).

[10] 422 U.S. 49 (1975). In *Rondeau* the Supreme Court required a showing of irreparable injury before injunctive relief would be granted for a violation of Section 13(d)(1).

[11] Where the members of the group together own 5 percent of the issuer's stock, the filing of a Schedule 13D would be required 10 days after the date on which the group was formed. This result follows

The same type of issue arises with respect to the term "beneficial owner." Individuals own some equity securities formally: They are the record owners of the securities. They own other securities informally: Even though others are the record owners, the securities *really* belong to them. Here Rule 13d–3 does provide some certainty, although the potential for ambiguity still remains. Note, for example, that subsection (a) of Rule 13d–3 speaks in terms of voting or investment power held "directly or indirectly, through any contract, arrangement, understanding, relationship, or otherwise . . . ." Thus, the same problem that created the uncertainty in connection with the term "group" reappears in connection with the term "beneficial owner."

Acquiring. On its face, Section 13(d)(1) seem to require that, to trigger a filing obligation, a person or group actually must make an acquisition of stock. If this were correct, the uncertainty concerning precisely when a group was formed would be substantially ameliorated. So long as all potential group members did not acquire stock while the terms of their relationship were being negotiated, there would be no danger of unknowingly triggering a filing obligation. The ten days would run only from a discernible event: an actual acquisition of securities. Thus, a brightline rule with respect to "acquiring" largely would make irrelevant the ambiguity with respect to "group."

It did not work out that way. Although an early case adopted this construction of the statute for the explicit purpose of providing some certainty,[12] later cases did not follow it.[13] In any event, the SEC resolved the matter in 1977 by the adoption of Rule 13d–5 which expressly provides that a group is deemed to acquire the securities of its members on the date the group is formed.

Equity Security and 5 Percent. Here the issues are ones of calculation. How are convertible securities counted? What if a person has an option to acquire securities? These issues are addressed in the context of the beneficial ownership provisions in Rule 13d–3.

Problems

What are the parties' Section 13(d) filing obligations in the following circumstances?

1. Susan Reynolds, a 22 year old law student, owns 3 percent ($150,000 face value) of the outstanding convertible subordinated debentures of GSSB, Inc., and 4 percent (40,000 shares) of its outstanding common stock. Both classes of securities are traded on a national securities exchange. The debentures are convertible into common stock at the rate of one share per $10 face value of debenture. Reynold's father, the original source of her GSSB holdings, owns 22 percent of GSSB's outstanding common stock and 10 percent of its outstanding debentures. As a Valentine Day's present Reynold's father presents her with an additional $150,000

---

from the construction of the term "acquiring" in Section 13(d)(1) considered infra.

[12] Bath Industries, Inc. v. Blot, 427 F.2d 97, 110 (7th Cir.1970).

[13] See, e.g., GAF Corp. v. Milstein, 453 F.2d 709 (2d Cir.1971), cert. denied 406 U.S. 910 (1972).

face value of GSSB convertible debentures. All of Reynold's securities are held in street name by the family broker.

2.   Ronald Davis is the President of TD, Inc., whose common stock is traded on a national securities exchange. One million shares are outstanding. Davis owns 25,000 shares of common stock and holds options to purchase 15,000 shares under the company's stock option plan. Davis also is (i) the beneficiary of a pledge of 7,500 shares of the company's common stock given as security for his loan of their purchase price to a company vice president; (ii) the trustee of an irrevocable trust for the benefit of his children (established by the children's grandfather) which holds 3,500 shares of the company's common stock.

(4) The Content of Required Disclosure

[Read Schedule 13D in Appendix A.]

For an acquirer, Item 4 of Schedule 13D poses the central Section 13(d) disclosure dilemma. Suppose that two acquirers each make a 5 percent acquisition that triggers the obligation to file a Schedule 13D— one a straightforward company that desires only to comply with applicable legal requirements, and one with a more strategic orientation that would like to minimize the extent to which disclosure interferes with achieving its aims. Item 4 requires disclosure of whether the offerer intends to seek control of the issuer.[14]   Now suppose that the straightforward company genuinely made its acquisition only as an investment and has no intention of seeking control. The problem with simply so stating in its Schedule 13D is twofold. First, some courts have viewed a substantial acquisition as itself evidence that the acquirer had an intent to seek control.[15]   Second, circumstances change. If the company later seeks control, the accuracy of its original statement of intent unavoidably will be determined in light of the fact that it turned out to be an inaccurate prediction.[16]

One approach to resolving this dilemma is what has been called "waffling"[17] or "kitchen sink" disclosure: Disclosure that covers all possibilities without disclosing the acquirer's estimate of their relative likelihood. Jewelcor's disclosure in connection with its acquisition of Lafayette stock is an example of this approach that passed judicial muster:

---

[14] Although item 4 does not by its terms explicitly require this disclosure, the courts have consistently held that it is required. Maiwurm & Tobin, Beachhead Acquisitions: Creating Waves in the Marketplace and Uncertainty in the Regulatory Framework, 38 Bus.Law. 419, 430 (1983).

[15] See, e.g., Dan River, Inc. v. Unitex Ltd., 624 F.2d 1216 (4th Cir.1980), cert. denied 449 U.S. 1101 (1981); Saunders Leasing System, Inc. v. Societe Holding Gray D'Albion, 507 F.Supp. 627 (N.D.Ala. 1981); General Steel Industries, Inc. v.

Walco National Corp., 529 F.Supp. 305 (E.D.Mo.), vacated per stipulation 676 F.2d 704 (8th Cir.1981).

[16] 1 Lipton & Steinberger, *Takeovers and Freezeouts* 85 (1978), reports that the SEC staff has stated informally that it "is inclining to a strict integration approach whereby later action taken by the acquirer with respect to the target company will be rebuttably presumed to have been intended at the time of the earlier filing."

[17] Maiwurn & Tobin, supra at 434-34.

Item 4: The Common Stock of Lafayette to which this statement relates was purchased by Jewelcor for the purpose of investment. Although Jewelcor has considered the possibility of a future acquisition of control of the business of Lafayette, whether by means of a tender offer, merger or other business combination, open market purchases, private transactions, or otherwise, Jewelcor has not made any definitive plans to attempt to acquire control of Lafayette, nor has Jewelcor entered into any contracts, arrangements or understandings with Lafayette or its affiliates for this purpose. * * *[18]

If, consistent with the discussion in Chapter Fifteen B.1.d., counsel for the acquirer is more risk averse than his client, what sort of disclosure would you expect him to recommend?

While the analysis is somewhat different in the case of the strategic acquirer, it may well lead to the same conclusion. Suppose that this acquirer is seriously considering seeking control of the target company, but would like to do so as cheaply as possible. To this end, the acquirer would like its Schedule 13D to have as little impact on the price of target company stock as possible consistent with disclosure that has a reasonable probability of being sustained if challenged. Empirical evidence indicates that Schedule 13D disclosures which state that the acquirer is considering additional investments in the target company's stock are associated with an average abnormal return of 7.74%, while Schedule 13D disclosures which state that the acquisition was only for investment are associated with an average abnormal return of 3.24%.[19] Would not the same form of disclosure that was best for the straightforward acquirer then also be best for the strategic acquirer?[20] How sensible is a system that leads to the same disclosure in situations that

---

[18] Jewelcor, Inc., v. Pearlman, 397 F.Supp. 221, 228 (S.D.N.Y.1975). A more extreme example is set forth in 1 Lipton & Steinberger, supra at 80–81:

Raider purchased the shares of Target's common stock presently owned by Raider to acquire an equity interest in Target. Raider has also considered, but has not decided whether or not to pursue, other possible courses of action with respect to Target, including (i) seeking control of Target by purchasing additional shares in brokerage transactions on the New York Stock Exchange, in private transactions, in a tender offer or exchange offer, or otherwise; (ii) proposing a merger or other form of combination between Raider and Target; and (iii) seeking representation on Target's Board of Directors.

* * *

Raider intends to review, from time to time, the possible courses of action referred to above and to take such action with respect to Target as Raider considers desirable in the light of the circumstances then prevailing. Pending Raider's decision whether or not to pursue

any of such possible courses of action, and depending on market conditions and other factors, Raider presently intends to continue to purchase shares of Target's common stock in brokerage transactions on the New York Stock Exchange or in private transactions, if appropriate opportunities to do so are available, on such terms and at such times as Raider considers desirable. Raider also may determine to continue to hold its shares of Target's common stock or to dispose of all or a portion of such shares.

Although the possibilities referred to above do exist, Raider has no plans or proposals to liquidate Target to sell its assets, to merge it with any other person or to make any other major change in its business or corporate structure.

[19] Mikkelson & Ruback, supra, Table 4.

[20] Ambiguous disclosure in the Schedule 13D, however, might be clarified by the identity of the purchaser. Would the market believe a statement by T. Boone Pickens that a purchase was made for investment?

are so different? Although the content of mandatory disclosure warrants more careful consideration, it will be deferred until we take up the same issues in connection with Section 14(d) in the following section.

b. *Disclosure and Substantive Regulation of Tender Offers*

Although an acquiring company's first encounter with the Williams Act likely will be with Section 13(d) following its predisclosure acquisition of target company stock, the disclosure required of both the acquiring company and the target company in connection with the tender offer, and the substantive terms of the tender offer itself, will be controlled by Sections 14(d) and (e). This combination of disclosure and substantive regulation is virtually unique in the universe of federal securities regulation. Other sections of the Securities Exchange Act of 1934 focus mainly on either requiring disclosure, as with registration under Section 12 and periodic reporting under Section 13(a), or on forbidding misleading disclosure as under Section 10(b). Similarly, the Securities Act of 1933 requires only disclosure of material facts bearing on whatever security the issuer proposes to offer to the public. Only the Williams Act seems to cross the boundary separating regulatory regimes that leave informed parties free to make whatever deal they choose, from those that limit the range of permissible deals available even to informed parties. As we will see, controversy over whether the Williams Act in fact crosses the boundary between disclosure regulation and substantive regulation has shaped debate over one of the statute's major jurisdictional limits.[21]

The general shape of Sections 14(d) and (e) is straightforward. Section 14(d)(1) prohibits making a tender offer that would result in the offerer holding more than 5 percent of a class of the target company's equity securities without filing a disclosure statement. Sections 14(d)(5) –(7) specify the minimum period that tender offers must be left open, the extent of a shareholder's right to withdraw shares after tender, the effect of over-subscription in a partial offer, and the effect of an offeror increasing the price during the pendency of a tender offer. Section 14(e) prohibits misrepresentation, nondisclosure and fraudulent, deceptive or manipulative acts or practices in connection with tender offers.

Note that all three aspects of the regulatory structure of Sections 14(d) and (e) share a common jurisdictional limited: They apply only to a "tender offer." This term, however, is nowhere defined in the statute or regulations. Thus, a natural place to begin our examination of the transactional aspects of the Williams Act would seem to be with the definition of the covered transactions: What is a tender offer? What kinds of transactions trigger the regulatory apparatus? For our purposes, however, this inquiry is a more fitting end than a beginning. A conventional tender offer is hardly difficult to recognize; the problem is with unconventional transactions—typically the work of planners

---

[21] This debate is posed in terms of whether the prohibition of "fraudulent, deceptive, or manipulative acts" in Section 14(e) extends to target company defensive tactics such as lock-ups, or is limited to acts of misrepresentation or nondisclosure. The subject is considered in Section A.1.d. of this Chapter, *infra*.

whose very purpose is to avoid the impact of Sections 14(d) and (e). As a result, it is necessary to understand the stakes for which the planners are playing—the collateral consequences of calling a transaction a tender offer—before evaluating the efforts of the courts and the SEC at defining a tender offer.

(1) Disclosure Under Sections 14(d) and (e).

(a) Introduction: The Statute and Regulations

(Read Securities Exchange Act Sections 14(d) and (e), and Regulations 14D and 14E in Appendix A.]

Prior to January 7, 1980, the Williams Act's requirement of mandatory disclosure in connection with a tender offer extended only to the offerer; the target company remained free to stone wall it. To be sure, if target management elected to comment on an offer or to make a recommendation to target shareholders, Rule 14d–9 required the filing of Schedule 14D–9, and Section 14(e) would apply to the content of the communication; however, there was no *requirement* that target management say anything. The January 7, 1980 effective date of Rule 14e–2 changed this imbalance. The Commission explained the reason for imposing a mandatory disclosure obligation on the target company as follows:

> The subject company's position with respect to a tender offer can have a determinative effect on the outcome of a tender offer and thus is material to security holders. The subject company therefore should not be permitted to state its position when it maximizes its tactical advantage and to remain silent when it does not. Such complete discretion increases the likelihood for hasty, illconsidered decision-making by security holders and the possibility for fraudulent, deceptive or manipulative acts or practices by a subject company and others.[22]

Is the case for the imposition of mandatory disclosure quite so easy? Suppose a tender offer were made and the target company did not comment. Would not the market infer that the failure of the target company to recommend against the offer meant that the target did not object to the offer? If that were the case, mandatory disclosure of a sort already existed in that the target company could not keep the market in doubt as to its view of the offer; silence would be read as tacit acceptance. Moreover, how significant a change does Rule 14e–2 effect? If the target company can limit its comment, as permitted by Rule 14e–2, to a statement that "it is unable to take a position with respect to the bidder's tender offer", and can explain the reasons for its inability by boilerplate,[23] has there been any gain over silence?

---

[22] Exchange Act Release No. 16384 (Nov. 29, 1979), reprinted in [1979–1980 Transfer Binder] Fed.Sec.L.Rep. (CCH) ¶ 82,373.

[23] For example, could the target company decline to take a position because it believes that target management has an inherent conflict of interest concerning any tender offer and therefore believes that the decision is appropriately one for shareholders?

(b) Standing and Remedies

PIPER v. CHRIS–CRAFT INDUSTRIES, INC.

Supreme Court of the United States, 1977.
430 U.S. 1.

Mr. Chief Justice BURGER delivered the opinion of the Court.

We granted certiorari in these cases to consider, among other issues, whether an unsuccessful tender offeror in a contest for control of a corporation has an implied cause of action for damages under § 14(e) of the Securities Exchange Act of 1934, as added by § 3 of the Williams Act of 1968, * * * based on alleged antifraud violations by the successful competitor, its investment adviser, and individuals constituting the management of the target corporation.

I

Background

The factual background of this complex contest for control, including the protracted litigation culminating in the cases now before us, is essential to a full understanding of the contending parties' claims.

The three petitions present questions of first impression, arising out of a "sophisticated and hard fought contest" for control of Piper Aircraft Corp., a Pennsylvania-based manufacturer of light aircraft. Piper's management consisted principally of members of the Piper family, who owned 31% of Piper's outstanding stock. Chris-Craft Industries, Inc., a diversified manufacturer of recreational products, attempted to secure voting control of Piper through cash and exchange tender offers for Piper common stock. Chris-Craft's takeover attempt failed, and Bangor Punta Corp. (Bangor or Bangor Punta), with the support of the Piper family, obtained control of Piper in September 1969. Chris-Craft brought suit under § 14(e) of the Securities Exchange Act of 1934 * * * alleging that Bangor Punta achieved control of the target corporation as a result of violations of the federal securities laws by the Piper family, Bangor Punta, and Bangor Punta's underwriter, First Boston Corp., who together had successfully repelled Chris-Craft's takeover attempt.

The struggle for control of Piper began in December 1968. At that time, Chris-Craft began making cash purchases of Piper common stock. By January 22, 1969, Chris-Craft had acquired 203,700 shares, or approximately 13% of Piper's 1,644,790 outstanding shares. On the next day, following unsuccessful preliminary overtures to Piper by Chris-Craft's president, Herbert Siegel, Chris-Craft publicly announced a cash tender offer for up to 300,000 Piper shares at $65 per share, which was approximately $12 above the then-current market price. Responding promptly to Chris-Craft's bid, Piper's management met on the same day with the company's investment banker, First Boston, and other advisers. On January 24, the Piper family decided to oppose Chris-Craft's tender offer. As part of its resistance to Chris-Craft's takeover campaign, Piper management sent several letters to the

company's stockholders during January 25–27, arguing against acceptance of Chris-Craft's offer. On January 27, a letter to shareholders
from W.T. Piper, Jr., president of the company, stated that the Piper
Board "has carefully studied this offer and is convinced that it is
inadequate and not in the best interests of Piper's shareholders."

In addition to communicating with shareholders, Piper entered into
an agreement with Grumman Aircraft Corp. on January 29, whereby
Grumman agreed to purchase 300,000 authorized but unissued Piper
shares at $65 per share. The agreement increased the amount of stock
necessary for Chris-Craft to secure control and thus rendered Piper less
vulnerable to Chris-Craft's attack. A Piper press release and letter to
shareholders announced the Grumman transaction but failed to state
either that Grumman had a "put" or option to sell the shares back to
Piper at cost, plus interest, or that Piper was required to maintain the
proceeds of the transaction in a separate fund free from liens.

Despite Piper's opposition, Chris-Craft succeeded in acquiring
304,606 shares by the time its cash tender offer expired on February 3.
To obtain the additional 17% of Piper stock needed for control, Chris-
Craft decided to make an exchange offer of Chris-Craft securities for
Piper stock. Although Chris-Craft filed a registration statement and
preliminary prospectus with the SEC in late February 1969, the exchange offer did not go into effect until May 15, 1969.

* * *

In the meantime, Chris-Craft made cash purchases of Piper stock
on the open market until Mr. Siegel, the company's president, was
expressly warned by SEC officials that such purchases, when made
during the pendency of an exchange offer, violated SEC Rule 10b–6. At
Mr. Siegel's direction, Chris-Craft immediately complied with the SEC's
directive and canceled all outstanding orders for purchases of Piper
stock.

While Chris-Craft's exchange offer was in registration, Piper in
March 1969 terminated the agreement with Grumman and entered into
negotiations with Bangor Punta. Bangor had initially been contacted
by First Boston about the possibility of a Piper takeover in the wake of
Chris-Craft's initial cash tender offer in January. With Grumman out
of the picture, the Piper family agreed on May 8, 1969, to exchange
their 31% stockholdings in Piper for Bangor Punta securities. Bangor
also agreed to use its best efforts to achieve control of Piper by means of
an exchange offer of Bangor securities for Piper common stock. A
press release issued the same day announced the terms of the agreement, including a provision that the forthcoming exchange offer would
involve Bangor securities to be valued, in the judgment of First Boston,
"at not less than $80 per Piper share."

While awaiting the effective date of its exchange offer, Bangor in
mid-May 1969 purchased 120,200 shares of Piper stock in privately
negotiated, off-exchange transactions from three large institutional
investors. * * *

With these three block purchases, amounting to 7% of Piper stock,
Bangor Punta in mid-May took the lead in the takeover contest. The

contest then centered upon the competing exchange offers. Chris-Craft's first exchange offer, which began in mid-May 1969, failed to produce tenders of the specified minimum number of Piper shares (80,000). Meanwhile, Bangor Punta's exchange offer, which had been announced on May 8, became effective on July 18. The registration materials which Bangor filed with the SEC in connection with the exchange offer included financial statements, reviewed by First Boston, representing that one of Bangor's subsidiaires, the Bangor & Aroostock Railroad (BAR), had a value of $18.4 million. This valuation was based upon a 1965 appraisal by investment bankers after a proposed sale of the BAR failed to materialize. The financial statements did not indicate that Bangor was considering the sale of the BAR or that an offer to purchase the railroad for $5 million had been received.[5]

In the final phase of the see-saw of competing offers, Chris-Craft modified the terms of its previously unsuccessful exchange offer to make it more attractive. The revised offer succeeded in attracting 112,089 additional Piper shares, while Bangor's exchange offer, which terminated on July 29, resulted in the tendering of 110,802 shares. By August 4, 1969, at the conclusion of both offers, Bangor Punta owned a total of 44.5%, while Chris-Craft owned 40.6% of Piper stock. The remainder of Piper stock, 14.9%, remained in the hands of the public.

After completion of their respective exchange offers, both companies renewed market purchases of Piper stock, but Chris-Craft, after purchasing 29,200 shares for cash in mid-August, withdrew from competition. Bangor Punta continued making cash purchases until September 5, by which time it had acquired a majority interest in Piper. The final tally in the nine-month takeover battle showed that Bangor Punta held over 50% and Chris-Craft held 42% of Piper stock.

II

Before either side had achieved control, the contest moved from the marketplace to the courts. Then began more than seven years of complex litigation growing out of the contest for control of Piper Aircraft.

* * *

III

* * *

The threshold issue in these cases is whether tender offerors such as Chris-Craft, whose activities are regulated by the Williams Act, have a cause of action for damages against other regulated parties under the statute on a claim that anti-fraud violations by other parties have frustrated the bidder's efforts to obtain control of the target corporation. * * *

---

[5] Shortly after the contest for control was completed, Bangor entered into an agreement to sell the BAR for $5 million, thereby resulting in a $13.8 million book loss.

IV

Our analysis begins, of course, with the statute itself. Section 14(e), like § 10(b), makes no provision whatever for a private cause of action, such as those explicitly provided in other sections of the 1933 and 1934 Acts. E.g., §§ 11, 12, 15 of the 1933 Act; §§ 9, 16, 18, 20 of the 1934 Act. This Court has nonetheless held that in some circumstances a private cause of action can be implied with respect to the 1934 Act's antifraud provisions, even though the relevant provisions are silent as to remedies. J.I. Case Co. v. Borak, 377 U.S. 426 (1964) (§ 14(a)); Superintendent of Ins. v. Bankers Life & Cas. Co., 404 U.S. 6, 13 n. 9 (1971) (§ 10(b)).

The reasoning of these holdings is that, where congressional purposes are likely to be undermined absent private enforcement, private remedies may be implied in favor of the particular class intended to be protected by the statute. For example, in J.I. Case Co. v. Borak, supra, recognizing an implied right of action in favor of a shareholder complaining of a misleading proxy solicitation, the Court concluded as to such a shareholder's right:

"While [§ 14(a)] makes no specific reference to a private right of action, among its chief purposes is *'the protection of investors,'* which certainly implies the availability of judicial relief *where necessary to achieve that result.*" 377 U.S., at 432. (Emphasis supplied.)

Indeed, the Court in *Borak* carefully noted that because of practical limitations upon the SEC's enforcement capabilities, "[p]rivate enforcement * * * provides *a necessary supplement to Commission action.*" Ibid. (Emphasis added.) Similarly, the Court's opinion in Blue Chip Stamps v. Manor Drug Stores, 421 U.S. 723, 730 (1975), in reaffirming the availability of a private right of action under § 10(b), specifically alluded to the language in *Borak* concerning the *necessity* for supplemental private remedies without which congressional protection of shareholders would be defeated. See also Rondeau v. Mosinee Paper Corp., 422 U.S. 49, 62 (1975).

Against this background we must consider whether § 14(e), which is entirely silent as to private remedies, permits this Court to read into the statute a damages remedy for unsuccessful tender offerors. To resolve that question we turn to the legislative history to discern the congressional purpose underlying the specific statutory prohibition in § 14(e). Once we identify the legislative purpose, we must then determine whether the creation by judicial interpretation of the implied cause of action asserted by Chris-Craft is necessary to effectuate Congress' goals.

A

Reliance on legislative history in divining the intent of Congress is, as has often been observed, a step to be taken cautiously. Department of Air Force v. Rose, 425 U.S. 352, 388–389 (1976) (BLACKMUN, J., dissenting); United States v. Public Utilities Comm'n, 345 U.S. 295, 319

(1953) (Jackson, J., concurring); Scripps-Howard Radio v. FCC, 316 U.S. 4, 11 (1942). In this case both sides press legislative history on the Court not so much to explain the meaning of the language of a statute as to explain the absence of any express provision for a private cause of action for damages. As Mr. Justice Frankfurter reminded us: "We must be wary against interpolating our notions of policy in the interstices of legislative provisions." Ibid. With that caveat, we turn to the legislative history of the Williams Act.

In introducing the legislation on the Senate floor, the sponsor, Senator Williams, stated:

> "This legislation will close a significant gap in *investor protection* under the Federal securities laws by requiring the disclosure of pertinent information *to stockholders* when persons seek to obtain control of a corporation by a cash tender offer or through open market or privately negotiated purchases of securities." 113 Cong. Rec. 854 (1967). (Emphasis supplied.)

* * *

The legislative history thus shows that Congress was intent upon regulating takeover bidders, theretofore operating covertly, in order to protect the shareholders of target companies. That tender offerors were not the intended beneficiaries of the bill was graphically illustrated by the statements of Senator Kuchel, cosponsor of the legislation, in support of requiring takeover bidders, whom he described as "corporate raiders" and "takeover pirates," to disclose their activities.

> "Today there are those individuals in our financial community who seek to reduce our proudest businesses into nothing but corporate shells. They seize control of the corporation with unknown sources, sell or trade away the best assets, and later split up the remains among themselves. The tragedy of such collusion is that the corporation can be financially raped without management *or shareholders* having any knowledge of the acquisitions. * * * The corporate raider may thus act under a cloak of secrecy while obtaining the shares needed to put him on the road to a successful capture of the company." 113 Cong.Rec. 857–858 (1967). (Emphasis supplied.)

* * *

The sponsors of this legislation were plainly sensitive to the suggestion that the measure would favor one side or the other in control contests; however, they made it clear that the legislation was designed solely to get needed information to the investor, the constant focal point of the committee hearings. Senator Williams articulated this singleness of purpose, even while advocating neutrality:

> "We have taken extreme care to avoid tipping the scales either in favor of management or in favor of the person making the takeover bids. *S.510 is designed solely to require full and fair disclosure for the benefit of investors.*" 113 Cong.Rec. 24664 (1967). (Emphasis supplied.)

Accordingly, the congressional policy of "evenhandedness" is nonprobative of the quite disparate proposition that the Williams Act was intended to confer rights for money damages upon an injured takeover bidder.

Besides the policy of evenhandedness, Chris-Craft emphasizes that the matter of implied private causes of action was raised in written submissions to the Senate Subcommittee. Specifically, Chris-Craft points to the written statements of Professors Israels and Painter, who made reference to J.I. Case Co. v. Borak, 377 U.S. 426 (1964). Chris-Craft contends, therefore, that Congress was aware that private actions were implicit in § 14(e).

But this conclusion places more weight on the passing reference to *Borak* than can reasonably be carried. Even accepting the value of written statements received without comment by the committee and without cross-examination, the statements do not refer to implied private actions by *offeror-bidders*. For example, Professor Israels' statement on this subject reads:

> "[A] private litigant could seek similar relief before or after the significant fact *such as the acceptance of his tender of securities.*"
> Senate Hearings 67. (Emphasis supplied.)

Similarly, Professor Painter in his written submission referred to "injured investors." Id., at 140. Neither Israels nor Painter discussed or even alluded to remedies potentially available to takeover bidders.

More important, these statements referred to a case in which the remedy was afforded to shareholders—the *direct* and *intended* beneficiaries of this legislation. In *Borak,* the Court emphasized that § 14(a), the proxy provision, was adopted expressly for "the protection of investors," 377 U.S., at 432, the very class of persons there seeking relief. The Court found no difficulty in identifying the legislative objective and concluding that remedies should be available if necessary "to make effective the congressional purpose." Id., at 433. *Borak* did not involve, and the statements in the legislative history relied upon by Chris-Craft do not implicate, the interests of parties such as offeror-bidders who are outside the scope of the concerns articulated in the evolution of this legislation.

* * *

The legislative history thus shows that the sole purpose of the Williams Act was the protection of investors who are confronted with a tender offer. As we stated in Rondeau v. Mosinee Paper Corp., 422 U.S., at 58: "The purpose of the Williams Act is to insure that public shareholders who are confronted by a cash tender offer for their stock will not be required to respond without adequate information * * *." We find no hint in the legislative history, on which respondent so heavily relies, that Congress contemplated a private cause of action for damages by one of several contending offerors against a successful bidder or by a losing contender against the target corporation.

* * *

B

Our conclusion as to the legislative history is confirmed by the analysis in Cort v. Ash, 422 U.S. 66 (1975). There, the Court identified four factors as "relevant" in determining whether a private remedy is implicit in a statute not expressly providing one. The first is whether the plaintiff is " 'one of the class for whose *especial* benefit the statute was enacted ＊ ＊ ＊.' " Id., at 78. (Emphasis in original.) As previously indicated, examination of the statute and its genesis shows that Chris-Craft is not an intended beneficiary of the Williams Act, and surely is not one "for whose *especial* benefit the statute was enacted." Ibid. To the contrary, Chris-Craft is a member of the class whose activities Congress intended to regulate for the protection and benefit of an entirely distinct class, shareholder-offerees. As a party whose previously unregulated conduct was purposefully brought under federal control by the statute, Chris-Craft can scarcely lay claim to the status of "beneficiary" whom Congress considered in need of protection.

Second, in Cort v. Ash we inquired whether there was "any indication of legislative intent, explicit or implicit, either to create such a remedy or to deny one." Ibid. Although the historical materials are barren of any express intent to deny a damages remedy to tender offerors as a class, there is, as we have noted, no indication that Congress intended to create a damages remedy in favor of the loser in a contest for control. Fairly read, we think the legislative documents evince the narrow intent to curb the unregulated activities of tender offerors. The expression of this purpose, which pervades the legislative history, negates the claim that tender offerors were intended to have additional weapons in the form of an implied cause of action for damages, particularly if a private damages action confers no advantage on the expressly protected class of shareholder-offerees, a matter we discuss later. Infra, at 39.

Chris-Craft argues, however, that Congress intended standing under § 14(e) to encompass tender offerors since the statute, unlike § 10(b), does not contain the limiting language, "in connection with the purchase or sale" of securities. Instead, in § 14(e), Congress broadly proscribed fraudulent activities "in connection with any tender offer ＊ ＊ ＊ or any solicitation ＊ ＊ ＊ in opposition to or in favor of any such offer. ＊ ＊ ＊"

The omission of the purchaser-seller requirement does not mean, however, that Chris-Craft has standing to sue for damages under § 14(e) in its capacity as a takeover bidder. It may well be that Congress desired to protect, among others, shareholder-offerees who decided not to tender their stock due to fraudulent misrepresentations by persons opposed to a takeover attempt. See generally 1 A. Bromberg, Securities Law: Fraud § 6.3 (1021), p. 122.17 (1969). See also Senate Report 2; House Report 3. These shareholders, who might not enjoy the protection of § 10(b) under Blue Chip Stamps v. Manor Drug Stores, 421 U.S. 723 (1975), could perhaps state a claim under § 14(e), even though they did not tender their securities.[25] But increased protection, if any, conferred upon the class of shareholder-offerees by the elimination of the purchaser-seller restriction can scarcely be

---

[25] These cases, of course, do not present that issue, and we express no view on it.

interpreted as giving protection to the entirely separate and unrelated class of persons whose conduct the statute is designed to regulate.

Third, Cort v. Ash tells us that we must ascertain whether it is "consistent with the underlying purposes of the legislative scheme to imply such a remedy for the plaintiff." 422 U.S., at 78. We conclude that it is not. As a disclosure mechanism aimed especially at protecting shareholders of target corporations, the Williams Act cannot consistently be interpreted as conferring a monetary remedy upon regulated parties, particularly where the award would not redound to the direct benefit of the protected class. Although it is correct to say that the $36 million damages award indirectly benefits those Piper shareholders who became Chris-Craft shareholders when they accepted Chris-Craft's exchange offer, it is equally true that the damages award injures those Piper shareholders who exchanged their shares for Bangor Punta's stock and who, as Bangor Punta shareholders, would necessarily bear a large part of the burden of any judgment against Bangor Punta. The class sought to be protected by the Williams Act are the shareholders of the *target* corporation; hence it can hardly be said that their interests as a class are served by a judgment in favor of Chris-Craft and against Bangor Punta. Moreover, the damages are awarded to the very party whose activities Congress intended to curb; Chris-Craft did not sue in the capacity of an injured Piper shareholder, but as a defeated tender offeror.

Nor can we agree that an ever-present threat of damages against a successful contestant in a battle for control will provide significant additional protection for shareholders in general. The deterrent value, if any, of such awards can never be ascertained with precision. More likely, however, is the prospect that shareholders may be prejudiced because some tender offers may never be made if there is a possibility of massive damages claims for what courts subsequently hold to be an actionable violation of § 14(e).[26] Even a contestant who "wins the battle" for control may well wind up exposed to a costly "war" in a later and successful defense of its victory. Or at worst—on Chris-Craft's damages theory—the victorious tender offeror or the target corporation might be subject to a large substantive judgment, plus high costs of litigation.

In short, we conclude that shareholder protection, if enhanced at all by damages awards such as Chris-Craft contends for, can more directly be achieved with other, less drastic means more closely tailored to the precise congressional goal underlying the Williams Act.

[26] The liability of the Piper family petitioners is instructive in this regard. Several able federal judges, including District Judges Tenney and Pollack and Chief Judge Lumbard of the Second Circuit, have expressly concluded that the Piper defendants did *not* violate the securities laws in their efforts to defeat Chris-Craft's bid. Judge Mansfield, while of the view that the Pipers had violated § 14(e), was convinced that their violations had not caused injury to Chris-Craft. The legal uncertainties that inevitably pervade this area of the law call into question whether "deterrence" of § 14(e) violations is a meaningful goal, except possibly with respect to the most flagrant sort of violations which no reasonable person could consider lawful. Such cases of flagrant misconduct, however, are not apt to occur with frequency, and to the extent that the violations are obvious and serious, injunctive relief at an earlier stage of the contest is apt to be the most efficacious form of remedy.

Fourth, under the Cort v. Ash analysis, we must decide whether "the cause of action [is] one traditionally relegated to state law * * *." 422 U.S., at 78. Despite the pervasiveness of federal securities regulation, the Court of Appeals concluded in these cases that Chris-Craft's complaint would give rise to a cause of action under common-law principles of interference with a prospective commercial advantage. Although Congress is, of course, free to create a remedial scheme in favor of contestants in tender offers, we conclude, as we did in Cort v. Ash, that "it is entirely appropriate in this instance to relegate [the offeror-bidder] and others in [that] situation to whatever remedy is created by state law," id., at 84, at least to the extent that the offeror seeks damages for having been wrongfully denied a "fair opportunity" to compete for control of another corporation.

C

What we have said thus far suggests that, unlike J.I. Case Co. v. Borak, supra, judicially creating a damages action in favor of Chris-Craft is unnecessary to ensure the fulfillment of Congress' purposes in adopting the Williams Act. Even though the SEC operates in this context under the same practical restraints recognized by the Court in *Borak,* institutional limitations alone do not lead to the conclusion that any party interested in a tender offer should have a cause of action for damages against a competing bidder. First, as Judge Friendly observed in Electronic Specialty Co. v. International Controls Corp., 409 F.2d 937, 947 (CA2 1969), in corporate control contests the stage of preliminary injunctive relief, rather than post-contest lawsuits, "is the time when relief can best be given." Furthermore, awarding damages to parties other than the protected class of shareholders has only a remote, if any, bearing upon implementing the congressional policy of protecting shareholders who must decide whether to tender or retain their stock.[28] Indeed, as we suggested earlier, a damages award of this nature may well be inconsistent with the interests of many members of the protected class and of only indirect value to shareholders who accepted the exchange offer of the defeated takeover contestant.

We therefore conclude that Chris-Craft, as a defeated tender offeror, has no implied case of action for damages under § 14(e).

* * *

Accordingly, the judgment of the Court of Appeals is Reversed.[*]

◆

Piper resolved one important issue concerning the remedies available under Sections 14(d) and 14(e) and the parties who are authorized to

---

[28] Our holding is a limited one. Whether shareholder-offerees, the class protected by § 14(e), have an implied cause of action under § 14(e) is not before us, and we intimate no view on the matter. Nor is the target corporation's standing to sue an issue in this case. We hold only that a tender offeror, suing in its capacity as a takeover bidder, does not have standing to sue for damages under § 14(e).

* * *

[*] Mr. Justice Blackmun concurred in the result. Mr. Justice Stevens, joined by Mr. Justice Brennan, dissented. [Ed.]

pursue them: Offerors do not have standing to pursue a damage remedy. The Court explicitly reserved the questions of whether target shareholders have an implied right of action, and the standing of the target company. 430 U.S. at 42 n. 28, 47 n. 33. In the context of transactional planning, however, the most critical question may be who has standing to seek *injunctive relief* during the period in which the fate of the offer is being determined in the market place. For this purpose, *Piper* has not deterred the courts from taking an expansive view of the standing requirements. In contrast to an action for damages, the courts have consistently held that both the offeror and the target company have standing to seek injunctive relief for violations of Section 14(e).[24]

This resolution—giving standing to both "contestants" in a hostile tender offer battle—is clearly correct even in light of the Supreme Court's insistence in *Piper* that the class protected by Section 14(e) was limited to target shareholders. While the contest is going on, target shareholders simply are in no position to assert their rights under the Williams Act. As the court stated in Mobil Corp. v. Marathon Oil with respect to the offerer:

> In a tender offer battle, events occur with explosive speed and require immediate response by a party seeking to enjoin illegal conduct. Issues such as incomplete disclosure and manipulative practices can only be effectively spotted and argued by parties with complete knowledge of the target, its business, and others in the industry. The tender offerer has frequently made intensive investigations before deciding to commence its offer and may often be the only party with enough knowledge and awareness to identify nondisclosure or manipulative practices in time to obtain a preliminary injunction.[25]

The situation is no different with respect to the target company's standing; no one else is in as good a position to monitor the offeror's compliance with Section 14(e). In this view, both the offeror and the target have standing, in effect, as surrogates for the target shareholders, rather than to protect their own interests.

What does this analysis suggest about the nature of the appropriate remedies for violations? The interests of neither surrogate completely correspond to those of the target shareholders; the offeror will be committed to the success of the transaction regardless of the benefits to the target shareholders, while target management may be committed to defeating the offer to protect their own positions regardless of the attractiveness of the offer to target shareholders. Thus, although it is helpful to rely upon surrogates to raise the issues, any remedy for violations discovered and pursued by a surrogate should be fashioned

[24] See, e.g., Mobil Corp. v. Marathon Oil Co., 669 F.2d 366 (6th Cir.1981), cert. denied 455 U.S. 982 (1982) (offerer); Whittaker Corp. v. Edgar, 535 F.Supp. 933 (N.D. Ill.1982) (offerer); Gearhart Industries v. Smith International, Inc., 741 F.2d 707 (5th Cir.1984) (target); Wellman v. Dickinson, 475 F.Supp. 783 (S.D.N.Y.1979), affirmed 682 F.2d 355 (2d Cir.1982), cert. denied sub nom. Dickinson v. SEC, 460 U.S. 1069 (1983) (target).

[25] 669 F.2d at 370–73.

with an eye only to giving the target shareholders the opportunity to make an intelligent decision concerning the offer and without concern for the interests of the particular surrogate. This approach would counsel in favor of heavy use of preliminary relief requiring amendment of previous disclosure, but little in the way of permanent relief—such as requiring an offeror either to divest stock acquired, or not to vote it, or to delay the offer for some "cooling off" period—that seriously would interfere with the offeror's ability, in the end, to put its offer before the shareholders.[26]

(c) The Triggers to Disclosure

The triggers of the filing and disclosure requirements under Section 14(d)(1) and regulation 14D substantially overlap those encountered in connection with Section 13D. Thus, the terms *person, equity security,* and *beneficial owner,* and the manner of calculating whether the tender offer would result in more than 5 percent ownership, are treated for purposes of Section 14(d) in the same way they are treated for purposes of Section 13(d). One triggering concept, however, is unique to Section 14(d): [27] The concept of when a tender offer commences. As well, the consequences of the trigger under Section 14(d) are also unique. Not only does the commencement of a tender offer trigger disclosure obligations, as does any acquisition that results in a person's holdings crossing the 5 percent threshold under Section 13(d), but it also serves as a critical benchmark for Sections 14(d) and 14(e)'s regulation of the substantive terms of tender offers: The various time periods governing the minimum length of the offer, and the withdrawal and proration periods, are measured from the commencement of the offer.

Prior to the effectiveness of present Rule 14d–2 in 1980, neither the statute nor the regulations defined the term "commencement of a tender offer." The principal drawback to this state of affairs was uncertainty; there was no bright line rule which allowed a planner to conform a transaction to the requirements of the statute. This problem is now addressed in Rule 14d–2(a). A tender offer commences on the day that the tender offer is first published or sent to shareholders in

---

[26] Judge Friendly's opinion in Electronic Specialty Co. v. International Controls Corp., 409 F.2d 937, 948 (2d Cir.1969), nicely captures this approach:

The likeness of tender offers to proxy contests is not limited to the feature of standing. They are alike in the fundamental feature that they generally are contests. This means that the participants on both sides act, not "in the peace of a quiet chamber," but under the stresses of the market place. They act quickly, sometimes impulsively, often in angry response to what they consider, whether rightly or wrongly, to be low blows by the other side. Probably there

will no more be a perfect tender offer than a perfect trial. Congress intended to assure basic honesty and fair dealing, not to impose an unrealistic requirement of laboratory conditions that might make the statute a potent tool for incumbent management to protect its own interests against the desires and welfare of the stockholders. These are the considerations to be applied in testing conduct—of both sides * * *.

[27] We continue to defer discussion of the definition of a tender offer, the most significant and difficult triggering concept, until Section A.1.c. of this Chapter, infra.

one of the specified ways. Thus, a planner now can achieve certainty simply by selecting one of the designated ways to announce its offer.

The adoption of a bright-line rule, however, does more than simply provide a guide for compliance; it also provides a blueprint for avoidance. In proposing a definition of the commencement of a tender offer, the SEC expressed concern over premature announcement of a tender offer:

> It has become a common practice for a bidder to publicly announce the material terms of a cash tender offer in advance of the offer's formal commencement. Such announcements trigger market mechanisms, such as arbitrageur activity, which are normally attendant to the tender offer itself. This practice has become a matter of increasing concern because it causes investors to make investment decisions with respect to a tender offer on the basis of incomplete information.[28]

Rule 14d–2(b) was adopted to deal with this problem. Under its terms, any public statement by an offeror which discloses the offerer's identity, the identity of the target company, the class of equity security the object of the offer, and the price or range of prices to be offered, constitutes the commencement of an offer. As a result the disclosure obligation is triggered and all time periods begin running.

There are two exceptions to this automatic commencement rule. First, an offer will be deemed never to have commenced if, within five business days after the public announcement triggering automatic commencement, the offeror announces that it will not proceed with the offer. Second, if within the same five day period the offeror files a Schedule 14D as required by Rule 14d–3 and contemporaneously with the filing disseminates to shareholders the information required by Rule 14d–6, the tender offer will be deemed to have commenced on the filing date, rather than on the date of automatic commencement.

Although the automatic commencement trigger was designed to prevent offerers from delaying compliance with the filing and disclosure requirements of the Williams Act, the nature of the solution has the potential to take from an offeror some of its control over when to commence its offer. Suppose, for example, that an enterprising analyst discovers that a company intends to make an offer and discloses that fact to the public along with the identity of the target company, the number of shares sought, and the price to be paid. Will the analyst's announcement—which contains all of the information specified in Rule 14d–2(c)—trigger the commencement of the offer? The SEC has taken the position, consistent with the language of the Rule, that the triggering announcement must be made by the offeror.[29] However, it remains the case that third parties can force the offeror's hand, the SEC having noted that, "[a]s a practical matter * * * if a bidder's intention

---

[28] Exchange Act Release No. 15548 (Feb. 5, 1978), reprinted in [1979 Transfer Binder] Fed. Sec. L. Rep. (CCH) ¶ 81,935 at 81,228.

[29] Exchange Act Rel. No. 16623, Interpretative Release Relating to Tender Offer Rules (March 5, 1980), 3 Fed.Sec.L.Rep. (CCH) ¶ 24,281. The same result would hold if the announcement were made by the target company in an effort to upset the offeror's plans. Id.

becomes generally known, the bidder may be unable to deny its intentions, and any affirmation of the information referred to in Rule 14d–2(c) by or on behalf of the bidder would cause the tender offer to start under Rule 14d–2(b)." [30]

A second problem with the operation of Rule 14d–2(b)'s automatic commencement trigger results from its interaction with other regulatory regimes. Suppose that the Federal Communications Commission must approve the transfer of control of any company that has a broadcast license. If the application for approval requires disclosure of the information that would automatically trigger the commencement of an offer, the offeror confronts a Catch 22: It would be required to commence an offer under one body of regulation that would be illegal under another. Could this problem be avoided by making the offer, but conditioning it on FCC approval? [31] The same kind of conflict can arise with other securities law disclosure requirements. What if an offeror discloses in Item 4 of its Schedule 13D that it intends to make an any or all offer at a designated price? Does accurate disclosure under Section 13(d) eliminate the offeror's discretion over when to commence an offer under Section 14(d)? See Ludlow Corp. v. Tyco Laboratories, Inc., 529 F.Supp. 62 (D.Mass.1981). Similarly, what if one party to a proxy contest discloses that if it is successful it will cause a tender offer to be made at a designated price? See Pabst Brewing Co. v. Jacobs, 549 F.Supp. 1068 (D.Del.1982).

How well does the SEC's concern with premature disclosure hold up to analysis? If an offeror is competently advised, it can avoid the automatic commencement trigger simply by delaying release of any information concerning the likelihood of its making an offer, thereby recapturing control over the timing of its offer. Why would this make target shareholders better off? Information concerning the offeror's intentions is clearly material, yet the SEC seems to take the position that the shareholders are better off without it. The trade-off seems to be between the interests of two potential groups of target shareholders: (i) those target shareholders who for other reasons have determined to sell their shares at the time disclosure would have been made in the absence of an automatic disclosure rule and who, with an automatic commencement rule, end up selling their shares in the market at a lower price because the rule results in the offeror delaying release of information concerning the prospective offer, and (ii) those target shareholders who, in the absence of an automatic commencement rule, would make one investment decision after public announcement of partial information, but would make a better decision had they been fully informed. In evaluating this trade-off, keep in mind that the automatic commencement rule does not really protect target shareholders from having to make an investment decision with only partial information concerning the prospective offer. Market rumors, or announcements of the imminence of the offer by third parties or the target company itself, cause precisely the same market activity and the same likelihood of shareholders making investment decisions "on the

---

[30] Id.   [31] See id.

basis of incomplete information" that motivated the SEC's adoption of the automatic commencement rule, yet do not operate as an automatic trigger.   Disclosure by the offeror, in response to third party statements, only makes *more* complete the information available to shareholders, but the effect of the automatic commencement rule denies shareholders access to information from the one party who actually knows the truth.

(d) The Content of Required Disclosure

The disclosure philosophy reflected in Sections 14(d) and (e), and the unique aspects of the disclosure issues raised under these sections, differ in two critical respects from the more familiar disclosure pattern associated with the Securities Act of 1933 and with Rule 10b–5.   First, mandatory disclosure is imposed not on the seller of securities, as under the Securities Act, nor with respect to nonpublic information originating with the issuer of the securities, as is commonly the case under Rule 10b–5.   Rather, the Williams Act requires the *offeror* to disclose, and the particular information Schedule 14D requires largely concerns not the current status of the target's business, the issuer of the securities in question, but the intentions of the offeror.   Second, disclosure is required in the context of an ongoing transaction to which the target company is a party.   As a result, the question of when disclosure must be made takes on unusual significance.   Required early disclosure will benefit those shareholders who would have traded at that time in any event;   however, the disclosure itself, coming during the course of complex negotiations, may have the effect of reducing the likelihood that the negotiations will succeed.   The common thread joining the two special characteristics of Williams Act disclosure is the tendency of courts to cloak their analysis under the guise of a traditional "materiality" inquiry.

Offeror Disclosure.   Suppose that an offeror, Alpha Corp., has extensively analyzed the business of a potential target company, the industry in which the target operates, and the potential for synergistic gains from combining the two companies.   Further suppose that this analysis persuades Alpha that if the target company could be acquired for no more than $20 per share above the then current market price, the acquisition would have a positive net present value.   The question posed by the Williams Act is why Alpha should be required to disclose this information to target shareholders.

The short answer to this question is that disclosure "protects" the target shareholder; as the Supreme Court put it in Piper v. Chris-Craft Industries, Inc., 430 U.S. 1, 35 (1977): "The purpose of the Williams Act is to insure that public shareholders who are confronted by a cash tender offer for their stock will not be required to respond without adequate information.   *   *   *"[32]   This formulation, however, begs the real questions.   From what must target shareholders be protected?

[32] Quoting Rondeau v. Mosinee Paper Corp., 422 U.S. 49, 58 (1975).

What information must be disclosed to provide the appropriate protection?

Continuing the hypothetical, suppose that Alpha makes a tender offer for any or all of the target company's stock at $10 per share above the market price immediately before the offer, and also announces that any shares not tendered would be acquired in a freezeout merger at the same price paid in the tender offer. What information is relevant to a target shareholder in deciding whether to tender? In particular, why would disclosure of Alpha's analysis of the target company's value, or of Alpha's plans to achieve synergistic gains following the acquisition, protect the target shareholders? From one perspective, information of this sort is of no value to target shareholders. Target shareholders need to compare the value of the two alternatives open to them: Either to accept the tender price or to continue to hold the target stock. Information about Alpha's plans for the transaction, or about Alpha's estimates of the value of the target after the transaction, is irrelevant because the announced freezeout cuts off a potential third alternative: Remaining shareholders in the target after Alpha's offer has been successful.

Target shareholders, however, might not be quite so willing to concede the irrelevance of this information. For them, disclosure of the information, although irrelevant to deciding between the two alternatives posed by the offer, does open up additional alternatives. The target company may use the information disclosed by Alpha to attract a competing bid at a higher price or use it by simply implementing some of the plans and ideas generated by Alpha's analysis. In either event, the result may be to increase the value of the target company either by altering (because of competitive bidding) the division of the synergistic gain in favor of the target, or by the target's independent adoption of some of Alpha's value enhancing ideas. From this perspective, however, it is somewhat difficult to describe offeror disclosure as serving to "protect" target shareholders. Rather, mandatory disclosure serves to benefit target shareholders by transferring to them a portion of the value of the offeror's investment in information.

When mandatory disclosure is analyzed in this way, judicial resolution of some difficult disclosure issues may seem more intelligible. Consider whether an offeror must disclose information—such as appraisals of the value of the target's assets or estimates of liquidation value—that it commissioned or otherwise acquired in making its decision to proceed with the offer. The manner in which the courts have approached this issue is described in the following case.

FLYNN v. BASS BROTHERS ENTERPRISES, INC.,
United States Court of Appeals, Third Circuit, 1984.
744 F.2d 978.

Before: SEITZ, ADAMS and HAYNSWORTH, Circuit Judges:

ADAMS, Circuit Judge: This appeal concerns the adequacy under federal securities law of disclosure in a tender offer by defendant Bass Brothers Enterprises, Inc. (Bass Brothers) for the outstanding shares of defendant National Alfalfa Dehydrating and Milling Company (National Alfalfa).

* * *

I.

The essential facts of the case are undisputed. Bass Brothers is a closely held Texas corporation. At the time of the tender offer its principal business was oil exploration with subsidiary interests in hydrocarbon production, radio, television, ranching and cattle-raising. In 1974 Bass Brothers was approached by the president of Prochemco, Inc. (Prochemco), a Texas corporation engaged in ranching and cattle-feeding, as a possible source of financing for a purchase by Prochemco of a large block of National Alfalfa's stock. National Alfalfa, a Delaware corporation whose stock was traded on the American Stock Exchange, was engaged in farming, farm supply operations and the sale of animal feed. Its former president, Charles Peterson, was seeking to sell his controlling interest in the company in order to raise sufficient capital to repay a large personal debt. To present its proposal to Bass Brothers and other potential sources of funding, Prochemco prepared two reports on National Alfalfa's history and operations, including an appraisal of its assets based in alternative hypothetical valuations.

Although Bass Brothers declined to finance such a purchase by Prochemco, it indicated that it might consider proceeding as a principal should Prochemco fail to obtain the necessary funding. In late 1975 Prochemco informed Bass Brothers that it had been unable to obtain financing and that Peterson's block of National Alfalfa stock was still available. In return for providing the detailed information about National Alfalfa contained in the Prochemco reports and for assistance in analyzing National Alfalfa's current and potential performance, Bass Brothers agreed to pay Prochemco a $130,000 finders fee.

In December 1975 Bass Brothers entered into an option agreement for the purchase of Peterson's 52% share of National Alfalfa's outstanding common stock. Thereafter, Bass Brothers exercised its option and bought the approximately 1.3 million shares from Peterson for a price of $8.44 million or $6.47 per share. A short time later, in a private sale, Bass Brothers was able to acquire an additional 226,673 shares of National Alfalfa, representing 9.1% of the outstanding shares, at $6.45 per share. This acquisition increased Bass Brothers' holding to 61.2% of the outstanding shares of National Alfalfa.

On March 2, 1976, Bass Brothers made public its tender offer for "any and all" outstanding shares of National Alfalfa at $6.45 per share. The reports prepared by Prochemco for Bass Brothers were not appended to the tender offer, nor did the tender offer refer to Prochemco's appraisal of the overall values per share of National Alfalfa which stated that:

> $6.40 could be realized through "liquidation [of National Alfalfa] under stress conditions";
>
> $12.40 could be realized through "liquidation in an orderly fashion over a reasonable period of time";

$16.40 represented National Alfalfa's value "as [an] ongoing venture."

Further, the tender offer did not refer to a second report prepared by Prochemco which gave two additional valuations: $17.28 representing the "Value per Peterson"; $7.60 representing the "Value per Prochemco." To the contrary, the tender offer stated in bold letters that "Offeror did not receive any material non-public information [National Alfalfa] with respect to its prior acquisitions of shares nor * * * does it believe it presently possesses any such information. Offeror has not been able to verify independently the accuracy or completeness of the information contained in Appendices A through E [furnished by National Alfalfa] and assumes no responsibility therefor."

On March 15, 1976, Bass Brothers did, however, issue a supplement to the tender offer describing the book value of "certain land owned or leased by" National Alfalfa and advising the shareholders that:

> While the Offeror has made no independent appraisal of the value of the Company's land and makes no representation with respect thereto, in view of the foregoing factors the aggregate current fair market value of the Company's agricultural land may be substantially higher than its original cost as reflected on the books of the Company. Depending upon the respective market values for such land, stockholders could receive, upon liquidation of the Company, an amount per share significantly higher than the current book value and possibly higher than the price of $6.45 per Share offered by Offeror in the Offer. The amount received by stockholders upon liquidation of the Company would also be dependent upon, among other things, the market value of the Company's other assets and the length of time allowed for such liquidation. The Offeror has no reason to believe that the Company's management has any present intention of liquidating the Company. As noted on page 8 of the Offer to Purchase under "Purpose of This Offer: Present Relationship of Company and Offeror". Offeror does not currently intend to liquidate the Company.

The supplement also extended the duration of the offer by one week "to afford stockholders an opportunity to evaluate" the new information. While the offer was in effect, the named plaintiffs tendered their shares to Bass Brothers for $6.45 per share. At the expiration of the extended offer, Bass Brothers owned more than 92% of the outstanding shares of National Alfalfa and took control of the company by removing the board of directors and electing a new board of directors. Shortly thereafter, a Delaware "short-form merger" was effected between National Alfalfa and Bass Brothers Farming Company, a wholly owned subsidiary of Bass Brothers. Emerging as the surviving entity, National Alfalfa became a wholly owned subsidiary of Bass Brothers.

On June 21, 1976, a group of former shareholders of National Alfalfa filed this class action for damages in the district court charging that the information disclosed in the tender offer was insufficient under federal and state securities law. Cross motions for summary judgment were denied. Flynn v. Bass Brothers Enterprises, Inc., 456 F.Supp. 484 (E.D.Pa.1978). * * * On September 15, 1983, at the close of plaintiffs' case, defendants moved for a directed verdict. The district judge concluded that "the information that was provided by the tender offeror was not materially misleading in any way" particularly because "the information that was contained in the Prochemco report is the kind that is not permitted to be disclosed to shareholders because it is not based on sufficient information * * * [T]he people who prepared it were interested in whatever transaction they were preparing it for at that time." * * * The district judge, determining that plaintiffs had not presented sufficient evidence of fraud under federal or state law to warrant sending the case to the jury, granted defendants' motion for a directed verdict.

* * *

III.

Plaintiffs allege that Bass Brothers and the management of National Alfalfa violated sections 10(b) and 14(e) of the 1934 Act and rule 10b–5 of the Securities and Exchange Commission (SEC) by not disclosing certain information with the tender offer. Specifically, plaintiffs maintain that defendants had a duty to disclose certain asset appraisal values because such information would have aided National Alfalfa's shareholders in deciding whether or not to accept Bass Brothers' tender offer. We must determine whether the district judge committed reversible error when he ruled that defendants had no duty to disclose the asset appraisal values they possessed.

In 1968, Congress enacted the Williams Act as an amendment to the Securities and Exchange Act of 1934. The purpose of the Williams Act was to protect investors confronted by a tender offer for their stock. See Piper v. Chris-Craft Industries, 430 U.S. 1, 22–27 (1977). Presenting the bill to the Senate, Senator Williams, its sponsor, stated:

> [t]his legislation will close a significant gap in investor protection under the Federal securities laws by requiring the disclosure of pertinent information to stockholders when persons seek to obtain control of a corporation by a cash tender offer or through open market or privately negotiated purchases of securities.

113 Cong.Rec. 854 (1967); see also id. at 24664.[2] Congress sought to ensure that public shareholders who are suddenly faced with a tender offer will not be forced to respond without adequate information regarding the qualifications and intentions of the offering party. See Rondeau v. Mosinee Paper Corp., 422 U.S. 49, 58 (1975). To that end, section 14(e) of the Williams Act prohibits the making of untrue statements of material fact or the omission of material facts in tender offers that could mislead the shareholders of a target company. Simi-

---

[2] Similarly, Manuel Cohen, the Chairman of the SEC when the Williams Act was enacted, testified to the Senate Subcommittee on Securities that "the general approach * * * of [the Williams Act] is to provide the investor, the person who is required to make a decision, an opportunity to examine and to assess the relevant facts * * *." Hearings on S. 510 before the Subcommittee on Securities of the Senate Committee on Banking and Currency, 90th Cong., 1st Sess., 15 (1967).

lar in thrust to rule 10b–5, this broadly worded anti-fraud provision protects target shareholders by subjecting tender offerors to advance disclosure requirements. See *Piper*, 430 U.S. at 22–27.

Where a "duty to speak" exists, therefore, federal securities law requires the disclosure of any "material fact" in connection with the purchase or sale of a security under rule 10b–5 or the tendering of an offer under section 14(e). Bass Brothers does not deny that at the time of the tender offer it was under a duty to make certain disclosures in its capacity as a majority shareholder of National Alfalfa as well as in its capacity as a tender offeror. Similarly, the management of National Alfalfa does not deny that it owed a duty of disclosure to its shareholders. Our task, then, is to determine whether the alleged nondisclosures were material omissions, and thus breached the duty to disclose.

This Court has previously noted that section 14(e) of the Williams Act makes unlawful the failure to disclose any "material fact" in connection with a tender offer. Rule 10b–5 similarly prohibits such omissions with regard to the purchase or sale of a security. The Supreme Court defined materiality in the context of an alleged violation of rule 14a–9, which governs disclosure requirements for proxy statements, in the following manner:

> An omitted fact is material if there is a substantial likelihood that a reasonable shareholder would consider it important in deciding how to vote. This standard is fully consistent with [Mills v. Electric Auto-Lite Co., 396 U.S. 375 (1970)] general description of materiality as a requirement that "the defect have a significant *propensity* to affect the voting process." It does not require proof of a substantial likelihood that disclosure of the omitted fact would have caused the reasonable investor to change his vote. What the standard does contemplate is a showing of a substantial likelihood that, under all the circumstances, the omitted fact would have assumed actual significance in the deliberations of the reasonable shareholder. Put another way, there must be a substantial likelihood that the disclosure of the omitted fact would have been viewed by the reasonable investor as having significantly altered the "total mix" of information made available.

TSC Industries, Inc. v. Northway, Inc., 426 U.S. 438, 449 (1976). This definition of "material" has been adopted for cases involving rule 10b–5 and we see no reason not to utilize the same formulation for evaluating materiality in the context of a tender offer.

As a matter of public policy, the SEC and the courts generally have not required the inclusion of appraised asset valuations, projects, and other "soft" information in proxy materials or tender offers. See e.g., South Coast Services Corp. v. Santa Ana Valley Irrigation Co., 669 F.2d 1265, 1271 (9th Cir.1982); Panter v. Marshall Field & Co., 646 F.2d 271 (7th Cir.), cert. denied, 454 U.S. 1092 (1982); Gerstle v. Gamble-Skogmo, Inc., 478 F.2d 1281, 1292–94 (2d Cir.1973); Kohn v. American Metal Climax, Inc., 458 F.2d 255, 265 (3d Cir.), cert. denied, 409 U.S. 874 (1972); Resource Exploration v. Yankee Oil and Gas, 566 F.Supp. 54 (N.D.Ohio 1983); Alaska Interstate Co. v. McMillian, 402 F.Supp. 532

(D.Del.1975); Denison Mines Ltd. v. Fibreboard Corp., 388 F.Supp. 812 (D.Del.1974). The reasons underpinning the SEC's longstanding policy against disclosure of soft information stem from its concern about the reliability of appraisals, its fear that investors might give greater credence to the appraisals or projections than would be warranted, and the impracticability of the SEC's examining such appraisals on a case by case basis to determine whether they are sufficiently reliable to merit disclosure. See *Gerstle*, 478 F.2d at 1294; see also 17 C.F.R. § 240.14a–9 (note following rule 14a–9) (1976).

Although the disclosure of soft information has not been prohibited as a matter of law, this Court in the past has followed the "general rule" that "presentations of future earnings, appraised asset valuations and other hypothetical data" are to be discouraged. *Kohn*, 458 F.2d at 265. In failing to require disclosure, courts have relied on a perceived SEC policy favoring nondisclosure of soft information, the lack of reliability of such information, and the reluctance to impose potentially huge liability for nondisclosure, even if desirable as a matter of public policy, because the law discouraged nondisclosure at the time of the alleged violation.

In assessing the need to disclose an appraised asset valuation courts have considered several indicia of reliability: the qualifications of those who prepared or compiled the appraisal; the degree of certainty of the data on which it was based; the purpose for which it was prepared; and evidence of reliance on the appraisal.

South Coast, for example, involved a shareholders' challenge to the adequacy of disclosure in a proxy statement. The board of directors of SAVI received several offers to sell all of the company's assets for cash. During negotiations, the SAVI board hired an expert appraiser to value two of SAVI's properties; the board prepared internal valuations for the remainder of the company's property. *South Coast,* 669 F.2d at 1267–69. In its proxy statement issued with the intent to elicit shareholder approval of a sale of SAVI's assets, the board revealed the expert's valuations with an appropriate disclaimer. The internal valuations for the remaining properties were not revealed, however, A divided panel of the Ninth Circuit held that the trial judge did not commit reversible error in determining that SAVI had no duty to disclose its internal appraisals. The court reasoned that none of the directors were expert appraisers and that no satisfactory basis upon which the estimates were made had been established. Id. at 1272.

At the time Bass Brothers was making its tender offer, although courts did not generally require the disclosure of asset valuations, such disclosure was not prohibited. In *Alaska Interstate,* the acquiring company, over the objection of the target management, included, with proper cautionary remarks, a range of hypothetic liquidation values made by the target management. The court approved the release of the valuations in spite of the "general rule" discouraging such disclosure which this Court announced in *Kohn, Alaska Interstate,* 402 F.Supp. at 572.

Recently, there have been indications that the law, in response to developing corporate trends, such as the increase in mergers, has begun to favor more disclosure of soft information. In this regard, we note that SEC policy—a primary reason courts in the past have not required the disclosure of soft information—has began to change. With respect to disclosure of projections of future earnings, the SEC in 1976 deleted future earnings from the list of examples of potentially misleading disclosures in the note which follows rule 14a–9.[15]

More importantly, in 1978 the SEC issued a safe harbor rule for "forward-looking" statements, such as future earnings, made in good faith, 17 C.F.R. § 230.175 (1983). And with respect to asset valuations, the SEC in 1980 authorized disclosure of good faith appraisals made on a reasonable basis in proxy contests in which a principal issue is the liquidation of all or a portion of a target company's assets. See SEC Release No. 34–16833, Fed.Sec.L.Rep. (CCH) ¶ 24,117 (May 23, 1980), codified at 17 C.F.R. § 241.16833 (1983). While SEC policy has not yet explicitly approved the disclosure of appraisal values when the target is to continue as a going concern rather than being liquidated, recent SEC promulgations herald a new view, more favorably disposed towards disclosure.

Part of the reason for this shift in policy is recognition of shareholders' need for such information. One rationale for the initial prohibition of soft information was the fear that potential *purchasers* of securities would be misled by overly optimistic claims by management. See *Gerstle,* 428 F.2d at 1294. An unintended by-product of such concern, however, was to keep valuable information from those shareholders who had to decide, within the context of a tender offer or merger, whether or not to *sell* their securities. See Kripke, *Rule 10b–5 Liability and "Material Facts,"* 46 N.Y.U.L. Rev. 1061, 1071 (1971). The present spate of proxy contests and tender offers was not anticipated when the SEC initially formulated its policy of nondisclosure of soft information.

At least one court has recognized that disclosure of asset valuations may be required. In *Radol,* plaintiffs challenged, among other things, the adequacy of disclosure in United States Steel's successful tender offer for Marathon Oil Company's stock in 1981. Rejecting the notion that "asset valuations are, as a matter of law, not material," the court held that such a determination was a matter for the jury to resolve in light of all the circumstances. *Radol,* 556 F.Supp. at 594; see also Weinberger v. UOP, Inc., 457 A.2d 701 (Del.1983).

The time lag between when a challenged tender offer or proxy statement is issued and when a trial or appellate court finally renders a decision on its sufficiency often can be considerable. This time lag has caused an unexpected side effect; it has retarded the evaluation of the law concerning disclosure. For example, the Second Circuit decided *Gerstle* in 1973, yet the challenged proxy statement has been issued in 1963.

---

[15] See Securities Act Release No. 5699. Notice of Adoption of an Amendment to Rule 14a–9, etc., [1975–1976 Transfer Binder] CCH Fed.Sec.L.Rep. ¶ 80,461 (1976).

In *Gerstle,* the SEC filed an amicus brief which set forth the view that notwithstanding the Commission's longstanding position that "in financial statements filed with the Commission, fixed assets should be carried at historical cost (less any depreciation)" and that "appraisals generally cannot be disclosed because they may be misleading," existing appraisals of current liquidating value must be disclosed if they have been made by a qualified expert and have a sufficient basis in fact. *Gerstle,* 478 F.2d at 1291, 1292. The Second Circuit stated, however, that in 1963 it had "long been an article of faith among lawyers specializing in the securities field that appraisals of assets could not be included in a proxy statement." Id. at 1293. The court also added that "[h]owever desirable such a policy may be, we do not believe this is what it was in 1963." Id. Holding that defendant Skogmo was not liable for its failure to disclose appraisals of the current market value of the merged company's plants which remained unsold at the time of the merger, the court candidly admitted that it "would be loath to impose a huge liability on Skogmo" because the law had evolved in the interim. Id. at 1294.

The Second Circuit's holding in 1973, admittedly influenced by the ten year time lapse between the proxy statement and the culmination of the litigation, became one basis for the Ninth Circuit's decision in *South Coast* in 1982. Once again, a court deciding a case a substantial time after the challenged acts felt compelled not to give full weight to changes in SEC policy and scholarly debate on disclosure. See *South Coast,* 669 F.2d at 1271–73.

In order to give full effect to the evolution in the law of disclosure, and to avoid in the future, at least in the Third Circuit, the problem caused by the time lag between challenged acts and judicial resolution, today we set forth the law for disclosure of soft information as it is to be applied from this date on. Henceforth, the law is not that asset appraisals are, as a matter of law, immaterial. Rather, in appropriate cases, such information must be disclosed. Courts should ascertain the duty to disclose asset valuations and other soft information on a case by case basis, by weighing the potential aid such information will give a shareholder against the potential harm, such as undue reliance, if the information is released with a proper cautionary note.

The factors a court must consider in making such a determination are: the facts upon which the information is based; the qualifications of those who prepared or compiled it; the purpose for which the information was originally intended; its relevance to the stockholders' impending decision; the degree of subjectivity or bias reflected in its preparation; the degree to which the information is unique; and the availability to the investor of other more reliable sources of information.

IV.

It is against the background set forth in Part III, supra, that we must determine whether the trial judge erred in ruling that Bass Brothers and the management of National Alfalfa had no duty to disclose the asset valuations at issue in this case. We note that despite our formulation of the current law applicable to corporate disclosure, we are constrained by the significant development in disclosure law since 1976 not to apply the announced standard retroactively,[19] but to evaluate defendants' conduct by the standards which prevailed in 1976.

Plaintiffs point to three sources of information that they believe should have been disclosed in the tender offer; the Prochemco reports; a report allegedly commissioned by Bass Brothers to corroborate the appraisals in the Prochemco reports; and an internal valuation prepared by National Alfalfa's accountant and vice-president, Carl Schweitzer.

A.

The shareholders contend that the Prochemco reports were material and should have been disclosed. However, employing the approach commonly followed by courts when Bass Brothers made its tender offer in early 1976, we do not find the Prochemco reports had sufficient indicia of reliability to require disclosure. Plaintiffs did not adequately establish that the reports were prepared by experts. Although Prochemco did have experience in acquisitions, there was scant evidence of the company's expertise in appraising the type of land involved in the present case. Moreover, plaintiffs did not establish that the reports had sufficient basis in fact to be reliable. Evidence introduced at trial demonstrated only that the first Prochemco report was based on a report prepared by one of the company's employees, but no basis for the reliability of this foundation report was established. The first Prochemco report itself merely stated that it "is our opinion, based on an evaluation by our staff as well as local interviews with those knowledgeable in farm real estate and with the Soil Conservation Service." No basis was established for the second report.

The purpose for which the Prochemco reports were prepared—to attract financing for its proposed purchase of Peterson's controlling block of National Alfalfa shares—also diminishes the reliability of the reports. Further, at the time of the tender offer the valuations in the Prochemco reports were outdated.

Plaintiffs assert that the reliability of the reports was amply demonstrated by Bass Brothers' reliance on them and by the payment of $130,000 to Prochemco for them. The shareholders reason that "if the Prochemco reports were reliable and accurate enough for Bass Brothers to use * * * in deciding to [purchase Peterson's stock] then the existence of and valuations in the Prochemco reports were material and should have been shared with National Alfalfa's shareholders" through the tender offer. To bolster their argument, the shareholders note that after buying Peterson's stock, Bass Brothers chose not to examine any of National Alfalfa's internal asset valuations before making the tender offer.

[19] Our reluctance to apply the new standard for disclosure retroactively is confined to the facts of this case. We do not intend to imply that in other cases based on actions occurring before the date of this opinion, the new standard necessarily is inapplicable.

Although it is not inconceivable that Bass Brothers may have relied on the Prochemco valuations, plaintiffs did not advance sufficient evidence to establish the point. Moreover, even if there had been some reliance on the reports, that alone would be insufficient to mandate disclosure in this case. The reports were not prepared by experts, had no adequately demonstrated basis in fact and were prepared to encourage financing to purchase Peterson's share. In light of the record before us, we cannot say that the district court erred in concluding that at the time of the tender offer Bass Brothers had no duty to disclose the Prochemco reports.

B.

Plaintiffs assert that Bass Brothers also should have disclosed its own internal valuations. To substantiate their belief that Bass Brothers commissioned a report to corroborate the information in the Prochemco report, the shareholders point to an informal typewritten list of "Items for Investigation" drawn up by Rusty Rose, a Bass Brothers consultant. The list sets forth a number of assignments to be performed by Rose. Item 2(a) states: "Have expert appraise farm land and equipment." A handwritten notation after this item states "Done—values confirmed." At trial it was revealed that Richard Rainwater, a Bass Brothers officer, had written the notation, although no evidence was produced concerning the circumstances under which the notation was made. The shareholders contend that this cryptic notation, without more, "confirms that Bass Brothers had obtained an 'expert' appraisal." Plaintiffs had ample opportunity during discovery to pursue this lead yet failed to turn up any additional evidence of a corroborating study. Presentation of this handwritten notation, alone, to the jury simply could not support a finding of fraudulent and material nondisclosure of information.

C.

The third piece of information that the shareholders claim should have been disclosed was a study prepared by Carl Schweitzer, a vice president of National Alfalfa, using various assumptions, such as the projected appreciation of National Alfalfa's land holdings, to arrive at a value per share of $12.95. At trial, Schweitzer's unrefuted testimony indicated that such a figure was, in fact, hypothetical because of the nature of the assumptions used in the calculation. Schweitzer stated that he used land values supplied by Peterson and some "unnamed people within or without of the company." Thus, plaintiffs have not established a sufficient factual basis for the valuations. Moreover, the purpose of some of these calculations was to help Peterson find a buyer for his stock. Schweitzer testified that the land values were inflated, or optimistic, so as to present the company in the best possible light to future investors. Moreover, Schweitzer admitted that neither he nor members of National Alfalfa's accounting staff had expertise with regard to land appraisal. Thus, plaintiffs were unable to produce evidence that the Schweitzer reports were sufficiently reliable to be material for shareholders confronted with the tender offer.

*   *   *

———————◆———————

Concluding that appraisals need not be disclosed because they are not "material" hardly seems convincing. What facts would be more likely to "have assumed actual significance in the deliberations of the reasonable investor" than the offeror's private information concerning the target's value? Nor does concern over the unreliability of appraisals provide a more persuasive rationale. Even if unsophisticated investors would systematically "give greater significance to the appraisals * * * than would be warranted," the arbitrage activity of sophisticated investors would cause the market price of the target's stock to reflect the actual value of the information.[33] Whatever justification there might be in restricting the use of appraisals and projections in the offer of securities under the Securities Act of 1933,[34] it does not seem to exend to the tender offer situation.

A different explanation for judicial reluctance to require disclosure of offerer estimates of target company value, such as appraisals, focuses not on materiality, but on the propriety character of the information at issue. To require disclosure of this offeror information is simply to transfer value from the offeror to target shareholders, and as a result to reduce the incentives for potential offerors to create it in the first place.[35] The target company, of course, could commission and disclose its own appraisals, but then it would have to pay for them. Thus, the issue is not materiality—target shareholders would like to know what the offeror thinks the target company is worth just as any negotiator would like to know the other side's reservation price—and not the protection of target shareholders. Rather, the issue is distributional: Is it appropriate to cause the transfer of wealth from the acquiring

---

[33] The claim of unreliability with respect to an appraisal may be particularly unpersuasive in *Flynn*. In many cases, the unreliability of an appraisal is based on the fact that it was prepared by an interested party. In *Flynn* the appraisal in question was the work of a third party.

[34] Easterbrook & Fischel, *Mandatory Disclosure and the Protection of Investors*, 70 Va.L.Rev. 669, 702–3 (1984), argue that because of the difficulty of verifying projections, fraud rules are more difficult to apply to them. This leads the authors to recommend that disclosure of projections be permissible but not mandatory, thereby allowing a seller to disclose projections only when it thinks the resulting increase in the value of the security it seeks to sell exceeds the risk of liability from the difficulty of demonstrating that projections which proved to be wrong (or else there would be no suit) were nevertheless reason-

able when disclosed. This approach does not extend to the tender offer situation because there the party with respect to which mandatory disclosure is at issue is the buyer, not the seller; its incentives are to keep the value of the securities low, not high.

In Starkman v. Marathon Oil Co., [Current Volume] Fed.Sec. L.Rep. (CCH) ¶ 92,200 (6th Cir.1985), the court rejected *Flynn's* balancing approach in favor of a rule requiring disclosure of "projections and asset appraisals based upon predictions regarding future economic and corporate events only if the predictions underlying the appraisal or prediction are substantially certain to hold."

[35] See, e.g., Kronman, *Mistake, Disclosure, Information, and the Law of Contracts*, 7 J.Leg.Stud. 1, 11–18 (1978).

company to target shareholders?[36]   If this analysis is followed, is Judge Adam's balancing test an improvement?[37]

Thus, all in all, offeror disclosure may be of value to target shareholders in the context of a particular transaction.   There is, however, serious question as to whether it improves the lot of potential target shareholders as a class.   Recalling Easterbrook and Fischel's analysis of the desirability of competitive bidding generally,[38] what should happen to the frequency and price of premium offers as a result of mandatory disclosure?   The average premium in successful offers should go up (reflecting the impact of competitive bidding and the target company's opportunity to implement some of the offeror's plans itself).   The number of offers, however, should decline.   The other side of an increase in the premium is a decrease in the return to the offeror on its investment in information concerning potential targets; a decrease in return should result in a decrease in investment.   If the reduced frequency effect exceeds the increased premium effect, mandatory disclosure has not protected target shareholders.[39]

Some tentative empirical evidence is available concerning the impact of the Williams Act's imposition of mandatory offerer disclosure.   Jarrell & Bradley, *The Economic Effects of Federal and State Regulations of Cash Tender Offers*, 23 J.L. & Econ. 371 (1980), report that tender offer premiums were twenty percent higher in a sample of offers completed after the adoption of the Williams Act than in a sample of pre-Williams Act offers.[40]   They also found some evidence of a decrease in frequency of offers, although the decrease became apparent only after the extension of the Williams Act to exchange offers in 1970.   Both of these results, however, are subject to alternative explanations.   With respect to the post-Williams Act increase in premium, what would be the impact of the parallel increase in the respectability of hostile tender offers, and the participation of major companies as acquirers in the market for corporate control?   With respect to the decrease in frequency of offers following the 1970 Amendments to the

[36] Where the offeror owes target shareholders some level of fiduciary duty, the result, though not the issue, may change. Compare Weinberger v. UPO, Inc. 457 A.2d 701 (Del.1983) with Rosenblatt v. Getty Oil Co., 493 A.2d 929 (Del.1985) with respect to whether the acquiring company in a freezeout transaction must disclose its reservation price.

[37] Another way to pose the issue is as a conflict between informational efficiency and allocational efficiency. Disclosure increases informational efficiency but, by reducing the incentives to engage in the transaction at all, reduces allocational efficiency. In this sense, the issue is identical to whether an issuer has an affirmative duty to disclose under Rule 10b–5, even in the absence of insider trading, where disclosure would interfere with the substantive operations of the company. The familiar example of this conflict is a mining company that has made a significant strike

but wishes to withhold disclosure while it purchases land in the vicinity of the strike.

[38] See Chapter Fourteen B.3.e., supra.

[39] Moreover, the arguments posed in favor of competitive bidding by Gilson in Chapter Fourteen B.3.e. do not extend to encouraging competitive bidding by forcing the offeror to disclose its information about the target. The point of Gilson's argument was that some information producers would be better off with competitive bidding and others would not; leaving target management free to seek competitive bids allowed each information producer to exploit its information in whatever manner it found most profitable. Mandatory disclosure, in contrast, eliminates producer choice about how to proceed.

[40] To isolate only the influence of the adoption of the Williams Act, the samples excluded offers which were also subject to state tender offer regulation.

Williams Act, why would the extension of Williams Act mandatory disclosure to exchange offers change anything in light of the fact that exchange offers always had been subject to the mandatory disclosure obligations of the Securities Act of 1933?

At this point in the discussion it is useful to recall that our analysis of mandatory offerer disclosure thus far has been limited to an any and all offer in which there is a commitment to freeze out any nontendering shareholders at the tender offer price. As was pointed out, under this circumstance target shareholders have only two alternatives—either (i) take the offer, or (ii) keep their target stock and, if the offer is unsuccessful, be left in the same position they were prior to the offer being made, or if the offer is successful, be frozen out and left in the same position they would have been had they taken the offer. As to both of these alternatives, much of the offeror disclosure required by Schedule 14D, dealing with the offeror's post-acquisition plans, is irrelevant. The analysis changes, however, if the terms of the hypothetical transaction are changed. Suppose now that the offer in question is instead only a partial offer intended simply to secure control, or even an any and all offer, but without a representation that non-tendering target shareholders will be frozen out. Under these circumstances shareholders have a third alternative: Keep their target stock but, if the offer is successful, in a company that is now controlled by the offeror. In fact, it was this situation that provided a major justification for mandatory offeror disclosure in the first place. As part of the campaign to pass the Williams Act in the first place, Manuel Cohen, then Chairman of the SEC, noted that "the shareholder to whom even a cash offer is made is, in a sense, a purchaser as well as a seller of a security. A change in control can result in what amounts to a new, or at least vastly changed, company. A decision not to accept the offer amounts to a decision to buy into that new Company." [41] If the real justification for mandatory offeror disclosure is this one, then two results follow. First, what first appears as unique offeror disclosure is in fact best understood as run of the mill seller disclosure; the offeror is really selling, and the target shareholder is really buying, a share in a corporation controlled by the offeror. Second, it follows that information like the offeror's post-acquisition plans for the company is important for target shareholders because the transaction consists, in part, of the target shareholders exchanging their old stock in the target for stock in the "new" target that will exist if the offeror achieves control of the target. Which parts of Schedule 14D can be supported on this basis? See generally Borden & Weiner, *An Investment Analysis of Cash Tender Offer Disclosure*, 23 N.Y.L.S.L.Rev. 553, 584–643 (1978).

Disclosure of Preliminary Negotiations. The second unusual aspect of tender offer disclosure is that it is transactional; it relates to an ongoing transaction to which the target company is a party. The problem posed is when during negotiation of the transaction must its existence be disclosed: When must shareholders be alerted that a

---

[41] Cohen, *A Note on Takeover Bids and Corporate Purchases of Stock,* 22 Bus.Law. 149, 152 (1966).

transaction may take place? The answer reached by the courts is at least clear. Disclosure is required only when there is a fair certainty that the transaction will—not may—take place. "[P]reliminary merger discussions are immaterial as a matter of law. * * * [But w]here an agreement in principle [to merge] has been reached a duty to disclose *does* exist." Greenfield v. Hublein, Inc., 742 F.2d 751, 756 (3d Cir.1983) (citations omitted, emphasis in the original), cert. denied 105 S.Ct. 1189 (1984).[42] What is equally clear, however, is that the answer's expressed rationale is problematic.

As with disclosure of appraisals, the rationale for nondisclosure is cast in terms of materiality, but the resolution appears to turn on something very different indeed. Under the *TSC* materiality standard described in *Bass Brothers,* supra, can there be any doubt that a reasonable shareholder "would consider it important" that a potential target company actually was engaged in negotiations concerning its acquisition? Thus, the courts stress not that information concerning preliminary merger discussions is unimportant, but that the information is subject to so much uncertainty that disclosure will do more harm than good:

> It does not serve the underlying purposes of the securities acts to compel disclosure of merger negotiations in the not unusual circumstances before us. * * * Such negotiations are inherently fluid and the eventual outcome is shrouded in uncertainty. Disclosure may in fact be more misleading than secrecy so far as investment decisions are concerned.

Reiss v. Pan American World Airways, supra, at 96,201.[43]

This analysis seems to take a quite limited view of the ability of professional analysts to factor probabilistic information into their estimates of price. To be sure, there would be a danger that particular individuals might misevaluate the significance of particular negotiations. But the lesson of the Efficient Capital Market Hypothesis, as developed in Chapter Five, is that the price of the security would reflect the *market's* evaluation of the significance of the negotiations—an aggregate of the individual assessments of market participants in which the misassessments of individuals would be factored out. Just as with the question of the mandatory disclosure of appraisals, the claim that disclosure of accurate information is undesirable solely because it is probabilistic is difficult to take seriously.

The result, in contrast to the rationale, nonetheless warrants further consideration. The problem with disclosure of preliminary

---

[42] Michaels v. Michaels, 767 F.2d 1185 (7th Cir.1985); accord Reiss v. Pan American World Airways, 711 F.2d 11 (2d Cir. 1983); Staffin v. Greenberg, 672 F.2d 1172 (3d Cir.1982); Missouri Portland Cement Co. v. H.K. Porter, 535 F.2d 388 (8th Cir. 1976); Susquehanna Corp. v. Pan American Sulphur Co., 423 F.2d 1075 (5th Cir. 1970).

[43] Accord Michaels v. Michaels, supra at 91,543–4 ("The need to protect shareholders from potentially misleading disclosure of preliminary merger negotiations * * * outweighs the rights of shareholders to have notice of corporate developments important to their investment decisions."); Staffin v. Greenberg, supra at 1206 ("The reason that preliminary merger discussions are immaterial as a matter of law is that disclosure of them may itself be misleading.").

negotiations is that the act of disclosure may alter the probability that the transaction will ever take place. The court in Staffin v. Greenberg, *supra*, had a sense of what was at stake. Arguing that disclosure of preliminary negotiations would "do more harm than good to shareholders", id. at 1206, the court quoted a statement made during the Senate hearings on the legislation that would become the Williams Act:

> Obviously, a company intending to make a tender offer strives to keep its plans secret. If word of the impending offer becomes public, the price of the stock will rise toward the expected tender price. Thus, the primary inducement to stockholders—an offer to purchase their shares at an attractive price above the market—is lost and the offerer may be forced to abandon its plans * * *.[44]

In fact, the difficulty associated with disclosure of preliminary negotiations is that there is a conflict of interest between different groups of shareholders, not that the information is so probabilistic as to be inherently misleading. Imagine two groups of target shareholders: One group who, because of personal reasons, will sell their shares in the target company during the period of negotiations before an agreement in principle is reached; and a second group, the remaining shareholders, who expect to hold their shares (at least until the negotiations have been resolved one way or the other). For the first group, disclosure of the preliminary negotiations is desirable however uncertain their outcome may be at that time. At least some portion of the expected premium thereby will be incorporated into the target's stock price at that time and, to that extent, the group of trading shareholders will have been benefited by disclosure. The non-trading group of shareholders, however, will have been injured by disclosure to the extent that disclosure reduces the likelihood of a successful transaction. For this group of shareholders, who by definition will not sell their shares until after the resolution of the negotiations, there is simply no benefit to having the market price early reflect the thereby lowered probability of a successful transaction. As the court in *Staffin* put it: "If the announcement is withheld until an agreement in principle on a merger is reached, the greatest good for the greatest number results." Id. at 1207.[45]

Whatever the underlying rationale for the rule, there are some mechanical difficulties associated with its application. The first concerns how can one tell when in the course of negotiations an agreement in principle actually has been reached. In the context of the negotia-

---

[44] Transcript, Hearings before the Subcommittee on Securities of the Committee on Banking and Currency, United States Senate, 90th Cong., 1st Sess., S. 510, p. 72 (statement of Mr. Calvin on behalf of the New York Stock Exchange, Inc.), quoted in Staffin v. Greenberg, *supra* at 1206. See SEC v. Gaspar, [Current Binder] Fed.Sec.L. Rep. (CCH) ¶ 92,004 at 90,980 (S.D.N.Y. 1985) ("[L]eaks of tender offer plans are a threat to the entire transaction because of the potential disruption of the ordinary market characteristics of the target company's stock."); United States v. Newman, 664 F.2d 12, 17–18 (2d Cir.1981), cert. denied 104 S.Ct. 166 (1983) (accord).

[45] It is interesting that in *Staffin* the two rationales for delaying when mandatory disclosure is required are intertwined, appearing, first one and then the other, in alternating sentences, as if in an effort to avoid choosing between them (or, perhaps, because the difference between them was not recognized).

tions themselves, the issue may become circular: An agreement in principle exists at the point one is disclosed. Once the matter moves into a litigation context, however, the court must have a means to evaluate the claim that disclosure came too late. In Greenfield v. Hublein, Inc., supra, the court rejected an intent test—had the parties reached an intent to merge—in favor of focusing on whether agreement had been reached on the "price and structure" of the transaction. 742 F.2d at 756–57. Note that the stress on the price term is consistent with the similar stress in the SEC's automatic commencement rule discussed in the previous section.

The second difficulty associated with the preliminary negotiations rule concerns what a party can say in response to an inquiry concerning indirect manifestations of the negotiations. The empirical evidence documents that there is typically a substantial increase in the price of and the trading volume in a potential target company's stock during the pre-disclosure negotiation period.[46] At least for an exchange listed stock, this usually triggers an inquiry from the exchange as to whether the company can explain the unusual activity in its stock. If the company does not know of any actual leakage of information concerning the negotiations, may it respond that "it is aware of no reason that would explain the activity in its stock" even though the only explanation it can imagine that would account for the trading activity is leakage of the ongoing negotiations? Compare Greenfield v. Hublein, Inc., supra (statement acceptable) with Schlanger v. Four-Phase Systems, Inc., 582 F.Supp. 128 (S.D.N.Y.1984) (if go beyond "no comment," disclosure required). The Securities and Exchange Commission considered the issue itself in In the Matter of Carnation Company, Securities Exchange Release No. 22214 (July 8, 1985).[47] During a period in which Carnation was negotiating its acquisition by Nestle, S.A., and in connection with which Nestle had advised Carnation that it would terminate negotiations if there was any public disclosure, Carnation was asked to explain unusual activity in its stock and directly was asked about rumors of a Nestle takeover. The company representative responded by saying: "[T]o the best of my knowledge there is nothing to substantiate * * * [it]. We are not negotiating with anyone." [48] A public announcement of the acquisition of Carnation by Nestle followed two weeks later. The Commission concluded that "an issuer statement that there is no corporate development that would account for unusual market activity in its stock, made while the issuer is engaged in acquisition discussions, may be materially false and misleading." [49] In an unusual comment, the Commission went on to state its view that Greenfield v. Hublein "was wrongly decided." [50]

[46] Keown & Pinkerton, *Merger Announcements and Insider Trading Activity: An Empirical Investigation,* 36 J.Fin. 855 (1981), found that the abnormal returns experienced by a target company in the 25 days *prior* to the public announcement of the transaction represented approximately half the total abnormal returns resulting from the transaction. Substantial increases in trading volume accompanied these returns.

[47] [Current Volume] Fed.Sec.L.Rep. (CCH) ¶ 83,801.

[48] Id. at 87,594.

[49] Id. at 87,596.

[50] Id. at 87,596 n. 8.

The *Four-Phase System* and Commission positions allow the company not to disclose as long as all they say is no comment. But would not any observer recognize that a "no comment" response is, in fact, a statement that negotiations were in process. If there were no negotiations, the company would be free to issue a denial. Only if there are negotiations is a "no comment" response required. From this perspective, the *Hublein* standard—a denial is lawful unless the company has actual knowledge of the leaks that resulted in the increased activity— may be best understood as a way to allow a company to avoid this implicit disclosure by telling a fib rather than a flat out lie.

(2) Substantive Regulation of Tender Offers Under Sections 14(d) and (e) and Section 10(b)

[Read Securities Exchange Act Sections 14(d)(5), (6) and (7) and Rules 14d–7, 14d–8, and 14e–1 in Appendix A.]

(a) Sections 14(d) and (e). The most unusual feature of the Williams Act is that it is not limited to disclosure. Under the Securities Act of 1933, it is at least technically true that an issuer can offer and sell a security with whatever substantive terms it can dream up as long as, in effect, it discloses that it does not own the Golden Gate Bridge and, in all events, is offering only a quit claim deed.[51] In contrast to this pure disclosure approach to the sale of securities, the Williams Act explicitly regulates the substantive terms under which securities can be purchased by tender offer. As originally enacted, the Williams Act's substantive regulation was contained in Sections 14(d) (5), (6) and (7). Section 14(d)(5) permits shareholders to withdraw their tendered securities within a tender offer's first seven calendar days and again after 60 calendar days from the offer's commencement. Section 14(d)(6) provides that when a partial offer—one for less than all of the outstanding securities of the class sought in the offer—is oversubscribed, shares tendered within the first ten calendar days must be purchased pro rata, rather than in the order they were tendered. Taken together, these two sections effectively established a minimum tender offer period: Seven days for any and all offers and ten days for partial offers. Finally, Section 14(d)(7) requires that any increase in price during a tender offer has to be paid with respect to all shares purchased, regardless of whether the shares are taken up prior to the price increase.

---

[51] This point easily can be overstated; the Securities and Exchange Commission has broad enough discretion in its administration of the disclosure system under the Securities Act of 1933 to accommodate a wide range of arm-twisting with respect to substantive matters. For example, the Commission has discretion whether to grant acceleration of the effectiveness of a registration statement. It has used this discretion, for example, to press its view that indemnification against statutory liabilities is unenforceable in certain situations by requiring, as a condition to acceleration, that the issuer undertake to present any claim for indemnification for judicial review prior to honoring it. See L. Loss, *Fundamentals of Securities Regulation* 131–36 (1983).

The Williams Act's substantive reach was significantly expanded in 1979 when the Securities and Exchange Commission took up the invitation to adopt regulations that always was contained in Section 14(d)(5), and that was added to Section 14(e) by the 1970 Amendments to the Williams Act. In Securities Exchange Act Release No. 16,384 [52] the Commission adopted regulations that substantially expanded target shareholder withdrawal rights and more than doubled the minimum length of a tender offer. Rule 14d–7 extends the initial withdrawal period from ten calendar days to 15 business days and creates a new withdrawal period—the ten business days following the commencement of a competing bid.[53] Rule 14e–1 prohibits any tender offer of less than twenty business days duration as well as any increase in the consideration to be paid to target shareholders (or an increase in the dealer's soliciting fee) unless the offer remains open for ten business days after the increase. This expansion in the scope of substantive regulation continued in 1982 when the Commission revised Rule 14d–8 to extend the ten day proration period specified in Section 14(d)(6) of the statute to the entire period of the offer.[54]

Both Congress and the Commission have been consistent in their explanation for the presence of these substantive aberrations in the Williams Act's otherwise pristinely disclosure-oriented structure. In its explanation for the adoption of a twenty business day minimum tender offer period in Rule 14e–1, the Commission stated: "Tender offers which do not stay open for a reasonable length of time increase the likelihood of hasty, ill-considered decision making on the basis of inadequate or incomplete information * * *." [55] From this perspective, these provisions are less substantive than supplementary. The idea is that disclosure of information about a tender offer is of little value if target shareholders do not have the time to evaluate the information. The movement toward a longer minimum tender offer period, and especially the extension of the pro rata period, serves to minimize pressure on shareholders either to tender promptly or miss out and, therefore, facilitates the shareholders' use of the information disclosed.[56]

[52] Reprinted in [1979–80 Transfer Binder] Fed.Sec. L. Rep. (CCH) ¶ 82,373 (Nov. 29, 1979).

[53] Release No. 16,384 specifies that when these periods overlapped, they would run concurrently. Thus, if a competing bid were made on business day five, the two periods would end on the same day. Id. at 82,591.

[54] Securities Exchange Act Release No. 19,336, reprinted in [1982–83 Transfer Binder] Fed.Sec.L.Rep. (CCH) ¶ 83,306 (Dec. 28, 1982). In the Release the Commission relied largely on its rulemaking authority under Section 14(e) to justify the adoption of a rule flatly inconsistent with the terms of Section 14(d)(6). Note, *SEC Tender Offer Timing Rules: Upsetting a Congressionally Selected Balance*, 68 Cornell L.Rev. 914 (1983), effectively presents the position, expressed by Commissioners Shad and Treadway in their dissent from the Rule's adoption, that the Commission lacks the statutory authority to alter Section 14(d)(6)'s proration period.

[55] Securities Exchange Act Release No. 16,384, supra, at 82,596. Similarly, the requirement that an offer remain open for at least ten business days following an increase in consideration was supported by the Commission's belief "that this provision will facilitate communication during tender offers and provide a reasonable time frame for security holders to evaluate certain increases before making an investment decision." Id.

[56] A different justification for longer minimum tender offer and proration periods—equal opportunity to participate—has also been advanced. Here the idea is that

As discussed in Chapter Fifteen A., it is in the interest of the offeror to design the terms of an offer to create pressure on a target shareholder to tender and to do so quickly. The problem with the Commission's justification is the link it establishes between time and information. Because of the existence of a sophisticated arbitrage community, very little time is necessary for the market to evaluate an offer and for that evaluation to be reflected in the market price of the security sought. Thus, the concern about time pressure resulting in ill-informed decisions seems somewhat attenuated. A better sense of what is really at stake with respect to the length of various tender offer periods comes from considering the effect of, in contrast to the expressed justification for, longer minimum periods, longer withdrawal periods, longer proration periods, and especially the extension of all periods when a competing offer is made or there is an increase in the offered compensation. From this perspective, the offeror's concerns described in Chapter Fifteen A. frame the issue correctly: Every increase in the various periods increases the likelihood of a competing bid. Giving the target company more time to solicit another offer, giving the target shareholders the confidence that they can withdraw their shares if there is another offer, and giving additional time for a competitive response each time one competing bidder increases its offer, all serve to facilitate an auction market for target companies. Thus, the central issue with respect to the "substantive" elements of the Williams Act seems to be resolution of the debate over the desirability of competitive bidding, as explored in Chapter Fourteen B.3.e., not concern over giving target shareholders the opportunity to thoughtfully evaluate the offeror's disclosure.[57]

What might explain the fixation of the Commission's rhetoric on the purported linkage between information and time periods? If Congress thought the Williams Act was *solely* a disclosure statute, the Commission's rulemaking authority would be similarly limited; it would then be difficult to find statutory justification for a preference for competitive bidding. Whether the reach of the Williams Act extends beyond disclosure was considered by the United States Supreme Court in a somewhat different context in Schreiber v. Burlington

---

small shareholders, especially unsophisticated individuals, are peculiarly disadvantaged by short time periods because it takes them longer to get their tender offer disclosure material, longer to evaluate the material, and longer simply to get their shares to the tender offer depository should they decide to tender. Longer time periods reduce their disadvantage as against sophisticated investors. See SEC Advisory Committee on Tender Offers, Report Recommendations 27–8, [Extra Addition No. 1028 (July 15, 1983)] Fed.Sec.L. Rep. (CCH). If this were the concern, however, why also extend the time periods for institutions and other sophisticated investors? One way to differentiate between sophisticated and unsophisticated investors

might be by the size of their holdings; under this approach, only small investors would get more time. Although there may be large investors who also are unsophisticated, they are in a position—and by definition have the means—to retain sophisticated advice.

[57] Lucian Bebchuk, for example, treats the principal function of the Williams Act as providing the time necessary for an auction market to develop. See Bebchuk, *The Case for Facilitating Tender Offers*, 95 Harv.L.Rev. 1028 (1982); Bebchuk, *The Case for Facilitating Tender Offers: A Reply and Extension*, 35 Stan.L.Rev. 51 (1982).

Northern, Inc., ＿ U.S. ＿, 105 S.Ct. 2458 (1985), and will be discussed in Section A.1.d. of this Chapter, infra.

Whatever underlying purpose the Commission has in mind for its substantive regulations, they do have one quite significant effect that has not yet been considered. It is quite easy to understand how the regulations are to be complied with in the context of a traditional tender offer. But what if the term "tender offer" is defined broadly? If, for example, a publicly announced series of open market purchases is a tender offer, then the substantive regulations operate, together with the definition of a tender offer, not as a means of regulating the transaction, but as a means of prohibiting it. How can the proration requirements of Section 14(d)(6) and Rule 14d–8 be met in the context of open market purchases? We will consider this issue in section A.1.c. of this Chapter where we confront the Williams Act's central, but entirely undefined, jurisdictional boundary: What is a tender offer?

(b) Section 10(b): Rules 10b–13 and 10b–4. In addition to direct regulation of the terms of tender offers under the Williams Act, the Securities and Exchange Commission in Rule 10b–13 has restricted the ability of offerors to acquire target shares other than pursuant to the offer, and in Rule 10b–4 has restricted the practice of short tendering through which sophisticated shareholders could avoid some of the impact of the proration requirements in partial offers. The operation of these rules are explained in the Releases announcing their adoption.

SECURITIES EXCHANGE ACT RELEASE NO. 8712
October 8, 1969.

The Securities and Exchange Commission today announced the adoption of Rule 10b–13 under the Securities Exchange Act of 1934 ("the Act") to prohibit a person who makes a cash tender offer or exchange offer for an equity security from purchasing that security (or any other security immediately convertible into or exchangeable for that security) otherwise than pursuant to the tender or exchange offer, during the period beginning with the public announcement or other commencement of the offering, whichever is earlier, and the time when the offer must by its terms be accepted or rejected.

* * *

Where securities are purchased for a consideration greater than that of the tender offer price, this operates to the disadvantage of the security holders who have already deposited their securities and who are unable to withdraw them in order to obtain the advantage of possible resulting higher market prices. Additionally, irrespective of the price at which such purchases are made, they are often fraudulent or manipulative in nature and they can deceive the investing public as to the true state of affairs. Their consequences can be various, depending upon conditions in the market and the nature of the purchases. They could defeat the tender offer, either by driving the market price above the offer price or by otherwise reducing the number of shares tendered below the stated minimum. Alternatively, they could further the tender offer by raising the market price to the point where ordinary investors sell in the market to arbitrageurs, who in turn tender. Accordingly, by prohibiting a person who makes a cash tender offer or exchange offer from purchasing equity securities of the same class during the tender offer period otherwise than pursuant to the offer itself, the rule accomplishes the objective of safeguarding the interests of the persons who have tendered their securities in response to a cash tender offer or exchange offer; moreover once the offer has been made, the rule removes any incentive on the part of holders of substantial blocks of securities to demand from the person making a tender offer or exchange offer a consideration greater than or different from that currently offered to public investors.

[Persons Affected]

Although the rule applies to purchases of securities immediately convertible into or exchangeable for securities of the same class which are the subject of the offer, it does not prohibit a person who, at the commencement of the offer, owns securities convertible into or exchangeable for securities of the class which are the subject of the offer from converting or exchanging such holdings into such securities.

The rule deals with purchases or arrangements to purchase, directly or indirectly, which are made from the time of public announcement or initiation of the tender offer or exchange offer, until the person making the offer is required either to accept or reject the tendered securities. As used in the rule an offer could be publicly announced or otherwise made known it the holders of the target security through a published advertisement, a news release, or other communication by or for the person making the offer to holders of the security being sought for cash tender or exchange. Moreover, any understanding or arrangement during the tender offer period, whether or not the terms and conditions thereof have been agreed upon, to make or negotiate such a purchase after the expiration of that period would be prohibited by the rule. Purchases made prior to the inception of that period are not specifically prohibited under the rule, although disclosure of such purchases within a specific prior period is required to be filed in schedules filed under Sections 13(d) and 14(d) of the Act. Of course, the general anti-fraud and anti-manipulation provisions could apply to such pre-tender purchases. The prohibition of Rule 10b–13 applies to exchange offers when publicly announced even though they cannot be made until the happening of a future event, such as the effectiveness of a registration statement under the Securities Act of 1933. As the Commission explained in Securities Exchange Act Release No. 8595, as applied to the offer by one company of its own securities in exchange for the securities of another issuer, the application of Rule 10b–13 to exchange offers in essentially a codification of existing interpretations under Rule 10b–6, which among other things, prohibits a person making a distribution from bidding for or purchasing the security being distributed or any right to acquire that security. These interpretations have pointed out that the security to be acquired in the exchange offer is, in substance, either a right to acquire the security being distributed or is brought within the rule under paragraph (b) thereof; and Rule

10b–6 prohibits the purchase of such security during the distribution except through the exchange offer, unless an exemption is available.

Since Rule 10b–13 applies to a cash tender offer or an offer of an exchange by an issuer to its own security holders of one class of its securities for another, if repurchase of the other security is subject to the prohibitions of Rule 10b-6, the issuer would have to obtain an exemption under paragraph (f) of that rule. Rule 10b-13 does, however, exempt from its prohibitions purchases if otherwise lawful, under specified conditions pursuant to "qualified stock options" or "employee stock purchase plans" as defined in Sections 422 and 423 of the Internal Revenue Code of 1954 as amended, or "restricted stock options" as defined in Section 424(b) of the Internal Revenue Code of 1954 as amended, as well as purchases under specified types of employee plans.

In addition, Rule 10b–13 contains a provision that the Commission may, unconditionally or on terms and conditions, exempt any transaction from the operation of the rule, if the Commission finds that the exemption would not result in the use of a manipulative or deceptive device or contrivance or of a fraudulent, deceptive or manipulative act or practice comprehended within the purpose of the rule. It is contemplated that this exemptive provision would be narrowly construed and that an exemption would be granted by the Commission only in cases involving very special circumstances.

* * *

By the Commission.

SECURITIES EXCHANGE ACT RELEASE NO. 20799
March 29, 1984.

I. BACKGROUND

In making a tender offer for securities of the corporation that is the subject of the offer, the bidder usually offers as consideration either cash, its own securities, or a combination of both. Tender offers can be for all the outstanding securities of the subject company or for a lesser amount.

Offers for less than all of the oustanding shares involve a risk to the securityholder of the subject company that not all of the securities that the securityholder tenders will be accepted.[3] Before the adoption of Rule 10b–4, certain securityholders tendered more securities than they owned in order to diminish this risk. By tendering a greater number of securities than they owned, and by guaranteeing their own tenders, market professionals were able to secure acceptance of a disproportionately larger number of the securities owned and tendered by them than could be secured by other persons who tendered only securities that they owned. Accordingly, the Commission adopted Rule 10b–4 in May 1968 for the specific purpose of prohibiting short tender-

[3] When tendered securities are accepted on a *pro rata* basis, the offeror accepts only a percentage of the securities tendered by each securityholder. The percentage is calculated from a fraction whose numera- tor represents the total number of securities accepted and whose denominator represents the total number of securities tendered.

ing. Rule 10b–4 makes it a "manipulative or deceptive device or contrivance," as used in Section 10(b) of the Act, for any person, in response to an offer or invitation for tenders of any security, to tender securities that he does not own. Ownership is defined in paragraph (b) of the Rule. The Rule applies to all tender offers whether made by a third party or by the issuer of the securities sought.

II. NEED FOR THE AMENDMENTS

By prohibiting short tendering, Rule 10b–4 was designed to promote equality of opportunity and risk for all tendering securityholders. In the years since the Rule's adoption, it has become apparent that simply requiring a tendering person to tender from a long position does not reach certain conduct that has the same purpose and effect as short tendering. Under the Rule, arbitrageurs are able to tender to an offer involving prorationing or selection by lot and then sell into a market that reflects the offer the portion of shares that they estimate will be returned unaccepted by the bidder. The shares sold may, in turn, be bought and tendered by another arbitrageur who may also hedge his tender by selling a portion of the shares. As a result, the same shares are effectively tendered by two (or more) shareholders and those shareholders who tender and do not engage in any hedging continue to experience the same dilution of their *pro rata* acceptance that occurred before the Rule was adopted.[7]

To address this concern, the Commission on August 21, 1981, published for comment a proposal to amend Rule 10b–4 to require that a tendering person own the tendered securities not only when they are tendered, but also at the end of the proration period. Since consistent treatment of short tendering and hedged tendering could also be achieved by deregulation and because it has been argued that deregulation might result in broader economic benefits, the Commission also requested comment on the effects, costs and benefits that would result from a deregulation of short tendering.

More recently, the Commission formed an Advisory Committee on Tender Offers ("Advisory Committee"). The Advisory Committee considered a wide range of matters relating to the regulation of tender

[7] For example, assume there is a tender offer for less than all the outstanding securities of the target and that A and B each owns 200 shares of the subject security and expects that the offeror will accept on a *pro rata* basis 60% of the securities tendered. If A tenders his 200 shares, and then sells 80 shares, he will (assuming the 60% expectation proves correct) have 120 shares accepted by the offeror, or 100% of the securities that he owns at the time the proration period ends. In contrast, if B simply tenders his 200 shares and does not engage in any hedging (possibly because he cannot borrow the subject security), he will have only 120 of his shares accepted and 80 shares will be returned unaccepted to him.

It seems anomalous that A, who would have engaged in a prohibited short tender if he had sold the 80 shares immediately before tendering 200 shares, can accomplish precisely the same result under the current Rule by waiting to sell the 80 shares until a moment after tendering. Furthermore, the 80 shares A tendered and then sold may be bought by an arbitrageur or other purchaser who will tender the same shares to the bidder and thereby increase the likelihood or degree of prorationing. If that occurred, it would reduce the number of tendered securities that would be accepted from other securityholders.

offers, including the appropriate regulatory treatment of short and hedged tendering. The Advisory Committee recommended that both short and hedged tendering should be prohibited.

* * *

A majority of the commentators believed that hedged tendering should be proscribed. A substantial minority of commentators argued that hedged tendering should not be curtailed. They asserted that hedged tendering enables arbitrageurs to minimize prorationing risks and therefore to bid higher for securities during a tender offer. This, in turn, benefits those securityholders who wish to avoid proration risk by selling all of their shares in the market at a known price.

The benefits to such securityholders, however, come at the expense of those shareholders who tender without hedging and thereby suffer from the expansion of the proration pool. The Commission believes that the impact of hedged tendering is unfair because, as a practical matter, hedged tendering is not available to most shareholders.
* * *

The Commission recognizes that hedged tendering and short tendering may be distinguished, largely because the hedged tenderor owns the tendered securities at the moment of tender. The Commission believes, however, that the two practices are closely analogous in terms of their purpose, availability, and effect on other shareholders who tender, and that hedged tendering should therefore be proscribed for essentially the same reasons that support the prohibition of short tendering.

III. SUMMARY OF AMENDED RULE

The amended Rule is designed to prohibit hedged tendering by the additional requirement that all tendering securityholders be "net long" the amount of securities tendered at the end of the proration period, or on the last day securities may be tendered in order to be accepted by lot where that method of acceptance is used. In addition, the Rule has been amended to clarify certain of its provisions and to limit its application to partial offers. The provisions of the rule are discussed below.

Paragraph (a)(1) sets forth the definition of ownership, which is essentially unchanged from current Rule 10b–4(2)(b), except for a revision to reflect the use of "equivalent security" as a defined term in paragraph (a)(2). The ownership definition has been refined to provide that a person who might otherwise tender securities will be deemed not to own the securities, and thus will be prohibited from tendering them, if he has entered into any arrangement or agreement (other than stock loans or the writing of exchange-traded call options) whereby another person can tender those securities under the Rule. Thus, for example, a person who has title to subject securities would not be permitted to tender them if he has (i) entered into an unconditional contract to sell them or (ii) written an over-the-counter call option on them and caused the holder to have the reasonable belief set forth in paragraph (a)(2) of the Rule.

Paragraph (a)(2) defines equivalent security to include (1) options, warrants, and rights issued by the person whose securities are the subject of the offer and (2) any other option to acquire the subject security, but only if the holder reasonably believes that the maker or writer of the option has title to and possession of the subject security and upon exercise will promptly deliver the subject security. This language tracks in all significant respects the proviso in existing Rule 10b–4(a)(1). An option traded on a national securities exchange would not be included within the definition of equivalent security since the holder of such an option cannot know that the maker or writer of the option has "title to and possession of" the underlying security within the meaning of the Rule. Since an unlimited number of options can be written on an uncovered basis, Rule 10b–4 does not permit listed options holders to tender unless they have exercised those options. The exclusion of options that are traded on a national securities exchange from the definition of equivalent securities represents a codification of prior staff interpretations of Rule 10b–4.

The term "tender" is defined in paragraph (a)(4) to encompass all methods by which a person can affirmatively respond to a request or invitation for tenders. Current Rule 10b–4(a)(1) refers to tendering for a person's own account; paragraph (a)(2) refers to tenders or guarantees on behalf of others. It has thus been possible to read Rule 10b–4 as prohibiting guarantees of delivery for a person's own account, although it is the Commission's understanding that market professionals routinely have employed so-called "self-guarantees" as a method of tendering securities purchased but not yet received. The definition of "tender" in paragraph (a)(4) specifically includes "guarantee" and thus eliminates any implication in the current Rule that self-guarantees are improper.[14]

Paragraph (b) of the Rule limits the substantive provisions to partial offers. In addition, new paragraph (c) would expressly exclude any partial offer where acceptance of tenders is not primarily by lot or on a *pro rata* basis for a specified period.[15]

Paragraph (b) of the amended Rule contains the substantive provisions of the Rule and covers acts by "any person acting alone or in concert with others, directly or indirectly." The phrase "directly or indirectly," together with the "in concert" language, is intended to make it clear that persons may not do indirectly what they may not do directly, and thereby to emphasize that indirect forms of short tender-

---

[14] If broker-dealers were unable to utilize self-guarantees, they could not tender securities purchased "regular-way" in the last five days of a partial offer, unless they secured the guarantee of another broker-dealer. There would not appear to be any regulatory rationale for imposing such a requirement.

[15] Incidental prorationing would not bring an offer within the coverage of the Rule. Such incidental prorationing might occur, for example, when some, but not all, securities at the highest acceptable price were accepted in an offer conducted on a "lowest price first" basis. Thus, Rule 10b–4, as amended, does not apply to most tender offers for municipal and corporate debt securities. Each of the commentators addressing the issue favored limiting the application of Rule 10b–4 to partial offers.

ing are prohibited. This does not, however, effect a substantive change in the Rule, in view of the provisions of Section 20(b) of the Act.[16]

Paragraph (b)(1) incorporates the ownership provisions of current Rule 10b-4(a)(1), considerably abbreviated through the use of defined terms. In addition, paragraph (b)(1) makes it unlawful for any person to tender any security unless he owns the securities tendered both at the time of tender and at the end of the proration acceptance period. This provision assures that the *pro rata* determination more fairly and accurately reflects actual ownership of tendered securities at that time. Securityholders who tender and do not thereafter sell the securities are unaffected by this amendment. A securityholder who tenders the subject security, and thereafter during the proration period sells all or a portion of the subject securities that constituted his net long position is required by this provision either to repurchase sufficient shares, or to withdraw shares from his tender, in order to comply with the net long proviso at the end of the proration period. The "end of the proration period" is the time after which securities would not be accepted by the bidder on a *pro rata* basis. Sales of subject securities occurring after the proration period are not prohibited since they do not affect the *pro rata* calculation.

In the case of a tender based upon ownership of an equivalent security, the Rule, as amended, clarifies the intent of the current Rule that equivalent securities need be converted, exchanged, or exercised only to the extent required by the bidder's terms of acceptance.

Paragraph (b)(2), which covers guarantees of tender, is largely comparable to current Rule 10b–4(a)(2), again simplified through the use of defined terms. The current standard of inquiry imposed upon guarantors by Rule 10b–4 remains unchanged. A guarantor must have "a reasonable belief that, upon information furnished by the person on whose behalf the tender is made," the person could tender in accordance with the provisions of the Rule.

Paragraph (b)(3) prohibits a tendering securityholder from tendering the same securities to more than one partial offer at the same time, i.e., multiple tendering. Some commentators believed that allowing multiple tendering would allow investors to have greater flexibility in choosing the best offer. The Advisory Committee, however, specifically recommended that multiple tendering be prohibited. The Commission agrees with the Advisory Committee and with the majority of commentators that prohibiting multiple tendering will prevent the confusion and possible deception to the market and to bidders that could otherwise arise, as well as the potential unfairness to certain securityholders for whom this practice may not be available.

Paragraph (d) provides a mechanism for obtaining exemptive relief to the extent that there may be factual situations that would justify the granting of an exemption upon a proper application.

*   *   *

[16] Section 20(b) of the Act [15 U.S.C. 78t(b)] makes it unlawful for "any person, directly or indirectly, to do any act or thing which it would be unlawful for such person to do under the provisions of [the Act] or any rule or regulation thereunder through or by means of any other person."

DISSENT OF COMMISSIONER COX

I respectfully dissent. From the standpoint of investor protection, I cannot agree to prohibit hedged tendering. My analysis leads me to conclude that a prohibition of hedged tendering arbitrarily favors one group of investors over another.

The Division of Market Regulation's ("Division") action memorandum recognizes the argument that the practice of hedged tendering benefits target shareholders who sell their shares rather than tender them during the interim period between announcement and execution of a tender offer. Unfortunately, the Division's analysis of that argument does not go far enough. Taken to its logical conclusion the analysis shows that hedged tendering merely transfers wealth between two groups of target shareholders. The Commission has no good reason, on the basis of investor protection, to say that one of these groups of target shareholders is more deserving than the other.

As it stands, the Division's analysis concludes that the benefits from hedged tendering accruing to target shareholders who sell into the market are at the expense of target shareholders who tender shares to the bidder without hedging those tenders. This is because hedged tendering expands the proration pool and thereby decreases the fraction of the tendered shares accepted. Let us briefly consider this redistribution of wealth from tenderors to sellers.

It is useful to divide target shareholders into three groups: (1) those who tender shares to the bidder but do not hedge the tenders, (2) those who sell shares into the market where the shares may be purchased and tendered by a market professional, a risk arbitrageur, who finds it worthwhile to hedge his tender, and (3) those who neither tender nor sell, that is, a group that does nothing. To understand the effect of hedged tendering, consider first the case of an oversubscribed partial tender offer when there is no hedged tendering. In this case, the larger is the group that does nothing, the better off are the shareholders who tender because a larger fraction of their shares is accepted by the bidder. This is to say that the inaction of those who do not tender benefits those who do tender.

Next, add the practice of hedged tendering to the market. This means adding a group of risk arbitrageurs who buy shares in the market, tender those shares, and then sell short the fraction of shares they estimate will be returned under prorationing. Note that the arbitrageurs buy these shares from target shareholders who prefer to sell at the interim price rather than go through the process of tendering the shares. The demand for shares by arbitrageurs who engage in hedged tendering bids up the market price, the price becomes closer to the tender premium offered by the bidder, and this benefits the target shareholders who sell into the market.

In order to accomplish hedged tendering, the arbitrageurs have to borrow shares to cover their short sales. Who will tend shares to these arbitrageurs without charging a premium, since the shares used to pay back the lender will be worth less than the shares lent? The answer is that target shareholders who neither tender nor sell their shares and who hold the shares in street name or a similar type of account "lend" the shares to the arbitrageurs. Arbitrageurs can borrow shares from these accounts as long as they stand ready to replace the shares immediately if the beneficial owner decides to tender or sell his shares.

Besides bidding up the interim price of shares, hedged tendering enlarges the proration pool and thereby decreases the fraction of shares accepted from target shareholders who tender. Now, however, the ultimate source of the wealth transfer is clear. When there is no hedged tendering, inaction by target shareholders who neither tender nor sell transfers wealth to target shareholders who tender their shares. This is to say, there is a redistribution of wealth from inactive target shareholders to those who tender. With hedged tendering, some of that wealth is redistributed away from the target shareholders who tender to the target shareholders who sell into the market. Put another way, target shareholders who tendered without hedged tendering gained greater benefits at the "expense" of those target shareholders who neither tendered nor sold. Hedged tendering allows target shareholders who sell to avail themselves of some of the gains otherwise enjoyed by the target shareholders who tendered.

The fact that some shareholders choose neither to tender nor to sell their shares creates a potential gain for target shareholders who tender or sell. There is no objective basis on which to judge that the group of shareholders that tenders is more worthy of the gains than the group of shareholders that sells into the market. To me, shareholder protection implies that both groups of target shareholders are equally worthy and the precise division of the tender premium is best left to market processes.

A helpful analogy is the sale of used cars. Is there any basis for deciding that people who choose to sell used cars to ultimate buyers by using such methods as newspaper advertisements (analogous to target shareholders who tender) are more deserving than people who choose to sell used cars to used car dealers (analogous to target shareholders who sell into the market)? I think not.

What about the risk arbitrageurs, the market professionals who have the ability to engage in hedged tendering? They supply a service to target shareholders who decide to sell at the interim price rather than bear the risk and go through the process of tendering. The professionals bear risk and provide other services to target shareholders who sell. In a competitive market they are compensated at a competitive rate. This is to say, they benefit the target shareholders who sell and they are compensated for it. There is neither reason to think nor evidence to show that they are compensated at a supracompetitive rate.

In summary, hedged tendering is a market practice that developed in response to a demand by target shareholders who do not want to bear the burdens of tendering shares. There is no basis for the Commission to judge these target shareholders less worthy of a share of the tender premium than target shareholders who choose to tender their shares. Prohibiting hedged tendering benefits target shareholders who tender and harms target shareholders who sell.   Overall investor protection is not increased by this change.

———————◆———————

c.   *What is a Tender Offer?*

The foregoing survey of the regulatory structure of the Williams Act makes the planner's task apparent.   The overall impact of the Williams Act is delay.[58]   Whether the transaction the planner has in mind is friendly or hostile, delay increases the likelihood of a competitive bid; and if the transaction is hostile, delay increases the target company's opportunity to take defensive actions.   The planner's task, then, is to structure a transaction that falls outside the jurisdictional boundary of the Williams Act—one that is not a statutory "tender offer"—while giving up as little as possible of the benefits of a tender offer's transactional form.   To put the problem more concretely, one critical benefit of a tender offer is that it bypasses target company management; in a hostile acquisition, the transaction simply cannot be accomplished without bypassing target management.   The Williams Act operates, in effect, to impose a tax—the delay necessitated by the substantive aspects of the Williams Act—on bypassing target management.   Can a transaction be designed that tiptoes past target management without awakening the regulatory guardian?   The effort to add content to the statutory term "tender offer" thus represents a strategic game between transaction planner and regulator.   The following case describes the development of the current rules of the game in the context of a transaction which was explicitly planned to fall outside what was perceived to be the definition of a "tender offer."

WELLMAN v. DICKINSON

United States District Court, Southern District of New York, 1979.
475 F.Supp. 783, affirmed 682 F.2d 355 (2d Cir.1982), denied sub nom.
Dickinson v. SEC, 460 U.S. 1069 (1983).

OPINION

ROBERT L. CARTER, District Judge.

I

Status of the Proceedings

This litigation stems from the acquisition by Sun Company, Inc. ("Sun"), a Pennsylvania corporation whose principal business is oil and gas, of roughly 34% of the stock of Becton, Dickinson & Company ("BD"), a New Jersey corporation which manufactures health care products and medical testing and research equipment.   Sun's brilliantly designed, lightning strike took place in January, 1978, and gave rise to seven separate actions which were consolidated for trial.   In 78 Civ.

---

[58] The combination of an extended minimum offering period and an extended proration period largely eliminates any pres- sure on target shareholders to tender their shares quickly.

1055, the Securities and Exchange Commission ("Commission") brings an enforcement action against Sun, L.H.I.W., Inc. (an acronym for *Lets Hope It Works*), the corporation Sun formed to receive the BD shares; Salomon Brothers ("Salomon"), a New York limited partnership engaged in the investment banking and brokerage business; F. Eberstadt & Co., Inc., ("Eberstadt"), a Delaware corporation engaged in investment banking, institutional stock brokerage and the management of pension funds and advisory accounts and which, along with Salomon, handled the Sun acquisition; F. Eberstadt & Co. Managers & Distributors, Inc. ("M & D"), a Delaware company 75% owned by Eberstadt and 25% owned by the estate of Ferdinand Eberstadt, which manages the two Eberstadt mutual funds involved in this proceeding; Robert Zeller, chief executive officer of Eberstadt and vice chairman of M & D; Fairleigh S. Dickinson, Jr., former chairman of BD and one of its principal stockholders; J.H. Fitzgerald Dunning, a former director and large stockholder in BD; and Kenneth Lipper, a partner in Salomon. The Commission charges the defendants with violating or aiding and abetting the violation of Sections 10(b), 13(d), 14(d) and 14(e) of the Securities Exchange Act of 1934; Rules 10b–5 and 10b–13 and Regulation 14D, promulgated thereunder.

In 78 Civ. 539, BD, its officers and several of its shareholders individually and derivatively sue Sun, L.H.I.W., Dickinson, Dunning, Salomon, Eberstadt, Chemical Fund, Inc., and Surveyor Fund, Inc., alleging violations of the Exchange Act similar to those charged in the Commission's case. * * * The Chemical and Surveyor Funds are open end investment companies managed by M & D and registered with the Commission under the Investment Company Act of 1940.

* * *

II

Findings of Fact

The background and governing facts in this complex drama embrace personality conflicts, animosity, distrust, and corporate politics, as well as a display of ingenuity and sophistication by brokers, investment bankers and corporate counsel.

Fairleigh S. Dickinson, Jr. was the son of one of the founders of BD. He held the reins of the company from 1948 until 1973. When he became BD chief in 1948, BD was a private family enterprise with gross sales of 10 million dollars annually. When he released the reins of the company in 1973, it was a public company with gross sales of $300 million annually. Dickinson loosened his hold on the helm but did not entirely let go. In 1974, he stepped upstairs to become Chairman of the Board, while Wesley Howe became Chief Executive and Marvin Asnes became Chief Operating Officer. Differences between the management team and the chairman became evident in late 1976 when Dickinson threatened to fire Asnes.

Sometime prior to January, 1977, Howe became interested in the acquisition by BD of National Medical Care Corp. Negotiations went well, and BD announced a proposed merger with the company in

January, 1977. Without advising the board or management, Dickinson engaged the services of Salomon and Eberstadt to look into the proposal and advise him about it. Dickinson was a personal friend of William Salomon, a senior partner of Salomon, and Eberstadt had been BD's investment banker. Robert Zeller, Eberstadt's chief executive, had arranged the first underwriting in 1962 when BD became a public company, and until 1975 had performed the same function when BD made additional public offerings. In addition, Zeller had advised Dickinson on the handling of some of his personal affairs. Both Salomon and Eberstadt filed negative reports on the National Medical Care proposal. Dickinson sent the Salomon report to BD board members in February, and on March 3 at a meeting of the Executive Committee, the proposal was abandoned.

Intrigue deepened at BD. Howe's secretary, Dorothy Matonti, began listening to telephone conversations that Dickinson's administrative assistant, Adele Piela, had with Jerome Lipper, Dickinson's attorney, and Board members. Matonti copied Piela's shorthand notes and material from Dickinson's appointment book, and Piela's secretary and Dickinson's driver kept Matonti informed of Dickinson's activities. This surveillance was duly recorded in memoranda given to Howe. On March 27, Dickinson held a meeting with Salomon attended by Kenneth Lipper, his brother Jerome Lipper, Dr. Edwards, an employee of BD, and several BD directors. At the meeting the participants discussed the financial community's reaction to changes in BD that Dickinson was contemplating. Dickinson apparently felt he had sufficient power in the company to bring about a change in management. Events, however, were soon to prove him wrong.

In early April, Dickinson, Howe, and Asnes met, presumably to bring their differences into the open and to resolve them. The meeting settled nothing. Howe and Asnes then decided on a show of strength. They canvassed the board, found enough votes to get rid of Dickinson, and on April 18 sent out notices for an April 20 meeting. Jerome Lipper knew the purpose of the meeting but Dickinson did not attend. Whether this was because Dickinson had also counted the votes, we do not know. At any rate, he spent part of the day in Washington, and part in Baltimore with Dunning. Howe prevailed. Dickinson was deposed as chairman and nudged out the back door with the title of Honorary Chairman.[16]

Obviously this must have been a terrible personal blow. Dickinson was now stripped of all power within what he must still have regarded as a family enterprise. On April 21, Dickinson had a meeting at Salomon to secure advice on how to proceed. Richard Rosenthal, John Gutfreund, and Kenneth Lipper of Salomon, two BD directors, Kane and Thompkins, Jerome Lipper and Salomon Brothers counsel, Martin Lipton were in attendance. The meeting centered on BD's trouble and the possibility of restoring Dickinson to power. A lawsuit based on procedural irregularities at the board meeting was ruled out. Nor was

---

[16] In September, 1977, Dickinson was terminated as a BD employee, and in December, 1977 he was dropped from the list of directors to be elected at the BD annual meeting in February.

a proxy fight considered a viable option when the small percentage of total BD shares Dickinson held was revealed. Although Dickinson and members of his family still held the largest segment of stock in the company, acquisitions, public offerings and the sale of some of their holdings had caused their aggregate portion to be reduced to approximately 5% of BD's outstanding shares. Discussion then turned to more practical solutions, e.g., for Dickinson to sell his shares on the open market to BD or to a third party, or to bring pressure on management through the outside directors. Dickinson vetoed the idea of selling his stock on the open market since he felt that that course would leave the shareholders of BD saddled with bad management. He accepted two remaining options—to vote with outside directors to bring pressure on management and to sell his stock to a company interested in a takeover of BD—and engaged Salomon for the latter purpose.

A few days later, on or about April 25, Dickinson advised Zeller that he was asking Salomon to involve Eberstadt in the effort to interest a company in acquiring his stock. Zeller confirmed these arrangements with Gutfreund.

At first, the relationship of Dickinson to Salomon and Zeller as principal and agent or broker for the sale of Dickinson's stock was merely an oral understanding. Events during the summer of 1977, however, caused the parties to alter the arrangement. By that time, there had been merger discussions with Avon Products Co. ("Avon") and American Home Products Corp. ("AHP"), and William LaPorte, chairman of the board of AHP, had met with Howe and Henry Becton, Dickinson's successor as chairman of the board of BD, seeking BD management's approval of an AHP acquisition. Howe was thus aware that Dickinson was seeking a takeover of BD by another company. Joseph Flom, BD counsel, called Lipton and threatened a lawsuit if Dickinson continued to try to secure a buyer for a large percentage of BD stock. Lipton suggested to Salomon that it secure an indemnification from Dickinson. Lipton drafted such a document for Dickinson to sign and sent it to Kenneth Lipper in July. Jerome Lipper and one of the senior partners of Salomon were opposed to the idea, but in late September or October, Flom renewed his threats to Lipton. Lipton again advised Lipper to have Dickinson sign the indemnification. This time Lipper took the document directly to Dickinson. He agreed to sign it, and after Jerome Lipper made some modifications, the revised document was signed by Dickinson and Kenneth Lipper. The letter of indemnification is dated October 12, 1977, and it confirms Dickinson's engagement of Salomon "in connection with seeking an offer for [his] shares" of BD stock. Dickinson agrees to indemnify Salomon against all claims relating to or arising out of the firm's acting on his behalf in securing a buyer for his stock.

From the spring of 1977 forward, Salomon and Eberstadt, particularly Lipper and Zeller, worked zealously to interest a company in acquiring a minority interest or in buying 100% of BD. Between April 25 and December, 1977, Salomon and Eberstadt arranged meetings with Avon, AHP, Monsanto Corp., ("Monsanto"), Hoffman-LaRoche,

Inc. ("Hoffman-LaRoche"), Shering-Plough Corp. ("Shering-Plough"), Squibb Corp. ("Squibb"), and Sun in an effort to interest those institutions in acquiring a position in BD. Dickinson himself participated in these activities until late December when he was hospitalized for about one month. In part, these efforts failed to bear fruit before Sun Company came on the scene because most of the other corporations were not interested in a takeover attempt in the face of hostile management. Since Sun's strategy was to move as quickly as possible, without public notice, the hostility of management was no deterrent.

* * *

Harry Sharbaugh, Sun's chief executive, had determined in 1977 that Sun needed to diversify by investing in institutions outside the energy field. Sun sought the acquisition of no less than a 20% interest and not more than a 50% interest in 3 or 4 companies over the succeeding two or three years by investing some 300–400 million dollars in each organization. Sun's corporate development committee was given responsibility for developing major acquisition opportunities for Sun. In August, Salomon was engaged to undertake some studies in connection with Sun's diversification program and Horace Kephart, a senior vice president concerned with corporate development and diversification, was given responsibility for dealing with Salomon. Kenneth Lipper was one of the Salomon partners in charge of the Sun account. Thus, the stage was now set for the main event.

Kephart discussed Sun's diversification program with Lipper, and in late November the two met at Salomon. Kephart was given a copy of BD's annual report, and Lipper suggested that Sun might consider BD as an acquisition possibility in its corporate development program. After studying the report, Kephart had further conversations with Lipper about BD. He learned about the rift between Dickinson and management, and about Salomon and Eberstadt's connection to Dickinson. In these discussions Kephart was told that a block of roughly 15% of BD shares was available, and that this included 1.2 million shares owned by Dickinson, 400,000 shares owned by Lufkin, 500,000 shares owned by Chemical Fund and 300–400,000 shares owned by Dunning. He also informed that BD was attempting to buy back Dickinson's stock, and that Dickinson had refused but would be willing to sell his shares to a major company. Kephart further learned that BD had publicly announced in June its desire to remain independent and had hired special counsel to assist it in resisting any takeover efforts. Moreover, Lipper told Kephart that a foreign company (Hoffman-LaRoche) and a domestic chemical company (Monsanto) were ready to move to acquire an interest in BD after the first of the year, giving Kephart the impression that speedy action was needed.

* * *

On December 22, Kephart assembled a study team of Sun executives to carry the analysis of the potential BD acquisition to "the next stage of sophistication." That is, this group "was to find out more about the health care products industry and [BD] in preparation for future reports to senior management [and] the board." In short, it was to provide top executives with necessary information to enable them to make an informed determination on whether to acquire an interest in BD.

On December 27, there was a meeting in New York attended by Sun's study team, Salomon, Eberstadt, Arthur Andersen and James Fogelson of Wachtell, Lipton (Salomon counsel), at which possible strategies for acquiring BD were discussed. Partial tender was dismissed as having a limited chance of success, and a friendly takeover bid was ruled out. There was discussion of soliciting individuals and institutions. Kephart was shown a list of available holdings including Dickinson's, Dunning's and Lufkin's. By this time he knew that a large percentage of BD shares were held by institutions, and he was assured that the Chemical Fund's 500,000 shares were available to Sun. Rosenthal proposed a two tier price—a higher price with no recourse and a lower figure with a guaranty to make up the difference between the lower price and the highest price eventually paid for any shares acquired. This was the so-called most favored nation clause, and the idea was accepted in principle. It was understood that a premium over the market was a prerequisite.

There was further discussion at Radnor, Pennsylvania on January 3 and 4 by the study team, Sun officials, Salomon, Eberstadt and Fogelson, all of whom were brought together by Kephart in preparation for a presentation on January 5 to Sun's board. Kephart prepared and Sharbaugh signed a personal and confidential letter for study by the board members at the January 5 meeting, which stated that a block of 15% of the shares of BD was available and an additional 10–20% could be quickly acquired. Kephart testified at trial that he had counted Dunning's, Lufkin's and Dickinson's in the 15% calculation. On January 5, Kephart presented the study team's findings to the corporate development committee at a meeting to which members of the board were invited to attend in informal session. The board heard the presentation. It was not asked to vote, but Kephart stated that a decision had to be made within a week. The consensus was that the matter should go forward. On the next day Wachtell, Lipton was employed as Sun's counsel and thereafter, Cleary, Gottlieb, Steen & Hamilton ("Cleary, Gottlieb") was employed by Salomon.

On January 9, there was a meeting of lawyers at Salomon. The lawyers indicated that the law regarding tender offers was still murky and that the concept of a tender offer had not been precisely defined. The lawyers wanted to structure a "privately negotiated" transaction. Fogelson and Charles Nathan of Cleary, Gottlieb felt this required that those solicited be limited in number. One felt that up to 60 solicitees was safe; the other argued for an upper limit of 40, but within those limits the lawyers felt there would be no problem.

Between December 22 and January 13 (when the executive committee authorized the acquisition and the expenditure of up to 350 million dollars), the study group was engaged in the examination of a myriad of alternatives. The study team knew that 10–13% of BD shares were held by non-management individuals who were willing to sell and that a large percentage of BD stock was in the hands of institutions. The study team concluded that the optimum percentage level for Sun to reach was over 33⅓%. At that level, Sun could utilize equity accounting and would have sufficient holdings to have a significant voice in BD's future direction. Even if BD increased the number of authorized shares, Sun's strength could not be diluted enough to frustrate these two objectives. The study team considered it acceptable for Sun to hold 20–30% of the stock for a short time, but a percentage in excess of 33⅓% was the basic objective.

On January 10 and 11, Kephart and the study team, augmented by Salomon (Rosenthal, Lipper, Gutfreund), Eberstadt (Zeller), Fogelson, Howard Blum, Sun's staff counsel, and Nathan met in Sun's headquarters to devise final recommendations to present to the Sun Board. There was an extended discussion of strategy. Kephart led the discussion, considering (1) open market purchases, (2) a conventional tender offer, and (3) private purchases. In the face of a hostile target, a conventional tender offer was not considered attractive. It was felt that it would lead to competitive bidding which would make the desired acquisition more expensive, and there was certain to be time consuming legal maneuvering to try to thwart the acquisition effort. What was needed was a procedure that would enable the acquisition to be effectuated quickly and put Sun in physical possession of the shares in the shortest possible time. There was a discussion of legal risk, but this was not a concern about the risk of litigation itself since everyone accepted that as inevitable. Rather, the participants were concerned with the chance that Sun's objective would be thwarted in mid-stream by legal maneuvers.

Four possible strategies were listed by Kephart on a blackboard and rated in terms of legal risk, quick control and price: (1) to seek shares sequentially first from individuals, then from institutions; (2) to seek shares simultaneously from these two groups; (3) to tender immediately; and (4) to contact management.

Simultaneous acquisition was considered the most desirable in terms of quick control and price, although there was a measurable legal risk that the effort would be aborted. Sun was advised by its lawyers that the exact boundary line between a private purchase and a tender offer had not been defined in the law. Nonetheless, the lawyers believed simultaneous purchases from large individual and institutional shareholders, carried out off the market after the New York Stock Exchange had closed and with as much secrecy as possible, constituted the strategy best suited to meet Sun's needs. The tender offer approach was rated best in terms of legal risk, but disadvantageous in terms of price. It would also give BD a wide opportunity to make counter moves. The lawyers felt it necessary to keep the solicitees limited in number in order for the acquisition to be considered a private transaction. There were discussions of the possibility of attaining the objective with purchases from 4 individuals and 6 institutions, but approaching as many as 40 solicitees was discussed. * * *

On January 11, these recommendations were presented to Sun senior officials. On January 13, the executive committee approved the "private transaction" proposal and authorized a $350 million expenditure for a 34% acquisition. Burtis testified that the maximum authorized was 38% of BD's outstanding shares, but Sharbaugh recalled the upper limit percentage as being 40%–50%. Salomon and Eberstadt were engaged at a fee of $350,000 each, conditioned on Sun's acquiring at least 20% of BD stock, and Sun provided each with a letter of indemnification.

On January 11, Fogelson, Nathan and Blum carefully considered the approach to be made to solicitees. When they learned that the strategy envisioned approaches to a number of individuals and institutions, they initially wanted Rosenthal to make all the solicitations. When he said that was impossible because there were too many solicitees, the lawyers decided on preparing two scripts: one for those soliciting individuals and a second one for those soliciting institutions.[19]

[19] OUTLINE FOR MAJOR INDIVIDUAL INVESTORS

1. Stress Need for Absolute Confidentiality

(a) To make transaction possible.

(b) To avoid liability under securities laws.

2. Provide outline of proposed transaction, including—

(a) Name of purchaser.

(b) General nature and scope of purchase program.

(c) Minimum number shares sought and ultimate goal.

3. Determine *precise* details of investor's shareholders and those of his family, including how registered, where securities located, whose approval needed for sale. Way shares held may affect ability to buy, since

—May not make offers to more than 10 shareholders resident in New Jersey—Assume that each member of family and each trust will count as separate New Jersey shareholder.

—Same true holdings of close friend (FD).

4. Terms of Offer

(a) Purchaser not able to make absolute commitment until minimum investment is assured. Thus final commitment from Purchaser must await results of institutional contacts.

(b) Price being offered and "most favored nation clause" [N.B. If raised by seller, no discussion of any kind concerning installment notes. Have lawyers work out all details].

(c) Because of restriction on offers to 10 N.J. residents, only want to discuss several biggest blocks. This to leave room to make offer to close friend.

(d) To avoid any possible breach of confidentiality, *no* offer to trust or other holdings where action or approval by a co-trustee or other party is required.

(e) Offer initially limited to 950,000 shares to avoid technical Section 13(d) questions re formation of family group. This not clear and lawyers still considering.

(f) Depending on reaction of friend and further evaluation by lawyers, may come back for additional shares, including trust shares.

(g) Goal of Purchaser is to acquire as many shares from investor and family as possible, consistent with law and interests of friend.

5. Approach to Friend

(a) Will he maintain absolute confidentiality? Any risk of his feeling obligated to inform target?

(b) Who can best make approach re:

—Friend's interest in selling

—How friend holds stock [needed because of 10 N.J. shareholder rule]

—Tax and estate planning considerations

(c) Note possible considerations re friend:

—approach may require joint filing under Williams Act because of argument have formed group

—target may sue everyone in sight, including sellers

(d) Any approach to friend must emphasize absolute need for total confidentiality.

(e) What is best timing re approach to friend?

—where he is now?

—where will he be this week?

The instructions stressed confidentiality and it was agreed that a lawyer would be at the side of each solicitor to monitor the latter's side of the conversation.

Rosenthal's two tiered price offer with a most favored nation clause was agreed upon. At his suggestion, solicitees were to be offered a top price of $45 per share with no recourse or $40 per share with the right to receive the highest price subsequently paid to any other solicitee. It was the understanding of Salomon, Sun and Eberstadt that all solicitees would get the benefit of the highest price paid.

Blum advised Rosenthal that the price should be negotiated, not fixed, and that if another price were suggested by solicitees, it should not be rejected but referred back to Sun. He told Rosenthal that there should be no specified time to respond, but Rosenthal said time deadlines would be set within the time frame normally allowable in block trading. Rosenthal was told that the principal was not to be disclosed

—what is his likely reaction time?

—how and from whom does he take tax and estate planning advice?

OUTLINE FOR INSTITUTIONS

I. *MANDATORY SELLING POINTS*

1. Emphasize that transaction cannot proceed unless absolute confidentiality is maintained by all parties. Also warn of risk of seller becoming member of a Williams Act group with filing responsibility if talks to others.

2. Emphasize that your principal will not finally commit to purchase until a block meeting its minimum requirements is assembled.

II. *PERMISSIBLE SELLING POINTS*

1. If institution expresses reluctance to agree because of future expectations, you may point out that its refusal to sell may preclude reaching minimum target and that your principal has no intention of going forward in such event. If this transaction is not consummated because principal can't assemble block, institution's expectations will be defeated.

2. As is customary in block transactions, you may state both the minimum size requirements for the block and the status of sellers' commitments at the time.

III. *DON'TS*

1. Do not characterize the price as a "take it or leave it" proposition. Be appropriately responsive to negotiating initiative by institution.

2. Do not impose a time constraint or institution's response shorter than is customary for institutional block purchases.

3. Do not disclose identity of principal unless absolutely necessary to consummate

the transaction and, in any event, not before the minimum size requirement for the block has been reached. If identity of principal is disclosed, make clear that purchase contract will be executed by subsidiary of principal.

4. Do not go beyond language in draft purchase agreement prefacing the "most favored nation" provision in response to questions regarding the intent of your principal.

IV. *POST–COMMITMENT INSTRUCTIONS*

1. If transaction with institution is *without* most favored nation clause, point out that contract will be amended by deleting last paragraph.

2. *Execution of Contract.* A representative of your principal will present a completed purchase contract (in form already submitted to institution with blanks filled in) for signature by the institution at the institution's office at the opening of business on the following morning. Determine whom the representative should ask to see.

3. *Proxy.* A form of proxy will be presented for signature by the institution together with the purchase contract.

4. *Settlement procedures.* Settlement will be C.O.D. as soon as possible. If institution willing to settle next day simultaneously with execution of purchase contract, arrange mechanics and form of payment (check, wire transfer, other). If settlement is not first thing in morning make arrangements to discuss details the next morning. Signature guarantees on stock powers will be required where appropriate.

and that solicitees should be told to keep the matter confidential, lest a 13(d) group develop as a result of leaks.

Kephart advised Lipper on January 13 that the executive committee had given the go ahead sign. He authorized the making of an offer to Dickinson and Dunning prior to January 16. In mid-December, Lipper had sent Dickinson Sun's annual report. Lipper, Zeller and Jerome Lipper arranged to see Dickinson in his hospital room the next day, January 14. Dickinson was told that the matter must be kept confidential and that Sun was the purchaser. After the price options were outlined, Dickinson indicated that he was ready to accept but only if the proposal was presented to Dunning as well. Dickinson chose the $45 price and asked that his shares be paid for with a cash down payment and the remainder in installments. He was told that the propriety of the installment payments would have to be referred to the lawyers.

After assuring them that he could vouch for Dunning's discretion, Dickinson called Dunning from his hospital room and spoke to him while Jerome and Kenneth Lipper and Zeller were still present. He told Dunning that Salomon and Eberstadt had brought him an attractive proposal for the sale of his BD stock but "he was conditioning his acceptance" on the same offer being made to Dunning. He identified Kenneth Lipper and Zeller to Dunning, indicated that they desired to go to Baltimore to talk to him as soon as possible about the sale of his stock, and requested that Dunning see them the next day. On completing the call, Dickinson advised Zeller and Lipper that Dunning would see them, and they agreed to get to Dunning's home in the early afternoon of January 15. Mrs. Turner then arrived in Dickinson's hospital room, and Zeller and Lipper offered her the same proposition offered to her father. Zeller and Lipper kept their appointment the next day with Dunning and made the proposal to him. Dunning liked the proposition and promised to advise them as soon as he talked to his brothers and to his co-trustee.

Kephart was authorized to go to New York on January 16 to supervise the solicitations, and he was instructed not to deviate from the agreed upon two tier price without getting prior approval from either Burtis or Sharbaugh. Kephart was told that Sun's acceptance should be conditioned on its securing a minimum of 25% of the total outstanding shares. When Rosenthal learned from Kephart on the morning of January 16, that Sun's minimum was 25%, he argued that it was too high a percentage to work to Sun's advantage. Rosenthal felt that many institutions might turn down the opportunity if Sun's acceptance were conditioned on its obtaining 25%, and he urged a 20% minimum. Kephart called Burtis and related Rosenthal's concerns to him, and Burtis agreed to the lower percentage.

* * *

At 4:00 P.M. [on January 16] all the persons assigned to do the solicitation met in the trading room of Salomon. Each solicitor had a script from which to read, and a lawyer was teamed up with each caller. Shortly after 4:00 P.M. the telephoning began. Some 30 institutions were contacted. The following institutions accepted the offer and sold their BD shares at $45 per share: American Security and Trust Co. sold 180,700 shares, Bank of America in California sold 143,400 shares, First National Bank of Boston sold 778,731 shares, First Wisconsin Trust Co. sold 96,625 shares, Hartford Fire Insurance Co. in Connecticut sold 99,300 shares, Home Indemnity Co. sold 10,000 shares, Home Insurance Company sold 28,600 shares, Investors Mutual Fund of Minnesota sold 200,000 shares, Investors Variable Fund of Minnesota sold 250,000 shares, Lincoln First Bank of Rochester sold 127,200 shares, Madison Fund sold 135,000 shares, Massachusetts Investors Growth Stock Fund sold 100,000 shares, Central Pension Fund of Massachusetts sold 15,000 shares, Seaboard Surety Co. sold 15,000 shares, State Street Research and Management Corp. of Massachusetts sold 508,300 shares, T. Rowe Price Growth Stock Fund of Maryland sold 461,000 shares, T. Rowe Price New Era Fund of Maryland sold 68,000 shares, T. Rowe Price Investment Counsel Account of Maryland sold 672,612 shares, Travellers Fund A for Variable Annuities of Connecticut sold 35,000 shares, the Massachusetts Fund sold 35,000 shares, Union Bank of California sold 1,100 shares, and the State of Wisconsin Investment Board sold 413,700 shares.

The following rejected the offer for various reasons: United States Trust Co. held 38,930 shares, North Carolina National Bank held 129,800 shares, Bankers Trust Co. held 394,880 shares, First National Bank of Chicago held 2,000 shares, First National Bank of Minneapolis held 2,000 shares. Morgan Guaranty Trust Co. was one of the institutions alerted to have someone available at 4:00 P.M., but it manifested no interest unless the offer was available to all of its accounts.

The calls from Boston were made only to the Massachusetts institutions, but the calls from Salomon's office in New York were made to cities throughout the United States.

The callers followed the script. There were slight variations, but each solicitee was told that a non-disclosed purchaser, sometimes identified as in the top fifty of Fortune Magazine's 500, was looking for 20% of BD stock; that no transaction would be final unless 20% of the shares were acquired; that the $45 option was a top final price and the $40 option could be accepted with protection in the event shares were later bought at a higher figure; and that the desired 20% goal was within reach or that the order was filling up fast and a hurried response was essential. Each solicitee was asked to respond within one hour or less, although some were given until the next day. Sun was identified to a few institutions, but to most the purchaser's specific identity was not revealed.

The institutions solicited had to consult with their in-house officials hurriedly. By 4:45 Kephart advised Burtis that verbal commitments for 3.1 million shares had been obtained. At 5:35 P.M. the total had reached 20%, and Kephart was given authorization to seal the bargain with these institutions that had committed their shares. Those institutions were called again, and Kephart was put on the phone. He identified himself, and after confirming that the solicitees were interested in selling at $45 a share, he accepted on behalf of Sun's subsidiary L.H.I.W. The project had gone so well that Kephart was concerned that the total might far exceed 34%, and he called Sharbaugh and asked whether he was to pro rate the shares if the 34% figure was exceeded. Sharbaugh replied that there would be no problem unless the figure was over 50%. Before retiring for the night on January 16, Sun officials knew that they had obtained their objective in that there were verbal commitments for at least 30% of BD's outstanding shares. Indeed, there was some concern that they might have overreached their goal by a wide margin.

* * *

Success had been achieved, but the lawyers were now concerned that the legal risks of the transaction were not entirely past. The solicitors had been in communication with a goodly number of individuals. To a few of these, Sun had been identified, and the solicitees had consulted with others in their organization to determine the institution's reaction to the offer. Thus, there was the likelihood that the transaction had already been traced to Sun, and the news would spread. Sun wanted to have physical possession of the stock certificates it had purchased before its identity was generally revealed. Blum feared that verbal commitments were not binding. The lawyers debated whether it was wiser to adopt a wait and see approach and react to the unfolding events or to seek to halt trading in BD stock on the NYSE. Fogelson and Nathan wanted trading halted.

The latter course was approved, but Sun executives forbade disclosure of Sun's identity to NYSE officials. At 9:20 on the morning of January 17, Fogelson called the NYSE and spoke to Richard Grasso, vice president for corporate services. Fogelson identified himself as a "partner of Wachtell, Lipton," said that "a client would be making a Williams Act filing with respect to [BD] by approximately noon the next day," and asked that trading be halted in BD. Grasso asked Fogelson to identify the client and reveal the purpose of the Williams Act filing, but Fogelson refused to give that information. Grasso told him that the NYSE could not order a halt in trading without further data. Some 15 minutes later Grasso received a second call from Fogelson. The latter said that rumors had come to his attention concerning BD. He repeated his earlier statement about a Williams Act filing the next day and requested that Grasso reconsider his trading halt request. Again Grasso asked Fogelson to identify the client and the nature of the Williams Act filing, and again Fogelson refused to provide the requested response. Grasso said trading could not be halted without further information and that he would have to communicate with BD. Fogelson suggested that he could confirm the rumors by speaking to Rosenthal, and Grasso said he would call him. Grasso then called Rosenthal and told the latter that the information Fogelson supplied him with was insufficient to warrant a halt in trading. Rosenthal said that there would be a material development announced upon the Williams Act filing and recommended that trading be halted.

Grasso reported the substance of the telephone conversations to the floor governor. Grasso again called Rosenthal, this time from the trading floor, and requested that he be given additional information. Rosenthal gave no additional information but repeated his request that trading be halted pending announcement of a Williams Act filing. Rosenthal told Grasso that "he and [the] senior partners in his firm were staking their credibility on the request that in fact a material development would be announced and therefore their recommendation was that we not trade in the stock." Rosenthal named Gutfreund and Salomon as the senior partners to whom he was referring. Grasso talked to the floor manager again, and the opening in trading was delayed. Trading in BD was officially halted at about 10:40 A.M. At 11:00 A.M., Leonard Quigley representing BD called Grasso to ascertain the reason for the halt in trading. BD at first wanted the trading halt lifted but then acquiesced, and on January 19 it requested the trading halt remain in effect. The halt continued until January 23.

Instead of the next day as promised, Sun's Williams Act filing did not take place until January 19 when its 13(d) was filed. Jerome Lipper, after discussion with his partner and Fogelson, advised Dickinson and Turner to file 13(d) statements. The statements were prepared and filed on January 19, the same day Sun's statements were filed. Dunning made a 13(d) filing on January 24.

* * *

III

Determination

Threshold Considerations

* * *

The next threshold inquiry concerns whether this was a privately negotiated transaction or series of such transactions or a public offering. There can be no disagreement that a purely private transaction is not subject to the pre-filing strictures under Section 14. Senator Williams, in stating the purpose of his proposed amendments, recognized that "[t]he essential problem in transfers of control resulting from cash tender offers or open market or privately negotiated purchases is that persons seeking control in these ways are able to operate in almost complete secrecy concerning their intentions, their commitments and even their identities." 113 Cong.Rec. 855 (1967). He recognized that a privately negotiated purchase may "relate to shifts in corporate control of which investors should be aware," id. at 856, and accepted the fact that a valid case could be made for requiring, as with a tender offer, that relevant information be filed before the securities are acquired. Nevertheless, Senator Williams concluded that requiring disclosure only after the privately negotiated or substantial open market transaction has been consummated "avoids upsetting the free and open auction market where buyer and seller normally do not disclose the extent of their interest and avoids prematurely disclosing the terms of privately negotiated transactions." Ibid. These activities are covered by Section 13(d) when 5% of a company's shares are acquired.

Although the difference between a privately negotiated transaction and a tender offer was alluded to on several occasions in the course of the debate on the Williams Act, the distinction was never articulated. As Judge Frankel said in Heine v. The Signal Companies, Inc., [1976–77] C.C.H.Fed.Sec.L.Rep. ¶ 95,898 at 91,320 (S.D.N.Y.1977), the "exact line of demarcation between a privately negotiated transaction and a public tender offer has not been *   *   * identified." Our first responsibility is therefore to distinguish a privately negotiated transaction, which is outside the scope of Section 14 of the Williams Act, from a public transaction, which may not be. While no differentiation between private and public has been spelled out in the Williams Act or the debates leading to its enactment, we have not been cast totally adrift. Some guidelines developed in defining a private offering exemption under Section 4(1) of the Securities Act of 1933 should be of aid in determining whether this transaction may properly be classified as one privately negotiated or publicly offered.

Arms-length negotiations between two persons epitomize a private transaction. As the number of actors increases, the identifiable characteristics of a private activity become blurred. "To determine the distinction between 'public' and 'private' in any particular context, it is essential to examine the circumstances under which the distinction is sought to be established and to consider the purposes sought to be achieved by such distinction." S.E.C. v. Sunbeam Gold Mines Co., 95 F.2d 699, 701 (9th Cir.1938), quoted with approval in S.E.C. v. Ralston Purina Co., 346 U.S. 119, 124, 73 S.Ct. 981, 984, 97 L.Ed. 1494 (1953).

In the latter case, the Court held that the proper way to interpret the private offering exemption provided under Section 4(1) of the Securities Act of 1933, was in the light of the statutory purpose. "Since exempt transactions are those as to which 'there is no practical need for *   *   * [the bill's] application,' the applicability of § 4(1) should turn on whether the particular class of persons affected need the protection of the Act. An offering to those who are shown to be able to fend for themselves is a transaction 'not involving any public offering.'" S.E.C. v. Ralston Purina Co., supra, 346 U.S. at 125, 73 S.Ct. at 984. The Court held that the statute applied to a public offering whether "few or many," and while it concluded the Commission could rightfully use a "numerical test in deciding when to investigate particular exemption claims," ibid, the Court did not favor embellishing the statute with the addition of a quantitative test as a means for defining a private offering. Finally, the Court stated that those claiming the private offering exemption properly have the burden of persuasion.

It must be conceded, of course, that *Ralston Purina* was concerned with the meaning of a private offering exemption under the 1933 Act, and we are faced with an entirely different statutory provision in the case at hand. Yet logic does make its demands. If statutory purpose gives proper definitional aid in distinguishing a public from a private offering under the 1933 Act, it would seem to follow that the purposes of the Williams Act would help define the contours of privately negotiated transactions exempted from the reach of Section 14.

Gloss has been added by case law developments since *Ralston Purina*. The number and relationship of the offers and the size and manner of the offering are all relevant in determining whether an offering qualifies for private exemption under the 1933 Act. See Doran v. Petroleum Management Corp., 545 F.2d 893, 900 (5th Cir.1977). An offering to a "diverse and unrelated group * * * would have the appearance of being public," Hill York Corp. v. American International Franchises, Inc., 448 F.2d 680, 688 (5th Cir.1971), and each offeree in a private transaction must be afforded the same information that would have been afforded a prospective investor in a public offering, or the offeree must be shown otherwise to have had such information or ready access to it. Woolf v. Cohn, 521 F.2d 591, 613 (5th Cir.1975). Nor does the "high degree of business or legal sophistication" of the offerees suffice to render a transaction private. Doran v. Petroleum Management Corp., supra, 545 F.2d at 902. Sophistication is not a substitute for access to the kind of information the 1933 Act requires. See Hill York Corp. v. American International Franchises, Inc., supra, 448 F.2d 680, 691. "[T]here must be a sufficient basis of accurate information upon which the sophisticated investor may exercise his skills." Doran v. Petroleum Management Corp., supra, 545 F.2d at 903. As in *Ralston Purina,* all the above cases place the burden of persuasion on the party who claims that it should not be subjected to the statute's pinch because the activity engaged in was private in nature. With these guidelines in mind, we now turn to the instant case.

Here, there were face to face transactions with four persons—Dickinson, Dunning, Turner and Lufkin. A total of 39 individuals and institutions were solicited with holdings involving a variety of discretionary accounts. There was no common characteristic binding the solicitees together except that they were uniformly shareholders with substantial BD holdings. Among those approached were highly knowledgeable individuals like Lufkin as well as unsophisticated investors like Smith, Willock and Drake. There were insurance companies, mutual funds, banks, a state entity, partnerships and corporations. The solicitation was nationwide. Some institutions held shares in their own account; others held shares in discretionary and non-discretionary accounts. While the Sun solicitors had been instructed by their lawyers to limit their offer to discretionary accounts, some institutions sold shares in non-discretionary accounts when faced with the demand to respond quickly to the offer lest the opportunity be lost, while others overlooked some of their shares held in discretionary accounts.

Defendants contend that here, unlike *Ralston Purina,* the private nature of the transaction cannot be determined by the solicitees' access to information because the distinction between 13(d) and 14(d) turns not on access to information, but on "which types of acquisition transactions should require prior, and which types subsequent, disclosure." They argue that a private offering in the 1933 Act and privately negotiated purchases in the Williams Act are not analogous.

It is true that a private or a public offering of an issuer concerns matters not relevant to considerations which would inform the boundaries separating a tender offer from a privately negotiated transaction. However, the present exercise is not yet an attempt to define a tender offer. Indeed that question need not be reached if what Sun did constituted a "privately negotiated" transaction. In determining the narrow threshold issue under consideration, it is submitted that *Ralston Purina* and cognate cases provide at least some rough guidance.

It should be noted that Senator Williams proposed exempting privately negotiated transactions from Section 14(d)'s pre-acquisition filing requirements to avoid requiring prematurely the disclosure of the terms of such transactions which the parties involved might prefer be kept secret. None of the solicitees involved here had any concern about any premature disclosure. That was solely Sun's anxiety.

Since these were undoutedly not "privately negotiated" transactions in which there was a mutual desire to avoid premature disclosure, the "access to information standard" derived from *Ralston Purina* and its cognate cases becomes even more relevant. The cases indicate that the supposed sophistication of the solicitees will not suffice to render the transaction private if they are given no information on which to exercise their skills. The procedure employed in this case required a hurried response on the basis of little information other than the price offered. The solicitors had no authorization to engage in negotiations with those they called. Their job was to obtain quick, oral commitments.

Plaintiffs argued in summation that the defendants chose from the list of shareholders "the ones they knew, they had done business with, hoped to do business with in the future, people they had reason to believe might not have challenged what they were doing." Defendants agree.

However, it is clear on this record that some solicitees were not previously known to defendants. *Vickers Guide* or some comparable publication was used to identify the institutional holders of BD shares. The information gleaned from these sources, not from Eberstadt or Salomon's private listing, determined who the solicitees were to be.

Defendants contend that the factors which decide whether a transaction is a "privately negotiated" purchase are the number of shareholders solicited, the way they are located, the publicity or lack thereof before the purchases are consummated and the procedures by which the sales terms are agreed upon and executed. They point to similarities between this transaction and those in Kennecott Copper Corp. v. Curtiss Wright Corp., supra. *Kennecott*, however, does not support defendants' definitional distinctions. The opinion never uses the phrase privately negotiated transaction and never attempts to distinguish a private from a public offering. Moreover, the transactions in *Kennecott* were in large part effectuated on the floor of the Exchange and it is clear that open market purchases are not subject to Section 14's pre-acquisition filing requirements. That certainly was not the case here.

This was a well structured, brilliantly conceived, and well executed project. The acquisition itself commenced Saturday, January 14 with the offer to Dickinson and Turner in confidence. Then Sunday, January 15, Dunning was approached, again with a pledge of confidentiality.

On Monday morning, January 16, Lufkin was brought in as an insider. On Monday afternoon before the close of the NYSE, calls were made to institutions around the country believed to possess large holdings in BD stock asking each to have someone available to receive an offer after 4:00 P.M., E.S.T., when the NYSE closes for trading. Some of these institutions had been sent earlier in the week a draft of the substance of the two tiered price agreement to be used (without the actual dollar figures). Shortly after 4:00 P.M., calls were made from Boston to Massachusetts based institutions and from New York to other solicitees around the country offering to purchase from each its holdings of BD stock. The solicitees were not told the name of the purchaser, except that it was in the top 50 of Fortune's 500, and the two tiered price was stated as $45 with no recourse or $40 with protection. The solicitees were told that the offer was contingent on the purchaser securing 20% of all the stock, and each was told that a response must be received within half an hour or an hour, although some were given until the next day. Additional pressure was placed on some who were told that acceptances were coming in very fast, inferring that the solicitee had better act quickly or be left out.

Based on the decided case law distinguishing "public" from "private" transactions, defendants have failed to carry their burden of showing that Sun's acquisition was "privately negotiated." Nor were these agreements a series of separate, independent contracts. This was a single intergrated project, planned and executed to secure for Sun some 33⅓% of outstanding BD shares, secretly and quickly so that the acquisition could not be aborted or halted at mid-point by legal action or other countermoves by BD. The institutions were solicited on the 4th market which, as I understand it, is the designation given transactions effectuated during the hours when the NYSE is not operating. Except for Turner and Dickinson, the same offer was made to each solicitee. There were no individual features to distinguish one confirmed solicitation from another except that the number of shares held by each institution varied. Nor, of course, is there any contention that these were open market purchases. Accordingly, the transaction fits neither of the traditional exceptions to Section 14.

This is not the end but merely the beginning of the inquiry. The conclusion that this was a public solicitation does not necessarily mean that the pre-acquisition filing requirements of the Williams Act apply. We now proceed to consider that issue.

Section 14(d) Claims

The Senate subcommittee introduced its report on the proposed Williams Act with a brief description of a typical tender offer:

> The offer normally consists of a bid by an individual or group to buy shares of a company—usually at a price above the market price. Those accepting the offer are said to tender their stock for purchase. The person making the offer obligates himself to purchase all or a specified portion of the tendered shares if certain specified conditions are met.

S.Rep.No. 550, 90th Cong., 1st Sess. 2 (1967). Thus, the Senate report
identified as attributes of a tender offer a bid, a premium price, tender
by the solicitees, and the conditional nature of the buyer's obligation.
The House subcommittee's definition of a tender offer was identical to
that adopted by its Senate counterpart. H.Rep.No. 1711, 90th Cong., 2d
Sess. 2 (1968), U.S.Code Cong. & Admin.News 1968, p. 2811.

The committee reports reflected statements made during the earlier committee hearings. For example, Commission Chairman, Manuel
F. Cohen, had testified that a tender offer typically involved the
solicitation by the buyer of options to purchase. The option would only
be exercised up to the maximum number of shares desired and would
not be exercised at all unless some minimum number of shares had
been tendered. *Full Disclosure of Corporate Equity Ownership and in
Corporate Takeover Bids: Hearings on S. 510 Before the Subcomm. on
Securities of the Comm. on Banking and Currency,* 90th Cong., 1st Sess.,
17 (1967). Chairman Cohen further indicated that the buyer usually
gave the impression that an immediate response was necessary but did
not disclose either what its intentions were with respect to the target
company or what the consequences might be for the investor who failed
to tender if the acquisition was successful. Ibid. Commission General
Counsel Phillip Loomis added to this definition his observation that
buyers frequently hurried the decision of the solicitees by indicating
that shares would be taken up on a first come, first served basis. Id. at
207. This general outline of the nature of a tender offer was reiterated
by Senator Kuchel, co-sponsor of the Williams Act. Id. at 72. Finally,
in opening the floor debate on the bill, Senator Williams alluded to
many of these same characteristics and added that buyers often hired
investment bankers and took out newspaper advertisements to facilitate the transactions. 113 Cong.Rec. 858 (1967).

The buyer need not seek one hundred percent or even a majority of
the stock of a company in order for its bid to qualify as a tender offer.
The Williams Act was drafted to cover only those tender offers resulting in ownership of more than 10% (now 5%) of the stock of a
corporation. Thus, the act recognizes the possibility that a purchase of
even less than 5% might be a tender offer, although exempted from
regulation. Senate Report No. 550, supra at 9.

A second characteristic common to many tenders but not an
essential element of Congress' definition is universal publicity of the
offer. Although the Senate recognized that use of a newspaper advertisement was one common tactic in making a tender offer, Senate
Hearings, supra at 2, it also understood that other means of publicity
were sometimes used. For example, the Senate Report refers to offers
that are "published or otherwise sent or given to security holders," id.
at 14, and in response to a question by Senator Williams, Robert Haack,
President of the National Association of Securities Dealers, indicated
that solicitations were sometimes made by telephone. Id. at 107.
Indeed, the practice of using newspaper advertisements was apparently
a phenomenon of recent origin that developed because the management
of target companies had begun to make it difficult for buyers to obtain

lists of shareholders which could be used to make direct individual solicitations. Id. at 229.

One of the chief concerns of Congress in enacting the Williams Act provisions was to remove the secrecy which had heretofore cloaked transactions involving a shift in corporate control. Defendants concede this purpose but contend that the transaction at issue here requires a post-acquisition Section 13(d) filing rather than a pre-acquisition Section 14(d) filing.

Senator Williams noted in the floor debate that the tender offer provisions were designed to remove the element of secrecy from transfers of control. 113 Cong.Rec. 855. According to the Senate report, no law prior to the Williams Act required that the person seeking control "disclose his identity, the source of his funds, who his associates are, or what he intends to do if he gains control of the corporation." Senate Report No. 550, supra at 2. Congress was also concerned that investors would choose to sell without the information necessary for a reasoned decision for fear that if they failed to tender quickly their shares would not be taken up at all. Ibid.

All of these elements—bid, premium price, obligation to purchase all or a specified portion of the tendered shares if certain specified conditions are met (in this instance, if 20% of the outstanding shares are acquired)—are present here. The above definition is set forth in *Kennecott,* supra, 584 F.2d at 1206, a case on which defendants rely as the "definition of a conventional tender offer [that] has received general recognition in the courts" (citations omitted). Defendants also assert, however, that publicity, the widespread solicitation of the general body of shareholders, and placement of the tendered shares in a depository are requisites for a conventional tender offer. However, there is no mention in *Kennecott* of these factors. The court there appeared to be concerned that the position taken by some courts and commentators would create an overlap between open market purchases and tender offers, thereby rendering § 14(d)(5)–(d)(7) unworkable. See Gulf & Western Industries, Inc. v. Great Atlantic & Pacific Tea Co., 356 F.Supp. 1066, 1073–74 (S.D.N.Y.) (Duffy, J.), aff'd, 476 F.2d 687 (2d Cir.1973). But there were open and off-the-market purchases involved in both *Kennecott* and *Gulf & Western Industries,* while there are no open market purchases involved in this case. This was a single cohesive transaction involving face to face transactions with Turner, Dickinson, Lufkin and Dunning, and 4th market telephone communication with institutional holders in which Sun received in hand roughly 6½ million shares and paid out 290 million dollars in about 5 days.

What is probably more important than the fact that this transaction has all the characteristics of a tender offer that were identified by Congress in the debates on consideration of the Williams Act is that Sun's acquisition is infected with the basic evil which Congress sought to cure by enacting the law. This purchase was designed in intent, purpose and effect to effectuate a transfer of at least a 20% controlling interest in BD to Sun in a swift, masked maneuver. It would surely undermine the remedial purposes of the Act to hold that this secret

operation, which in all germane respects meets the accepted definition
of a tender offer, is not covered by Section 14(d)'s pre-acquisition filing
requirements because Sun's coup was not heralded by widespread
publicity and because no shares were placed in a depository. Sun
wanted no publicity. It deliberately chose to keep its moves hidden
because as Kephart stated, Sun executives were fearful that they might
have large sums of corporate funds committed before having in hand
shares and proxies representing a 33⅓% controlling interest in BD.
Nor did Sun put trust in a depository. It wanted to have physical
possession of the stock certificates purchased as quickly as possible.

The argument that the solicitees were sophisticated investors and
therefore did not need Section 14 disclosure is no more convincing in
this connection than it was in relation to the issue of whether this was
merely a private transaction. Sophistication serves no purpose unless
it can be applied to the particulars of an investment or sale decision.
Therefore, sophistication and expertise cannot be relied on here to
exempt this transaction from the reach of Section 14(d). See Aronow,
Einhorn & Berlstein, *Developments in Tender Offers For Corporate
Control* 8 (1977).

* * *

The central thesis of the federal securities laws is that full disclosure is a necessary element of public protection. In S.E.C. v. Capital
Gains Research Bureau, Inc., 375 U.S. 180, 186, 84 S.Ct. 275, 11 L.Ed.2d
237 (1963), while referring to the Securities Act, the Exchange Act, the
Investment Company Act and a statute not of concern to us here, the
Court said, "A fundamental purpose, common to these statutes, was to
substitute a philosophy of full disclosure for the philosophy of *caveat
emptor* and thus to achieve a high standard of business ethics in the
securities industry." The institutional solicitees approached in this
transaction, while for the most part concededly sophisticated and experienced in market transactions, were in no position to put their sophistication and experience to use.

Even if this transaction were not seen as a *conventional* tender
offer, it would not necessarily fall outside the ambit of Section 14(d).
As discussed above, the concept of a tender offer has never been
precisely defined either in the Williams Act itself or by the Commission. Congress left to the Commission the task of providing through its
experience concrete meaning to the term. The Commission has not yet
created an exact definition, but in this case and in others, it suggests
some seven elements as being characteristic of a tender offer: (1) active
and widespread solicitation of public shareholders for the shares of an
issuer; (2) solicitation made for a substantial percentage of the issuer's
stock; (3) offer to purchase made at a premium over the prevailing
market price; (4) terms of the offer are firm rather than negotiable; (5)
offer contingent on the tender of a fixed number of shares, often subject
to a fixed maximum number to be purchased; (6) offer open only a
limited period of time; (7) offeree subjected to pressure to sell his stock.
These characteristics were recently accepted as appropriately describing the nature of a tender offer. See Hoover v. Fuqua Industries, Inc.,
C. 79–1062A (N.D.Ohio June 11, 1979). In that case, the Commission

also had listed an 8th characteristic not included here—whether the public announcements of a purchasing program concerning the target company precede or accompany rapid accumulation of large amounts of the target company's securities. The reason this last characteristic was left out undoubtedly was because publicity was not a feature of this transaction.

At any rate, it seems to me that the list of characteristics stressed by the Commission are the qualities that set a tender offer apart from open market purchases, privately negotiated transactions or other kinds of public solicitations. With the exception of publicity, all the characteristics of a tender offer, as that term is understood, are present in this transaction. The absence of one particular factor, however, is not necessarily fatal to the Commission's argument because depending upon the circumstances involved in the particular case, one or more of the above features may be more compelling and determinative than the others.

There was certainly "active and widespread solicitation" involved. Defendants contend that there was no widespread public solicitation of the general body of shareholders. But institutional holdings accounted for roughly 40% of all BD's outstanding shares as of January 16, and there was surely widespread solicitation of this class of shareholders. In addition, there was solicitation of individual shareholders holding a considerable percentage of BD shares. Measured by the size of the holdings solicited (34%), the geographic dimensions of the effort (from New York to California and from Massachusetts to North Carolina) and by the number of solicitees approached (30 institutions and 9 individuals, not including 3 institutions that were approached earlier and either indicated no interest, as did Morgan Guaranty Co., or were forgotten, as was Allendale Insurance Co.), there was widespread solicitation of BD's shareholders. See Hoover v. Fuqua Industries, supra; Cattlemen's Investment Co. v. Fears, 343 F.Supp. 1248, 1251–52 (W.D.Okl.1972).

The second characteristic, substantial percentage, does not move us very far, for unless the solicitation embraces at least 5% of the issuer's stock, the Act would not be called into play. The third element, premium over market, is regarded as one of the typical indicia of a conventional tender offer and was certainly present here. See Kennecott Copper Corp. v. Curtiss-Wright Corp., supra, 584 F.2d at 1206.

The fourth element—the firm terms of the offer and the absence of opportunity for negotiation—is stressed by the Commission. Defendants argue that the solicitees were not told that negotiations were barred, but the price was so attractive that none sought to negotiate. No negotiation took place and indeed if any had occurred, the whole project would have been derailed. It is undisputed that the solicitors could not barter about the terms of the offer. Any desire by a solicitee to deviate from the proffered terms had to be referred to Kephart. He, in turn, had to call Radnor to obtain permission to accept such a variation. That time-consuming process would have slowed the project and increased the legal risk of BD's being able to abort the acquisition. This project was structured so that there would be no individualized negotiations. The hope and expectation were that the price would be so attractive that negotiation would be unnecessary.

The fifth, sixth, and seventh elements were also present. The offer was contingent on Sun's achieving a stated percentage of BD shares—another characteristic of a typical tender offer. See Kennecott Copper Corp. v. Curtiss-Wright Corp., supra, 584 F.2d at 1206; Smallwood v. Pearl Brewing Co., supra, 489 F.2d at 597 n. 22. Time constraints were placed on each solicitee, and although some were given additional time to respond, most felt that they had to reply within the time constraints imposed. See Great Western United Corp. v. Kidwell, 577 F.2d 1256, 1261 n. 2 (5th Cir.1978), rev'd on other grounds __ U.S. __, 99 S.Ct. 2710, 61 L.Ed.2d 464 (1979). The solicitors tried to exert a maximum amount of pressure on the solicitees they contacted. The latter were told that favorable responses were coming in fast, and it was implied that either they had better make a hurried acceptance of this attractive offer or their chance would be gone.

The one element missing is publicity. Lack of publicity, however, should be no deterrent to classifying this transaction as a tender offer since, as has been stated, a principal objective of the Williams Act was to prevent secret corporate takeovers. Congress intended the Williams Act "to be construed * * * not technically and restrictively, but flexibly to effectuate its remedial purposes," S.E.C. v. Capital Gains Research Bureau, supra, 375 U.S. at 195, 84 S.Ct. at 284–85; S.E.C. v. National Securities, Inc., 393 U.S. 453, 89 S.Ct. 564, 21 L.Ed.2d 668 (1969), and it has long been the rule that all the federal securities laws must be given a construction which effectuates their remedial objectives. S.E.C. v. National Securities, Inc., supra. While Piper v. Chris-Craft Industries, Inc., supra, may have narrowed the presumed scope of the Williams Act in respect to who may claim its protection, particularly in suits for damages, there is nothing in that opinion to indicate a retreat from the long accepted doctrine that the substance of the federal securities laws must be broadly construed. Public investors are the intended beneficiaries of the Williams Act; accordingly, its provisions should be construed to facilitate their coverage.

Defendants contend, in effect, that acceptance of the Commission's characterization of this transaction as a tender offer would offend due process. That argument is devoid of merit in any event, but coming from counsel in this case, it is particularly disingenuous. Throughout the trial and in their post trial briefs defendants have placed heavy emphasis on the high quality of the legal advice which informed this transaction. The record shows that counsel realized that the concept of a tender offer had not been precisely defined, and Sun executives were advised of this lack of certainty in the law. Indeed, a quotation from Martin Lipton illustrates that knowledgeable lawyers, such as defendants' counsel, surely cannot be caught by surprise by a holding that this transaction is a tender offer. In a piece written in 1977, *Open Market Purchases,* 32 Bus.Law 1321 (1977), Lipton noted that "tender offer" was not defined by Congress in drafting the Williams Act, nor by the Commission in adopting implementing rules. The Commission in the proposed new tender offer rules, Securities Act Release No. 5731, August 2, 1976, declined to define "tender offer." "Case law, in defining 'tender offer,' has followed the Williams Act's legislative history, which makes it clear that the Williams Act was not intended to be restricted to conventional tender offers but rather was meant to encompass all methods of takeover by a large-scale stock purchase program."

To the same effect, see Aronow, Einhorn & Berlstein, *Developments in Tender Offers For Corporate Control* 1 (1977), where the authors suggest that the absence of a definition apparently was due to the fact that Congress and the Commission believed that, for purposes of the federal regulatory scheme, the term "tender offer" might well encompass transactions yet unborn with characteristics not typical of the transactions then identified in general custom and usage as tender offers. Thus, the question of just what was encompassed by the term "tender offer" was intentionally left open in an effort to preserve the flexibility of both the Commission and the courts in making determinations on a case-by-case basis. Both counsel and Sun executives knew that no court had accepted the simplistic definition now urged by defendants.

Sun wanted to achieve a 33% holding without being cut off in midstream. The pre-filing requirements of Section 14(d) would have given BD warning and insured its interference with Sun's objective. Defendants' lawyers simply sought to devise a strategy to meet Sun's needs and those of the investment bankers whose fee was contingent on a successful acquisition. The strategy was purposed to avoid the pitfalls which compliance with the Act mandated. There is nothing necessarily wrong with creating a *sui generis* approach to suit the particular needs of a client. But, when knowledgeable lawyers advise their clients to take an action which falls within the periphery of the law's proscriptions, due process considerations do not come into play simply because of miscalculation.

*   *   *

There are, therefore, no due process constraints barring the court from holding that the Sun transaction was a tender offer within the meaning of the Williams Act. None of the cases in which it was held that there had been no tender offer, e.g., *Kennecott*, supra; *Brascan*, supra, has all the definitional features that courts have traditionally used to describe a tender offer. As noted above, however, the important elements are present here. Accordingly, in acquiring 34% of BD stock in the transaction at issue here, Sun made a tender offer for BD stock without a pre-acquisition filing in violation of Section 14(d) of the Williams Act.

*   *   *

As the *Wellman* court recognized, some forms of "private" purchases had to be excluded from the definition of a tender offer. In the absence of such an exclusion, a simple negotiated sale between a purchaser and a controlling shareholder would be drawn into the statute's regulatory orbit. The result, through the application of the statute's best price and proration requirements, would be to impose an equal access resolution of the Perlman v. Feldmann issue [59] as a matter of federal law. The more difficult problem is to identify the exclusion's breadth.

The *Wellman* court approached this problem in a traditional way; it used the statute's purpose to define the limits of its application. An important purpose of the Williams Act was to provide information to target shareholders. Relying on a line of Fifth Circuit cases defining the scope of the private offering exemption in Section 4(2) of the Securities Act of 1933, the court held that the mere sophistication of the offerees did not eliminate the need for the information that compliance with the Williams Act would have provided. But why not? A sophisticated investor should know what information he needs to make a decision and whether or not he has it. Is there any reason to deny that investor the opportunity to make his decision with less information if he thinks the return is worth the extra risk? Interestingly, the Securities and Exchange Commission in its rulemaking has not interpreted the scope of the private offering exemption in the same way as the Fifth Circuit. Regulation D under the Securities Act of 1933 defines a safe harbor that, if met, assures the availability of the private offering exemption from registration under Section 4(2). There is no requirement that particular information be given investors so long as the offer is made only to "accredited investors," [60] defined, *inter alia,* to include any organization with total assets in excess of $5 million, any person who purchases at least $150,000 of the offered securities so long as the total price does not exceed 20 percent of the person's net worth, and any individual whose net worth exceeds $1 million or whose income has been in excess of $200,000 for the two previous years.[61] If the analogy to the Securities Act of 1933 carries the weight the *Wellman* court gave it, and if the offerees would have been accredited investors under the terms of Regulation D, then was the case incorrectly decided? Keep in mind that the thrust of the Fifth Circuit cases as the *Wellman* court read them—"that the supposed sophistication of the solicitees will not suffice to render the transaction private if they are given no information on which to exercise their skills"—was rejected by the Commission in drafting Regulation D.[61a]

This, in turn, leads to a different question. If the Commission had rejected the Fifth Circuit's absolute information requirement in Regulation D, why did it bring an enforcement action against Sun Co. in the first place? One answer might be that disclosure of information has an additional function under the Williams Act that it does not have under

[59] See Chapter Fourteen A., supra.

[60] Rule 502(b)(1).

[61] Rule 501(a).

[61a] That large scale private purchases can fall outside the definition of a tender offer was again demonstrated by Hanson Trust PLC v. SCM Corp., 774 F.2d 47 (2d Cir.1985). There Hanson Trust terminated a conventional tender offer and immediately thereafter purchased 25 percent of the target company's outstanding stock from five sophisticated institutional investors and in one open market transaction. The Second Circuit held that the purchases did not constitute a tender offer.

the Securities Act of 1933. Not only does it inform the offerees about the transaction, it also informs the market. The problem with this explanation, however, is that it runs headlong into the structure of the statute. The filing required by Section 13(d), whether the transaction is a tender offer or not, serves to inform the market—albeit only 10 days *after* the transaction, but that is all Congress required—while Section 14(d) is concerned with informing the offeree *prior* to the transaction.

That leaves as a source of Commission motivation not lack of offeree information, but lack of fairness. In February 1980, the Commission responded to an inquiry by Senator Proxmire and others concerning the operation of the Williams Act with a series of memoranda and a proposed revision of the Williams Act that would have defined the Act's jurisdictional boundary not by reference to a tender offer, but by reference to a "statutory offer": Any offer by a person who could thereby become the owner of more than 10 percent of the class of securities subject to the offer.[62] The Commission explained the need for the revision as follows:

MEMORANDUM OF THE SECURITIES AND EXCHANGE COMMISSION TO THE SENATE COMMITTEE ON BANKING, HOUSING AND URBAN AFFAIRS PROPOSING AMENDMENTS TO THE WILLIAMS ACT

*   *   *

At the time Section 14(d) was enacted, the prevailing business practice was for public acquisitions of controlling stock interests in contested situations to be conducted as tender offers. Therefore the legislation, which was written to respond to the abuses associated with that prevailing practice, was drafted in terms of regulation of tender offers. *   *   * Whereas the conventional tender offer was the preferred method of acquisition in the 1960's and early 1970's, new techniques have evolved which are designed to avoid the literal application of Section 14(d). If successful, these techniques deprive investors, confronted with a takeover bid, of the protections afforded by the provisions of Section 14(d).

*   *   * In light of the Commission's experience in the tender offer area, it is our conclusion that the most suitable and workable alternative to Section 14(d) would be a provision whose application was triggered by the acquisition in the aggregate of a fixed percentage of the voting securities of a company, which represents the ability to exert or influence control of a company. *   *   *

The overall effect of a statute based upon the acquisition of a fixed percentage of securities would be to channel stock purchase programs into a regulatory mold similar to that now used to govern "tender offers." As a policy matter, such a statute would further the goal of

---

[62] The Commission's response to Senator Proxmire appears in Securities Regulation & Law Report (BNA), No. 542 (Special Supplement) (Feb. 27, 1980). Under the Commission's proposal, acquisitions from no more than 10 persons in any twelve month period would have been exempted.

providing all security holders an equal opportunity to participate in the sale of controlling interests in public issuers. *   *   *

◆

Where in the Williams Act does the Commission find an equal opportunity goal?[63] Section 14(d)(6) does require proration, but says nothing about whether the offer must be made to all offerees. Moreover, the proration requirement is typically treated as a means of diminishing time pressure on target shareholders to the end of making disclosure more effective, not as an independent goal in itself. Of course, if equal opportunity is an independent goal, then the statute is not limited to disclosure and careful (and creative) inspection might uncover other policy goals.[64]

The private solicitation exclusion is not the only significant judicial exclusion from the concept of a tender offer. There is also substantial support for the proposition that open market purchases are not tender offers subject to the Williams Act.[65] As with the private solicitation exclusion, the problem is to define the breadth of the exclusion, rather than to justify the concept. At one extreme, it seems clear that simply purchasing shares on a securities exchange in normal market transactions without publicity or solicitations is not a tender offer. If it were, the statute would operate not as a regulation but as a prohibition; there is no way in which market purchases can be made to comply with the withdrawal, proration and best price rules of Sections 14(d)(5), (6) and (7), let alone their expansion by Commission rules. The other extreme seems equally clear. Suppose that after the exchange closed one evening an offerer publicly announced that it would place a buy order the next morning to purchase 30 percent of the target company's outstanding stock at a 50 percent premium over that evening's closing price. In this situation, it is hardly persuasive to argue that the transaction is not a tender offer because it is impossible to satisfy the terms of the statute in connection with market purchases. There is simply no reason to use the exchange as a means to effect the purchases in preference to the use of a depository as in the typical tender offer. Between the extremes, however, is a substantial expanse of gray.

There have been a number of efforts to spell out in greater detail the definition of a tender offer so as to eliminate the uncertainty

---

[63] That the Commission remains committed to this equal opportunity goal is clear from its proposal of Rule 14d–10(6) which provides that third-party tender offers must be open to all holders of the class of securities sought, thus imposing the Perlman v. Feldmann rule on acquisitions cast in the form of tender offers. Securities Exchange Release No. 22,198 (July 1, 1985), reprinted in [Current Volume] Fed. Sec. L.Rep. (CCH) ¶83,797. In the release announcing the proposal, the Commission reiterated its view, held "since the Williams Act was enacted," that "the Williams Act * * * [contains] an implicit requirement for equal treatment of security holders." Id. at 87,562.

[64] The availability of this enterprise turns on the Supreme Court's interpretation of the scope of the Williams Act, which we consider in Section A.1.d. of this Chapter.

[65] See, e.g., Kennecott Copper Corp. v. Curtiss-Wright Corp., 584 F.2d 1195 (2d Cir.1978); Brascan v. Edper Equities, Ltd., 477 F.Supp. 773 (S.D.N.Y.1979).

concerning the scope of the private solicitation and open market exclusions, as well as to delineate more precisely the application of the Williams Act to a varied range of unconventional transactions such as block purchases.[66] Although the Commission at one time proposed a rule defining a tender offer [67] the effort at clarification that has achieved the greatest prominence is the Commission's eight factor analysis, discussed in *Wellman,* that originated in the Commission's litigation briefs and found a ready audience among courts who were otherwise without guidance. This factor analysis hardly provides certainty because, as *Wellman* emphasizes, it is apparent that not all of the factors need be met in any single case; [68] indeed, some of the factors may be redundant. For example, if factor 8—public announcements of a purchasing program—is present, what does factor 1—active and widespread solicitation of public shareholders—add? It may be that factor 8 is concerned with open market purchases while factor 1 is concerned with private solicitations, but the general problem remains: There is no guidance concerning how many factors must be present for there to be a tender offer or concerning the relative importance of the individual factors. Additionally, many of the factors are ambiguous. Some of the ambiguity is obvious: Is an offer firm or negotiable if the

[66] See In the Matter of Paine Webber Jackson & Curtis, Inc., [1982–83 Transfer Binder] Fed.Sec.L. Rep. (CCH) ¶83,310 (Dec. 30, 1982).

[67] In Securities Exchange Act Release No. 16,385, [1979–80 Transfer Binder] Fed. Sec.L. Rep. (CCH) ¶82,374 (Nov. 29, 1979), the Commission proposed to add the following definition of a tender offer to Regulation 14D:

(1) The term 'tender offer' includes a 'request or invitation for tenders' and means one or more offers to purchase or solicitations of offers to sell securities of a single class, whether or not all or any portion of the securities sought are purchased, which

(i) during any 45-day period are directed to more than 10 persons and seek the acquisition of more than 5% of the class of securities, except that offers by a broker (and its customer) or by a dealer made on a national securities exchange at the then current market or made in the over-the-counter market at the then current market shall be excluded if in connection with such offers neither the person making the offers nor such broker or dealer solicits or arranges for the solicitation of any order to sell such securities and such broker or dealer performs only the customary functions of a broker or dealer and receives no more than the broker's usual and customary commission or the dealer's usual and customary mark-up; or

(ii) are not otherwise a tender offer under paragraph (1)(i) of this section, but which (A) are disseminated in a widespread manner, (B) provide for a price which represents a premium in excess of the greater of 5% or $2 above the current market price and (C) do not provide for a meaningful opportunity to negotiate the price and terms.

The American Law Institute, Federal Securities Code § 202 (166) (Official Draft, 1980) made a similar effort:

(A) GENERAL.—'Tender offer' means an offer to buy a security, or a solicitation of an offer to sell a security, that is directed to more than 35 persons, unless—

(i) it (I) is incidental to the execution of a buy order by a broker, or to a purchase by a dealer, who performs no more than the usual function of a broker or dealer, or (II) does no more than state an intention to make such an offer or solicitation; and

(ii) it satisfies any additional conditions that the Commission imposes by rule.

What explains the Commission's emphasis on solicitation and premium?

[68] See SEC v. Carter Hawley Hale Stores, Inc., 760 F.2d 945 (9th Cir.1985); Zuckerman v. Franz, 573 F.Supp. 351 (S.D.Fla. 1983); Hoover Co. v. Fuqua Indus., Inc., [1979–80 Transfer Binder] Fed.Sec.L. Rep. (CCH) ¶97,107 (N.D.Ohio, 1979).

offerer provides the opportunity to negotiate but then elects not to make concessions?[69] Other ambiguity is less obvious but more complex.

In SEC v. Carter Hawley Hale Stores, Inc., 760 F.2d 945 (9th Cir. 1985), The Limited had made a cash tender offer for some 55 percent of Carter Hawley Hale (CHH) common stock at $30 per share at a time when CHH stock was trading at $23.78 per share. After the offer was announced, CHH stock rose to $29.25 per share. CHH did not favor the offer and, in response, took a number of defensive actions among which was to announce that it would repurchase 15 million of its outstanding shares in market purchases.[70] Thereafter, the price of CHH stock fell, reflecting the reduced likelihood that The Limited's offer would be successful. CHH then carried out its repurchase, succeeding in repurchasing some 17.5 million shares—over 50 percent of its outstanding stock—in market transactions at prices between $25 and $26 per share. The Limited ultimately withdrew its offer and the price of CHH stock fell to $20.62 per share, slightly more than $3.00 per share below the pre-tender price.

Following the completion of CHH's repurchase program, the SEC filed an action against CHH alleging that the repurchases were an illegal tender offer in violation of Section 13(e)(1) of the Securities Exchange Act of 1934[71] and Rule 13e–4 promulgated thereunder. Under Rule 13e–1, a target company is allowed to make open market repurchases in response to a hostile tender offer subject only to filing with the Commission a Rule 13e–1 Transaction Statement describing the relevant facts.[72] Under Rule 13e–4, however, an issuer *tender offer* is subject to withdrawal, proration and minimum length requirements that are similar to those governing third party tender offers.[73] CHH had complied with Rule 13e–1, but not with Rule 13e–4; the legality of its repurchase program thus turned on whether it was a tender offer.[74]

---

[69] For example, the *Wellman* script could be altered to have the solicitor recite that the offer was negotiable but remain unwilling to alter the offer more than a minimal amount. Some negotiations prove unsuccessful although meaningful discussions actually took place; others are a charade despite all the talking. There is no bright line rule that distinguishes between the two.

[70] CHH also sold to General Cinema Corporation one million shares of convertible preferred stock representing 22 percent of the CHH voting securities then outstanding. The effect of the CHH repurchase was to raise General Cinema's voting power to 38 percent. Additionally, CHH granted General Cinema an option to buy its Walden Book subsidiary.

[71] Section 13(e)(1) prohibits issuer repurchases in contravention of rules and regulations adopted by the Securities and Exchange Commission.

[72] These include the amount of securities purchased, from whom purchased, and the purpose of the purchase.

[73] Although similar, the correspondence is not precise. For example, Rules 13e–4(f)(2) and 13e–4(f)(3) impose, respectively, ten-business day withdrawal and proration periods while Rules 14d–7 and 14d–8 impose a 15-business day withdrawal period and a proration period matching the length of the offer. Additionally, Rule 13e–4(f)(1) imposes a 15-business day minimum offer period for issuer tender offers while Rule 14e–1(a) imposes a 20-business day minimum for third party tender offers. The Commission has proposed to amend the rules governing issuer tender offers to correspond to those in Regulation 14D that apply to third-party offers. Exchange Act Release No. 22,199 [Current Volume] Fed. Sec.L. Rep. (CCH) ¶83,798 (July 1, 1985).

[74] The regulatory pattern reflected in the Commission's issuer repurchase rules is rather bizarre. The acquirer, seeking control of the target company, is subject to the restraints imposed by Regulation 14D. Target management, who by adopting defensive tactics like repurchases is also competing for control of the target company, is subject to no effective restraints so long as

In determining whether the CHH repurchases were a tender offer, both the district court [75] and the Court of Appeals applied the 8 factor analysis described in *Wellman*. Among other factors determined not to be present in the CHH repurchases, both courts found that the repurchases did not take place at a premium price.[76] The ambiguity concerning this factor was whether the existence of a premium was to be measured by comparison with the market price at the time CHH began its market purchases, or by comparison with the pre-tender offer price. Over the Commission's argument that the relevant comparison was the pre-tender price, the Court of Appeals held that the proper measure of a premium was by comparison with the market price at the time of the repurchase, even if it had increased as a result of the hostile offer.[77] Because the market price of a target's stock always increases after a premium third party offer, the court reasoned that to adopt the pre-tender comparison would eliminate "consideration of this *Wellman* factor in the context of issuer repurchases during a tender offer" [78] because it would always be met. Accordingly, it adopted the current market price definition of the premium factor.[79]

Is the court's reliance on the determinist character of a pre-tender price comparison persuasive? Market purchases are by definition at the then market price; in the absence of a complicated theory about the influence of the issuer's purchases on the market price,[80] a market price comparison is no less tautological. Perhaps the court felt more troubled by one tautology than the other because the existence of Rule 13e–1 holds out the potential that some open market repurchases are not tender offers; however, the issue should have been less the coherence of the SEC's regulatory pattern, than what the statutory term meant.

There is a fourth approach to defining a tender offer that also has drawn some attention. In S–G Securities Inc. v. Fuqua Investment Co., 466 F.Supp. 1114 (D.Mass.1978), the court held that a tender offer is present if there is "(1) a publicly announced intention by the purchaser to acquire a block of the stock of the target company for purposes of acquiring control thereof, and (2) a subsequent rapid acquisition by the purchaser of large blocks of stock through open market and privately negotiated purchases." [81] Interestingly, the Commission urged the application of this definition in *Carter Hawley Hale* in preference to the 8 factor test it had itself developed. The reason for the Commission's preference is clear enough; CHH's repurchase program could hardly

---

Rule 13e–1 applies. The result is to give target management an important strategic advantage. Indeed, Bradley & Rosenzweig persuasively argue that an issuer repurchase not subject to the requirements of Rule 13e–4 will dominate even a value increasing third party offer. Bradley & Rosenzweig, *The Law and Economics of Defensive Stock Repurchases and Defensive Self-Tender Offers*, 98 Harv.L.Rev. (forthcoming 1986).

[75] 587 F.Supp. 1248 (C.D.Cal.1984).

[76] 587 F.Supp. at 1254; 760 F.2d at 951.

[77] Is it clear which comparison the Commission had in mind in its proposed Rule defining a tender offer?

[78] 760 F.2d at 951.

[79] Accord, LTV v. Grumman Corp., 526 F.Supp. 106 (E.D.N.Y.1981).

[80] Should it matter whether this influence is a result of the increase in market demand resulting only from the issuer's purchases or whether the price was also affected by the derivatively derived trading mechanism?

[81] 466 F.Supp. at 1126–27.

fail to satisfy the S–G Securities test in light of the clear intention to move control of CHH to a coalition composed of CHH management and General Cinema. The Court of Appeals had little pause in rejecting this test, finding that it offered little guidance to the issuer in determining whether Rule 13e–4 or Rule 13e–1 governed its conduct.[82]

Why has defining a tender offer proved so difficult? The Commission's proposed Rule and the definition contained in the Federal Securities Code rely upon purely objective standards—the number of offers during a specified period and the normal functions of brokers and dealers—and draw the boundary quite expansively. The S–G Securities test also draws the boundary broadly, but relies on more subjective criteria like "substantial," "for the purpose of acquiring control," and "rapid." The 8 factor analysis, in contrast, is less a test than a checklist and is itself neither broad nor narrow; its boundaries depend entirely on how the ambiguities concerning the various factors are resolved and how the presence or absence of particular factors are balanced. A different approach might be to treat the problem in its strategic context. As each body that has confronted the definition problem has noted, there has been no difficulty defining a conventional tender offer. The definitional problem arose when acquirers, acting strategically, designed their offers to avoid the conventional form in order to avoid the Williams Act's regulatory restrictions. The ball was then in the regulators' court for a response. Suppose one began the definitional effort not by trying to identify the abstract characteristics of a tender offer, but by focusing on those transactional characteristics that are central to the acquirer's efforts. Here we would be looking for those elements of a transaction that a planner could not change—even to avoid regulatory restrictions—without giving up the very advantages the planning exercise seeks to preserve.

Approaching the issue from this perspective draws us back to the analysis of the offerer's motives in Chapter Fifteen C.—how to avoid competitive bidding. The point, it will be recalled, was to structure the offer so that target shareholders had an incentive to tender and to do so promptly.[83] A definition of a tender offer that recognized the strategic character of the ongoing game between planners and regulators, would feature those characteristics of a transaction that could not be changed without losing its central substantive element. For example, with respect to open market purchases publicity seems to be critical; target shareholders must know about the source of the new demand—and the implicit "or else" if they do not participate—for the desired incentive to be present. What other characteristics are sacrosanct to a planner? Does the emphasis on a premium in other formulations hold up to this kind of analysis?

d. Litigation Under Section 14(e)

Litigation is a central element of the current tender offer environment. If the offer is hostile, we have already seen in Chapter Fourteen

---

[82] 760 F.2d at 953.

[83] In this regard, the two-tier, front-end loaded offer was simply an effort to impose some pressure to tender despite the Williams Act's best price, proration and withdrawal provisions.

B.1.b. that target management's first step typically will be to commence litigation against the offerer.[84] Even if the offer is friendly, the potential exists for pre-transaction litigation by target shareholders who are seeking a better deal, as well as for post-transaction litigation by tendering or nontendering shareholders who turn out to be unhappy with their decision because, depending on what choice they made, the market has turned sharply up or down. In all events, Williams Act Section 14(e) is certain to figure prominently in the litigation.

Section 14(e) makes it unlawful "in connection with any tender offer"

> to make any untrue statement of a material fact or omit to state any material fact necessary in order to make the statements made, in the light of the circumstances under which they are made, not misleading, or to engage in any fraudulent, deceptive, or manipulative acts or practices.[85]

Rather obviously, this language is patterned after Rule 10b–5 which makes it unlawful, "in connection with the purchase or sale of any security"

> (a) to employ any device, scheme, or artifice to defraud,
>
> (b) to make any untrue statement of a material fact or omit to state a material fact necessary in order to make the statements made, in the light of circumstances under which they were made, not misleading, or
>
> (c) to engage in any act, practice, or course of business which operates or would operate as a fraud or deceit upon any person
>
> * * *

Because of this commonality of language, and because of the federal courts' vast store of precedents concerning the scope and elements of a Rule 10b–5 cause of action, it is hardly surprising that Rule 10b–5 solutions have been applied to Section 14(e) problems. Although this transposition is understandable, it merits careful consideration. Issues under Rule 10b–5 arise in a wide variety of contexts; the only common thread is a purchase or sale of securities. In contrast, issues under Section 14(e) arise in the context of a special transaction: a tender offer. Thus, the task is to evaluate how much reliance should be placed on Rule 10b–5 precedent when, despite the similarity in language between Rule 10b–5 and Section 14(e), there is a substantial transactional difference.

We focus on two inquiries that may best be characterized as jurisdictional. First, what type of misconduct is covered by Section 14(e)? Does it, like Rule 10b–5, reach only misrepresentation and

[84] Describing the job of counsel for the target company following a hostile tender offer, Herbert Wachtell states: "He brings a lawsuit. We all agree about that. And he brings it fast." Wachtell, *Special Tender Offer Litigation Tactics*, 32 Bus.Law. 1433, 1437 (1977).

[85] Section 14(e), goes on to authorize the Securities and Exchange Commission to adopt regulations "reasonably designed to prevent such practices as are fraudulent, deceptive, or manipulative." This rulemaking authority was added by the 1970 Amendments to the Williams Act. Recall that the twenty-business day minimum offering period in Rule 14e–1 was adopted pursuant to this authority.

nondisclosure, or does it extend more broadly, perhaps to encompass such matters as defensive tactics or lock-ups? Second, assuming the particular misconduct is covered, how far must the transaction have progressed before that misconduct is "in connection with any tender offer?" Thereafter we consider the treatment of another possible element of a cause of action under Section 14(e), scienter, that also has figured prominently in the development of Rule 10b–5.

(1) What Types of Misconduct are Covered by Section 14(e)?

The parallel development of Rule 10b–5 and Section 14(e) has been especially striking with respect to the range of misconduct each provision has been held to encompass. In the early 1970's, the failure of state law litigation efforts to restrain minority freezeouts led plaintiffs to what was, for a time at least, a more sympathetic forum. Reaching its apogee in the opinion of the Second Circuit in Santa Fe Industries, Inc. v. Green,[86] Rule 10b–5 was held to cover "breaches of fiduciary duty by majority against minority shareholders without any charge of misrepresentation or lack of disclosure."[87] At the same time, state courts were equally unreceptive to efforts to restrict a target company's use of defensive tactics to defeat a tender offer.[88] As with freezeouts, plaintiffs moved to federal court and their early success with Section 14(e) matched that experienced with Rule 10b–5. Expressly relying on the Second Circuit decision in *Santa Fe,* the court in Applied Digital Data Systems v. Milgo Electronic [89] held that the issuance of a large block of stock to a friendly suitor to block a hostile offer may violate Section 14(e).[90]

The bubble burst for Rule 10b–5 when the Supreme Court reversed the Second Circuit in *Santa Fe.*

SANTA FE INDUSTRIES v. GREEN
Supreme Court of the United States, 1977.
430 U.S. 462.

Mr. Justice WHITE delivered the opinion of the Court.

The issue in this case involves the reach and coverage of § 10(b) of the Securities Exchange Act of 1934 and Rule 10b–5 thereunder in the context of a Delaware short-form merger transaction used by the majority stockholder of a corporation to eliminate the minority interest.

---

[86] 533 F.2d 1283 (2d Cir.1976), reversed 430 U.S. 462 (1977).

[87] 533 F.2d at 1287. The history of state law efforts to restrict freezeouts is traced in Chapter Fifteen B., supra.

[88] See Chapter Fourteen B.3., supra.

[89] 425 F.Supp. 1145 (S.D.N.Y.1977). The court stated that "Section 14(e) was intended to make Rule 10b–5 applicable to the tender offer or exchange offer situation." Id. at 1157.

[90] Accord, Royal Industries v. Monogram Industries, [1976–1977 Transfer Binder] Fed.Sec.L. Rep. (CCH) ¶95,863 (C.D.Cal. 1976) (acquisition of a corporation solely to defeat a hostile tender offer violated Section 14(e); Crane Co. v. Anaconda Co., 411 F.Supp. 1208 (S.D.N.Y.1975) (complaint that sole purpose of acquisition by target was to defeat tender offer would state cause of action).

I

In 1936, petitioner Santa Fe Industries, Inc. (Santa Fe), acquired control of 60% of the stock of Kirby Lumber Corp. (Kirby), a Delaware corporation. Through a series of purchases over the succeeding years, Santa Fe increased its control of Kirby's stock to 95%; the purchase prices during the period 1968–1973 ranged from $65 to $92.50 per share. In 1974, wishing to acquire 100% ownership of Kirby, Santa Fe availed itself of § 253 of the Delaware Corporation Law, known as the "short-form merger" statute. Section 253 permits a parent corporation owning at least 90% of the stock of a subsidiary to merge with that subsidiary, upon approval by the parent's board of directors, and to make payment in cash for the shares of the minority stockholders. The statute does not require the consent of, or advance notice to, the minority stockholders. However, notice of the merger must be given within 10 days after its effective date, and any stockholder who is dissatisfied with the terms of the merger may petition the Delaware Court of Chancery for a decree ordering the surviving corporation to pay him the fair value of his shares, as determined by a court-appointed appraiser subject to review by the court.

Santa Fe obtained independent appraisals of the physical assets of Kirby—land, timber, buildings, and machinery—and of Kirby's oil, gas, and mineral interests. * * * Kirby's physical assets were appraised at $320 million (amounting to $640 for each of the 500,000 shares); Kirby's stock was valued by Morgan Stanley at $125 per share. Under the terms of the merger, minority stockholders were offered $150 per share.

The provisions of the short-form merger statute were fully complied with. The minority stockholders of Kirby were notified the day after the merger became effective and were advised of their right to obtain an appraisal in Delaware court if dissatisfied with the offer of $150 per share. They also received an information statement containing, in addition to the relevant financial data about Kirby, the appraisals of the value of Kirby's assets and the Morgan Stanley appraisal concluding that the fair market value of the stock was $125 per share.

Respondents, minority stockholders of Kirby, objected to the terms of the merger, but did not pursue their appraisal remedy in the Delaware Court of Chancery. Instead, they brought this action in federal court on behalf of the corporation and other minority stockholders, seeking to set aside the merger or to recover what they claimed to be the fair value of their shares. The amended complaint asserted that * * * the purpose of the merger was to appropriate the difference between the "conceded pro rata value of the physical assets," * * * and that Santa Fe, knowing the appraised value of the physical assets, obtained a "fraudulent appraisal" of the stock from Morgan Stanley and offered $25 above that appraisal "in order to lull the minority stockholders into erroneously believing that [Santa Fe was] generous."

This course of conduct was alleged to be "a violation of Rule 10b–5 because defendants employed a 'device, scheme, or artifice to defraud' and engaged in an 'act, practice or course of business which operates or would operate as a fraud or deceit upon any person, in connection with the purchase or sale of any security.' " * * *

The District Court dismissed the complaint for failure to state a claim upon which relief could be granted. 391 F.Supp. 849 (SDNY 1975). As the District Court understood the complaint, respondents' case rested on two distinct grounds. First, federal law was assertedly violated because the merger was for the sole purpose of eliminating the minority from the company, therefore lacking any justifiable business purpose, and because the merger was undertaken without prior notice to the minority shareholders. Second, the low valuation placed on the shares in the cash-exchange offer was itself said to be a fraud actionable under Rule 10b–5. In rejecting the first ground for recovery, the District Court reasoned that Delaware law required neither a business purpose for a short-form merger nor prior notice to the minority shareholders who the statute contemplated would be removed from the company, and that Rule 10b–5 did not override these provisions of state corporate law by independently placing a duty on the majority not to merge without prior notice and without a justifiable business purpose.

As for the claim that actionable fraud inhered in the allegedly gross undervaluation of the minority shares, the District Court observed that * * * the physical asset appraisal, along with other information relevant to Morgan Stanley's valuation of the shares, had been included with the information statement sent to respondents within the time required by state law. It thought that if "full and fair disclosure is made, transactions eliminating minority interests are beyond the purview of Rule 10b–5," and concluded that the "complaint fail[ed] to allege an omission, misstatement or fraudulent course of conduct that would have impeded a shareholder's judgment of the value of the offer." Id., at 854. The complaint therefore failed to state a claim and was dismissed.

A divided Court of Appeals for the Second Circuit reversed. 533 F.2d 1283 (1976). It first agreed that there was a double aspect to the case: first, the claim that gross undervaluation of the minority stock itself violated Rule 10b–5; and second, that "without any misrepresentation or failure to disclose relevant facts, the merger itself constitutes a violation of Rule 10b–5" because it was accomplished without any corporate purpose and without prior notice to the minority stockholders. Id., at 1285. As to the first aspect of the case, the Court of Appeals did not disturb the District Court's conclusion that the complaint did not allege a material misrepresentation or nondisclosure with respect to the value of the stock; and the court declined to rule that a claim of gross undervaluation itself would suffice to make out a Rule 10b–5 case. With respect to the second aspect of the case, however, the court fundamentally disagreed with the District Court as to the reach and coverage of Rule 10b–5. The Court of Appeals' view was that, although the Rule plainly reached material misrepresentations and nondisclosures in connection with the purchase or sale of securities, neither misrepresentation nor nondisclosure was a necessary element of a Rule 10b–5 action; the Rule reached "breaches of fiducia-ry duty by a majority against minority shareholders without any charge of misrepresentation or lack of disclosure." Id. at 1287.[8] The court went on to hold that the complaint, taken as a whole, stated a cause of action under the Rule *   *   *

We reverse.

II

Section 10(b) of the 1934 Act makes it "unlawful for any person *   *   * to use or employ *   *   * any manipulative or deceptive device or contrivance in contravention of [Securities and Exchange Commis-sion rules]"; Rule 10b–5, promulgated by the SEC under § 10(b), prohibits, in addition to nondisclosure and misrepresentation, any "arti-fice to defraud" or any act "which operates or would operate as a fraud or deceit." The court below construed the term "fraud" in Rule 10b–5 by adverting to the use of the term in several of this Court's decisions in contexts other than the 1934 Act and the related Securities Act of 1933, 15 U.S.C. § 77a et seq. The Court of Appeals' approach to the interpretation of Rule 10b–5 is inconsistent with that taken by the Court last Term in Ernst & Ernst v. Hochfelder, 425 U.S. 185 (1976).

Ernst & Ernst makes clear that in deciding whether a complaint states a cause of action for "fraud" under Rule 10b–5, "we turn first to the language of § 10(b), for '[t]he starting point in every case involving construction of a statute is the language itself.'" Id., at 197, quoting Blue Chip Stamps v. Manor Drug Stores, 421 U.S. 723, 756 (1975) (Powell, J., concurring). In holding that a cause of action under Rule 10b–5 does not lie for mere negligence, the Court began with the principle that "[a]scertainment of congressional intent with respect to the standard of liability created by a particular section of the [1933 and 1934] Acts must *   *   * rest primarily on the language of that section," 425 U.S., at 200, and then focused on the statutory language of § 10(b)—"[t]he words 'manipulative or deceptive' used in conjunction with 'device or contrivance.'" Id., at 197. The same language and the same principle apply to this case.

To the extent that the Court of Appeals would rely on the use of the term "fraud" in Rule 10b–5 to bring within the ambit of the Rule all breaches of fiduciary duty in connection with a securities transac-tion, its interpretation would, like the interpretation rejected by the Court in *Ernst & Ernst,* "add a gloss to the operative language of the statute quite different from its commonly accepted meaning." Id., at 199. But, as the Court there held, the language of the statute must control the interpretation of the Rule:

"Rule 10b–5 was adopted pursuant to authority granted the [Secur-ities and Exchange] Commission under § 10(b). The rulemaking

---

[8] The court concluded its discussion thus:

"Whether full disclosure has been made is not the crucial inquiry since it is the merger and the undervaluation which constituted the fraud, and not whether or not the majority determines to lay bare their real motives. If there is no valid corporate purpose for the merger, then even the most brazen disclosure of that fact to the minority shareholders in no way mitigates the fraudulent con-duct." 533 F.2d, at 1292.

power granted to an administrative agency charged with the administration of a federal statute is not the power to make law. Rather, it is ' "the power to adopt regulations to carry into effect the will of Congress as expressed by the statute." ' * * * [The scope of the Rule] cannot exceed the power granted the Commission by Congress under § 10(b)."   Id., at 212–214.

The language of § 10(b) gives no indication that Congress meant to prohibit any conduct not involving manipulation or deception. Nor have we been cited to any evidence in the legislative history that would support a departure from the language of the statute. "When a statute speaks so specifically in terms of manipulation and deception, * * * and when its history reflects no more expansive intent, we are quite unwilling to extend the scope of the statute * * *." Id., at 214. Thus the claim of fraud and fiduciary breach in this complaint states a cause of action under any part of Rule 10b–5 only if the conduct alleged can be fairly viewed as "manipulative or deceptive" within the meaning of the statute.

III

It is our judgment that the transaction, if carried out as alleged in the complaint, was neither deceptive nor manipulative and therefore did not violate either § 10(b) of the Act or Rule 10b–5.

As we have indicated, the case comes to us on the premise that the complaint failed to allege a material misrepresentation or material failure to disclose. * * *

We therefore find inapposite the cases relied upon by respondents and the court below, in which the breaches of fiduciary duty held violative of Rule 10b–5 included some element of deception.[15] Those cases forcefully reflect the principle that "[§]10(b) must be read flexibly, not technically and restrictively" and that the statute provides a cause of action for any plaintiff who "suffer[s] an injury as a result of deceptive practices touching its sale [or purchase] of securities * * *." Superintendent of Insurance v. Bankers Life & Cas. Co., 404 U.S. 6, 12–13 (1971). But the cases do not support the proposition, adopted by the Court of Appeals below and urged by respondents here, that a breach of

---

[15] The decisions of this Court relied upon by respondents all involved deceptive conduct as part of the Rule 10b–5 violation alleged. Affiliated Ute Citizens v. United States, 406 U.S. 128 (1972) (misstatements of material fact used by bank employees in position of market maker to acquire stock at less than fair value); Superintendent of Insurance v. Bankers Life & Cas. Co., 404 U.S. 6, 9 (1971) ("seller [of bonds] was duped into believing that it, the seller, would receive the proceeds").

We have been cited to a large number of cases in the Courts of Appeals, all of which involved an element of deception as part of the fiduciary misconduct held to violate Rule 10b–5. E.g., Schoenbaum v. First-

brook, 405 F.2d 215, 220 (CA2 1968) (en banc), cert. denied, 395 U.S. 906 (1969) (majority stockholder and board of directors "were guilty of deceiving" the minority stockholders); Pappas v. Moss, 393 F.2d 865, 869 (CA3 1968) ("if a 'deception' is required in the present context [of § 10(b) and Rule 10b–5], it is fairly found by viewing this fraud as though the 'independent' stockholders were standing in the place of the defrauded corporate entity," where the board of directors passed a resolution containing at least two material misrepresentations and authorizing the sale of corporate stock to the directors at a price below fair market value).

fiduciary duty by majority stockholders, without any deception, misrepresentation, or nondisclosure, violates the statute and the Rule.

It is also readily apparent that the conduct alleged in the complaint was not "manipulative" within the meaning of the statute. "Manipulation" is "virtually a term of art when used in connection with securities markets." Ernst & Ernst, 425 U.S., at 199. The term refers generally to practices, such as wash sales, matched orders, or rigged prices, that are intended to mislead investors by artificially affecting market activity. See, e.g., § 9 of the 1934 Act, 15 U.S.C. § 78i (prohibiting specific manipulative practices); Ernst & Ernst, supra, at 195, 199 n. 21, 205; Piper v. Chris-Craft Industries, Inc., ante, at 43 (Rule 10b–6, also promulgated under § 10(b), is "an antimanipulative provision designed to protect the orderliness of the securities market during distributions of stock" and "to prevent stimulative trading by an issuer in its own securities in order to create an unnatural and unwarranted appearance of market activity"). Section 10(b)'s general prohibition of practices deemed by the SEC to be "manipulative"—in this technical sense of artifically affecting market activity in order to mislead investors—is fully consistent with the fundamental purpose of the 1934 Act " 'to substitute a philosophy of full disclosure for the philosophy of *caveat emptor* * * *.' " Affiliated Ute Citizens v. United States, 406 U.S. 128, 151 (1972), quoting SEC v. Capital Gains Research Bureau, 375 U.S. 180, 186 (1963). Indeed, nondisclosure is usually essential to the success of a manipulate scheme. No doubt Congress meant to prohibit the full range of ingenious devices that might be used to manipulate securities prices. But we do not think it would have chosen this "term of art" if it had meant to bring within the scope of § 10(b) instances of corporate mismanagement such as this, in which the essence of the complaint is that shareholders were treated unfairly by a fiduciary.

IV

The language of the statute is, we think, "sufficiently clear in its context" to be dispositive here, Ernst & Ernst, supra, at 201; but even if it were not, there are additional considerations that weigh heavily against permitting a cause of action under Rule 10b–5 for the breach of corporate fiduciary duty alleged in this complaint. Congress did not expressly provide a private cause of action for violations of § 10(b). Although we have recognized an implied cause of action under that section in some circumstances, Superintendent of Insurance v. Bankers Life & Cas. Co., supra, at 13 n. 9, we have also recognized that a private cause of action under the antifraud provisions of the Securities Exchange Act should not be implied where it is "unnecessary to ensure the fulfillment of Congress' purposes" in adopting the Act. As we noted earlier, the Court repeatedly has described the "fundamental purpose" of the Act as implementing a "philosophy of full disclosure"; once full and fair disclosure has occurred, the fairness of the terms of the transaction is at most a tangential concern of the statute. As in Cort v. Ash, 422 U.S. 66, 80 (1975), we are reluctant to recognize a cause of action here to serve what is "at best a subsidiary purpose" of the federal legislation.

A second factor in determining whether Congress intended to create a federal cause of action in these circumstances is "whether 'the cause of action [is] one traditionally relegated to state law * * *.' " Piper v. Chris-Craft Industries, Inc., ante, at 40, quoting Cort v. Ash, supra, at 78. The Delaware Legislature has supplied minority shareholders with a cause of action in the Delaware Court of Chancery to recover the fair value of shares allegedly undervalued in a short-form merger. Of course, the existence of a particular state-law remedy is not dispositive of the question whether Congress meant to provide a similar federal remedy, but as in *Cort* and *Piper,* we conclude that "it is entirely appropriate in this instance to relegate respondent and others in his situation to whatever remedy is created by state law."

The reasoning behind a holding that the complaint in this case alleged fraud under Rule 10b–5 could not be easily contained. It is difficult to imagine how a court could distinguish, for purposes of Rule 10b–5 fraud, between a majority stockholder's use of a short-form merger to eliminate the minority at an unfair price and the use of some other device, such as a long-form merger, tender offer, or liquidation, to achieve the same result; or indeed how a court could distinguish the alleged abuses in these going private transactions from other types of fiduciary self-dealing involving transactions in securities. The result would be to bring within the Rule a wide variety of corporate conduct traditionally left to state regulation. In addition to posing a "danger of vexatious litigation which could result from a widely expanded class of plaintiffs under Rule 10b–5," Blue Chip Stamps v. Manor Drug Stores, 421 U.S., at 740, this extension of the federal securities laws would overlap and quite possibly interfere with state corporate law. Federal courts applying a "federal fiduciary principle" under Rule 10b–5 could be expected to depart from state fiduciary standards at least to the extent necessary to ensure uniformity within the federal system.[16] Absent a clear indication of congressional intent, we are reluctant to federalize the substantial portion of the law of corporations that deals with transactions in securities, particularly where established state policies of corporate regulation would be overridden. As the Court stated in Cort v. Ash, supra: "Corporations are creatures of state law, and investors commit their funds to corporate directors on the understanding that, except where federal law *expressly* requires certain responsibilities of directors with respect to stockholders, state law will govern the internal affairs of the corporation." 422 U.S., at 84 (emphasis added).

We thus adhere to the position that "Congress by § 10(b) did not seek to regulate transactions which constitute no more than internal corporate mismanagement." Superintendent of Insurance v. Bankers Life & Cas. Co., 404 U.S., at 12. There may well be a need for uniform federal fiduciary standards to govern mergers such as that challenged

---

[16] For example, some States apparently require a "valid corporate purpose" for the elimination of the minority interest through a short-form merger, whereas other States do not. Thus to the extent that Rule 10b–5 is interpreted to require a valid corporate purpose for elimination of minority shareholders as well as a fair price for their shares, it would impose a stricter standard of fiduciary duty than that required by the law of some States.

in this complaint. But those standards should not be supplied by judicial extension of § 10(b) and Rule 10b–5 to "cover the corporate universe." [17]

The judgment of the Court of Appeals is reversed, and the case is remanded for further proceedings consistent with this opinion.[*]

So ordered.

◆

The lower federal courts responded to the Supreme Court's decision in *Santa Fe* by continuing their simple application of Rule 10b–5 precedent to the interpretation of Section 14(e), only now with the effect of restricting the scope of the Section; claims that target company defensive tactics violated Section 14(e) were routinely defeated by simple reference to *Santa Fe*.[91] So matters stood until the decision of the Sixth Circuit in Mobil Corp. v. Marathon Oil Co.

MOBIL CORP. v. MARATHON OIL CO.

United States Court of Appeals, Sixth Circuit, 1981.
669 F.2d 366, cert. denied 455 U.S. 982 (1982).

Before EDWARDS, Chief Judge and ENGEL and MERRITT, Circuit Judges.

ENGEL, Circuit Judge.

On October 30, 1981, Mobil Corporation ("Mobil") announced its intention to purchase up to 40 million outstanding common shares of stock in Marathon Oil Company ("Marathon") for $85 per share in cash. Mobil conditioned that purchase upon receipt of at least 30 million shares, just over one-half of the outstanding shares. It further stated its intention to acquire the balance of Marathon by merger following its purchase of those shares.

Marathon directors were concerned about the effects of a merger with Mobil, and they immediately held a board meeting. The directors determined that, together with consideration of other alternatives, they would seek a "white knight"—a more attractive candidate for merger.

---

[17] Cary, *Federalism and Corporate Law: Reflections Upon Delaware*, 83 Yale L.J. 663, 700 (1974) (footnote omitted). Professor Cary argues vigorously for comprehensive federal fiduciary standards, but urges a "frontal" attack by a new federal statute rather than an extension of Rule 10b–5. He writes: "It seems anomalous to jig-saw every kind of corporate dispute into the federal courts through the securities acts as they are presently written." Ibid.

[*] Dissenting opinion of Justice BRENNAN and concurring opinions of Justices BLACKMUN and STEVENS omitted. [Ed.]

[91] E.g., In re Sunshine Mining Securities Litigation, 496 F.Supp. 9, 11 (S.D.N.Y.1979)

("In order for the plaintiff's complaint to withstand this motion to dismiss, we must find that the wrongful withholding of support for a proposed tender offer amounts to a fraudulent, deceptive, or manipulative act or practice. After Santa Fe v. Green, such a finding is untenable."); Altman v. Knight, 431 F.Supp. 309, 313–14 (S.D.N.Y. 1977) ("After the United States Supreme Court's decision in Santa Fe v. Green, it is clear that Anaconda's acquisition of Walworth, even if for no valid business purpose, does not alone constitute a manipulative or deceptive device, as is necessary to state a claim under Section 14(e) of the Act.")

Negotiations developed between Marathon and several companies.
* * * United States Steel Corporation ("U.S. Steel") indicated its
interest, and on November 18, 1981, offered what it termed a "final
proposal" to be acted upon that day. By that proposal U.S. Steel
offered $125 per share for 30 million shares of Marathon stock, with a
plan for a follow-up merger with its subsidiary, U.S.S. Corporation
("USS").

The Marathon directors voted to recommend the U.S. Steel offer to
the shareholders on November 18, 1981. Marathon, U.S. Steel and
USS executed a formal merger agreement on that day. USS made its
tender offer on November 19, 1981. Both USS and Marathon filed the
appropriate documents with the Securities Exchange Commission.

The USS offer, and subsequently the merger agreement, had two
significant conditions. First, they required a present, irrevocable option to purchase ten million authorized but unissued shares of Marathon common stock for $90 per share ("stock option"). These shares
equalled approximately 17% of Marathon's outstanding shares. Next,
they required an option to purchase Marathon's 48% interest in oil and
mineral rights in the Yates Field for $2.8 billion. ("Yates Field
option"). The latter option could be exercised only if USS's offer did
not succeed and if a third party gained control of Marathon. Thus, in
effect, a potential competing tender offeror could not acquire Yates
Field upon a merger with Marathon.

The value of Yates Field to Marathon and to potential buyers is
significant; Marathon has referred to the field as its "crown jewel."

> One of the world's most remarkable oil fields is the Yates Field in
> Pecos County (of the Permian basin province of West Texas).
> Producing from an unusually prolific and highly permeable reser-
> voir rock, under natural hydraulic pressure, the potential produc-
> tion of 313 wells distributed over 17,000 acres in this field was in
> 1929 estimated to be in excess of 5 million bbl. per day. This was
> more than the total daily production of all United States fields;
> however, production has been drastically curtailed. (Footnote
> omitted.)

L.C. Uren, *Petroleum Production Engineering* (1950) quoted at p. 5
of the first Boston Corporation, *Yates Field: Another Look* (August 14,
1980). Judge Kinneary observed the unique characteristics of the
Yates Field:

> [E]ven though the Yates Field has been producing oil for more than
> fifty years, petroleum engineers consider the field to be in the
> intermediate state of depletion, that is, they expect the field to
> continue producing oil for ninety years; in that there are between
> 3 and 3.5 billion barrels of oil still in place, the Yates Field holds
> the promise of providing additional reserves of oil that could be
> recovered; and cumulative production, as of the date of the report,
> accounted for only 39 percent of the conservatively estimated
> recoverable reserves of 2.0 billion barrels.

* * *

Mobil Corp. v. Marathon Co., C–2–81–1402 at 27–28.

The importance of Yates to a potential tender offeror is illustrated by the fact that both Gulf Oil and Allied indicated that they would propose a tender offer only upon assurances that they would have an option to buy Marathon's interest in the Yates Field. Such requests are a recent but recurring phenomenon in connection with tender offers.

Following this agreement, Mobil filed suit in the United States District Court for the Southern District of Ohio, seeking to enjoin the exercise of the options and any purchase of shares in accordance with the tender offer. Named as defendants were Marathon, its directors, and USS. Mobil alleged that the options granted to USS served as a "lock-up" arrangement to defeat any competitive offers of Mobil or third parties, thereby constituting a "manipulative" practice "in connection with a tender offer," in violation of section 14(e) of the Williams Act. It claimed further that Marathon failed to disclose material information regarding the purpose of the options to its shareholders, also in violation of section 14(e). It also complained of various violations of state law. * * *

On November 24, 1981, Judge Kinneary granted in part Mobil's motion for a temporary restraining order, prohibiting Marathon and USS from taking any action in connection with the tender offer or the Yates Field option agreement. Mobil announced a new tender offer on November 25, 1981, offering to purchase at least 30 million common shares of Marathon at $126 per share in cash. This offer was conditioned on a finding that the USS stock option and the Yates Field option were invalid. * * * Mobil again indicated its intention to merge with Marathon if the tender offer were successful, proposing to purchase remaining shares with Mobil debentures having a value of $90 in cash.

Following that offer, Judge Kinneary considered Mobil's application for a preliminary injunction. In an opinion dated December 7, 1981, he denied a preliminary injunction. * * *

This appeal followed. Because there appears to be a substantial likelihood that Mobil will succeed on its claim that execution of the Yates Field and stock options are "manipulative acts or practices, in connection with [a] tender offer" in violation of section 14(e), § 78n(e) [3], * * * and accordingly, we reverse.

* * *

III.

Having determined that Mobil has an implied cause of action under the Williams Act, we now consider Mobil's claim that the Yates Field and stock options granted by Marathon to USS, the wholly owned subsidiary of U.S. Steel, constitute a "manipulative act or practice" in connection with the USS tender offer of November 19, 1981, in violation of section 14(e). * * * The district court found no substantial

---

[3] Our holding makes unnecessary for purposes of this appeal any consideration of whether Marathon acted in violation of state law or violated disclosure requirements of section 14 of the Williams Act, 15 U.S.C. § 78n(e).

likelihood of success by Mobil on the merits of this claim, holding that it "amounts to no more than a claim that the Marathon directors acted unfairly and breached their fiduciary [duty] to Marathon and its shareholders," and as such fails to state a cause of action under section 14(e). The district court relied on Santa Fe Industries, Inc. v. Green, 430 U.S. 462, 97 S.Ct. 1292, 51 L.Ed.2d 480 (1977), in which the Supreme Court held that a mere breach of corporate fiduciary duty does not violate section 10(b) of the Securities Exchange Act of 1934. We believe the district court's interpretation of the *Santa Fe* case and its characterization of Mobil's claim as nothing more than a breach of fiduciary duty were erroneous.

Santa Fe involved a claim under section 10(b) of the Securities Exchange Act of 1934 and S.E.C. Rule 10b–5. Section 10(b) concerns the sale and purchase of securities rather than tender offers, but its anti-manipulation language is similar to that of section 14(e), and provides:

> It shall be unlawful for any person * * *
>
> > To use or employ, in connection with the purchase or sale of any security, any manipulative or deceptive device or contrivance in contravention of such rules and regulations as the Commission may prescribe as necessary or appropriate in the public interest or for the protection of investors.

Santa Fe held that a mere allegation of unfair treatment of minority shareholders, corporate mismanagement, or breach of corporate fiduciary duty by majority shareholders or corporate directors does not state a cause of action under section 10(b), and particularly that such conduct, standing alone, does not constitute a "manipulative device or contrivance" under the statute. 430 U.S. at 474–77, 97 S.Ct. at 1301.

Although Mobil alleges a breach of fiduciary duty by the Marathon directors as one of its pendent state law claims, this claim is not the only basis upon which it complains. We offer no opinion regarding the merits of the fiduciary duty claim, but we conclude that the Yates Field option and the stock option individually and together are "manipulative" as that term is used in section 14(e).

The term "manipulative" is not defined in either the Securities Exchange Act or the Williams Act. "Manipulation" in securities markets can take many forms, see, e.g., 15 U.S.C. §§ 78i, 78j (proscribing certain forms of manipulation), but the Supreme Court has recently indicated that manipulation is an affecting of the market for, or price of, securities by *artificial* means, i.e., means unrelated to the natural forces of supply and demand.

> Use of the word "manipulative" is especially significant. It is and was virtually a term of art when used in connection with securities markets. It connotes intentional or willful conduct designed to deceive or defraud investors by controlling or artificially affecting the price of securities.

Ernst & Ernst v. Hochfelder, 425 U.S. 185, 199, 96 S.Ct. 1375, 1383, 47 L.Ed.2d 668 (1976) (footnote omitted).

"Manipulation" is "virtually a term of art when used in connection with securities markets." *Ernst & Ernst,* 425 U.S., at 199. The term refers generally to practices, such as wash sales, matched orders, or rigged prices, that are intended to mislead investors by artificially affecting market activity.

Santa Fe Industries, Inc. v. Green, 430 U.S. 462, 476, 97 S.Ct. 1292, 1302, 51 L.Ed.2d 480 (1977). In our view, it is difficult to conceive of a more effective and manipulative device than the "lock-up" options employed here, options which not only artificially affect, but for all practical purposes completely block, normal healthy market activity and, in fact, could be construed as expressly designed solely for that purpose.

The types of options demanded and received by USS in this case are relatively new to the world of tender offer takeover contests, and we are unaware of any Supreme Court or Court of Appeals case confronting the question of whether these particular techniques are "manipulative" within the meaning of section 14(e) of the Williams Act. However, courts have recognized that the term "manipulative" must remain flexible in the face of new techniques which artificially affect securities markets. "No doubt Congress meant to prohibit the full range of ingenious devices that might be used to manipulate securities prices." Santa Fe Industries, Inc. v. Green, supra, 430 U.S. at 477, 97 S.Ct. at 1302 (Section 10(b)). * * *

We are of the opinion that under the circumstances of this particular case, Mobil has shown a sufficient likelihood of ultimately establishing that the Yates Field option and the stock option had the effect of creating an artificial price ceiling in the tender offer market for Marathon common shares, and that the options therefore are "manipulative acts or practices" in connection with a tender offer in violation of section 14(e) of the Williams Act.

There is ample evidence in the record to support Judge Kinneary's finding that Marathon's Yates Field interest is a unique and significant asset. We believe there is also sufficient evidence in the record to indicate that this asset is a very important attraction to Mobil and other potential bidders for control of Marathon. The Yates Field option which USS demanded and received in connection with its tender offer of $125 per share greatly dampens the demand by Mobil and other potential bidders in the tender offer market, because a successful takeover by any bidder other than USS will give USS the right to exercise its option and purchase the Yates Field interest for $2.8 billion. This presents a significant threat to other bidders that even if they gain control of Marathon they will lose the Yates Field oil reserves.

The district court found that the $2.8 billion which Marathon would receive from USS in exchange for the Yates Field oil reserves is a fair price, but there was evidence that the field might be worth as much as $3.639 billion. We point this out not to disturb the district court's finding, but to illustrate that potential tender offerors may value the Yates Field reserves at a higher figure than $2.8 billion, especially in today's world of ever-depleting oil supplies and the volatile, unpredictable nature of oil prices over the long term. Oil companies and other companies like USS seeking to invest in the oil industry may believe that long-term oil reserves, not cash or other assets, will best ensure long-term profits. As a result, we cannot say that Mobil and other potential bidders for control of Marathon would not be willing to make tender offers reflecting a Yates Field valuation far greater than $2.8 billion, were it not for the Yates Field option which USS possesses. Only the open market contemplated by the Act provides a means to measure its value.

The Yates Field option is exercisable if, and only if, control of Marathon is obtained by a third party. The only effect of this option can be to deter Mobil and any other potential tender offerors from competing with USS in an auction for control of Marathon. Others cannot compete on a par with USS; its bid of $125 per share thus amounts to an artificial ceiling on the value Marathon shareholders can receive for their shares. Therefore, there is a substantial likelihood that the option is manipulative under section 14(e) of the Williams Act.

The particular facts before us also indicate that the stock option that USS demanded and received in connection with its tender offer prevents all others from competing on a par with USS for control of Marathon. In our opinion, the stock option was large enough in this takeover contest to serve as an artificial and significant deterrent to competitive bidding for a controlling block of Marathon shares.

The stock option gave USS the right to purchase 10 million authorized but unissued shares of Marathon for $90 per share. USS could exercise its option at any time during the takeover contest and acquire 10 million newly issued shares; presently there are 58,685,906 Marathon common shares outstanding. The original Mobil tender offer was for 40 million shares at a price of $85 per share. The USS tender offer was for 30 million shares at $125 per share. An estimate prepared by the First Boston Corporation, Marathon's investment banker, calculated that because of the stock option, it would cost Mobil (or any other outside bidder seeking 40 million shares of Marathon) 1.1 to 1.2 billion additional dollars to match the USS tender offer. A chart contained in page six of the First Boston report discloses that every dollar raise in the bid by USS would cost USS $30 million, while each such dollar raise would cost Mobil $47 million. * * *

The size and price of the stock option, together with the fact that it was granted to USS, a tender offeror, prevented all others from competing on a par with USS for a controlling block of Marathon shares, and tipped the scales decidedly in favor of USS. In our opinion, the stock option artificially and significantly discouraged competitive bidding for the Marathon stock.

The Yates Field option and the stock option, both individually and in combination, have the effect of circumventing the natural forces of market demand in this tender offer contest. Were this contest a straight price-per-share auction, tender offers well in excess of the USS offer of $125 per share may have been forthcoming. Of course, Mobil itself has offered $126 per share, conditional on the judicial removal of the options. Our task under the Williams Act is not to speculate about what price the Marathon shareholders might have been offered if the natural market forces existed in this tender offer contest, but rather to enforce the mandate of section 14(e) against manipulation of the market. The purpose of the Williams Act, protection of the target shareholders, requires that Mobil and any other interested bidder be permitted an equal opportunity to compete in the marketplace and persuade the Marathon shareholders to sell their shares to them.

The defendants argue that section 14(e) requires full disclosure and nothing more. They point to the following language in the Supreme Court's opinion in *Santa Fe,* concerning section 10(b):

> [T]he Court repeatedly has described the "fundamental purpose" of the [Securities Exchange] Act as implementing a "philosophy of full disclosure"; once full and fair disclosure has occurred, the fairness of the terms of the transaction is at most a tangential concern of the statute.

430 U.S. at 477–78, 97 S.Ct. at 1302–03. The defendants read too much into this language. *Santa Fe* held that mere allegations of unfairness and breach of fiduciary duty by majority shareholders to the minority did not violate section 10(b). It did not find that nondisclosure was the only ground upon which to base a 10(b) claim. Instead, the Court expressly made a factual determination that "the conduct * * * alleged in the complaint was not 'manipulative' * * *" 430 U.S. at 476, 97 S.Ct. at 1302. *Santa Fe* thus cannot be taken to mean that conduct that falls within the special meaning of the term "manipulation" is legal so long as it is fully disclosed. "[N]ondisclosure is usually essential to the success of a manipulative scheme," id. at 477, 97 S.Ct. at 1302, but this case illustrates that disclosure alone does not always mean that there is no manipulation. It may be that the Marathon shareholders in this case have now been fully informed that their management granted USS the Yates Field option and the stock option. They may now understand fully how these options deter any tender offers higher than $125 per share. Yet, they have had no real alternative to accepting the USS offer, because Mobil's offer of $126 is conditional upon the invalidity of the options, and there is and could be no other comparable tender offer as long as the "lock-up" options remain in effect. The artificial ceiling on the price of their shares at $125 is manipulation to which they must submit whether it is disclosed to them or not, since in not tendering their shares to USS they risk being relegated to the "back end" of USS's takeover proposal and receiving only $90 per share.

In short, to find compliance with section 14(e) solely by the full disclosure of a manipulative device as a *fait accompli* would be to read the "manipulative acts and practices" language completely out of the Williams Act.

The district court found that the Marathon directors' decision on November 18, 1981 to accept USS's proposed merger agreement, including the Yates Field and stock options, was not a breach of fiduciary duty. The district court's holding was based in part on its finding that the Marathon directors were faced with a non-negotiable package proposal from USS which had to be accepted or rejected in less than a day, and which they accepted because they felt it was the only way they could get the USS $125 bid for their shareholders. (Mobil's bid at that time was $85.) In holding today that the option agreements were manipulative under section 14(e) of the Williams Act, we need not disturb the district court's finding of good faith and loyalty by the Marathon directors. Section 14(e) prohibits manipulation by "*any* person," and thereby covers the conduct of USS in demanding and obtaining the options, as well as any manipulative conduct by the Marathon directors. The Williams Act protects the target shareholders regardless of who did the manipulating.

In conclusion, it is apparent to us that the particular options granted to USS by Marathon under the circumstances of this tender offer contest constitute "manipulative acts" in connection with the tender offer, violative of section 14(e) of the Williams Act. In so ruling, we do not purport to define a rule of decision for all claims of manipulation under the Williams Act, or indeed for all forms of options which might be claimed to "lock up" takeover battles or otherwise discourage competing tender offers. We leave these issues to developing law in this new and difficult area of securities regulation.*

The holding in *Mobil* attracted no following in other circuits.[92] Yet, its underlying premise—that, whatever the result reached, determination of the breadth of misconduct covered by Section 14(e) could not be resolved by simple reference to Rule 10b–5 precedent—had an inviting logic. Indeed, although the cases remained almost unanimously opposed to the proposition that Section 14(e) extended to substantive conduct, the first round of academic comment largely favored the *Mobil* result, if not its rationale.[93] The resulting uncertainty meant that the scope of Section 14(e) would be litigated in every contested tender offer until the issue was definitively resolved. The Supreme Court undertook this effort in the following case.

* Judge Merritt dissented on the grounds that the Sixth Circuit's separate decision against Mobil on an antitrust issue made the case moot. [Ed.]

[92] See, e.g., Feldbaum v. Avon Products, Inc., 741 F.2d 234 (8th Cir.1984); Data Probe Acquisition Corp. v. Datatab, Inc., 722 F.2d 1 (2d Cir.1983), cert. denied 465 U.S. 1052 (1984); Buffalo Forge Co. v. Ogden Corp., 717 F.2d 757 (2d Cir.1983), cert. denied, 464 U.S. 1018 (1983); Schreiber v. Burlington Northern Inc., 731 F.2d 163 (3d Cir.1984), rev'd, ___ U.S. ___ (1985).

[93] See Junewicz, *The Appropriate Limits of Section 14(e) of the Securities Exchange Act of 1934,* 62 Texas L.Rev. 1171 (1984); Note, *Target Defensive Tactics as Manipulative under Section 14(e),* 84 Col.L.Rev. 228 (1984); Loewenstein, *Section 14(e) of the Williams Act and the Rule 10b–5 Comparisons,* 71 Georgetown L.Rev. 1311 (1983); Weiss, *Defensive Responses to Tender Offers and the Williams Act's Prohibition Against Manipulation,* 35 Vand.L.Rev. 1087 (1982).

SCHREIBER v. BURLINGTON NORTHERN, INC.

Supreme Court of the United States, 1985.
— U.S. —, 105 S.Ct. 2458.

Chief Justice BURGER delivered the opinion of the Court.

We granted certiorari to resolve a conflict in the Circuits over whether misrepresentation or nondisclosure is a necessary element of a violation of § 14(e) of the Securities Exchange Act of 1934, 15 U.S.C. § 78n(e).

I

On December 21, 1982, Burlington Northern, Inc., made a hostile tender offer for El Paso Gas Co. Through a wholly owned subsidiary, Burlington proposed to purchase 25.1 million El Paso shares at $24 per share. Burlington reserved the right to terminate the offer if any of several specified events occurred. El Paso management initially opposed the takeover, but its shareholders responded favorably, fully subscribing the offer by the December 30, 1982 deadline.

Burlington did not accept those tendered shares; instead, after negotiations with El Paso management, Burlington announced on January 10, 1983, the terms of a new and friendly takeover agreement. Pursuant to the new agreement, Burlington undertook, *inter alia,* to (1) rescind the December tender offer, (2) purchase 4,166,667 shares from El Paso at $24 per share, (3) substitute a new tender offer for only 21 million shares at $24 per share, (4) provide procedural protections against a squeeze-out merger of the remaining El Paso shareholders, and (5) recognize "golden parachute" contracts between El Paso and four of its senior officers. By February 8, more than 40 million shares were tendered in response to Burlington's January offer, and the takeover was completed.

The rescission of the first tender offer caused a diminished payment to those shareholders who had tendered during the first offer. The January offer was greatly oversubscribed and consequently those shareholders who retendered were subject to substantial proration. Petitioner Barbara Schreiber filed suit on behalf of herself and similarly situated shareholders, alleging that Burlington, El Paso, and members of El Paso's board violated § 14(e)'s prohibition of "fraudulent, deceptive or manipulative acts or practices * * * in connection with any tender offer." She claimed that Burlington's withdrawal of the December tender offer coupled with the substitution of the January tender offer was a "manipulative" distortion of the market for El Paso stock. * * *

The District Court dismissed the suit for failure to state a claim. 568 F.Supp. 197 (Del.1983). The District Court reasoned that the alleged manipulation did not involve a misrepresentation, and so did not violate § 14(e). The District Court relied on the fact that in cases involving alleged violations of § 10(b) of the Securities Exchange Act,

15 U.S.C. § 78j(b), this Court has required misrepresentation for there to be a "manipulative" violation of the section. 568 F.Supp. at 202.

The Court of Appeals for the Third Circuit affirmed. 731 F.2d 163 (1984). The Court of Appeals held that the acts alleged did not violate the Williams Act, because "§ 14(e) was not intended to create a federal cause of action for all harms suffered because of the proffering or the withdrawal of tender offers." Id., at 165. The Court of Appeals reasoned that § 14(e) was "enacted principally as a disclosure statute, designed to insure that fully-informed investors could intelligently decide how to respond to a tender offer." Id., at 165–166. It concluded that the "arguable breach of contract" alleged by petitioner was not a "manipulative act" under § 14(e).

We granted certiorari to resolve the confict,[3] 469 U.S. ___ (1984). We affirm.

II

A

We are asked in this case to interpret § 14(e) of the Securities Exchange Act.

The starting point is the language of the statute. Section 14(e) provides:

"It shall be unlawful for any person to make any untrue statement of a material fact or omit to state any material fact
necessary in order to make the statements made, in the light of
the circumstances under which they are made, not misleading, or
to engage in any fraudulent, deceptive or manipulative acts or
practices, in connection with any tender offer or request or
invitation for tenders, or any solicitation of security holders in
opposition to or in favor of any such offer, request, or invitation.
The Commission shall, for the purposes of this subsection, by
rules and regulations define, and prescribe means reasonably
designed to prevent, such acts and practices as are fraudulent,
deceptive, or manipulative."

Petitioner relies on a construction of the phrase, "fraudulent, deceptive or manipulative acts or practices." Petitioner reads the phrase "fraudulent, deceptive or manipulative acts or practices" to include acts which, although fully disclosed, "artificially" affect the price of the takeover target's stock. Petitioner's interpretation relies on the belief that § 14(e) is directed at purposes broader than providing full and true information to investors.

---

[3] The Court of Appeals for the Sixth Circuit has held that manipulation does not always require an element of misrepresentation or nondisclosure. Mobil Corp. v. Marathon Oil Co., 669 F.2d 366 (1981), cert. denied, 455 U.S. 982 (1982). The Court of Appeals for the Second and Eighth Circuits have applied an analysis consistent with the one we apply today. Feldbaum v. Avon Products, Inc., 741 F.2d 234 (CA8 1984); Buffalo Forge Co. v. Ogden Corp., 717 F.2d 757 (CA2), cert. denied, 464 U.S. 1018 (1983); Data Probe Acquisition Corp. v. Datalab, Inc., 722 F.2d 1 (CA2 1983), cert. denied 465 U.S. 1052 (1984).

Petitioner's reading of the term "manipulative" conflicts with the normal meaning of the term. We have held in the context of an alleged violation of § 10(b) of the Securities Exchange Act:

"Use of the word 'manipulative' is especially significant. It is and was virtually a term of art when used in connection with the securities markets. It connotes intentional or willful conduct *designed to deceive or defraud* investors by controlling or artificially affecting the price of securities." Ernst & Ernst v. Hochfelder, 425 U.S. 185, 199 (1976) (emphasis added).

Other cases interpreting the term reflect its use as a general term comprising a range of misleading practices:

"The term refers generally to practices, such as wash sales, matched orders, or rigged prices, that are intended to mislead investors by artificially affecting market activity. * * * Section 10(b)'s general prohibition of practices deemed by the SEC to be 'manipulative'—in this technical sense of artificially affecting market activity in order to mislead investors—is fully consistent with the fundamental purpose of the 1934 Act ' "to substitute a philosophy of full disclosure for the philosophy of *caveat emptor* * * *." ' * * * Indeed, nondisclosure is usually essential to the success of a manipulative scheme. * * * No doubt Congress meant to prohibit the full range of ingenious devices that might be used to manipulate securities prices. But we do not think it would have chosen this 'term of art' if it had meant to bring within the scope of § 10(b) instances of corporate mismanagement such as this, in which the essence of the complaint is that shareholders were treated unfairly by a fiduciary." Santa Fe Industries, Inc. v. Green, 430 U.S. 462, 476–477 (1977).

The meaning the Court has given the term "manipulative" is consistent with the use of the term at common law,[4] and with its traditional dictionary definition.[5]

She argues, however, that the term manipulative takes on a meaning in § 14(e) that is different from the meaning it has in § 10(b). Petitioner claims that the use of the disjunctive "or" in § 14(e) implied that acts need not be deceptive or fraudulent to be manipulative. But Congress used the phrase "manipulative or deceptive" in § 10(b) as well, and we have interpreted "manipulative" in that context to require misrepresentation.[6] Moreover, it is a " 'familiar principle of statutory

---

[4] See generally, L. Loss, Securities Regulation 984–989 (3d ed.1983). For example, the seminal English case of Scott v. Brown, Doering, McNab & Co., [1892] 2 Q.B. 724, 724 (C.A.), which broke new ground in recognizing that manipulation could occur without the dissemination of false statements, nonetheless placed emphasis on the presence of deception. As Lord Lopes stated in that case, "I can see no substantial distinction between false rumours and false and fictitious acts." Id., at 730. See also, United States v. Brown, 5 F.Supp. 81, 85 (SDNY 1933) ("[E]ven a speculator is entitled not to have any present fact involving the subject matter of his speculative purchase or the price thereof misrepresented by word or act").

[5] See Webster's Third New International Dictionary 1376 (1971) (Manipulation is "management with use of unfair, scheming, or underhanded methods").

[6] Santa Fe Industries, Inc. v. Green, 430 U.S. 462, 476–477 (1977); Piper v. Chris-Craft Industries, 430 U.S. 1, 43 (1977); Ernst & Ernst v. Hochfelder, 425 U.S. 185, 199 (1976).

construction that words grouped in a list should be given related meaning.'" Securities Indus. Assn. v. Board of Governors, 468 U.S. ___, ___ (1984). All three species of misconduct, i.e., "fraudulent, deceptive or manipulative," listed by Congress are directed at failures to disclose. The use of the term "manipulative" provides emphasis and guidance to those who must determine which types of acts are reached by the statute; it does not suggest a deviation from the section's facial and primary concern with disclosure or Congressional concern with disclosure which is the core of the Act.

B

Our conclusion that "manipulative" acts under § 14(e) require misrepresentation or nondisclosure is buttressed by the purpose and legislative history of the provision. Section 14(e) was originally added to the Securities Exchange Act as part of the Williams Act. "The purpose of the Williams Act is to insure that public shareholders who are confronted by a cash tender offer for their stock will not be required to respond without adequate information." Rondeau v. Mosinee Paper Corp., 422 U.S. 49, 58 (1975).

It is clear that Congress relied primarily on disclosure to implement the purpose of the Williams Act. Senator Williams, the Bill's Senate sponsor, stated in the debate:

> "Today, the public shareholder in deciding whether to accept or reject a tender offer possesses limited information. No matter what he does, he acts without adequate knowledge to enable him to decide rationally what is the best course of action. This is precisely the dilemma which our securities laws are designed to prevent." 113 Cong.Rec. 24664 (1967) (Remarks of Sen. Williams).

The expressed legislative intent was to preserve a neutral setting in which the contenders could fully present their arguments.[8] The Senate sponsor went on to say:

> "We have taken extreme care to avoid tipping the scales either in favor of management or in favor of the person making the takeover bids. S. 510 is designed solely to require full and fair disclosure for the benefit of investors. The bill will at the same time provide the offeror and management equal opportunity to present their case." Ibid.

[8] The process through which Congress developed the Williams Act also suggests a calculated reliance on disclosure, rather than court-imposed principles of "fairness" or "artificiality," as the preferred method of market regulation. For example, as the bill progressed through hearings, both Houses of Congress became concerned that corporate stock repurchases could be used to distort the market for corporate control. Congress addressed this problem with § 13(e), which imposes specific disclosure duties on corporations purchasing stock and grants broad regulatory power to the Securities Exchange Commission to regulate such repurchases. Congress stopped short, however, of imposing specific substantive requirements forbidding corporations to trade in their own stock for the purpose of maintaining its price. The specific regulatory scheme set forth in § 13(e) would be unnecessary if Congress at the same time had endowed the term "manipulative" in § 14(e) with broad substantive significance.

To implement this objective, the Williams Act added §§ 13(d), 13(e), 14(d), 14(e), and 14(f) to the Securities Exchange Act. Some relate to disclosure; §§ 13(d), 14(d) and 14(f) all add specific registration and disclosure provisions. Others—§§ 13(e) and 14(d)—require or prohibit certain acts so that investors will possess additional time within which to take advantage of the disclosed information.[9]

Section 14(e) adds a "broad antifraud prohibition," Piper v. Chris Craft Industries, 430 U.S. 1, 24 (1977), modeled on the antifraud provisions of § 10(b) of the Act and Rule 10b–5.[10] It supplements the more precise disclosure provisions found elsewhere in the Williams Act, while requiring disclosure more explicitly addressed to the tender offer context than that required by § 10(b).

While legislative history specifically concerning § 14(e) is sparse, the House and Senate Reports discuss the role of § 14(e). Describing § 14(e) as regulating "fraudulent transactions," and stating the thrust of the section:

"This provision would affirm the fact that persons engaged in making or opposing tender offers or otherwise seeking to influence the decision of investors or the outcome of the tender offer are under an obligation to make *full disclosure* of material information to those with whom they deal." H.R.Rep. No. 1711, 90th Cong., 2d Sess., 11 (1968) (emphasis added); S.R.Rep. No. 550, 90th Cong., 1st Sess., 11 (1967) (emphasis added).

Nowhere in the legislative history is there the slightest suggestion that § 14(e) serves any purpose other than disclosure,[11] or that the term

[9] Section 13(d) requires those acquiring a certain threshold percentage of a company's stock to file reports disclosing such information as the purchaser's background and identity, the source of the funds to be used in making the purchase, the purpose of the purchase, and the extent of the purchaser's holdings in the target company. Section 13(e) imposes restrictions on certain repurchases of stock by corporate issuers. Section 14(d) imposes specific disclosure requirements on those making a tender offer. Section 14(d) also imposes specific substantive requirements on those making a tender offer. These requirements include allowing shareholders to withdraw tendered shares at certain times during the bidding process, 15 U.S.C. § 78n(d)(5), the proration of share purchases when the number of shares tendered exceeds the number of shares sought, and the payment of the same price to all those whose shares are purchased. Section 14(f) imposes disclosure requirements when new corporate directors are chosen as the result of a tender offer.

[10] * * * Because of the textual similarities, it is often assumed that § 14(e) was modeled on § 10(b) and Rule 10b–5. See, e.g., Panter v. Marshall Field & Co., 646 F.2d 271, 283 (CA7), cert. denied 454 U.S.

1092 (1981). For the purpose of interpreting the term "manipulative," the most significant changes from the language of § 10(b) were the addition of the term "fraudulent," and the reference to "acts" rather than "devices." Neither change bears in any obvious way on the meaning to be given to "manipulative."

Similar terminology is also found in § 15(c) of the Securities Exchange Act, 15 U.S.C. § 780(c), § 17(a) of the Securities Act of 1933, 15 U.S.C. § 77q, and § 206 of the Investment Advisers Act of 1940, 15 U.S.C. § 80b–6.

[11] The Act was amended in 1970, and Congress added to § 14(e) the sentence, "The Commission shall, for the purposes of this subsection, by rules and regulations define, and prescribe means reasonably designed to prevent, such acts and practices as are fraudulent, deceptive, or manipulative." Petitioner argues that this phrase would be pointless if § 14(e) was concerned with disclosure only.

We disagree. In adding the 1970 amendment, Congress simply provided a mechanism for defining and guarding against those acts and practices which involve material misrepresentation or nondisclosure. The amendment gives the Securities and

"manipulative" should be read as an invitation to the courts to oversee the substantive fairness of tender offers; the quality of any offer is a matter for the marketplace.

To adopt the reading of the term "manipulative" urged by petitioner would not only be unwarranted in light of the legislative purpose but would be at odds with it. Inviting judges to read the term "manipulative" with their own sense of what constitutes "unfair" or "artificial" conduct would inject uncertainty into the tender offer process. An essential piece of information—whether the court would deem the fully disclosed actions of one side or the other to be "manipulative"—would not be available until after the tender offer had closed. This uncertainty would directly contradict the expressed Congressional desire to give investors full information.

Congress' consistent emphasis on disclosure persuades us that it intended takeover contest to be addressed to shareholders. In pursuit of this goal, Congress, consistent with the core mechanism of the Securities Exchange Act, created sweeping disclosure requirements and narrow substantive safeguards. The same Congress that placed such emphasis on shareholder choice would not at the same time have required judges to oversee tender offers for substantive fairness. It is even less likely that a Congress implementing that intention would express it only through the use of a single word placed in the middle of a provision otherwise devoted to disclosure.

C

We hold that the term "manipulative" as used in § 14(e) requires misrepresentation or nondisclosure. It connotes "conduct designed to deceive or defraud investors by controlling or artificially affecting the price of securities." Ernst & Ernst v. Hochfelder, 425 U.S., at 199. Without misrepresentation or nondisclosure, § 14(e) has not been violated.

Applying that definition to this case, we hold that the actions of respondents were not manipulative. The amended complaint fails to allege that the cancellation of the first tender offer was accompanied by any misrepresentation, nondisclosure or deception. The District Court correctly found, "All activity of the defendants that could have conceivably affected the price of El Paso shares was done openly." 568 F.Supp., at 203.

III

The judgment of the Court of Appeals is affirmed.

Justice POWELL took no part in the decision of this case.

Justice O'CONNOR took no part in the consideration or decision of this case.

◆

The Supreme Court's resolution of the breadth of Section 14(e) is clear enough: "We hold that the term 'manipulative' as used in Section 14(e) requires misrepresentation or nondisclosure." What is less clear, however, is why the Court came out the way that it did.

The bulk of the Court's analysis is a parsing of the precise language chosen by Congress for Section 14(e). Yet while the Court's treatment of the statutory language is a possible interpretation, it is hardly the only interpretation or even the most persuasive. For example, the operative part of Section 14(e) breaks down into two components: The first prohibiting untrue statements and material omissions; and the second prohibiting fraudulent, deceptive, or manipulative acts or practices. Does the Supreme Court's holding that manipulative acts require misrepresentation or nondisclosure make Section 14(e)'s second component redundant? Would not any manipulative act that violated the second component because it involved misrepresentation or nondisclosure also violate the first component? [94] Additionally, the phrase "fraudulent, deceptive or manipulative" in Section 14(e)'s second component is in the disjunctive. The implication is that an act need not be deceptive or fraudulent—and therefore need not involve misrepresentation and nondisclosure—to be manipulative.[95] To be sure, there is nothing in the phrase that is inconsistent with the Court's rejection of a disjunctive construction in favor of treating the phrase as simply a legal litany of synonyms whose juxtaposition indicates a similarity rather than a difference in meaning, much as a traditional form of bill of sale would "sell, grant, and devise" some piece of personal property. But there is also nothing in the Court's opinion that explains *why* it chose its interpretation from among the possible alternatives.[96]

Some understanding of what may have motivated the Court's narrow construction of the breadth of Section 14(e) comes from more careful examination of the Court's opinion in *Santa Fe* whose holding— that Rule 10b–5 requires misrepresentation or nondisclosure—*Schreiber* extended to Section 14(e). Justice White's concern that the Second Circuit was creating a federal law of fiduciary duty seems well placed— was not the Second Circuit quite explicitly doing that? For about a fifteen year period from 1960 to 1975, Rule 10b–5 seemed increasingly "like the medieval alchemist's 'universal solvent' which was so potent that it dissolved every container employed to hold it." [97] The Second Circuit decision in *Sante Fe*, quoted in the Supreme Court opinion, seemed a natural extension of prior case law. At that point, however,

---

[94] See Junewicz, supra at 1174–74.

[95] See Weiss, supra at 1096.

[96] The Court does briefly argue that the legislative history of the Williams Act supports its statutory construction. A more detailed review of the legislative history leads to the same conclusion as the linguistic analysis: The Court's interpretation of the statute's legislative history is plausible, but is neither compelled nor even the most convincing of the alternatives. See the sources cited in note 85, supra, for more thorough discussions of the legislative history of the Williams Act. As with its linguistic analysis, the Court offers no explanation for its choice among competing histories.

[97] Kaplan, *Fiduciary Responsibility in the Management of the Corporation*, 31 Bus. Law 883, 885 (1976).

the tide turned. The unifying theme of the Supreme Court's securities law decisions of the mid-1970's was to reverse the trend and more narrowly confine the application of federal securities law.[98] The significance of the Supreme Court's linguistic analysis of Section 10(b) in *Santa Fe* can be understood only in that context.

In Part IV of the *Santa Fe* opinion, Justice White stressed that a broad reading of Rule 10b–5 would "bring within the Rule a wide variety of corporate conduct traditionally left to state regulation. * * * Absent a clear indication of congressional intent, we are reluctant to federalize the substantial portion of the law of corporations that deals with transactions in securities, particularly where established state policies of corporate regulation would be overridden." Does Section 14(e) present the same federalism concerns that seem to have motivated the Court's linguistic analysis in *Santa Fe*? Section 10(b) concerns trading in securities generally; the Court is thus correct that a broad reading of it "could not be easily contained." The range of activities covered by Section 14(e), however, is self-limiting: It concerns only tender offers. Moreover, the imposition on state prerogatives by a broader construction of Section 14(e) is similarly limited; it extends to but a narrow slice of state corporate law, and one which has not been an area of major state law concern. Finally, in this narrow area Congress has explicitly expressed a federal interest.[99]

The upshot of this analysis is that the Court's decision in *Schreiber* seems curiously unexplained; deprived of the support provided by the federalism analysis in *Santa Fe*, the opinion amounts to mere fiat. What, then, was going on?

An explanation for both the *Schreiber* result and the opinion's lack of explicit justification for it may come from recognizing the difficulty of articulating a broader construction of Section 14(e). Among the alternatives suggested by commentators who support a broader reach for the Section are:

> (1) Section 14(e) is violated by "[c]onduct by the target that interferes with the shareholders' right to decide the fate of the offer or with the bidder's opportunity to present its case * * * * " [100]

> (2) Section 14(e) is violated by "any arrangements that artificially impair the tender offer market for a company's shares." [101]

---

[98] See Blue Chip Stamps v. Manor Drug Stores, 421 U.S. 723 (1975) (standing under Rule 10b–5 requires actual purchase or sale of securities); Rondeau v. Mosinee Paper Corp., 422 U.S. 49 (1975) (narrowed availability of injunctive relief under Section 13(d)); Ernst & Ernst v. Hochfelder, 425 U.S. 185 (1976) (proof of scienter required under Rule 10b–5); Piper v. Chris-Craft Industries, 430 U.S. 1 (1977) (tender offerer lacks standing to recover damages under Section 14(e)); Green v. Santa Fe Industries, supra (misrepresentation or nondisclosure required under Rule 10b–5).

[99] Indeed, in Edgar v. MITE Corp., 457 U.S. 624 (1982), the one case where issues of federalism with respect to the overlap of state and federal law covering tender offers was explicitly considered, the federal interest prevailed. This case is discussed in Section B of this Chapter, infra.

[100] Note, *Target Defensive Tactics as Manipulative Under Section 14(e)*, supra at 253.

[101] Weiss, supra at 1100.

(3) Section 14(e) is violated when target "management breaches its fiduciary duty to its shareholders and the effect of that breach is to thwart the offeror's efforts." [102]

Although the application of Section 14(e) to tender offers may be self-limiting, the range of conduct to which any of these definitions apply may not be. The Court could well have been hesitant to impose such open-ended definitions of liability on a type of transaction that was already overly burdened with litigation.[103]

If this analysis explains the Court's holding, does not the opinion go too far? The Court's reading of Section 14(e) may not be of much concern if the Securities and Exchange Commission still can adopt rules defining manipulation pursuant to the last sentence of Section 14(e). Indeed, because of the Commission's expertise, such rules likely would cause less uncertainty than a general court-made rule. In all events, Commission rules could be changed more easily in light of experience and the fast changing transactional world of tender offers than could the Court's construction of the terms of the statute. To change the Court's construction, of course, would require either another Supreme Court decision or Congressional action. The problem, however, is that if the statutory term "manipulation" is as limited as the Court holds, is not the Commission's rulemaking authority similarly limited? [104] Moreover, if the Commission's rulemaking authority is so limited, substantial questions are raised concerning the validity of some of the Rules the Commission has already adopted pursuant to Rule 14(e). What misrepresentation or nondisclosure, for example, justifies the Commission's prohibition in Rule 14e–1(a) of tender offers less than 20 days in length? Similarly, what misrepresentation or nondisclosure justifies the Commission's prohibition in Rule 14d–8, in reliance on Section 14(e), of proration periods shorter than the full length of the offer?

The argument that the Court's holding in *Schreiber* is explained by its desire to defer to the expertise and flexibility of the Commission in the regulation of tender offer conduct finds support in the Court's more generous construction of Section 14(e)'s grant of rulemaking authority to the Commission. In footnote 11 the Court held that the last sentence of Section 14(e) "gives the Securities and Exchange Commission latitude to regulate *nondeceptive* activities as a 'reasonably designed' means of preventing manipulative acts * * *." (emphasis added). To what manipulative acts could you link Rules 14e–1(a) and 14d–8 in order to demonstrate their post-*Schreiber* validity? How broad an invitation to the Commission does footnote 11 convey?

[102] Loewenstein, supra at 1352.

[103] The Court did stress that "[i]nviting judges to read the term 'manipulative' with their own sense of what constitutes 'unfair' or 'artificial' conduct would inject uncertainty into the tender offer process." To say that the Court may have seen these definitions as injecting undesirable uncertainty is not necessarily to agree with it. For a favorable discussion of the uncertain-ty issue with respect to the first definition in the text, see Gilson, *A Structural Approach to Corporations: The Case Against Defensive Tactics in Tender Offers*, 33 Stan. L.Rev. 819, 881–90 (1981).

[104] Recall that in *Santa Fe* the Court stressed that the scope of Rule 10b–5 was limited by the scope of Section 10(b)—the source of the Commission's authority to adopt the Rule.

(2) "In Connection With Any Tender Offer": The Problem of Causation in an Aborted Offer

Sometimes target management successfully defeats a tender offer. Suppose that an offerer carries an offer through to completion, but the offer fails because target management's misrepresentations convince too many of its shareholders not to tender. In this situation it is clear that target management's misrepresentations were "in connection with" a tender offer as required by Section 14(e) and that target shareholders could bring a Section 14(e) action against their management. A more common situation, however, is one in which a bidder announces a tender offer, but target management's defensive activity— again assume it consists of misrepresentations—causes the bidder to withdraw the offer *before* target shareholders are able to tender. In this situation two barriers confront target shareholders who wish to sue their management under Section 14(e) to recover the now lost premium. First, were target management's misrepresentation's "in connection with" a tender offer? Put differently, what is Section 14(e)'s temporal jurisdiction? Second, assuming that the transaction had gone far enough to meet jurisdictional requirements, how can target shareholders prove reliance on the misrepresentations when the tender offer's withdrawal prevented them from acting with respect to them at all?

PANTER v. MARSHALL FIELD & CO.,
United States Court of Appeals, Seventh Circuit, 1981.
646 F.2d 271, cert. denied, 454 U.S. 1092 (1981).

[The facts leading up to the withdrawal of Carter Hawley Hale's (CHH) tender offer for Marshall & Field Co. are set forth in detail in an earlier excerpt from the case in Chapter Fourteen B.3.a. For present purposes, recall that CHH announced its intention to make an exchange offer of $42.00 per share in cash and CHH stock for each share of Field's stock tendered, conditioned on the satisfaction of some twenty conditions. Three weeks later, after Field's had engaged in a variety of defensive maneuvers, CHH withdrew its proposed offer before it became effective. None of the events that conditioned CHH's offer had occurred by the date of the withdrawal. Following the withdrawal, Field stock traded at $19.00 per share. Field shareholders then sued the company and its directors.]

Before PELL and CUDAHY, Circuit Judges, and DUMBAULD, Senior District Judge.

PELL, Circuit Judge.

* * *

III. THE FEDERAL SECURITIES LAW CLAIMS

The plaintiffs * * * claim the defendants violated § 14(e) of the Williams Act, which prohibits deception "in connection with any tender offer." * * * [Section 14(e) and Rule 10b–5] are coextensive in their antifraud prohibitions, and are therefore construed *in pari materia* by courts. Both provisions are manifestations of the "philosophy of full disclosure" embodied in the Securities Exchange Act of 1934. Santa Fe Industries, Inc. v. Green, 430 U.S. 462 (1977). However, * * * the "in connection with any tender offer" language of the Williams Act provision presents special concerns not present in analysis under Rule 10b–5 * * *.

A. *The Williams Act Claims*

Section 14(e) of the Williams Act is a broad antifraud provision modeled after SEC Rule 10b–5, and is designed to insure that shareholders confronted with a tender offer have adequate and accurate information on which to base the decision whether or not to tender their shares. Piper v. Chris-Craft Industries, Inc., 430 U.S. 1, 35 (1977); Rondeau v. Mosinee Paper Corp., 422 U.S. 49, 58 (1975); Lewis v. McGraw, 619 F.2d 192 (2d Cir.), cert. denied, 449 U.S. 941 (1980).

Upon the announcement of a tender offer proposal a target company shareholder is presented with three options: he may retain his shares; he may tender them to the tender offeror if the offer becomes effective; or he may dispose of them in the securities market for his shares, which generally rises on the announcement of a tender offer. The plaintiffs have alleged that the defendants violated § 14(e) both by depriving them of their opportunity to tender their shares to CHH, the tender offeror, and by deceiving them as to the attractiveness of disposing of their shares in the rising market.

1. The Lost Tender Offer Opportunity

By denying the plaintiffs the opportunity to tender their shares to CHH, the plaintiffs claim the defendants deprived them of the difference between $42.00, the amount of the CHH offer, and $19.76, the amount at which Field's shares traded in the market after withdrawal of the CHH proposal. Total damages under this theory would exceed $200,000,000.00.

Because § 14(e) is intended to protect shareholders from making a tender offer decision on inaccurate or inadequate information, among the elements of § 14(e) plaintiff must establish is "that there was a misrepresentation upon which the target corporation shareholders relied. * * * " Chris-Craft Industries, Inc. v. Piper Aircraft Corp., 480 F.2d 341, 373 (2d Cir.), cert. denied, 414 U.S. 910 (1973). Because the CHH tender offer was withdrawn before the plaintiffs had the opportunity to decide whether or not to tender their shares, it was impossible for the plaintiffs to rely on any alleged deception in making the decision to tender or not. Because the plaintiffs were never presented with that critical decision and therefore never relied on the defendants' alleged misrepresentations, they fail to establish a vital element of a § 14(e) claim as regards the CHH $42.00 offer.

In the recent case of Lewis v. McGraw, 619 F.2d 192 (2d Cir.), cert. denied, 449 U.S. 941 (1980), the Second Circuit similarly held that when a proposed tender offer fails to become effective, shareholders of the target company cannot state a cause of action for alleged misstatements under § 14(e) because of the absence of this crucial element of reliance. Id. at 195–96.

It is difficult indeed to imagine a case more directly to the point here than the *Lewis* decision. In that case the American Express Company proposed a "friendly business combination" with McGraw-Hill. McGraw-Hill's directors rejected the offer in a public letter as reckless, illegal, and improper. American Express then filed a proposed tender offer with the SEC, revealing its intention to make a second offer for the McGraw-Hill stock. The offer would not become effective unless McGraw-Hill agreed not to oppose it. McGraw-Hill's directors rejected the second offer, however, which therefore expired before becoming effective. McGraw-Hill shareholders sued for damages under § 14(e) of the Williams Act. In affirming the district court's dismissal for failure to state a cause of action, the court noted that "[i]n the instant case, the target's shareholders simply could not have relied upon McGraw-Hill's statements, whether true or false, since they were never given an opportunity to tender their shares." Id. at 195. The plaintiffs here seek to distinguish *Lewis* on its "unique facts." The two cases, however, are the same in all material aspects: both involve shareholders' allegations that incumbent management and directors prevented the plaintiffs from accepting a tender offer by issuing false and misleading statements or by breaching the fiduciary duties owed to the shareholders. In both cases the requisite element of reliance is absent.

The plaintiffs seek to establish that reliance is presumed from materiality in a case involving primarily a failure to disclose, relying on a line of cases culminating in Affiliated Ute Citizens v. United States, 406 U.S. 128, 153–54 (1972). As the court pointed out, however, in *Lewis,* neither Mills v. Electric Auto-Lite Co., 396 U.S. 375 (1970), nor *Affiliated Ute* abolished the reliance requirement, but "[r]ather * * * held that in cases in which reliance is possible, and even likely, but is unduly burdensome to prove, the resulting doubt would be resolved in favor of the class the statute was designed to protect." *Lewis* at 195.

The *Mills-Ute* presumption is essentially a rule of judicial economy and convenience, designed to avoid the impracticality of requiring that each plaintiff shareholder testify concerning the reliance element. However, when the logical basis on which the presumption rests is absent, it would be highly inappropriate to apply the *Mills-Ute* presumption. "[W]here no reliance [is] possible under any imaginable set of facts, such a presumption would be illogical in the extreme." *Lewis* at 195.

The plaintiffs here pose two additional arguments to application of the *Lewis* holding; first, that it allows a target company management to profit by their own wrong if they are successful in driving off a tender offeror with misrepresentations or omissions otherwise violative of the Act.

Courts seeking to construe the provisions of the Williams Act have also noted that its protections are required by the peculiar nature of a tender offer, which forces a shareholder to decide whether to dispose of his shares at some premium over the market, or retain them with knowledge that the offeror may alter the management of the target company to its detriment. See Piper v. Chris-Craft Industries, Inc., 430 U.S. at 35.

In another context, courts seeking to determine whether unconventional means of acquisition of controlling blocks of shares constitute a "tender offer" within the meaning of the Williams Act (which leaves the term undefined) have determined that the distinguishing characteristic of the activity the Williams Act seeks to regulate is the exertion of pressure on the shareholders to make a hasty, ill-considered decision to sell their shares. See, e.g., Wellman v. Dickinson, 475 F.Supp. 783 (S.D. N.Y.1979) (intensive private solicitation plus premium plus strict time constraints on acceptance created tender offer); S–G Securities, Inc. v. Fuqua Investment Co., 466 F.Supp. 1114 (D.Mass.1978) (widespread publicity campaign plus massive open market purchases created tender offer pressures). Here there was no deadline by which shareholders were forced to tender, and by hypothesis when we are discussing market transactions, no premium over the market. Therefore Field's shareholders were simply not subjected to the proscribed pressures the Williams Act was designed to alleviate. See Kennecott Copper Corp. v. Curtiss-Wright Corp., 584 F.2d 1195, 1207 (2d Cir.1978) (solicitations to sell on national exchange where shareholders were offered no premium over the market and given no deadline by which to make their decision created "no pressure * * * on sellers other than the normal pressure of the marketplace," although the purchaser sought to obtain and exercise control of the company).

* * *

We hold that § 14(e) of the Williams Act does not give a damages remedy for alleged misrepresentations or omissions of material fact when the proposed tender offer never becomes effective. The brief filed by the SEC as *amicus curiae* contends that failure to afford investors a damages remedy under § 14(e) in situations where a tender offer proposal is withdrawn before it becomes effective might lead to abuses. It poses the hypothetical situation "where a person announces a proposed tender offer that he never intends to make in order to dispose of securities of the subject company at artificially inflated prices. * * *" We note that such conduct would fall within the ambit of the prohibitions of Rule 10b–5 * * *

The SEC also suggests that without such a remedy, persons could announce tender offers, again without intending to make them, to put pressure on management to consider merger proposals. Although the present case does not present such a situation, we believe that preliminary injunctive relief would be the appropriate remedy for such conduct. * * * The rule urged by the SEC would only serve to intensify the pressure such spurious offers would exert on incumbent management, by confronting them with the spectre of shareholder damage suits which could result from the withdrawal of even a sham tender offer.

* * *

CUDAHY, Circuit Judge, concurring in part and dissenting in part:

* * *

I disagree with the majority's view that misleading and deceptive representations about an offeror's proposal are immunized from the proscriptions of Section 14(e) if the offer is withdrawn before the shareholders have an opportunity to tender. * * * The type of rule which the majority advocates is simply an invitation to incumbent management to make whatever claims and assertions may be expedient to force withdrawal of an offer. Management could speak without restraint knowing that once withdrawal is forced there is no Securities Act liability for deception practiced before withdrawal took place. Such a rule provides a major loophole for escaping the provisions of Section 14(e) and obviously frustrates the remedial purpose of the Act. * * * The management of a company subject to a tender offer proposal is in a unique position to take steps and make representations that may have a significant impact on the likelihood that the proposal will be frustrated. For example, in the instant case, Field's undertook a hasty acquisition program which may have made Field's significantly less attractive and contributed to the withdrawal of the proposal. Admittedly, this was a course of action rather than primarily a course of representation—but the effect of the latter could be the same.

Compelled by the logic of its position that Section 14(e) provides no protection with respect to offers which are withdrawn before stockholders have an opportunity to tender, the majority also concludes that Section 14(e) does not apply to decisions not to sell into markets which are rising on news of a tender offer announcement. But in [Berman v. Gerber Products Co., 454 F.Supp. 1310 (W.D.Mich.1978)] the court said that claims based on the interim market price of stock were actionable even where a proposed tender offer is withdrawn without becoming effective:

> The requisite causation does exist, however, to the extent that [shareholders] were misled into retaining their holdings when they could have sold them on the market at a higher price. The legislative history of the Williams Act indicates that the legislation was intended to reach such transactions as well as those involving the actual tender of a stockholder's shares. * * * If [the board of directors] misrepresented or omitted material facts in connection with their opposition to the [tender offer] proposal so that [the shareholders] were induced to retain their shares in reliance upon the integrity and good judgment of the board of directors, but had they known the truth they would have sold their stock in the rising market, a direct causative link exists between [the board of directors'] acts and [the shareholders'] investment decision.

Berman, 454 F.Supp. at 1325.

The majority places heavy reliance on Lewis v. McGraw, 619 F.2d 192 (2d Cir.) (per curiam), cert. denied, 449 U.S. 941 (1980) where the Court of Appeals for the Second Circuit dismissed the stockholders' Section 14(e) claim for failure to establish reliance or causation. There a tender offer, conditioned on the approval of target management, never became effective because the board of the target corporation rejected the proposal. The district court in *Lewis* concluded that the complaint sufficiently alleged deception "in connection with the tender offer" because "the prospective offeror [had] made a public announcement of a proposed tender offer and [plaintiff had alleged] a clear and definite intent to make a tender offer." Lewis v. McGraw, [1979–1980 Transfer Binder] Fed.Sec.L.Rep. (CCH) ¶ 97,195, 96,568 (S.D.N.Y.1979). Although the complaint was dismissed for failure to allege causation and reliance, the district court emphasized that "it would be inconsistent with the purpose of Section 14(e) to preclude an action for damages relating to pre-tender offer violations in cases where no tender offer was in fact made. Such [a rule] would have the effect of providing a safe harbor for target companies who were successful in their use of misstatements or deception to discourage the making of tender offers." Id. at 96,568. I find the district court's mode of analysis reflective of the economic realities of the situation and consistent with the thrust of prior case law. See Berman v. Gerber Products Co., supra; Applied Digital Data Systems, Inc. v. Milgo Electronic Corp., 425 F.Supp. 1145 (S.D.N.Y.1977).[34] If, therefore, *Lewis* is to be construed as the majority would have it here, I am quite unpersuaded by what would seem to be the Second Circuit's unexplained and summary departure from a well-established line of analysis.

* * * From the perspective of a public shareholder, once announcement of a tender offer proposal is made, it matters little whether fraud occurs before or after shareholders are given the opportunity to tender to the bidder, or whether they are ever given that opportunity. A shareholder, who, in the face of a proposed tender offer elects not to sell into the market in reliance on management's misleading statements, is in a position similar to that of a shareholder who elects not to tender to the bidder in reliance upon such statements. Congress clearly protected the latter, as well as, I believe, the former.

* * *

⸻♦⸻

As Judge Cudahy's dissent stresses, the majority opinion in *Panter* conflates two quite different issues. First, a tender offer may have been aborted so early that the misconduct complained of was not "in connection with any tender offer." Here the issue is jurisdictional; regardless of what plaintiffs prove about the materiality of any misrepresentation or their reliance upon it, Section 14(e) simply does not apply. Second, even if the temporal jurisdiction requirement of Section 14(e) is met, plaintiffs may not have proven that the misrepresentations by the target company caused their damage. Here the issue is factual; the plaintiffs have the opportunity to offer proof on the issue of causation.

With respect to the jurisdictional issue, the District Court's formulation in Lewis v. McGraw that Judge Cudahy relied upon seems clearly

---

[34] "When * * * a public announcement of a proposed offer has been made, the very dangers that the Act was intended to guard against come into play, and the application of section * * * 14(e) is thus appropriate." *Applied Digital*, 425 F.Supp. at 1155 (footnote omitted).

correct. To exclude from the scope of Section 14(e) misrepresentations made after the announcement, but before the effectiveness, of a tender offer would serve to provide antifraud immunity for misrepresentations that are serious enough—and made early enough—to cause the offer's withdrawal. The *Panter* majority responds to a similar argument by suggesting that an action under Rule 10b–5 might still be available. Would a Rule 10b–5 action be available when the misrepresentation prevented the target shareholders from selling their shares? What transaction could be relied upon to satisfy the *Blue Chip* purchase or sale requirement?

Does the majority opinion really hold that Section 14(e)'s jurisdictional requirement—that the misrepresentation be in connection with a tender offer—was not met? In its *amicus* brief in *Panter* the Securities and Exchange Commission expressed its fear that a narrow construction of Section 14(e)'s temporal jurisdiction would allow acquirers to pressure target companies into friendly transactions by announcing tender offers that they never intended to pursue. The majority responded to this fear by suggesting that preliminary injunctive relief, although not damages, would be available in that situation. But the availability of any relief under Section 14(e) requires that the claim be within the statute's jurisdiction. Perhaps the court did not mean to rest its decision on the jurisdictional ground at all.

In any event, the jurisdictional issue effectively may have been resolved by the Commission's 1979 adoption of the automatic commencement trigger in Rule 14d–2(b). Can misrepresentations made after the offeror publicly announces the identity of the target company, the securities sought and the price to be paid, and thereby triggers the commencement of a tender offer, not be "in connection with" a tender offer?

That leaves the issue of causation. Plaintiffs made two claims: That the withdrawal of the tender offer prevented them from receiving the offered premium; and that Field's misrepresentations deceived plaintiffs into not selling their shares in the market when the market price of Field's stock still reflected the pendency of the CHH offer. The court resolved the first claim against plaintiffs on the absence of a showing of reliance. Plaintiffs could not show that they relied upon Field's misrepresentations because they never had the opportunity to rely on the misrepresentations; the offer was withdrawn before the plaintiffs could act at all. Does not this analysis misunderstand the function of the reliance requirement? The real issue is causation: Did the misrepresentation cause plaintiffs' injury? Where the injury requires that the plaintiffs take some affirmative action, as will always be the case in a Rule 10b–5 action because of the *Blue Chip* purchase or sale requirement, the reliance requirement causally links the defendant's misrepresentations to the plaintiffs' actions—in a Rule 10b–5 case the purchase or sale of the security—that caused the damage. In the case of an aborted tender offer, however, the damage is inflicted by the withdrawal of the offer without any action by plaintiffs. There is simply no causal link that reliance by plaintiffs must provide.[105]

---

[105] See Loewenstein, supra at 1343.

That does not mean that the issue of cause is without difficulty. The critical causal issue is whether defendant's misrepresentations caused the tender offer to be withdrawn: Did the *offeror* rely on the misrepresentations? To be sure, the court notes that it was Field's defensive actions, not its misrepresentations, that caused CCH to withdraw the tender offer, and that this form of misconduct is not covered by Section 14(e). But that just indicates that plaintiffs did not prove their case. Suppose that in Lewis v. McGraw plaintiffs could prove that American Express withdrew its tender offer for McGraw-Hill because McGraw-Hill falsely represented that all of its editorial employees would quit if the offer were successful. Why is plaintiffs' inaction relevant to the issue of causation?

The court's treatment of the reliance issue in connection with plaintiffs' claim that Field's misrepresentations dissuaded them from selling their shares into the market prior to the offer's withdrawal is even more puzzling. Here there is no question that plaintiffs relied on the misrepresentations. At best the court's argument seems to be that such reliance was inadequate as a matter of law because it was not "in connection with any tender offer." Referring to the statutory language, the court states "[t]he language is not unambiguous, but it does seem to contemplate the existence of an offer capable of acceptance by the shareholders." Is this argument plausible after the adoption of Rule 14d–2(b)?

(3) Is Scienter Required Under Section 14(e)?

In Ernst & Ernst v. Hochfelder, 425 U.S. 185 (1976), the Supreme Court held that Rule 10b–5 requires proof of scienter. Consistent with the lower courts' pattern of incorporating Rule 10b–5 concepts directly into the jurisprudence of Section 14(e), scienter quickly was treated as a necessary element of a Section 14(e) cause of action.[106] Rule 10b–5, however, is not the only possible analogy. Rule 14a–9 prohibits proxy statements "which are false or misleading with respect to any material fact, or which omits to state any material fact necessary in order to make the statements therein not false or misleading * * *." In Gerstle v. Gamble-Skogmo, Inc.,[107] Judge Friendly held that scienter was not required under Rule 14a–9. In the following, Professor Loewenstein tracks the three cornered comparison between Rule 10b–5, Rule 14a–9 and Section 14(e) on the issue of scienter.

LOEWENSTEIN, SECTION 14(e) OF THE WILLIAMS ACT AND THE RULE 10b–5 COMPARISONS
71 Georgetown L.Rev. 1311 (1983).

[*Gerstle*] concluded that scienter was not required under rule 14a–9, noting as support several differences between section 14(a), on the one hand, and section 10(b) and rule 10b–5, on the other hand—differences

---

[106] E.g., Bell v. Cameron Land Co., 669 F.2d 1278 (9th Cir.1982); see E. Aranow, H. Einhorn & G. Bernstein, *Developments in* *Tender Offers for Corporate Control* 118–22 (1977).

[107] 478 F.2d 1281 (2d Cir.1973).

that are equally applicable to a comparison of section 14(e) and rule 10b–5. For instance, the *Gerstle* court first concluded that the statutory language of section 14(a), unlike that of section 10(b), does not emphasize the prohibition of fraudulent conduct but rather indicates a congressional concern with "protection of the outsider whose proxy is being solicited." [217] Similarly, at least with respect to material misstatements and omissions, section 14(e) is not concerned with fraudulent conduct, but with protecting shareholders confronted with a tender offer.

* * *

Finally, the court in *Gerstle* assessed the effect of permitting a negligence standard under section 14(a), again comparing it to rule 10b–5. In concluding that negligence was the appropriate standard for actions based on section 14(a), the court said:

> [A] broad standard of culpability here will serve to reinforce the high duty of care owed by a controlling corporation to minority shareholders in the preparation of a proxy statement seeking their acquiescence in this sort of transaction, a consideration which is particularly relevant since liability in this case is limited to the stockholders whose proxies were solicited. While "privity" is not required for most actions under the securities laws, its existence may bear heavily on the appropriate standard of culpability.[226]

The court contrasted this assessment with the effect of allowing a negligence standard under rule 10b–5, which, the court surmised, would deter the laudable corporate policy of publicly disclosing important business and financial developments. Although the court's conjecture regarding rule 10b–5 may be questioned,[227] its conclusion with respect to section 14(a) seems sound and equally applicable to section 14(e).

Providing a negligence standard under the first clause of section 14(e) is particularly appropriate since an obvious use of this provision would be in suits by target stockholders against target management claiming that a tender offer was defeated as a result of management's allegedly false statements. In such a suit, a number of factors justify a strict standard of liability: Requiring a high duty of care is not unreasonable because management owes a fiduciary duty to its stockholders; individuals in management would gain personally if the tender offer is defeated and, therefore, they should proceed cautiously when advising stockholders; and management is under no obligation to

---

[217] 478 F.2d at 1299.

[226] 478 F.2d at 1300 (footnote omitted).

[227] The New York Stock Exchange rules require listed companies to promptly release to the public material information. New York Stock Exchange Company Manual, § A–6. Thus, for listed companies, the incentive to release information is unaffected by the standard of culpability in a subsequent fraud action. See generally Industrial Fund, Inc. v. McDonnell Douglas Corp., 474 F.2d 514, 521–22 (10th Cir.1973) (recognizing corporate duty to disclose, but holding that timing of disclosure is subject to the business judgment rule). [If there is no private cause of action for violating NYSE rules, and if the NYSE does not itself enforce the provision by delisting offending companies, would not exactly the converse be true—that a company's incentive to disclose would be affected *only* by the standard of culpability in a later fraud action. Ed.]

express any opinion with respect to a tender offer, so that when it undertakes to do so it should exercise care.[231]

Damage actions might also be brought by target stockholders against the bidder alleging material misstatements or omissions. These actions may include allegations that the bidder sought to discourage stockholders from tendering to a rival bidder * * * or that the bidder made a misrepresentation in its tender offer materials regarding the value of the deal to the stockholders. In any of these situations, liability should be imposed even if the misstatement or omission was only negligent since a bidder who seeks to discourage tenders to a rival bidder is, in some respects, like target management seeking to discourage its stockholders from tendering to a bidder. Like management, the dissuading bidder stands to gain from successful influence, and, like management, the dissuading bidder is under no obligation to make any statements regarding its rival. Although the bidder may not owe a fiduciary duty to the shareholder-offerees, these other factors suggest that, like management, a tender offeror should be held to a high standard of care in its communications with target stockholders.
* * *

Finally, if the offering materials include a material misrepresentation, a case can be made that liability ought to be imposed without regard to fault, at least with respect to those matters within the knowledge or control of the bidder. If, for instance, the bidder misrepresents the value of securities to be delivered to stockholders in a post-offer merger, the effect of such a misrepresentation is analogous to a misrepresentation by an issuer in a registration statement. In both cases the investor is asked to make an investment decision based on inaccurate or incomplete information furnished by a party who seeks a certain response from the investor. Section 11(a) of the Securities Act imposes virtually absolute liability on the issuer for deficiencies in the registration statement, presumably because some party must be responsible for the contents of a registration statement. This same rationale would apply to tender offer materials prepared by the bidder.

◆

Another way in which Section 14(e) seems more like Rule 14a–9 than Rule 10b–5 is that both Section 14(e) and Rule 14a–9 have a common transactional focus—a contest for control. Indeed, the two forms of transactions—tender offers and proxy fights—are alternative means of achieving the same goal. Should the standard of liability for misstatements depend on the form in which the transaction is cast?

---

[231] Rule 14e–2 [allows target management to take no position on an offer so long as it explains why it is unable to do so.]

2. Federal Securities Regulation of Alternative Transactional Forms: The Securities Act of 1933 and the Use of Non-cash Consideration

The central task in devising a regulatory structure that minimizes a planner's ability to avoid it by manipulation of the formal characteristics of the transaction is to define the object of the regulation so that it encompasses the substantive matters of concern to the planner regardless of the form in which it is cast. We have already seen two regulatory efforts that have encountered difficulty at this level—the courts' problems with the de facto merger doctrine when the legislature defined the regulated transaction in purely formal terms,[108] and the continuing debate over the definition of a tender offer as a result of the absence of any definition at all.[109] Even greater difficulties arise, however, when the regulators lack a coherent idea of the substance of the transaction they seek to control. There are two parallel, and sometimes overlapping, patterns of federal securities regulation generally applicable to corporate acquisitions. The Williams Act, which we have just reviewed, treats the relevant transaction for regulatory purposes as a particular means of effecting an acquisition—a tender offer. The Securities Act of 1933, in contrast, defines the object of its attention more generally: The issuance of securities, whether in a corporate acquisition or otherwise. This difference in the specificity with which the regulatory object is described allows planners to choose which of the two regulatory patterns will govern their transaction. If the consideration used is cash, only the Williams Act applies; if the consideration includes securities to be issued by the acquirer, the Securities Act applies.[110] Because differences in the two regulatory patterns have come to have very important transactional impacts, an acquirer's decision to offer cash or stock as consideration—essentially the choice of how to finance its capital budgeting decision—will be determined in important measure by considerations other than selecting the acquirer's optimal capital structure. In this section we will review how this disparity in regulatory patterns came about, the resulting bias in transactional form it creates, and some recommendations for its elimination.

That the current federal securities regulation of corporate acquisitions lacks coherence is hardly surprising in light of its history. Prior to 1967 there was virtually no federal securities regulation of corporate acquisitions at all. From the outset, the Securities and Exchange Commission took the position that a merger or sale of assets in which the consideration was the acquirer's securities was not an "offer" or "sale" of the securities. Because they were issued as a result of corporate acts authorized by a vote of shareholders, the issuance was believed to lack the individual volition by shareholders thought necessary under Section 2(11) of the Securities Act.[111] As a result of this

---

[108] See Chapter Thirteen E., supra.

[109] See Section A.1.c. of this Chapter.

[110] The Williams Act also applies if the transaction is cast as an exchange offer—a tender offer in which the consideration is the acquirer's securities rather than cash.

[111] The Commission's position was formalized in Rule 133 under the Securities

interpretation, and because the Williams Act had not yet been enacted, the principal way in which a corporate acquisition could be subject to any federal securities regulation at all was for the transaction to be structured as an exchange offer, thereby triggering the registration provisions of the Securities Act. For the planner, the combination of regulatory patterns made the application of any securities regulation to the transaction entirely optional.

By 1972, federal securities regulation had been broadened to cover, with quite different levels of vigor, essentially all forms of acquisitions. The adoption of the Williams Act in 1967 brought cash tender offers under regulatory supervision, and the replacement of Rule 133 with Rule 145 (which specified that a "sale" did occur when securities were issued in an acquisition pursuant to the vote of target shareholders) in 1972, brought mergers and sales of assets in which the consideration was securities within the scope of the Securities Act. This expansion of the reach of federal regulation, however, did not eliminate the differences in the patterns of regulation reflected in the Williams Act and the Securities Act. These differences, made prominent by a change in the substantive character of the market for corporate acquisitions, greatly increased the impact of the planner's strategic choice between the two regulatory patterns on the form in which a transaction was cast and even on the transaction's feasibility.

At this point in the development of federal securities regulation of acquisitions, which regulatory pattern applies to a transaction—the Williams Act or the Securities Act—depends on the form of consideration chosen by the planners. If the consideration chosen is cash, the natural transactional form is a tender offer, regulated by the Williams Act. For this purpose, the Williams Act's most important characteristic is that there is no waiting period. Once the disclosure requirements of the statute and Regulation 14D are met by filing with the Commission and otherwise disseminating the required information, the offer can commence and the bidder can begin purchasing target shares.[112] If, however, the consideration selected is stock, the transaction is subject to the Securities Act, the most important characteristic of which is that no offer can be made until a registration statement is filed with the Commission [113] and no sale can be made—the transaction cannot be closed—until the Commission declares the registration statement effective. If the registration statement is given full review by the Commission staff, the experience in 1969 was that an average of 49 days would pass before the issuer received a letter of comments,[114] and some additional delay would result before the terms of the predictable

Act, adopted in Securities Act Release No. 3846 (Oct. 8, 1957). Solicitation of proxies with respect to the shareholder vote, however, was subject to proxy regulation under Section 14 of the Williams Act.

[112] In anything but an any or all offer, purchasing would have to await the end of the applicable proration period.

[113] Under Rule 145(b), the only information that may be disclosed about the trans-

action before the registration statement is filed is the identity of the parties and their businesses, the date of the shareholders' meeting, and a skeletal description of the transaction.

[114] L. Loss, *Fundamentals of Securities Regulation* 129 (1983).

revisions were negotiated and before the registration statement could be declared effective.[115]

With a change in the market for corporate acquisitions, the timing difference between the Williams Act and the Securities Act of 1933 became critical. By 1979, it was recognized that "we are in the midst of an era of intense competition for desirable acquisition candidates— where auctions and bidding contests are very much the 'in' thing. Just as third parties invade hostile takeover territory—either invited in by the beleaguered target or simply attracted by the noise of the scuffle— uninvited acquirers are likely to barge in on friendly situations." [116] If one contestant can offer cash, while the other must use securities, the timing advantage to the more liquid bidder is substantial: Its entire twenty day cash tender offer can be completed and the contest ended before its opponent is in a position to move forward. Not surprisingly, both contested and friendly acquisitions were increasingly structured so that at least the first step of the transaction involved a cash tender offer.[117]

This regulatory bias in favor of using cash as consideration is difficult to justify and results from a regulatory pattern that does not correspond to the transaction the planners have in mind. From the planners' perspective, what is at issue is an acquisition. If because of the accidents of history the regulatory pattern treats an acquisition differently depending on whether cash or securities are used as the consideration then, subject to non-regulatory constraints, the planners will cast their transactions in the form least burdened by regulation. In this sense, the problem is of the same character as the de facto merger doctrine, only more troubling. In the de facto merger setting, the planners' strategic response involves only changing the form of the transaction; no costs are incurred by the parties or society other than the regulation's failure to achieve its purpose. If regulatory failure were the only cost associated with the strategic use of cash as consideration in order to avoid the delay the Securities Act imposes on the use of securities as consideration, little would be lost because there is little reason to differentiate between cash and securities for this purpose.[118] The problem, however, is that the planners' strategic response imposes another cost: The preference for the use of debt rather than equity financing. Is there any justification for a regulatory pattern that

[115] In 1979, Freund & Easton, *The Three-Piece Suitor: An Alternative Approach to Negotiated Corporate Acquisitions,* 34 Bus. Law. 1679, 1690 (1979), stated that review of a merger proxy statement (under Rule 145 the same as a registration statement) "can easily take a month before final clearance."

[116] Freund & Easton, supra at 1683.

[117] See the portion of the Freund & Easton article reprinted in Chapter Fifteen A. 1.a., supra.

[118] One might argue that shareholders receiving stock in a new corporation need more time to evaluate the transaction than one offered cash. Yet if the shareholder offered cash rejects the offer, he receives, in effect, stock in a new corporation if a sufficient number of other shareholders accept the offer. Moreover, even in a tender offer, target shareholders get twenty days, the minimum offer period under the Williams Act, to evaluate the offer. Finally, in light of the foregoing, is there any reason to believe that Commission staff review is more important when the consideration is stock than when it is cash?

creates an incentive favoring a particular means of financing an acquisition?

One approach to eliminating the disparate treatment of acquisitions depending on the type of consideration used was set forth in Recommendation 12 of the SEC Advisory Committee on Tender Offers. Concluding that "the regulations applicable to exchange offers under the Securities Act are a major disincentive to using securities as consideration in a tender offer" and that "deterrence of exchange offers are not in the best interests of shareholders," [119] the Committee recommended that:

> Bidders should be permitted to commence their bids upon filing of a registration statement and receive tenders prior to the effective date of the registration statement. Prior to effectiveness, all tendered shares would be withdrawable. Effectiveness of the registration statement would be a condition to the exchange offer. If the final prospectus were materially different from the preliminary prospectus, the bidder would be required to maintain, by extension, a 10 day period between mailing of the amended prospectus and expiration, withdrawal and proration dates. This period would assure adequate dissemination of information to shareholders and opportunity to react prior to incurring any irrevocable duties.[120]

The Commission has not acted on this recommendation.[121]

Would adoption of the Advisory Committee's recommendation entirely eliminate the advantage of using cash as consideration? What if the security to be offered was new and had no previous trading market? Would it help if a bidder who desired to use such securities secured the equivalent of a standby commitment with respect to them?

B. State Regulation of Tender Offers

It was not surprising that state legislatures took an interest in the growth of hostile tender offers. Target companies are always "local" in the states in which their headquarters are located or in which they have substantial facilities. A takeover, with the potential for management restructuring, the relocation of executive offices, plant closings,

[119] SEC Advisory Committee on Tender Offers, Report of Recommendations, reprinted in [Special Report No. 1028] Fed. Sec. L. Rep. (CCH) (July 15, 1983) at 20.

[120] Id. at 21.

[121] The historical distinction between the Williams Act and the Securities Act, together with a lack of recognition of the differences between friendly and hostile transactions has led to another anomaly— a substantial difference in the content and timing of disclosure to shareholders and the market depending on the nature of the consideration selected by the planner. See Freund & Greene, *Substance over Form S-14: A Proposal to Reform SEC Regulation of Negotiated Acquisitions,* 36 Bus.Law. 1483 (1981). A part of this anomaly was

the subject of Advisory Committee Recommendation 11 which suggested the extension of the Commission's efforts at integrating disclosure under the Securities and Exchange Act of 1934 and the Securities Act of 1933, see L. Loss, supra at 148–545, to exchange offers. Advisory Committee Report, supra at 21. The Commission has responded to this recommendation by the adoption of a new registration form under the Securities Act of 1933—Form S-4— which allows for substantial incorporation by reference of Exchange Act filings in registration statements filed with respect to securities to be issued in an acquisition. Securities Act Release No. 6578, [Current Volume] Fed.Sec.L.Rep. ¶72,418 (April 23, 1985).

the loss of jobs and the like, pose an obvious threat to local interests. From this perspective, state legislation that strengthens target management's hand in a hostile tender offer makes perfect sense: The interests of target management and the state correspond even if those of target management and target shareholders may not.[122] A state statute that reduces the likelihood of takeovers makes shareholders as a class worse off, and likely also has a negative impact on the national economy by reducing managerial incentives to maximize the efficiency of their enterprises. From the perspective of the state, however, its share of these costs would not outweigh its share of the benefits. The costs—to shareholders and the overall economy—are shared across the nation; the benefits, in contrast, are entirely local.[123]

Consistent with this cost-benefit analysis, state takeover laws spread widely. Virginia acted first in 1968,[124] some four months before the Williams Act was enacted by Congress. By 1979, every state except California that accounted for more than 1 percent of the national total of main offices or incorporation headquarters had adopted takeover legislation; [125] by 1981, the total of states had reached 37.[126] A response to this movement was predictable. Acquiring companies had the incentive and resources to challenge these statutes and the same cost-benefit analysis that explains their adoption suggests one of the legal bases for the challenge. Efforts by one state to benefit its economy at the expense of that of other states or of the nation call to mind the Commerce Clause. The second basis for challenge grew out of the Williams Act: If state takeover legislation could be shown to conflict with Congress' approach to takeover regulation, the Supremacy Clause would invalidate state efforts.

The ensuing litigation resulted in the invalidation cf a large number of state takeover statutes on Commerce Clause and Supremacy Clause grounds.[127] After one abortive effort to resolve the federal-state conflict,[128] the Supreme Court reached, but may not have entirely resolved the merits of the conflict, in the following case.

---

[122] The coincidence is not, however, perfect. A state could control the feared local impact of hostile takeovers directly by plant closing legislation or by contractual restrictions as a condition for local assistance to companies. Moreover, these efforts would protect local interests whether or not control of a company changes. Which approach—indirect and partial protection through antitakeover legislation or direct and complete protection through generally applicable substantive statutes— would be more likely to attract the political support of the local business community?

[123] See Levmore, *Interstate Exploitation and Judicial Intervention,* 69 Va.L.Rev. 563, 622–24 (1983); cf. Rose-Ackerman, *Does Federalism Matter? Political Choice in Federal Republic,* 89 J.Pol.Econ. 152 (1981) (social choice approach to state-federal conflict).

[124] Va. Code Sec. 13.1–528 to –541 (1978).

[125] Smiley, *The Effect of State Securities Statutes on Tender Offer Activity,* 19 Econ. Inquiry 426, 432 (1981).

[126] These states are listed in Sargent, *On the Validity of State Takeover Regulation: Responses to MITE and Kidwell,* 42 Ohio State L.J. 689, 690 n. 7 (1981).

[127] A sampling of these cases is set out in Warren, *Developments in State Takeover Regulation: MITE and its Aftermath,* 40 Bus.Law. 671, 678 n. 52 (1985).

[128] Great Western United Corp. v. Kidwell, 577 F.2d 1256 (5th Cir.1978) (Idaho takeover statute invalidated on Commerce Clause and Supremacy Clause grounds), reversed on other grounds sub. nom. Leroy v. Great Western United Corp., 443 U.S. 173 (1979).

EDGAR v. MITE CORP.
Supreme Court of the United States, 1982.
457 U.S. 624.

Justice WHITE delivered an opinion, Parts I, II, and V–B of which are the opinion of the Court.[†]

The issue in this case is whether the Illinois Business Take-Over Act, Ill.Rev.Stat., ch. 121½, ¶ 137.51 et seq. (1979), is unconstitutional under the Supremacy and Commerce Clauses of the Federal Constitution.

I

Appellee MITE Corp. and its wholly owned subsidiary, MITE Holdings, Inc., are corporations organized under the laws of Delaware with their principal executive offices in Connecticut. Appellant James Edgar is the Secretary of State of Illinois and is charged with the administration and enforcement of the Illinois Act. Under the Illinois Act any takeover offer[1] for the shares of a target company must be registered with the Secretary of State. Ill.Rev.Stat., ch. 121½, ¶ 137.54.A (1979). A target company is defined as a corporation or other issuer of securities of which shareholders located in Illinois own 10% of the class of equity securities subject to the offer, or for which any two of the following three conditions are met: the corporation has its principal executive office in Illinois, is organized under the laws of Illinois, or has at least 10% of its stated capital and paid-in surplus represented within the State. ¶ 137.52–10. An offer becomes registered 20 days after a registration statement is filed with the Secretary unless the Secretary calls a hearing. ¶ 137.54.E. The Secretary may call a hearing at any time during the 20-day waiting period to adjudicate the substantive fairness of the offer if he believes it is necessary to protect the shareholders of the target company, and a hearing must be held if requested by a majority of a target company's outside directors or by Illinois shareholders who own 10% of the class of securities subject to the offer. ¶ 137.57.A. If the Secretary does hold a hearing, he is directed by the statute to deny registration to a tender offer if he finds that it "fails to provide full and fair disclosure to the offerees of all material information concerning the take-over offer, or that the take-over offer is inequitable or would work or tend to work a fraud or deceit upon the offerees * * *." ¶ 137.57.E.

On January 19, 1979, MITE initiated a cash tender offer for all outstanding shares of Chicago Rivet & Machine Co., a publicly held

---

[†] THE CHIEF JUSTICE joins the opinion in its entirety; Justice Blackmun joins Parts I, II, III, and IV: Justice Powell joins Parts I and V–B; and Justice Stevens and Justice O'Connor join Parts I, II, and V.

[1] The Illinois Act defines "take-over offer" as "the offer to acquire or the acquisition of any equity security of a target company, pursuant to a tender offer * * *." Ill.Rev.Stat., ch. 121½, ¶ 137.52–9 (1979).

"A tender offer has been conventionally understood to be a publicly made invitation addressed to all shareholders of a corporation to tender their shares for sale at a specified price." Note, The Developing Meaning of "Tender Offer" Under the Securities Exchange Act of 1934, 86 Harv.L. Rev. 1250, 1251 (1973) (footnotes omitted). The terms "tender offer" and "takeover offer" are often used interchangeably.

Illinois corporation, by filing a Schedule 14D-1 with the Securities and
Exchange Commission in order to comply with the Williams Act. The
Schedule 14D-1 indicated that MITE was willing to pay $28 per share
for any and all outstanding shares of Chicago Rivet, a premium of
approximately $4 over the then-prevailing market price. MITE did not
comply with the Illinois Act, however, and commenced this litigation on
the same day by filing an action in the United States District Court for
the Northern District of Illinois. The complaint asked for a declaratory
judgment that the Illinois Act was pre-empted by the Williams Act and
violated the Commerce Clause. In addition, MITE sought a temporary
restraining order and preliminary and permanent injunctions prohibiting the Illinois Secretary of State from enforcing the Illinois Act.

Chicago Rivet responded three days later by bringing suit in
Pennsylvania, where it conducted most of its business, seeking to enjoin
MITE from proceeding with its proposed tender offer on the ground
that the offer violated the Pennsylvania Takeover Disclosure Law, Pa.
Stat.Ann., Tit. 70, § 71 et seq. (Purdon Supp.1982–1983). After Chicago
Rivet's efforts to obtain relief in Pennsylvania proved unsuccessful,
both Chicago Rivet and the Illinois Secretary of State took steps to
invoke the Illinois Act. On February 1, 1979, the Secretary of State
notified MITE that he intended to issue an order requiring it to cease
and desist further efforts to make a tender offer for Chicago Rivet. On
February 2, 1979, Chicago Rivet notified MITE by letter that it would
file suit in Illinois state court to enjoin the proposed tender offer.
MITE renewed its request for injunctive relief in the District Court and
on February 2 the District Court issued a preliminary injunction
prohibiting the Secretary of State from enforcing the Illinois Act
against MITE's tender offer for Chicago Rivet.

MITE then published its tender offer in the February 5 edition of
the Wall Street Journal. The offer was made to all shareholders of
Chicago Rivet residing throughout the United States. The outstanding
stock was worth over $23 million at the offering price. On the same
day Chicago Rivet made an offer for approximately 40% of its own
shares at $30 per share.[4] The District Court entered final judgment on
February 9, declaring that the Illinois Act was pre-empted by the
Williams Act and that it violated the Commerce Clause. Accordingly,
the District Court permanently enjoined enforcement of the Illinois
statute against MITE. Shortly after final judgment was entered, MITE
and Chicago Rivet entered into an agreement whereby both tender
offers were withdrawn and MITE was given 30 days to examine the
books and records of Chicago Rivet. Under the agreement MITE was
either to make a tender offer of $31 per share before March 12, 1979,
which Chicago Rivet agreed not to oppose, or decide not to acquire
Chicago Rivet's shares or assets. On March 2, 1979, MITE announced
its decision not to make a tender offer.

The United States Court of Appeals for the Seventh Circuit affirmed sub nom. MITE Corp. v. Dixon, 633 F.2d 486 (1980). It agreed

---

[4] Chicago Rivet's offer for its own shares
was exempt from the requirements of the
Illinois Act pursuant to Ill.Rev.Stat., ch.
121½, ¶ 137.52–9(4) (1979).

with the District Court that several provisions of the Illinois Act are pre-empted by the Williams Act and that the Illinois Act unduly burdens interstate commerce in violation of the Commerce Clause. We noted probable jurisdiction, 451 U.S. 968 (1981), and now affirm.

II

The Court of Appeals specifically found that this case was not moot, 633 F.2d, at 490, reasoning that because the secretary has indicated he intends to enforce the Act against MITE, a reversal of the judgment of the District Court would expose MITE to civil and criminal liability [5] for making the February 5, 1979, offer in violation of the Illinois Act. We agree. * * *

Accordingly, the case is not moot.

III

We first address the holding that the Illinois Take-Over Act is unconstitutional under the Supremacy Clause. We note at the outset that in passing the Williams Act, which is an amendment to the Securities Exchange Act of 1934, Congress did not also amend § 28(a) of the 1934 Act.[6] In pertinent part, § 28(a) provides as follows:

"Nothing in this title shall affect the jurisdiction of the securities commission (or any agency or officer performing like functions) of any State over any security or any person insofar as it does not conflict with the provisions of this title or the rules and regulations thereunder." 48 Stat. 903.

Thus Congress did not explicitly prohibit States from regulating takeovers; it left the determination whether the Illinois statute conflicts with the Williams Act to the courts. Of course, a state statute is void to the extent that it actually conflicts with a valid federal statute; and

"[a] conflict will be found 'where compliance with both federal and state regulations is a physical impossibility * * *,' Florida Lime & Avocado Growers, Inc. v. Paul, 373 U.S. 132, 142–143 (1963), or where the state 'law stands as an obstacle to the accomplishment and execution of the full purposes and objectives of Congress.' Hines v. Davidowitz, 312 U.S. 52, 67 (1941); Jones v. Rath Packing Co., [430 U.S. 519,] 526, 540–541 [(1977)]. Accord, De Canas v. Bica, 424 U.S. 351, 363 (1976)." Ray v. Atlantic Richfield Co., 435 U.S. 151, 158 (1978).

Our inquiry is further narrowed in this case since there is no contention that it would be impossible to comply with both the provisions of

[5] The Secretary of State may bring an action for civil penalties for violations of the Illinois Act., Ill.Rev.Stat., ch. 121½, ¶ 137.65 (1979), and a person who willfully violates the Act is subject to criminal prosecution. ¶ 137.63.

[6] There is no evidence in the legislative history that Congress was aware of state takeover laws when it enacted the Williams Act. When the Williams Act was enacted in 1968, only Virginia had a takeover statute. The Virginia statute, Va. Code § 13.1–528 (1978), became effective March 5, 1968; the Williams Act was enacted several months later on July 19, 1968. Takeover statutes are now in effect in 37 States. Sargent, *On the Validity of State Takeover Regulation: State Responses to MITE and Kidwell*, 42 Ohio St. L.J. 689, 690, n. 7 (1981).

the Williams Act and the more burdensome requirements of the Illinois law. The issue thus, is, as it was in the Court of Appeals, whether the Illinois Act frustrates the objectives of the Williams Act in some substantial way.

The Williams Act, passed in 1968, was the congressional response to the increased use of cash tender offers in corporate acquisitions, a device that had "removed a substantial number of corporate control contests from the reach of existing disclosure requirements of the federal securities laws." Piper v. Chris-Craft Industries, Inc., 430 U.S. 1, 22 (1977). The Williams Act filled this regulatory gap. The Act imposes several requirements. First, it requires that upon the commencement of the tender offer, the offeror file with the SEC, publish or send to the shareholders of the target company, and furnish to the target company detailed information about the offer.

The offeror must disclose information about its background and identity; the source of the funds to be used in making the purchase; the purpose of the purchase, including any plans to liquidate the company or make major changes in its corporate structure; and the extent of the offeror's holdings in the target company.

Second, stockholders who tender their shares may withdraw them during the first 7 days of a tender offer and if the offeror has not yet purchased their shares, at any time after 60 days from the commencement of the offer.

Third, all shares tendered must be purchased for the same price; if an offering price is increased, those who have already tendered receive the benefit of the increase.

There is no question that in imposing these requirements, Congress intended to protect investors. Piper v. Chris-Craft Industries, Inc., supra, at 35; Rondeau v. Mosinee Paper Corp., 422 U.S. 49, 58 (1975); S.Rep. No. 550, 90th Cong., 1st Sess., 3–4 (1967) (Senate Report). But it is also crystal clear that a major aspect of the effort to protect the investor was to avoid favoring either management or the takeover bidder. As we noted in *Piper,* the disclosure provisions originally embodied in S. 2731 "were avowedly pro-management in the target company's efforts to defeat takeover bids." 430 U.S., at 30. But Congress became convinced "that takeover bids should not be discouraged because they serve a useful purpose in providing a check on entrenched but inefficient management." Senate Report, at 3.[9] It also became apparent that entrenched management was often successful in defeating takeover attempts. As the legislation evolved, therefore, Congress disclaimed any "intention to provide a weapon for management to discourage takeover bids," Rondeau v. Mosinee Paper Corp., supra, at 58, and expressly embraced a policy of neutrality. As Senator Williams explained: "We have taken extreme care to avoid tipping the scales either in favor of management or in favor of the person making

[9] Congress also did not want to deny shareholders "the opportunities which result from the competitive bidding for a block of stock of a given company," name- ly, the opportunity to sell shares for a premium over their market price. 113 Cong.Rec. 24666 (1967) (remarks of Sen. Javits).

the takeover bids." 113 Cong.Rec. 24664 (1967). This policy of "even-handedness," Piper v. Chris-Craft Industries, Inc., supra, at 31, represented a conviction that neither side in the contest should be extended additional advantages vis-a-vis the investor, who if furnished with adequate information would be in a position to make his own informed choice. We, therefore, agree with the Court of Appeals that Congress sought to protect the investor not only by furnishing him with the necessary information but also by withholding from management or the bidder any undue advantage that could frustrate the exercise of an informed choice. 633 F.2d, at 496.

To implement this policy of investor protection while maintaining the balance between management and the bidder, Congress required the latter to file with the Commission and furnish the company and the investor with all information adequate to the occasion. With that filing, the offer could go forward, stock could be tendered and purchased, but a stockholder was free within a specified time to withdraw his tendered shares. He was also protected if the offer was increased. Looking at this history as a whole, it appears to us, as it did to the Court of Appeals, that Congress intended to strike a balance between the investor, management, and the takeover bidder. The bidder was to furnish the investor and the target company with adequate information but there was no "inten[tion] to do * * * more than give incumbent management an opportunity to express and explain its position." *Rondeau v. Mosinee Paper Corp.,* supra, at 58. Once that opportunity was extended, Congress anticipated that the investor, if he so chose, and the takeover bidder should be free to move forward within the time frame provided by Congress.

IV

The Court of Appeals identified three provisions of the Illinois Act that upset the careful balance struck by Congress and which therefore stand as obstacles to the accomplishment and execution of the full purposes and objectives of Congress. We agree with the Court of Appeals in all essential respects.

A

The Illinois Act requires a tender offeror to notify the Secretary of State and the target company of its intent to make a tender offer and the material terms of the offer 20 business days before the offer becomes effective. Ill.Rev.Stat., ch. 121½, ¶¶ 137.54.E, 137.54.B (1979). During that time, the offeror may not communicate its offer to the shareholders. ¶ 137.54.A. Meanwhile, the target company is free to disseminate information to its shareholders concerning the impending offer. The contrast with the Williams Act is apparent. Under that Act, there is no precommencement notification requirement; the critical date is the date a tender offer is "first published or sent or given to security holders." 15 U.S.C. § 78n(d)(1). See also [Rule] 14d–2.

We agree with the Court of Appeals that providing the target company with additional time within which to take steps to combat the offer, the precommencement notification provisions furnish incumbent management with a powerful tool to combat tender offers, perhaps to the detriment of the stockholders who will not have an offer before them during this period.[10] These consequences are precisely what Congress determined should be avoided, and for this reason, the precommencement notification provision frustrates the objectives of the Williams Act.

It is important to note in this respect that in the course of events leading to the adoption of the Williams Act, Congress several times refused to impose a precommencement disclosure requirement. In October 1965, Senator Williams introduced S. 2731, a bill which would have required a bidder to notify the target company and file a public statement with the Securities and Exchange Commission at least 20 days before commencement of a cash tender offer for more than 5% of a class of the target company's securities. 111 Cong.Rec. 28259 (1965). The Commission commented on the bill and stated that "the requirement of a 20-day advance notice to the issuer and the Commission is unnecessary for the protection of security holders * * *." 112 Cong. Rec. 19005 (1966). Senator Williams introduced a new bill in 1967, S. 510, which provided for a confidential filing by the tender offeror with the Commission five days prior to the commencement of the offer. S. 510 was enacted as the Williams Act after elimination of the advance disclosure requirement. As the Senate Report explained:

> "At the hearings it was urged that this prior review was not necessary and in some cases might delay the offer when time was of the essence. In view of the authority and responsibility of the Securities and Exchange Commission to take appropriate action in the event that inadequate or misleading information is disseminated to the public to solicit acceptance of a tender offer, the bill as approved by the committee requires only that the statement be on file with the Securities and Exchange Commission at the time the tender offer is first made to the public." Senate Report, at 4.

Congress rejected another precommencement notification proposal during deliberations on the 1970 amendments to the Williams Act.[11]

B

For similar reasons, we agree with the Court of Appeals that the hearing provisions of the Illinois Act frustrate the congressional pur-

---

[10] See n. 11 and accompanying text, infra.

[11] H.R. 4285, 91st Cong., 2d Sess. (1970). The bill was not reported out of the Subcommittee. Instead, the Senate amendments to the Williams Act, which did not contain precommencement notification provisions, were adopted. Pub.L. 91–567, 84 Stat. 1497.

The Securities and Exchange Commission has promulgated detailed rules governing the conduct of tender offers. Rule 14d–2(b), requires that a tender offeror

make its offer effective within five days of publicly announcing the material terms of the offer by disseminating specified information to shareholders and filing the requisite documents with the Commission. Otherwise the offeror must announce that it is withdrawing its offer. The events in this litigation took place prior to the effective date of Rule 14d–2(b), and because Rule 14d–2(b) operates prospectively only, see 44 Fed.Reg. 70326 (1979), it is not at issue in this case.

pose by introducing extended delay into the tender offer process. The Illinois Act allows the Secretary of State to call a hearing with respect to any tender offer subject to the Act, and the offer may not proceed until the hearing is completed. Ill.Rev.Stat. ch. 121½, ¶¶ 137.57A and B (1979). The Secretary may call a hearing at any time prior to the commencement of the offer, and there is no deadline for the completion of the hearing. ¶¶ 137.57.C and D. Although the Secretary is to render a decision within 15 days after the conclusion of the hearing, that period may be extended without limitation. Not only does the Secretary of State have the power to delay a tender offer indefinitely, but incumbent management may also use the hearing provisions of the Illinois Act to delay a tender offer. The Secretary is required to call a hearing if requested to do so by, among other persons, those who are located in Illinois "as determined by post office address as shown on the records of the target company and who hold of record or beneficially, or both, at least 10% of the outstanding shares of any class of equity securities which is the subject of the take-over offer." ¶ 137.57.A. Since incumbent management in many cases will control, either directly or indirectly, 10% of the target company's shares, this provision allows management to delay the commencement of an offer by insisting on a hearing. As the Court of Appeals observed, these provisions potentially afford management a "powerful weapon to stymie indefinitely a takeover." 633 F.2d, at 494.[12] In enacting the Williams Act, Congress itself "recognized that delay can seriously impede a tender offer" and sought to avoid it. Great Western United Corp. v. Kidwell, 577 F.2d 1256, 1277 (CA5 1978); Senate Report, at 4.[13]

Congress reemphasized the consequences of delay when it enacted the Hart-Scott-Rodino Antitrust Improvements Act of 1976, Pub.L. 94–435, 90 Stat. 1397, 15 U.S.C. § 12 et seq.

"[I]t is clear that this short waiting period [the 10-day period for proration provided for by § 14(d)(6) of the Securities Exchange Act, which applies only after a tender offer is commenced] was founded on congressional concern that a longer delay might unduly favor the target firm's incumbent management, and permit them to frustrate many pro-competitive cash tenders. This ten-day waiting period thus underscores the basic purpose of the Williams Act—to maintain a neutral policy towards cash tender offers, by avoiding

---

[12] Delay has been characterized as "the most potent weapon in a tender-offer fight." Langevoort, *State Tender-Offer Legislation: Interests, Effects, and Political Competency,* 62 Cornell L.Rev. 213, 238 (1977). See also Wachtell, *Special Tender Offer Litigation Tactics,* 32 Bus.Law. 1433, 1437–1442 (1977); Wilner & Landy, *The Tender Trap: State Takeover Statutes and Their Constitutionality,* 45 Ford.L.Rev. 1, 9–10 (1976).

[13] According to the Securities and Exchange Commission, delay enables a target company to:

"(1) repurchase its own securities;

"(2) announce dividend increases or stock splits;

"(3) issue additional shares of stock;

"(4) acquire other companies to produce an antitrust violation should the tender offer succeed;

"(5) arrange a defensive merger;

"(6) enter into restrictive loan agreements; and

"(7) institute litigation challenging the tender offer." Brief for Securities and Exchange Commission as *Amicus Curiae* 10, n. 8.

lengthy delays that might discourage their chances for success." H.R. Rep. No. 94–1373, p. 12 (1976).[14]

As we have said, Congress anticipated that investors and the takeover offeror would be free to go forward without unreasonable delay. The potential for delay provided by the hearing provisions upset the balance struck by Congress by favoring management at the expense of stockholders. We therefore agree with the Court of Appeals that these hearing provisions conflict with the Williams Act.

C

The Court of Appeals also concluded that the Illinois Act is preempted by the Williams Act insofar as it allows the Secretary of State of Illinois to pass on the substantive fairness of a tender offer. Under ¶ 137.57.E of the Illinois law, the Secretary is required to deny registration of a takeover offer if he finds that the offer "fails to provide full and fair disclosure to the offerees * * * *or that the take-over offer is inequitable* * * *" (emphasis added).[15] The Court of Appeals understood the Williams Act and its legislative history to indicate that Congress intended for investors to be free to make their own decisions. We agree. Both the House and Senate Reports observed that the Act was "designed to make the relevant facts known so that shareholders have a fair opportunity to make their decision." H.R. Rep. No. 1711, 90th Cong., 2d Sess., 4 (1968); Senate Report, at 3. Thus, as the Court of Appeals said, "[t]he state thus offers investor protection at the expense of investor autonomy—an approach quite in conflict with that adopted by Congress." 633 F.2d, at 494.

V

The Commerce Clause provides that "Congress shall have Power * * * [t]o regulate Commerce * * * among the several States." U.S. Const., Art. I, § 8, cl. 3. "[A]t least since Cooley v. Board of

[14] Representative Rodino set out the consequences of delay in greater detail when he described ther relationship between the Hart-Scott-Rodino Act and the Williams Act:

"In the case of cash tender offers, more so than in other mergers, the equities include time and the danger of undue delay. This bill in no way intends to repeal or reverse the congressional purpose underlying the 1968 Williams Act, or the 1970 amendments to that act. * * * Lengthier delays will give the target firm plenty of time to defeat the offer, by abolishing cumulative voting, arranging a speedy defensive merger, quickly incorporating in a State with an antitakeover statute, or negotiating costly lifetime employment contracts for incumbent management. And the longer the waiting period, the more the target's stock may be bid up in the market, making the offer more costly—and less successful. Should this happen, it will mean that shareholders of the target firm will be effectively deprived of the choice that cash tenders given to them: Either accept the offer and thereby gain the tendered premium, or reject the offer. Generally, the courts have construed the Williams Act so as to maintain these two options for the target company's shareholders, and the House conferees contemplate that the courts will continue to do so." 122 Cong.Rec. 30877 (1976).

[15] Appellant argues that the Illinois Act does not permit him to adjudicate the substantive fairness of a tender offer. Brief for Appellant 21–22. On this state-law issue, however, we follow the view of the Court of Appeals that ¶ 137.57.E allows the Secretary of State "to pass upon the substantive fairness of a tender offer * * *." 633 F.2d 486, 493 (1980).

Wardens, 12 How. 299 (1852), it has been clear that 'the Commerce Clause * * * even without implementing legislation by Congress is a limitation upon the power of the States.' " Great Atlantic & Pacific Tea Co. v. Cottrell, 424 U.S. 366, 370–371 (1976), quoting Freeman v. Hewitt, 329 U.S. 249, 252 (1946). See also Lewis v. BT Investment Managers, Inc., 447 U.S. 27, 35 (1980). Not every exercise of state power with some impact on interstate commerce is invalid. A state statute must be upheld if it "regulates evenhandedly to effectuate a legitimate local public interest, and its effects on interstate commerce are only incidental * * * unless the burden imposed on such commerce is clearly excessive in relation to the putative local benefits." Pike v. Bruce Church, Inc., 397 U.S. 137, 142 (1970), citing Huron Cement Co. v. Detroit, 362 U.S. 440, 443 (1960). The Commerce Clause, however, permits only *incidental* regulation of interstate commerce by the States; direct regulation is prohibited. Shafer v. Farmers Grain Co., 268 U.S. 189, 199 (1925). See also Pike v. Bruce Church, Inc., supra, at 142. The Illinois Act violates these principles for two reasons. First, it directly regulates and prevents, unless its terms are satisfied, interstate tender offers which in turn would generate interstate transactions. Second, the burden the Act imposes on interstate commerce is excessive in light of the local interests the Act purports to further.

A

States have traditionally regulated intrastate securities transactions,[16] and this Court has upheld the authority of States to enact "blue-sky" laws against Commerce Clause challenges on several occasions. Hall v. Geiger-Jones Co., 242 U.S. 539 (1917); Caldwell v. Sioux Falls Stock Yards Co., 242 U.S. 559 (1917); Merrick v. N.W. Halsey & Co., 242 U.S. 568 (1917). The Court's rationale for upholding blue-sky laws was that they only regulated transactions occurring within the regulating States. "The provisions of the law * * * apply to dispositions of securities *within* the State and while information of those issued in other States and foreign countries is required to be filed * * *, they are only affected by the requirement of a license of one who deals with them *within* the State. * * * Such regulations affect interstate commerce in [securities] only incidentally." Hall v. Geiger-Jones Co., supra, at 557–558 (citations omitted). Congress has also recognized the validity of such laws governing intrastate securities transactions in § 28(a) of the Securities Exchange Act, a provision "designed to save state blue-sky laws from pre-emption." Leroy v. Great Western United Corp., 443 U.S. 173, 182, n. 13 (1979).

The Illinois Act differs substantially from state blue-sky laws in that it directly regulates transactions which take place across state lines, even if wholly outside the State of Illinois. A tender offer for securities of a publicly held corporation is ordinarily communicated by the use of the mails or other means of interstate commerce to shareholders across the country and abroad. Securities are tendered and

---

[16] For example, the Illinois blue-sky law, Ill.Rev.Stat., ch. 121½, ¶ 137.1 et seq. (1979 and Supp.1980), provides that securities subject to the law must be registered "prior to sale in this State * * *." ¶ 137.5.

transactions closed by similar means. Thus, in this case, MITE Corp., the tender offeror, is a Delaware corporation with principal offices in Connecticut. Chicago Rivet is a publicly held Illinois corporation with shareholders scattered around the country, 27% of whom live in Illinois. MITE's offer to Chicago Rivet's shareholders, including those in Illinois, necessarily employed interstate facilities in communicating its offer, which, if accepted, would result in transactions occurring across state lines. These transactions would themselves be interstate commerce. Yet the Illinois law, unless complied with, sought to prevent MITE from making its offer and concluding interstate transactions not only with Chicago Rivet's stockholders living in Illinois, but also with those living in other States and having no connection with Illinois. Indeed, the Illinois law on its face would apply even if not a single one of Chicago Rivet's shareholders were a resident of Illinois, since the Act applies to every tender offer for a corporation meeting two of the following conditions: the corporation has its principal executive office in Illinois, is organized under Illinois laws, or has at least 10% of its stated capital and paid-in surplus represented in Illinois. Ill.Rev.Stat., ch. 121½, ¶ 137.52–10(2) (1979). Thus the Act could be applied to regulate a tender offer which would not affect a single Illinois shareholder.

It is therefore apparent that the Illinois statute is a direct restraint on interstate commerce and that it has a sweeping extraterritorial effect. Furthermore, if Illinois may impose such regulations, so may other States; and interstate commerce in securities transactions generated by tender offers would be thoroughly stifled. In Shafer v. Farmers Grain Co., supra, at 199, the Court held that "a state statute which by its necessary operation directly interferes with or burdens [interstate] commerce is a prohibited regulation and invalid, regardless of the purpose with which it was enacted." See also Hughes v. Alexandria Scrap Corp., 426 U.S. 794, 806 (1976). The Commerce Clause also precludes the application of a state statute to commerce that takes place wholly outside of the State's borders, whether or not the commerce has effects within the State. In Southern Pacific Co. v. Arizona, 325 U.S. 761, 775 (1945), the Court struck down on Commerce Clause grounds a state law where the "practical effect of such regulation is to control [conduct] beyond the boundaries of the state * * *." The limits on a State's power to enact substantive legislation are similar to the limits on the jurisdiction of state courts. In either case, "any attempt 'directly' to assert extraterritorial jurisdiction over persons or property would offend sister States and exceed the inherent limits of the State's power." Shafer v. Heitner, 433 U.S. 186, 197 (1977).

Because the Illinois Act purports to regulate directly and to interdict interstate commerce, including commerce wholly outside the State, it must be held invalid as were the laws at issue in Shafer v. Farmers Grain Co. and *Southern Pacific.*

B

The Illinois Act is also unconstitutional under the test of Pike v. Bruce Church, Inc., 397 U.S., at 142, for even when a state statute regulates interstate commerce indirectly, the burden imposed on that commerce must not be excessive in relation to the local interests served by the statute. The most obvious burden the Illinois Act imposes on interstate commerce arises from the statute's previously described nationwide reach which purports to give Illinois the power to determine whether a tender offer may proceed anywhere.

The effects of allowing the Illinois Secretary of State to block a nationwide tender offer are substantial. Shareholders are deprived of the opportunity to sell their shares at a premium. The reallocation of economic resources to their highest valued use, a process which can improve efficiency and competition, is hindered. The incentive the tender offer mechanism provides incumbent management to perform well so that stock prices remain high is reduced. See Easterbrook & Fischel, *The Proper Role of a Target's Management in Responding to a Tender Offer,* 94 Harv.L.Rev. 1161, 1173–1174 (1981); Fischel, *Efficient Capital Market Theory, the Market for Corporate Control, and the Regulation of Cash Tender Offers,* 57 Texas L.Rev. 1, 5, 27–28, 45 (1978); H.R. Rep. No. 94–1373, p. 12 (1976).

Appellant claims the Illinois Act furthers two legitimate local interests. He argues that Illinois seeks to protect resident security holders and that the Act merely regulates the internal affairs of companies incorporated under Illinois law. We agree with the Court of Appeals that these asserted interests are insufficient to outweigh the burdens Illinois imposes on interstate commerce.

While protecting local investors is plainly a legitimate state objective, the State has no legitimate interest in protecting nonresident shareholders. Insofar as the Illinois law burdens out-of-state transactions, there is nothing to be weighed in the balance to sustain the law. We note, furthermore, that the Act completely exempts from coverage a corporation's acquisition of its own shares. Ill.Rev.Stat., ch. 121½, ¶ 137.52–9(4) (1979). Thus Chicago Rivet was able to make a competing tender offer for its own stock without complying with the Illinois Act, leaving Chicago Rivet's shareholders to depend only on the protections afforded them by federal securities law, protections which Illinois views as inadequate to protect investors in other contexts. This distinction is at variance with Illinois' asserted legislative purpose, and tends to undermine appellant's justification for the burdens the statute imposes on interstate commerce.

We are also unconvinced that the Illinois Act substantially enhances the shareholders' position. The Illinois Act seeks to protect shareholders of a company subject to a tender offer by requiring disclosures regarding the offer, assuring that shareholders have adequate time to decide whether to tender their shares, and according shareholders withdrawal, proration, and equal consideration rights. However, the Williams Act provides these same substantive protections, compare Ill.Rev.Stat., ch. 121½, ¶¶ 137.59.C, D, and E (1979) (withdrawal, proration, and equal consideration rights), with [Sections] 14(d)(5), (6), and (7) and [Rule] 14d–7 (1981) (same). As the Court of Appeals noted, the disclosures required by the Illinois Act which go beyond those mandated by the Williams Act and the regulations pursuant to it may not substantially enhance the shareholders' ability to make informed decisions. 633 F.2d, at 500. It also was of the view that the possible benefits of the potential delays required by the Act may be outweighed by the increased risk that the tender offer will fail due to defensive tactics employed by incumbent management. We are unprepared to disagree with the Court of Appeals in these respects, and conclude that the protections the Illinois Act affords resident security holders are, for the most part, speculative.

Appellant also contends that Illinois has an interest in regulating the internal affairs of a corporation incorporated under its laws. The internal affairs doctrine is a conflict of laws principle which recognizes that only one State should have the authority to regulate a corporation's internal affairs—matters peculiar to the relationships among or between the corporation and its current officers, directors, and shareholders—because otherwise a corporation could be faced with conflicting demands. See Restatement (Second) of Conflict of Laws § 302, Comment *b*, pp. 307–308 (1971). That doctrine is of little use to the State in this context. Tender offers contemplate transfers of stock by stockholders to a third party and do not themselves implicate the internal affairs of the target company. Great Western United Corp. v. Kidwell, 577 F.2d, at 1280, n. 53; Restatement, supra, § 302, Comment *e*, p. 310. Furthermore, the proposed justification is somewhat incredible since the Illinois Act applies to tender offers for any corporation for which 10% of the outstanding shares are held by Illinois residents, Ill. Rev.Stat., ch. 121½, ¶ 137.52–10 (1979). The Act thus applies to corporations that are not incorporated in Illinois and have their principal place of business in other States. Illinois has no interest in regulating the internal affairs of foreign corporations.

We conclude with the Court of Appeals that the Illinois Act imposes a substantial burden on interstate commerce which outweighs its putative local benefits. It is accordingly invalid under the Commerce Clause.

The judgment of the Court of Appeals is affirmed.

Justice POWELL, concurring in part.

I agree with Justice Marshall that this case is moot. In view, however, of the decision of a majority of the Court to reach the merits, I join Parts I and V–B of the Court's opinion.

I join Part V–B because its Commerce Clause reasoning leaves some room for state regulation of tender offers. This period in our history is marked by conglomerate corporate formations essentially unrestricted by the antitrust laws. Often the offeror possesses resources, in terms of professional personnel experienced in takeovers as well as of capital, that vastly exceed those of the takeover target. This disparity in resources may seriously disadvantage a relatively small or regional target corporation. Inevitably there are certain adverse consequences in terms of general public interest when corporate headquarters are moved away from a city and State.*

The Williams Act provisions, implementing a policy of neutrality, seem to assume corporate entities of substantially equal resources. I agree with Justice Stevens that the Williams Act's neutrality policy does not necessarily imply a congressional intent to prohibit state legislation designed to assure—at least in some circumstances—greater protection to interests that include but often are broader than those of incumbent management.

Justice STEVENS, concurring in part and concurring in the judgment.

[In Part I of his opinion, Justice Stevens concluded that the case was not moot.]

II

On the merits, I agree with the Court that the Illinois Take-Over Act is invalid because it burdens interstate commerce. I therefore join Part V of its opinion. I am not persuaded, however, that Congress' decision to follow a policy of neutrality in its own legislation is tantamount to a federal prohibition against state legislation designed to provide special protection for incumbent management. Accordingly, although I agree with the Court's assessment of the impact of the Illinois statute, I do not join its pre-emption holding.

Justice O'CONNOR, concurring in part.

I agree with the Court that the case is not moot, and that portions of the Illinois Business Take-Over Act, Ill.Rev.Stat., ch. 121½, ¶ 137.51 et seq. (1979), are invalid under the Commerce Clause. Because it is not necessary to reach the pre-emption issue, I join only Parts I, II, and V of the Court's opinion, and would affirm the judgment of the Court of Appeals on that basis.

[Justice MARSHALL, in an opinion joined by Justice BRENNAN, and Justice REHNQUIST in a separate opinion, would have found the case moot.]

◆

The plethora of opinions in *MITE* make it somewhat difficult to specify the breadth of its invalidation of state efforts to regulate takeovers. Professor Loss points out that even though only the Chief Justice and Justice Blackmun joined Justice White in the preemption portion of the opinion, only Justice Stevens clearly stated that he disagreed with Justice White's position. The remaining Justices simply

---

* The corporate headquarters of the great national and multinational corporations tend to be located in the large cities of a few States. When corporate headquarters are transferred out of a city and State into one of these metropolitan centers, the State and locality from which the transfer is made inevitably suffer signifi- cantly. Management personnel—many of whom have provided community leadership—may move to the new corporate headquarters. Contributions to cultural, charitable, and educational life—both in terms of leadership and financial support—also tends to diminish when there is a move of corporate headquarters.

did not reach the issue.[129] Thus, Loss concludes that "the preemption issue is still altogether open, and even the Commerce Clause holding might be distinguished with respect to statutes, of narrower scope." [130] Nonetheless, the federal courts have generally treated *MITE* as invalidating all "first generation" state takeover statutes [131] on Commerce Clause grounds.[132] The critical issue, then, is what room for state takeover regulation remains after *MITE*.

One approach a state might take would be to follow Professor Loss' suggestion and pare down a first generation statute to the point where a balance of the local benefits and the burdens on interstate commerce favor the validity of the statute. This could be accomplished by restricting the statute's application to only offers to in-state shareholders of companies closely connected with the state, and by eliminating pre-offer filing,[133] pre-offer hearings, and substantive review of the fairness of the terms of the offer.[134] One might well ask, however, whether the game is worth the candle. Recall that the state's interest in regulating the takeover process is to strengthen the hands of local management. If the scope of first generation statutes after *MITE* is limited to some expansion of the scope of disclosure, perhaps to include a statement of the acquisition's impact on local interests,[135] the state's goal in adopting any statute at all will hardly be met.

As a practical matter, then, *MITE* did sound the death knell for the first generation of state takeover statutes.[136] Any hope of protecting local companies in a fashion that would survive constitutional challenge then requires a new approach. After *MITE*, Ohio, Maryland, and Pennsylvania each adopted variants of such an approach.

The three statutes share a common theme. The Williams Act, and the first generation state statutes, treat tender offers as a unique type of transaction. In contrast, all three post-*MITE* states recognize that a

[129] L. Loss, *Fundamentals of Securities Regulation* 602–03 (1983). Justices Brennan, Marshall, Powell & Rehnquist thought the case moot; Justice O'Connor thought that the Court's Commerce Clause holding made it unnecessary to decide the preemption issue.

[130] Id. at 603.

[131] These statutes generally share a number of the characteristics emphasized by Justice White in *MITE*. For a description of the range of characteristics see Wilner & Landy, *The Tender Trap: State Takeover Statutes and Their Constitutionality*, 45 Ford.L.Rev. 1, 5–9 (1976).

[132] See, e.g., Mesa Petroleum Co. v. Cities Service Co., 715 F.2d 1425 (10th Cir.1983) (Oklahoma statute); Telvest, Inc. v. Bradshaw, 697 F.2d 576 (4th Cir.1983) (Virginia statute); Martin-Marietta Corp. v. Bendix Corp., 690 F.2d 558 (6th Cir.1982) (Michigan statute); National City Lines, Inc. v. LLC Corp., 687 F.2d 1122 (8th Cir.1982) (Missouri statute). The *National City* court also relied upon preemption.

[133] The SEC's 1979 adoption of Rule 14d–2 makes clear that state statutes that require public filings to be made a specified period prior to commencing an offer have been preempted because they conflict with the requirement of Rule 14d–2(b) that an offer commence within 5 business days after publication of the information typically required in a state filing. Securities Exchange Act Release No. 34–16623, Interpretive Release Relating to Tender Offer Rules (March 5, 1980), reprinted in 3 Fed. Sec.L. Rep. (CCH) ¶24,284l.

[134] See Cardiff Acquisitions, Inc. v. Hatch, 751 F.2d 917 (8th Cir.1984) (Upholding validity of Minnesota statute narrowly circumscribed by 1984 amendment in light of *MITE*).

[135] See Cardiff Acquisitions, Inc. v. Hatch, supra at 90,260.

[136] Kozyris, *Corporate Wars and Choice of Laws*, 1985 Duke L.J. 1, 76 (1985) ("The typical state takeover statute that ran into early trouble in the lower courts and finally fared so badly in *MITE* is rapidly disappearing.")

tender offer is only one of the ways to make an acquisition; each is an effort to ameliorate problems facing target shareholders in tender offers that are not present in other acquisition techniques. The Ohio statute, the first of the second generation of state takeover statutes,[137] requires the approval of a majority of disinterested target company shareholders [138] before consummation of a tender offer, or an open market or private purchase, that would cause the acquiring company's holdings to exceed 20 percent, 33⅓ percent or 50 percent.[139] The idea is to require the same kind of shareholder approval in tender offers as in other forms of acquisitions. Maryland approached the problem somewhat differently, focusing not on a tender offer at all, but on the subsequent second-step transaction. In effect the statute imposes a statutory fair price charter amendment [140] for Maryland corporations. Unless shareholders receive a fair price as calculated under the statutory formula, "business combinations," broadly defined to include mergers, sales of assets, liquidations and recapitalizations, with an "interested shareholder" must be approved by 80 percent of the outstanding shares and 66⅔ percent of the shares held by disinterested shareholders.[141] Pennsylvania, in turn, created a statutory right of redemption, like the charter amendment of the same character,[142] that requires persons acquiring thirty percent or more of the stock of a Pennsylvania corporation to pay to the remaining shareholders the "fair value" of their shares.[143]

The strategy reflected in each of these three approaches is to cast the statute as part of the state's corporate law and, thus, no more in conflict with the Williams Act than the familiar requirement under state corporate law that target shareholders approve a statutory merg-

[137] The second generation characterization is that of Sargent, *Do Second-Generation State Takeover Statutes Violate the Commerce Clause?*, 8 Corp.L.Rev. 3 (1985).

[138] The exclusion of interested·shareholders encompasses largely the acquiring company and its affiliates.

[139] Ohio Rev.Code Ann. Section 1701.831 (Page Supp.1984). See Kreider, *Fortress without Foundation? Ohio Takeover Act II,* 52 U.Cinn.L.Rev. 108 (1983). Minnesota, Minn.Stat.Ann. Section 302A.671 (West Supp.1985), and Wisconsin, Wis.Stat.Ann. Section 180.69 (West Supp. 1984–85), have adopted statutes which include similar provisions. Cardiff v. Hatch, supra, did not reach the constitutionality of this aspect of the Minnesota statute.

[140] See Chapter Fourteen B.1.(a).(2)., supra, for a discussion of fair price charter amendments.

[141] Md. Corps. & Ass'ns Code Ann. Secs 3–601 to 3–603 (Supp.1984). The board of directors retains some discretion with respect to whom the super majority will apply, and the corporation can adopt a charter amendment electing not to be governed by the statute. See Scriggins & Clarke,

Takeovers and the 1983 Maryland Fair Price Legislation, 43 Md.L.Rev. 266 (1984); Note, *Second Generation State Takeover Legislation: Maryland Takes a New Tack,* 83 Mich.L.Rev. 443 (1984). Connecticut, 1984 Conn. Acts Section 84–431 (Reg.Sess.), Kentucky, Ky.Rev.Stat.Ann. Sections 271A.397–.399 (Baldwin 1984), Michigan, Mich.Comp.Laws Ann. Secs. 450.1775–.1784 (1984), New York, New York Business Corp. Act. Sec. 912 (enacted Dec. 10, 1985), and Wisconsin, Wis.Stat.Ann. Sec. 180.725 (West Supp.1984–84), have adopted statutes which include similar provisions.

[142] See Chapter Fourteen B.1.(a).(2)., supra, for a discussion of right of redemption charter amendments.

[143] Pa.Stat.Ann. tit. 15, sec. 1910 (Purdon Supp.1984–85). As with the Ohio and Maryland statutes, the board of directors has significant discretion with respect to the application of the statute and a corporation may elect not to be covered by the statute by adopting a charter amendment. See Newlin & Gilmer, *The Pennsylvania Shareholder Protection Act: A New Approach to Deflecting Corporate Takeover Bids,* 40 Bus.Law. 111 (1984).

er. Further buttressing the corporate law characterization of these statutes, none provide for a state administrative role; like the rest of state corporate law, it is self-administering. The explanation for this common emphasis on state corporate law is *MITE*'s treatment of the internal affairs doctrine: The conflict of laws principle that the state of incorporation has the authority to regulate a corporation's internal affairs. Justice White disposed of Illinois' reliance on this doctrine in the Commerce Clause balance by treating tender offers as an external matter: "Tender offers contemplate transfers of stock by stockholders to a third party and do not themselves implicate the internal affairs of the target company." [144] How successful are the three statutes in invoking the internal affairs doctrine? The three statutes do differ with respect to their placement on an internal-external continuum. The Maryland statute concerns only intra-corporate transactions, like liquidations, or transactions to which the corporation is a party, like mergers. The Pennsylvania statute, in contrast, creates an obligation between a third party and shareholders, and the Ohio statute imposes a pre-condition, albeit a shareholder vote, on precisely the "transfers of stock by stockholders to a third party" referred to by Justice White.[145]

Even if the internal affairs doctrine is successfully invoked, must it still be balanced against the impact of the statute on interstate commerce? For example, would the weight of Delaware's interest in regulating the internal affairs of Delaware corporations be diminished by the fact that Delaware citizens own only a tiny portion of the shares of Delaware corporations? If the weight of the internal affairs doctrine is not limited by the number of shareholders located within the state, what precisely is the state's interest in the matter? Delaware could argue that it has an important local interest in remaining the leading state of incorporation for major corporations.[146] To remain the leader, the argument would run, Delaware has to be able to offer laws at least as desirable as any other state. If only more populous states (in which a larger percentage of shareholders reside and which therefore have a greater interest in the internal affairs of their corporations) could offer laws, like antitakeover provisions, that corporate management finds attractive, Delaware would be at a significant disadvantage.

From this perspective, giving weight to the internal affairs doctrine, and thereby allowing states to compete for the opportunity to "protect" non-resident shareholders, is the central legal underpinning for the existence of a market for corporate charters in which states

---

[144] Justice White also noted that the Illinois statute applied to corporations chartered in other states and that Illinois could have "no interest in regulating the internal affairs of foreign corporations." The application of each of the three statutes is limited to corporations chartered in that state.

[145] For a comprehensive treatment of the application of the internal affairs doctrine to corporate control contests generally, and to the second generation statutes, see Kozyris, supra at 15–45, 76–85.

[146] For example, 55 percent of the top 200 American corporations by sales in 1981 were incorporated in Delaware. Romano, *Some Pieces of the Incorporation Puzzle* at n. 50, Working Paper No. 19, Stanford Law School Law and Economics Program (Dec. 1984). Over the period from 1960 to 1981, the percentage of Delaware's total tax collections that came from its corporate franchise tax ranged from 10.9 percent to 24.9 percent. Id. at Table 2.

compete for incorporation business. The idea is that so long as a corporation can choose in which state to incorporate regardless of where it actually does business, and so long as the internal affairs doctrine assures that its choice will be respected, states seeking the revenue from incorporation will adopt laws that corporations find attractive. The competitive process would have no detrimental impact on interstate commerce because corporations would select the corporate statute most beneficial to its shareholders,[147] the great majority of whom will live in states *other* than the state of incorporation, thereby preventing any state from adopting a purely local perspective.

Does the argument that competition among states leads to the survival of the most efficient corporate laws, and therefore benefits rather than burdens interstate commerce, apply with respect to state regulation of takeovers? If, as argued in Chapter Fourteen B.3.b., management and shareholders have a conflict of interest with respect to takeovers, would not management select the state law that on this point served its interests rather than those of the shareholders? [148] And if the interests of the state and those of management coincide, then the argument, in the end, describes precisely the pattern with which we began this section: States restricting takeovers to further their local economic interests, despite the costs imposed on the national economy.[149]

How do the second generation statutes fare with respect to preemption? If the Congressional purpose in the Williams Act was neutrality, with the intent of freezing the balance between offerers and target management where it stood in July, 1967, then virtually any subse-

---

[147] Among the scholars associated with this view are R. Winter, *Government and the Corporation* (1978); Easterbrook & Fischel, *Voting in Corporate Law,* 26 J.L. & Econ. 395 (1983). Others have recognized the existence of competition, but argued that the outcome was not efficiency, but a "race to the bottom." See Cary, *Federalism and Corporate Law: Reflections upon Delaware,* 83 Yale L.J. 663 (1974). Romano, supra, and Dodd & Leftwich, *The Market for Corporate Charters: "Unhealthy Competition" versus Federal Regulation,* 53 J.Bus. 259 (1980) subject these competing hypotheses to empirical tests.

[148] Romano, supra, has attempted an empirical test of the proposition that the management decision to incorporate in a state that protects management against takeovers is harmful to shareholders. Using a sample of firms that reincorporated in another state to obtain protection against hostile takeovers, Romano found a positive but statistically insignificant CAR of 1.3 percent over the 99 day period before and after the reincorporation proposal first became public. Id. at Tables 13 & 14; Figure 4. Romano describes this evidence as inconsistent with the claim that management antitakeover tactics injure sharehold-

ers. Query, however, whether the CAR reported is subject to other interpretations. Suppose the market interpreted the reincorporation announcement as a signal that management had information indicating a higher likelihood of a premium takeover in the future. In that event, the CAR on announcement would reflect the market's balance of the negative effect of the unfavorable new state law and the positive effect of the new information. Approached in this way, the empirical result is simply ambiguous. Recall that this is the same problem we encountered in evaluating CAR studies of the adoption of shark repellant amendments in Chapter Fourteen B. 2.(a).(2)., supra.

[149] How much of the constitutional problem confronting state legislative efforts results from the choice to control the local impact of corporate business decisions partially and indirectly by antitakeover statutes under the guise of shareholder protection? For a thoughtful analysis of the different Commerce Clause analysis that would apply to direct restriction of plant closings and other workplace restrictions, see Buxbaum, *Federalism and Corporate Law,* 82 Mich.L.Rev. 1163, 1171–78 (1984).

quent state action affecting the success of tender offers would be suspect. If, alternatively, the Congressional purpose was to preserve shareholder autonomy, then might not the Maryland and Ohio statutes, by reducing the prisoners' dilemma pressure on individual shareholders to tender even when shareholders as a group would be better off not tendering,[150] serve to further Congress' goal? If it is difficult to determine whether Congress had either goal in mind exclusively, then would the appropriate preemption analysis after *MITE* simply be to allow the states to try new approaches—certainly less burdensome with respect to *both* goals than the first generation statutes struck down in *MITE*— until Congress or the SEC make their intent more clear?

A final issue with respect to the second generation statutes, now concerning their wisdom rather than their constitutionality, is also worth raising. Regardless of whether the substance of the statutes is desirable, do they not put the burden of initiating action on the wrong party? Assume that management will tend to protect itself from takeovers even if it is not in the shareholders' best interests. Would it not be better to draft the statutes to authorize corporations to opt *into* the statutory scheme by charter amendment, rather than to opt *out* of it? If the statutes were structured this way, management would still be able to use corporate funds to propose the amendment and solicit votes in its favor, but shareholders would at least have the opportunity to reject it. As the statutes are actually structured, it is not in management's interests to propose the opt-out amendment so that, at best, a shareholder would have to overcome free rider problems and take the initiative to remove it. At worst, in some states the opt-out amendment could never be proposed because any charter amendment requires the prior approval of the board of directors.

[150] See Chapters Fourteen B.3.d. and Fifteen B., *supra*.

CHAPTER SEVENTEEN. THE HART–SCOTT–RODINO ANTITRUST IMPROVEMENTS ACT

In the early 1970's, an unusual concern was being raised about the effectiveness of Section 7 of the Clayton Act,[1] the principal federal antitrust restriction on corporate acquisitions. Unlike more familiar criticism of the antitrust laws, the concern was not substantive—that the measure of whether an acquisition violated the statute was too lenient or not lenient enough—although there was plenty of that. Rather, it was that in cases where courts ultimately found a violation, the relief actually achieved did not restore competition to preacquisition levels. In particular, two studies of the actual relief obtained following successful government Clayton Act prosecutions concluded that in the overwhelming percentage of cases, relief was ineffective.[2] The principal explanation for this phenomenon was the government's difficulty in obtaining a preliminary injunction preventing the transaction while its legality was resolved.[3] Where preliminary relief was not obtained, divestiture could come as much as 10 years after the complaint was filed,[4] and in a number of cases never took place at all;[5] the difficulties in recreating an independent competitor that for years had not existed at all were substantial. Part of the explanation for the failure to obtain preliminary relief was that the Antitrust Division of the Justice Department and the Federal Trade Commission, the federal government's two antitrust enforcement arms, lacked an effective means of securing the information about a proposed acquisition necessary to establish that a preliminary injunction was appropriate.[6]

It was against this background that Congress enacted Title II of the Hart-Scott-Rodino Antitrust Improvements Act of 1976 (the Act),[7] adding a new Section 7A to the Clayton Act.[8]

---

[1] 15 U.S.C. § 18 (1983). Section 7 provides that no corporation "shall acquire, directly or indirectly, the whole or any part of the stock * * * [or] the whole or any part of the assets of another corporation * * *, where in any line of commerce in any section of the country, the effect of such acquisition may be substantially to lessen competition, or to tend to create a monopoly."

[2] Pfunder, Plaine & Whittemore, *Compliance with Divestiture Orders under Section 7 of the Clayton Act: An Analysis of Relief Obtained,* 17 Antitrust Bull. 19 (1972); Elzinga, *The Antimerger Law: Pyrrhic Victories?,* 12 J.L. & Econ. 43 (1969).

[3] "In most cases where preliminary injunctions were denied and divestiture was subsequently ordered, the divestiture which was ordered did not prove to be an adequate remedy." Pfunder, Plaine & Whittemore, supra at 117.

[4] S. Axnin, B. Fogg & N. Stoll, *Acquisitions Under the Hart-Scott-Rodino Antitrust Improvements Act* § 3 (1984).

[5] In the Pfunder, Plaine & Whittemore sample of 103 cases, the ordered divestiture never took place at all in 8 cases, and in 4 others there was a substantial reduction in the scope of divestiture.

[6] Private parties fared even worse with respect to preliminary relief. In their cases, the public interest and balance of equities factors consistently were found lacking. It seemed that only the government could represent the public interest. Consistent with this problem, no private party had ever obtained divestiture relief, as opposed to damages, under Section 7 of the Clayton Act.

[7] P.L. No. 94–435, 90 Stat. 1383 (1976).

[8] 15 U.S.C. § 18a (1983).

"Sec. 7A. (a) Except as exempted pursuant to subsection (c), no person shall acquire, directly or indirectly, any voting securities or assets of any other person, unless both persons (or in the case of a tender offer, the acquiring person) file notification pursuant to rules under subsection (d)(1) and the waiting period described in subsection (b)(1) has expired, if—

"(1) the acquiring person, or the person whose voting securities or assets are being acquired, is engaged in commerce or in any activity affecting commerce:

"(2)(A) any voting securities or assets of a person engaged in manufacturing which has annual net sales or total assets of $10,000,000 or more are being acquired by any person which has total assets or annual net sales of $10,000,000 or more;

"(B) any voting securities or assets of a person not engaged in manufacturing which has total assets of $10,000,000 or more are being acquired by any person which has total assets or annual net sales of $100,000,000 or more; or

"(C) any voting securities or assets of a person with annual net sales or total assets of $100,000,000 or more are being acquired by any person with total assets or annual net sales of $10,000,000 or more; and

"(3) as a result of such acquisition, the acquiring person would hold—

"(A) 15 per centum or more of the voting securities or assets of the acquired person, or

"(B) an aggregate total amount of the voting securities and assets of the acquired person in excess of $15,000,000.

In the case of a tender offer, the person whose voting securities are sought to be acquired by a person required to file notification under this subsection shall file notification pursuant to rules under subsection (d).

"(b)(1) The waiting period required under subsection (a) shall—

"(A) begin on the date of the receipt by the Federal Trade Commission and the Assistant Attorney General in charge of the Antitrust Division of the Department of Justice (hereinafter referred to in this section as the 'Assistant Attorney General') of—

"(i) the completed notification required under subsection (a), or

"(ii) if such notification is not completed, the notification to the extent completed and a statement of the reasons for such noncompliance, from both persons, or, in the case of a tender offer, the acquiring person; and

"(B) end on the thirtieth day after the date of such receipt (or in the case of a cash tender offer, the fifteenth day), or on such later date as may be set under subsection (e)(2) or (g)(2).

"(2) The Federal Trade Commission and the Assistant Attorney General may, in individual cases, terminate the waiting period specified in paragraph (1) and allow any person to proceed with any acquisition subject to this section, and promptly shall cause to be published in the FEDERAL REGISTER a notice that neither intends to take any action within such period with respect to such acquisition.

"(3) As used in this section—

"(A) The term 'voting securities' means any securities which at present or upon conversion entitle the owner or holder thereof to vote for the election of directors of the issuer or, with respect to unincorporated issuers, persons exercising similar functions.

"(B) The amount of percentage of voting securities or assets of a person which are acquired or held by another person shall be determined by aggregating the amount or percentage of such voting securities or assets held or acquired by such other person and each affiliate thereof.

"(c) The following classes of transactions are exempt from the requirements of this section—

"(1) acquisitions of good or realty transferred in the ordinary course of business;

"(2) acquisitions of bonds, mortgages, deeds of trust, or other obligations which are not voting securities;

"(3) acquisitions of voting securities of an issuer at least 50 per centum of the voting securities of which are owned by the acquiring person prior to such acquisitions;

"(4) transfers to or from a Federal agency or a State or political subdivision thereof;

"(5) transactions specifically exempted from the antitrust laws by Federal statute;

"(6) transactions specifically exempted from the antitrust laws by Federal statute if approved by a Federal agency, if copies of all information and documentary material filed with such agency are contemporaneously filed with the Federal Trade Commission and the Assistant Attorney General;

"(7) transactions which require agency approval under section 18(c) of the Federal Deposit Insurance Act (12 U.S.C. 1828(c)), or section 3 of the Bank Holding Company Act of 1956 (12 U.S.C. 1842);

"(8) transactions which require agency approval under section 4 of the Bank Holding Company Act of 1956 (12 U.S.C. 1843), sections 403 and 408(e) of the National Housing Act (12 U.S.C. 1726 and 1730(a), or section 5 of the Home Owners' Loan Act of 1933 (12 U.S.C. 1464), if copies of all information and documentary material filed with any such agency are contemporaneously filed with the Federal Trade Commission and the Assistant Attorney General at least 30 days prior to consummation of the proposed transaction;

"(9) acquisition, solely for the purpose of investment, of voting securities, if, as a result of such acquisition, the securities acquired or held do not exceed 10 per centum of the outstanding voting securities of the issuer;

"(10) acquisitions of voting securities, if, as a result of such acquisition, the voting securities acquired do not increase, directly or indirectly, the acquiring person's per centum share of outstanding voting securities of the issuer;

"(11) acquisitions, solely for the purpose of investment, by any bank, banking association, trust company, investment company, or insurance company, of (A) voting securities pursuant to a plan of reorganization or dissolution; or (B) assets in the ordinary course of its business; and

"(12) such other acquisitions, transfers, or transactions, as may be exempted under subsection (d)(2)(B).

"(d) The Federal Trade Commission, with the concurrence of the Assistant Attorney General and by rule in accordance with section 553 of title 5, United States Code, consistent with the purposes of this section—

"(1) shall require that the notification required under subsection (a) be in such form and contain such documentary material and information relevant to a proposed acquisition as is necessary and appropriate to enable the Federal Trade Commission and the Assistant Attorney General to determine whether such acquisitions may, if consummated, violate the antitrust laws; and

"(2) may—

"(A) define the terms used in this section;

"(B) exempt, from the requirements of this section, classes of persons, acquisitions, transfers, or transactions which are not likely to violate the antitrust laws; and

"(C) prescribe such other rules as may be necessary and appropriate to carry out the purposes of this section.

"(e)(1) The Federal Trade Commission or the Assistant Attorney General may, prior to the expiration of the 30-day waiting period (or in the case of a cash tender offer, the 15-day waiting period) specified in subsection (b)(1) of this section, require the submission of additional information or documentary material relevant to the proposed acquisition, from a person required to file notification with respect to such acquisition under subsection (a) of this section prior to the expiration of the waiting period specified in subsection (b)(1) of this section, or from any officer, director, partner, agent, or employee of such person.

"(2) The Federal Trade Commission or the Assistant Attorney General, in its or his discretion, may extend the 30-day waiting period (or in the case of a cash tender offer, the 15-day waiting period) specified in subsection (b)(1) of this section for an additional period of not more than 20 days (or in the case of a cash tender offer, 10 days) after the date on which the Federal Trade Commission or the Assistant Attorney General, as the case may be, receives from any person to whom a request is made under paragraph (1).

* * *

"(f) If a proceeding is instituted or an action is filed by the Federal Trade Commission, alleging that a proposed acquisition violates section 7 of this Act or section 5 of the Federal Trade Commission Act, or an action is filed by the United States, alleging that a proposed acquisition violates such section 7 or section 1 or 2 of the Sherman Act, and the Federal Trade Commission or the Assistant Attorney General (1) files a motion for a preliminary injunction against consummation of such acquisition pendente lite, and (2) certifies to the United States district court for the judicial district within which the respondent resides or carries on business, or in which the action is brought, that it or he believes that the public interest requires relief pendente lite pursuant to this subsection—

"(A) upon the filing of such motion and certification, the chief judge of such district court shall immediately notify the chief judge of the United States court of appeals for the circuit in which such district court is located, who shall designate a United States district judge to whom such action shall be assigned for all purposes; and

"(B) the motion for a preliminary injunction shall be set down for hearing by the district judge so designated at the earliest practicable time, shall take precedence over all matters except older matters of the same character and trials pursuant to section 3161 of title 18, United States Code, and shall be in every way expedited.

"(g)(1) Any person, or any officer, director, or partner thereof, who fails to comply with any provision of this section shall be liable to the United States for a civil penalty of not more than $10,000 for each day during which such person is in violation of this section. Such penalty may be recovered in a civil action brought by the United States.

* * *

The requirement that pre-transaction information concerning an acquisition be given to the enforcement agencies, the creation of a waiting period to provide the time necessary to evaluate the information received, and the specification in Section 7A(f) that a government motion for preliminary injunction be given priority in federal court, were designed to improve the likelihood that an acquisition likely to violate the Clayton Act would be prevented from ever taking place.[9] This, in turn, would reduce the need to resort to post-acquisition divestiture relief, believed to be generally ineffective at restoring competition.

As is apparent, the principal terms of the Act itself are quite skeletal. Although jurisdictional limits are specified, no effort was made to provide definitions for the terms used or otherwise to flesh out the detail of how the Act would apply to a transaction whose metamorphic character has been repeatedly stressed in previous Chapters. This detail is provided by an extraordinary set of Rules [10] developed by the

---

[9] The Act also imposes non-trivial penalties. Section 7A(g) provides for a fine of up to $10,000 a day for noncompliance.

[10] 16 C.F.R. §§ 801–803 (1985).

FTC pursuant to the direction of Section 7A(d). These Rules and an accompanying Statement of Bases and Purposes, taking up over 100 pages of the Federal Register when adopted,[11] represent an advanced evolutionary form of the regulator's craft. The problem was, simultaneously, (i) to cast a net broad enough that planners could not avoid the Act merely by altering the formal characteristics of the transaction, yet at the same time to treat some forms of transactions differently when their substance warranted it; (ii) to provide sufficient detail that planners could structure their transactions with some certainty of how the Act would apply; and (iii) to avoid conflict with the terms of the other bodies of regulation, principally the federal securities laws, that also would apply to the same transactions.

From the perspective of a transaction planner, the starting point for analysis of the Act is to recognize that, despite the legislative intent and the Act's codification as part of the Clayton Act, it is *not* an antitrust statute. The substantive content of the antitrust laws changed not one whit as a result of its passage.[12] For the planner, the task is to understand how the Act and the Rules, independently and in their interaction with federal securities regulation, influence the optimal transaction forms and acquisition strategies.

A. An Overview of the Act and Rules

The Act itself requires that a pre-acquisition filing be made if the persons who are parties to the transaction, and the assets or stock acquired in it, are of the requisite size. The size-of-person requirement is satisfied if one party to the transaction has sales or assets of $100 million or more and the other party, if engaged in manufacturing, has sales or assets of $10 million or, if not engaged in manufacturing, has assets of $10 million. Section 7A(a)(2).[13] Under the statute, the size-of-transaction test is satisfied if, as a result of the transaction, the

[11] See 43 Fed.Reg. 33450–35562 (July 31, 1978). Charitably, it has been the practice of the Federal Trade Commission staff to provide advice on compliance with the Act and Rules in any given or hypothetical case without requiring disclosure of the identity of the principal.

[12] Titles I and III of the Act also were directed at improving enforcement rather than changing substantive standards. Title I expanded the authority of the Antitrust Division to use the Civil Investigative Demand authorized by the Antitrust Civil Process Act, 15 U.S.C. §§ 1311–1314 (1983), prior to the commencement of an action. Title III amended § 4 of the Clayton Act, 15 U.S.C. §§ 15c–h (1983) to give state attorneys general a damage action on behalf of state citizens.

[13] In order to implement the size-of-person test the drafter of the Rules had to define the term "person" in a way that prevented the planner from using a small related entity, distantly controlled by the "real" acquirer, to avoid the Act. This effort provides a good example of how com-

plicated it is to fully anticipate the planner's full range of options. The Rules proceed by defining three terms in Section 801.1(a): Person, entity and ultimate parent entity. A person is defined as an ultimate parent entity—an entity which is not controlled by any other entity—and all entities, including natural persons, any type of organization, any group however organized, partnerships and joint ventures, which it controls. Thus, in determining whether the size-of-person test is met, the aggregate size of the entire group of related entities must be determined. Some indication of the resulting complexity—keep in mind that the term control is also the subject of a complex definition in section 801.1(b) and that the notion of when a group exists is itself complex—can be seen from an example. In the following diagram, the percentages and arrows represent ownership interests, UPE stands for ultimate parent entity, and Mr. and Mrs. A are husband and wife. Assume entity S-1 is making an acquisition. Who is the acquiring person (assuming, as provided in

acquiring person will hold 15 percent of the voting stock or assets of the acquired person or voting stock or assets with a value in excess of $15 million. Section 7A(a)(3). The Rules, however, first substantially expand, then even more substantially contract, and finally entirely reshape the events that trigger a filing obligation under the Act.

The expansion results from the treatment of "creeping acquisitions" in Section 801.13. The problem is to identify which transactions are to be taken into account in determining whether the size-of-transaction test is met. In statutory terms, the question is posed in terms of what stock or assets are held "as a result of" the acquisition. In substance, however, the inquiry is simply another variation of the familiar step transaction doctrine from tax law: Can the regulatory apparatus be avoided by dividing one transaction into a number of "separate" transactions? The thrust of the Rules is to eliminate this response from the planner's repertoire. For stock acquisitions, Section 801.13(a) provides that all stock of the acquired party that will be held by the acquiring person after the transaction is held "as a result of" the acquisition. Thus, a succession of entirely separate stock acquisitions will trigger a filing obligation when the aggregate of the transactions meet the size-of-transaction test. Asset acquisitions are also subject to aggregation, but in a much more limited way. Section 801.13(b) treats assets acquired within the 180 days preceding the execution of the contract, agreement in principle, or letter of intent with respect to the current transaction, as acquired "as a result of" the current transaction, but only for purposes of the $15 million test. There is no asset aggregation for purposes of the 15 percent test.

From the perspective of the drafter of the Rules, what explains the different treatment of creeping stock, as opposed to creeping asset, acquisitions? Keep in mind that a planner's ability to manipulate the form of the transaction for regulatory purposes is constrained by the non-regulatory costs associated with the manipulation. What costs are imposed by acquiring a target company's stock over a period of time rather than in one transaction? Is your answer different with respect

section 801.1(c), that the ownership of one spouse is imputed to the other)? The answer is that there are *four* chains of acquiring persons: 1) S-1, P, UPE-1, and X; 2) S-1, Mrs. A, and S-2; 3) S-1, P, and UPE-2; and 4) S-1, Mr. A, and S-2; and the size of each link in each chain must be aggregated with that of each other link in the chain to determine the size of the acquiring person. Figure it out.

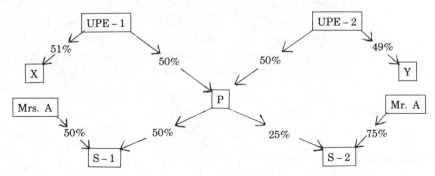

to acquisitions of a target's assets? Changes in stock ownership affect only the ownership of the target. Changes in the ownership of the target's assets change the company's productive capability which may have real competitive consequences. Thus, the existence of real consequences to the target company from having to operate without the assets disposed of for at least 180 days makes a creeping asset acquisition a less likely planning vehicle for regulatory avoidance.

The contraction in the Act's coverage results from the exemption from the filing and waiting period requirements contained in Section 802.20. Under Section 7A(a)(3) of the Act, an asset acquisition is covered if it represents 15 percent of the acquired person's assets *or* if the assets acquired have a value in excess of $15 million. Thus, even a small asset acquisition measured in dollar value is subject to the Act if it meets the percentage-of-assets requirement. Section 820.20(a) recognizes that some acquisitions that meet the percentage of assets requirement of the Act are simply too small to have an anticompetitive effect. For example, if a $100 million person acquired 15 percent of the assets of a $10 million person, the Act is triggered by an acquisition of only $1.5 million in assets.[14] This problem is met by exempting from the Act all asset acquisitions of less than $15 million. A somewhat broader exemption is provided for small stock acquisitions. First, acquisitions of more than 50 percent of an acquired person's stock are exempted from the Act if the acquired person has both sales and earnings of less than $25 million and if the stock acquired is valued at less than $15 million. Second, acquisitions of less than 50 percent of an acquired person's stock are exempt, regardless of the size of the person, if the stock acquired is valued at less than $15 million.[15] The Section 802.20 exemption can have significant transactional importance. Because of the exemption, "it may be possible to obtain *de facto* control of many smaller publicly held companies without filing and observing the preacquisition waiting period." [16]

Finally, the Rules change the structure of the Act by introducing the concept of "notification thresholds." These are defined in Section 801.1(h) as:

> (h) *Notification threshold.* The term "notification threshold" means:

> (1) Fifteen percent of the outstanding voting securities of an issuer, or an aggregate total amount of voting securities and assets of the acquired person valued in excess of $15 million;

> (2) Fifteen percent of the outstanding voting securities of an issuer, if valued in excess of $15 million;

> (3) Twenty-five percent of the outstanding voting securities of an issuer; or

---

[14] Statement of Background and Purposes, Background Information to Section 802.20, 43 Fed.Reg. 33,490 (July 31, 1978).

[15] As with implementation of all of the Act, the determination of the value of stock and assets is quite complex. See

Tomlinson, *Premerger Notification under Hart-Scott-Rodino: Valuation of Assets and Voting Securities*, 26 U.C.L.A.L.Rev. 1321 (1979).

[16] S. Axnin, B. Fogg, & N. Stoll, supra at 274.6–.7.

(4) Fifty percent of the outstanding voting securities of an issuer.

The concept is implemented by the exemption provided in Section 802.21 which generally relieves acquisitions of the Act's filing and waiting periods obligations if "[t]he acquisition will not increase the holdings of the acquiring person to meet or exceed a notification threshold greater than the greatest notification threshold met or exceeded in [an] earlier acquisition." The exemption's operation is explained in the Statement of Bases and Purposes to 'Section 802.21 and illustrated in the examples set forth following Section 802.21.

Background Information to § 802.21

The language of the act indicates that Congress contemplated agency review of stock acquisitions not only at the 15 percent or $15 million level, but also at additional, higher levels of ownership. Further review is desirable because holdings that may be innocuous at low levels may pose antitrust concerns at higher levels. Section 801.13 construes the phrase "as a result of" to fulfill this congressional purpose.

However, this principle would not justify notification and a waiting period prior to every acquisition above the 15 percent or $15 million level. The delay and expense of repeated filings would be extremely burdensome to reporting persons and would present too substantial an administrative burden for the enforcement agencies. Nor would such notifications serve any enforcement purpose. Percentage holdings varying by a few percentage points will in most cases have equivalent antitrust significance, and periodic review at the levels of the notification thresholds, or within the timing constraints of § 802.21, should be sufficient. The rule insures that the agencies learn of appreciable increases in holdings by imposing the reporting requirements at the prescribed notification thresholds, and insures that the agencies learn of changed circumstances by imposing the reporting requirement in any event after 5 years. Of course, in a particular case an acquisition exempted by the rule may prove to have antitrust significance, and the fact that the acquisition was exempt under this (or any other) rule does not preclude either agency from challenging the acquisition. See section 7A(i).

* * *

[Examples to Section 8.] 1. Corporation A acquires 15 percent of the voting securities of corporation B and both "A" and "B" file notification as required. Within five years of the expiration of the original waiting period, "A" acquires additional voting securities of B but not in an amount sufficient to meet or exceed 25 percent of the voting securities of B. No additional notification is required.

2. In example 1, "A" continues to acquire B's securities. Before "A's" holdings meet or exceed 25 percent of B's outstanding voting securities, "A" and "B" must file notification and wait the prescribed period, regardless of whether the acquisition occur within five years after the expiration of the earlier waiting period.

3. In example 2, suppose that "A" and "B" file notification at the 25 percent level and that, within 5 years after expiration of the waiting period, "A" continues to acquire voting securities of B. No further notification is required until "A" plans to make the acquisition that will give it 50 percent ownership of B. (Once "A" holds 50 percent, further acquisitions of voting securities are exempt under section 7A(c) (3).

♦

The combination of the notification threshold and aggregation concepts is a clever resolution of a problem inherent in the Act. As written, the Act requires filing when an acquiring person's stake hits 15 percent. Absent some creative interpretation, however, compliance with the filing and waiting period requirements at that time eliminates any obligation for further filings when the acquiring person later increases its stake. Literally, the acquiring person would not hold 15 percent of the acquired person's stock "as a result of" the later, in contrast to the earlier, acquisition. The result would be that the later acquisition, when control shifted and the potential for an anticompetitive effect arose, would not be subject to the Act. The aggregation principle in Section 801.13(a) meets this problem by treating all stock held by an acquiring person as held as a result of *any* acquisition. The notification threshold concept avoids the potential problem created by the solution—that the acquisition of even a small number of shares by an acquiring person that already held 15 percent always would trigger the filing and waiting period requirements.

B. The Length of the Waiting Period and the Impact on Transactional Form

In the end, the importance of the Act and Rules to the planner is how they impact on the selection of the optimal transaction form. For this purpose, the critical aspect of the regulation is the waiting period. Preparing and filing the information required may be expensive and may tip the Justice Department or the FTC to an upcoming transaction with which they should be concerned; however, the costs of complying with these obligations would warrant little effort in avoidance. Standing alone, they do not affect the planner's real strategic concern: Causing the transaction to be completed as quickly as possible so as to minimize the possibility of defensive conduct in unfriendly transactions, or of competitive bids whether the transaction is friendly or unfriendly. This concern is affected only when the Act's principal impact on a potential transaction is considered: The delay associated with the waiting period.

In specifying the waiting period applicable to different forms of transactions, the Act and Rules draw two important distinctions, one dealing with the length of the waiting period, and the second dealing with the date on which the waiting period begins to run. Sections 7A(b)(1) and 7A(e) of the statute establish the length of the waiting period. Both distinguish between cash tender offers and all other transactions. For cash tender offers, Section 7A(b)(1) sets the initial waiting period at 15 days, and Section 7A(e) limits to 10 days the extension of the waiting period that results from a request for additional information from the enforcement agency. For all other acquisitions, the initial waiting period is 30 days and the extension following a request for additional information is 20 days. The justification for this distinction is set forth in the legislative history of the Act quoted by Justice White in his opinion in Edgar v. MITE Corp.[17] Congressman Rodino, speaking with respect to the shorter waiting period for cash tender offers, noted that "[i]n cash tender offers, more so than in other mergers, the equities include time and the danger of undue delay." [18] In this regard, the Act maintains, in direction, if not precisely in magnitude, the timing difference between cash tender offers and transactions where the consideration is the acquiring company's securities created by the jurisdictional boundaries of the Williams Act and the Securities Act of 1933.[19]

Section 7A(b)(1) of the Act also distinguishes between cash tender offers and other acquisition forms with respect to the date on which the waiting period begins to run. For all transactions except cash tender offers, the waiting period commences on the date when both the acquiring and the acquired persons have filed their reports. For cash tender offers, the waiting period commences when the acquiring person files its report. Although the Act carves out only cash tender offers for special treatment with respect to commencement of the waiting period, the problem at which the statutory distinction is directed has broader application. In setting different waiting period lengths, the Act properly focused on the type of consideration used in the transaction because that distinction determined a parallel timing difference under the federal securities law; to do otherwise would have negated a seemingly important difference in treatment under a regulatory structure applicable to the same range of transactions. The distinction between types of transactions with respect to the commencement of the waiting period, however, has nothing to do with the meshing of the Act with other bodies of regulation. Rather, it is intended to solve a problem associated not with the form of the transaction, but with whether the transaction is friendly or unfriendly. If the transaction is friendly, then there is no difficulty in the waiting period commencing only after both parties make the required filing because target management, by definition, is cooperative. But when the transaction is hostile, the effect of delaying the commencement of the waiting period until the target company has filed its report would be to give the target company the

---

[17] 457 U.S. 624 (1982). The relevant portion of the opinion appears in Chapter Sixteen B., supra.

[18] 122 Cong.Rec. 30877 (1976). The legislative history of the shorter waiting period for cash tender offers is set out in detail in S. Axnin, B. Fogg & N. Stoll, supra at 51–56.

[19] See Chapter Sixteen A.3., supra. As of this writing, several bills are pending in Congressional committees to eliminate this timing difference in the Act. The rationale appears to be that no distinction relevant to antitrust concerns turns on the form of consideration offered, but that the difference in time periods favors a cash offer. Does this rationale counsel in favor of increasing the waiting period for cash tender offers or decreasing it for stock transactions? Also, several bills propose a 60-day second waiting period for acquisitions of very large size.

ability to substantially delay the acquisition, simply by not making the required filing, at the cost of no more than $10,000 a day in penalties. Where the daily fees of the target company's lawyers in takeover litigation can run substantially in excess of that amount, the price of delay might not appear excessive to a hard pressed target.

The Act's distinction with respect to the commencement of the waiting period thus is best understood as intending to distinguish between friendly and hostile transactions, using the cash tender offer as a shorthand definition of an unfriendly transaction. Although the shorthand definition may be somewhat overinclusive—some cash tender-er offers are friendly transactions [20]—the more serious problem is that it is significantly underinclusive. Some hostile transactions—for example, an exchange offer—take a form other than a cash tender offer, and under the terms of the Act, the waiting period for these transactions will not begin until the acquired person makes its filing. As a result, "an apathetic or hostile issuer could frustrate the transaction merely by neglecting to file notification." [21] The Rules attempt to remedy this statutory shortcoming in Section 801.30 which "extends to analogous types of transactions the treatment accorded tender offers" [22] with respect to the commencement of the waiting period.[23] The result is to distinguish between acquisitions of securities from third parties and acquisitions of securities from the issuer. The waiting period for the former commences with the filing by the acquiring person; only when the issuer is a party to the transaction does commencement await the filing by both parties.[24]

The terms of the waiting period dictate the transactional impact of the Act. For our purposes, however, the critical concern is not simply whether the Act imposes a delay. Rather, it is whether the Act's waiting period has planning implications: Can a timing advantage be secured by casting a transaction in one form or another? Most generally, the application of the Act's waiting period reinforces the bias in favor of cash consideration created by the Williams Act. An acquiring person making a cash tender offer will be free to begin purchasing shares 15 to 25 days before an acquiring person whose proposed transaction, whether an exchange offer or a merger, involves the issuance of securities. In an acquisition market in which an acquirer must anticipate the possibility of a competitive bid whether the initial

---

[20] See the excerpt from Freund & Easton, Chapter Fifteen A., supra.

[21] Statement of Bases and Purpose, Section 801.30—Tender Offers and Acquisitions of Voting Securities from Third Parties, 43 Fed.Reg. 33483 (July 31, 1978).

[22] Id.

[23] The principal transactions covered by Section 801.30 are "exchange offers, open-market purchases, private purchases, and conversions of non-voting securities." The central theme of the list is to include all "transactions that may be initiated by the acquiring person without the agreement of the acquired person." Id.

[24] Although the acquired person's filing need not be made in order for the waiting period to commence in a Section 801.30 transaction, Section 801.30(b)(2) does impose an obligation on the acquired person to make the filing within 15 days (10 days in a cash tender offer) after receiving notice from the acquiring person. Section 803.5 in turn requires that the acquiring person's filing in a Section 801.30 transaction include an affidavit that the acquiring person has notified the acquired person of the transaction.

transaction is friendly or hostile, the bias in favor of cash, and in favor of a two step transaction when the use of some stock as consideration is anticipated, is substantial.

The Act does more, however, than reinforce existing biases. With respect to the two most important forms of unconventional transactions—securing control through private purchases or open market purchases—the Act may significantly impair their attractiveness.

We can examine the Act's impact on efforts to take control of a company through privately negotiated stock purchases by seeing how the Act would have applied to the transaction involved in Wellman v. Dickinson [25]—the purchase by Sun Company, in a single day, of 34 percent of the voting stock of Becton, Dickinson & Company from some 30 institutions and individuals.[26] The Act's requirement that one party be involved in commerce and the size-of-person test were clearly satisfied. What is the relevant transaction for purposes of the size-of-transaction test? If each of the purchases involved less than 15 percent of the outstanding Becton, Dickinson stock, when would the Act's filing and waiting period requirements be triggered? Recall that Section 801.13(a) provides that all stock held by an acquiring person is deemed acquired in each acquisition of additional stock.

Once the filing requirement is triggered, who must file as the acquired person: Becton, Dickinson or each of the individual sellers? If the sellers were required to file, a substantial coordination problem could be created. In this regard, consider the following example that appears in Rule 801.2(b):

> 1. Assume that person "Q" will acquire voting securities of corporation X held by "P" and that X is not included within person "P." Under this section, the acquired person is the person within which X is included, and is not "P." [27]

The most critical strategic issue is the length of the waiting period that would apply to the transaction.[28] Under the Act, all acquisitions other than a cash tender offer have a 30-day waiting period, with the possibility of a 20-day extension if the enforcement agency requests additional information. For cash tender offers, the waiting period is only fifteen days with the possibility of a ten day extension. Is the *Wellman* transaction a cash tender offer for purposes of the Act? The possibility of a clever planner crafting a transaction that was a cash tender offer for purposes of Hart-Scott-Rodino, and thereby subject only to the shorter waiting period, but not a tender offer for purposes of the

---

[25] 475 F.Supp. 783 (S.D.N.Y.1979), affirmed 682 F.2d 355 (2d Cir.1982), cert. denied 460 U.S. 1069 (1983).

[26] The Act did not, in fact, apply to the transaction in *Wellman*. Although the Act became law on September 30, 1976, a Federal Trade Commission transitional rule exempted all acquisitions completed prior to the adoption of the FTC Rules on September 5, 1978. The *Wellman* transaction took place in January, 1978, and therefore was exempt.

[27] In the examples to the Rules, persons are designated by letters within quotation marks and entities are designated by letters without quotation marks.

[28] When the waiting period would commence is not in doubt. Because the transaction is one "in which voting securities are to be acquired from a holder or holders other than the issuer," Section 801.30 provides that the waiting period is commenced by the acquiring person's filing.

Williams Act, was eliminated by the Rules' cross reference to the Williams Act for a definition of a tender offer.[29]   Thus, a planner is put to a choice: The price of the shorter waiting period under Hart-Scott-Rodino is compliance with the Williams Act.

How one makes this choice depends on the importance of the extra 15 days of initial waiting period, given that there will be a minimum 15 day period in practically all events.[30]   Answering this question, in turn, requires resolution of two additional inquiries.   As a threshold matter, can the transaction even be mechanically accomplished in light of the waiting period?   If so, do any benefits of a *Wellman* type transaction survive the imposition of any waiting period?

With respect to the threshold inquiry, the planner's principal concern is that the acquiring company be able to enter into a binding purchase contract with the seller prior to the expiration of the waiting period so that it does not have to tip its hand to other potential sellers before it has completed its purchasing activity.[31]   One approach would be to enter into binding purchase contracts the closing of which are conditioned on compliance with the Act.   By entering into such a contract, does one "acquire" the security within the meaning of the Act?   Under the Rules, the answer depends on whether the contract transfers beneficial ownership of the stock.[32]   What provisions should be included in the contract concerning such matters as voting and dividend rights pending the closing of the transaction?

Assuming that the contract could be drafted to avoid the passage of beneficial ownership until the expiration of the waiting period, would the transaction still be worth doing?   The point of the transaction's structure, after all, is to be able to pressure the institutions to make a decision and tender quickly.   Would the pressure imposed be reduced if the purchases could not be closed for 30 days?   This problem, of course, would not be present in connection with private purchases entered into as part of a negotiated transaction as described by Freund & Easton.[33] There the point was only to discourage competitive bidders by securing a significant stock holding before public disclosure.   So long as the contracts were conditioned *only* on the running of the waiting period, the impact on competitive bidders should be the same.

[29] Rule 801.1(g) defines a tender offer as "any offer to purchase voting securities which is a tender offer within the meaning of section 14 of the Securities Exchange Act."

[30] The Rules provide for early termination of the initial or subsequent waiting periods upon the discretion of the FTC or Justice Department.   This discretion is subject to judicial review.   See Hublein, Inc. v. FTC, 539 F. Supp. 123 (D.Conn. 1982).

[31] The enforcement agencies are obligated to keep filings under the Act, including the identity of the parties, confidential throughout the process until an injunction is sought or early termination of the waiting period is granted.

[32] Technically, neither the statute nor the rules define the term "acquire."   Section 801.1(c) defines "holds" to mean "beneficial ownership" and § 801.13 uses the word "held" in the phrase "held by the acquiring person as a result of the acquisition."   Taken together, one holds securities as a result of an acquisition when one acquires beneficial ownership of them.   It should follow that one acquires securities when one becomes the beneficial owner of them.   Accord S. Axnin, B. Fogg & N. Stoll, supra at 82–83.

[33] See Chapter Fifteen A., supra.

The technique of acquiring a significant ownership position by means of open market purchases fares worse under the Act's regulatory regime than do private acquisitions. Recall that open market purchases could not be carried out if the Williams Act applied because it would be mechanically impossible to comply with the proration, withdrawal and length of offer requirements. A similar problem arises under Hart-Scott-Rodino. If Hart-Scott-Rodino applies, the open market purchase cannot be consummated until the 30-day waiting period has run but, unlike in private purchases, there is no way in which open market purchases can be conditioned on the expiration of the waiting period. Thus, the Act effectively reduces to $15 million the amount of stock an acquiring company can purchase without any public disclosure. This may have a much more significant impact on acquiring company strategy than simply making it impossible to secure working control through a campaign of large open market purchases. As described in Chapter Fourteen B.3.e., one of the means by which an initial bidder can protect itself against the risk of losing the target to a competitive bidder, and thereby losing its investment in discovering the target in the first place, is to take a position in the target's stock as a hedge. So long as the hedge was purchased before disclosure of the first offer caused the price of the target's stock to rise, the gain on its sale to the winning bidder would offset the loss on the investment in information. The effect of the Act is to cap the size of the hedge possible and, as a result, to increase the risk of a competitive bidder that the initial bidder actually must bear. To that extent, the Act reduces the incentives to make an initial bid to the detriment of target shareholders.[34]

This final point—that the Act may reduce the absolute number of acquisitions to the detriment of target shareholders and, perhaps, the economy as a whole, poses an interesting issue concerning the Act's overall value. If the problems which led to the Act could be solved without imposing costs beyond the simple transaction costs of compliance such as filling out the notification form, the overall value of the Act would be subject to little debate. The problem, however, is that the Act does impose other costs. Most importantly, the effect of the

[34] The potential acquiring company could file under the Act with respect to anticipated open market purchases with the intent of not beginning to purchase until the waiting period had expired. The problem, however, is that under Section 801.30 the waiting period will not commence until the target company is notified of the information specified in section 803.5, including the amount of securities intended to be purchased. So long as the target company made this information public prior to the expiration of the waiting period, the market price of the target's stock would rise in anticipation and, by reducing the potential profit from reselling the stock to a higher bidder, to that extent reduce the value of the hedge.

The practical application of the Act creates an additional disincentive to identifying a takeover target when a competitive bid is possible. The first filing under the Act requires the FTC or the Antitrust Division to learn about the two companies and their competitive overlap. A subsequent filing by a competitive bidder requires study of only that company; the target has already been analyzed. As a practical matter, the request for additional information often issues only to buy the enforcement agencies more time to analyze the information they have, as much as to acquire more information. Thus, the initial bidder—the first filer—is taxed with the time to learn about the target and, often, with an additional waiting period and document production cost.

waiting period is to reduce the incentive to make acquisitions. This is especially troublesome because the Act is terribly over-inclusive from the perspective of preserving competition. The disincentive created does not depend on whether an acquisition has the potential to be anticompetitive; it applies equally to conglomerate and horizontal acquisitions. Is it possible to balance in any meaningful way the cost of discouraging some perfectly desirable acquisitions against the gains from avoiding later failures in obtaining effective divestiture by facilitating the issuance of a preliminary injunction? Would it be helpful to know how many times the Department of Justice and the FTC have sought pre-transaction preliminary injunctions in transactions where notification was filed? [35] One way in which the overinclusive nature of the statute could be ameliorated is through the authority of the Federal Trade Commission and the Assistant Attorney General in charge of the Antitrust Division under Section 7A(b)(2) of the Act to terminate the waiting period prior to its expiration "in individual cases" if neither intends to take any action. Would the adoption of a rule specifying the circumstances under which requests for early termination would be allowed reduce the disincentive to make acquisitions that do not pose antitrust problems? Would the statutory phrase "in individual cases" limit the extent to which a rule might authorize blanket early termination in specified categories of acquisitions?

[35] In 1983, neither the Antitrust Division nor the FTC sought a single preliminary injunction in a merger case, although the Antitrust Division did inform parties on four occasions that it would challenge the transaction unless it were restructured to eliminate competitive overlap or abandoned. In each case the parties complied.

Also interesting is the percentage of reportable transactions in which either enforcement agency made a request for additional information:

1979 – 12.9%
1980 – 9.0%
1981 – 7.5%
1982 – 4.3%
1983 – 4.3%

Seventh Annual Report to Congress Pursuant to Section 201 of the Hart-Scott-Rodino Antitrust Improvements Act of 1976 at 3 (May 31, 1984).

This data is subject to differing interpretations. The Report itself states:

[T]his persistent downward trend may in part reflect a beneficial deterrent effect to the premerger notification program. Because the program enables the enforcement agencies to detect and challenge virtually all sizeable anticompetitive acquisitions before they are consummated, businesses may be increasingly avoiding transactions that approach the line of illegality.

The drop in the second request issue rate since 1981 may also reflect the impact of the Justice Department's 1982 Merger Guidelines and the Federal Trade Commission's contemporaneous Statement Concerning Horizontal Mergers. These documents have provided business decision-makers with a better understanding of the types of transactions that are likely to be challenged as well as the factors the enforcement agencies will consider in making their decisions. With this knowledge, business decision-makers can more easily avoid transactions of questionable legality. In addition, because of these documents, parties involved in transactions that appear to raise antitrust issues have been better able to identify areas of concern and have, on several occasions, voluntarily provided information addressing these concerns. Thus, the agencies have been able to resolve some concerns without resorting to a second request.

In contrast, FTC Commissioner Pertschuk, in a separate statement concerning the Seventh Annual Report, challenged the Report's evaluation of the data. In response to the above-quoted analysis, Commissioner Pertschuk noted that "the number of acquisitions during 1983 [was] a nine-year high and the number of large mergers [was] an all time high" and went on to state that he "simply cannot accept the [Report's] Panglossian vision of what is actually happening."

CHAPTER EIGHTEEN. SUCCESSOR LIABILITY OF THE ACQUIRING COMPANY

The survey of alternative acquisition techniques in Chapter Thirteen disclosed substantial differences in the protections provided shareholders and creditors by different techniques. A statutory merger provides the most protection. Shareholders of both the acquiring and target companies typically have voting and appraisal rights. In turn, creditors of the target company are protected because the surviving company in a merger assumes as a matter of law all of the target's liabilities, including unknown or contingent liabilities. Because these protections are costly, planners responded by casting their transactions in an alternative form which provided fewer protections. The alternative most often chosen is a purchase of the target company's assets. When the transaction is cast in this form, acquiring company shareholders lose their vote, in many jurisdictions target shareholders lose their appraisal rights, and, in all jurisdictions, the general rule is that the acquiring company is responsible for only those liabilities of the target company that it expressly agrees to assume. Creditors of the target company then run the post-acquisition risk that the target company, now a shell holding only the consideration received in the transaction, quickly will dissolve, leaving creditors unpaid and without other recourse. It was predictable that in precisely those circumstances in which the planners thought it advantageous to eliminate the protections given shareholders and creditors in a statutory merger, those denied the protections would complain. Chapter Thirteen E. examined the de facto merger doctrine—the claim by *shareholders* that they are entitled to just those protections planners sought to eliminate by choosing a particular form of acquisition. This Chapter considers the parallel doctrine of successor liability—the claim by *creditors* of the target company that the acquiring company should be deemed to have assumed their claims, as would have been the case if the transaction had been structured as a merger rather than as a sale of assets.

It is helpful at the outset to identify more precisely those target company creditors whose claims are particularly vulnerable to reduction in value as a result of the form in which an acquisition is cast. Although corporate law does not give traditional lenders, such as bondholders or banks, a vote on acquisitions as a means of protecting their interests,[1] they can, and typically do, protect themselves against this risk by contracting for a veto over major corporate changes like acquisitions.[2] The borrowing company will be willing to provide such protection in order to secure a lower interest rate—one that does not reflect the risk of a future acquisition structured to disadvantage creditors. Moreover, neither the contracting nor monitoring costs

---

[1] See Chapter Thirteen A.2. and B.3., supra.

[2] See Am.B.Found., *Commentaries on Model Debenture Identure Provisions* 290– 301 (§ 801) (1971); Smith & Warner, *On Financial Contracting: An Analysis of Bond Covenants*, 7 J.Fin.Econ. 117, 126–27 (1979).

associated with this form of creditor protection are likely to be significant. The marginal costs of contracting for the protection are low because negotiations already will be under way concerning the loan itself, and monitoring the debtor's behavior for violations of the contractual restrictions should not be burdensome given the specialized character of these types of lenders. Finally, state corporate law substantially restricts the ability of target shareholders to disadvantage this class of creditors by absconding with the proceeds of an asset sale by promptly dissolving the target corporation. State law typically requires that known debts, obviously including debts of this character, must either be paid or otherwise adequately provided for as a condition to dissolution.[3]

Trade creditors, in contrast, will not be protected by elaborate contractual provisions because the costs of contracting and monitoring are too high given the typical size of the debt and the character of the creditor. They are not, however, unprotected. Just like specialized lenders, trade creditors must be paid prior to dissolution because their debts are known. Thus, even though the acquiring company does not assume their debt, the consideration paid to the target company remains subject to it. Moreover, because trade credit is typically short term, creditors often will have sufficient notice of a sale of assets that would increase the debtor's default risk that they can protect themselves simply by declining further business with the debtor or by altering their terms of trade.

Contingent unknown creditors—those who are not yet aware that they may have a claim against the target company—are in a radically different position. They cannot protect themselves by a tailored contractual provision because their claims typically do not arise out of a negotiated contract. And precisely because the claim is contingent and unknown, the dissolution of the target company can deprive the potential creditor of its only potential defendant. State corporate statutes commonly require either that only known debts and claims be paid or provided for as a condition to dissolution, or provide for a post-dissolution period in which creditors can bring suit. If suit is not brought within this period, because the claim is still unknown, it is cut off.[4]

The prototype of such a contingent creditor—and the major concern of planners with respect to the successor liability of an acquiring company—is the future products liability plaintiff. First, potential products liability claims are often large enough to get the attention of planners; there is sufficient incentive for planners to devote their

---

[3] See, e.g., Cal.Corp.Code § 1905. Other states provide a two or three year post-dissolution period in which claims can be brought. See, e.g., Model Bus. Corp. Act § 105 (1971); Del.Code Ann. tit. 8, § 278; Mass.Gen.Laws Ann., C. 156B, § 102. This approach provides effectively identical protection for known creditors.

[4] See, e.g., Henn & Alexander, *Effect of Corporate Dissolution on Products Liability Claims,* 56 Cornell L.Rev. 865 (1971); Wallach, *Products Liability: A Remedy in*

Search of a Defendant—The Effect of a Sale of Assets and Subsequent Dissolution on Product Dissatisfaction Claims, 41 Mo. L.Rev. 321 (1976); Note, *Continuing Corporate Existence for Post-Dissolution Claims: The Defective Products Dilemma,* 13 Pac. L.J. 1227 (1982). One court has held that dissolution under the California statute does not cut off unknown claims if the injury occurred prior to dissolution. Abington Heights School Dist. v. Speedspace Corp., 693 F.2d 284 (3d Cir.1982).

attention to avoiding them. Second, defective or unsafe products can create claims far in the future. The effects of chemicals and drugs may take years to appear; even a mundane product like a ladder can cause injuries in the future when someone falls off of it years after it was manufactured. Thus, there is both an incentive for planners to structure their transaction to avoid these liabilities and, because the dissolution statutes effectively protect only known creditors, a real potential for tort victims to be left uncompensated. In the absence of successor liability, a tort victim simply may have no available defendant because the manufacturer of the product that caused the injury will have ceased to exist before the victim was injured.

In this Chapter we begin by examining the doctrine of successor liability in its most prominent manifestation: What is the effect of an acquisition on the target company's as yet unasserted products liability claims? We first consider the traditional rules governing successor liability and attempt to understand the real nature of the problem at which successor liability is directed. We then evaluate the different approaches courts have used to expand the doctrine of successor liability, largely in response to the problem of products liability claims, and suggest an alternative approach. Next, we examine what room remains for planners to limit the acquiring company's liability for the target company's potential products liability claims. Finally, we briefly survey two other areas of potential successor liability—labor union contracts and pension fund obligations.

A. "Buy Assets—Sell Stock": Traditional Distinctions Between Acquisition Techniques

The traditional expression of the acquisition planner's decision rule was to buy assets and sell stock. The principal explanation for the preference was the problem of contingent and unknown liabilities: In an asset acquisition one assumed only those liabilities specified in the contract, while in a stock acquisition (or a merger) all liabilities, including contingent and unknown liabilities, became the responsibility of the acquiring company. Thus, an acquiring company would like to buy assets and leave unwanted liabilities to target shareholders; symmetrically, target shareholders would like to sell stock (or merge) and thereby be relieved of them.

This formulation of the decision rule obscures the real nature of the problem. As expressed, the traditional decision rule posits a conflict between the acquiring company and the target company—one or the other ends up holding the liability bag. The real problem associated with the successor liability doctrine becomes apparent only after it is realized that, if the acquirer and target cooperate, neither need end up with the unwanted liabilities. Suppose a target company has a value of $5 million if future products liability claims are ignored, but both it and the acquiring company believe that it is subject to $2 million of such claims. In this event, the target company is worth $3 million if it is subject to the products liability claims. The choice of the acquisition technique does not alter this valuation one bit. If the acquisition is structured as a sale of assets so that the acquiring company does not assume the future products liabilities claims, it will be willing to pay $5 million—the value of the assets it receives—but the target company will still be worth only $3 million because its assets, albeit now consisting of only the $5 million consideration, remain subject to $2 million in future products liabilities claims. If, alternatively, the acquisition is structured as a merger so that the acquiring company assumes the future products liability claims, it will pay only $3 million. The target shareholders, however, will retain all of the consideration because the consideration is no longer subject to the future claims. Thus, the acquiring and target companies end up in precisely the same position whether assets are bought or stock is sold. To be sure, one or the other party ends up bearing the future liabilities, but that party is compensated for it. As well, the future products liability claimants end up no worse off as a result of the transaction; either way the transaction is structured, $5 million in assets are subject to their claims, just as before the transaction took place.

This analysis does not, however, demonstrate that planners cannot improve the position of the acquiring and target companies. If we assume that the traditional rule governing dissolution prevails—that a company can liquidate without provision for unknown contingent claims like future products liability claims and that shareholders cannot later be charged with these claims even to the extent of their liquidation distributions—then both the acquiring company and the target company will want the transaction structured in precisely the same way. If the transaction is structured as an asset acquisition following which the target company is dissolved, the value of the target company's assets is increased by $2 million. This result follows from the combination of the dissolution rule and the ability of the acquiring company to specify which liabilities it will assume in an asset acquisition. The assets are worth $5 million to the acquiring company in an asset acquisition because they will not be subject to the future products liability claims. If the target company promptly liquidates, before the future claims are made, its shareholders get to keep all of the consideration. The target company is thus worth $2 million dollars more because the effect of structuring the transaction as a sale of assets and a dissolution is to eliminate $2 million dollars in liabilities. Although the target and acquiring companies may disagree about how this windfall should be shared, they *will* agree that the transaction should be structured so as to create it. An accurate statement of the decision rule then is buy assets, liquidate the target, and cut off the future products liability claimants.[5]

The doctrine of successor liability is thus directed at the ability of planners to use a corporate acquisition to externalize products liability risks—to leave the victims uncompensated and thereby allow manufacturers to make product safety decisions without taking into account the

---

[5] See Roe, *Mergers, Acquisitions, and Tort: A Comment on the Problem of Successor Corporate Liability*, 70 Va.L.Rev. 1559, 1565 (1984); D. Phillips, *Products Liability of Successor Corporations: A Corporate and Commercial Law Perspective*, 11 Hofstra L.Rev. 249, 264 (1982).

costs of defective products. So understood, it is hardly surprising that the doctrine historically took a quite restrictive form. Prior to the rapid development of products liability law, few circumstances posed the risk of large contingent future liabilities. In this setting, the successor liability doctrine—the statement of when an acquiring company would be deemed to have assumed target company liabilities in an asset acquisition—consisted of the following four elements:

(1) the acquiring company explicitly or implicitly agreed to assume the target company's liabilities;

(2) the acquiring company was a mere continuation of the target company;

(3) the target company's transfer of assets was fraudulent in that its only purpose was to escape liability for its debts; or

(4) the transaction constituted a de facto merger.[6]

From a planning perspective, only one of the four elements is of special concern. The first—contractual assumption—is of little interest in a planning setting. There has never been any doubt that an acquiring company *could* assume the target company's contingent future liabilities; the successor liability doctrine takes on planning significance only to the extent it limits the acquiring company's ability *not* to assume them. The second and third elements—mere continuation and fraud on creditors—do have some general planning implications; however, they are directed not at arm's length transactions, but merely at contrivances without substance independent of the impact on creditors. In this sense, they are corporate law restatements of the traditional prohibitions on fraudulent conveyances reflected in the Uniform Fraudulent Conveyance Act.[7] That leaves the de facto merger element as the focus of traditional successor liability doctrine.

This result is entirely understandable. For a court faced with a creditor's claim that the form of an arms-length acquisition should be disregarded and the creditor given the same protections as if the acquisition had been cast in a different form, the obvious analogy was the de facto merger doctrine. The difficulty, however, was that the analogy, although facially accurate, was empty. First, as we saw in Chapter Thirteen E., the de facto merger doctrine that developed in response to shareholder claims itself lacked a coherent core. There was no clear statement of the circumstances when the planner's choice

---

[6] See, e.g., J. Phillips, *Product Line Continuity and Successor Corporate Liability*, 58 N.Y.U.L.Rev. 906, 908–12 (1983); Heitland, *Survival of Products Liability Claims in Asset Acquisitions*, 34 Bus.Law. 489–90 (1979).

[7] Uniform Fraudulent Conveyance Act, 7A U.L.A. (1978); see Clark, *The Duties of the Corporate Debtor to its Creditors*, 90 Harv.L.Rev. 505 (1977) (relationship between Uniform Fraudulent Conveyance Act and corporate law principles); D. Phillips, supra, at 261–64. It is possible to treat the mere continuation element as the equivalent of de facto merger, see J. Phil-

lips, supra, at 909, but the better reading treats it as a species of non-arms length contrivance. For example, the California Supreme Court has held that proof of mere continuation requires "a showing of one or both of the following factual elements: (1) no adequate consideration was given for the predecessor corporation's assets and made available for meeting the claims of its unsecured creditors; (2) one or more persons were officers, directors, or stockholders of both corporations." Ray v. Alad Corp., 19 Cal.3d 22, 29, 136 Cal.Rptr. 574, 578, 560 P.2d 3, 7 (1977).

would be respected and of those when it would be disregarded. Thus, the analogy served not to answer the successor liability question, but merely to move the uncertainty down one level. Second, and more important, the analogy did not recognize that target shareholders, for whom the de facto merger doctrine was created, and target creditors, for whom the successor liability doctrine was created, are in quite different situations. Although the same transactional trigger—the planner's selection of an asset acquisition instead of a merger—creates the problem in both cases, there is no a priori reason to think that the solution, or even the mode of analysis, should be the same in both.

B. Judicial Responses to Products Liability Claims

By the time the products liability onslaught hit the courts, it was increasingly clear that the traditional formulation of the successor liability doctrine provided little guidance concerning how to deal with products liability claims against a target company that no longer existed. Plaintiffs, of course, had no difficulty deciding where to turn; they sued the acquiring company, the only deep pocket in sight. The courts, however, faced a more complicated choice in deciding how to respond to these new claims. They could have stayed within the traditional vocabulary of the successor liability doctrine, trying to add products liability content to the empty vessel of de facto merger analysis. Alternatively, the courts could forge a new approach to the problem in recognition of the fact that when plaintiffs were tort victims instead of target shareholders, the traditional formulation of the successor liability doctrine, and especially reliance on the de facto merger concept, were simply beside the point. Both approaches were tried.

1. Expanding Traditional Doctrine to Cope With Products Liability

KNAPP v. NORTH AMERICAN ROCKWELL CORP.

United States Court of Appeals, Third Circuit, 1974.
506 F.2d 361, cert. denied 421 U.S. 965 (1975).

Before ALDISERT, ADAMS and ROSENN, Circuit Judges.

OPINION OF THE COURT

ADAMS, Circuit Judge.

The principal question here is whether it was error to grant summary judgment on the ground that one injured by a defective machine may not recover from the corporation that purchased substantially all the assets of the manufacturer of the machine because the transaction was a sale of assets rather than a merger or consolidation.

I.

Stanley Knapp, Jr., an employee of Mrs. Smith's Pie Co., was injured on October 6, 1969, when, in the course of his employment, his hand was caught in a machine known as a "Packomatic." The machine had been designed and manufactured by Textile Machine Works (TMW) and had been sold to Mrs. Smith's Pie Co. in 1966 or 1967.

On April 5, 1968, TMW entered into an agreement with North American Rockwell whereby TMW exchanged substantially all its assets for stock in Rockwell. TMW retained only its corporate seal, its articles of incorporation, its minute books and other corporate records, and $500,000. in cash intended to cover TMW's expenses in connection with the transfer. TMW also had the right, prior to closing the transaction with Rockwell, to dispose of land held by TMW or its subsidiary. Among the assets acquired by Rockwell was the right to use the name "Textile Machine Works." TMW was to change its name on the closing date, then to distribute the Rockwell stock to its shareholders and to dissolve TMW "[a]s soon as practicable after the last of such distributions."

The accord reached by Rockwell and TMW also stipulated that Rockwell would assume specified obligations and liabilities of TMW, but among the liabilities not assumed were: "(a) liabilities against which TMW is insured or otherwise indemnified to the extent of such insurance or indemnification unless the insurer or indemnitor agrees in writing to insure and indemnify [Rockwell] to the same extent as it was so insuring and indemnifying TMW."

Closing took place pursuant to the agreement on August 29, 1968. Plaintiff sustained his injuries on October 6, 1969. TMW was dissolved on February 20, 1970, almost 18 months after the bulk of its assets had been exchanged for Rockwell stock.

Plaintiff filed this suit against Rockwell in the district court on March 22, 1971. He alleged that his injuries resulted from the negligence of TMW in designing and manufacturing the machine and that Rockwell, as TMW's successor, is liable for such injuries. Rockwell joined plaintiff's employer, Mrs. Smith's Pie Co., as a third-party defendant.[3]

Rockwell moved for summary judgment in the district court on June 19, 1973. On September 6, 1973, the district court granted the motion, ruling that Rockwell had neither merged nor consolidated with TMW, that Rockwell was not a continuation of TMW, and that Rockwell had not assumed TMW's liability to Knapp. * * *

II.

Both parties agree that this case is controlled by the following principle of law:

The general rule is that "a mere sale of corporate property by one company to another does not make the purchaser liable for the liabilities of the seller not assumed by it." * * * There are,

[3] On July 13, 1972, after Rockwell had denied responsibility for any liability TMW may have had to Knapp, Knapp sued TMW in a Pennsylvania state court to recover for his injuries. That suit was barred, however, either by the two year statute of limitations on personal injury actions [12 Pa. Stat.Ann. § 31] or by the statute requiring that suits against a dissolved corporation be commenced within two years of the date of dissolution [15 Pa.Stat.Ann. § 2111 (Supp.1974)].

however, certain exceptions to this rule. Liability for obligations of a selling corporation may be imposed on the purchasing corporation when (1) the purchaser expressly or impliedly agrees to assume such obligations; (2) the transaction amounts to a consolidation or merger of the selling corporation with or into the purchasing corporation; (3) the purchasing corporation is merely a continuation of the selling corporation; or (4) the transaction is entered into fraudulently to escape liability for such obligations.

Shane v. Hobam, Inc., 332 F.Supp. 526, 527–528 (E.D.Pa.1971) (citations omitted) (decided under New York law).

In light of this language, Knapp contends that the transaction in question "amounts to a consolidation or merger of [TMW] with or into the purchasing corporation [Rockwell]" or, alternatively, that Rockwell is a "continuation" of TMW. Although the TMW corporation technically continued to exist until its dissolution approximately 18 months after the consummation of the transaction with Rockwell, TMW was, Knapp argues, a mere shell during that period. It had none of its former assets, no active operations, and was required by the contract with Rockwell to dissolve itself "as soon as practicable." Knapp urges in effect that the transaction between TMW and Rockwell should be considered a de facto merger.

* * *

III

In a diversity case, the federal court must apply the rule of law which would govern if suit were brought in a court of the forum state.

* * *

No prior cases decided under Pennsylvania law have addressed the problem presently before this Court. However, when courts from other jurisdictions have considered similar questions, they have ascertained the existence *vel non* of a merger, a consolidation or a continuation on the basis of whether, immediately after the transaction, the selling corporation continued to exist as a corporate entity and whether, after the transaction, the selling corporation possessed substantial assets with which to satisfy the demands of its creditors.

Thus, in Bazan v. Kux Machine Co.,[12] the plaintiff was injured in 1966 by a machine purchased by his employer from Kux Machine Co. in 1961. In 1963, after the sale of the machine to plaintiff's employer but prior to the accident, Kux sold to the Wickes Corporation the bulk of Kux's assets, retaining only its accounts receivable, its prepaid insurance and its real estate. Wickes acquired Kux' tangible personal property, licenses, trademarks, patents, good will, and the exclusive right to use the name "Kux Machine." Kux, after changing its name, remained in existence for ten months before dissolving as required by the contract with Wickes. The court held that the transaction was not a merger, consolidation or continuation. It reasoned that Kux continued to exist for a substantial period after the exchange, that the transaction was a cash sale rather than an exchange of stock, and that

---

[12] 358 F.Supp. 1250 (E.D.Wis.1973).

none of the owners or management of the seller acquired any interest in the buyer.

Similarly, in McKee v. Harris-Seybold Co.[13] the court held that there had been no merger or consolidation between the alleged tort-feasor and the purchaser of its assets. The plaintiff was injured in 1968 by a paper-cutting machine manufactured in 1916 by the Seybold Machine Co. In 1926, Seybold agreed to sell its assets to Harris Automatic Press Co. In exchange, Harris agreed to give Seybold cash plus common stock in Harris, and to assume certain of Seybold's liabilities. Harris acquired all the assets of Seybold including its good will and the exclusive use of the name "Seybold Machine Co." Seybold agreed to change its name and not to engage in any manufacturing activities. Seybold continued to exist under a different name for one year after the exchange. Prior to the consummation of the transaction Harris assigned its interest in the contract to a new corporation formed for the purpose. The new corporation was later renamed the Harris-Seybold Co. The court held that Harris-Seybold was not liable for the plaintiff's injuries because there had been no merger or consolidation between the Harris and Seybold corporations. Nor, the court ruled, was Harris or Harris-Seybold a continuation of Seybold. After observing that this was not an exchange for securities alone, the court stressed that "[t]he identity of the [Seybold] corporation and of its stockholders as an integral part of the corporate identity was not eradicated by the transfer." 264 A.2d at 104. * * * The court's analysis was that "[i]f the vendor corporation receives the consideration for the transfer, as opposed to those situations where the stockholders directly receive the same, and that corporation is thereby kept alive, there seems to be nothing in the nature of a merger or consolidation." Id.

The Nevada Supreme Court reached the same conclusion in Lamb v. Leroy Corp.[14] There, a contract creditor of Nevada Land and Mortgage Co. sought to enforce his claim against the Leroy Corp. Shares in Leroy were exchanged in 1965 for all the assets of Nevada Land exclusive of two items of real estate Leroy did not want and some incidental cash. A certificate representing the stock was delivered to Nevada Land. "Soon after the consummation of [the] transaction," Nevada Land distributed the Leroy shares to its shareholders and dissolved, without satisfying Lamb's claim. The court concluded that the transaction was not a merger or a consolidation, on the basis that the consideration was adequate, that Leroy delivered the shares to Nevada Land rather than to its shareholders, and that the subsequent dissolution was a separate transaction.

This cluster of cases [16] illustrates the significance which the decisions from other jurisdictions accord to corporate theory and the

---

[13] 109 N.J.Super. 555, 264 A.2d 98 (L.Div. 1970) aff'd per curiam, 118 N.J.Super. 480, 288 A.2d 585 (1972).

[14] 85 Nev. 276, 454 P.2d 24 (1969).

[16] See also, Forest Laboratories v. Pillsbury Co., 452 F.2d 621 (7th Cir.1971); West

Texas Refining & Dev. Co. v. Commissioner of Internal Revenue, 68 F.2d 77 (10th Cir. 1933); Kloberdanz v. Joy Mfg. Co., 288 F.Supp. 817 (D.Colo.1968); Copease Mfg. Co. v. Cormac Photocopy Corp., 242 F.Supp. 993 (S.D.N.Y.1965); J.F. Anderson

continued existence of the corporate entity. The adequacy of the consideration received by the selling corporation has also been given great weight in deciding the existence of a sale as contrasted with a merger or continuation. In *Lamb*, supra, the court pointed out that the consideration was adequate, since the selling corporation received a valuable asset—the purchaser's stock—which for the remainder of the life of the corporation was exposed to the claims of the seller's creditors. Similarly, the court emphasized in *McKee*, supra, that the selling corporation had received substantial value for its assets, and that there was no hint the selling corporation was being denuded of assets with which it might satisfy the claims of its creditors. The district court for the District of Colorado, in Kloberdanz v. Joy Mfg. Co.,[17] stated that "the emphasis should be on whether the sale was a bona fide one involving the payment of money or property to the selling corporation whereby it can respond [in damages] in actions like the present one."

In Jackson v. Diamond T. Trucking Co.,[18] the court found the purchasing corporation to be a continuation of the selling corporation because the "purchaser" took all the assets of the "seller" in return for nominal consideration only. Similarly, in Ruedy v. Toledo Factories Co.[19] and Hoche Productions v. Jayark Films Corp.,[20] the courts concluded that the transactions were mergers after the "selling" corporations were left without appreciable assets to satisfy the claims of their creditors.

IV.

The cases discussed above, all decided under the law of jurisdictions other than Pennsylvania, may suggest that the arrangement between Rockwell and TMW should be considered a sale rather than a merger or a continuation, since TMW did not officially terminate its corporate existence for 18 months after the exchange, and throughout that period possessed valuable assets with which to respond to tort claims similar to the one now advanced. However, a number of considerations indicate the insubstantiality of the continued existence of TMW, including the brevity of the corporation's continued life, the contractual requirement that TMW be dissolved as soon as possible, the prohibition on engaging in normal business transactions, and the character of the assets TMW controlled. Although each of these factors was present in one or more of the above cases, the present appeal is unique in combining all these elements. In addition, the better-reasoned result would be to conclude that, for the purpose of determining liability to tortiously injured parties, the Rockwell-TMW transaction should be treated as a merger, thereby subjecting Rockwell to liability for injuries caused by defective products distributed by TMW prior to the transaction.

Lumber Co. v. Myers, 296 Minn. 33, 206 N.W.2d 365 (1973); Schwartz v. McGraw-Edison Co., 14 Cal.App.3d 767, 92 Cal.Rptr. 776 (1971); Buis v. Peabody Coal Co., 41 Ill. App.2d 317, 190 N.E.2d 507 (1963).

[17] 288 F.Supp. 817, 820 (D.Colo.1968).

[18] 100 N.J.Super. 186, 241 A.2d 471 (L.Div.1968).

[19] 61 Ohio App. 21, 22 N.E.2d 293 (1939).

[20] 256 F.Supp. 291 (S.D.N.Y.1966).

We must, of course, apply the rule we believe a Pennsylvania appellate tribunal would adopt if the case arose in the state courts. In resolving issues relating to the recognition of a cause of action in favor of an injured party, the Pennsylvania courts have emphasized the public policy considerations served by imposing liability on the defendant rather than formal or technical requirements.[21]

* * *

In Farris v. Glen Alden Corp.,[24] a shareholder of Glen Alden sought to enjoin a meeting of Glen Alden shareholders called to approve a "reorganization agreement" with List Industries. Plaintiff asked that the meeting be enjoined because management had failed to inform the shareholders that the purpose of the meeting was the approval of a merger and that the shareholders had a right to dissent from the merger and obtain a valuation of their stock. Management responded that the shareholders had no valuation rights because the transaction did not conform to the statutory merger procedures and therefore was not a merger, but a sale of assets to which valuation rights did not apply. Pursuant to the plan of reorganization, Glen Alden was to acquire all the assets of List except a small amount of cash reserved for payment of expenses in connection with the transaction. In exchange, Glen Alden was to assume all List's liabilities and to issue stock to List that List would distribute to its stockholders. List was then to dissolve and Glen Alden to change its name to List Alden.

The Court expressed the view in *Farris* that because of the complexities of modern corporate reorganizations,

> it is no longer helpful to consider an individual transaction in the abstract and solely by reference to the various elements therein determine whether it is a "merger" or a "sale". Instead, to determine properly the nature of a corporate transaction, we must refer not only to all the provisions of the agreement, but also to the consequences of the transaction and to the purposes of the provisions of the corporation law said to be applicable.

The rationale of dissenting shareholders' rights, the Court stated, is to allow shareholders to treat their membership in the original corporation as terminated when the corporation, in combining with another, "lose[s] its original nature." The List-Glen Alden agreement, the Court held, fundamentally altered the relationship between Glen Alden and its shareholders, and therefore the provisions relating to dissenting shareholders' rights should apply.

The present case, like *Farris,* involves a transaction which resembles a merger but does not possess all the formal characteristics of one. It seems appropriate to infer from *Farris* that in deciding whether to

---

[21] Some indication of the probable reaction of the Pennsylvania Supreme Court to the issue posed by this case may perhaps be gleaned from that Court's discussion in Kassab v. Central Soya, 432 Pa. 217, 246 A.2d 848 (1968), and Salvador v. Atlantic Steel Boiler Co., Pa., 319 A.2d 903 (1974). Although the issues presented in *Kassab* and *Salvador* turned on the doctrine of privity, which is not present here, the reasoning utilized by the Supreme Court in those cases dealt with the economic reality of the relationship between manufacturers and the users of the allegedly defective products.

[24] 393 Pa. 427, 143 A.2d 25 (1958).

treat such an arrangement as a merger the Pennsylvania courts would consider the purposes which would be served by imposing liability on Rockwell for the tortious conduct of TMW.[27]

In the present case, Knapp is confronted with the melancholy prospect of being barred from his day in court unless Rockwell is held subject to suit. And quite significantly, if Knapp had been injured more than two years after the dissolution of TMW, Knapp would never have had any opportunity to recover at law, since under Pennsylvania law a dissolved corporation is subject to suit for only two years after the date of dissolution.

Denying Knapp the right to sue Rockwell because of the barren continuation of TMW after the exchange with Rockwell would allow a formality to defeat Knapp's recovery. Although TMW technically existed as an independent corporation, it had no substance. The parties clearly contemplated that TMW would terminate its existence as a part of the transaction. TMW had, in exchange for Rockwell stock, disposed of all the assets it originally held, exclusive of the cash necessary to consummate the transaction. It could not undertake any active operations. * * * Most significantly, TMW was requried by the contract with Rockwell to dissolve "as soon as practicable."

On the other hand, Rockwell acquired all the assets of TMW, exclusive of certain real estate that Rockwell did not want, and assumed practically all of TMW's liabilities. Further, Rockwell required that TMW use its "best efforts," prior to the consummation of the transaction, to preserve TMW's business organization intact for Rockwell, to make available to Rockwell TMW's existing officers and employees, and to maintain TMW's relationship with its customers and suppliers. After the exchange, Rockwell continued TMW's former business operations.

If we are to follow the philosophy of the Pennsylvania courts that questions of an injured party's right to seek recovery are to be resolved by an analysis of public policy considerations rather than by a mere procrustean application of formalities, we must, in considering whether the TMW-Rockwell exchange was a merger, evaluate the public policy implications of that determination.

In resolving, where the burden of a loss should be imposed, the Pennsylvania Supreme Court has considered which of the two parties is better able to spread the loss. * * *

[N]either Knapp nor Rockwell was ever in a position to prevent the occurrence of the injury, inasmuch as neither manufactured the defective device. As between these two parties, however, Rockwell is better able to spread the burden of the loss. Prior to the exchange with Rockwell, TMW had procured insurance that would have indemnified TMW had it been held liable to Knapp for his injuries. Rockwell could

---

[27] Although the facts of the present case are admittedly a step beyond those in *Farris*, in view of the legislative intent deduced by the Pennsylvania courts in the field of dissenting shareholders' rights, it might be contended that the Pennsylvania Supreme Court would find that the legislature intended to permit tort liability in cases like the one sub judice.

have protected itself from sustaining the brunt of the loss by securing from TMW an assignment of TMW's insurance. There is no indication in the record that such an assignment would have placed a burden on either Rockwell or TMW since TMW had already purchased the insurance protection, and the insurance was of no continuing benefit to TMW after its liability to suit was terminated by Pennsylvania statute. Rockwell has adduced no explanation, either in its brief or at oral argument, why it agreed in the contract not to take an assignment of TMW's prepaid insurance. Rockwell therefore should not be permitted to impose the weight of the loss upon a user of an allegedly defective product by delaying the formal dissolution of TMW. In the absence of contrary controlling decisions by the Pennsylvania courts, we conclude that the state judiciary would adopt the rule of law that appears to be better reasoned and more consistent with the social policy set forth in recent Pennsylvania cases.

The judgment of the district court will therefore be reversed and the case remanded for further proceedings consistent with this opinion.

ROSENN, Circuit Judge (concurring).

The majority holds that, under certain circumstances, a corporation which acquires substantially all the assets of another corporation may be held liable for injuries caused by defective products manufactured by the other corporation before the date of acquisition. In the present case, they conclude that, even though the transaction was structured as a sale of assets, it should be "treated as a merger" for the purpose of imposing tort liability. Although I concur in the result reached by the majority, I wish to clarify the basis upon which I would impose such liability.

* * *

In the present day of complex corporate reorganizations and acquisitions, the intrinsic nature of a transaction cannot be ascertained merely from the form in which it is structured. Courts therefore must examine the substance of the transaction to ascertain its purpose and true intent.

* * *

The Pennsylvania Supreme Court has had occasion to examine the rights of dissenting shareholders when a transfer of the business operations of one corporation to another is effectuated by sale rather than by utilization of the statutory procedures provided for merger. Farris v. Glen Alden Corp., supra.

* * *

If, in protecting dissenting shareholders, a court should scrutinize a corporate transaction to ascertain the presence of certain attributes of merger relevant to the enforcement of appraisal rights, it should do no less in protecting tort claimants. Both dissenting shareholders under section 805 and tort claimants under section 803 are the intended beneficiaries of protective legislation. Although a transaction should be scrutinized to protect both shareholders and tort claimants, a court should search for somewhat different attributes of merger for purposes of imposing tort liability. This difference in relevant attributes stems from the distinct relationships to the corporation of the persons whom the legislature has sought to protect. While dissenting shareholders need protection against alteration of their investment rights, tort claimants need protection against attempts by ongoing businesses to avoid liability through transfer of their operations to another legal entity.

I believe that, where a corporation purchases substantially all the assets of a second corporation, the legislature intended to impose the second corporation's tort liabilities on the acquiring corporation at least if the following attributes of merger are present:

(1) an ongoing business, including its name and good will, is transferred to the acquiring corporation; and

(2) the corporation whose assets are acquired is dissolved after distribution to its shareholders of the consideration received from the acquiring corporation.

In the present case, TMW transferred to Rockwell almost all its assets, retaining only its corporate records and a limited amount of cash to effectuate the transaction. The "Agreement and Plan of Reorganization" specifically provided for the transfer of TMW's business "as a going concern," including good will, the exclusive right to use the name "Textile Machine Works," and the "permits or licenses to conduct [TMW's] business as now carried on." TMW also agreed to change its name and dissolve.

* * *

In addition, this transaction has another characteristic of a statutory merger. The consideration given for TMW's assets was Rockwell stock, which in turn was to be distributed to TMW's shareholders on TMW's liquidation and dissolution. Thus, TMW shareholders became shareholders in Rockwell just as if they had exchanged their shares directly with Rockwell under the statutory merger procedure.

* * *

While I recognize the rightful prerogative of a corporation to rearrange its business or go out of business entirely, there is also a practical and reasonable basis for construing this transaction as a merger. Were we in the circumstances of this case to absolve of liability a corporation which acquires a functioning business by purchasing substantially all the assets of another corporation, many injured parties would be unable to maintain products liability actions after the former corporate owner of the business has been dissolved. Although by statute Pennsylvania corporations are amenable to suit for two years after dissolution, a defect in a product manufactured by a dissolved corporation may not come to light until long after the two-year period. Because the statute of limitations generally does not begin to run until the defect is discovered, such an action probably would not be time-barred.

In imposing liability for the torts of the acquired corporation, I realize that the acquiring corporation was not a party to any tortious act and had no connection with the acquired corporation at the time the allegedly defective product was manufactured. The acquiring corporation, however, is in a position both before and after the acquisition to take necessary measures for its protection against potential products liability claims.

◆

Knapp and a number of other cases explicitly stretched, but did not quite break, the bounds of traditional successor liability doctrine in an effort to accommodate the public policy underpinnings of products liability and the corporate law origins of the de facto merger and mere continuation elements.[8]   These opinions are laudable in that they clearly recognized that it was the products liability aspect of the cases that made them difficult.   The problem, however, is understanding the scope of their holdings.   The opinions reflect an uneasy mix of (a) seeing how closely the transaction fits the traditional de facto merger mold; and (b) policy analysis focusing on the usual reasons for imposing strict products liability, including the acquiring company's ability to spread the loss, to insure, and to improve the product in the future. There is nothing in the *Knapp* opinion that explains how one "balances" in a particular case the power of products liability policy against the extent to which the facts deviate from those usually necessary to finding a de facto merger—we do not learn how much policy buys how much deviation.   For example, the transaction in *Knapp* did meet one of the traditional requirements of the de facto merger doctrine: The consideration received by the target company was stock.[9]   Would the result in *Knapp* have been different if the consideration had been cash?

In Turner v. Bituminous Casualty Co., supra, the court imposed successor liability despite the fact that the consideration was cash rather than stock, listing the following elements of a "prima facie case" for successor liability: (1) a basic continuity of the enterprise of the target company, including a retention of key personnel, assets, and general business operations; (2) dissolution of the target company after distribution of the consideration; (3) assumption by the acquiring company of those liabilities necessary to the continuation of the target company's business; and (4) the acquiring company held itself out as the effective continuation of the target company.   *Turner*, 244 N.W.2d at 883–84.   Under this quasi-traditional analysis, would the result in *Turner* have been different if the acquiring company manufactured the product line acquired under its own name rather than under the name of the target company?

2.   The Product Line Theory of Successor Liability

In light of the analytic difficulty of balancing the public policy favoring products liability against the traditional corporate law limits on successor liability, it was not surprising that other courts soon

---

[8] See, e.g., Cyr v. B. Offen & Co., 501 F.2d 1145 (1st Cir.1974) (expansion of mere continuation exception); Turner v. Bituminous Casualty Co., 397 Mich. 406, 244 N.W.2d 873 (1976) (expansion of de facto merger analysis).

[9] See, e.g., Kloberdanz v. Joy Mfg. Co., 288 F.Supp. 817 (D.Colo.1968); McKee v. Harris-Seybold Co., 109 N.J.Super. 555, 264 A.2d 98 (1970), affirmed 118 N.J.Super. 480, 288 A.2d 585 (1972).

developed an entirely new doctrine of successor liability designed especially for products liability cases. Indeed, it is entirely possible that the efforts in *Knapp* and Cyr v. B. Offen & Co., supra, to stretch traditional doctrine rather than discard it were artifacts of the limits of diversity jurisdiction: Federal courts required under Erie Railroad v. Tompkins [10] to apply state law can stretch existing doctrine but are limited in their freedom to announce entirely new doctrine in the face of contrary state precedent.[11]

RAMIREZ v. AMSTED INDUSTRIES

Supreme Court of New Jersey (1981).
86 N.J. 332, 431 A.2d 811.

CLIFFORD, J.

This products liability case implicates principles of successor corporation liability. We are called upon to formulate a general rule governing the strict tort liability of a successor corporation for damages caused by defects in products manufactured and distributed by its predecessor. The Appellate Division, in an opinion reported at 171 N.J. Super. 261, 408 A.2d 818 (1979), devised the following test, based essentially on the holding of the Supreme Court of California in Ray v. Alad Corp., 19 Cal.3d 22, 560 P.2d 3, 136 Cal.Rptr. 574 (1977):

> [W]here, as in the present case, the successor corporation acquires all or substantially all the assets of the predecessor corporation for cash and continues essentially the same manufacturing operation as the predecessor corporation the successor remains liable for the product liability claims of its predecessor. [171 N.J.Super. at 278, 408 A.2d 818.]

In affirming the judgment below we adopt substantially this test for determining successor corporation liability in the factual context presented.

I

On August 18, 1975 plaintiff Efrain Ramirez was injured while operating an allegedly defective power press on the premises of his employer, Zamax Manufacturing Company, in Belleville, New Jersey. The machine involved, known as a Johnson Model 5, sixty-ton punch press, was manufactured by Johnson Machine and Press Company (Johnson) in 1948 or 1949. As a result of the injuries sustained plaintiffs filed suit against Amsted Industries, Inc. (Amsted) as a successor corporation to Johnson, seeking to recover damages on theories of negligence, breach of warranty and strict liability in tort for defective design and manufacturing. After discovery had been completed, Amsted moved for summary judgment on the ground that the mere purchase of Johnson's assets for cash in 1962 did not carry with it tort

---

[10] 304 U.S. 64 (1938).

[11] The requirement that federal courts apply state law has been an explicit factor in the decision of some federal courts to reject any broadening of successor liability.

See Leannais v. Cincinnati, Inc., 565 F.2d 437 (7th Cir.1977) (applying Wisconsin law); Travis v. Harris Corp., 565 F.2d 443 (7th Cir.1977) (applying Ohio and Indiana law).

liability for damages arising out of defects in products manufactured by Johnson. The trial court granted summary judgment for Amsted, holding that there is no assumption of liability when the successor purchases the predecessor's assets for cash and when the provisions of the purchase agreement between the selling and purchasing corporations indicate an intention to limit the purchaser's assumption of liability. That holding was consistent with the traditional rule governing the liability of successor corporations. See McKee v. Harris-Seybold Co., 109 N.J.Super. 555, 264 A.2d 98 (Law Div.1970), aff'd 118 N.J.Super. 480, 288 A.2d 585 (App.Div.1972).

On their appeal to the Appellate Division plaintiffs argued that a corporation that purchases the assets of a manufacturer and continues the business of the selling corporation in an essentially unchanged manner should not be allowed to use exculpatory contractual language to avoid liability for contingent personal injury claims arising out of defects in the predecessor's product. The Appellate Division agreed and reversed the trial court. Although it recognized that the purchase agreement manifested a clear intent to negate any assumption of liability by Amsted for contingent product claims, the court below took notice of "[t]he recent trend towards a rule imposing liability on the successor corporation without regard to the niceties of corporate transfers where the successor has acquired and has continued the predecessor's commercial activity in an essentially unchanged manner." 171 N.J.Super. at 269–70, 408 A.2d 818. Taking cognizance of New Jersey's position "in the vanguard" advancing the principle of enterprise liability and the philosophy of spreading the risk to society for the cost of injuries from defective products, the Appellate Division reasoned that the result in this troublesome area of products liability law should not be controlled by the form of the corporate transfer nor by exculpatory language in the purchase agreement. Id. at 275–76, 408 A.2d 818. It concluded that because Amsted ultimately acquired all or substantially all the assets of Johnson and continued essentially the same manufacturing operation, Amsted could not as a matter of law avoid potential liability for injuries caused by defects in the Johnson product line, notwithstanding an intervening ownership by an intermediate corporation. Id. at 278, 408 A.2d 818. It therefore remanded the cause for trial. We granted Amsted's petition for certification. 82 N.J. 298, 412 A.2d 804 (1980).

II

* * *

As indicated above, the machine that caused the injury was manufactured in 1948 or 1949 by Johnson Machine and Press Company of Elkhart, Indiana. In 1956 Johnson transferred all of its assets and liabilities to Bontrager Construction Company (Bontrager), another Indiana corporation. Johnson transacted no business as a manufacturing entity following its acquisition by Bontrager, but Bontrager did retain a single share of Johnson common stock in order to continue the Johnson name in corporate form. Bontrager's primary activity then became the manufacture of the Johnson press line.

By purchase agreement dated August 29, 1962, Amsted acquired all of the assets of Bontrager, including all the Johnson assets that Bontrager had acquired in 1956, plus the one share of Johnson stock. The purchase price was $1,200,406 in cash.[2] The assets purchased by Amsted in the 1962 transaction included the manufacturing plant in Elkhart, which had been operated by Johnson prior to its transfer to Bontrager in 1956. Amsted also required all of Bontrager's inventory, machinery and equipment, patents and trademarks, pending contracts, books and records, and the exclusive right to adopt and use the trade name "Johnson Machine and Press Corporation." Bontrager further agreed to "use its best efforts to make available" to Amsted the services of all of its present employees except its three principals, who covenanted not to compete with Amsted for a period of five years.

In addition, the August 1962 agreement provided that Amsted would assume responsibility for certain specified debts and liabilities necessary to an uninterrupted continuation of the business. Included, however, was the following reservation:

> It is understood and agreed that Purchaser shall not assume or be liable for any liability or obligations other than those herein expressly assumed by Purchaser.

* * *

Thus it is clear that Amsted expressly declined to assume liability for any claims arising out of defects in products manufactured by its predecessors.

Following the 1962 acquisition Amsted manufactured the Johnson press line through its wholly-owned subsidiary, South Bend Lathe, Inc. (South Bend I), in the original Johnson plant in Elkhart.

* * *

In September 1965 South Bend I, the Amsted subsidiary that had been manufacturing the Johnson product line, was dissolved and its assets and liabilities were assumed by Amsted. The manufacturing business was operated by Amsted until June 1975, at which time the business was sold to a newly-formed Indiana corporation also named South Bend Lathe, Inc. (South Bend II). As part of this transaction Amsted agreed to indemnify South Bend II for any losses arising out of machinery manufactured and sold prior to the date of closing. Amsted acknowledges that by virtue of this indemnity agreement, it is responsible for the defense against and payment of any liability claims against South Bend II arising out of any defects in the Johnson product line.

III

Amsted urges this Court to judge its potential liability for defective Johnson products on the basis of the traditional analysis of corporate successor liability.

---

[2] Although as noted by the Appellate Division, 171 N.J.Super. at 265, 408 A.2d 818 "[t]he fate of Bontrager is not revealed by the present record," other courts analyzing the very same corporate transaction have determined that Bontrager distributed the cash proceeds of the transaction to its shareholders and dissolved its inert corporate existence not long thereafter. See Korzetz v. Amsted Industries, Inc., 472 F.Supp. 136, 144 (E.D.Mich.1979); Ortiz v. South Bend Lathe Co., 46 Cal.App.2d 842, 846, 120 Cal.Rptr. 556, 558 (Dist.Ct.App. 1975).

* * *

In recent years, however, the traditional corporate approach has been sharply criticized as being inconsistent with the rapidly developing principles of strict liability in tort and unresponsive to the legitimate interests of the products liability plaintiff. Courts have come to recognize that the traditional rule of nonliability was developed not in response to the interests of parties to products liability actions, but rather to protect the rights of commercial creditors and dissenting shareholders following corporate acquisitions, as well as to determine successor corporation liability for tax assessments and contractual obligations of the predecessor. Turner v. Bituminous Cas. Co., 397 Mich. 406, 418, 244 N.W.2d 873, 878 (1976); see Cyr v. B. Offen & Co., Inc., 501 F.2d 1145, 1152 & n. 12 (1st Cir.1974).

Strict interpretation of the traditional corporate law approach leads to a narrow application of the exceptions to nonliability, and places unwarranted emphasis on the form rather than the practical effect of a particular corporate transaction. The principal exceptions to nonliability outlined in *McKee,* supra, condition successor liability on a determination of whether the transaction an be labeled as a merger or a de facto merger, or whether the purchasing corporation can be described as a mere continuation of the selling corporation. Traditionally, the triggering of the "de facto merger" exception has been held to depend on whether the assets were transferred to the acquiring corporation for shares of stock or for cash—that is, whether the stockholders of the selling corporation become the stockholders of the purchasing corporation. See Travis v. Harris Corp., 565 F.2d 443, 447 (7th Cir. 1977); Shannon v. Samuel Langston Co., 379 F.Supp. 797, 801 (W.D. Mich.1974). Under a narrow application of the *McKee* exception of de facto merger no liability is imposed where the purchasing corporation paid for the acquired assets principally in cash. Id.

In like manner, narrow application of *McKee's* "continuation" exception causes liability *vel non* to depend on whether the plaintiff is able to establish that there is continuity in management, shareholders, personnel, physical location, assets and general business operation between selling and purchasing corporations following the asset acquisition. See, e.g., Travis v. Harris Corp., supra, 565 F.2d at 447; Freeman v. White Way Sign & Maintenance Co., 82 Ill.App.3d 884, 892, 403 N.E.2d 495, 502 (App.Ct.1980). Where the commonality of corporate management or ownership cannot be shown, there is deemed to have been no continuation of the seller's corporate entity. Id.

When viewed in this light, narrow application of the *McKee* approach to corporate successor liability is indeed inconsistent with the developing principles of strict products liability and unresponsive to the interests of persons injured by defective products in the stream of commerce. The Supreme Court of Michigan has offered this insight:

> To the injured persons the problem of recovery is substantially the same, no matter what corporate process led to transfer of the first corporation and/or its assets. Whether the corporate transaction was (1) a traditional merger accompanied by exchange of stock

of the two corporations, or (2) a de facto merger brought about by the purchase of one corporation's assets by part of the stock of the second, or (3) a purchase of corporate assets for cash, the injured person has the same problem, so long as the first corporation in each case legally and/or practically becomes defunct. He has no place to turn for relief except to the second corporation. Therefore, as to the injured person, distinctions between types of corporate transfers are wholly unmeaningful. [Turner v. Bituminous Cas. Co., supra, 244 N.W.2d at 878.]

We likewise refuse to decide this case through a narrow application of *McKee*. The form of the corporate transaction by which Amsted acquired the manufacturing assets of Bontrager should not be controlling as to Amsted's liability for the serious injury suffered by plaintiff some thirteen years after that transaction. We therefore must consider the alternative approaches to successor corporation liability that have been adopted by other reviewing courts in an effort to arrive at the standard most consistent with the principles underlying the New Jersey law of strict products liability.

IV

In an effort to make the traditional corporate approach more responsive to the problems associated with the developing law of strict products liability several courts have broadened the *McKee* exceptions of "de facto merger" and "mere continuation" in order to expand corporate successor liability in certain situations. See, e.g., Knapp v. North American Rockwell Corp., 506 F.2d 361 (3rd Cir.1974); *Cyr,* supra, *Shannon,* supra, *Turner,* supra.

The "mere continuation" exception was first expanded by a federal court applying New Hampshire law in Cyr v. B. Offen & Co., Inc., supra.   *   *   *

The *Cyr* court based the justification for its holding on the public policy considerations underlying strict products liability. It recognized that the successor corporation, not being the original manufacturer, is not the specific legal entity that placed the defective product in the stream of commerce or made implied representations as to its safety. Nonetheless, there were several other policy justifications for imposing strict products liability on the successor. The first was in essence the risk-spreading approach:

> The very existence of strict liability for manufacturers implies a basic judgment that the hazards of predicting and insuring for risk from defective products are better borne by the manufacturer than by the consumer. The manufacturer's successor, carrying over the experience and expertise of the manufacturer, is likewise in a better position than the consumer to gauge the risks and the costs of meeting them. The successor knows the product, is as able to calculate the risk of defects as the predecessor, is in position to insure therefor and reflect such cost in sale negotiations, and is the

only entity capable of improving the quality of the product. [Id. at 1154.]

The court also reasoned that the successor corporation, having reaped the benefits of continuing its predecessor's product line, exploiting its accumulated good will and enjoying the patronage of its established customers, should be made to bear some of the burdens of continuity, namely, liability for injuries caused by its defective products.

Perhaps the most significant decision expanding the "mere continuation" exception to the traditional rule of corporate successor nonliability is Turner v. Bituminous Cas. Co., 397 Mich. 406, 244 N.W.2d 873 (1976). The defendant in *Turner* contended that where manufacturing assets are acquired by a purchasing corporation for cash rather than for stock, there is no continuity of shareholders and therefore no corporate successor liability. However, the court looked upon the kind of consideration paid for assets as but "one factor to use to determine whether there exists a sufficient nexus between the successor and predecessor corporations to establish successor liability." It reasoned that there was no practical basis for treating a cash purchase of corporate assets any differently from an acquisition of assets for stock, concluding that "[i]t would make better sense if the law had a common result and allowed products liability recovery in each case."

Accordingly, the *Turner* court held that in applying the "mere continuation" exception to situations involving the sale of corporate assets for cash, continuity of shareholders between selling and purchasing corporations is not a relevant criterion for the purposes of determining successor liability for injury caused by defective products. Rather, it adopted a less stringent version of the "mere continuation" exception in the sale-of-assets-for-cash context, jettisoning the criterion of continuity of shareholders and emphasizing continuity of the enterprise of the predecessor corporation. Applying the rule it had adopted to the record before it, the court concluded that all relevant elements of continuation were present.

In the instant case plaintiffs contend that Amsted can be held responsible for liability arising out of defective Johnson products based upon *Turner*'s expanded "continuation" approach. To support this line of attack they rely on Korzetz v. Amsted Industries, Inc., 472 F.Supp. 136 (E.D.Mich.1979). In *Korzetz*, a federal court in Michigan applied the *Turner* analysis to the very same corporate succession involved in the instant case (Johnson to Bontrager to Amsted), and determined that Amsted could be held liable for injuries caused by presses manufactured by Johnson well before Amsted acquired the Johnson assets from Bontrager. * * *

We agree with plaintiffs that under *Turner*, which simply expands the "continuation" exception to the traditional *McKee* approach, Amsted may be held to be the mere continuation of Johnson for the purpose of imposing corporate successor liability for injuries caused by defective Johnson products. However, the Appellate Division actually based its decision below and its ultimate test of successor corporation liability not on the *Turner* analysis but rather on the so-called "product line exception" developed by the California Supreme Court in Ray v. Alad Corp., 19 Cal.3d 22, 560 P.2d 3, 136 Cal.Rptr. 574 (1977).

There are fundamental practical and analytical differences between *Turner*'s expanded "mere continuation" exception and *Ray*'s "product line" approach. *Turner* merely broadens the inroads into the traditional principles of corporate successor nonliability expressed in *McKee* and related cases, while *Ray* completely abandons the traditional rule and its exceptions, utilizing instead the policies underlying strict liability in tort for injuries caused by defective products. Whereas the *Turner* variation on continuation of the enterprise contemplates such factors as the ownership and management of the successor's corporate entity, its personnel, physical location, assets, trade name, and general business operation, the *Ray* test is concerned not with the continuation of the corporate entity as such but rather with the successor's undertaking to manufacture essentially the same line of products as the predecessor.

Because we believe that the focus in cases involving corporate successor liability for injuries caused by defective products should be on the successor's continuation of the actual manufacturing operation and not on commonality of ownership and management between the predecessor's and successor's corporate entities, and because the traditional corporate approach, even as broadened by *Turner* and its progeny, renders inconsistent results,[3] we adopt substantially *Ray*'s product line analysis.

V

In Ray v. Alad Corp., supra, the plaintiff was injured in a fall from a defective ladder on which he had been working. One year prior to plaintiff's injury the manufacturer of the ladder, Alad Corporation (Alad I), had sold to Lighting Maintenance Corporation its assets, stock in trade, trade name and goodwill. As part of the transaction Alad I agreed to dissolve its corporate existence as soon as practical and to assist the purchasing corporation in the organization of a new business entity under the name of Alad Corporation (Alad II). The principal stockholders of Alad I agreed not to compete with Alad II for forty-two months and to render nonexclusive consulting services during that

---

[3] For example, in Hernandez v. Johnson Press Corp., 70 Ill.App.3d 664, 26 Ill.Dec. 777, 388 N.E.2d 778 (App.Ct.1979), an Illinois appellate court applied the *Turner* analysis to the very same corporate genealogy as involved herein, and determined that there was no de facto merger between Johnson and Amsted. The court's findings of fact, however, indicate that the plaintiff presented a shamefully weak record, as the court was unable to point to facts indicating continuity of management, personnel, physical location, assets and general business operation. 388 N.E.2d at 780. In *Korzetz*, supra, *Turner*'s continuity rationale was applied to the identical factual situation and the court found "strong and convincing evidence of continuity of enterprise" from Johnson to Amsted, emphasizing continuity of personnel, physical location, assets, trade name, sales contract, customer lists, and general business operations. 472 F.Supp. at 144. While the record in the present case clearly supports the *Korzetz* court's result, the point is that the *Turner* analysis lends itself to inconsistency and ambiguity. *Ray*'s product line analysis, focusing primarily on the continuation of the general business operations, not only can be applied with greater consistency, but better reflects the underlying policy in New Jersey that liability for defective products attaches to the manufacturing enterprise.

period. The principal stockholder of Alad I was employed as a salaried consultant for the initial five months of Alad II's organization. Once in operation Alad II continued to manufacture the same line of Alad I ladders, under the same name, using the same equipment, employees and customer lists. No contractual provisions were made for the assumption of liability by Alad II for defects in products manufactured or sold by Alad I prior to the asset acquisition. The injured plaintiff in *Ray* sued Alad II on the theory of strict liability in tort.

The California Supreme Court reversed a trial court's summary judgment in favor of Alad II. It determined that none of the four stated exceptions to the general rule of nonliability under the traditional corporate law approach was sufficient basis for imposing liability on the purchasing corporation, Alad II. Nevertheless, the court determined that a special departure from that traditional approach was called for by the policies underlying strict tort liability for injuries caused by defective products. Rather than adopt the expanded "mere continuation" exception to the corporate law approach as developed in *Cyr,* supra, and *Turner,* supra, the *Ray* court abandoned the traditional analysis. It developed instead the following formulation, which has since come to be known as the "product line" approach to successor corporation liability for injuries caused by defective products:

> We * * * conclude that a party which acquires a manufacturing business and continues the output of its line of products under the circumstances here presented assumes strict tort liability for defects in units of the same product line previously manufactured and distributed by the entity from which the business was acquired.

The *Ray* court offered a three-fold justification for its imposition of potential liability upon a successor corporation that acquires the assets and continues the manufacturing operation of the predecessor:

> (1) The virtual destruction of the plaintiff's remedies against the original manufacturer caused by the successor's acquisition of the business, (2) the successor's ability to assume the original manufacturer's risk-spreading role, and (3) the fairness of requiring the successor to assume a responsibility for defective products that was a burden necessarily attached to the original manufacturer's good will being enjoyed by the successor in the continued operation of the business.

In our view these policy considerations likewise justify the imposition of potential strict tort liability on Amsted under the circumstances here presented. First, the plaintiff's potential remedy against Johnson, the original manufacturer of the allegedly defective press, was destroyed by the purchase of the Johnson assets, trade name and good will, and Johnson's resulting dissolution. It is true that there was an intermediate transaction involved, namely, the acquisition of the Johnson assets by Bontrager in 1956. But the acquisition of these assets by Amsted in 1962 directly brought about the ultimate dissolution of Bontrager's corporate existence. Accordingly, the Bontrager acquisition destroyed whatever remedy plaintiff might have had against Johnson, and the Amsted acquisition destroyed the plaintiff's potential cause of action against Bontrager. What is most important, however, is that there was continuity in the manufacturing of the Johnson product line throughout the history of these asset acquisitions.

Second, the imposition of successor corporation liability upon Amsted is consistent with the public policy of spreading the risk to society at large for the cost of injuries from defective products. The progressive character of New Jersey decisional law in the area of strict products liability is well known, and its development need not be retraced here. See Suter v. San Angelo Foundry and Machine Co., 81 N.J. 150, 169–72, 406 A.2d 140 (1979). * * *

In essence, Amsted contends that because it had no physical control over the allegedly defective Johnson press when it was placed into the stream of commerce, it is not the maker of the product who put it in the channels of trade. But to argue that a successor corporation can not be liable for injuries arising out of defects in certain products because it is not the same corporate entity that actually manufactured or distributed those products is to beg the underlying question involved in downstream corporate liability cases in the products liability context. No one asserts that Amsted was responsible for actually placing the allegedly defective press into the commercial stream. This was done by Johnson, the original manufacturer. But the injured plaintiff obviously cannot look to Johnson for a recovery of the damages occasioned by the accident involving the defective press. Rather, he looks to a viable successor corporation that continued to manufacture and sell the line of products that injured him. Strict liability for injuries caused by defective products placed into the stream of commerce is "an enterprise liability" one that continues so long as the defective product is present on the market. The successor corporation that continues the manufacturing enterprise of its predecessor may not have had the means available for avoiding the risk of placing a defective product into the stream of commerce initially, but it does have the means available for avoiding the risk of harm caused by its predecessor's defective products still present on the market.

As stated by Justice Schreiber for the Court in *Suter,* supra:

> Strict liability in a sense is but an attempt to minimize the cost of accidents and to consider who should bear those costs. See the discussion in Calabresi & Hirschoff, "Toward a Test for Strict Liability in Torts," 81 Yale L.J. 1055 (1972), in which the authors suggest that the strict liability issue is to decide which party is the "cheapest cost avoider" or who is in the best position to make the cost-benefit analysis between accident costs and accident avoidance costs and to act on that decision once it is made. Id. at 1060. Using this approach, it is obvious that the manufacturer rather than the factory employee is "in the better position both to judge whether avoidance costs would exceed foreseeable accident costs and to act on that judgment." Id.

Similarly, because the manufacturer transfers to its successor corporation "the resources that had previously been available to [the manufacturer] for meeting its responsibilities to persons injured by defects in [products] it had produced," Ray v. Alad, supra, the successor rather than the user of the product is in the better position to bear accident-avoidance costs. By the terms of the 1962 purchase agreement with Bontrager, Amsted acquired the Johnson trade name, physical plant, manufacturing equipment, inventory, records of manufacturing designs, patents and customer lists. Amsted also sought the continued employment of the factory personnel that had manufactured the Johnson presses for Bontrager. "With these facilities and sources of information, [Amsted] had virtually the same capacity as [Johnson] to estimate the risks of claims for injuries from defects in previously manufactured [presses] for purposes of obtaining [liability] insurance coverage or planning self-insurance."

Amsted was in the same position as its predecessors to avoid the costs and to spread the risk of accident injuries to users of defective Johnson power presses.

Third, the imposition upon Amsted of responsibility to answer claims of liability for injuries allegedly caused by defective Johnson presses is justified as a burden necessarily attached to its enjoyment of Johnson's trade name, good will and the continuation of an established manufacturing enterprise. See Ray v. Alad, supra. Through acquisition of the Johnson trade name, plant, employees, manufacturing equipment, designs and customer lists, and by holding itself out to potential customers as the manufacturer of the same line of Johnson power presses, Amsted benefited substantially from the legitimate exploitation of the accumulated good will earned by the Johnson product line. Public policy requires that having received the substantial benefits of the continuing manufacturing enterprise, the successor corporation should also be made to bear the burden of the operating costs that other established business operations must ordinarily bear. By acquiring all of the Johnson assets and continuing the established business of manufacturing and selling Johnson presses, Amsted "became 'an integral part of the overall producing and marketing enterprise that should bear the cost of injuries resulting from defective products.' "

VI

Defendant contends that the imposition of strict products liability on corporations that purchase manufacturing assets for cash will have a chilling—even a crippling—effect on the ability of the small manufacturer to transfer ownership of its business assets for a fair purchase price rather than be forced into liquidation proceedings. Business planners for prospective purchasing corporations will be hesitant to acquire "a potential can of worms that will open with untold contingent products liability claims." In order to divest itself of its business assets, the small manufacturing corporation will be forced to sacrifice such a substantial deduction from a fair purchase price that it would lose the ability to net a sum consistent with the true worth of the business assets.

These contentions raise legitimate concerns. We do not look upon them as "cassandrian arguments," see *Turner,* supra.

However, in light of the social policy underlying the law of products liability, the true worth of a predecessor corporation must reflect the potential liability that the shareholders have escaped through the sale of their corporation. Thus, a reduction of the sale price by an amount calculated to compensate the successor corporation for the potential liability it has assumed is a more, not less, accurate measure of the true worth of the business.

Furthermore, a corporation planning the acquisition of another corporation's manufacturing assets has certain protective devices available to insulate it from the full costs of accidents arising out of defects in its predecessor's products. In addition to making adjustments to the purchase price, thereby spreading the potential costs of liability between predecessor and successor corporations, it can obtain products liability insurance for contingent liability claims, and it can enter into full or partial indemnification or escrow agreements with the selling corporation. True, the parties may experience difficulties in calculating a purchase price that fairly reflects the measure of risk of potential liabilities for the predecessor's defective products present in the market at the time of the asset acquisition. Likewise do we acknowledge that small manufacturing corporations may not find readily available adequate and affordable insurance coverage for liability arising out of injuries caused by the predecessor's defective products. However, these concerns, genuine as they may be, cannot be permitted to overshadow the basic social policy, now so well-entrenched in our jurisprudence, that favors imposition of the costs of injuries from defective products on the manufacturing enterprise and consuming public rather than on the innocent injured party. In time, the risk-spreading and cost avoidance measures adverted to above should become a normal part of business planning in connection with the corporation acquisition of the assets of a manufacturing enterprise.

VII

Defendant further asserts that it is unfair to impose on it liability for defects in a predecessor's product manufactured and placed into the stream of commerce twenty eight years and two corporate transactions before the accidental injury occurred. This argument, however, goes essentially to a question of repose, namely, whether there should be a limitation on the time period during which a party may bring suit for injury arising out of a defective product. As the Appellate Division correctly concluded, only the legislature is authorized to establish a limitation on the period during which suit may be commenced against a manufacturer, its successor, or seller of allegedly defective products. * * * With the expanded potential liability of successor corporations for injuries arising out of defects in their predecessors' products, legislative response may be in order with respect to product liability claims.

VIII

Finally, Amsted contends that a new standard of liability for successor corporations in the acquisition-of-assets-for-cash context should be limited to solely prospective application and not applied to the instant case. * * * Defendant urges that its corporate business planners relied on the general rule of nonliability as expressed in *McKee* and its progeny when drafting the appropriate provisions to be included in the 1962 purchase agreement and in determining what financial protection they would need thereafter to insure against the risk entailed in the liabilities assumed. In addition, Amsted argues that insurers providing that protection have relied on the existing state of the law in determining the degree of risk involved and the rates of premiums to charge in providing coverage for injuries caused by defects in the insured corporation's products.

While we agree that there was a reasonable basis for reliance by successor corporations and their insurance carriers on the general rule of nonliability under the *McKee* approach, the plaintiffs in this case should not be denied the reward for their efforts and expense in challenging the traditional corporate law principles expressed by *McKee*. Therefore, we apply the new rule to the present case and its companion, Nieves v. Bruno-Sherman Corp. and Harris Corp., 86 N.J. 361, 431 A.2d 826. Moreover, we conclude that on balance and as a matter of fundamental fairness, the benefit of today's rule should be extended to other similarly situated plaintiffs with products liability suits against successor manufacturers affected by this rule, which suits were in progress as of November 15, 1979, the date of the Appellate Division decision.

* * *

This limitation on the application of the product-line theory will provide concerned parties the opportunity to adjust their future conduct and relationships, particularly with regard to the procurement of adequate products liability insurance and other available risk-spreading and cost avoidance arrangements.

IX

Under today's determination the *McKee* approach is no longer the standard to be applied in determining the liability of a successor corporation for injuries caused by a defective product manufactured and placed in the stream of commerce by a predecessor. Rather, we hold that where one corporation acquires all or substantially all the manufacturing assets of another corporation, even if exclusively for cash, and undertakes essentially the same manufacturing operation as the selling corporation, the purchasing corporation is strictly liable for injuries caused by defects in units of the same product line, even if previously manufactured and distributed by the selling corporation or its predecessor. The social policies underlying strict products liability in New Jersey are best served by extending strict liability to a successor corporation that acquires the business assets and continues to manufacture essentially the same line of products as its predecessor, particularly where the successor corporation benefits from trading its product line on the name of the predecessor and takes advantage from its accumulated good will, business reputation and established customers.

*   *   *

Affirmed.

SCHREIBER, J., concurring.

The Court today has fashioned a remedy for persons injured due to a defective product against a successor to the manufacturer of the product, irrespective of the form of that succession. I agree with the functional approach embraced by the majority. The central thesis of this methodology is premised on the elimination by the successor of an effective remedy. That is an essential condition precedent to recovery.

It is with the retrospectiveness of the new rule that I have difficulty. It is inequitable to saddle, as the majority does, all previous purchasers of assets, who have not assumed the liabilities arising out of defects of previously manufactured products, with those liabilities when the accident occurs after November 15, 1979. This injustice is apparent.

A crucial element in a product liability action against a manufacturer is that it placed a defective product in the stream of commerce. Yet here the defendant manufacturer is completely innocent. *   *   *

Moreover, the purchaser of the manufacturing assets has entered into a contract in good faith fully relying upon the law that it would not be responsible for defective products made by the seller. When the price of acquisitions, whether by merger, consolidation or purchase of assets, is determined, the parties in fixing value consider, among other things, the liabilities which the buyer is assuming. One factor motivating acquisition of the seller's assets rather than its securities has been to avoid known and unknown liabilities. *   *   *

Lastly, it is unfair to impose the economic monetary consequences on the purchaser. Not only has the purchaser paid more than it would have, it has also been deprived of any opportunity for contractually providing for indemnification from the seller or for some other protective device, such as an escrow. Thus the purchaser will have the cumulative loss of overpaying for the assets and of satisfying the claims of injured persons.* Moreover, it is questionable whether purchasers may realistically be able to acquire insurance policies covering them for future accidents caused by defective products made and sold prior to acquisition. See *Senate Select Comm. on Small Business, 28th Annual Rept.*, ch. 18, "Impact of Product Liability on Small Business," 167–171, S.Rept.No. 629, 95th Cong., 1st Sess. (1977); Dep't of Commerce, *Interagency Task Force on Product Liability: Final Report* at VI–2 to VI–38 (1977). For testimony to the effect that 21.6% of those businesses seeking products liability insurance could not obtain it, see *Products Liability Insurance: Hearings Before the Subcomm. on Capital, Invest-*

---

* [This is, of course, the same loss, seen once ex ante and the second time ex post. Ed.]

ment and Business of the House Comm. on Small Business, 95th Cong., 1st Sess. (Part 1) 4 (1977). See also Kadens, supra, 10 *U.Tol.L.Rev.* at 22–25; Comment, "Products Liability and Successor Corporations: Protecting the Product User and the Small Manufacturer Through Increased Availability of Products Liability Insurance," *U.Calif.D.L.Rev.* 1000, 1002–1004, 1022–1024 (1980). There is nothing in the record which is of assistance in answering this question. If such a policy may not feasibly be obtainable, the exposures of many small and moderate size companies would be immense. The economic consequences could be disastrous as well as inequitable and unjust.

On the other hand, the injured persons may not have been left totally unrecompensed. Workers' compensation, accident and health insurance policies, and liability of the manufacturer of the defective product or its insurer are some monetary sources which may be available to compensate the injured plaintiff.

An equitable resolution of retrospectiveness should focus on the date of acquisition rather than the date of the accident. Thus only purchasers of assets whose contracts were entered into after November 15, 1979 should be subject to the rule announced today.

◆

The product line approach to successor liability generally has met a favorable response from the commentators,[12] but a number of states have refused to follow the lead of New Jersey and California.[13] Although it is easy enough to cheer the rejection of the traditional successor liability doctrine because it gave no weight to the public policy underlying products liability law, the attractiveness of the product line approach depends on the persuasiveness of the justifications for it. The *Ramirez* court offers four justifications, each of which warrants attention.

The court first notes that in the absence of successor liability, the plaintiff will have no one to sue because the actual manufacturer of the defective press dissolved following the acquisition. The point is accurate, but why does it dictate *successor* liability in contrast to no liability or liability on the part of the entire industry?[14]

[12] See, e.g., Note, 12 Seton Hall L.Rev. 327 (1982); Note, *Successor Liability for Defective Products: A Tort Exception to a Corporate Rule,* 10 Hofstra L.Rev. 831 (1982); Note, *Postdissolution Product Claims and the Emerging Rule of Successor Liability,* 64 Va.L.Rev. 861 (1978).

[13] See, e.g., Stratton v. Garvey Int'l, Inc., 9 Kan.App.2d 254, 676 P.2d 1290 (1984); Tucker v. Paxson Machine Co., 645 F.2d 620 (8th Cir.1981) (applying Missouri law); Rhynes v. Branick Mfg. Corp., 629 F.2d 409 (5th Cir.1980) (applying Texas law); Leannais v. Cincinnati, Inc., supra (applying Wisconsin law); Travis v. Harris Corp., supra (applying Ohio and Indiana law); Bernard v. Kee Mfg. Co., 394 So.2d 552 (Fla. App.1981); Domaine v. Fulton Iron Works,

76 Ill.App.3d 253, 32 Ill.Dec. 72, 395 N.E.2d 19 (1979); cf. Andrews v. John E. Smith's Sons, Co., 369 So.2d 781 (Ala.1979) (rejecting product line theory, but accepting a modified de facto merger analysis).

[14] Industry-wide liability might be argued by analogy to Sindell v. Abbott Laboratories, 26 Cal.3d 588, 163 Cal.Rptr. 132, 607 P.2d 924, cert. denied 449 U.S. 912 (1980), in which the court allowed victims of DES to sue all DES manufacturers when the victims could not prove which manufacturer was associated with a victim's injury. There, industry wide liability was created to protect victims against the absence of a defendant; in the successor liability setting, industry liability would serve the same purpose.

The court then stresses the successor's ability to assume the original manufacturer's risk-spreading role: To help spread "the risk to society at large for the cost of injuries from defective products." Again, however, does the justification meet its goal? Would not imposing liability on almost any entity or group of entities, including the entire industry or even the federal government, serve to spread the risk equally as well as imposing liability on the successor?

The court's next justification does at least focus on a factor peculiar to the successor. The court notes that one justification for products liability is to place the cost of accidents on the "cheapest cost avoider" so that the optimum investment in safety is undertaken. Because the acquiring company presumably will continue to manufacture the product that caused the injury, placing the costs on it will guide it in evaluating the safety of the product's design. Is it necessary, however, to impose successor liability to accomplish this? Suppose instead of having liability imposed on it, the successor merely was told that a court had determined that the current design of the product was defective. Would not the fact that the successor would be liable for all injuries due to the products that *it* manufactured be sufficient for it to determine the optimal investment in safety? Indeed, might not imposing the costs of prior defects on the successor cause it to invest too much in safety? A second problem with this justification is that it imposes a limit on successor liability doctrine that the court does not acknowledge and may not even recognize. If the justification for successor liability is to influence the successor's decision about how it manufactures the product in question, then should successor liability be imposed where the successor did not continue to manufacture the product? See Gee v. Tennaco, Inc., 615 F.2d 857 (9th Cir.1980) (applying California law). Note that the other justifications considered thus far are not affected by whether the successor continues to manufacture the product.[15]

The final justification offered by the court also applies uniquely to the successor. The court stressed that because the successor "benefited substantially from the legitimate exploitation of the accumulated goodwill" of the original manufacturer, it is only fair that it bear the costs associated with that goodwill. The goodwill to which the court referred is presumably the manufacturer's reputation for a quality product; the idea is that one should not be able to rely on that reputation without having to bear the cost when its reputation proves incorrect.[16] The difficulty with this analysis is that the successor already bears this cost. The successor paid for the manufacturer's good will in the acquisition. The effect of revelation of the defective product is to reduce the value of the good will; certainly the successor would not have paid as much for the manufacturer's reputation had it known it was not justified.[17] The

[15] If the product line that caused the injury is purchased, does it make any difference if the selling company remains in business manufacturing other products? See Kline v. Johns-Manville, 745 F.2d 1217 (9th Cir.1984) (applying California law).

[16] This justification also contains its own limitation. What if the successor company

made substantial efforts to disclose that it, and not the predecessor, now manufactures the product line acquired? See Kline v. Johns-Manville, supra.

[17] See D. Phillips, supra, at 255–56; Note, *Imposing Strict Liability Upon a Successor Corporation for the Defective Products of its Corporate Predecessor: Proposed*

successor thus bears the cost of the defective product through the reduction in the value of the asset it purchased. What is added by imposing the additional cost of liability to the victim?

There is a common thread to the difficulties encountered with all of the court's justifications for successor liability. Grounded as they are in the public policy of products liability, each of them makes sense as applied to the original manufacturer. None, however, explains why the public policy underlying products liability dictates *successor* liability. And if products liability policy does not solve the problem, then perhaps we were too facile in applauding the courts turn away from corporate law analysis—i.e., analysis focusing on the character of the particular transaction. This approach to making sense out of the doctrine of successor liability is considered in the next section.

C. An Internalization Approach to Successor Liability

In Section A of this Chapter we saw that the issue really posed by the doctrine of successor liability was whether the acquiring company and the target company would be allowed to structure the acquisition transaction to serve their *joint* goal of cutting off—externalizing in the vocabulary of products liability—contingent future products liability claims. The goal of products liability policy is to insure that the manufacturer takes into account—internalizes—the cost of injuries caused by the product in making decisions about product safety. From this perspective, the function of successor liability is straightforward. Imposing liability on any future purchaser of the manufacturer's business means that the manufacturer must take the cost of future products liability claims into account currently because it will always bear them. If it continues to operate the business, it will bear the costs directly through products liability litigation; if it sells the business, it will bear the costs indirectly through a reduction in the price a purchaser will be willing to pay for the business. Thus, the point of successor liability is not to cause the *successor* to bear the costs of the predecessor's defective products, but as a tool to insure that the *predecessor* bears the cost.[18] In the absence of internalization, there is an incentive to operate the company in a manner that maximizes current profits at the expense of future injuries because the company can be

Alternatives to the Product Line Theory of Liability, 23 Bos.Col.L.Rev. 1397, 1421–22 (1982).

[18] Schwartz, *Products Liability, Corporate Structure and Bankruptcy: Toxic Substances and the Remote Risk Relationship,* Social Science Working Paper No. 542, California Institute of Technology (July, 1984); Roe, *Mergers, Acquisitions and Tort: A Comment on the Problem of Successor Corporate Liability,* 70 Va.L.Rev. 1559 (1984). D. Phillips, supra, reaches the same conclusion by examining comparable commercial law doctrines. In particular, he notes that the section 6–106 of the Uniform Commer-

cial Code, dealing with bulk sales, imposes a duty on the purchaser in a bulk sale "to assure that such consideration [paid for the business] is applied so far as necessary to pay those debts of the transferor." Id. at 265–66. Both applications build on the Coase Theorem's insight that, as long as the parties are in a bargaining relationship, it makes no difference on which party liability is initially imposed; the parties will reallocate the burden by contract in the most efficient way. For an accessible introduction to Coasean analysis, see A.M. Polinsky, *An Introduction to Law and Economics* 11–14 (1983).

sold free of claims so long as the sale takes place in time.[19]   Moreover, the absence of internalization may lead not only to unreasonably dangerous operations, but inefficient operations as well.   A rule of predecessor liability but no successor liability means that externalization can be accomplished only by selling the company.   Thus, an incentive is created to sell the company even if management of the acquiring company is less efficient.[20]

This analysis suggests a rule of absolute successor liability.   Does such an internalization approach to products liability provide sufficient guidance concerning the types of transactions which would be subject to an absolute successor liability rule?   For example, in light of the court's reliance in *Ramirez* on the successor's ability to make the product line safer, a powerful argument can be made that the product line approach would not impose liability on a successor company if it did not continue to produce the particular product line.   How would such a case come out under an internalization approach? [21]   Are there other differences in result between an internalization approach and the various judicial approaches to the problem?

D. Limits on an Internalization Approach to Successor Liability

An internalization approach to successor liabilities is subject to a number of objections.   One raises the issue of its fairness; the remainder concern its feasibility.

1. The Fairness of an Internalization Approach

An acquiring company on whom successor liability is imposed based on an internalization approach might well object on the simple basis of fairness.   It did not manufacture the product which caused the injury—as the court stated in *Ramirez:* "No one asserts that Amsted was responsible for actually placing the allegedly defective press into the commercial stream."   It is correct that the acquiring company has the means to make the product safer in the future.   But that effort to link liability if not to the past conduct of the successor, at least to the possibility of its future action, is a sham.   An internalization approach contemplates absolute successor liability; even if the defect that caused the injury has already been corrected, so that no future action by the successor was necessary, successor liability would still be imposed.   Finally, and perhaps most troubling from the perspective of an "innocent" successor, a morally culpable defendant does exist: The individuals who, as shareholders of the target company, presumably reaped the benefits of having placed the unsafe product into commerce.   Even conceding the overall validity of an internalization approach, the successor would object that the desired internalization could be effected by imposing liability on the morally culpable party rather than on a stranger.   Imposing personal liability on the former shareholders of a dissolved company to the extent of dissolution distributions also forces

---

[19] See Schwartz, supra.   [21] See D. Phillips, supra at 270–71.

[20] Roe, supra at 1565.

the target company to internalize the costs of expected products liability claims. Because the goal of internalization can be satisfied by imposing liability on either the successor or the former shareholders, the argument concludes, simple fairness dictates that it be placed on the parties who actually caused, or benefitted from, the harm.

The short response to this concern is that imposing liability on the former shareholders of a dissolved company is not feasible. Precisely because products liability claims may arise long after the dissolution of the target company, it would be difficult and expensive to discover the identity of the former shareholders, trace the proceeds if, as can be expected, the passage of time has allowed the proceeds to move to new holders by gift, inheritance and the like, and to bring multiple actions against multiple defendants in order to recover an amount sufficient to cover plaintiff's damages. To the extent that these transaction costs reduce the likelihood that actual, as opposed to theoretical, liability will be imposed on the former shareholders, the extent of internalization achieved is reduced.

Does the principle of matching culpability and liability warrant this reduction in internalization, especially when imposition of successor liability on the acquiring company does not determine the incidence of that liability? The point of successor liability is not to impose liability on the successor, but to use the successor as a tool to impose liability—through bargaining over the acquisition price—on the target company. The acquiring company may still object that there is something morally offensive about using it as a tool to get at the culpable party, but that type of liability strategy is not unusual. For example, the Securities Act of 1933 imposes near identical liability for misrepresentations in a registration statement on the issuer and on the underwriter, despite the fact that the underwriter does not retain the proceeds of the offering. Liability is imposed on the underwriter to give it an incentive to police the issuer—in essence, to use the underwriter as an enforcement tool. Kraakman, *Corporate Liability Strategies and the Costs of Legal Controls,* 93 Yale L.J. 857 (1984), provides a thoughtful analysis of this type of liability strategy.

2. Strategic Reponses to an Internalization Approach

A second, and more telling, criticism of successor liability as a means to force internalization of expected products liability costs is that it will not work; that is, it will not be sufficient to achieve the desired internalization. It has been repeatedly stressed in prior Chapters that planners and regulators are engaged in a multi-round strategic game. If planners can reformulate their transactions to avoid new regulation, then nothing has been gained. Thus, the case for successor liability is compromised if planners can devise techniques other than selling the company by which to externalize the future costs of products liability. Two such techniques come to mind: A piecemeal sale of assets followed by dissolution; and bankruptcy.

At least on the surface, a piecemeal sale of assets followed by dissolution will serve to externalize future products liability claims. First, as has been stressed, distributions in dissolution generally are not subject to recapture from former shareholders if previously unknown liabilities arise. Second, successor liability is unworkable in a true piecemeal sale of assets because there simply is no successor. To be sure, if the company is sold division by division or product line by product line, successor liability could be applied on that basis. But if the sale is truly piecemeal, so that no aspect of the business is sold as a going concern, successor liability would be quite difficult to apply.

What practical limitations constrain the use of piecemeal sales of assets to avoid forced internalization through successor liability? It is important to keep in mind that a planner does not have an entirely free hand in manipulating transaction form to avoid regulatory constraints; the alteration in transaction form may have real non-regulatory costs. A piecemeal sale of assets has the potential of imposing a very substantial non-regulatory cost: The loss of the company's goodwill, the difference between the company's going concern value and its liquidation value. Thus, avoiding internalization by means of a piecemeal sale of assets will be desirable only when the present value of the future products liability claims, eliminated by the sale, exceed the value of the company's goodwill, also eliminated by the sale.

The necessary relation between future products liability claims and goodwill may exist where, in anticipation of the availability of a piecemeal sale, the owners of the company treat their ownership as an option and systematically underinvest in product safety. If they are lucky—they end up on the "safe" side of the probability distribution of future injury caused by their product—they can sell the business as a going concern and reap the benefits of their goodwill even in the face of successor liability. If they are unlucky and end up with a product that looks like it will cause substantial injury, they can sell the assets piecemeal. In option terms, they get the upside, the potential victims bear the downside. This situation, however, is only one manifestation of the general problem created by limited liability for shareholders. So long as shareholders' responsibility for injuries inflicted by the company's products cannot exceed their investment in the company, there is an incentive to underinvest in safety and insurance. To that extent, products liability risks are externalized.[22] Successor liability thus does not solve the problem of asset insufficiency that is associated with limited liability generally,[23] but it does narrow the extent to which externalization is possible. Put differently, the planner's freedom of action is substantially constrained.[24]

[22] Schwartz, supra; Stone, *The Place of Enterprise Liability in the Control of Corporate Conduct,* 90 Yale L.J. 857 (1980).

[23] Schwartz, supra; Kraakman, supra at 868–76.

[24] In situations where asset insufficiency allows externalization of risks, the use of liability as an indirect technique of controlling conduct gives way to direct regulation with specified standards and penalties and imprisonment for violations. See Shavell, *Liability for Harm Versus Regulation of Safety,* 13 J.Leg.Stud. 357 (1984). While this approach has its own limitations, it does avoid the critical problem posed by the alternative of eliminating limited liability altogether: The need to balance the benefits from eliminating externalization

The second means of avoiding successor liability—bankruptcy—is really a variation on the piecemeal sale theme. A piecemeal sale of assets followed by dissolution functions as an informal bankruptcy liquidation: A company resorts to it only if it is worth more in pieces than as a going concern, *or* if the process cuts off the claims of enough creditors—future products liability claimants—that the loss of goodwill is outweighed. It follows that a formal bankruptcy liquidation may also be a means of avoiding successor liability. If future products liability plaintiffs are not treated as creditors for purposes of bankruptcy—in technical terms, if they are not holders of *claims* under Section 726 of the Bankruptcy Act—then they are excluded from any distribution to creditors.[25] Thus a formal as well as an informal bankruptcy liquidation has the potential to allow some externalization.

What if substantially all of the assets of the bankrupt company were sold in the bankruptcy proceeding as a going concern rather than piecemeal? Would successor liability extend to a purchaser from the trustee in bankruptcy? Should the answer depend on whether future products liability victims are treated as having "claims"? See Jackson, *Translating Assets and Liabilities to the Bankruptcy Forum,* 14 J.Leg. Stud. 73, 94–97 (1985).

3. Uncertainty and the Failure of Internalization

An additional objection to an internalization approach goes to its very heart. Suppose that the defect that caused the injuries in question was not foreseeable at the time the product was designed or produced. A rule that imposes successor liability for injuries caused by this type of defect will not cause the predecessor to take the expected costs of future liability into account in making design or production decisions; by definition, costs that cannot be anticipated cannot be internalized.[26] What is the effect of imposing successor liability with respect to unforeseeable product defects? One response to the objection

against the cost of the reduction in capital market efficiency that would result from eliminating limited liability. See Halpern, Trebilcock & Turnbull, *An Economic Analysis of Limited Liability in Corporation Law,* 70 U.Toronto L.J. 117 (1980); Easterbrook & Fischel, *Limited Liability and the Corporation,* 52 U.Chi.L.Rev. 89 (1985).

[25] T. Jackson, *The Logic and Limits of Bankruptcy Law: The Implications of Collective Action and Discharge Policy,* Ch. 4 (forthcoming, Harvard University Press). Professor Jackson points out that, in addition to facilitating some amount of externalization, a rule barring future products liability plaintiffs from participating as creditors in the bankruptcy proceeding has the perverse effect of leading to a liquidation even though the company is worth more as a going concern. If the plaintiffs do not hold "claims", then whatever we call what they do have is not discharged in bankruptcy; any reorganized company would remain subject to them. Thus, existing creditors may well prefer to liquidate, thereby getting 100 percent of a smaller pie, rather than share a larger pie, the reorganized company, with an additional group of claimants. If the future products liability plaintiffs were treated as having claims, so that they could not be excluded from participation in the bankrupt's assets, existing creditors would make the socially correct choice: To maintain the company as a going concern through reorganization because that maximizes the size of the pie. These issues are at the heart of the controversy over the role of asbestos victims in the Johns-Manville bankruptcy. See In re UNR Industries, Inc. 725 F.2d 1111 (7th Cir.1984); In re Johns-Manville Corp., 36 B.R. 743 (S.D.N.Y.1984). See generally Roe, *Bankruptcy and Tort,* 84 Colum.L.Rev. 846 (1984); Note, *The Manville Bankruptcy: Treating Mass Tort Claims in Chapter 11 Proceedings,* 96 Harv.L.Rev. 1121 (1983).

[26] Schwartz, supra.

that successor liability was unfair to the successor was that the successor did not bear the incidence of the liability; the successor is merely a convenient place to put initial liability because the successor will shift the liability to the target company through bargaining. Can this liability shifting work if neither the successor nor the predecessor can anticipate, even probabilistically, the potential for future liability? From the perspective of the acquiring company, where successor liability for unforeseeable defects exists, an acquisition takes on something of the character of a game of Russian roulette, but played without any knowledge of the number of chambers in the cylinder, nor the number of bullets that have been inserted. Under these circumstances, a rule of absolute successor liability would prevent anything but a piecemeal transfer of the predecessor's assets.[27]

Is the problem in this situation with an internalization approach to successor liability, or with the basic products liability rule that imposes liability on the predecessor in the first place?[28] If the problem lies with the initial imposition of products liability, and if that result is treated as given, as it might be in judicial consideration of a case that raised only the successor liability issue, how should the internalization approach be applied? One choice would be to recognize that internalization is impossible with respect to unforeseeable risks, and, as a result, that the justification for successor liability was not present. The internalization approach thus would define its own limits: Successor liability would not be imposed when internalization would be impossible. An alternative would be to opt for consistency—to impose successor liability whenever the predecessor would have been liable—even though an internalization approach would not require it. Would this result benefit future products liability claimants on an *ex ante* basis? If the anticipation of successor liability for unforeseeable claims prevents the company from being sold at all, so that no successor will exist, claimants are left with recourse only to the original company, subject to a piecemeal sale of assets and bankruptcy.[29] Which way are products liability claimants better off?

How easily could a court determine whether or not a particular risk was or should have been foreseeable? Could a court determine with any accuracy whether a reasonable person would have done more research, and thereby would have discovered the product defect that later caused injury? If this type of determination is subject to error, then what will be the impact on behavior? Will it result in too much research or not enough?

If it is difficult to determine long after the fact whether a particular risk was foreseeable at the time the product was designed, would a statute of limitations—measured from the date the product was pur-

---

[27] See Roe, *Mergers, Acquisitions, and Tort,* supra at 1573–74.

[28] See Schwartz, supra.

[29] Professor Roe reports that "GAF, a co-defendant in the massive asbestos litigation, recently attempted to sell a chemical division to Allied Corporation. The two firms were reported to have reached preliminary agreement about the transfer, but the deal collapsed with Allied claiming it could not be assured it would not be subject to GAF's potentially large asbestos liability." Roe, *Mergers, Acquisitions, and Torts,* supra at 1561.

chased rather than the date of injury—serve as a more certain proxy for foreseeability? The idea would be that a successor would always know at least the period of exposure, if not its size. Are there some risks—for example, with respect to toxic substances—where the injury is foreseeable but nonetheless would not occur for a significant period of time?

E. Planning for Successor Liability for Future Products Claims

What are the planning implications of the expansion of successor liability for future products liability claims? One clear message is that an acquiring company must make a substantial investment in investigating the potential for future liability with respect to products previously manufactured by the target. To be sure, this has always been necessary because, in estimating the target company's future cash flows, the acquiring company has to estimate the likelihood of future liability with respect to *post*-acquisition production, an estimate that would depend heavily on past experience. Now, however, the estimate not only would help set the price, it would also help set the bounds of any contractual protection the acquiring company might seek from the target company concerning the maximum amount of future liability.

Up to this point, we have not considered the character of the actual negotiations between the acquiring company and the target company that would cause the target to internalize products liability costs. Would not the target company have an incentive to understate the potential for future liability? And to the extent that the target company succeeds in fooling the acquiring company, the incidence of successor liability then remains on the successor. We consider the range of contractual techniques which might be used to protect against the target company's understatement of future risk in connection with Chapter Nineteen's examination of the content of a typical acquisition agreement.

Assuming that an internalization approach to sucessor liability limits the planner's ability to avoid future product liability entirely, and further assuming that the target company has provided as much contractual protection as possible, can anything be done to protect against disaster? Suppose that both the acquiring company and the target company greatly underestimate the potential of future liability, perhaps because the particular jurisdiction imposes both primary and successor liability for products liability even if the risk was unforeseeable. Here the need for protection is critical; as suggested above, in the absence of protection, the acquisition becomes a game of Russian roulette. In the past, disaster insurance was provided either by making a triangular acquisition, so that the target company remained a wholly owned subsidiary of the acquiring company, or, particularly in a close corporation, achieving the same result by simply buying all of the target company's outstanding stock.[30] The advantage sought was limit-

---

[30] In a public company, an exchange offer would be unlikely to garner 100 percent of the target's outstanding shares, thereby requiring recourse to a triangular technique in any case.

ed liability. Although the assets of the target company would remain subject to future products liability claims, the parent's assets would be shielded because, as a shareholder, the parent's liability would be limited.[31]

As yet, the momentum of products liability law has not breached the parent-subsidiary boundary, at least when the subsidiary has not been systematically stripped of its assets. Thus, the rule governing parent liability for the torts of its subsidiary has remained largely a creature of corporate law, technical and restrictive much as was the original successor liability doctrine. See, e.g., C.M. Corp. v. Oberer Development Corp., 631 F.2d 536 (7th Cir.1980); Note, *Piercing the Corporate Veil: The Alter Ego Doctrine Under Federal Common Law*, 95 Harv.L.Rev. 853 (1982). Does an internalization approach require treating the parent company as the successor in this setting? Have future products liability plaintiffs been made worse off by the acquisition? Prior to the transaction, the doctrine of limited liability imposed on the plaintiff the risk that the target company's assets would be insufficient to pay the plaintiff's claim at the time of judgment; after the transaction, the plaintiff is subject to the identical risk. In both cases, the claim is protected by the same amount of assets. An argument that an internalization approach should make it easier to pierce the corporate veil following an acquisition would require demonstrating that the acquisition—the target's shift from an independent company to a subsidiary—increases the risk of asset insufficiency.

Would it be enough to show that the parent generally has an incentive to keep the subsidiary undercapitalized and to try to increase the risks of all creditors? Do not these incentives also exist for shareholders of an independent company? Could it be shown that externalization is easier to accomplish in a parent-subsidiary relationship? Suppose the comparison was between the pre-acquisition behavior of a publicly held company and its post-acquisition behavior as a wholly owned subsidiary. Would the existence of separation with respect to the public company, so that all shareholders desired to maximize the value of the company,[32] distinguish that situation from the sole shareholder setting of the parent-subsidiary, where what would be maximized would be the value of the parent's entire portfolio, not the value of the subsidiary alone?[33] For a debate on the merits of

---

[31] See, e.g., Heitland, *Survival of Products Liability Claims in Asset Acquisitions*, 34 Bus.Law. 489 (1979).

[32] See Chapter Four B., supra.

[33] For example, below market rate loans from parent to subsidiary, overattribution of corporate overhead to the subsidiary, diversion of profitable opportunities to the parent, and transfer pricing favorable to the parent are available to divert assets in the subsidiary setting in a way not possible for a publicly held company (although they would be available to a privately held company). Additionally, the parent-subsidiary relationship may eliminate some of the collateral costs of increasing the risk to creditors. Dividends to individuals, likely a significant portion of the publicly held company's shareholders, are taxed at ordinary income rates. Dividends to a corporation are subject to an 85 percent dividend deduction under IRC § 243, which reduces the effective rate to 6.6 percent. For a wholly owned subsidiary filing a consolidated return pursuant to IRC § 1501, there is no tax at all. Thus, the cost of moving assets out of the company, and out of the grasp of creditors, is reduced.

piercing the parent-subsidiary veil with respect to trade and other contract creditors, see Landers, *A Unified Approach to Parent, Subsidiary, and Affiliate Questions in Bankruptcy,* 42 U.Chi.L.Rev. 589 (1975); Posner, *The Rights of Creditors of Affiliated Corporations,* 43 U.Chi.L. Rev. 499 (1876); Landers, *Another Word on Parents, Subsidiaries, and Affiliates in Bankruptcy,* 43 U.Chi.L.Rev. 526 (1976).

Insurance is a final method of dealing with the risk of successor products liability. "Claims made" insurance, a policy that covers any claims made while the policy is in force, regardless of when the product was manufactured, and "tail" coverage, covering claims with respect to products no longer manufactured, are helpful.[34] The problem, however, is that such insurance may not be available at all, or only at an unacceptable price. An important part of what is typically referred to as the products liability crisis is that such insurance is unavailable to large numbers of manufacturers.[35]

F. Other Areas of Successor Liability

Future products liability claims are not the only target company obligations that pose the risk of successor liability. Obligations relating to the target company's collective bargaining agreements and its pension plans also raise the problem in important ways. Where, for example, an acquisition is motivated by synergy, the imposition of a duty to bargain on the acquiring company may interfere with the changes in production techniques, plant location or employment levels necessary to achieve the contemplated synergy. The importance of successor liability for target company pension fund obligations is even more straightforward: Liability for underfunding can be as high as 30 percent of the combined net worth of the acquiring company and its affiliates.

1. Successor Liability With Respect to Collective Bargaining Agreements

The acquisition of a target company subject to a collective bargaining agreement raises the question of whether, and to what extent, the acquiring company succeeds to the target's collective bargaining obligations.[36] As with future products liability claims, issues of public policy—in this case the policy of discouraging labor strife embodied in the National Labor Relations Act—have led to the development of a doctrine of successor liability peculiar to the context. Unlike in the products liability context, however, the issue is not limited to the single

[34] For a general discussion of products liability insurance coverage, see Kadens. *Practitioner's Guide to Treatment of Seller's Products Liabilities in Asset Acquisitions,* 16 U.Tol.L.Rev. 1, 32–44 (1978).

[35] See United States Dept. of Commerce Interagency Task Force on Product Liability, Final Report VI 2–13 (1977).

[36] The area has generated a substantial literature. See, e.g., Crawford, Collective Bargaining Agreement's and Employee's Rights, in II Business Acquisitions 873 (J. Herz & C. Baller eds., 2nd ed. 1981); Silver, *Reflections on the Obligations of a Successor Employer,* 2 Cardozo L.Rev. 545 (1981); Morris & Gaus, *Successorship and the Collective Bargaining Agreement: Accommodating Wiley and Burns,* 59 Va.L. Rev. 1359 (1973).

matter of monetary responsibility for damages. In the collective bargaining context, successor liability is possible with respect to four different target obligations: Does the acquiring company succeed

> (1) to the target's recognition of a union and obligation to bargain with it? [37]

> (2) to the target's obligations under the collective bargaining agreement with the union? [38]

> (3) to the target's contractual obligation to arbitrate grievances? [39]

> (4) to the target's obligations to remedy past unfair labor practices? [40]

Both the federal courts' analysis of these questions and the answers reached differ depending on which issue is considered. However, all four pose interesting contrasts to the performance of state courts in developing the doctrine of successor liability with respect to products liability [41] and, in all events, the answers to these questions may be critical to the success of an acquisition. As already noted, whether the acquiring company succeeds to some or all of the collective bargaining obligations of the target company may determine whether the synergy anticipated from the transaction can be accomplished or whether a reduction in wages, in order to make the company more competitive, is possible.

Historically, the federal courts have dealt with these issues in terms that recall the state courts' development of the de facto merger doctrine. Successorship depended on the finding of "a substantial continuity of identity in the business enterprise" [42] as evidenced by a litany of factors including whether a majority of the post-acquisition employees had been employees of the target, and whether, after the acquisition, the same business operations were continued, the same supervisors were employed, the same methods of production were maintained, and the same products or services were manufactured.[43] At the same time, however, the Supreme Court has stressed that no simple tallying of the factors is possible. In Howard Johnson Co. v. Detroit Local Joint Executive Board, 417 U.S. 249, 262 n. 9 (1974), the Court stated:

> The question of whether Howard Johnson [the acquirer] is a "successor" is simply not meaningful in the abstract. Howard Johnson is of course a successor employer in the sense that it succeeded to operation of a restaurant and motor lodge formerly operated by the

[37] See NLRB v. Burns Int'l Security Serv., 406 U.S. 272 (1972).

[38] See id.

[39] See John Wiley & Sons v. Livingston, 376 U.S. 543 (1964); Howard Johnson Co., Inc., v. Detroit Local Joint Executive Bd., 417 U.S. 249 (1974).

[40] See Golden State Bottling Co. v. NLRB, 414 U.S. 168 (1973).

[41] The status of an acquiring company employer with respect to the target company's collective bargaining obligations is a matter of federal law under the National Labor Relations Act. Products liability remains an issue of state law. See Section C. of this Chapter, supra.

[42] John Wiley & Sons v. Livingston, 376 U.S. 543, 551 (1964).

[43] See generally, Slicker, A Reconsideration of the Doctrine of Employer Successorship—A Step Toward a Rational Approach, 57 Minn.L.Rev. 1051 (1973).

[target]. But the real question in each of these successor cases is, on the particular facts, what are the legal obligations of the new employer to the employees of the former owner * * *. The answer to this inquiry requires analysis of the interests of the new employer and the employees and of the policies of the labor laws in light of the facts of each case and the particular legal obligation at issue, whether it be the duty to recognize and bargain with the union, the duty to remedy unfair labor practices, the duty to arbitrate, etc. There is, and can be, no single definition of "successor" which is applicable in every legal context. A new employer, in other words, may be a successor employer for some purposes and not for others.

Without excluding the possibility that unique labor law considerations dictate the result with respect to one or more of the four central issues, it is interesting to see how each would be evaluated under an internalization approach to successor liability. Recall that under this approach, successor liability is justified to prevent the acquiring and target companies from combining to externalize risks on creditors—like future products liability claimants—who cannot protect themselves. Thus, contract creditors who can negotiate the terms of their relationship directly with the target company and, as a result, can force the target company to take into account the cost to them of an unexpected termination of the contract, generally are not protected by the successor liability doctrine. In contrast, where creditors cannot themselves negotiate with the target company, as with future products liability claimants, an internalization approach to the successor liability doctrine imposes liability on the successor so that the successor acts as a surrogate for the interests of the creditors in its negotiations with the target.

Under an internalization approach, might not the Supreme Court's fragmentation of the problem of successorship in labor law be wrong? In any case in which a successorship issue is raised, the target company and the union were, by definition, already in a contractual relationship out of which a contract determining their rights and responsibilities— the collective bargaining agreement—was negotiated. One matter that could have been negotiated was what would happen if the company were sold; the successorship issue could have been resolved by contract in a labor setting just as the successorship issue is resolved by contract in a bond indenture. Indeed, it appears that a significant number of collective bargaining agreements do contain a successorship clause.[44] And where such a contract exists, the courts have held that a pending

44 BNA, *Basic Patterns of Union Contracts* 8 (8th ed. 1975), reports that 22 percent of a sample of collective bargaining agreements contained a successorship clause. One such clause provided that:

This agreement shall be binding upon the successors and assigns of the parties hereto, and no provisions, terms or obligations herein contained shall be affected, modified, altered or changed in any respect whatsoever by consolidation, merger, sale, transfer or assignment of either party hereto or affected, modified, altered or changed in any respect whatsoever, by any change of any kind of the legal status, ownership or management of either party hereto.

11 *Collective Bargaining Agreement Negotiations and Contracts* (BNA) 70:182 (1981) (Fairchild Republic Co. and United Auto Workers).

acquisition of the target can be enjoined unless the acquiring company satisfies the contract.[45]

In light of the opportunity for the union to bargain with respect to successorship, what reason is there to create *any* labor law successor liability doctrine? When some unions bargain for successor protection and others do not, one inference is that the unions which did not secure a successorship clause chose to take the consideration the employees' bargaining position could command in a different currency. For example, a decision to give up a successorship clause in favor of higher wages is, in effect, a decision to prefer current benefits to future benefits. Unless we believe that the union systematically applied an erroneously high discount rate to future benefits, why as a matter of federal labor policy should we override the union's choice of the timing of benefits? [46]

One explanation for such a bias might be that labor unions, like any other representative organization, are subject to agency costs: Those representing employees in the bargaining may pursue the goals of some subgroup of employees rather than what makes the entire group of affected employees best off. From this perspective, a union bias against the future may be perfectly understandable. In negotiating a successorship clause, the union represents two groups of potentially different employees: present employees, who will benefit from higher current wages; and future employees, who will be present when the company is acquired and who would be benefitted by a successorship clause. Only if it is certain that the two groups will be identical can there be confidence that the union will apply the correct discount rate. The higher the turnover in the particular workforce, the greater the likelihood that the makeup of the two groups of employees will differ, and the greater the likelihood that the union will honor the preference of current employees, whose vote is required to approve the contract, for higher current wages even if the joint welfare of both groups of employees would be maximized by trading current wages for a successorship clause.[47]

There may be circumstances in other labor related areas where an internalization approach might favor successor liability. For example, suppose a company that systematically engaged in employment discrimination sought, as with products liability claims, to cut off future employment discrimination claims by selling its assets and dissolving. Subject to the requirement that the claims be foreseeable, the imposition of successor liability in this circumstance would serve to force the target to internalize the costs of employment discrimination.[48]

[45] Local Lodge No. 1266, IAM, v. Panoramic Corp., 668 F.2d 276 (7th Cir.1981).

[46] Cf. Jackson, *Fresh-Start Policy in Bankruptcy Law,* 98 Harv.L.Rev. 1393 (1985) (individual discharge under federal bankruptcy law justified by systematic biases in consumer decision-making).

[47] See Leslie, *Labor Bargaining Units,* 70 Va.L.Rev. 353 (1984) (development of a collective goods model of labor unions).

[48] The requirement in the case law that the successor employer have notice of the claims of employment discrimination could be read as a foreseeability requirement. See Wiggins v. Spector Freight Systems, 583 F.2d 882 (6th Cir.1978). *Wiggins,* however, has been read to exonerate a successor if charges had not been filed with the EEOC at the time the acquisition took place. Rabidue v. Osceola Refining Co., 584 F.Supp. 419, 424 (E.D.Mich.1984). Un-

From a planning perspective, what elements of the litany of factors the courts have described as relevant to successorship are subject to control? Would it be worthwhile to try to minimize the number of target employees who are hired? If so, does the successorship doctrine protect employees?

A final consideration is whether the imposition of successor liability can be avoided by restructuring the transaction. A piecemeal sale of assets would seem to work to avoid successor liability; however, it would be subject to the same non-regulatory costs as were noted with respect to products liability claims. Is anything gained if the target company is first put into bankruptcy and the acquisition is made as part of a plan of reorganization? In NLRB v. Bildisco & Bildisco, 465 U.S. 513 (1984), the Supreme Court held that a debtor could reject a collective bargaining agreement under Section 365 of the Bankruptcy Reform Act [49] "if the debtor can show that the collective-bargaining agreement burdens the estate, and that after careful scrutiny, the equities balance in favor of rejecting the labor contract." 465 U.S. at 526. The Court's decision was widely viewed as an invitation to otherwise healthy companies to enter bankruptcy in order to shed their collective bargaining agreements.[50] After a tortured legislative process that coincided with Congressional efforts to resurrect bankruptcy court jurisdiction after the Supreme Court had held a significant portion of it unconstitutional,[51] Congress responded to *Bildisco* by adding Section 1113 to the Bankruptcy Act. Under Section 1113, a trustee can reject a collective bargaining agreement, but the section requires that the court make the presumably more stringent finding that the equities "clearly" favor rejection and that "all of the affected parties are treated fairly and equitably." [52] Assuming that the trustee retains relative freedom to reject collective bargaining agreements,[53] how likely is it that, for companies that are not in serious financial trouble, the advantages of rejecting a collective bargaining agreement will outweigh the collateral costs of bankruptcy?

2. Successor Liability With Respect to Defined Benefit Pension Plan Obligations

Successor liability with respect to the target company's defined benefit pension plan obligations is both an important and an interesting issue.[54] Its importance derives from the size of the stakes; in the

der an internalization approach, all that is necessary is that the employment discrimination claims be foreseeable on a probabilistic basis; they need not be certain. What incentive would a bright line rule like that of *Rabidue* create?

[49] 11 U.S.C. Sec. 365 (1982) (Trustee, subject to court's approval, may assume or reject any executory contract of the debtor.).

[50] See White, *The Bildisco Case and the Congressional Response*, 30 Wayne L.Rev. 1169, 1181–82 (1984).

[51] Marathon Pipeline Co. v. Northern Pipeline Co., 458 U.S. 50 (1982).

[52] Section 1113(d)(1)(A).

[53] See White, supra at 1201–02 (Section 1113 somewhat more restrictive than *Bildisco* test but less restrictive than pre-*Bildisco* law.).

[54] A defined benefit pension plan is one that promises the employee a fixed benefit on retirement. In contrast, a defined contribution plan promises the employee only the money that has been contributed to the employee's account augmented or dimin-

worst case scenario, the acquiring company's liability could reach 30 percent of the aggregate net worth of the company and its affiliates. The subject's interest derives from the fact that successor liability for pension plan obligations is an anomaly in two respects. First, in contrast to the common law development of the standards for successor liability for products liability and collective bargaining obligations, successor liability for pension fund obligations is determined by statute, part of the complex legislative scheme adopted by the Employment Retirement Income Security Act of 1974 (ERISA),[55] as amended by the Multiemployer Pension Plan Amendments Act of 1980,[56] and as influenced by the detailed requirements governing the federal income tax treatment of pension funds under the Internal Revenue Code (IRC). Second, the manner in which Congress resolved the successor liability issue stands in stark contrast to the manner in which the courts have dealt with successor liability for products liability and collective bargaining obligations. With respect to pension plan obligations, Congress chose to forgo successor liability in favor of what may be called predecessor liability. This manner of dealing with the problem provides a useful counterpoint in understanding the bases for the internalization approach developed earlier in this Chapter.

An acquisition poses the risk of three general categories of liability with respect to the target company's defined benefit pension plan:[57]

(1) liability under ERISA and the IRC to fund already vested benefits under the plan:

(2) liability under ERISA if the plan is terminated; and

(3) liability under the IRC for back income taxes if the plan retroactively loses its qualification for special tax treatment.

With respect to each of these categories of liability, the obligation of the acquiring company is determined by the form of the transaction. If the acquisition is structured as a merger, the acquiring company assumes all obligations of the target company, including pension obligations, as a matter of state law. If the transaction is structured as a stock acquisition, the assets of the target remain subject to its pension

---

ished by investment performance since its contribution. In a defined benefit plan, the company bears the risk that the plan will have insufficient funds to pay the benefits; in a defined contribution plan, such a shortfall is impossible. Because pension liability, and therefore successor liability, focuses on this shortfall, our concern here is only with defined benefit plans.

[55] 29 U.S.C. §§ 1001–1381 (1982).

[56] Pub.L. No. 96–364, 94 Stat. 1208 (1980).

[57] What follows is a general description of an enormously complicated problem. Although the successor liability problem can be described straightforwardly, the manner in which the size of the liability is calculated, and the details of the rules governing the precise circumstances in which

the liability is created, are extraordinarily complex and beyond the scope of this Chapter. For more detailed discussions of some of these issues, see, e.g., L. Laarman & D. Hildebrandt, *Plan Terminations and Mergers,* 357 Tax Management Portfolios (1983); Reichler, *Handling Significant Benefit Plans in Mergers and Acquisitions,* in II Business Acquisitions 831 (J. Herz & C. Baller eds., 2d ed. 1981); Novikoff & Polebaum, *Pension Related Claims in Bankruptcy Code Cases,* 40 Bus.Law. 373 (1985); Krueger, *Corporate Transactions— Retirement Plan Issues,* 61 Taxes 147 (1983); Miller, *The Employee Benefit Aspects of Acquisitions and Divestitures: The Liabilities,* 4 Corp.L.Rev. 91 (1981); Kladder, *Asset Sales after MPPAA—An Analysis of ERISA Section 4204,* 39 Bus.Law. 101 (1983).

obligations and, at least for purposes of termination liabilities, the assets of the acquiring company and all members of its affiliated group also may become subject to the liabilities. Finally, and most importantly from planning a perspective, if the transaction is structured as a sale of assets, the traditional rule is retained: The acquiring company succeeds to only those of the target company's liabilities, including pension obligations, as are expressly assumed in the acquisition agreement.

Liability for unfunded vested benefits—benefits already earned by plan participants but for which employer contributions have not yet been made—has two aspects. The first is a tax liability. Under IRC Section 412 and ERISA Section 302, an employer has the obligation to meet minimum annual funding standards. If the standards are not met, IRC Section 4791(a) imposes an annual 5 percent excise tax on the accumulated funding deficiency and, if the deficiency is not eliminated during a specified correction period, IRC Section 4791(b) imposes an excise tax equal to 100 percent of the remaining accumulated funding deficiency. The Internal Revenue Code does not impose liability on the acquiring company in an asset acquisition for excise taxes owed by the target;[58] as a result, there are no limits short of a sham transaction attack on a planner's efforts to use an asset acquisition to avoid assuming excise taxes owed by the target company.

The second aspect of liability for unfunded vested benefits is the obligation ultimately to pay the benefits. If the pension plan is assumed by the acquirer, the funding and payment obligations are, of course, also assumed. If the acquiring company does not assume the pension plan, because the acquisition is in the form of a sale of assets and the acquisition agreement does not provide for assumption, the target company retains liability for unfunded vested benefits. The problem, however, is that a target company typically goes out of business following a sale of its assets. This results in a termination of the plan with the consequence that, under Title IV of ERISA, the Pension Benefit Guaranty Corporation (PBGC) guarantees the payment to employees of certain vested plan benefits. If the assets of the plan are insufficient to pay the benefits guaranteed by the PBGC—if the plan is underfunded—the target company is liable to the PBGC for the shortfall in an amount up to 30 percent of the combined net worth of the target and its affiliates.[59] Of critical importance to the acquiring company, no successor liability attaches to the acquiring company if the target's assets are insufficient to satisfy the PBGC's claim.[60]

[58] Successor liability will exist only where imposed by applicable state law such as the Uniform Fraudulent Conveyances Act or a bulk sales act. Miller, supra at 114–16.

[59] ERISA Section 4062.

[60] ERISA Section 4062(d); PBGC Opinion Letter 78–10 (June 21, 1978). Two qualifications are necessary. If the transfer was a subterfuge to shield target company assets, liability may attach to the transferee.

Additionally, the PBGC has a lien against the target company's assets to secure payment of the target's liability to the PBGC. From the acquiring company's perspective, the critical date is that on which the PBGC files a claim similar to that filed with respect to a federal tax lien. Property acquired from the target before the filing is not subject to the lien. See Miller, supra at 110.

A second form of termination liability arises when the target company is a member of a multiemployer pension plan. Under the MPPA, an employer who withdraws from a multiemployer pension plan is immediately liable for a portion of the plan's unfunded vested benefits. An acquisition of the target company operates as a withdrawal unless the acquisition is a merger, ERISA Section 4218, or unless in a sale of assets the acquiring company assumes the target's obligations under the plan and posts a bond or sets up an escrow to secure against liability for future withdrawals. ERISA Section 4204. As with liability for termination of a single employer plan, the acquiring company has no successor obligation in a sale of assets unless there has been an explicit assumption.[61]

The final category of liability is the target company's obligations for back taxes if a plan is retroactively disqualified because of an acquisition. This will have the effect of making unavailable the income tax deduction taken by the target in previous years for contributions to the plan.[62] The standards which determine disqualification are complex;[63] however, for our purpose the important point is that in an asset acquisition no successor liability is imposed for deficiencies resulting from retroactive disqualification.[64]

The common thread that joins each category of potential liability is the fact that the planner's decision to cast the transaction as a sale of assets, so that the acquiring company does not assume the target's liabilities, will be respected. That result, quite different from the results encountered earlier in this Chapter, poses a question. If successor liability is necessary to force internalization of future products liability costs, why is it not necessary with respect to future pension costs? Recall that what allowed externalization of future products liability costs was the target company's ability to dissolve under state corporate law and thereby cut off future claims. Because pension obligations are known—the amount of future claims can be determined actuarially—they must be paid or adequately provided for prior to dissolution; externalization in this sense is not possible. Indeed, in some circumstances, ERISA imposes "predecessor liability" on the target company with respect to obligations explicitly assumed by the acquiring company. In connection with both liability arising from the termination of a single employer pension plan,[65] and liability arising from withdrawal from a multiemployer pension plan,[66] the target company remains secondarily liable if the acquiring company fails to discharge the assumed obligation.[67] But why would Congress worry about predecessor liability if a successor has already assumed the

[61] See generally Kladder, *supra.*

[62] An assessment would be possible with respect to all years for which the statute of limitations, under IRC Section 6501(a) generally three years after the filing of a return, has not run.

[63] See Reichler, *supra* at 837–42.

[64] The liability could create a federal tax lien. Prior to the filing of the lien, however, an acquirer would be protected in the same manner as discussed earlier with respect to excise taxes owed by the target.

[65] Miller, *supra,* at 112–13.

[66] ERISA Section 4204.

[67] In the multiemployer setting, ERISA Section 4204(a)(1)(C) requires that the contract of sale explicitly provide for secondary liability, and Section 4204(a)(3) requires that a bond be posted or an escrow

predecessor's obligations? So long as the liability is not externalized, because the successor has assumed it, what does predecessor liability add?

Might not ERISA be concerned with the risk of underfunding being externalized not to employees—they are protected by the guarantee of the PBGC—but to the PBGC itself? The PBGC is essentially an insurance company to which companies that maintain covered plans pay premiums. If a company can avoid potential liability by shifting the obligation to a riskier company, perhaps one with a net worth below what would have been the target's 30 percent obligation, the risk to that extent has been externalized to the PBGC.[68] The maintenance of predecessor liability thus functions to protect the 30 percent of net worth rule.

It is a mistake, however, to overestimate the planning flexibility that the absence of successor liability provides.[69] Quite often there will be substantive reasons for the acquiring company to assume the target's pension liabilities.[70] In this situation, ERISA eliminates one of the planning techniques that remains available with respect to future products liability claims despite the expansion of successor liability. The acquiring company's assets can be shielded from the target company's future products liability claims, even if the target's assets cannot be, either by acquiring the stock of the target and keeping it as a separate subsidiary, or by casting the transaction in triangular form. Under ERISA, a parent's liability for the pension obligations of its subsidiary is *not* limited; the net worth of all businesses under "common control" as determined under IRC Sections 414(b) and (c) are aggregated for purposes of determining the maximum liability to the PBGC.[71]

The message to planners is that investigation and contractual protection is critical here. That the liability cannot be externalized means that, for this item, the acquiring and target companies will be engaged in distributive bargaining. Thus, allocation of the burden of pension liability by, for example, the manner in which the purchase price is calculated and by contractual representations, warranties and indemnification, requires consideration of techniques of private, rather than public ordering. This is the subject of Part V, to which we now turn.

created if the target is to be liquidated before its secondary liability terminates.

[68] See Bulow, Scholes & Menell, *Economic Implications of ERISA* in Financial Aspects of the U.S. Pension System 37 (Z. Bodie & J. Shaven eds. 1984) (right to terminate PBGC insured plan as put option).

[69] For discussion of the ability to use bankruptcy to cut off pension fund obligations, see Novikoff & Polebaum, supra.

[70] See Kruger, supra at 152–54.

[71] Not surprisingly given the stakes, the precise contours of the phrase "common control" has generated a substantial amount of litigation. See, e.g., Pension Benefit Guaranty Corp. v. Dickens, 535 F.S. 922 (D.C.Mich.1982); Pension Benefit Guaranty Corp. v. Ouimet Corp., 630 F.2d 4 (1st Cir.1980), cert. denied 450 U.S. 914 (1981); Pension Benefit Guaranty Corp. v. Anthony Co., 575 F.Supp. 953 (N.D.Ill. 1983). The manner of calculating the aggregate net worth of a controlled group can serve to expose more than 30 percent of the group's net worth. A negative net worth of one member of the group is disregarded and does not serve to reduce the net worth of other group members. PBGC v. Diamond Reo Trucks, Inc., 509 F.Supp. 1191 (W.D.Mich.1981).

*

PART V. PRIVATE ORDERING ASPECTS OF CORPORATE ACQUISITIONS

We began this book in Chapter One A. with the goals of understanding the relationship between what business lawyers do in a transaction and the value of the transaction, of developing analytical techniques that identify what activities have the potential for creating value, and of exploring professional approaches that make business lawyers better at achieving this potential. In Parts III and IV we pursued these goals in connection with the public ordering aspects of business transactions—the influence of various regulatory regimes on the structure of a transaction. Now in Part V we turn to the private ordering aspects of business transactions—matters bearing on transactional structure that would be important even in a world with *no* regulation and that are equally important in a world where regulation imposes liability on one party, but allows the parties to alter the incidence of liability by contract. Passing now the easier task of structuring a transaction to minimize the cost of regulation, how else can a business lawyer help private parties order their relationship in a way that increases the value of the transaction? Chapter Nineteen focuses on this question in the context of a corporate acquisition agreement.

CHAPTER NINETEEN. THE CORPORATE ACQUI-SITION AGREEMENT: THE PRIVATE ORDERING ROLE OF BUSINESS LAWYERS *

[Read the form of corporate acquisition agreement
in Appendix B]

The subject of a business transaction is typically a capital asset. The transaction itself typically consists of the transfer of that asset from one party to another [1] where the critical issue is the value—the price—of the asset to be transferred. The capital asset pricing model, it will be recalled from Chapter Four, specifies that the asset to be transferred will be priced based on the systematic risk associated with it. As long as the capital market is relatively efficient in informational terms, arbitrage activity by traders who identify an asset the market price of which is different than what would be expected based on the asset's systematic risk, keeps asset prices from diverging from their predicted level.

Although there have been important criticisms of this formulation of capital asset pricing theory,[2] they do not blunt its central insight for our purposes: *In a world in which assets are valued according to any version of capital asset pricing theory, there is little role for business lawyers.* Because capital assets will be priced correctly as a result of market forces, business lawyers *cannot* increase the value of a transaction. Absent regulatory-based explanations, the fees charged by business lawyers would *decrease* the net value of the transaction.

The matter, of course, cannot be left there. Simple principles of survivorship strongly suggest a more positive role for business lawyers. Identifying it, or at least establishing its absence, requires another look at capital asset pricing theory.

Like many economic models, capital asset pricing theory can be derived only after a number of important simplifying assumptions are made. The reason for such assumptions in economic models is straight-forward enough: Reality is too complicated and admits of too many interactions to be modeled. The assumptions function to eliminate those complications not critical to understanding the relationship under study. To be sure, when one makes these assumptions, the examined relationship no longer corresponds exactly to the real-world relationship, curiosity about which originally gave rise to the inquiry. The value of the model, however, rests not on how well it describes reality,

---

* Much of this Chapter originally appeared in Gilson, *Value Creation by Business Lawyers: Legal Skills and Asset Pricing*, 94 Yale L.J. 239 (1984).

[1] See Chapter One A., supra.

[2] These criticisms, surveyed in Chapter Four C.2., supra, focus on the capital asset pricing model's claim that systematic risk is the only determinant of asset value. For present purposes, however, disagreement over the number of factors that determine value is less important than the general agreement that in a perfectly functioning market arbitrage will cause all assets to be correctly priced.

but on whether it allows us better to understand it.[3]   And as has been the case with capital asset pricing theory, the effect of relaxing the assumptions can also be modeled once the structure of the simple relationship is understood.

The difference between the simple world of capital asset pricing theory and the complex world in which transactions actually take place provides the focus for developing a hypothesis concerning the potential for a business lawyer to increase a transaction's value.   In the world described by capital asset pricing theory's simplifying assumptions, the lawyer has no function.   What happens, however, when we relax the assumptions on which capital asset pricing theory is based?   Is there a value creating role for the business lawyer in this less orderly world?

At this point we need to look more carefully at the assumptions on which capital asset pricing theory is built.   Of particular importance to our inquiry are four:

1.   All investors have a common time horizon—i.e., they measure the return to be earned from the asset in question over the same period of time.

2.   All investors have the same expectations about the future, in particular, about the future risk and return associated with the asset in question.

3.   There are no transaction costs.

4.   All information is costlessly available to all investors.[4]

These assumptions, of course, do not describe the real world. Investors do not have the same time horizons; indeed, it is often precisely because they do not—for example, an older person may wish to alter the composition of his portfolio in favor of assets whose pattern of returns more closely match his remaining life span—that a transaction occurs in the first place.   Similarly, investors do not have homogeneous expectations; the phenomenon of conflicting forecasts of earnings or value even among reputed experts is too familiar for that assump-

---

[3] This is a rather different statement than the positivist approach typically associated with the views of Milton Friedman—that the measure of a theory is purely its ability to make accurate predictions. See M. Friedman, *The Methodology of Positive Economics*, in Essays in Positive Economics 3 (1953); Gibbard & Barian, *Economic Models*, 75 J. Phil. 664 (1978). In the context of asset pricing theory, substantial questions exist about how, or even whether, the predictions of the two-parameter CAPM or the alternative, the arbitrage pricing theory, can be tested. See, e.g., Dhrymes, Friend & Gultekin, *A Critical Re-Examination of the Empirical Evidence on the Arbitrage Pricing Theory*, 39 J. Fin. 323 (1984); Roll, *A Critique of the Asset Pricing Theory's Tests*, 4 J. Fin. Econ. 129 (1977) (testability of two-parameter CAPM); Shanken, *The Arbitrage Pricing Theory: Is It Testable?*, 37 J. Fin. 1129 (1982). In this setting, empirical testing of predictions necessarily must be supplemented with subjective tests of the fit between theory and reality.

[4] These assumptions are common to both the CAPM and the Arbitrage Pricing Model (APM). See Ross, *The Current Status of the Capital Asset Pricing Model*, 33 J. Fin. 885 (1978). Thus, the distinctions between the two are not critical for purposes of this analysis.

There are additional assumptions not listed in the text which are necessary to derive the two-parameter CAPM, such as the ability to borrow and to lend at the same rate, no differential taxes, risk aversion, normal distribution of returns, and risk measured by standard deviation, not all of which are necessary to derive the APM. These, however, can be relaxed without invalidating the approach. See Chapter Four C.2., supra.

tion to stand. Transaction costs, of course, are pervasive. Finally, information is often one of the most expensive and poorly distributed commodities.[5] In short, the world in which capital assets are priced and transactions actually carried out differs in critical respects from the world of perfect markets in which capital asset pricing theory operates.

For a business lawyer, however, the unreality of these perfect market assumptions is not cause for despair. Rather, it is in the very failure of these assumptions to describe the real world that the potential for value creation by lawyers is to be found. When markets fall short of perfection, incentives exist for private innovations that improve market performance. As long as the costs of innovation are less than the resulting gains, private innovation to reduce the extent of market failure creates value. It is in precisely this fashion that opportunity exists for business lawyers to create value.

A. A Hypothesis Concerning Value Creation: Business Lawyers as Transaction Cost Engineers

The basic assumptions on which capital asset pricing theory is built can be reduced to the simple statement that there are no costs of transacting; there are neither informational disparities between the parties, nor any of the more traditional forms of transaction costs. In such a setting, even one unfamiliar with capital asset pricing theory hardly would be surprised that assets would be correctly priced. In this Coasean world, private outcomes are always optimal,[6] and capital asset pricing theory is no more than the inevitable result of the investor's ability costlessly and thoroughly to diversify his portfolio in a frictionless world. The accuracy of capital asset prices, however, is reduced to the extent there are deviations from capital asset pricing theory's perfect market assumptions. For assets to be correctly priced, the real-world deviations from these assumptions must be constrained. This insight is the first step toward a hypothesis explaining how business lawyers might create value.

The next step, then, is to focus on the mechanisms which reduce real-world deviations from capital asset pricing theory's central assumptions. From this perspective, the variance between assumption and reality is, in effect, a form of market failure. Our concern here is with the character of the market response to that failure. Just as competitive conditions create incentives that encourage reduction of

---

[5] See Chapter Five B., supra.

[6] See, e.g., Calabresi, *Transaction Costs, Resource Allocation and Liability Rules— A Comment*, 11 J.L. & Econ. 67, 68 (1968) ("[A]ll misallocations ＊ ＊ ＊ can be remedied by the market, except to the extent that transactions cost money ＊ ＊ ＊."); Dahlman, *The Problem of Externality*, 22 J.L. & Econ. 141, 142 (1979) ("[I]f there were no costs of transacting, then the potential Pareto improvement could be realized by costless bargaining between self-interested economic agents.") Such a

world, of course, is quite unfamiliar. George Stigler puts the point nicely:

> If this [world] strikes you as incredible on first hearing, join the club. The world of zero transaction costs turns out to be as strange as the physical world would be with zero friction. Monopolies would be compensated to act like competitors, and insurance companies and banks would not exist.

Stigler, *The Law and Economics of Public Policy: A Plea to the Scholars*, 1 J. Legal Stud. 1, 12 (1972).

production costs, the market also encourages private efforts to reduce transaction costs. A service that reduces a good's costs—transaction or other—will earn a positive return. To the extent that private economizing successfully reduces transaction costs, the deviation between the real world in which assets are transferred and the frictionless world of the capital asset pricing theory is minimized. The continued presence of a voluntary social convention—for example, the pervasive use of business lawyers—raises an inference that it is a cost-saving, in our terms value-creating, phenomenon.[7]

Formulating a hypothesis about how business lawyers create value, however, requires more than establishing the importance of private innovation as an important method of reducing transaction costs. Two steps are necessary: The specification of precisely how business lawyers can reduce transaction costs, and the tie between their activities and transaction value.

It is useful at this point to return to the idea that a business transaction is the transfer of a capital asset in which the central aspect of the transaction is the asset's valuation. And the role of the business lawyer is precisely as Vonnegut described it in Chapter One A.: To look "for situations where large amounts of money are about to change hands." The lawyer places himself strategically in the transfer of valuable assets so as to control the process. He will survive economically—be allowed to take a little of the treasure before passing it on—as long as the gains to the parties exceed his fees. Completing the hypothesis of how business lawyers create value now requires only specifying from where these gains come.

This suggests that the tie between legal skills and transaction value is the business lawyer's ability to create a transactional structure that reduces transaction costs and therefore results in more accurate asset pricing. Put in terms of capital asset pricing theory, the business lawyer acts to constrain the extent to which conditions in the real world deviate from the theoretical assumptions of capital asset pricing. The hypothesis about how business lawyers can create value is simply this: Lawyers function as *transaction cost engineers*, devising efficient mechanisms that bridge the gap between capital asset pricing theory's hypothetical world of perfect markets and the less-then-perfect reality of effecting transactions in this world. Value is created when the transactional structure designed by the business lawyer allows the parties to act, *for that transaction*, as if the assumptions on which capital asset pricing theory is based were accurate.

The central role of transaction cost economizing in private ordering is, by now, no longer surprising.[8] What has received less attention is

---

[7] For a discussion of the use of evidence of survival in economic theory, see Jensen, *Organization Theory and Methodology*, 58 Acct.Rev. 319, 331–33 (1983).

[8] Oliver Williamson put the matter aptly: "The overall object of the exercise essentially comes down to this: for each abstract description of a transaction, identify the most economical governance structure—where by governance structure I refer to the institutional framework within which the integrity of a transaction is decided." Williamson, *Transaction-Cost Economics: The Governance of Contractual Relations*, 22 J.L. & Econ. 233, 234–234 (1979).

the link between capital asset pricing theory and transaction cost economics, and the institutional framework in which transaction cost economizing takes place. The hypothesis—the business lawyer as transaction cost engineer—thus asserts the dual claim that skilled structuring of the transaction's form can create transaction value *and* that business lawyers are primary players at the game. In the next section, we evaluate both the positive and normative implications of the hypothesis using a standard corporate acquisition agreement as the text. If the hypothesis is correct, the traditional contractual approaches reflected in the agreement should be explainable by their relation to one or more of the perfect market assumptions on which capital asset pricing theory is based. And if major elements of a corporate acquisition agreement can be understood by reference to their impact on these assumptions, then this discovery would constitute substantial empirical evidence of business lawyers' potential to create value. Moreover, we would not only better understand the function of different portions of the agreement, but also be better able to draft and negotiate them.

B. The Acquisition Agreement

1. An Overview of the Acquisition Agreement

Acquisition agreements have become forms, not in the sense of becoming boilerplate—enormous amounts of time still are spent on their negotiation—but in the sense that the general contents of the agreement have by now become pretty much standardized.[9] This is not to say that the distributive consequences of acquisition agreements are likely to be the same. Rather, it is that the problems confronted and the mechanics of the solutions adopted are similar, even if the impact of the specific application of the solution to the parties will differ from transaction to transaction. The form of agreement set forth in Appendix B, to which reference will be made throughout this discussion, was selected for use not because it is necessarily the best the profession can offer or even a recommended form, but because it is typical and because it illustrates some of the points we will consider.

---

[9] James Freund, a leading practitioner in the mergers and acquisition area, makes this point explicitly: "[M]ost agreements utilized in the mergers and acquisition field do manage to cover pretty much the same ground and contain relatively similar provisions. I'll go further; there are abundant instances of nearly identical words, phrases and clauses, suggesting that respectful plagiarism is indeed the order of the day." J. Freund, *Anatomy of a Merger: Strategies and Techniques for Negotiating Corporate Acquisitions* 140 (1975) (footnote omitted). The similarity can also be seen by comparing a number of agreements contained in form books. See *Business Acquisitions* 55–60, 84–165, 240–343 (P. Gaynor, 2d ed. 1981); *California Continuing Education of the Bar, Drafting Agreements for the Sale of Businesses* (1971) [hereinafter cited as *Drafting Agreements*]; *California Continuing Education of the Bar, Drafting Agreements for the Sale of Business—Supplement* (1983) [hereinafter cited as *Drafting Agreements Supp.*]; *4 West's Legal Forms* (P. Lieberman 2d ed. 1982).

Freund also captures something of the process by which the pattern of practice develops: "I freely confess, in small point, to having lifted from the drafts of my friends and adversaries a number of valuable nuggets for further utilization." J. Freund, supra at 140 n. 2. The existence of commercial form books, as well as the conscious practice of law firms to create and urge the use of in-house form files, id. at 140–141, also reflect the systematization of the process.

A description of the subject necessarily precedes an examination of the functional significance of its parts. A skeletal outline of the form of a typical agreement provides a representative picture.

Description of the Transaction. The initial, and usually most straightforward, portion of the agreement provides an overall description of the transaction. The parties are identified, the structure of the transaction—for example, a purchase of stock or assets, or some triangular variation—is described, and details concerning such matters as the timing and location of the closing of the transaction are set forth.

Price and Terms of Payment. The next portion of the agreement typically focuses on the price to be paid and the medium and timing of payment. The text is most straightforward when the medium of payment is cash and the entire amount is to be paid on closing.[10] But where the transaction contemplates other than immediate payment of the entire purchase price, the document inevitably becomes a great deal more complicated. For example, at the time the agreement is prepared, it may be possible to describe the purchase price only by reference to a formula because its amount depends on the performance of the business over some period following the agreement's execution.[11] As discussed shortly, the need to specify the appropriate performance measure and to protect against manipulation of the indicia of performance makes for a more expansive discussion in the document. Similarly, when the medium of payment is other than cash, the need to address valuation issues—for example, if the consideration will be shares of the acquirer's stock, how the effects of pre-closing changes in the market price of the stock will be shared—also expands the document's text.[12] Of course, if the timing of the payment will be delayed—for example, if the medium of payment will be the acquirer's note—the agreement must cover what is, in effect, an additional transaction: A loan from the target to the acquirer.[13]

[10] There are complications, however, even in an all-cash transaction. For example, if the purchase price is not literally to be paid in cash, but by the transfer of bank funds, then specification of the character of the funds to be provided—e.g., Clearinghouse Funds, same-day funds—can affect the availability of overnight investment, the interest on which can be a substantial amount in a major transaction.

[11] If the period extends beyond the closing of the agreement, as well as beyond its execution, the technique is commonly referred to as a contingent-price formula or simply as an "earnout." This technique is considered in detail in Section B.2. of this Chapter, infra.

[12] Suppose that the acquisition agreement provides that the consideration for the purchase of the target's assets will be one million shares of the acquirer's common stock that, at the time of the agreement's execution, trade for $50 per share— a $50 million transaction. If the price of the acquirer's stock changes during the post-execution/pre-closing period, however, the value of the transaction will change accordingly. Thus, the acquisition agreement typically will allocate the risk of such price fluctuation between the parties. There is typically not a parallel problem with movements in the price of the target's stock because the potential for arbitrage will cause its value to be a function of the value of the acquirer's stock unless there is a possibility either that the transaction will not occur, or that a higher offer for the target will be made. In those cases, the price of the target's stock would likewise reflect these possibilities through the action of risk arbitraguers. See 1 M. Lipton & E. Steinberger, *Takeovers and Freezeouts* 19–20 (1978).

[13] Thus, matters such as the interest rate, security, payment schedule, and acceleration terms all must be negotiated just as in a transaction involving *only* a loan. Where the note is big enough (a rather frequent occurrence in the increasingly common divestiture transaction

Representations and Warranties. The next major portion of the agreement consists of representations and warranties made by the target and, typically to a much lesser extent, by the acquirer.[14] These provisions consist of a series of detailed statements of fact concerning the relevant business. The target commonly will warrant, *inter alia,* the accuracy of its financial statements; the absence of any liabilities for taxes or other matters accruing after the date of its most recent audited financial statements including, most importantly, the absence of contingent liabilities; the ownership and condition of various assets of importance to the operation of the target's business; the existence of litigation against the target, whether actual or threatened; and the extent to which the target's operations are unionized.[15] Thoroughly done, this portion of the acquisition agreement paints a detailed picture of the target—the capital asset that is being acquired.

Covenants and Conditions. The two final steps in the survey of the major portions of a typical acquisition agreement result from the fact that many acquisition transactions contemplate a significant gap between the date on which the acquisition agreement is signed and the date on which the transaction is closed. Whether delay is caused by regulatory necessity, such as the requirement that a proxy statement seeking the approval of the transaction by the target's shareholders be filed and reviewed by the Securities and Exchange Commission, by regulatory convenience, such as the need for an Internal Revenue Service ruling as to the income tax consequences of the transaction, or simply by the acquirer's need for additional time to complete its investigation of the target,[16] the temporal gap between execution and

where the subject of the acquisition is a division of a larger company), the transaction may make the divesting company one of the acquirer's major creditors with the same need for protection as other major lenders. As a result, one would expect the acquisition agreement to contain the same type of detailed operating covenants as a standard institutional loan agreement.

[14] The asymmetry between the extent of the acquirer's and target's representations and warranties results from the different character of their roles in the transaction. At the extreme, in an all-cash transaction that is both executed and closed at the same time, the only fact concerning the acquirer that will be of interest to the target is that the check be good. As the time between execution and closing grows, and as the character of the consideration moves from cash to a form like stock or debt, the value of which depends on the future performance of the acquirer, the target begins to take on some of the attributes of an acquirer and the asymmetry in the extent of representations and warranties is reduced.

[15] See *Drafting Agreements,* supra at 53–182; *Drafting Agreements Supp.,* supra at 45–64; J. Freund, supra at 248–53; J. McGaffey, *Buying, Selling, and Merging Busi-*

nesses, 37–41 (1979); Weinreich, *Contract of Sale,* in 1 *Business Acquisitions* 145, 170–86 (J. Herz & C. Baller 2d ed. 1981).

[16] The critical role of the investigation that occurs in the post-agreement/pre-closing period is illustrated by the course of the transaction in which American Express Co. purchased Investors Diversified Services, Inc. ("IDS"), the principal subsidiary of Alleghany Corp. On July 13, 1983, American Express announced the transaction, at a purchase price of $1.01 billion in American Express common stock. *Alleghany to Sell Most of Its Assets for $1.01 Billion,* Wall St. J., July 13, 1983, at 3, col. 1. By August 12, 1983, the intensive investigation of IDS by American Express had raised doubts about whether American Express would actually proceed with the transaction. *Some Officials at American Express Fear Problems if IDS Purchase Goes Through,* Wall St. J., August 12, 1983, at 3, cols. 2–3. These doubts proved correct when, on August 17, 1983, American Express announced that it would not proceed with the acquisition of IDS "after a review of the company disclosed potential problems in absorbing it." *American Express Abandons Plan to Buy Alleghany Assets After Operations Check,* Wall St. J., Aug. 17, 1983, at 3, cols. 2–3. Abandon-

closing requires contractual bridging. This is accomplished by two complementary techniques: *Covenants* governing the operation of the business during the gap period, and *conditions* which, if not satisfied, relieve a party of its obligation to complete the transaction. Typically these two techniques combine with the representations and warranties to operate as a unit, providing a hierarchy of obligations and the potential for a hierarchy of remedies if one or more of the other party's obligations are not met.[17] Thus a covenant may require that the target maintain working capital above a specified level pending closing. At the same time, the target also may have warranted that working capital was, and at closing will be, above the specified level, and the acquirer's obligation to close the transaction may be conditioned generally on the accuracy of the target's representations and warranties as of the date of closing, on the target's satisfaction of all covenants during the pre-closing period, and, specifically, on the required level of working capital at the closing date. A failure to maintain adequate working capital will then constitute both a breach of warranty and a violation of a covenant, as well as providing the acquirer with a number of justifications for not completing the transaction.[18]

In formal terms, then, the acquisition agreement is simply a more complicated version of what one would expect in any sales agreement: It states the form and terms of the transaction, describes the asset to be transferred, and specifies the manner in which the asset will be preserved pending the completion of the transaction. The possibility that this contractual structure has the potential to create value, however, arises not from a formal overview, but from the manner in which different elements of the agreement respond to the problem of constraining the effect of real world deviations from capital asset pricing theory's perfect market assumptions. For this purpose, it is necessary to focus attention directly on the assumptions themselves, particularly the assumptions that all investors have homogeneous expectations, that

ment proved only temporary as by late September American Express and Alleghany had renegotiated the transaction at a price of $773 million, some $237 million lower than the original price. *Alleghany to Sell IDS to American Express Co.*, Wall St. J., Sept. 27, 1983, at 2, col. 2.

Available data suggest that the cancellation of a friendly acquisition by the acquirer after initial announcement of the transaction is not an isolated phenomenon. According to one study of all announced mergers among New York Stock Exchange listed companies from 1971 through 1977, 36% were cancelled by the acquirer prior to their consumation. Dodd, *Merger Proposals, Management Discretion and Stockholder Wealth*, 8 J. Fin. Econ. 105 (1980). Thus, the acquirer's post-announcement investigation seems to be of major importance.

There also are other non-regulatory reasons for a delay between execution of an agreement and the closing of the transac-

tion. For example, where the seller's lease or contract rights require consent for assignment or assumption, these must be secured during the period.

[17] The importance of the interaction of these elements of the agreement is thoughtfully canvassed in J. Freund, supra, at 153–61.

[18] Having alternative and, indeed, cumulative remedies for a particular event can be of substantial benefit to an acquirer. For example, the failure of a condition would provide only an excuse not to close. A breach of warranty or a violation of a covenant would additionally give rise to a damage action for expenses if the decision were made not to close and, depending on the terms of the agreement, perhaps a damage action for the reduced value of the target even if the acquirer went forward with the acquisition. See J. Freund, supra at 287–89; Dillport, *Breaches and Remedies*, in 2 *Business Acquisitions*, supra at 1249.

they share a common time horizon, that information is costlessly available to all, and that there are no other transaction costs. It is in response to the potential impact of this unholy host that the hypothesis holds out the potential for a value-creating role for business lawyers.

2. The Failure of the Homogeneous-Expectations Assumption: The Earnout Response

a. *Conceptual Analysis*

We can begin with the assumption that can be most clearly examined from this perspective: The assumption that all investors have homogeneous expectations. The critical place in asset pricing theory of the assumption that all investors share the same beliefs about the future risk and return associated with owning the asset in question, in our case a business, is obvious: As long as we all agree about the future income stream associated with owning that business and about the systematic risk associated with that income, there is no reason to expect potential buyers and sellers of the business to disagree about its price. But it is also obvious that buyers and sellers often *do not* share common expectations concerning the business future.

Imagine a negotiation between the presidents of an acquirer and a target concerning the price at which the transaction will take place. Imagine further that the negotiations have progressed to the point where agreement has been reached on an abstract, but nonetheless important, pricing principle, that the appropriate way to value the target's business is $1 in purchase price for each $1 in annual sales.[19] The critical nature of the homogeneous-expectations assumption should be apparent. Even after agreement on a valuation principle, the parties will agree on price *only* if they share the same expectations about the target's future sales. The problem, of course, is that they will not. The negotiating dance that results is familiar to practitioners.

Now suppose that the acquirer's president, having done his homework, believes that there is a 50% chance the target will do $10 million in sales next year and a 50% chance that it will do only $5 million. The expected value of the alternatives is $7.5 million [20] which the acquirer's president offers as the purchase price that the agreed-upon valuation principle dictates. The president of the target, not surprisingly, has different expectations. He is much more optimistic about the probabilities associated with next year's sales. His homework suggests an 85% chance of $10 million in sales and only a 15% chance of sales as low as $5 million. These figures, yield an expected value,

---

[19] The example could be restated directly in the terms of capital asset pricing theory without much difficulty. Suppose that we could establish the systematic risk associated with the target's business. This would allow us to determine the return which the market deems necessary to bear such risk. The purchase price would then represent the capitalized value of that return. The issue in doubt would remain, as in the text, whether the target's future performance would generate the necessary results. The application of capital asset pricing theory to capital budgeting is examined in Chapter Four D., supra.

[20] The calculation is:

$10 million x .50 = $5.0 million
5 million x .50 = 2.5 million
 $7.5 million

and a purchase price under the agreed valuation principle, of $9.25 million.[21] The result is inaccurate pricing at best and, because of the resulting conflict over the purchase price, at worst no transaction at all if the parties are unable to resolve their differences.

It is important to emphasize at this point that the problem that "kills" our hypothetical deal is not distributional conflict—disagreement over sharing the gains from the transaction. The distributional principle in the form of a valuation formula has already been approved. Rather, the problem is an example of the failure of the homogeneous-expectations assumption: The parties simply have different expectations concerning the future performance of the business. If this problem could be solved, a deal could be made. Tautologically, the value of the transaction would be increased. And if the hypothesis about what business lawyers do is correct, a particularly inviting opportunity then exists for value creation by a business lawyer. The lawyer can increase the value of the transaction if he can devise a transactional structure that creates homogeneous expectations.

As the hypothesis predicts, there is a familiar remedy, commonly called an "earnout" or "contingent price" deal, for this failure of the homogeneous-expectations assumption. It is intended, as a prominent practitioner has put it, to "bridge the negotiating gap between a seller who thinks his business is worth more than its historical earnings justify and a purchaser who hails from Missouri."[22] The solution that business lawyers resort to for this problem is one that economists refer to as state-contingent contracting.[23] Its central insight is that the difference in expectations between the parties as to the probabilities assigned to the occurrence of future events will ultimately disappear as time transforms a prediction of next year's sales into historical fact. If determination of the purchase price can be delayed until next year's sales are known with certainty, the deal can be made. The solution, therefore, is to formulate the purchase price as an initial payment, here $7.5 million, to be followed by an additional payment at the close of the next fiscal year equal, in this case, to $1 for each $1 of sales in excess of $7.5 million. The problem of non-homogeneous expectations is avoided by making the failure irrelevant. Only uncertainty concerning the future forced the parties to rely on expectations about the future; the earnout solution allows the purchase price to be set after that uncertainty has been resolved. That is, each party is allowed to act *as if* his expectation was shared by the other. In effect he bets on the accuracy of his expectation, with a settling up only after the uncertainty has been eliminated and the parties really do have homogeneous beliefs concerning the matter.

[21] The calculation is:

$10 million x .85 = $8.50 million
5 million x .15 = $0.75 million
                   $9.25 million

[22] J. Freund, supra at 205.

[23] See K. Arrow, *Essays in the Theory of Risk-Bearing* 121–43 (1971); O. Williamson, *Markets and Hierarchies: Analysis and Antitrust Implications* 21–23 (1975). The idea is that a contract will specify a different result for each possible outcome of an uncertain future event. The result called for by the contract is thus contingent on the actual outcome of the uncertain event—i.e., which "state" of the world actually occurs.

The business lawyer's traditional response to failure of the homogeneous-expectations assumption can thus create value by allowing a transaction to go forward that might otherwise not have occurred. But the technique's potential for value creation is greater than just allowing the deal to be made; it also may increase the total value of the deal beyond that which would have resulted even if the parties were capable of compromising their differences. Recall that under capital asset pricing theory the value of the business turns on both the expected return—the weighted average of the possible sales for the next year in our hypothetical—and the systematic risk associated with that return. The effect of the contingent price arrangement is to reduce the acquirer's risk by transforming the price from a function of expected—risky—returns to one of certain returns. Thus, the acquirer should be willing to pay a higher price per unit of sales because there is no risk associated with that return.[24]

Thus far, the hypothesis about what business lawyers do and how they create value seems confirmed. At least with respect to the failure of the homogeneous-expectations assumption, business lawyers create a transactional structure which bridges the gap between the perfect market assumptions of capital asset pricing theory and the imperfect reality of transacting.

b. *Regulatory Constraints*

Despite the potential value of an earnout in mitigating the parties' differing expectations, regulatory constraints significantly limit the manner in which the technique can be implemented and, in some cases, make its use undesirable. These limitations result from the impact of an earnout on the tax and accounting treatment of the transaction.

The critical tax constraints apply to transactions that are intended to qualify as reorganizations.[25] For an acquisition to qualify as any of the forms of reorganization, the selling shareholders must receive all or a significant portion of their consideration in the form of the acquiring company's voting stock. The issue posed by an earnout arrangement is whether the contingent right to receive voting stock if the conditions of the earnout are met counts as voting stock.[26] The Internal Revenue Service has established guidelines specifying the circumstances under which it will issue a ruling that an earnout will be treated as voting

---

[24] The target also benefits because the target is inevitably better informed than the acquirer about its prospects and, as a result, is better able to "price" the risk associated with its future sales. Thus, the target is likely to be the best risk bearer. This need not, however, always be the case. Where the target is more risk averse than the acquirer, as frequently may be the case in the acquisition of a privately held company by a publicly held company, and where the target's future depends on information to which the acquirer has better access—the potential for synergy comes to mind as an example—it becomes more difficult to determine the party best able to price and bear the risk.

[25] The general requirements for qualification as a reorganization are reviewed in Chapter Twelve A.1., supra.

[26] For example, in a B reorganization the consideration must be solely voting stock. If the shareholders' rights under the earnout are not treated as voting stock, the entire transaction will not qualify as a reorganization.

stock.[27] For planning purposes, the most important of the ruling requirements are:

(1) At least 50 percent of the maximum number of shares issuable in the transaction must be issued at the outset.

(2) The earnout must terminate and all stock earned must be issued within five years after the closing of the transaction.

(3) The right to receive earnout stock cannot be assignable.

The prohibition of assignable interests in earnout shares has a critical impact on the use of the earnout technique in the acquisition of public companies. Despite the attraction of the technique as a response to divergent beliefs about the future of the target company's business, it may well be difficult to persuade public shareholders to accept an entirely illiquid investment. In response to a different problem, T. Ness & W. Indoe, *Tax Planning for Dispositions of Business Interests* 6–30 (1985), suggest as an alternative to an earnout the issuance of a voting convertible preferred stock whose conversion ratio is adjusted to increase the number of shares into which the preferred may be converted based on the same formula as a traditional earnout would have specified.[28] Ness and Indoe report that the Internal Revenue Service has ruled that adjustment of the conversion rate to implement an earnout will not result in the shareholders being treated as having received a taxable stock dividend under IRC § 305(c). Would this approach also serve to avoid the restriction on making rights under an earnout nontransferable?

Where the earnout is created in connection with a taxable transaction, the critical issue is whether a cash basis shareholder must report the value of the earnout right as income in the year the transaction closes despite the fact that actual payment pursuant to the earnout is both deferred and contingent. Prior to the amendments to IRC § 453 by the Installment Sales Revision Act of 1980,[29] installment sales treatment was not available for contingent payments; the Internal Revenue Service required immediate valuation and recognition. Under the regulations adopted under Section 453 following amendment, earnout payments can be reported on the installment basis.

The constraint imposed on the use of an earnout by accounting rules results from the earnout's impact on the availability of the pooling of interests method of accounting for the acquisition. Under Paragraph 47–g of Accounting Principles Board Opinion No. 16, the pooling of interests method cannot be used if the transaction contem-

---

[27] Rev.Proc. 77–37, Section 3.03, 1977–2 CB 568, as amplified by Rev.Proc. 84–42, 1984–20 IRB 12.

[28] The solution was directed at the problem of how to avoid original issue discount under IRC § 1274, or imputed interest under IRC § 483, caused by an earnout's deferral of the receipt of consideration. An alternative approach to this problem is to issue the stock at the outset, but place it in escrow subject to forfeiture if the earnout conditions are not met. T. Ness &

W. Indoe, supra at 6–29. The Internal Revenue Service has ruled that, so long as shareholders are allowed to vote and receive dividends on the escrowed stock, no stock released from escrow will be treated as imputed interest or original issue discount. Rev.Rul. 70–120, 1970–1 CB 124. For an example of such an approach see Section II.B of the form of acquisition agreement in Appendix B.

[29] Pub.L. No. 96–471, 94 Stat. 2247 (1980).

plates the issuance of contingent stock in an earnout.[30] Despite the evidence that the manner of accounting for an acquisition does not effect the post-acquisition price of the acquiring company's stock,[31] experienced practitioners report that the adoption of Accounting Principles Board Opinion No. 16 in 1970 resulted in a sharp reduction in the use of earnouts.[32]

3. The Failure of the Common-Time-Horizon Assumption: Conduct of the Business During the Earnout Period

The failure of a second assumption—this time that investors measure risk and return over the same period—provides an additional opportunity for business lawyers to create value. This can be seen most easily by pursuing discussion of the earnout solution just considered. The earnout concept responds to the failure of the homogeneous-expectations assumption. Efforts to make the concept operational, however, highlight the absence of a common time horizon and the resulting potential for strategic, opportunistic behavior. Where the parties do have different time horizons, each has an incentive to maximize value in the period relevant to the other party. This conflict reduces the value of the transaction.[33]

Consider first what behavior we would expect during the earnout's one-year measuring period if the target's original management were allowed to run the company for that time. From the target's perspective, the earnout formula reduces to one year the relevant period over which asset value is to be determined; at the end of that year the target's shareholders will receive whatever payment is due under the earnout formula. At least for them, the asset will cease to exist. To the target's shareholders, therefore, the asset is worth only what it can earn for them in a year's time. Their goal is to maximize value over that short period. The acquirer, in contrast, is concerned with the value of the business over a much longer period: The entire time it expects to operate the target's business. Accordingly, the acquirer's behavior will differ substantially from that which would be dictated by the target's short-term orientation.

Returning to the terms of the hypothetical earnout formula—an additional $1 in purchase price for each $1 in sales over $7.5 million— the target would maximize sales during the one-year measuring period. For example, prices might be cut and advertising expenditures substan-

---

[30] Accounting Principles Board Opinion No. 16 appears in Chapter Eight A.1., supra.

[31] See Chapter Eight C., supra.

[32] J. Freund, supra at 205; see Chapter Eight D., supra.

[33] We are taking some liberties in our treatment of this assumption. The requirement that investors maximize end-of-period wealth results in a one-period model that avoids difficult statistical problems associated with compounding returns over multiple periods. See Merton, *An Intertemporal Capital Asset Pricing Model,* 41 Econometrica 867 (1973). In the absence of an impersonal market, as in a corporate acquisition, a shift to a multi-period setting, where buyers and sellers may maximize over different periods, also causes serious strategic problems. These, rather than the statistical problems, are the object of concern here.

tially increased, even if these actions meant that the company actually suffered a loss. In contrast, the acquirer, which would ultimately bear the loss because it continues to own the company after the one year period, has a very different interest. And the conflict is not merely the result of a poorly specified earnout formula. Stating the formula in terms of profits rather than sales, thus eliminating the target's incentive to maximize sales at the expense of the acquirer's long term interest in earnings, would be a possible improvement. But even then the different time horizons would create an incentive for the target's management to behave opportunistically. Short-term profits could be maximized by eliminating research and development expenditures, cutting maintenance, and, in general, deferring expenses to later periods.

This failure of the common-time-horizon assumption reduces the value of the transaction. So long as the acquirer anticipates that the target's management will behave opportunistically—which hardly requires a crystal ball—it will reduce its offer accordingly. The business lawyer then has the opportunity to create value by devising a transaction structure that constrains the target's ability to maximize the value of the business over a period different from that relevant to the acquirer.[34] The typical earnout agreement responds to precisely this challenge.

Stated most generally, a complete earnout formula is a complicated state-contingent contract, that, by carefully specifying in advance the impact on the purchase price of all events that might occur during the earnout period, substantially reduces the incentives and opportunity for the parties to behave strategically. Actually creating such a formula, however, poses difficult problems of design and drafting. Consider, for example, the following issues.

How do you eliminate the perverse incentives caused by an earnout formula that specifies either sales or earnings as the sole measure of success? Put differently, how do you prevent the existence of the earnout from influencing the outcome of a business decision that poses

---

[34] The problem is not avoided if the acquirer undertakes to operate the business. Rather, the opportunity to behave strategically merely shifts to the acquirer. From its perspective, value is maximized by deferring sales or earnings to the following year, thereby reducing the purchase price of the business. This behavior, of course, would be anticipated by the target and, unless the behavior were prohibited by contract, would alter the terms on which it would be willing to sell the business.

One might argue that if the acquirer could fully anticipate the target's opportunistic behavior in setting the purchase price, no potential for value creation would exist because the net purchase price to the acquirer—the reduced purchase price plus the cost of the target's opportunistic behavior—would remain the same, i.e., it would be a zero-sum game. In fact, the game is negative-sum in the absence of a transactional structure that responds to the failure of the common-time-horizon assumption. First, it is likely to be quite difficult to estimate the cost of allowing the target to behave opportunistically: The lack of precision results in greater risk for the acquirer and a lower value for the transaction. Second, the target's or acquirer's short-run behavior may result in a *decrease* in the value of the business. For example, if research and development is deferred, opportunities may be lost that cannot be recovered. Although the acquirer may not be cheated—the price of the business would be reduced to reflect the reduction in value—the business would be worth more to both parties if a transactional structure could be designed that prevents value-reducing behavior.

a short run tradeoff between sales and earnings? The acquisition agreement in Appendix B confronts this problem in Section II.B. by requiring both sales growth *and* an increase in profits as a percentage of sales. How effectively does that combination constrain strategic behavior? Could a cut in the research and development budget of a research oriented company serve to increase profits as a percentage of sales without, at least in the short run, adversely affecting sales growth? How do you determine which variables bearing on the target company's operation must be specified in the formula to prevent their manipulation? Could sensitivity analysis [35] (together with a good spread sheet program) help answer this question?

How long should be the earnout period? From the target's perspective, a multi-year period may be preferable to avoid the impact of a single unpredictable event adversely affecting the target company's chances under a one year earnout. Additionally, a multi-year period reduces the influence of the existence of the earnout on operating decisions. If the target will get a number of bites at the apple, the acquirer has less incentive to influence the target's operations so as to reduce the target's chance of success in any one year; an effort to reduce the target's chance of success over a number of years likely poses too great a risk of damaging the target in a way that will not disappear after the earnout is over.

The choice of a multi-year period, however, raises other issues. For example, are the years independent or cumulative? If the earnout is not met in one year, must the deficit be made up before the earnout can be met in a subsequent year? Is the portion of the earnout not made in one year lost forever, or may it be made up in subsequent years? If the earnout formula is exceeded in one year, does the excess carry over to give the target a head start in the next period?

How does the acquisition agreement in Appendix B handle these problems? Note that under Section II.B. nothing cumulates until the end of the third year at which point the trigger for release of the remainder of the earnout is meeting the sales and earnings requirements for the third year *plus* the appropriate earnings percentage of whatever sales were in the first two years. What kind of a compromise between the acquirer and the target does this resolution suggest?

How are earnings defined for purposes of the formula? Most importantly, is there a way to segregate the earnings of what constituted the pre-acquisition target company? Even though the acquisition agreement in Appendix B contemplates that the target will remain a separate subsidiary, the agreement anticipates the possibility that additional operations may be added or some removed; Section II.B.2.e. defines the relevant earnings as those of the "business operations which constituted the Target on the date of closing."

Assuming that the business of the target can be segregated, how will earnings be computed? Is it sufficient simply to refer to earnings "computed in accordance with generally accepted accounting principles consistently applied"? Would this definintion include non-operating

---

[35] See Chapter Six A., supra.

gains? If there are assets that the target does not need to conduct its business, should gain on their sale count toward the earnout? Suppose that the consideration paid is greater than the book value of the target's assets, and that Accounting Principles Board Opinion No. 16 requires that the acquisition be accounted for as a purchase. Will earnings be reduced by the higher depreciation associated with the increase in asset value resulting from purchase accounting? Does GAPP resolve how large an overhead or central office allocation can be charged against the target's earnings?

Finally, who gets to run the business during the earnout period? If it is target management, under what circumstances can the acquirer intervene? After all, the purpose of making the acquisition was not just to facilitate the earnout; one can easily imagine that competitive conditions could put the acquirer in a position where it had to take action even though it would interfere with the operation of the earnout.

A thoroughly specified earnout formula is thus extraordinarily complex and, in any event, cannot entirely eliminate the potential for strategic behavior. To be fully effective, a formula would have to specify not only the complete production function for the business, but all possible exogenous events that might occur during the earnout period and the impact of such events on the formula. Neither, of course, is possible. Moreover, the cost of detailed contracting—not just in lawyers' fees, but in the time and goodwill of the parties—will be substantial and in many cases prohibitive. There will be times, then, where the gain in transaction value resulting from ameliorating the failure of the homogeneous-expectations or common-time-horizons assumptions will be outweighed by the cost of the cure. But this possibility merely constrains, rather than eliminates, the potential for value creation by business lawyers. That transaction costs are, at some level, irreducible hardly diminishes the value of efforts to keep costs at that level. It is value creation of the sort that reflects what clients may mean by the comment that a particular lawyer has good "judgment," to know when the game is not worth the candle.[36]

4. The Failure of the Costless-Information Assumption: Representations, Warranties, Indemnification, and Opinions

Perhaps the most important assumption of all is that information is costlessly available to all parties. Its central importance derives in

[36] There has been a spate of continuing education programs emphasizing the cost-effective use of lawyers. See, e.g., R. Gilson & R. Mnookin, *The Cost Effective Use of Counsel: Strategies for Controlling Your Company's Legal Costs* (June 24, 1982); R. Gilson & R. Mnookin, *Reducing the Cost of Outside Counsel: Strategies for Controlling Your Company's Legal Costs* (June 5, 1981). A central theme in this movement is that the quality of legal services cannot be evaluated in the abstract, but only in a particu- lar context. Thus, careful and detailed contract drafting or litigation discovery is "good" work *only* if the matter warrants the expense. In this sense, clients increasingly seem to be equating a lawyer's judgment with the wisdom of knowing when not to "over-lawyer" a transaction or lawsuit. Cf. Shavell, *The Design of Contracts and Remedies for Breach*, 99 Q.J.Econ. 121 (1984) (costs of contracting must be incorporated into a model for determining optimal contractual provisions).

part because it is, in a sense considered shortly, a *master* assumption that controls the other assumptions we have considered, and in part because it is in response to its failure that business lawyers have been most creative.

The relation between the costless-information assumption and the homogeneous-expectations assumption illustrates the central role for information problems in our analysis. For our purposes, information is data that can alter the parties' beliefs about the price of an asset. But it is also useful to characterize information in terms of a second attribute: To distinguish between the "hard" information of known "facts" and the "soft" information of forecasts and predictions.

This fact/forecast dichotomy rests on the simple difference between the fixed past and the uncertain future, a distinction that can be illustrated by reference to a hypothetical fully informed trader.[37] Imagine a trader who has knowledge of all past events—"hard" information because it concerns events that have already occurred—relevant to pricing an asset. Even so thoroughly endowed a trader would still lack a type of information critical to asset pricing. Because asset value ultimately depends on predictions of *future* earnings, hard information about *past* events alone is insufficient for accurate pricing. Soft information—forecasts of future events—is also necessary.

The homogeneous-expectations assumption considered earlier is thus really an assumption that all parties have the same soft information. Understanding the relation between soft and hard information then should also disclose the relation between the homogeneous-expectations assumption and the costless-information assumption. The critical point is that our forecasts of the future are based, in significant part, on our knowledge of the past; if we know, for example, that high interest rates adversely affected performance of a company in the past, our prediction of future performance will be substantially influenced by that fact. Changes in hard facts will change soft projections.

So understood, a major part of the reason for the failure of the homogeneous-expectations assumption—potential acquirers and targets have different soft facts—is that they base their expectations on different hard facts.[38] In this sense, the costless-information assumption might be rephrased as the assumption of *homogeneous retrospection*. The assumption of homogeneous *expectations* would require that the parties share common soft facts; that of homogeneous *retrospection* would require common hard facts. And if acquisition of hard facts is not only costly, but differentially so, the impact on asset pricing is clear: There will be greater disagreement about the price of an asset, and the resulting pattern of prices will be suboptimal.

The business lawyer's response to the failure of the homogeneous-expectations assumption has been to devise a structure—state-contin-

---

[37] The discussion of the character of information that follows in the text is based on Gilson & Kraakman, *The Mechanisms of Market Efficiency,* 70 Va.L.Rev. 549, 560–64 (1984), reprinted in Chapter Five, supra.

[38] There also may be differences in forecasting ability, because of differences in training or in inherent ability of the forecasters, even given identical hard facts.

gent pricing—which does not *eliminate* the parties' differences in expectations, but merely reduces the *impact* of the disagreement. Because the disagreement in significant measure results from differences in hard information held by the parties, efforts to constrain the extent of the conflict in expectations (in contrast to efforts to minimize the impact of the conflict) respond to the failure of the costless-information assumption. And because these differences result from differential information costs for the acquirer and target, if business lawyers do function to alleviate failures of the perfect market assumptions underlying capital asset pricing theory, we would then expect the typical corporate acquisition agreement to contain provisions designed to reduce the extent of information asymmetry—information differences between the acquirer and target.[39]

The portion of the acquisition agreement dealing with representations and warranties—commonly the longest part of a typical acquisition agreement and the portion that usually requires the most time for a lawyer to negotiate [40]—has as its primary purpose to remedy conditions of asymmetrical information in the least-cost manner. To understand the way in which the device of representations and warranties operates to reduce information asymmetry between the acquirer and the target, it is helpful to distinguish between the costs of acquiring new information and the costs of verifying previously acquired information.

a. Costs of Acquiring Information

During the negotiation, the acquirer and target will face different costs of information acquisition for two important reasons. First, as a simple result of its prior operation of the business, the target will already have large amounts of information concerning the business that the acquirer does not have, but would like to acquire. Second, there usually will be information that neither party has, but that one or both would like and which one or the other can acquire more cheaply. The question is then how both of these situations are dealt with in the acquisition agreement so as to reduce the informational differences between the parties at the lowest possible cost.

At first, one might wonder why any cooperative effort is necessary. Assuming that the target did not affirmatively block the acquirer's efforts to acquire the information the acquirer wanted (and the target already had), nothing would prevent the acquirer from independently acquiring the desired information. Similarly, assuming both parties

---

[39] If information costs were not different, then the parties would hold the same facts and, subject to the conditions of the previous note, reach the same predictions. To be sure, they would still be less accurate than if information were costless, but then the role of the business lawyer would be to lower the cost of information generally, rather than, as the discussion will emphasize, to reduce the cost differential between the parties. While the lawyer can accomplish this with respect to particular types of information, this function is likely to be best performed by a different professional—the accountant.

[40] James Freund observes: "There are no known statistics on the subject, but I'm willing to bet my briefcase that lawyers spend more time negotiating 'Representations and Warranties of the Seller' than any other single article in the typical acquisition agreement." J. Freund, supra at 229.

had the opportunity to acquire the desired new information, nothing would prevent both parties from independently acquiring it.

Actually, however, it is in the target's best interest to make the information that the target already has available to the acquirer as cheaply as possible. Suppose the target refused to assist the acquirer in securing a particular piece of information that the target already had. If the information could have either a positive or negative value on the acquirer's evaluation of the worth of the business, a rational acquirer would infer from the target's refusal to cooperate that the information must be unfavorable. Thus, the target has little incentive to withhold the information.[41] Indeed, the same result would follow even if the information in question would not alter the acquirer's estimate of the value of the business, but only increase the certainty with which that estimate was held.[42] Once we have established that the target wants the acquirer to have the information, the only issue that remains is which party can produce it most cheaply. The total price the acquirer will pay for the business is the sum of the amount to be paid to the target and the transaction costs incurred by the acquirer in effecting the transaction. To the extent that the acquirer's information costs are reduced, there simply is more left over for division between the acquirer and the target.

Precisely the same analysis holds for information that neither party has yet acquired. The target could refuse to cooperate with the acquirer in its acquisition. To do so, however, would merely increase the information costs associated with the transaction to the detriment of both parties.

There is thus an incentive for the parties to cooperate both to reduce informational asymmetries between them and to reduce the costs of acquiring information either believes necessary for the transaction. As a result, we would expect an acquisition agreement to contain provisions for three kinds of cooperative behavior concerning information acquisition costs. First, the agreement would facilitate the transfer of information the target already has to the acquirer. Second, the

---

[41] See Grossman, *The Informational Role of Warranties and Private Disclosure About Product Quality*, 24 J.L. & Econ. 461, 479 (1981); Grossman & Hart, *Disclosure Laws and Takeover Bids*, 35 J.Fin. 323 (1980). The analysis becomes more complicated, however, if disclosure imposes other kinds of costs on the target—for example, disclosure of some accounting data might provide to competitors insights into the target's future strategy, and disclosure of product information might allow competitors more easily to duplicate the target's product. Where there are such proprietary costs to disclosure, the signal conveyed by nondisclosure becomes "noisy": Nondisclosure may mean that the information kept private is negative; less ominously, it may mean that disclosure of the information would be costly. The result would be an equilibrium amount of nondisclosure.

R. Verrecchia, *Discretionary Disclosure*, Working Paper No. 101, Center for Research in Security Prices (August, 1983). While Verrecchia's argument has important insights for the issue of voluntary disclosure in the setting of organized securities markets, it is much less relevant in the acquisition setting. There the opportunity for face-to-face bargaining allows the use of techniques such as confidentiality agreements, see 3 Business Acquisitions, *supra* at 399–401 (form of confidentiality agreement), that can substantially reduce such proprietary disclosure costs and, as a result, reduce the noise associated with failure to disclose.

[42] In other words, the new information would not alter the mean estimate of value but would reduce the variance associated with the distribution of possible values.

agreement would allocate the responsibility of producing information that neither the target nor the acquirer already has to the party who can acquire it most cheaply, thereby both avoiding duplication of costs and minimizing those that must be incurred. Finally, the agreement would try to control overspending on information acquisition by identifying not only the type of information that should be acquired, but also how much should be spent on its acquisition.

(1) Facilitating the Transfer of Information to the Acquirer

In the course of negotiating an acquisition, there is an obvious and important information asymmetry between the acquirer and the target. The acquirer will have expended substantial effort in selecting the target from among the number of potential acquisitions considered at a preliminary stage and, in doing so, may well have gathered all the available public information concerning the target. Nonetheless, the target will continue to know substantially more than the acquirer about the business. Much detailed information about the business, of interest to an acquirer but not, perhaps, to the securities market generally, will not have been previously disclosed by the target.[43]

It is in the target's interest, not just in the acquirer's, to reduce this asymmetry. If the target's private information is not otherwise available to the acquirer at all, the acquirer must assume that the undisclosed information reflects unfavorably on the value of the acquirer's business, an assumption that will be reflected to the target's disadvantage in the price the acquirer offers. Alternatively, even if the information could be gathered by the acquirer (a gambit familiar to business lawyers is the target's statement that it will open all its facilities to the acquirer, that the acquirer is welcome to come out and "kick the tires," but that there will be no representations and warranties), it will be considerably cheaper for the target, whose marginal costs of production are very low,[44] to provide the information than for the acquirer to produce it alone. From the acquirer's perspective, the cost of acquiring information is part of its overall acquisition cost; amounts spent on information reduce the amount left over for the target.

This analysis seems to account for the quite detailed picture of the target's business that the standard set of representations and warranties presents. Among other facts covered by Section III of the acquisition agreement in Appendix B., the identity, location and condition of

[43] For example, the potential for synergy between the target's business and that of a particular potential acquirer will become of interest to the market only at the point where the possibility of the acquisition comes to the market's attention.

[44] The costs are still *not* zero. While the information exists, there are still costs associated with finding out where within the target's organization the information is located, putting it in a form that is useful to the acquirer, and verifying it. As a result, even some information that already exists may not be worthwhile to locate and transmit. See Section B.4.a.(3). of this Chapter, infra (limitations on for what, and how hard, to look). Additionally, there will be situations where a third party will be able to produce the information even more cheaply than the target. See Section B. 4.a.(2). of this Chapter, infra (lawyers' opinions).

the assets of the business are described; [45] the nature and extent of liabilities are specified; [46] and the character of employee relationships—from senior management to production employees—is described.[47] This is information that the acquirer wants and the target already has; provision by the target minimizes its acquisition costs to the benefit of both parties.

What remains puzzling, however, is the apparent failure by both business lawyers and clients to recognize that the negotiation of representations and warranties, at least from the perspective of information acquisition costs, presents the occasion for cooperative rather than distributive bargaining.[48] Reducing the cost of acquiring information needed by either party makes both better off. Yet practitioners report that the negotiation of representations and warranties is the most time-consuming aspect of the transaction; it is termed "a nit-picker's delight, a forum for expending prodigious amounts of energy in debating the merits of what sometimes seem to be relatively insignificant items." [49] And it is not merely lawyers who are seduced by the prospect of combat; acquirers also express repugnance for a "three pound acquisition agreement" [50] whose weight and density owe much to the detail of the article titled "Representations and Warranties of the Target." As a result, targets' lawyers are instructed to negotiate ferociously to keep the document—especially the representations and warranties—short. Increased information costs needlessly result. Indeed, a business lawyer's inability to explain the actual function of these provisions can often cause the acquirer incorrectly to attribute the document's length to its own lawyer's preference for verbosity and unnecessary complexity. This failure to explain can prevent recognition of value-creating activity even when it occurs.

(2) Facilitating the Production of Previously Nonexistent Information

A similar analysis applies when the acquirer needs information that the target has not already produced. For example, the acquirer may desire information about aspects of the target's operation that bear on the opportunity for synergy between its own business and that of the target and that, prior to the negotiation, the target had no reason to create. Alternatively, the acquirer may be interested in the impact of

[45] See *Drafting Agreements,* supra at 81–94 (warranties disclosing identity and condition of real property and leases; compliance with zoning; composition, condition, and marketability of inventory; personal property and condition; accounts receivable and collectability; trade names, trademarks, and copyrights; patent and patent rights; trade secrets; insurance policies; and employment contracts).

[46] See id. at 76–81, 94–96, 118 (warranties concerning undisclosed liabilities, tax liabilities, compliance with laws, accuracy of financial statements, and pending or threatened litigation).

[47] See id. at 93 (disclosure of all employment, collective bargaining, bonus, profit-sharing, or fringe benefit agreements).

[48] We will put off for the moment the question of what happens when one of the target's representations and warranties turns out to be incorrect. The issue of indemnification for breach of warranty will be taken up in connection with the verification function. See Section B.4. of this Chapter, infra.

[49] J. Freund, supra at 229.

[50] Id. at 233.

the transaction itself on the target's business; whether the target contracts can be assigned or assumed; whether, for example, the transaction would accelerate the target's obligations. Like the situation in which the acquirer has already produced the information desired by the target, the only issue here should be to minimize the acquisition cost of the information in question.

While the analysis is similar to the situation in which the target had previously produced the information, the result of the analysis is somewhat different. Not only will the target not always be the least-cost information producer, but there will also be a substantial role for third-party information producers. Returning to the synergy example, a determination of the potential for gain from the combination of the two businesses requires information about both. The particular character of the businesses, as well as the skills of their managers, will determine whether such a study is better undertaken by the target, which knows its own business but will be required to learn about the acquirer's business or by the acquirer, which knows about its own business and is in the process of learning about the target's.[51]

The more interesting analysis concerns the potential role for third-party information producers. This can be seen most clearly with respect to information concerning the impact of the transaction itself on the target's business. As between the acquirer and the target, the target will usually be the least-cost producer of information concerning the impact of the transaction on, for example, the target's existing contracts. Although there is no reason to expect that either party routinely will have an advantage in interpreting the contracts, it is predictable that the target can more cheaply assemble the facts on which the interpretation will be based. The real issue, however, is not whether the target is the lower-cost producer out of a group of candidates artificially limited to the target and acquirer. Rather, the group of candidates must be expanded to include third parties.

The impact of including third-party information production in the analysis can be seen by examining the specialized information production role for lawyers in acquisition transactions. Even with respect to the production of information concerning the target's assets and liabilities, the area where our prior analysis demonstrated the target's prominence as an information producer, there remains a clear need for a specialized third party. Production of certain information concerning the character of the target's assets and liabilities simply requires legal analysis. For example, the target will know whether it has been cited for violation of environmental or health and safety legislation in the

---

[51] The least-cost producer typically will be the acquirer. Although the acquirer will already know something about the target, the target will have had little reason to learn about the acquirer's business prior to initiation of negotiations. As a result, the amount that still must be learned about the other party's business in order to evaluate the potential for synergy is likely to be smaller for the acquirer than for the target. This yields a prediction that should be subject to empirical testing. If this hypothesis is correct, we would expect to find few representations and warranties by the target that could be understood to speak to conditions directly related to the manner in which the two entities could be combined. The *absence* of a representation by the target, of course, leaves the information-production function with the acquirer.

past, but it may require legal analysis to determine whether continued operation of the target's business likely will result in future prosecution.

The need for third-party assistance is even more apparent with respect to information about the impact of the transaction itself on the target's business. Again, however, much of the information requires legal analysis; there exists a specialized information-production role for third parties. For example, it will be important to know whether existing contracts are assignable or assumable: The continued validity of the target's leasehold interests will depend on whether a change in the control of the target operates—as a matter of law or because of the specific terms of the lease—as an assignment of the leasehold,[52] and the status of the target's existing liabilities, such as its outstanding debt, will depend on whether the transaction can be undertaken without the creditor's consent.

In both cases, the target's lawyer appears to be the lowest-cost producer of such information.[53] As a result, we would expect the typical acquisition agreement to assign lawyers this information-production role. And it is from this perspective that important elements of the common requirement of an "Opinion of Counsel for the Target" are best understood.

Any significant acquisition agreement requires, as a condition to the buyer's obligation to complete the transaction, that the acquirer receive an opinion of target's counsel with respect to a substantial number of items.[54] Consistent with our analysis, most of the matters on which legal opinions are required reflect the superiority of the target's lawyer as an information producer. For example, determination of the target's proper organization and continued good standing under state law, the appropriate authorization of the transaction by target, the existence of litigation against the target, the impact of the transaction on the target's contracts and commitments, and the extent to which the current operation of the target's business violates any law or regulation, represent the production of information which neither

[52] For example, would a general clause prohibiting assignment of a lease by a corporate tenant prohibit the sale of all the tenant's stock, or a merger of the tenant, or even the dissolution of the tenant and the succession to the tenancy by the tenant's shareholders? See 1 M. Friedman, *Friedman on Leases* 244–52 (2d ed. 1983).

[53] The target's lawyer will likely have been involved in the original preparation of the documents and, as a result, will have much better information concerning their contents and the context in which they were negotiated.

[54] See Section VI.C. of the acquisition agreement in Appendix B. There is a substantial practical literature concerning opinions of counsel. See A. Jacobs, *Opinion Letters in Securities Matters: Text—Clauses—Law* (1983); Babb, Barnes Gordon & Kjellenberg, *Legal Opinions to*

Third Parties in Corporate Transactions, 32 Bus.Law. 553 (1977); Bermant, *The Role of the Opinion of Counsel—A Tentative Reevaluation*, 49 Cal.St.B.J. 132 (1974); Committee on Corporations of the Business Law Section of the State Bar of California, *Report of the Committee on Corporations Regarding Legal Opinions in Business Transactions*, 14 Pac.L.J. 1001 (1983) [hereinafter cited as *California State Bar Report*]; Committee on Developments in Business Financing, *Legal Opinions Given in Corporate Transactions*, 33 Bus.Law. 2389 (1978); Fuld, *Legal Opinions in Business Transactions—An Attempt to Bring Some Order Out of Some Chaos*, 28 Bus.Law. 915 (1973); Special Comm. on Legal Opinions on Commercial Transactions, N.Y. County Lawyers' Association, *Legal Opinions to Third Parties: An Easier Path*, 34 Bus. Law. 1891 (1979).

the acquirer nor the target previously had, by a third party—the lawyer—who is the least-cost producer.[55]

Just as was the case in our examination of the function of representations and warranties, this focus on the information production role for lawyers' opinions also provides a nonadversarial approach to resolving the conflict over their content. Because reducing the cost of information necessary to the correct pricing of the transaction is beneficial to both acquirer and target, determination of the matters to be covered by the opinion of counsel for the target [56] should be in large measure a cooperative, rather than a competitive, opportunity. Debate over the scope of the opinion, then, should focus explicitly on the cost of producing the information. For example, where a privately owned business is being sold, the target may retain special counsel to handle the acquisition transaction, either because the company has had no regular counsel prior to the transaction, or because its regular counsel is not experienced in acquisition transactions. In this situation, recognition of the informational basis of the subject matter usually covered by legal opinions not only suggests that a specialized third-party producer is appropriate, but also provides guidance about *whose* third party should actually do the production.

From this perspective, target's counsel typically will be the least-cost producer of the information in question. Past experience with the target will eliminate the need for much factual investigation that would be necessary for someone who lacked a prior professional relation to the target. Similarly, target's counsel may well have been directly involved in some of the matters of concern—such as the issuance of the securities which are the subject of an opinion concerning the target's capitalization, or the negotiation of the lease which is the subject of an opinion concerning the impact of the transaction on the target's obligations. Where the target has retained special counsel for the transaction, however, the production-cost advantage in favor of target's counsel will be substantially reduced, especially with respect to past matters. In those cases, focus on the cost of information production provides a method for cooperative resolution of the frequently contentious issue of the scope of the opinion.[57]

---

[55] The opinion of counsel also serves an important verification function. See Section B.4.b.(2). of this Chapter, infra.

[56] Typically there will be occasions that call for an opinion of *acquirer's* counsel as well. See Section VII.C. of the acquisition agreement in Appendix B. Consistent with an information-cost analysis, the scope of the opinion of acquirer's counsel increases as information about the acquirer becomes important to pricing the transaction. This would be the case, for example, where the two parties are so close in size that the transaction is really a merger, or where the consideration to be given by the seller is the acquirer's stock. In virtually all transactions, the opinion of the acquirer's counsel will be required with respect to the impact of the transaction

itself, such as proper authorization of the transaction by the acquirer.

[57] The role of information-producer also may be played by another third-party specialist: The public accountant. The accountant typically also renders an opinion concerning the transaction—the cold comfort letter—and easily can be imagined having an information-production role. The common presence of an internal accounting staff within the seller, however, is persuasive evidence that the transactional function of the public accountant is one of verification. See section B.4.b.(2). of this Chapter, infra. Whether or not there is also an information-production role for the public accountant depends on the comparative information-production costs of the

(3) Controls Over What Information to Look for and How Hard to Try

Emphasis on the information-production role of the target's representations and warranties and the opinion of counsel for the target leads to the conclusion that determination of the least-cost information producer provides a cooperative focus for negotiating the content of those provisions. The same emphasis on information production also raises a related question. The demand for information, as for any other good, is more or less price elastic. Information production is costly even for the most efficient producer, and the higher the cost, the less the parties will choose to produce. Thus, some fine tuning of the assignment of information-production roles would seem to be necessary. We would expect some specific limits on the kind of information required to be produced. And we would also expect some specific limits on how much should be spent even for information whose production is desired.

Examination of an acquisition agreement from this perspective identifies provisions which impose precisely these kinds of controls. Moreover, explicit recognition of the function of these provisions, as with our analysis of representations and warranties and opinions of counsel, can facilitate the negotiation of what traditionally have been quite difficult issues.

Consider first the question of limiting the type of information that must be produced in light of the cost of production. To put the problem in a context, we can focus on the standard representation concerning the target's existing contracts. The acquirer's initial draft typically will require the target to represent that an attached schedule lists "all agreements, contracts, leases, and other commitments to which the target is a party or by which any of its property is bound." In fact, it is quite unlikely that the acquirer really wants the target to incur the costs of producing all the information specified. In a business of any significant size, there will be a large number of small contracts—for office plant care, coffee service, addressographs, and the like—the central collection and presentation of which would entail substantial cost. Moreover, to the extent these contracts are all in the normal course of the target's business, the information may have little bearing on the pricing of the transaction. As a result, it would be beneficial to both parties to limit the scope of the target's search.

It is from this perspective that the function of certain common qualifications of the representations and warranties of the target are best understood. The expected response of a target to a representation as to existing contracts of the breadth of that described above would be to qualify the scope of the information to be produced: To limit the obligation to only *material* contracts.[58] If the contracts themselves are not important, then there is no reason to incur the cost of producing information about them. Variations on the theme include qualifica-

---

public accountant and the target's internal accounting staff.

[58] See J. Freund, supra at 272–74.

tions based on the dollar value of the contracts,[59] or on the relationship of the contracts to "the ordinary course of business." [60]

A second common form of qualification—a limit on the information costs to be incurred—is best understood as an instruction concerning how hard to look for information whose subject matter cannot be excluded as unimportant ahead of time. Here the idea is to qualify not the object of the inquiry, but the diligence of the search.[61] Consider, for example, the common representation concerning the absence of defaults under disclosed contracts.[62] While it might involve little cost to determine whether the target, as lessee, has defaulted under a lease, it may well be quite expensive to determine whether the lessor is in default. In that situation, the acquirer might consider it sufficient to be told everything that the target had thought appropriate to find out for its own purposes, without regard to the acquisition, but not to require further investigation.

This type of qualification, limiting the representation to information the target already has and requiring no further search, is the domain of the familiar "knowledge" qualification. In form, the representation concerning the existence of breaches is qualified by the phrase "to target's knowledge." In function, the qualification serves to limit the scope of the target's search to information already within its possession; no new information need be sought.[63]

---

[59] See Section III.A.(16) of the acquisition agreement in Appendix B.; 3 *Business Acquisitions*, supra at 96–97 ("Set forth as Schedule G hereto are complete and accurate lists of the following: (i) all arrangements of the Seller, except for purchase and sales order that involve future payments of less than $250,000 * * *.").

[60] See *Drafting Agreements*, supra at 94 ("Neither corporation nor subsidiary is a party to, nor is the property of either bound by * * * any agreement not entered into in the ordinary course of business * * * except the agreements listed in Exhibit —— * * *.").

[61] This analysis, and that concerning the object of the inquiry, applies as well to the role of third-party information producers.

[62] See Section III.A.(16) of the acquisition agreement in Appendix B.; *Drafting Agreements*, supra at 94 ("There is no default or event that with notice or lapse of time, or both, would constitute a default by any party to any of these agreements.").

[63] James Freund identifies another function for representations and warranties that suggests a different role for the knowledge qualification. Freund points out that an unqualified representation serves, in effect, as an insurance policy. Thus, an unqualified representation may be made even though the target is aware of a possibility that the representation is incorrect, because the parties have determined that the target should bear the risk and the abso-

lute representation serves to allocate that risk to the target. J. Freund, supra at 247–48. From an information perspective, however, Freund's point is part of an approach to dealing with the problem of information asymmetry. Suppose both the acquirer and the target are aware that certain of the target's trade secrets may be subject to a misappropriation claim, and that such a claim, if successful, would reduce the value of the target's business by $1,000,000. It would hardly be surprising if the acquirer and the target had different estimates of the probability of a successful misappropriation claim; after all, the target has vastly more information concerning the circumstances in which the trade secrets were developed than does the acquirer. Suppose further that the acquirer, based on its information, estimates the probability of liability at .5, and therefore argues that the purchase price should be reduced by $500,000. The target, however, based on its information, estimates the probability at only .15, which would justify only a 150,000 reduction in the purchase price. The effect of the target's making an unqualified warranty concerning ownership of trade secrets is to allocate the risk of liability to the seller, the party with the best information and, therefore, the party best able to price the risk. From the acquirer's perspective, the risk has been eliminated. From the target's perspective, $350,000 has been gained: The expected value of the purchase price—total price

Recognizing the function of the knowledge qualification also raises another question concerning the variation in form that the qualification takes in typical acquisition agreements. In fact, the knowledge qualification—the limit on how hard the target must search for information—comes in a variety of forms. Often within the same agreement one will see all of the following variations:

"to target's knowledge"; [64]

"to the best of target's knowledge"; [65]

"to the best of target's knowledge and after diligent investigation." [66]

What seems to be at work, at least implicitly, is the creation of a hierarchy of search effort that must be undertaken with respect to information of different levels of importance.[67]

This result is perfectly consistent with a view of the business lawyer as a transaction cost engineer, and with a view of representations and warranties as a means of producing the information necessary to pricing the transaction at the lowest cost. However, it also raises the question of whether implicit recognition of the information-cost function of these qualifications might not facilitate the design of more effective cost reduction techniques. Although this is not the ocassion to detail the changes in the form of acquisition agreements that might result from conscious attention to issues of information cost, it seems quite clear that once we understand more precisely what it is we are about, we should be able to do a more effective job.

Consider, for example, the qualifications that we have just discussed concerning how hard the target must look. Given our understanding of their purpose, the problem of limiting the scope of the target's investigation might be better approached explicitly, rather than implicitly through a variety of undefined adjectives. If, for example, the concern is whether the lessor of a real estate lease, under which the target is the lessee, has breached the lease, as in Section III.A.(10) of the acquisition agreement in Appendix B., why not specify the actual investigation the target should make? Do we want the target to go directly to the lessor to secure a statement by the lessor as to the lessor's satisfaction of its obligations? [68] Different levels of cost

less expected liability—is $350,000 higher than if the acquirer's estimate was used. Thus, unqualified representations and warranties can serve, as Freund perceptively suggests, as insurance policies. However, the determination of which party should be the insurer turns on the determination of which party has better information and, as a result, is better able to price the risk.

[64] See Sections III.A.(14), (15), and (25) of the acquisition agreement in Appendix B.

[65] See id. at Sections III.A.(10), (13), and (16).

[66] See id. at Section VI.C.(v).

[67] This proposition—that different forms of qualification reflect the different levels

of intended search effort—also may be subject to empirical evaluation. If one of the parties to an acquisition agreement is a reporting company under the Securities Exchange Act, its Form 10K Annual Report typically would contain the agreement as an exhibit. Thus, one could gather a substantial sample of acquisition agreements to analyze whether there was a pattern to the types of information subject to qualification and to the form of qualification used.

[68] If information is too costly to produce, the issue shifts to who is best able to price and bear the risk, again information-cost issues.

obviously are associated with the different inquiries; specificity about the desired level of cost, however, should allow further minimization of information costs. To make the point in a slightly different way, is it possible to say with any assurance which of the forms of qualification listed above imposes an obligation to inspect the premises, but no obligation to inquire directly of the lessor?

b. Costs of Verifying Information

Problems of information cost do not end when the information is acquired. Even if cooperative negotiation between the acquirer and target minimizes the costs of reducing the informational asymmetry confronting the acquirer, another information-cost dilemma remains: How can the acquirer determine whether the information it has received is accurate? After all, the target, who has probably provided most of the information, has a clear incentive to mislead the acquirer into overvaluing the business.

Just as the market provides incentives that offset a target's inclination to withhold unfavorable information, the market also provides incentives that constrain a target's similar inclination to proffer falsely favorable information. If, before a transaction, an acquirer can neither itself determine the quality of the target's product nor evaluate the accuracy of the target's representations about product quality, the acquirer has no alternative but to treat the target's product as being of low quality, regardless of the target's protestations.[69] To avoid this problem, a high quality target has a substantial incentive to demonstrate to an acquirer that its representations about the quality of its business are accurate and can be relied upon. And because it is in the target's interest to keep all information costs at a minimum, there is also an incentive to accomplish this verification in the most economical fashion.

Verification techniques, then, are critical means of reducing total information costs. Like efforts to reduce acquisition costs, verification techniques can be implemented both by the parties themselves and through the efforts of third parties. It is helpful to consider each approach to verification separately.

(1) Economizing by the Parties

Perhaps the cheapest verification technique is simply an expectation of future transactions between the acquirer and target. When the target's misrepresentation in one transaction will be taken into account by the acquirer in decisions concerning future transaction, whether by

---

[69] In the absence of some method by which the seller of a high quality product can demonstrate to potential buyers that its product is in fact of high quality, the seller may have no incentive to provide a high quality product at all. If a buyer cannot tell a good product from a bad one, all products will be treated, and priced, as if they were of low quality. The result is the standard "lemon problem": Poor quality products drive higher quality products from the market. See Ackerlof, *The Market for "Lemons": Quality Uncertainty and the Market Mechanism*, 84 Q.J.Econ. 488, 489–90 (1970); Grossman, supra; Wilson, *The Nature of Equilibrium in Markets with Adverse Selection*, 11 Bell J.Econ. 108 (1980).

reducing the price to reflect lowered expectations, or, at the extreme, by withdrawing patronage altogether, the target will have little incentive to mislead.[70] In a corporate acquisition, however, the target has no expectation of future transactions; for the target, a corporate acquisition is, virtually by definition, a one-shot transaction. Thus, the expectation of future transactions is simply not available as a constraint on the target's incentive to misrepresent the information provided.[71]

Nonetheless, the insight gleaned from understanding how an expectation of future transactions serves to validate a target's information can be used to create an inexpensive verification technique that will work even in the one-period world of a corporate acquisition. The expectation technique works because of the existence of additional periods; the insight is simply to devise what Oliver Williamson has called a "hostage" strategy,[72] i.e., an artificial second period in which misrepresentations in the first period—the acquisition transaction—are penalized. If any of the target's information turns out to be inaccurate, the target will be required to compensate the acquirer; in effect, the target posts a bond that it has provided accurate information. This technique has the advantage of being quite economical: Beyond the negotiating cost involved in agreeing to make the acquirer whole, there is no cost to the target *unless* the information proves inaccurate.[73]

This technique is among the most common approaches to verification that appear in corporate acquisition agreements. The target verifies the accuracy of the information it has provided through its representations and warranties by agreeing to indemnify the acquirer if the information turns out to be wrong, i.e., if a breach of representation

[70] The expectation of future transactions can serve as a means to facilitate low-cost verification even if the seller has no reason to believe that it will deal with a particular buyer again. So long as any discrepancy between the represented and actual quality of a seller's product can be easily communicated to potential buyers by a buyer who has been misled, a seller can effectively signal to potential buyers that it is a high quality producer—that the disclosed information concerning product quality is correct—by making investments in form-specific capital, like reputation and advertising, that would be lost if the seller's product turned out to be of lower quality than represented. See Klein & Leffler, *The Role of Market Forces in Assuring Contractual Performance*, 89 J.Pol.Econ. 615 (1981).

[71] Final-period problems of the sort described in the text may still be present even in the unusual situation when the target in an acquisition transaction in fact can be anticipated to engage in future transactions. Suppose a target is engaged in a divestiture program, trying to shed previously acquired businesses that have not worked out. While a misrepresenta-

tion in a particular transaction may make it more expensive for a target to verify the quality of its information in a subsequent transaction, the extent of the constraint is limited for a number of reasons. First, the misrepresentation may not become known before the target has completed the divestiture program, after which point the target can no longer be penalized through future transactions. In this sense, a final period may be long enough to shelter a number of transactions. Second, the transactions may not be of equal magnitude. A successful misrepresentation in a particularly large transaction may more than offset the resulting penalty with respect to a number of small transactions.

[72] Williamson, *Credible Commitments: Using Hostages to Support Exchange*, 73 Am.Econ.Rev. 519 (1983).

[73] Williamson provides a number of other examples of how this approach has been used. Id. at 532–33. Additional examples can be found in Knoeber, *An Alternative Mechanism to Assure Contractual Reliability*, 12 J.Legal Stud. 333, 337–38, 342–43 (1983).

or warranty occurs.[74] And the hostage metaphor rings especially true because the target's promise to indemnify the acquirer is frequently backed by the acquirer's or a neutral third party's retention of a portion of the consideration as a fund to assure the target's performance of its indemnification obligation.[75]

Emphasis on verification costs also highlights that indemnification, like the target's representations and warranties, ultimately works principally to the target's advantage. As long as the target recognizes that the perceived quality, as well as the amount, of the information provided by the target will be reflected in the price the acquirer is willing to pay, the subject provides the opportunity for cooperative, rather than merely distributive, bargaining.[76]

The common appearance of target indemnification against inaccuracies in the information contained in the target's representations and warranties is persuasive evidence of the information-cost basis for the technique. But it is also true that use of the technique is not universal. There are a significant number of acquisitions containing no contractual provision for indemnification. Even more troubling, its presence or absence follows a predictable pattern: Indemnification is typically used if the target is a private company, but not if the target is a public company.[77] A complete information-cost explanation for indemnification in acquisition agreements thus also must explain why indemnification provisions are rarely, if ever, used when the target is a public company. And the range of possible explanations is limited in an important respect: There is no reason to believe that the need for verification is any less significant when the target is a public rather than a private company. The real task is to identify the alternative means of verification that are available in the acquisition of a public company and to understand why their comparative cost advantage does not extend to private companies.

[74] See Section V. of the acquisition agreement in Appendix B.

[75] See section II and appendix A of the acquisition agreement in Appendix B; J. Freund, supra at 363–88; Weinreich, *Contract of Sale,* in 1 *Business Acquisitions,* supra at 191–194 (discussion of escrow arrangements).

The negotiation of indemnification and "hold back" funds is quite complicated. See J. Freund, supra at 383–84. Nonetheless, the common elements out of which a solution is built—for example, "baskets" that require a minimum amount before any claim can be made and "cut-offs" that limit claims to breaches discovered during a specified period—have become standard.

[76] It is hard to know what to make of the anecdotal evidence that can be marshalled in response to the claim that indemnification presents a target with the opportunity for cooperative bargaining. Practicing business lawyers will recount that the price is set by the clients long prior to the negotiation over whether there will be indemnification; as a result, they may argue that the presence or absence of provisions for indemnification have *no* effect on the price of the transaction. Evaluation of the argument requires information about the expectations of the acquirer when the price was negotiated and about whether price and other provisions were negotiated at the same time by sophisticated clients. In any event, the core of the argument is that understanding the function of such provisions can make for different and better results.

[77] See J. Freund, supra at 160. Indemnification is absent if the acquisition agreement states that the target's representations and warranties do not survive the closing of the transaction. See Weinreich, *Contract of Sale,* in 1 *Business Acquisitions,* supra at 187.

Two significant differences seem to account for the absence, in the acquisition of public companies, of the dominant verification technique in acquisitions of private companies. First, less costly verification techniques are available in the public setting but unavailable in a private transaction. Second, the indemnification technique is more costly to implement in a public than in a private transaction.

Consider first the verification techniques that are available to public, but not to private, companies as alternatives to indemnification. One, which functions to reduce the incentives of the target's management to provide misleading information in the first place, is not an innovative contractual technique that cleverly alters incentives. Rather it simply reflects that the differences in transactional setting and in the cast of characters between the acquisition of a public and private company result in different incentives with respect to the provision of inaccurate information by the target. Here the critical players are the target's management, who will negotiate the transaction and actually provide the information whose verification is required. And the central point is that the managers' incentives to provide accurate information differ critically depending on whether the target is privately or publicly owned. Where the target is private, management is typically dominated by the principal shareholders who also will receive the lion's share of the proceeds from the acquisition. The transaction enables these individuals to diversify their previously undiversified portfolio. Prior to the transaction, most of their wealth was tied up in their private company;[78] after the transaction, their wealth has been transformed into either cash or the publicly traded stock of the acquirer, either of which allows portfolio diversification. To be sure, these owner-managers will also have an undiversifiable *human* capital investment in the company they manage, and this investment may remain after the transaction through a post-acquisition employment relationship. But this benefit will constitute so small a portion of the total benefits from the transaction that the owner-managers will see the transaction as a one-time event that presents the incentives to mislead associated with any final period situation.

Separation of ownership and management in public companies puts management of a publicly held target in a quite different position. Even if these employee-managers have some ownership position in the target as a result of stock option or bonus plans, their principal investment in the company is typically their human capital. As a result, a post-acquisition employment contract is of much greater importance both in absolute terms and, because their human capital investment cannot be diversified, in relative terms as well. These factors combine to create an interesting verification technique. For the employee-managers, the acquisition transaction is a two-period rather

---

[78] The critical financial characteristic of private corporations is that the absence of a public market prevents their owners from achieving optimally diversified portfolios by selling off a portion of the ownership of the private company. As a result, the company may well be worth more to a publicly held acquiring company, whose shareholders can optimally diversify, than to the private owners of the company. See Fama & Jensen, *Organizational Forms and Investment Decisions*, 14 J.Fin.Econ. 101, 103–07 (1985).

than a single-period game. During the first period, in which the actual transaction takes place, the employee-managers provide the acquirer with information bearing on the target's value. However, their compensation from the transaction, post-transaction employment contracts, unlike the compensation of the shareholders of the target, comes not in the first period but later, as payments are received under the employment contracts. These second-period payments serve as a bond of the accuracy of the information provided by the employee-managers in the first period: If misrepresentations are discovered, their employment can be terminated.[79] Precisely because post-transaction employment is substantially less valuable to owner-managers, this verification technique is simply not available to private companies [80] which, as a result, must rely on indemnification.

Some evidence supports this explanation of the different transactional structures found in the acquisitions of public and private companies. A familiar type of company is neither truly public nor truly private. Such a company is public in that its stock is freely traded on a national securities exchange or in the over-the-counter market, but private in that there is a single dominant shareholder, or group of shareholders, whose own situation is much closer to that of the owner-managers in the prototypical private company than to that of the employee-managers in a truly public company. Because the operative factor in the analysis is the character of the managers' portfolios—the public/private distinction is only the common shorthand characterization—one would expect acquirers of these quasi-public companies to treat them more like private than public companies. This prediction appears to be correct. The literature treats the situation of a public company with a dominant shareholder as an exception to the general rule that indemnification is not appropriate in the acquisition of a

---

[79] Management buyouts, see Chapter Fifteen B.4., supra, are an extreme example of this verification technique: Management demonstrates to the third parties (or their lenders) who are putting up the bulk of the investment the accuracy of the information provided, including, most importantly, projections of post-transaction cash flows, by making a substantial personal investment in the post-transaction company.

[80] This analysis suggests that "golden parachutes" employment arrangements create a perverse incentive in addition to the anti-takeover motive discussed in Chapter Fourteen B.1.b.(5), supra. Golden parachute arrangements are commonly justified as reducing the conflict of interest between employee-managers and shareholders with respect to acquisition offers by providing a benefit to management that offsets the loss of management's control if an acquisition takes place. But it also has been recognized that too high a payoff under the arrangement creates a moral hazard: The employee-manager may be better off if an acquisition takes place even on terms that make the shareholders worse off. The conflict of interest has not been eliminated; it has merely been reshaped. Golden parachute arrangements thus can interfere with the verification technique of reducing information costs. The engine that drives the technique is the risk that the value of the employee-manager's most important asset—his post-transaction employment relationship—will be reduced if he is discovered to have made misrepresentations to the acquirer. But that risk can be eliminated, and the effectiveness of the information-cost reducing technique impaired, if the manager acquires a hedge—another asset that will increase in value as a result of the same event that causes the decrease in the value of the employment relationship. A golden parachute arrangement provides precisely such a hedge. It pays off only on post-transaction termination, precisely the event that reduces the value of the manager's employment relationship. Golden parachutes, then, should increase an acquirer's verification costs even in friendly transaction.

public company: An explicit agreement by the dominant shareholder of a quasi-public company to indemnify the acquirer for breaches of representations and warranties is a quite familiar transactional structure.[81]

The second verification technique that is uniquely available in the acquisition of a public company results from the continuing disclosure obligations imposed by the Securities Exchange Act of 1934[82] only on public companies. In the course of compliance with its regulatory obligations, the target will previously have disclosed substantial amounts of the information covered by the representations and warranties contained in the acquisition agreement. The critical point, however, is not that the information was previously produced—we have already seen that the target is typically the least-cost information producer—but that it was produced subject to a powerful verification technique. Material misrepresentations and omissions in disclosures made pursuant to 1934 Act requirements subject both a company and its management to potential civil and criminal penalties.[83] This potential liability serves further to bond the accuracy of the representations made by employee-managers and, thus, further to reduce both the incentives and the opportunity to mislead the acquirer. In this sense, the 1934 Act serves to collectivize the verification problem.[84]

The operation of these two verification techniques in the acquisition of a public company thus goes a long way toward explaining why indemnification, the central verification technique in the acquisition of a private company, is not observed in the public setting. An additional point should also be made, however, bearing not on the availability of alternatives to indemnification as a means of verification, but on the differential costs of using indemnification in acquisitions of public, as opposed to private, companies. An indemnification arrangement is costly to administer. If a claim of breach of warranty arises, it must be resolved. This resolution, whether by litigation or some alternative method of dispute resolution such as arbitration, is expensive. Moreover, there are significant collective action problems: Someone must

---

[81] See section V of the acquisition agreement in Appendix B; J. Freund, supra at 161, 365.

[82] 15 U.S.C. § 78m. The obligation to file periodic quarterly and annual reports under § 13 of the Securities Exchange Act, 15 U.S.C. § 78m (1982), is triggered either by registration pursuant to § 12, 15 U.S.C. § 78l (1982), or by the filing of a registration statement under the Securities Act of 1933, pursuant to § 15(d), 15 U.S.C. § 78o(d) (1982).

[83] In addition to standard civil remedies, § 32(a), 15 U.S.C. § 77ff(a) (1982), provides for fines of up to $10,000 and imprisonment for up to five years (although § 32(b), 15 U.S.C. § 77ff(b) (1982), reduces the maximum penalty for failure to file, as opposed to filing an inaccurate report for companies whose reporting obligation arises under § 15(d), 15 U.S.C. § 79o(d) (1982)).

[84] The idea of legislation serving as a collective response to problems of verification cost is developed in Gilson & Kraakman, supra at 605. It should be stressed that employee-managers are likely to be quite risk averse with respect to incurring such penalties. The simple fact is that most of the benefits from "successful" violations go to the shareholders, while the costs of getting caught are borne more than proportionally by the managers, absent an effective indemnification arrangement. For a comprehensive analysis of the impact of managers' attitudes toward risk on corporate compliance with regulatory obligations, see Kraakman, *Corporate Liability Strategies and the Costs of Legal Controls*, 93 Yale L.J. 857 (1984).

act on behalf of the target in responding to the acquirer's claim. Where the target is privately held, the collective action problem is minimal; the shareholder group is small enough that it can play that role directly. Where the target is publicly held, however, the collective action problem is quite real. Dispersal of ownership among numerous shareholders dilutes the incentive for any single shareholder to monitor the indemnification process; a collective solution is required to overcome the free-rider problem. Thus, a trustee, typically a commercial bank, is appointed.[85] The cost of this arrangement includes not merely the amount the trustee must be paid, but also the dilution of incentives to oppose an acquirer's claim that results from the inevitable divergence in interests between the target's shareholders and the appointed trustee.[86]

In short, an information-cost approach to the problem of verification explains a good deal about the presence or absence of indemnification provisions in acquisition agreements. But the range of verification techniques available is not limited to those involving participation only by the acquirer and target. Just as with the production of the information in the first place, there are verification techniques that depend upon participation by third parties. And these also help to demonstrate the information-cost basis for additional provisions of the typical agreement.

(2) Third-Party Verification Techniques

Regardless of whether the target is a public or private company, there is a common limit on the effectiveness of all of the verification techniques discussed thus far; the possibility of misleading statements remains. Consider first the limits on the verification techniques associated with the sale of a public company: Senior management may not expect their misrepresentations to be discovered at all; they may be far enough along in their careers that they expect to retire before discovery; golden-parachute agreements may have reversed senior management's incentives; and, ultimately, the possibility remains that the particular misleading disclosure, or failure to disclose, masks information which is so damaging that senior manage-

---

[85] J. Freund, supra at 387.

[86] The agreement with the trustee typically holds the trustee harmless from claims by the target's shareholders, as long as the trustee has acted in good faith. See appendix A to the acquisition agreement in Appendix B. Additionally, the trustee's fee is usually fixed, although all costs—especially attorney's fees in the event of litigation—are reimbursed. The result is that the trustee bears a significant portion of the cost of resisting, through the extra work for its personnel, while the target's shareholders receive all the benefits. The divergence in interests creates a clear bias on the part of the trustee in favor of early settlement.

Just as was the case with respect to the differential impact of post-acquisition employment on the incentives of target management to misrepresent depending on whether the target is publicly or privately held, the intermediate case of a publicly held company with a dominant shareholder is more like the privately held company than the publicly held company with respect to the need for a third party to monitor the indemnification process. The concentration in holdings represented by the dominant shareholder overcomes the free-rider problem inherent in diverse public ownership. Again, the result is to suggest a greater role for indemnification in this setting.

ment is better off with misleading disclosure even in the face of possible future penalties.[87]

Even the more direct verification technique associated with the sale of a private company—indemnification arrangements backed by the withholding of a portion of the purchase price—will not be completely effective. The indemnification obligation often is limited to an amount lower than the purchase price.[88] Moreover, the obligation is typically limited in time; a contractual statute of limitations limits the period in which claims for indemnification may be asserted.[89] If the reduction in value resulting from complete disclosure exceeds the limit on indemnification, then indemnification operates not as bond, but as bait; a piece of the proceeds is given up in order to increase the net take. Most troubling to a potential acquirer, the balance of incentives facing owner-managers of a private target favors misrepresentation or nondisclosure in precisely those situations where the information in question would result in the greatest downward adjustment in the purchase price. Verification fails in the situation where it is most needed.

Ultimately, all of these verification techniques are imperfect because they do not entirely eliminate the potential for opportunism inherent in one-time transactions. The techniques examined—indemnification, employment contracts, liability under the Securities Exchange Act—operate to reduce final-period problems by adding an artificial second round to the transaction. For this reason, all share a common limit on their effectiveness: As long as the gain from cheating in the first round can exceed the penalties if caught in the second— whether because the probability of detection is less than 1.0, or because the financial risk borne by the target in the second round is too low, since the solutions to other kinds of problems conflict with what would be the optimal resolution of the verification problem [90]—the acquirer

---

[87] The analysis can be generalized. Most unfavorable disclosure reduces the value of the target by shifting the acquirer's estimate of the probable distribution of future earnings. For the target, the disclosure calculus compares the certain reduction in value that results from disclosure (the acquirer's expected value is lowered), with the penalty for making a misrepresentation or non-disclosure discounted by the possibility that the actual result will still fall on a part of the probability distribution that exceeds the acquirer's uncorrected expected value, and by the possibility that the misrepresentation or nondisclosure will remain undetected. From this perspective, for example, the decision by senior management of National Telephone Co. not to disclose the company's violation of its loan agreements may be understandable. See In re Carter, [1981 Transfer Binder] Fed.Sec.L.Rep. (CCH) ¶ 82,847 (S.E.C.Admin.). Alternatively, the size of the penalties that can be imposed may be bounded because of bankruptcy or retirement or, as in the Equity Funding

scandal, see Dirks v. S.E.C., 463 U.S. 646 (1983), because the fraud is so large as to dwarf the potential penalties, i.e., the penalties are insufficient to eliminate the final period problem by creating an artificial second round.

[88] It is not uncommon to limit the target's total exposure for indemnification to the amount of the purchase price that has been withheld as a hostage. J. Freund, supra at 385–86.

[89] Id. at 386.

[90] One response might be that any reluctance by the target to take full advantage of available verification techniques—for example, by attempting to limit its indemnification obligation to an amount less than the total proceeds to be received— would be understood by the acquirer as a signal that the target's information was inaccurate, and would result in an equivalent reduction in the offered purchase price, thereby eliminating any gain to the target from the gambit. The problem, however, is that the information content of

lacks the assurance that the information provided by the target can be entirely trusted.

At this point, further efforts at verification by the acquirer or target are unlikely to be successful.[91] A critical role is thus created for third parties to act to close the verification gap left by the target's residual final-period problems. Suppose one could discover what can be called a reputational intermediary: Someone paid to verify another party's information.[92] When residual final-period problems prevent a target from completely verifying the information it provides, a third party can offer *its* reputation as a bond that the target's information is accurate. The value of the transaction then increases because information costs are reduced, and the reputational intermediary is paid some portion of the increase as compensation for the pledge of its reputation.

The third party's role will be successful, however, only if there are no final-period problems associated with its verification. The intermediary is paid only because its reputation renders it trustworthy in circumstances when a party to the transaction could not be trusted. Unlike the target, the intermediary expects future transactions in which it again will pledge its reputation. If the intermediary cheats in one transaction—by failing to discover or disclose seller misrepresentations [93]—its reputation will suffer and, in a subsequent transaction, its

the signal—in the example, the target's desire to put a ceiling on the indemnification obligation—is noisy. If reasons other than the inaccuracy of the information could explain why the target might want to limit indemnification, then the acquirer will have difficulty sorting out how much of a price reduction is warranted. See Verrecchia, supra. For example, the target might want to limit the indemnification obligation because of a fear that the acquirer will behave opportunistically with respect to claims of breach, i.e., if the business performs poorly after the transaction, the acquirer may claim that the poor performance resulted from facts that were not disclosed—the buyer's probability distribution of future performance was skewed because of misleading disclosure—rather than from the mere bad luck of ending up on an unfavorable portion of an accurately disclosed probability distribution. Alternatively, the target may want to keep the size of the holdback low, even though this may be seen by the acquirer as an effort to limit the "real" exposure for indemnification and, therefore, as a negative signal about the accuracy of the information, in order to allow desirable diversification of what had previously been an undiversifiable investment. Where there is this kind of noise surrounding a signal, it can be expected that a full discount will not occur: That is, there will be some equilibrium amount of misleading disclosure. Id. at 18.

The noisiness of the signal of inaccuracy also suggests that some of the costs to target's management from misleading disclosure are not scale related. If any misrepresentation signals that the information provided is inaccurate, but without providing guidance as to the extent of the problem, there will be a greater incentive to tell only the "big lie." Put differently, there may be economics of scale in misrepresentation.

[91] The target has already pledged all of its assets—both tangible physical property and the intangible values associated with the reputations of its managers—so little else can be done in the absence of inventive means to reduce the noise associated with the target's signals. Cf. Thakor, *An Exploration of Competitive Signaling Equilibria with "Third Party" Information Production: The Case of Debt Insurance,* 37 J.Fin. 717 (1982) (problem of additional verification when issuer of debt has already pledged its assets to repay).

[92] The concept of a reputational intermediary is developed in Gilson & Kraakman, supra at 604–07, 618–21.

[93] The intermediary can cheat in two quite different ways. First, the intermediary may discover that the target's information is misleading, but because of payments received from the target, may not disclose to the acquirer. In this setting it is the acquirer who is being cheated. Second, the intermediary may simply shirk its responsibilities to investigate the accuracy of the target's information. In this setting both the acquirer and target are being cheated,

verification will be less completely believed. The result will be a smaller increase in the value of the subsequent transaction because of the intermediary's participation and, in turn, a lower payment to the intermediary.[94] And as long as the intermediary will be penalized in subsequent periods for cheating in this period, there will be no final-period problems to dilute the intermediary's signal of accuracy.[95]

In fact, lawyers and accountants commonly play the role of reputational intermediary. And once we think of them as being in the business of selling—more accurately, renting—their reputations,[96] a number of examples readily come to mind in which this phenomenon seems to be at work. Practicing lawyers will recall instances when, having been advised that they were to represent their client in a transaction with an unfamiliar party on the other side, their initial question to their client concerned the identity of the other side's lawyers. Implicit in the question is that the identity of the lawyer conveyed information about the lawyer's client; i.e., a reputable business lawyer would not risk his reputation by representing an untrustworthy client.[97] Similarly, it is a common occurrence for companies about to make an initial public offering to switch to a Big Eight auditor.[98] Since the previous audit firm apparently satisfied *management's* need for information, the discovery of systematic switching when the company is, in effect, to be sold to the public, strongly suggests a reputational explanation.[99]

the acquirer because it has been misled about the accuracy of the target's information by the behavior of the intermediary, and the target because it has paid for verification that was not actually performed, with the resulting risk that it will be blamed by the acquirer for future failures of the business. The latter conclusion is limited to cases where the loss to the target resulting from the risk of future blame exceeds the gain to the target from the nondisclosure.

[94] The intermediary may pledge more than its reputation depending on whether it also incurs liability if the target's information behind which it has stood proves inaccurate. The liability standards with respect to lawyers are considered infra. For discussion of liability for accountants acting as reputational intermediaries, see Filflis, *Current Problems of Accountants' Responsibilities to Third Parties*, 28 Vand. L.Rev. 31 (1975); Gruenbaum & Steinberg, *Accountants' Liability and Responsibility: Securities, Criminal and Common Law*, 13 Loy.L.A.L.Rev. 247 (1980).

[95] To say that there are *no* final-period problems is something of an overstatement. The analysis is really an application of the insight that when product quality is difficult to determine ex ante, as here with the verification role of an intermediary, but easy to determine ex post, as here when the passage of time will demonstrate whether the target's information was inac-

curate, the provider of the good or service will make investments in firm-specific capital—like reputation—that will be devalued if actual quality turns out to be lower than that represented. Cf. DeAngelo, *Auditor Size and Audit Quality*, 3 J.Acct. & Econ. 183 (1981) (value of audit depends on size of investment in firm-specific assets made by particular auditor; larger accounting firms offer a more believable signal of accuracy to third parties than smaller firms).

[96] The role of lawyers as reputational intermediaries is developed in Gilson & Mnookin, *Sharing Among the Human Capitalists: An Economic Inquiry into the Corporate Law Firm and How Partners Split Profits*, 37 Stan.L.Rev. 313 (1985).

[97] See Gilson & Mnookin, supra at 366–68.

[98] Carpenter & Strawser, *Displacement of Auditors When Clients Go Public*, 131 J.Acct., June, 1971, at 55; cf. DeAngelo, supra (verification-based explanation for phenomenon).

[99] The reputational role of public accountants generally is discussed in a substantial literature, with particular emphasis on the need for and function of the independence requirement. See Benston, *The Market for Public Accounting Services: Demand, Supply and Regulation*, 2 Acct.J. 2 (1979); DeAngelo, supra note 131; Watts & Zimmerman, *Agency Problems, Auditing,*

It is from this perspective that an important part of the role for lawyers and accountants described in the acquisition agreement can best be understood. As already discussed, acquisition agreements commonly require that an opinion of the target's counsel be delivered to the acquirer as a condition to the acquirer's obligation to complete the transaction. It is also common further to condition the acquirer's obligation on receipt of an opinion of the target's independent accountant—the "cold comfort" letter.[100] While we cannot examine here the entire range of third-party opinions given in acquisition transactions, a particular opinion often required of the target's lawyer and the accountant's cold comfort letter most prominently highlight the reputational intermediary role played by both professionals.

The opinion commonly requested from the target's lawyer that "we are not aware of any factual information that would lead us to believe that the agreement contains an untrue statement of a material fact or omits to state a fact necessary to make the statements made therein not misleading,"[101] and the cold comfort opinion typically requested of the target's accountant to the effect that there have been no changes in specified financial statement items since the last audited financial statements,[102] share a common conceptual underpinning that is reputationally based. The central characteristic of both opinions is that neither alters the total *quantity* of information that has been produced for the buyer. Rephrased, the lawyer's statement is simply that a third party who has been intimately involved in the *target's* production of information for the acquirer does not believe the target has misled the acquirer. It is quite clearly the *lawyer's* reputation [103] for diligence and honesty—that is intended to be placed at risk.[104] Similarly, the cold

---

and the Theory of the Firm: Some Evidence, 26 J.L. & Econ. 613 (1983); R. Watts & J. Zimmerman, *The Market for Independence and Independent Auditors,* Working Paper No. GPB 80–10, University of Rochester Center for Research in Government Policy & Business (Mar.1981); Wilson, *Auditing: Perspectives from Multi-Person Decision Theory,* 58 Acctng.Rev. 305 (1983).

[100] See J. Freund, supra at 301–04.

[101] See Bermant, supra at 190; *California State Bar Report,* supra at 1012.

[102] Prior to 1971, the language of the accountants' cold comfort letter was quite similar to that of the lawyers' opinion: Based on a limited review, nothing had come to their attention that gave them reason to believe that there had been any material adverse change in the company's financial position. This correspondence changed with the issuance of Statement on Auditing Procedures No. 48 (October, 1971), codified as American Institute of Certified Public Accountants, Statements on Auditing Standards § 630 (1973), which limits the letter to identifying decreases in the amounts of specified items—such as net current assets, net sales and net assets. See J. Freund, supra at 302–03.

[103] There is also a small risk of liability based on the rendering of an incorrect opinion. The standards for the imposition of liability to third parties based on incorrect legal opinions are discussed in, e.g., *California State Bar Report,* supra note 89, at 1006–07; Fuld, *Lawyers' Standards and Responsibilities in Rendering Opinions,* 33 Bus.Law. 1295 (1978). It is also interesting that the legal profession has developed ethical prohibitions barring misrepresentation of facts by lawyers. See *Model Rules of Professional Conduct* ¶ 4.1 (1983) (a lawyer shall not knowingly make a false statement of material fact to a third person or fail to disclose a material fact when nondisclosure would be equivalent to a material misrepresentation). This prohibition may be best understood as an effort to extend a reputational role to lawyers generally, by reducing the incentives for a lawyer to free ride—by making misrepresentations to help a client—because he did not bear the full cost of the reduction in the profession's reputation that would result from his action.

[104] The importance of the lawyer's reputation in shaping the character of the expected opinion can be clearly seen in the familiar debate over from whom the ac-

comfort letter adds no new facts to those that have already been produced by means of the target's representations and warranties; the accountant's letter adds only the imprimatur of a respectable third party by attesting to the accuracy of the information produced by the target.

The care with which both of these third-party opinions are qualified further demonstrates their information-verification function. The lawyer's opinion typically will state explicitly that the firm has made no independent investigation of the facts—i.e., that it has engaged in no information production concerning the accuracy of the information provided by the target.[105] The accountant's opinion, in turn, will set out in detail the procedures that were undertaken, and stress that they are far more limited than what would be required for an audit.[106]

C. Normative Implications: How to Create Value

In Section B. of this Chapter, we examined the central elements of a typical corporate acquisition agreement for evidence that business lawyers do serve as transaction cost engineers, and that this function has the potential for creating value. If business lawyers do act to bridge the gap between the perfect market assumptions of capital asset pricing theory and the drastically less-than-perfect market conditions of the world in which transactions actually take place, this activity should be visible from examination of a by now standardized document—the acquisition agreement—that creates the structure for the transfer of a significant capital asset. From this perspective, the traditional contractual approaches reflected in the agreement should act to ameliorate the failure of one or more of the key perfect market assumptions.

We found, consistent with the transaction cost engineer hypothesis, that important elements of the acquisition agreement serve to remedy failures of the perfect market assumptions on which capital asset

---

quirer will accept an opinion on behalf of the target. For example, acquirers will frequently object to receiving the opinion of the target's in-house counsel with respect to certain items. Identifying the matters for which the acquirer will or will not accept the opinion of the target's in-house counsel is a good way to distinguish those aspects of the opinion of counsel that serve primarily an information-production function from those that serve primarily a verification function. In-house counsel will often have a cost advantage with respect to the information-production function because of their more intimate knowledge of their client. With respect to the verification function, however, the ability to serve as a reputational intermediary requires a sufficient diversity of clients such that a penalty will be imposed in future dealings if the intermediary cheats. See Gilson & Mnookin, supra at 368. As a result, opinions that serve a verification function are largely limited to outside counsel, while those that serve an information-production function are often accepted from in-house counsel.

Similarly, where the target's counsel wishes to deliver the opinion of another lawyer, as with respect to a matter governed by the law of a foreign jurisdiction, the acquirer often will require either that the target's counsel nonetheless render his opinion, albeit with explicit reference to reliance on the supplemental opinion, or give the opinion that the acquirer is justified in relying on the supplemental opinion. See J. Freund, supra at 310–11. Here the underlying assumption seems to be that an out-of-state lawyer is not likely to be a repeat player in the acquirer's state and, thus, has not really put his reputation at stake. This analysis would suggest that when a "national" firm renders a foreign law opinion, the acquirer would not require a covering opinion by the target's counsel.

[105] See *California State Bar Report,* supra at 1012.

[106] See American Institute of Certified Public Accountants, Statement on Auditing Standards ¶ 630 (1973).

pricing theory is based. Earnout or contingent pricing techniques respond to the failure of the homogeneous expectations assumption; controls over operation of the target's business during the period in which the determinants of the contingent price are measured respond to the failure of the common-time-horizon assumption; and the panoply of representations and warranties, together with provisions for indemnification and other verification techniques, respond to the failure of the costless-information assumption.

The next step is to emphasize the normative implications of identifying how a business lawyer can create value. The discussion of the acquisition agreement in Sections A. and B. of this Chapter highlighted a variety of ways in which recognition of the business lawyer's transaction cost engineering role and its theoretical underpinnings can make devising and negotiating responses to market imperfections easier and more effective. For example, understanding the function of the different elements of the agreement exposed the cooperative character of some matters—like warranties and indemnification—that traditionally have been considered as involving only distributive bargaining. Similarly, understanding the function of the variety of knowledge qualifications found in typical representations and warranties suggests a more effective way of achieving that end.

An additional value to understanding the theoretical underpinnings of transactional structure should also be stressed. Theory is an extremely efficient way of conveying and storing information. Suppose a client asks a lawyer to represent him in a transaction. One way the lawyer might analyze the transaction is first to categorize it—as a corporate, or real estate, or venture capital deal—and then look to alternative structural techniques commonly used in the relevant category. More prosaicly, the lawyer would look in the index to his firm's form file under the heading of the category of the particular transaction. Because this approach treats each technique as unique to a category—solutions used in venture capital deals—it requires the lawyer to learn and retain an amount of information equal to the sum of the techniques available in each category. A transaction cost engineering approach to the analysis defines structural techniques in a way—as responses to failures of perfect market assumptions—that they are applicable to all categories of transactions. One thus analyzes a transaction by, for example, first locating the inevitable information-cost problem and then selecting an information-cost technique to solve it, rather than by pigeonholing the transaction and then limiting the techniques considered to those traditionally associated with a particular category. Not only does this approach make it easier to teach new lawyers how to analyze a transaction, but it also facilitates creative responses to new forms of transactions that do not fit within traditional categories.

A final point should also be stressed. We have focused in this Chapter on bringing capital asset pricing theory to bear on the general structure of the acquisition agreement. It can also have significant value in shaping the substance of the transaction itself. Suppose the seller of a business agrees to take an installment note as part of the consideration to be received. In the absence of a market for that note, so that it can be sold and the proceeds invested in a diversified portfolio, capital asset pricing theory tells us that the seller bears more than systematic risk; he bears the unsystematic, firm specific, risk that the buyer will default. If that risk can be eliminated, the value of the installment note to the seller will be increased; the lawyer will have created value. How should the seller's lawyer determine what kind of security best protects the seller against the risk of default? Understanding that the problem is one of portfolio diversification facilitates design of an appropriate transactional structure. The seller in the first instance holds a portfolio composed of a single asset: The buyer's note. The analytic problem is devising additional assets that can be added to the portfolio so as to cause its value to be invariant to the buyer's default.

The importance of understanding the opportunity for business lawyers to create value by acting as transaction cost engineers is underscored by recognition that this function is not traditionally "legal," nor are there any special requirements peculiar to lawyers necessary to play this role. One need not be able to recite ancient Latin incantations to bless the union of the parties' interests through exchange.[107] The fact is that formal distinctions between professions which protected the lawyer's central role in transactional structuring have been and are likely to continue to break down.[108] There has been a substantial growth in competition for transactional responsibility—not among lawyers, although that, to be sure, has also grown—but with other professions. Increasingly, other institutions, like investment banking and public accounting firms, are recognizing that the role of transaction cost engineer, long dominated by the legal profession,[109] is contestable. Even if the imprimatur of a lawyer remains necessary to convince a client that all bases have been touched, lawyers can be employed by investment banking and accounting firms without fear of being charged with unlawful practice.[110] In a competitive market, those who are best succeed. Bringing theory to bear on practice can make business lawyers better at what they do.

[107] One might, however, need a license; legislation providing that only a lawyer can provide a specified service may result in lawyers providing the service even though non-lawyers could also provide it. See Rhode, *Policing the Professional Monopoly: A Constitutional and Empirical Analysis of Unauthorized Practice Prohibitions,* 34 Stan.L.Rev. 1 (1981). Yet the very fact that non-lawyers could provide the service belies the fact that it is peculiarly legal. In any event, such restrictive licensing regimes have not been the basis for direct protection of the lawyer's role as transaction cost engineer.

[108] James Freund has noted this blurring of professional roles in an acquisition setting:

There is a great intermeshing of disciplines in connection with a merger negotiation. My experience is that everyone else involved—accountants, businessmen, investment bankers—contributes ideas that could be termed "legal," while the

lawyer himself is frequently pointing out considerations that could be considered "accounting" or "business" or "financial."

J. Freund, supra at 4–5.

[109] See Gilson, *Value Creation by Business Lawyers: Legal Skills and Asset Pricing,* 94 Yale L.J. 239, 296–300 (1984).

[110] For example, in the area of corporate acquisitions, Bruce Wasserstein, formerly a lawyer at Cravath, Swaine & Moore, heads First Boston's mergers and acquisitions department. Bruce A. Mann, formerly a partner at Pillsbury, Madison & Sutro; Charles Nathan, until recently a partner at Cleary, Gottlieb, Steen & Hamilton; and Allen Finkelson, previously a partner at Cravath, Swaine & Moore, hold similar positions at L.F. Rothchild, Unterberg, Towbin, A.G. Becker Paribas, Inc., and Lehman Brothers Kuhn Loeb, Inc. Lempert, *Business Lures Lawyers From Law,* Legal Times, Mar. 5, 1984, at 1, col. 6.

APPENDIX A

SELECTED PROVISIONS OF THE SECURITIES EXCHANGE ACT OF 1934 AND RELATED REGULATIONS

Table of Contents

SECTIONS 13(d), (e), (f) and (g)

(d)(1) Any person who, after acquiring directly or indirectly the beneficial ownership of any equity security of a class which is registered pursuant to section 12 of this title, or any equity security of an insurance company which would have been required to be so registered except for the exemption contained in section 12(g)(2)(G) of this title, or any equity security issued by a closed-end investment company registered under the Investment Company Act of 1940, is directly or indirectly the beneficial owner of more than 5 per centum of such class shall, within ten days after such acquisition, send to the issuer of the security at its principal executive office, by registered or certified mail, send to each exchange where the security is traded, and file with the Commission, a statement containing such of the following information, and such additional information, as the Commission may by rules and regulations prescribe as necessary or appropriate in the public interest or for the protection of investors—

* (A) the background, and identity, residence, and citizenship of, and the nature of such beneficial ownership by, such person and all other persons by whom or on whose behalf the purchases have been or are to be effected;

(B) the source and amount of the funds or other consideration used or to be used in making the purchases, and if any part of the purchase price is represented or is to be represented by funds or other consideration borrowed or otherwise obtained for the purpose of acquiring, holding, or trading such security, a description of the transaction and the names of the parties thereto, except that where a source of funds is a loan made in the ordinary course of business by a bank, as defined in section 3(a)(6) of this title, if the person filing such statement so requests, the name of the bank shall not be made available to the public;

(C) if the purpose of the purchases or prospective purchases is to acquire control of the business of the issuer of the securities, any plans or proposals which such persons may have to liquidate such issuer, to sell its assets to or merge it with any other persons, or to make any other major change in its business or corporate structure;

(D) the number of shares of such security which are beneficially owned, and the number of shares concerning which there is a right to acquire, directly or indirectly, by (i) such person, and (ii) by each associate of such person, giving the background, identity, residence, and citizenship of each such associate; and

(E) information as to any contracts, arrangements, or understandings with any person with respect to any securities of the issuer, including but not limited to transfer of any of the securities, joint ventures, loan or option arrangements, puts or calls, guaranties of loans, guaranties against loss or guaranties of profits, division of losses or profits, or the giving or withholding of proxies, naming the persons with whom such contracts, arrangements, or understandings have been entered into, and giving the details thereof.

(2) If any material change occurs in the facts set forth in the statements to the issuer and the exchange, and in the statement filed with the Commission, an amendment shall be transmitted to the issuer and the exchange and shall be filed with the Commission, in accordance with such rules and regulations as the Commission may prescribe as necessary or appropriate in the public interest or for the protection of investors.

(3) When two or more persons act as a partnership, limited partnership, syndicate, or other group for the purpose of acquiring, holding, or disposing of securities of an issuer, such syndicate or group shall be deemed a "person" for the purposes of this subsection.

(4) In determining, for purposes of this subsection, any percentage of a class of any security, such class shall be deemed to consist of the amount of the outstanding securities of such class, exclusive of any securities of such class held by or for the account of the issuer or a subsidiary of the issuer.

(5) The Commission, by rule or regulation or by order, may permit any person to file in lieu of the statement required by paragraph (1) of this subsection or the rules and regulations thereunder, a notice stating the name of such person, the number of shares of any equity securities subject to paragraph (1) which are owned by him, the date of their acquisition and such other information as the Commission may specify, if it appears to the Commission that such securities were acquired by such person in the ordinary course of his business and were not acquired for the purpose of and do not have the effect of changing or influencing the control of the issuer nor in connection with or as a participant in any transaction having such purpose or effect.

(6) The provisions of this subsection shall not apply to—

(A) any acquisition or offer to acquire securities made or proposed to be made by means of a registration statement under the Securities Act of 1933;

(B) any acquisition of the beneficial ownership of a security which, together with all other acquisitions by the same person of securities of the same class during the preceding twelve months, does not exceed 2 per centum of that class;

(C) any acquisition of an equity security by the issuer of such security;

(D) any acquisition or proposed acquisition of a security which the Commission, by rules or regulations or by order, shall exempt from the provisions of this subsection as not entered into for the purpose of, and not having the effect of, changing or influencing the control of the issuer or otherwise as not comprehended within the purposes of this subsection.

(e)(1) It shall be unlawful for an issuer which has a class of equity securities registered pursuant to section 12 of this title, or which is a closed-end investment company registered under the Investment Company Act of 1940, to purchase any equity security issued by it if such purchase as in contravention of such rules and regulations as the Commission, in the public interest or for the protection of investors, may adopt (A) to define acts and practices which are fraudulent, deceptive, or manipulative, and (B) to prescribe means reasonably designed to prevent such acts and practices. Such rules and regulations may require such issuer to provide holders of equity securities of such class with such information relating to the reasons for such purchase, the source of funds, the number of shares to be purchased, the price to be paid for such securities, the method of purchase, and such additional information, as the Commission deems necessary or appropriate in the public interest or for the protection of investors, or which the Commission deems to be material to a determination whether such security should be sold.

(2) For the purpose of this subsection, a purchase by or for the issuer or any person controlling, controlled by, or under common control with the issuer, or a purchase subject to control of the issuer or any such person, shall be deemed to be a purchase by the issuer. The Commission shall have power to make rules and regulations implementing this paragraph in the public interest and for the protection of investors, including exemptive rules and regulations covering situations in which the Commission deems it unnecessary or inappropriate that a purchase of the type described in this paragraph shall be deemed to be a purchase by the issuer for purposes of some or all of the provisions of paragraph (1) of this subsection.

(3) At the time of filing such statement as the Commission may require by rule pursuant to paragraph (1) of this subsection, the person making the filing shall pay to the Commission a fee of $\frac{1}{50}$ of 1 per centum of the value of securities proposed to be purchased. The fee shall be reduced with respect to securities in an amount equal to any fee paid with respect to any securities issued in connection with the proposed transaction under section 6(b) of the Securities Act of 1933, or the fee paid under that section shall be reduced in an amount equal to the fee paid to the Commission in connection with such transaction under this paragraph.

(f)(1) Every institutional investment manager which uses the mails, or any means or instrumentality of interstate commerce in the course of its business as an institutional investment manager and which exercises investment discretion with respect to accounts holding equity securities of a class described in section 13(d)(1) of this title having an aggregate fair market value on the last trading day in any of the preceding twelve months of at least $100,000,000 or such lesser amount (but in no case less than $10,000,000) as the Commission, by rule, may determine, shall file reports with the Commission in such form, for such periods, and at such times after the end of such periods as the

Commission, by rule, may prescribe, but in no event shall such reports be filed for periods longer than one year or shorter than one quarter. Such reports shall include for each such equity security held on the last day of the reporting period by accounts (in aggregate or by type as the Commission, by rule, may prescribe) with respect to which the institutional investment manager exercises investment discretion (other than securities held in amounts which the Commission, by rule, determines to be insignificant for purposes of this subsection), the name of the issuer and the title, class, CUSIP number, number of shares or principal amount, and aggregate fair market value of each such security. Such reports may also include for accounts (in aggregate or by type) with respect to which the institutional investment manager exercises investment discretion such of the following information as the Commission, by rule, prescribes—

(A) the name of the issuer and the title, class, CUSIP number, number of shares or principal amount, and aggregate fair market value or cost or amortized cost of each other security (other than an exempted security) held on the last day of the reporting period by such accounts;

(B) the aggregate fair market value or cost or amortized cost of exempted securities (in aggregate or by class) held on the last day of the reporting period by such accounts;

(C) the number of shares of each equity security of a class described in section 13(d)(1) of this title held on the last day of the reporting period by such accounts with respect to which the institutional investment manager possesses sole or shared authority to exercise the voting rights evidenced by such securities;

(D) the aggregate purchases and aggregate sales during the reporting period of each security (other than an exempted security) effected by or for such accounts; and

(E) with respect to any transaction or series of transactions having a market value of at least $500,000 or such other amount as the Commission, by rule, may determine, effected during the reporting period by or for such accounts in any equity security of a class described in section 13(d)(1) of this title—

(i) the name of the issuer and the title, class, and CUSIP number of the security;

(ii) the number of shares or principal amount of the security involved in the transaction;

(iii) whether the transaction was a purchase or sale;

(iv) the per share price or prices at which the transaction was effected;

(v) the date or dates of the transaction;

(vi) the date or dates of the settlement of the transaction;

(vii) the broker or dealer through whom the transaction was effected;

(viii) the market or markets in which the transaction was effected; and

(ix) such other related information as the Commission, by rule, may prescribe.

(2) The Commission, by rule or order, may exempt, conditionally or unconditionally, any institutional investment manager or security or any class of institutional investment managers or securities from any or all of the provisions of this subsection or the rules thereunder.

* * *

(4) In exercising its authority under this subsection, the Commission shall determine (and so state) that its action is necessary or appropriate in the public interest and for the protection of investors or to maintain fair and orderly markets or, in granting an exemption, that its action is consistent with the protection of investors and the purposes of this subsection. In exercising such authority the Commission shall take such steps as are within its power, including consulting with the Comptroller General of the United States, the Director of the Office of Management and Budget, the appropriate regulatory agencies, Federal and State authorities which, directly or indirectly, require reports from institutional investment managers of information substantially similar to that called for by this subsection, national securities exchanges, and registered securities associations, (A) to achieve uniform, centralized reporting of information concerning the securities holdings of and transactions by or for accounts with respect to which institutional investment managers exercise investment discretion, and (B) consistently with the objective set forth in the preceding subparagraph, to avoid unnecessarily duplicative reporting by, and minimize the compliance burden on, institutional investment managers. Federal authorities which, directly or indirectly, require reports from institutional investment managers of information substantially similar to that called for by this subsection shall cooperate with the Commission in the performance of its responsibilities under the preceding sentence. An institutional investment manager which is a bank, the deposits of which are insured in accordance with the Federal Deposit Insurance Act, shall file with the appropriate regulatory agency a copy of every report filed with the Commission pursuant to this subsection.

(5)(A) For purposes of this subsection the term "institutional investment manager" includes any person, other than a natural person, investing in or buying and selling securities for its own account, and any person exercising investment discretion with respect to the account of any other person.

(B) The Commission shall adopt such rules as it deems necessary or appropriate to prevent duplicative reporting pursuant to this subsection by two or more institutional investment managers exercising investment discretion with respect to the same amount.

(g)(1) Any person who is directly or indirectly the beneficial owner of more than 5 per centum of any security of a class described in subsection (d)(1) of this section shall send to the issuer of the security and shall file with the Commission a statement setting forth, in such form and at such time as the Commission may, by rule, prescribe—

(A) such person's identity, residence, and citizenship; and

(B) the number and description of the shares in which such person has an interest and the nature of such interest.

(2) If any material change occurs in the facts set forth in the statement sent to the issuer and filed with the Commission, an amendment shall be transmitted to the issuer and shall be filed with the Commission, in accordance with such rules and regulations as the Commission may prescribe as necessary or appropriate in the public interest or for the protection of investors.

(3) When two or more persons act as a partnership, limited partnership, syndicate, or other group for the purpose of acquiring, holding, or disposing of securities of an issuer, such syndicate or group shall be deemed a "person" for the purposes of this subsection.

(4) In determining, for purposes of this subsection, any percentage of a class of any security, such class shall be deemed to consist of the amount of the outstanding securities of such class, exclusive of any securities of such class held by or for the account of the issuer or a subsidiary of the issuer.

(5) In exercising its authority under this subsection, the Commission shall take such steps as it deems necessary or appropriate in the public interest or for the protection of investors (A) to achieve centralized reporting of information regarding ownership, (B) to avoid unnecessarily duplicative reporting by and minimize the compliance burden on persons required to report, and (C) to tabulate and promptly make available the information contained in any report filed pursuant to this subsection in a manner which will, in the view of the Commission, maximize the usefulness of the information to other Federal and State agencies and the public.

(6) The Commission may, by rule or order, exempt, in whole or in part, any person or class of persons from any or all of the reporting requirements of this subsection as it deems necessary or appropriate in the public interest or for the protection of investors.

* * *

REGULATION 13D–G

Rule 13d–1. Filing of Schedule 13D and 13G

(a) Any person who, after acquiring directly or indirectly the beneficial ownership of any equity security of a class which is specified in paragraph (d), is directly or indirectly the beneficial owner of more than 5 percent of such class shall, within 10 days after such acquisition, send to the issuer of the security at its principal executive office, by registered or certified mail, and to each exchange where the security is traded, and file with the Commission, a statement containing the information required by Schedule 13D. Six copies of the statement, including all exhibits, shall be filed with the Commission.

(b)(1) A person who would otherwise be obligated under paragraph (a) to file a statement on Schedule 13D may, in lieu thereof, file with the Commission, within 45 days after the end of the calendar year in which such person became so obligated, six copies, including all exhibits, of a short form statement on Schedule 13G and send one copy each of such schedule to the issuer of the security at its principal executive office, by registered or certified mail, and to the principal national securities exchange where the security is traded: *Provided,* That it shall not be necessary to file a Schedule 13G unless the percentage of the class of equity security specified in paragraph (d) of this section beneficially owned as of the end of the calendar year is more than 5 percent: *And provided further,* That:

(i) Such person has acquired such securities in the ordinary course of his business and not with the purpose nor with the effect of changing or influencing the control of the issuer, nor in connection with or as a participant in any transaction having such purpose or effect, including any transaction subject to Rule 13d–3(b); and

(ii) Such person is:

(A) A broker or dealer registered under section 15 of the Act;

(B) A bank as defined in Section 3(a)(6) of the Act;

(C) An insurance company as defined in Section 3(a)(19) of the Act;

(D) An investment company registered under Section 8 of the Investment Company Act of 1940;

(E) An investment adviser registered under Section 203 of the Investment Advisers Act of 1940;

(F) An employee benefit plan, or pension fund which is subject to the provisions of the Employee Retirement Income Security Act of 1974 ("ERISA") or an endowment fund;

(G) A parent holding company, provided the aggregate amount held directly by the parent, and directly and indirectly by its subsidiaries which are not persons specified in Rule 13d–1(b)(ii)(A) through (F), does not exceed one percent of the securities of the subject class;

(H) A group, provided that all the members are persons specified in Rule 13d–1(b)(1)(ii)(A) through (G); and

(iii) Such person has promptly notified any other person (or group within the meaning of Section 13(d)(3) of the Act) on whose behalf it holds, on a discretionary basis, securities exceeding five percent of the class, of any acquisition or transaction on behalf of such other person which might be reportable by the person under Section 13(d) of the Act. This paragraph only requires notice to the account owner of information which the filing person reasonably should be expected to know and which would advise the account owner of an obligation he may have to file a statement pursuant to Section 13(d) of the Act or an amendment thereto.

(2) Any person relying on Rules 13d–1(b)(1) and 13d–2(b) shall, in addition to filing any statements required thereunder, file a statement on Schedule 13G, within ten days after the end of the first month in which such person's direct or indirect beneficial ownership exceeds ten percent of a class of equity securities specified in Rule 13d–1(c) computed as of the last day of the month, and thereafter within ten days after the end of any month in which such person's beneficial ownership of securities of such class, computed as of the last day of the month, increases or decreases by more than five percent of such class of equity securities. Six copies of such statement, including all exhibits, shall be filed with the Commission and one each sent, by registered or certified mail, to the issuer of the security at its principal executive office and to the principal national securities exchange where the security is traded. Once an amendment has been filed reflecting beneficial ownership of five percent or less of the class of securities, no additional filings are required by this paragraph (b)(2) unless the person thereafter becomes the beneficial owner of more than ten percent of the class and is required to file pursuant to this provision.

(3)(i) Notwithstanding paragraphs (b)(1) and (2) and Rule 13d–2(b), a person shall immediately become subject to Rules 13d–1(a) and 13d–2(a) and shall promptly, but not more than 10 days later, file a statement on Schedule 13D if such person:

(A) Has reported that it is the beneficial owner of more than five percent of a class of equity securities in a statement on Schedule 13G pursuant to paragraph (b)(1) or (b)(2), or is required to report such acquisition but has not yet filed the schedule;

(B) Determines that it no longer has acquired or holds such securities in the ordinary course of business or not with the purpose nor with the effect of changing or influencing the control of the issuer, nor in connection with or as a participant in any transaction having such purpose or effect, including any transaction subject to Rule 13d–3(b); and

(C) is at that time the beneficial owner of more than five percent of a class of equity securities described in Rule 13d–1(c).

(ii) For the ten day period immediately following the date of the filing of a Schedule 13D pursuant to this paragraph (b)(3), such person shall not: (A) Vote or direct the voting of the securities described in paragraph (b)(3)(i)(A); nor, (B) Acquire an additional beneficial ownership interest in any equity securities of the issuer of such securities, nor of any person controlling such issuer.

(4) Any person who has reported an acquisition of securities in a statement on Schedule 13G pursuant to paragraph (b)(1) or (b)(2) and thereafter ceases to be a person specified in paragraph (b)(1)(ii) shall immediately become subject to Rules 13d–1(a) and 13d–2(a) and shall file, within ten days thereafter, a statement on Schedule 13D, in the

event such person is a beneficial owner at that time of more than five percent of the class of equity securities.

(c) Any person who, as of December 31, 1978, or as of the end of any calendar year thereafter, is directly or indirectly the beneficial owner of more than 5 percent of any equity security of a class specified in paragraph (d) and who is not required to file a statement under paragraph (a) by virtue of the exemption provided by Section 13(d)(6)(A) or (B) of the Act, or because such beneficial ownership was acquired prior to December 20, 1970, or because such person otherwise (except for the exemption provided by Section 13(d)(6)(c) of the Act) is not required to file such statement, shall, within 45 days after the end of the calendar year in which such person became obligated to report under this paragraph, send to the issuer of the security at its principal executive office, by registered or certified mail, and file with the Commission a statement containing the information required by Schedule 13G. Six copies of the statement, including all exhibits, shall be filed with the Commission.

(d) For the purpose of this regulation, the term "equity security" means any equity security of a class which is registered pursuant to Section 12 of that Act, or any equity security of any insurance company which would have been required to be so registered except for the exemption contained in Section 12(g)(2)(G) of the Act, or any equity security issued by a closed-end investment company registered under the Investment Company Act of 1940; *Provided,* Such term shall not include securities of a class of non-voting securities.

(e) For the purpose of Sections 13(d) and 13(g), any person, in determining the amount of outstanding securities of a class of equity securities, may rely upon information set forth in the issuer's most recent quarterly or annual report, and any current report subsequent thereto, filed with the Commission pursuant to this Act, unless he knows or has reason to believe that the information contained therein is inaccurate.

* * *

Rule 13d–2. Filing of Amendments to Schedules 13D or 13G

(a) *Schedule 13D.* If any material change occurs in the facts set forth in the statement required by Rule 13d–1(a), including, but not limited to, any material increase or decrease in the percentage of the class beneficially owned, the person or persons who were required to file such statement shall promptly file or cause to be filed with the Commission and send or cause to be sent to the issuer at its principal executive office, by registered or certified mail, and to each exchange on which the security is traded an amendment disclosing such change. An acquisition or disposition of beneficial ownership of securities in an amount equal to one percent or more of the class of securities shall be deemed "material" for purposes of this rule; acquisitions or dispositions of less than such amounts may be material, depending upon the facts and circumstances. Six copies of each such amendment shall be filed with the Commission.

(b) *Schedule 13G.* Notwithstanding paragraph (a) of this rule, and provided that the person or persons filing a statement pursuant to Rule 13d–1(b) continues to meet the requirements set forth therein, any person who has filed a short form statement on Schedule 13G shall amend such statement within forty-five days after the end of each calendar year if, as of the end of such calendar year, there are any changes in the information reported in the previous filing on that Schedule; *Provided, however,* that such amendment need not be filed with respect to a change in the percent of class outstanding previously reported if such change results solely from a change in the aggregate number of securities outstanding. Six copies of such amendment, including all exhibits, shall be filed with the Commission and one each sent, by registered or certified mail, to the issuer of the security at its principal executive office and to the principal national securities exchange where the security is traded. Once an amendment has been filed reflecting beneficial ownership of five percent or less of the class of securities, no additional filings are required unless the person thereafter becomes the beneficial owner of more than five percent of the class and is required to file pursuant to Rule 13d–1.

NOTE: For persons filing a short form statement pursuant to Rule 13d–1(b), See also Rule 13d–1(b)(2), (3) and (4).

Rule 13d–3. Determination of Beneficial Owner

(a) For the purposes of section 13(d) and 13(g) of the Act a beneficial owner of a security includes any person who, directly or indirectly, through any contract, arrangement, understanding, relationship, or otherwise has or shares:

(1) *Voting power* which includes the power to vote, or to direct the voting of, such security; and/or,

(2) *Investment power* which includes the power to dispose, or to direct the disposition, of such security.

(b) Any person who, directly or indirectly, creates or uses a trust, proxy, power of attorney, pooling arrangement or any other contract, arrangement, or device with the purpose or effect of divesting such person of beneficial ownership of a security or preventing the vesting of such beneficial ownership as part of a plan or scheme to evade the reporting requirements of section 13(d) or 13(g) of the Act shall be deemed for purposes of such section to be the beneficial owner of such security.

(c) All securities of the same class beneficially owned by a person, regardless of the form which such beneficial ownership takes, shall be aggregated in calculating the number of shares beneficially owned by such person.

(d) Notwithstanding the provisions of paragraphs (a) and (c) of this rule:

(1)(i) A person shall be deemed to be the beneficial owner of a security, subject to the provisions of paragraph (b) of this rule, if that person has the right to acquire beneficial ownership of such security, as defined in Rule 13d–3(a) within sixty days, including but not limited to any right to acquire: (A) through the exercise of any option, warrant or right; (B) through the conversion of a security; (C) pursuant to the power to revoke a trust, discretionary account, or similar arrangement; or (D) pursuant to the automatic termination of a trust, discretionary account or similar arrangement; *Provided, however,* any person who acquires a security or power specified in paragraphs (A), (B) or (C), above, with the purpose or effect of changing or influencing the control of the issuer, or in connection with or as a participant in any transaction having such purpose or effect, immediately upon such acquisition shall be deemed to be the beneficial owner of the securities which may be acquired through the exercise or conversion of such security or power. Any securities not outstanding which are subject to such options, warrants, rights or conversion privileges shall be deemed to be outstanding for the purpose of computing the percentage of outstanding securities of the class owned by such person but shall not be deemed to be outstanding for the purpose of computing the percentage of the class by any other person.

(ii) Paragraph (i) remains applicable for the purpose of determining the obligation to file with respect to the underlying security even though the option, warrant, right or convertible security is of a class of equity security, as defined in Rule 13d–1(c), and may therefore give rise to a separate obligation to file.

(2) A member of a national securities exchange shall not be deemed to be a beneficial owner of securities held directly or indirectly by it on behalf of another person solely because such member is the record holder of such securities and, pursuant to the rules of such exchange, may direct the vote of such securities, without instruction, on other than contested matters or matters that may affect substantially the rights or privileges of the holders of the securities to be voted, but is otherwise precluded by the rules of such exchange from voting without instruction.

(3) A person who in the ordinary course of business is a pledgee of securities under a written pledge agreement shall not be deemed to be the beneficial owner of such pledged securities until the pledgee has taken all formal steps necessary which are required to declare a default and determines that the power to vote or to direct the vote or to dispose or to direct the disposition of such pledged securities will be exercised, provided that:

(i) The pledgee agreement is bona fide and was not entered into with the purpose nor with the effect of changing or influencing the control of the issuer, nor in connection with any transaction having such purpose or effect, including any transaction subject to Rule 13d–3(b);

(ii) The pledgee is a person specified in Rule 13d–1(b)(ii), including persons meeting the conditions set forth in paragraph (G) thereof; and

(iii) The pledgee agreement, prior to default, does not grant to the pledgee:

(A) The power to vote or to direct the vote of the pledged securities; or

(B) The power to dispose or direct the disposition of the pledged securities, other than the grant of such power(s) pursuant to a pledge agreement under which credit is extended subject to Regulation T and in which the pledgee is a broker or dealer registered under section 15 of the Act.

(4) A person engaged in business as an underwriter of securities who acquires securities through his participation in good faith in a firm commitment underwriting registered under the Securities Act of 1933 shall not be deemed to be the beneficial owner of such securities until the expiration of forty days after the date of such acquisition.

Rule 13d–4. Disclaimer of Beneficial Ownership

Any person may expressly declare in any statement filed that the filing of such statement shall not be construed as an admission that such person is, for the purposes of section 13(d) or 13(g) of the Act, the beneficial owner of any securities covered by the statement.

Rule 13d–5. Acquisition of Securities

(a) A person who becomes a beneficial owner of securities shall be deemed to have acquired such securities for purposes of Section 13(d)(1) of the Act, whether such acquisition was through purchase or otherwise. However, executors or administrators of a decedent's estate generally will be presumed not to have acquired beneficial ownership of the securities in the decedent's estate until such time as such executors or administrators are qualified under local law to perform their duties.

(b)(1) When two or more persons agree to act together for the purpose of acquiring, holding, voting or disposing of equity securities of an issuer, the group formed thereby shall be deemed to have acquired beneficial ownership, for purposes of Sections 13(d) and 13(g) of the Act, as of the date of such agreement, of all equity securities of that issuer beneficially owned by any such persons.

(2) Notwithstanding the previous paragraph, a group shall be deemed not to have acquired any equity securities beneficially owned by the other members of the group solely by virtue of their concerted actions relating to the purchase of equity securities directly from an issuer in a transaction not involving a public offering, provided that:

(i) All the members of the group are persons specified in Rule 13d–1(b)(1)(ii);

(ii) The purchase is in the ordinary course of each member's business and not with the purpose nor with the effect of changing or influencing control of the issuer, nor in connection with or as a participant in any transaction having such purpose or effect, including any transaction subject to Rule 13d–3(b);

(iii) There is no agreement among, or between any members of the group to act together with respect to the issuer or its securities except for the purpose of facilitating the specific purchase involved; and

(iv) The only actions among or between any members of the group with respect to the issuer or its securities subsequent to the closing date of the non-public offering are those which are necessary to conclude ministerial matters directly related to the completion of the offer or sale of the securities.

Rule 13d–6. Exemption of Certain Acquisitions

The acquisition of securities of an issuer by a person who, prior to such acquisition, was a beneficial owner of more than five percent of the outstanding securities of the same class as those acquired shall be exempt from section 13(d) of the act, *provided that:*

(a) The acquisition is made pursuant to preemptive subscription rights in an offering made to all holders of securities of the class to which the preemptive subscription rights pertain;

(b) Such person does not acquire additional securities except through the exercise of his pro rata share of the preemptive subscription rights; and

(c) The acquisition is duly reported, if required, pursuant to section 16(a) of the Act and the rules and regulations thereunder.

* * *

SCHEDULE 13D—INFORMATION TO BE INCLUDED IN STATEMENTS FILED PURSUANT TO RULE 13d–1(a) AND AMENDMENTS THERETO FILED PURSUANT TO RULE 13d–2(a)

* * *

GENERAL INSTRUCTIONS

* * *

C. If the statement is filed by a general or limited partnership, syndicate, or other group, the information called for by Items 2-6, inclusive, shall be given with respect to (i) each partner of such general partnership; (ii) each partner who is denominated as a general partner or who functions as a general partner of such limited partnership; (iii) each member of such syndicate or group; and (iv) each person controlling such partner or member. If the statement is filed by a corporation or if a person referred to in (i), (ii), (iii) or (iv) of this Instruction is a corporation, the information called for by the above mentioned items shall be given with respect to (a) each executive officer and director of such corporation; (b) each person controlling such corporation; and (c) each executive officer and director of any corporation or other person ultimately in control of such corporation.

Item 1. Security and Issuer

State the title of the class of equity securities to which this statement relates and the name and address of the principal executive offices of the issuer of such securities.

Item 2. Identity and Background

If the person filing this statement or any person enumerated in Instruction C of this statement is a corporation, general partnership, limited partnership, syndicate or other group of persons, state its name, the state or other place of its organization, its principal business, the address of its principal business, the address of its principal office and the information required by (d) and (e) of this Item. If the person filing this statement or any person enumerated in Instruction C is a natural person, provide the information specified in (a) through (f) of this Item with respect to such person(s).

(a) Name;

(b) Residence or business address;

(c) Present principal occupation or employment and the name, principal business and address of any corporation or other organization in which such employment is conducted;

(d) Whether or not, during the last five years, such person has been convicted in a criminal proceeding (excluding traffic violations or similar misdemeanors) and, if so, give the dates, nature of conviction, name and location of court, any penalty imposed, or other disposition of the case;

(e) Whether or not, during the last five years, such person was a party to a civil proceeding of a judicial or administrative body of competent jurisdiction and as a result of such proceeding was or is subject to a judgment, decree or final order enjoining future violations of, or prohibiting or mandating activities subject to, federal or state securities laws or finding any violation with respect to such laws; and, if so, identify and describe such proceedings and summarize the terms of such judgment, decree or final order; and

(f) Citizenship.

Item 3. Source and Amount of Funds or Other Consideration

State the source and the amount of funds or other consideration used or to be used in making the purchases, and if any part of the purchase price is or will be represented by funds or other consideration borrowed or otherwise obtained for the purpose of acquiring, holding, trading or voting the securities, a description of the transaction and the names of the parties thereto. Where material, such information should also be provided with respect to prior acquisitions not previously reported pursuant to this regulation. If the source of all or any part of the funds is a loan made in the ordinary course of business by a bank, as defined in Section 3(a)(6) of the Act, the name of the bank shall not be made available to the public if the person at the time of filing the statement so requests in writing and files such request, naming such bank, with the Secretary of the Commission. If the securities were acquired other than by purchase, describe the method of acquisition.

Item 4. Purpose of Transaction

State the purpose or purposes of the acquisition of securities of the issuer. Describe any plans or proposals which the reporting persons may have which relate to or would result in:

(a) The acquisition by any person of additional securities of the issuer, or the disposition of securities of the issuer;

(b) An extraordinary corporate transaction, such as a merger, reorganization or liquidation, involving the issuer or any of its subsidiaries;

(c) A sale or transfer of a material amount of assets of the issuer or of any of its subsidiaries;

(d) Any change in the present board of directors or management of the issuer, including any plans or proposals to change the number or term of directors or to fill any existing vacancies on the board;

(e) Any material change in the present capitalization or dividend policy of the issuer;

(f) Any other material change in the issuer's business or corporate structure, including but not limited to, if the issuer is a registered closed-end investment company, any plans or proposals to make any changes in its investment policy for which a vote is required by section 13 of the Investment Company Act of 1940;

(g) Changes in the issuer's charter, bylaws or instruments corresponding thereto or other actions which may impede the acquisition of control of the issuer by any person;

(h) Causing a class of securities of the issuer to be delisted from a national securities exchange or to cease to be authorized to be quoted in an inter-dealer quotation system of a registered national securities association;

(i) A class of equity securities of the issuer becoming eligible for termination of registration pursuant to Section 12(g)(4) of the Act; or

(j) Any action similar to any of those enumerated above.

Item 5. Interest in Securities of the Issuer

(a) State the aggregate number and percentage of the class of securities identified pursuant to Item 1 (which may be based on the number of securities outstanding as contained in the most recently available filing with the Commission by the issuer unless the filing person has reason to believe such information is not current) beneficial- ly owned (identifying those shares which there is a right to acquire) by each person named in Item 2. The above mentioned information should also be furnished with respect to persons who, together with any of the persons named in Item 2, comprise a group within the meaning of Section 13(d)(3) of the Act;

(b) For each person named in response to paragraph (a), indicate the number of shares as to which there is sole power to vote or to direct the vote, shared power to vote or to direct the vote, sole power to dispose or to direct the disposition. Provide the applicable information required by Item 2 with respect to each person with whom the power to vote or to direct the vote or to dispose or direct the disposition is shared;

(c) Describe any transactions in the class of securities reported on that were effected during the past sixty days or since the most recent filing on Schedule 13D (§ 240.13d–101), whichever is less, by the per- sons named in response to paragraph (a).

Instruction. The description of a transaction required by Item 5(c) shall include, but not necessarily be limited to: (1) the identity of the person covered by Item 5(c) who effected the transaction; (2) the date of the transaction; (3) the amount of securities involved; (4) the price per share or unit; and (5) where and how the transaction was effected.

(d) If any other person is known to have the right to receive or the power to direct the receipt of dividends from, or the proceeds from the sale of, such securities, a statement to that effect should be included in response to this time and, if such interest relates to more than five percent of the class, such person should be identified. A listing of the shareholders of an investment company registered under the Invest- ment Company Act of 1940 or the beneficiaries of an employee benefit plan, pension fund or endowment fund is not required.

(e) If applicable, state the date on which the reporting person ceased to be the beneficial owner of more than five percent of the class of securities.

Instruction. For computations regarding securities which repre- sent a right to acquire an underlying security, see Rule 13d–3(d)(1) and the note thereto.

Item 6. Contracts, Arrangements, Understandings or Relation- ships With Respect to Securities of the Issuer

Describe any contracts, arrangements, understandings or relation- ships (legal or otherwise) among the persons named in Item 2 and between such persons and any person with respect to any securities of the issuer, including but not limited to transfer or voting of any of the securities, finder's fees, joint ventures, loan or option arrangements, puts or calls, guarantees of profits, division of profits or loss, or the giving or withholding of proxies, naming the persons with whom such contracts, arrangements, understandings or relationships have been entered into. Include such information for any of the securities that are pledged or otherwise subject to a contingency the occurrence of which would give another person voting power or investment power over such securities except that disclosure of standard default and similar provisions contained in loan agreements need not be included.

Item 7. Material to Be Filed as Exhibits

The following shall be filed as exhibits: Copies of written agreements relating to the filing of joint acquisition statements as required by Rule 13d–1(f) (§ 240.13d–1(f)) and copies of all written agreements, contracts, arrangements, understandings, plans, or proposals relating to: (1) The borrowing of funds to finance the acquisition as disclosed in Item 3; (2) the acquisition of issuer control, liquidation, sale of assets, merger, or change in business or corporate structure, or any other matter as disclosed in Item 4; and (3) the transfer or voting of the securities, finder's fees, joint ventures, options, puts, calls, guarantees of loans, guarantees against loss or of profit, or the giving or withholding of any proxy as disclosed in Item 6.

*   *   *

Rule 13e–1. Purchase of Securities by Issuer Thereof

When a person other than the issuer makes a tender offer for, or request or invitation for tenders of, any class of equity securities of an issuer subject to section 13(e) of the Act, and such person has filed a statement with the Commission pursuant to Rule 14d–1 and the issuer has received notice thereof, such issuer shall not thereafter, during the period such tender offer, request or invitation continues, purchase any equity securities of which it is the issuer unless it has complied with both of the following conditions:

(a) The issuer has filed with the Commission eight copies of a statement containing the information specified below with respect to the proposed purchases:

(1) The title and amount of securities to be purchased, the names of the persons or classes of persons from whom, and the market in which, the securities are to be purchased, including the name of any exchange on which the purchase is to be made;

(2) The purpose for which the purchase is to be made and whether the securities are to be retired, held in the treasury of the issuer or otherwise disposed of, indicating such disposition; and

(3) The source and amount of funds or other consideration used or to be used in making the purchases, and if any part of

the purchase price or proposed purchase price is represented by funds or other consideration borrowed or otherwise obtained for the purpose of acquiring, holding, or trading the securities, a description of the transaction and the names of the parties thereto; and

(b) The issuer has at any time within the past 6 months sent or given to its equity security holders the substance of the information contained in the statement required by paragraph (a).

Provided, however, That any issuer making such purchases which commenced prior to July 30, 1968, shall, if such purchases continue after such date, comply with the provisions of this rule on or before August 12, 1968.

Rule 13e–3. Going Private Transactions by Certain Issuers or Their Affiliates

(a) *Definitions.* Unless indicated otherwise or the context otherwise requires, all terms used in this section and in Schedule 13E–3 shall have the same meaning as in the Act or elsewhere in the General Rules and Regulations thereunder. In addition, the following definitions apply:

(1) An "affiliate" of an issuer is a person that directly or indirectly through one or more intermediaries controls, is controlled by, or is under common control with such issuer. For the purposes of this section only, a person who is not an affiliate of an issuer at the commencement of such person's tender offer for a class of equity securities of such issuer will not be deemed an affiliate of such issuer prior to the stated termination of such tender offer and any extensions thereof;

(2) The term "purchase" means any acquisition for value including, but not limited to, (i) any acquisition pursuant to the dissolution of an issuer subsequent to the sale or other disposition of substantially all the assets of such issuer to its affiliate, (ii) any acquisition pursuant to a merger, (iii) any acquisition of fractional interests in connection with a reverse stock split, and (iv) any acquisition subject to the control of an issuer or an affiliate of such issuer;

(3) A "Rule 13e–3 transaction" is any transaction or series of transactions involving one or more of the transactions described in paragraph (a)(3)(i) of this section which has either a reasonable likelihood or a purpose of producing, either directly or indirectly, any of the effects described in paragraph (a)(3)(ii) of this section;

(i) The transactions referred to in paragraph (a)(3) of this section are:

(A) A purchase of any equity security by the issuer of such security or by an affiliate of such issuer;

(B) A tender offer for or request or invitation for tenders of any equity security made by the issuer of such class of securities or by an affiliate of such issuer; or

(C) A solicitation subject to Regulation 14A of any proxy, consent or authorization of, or a distribution subject to Regulation 14C of information statements to, any equity security holder by the issuer of the class of securities or by an affiliate of such issuer, in connection with: a merger, consolidation, reclassification, recapitalization, reorganization or similar corporate transaction of an issuer or between an issuer (or its subsidiaries) and its affiliate; a sale of substantially all the assets of an issuer to its affiliate or group of affiliates; or a reverse stock split of any class of equity securities of the issuer involving the purchase of fractional interests.

(ii) The effects referred to in paragraph (a)(3) of this section are:

(A) Causing any class of equity securities of the issuer which is subject to section 12(g) or section 15(d) or the Act to be held of record by less than 300 persons; or

(B) Causing any class of equity securities of the issuer which is either listed on a national securities exchange or authorized to be quoted in an inter-dealer quotation system of a registered national securities association to be neither listed on any national securities exchange nor authorized to be quoted on an inter-dealer quotation system of any registered national securities association.

(4) An "unaffiliated security holder" is any security holder of an equity security subject to a Rule 13e–3 transaction who is not an affiliate of the issuer of such security.

(b) *Application of Section to an Issuer (or an Affiliate of Such Issuer) Subject to Section 12 of the Act.*

(1) It shall be a fraudulent, deceptive or manipulative act or practice, in connection with a Rule 13e–3 transaction, for an issuer which has a class of equity securities registered pursuant to Section 12 of the Act or which is a closed-end investment company registered under the Investment Company Act of 1940, or an affiliate of such issuer, directly or indirectly

(i) To employ any device, scheme or artifice to defraud any person;

(ii) To make any untrue statement of a material fact or to omit to state a material fact necessary in order to make the statements made, in light of the circumstances under which they were made, not misleading; or

(iii) To engage in any act, practice or course of business which operates or would operate as a fraud or deceit upon any person.

(2) As a means reasonably designed to prevent fraudulent, deceptive or manipulative acts or practices in connection with any Rule 13e–3 transaction, it shall be unlawful for an issuer which has a class of equity securities registered pursuant to Section 12 of the Act, or an affiliate of such issuer, to engage, directly or indirectly, in a Rule 13e–3 transaction unless:

(i) Such issuer or affiliate complies with the requirements of paragraphs (d), (e) and (f) of this Section; and

(ii) The Rule 13e–3 transaction is not in violation of paragraph (b)(1) of this section.

(c) *Application of Section to an Issuer (or an Affiliate of Such Issuer) Subject to Section 15(d) of the Act.*

(1) It shall be unlawful as a fraudulent, deceptive or manipulative act or practice for an issuer which is required to file periodic reports pursuant to Section 15(d) of the Act, or an affiliate of such issuer, to engage, directly or indirectly, in a Rule 13e–3 transaction unless such issuer or affiliate complies with the requirements of paragraphs (d), (e) and (f) of this section.

(2) An issuer or affiliate which is subject to paragraph (c)(1) of this section and which is soliciting proxies or distributing information statements in connection with a transaction described in paragraph (a)(3)(i)(A) of this section may elect to use the timing procedures for conducting a solicitation subject to Regulation 14A (Rules 14a–1 to 14a–103) or a distribution subject to Regulation 14C (Rules 14c–1 to 14c–101) in complying with paragraphs (d), (e) and (f) of this section, *provided,* That if an election is made, such solicitation or distribution is conducted in accordance with the requirements of the respective regulations, including the filing of preliminary copies of soliciting materials or an information statement at the time specified in Regulation 14A or 14C, respectively.

(d) *Material Required to Be Filed.* The issuer or affiliate engaging in Rule 13e–3 transaction shall, in accordance with the General Instructions to the Rule 13e–3 Transaction Statement on Schedule 13E–3:

(1) File with the Commission eight copies of such schedule, including all exhibits thereto;

(2) Report any material change in the information set forth in such schedule by promptly filing with the Commission eight copies of an amendment on such schedule; and

(3) Report the results of the Rule 13e–3 transaction by filing with the Commission promptly but no later than ten days (ten business days if Rule 13e–4 is applicable) after the termination of such transaction eight copies of a final amendment to such schedule.

(e) *Disclosure of Certain Information.*

(1) The issuer or affiliate engaging in the Rule 13e–3 transaction, in addition to any other information required to be disclosed pursuant to any other applicable rule or regulation under the federal securities laws, shall disclose to security holders of the class of equity securities which is the subject of the transaction, in the manner prescribed by paragraph (f) of this section, the information required by Items 1, 2, 3, 4, 5, 6, 10, 11, 12, 13, 14, 15 and 16 of Schedule 13e–3, or a fair and adequate summary thereof, and Items 7, 8 and 9 and include in the document which contains such information the exhibit required by Item 17(e) of such Schedule. If the Rule 13e–3 transaction involves (i) a transaction subject to Regulation 14A or 14C of the Act, (ii) the registration of securities pursuant to the Securities Act of 1933 and the General Rules and Regulations promulgated thereunder, or (iii) a tender offer subject to Regulation 14D or Rule 13e–4 such information shall be included in the proxy statement, the information statement, the registration statement or the tender offer for or request or invitation for tenders of securities published, sent or given to security holders, respectively.

(2) If any material change occurs in the information previously disclosed to security holders of the class of equity securities which is the subject of the transaction, the issuer or affiliate shall promptly disclose such change to such security holders in the manner prescribed by paragraph (f) (iii) of this section.

(3) Any document transmitted to such security holders which contains the information required by paragraph (e)(1) of this section shall:

(i) set forth prominently the information required by Items 7, 8 and 9 of the Rule 13e–3 Transaction Statement on Schedule 13E–3 in a Special Factors section to be included in the forepart of such document; and

(ii) set forth on the outside front cover page, in capital letters printed in bold face roman type at least as large as ten point modern type and at least two points leaded, the statement in paragraph (e)(3)(ii)(A) of this section, if the Rule 13e–3 transaction does not involve a prospectus, or the statement in paragraph (e)(3)(ii)(B) of this section, if the Rule 13e–3 transaction involves a prospectus, and in the latter case such statement shall be used in lieu of that required by Item 501(c)(5) of Regulation S–K.

(A) THIS TRANSACTION HAS NOT BEEN APPROVED OR DISAPPROVED BY THE SECURITIES AND EXCHANGE COMMISSION NOR HAS THE COMMISSION PASSED UPON THE FAIRNESS OR MERITS OF SUCH TRANSACTION NOR UPON THE ACCURACY OR ADEQUACY OF THE INFORMATION CONTAINED

IN THIS DOCUMENT. ANY REPRESENTATION TO THE CONTRARY IS UNLAWFUL.

(B) NEITHER THIS TRANSACTION NOR THESE SECURITIES HAVE BEEN APPROVED OR DISAPPROVED BY THE SECURITIES AND EXCHANGE COMMISSION. THE COMMISSION HAS NOT PASSED UPON THE FAIRNESS OR MERITS OF THIS TRANSACTION NOR UPON THE ACCURACY OR ADEQUACY OF THE INFORMATION CONTAINED IN THIS PROSPECTUS. ANY REPRESENTATION TO THE CONTRARY IS UNLAWFUL.

* * *

(f) *Dissemination of Disclosure.*

(1) If the Rule 13e–3 transaction involves a purchase as described in paragraph (a)(3)(i)(A) of this section or a vote, consent, authorization, or distribution of information statements as described in paragraph (a)(3)(i)(C) of this section, the issuer or affiliate engaging in the Rule 13e–3 transaction shall:

(i) Provide the information required by paragraph (e) of this section: (A) in accordance with the provisions of any applicable federal or state law, but in no event later than 20 days prior to: any such purchase; any such vote, consent or authorization; or with respect to the distribution of information statements, the meeting date, or if corporate action is to be taken by means of the written authorization or consent of security holders, the earliest date on which corporate action may be taken: *Provided, however,* That if the purchase subject to this section is pursuant to a tender offer excepted from Rule 13e–4 by paragraph (g)(5) of Rule 13e–4, the information required by paragraph (e) of this section shall be disseminated in accordance with paragraph (e) of Rule 13e–4 no later than 10 business days prior to any purchase pursuant to such tender offer, (B) to each person who is a record holder of a class of equity security subject to the Rule 13e–3 transaction as of a date not more than 20 days prior to the date of dissemination of such information;

(ii) If the issuer or affiliate knows that securities of the class of securities subject to the Rule 13e–3 transaction are held of record by a broker, dealer, bank or voting trustee or their nominees, such issuer or affiliate shall (unless Rule 14a–3(d) or 14c–7 is applicable) furnish the number of copies of the information required by paragraph (e) of this section that are requested by such persons (pursuant to inquiries by or on behalf of the issuer or affiliate), instruct such persons to forward such information to the beneficial owners of such securities in a timely manner and undertake to pay the reasonable expenses incurred by such persons in forwarding such information; and

(iii) Promptly disseminate disclosure of material changes to the information required by paragraph (d) of this section in a manner reasonably calculated to inform security holders.

(2) If the Rule 13e–3 transaction is a tender offer or a request or invitation for tenders of equity securities which is subject to Regulation 14D or Rule 13e–4, the tender offer containing the information required by paragraph (e) of this section, and any material change with respect thereto, shall be published, sent or given in accordance with Regulation 14D or Rule 13e–4, respectively, to security holders of the class of securities being sought by the issuer or affiliate.

(g) *Exceptions.* This section shall not apply to:

(1) Any Rule 13e–3 transaction by or on behalf of a person which occurs within one year of the date of termination of a tender offer in which such person was the bidder and became an affiliate of the issuer as a result of such tender offer *provided* that the consideration offered to unaffiliated security holders in such Rule 13e–3 transaction is at least equal to the highest consideration offered during such tender offer and *provided further,* That:

(i) If such tender offer was made for any or all securities of a class of the issuer;

(A) Such tender offer fully disclosed such person's intention to engage in a Rule 13e–3 transaction, the form and effect of such transaction and, to the extent known, the proposed terms thereof; and

(B) Such Rule 13e–3 transaction is substantially similar to that described in such tender offer; or

(ii) If such tender offer was made for less than all the securities of a class of the issuer:

(A) Such tender offer fully disclosed a plan of merger, a plan of liquidation or a similar binding agreement between such person and the issuer with respect to a Rule 13e–3 transaction; and

(B) Such Rule 13e–3 transaction occurs pursuant to the plan of merger, plan of liquidation or similar binding agreement disclosed in the bidder's tender offer.

(2) Any Rule 13e–3 transaction in which the security holders are offered or receive only an equity security *provided,* That:

(i) such equity security has substantially the same rights as the equity security which is the subject of the Rule 13e–3 transaction including, but not limited to, voting, dividends, redemption and liquidation rights except that this requirement shall be deemed to be satisfied if unaffiliated security holders are offered common stock;

(ii) such equity security is registered pursuant to section 12 of the Act or reports are required to be filed by the issuer thereof pursuant to section 15(d) of the Act; and

(iii) if the security which is the subject of the Rule 13e–3 transaction was either listed on a national securities exchange or authorized to be quoted in an inter-dealer quotation system of a registered national securities association, such equity security is either listed on a national securities exchange or authorized to be quoted in an inter-dealer quotation system of a registered national securities association.

(3) Transactions by a holding company registered under the Public Utility Holding Company Act of 1935 in compliance with the provisions of that Act;

(4) Redemptions, calls or similar purchases of an equity security by an issuer pursuant to specific provisions set forth in the instrument(s) creating or governing that class of equity securities; or

(5) Any solicitation by an issuer with respect to a plan of reorganization under Chapter X of the Bankruptcy Act, as amended, if made after the entry of an order approving such plan pursuant to section 174 of that Act and after, or concurrently with, the transmittal of information concerning such plan as required by section 175 of the Act.

Rule 13e–100. Schedule 13E–3 Transaction Statement Pursuant to Section 13(e) of the Securities Exchange Act of 1934 and Rule 13e–3 Thereunder

* * *

GENERAL INSTRUCTIONS

* * *

C. If the statement is filed by a general or limited partnership, syndicate or other group the information called for by Items, 2, 3, 5, 6, 10, and 11 shall be given with respect to: (i) each partner of such general partnership; (ii) each partner who is denominated as a general partner or who functions as a general partner of such limited partnership; (iii) each member of such syndicate or group; and (iv) each person controlling such partner or member. If the statement is filed by a corporation or if a person referred to in (i), (ii), (iii) or (iv) of this Instruction is a corporation, the information called for by the above mentioned items shall be given with respect to: (a) each executive officer and director of such corporation; (b) each person controlling such corporation; and (c) each executive officer and director of any corporation ultimately in control of such corporation.

* * *

E. The information required by the items of this statement is intended to be in addition to any disclosure requirements of any other form or schedule which may be filed with the Commission in connection with the Rule 13e–3 transaction. To the extent that the disclosure requirements of this statement are inconsistent with the disclosure requirements of any such forms or schedules, the requirements of this statement are controlling.

F. If the Rule 13e–3 transaction involves a transaction subject to Regulation 14A of the Act, the registration of securities pursuant to the Securities Act of 1933 and the General Rules and Regulations promulgated thereunder, or a tender offer subject to Regulation 14D or Rule 13e–4, the information contained in the proxy or information statement, the registration statement, the Schedule 14D–1, or the Schedule 13E–4, respectively, which is filed with the Commission shall be incorporated by reference in answer to the items of this statement or amendments thereto; this statement shall include an express statement to that effect and a cross reference sheet showing the location in the proxy or information statement, the registration statement, the Schedule 14D–1 or the Schedule 13E–4 of the information required to be included in response to the items of this statement. If any such item is inapplicable or the answer thereto is in the negative and is omitted from the proxy or the information statement, the registration statement, the Schedule 14D–1, or the Schedule 13E–4, a statement to that effect shall be made in the cross reference sheet.

G. If the Rule 13e–3 transaction involves a proxy or an information statement subject to Regulation 14A or Regulation 14C and if preliminary copies of such materials have been incorporated by reference into this statement pursuant to Instruction F of this statement, this Schedule 13E–3 shall be deemed to constitute "Preliminary Copies" within the meaning of Rule 14a–6(e) and Rule 14c–5 and shall not be available for public inspection before an amendment to this statement containing definitive material has been filed with the Commission.

H. Amendments disclosing a material change in the information set forth in this statement may omit any information previously disclosed in this statement.

Item 1. Issuer and Class of Security Subject to the Transaction

(a) State the name of the issuer of the class of equity security which is the subject of the Rule 13e–3 transaction and the address of its principal executive offices.

(b) State the exact title, the amount of securities outstanding of the class of security which is the subject of the Rule 13e–3 transaction as of the most recent practicable date and the approximate number of holders of record of such class as of the most recent practicable date.

(c) Identify the principal market in which such securities are being traded and, if the principal market is an exchange, state the high and low sales prices for such securities as reported in the consolidated transaction reporting system or, if not so reported, on such principal exchange for each quarterly period during the past two years. If the principal market is not an exchange, state the range of high and low bid quotations for each quarterly period during the past two years, the source of such quotations and, if there is currently no established trading market for such securities (excluding limited or sporadic quotations); furnish a statement to that effect.

(d) State the frequency and amount of any dividends paid during the past two years with respect to such class of securities and briefly describe any restriction on the issuer's present or future ability to pay such dividends.

Instruction. If the person filing this statement is an affiliate of the issuer, the information required by Item 1(d) should be furnished to the extent known by such affiliate after making reasonable inquiry.

(e) If the issuer and/or affiliate filing this statement has made an underwritten public offering of such securities for cash during the past three years which was registered under the Securities Act of 1933 or exempt from registration thereunder pursuant to Regulation A, state the date of such offering, the amount of securities offered, the offering price per share (which should be appropriately adjusted for stock splits, stock dividends, etc.) and the aggregate proceeds received by such issuer and/or such affiliate.

(f) With respect to any purchases of such securities made by the issuer or affiliate since the commencement of the issuer's second full fiscal year preceding the date of this schedule, state the amount of such securities purchased, the range of prices paid for such securities and the average purchase price for each quarterly period of the issuer during such period.

Instruction. The information required by Item 1(f) need not be given with respect to purchases of such securities by a person prior to the time such person became an affiliate.

Item 2. Identity and Background

If the person filing this statement is the issuer of the class of equity securities which is the subject of the Rule 13e–3 transaction, make a statement to that effect. If this statement is being filed by an affiliate of the issuer which is other than a natural person or if any person enumerated in Instruction C to this statement is a corporation, general partnership, limited partnership, syndicate or other group of persons, state its name, the state or other place of its organization, its principal business, the address of its principal executive offices and provide the information required by (e) and (f) of this Item. If this statement is being filed by an affiliate of the issuer who is a natural person or if any person enumerated in Instruction C of this statement is a natural person, provide the information required by (a) through (g) of this Item with respect to such person(s).

(a) Name;

(b) Residence or business address;

(c) Present principal occupation or employment and the name, principal business and address of any corporation or other organization in which such employment or occupation is conducted;

(d) Material occupations, positions, offices or employments during the last 5 years, giving the starting and ending dates of each and the name, principal business and address of any business corporation or other organization in which such occupation, position, office or employment was carried on;

(e) Whether or not, during the last 5 years, such person has been convicted in a criminal proceeding (excluding traffic violations or similar misdemeanors) and, if so give the dates, nature of conviction, name and location of court, and penalty imposed or other disposition of the case;

(f) Whether or not, during the last 5 years, such person was a party to a civil proceeding of a judicial or administrative body of competent jurisdiction and as a result of such proceeding was or is subject to a judgment, decree or final order enjoining further violations of, or prohibiting activities subject to, federal or state securities laws or finding any violation of such laws; and, if so, identify and describe such proceeding and summarize the terms of such judgment, decree or final order;

Instruction. While negative answers to Items 2(e) and 2(f) are required in this schedule, they need not be furnished to security holders.

(g) Citizenship(s).

Item 3. Past Contacts, Transactions or Negotiations

(a) If this schedule is filed by an affiliate of the issuer of the class of securities which is the subject of the Rule 13e–3 transaction:

(1) Briefly state the nature and approximate amount (in dollars) of any transaction, other than those described in Item 3(b) of this schedule, which has occurred since the commencement of the issuer's second full fiscal year preceding the date of this schedule between such affiliate (including subsidiaries of the affiliate and those persons enumerated in Instruction C of this schedule) and the issuer: *Provided, however,* That no disclosure need be made with respect to any transaction if the aggregate amount involved in such transaction was less than one percent of the issuer's consolidated revenues (which may be based upon information contained in the most recently available filing with the Commission by the issuer unless such affiliate has reason to believe otherwise) (i) for the fiscal year in which such transaction occurred or (ii) for the portion of the current fiscal year which has occurred, if the transaction occurred in such year; and

(2) Describe any contacts, negotiations or transactions which have been entered into or which have occurred since the commencement of the issuer's second full fiscal year preceding the date of this schedule between such affiliate (including subsidiaries of the affiliate and those persons enumerated in Instruction C of this schedule) and the issuer concerning: a merger, consolidation or

acquisition; a tender offer for or other acquisition of securities of any class of the issuer; an election of directors of the issuer; or a sale or other transfer of a material amount of assets of the issuer or any of its subsidiaries.

(b) Describe any contacts or negotiations concerning the matters referred to in Item 3(a)(2) which have been entered into or which have occurred since the commencement of the issuer's second full fiscal year preceding the date of this schedule (i) between any affiliates of the issuer of the class of securities which is the subject of the Rule 13e–3 transaction; or (ii) between such issuer or any of its affiliates and any person who is not affiliated with the issuer and who would have a direct interest in such matters. Identify the person who initiated such contacts or negotiations.

Item 4. Terms of the Transaction

(a) State the material terms of the Rule 13e–3 transaction.

(b) Describe any term or arrangement concerning the Rule 13e–3 transaction relating to any security holder of the issuer which is not identical to that relating to other security holders of the same class of securities of the issuer.

Item 5. Plans or Proposals of the Issuer or Affiliate

Describe any plan or proposal of the issuer or affiliate regarding activities or transactions which are to occur after the Rule 13e–3 transaction which relate to or would result in:

(a) An extraordinary corporate transaction, such as a merger, reorganization or liquidation, involving the issuer or any of its subsidiaries;

(b) A sale or transfer of a material amount of assets of the issuer or any of its subsidiaries;

(c) Any change in the present board of directors or management of the issuer including, but not limited to, any plan or proposal to change the number or term of directors, to fill any existing vacancy on the board or to change any material term of the employment contract of any executive officer;

(d) Any material change in the present dividend rate or policy or indebtedness or capitalization of the issuer;

(e) Any other material change in the issuer's corporate structure or business;

(f) A class of equity securities of the issuer becoming eligible for termination of registration pursuant to Section 12(g)(4) of the Act; or

(g) The suspension of the issuer's obligation to file reports pursuant to Section 15(d) of the Act.

Item 6. Source and Amounts of Funds or Other Consideration

(a) State the source and total amount of funds or other consideration to be used in the Rule 13e–3 transaction.

(b) Furnish a reasonably itemized statement of all expenses incurred or estimated to be incurred in connection with the Rule 13e–3 transaction including, but not limited to, filing fees, legal, accounting and appraisal fees, solicitation expenses and printing costs and state whether or not the issuer has paid or will be responsible for paying any or all of such expenses.

(c) If all or any part of such funds or other consideration is, or is expected to be, directly or indirectly borrowed for the purpose of the Rule 13e–3 transaction,

(1) Provide a summary of each such loan agreement containing the identity of the parties, the term, the collateral, the stated and effective interest rates, and other material terms or conditions; and

(2) Briefly describe any plans or arrangements to finance or repay such borrowings, or, if no such plans or arrangements have been made, make a statement to that effect.

(d) If the source of all or any part of the funds to be used in the Rule 13e–3 transaction is a loan made in the ordinary course of business by a bank as defined by Section 3(a)(6) of the Act and Section 13(d) or 14(d) is applicable to such transaction, the name of such bank shall not be made available to the public if the person filing the statement so requests in writing and files such request, naming such bank, with the Secretary of the Commission.

Item 7. Purpose(s), Alternatives, Reasons and Effects

(a) State the purpose(s) for the Rule 13e–3 transaction.

(b) If the issuer or affiliate considered alternative means to accomplish such purpose(s), briefly describe such alternative(s) and state the reason(s) for their rejection.

(c) State the reasons for the structure of the Rule 13e–3 transaction and for undertaking such transaction at this time.

(d) Describe the effects of the Rule 13e–3 transaction on the issuer, its affiliates and unaffiliated security holders, including the federal tax consequences.

Instructions.   (1) Conclusory statements will not be considered sufficient disclosure in response to Item 7.

(2) The description required by Item 7(d) should include a reasonably detailed discussion of the benefits and detriments of the Rule 13e–3 transaction to the issuer, its affiliates and unaffiliated security holders. The benefits and detriments of the Rule 13e–3 transaction should be quantified to the extent practicable.

(3) If this statement is filed by an affiliate of the issuer, the description required by Item 7(d) should include but not be limited to,

the effect of the Rule 13e–3 transaction on the affiliate's interest in the net book value and net earnings of the issuer in terms of both dollar amounts and percentages.

Item 8. Fairness of the Transaction

(a) State whether the issuer or affiliate filing this schedule reasonably believes that the Rule 13e–3 transaction is fair or unfair to unaffiliated security holders. If any director dissented to or abstained from voting on the Rule 13e–3 transaction, identify each such director, and indicate, if known, after making reasonable inquiry, the reasons for each dissent or abstention.

Instruction. A statement that the issuer or affiliate has no reasonable belief as to the fairness of the Rule 13e–3 transaction to unaffiliated security holders will not be considered sufficient disclosure in response to Item 8(a).

(b) Discuss in reasonable detail the material factors upon which the belief stated in Item 8(a) is based and, to the extent practicable, the weight assigned to each such factor. Such discussion should include an analysis of the extent, if any, to which such belief is based on the factors set forth in instruction (1) to paragraph (b) of this Item, paragraphs (c), (d), and (e) of this Item, and Item 9.

Instructions. (1) The factors which are important in determining the fairness of a transaction to unaffiliated security holders and the weight, if any, which should be given to them in a particular context will vary. Normally such factors will include, among others, those referred to in paragraphs (c), (d) and (e) of this Item and whether the consideration offered to unaffiliated security holders constitutes fair value in relation to:

(i) current market prices

(ii) historical market prices

(iii) net book value

(iv) going concern value

(v) liquidation value

(vi) the purchase price paid in previous purchases disclosed in Item 1(f) of Schedule 13e–3

(vii) any report, opinion, or appraisal described in Item 9 and

(viii) firm offers of which the issuer or affiliate is aware made by any unaffiliated person, other than the person filing this statement, during the preceding eighteen months for (A) the merger or consolidation of the issuer into or with such person or of such person into or with the issuer, (B) the sale or other transfer of all or any substantial part of the assets of the issuer or (C) securities of the issuer which would enable the holder thereof to exercise control of the issuer.

(2) Conclusory statements, such as "The Rule 13e–3 transaction is fair to unaffiliated security holders in relation to net book value, going

concern value and future prospects of the issuer" will not be considered sufficient disclosure in response to Item 8(b).

(c) State whether the transaction is structured so that approval of at least a majority of unaffiliated security holders is required.

(d) State whether a majority of directors who are not employees of the issuer has retained an unaffiliated representative to act solely on behalf of unaffiliated security holders for the purposes of negotiating the terms of the Rule 13e–3 transaction and/or preparing a report concerning the fairness of such transaction.

(e) State whether the Rule 13e–3 transaction was approved by a majority of the directors of the issuer who are not employees of the issuer.

(f) If any offer of the type described in instruction (vii) to Item 8(b) has been received, describe such offer and state the reason(s) for its rejection.

Item 9. Reports, Opinions, Appraisals and Certain Negotiations

(a) State whether or not the issuer or affiliate has received any report, opinion (other than an opinion of counsel) or appraisal from an outside party which is materially related to the Rule 13e–3 transaction including, but not limited to, any such report, opinion or appraisal relating to the consideration or the fairness of the consideration to be offered to security holders of the class of securities which is the subject of the Rule 13e–3 transaction or the fairness of such transaction to the issuer or affiliate or to security holders who are not affiliates.

(b) With respect to any report, opinion or appraisal described in Item 9(a) or with respect to any negotiation or report described in Item 8(d) concerning the terms of the Rule 13e–3 transaction:

(1) Identify such outside party and/or unaffiliated representative;

(2) Briefly describe the qualifications of such outside party and/or unaffiliated representative;

(3) Describe the method of selection of such outside party and/or unaffiliated representative;

(4) Describe any material relationship between (i) the outside party, its affiliates, and/or unaffiliated representative, and (ii) the issuer or its affiliates, which existed during the past two years or is mutually understood to be contemplated and any compensation received or to be received as a result of such relationship;

(5) If such report, opinion or appraisal relates to the fairness of the consideration, state whether the issuer or affiliate determined the amount of consideration to be paid or whether the outside party recommended the amount of consideration to be paid.

(6) Furnish a summary concerning such negotiation report, opinion or appraisal which shall include, but not be limited to, the procedures followed; the findings and recommendations; the bases

for and methods of arriving at such findings and recommendations; instructions received from the issuer or affiliate; and any limitation imposed by the issuer or affiliate; and any limitation imposed by the issuer or affiliate on the scope of the investigation.

Instruction. The information called for by subitem 9(b)(1), (2) and (3) should be given with respect to the firm which provides the report, opinion or appraisal rather than the employees of such firm who prepared it.

(c) Furnish a statement to the effect that such report, opinion or appraisal shall be made available for inspection and copying at the principal executive offices of the issuer or affiliate during its regular business hours by any interested equity security holder of the issuer or his representative who has been so designated in writing. This statement may also provide that a copy of such report, opinion or appraisal will be transmitted by the issuer or affiliate to any interested equity security holder of the issuer or his representative who has been so designated in writing upon written request and at the expense of the requesting security holder.

Item 10. Interest in Securities of the Issuer

(a) With respect to the class of equity security to which the Rule 13e–3 transaction relates, state the aggregate amount and percentage of securities beneficially owned (identifying those securities for which there is a right to acquire) as of the most recent practicable date by the person filing this statement (unless such person is the issuer), by any pension, profit sharing or similar plan of the issuer or affiliate, by each person enumerated in Instruction C of this Schedule or by any associate or majority owned subsidiary of the issuer or affiliate giving the name and address of any such associate or subsidiary.

Instructions. 1. For the purpose of this Item, beneficial ownership shall be determined in accordance with Rule 13d–3 under the Exchange Act.

2. The information required by this paragraph should be given with respect to officers, directors and associates of the issuer to the extent known after making reasonable inquiry.

(b) Describe any transaction in the class of equity securities of the issuer which is the subject of a Rule 13e–3 transaction that was effected during the past 60 days by the issuer of such class or by the persons named in response to paragraph (a) of this Item.

Instructions. 1. The description of a transaction required by Item 10(b) shall include, but not necessarily be limited to: (i) the identity of the person covered by Item 10(b) who effected the transaction; (ii) the date of the transaction; (iii) the amount of securities involved; (iv) the price per security; and (v) where and how the transaction was effected.

2. If the information required by Item 10(b) is available to the person filing this statement at the time this statement is initially filed with the Commission, the information shall be included in the initial

filing. However, if the information is not available to such person at the time of such initial filing, it shall be filed with the Commission promptly but in no event later than seven days (or 2 business days with respect to a tender subject to Regulation 14D or 10 business days with respect to a tender offer subject to Rule 13e–4 [§ 240.13e–4]) after the date of such filing and, if material, disclosed to security holders of the issuer pursuant to Rule 13e–3(e), and disseminated to them in a manner reasonably calculated to inform security holders.

Item 11. Contracts, Arrangements or Understandings With Respect to the Issuer's Securities

Describe any contract, arrangement, understanding or relationship (whether or not legally enforceable) in connection with the Rule 13e–3 transaction between the person filing this statement (including any person enumerated in Instruction C of this schedule) and any person with respect to any securities of the issuer (including, but not limited to, any contract, arrangement, understanding or relationship concerning the transfer or the voting of any of such securities, joint ventures, loan or option arrangements, puts or calls, guaranties of loans, guaranties against loss or the giving or withholding of proxies, consents or authorizations), naming the persons with whom such contracts, arrangements, understandings or relationships have been entered into and giving the material provisions thereof. Include such information for any of such securities that are pledged or otherwise subject to a contingency, the occurrence of which would give another person the power to direct the voting or disposition of such securities, except that disclosure of standard default and similar provisions contained in loan agreements need not be included.

Item 12. Present Intention and Recommendation of Certain Persons With Regard to the Transaction

(a) To the extent known by the person filing this statement after making reasonable inquiry, furnish a statement of present intention with regard to the Rule 13e–3 transaction indicating whether or not any executive officer, director or affiliate of the issuer or any person enumerated in Instruction C of this statement will tender or sell securities of the issuer owned or held by such person and/or how such securities, and securities with respect to which such person holds proxies, will be voted and the reasons therefor.

Instruction. If the information required by Item 12(a) is available to the person filing this statement at the time this statement is initially filed with the Commission, the information shall be included in the initial filing. However, if the information is not available to such person at the time of such initial filing, it shall be filed with the Commission promptly but in no event later than seven days (or two business days with respect to a tender offer subject to Regulation 14D or ten business days with respect to a tender offer subject to Rule 13e–4) after the date of such filing and, if material, disclosed to security holders of the issuer pursuant to Rule 13e–3(e), and disseminated to them in a manner reasonably calculated to inform security holders.

(b) To the extent known by the person filing this statement after making reasonable inquiry, state whether any person named in paragraph (a) of this item has made a recommendation in support of or opposed to the Rule 13e–3 transaction and the reasons for such recommendation. If no recommendation has been made by such persons, furnish a statement to that effect.

Item 13. Other Provisions of the Transaction

(a) State whether or not appraisal rights are provided under applicable state law or under the issuer's articles of incorporation or will be voluntarily accorded by the issuer or affiliate to security holders in connection with the Rule 13e–3 transaction and, if so, summarize such appraisal rights. If appraisal rights will not be available under the applicable state law, to security holders who object to the transaction, briefly outline the rights which may be available to such security holders under such law.

(b) If any provision has been made by the issuer or affiliate in connection with the Rule 13e–3 transaction to allow unaffiliated security holders to obtain access to the corporate files of the issuer or affiliate or to obtain counsel or appraisal services at the expense of the issuer or affiliate, describe such provision.

(c) If the Rule 13e–3 transaction involves the exchange of debt securities of the issuer or affiliate for the equity securities held by security holders of the issuer who are not affiliates, describe whether or not the issuer or affiliate will take steps to provide or assure that such securities are or will be eligible for trading on any national securities exchange or an automated inter-dealer quotation system.

Item 14. Financial Information

(a) Furnish the following financial data concerning the issuer:

(1) Audited financial statements for the two fiscal years required to be filed with the issuer's most recent annual report under sections 13 and 15(d) of the Act;

(2) Unaudited balance sheets and comparative year-to-date income statements and statements of changes in financial position and related earnings per share amounts required to be included in the issuer's most recent quarterly report filed pursuant to the Act;

(3) Ratio of earnings to fixed charges for the two most recent fiscal years and the interim periods provided under Item 14(a)(2); and

(4) Book value per share as of the most recent fiscal year end and as of the date of the latest interim balance sheet provided under Item 14(a)(2).

(b) If material, provide pro forma data disclosing the effect of the Rule 13e–3 transaction on:

(1) The issuer's balance sheet as of the most recent fiscal year end and the latest interim balance sheet provided under Item 14(a)(2);

(2) The issuer's statement of income, earnings per share amounts, and ratio of earnings to fixed charges for the most recent fiscal year and the latest interim period provided under Item 14(a)(2); and

(3) The issuer's book value per share as of the most recent fiscal year end and as of the latest interim balance sheet date provided under Item 14(a)(2).

Item 15. Persons and Assets Employed, Retained or Utilized

(a) Identify and describe the purpose for which any officer, employee, class of employees or corporate asset of the issuer (excluding corporate assets which are proposed to be used as consideration for purchases of securities which are disclosed in Item 6 of this schedule) has been or is proposed to be employed, availed of or utilized by the issuer or affiliate in connection with the Rule 13e–3 transaction.

(b) Identify all persons and classes of persons (excluding officers, employees and class of employees who have been identified in Item 15(a) of this Schedule) employed, retained or to be compensated by the person filing this statement, or by any person on behalf of the person filing this statement, to make solicitations or recommendations in connection with the Rule 13e–3 transaction and provide a summary of the material terms of such employment, retainer or arrangement for compensation.

Item 16. Additional Information

Furnish such additional material information, if any, as may be necessary to make the required statements in the light of the circumstances under which they are made, not materially misleading.

Item 17. Material to Be Filed as Exhibits

Furnish a copy of:

(a) Any loan agreement referred to in Item 6 of this Schedule;

Instruction. The identity of any bank which is a party to a loan agreement need not be disclosed if the person filing the statement has requested that the identity of such bank not be made available to the public pursuant to Item 6 of this schedule.

(b) Any report, opinion or appraisal referred to in Items 8(d) or 9 of this schedule;

(c) Any document setting forth the terms of any contract, arrangements or understandings or relationships referred to in Item 11 of this schedule; and

(d) Any disclosure materials furnished to security holders in connection with the transaction pursuant to Rule 13e–3(d).

(e) A detailed statement describing the appraisal rights and the procedures for exercising such appraisal rights which are referred to in Item 13(a) of this schedule.

(f) If any oral solicitation of or recommendations to security holders referred to in Item 15(b) are to be made by or on behalf of the person filing this statement, any written instruction, form or other material which is furnished to the persons making the actual oral solicitation or recommendation for their use, directly or indirectly, in connection with the Rule 13e–3 transaction.

* * *

Rule 13e–4. Tender Offers by Issuers

(a) *Definitions.* Unless the context otherwise requires, all terms used in this section and in Schedule 13E–4 shall have the same meaning as in the Act or elsewhere in the General Rules and Regulations thereunder. In addition, the following definitions shall apply:

(1) The term "issuer" means any issuer which has a class of equity security registered pursuant to section 12 of the Act, or which is required to file periodic reports pursuant to section 15(d) of the Act, or which is a closed-end investment company registered under the Investment Company Act of 1940.

(2) The term "issuer tender offer" refers to a tender offer for, or a request or invitation for tenders of, any class of equity security, made by the issuer of such class of equity security or by an affiliate of such issuer.

(3) The term "business day" means any day, other than Saturday, Sunday or a federal holiday, on which the principal office of the Commission at Washington, D.C. is scheduled to be open for business. In computing any time period under this section, the date of commencement of the issuer tender offer shall be included.

(4) The term "commencement" means the date an issuer tender offer is first published, sent or given to security holders.

(5) The term "termination" means the date after which securities may not be tendered pursuant to an issuer tender offer.

(6) The term "security holders" means holders of record and beneficial owners of securities of the class of equity security which is the subject of an issuer tender offer.

(7) The term "security position listing" means, with respect to the securities of any issuer held by a registered clearing agency in the name of the clearing agency or its nominee, a list of those participants in the clearing agency on whose behalf the clearing agency holds the issuer's securities and of the participants' respective positions in such securities as of a specified date.

(b)(1) It shall be a fraudulent, deceptive or manipulative act or practice, in connection with an issuer tender offer, for an issuer or an affiliate of such issuer, in connection with an issuer tender offer:

(i) to employ any device, scheme or artifice to defraud any person;

(ii) to make any untrue statement of a material fact or to omit to state a material fact necessary in order to make the statements made, in the light of the circumstances under which they were made, not misleading; or

(iii) to engage in any act, practice or course of business which operates or would operate as a fraud or deceit upon any person.

(2) As a means reasonably designed to prevent fraudulent, deceptive or manipulative acts or practices in connection with any issuer tender offer, it shall be unlawful for an issuer or an affiliate of such issuer to make an issuer tender offer unless:

(i) such issuer or affiliate complies with the requirements of paragraphs (c), (d), (e) and (f) of this section; and

(ii) the issuer tender offer is not in violation of paragraph (b)(1) of this section.

(c) *Material Required to Be Filed.* The issuer or affiliate making the issuer tender offer shall, in accordance with the General Instructions to the Issuer Tender Offer Statement on Schedule 13E–4.

(1) File with the Commission ten copies of such schedule, including all exhibits thereto, prior to or as soon as practicable on the date of commencement of the issuer tender offer;

(2) Report any material change in the information set forth in such schedule by promptly filing with the Commission ten copies of an amendment on such schedule;

(3) Report the results of the issuer tender offer by filing with the Commission no later than ten business days after the termination of the issuer tender offer ten copies of a final amendment to such schedule.

(d) *Disclosure of Certain Information.*

(1) The issuer or affiliate making the issuer tender offer shall publish, send or give to security holders in the manner prescribed in paragraph (e)(1) of this section a statement containing the following information:

(i) the scheduled termination date of the issuer tender offer and whether it may be extended;

(ii) the specified dates prior to which, and after which, persons who tender securities pursuant to the issuer tender offer may withdraw their securities pursuant to paragraph (f)(2) of this section;

(iii) if the issuer tender offer is for less than all the securities of a class, the exact dates of the period during which securities will be accepted on a pro rata basis pursuant to paragraph (f)(3) of this section and the manner in which securities will be accepted for payment and in which securities may be withdrawn; and

(iv) the information required by Items 1 through 8 of Schedule 13E–4 or a fair and adequate summary thereof.

Provided, however, That if the issuer tender offer involves the registration of securities pursuant to the Securities Act of 1933 and the General Rules and Regulations promulgated thereunder, any prospectus relating to such securities shall include all of the information, not otherwise required to be included therein, required by this paragraph.

(2) If any material change occurs in the information previously disclosed to security holders, the issuer or affiliate shall disclose promptly such change in the manner prescribed by paragraph (e)(2) of this section.

* * *

(3) If an issuer or an affiliate publishes, sends or gives the issuer tender offer to security holders by means of a summary publication in the manner prescribed in paragraph (e)(1)(iii) of this section, the summary advertisement shall not contain a transmittal letter pursuant to which securities which are sought in the issuer tender offer may be tendered, and shall disclose only the following information:

(i) the identity of the issuer or affiliate making the issuer tender offer;

(ii) the amount and class of securities being sought and the price being offered;

(iii) the information required by paragraphs (d)(1)(i)-(iii) of this section;

(iv) a statement of the purpose of the issuer tender offer;

(v) appropriate instructions for security holders regarding how to obtain promptly, at the expense of the issuer or affiliate making the issuer tender offer, the statement required by paragraph (d)(1) of this section; and

(vi) a statement that the information contained in the statement required by paragraph (d)(1) of this section is incorporated by reference.

(e) *Dissemination of Tender Offers.*

(1) The issuer or affiliate making the issuer tender offer will be deemed to have published, sent or given the issuer tender offer to security holders if such issuer or affiliate complies fully with one or more of the following methods of dissemination. Depending on the facts and circumstances involved, and for purposes of paragraphs (e)(1)(i) and (e)(1)(iii) of this section, adequate publication of the issuer tender offer may require publication in a newspaper with a national circulation or may require only publication in a newspaper with metropolitan or regional circulation or may require publication in a combination thereof.

(i) *Dissemination of Cash Issuer Tender Offers by Long-Form Publication:* By making adequate publication in a newspaper or newspapers, on the date of commencement of the issuer tender offer, of the statement required by paragraph (d)(1) of this section.

(ii) *Dissemination of Any Issuer Tender Offer by Use of Shareholder and Other Lists:*

(A) By mailing the statement required by paragraph (d)(1) of this section to each security holder whose name appears on the most recent shareholder list of the issuer;

(B) By contacting each participant named on the most recent security position listing of any clearing agency within the possession or access of the issuer or affiliate making the tender offer, and making inquiry of each such participant as to the approximate number of beneficial owners of the securities for which the issuer tender offer is made which are held by such participant;

(C) By furnishing to each such participant a sufficient number of copies of the statement required by paragraph (d)(1) of this section for transmittal to the beneficial owners; and

(D) By agreeing to reimburse promptly each such participant for reasonable expenses incurred by it in forwarding such statement to the beneficial owners.

(iii) *Dissemination of Certain Cash Issuer Tender Offers by Summary Publication:*

(A) If the issuer tender offer is not subject to Rule 13e–3, by making adequate publication in a newspaper or newspapers, on the date of commencement of the issuer tender offer, of a summary advertisement containing the information required by paragraph (d)(3) of this section; and

(B) By mailing or otherwise furnishing promptly the statement required by paragraph (d)(1) of this section and a transmittal letter to any security holder who requests either a copy of such statement or a transmittal letter.

(2) If a material change occurs in the information published, sent or given to security holders, the issuer or affiliate shall disseminate promptly disclosure of such change in a manner reasonably calculated to inform security holder of such change.

(f) *Manner of Making Tender Offer.*

(1) The issuer tender offer, unless withdrawn shall remain open until the expiration of at least fifteen business days from its commencement.

(2) The issuer or affiliate making the issuer tender offer shall permit securities tendered pursuant to the issuer tender offer to be withdrawn

(i) at any time until the expiration of ten business days from the commencement of the issuer tender offer;

(ii) if not yet accepted for payment, at any time until the expiration of seven business days from the date another tender offer for securities of the same class is first published, sent or given to security holders, pursuant to Section 14(d)(1) of the Act or otherwise; and

(iii) if not yet accepted for payment after the expiration of forty business days from the commencement of the issuer tender offer.

(3) The issuer of affiliate making the issuer tender offer shall accept tendered securities as nearly as practicable on a pro rata basis (disregarding fractions) according to the amount of securities tendered by each security holder if the amount of securities tendered within ten business days (or such longer period as may be specified) from the commencement of the issuer tender offer exceeds the amount of securities that will be accepted. The provisions of this paragraph shall also apply to securities tendered within ten business days (or such longer period as may be specified) from the date notice of an increase in the consideration offered to security holders, as described in paragraph (f)(4) of this section, is first published, sent or given to security holders; *Provided, however, That* this provision shall not prohibit the issuer or affiliate making the issuer tender offer from

(i) accepting all securities tendered by persons who own, beneficially or of record, an aggregate of not more than a specified number which is less than one hundred shares of such security and who tender all their securities, before prorating securities tendered by others, or

(ii) accepting by lot securities tendered by security holders who tender all securities held by them and who, when tendering their securities, elect to have either all or none accepted, if the issuer or affiliate first accepts all securities tendered by security holders who do not so elect;

(4) In the event the issuer or affiliate making the issuer tender increases the consideration offered after the issuer tender offer has commenced, such issuer or affiliate shall pay such increased consideration to all security holders whose tendered securities are accepted for payment by such issuer or affiliate.

(5) The issuer or affiliate making the tender offer shall either pay the consideration offered, or return the tendered securities, promptly after the termination or withdrawal of the tender offer.

(6) Until the expiration of at least ten business days after the date of termination of the issuer tender offer, neither the issuer nor

any affiliate shall make any purchases, otherwise than pursuant to the tender offer, of:

(i) any security which is the subject of the issuer tender offer, or any security of the same class and series, or any right to purchase any such securities; and

(ii) in the case of an issuer tender offer which is an exchange offer, any security being offered pursuant to such exchange offer, or any security of the same class and series, or any right to purchase any such security.

(g) This section shall not apply to:

(1) Calls or redemptions of any security in accordance with the terms and conditions of its governing instruments;

(2) Offers to purchase securities evidenced by a scrip certificate, order form or similar document which represents a fractional interest in a share of stock or similar security;

(3) Offers to purchase securities pursuant to a statutory procedure for the purchase of dissenting security holders' securities;

(4) Any tender offer which is subject to section 14(d) of the Act; or

(5) Offers to purchase from security holders who own an aggregate of not more than a specified number of shares that is less than one hundred: *Provided, however,* That the offer is made to all record and beneficial holders (other than participants in an issuer's plan, as that term is defined in Rule 10b–6(c)(4) under the Act, if the issuer elects not to extend the offer to such participants) who own that number of shares as of a specified date prior to the announcement of the offer; or

(6) Any other transaction or transactions, if the Commission, upon written request or upon its own motion, exempts such transaction or transactions, either unconditionally, or on specified terms and conditions, as not constituting a fraudulent, deceptive or manipulative act or practice comprehended within the purpose of this section.

Rule 13e–101. Schedule 13E–4. Tender Offer Statement Pursuant to Section 13(e)(1) of the Securities Exchange Act of 1934 and Rule 13e–4 Thereunder.

* * *

GENERAL INSTRUCTIONS

* * *

C. If the statement is filed by a general or limited partnership, syndicate or other group, the information called for by Items 2–5, inclusive, shall be given with respect to (i) each partner of such general partnership; (ii) each partner who is denominated as a general partner or who functions as a general partner of such limited partnership; (iii) each member of such syndicate or group; and (iv) each person controlling such partner or member. If the statement is filed by a corporation, or if a person referred to in (i), (ii), (iii) or (iv) of this Instruction is a corporation, the information called for by Items 2–5, inclusive, shall be given with respect to (a) each executive officer and director of such corporation; (b) each person controlling such corporation; and (c) each executive officer and director of any corporation ultimately in control of, such corporation.

D.   Upon termination of the tender offer, the person filing this statement shall promptly, but in no event later than ten business days after the termination of the tender offer, file a final amendment to Schedule 13E–4 disclosing all material changes in the information set forth in such statement and stating that the tender offer has terminated, the date of such termination and the results of such tender offer.

E.   Amendments disclosing a material change in the information set forth in this statement may omit information previously disclosed in this statement.

Item 1.   Security and Issuer

(a) State the name of the issuer and the address of its principal executive office;

(b) State the exact title and the amount of securities outstanding of the class of security being sought as of the most recent practicable date; the exact amount of such securities being sought and the consideration being offered therefor; whether any such securities are to be purchased from any officer, director or affiliate of the issuer, and the details of each such transaction; and

(c) Identify the principal market in which such securities are being traded and, if the principal market is an exchange, state the high and low sales prices for such securities as reported in the consolidated transaction reporting system or, if not so reported, on such principal exchange for each quarterly period during the past two years. If the principal market is not an exchange, state the range of high and low bid quotations for each quarterly period during the past two years, the source of such quotations, and if there is currently no established trading market for such securities (excluding limited or sporadic) furnish a statement to that effect.

(d) State the name and address of the person filing this statement, if other than the issuer, and the nature of the affiliation between such person and the issuer.

Item 2.   Source and Amount of Funds or Other Consideration

(a) State the source and total amount of funds or other consideration for the purchase of the maximum amount of securities for which the tender offer is being made.

(b) If all or any part of such funds or other consideration is, or is expected to be borrowed, directly or indirectly, for the purpose of the tender offer:

(1) Provide a summary of each such loan agreement or arrangement containing the identity of the parties, the term, the collateral, the stated and effective interest rates, and other material terms or conditions relative to such loan agreement; and

(2) Briefly describe any plans or arrangements to finance or repay such borrowings, or if no such plans or arrangements have been made, make a statement to that effect.

Item 3. Purpose of the Tender Offer and Plans or Proposals of the Issuer or Affiliate

State the purpose or purposes of the tender offer, and whether the securities are to be retired, held in the treasury of the issuer, or otherwise disposed of, indicating such disposition, and any plans or proposals which relate to or would result in:

(a) The acquisition by any person of additional securities of the issuer, or the disposition of securities of the issuer;

(b) An extraordinary corporate transaction, such as a merger, reorganization or liquidation, involving the issuer or any of its subsidiaries;

(c) A sale or transfer of a material amount of assets of the issuer or any of its subsidiaries;

(d) Any change in the present board of directors or management of the issuer including, but not limited to, any plans or proposals to change the number or the term of directors, to fill any existing vacancy on the board or to change any material term of the employment contract of any executive officer;

(e) Any material change in the present dividend rate or policy, or indebtedness or capitalization of the issuer;

(f) Any other material change in the issuer's corporate structure or business, including, if the issuer is a registered closed-end investment company, any plans or proposals to make any changes in its investment policy for which a vote would be required by Section 13 of the Investment Company Act of 1940;

(g) Changes in the issuer's charter, bylaws or instruments corresponding thereto or other actions which may impede the acquisition of control of the issuer by any person;

(h) Causing a class of equity security of the issuer to be delisted from a national securities exchange or to cease to be authorized to be quoted in an inter-dealer quotation system of a registered national securities association;

(i) A class of equity security of the issuer becoming eligible for termination of registration pursuant to Section 12(g)(4) of the Act; or

(j) The suspension of the issuer's obligation to file reports pursuant to Section 15(d) of the Act.

Item 4. Interest in Securities of the Issuer

Describe any transaction in the class of subject security that was effected during the past 40 business days by the issuer or the person filing this statement, by any person referred to in Instruction C of this schedule or by any associate or subsidiary of any such person, including any executive officer or director of any such subsidiary.

Instructions. 1. The description of a transaction required by this Item shall include, but not necessarily be limited to: (1) the identity of the person covered by this Item who effected the transaction; (2) the date of the transaction; (3) the amount of securities involved; (4) the price per security; and (5) where and how the transaction was effected.

2. If the information required by this Item is available to the person filing this statement at the time this statement is initially filed with the Commission, the information should be included in the initial filing. However, if the information is not available to such person at the time of such initial filing, it shall be filed with the Commission promptly but in no event later than ten business days after such date of the filing and, if material, should be disclosed to security holders of the issuer in a manner reasonably calculated to inform security holders.

Item 5. Contracts, Arrangements, Understandings or Relationships With Respect to the Issuer's Securities

Describe any contract, arrangement, understanding or relationship relating, directly or indirectly, to the tender offer (whether or not legally enforceable) between the person filing this statement (including any person enumerated in Instruction C of this schedule) and any person with respect to any securities of the issuer (including, but not limited to, any contract, arrangement, understanding or relationship concerning the transfer or the voting of any such securities, joint ventures, loan or option arrangements, puts or calls, guaranties of loans, guaranties against loss, or the giving or withholding of proxies, consents or authorizations) naming the persons with whom such contracts, arrangements, understandings or relationships have been entered into and giving the material provisions thereof. Include such information for any of such securities that are pledged or otherwise subject to a contingency, the occurrence of which would give another person the power to direct the voting or disposition of such securities, except that disclosure of standard default and similar provisions contained in loan agreements need not be included.

Item 6. Persons Retained, Employed or to Be Compensated

Identify all persons and classes of persons employed, retained or to be compensated by the person filing this statement, or by any person on behalf of the person filing this statement, to make solicitations or recommendations in connection with the tender offer, and provide a summary of the material terms of such employment, retainer or arrangement for compensation.

Item 7. Financial Information

(a) If Material, furnish the following financial data of the issuer:

(1) Audited financial statements for the two fiscal years required to be filed with the issuer's most recent annual report under Sections 13 and 15(d) of the Act;

(2) Unaudited balance sheets and comparative year-to-date income statements and statements of changes in financial position and related earnings per share amounts required to be included in the issuer's most recent quarterly report filed pursuant to the Act;

(3) Ratio of earnings to fixed charges for the two most recent fiscal years and the interim periods provided under Item 7(a)(2); and

(4) Book value per share as of the most recent fiscal year end and as of the date of the latest interim balance sheet provided under Item 7(a)(2).

(b) If material, provide pro forma data disclosing the effect of the tender offer on:

(1) The issuer's balance sheet as of the most recent fiscal year end and the latest interim balance sheet provided under Item 7(a)(2);

(2) The issuer's statement of income, earnings per share amounts, and ratio of earnings to fixed charges for the most recent fiscal year and the latest interim period provided under Item 7(a)(2); and

(3) The issuer's book value per share as of the most recent fiscal year end and as of the latest interim balance sheet date provided under Item 7(a)(2).

Item 8. Additional Information

If material to a decision by a security holder whether to sell, tender or hold securities being sought in the tender offer, furnish information including, but not limited to, the following:

(a) Any present or proposed contracts, arrangements, understandings or relationships between the issuer and its executive officers, directors or affiliates (other than any contract, arrangement or understanding required to be disclosed pursuant to Item 5 of this schedule);

(b) Any applicable regulatory requirements which must be complied with or approvals which must be obtained in connection with the tender offer;

(c) The applicability of the margin requirements of Section 7 of the Act and the regulation promulgated thereunder;

(d) Any material pending legal proceedings relating to the tender offer, including the name and location of the court or agency in which the proceedings are pending, the date instituted, the principal parties thereto and a brief summary of the proceedings and the relief sought; and

Instruction. In connection with sub-item(d), a copy of any document relating to a major development (such as pleadings, an answer, complaint, temporary restraining order, injunction, opinion, judgment or order) in a material pending legal proceeding should be furnished promptly to the Commission on a supplemental basis.

(e) Such additional material information, if any, as may be necessary to make the required statements, in light of the circumstances under which they are made, not materially misleading.

Item 9. Material to be Filed as Exhibits

Furnish a copy of:

(a) Tender offer material which is published, sent or given to security holders by or on behalf of the person filing this statement in connection with the tender offer;

(b) Any loan agreement referred to in Item 2 of this schedule.

(c) Any document setting forth the terms of any contract, arrangements, understandings or relationships referred to in Items 5 or 8(a) of this Schedule;

(d) Any written opinion prepared by legal counsel at the request of the person filing this statement and communicated to such person pertaining to the tax consequences of the tender offer;

(e) In an exchange offer where securities of the issuer have been or are to be registered under the Securities Act of 1933, any prospectus filed with the Commission in connection with the registration statement; and

(f) If any oral solicitation of security holders is to be made by or on behalf of the person filing this statement, any written instruction, form or other material which is furnished to the persons making the actual oral solicitation for their use, directly or indirectly, in connection with the tender offer.

* * *

Rule 13f–1. Reporting by Institutional Investment Managers of Information With Respect to Accounts Over Which They Exercise Investment Discretion

(a) Every institutional investment manager which exercises investment discretion with respect to accounts holding section 13(f) securities, as defined in paragraph (c) of this section, having an aggregate fair market value on the last trading day of any month of any calendar year of at least $100,000,000 shall file a report on Form 13F with the Commission within 45 days after the last day of such calendar year and within 45 days after the last day of each of the first three calendar quarters of the subsequent calendar year.

(b) For the purposes of this rule, "investment discretion" has the meaning set forth in section 3(a)(35) of the Act. An institutional investment manager shall also be deemed to exercise "investment discretion" with respect to all accounts over which any person under its control exercises investment discretion.

(c) For purposes of this rule "section 13(f) securities" shall mean equity securities of a class described in section 13(d)(1) of the Act that are admitted to trading on a national securities exchange or quoted on the automated quotation system of a registered securities association. In determining what classes of securities are section 13(f) securities, an institutional investment manager may rely on the most recent list of such securities published by the Commission pursuant to section 13(f)(3) of the Act. Only securities of a class on such list shall be counted in determining whether an institutional investment manager must file a report under this rule and only those securities shall be reported in such report. Where a person controls the issuer of a class of equity securities which are "section 13(f) securities" as defined in this rule, those securities shall not be deemed to be "section 13(f) securities" with respect to the controlling person, provided that such person does not otherwise exercise investment discretion with respect to accounts with fair market value of at least $100,000,000 within the meaning of paragraph (a) of this section.

* * *

SCHEDULE 13G. Information to Be Included in Statements Filed Pursuant to 13d–1(b) and Amendments Thereto Filed Pursuant to 13d–2(b)

* * *

Item 1(a). Name of Issuer

Item 1(b). Address of Issuer's Principal Executive Offices

Item 2(a). Name of Person Filing

Item 2(b). Address of Principal Business Office or, if None, Residence

Item 2(c). Citizenship

Item 2(d). Title of Class of Securities

Item 2(e). CUSIP No.

Item 3. If This Statement Is Filed Pursuant to Rules 13d–1(b), or 13d–2(b), Check Whether the Person Filing Is a

    (a) [   ] Broker of Dealer registered under Section 15 of the Act

    (b) [   ] Bank as defined in section 3(a)(6) of the Act

(c) [   ] Insurance Company as defined in section 3(a)(19) of the Act

(d) [   ] Investment Company registered under section 8 of the Investment Company Act

(e) [   ] Investment Adviser registered under section 203 of the Investment Advisers Act of 1940

(f) [   ] Employee Benefit Plan, Pension Fund which is subject to the provisions of the Employee Retirement Income Security Act of 1974 or Endowment Fund; see Rule 13d–1(b)(1)(ii)(F)

(g) [   ] Parent Holding Company, in accordance with Rule 13d–1(b)(ii)(G) (Note: See Item 7)

(h) [   ] Group, in accordance with Rule 13d–1(b)(1)(ii)(H)

Item 4. Ownership

If the percent of the class owned, as of December 31 of the year covered by the statement, or as of the last day of any month described in Rule 13d–1(b)(2), if applicable, exceeds five percent, provide the following information as of that date and identify those shares which there is a right to acquire.

(a) Amount Beneficially Owned:

_____

(b) Percent of Class:

_____

(c) Number of shares as to which such person has:

(i) sole power to vote or to direct the vote _____

(ii) shared power to vote or to direct the vote _____

(iii) sole power to dispose or to direct the disposition of

_____

(iv) shared power to dispose or to direct the disposition of

_____

Instruction. For computations regarding securities which represent a right to acquire an underlying security see Rule 13d–3(d)(1).

Item 5. Ownership of Five Percent or Less of a Class

If this statement is being filed to report the fact that as of the date hereof the reporting person has ceased to be the beneficial owner of more than five percent of the class of securities, check the following [ ].

Instruction. Dissolution of a group requires a response to this item.

Item 6. Ownership of More than Five Percent on Behalf of Another Person

If any other person is known to have the right to receive or the power to direct the receipt of dividends from, or the proceeds from the sale of, such securities, a statement to that effect should be included in response to this item and, if such interest relates to more than five percent of the class, such person should be identified. A listing of the shareholders of an investment company registered under the Investment Company Act of 1940 or the beneficiaries of employee benefit plan, pension fund or endowment fund is not required.

Item 7. Identification and Classification of the Subsidiary Which Acquired the Security Being Reported on By the Parent Holding Company

If a parent holding company has filed this schedule, pursuant to Rule 13d–1(b)(ii)(G), so indicate under Item 3(g) and attach an exhibit stating the identity and the Item 3 classification of the relevant subsidiary. If a parent holding company has filed this schedule pursuant to Rule 13d–1(c), attach an exhibit stating the identification of the relevant subsidiary.

Item 8. Identification and Classification of Members of the Group

If a group has filed this schedule pursuant to Rule 13d–1(b)(ii)(H), so indicate under Item 3(h) and attach an exhibit stating the identity and Item 3 classification of each member of the group. If a group has filed this schedule pursuant to Rule 13d–1(c), attach an exhibit stating the identity of each member of the group.

Item 9. Notice of Dissolution of Group

Notice of dissolution of a group may be furnished as an exhibit stating the date of the dissolution and that all further filings with respect to transactions in the security reported on will be filed, if required, by members of the group, in their individual capacity. See Item 5.

Item 10. Certification

The following certification shall be included if the statement is filed pursuant to Rule 13d–1(b):

> By signing below I certify that, to the best of my knowledge and belief, the securities referred to above were acquired in the ordinary course of business and were not acquired for the purpose of and do not have the effect of changing or influencing the control of the issuer of such securities and were not acquired in connection with or as a participant in any transaction having such purposes or effect.

* * *

SECTIONS   14(d), (e) and (f)

(d)(1) It shall be unlawful for any person, directly or indirectly, by use of the mails or by any means or instrumentality of interstate commerce or of any facility of a national securities exchange or otherwise, to make a tender offer for, or a request or invitation for tenders of, any class of any equity security which is registered pursuant to section 12 of this title, or any equity security of an insurance company which would have been required to be so registered except for the exemption contained in section 12(g)(2)(G) of this title, or any equity security issued by a closed-end investment company registered under the Investment Company Act of 1940, if, after consummation thereof, such person would, directly or indirectly, be the beneficial owner of more than 5 per centum of such class, unless at the time copies of the offer or request or invitation are first published or sent or given to security holders such person has filed with the Commission a statement containing such of the information specified in section 13(d) of this title, and such additional information as the Commission may by rules and regulations prescribed as necessary or appropriate in the public interest or for the protection of investors. All requests or invitations for tenders or advertisements making a tender offer or requesting or inviting tenders of such a security shall be filed as a part of such statement and shall contain such of the information contained in such statement as the Commission may by rules and regulations prescribe. Copies of any additional material soliciting or requesting such tender offers subsequent to the initial solicitation or request shall contain such information as the Commission may by rules and regulations prescribe as necessary or appropriate in the public interest or for the protection of investors, and shall be filed with the Commission not later than the time copies of such material are first published or sent or given to security holders. Copies of all statements, in the form in which such material is furnished to security holders and the Commission, shall be sent to the issuer not later than the date such material is first published or sent or given to any security holders.

(2) When two or more persons act as a partnership, limited partnership, syndicate, or other group for the purpose of acquiring, holding, or disposing of securities of an issuer, such syndicate or group shall be deemed a "person" for purposes of this subsection.

(3) In determining, for purposes of this subsection, any percentage of a class of any security, such class shall be deemed to consist of the amount of the outstanding securities of such class, exclusive of any securities of such class held by or for the account of the issuer or a subsidiary of the issuer.

(4) Any solicitation or recommendation to the holders of such a security to accept or reject a tender offer or request or invitation for tenders shall be made in accordance with such rules and regulations as the Commission may prescribe as necessary or appropriate in the public interest or for the protection of investors.

(5) Securities deposited pursuant to a tender offer or request or invitation for tenders may be withdrawn by or on behalf of the depositor at any time until the expiration of seven days after the time definitive copies of the offer or request or invitation are first published or sent or given to security holders, and at any time after sixty days from the date of the original tender offer or request or invitation,

except as the Commission may otherwise prescribe by rules, regulations, or order as necessary or appropriate in the public interest or for the protection of investors.

(6) Where any person makes a tender offer, or request or invitation for tenders, for less than all the outstanding equity securities of a class, and where a greater number of securities is deposited pursuant thereto within ten days after copies of the offer or request or invitation are first published or sent or given to security holders than such person is bound or willing to take up and pay for the securities taken up shall be taken up as nearly as may be pro rata, disregarding fractions, according to the number of securities deposited by each depositor. The provisions of this subsection shall also apply to securities deposited within ten days after notice of an increase in the consideration offered to security holders, as described in paragraph (7), is first published or sent or given to security holders.

(7) Where any person varies the terms of a tender offer or request or invitation for tenders before the expiration thereof by increasing the consideration offered to holders of such securities, such person shall pay the increased consideration to each security holder whose securities are taken up and paid for pursuant to the tender offer or request or invitation for tenders whether or not such securities have been taken up by such person before the variation of the tender offer or request or invitation.

(8) The provisions of this subsection shall not apply to any offer for, or request or invitation for tenders of, any security—

(A) if the acquisition of such security, together with all other acquisitions by the same person of securities of the same class during the preceding twelve months, would not exceed 2 per centum of that class;

(B) by the issuer of such security; or

(C) which the Commission, by rules or regulations or by order, shall exempt from the provisions of this subsection as not entered into for the purpose of, and not having the effect of, changing or influencing the control of the issuer or otherwise as not comprehended within the purposes of this subsection.

(e) It shall be unlawful for any person to make any untrue statement of a material fact or omit to state any material fact necessary in order to make the statements made, in the light of the circumstances under which they are made, not misleading, or to engage in any fraudulent, deceptive, or manipulative acts or practices, in connection with any tender offer or request or invitation for tenders, or any solicitation of security holders in opposition to or in favor of any such offer, request, or invitation. The Commission shall, for the purposes of this subsection, by rules and regulations define, and prescribe means reasonably designed to prevent, such acts and practices as are fraudulent, deceptive, or manipulative.

(f) If, pursuant to any arrangement or understanding with the person or persons acquiring securities in a transaction subject to subsection (d) of this section or subsection (d) of section 13 of this title, any persons are to be elected or designated as directors of the issuer, otherwise than at a meeting of security holders, and the persons so elected or designated will constitute a majority of the directors of the issuer, then, prior to the time any such person takes office as a director, and in accordance with rules and regulations prescribed by the Commission, the issuer shall file with the Commission, and transmit to all holders of record of securities of the issuer who would be entitled to vote at a meeting for election of directors, information substantially equivalent to the information which would be required by subsection (a) or (c) of this section to be transmitted if such person or persons were nominees for election as directors at a meeting of such security holders.

* * *

REGULATION 14D

Rule 14d–1. Scope of and Definitions Applicable to Regulations 14D and 14E

(a) *Scope.* Regulation 14D shall apply to any tender offer which is subject to section 14(d)(1) of the Act, including, but not limited to, any tender offer for securities of a class described in that section which is made by an affiliate of the issuer of such class. Regulation 14E shall apply to any tender offer for securities (other than exempted securities) unless otherwise noted therein.

(b) *Definitions.* Unless the context otherwise requires, all terms used in Regulation 14D and Regulation 14E have the same meaning as in the Act and in Rule 12b–2 promulgated thereunder. In addition, for purposes of sections 14(d) and 14(e) of the Act and Regulations 14D and 14E, the following definitions apply:

(1) The term "bidder" means any person who makes a tender offer or on whose behalf a tender offer is made: *Provided, however,* That the term does not include an issuer which makes a tender offer for securities of any class of which it is the issuer;

(2) The term "subject company" means any issuer of securities which are sought by a bidder pursuant to a tender offer;

(3) The term "security holders" means holders of record and beneficial owners of securities which are the subject of a tender offer;

(4) The term "beneficial owner" shall have the same meaning as that set forth in Rule 13d–3: *Provided, however,* That, except with respect to Rule 14d–3, Rule 14d–9(d) and Item 6 of Schedule 14D–1, the term shall not include a person who does not have or share investment power or who is deemed to be a beneficial owner by virtue of Rule 13d–3(d)(1);

(5) The term "tender offer material" means:

(i) The bidder's formal offer, including all the material terms and conditions of the tender offer and all amendments thereto;

(ii) The related transmittal letter (whereby securities of the subject company which are sought in the tender offer may be transmitted to the bidder or its depositary) and all amendments thereto; and

(iii) Press releases, advertisements, letters and other documents published by the bidder or sent or given by the bidder to security holders which, directly or indirectly, solicit, invite or request tenders of the securities being sought in the tender offer;

(6) The term "business day" means any day, other than Saturday, Sunday or a federal holiday, and shall consist of the time period from 12:01 a.m. through 12:00 midnight Eastern time. In computing any time period under section 14(d)(5) or section 14(d)(6) of the Act or under Regulation 14D or Regulation 14E, the date of the event which begins the running of such time period shall be included *except that* if such event occurs on other than a business day such period shall begin to run on and shall include the first business day thereafter; and

(7) The term "security position listing" means, with respect to securities of any issuer held by a registered clearing agency in the name of the clearing agency or its nominee, a list of those participants in the clearing agency on whose behalf the clearing agency holds the issuer's securities and of the participants' respective positions in such securities as of a specified date.

Rule 14d–2. Date of Commencement of a Tender Offer

(a) *Commencement.* A tender offer shall commence for the purposes of section 14(d) of the Act and the rules promulgated thereunder at 12:01 a.m. on the date when the first of the following events occurs:

(1) The long form publication of the tender offer is first published by the bidder pursuant to Rule 14d–4(a)(1);

(2) The summary advertisement of the tender offer is first published by the bidder pursuant to Rule 14d–4(a)(2);

(3) The summary advertisement or the long form publication of the tender offer is first published by the bidder pursuant to Rule 14d–4(a)(3);

(4) Definitive copies of a tender offer, in which the consideration offer by the bidder consists of securities registered pursuant to the Securities Act of 1933, are first published or sent or given by the bidder to security holders; or

(5) The tender offer is first published or sent or given to security holders by the bidder by any means not otherwise referred to in paragraphs (a)(1) through (a)(4) of this section.

(b) *Public Announcement.* A public announcement by a bidder through a press release, newspaper advertisement or public statement which includes the information in paragraph (c) of this section with respect to a tender offer in which the consideration consists solely of cash and/or securities exempt from registration under section 3 of the Securities Act of 1933 shall be deemed to constitute the commencement of a tender offer under paragraph (a)(5) of this section *except that* such tender offer shall not be deemed to be first published or sent or given to security holders by the bidder under paragraph (a)(5) of this section on the date of such public announcement if within five business days of such public announcement, the bidder either:

(1) Makes a subsequent public announcement stating that the bidder has determined not to continue with such tender offer, in which even paragraph (a)(5) of this section shall not apply to the initial public announcement; or

(2) Complies with Rule 14d–3(a) and contemporaneously disseminates the disclosure required by Rule 14d–6 to security holders pursuant to Rule 14d–4 or otherwise in which event:

(i) The date of commencement of such tender offer under paragraph (a) of this section will be determined by the date of information required by Rule 14d–6 is first published or sent or given to security holders pursuant to Rule 14d–4 or otherwise; and

(ii) Notwithstanding paragraph (b)(2)(i) of this section, section 14(d)(7) of the Act shall be deemed to apply to such tender offer from the date of such public announcement.

(c) *Information.* The information referred to in paragraph (b) of this section is as follows:

(1) The identity of the bidder;

(2) The identity of the subject company; and

(3) The amount and class of securities being sought and the price or range of prices being offered therefor.

(d) *Announcements Not Resulting in Commencement.* A public announcement by a bidder through a press release, newspaper advertisement or public statement which only discloses the information in paragraphs (d)(1) through (d)(3) of this section concerning a tender offer in which the consideration consists solely of cash and/or securities exempt from registration under section 3 of the Securities Act of 1933 shall not be deemed to constitute the commencement of a tender offer under paragraph (a)(5) of this section.

(1) The identity of the bidder;

(2) The identity of the subject company; and

(3) A statement that the bidder intends to make a tender offer in the future for a class of equity securities of the subject company which statement does not specify the amount of securities of such class to be sought or the consideration to be offered therefor.

(e) *Announcement Made Pursuant to Rule 135.* A public announcement by a bidder through a press release, newspaper advertisement or public statement which discloses only the information in Rule 135(a)(4) concerning a tender offer in which the consideration consists solely or in part of securities to be registered under the Securities Act of 1933 shall not be deemed to constitute the commencement of a tender offer under paragraph (a)(5) of this section: *Provided,* That such bidder files a registration statement with respect to such securities promptly after such public announcement.

Rule 14d–3. Filing and Transmission of Tender Offer Statement

(a) *Filing and Transmittal.* No bidder shall make a tender offer if, after consummation thereof, such bidder would be the beneficial owner of more than 5 percent of the class of the subject company's securities for which the tender offer is made, unless as soon as practicable on the date of the commencement of the tender offer such bidder:

(1) Files with the Commission ten copies of a Tender Offer Statement on Schedule 14D–1, including all exhibits thereto;

(2) Hand delivers a copy of such Schedule 14D–1, including all exhibits thereto:

    (i) To the subject company at its principal executive office; and

    (ii) To any other bidder, which has filed a Schedule 14D–1 with the Commission relating to a tender offer which has not yet terminated for the same class of securities of the subject company, at such bidder's principal executive office or at the address of the person authorized to receive notices and communications (which is disclosed on the cover sheet of such other bidder's Schedule 14D–1);

(3) Gives telephonic notice of the information required by Rule 14d–6(e)(2)(i) and (ii) and mails by means of first class mail a copy of such Schedule 14D–1, including all exhibits thereto:

    (i) To each national securities exchange where such class of the subject company's securities is registered and listed for trading (which may be based upon information contained in the subject company's most recent Annual Report on Form 10–K filed with the Commission unless the bidder has reason to believe that such information is not current) which telephonic notice shall be made when practicable prior to the opening of each such exchange; and

    (ii) To the National Association of Securities Dealers, Inc. ("NASD") if such class of the subject company's securities is authorized for quotation in the NASDAQ interdealer quotation system.

(b) *Additional Materials.* The bidder shall file with the Commission ten copies of any additional tender offer materials as an exhibit to the Schedule 14D–1 required by this section, and if a material change occurs in the information set forth in such Schedule 14D–1, ten copies of an amendment to Schedule 14D–1 (each of which shall include all exhibits other than those required by Item 11(a) of Schedule 14D–1) disclosing such change and shall send a copy of such additional tender offer material or such amendment to the subject company and to any exchange and/or the NASD, as required by paragraph (a) of this section, promptly but not later than the date such additional tender offer material or such change is first published, sent or given to security holders.

(c) *Certain Announcements.* Notwithstanding the provisions of paragraph (b) of this section, if the additional tender offer material or an amendment to Schedule 14d–1 discloses only the number of shares deposited to date, and/or announces an extension of the time during which shares may be tendered, then the bidder may file such tender offer material or amendment and send a copy of such tender offer material or amendment to the subject company, any exchange and/or the NASD, as required by paragraph (a) of this section, promptly after the date such tender offer material is first published or sent or given to security holders.

Rule 14d–4. Dissemination of Certain Tender Offers

(a) *Materials Deemed Published or Sent or Given.* A tender offer in which the consideration consists solely of cash and/or securities exempt from registration under section 3 of the Securities Act of 1933 shall be deemed "published or sent or given to security holders" within the meaning of section 14(d)(1) of the Act if the bidder complies with all of the requirements of any one of the following sub-paragraphs: *Provided, however,* That any such tender offers may be published or sent or given to security holders by other methods, but with respect to summary publication, and the use of stockholder lists and security position listings pursuant to Rule 14d–5, paragraphs (a)(2) and (a)(3) of this section are exclusive.

(1) *Long-Form Publication.* The bidder makes adequate publication in a newspaper or newspapers of long-form publication of the tender offer.

(2) *Summary publication.*

(i) If the tender offer is not subject to Rule 13e–3, the bidder makes adequate publication in a newspaper or newspapers of a summary advertisement of the tender offer; and

(ii) Mails by first class mail or otherwise furnishes with reasonable promptness the bidder's tender offer materials to any security holder who requests such tender offer materials pursuant to the summary advertisement or otherwise.

(3) *Use of Stockholder Lists and Security Position Listings.* Any bidder using stockholder lists and security position listings pursuant to Rule 14d–5 shall comply with paragraphs (a)(1) or (a)(2) of this section on or prior to the date of the bidder's request for such lists or listing pursuant to Rule 14d–5(a).

(b) *Adequate Publication.* Depending on the facts and circumstances involved, adequate publication of a tender offer pursuant to this section may require publication in a newspaper with a national circulation or may only require publication in a newspaper with metropolitan or regional circulation or may require publication in a combination thereof: *Provided, however,* That publication in all editions of a daily newspaper with a national circulation shall be deemed to constitute adequate publication.

(c) *Publication of Changes.* If a tender offer has been published or sent or given to security holders by one or more of the methods enumerated in paragraph (a) of this section, a material change in the information published, sent or given to security holders shall be promptly disseminated to security holders in a manner reasonably designed to inform security holders of such change; *Provided, however,* That if the bidder has elected pursuant to Rule 14d–5(f)(1) of this section to require the subject company to disseminate amendments disclosing material changes to the tender offer materials pursuant to Rule 14d–5, the bidder shall disseminate material changes in the information published or sent or given to security holders at least pursuant to Rule 14–5.

Rule 14d–5. Dissemination of Certain Tender Offers by the Use of Stockholder Lists and Security Position Listings

(a) *Obligations of the Subject Company.* Upon receipt by a subject company at its principal executive offices of a bidder's written request, meeting the requirements of paragraph (e) of this section, the subject company shall comply with the following sub-paragraphs.

(1) The subject company shall notify promptly transfer agents and any other person who will assist the subject company in complying with the requirements of this section of the receipt by the subject company of a request by a bidder pursuant to this section.

(2) The subject company shall promptly ascertain whether the most recently prepared stockholder list, written or otherwise, within the access of the subject company was prepared as of a date earlier than ten business days before the date of the bidder's request and, if so, the subject company shall promptly prepare or cause to be prepared a stockholder list as of the most recent practicable date which shall not be more than ten business days before the date of the bidder's request.

(3) The subject company shall make an election to comply and shall comply with all of the provisions of either paragraph (b) or paragraph (c) of this section. The subject company's election once made shall not be modified or revoked during the bidder's tender offer and extensions thereof.

(4) No later than the second business day after the date of the bidder's request, the subject company shall orally notify the bidder, which notification shall be confirmed in writing, of the subject company's election made pursuant to paragraph (a)(3) of this section. Such notification shall indicate (i) the approximate number of security holders of the class of securities being sought by the bidder and, (ii) if the subject company elects to comply with paragraph (b) of this section, appropriate information concerning the location for delivery of the bidder's tender offer materials and the approximate direct costs incidental to the mailing to security holders of the bidder's paragraph (g)(2) of this section.

(b) *Mailing of Tender Offer Materials by the Subject Company.* A subject company which elects pursuant to paragraph (a)(3) of this section to comply with the provisions of this paragraph shall perform the acts prescribed by the following subparagraphs.

(1) The subject company shall promptly contact each participant named on the most recent security position listing of any clearing agency within the access of the subject company and make inquiry of each such participant as to the approximate number of beneficial owners of the subject company securities being sought in the tender offer held by each such participant.

(2) No later than the third business day after delivery of the bidder's tender offer materials pursuant to paragraph (g)(1) of this section, the subject company shall begin to mail or cause to be mailed by means of first class mail a copy of the bidder's tender offer materials to each person whose name appears as a record holder of the class of securities for which the offer is made on the most recent stockholder list referred to in paragraph (a)(2) of this section. The subject company shall use its best efforts to complete the mailing in a timely manner but in no event shall such mailing be completed in a substantially greater period of time than the subject company would complete a mailing to security holders of its own materials relating to the tender offer.

(3) No later than the third business day after the delivery of the bidder's tender offer materials pursuant to paragraph (g)(1) of this section, the subject company shall begin to transmit or cause to be transmitted a sufficient number of sets of the bidder's tender offer materials to the participants named on the security position listings described in paragraph (b)(1) of this section. The subject company shall use its best efforts to complete the transmittal in a timely manner but in no event shall such transmittal be completed in a substantially greater period of time than the subject company would complete a transmittal to such participants pursuant to

security position listings of clearing agencies of its own material relating to the tender offer.

(4) The subject company shall promptly give oral notification to the bidder, which notification shall be confirmed in writing, of the commencement of the mailing pursuant to paragraph (b)(2) of this section and of the transmittal pursuant to paragraph (b)(3) of this section.

(5) During the tender offer and any extension thereof the subject company shall use reasonable efforts to update the stockholder list and shall mail or cause to be mailed promptly following each update a copy of the bidder's tender offer materials (to the extent sufficient sets of such materials have been furnished by the bidder) to each person who has become a record holder since the later of (i) the date of preparation of the most recent stockholder list referred to in paragraph (a)(2) of this section or (ii) the last preceding update.

(6) If the bidder has elected pursuant to paragraph (f)(1) of this section to require the subject company to disseminate amendments disclosing material changes to the tender offer materials pursuant to this section, the subject company, promptly following delivery of each such amendment, shall mail or cause to be mailed a copy of each such amendment to each record holder whose name appears on the shareholder list described in paragraphs (a)(2) and (b)(5) of this section and shall transmit or cause to be transmitted sufficient copies of such amendment to each participant named on security position listings who received sets of the bidder's tender offer materials pursuant to paragraph (b)(3) of this section.

(7) The subject company shall not include any communication other than the bidder's tender offer materials or amendments thereto in the envelopes or other containers furnished by the bidder.

(8) Promptly following the termination of the tender offer, the subject company shall reimburse the bidder the excess, if any, of the amounts advanced pursuant to paragraph (f)(3)(iii) over the direct costs incidental to compliance by the subject company and its agents in performing the acts required by this section computed in accordance with paragraph (g)(2) of this section.

(c) *Delivery of Stockholder Lists and Security Position Listings.* A subject company which elects pursuant to paragraph (a)(3) of this section to comply with the provisions of this paragraph shall perform the acts prescribed by the following subparagraphs.

(1) No later than the third business day after the date of the bidder's request, the subject company shall furnish to the bidder at the subject company's principal executive office a copy of the names and addresses of the record holders on the most recent stockholder list referred to in paragraph (a)(2) of this section and a copy of the names and addresses of participants identified on the

most recent security position listing of any clearing agency which is within the access of the subject company.

(2) If the bidder has elected pursuant to paragraph (f)(1) of this section to require the subject company to disseminate amendments disclosing material changes to the tender offer materials, the subject company shall update the stockholder list by furnishing the bidder with the name and address of each record holder named on the stockholder list, and not previously furnished to the bidder, promptly after such information becomes available to the subject company during the tender offer and any extensions thereof.

(d) *Liability of Subject Company and Others.* Neither the subject company nor any affiliate or agent of the subject company nor any clearing agency shall be:

(1) Deemed to have made a solicitation or recommendation respecting the tender offer within the meaning of section 14(d)(4) based solely upon the compliance or noncompliance by the subject company or any affiliate or agent of the subject company with one or more requirements of this section;

(2) Liable under any provision of the Federal securities laws to the bidder or to any security holder based solely upon the inaccuracy of the current names or addresses on the stockholder list or security position listing, unless such inaccuracy results from a lack of reasonable care on the part of the subject company or any affiliate or agent of the subject company;

(3) Deemed to be an "underwriter" within the meaning of section (2)(11) of the Securities Act of 1933 for any purpose of that Act or any rule or regulation promulgated thereunder based solely upon the compliance or noncompliance by the subject company or any affiliate or agent of the subject company with one or more of the requirements of this section;

(4) Liable under any provision of the Federal securities laws for the disclosure in the bidder's tender offer materials, including any amendment thereto, based solely upon the compliance or noncompliance by the subject company or any affiliate or agent of the subject company with one or more of the requirements of this section.

(e) *Content of the Bidder's Request.* The bidder's written request referred to in paragraph (a) of this section shall include the following:

(1) The identity of the bidder;

(2) The title of the class of securities which is the subject of the bidder's tender offer;

(3) A statement that the bidder is making a request to the subject company pursuant to paragraph (a) of this section for the use of the stockholder list and security position listings for the purpose of disseminating a tender offer to security holders;

(4) A statement that the bidder is aware of and will comply with the provisions of paragraph (f) of this section;

(5) A statement as to whether or not it has elected pursuant to paragraph (f)(1) of this section to disseminate amendments disclosing material changes to the tender offer materials pursuant to this section; and

(6) The name, address and telephone number of the person whom the subject company shall contact pursuant to paragraph (a) (4) of this section.

(f) *Obligations of the Bidder.* Any bidder who requests that a subject company comply with the provisions of paragraph (a) of this section shall comply with the following sub-paragraphs.

(1) The bidder shall make an election whether or not to require the subject company to disseminate amendments disclosing material changes to the tender offer materials pursuant to this section, which election shall be included in the request referred to in paragraph (a) of this section and shall not be revocable by the bidder during the tender offer and extensions thereof.

(2) With respect to a tender offer subject to section 14(d)(1) of the Act in which the consideration consists solely of cash and/or securities exempt from registration under section 3 of the Securities Act of 1933, the bidder shall comply with the requirements of Rule 14d–4(a)(3).

(3) If the subject company elects to comply with paragraph (b) of this section,

(i) The bidder shall promptly deliver the tender offer materials after receipt of the notification from the subject company as provided in paragraph

(ii) The bidder shall promptly notify the subject company of any amendment to the bidder's tender offer materials requiring compliance by the subject company with paragraph (b) (6) of this section and shall promptly deliver such amendment to the subject company pursuant to paragraph (g)(1) of this section;

(iii) The bidder shall advance to the subject company an amount equal to the approximate cost of conducting mailings to security holders computed in accordance with paragraph (g) (2) of this section;

(iv) The bidder shall promptly reimburse the subject company for the direct costs incidental to compliance by the subject company and its agents in performing the acts required by this section computed in accordance with paragraph (g)(2) of this section which are in excess of the amount advanced pursuant to paragraph (f)(2)(iii) of this section; and

(v) The bidder shall mail by means of first class mail or otherwise furnish with reasonable promptness the tender offer materials to any security holder who requests such materials.

(4) If the subject company elects to comply with paragraph (c) of this section,

(i) The subject company shall use the stockholder list and security position listings furnished to the bidder pursuant to paragraph (c) of this section exclusively in the dissemination of tender offer materials to security holders in connection with the bidder's tender offer and extensions thereof;

(ii) The bidder shall return the stockholder lists and security position listings furnished to the bidder pursuant to paragraph (c) of this section promptly after the termination of the bidder's tender offer;

(iii) The bidder shall accept, handle and return the stockholder lists and security position listings furnished to the bidder pursuant to paragraph (c) of this section to the subject company on a confidential basis;

(iv) The bidder shall not retain any stockholder list or security position listing furnished by the subject company pursuant to paragraph (c) of this section, or any copy thereof, nor retain any information derived from any such list or listing or copy thereof after the termination of the bidder's tender offer;

(v) The bidder shall mail by means of first class mail, at its own expense, a copy of its tender offer materials to each person whose identity appears on the stockholder list as furnished and updated by the subject company pursuant to paragraphs (c)(1) and (c)(2) of this section;

(vi) The bidder shall contact the participants named on the security position listing of any clearing agency, make inquiry of each participant as to the approximate number of sets of tender offer materials required by each such participant, and furnish, at its own expense, sufficient sets of tender offer materials and any amendment thereto to each such participant for subsequent transmission to the beneficial owners of the securities being sought by the bidder;

(vii) The bidder shall mail by means of first class mail or otherwise furnish with reasonable promptness the tender offer materials to any security holder who requests such materials; and

(viii) The bidder shall promptly reimburse the subject company for direct costs incidental to compliance by the subject company and its agents in performing the acts required by this section computed in accordance with paragraph (g)(2) of this section.

(g) *Delivery of Materials, Computation of Direct Costs.*

(1) Whenever the bidder is required to deliver tender offer materials or amendments to tender offer materials, the bidder shall deliver to the subject company at the location specified by the subject company in its notice given pursuant to paragraph (a)(4) of this section a number of sets of the materials or of the amendment, as the case may be, at least equal to the approximate number of security holders specified by the subject company in such notice, together with appropriate envelopes or other containers therefor; *Provided, however,* That such delivery shall be deemed not to have been made unless the bidder has complied with paragraph (f)(3)(iii) of this section at the time the materials or amendments, as the case may be, are delivered.

(2) The approximate direct cost of mailing the bidder's tender offer materials shall be computed by adding (i) the direct cost incidental to the mailing of the subject company's last annual report to shareholders (excluding employee time), less the costs of preparation and printing of the report, and postage, plus (ii) the amount of first class postage required to mail the bidder's tender offer materials. The approximate direct costs incidental to the mailing of the amendments to the bidder's tender offer materials shall be computed by adding (iii) the estimated direct costs of preparing mailing labels, of updating shareholders lists and of third party handling charges plus (iv) the amount of first class postage required to mail the bidder's amendment. Direct costs incidental to the mailing of the bidder's tender offer materials and amendments thereto when finally computed may include all reasonable charges paid by the subject company to third parties for supplies or services, including costs attendant to preparing shareholder lists, mailing labels, handling the bidder's materials, contacting participants named on security position listings and for postage, but shall exclude indirect costs, such as employee time which is devoted to either contesting or supporting the tender offer on behalf of the subject company. The final billing for direct costs shall be accompanied by an appropriate accounting in reasonable detail.

Rule 14d–6. Disclosure Requirements With Respect to Tender Offers

(a) *Information Required on Date of Commencement.*

(1) *Long-Form Publication.* If a tender offer is published, sent or given to security holders on the date of commencement by means of long-term publication pursuant to Rule 14d–4(a)(1), such long-form publication shall include the information required by paragraph (e)(1) of this section.

(2) *Summary Publication.* If a tender offer is published, sent or given to security holders on the date of commencement by means of summary publication pursuant to Rule 14d–4(a)(2),

(i) The summary advertisement shall contain and shall be limited to, the information required by paragraph (e)(2) of this section; and

(ii) The tender offer materials furnished by the bidder upon the request of any security holder shall include the information required by paragraph (e)(1) of this section.

(3) *Use of Stockholder Lists and Security Position Listings.* If a tender offer is published or sent or given to security holders on the date of commencement by the use of stockholder lists and security position listings pursuant to Rule 14d–4(a)(3).

(i) Either (A) the summary advertisement shall contain, and shall be limited to the information required by paragraph (e)(2) of this section, or (B) if long form publication of the tender offer is made, such long form publication shall include the information required by paragraph (e)(1) of this section; and

(ii) The tender offer materials transmitted to security holders pursuant to such lists and security position listings and furnished by the bidder upon the request of any security holder shall include the information required by paragraph (e)(1) of this section.

(4) *Other Tender Offers.* If a tender offer is published or sent or given to security holders other than pursuant to Rule 14d–4(a), the tender offer materials which are published or sent or given to security holders on the date of commencement of such offer shall include the information required by paragraph (e)(1) of this section.

(b) *Information Required in Summary Advertisement Made After Commencement.* A summary advertisement published subsequent to the date of commencement of the tender offer shall include at least the information specified in paragraphs (e)(1)(i)–(iv) and (e)(2)(iv) of this section.

(c) *Information Required in Other Tender Offer Materials Published After Commencement.* Except for summary advertisements described in paragraph (b) of this section and tender offer materials described in paragraphs (a)(2)(ii) and (a)(3)(ii) of this section, additional tender offer materials published, sent or given to security holders subsequent to the date of commencement shall include the information required by paragraphs (e)(1) and may omit any of the information required by paragraphs (e)(1)(v)–(viii) of this section which has been previously furnished by the bidder in connection with the tender offer.

(d) *Material Changes.* A material change in the information published or sent or given to security holders shall be promptly disclosed to security holders in additional tender offer materials.

(e) *Information to Be Included.*

(1) *Long-Form Publication and Tender Offer Materials.* The information required to be disclosed by paragraphs (a)(1), (a)(2)(ii), (a)(3)(i)(B) and (a)(4) of this section shall include the following:

(i) The identity of the holder;

(ii) The identity of the subject company;

(iii) The amount of class of securities being sought and the type and amount of consideration being offered therefor;

(iv) The scheduled expiration date of the tender offer, whether the tender offer may be extended and, if so, the procedures for extension of the tender offer;

(v) The exact dates prior to which, and after which, security holders who deposit their securities will have the right to withdraw their securities pursuant to section 14(d)(5) of the Act and Rule 14d–7 and the manner in which shares will be accepted for payment and in which withdrawal may be effected;

(vi) If the tender offer is for less than all the outstanding securities of a class of equity securities and the bidder is not obligated to purchase all of the securities tendered, the period or periods, and in the case of the period from the commencement of the offer, the date of the expiration of such period during which the securities will be taken up pro rata pursuant to Section 14(d)(6) of the Act or Rule 14d–8, and the present intention or plan of the bidder with respect to the tender offer in the event of an over subscription by security holders;

(vii) The disclosure required by Items 1(c); 2 (with respect to persons other than the bidder, excluding sub-items (b) and (d); 3; 4; 5; 6; 7; 8; and 10 of Schedule 14D–1 or a fair and adequate summary thereof; *Provided, however,* That negative responses to any such item or sub-item or Schedule 14D–1 need not be included; and

(viii) The disclosure required by Item 9 of Schedule 14D–1 or a fair and adequate summary thereof. ＊ ＊ ＊

(ix) If the financial statements are prepared according to a comprehensive body of accounting principles other than those generally accepted in the United States, the summary financial information shall be accompanied by a reconciliation to generally accepted accounting principles of the United States.

(2) *Summary Publication.* The information required to be disclosed by paragraphs (a)(2)(i) and (a)(3)(i)(A) of this section in a summary advertisement is as follows:

(i) The information required by paragraph (e)(1)(i) through (vi) of this section;

(ii) If the tender offer is for less than all the outstanding securities of a class of equity securities, a statement as to whether the purpose or one of the purposes of the tender offer is to acquire or influence control of the business of the subject company;

(iii) A statement that the information required by paragraph (e)(1)(vii) of this section is incorporated by reference into the summary advertisement;

(iv) Appropriate instructions as to how security holders may obtain promptly, at the bidders expense, the bidder's tender offer materials; and

(v) In a tender offer published or sent or given to security holders by the use of stockholders lists and security position listings pursuant to Rule 14d–4(a)(3), a statement that a request is being made for such lists and listings and that tender offer materials will be mailed to record holders and will be furnished to brokers, banks and similar persons whose name appears or whose nominee appears on the list of stockholders or, if applicable, who are listed as participants in a clearing agency's security position listing for subsequent transmittal to beneficial owners of such securities.

(3) *No Transmittal Letter.* Neither the initial summary advertisement nor any subsequent summary advertisement shall include a transmittal letter (whereby securities of the subject company which are sought in the tender offer may be transmitted to the bidder or its depository) or any amendment thereto.

Rule 14d–7. Additional Withdrawal Rights

(a) *Rights.* In addition to the provisions of section 14(d)(5) of the Act, any person who has deposited securities pursuant to a tender offer has the right to withdraw any such securities during the following periods:

(1) At any time until the expiration of fifteen business days from the date of commencement of such tender offer; and

(2) On the date and until the expiration of ten business days following the date of commencement of another bidder's tender offer other than pursuant to Rule 14d–2(b) for securities of the same class, *Provided,* That the bidder has received notice or otherwise has knowledge of the commencement of such other tender offer and, *Provided further,* That withdrawal may only be effected with respect to securities which have not been accepted for payment in the manner set forth in the bidder's tender offer prior to the date such other tender offer is first published, sent or given to security holders.

(b) *Computation of Time Periods.* The time periods for withdrawal rights pursuant to this section shall be computed on a concurrent, as opposed to a consecutive basis.

(c) *Knowledge of Competing Offer.* For the purposes of this section, a bidder shall be presumed to have knowledge of another tender offer, as described in paragraph (a)(2) of this section, on the date such bidder receives a copy of the Schedule 14D–1 pursuant to Rule 14d–2 from such other bidder.

(d) *Notice of Withdrawal.* Notice of withdrawal pursuant to this section shall be deemed to be timely upon the receipt by the bidder's depositary of a written notice of withdrawal specifying the name(s) of the tendering stockholder(s), the number or amount of the securities to be withdrawn and the name(s) in which the certificate(s) is (are) registered, if different from that of the tendering security holder(s). A bidder may impose other reasonable requirements, including certificate numbers and a signed request for withdrawal accompanied by a signature guarantee, as conditions precedent to the physical release of withdrawn securities.

Rule 14d–8. Exemption From Statutory Pro Rata Requirements

Notwithstanding the pro rata provisions of Section 14(d)(6) of the Act, if any person makes a tender offer or request or invitation for tenders, for less than all of the outstanding equity securities of a class, and if a greater number of securities are deposited pursuant thereto than such person is bound or willing to take up and pay for, the securities taken up and paid for shall be taken up and paid for as nearly as may be pro rata, disregarding fractions, according to the number of securities deposited by each depositor during the period such offer, request or invitation remains open.

Rule 14d–9. Solicitation/Recommendation Statements With Respect to Certain Tender Offers

(a) *Filing and Transmittal of Recommendation Statement.* No solicitation or recommendation to security holders shall be made by any person described in paragraph (d) of this section with respect to a tender offer for such securities unless as soon as practicable on the date such solicitation or recommendation is first published or sent or given to security holders such person complies with the following subparagraphs.

(1) Such person shall file with the Commission eight copies of a Tender Offer Solicitation/Recommendation Statement on Schedule 14D–9, including all exhibits thereto; and

(2) If such person is either the subject company or an affiliate of the subject company,

(i) Such person shall hand deliver a copy of the Schedule 14D–9 to the bidder at its principal office or at the address of the person authorized to receive notices and communications (which is set forth on the cover sheet of the bidder's Schedule 14D–1 filed with the Commission; and

(ii) Such person shall give telephonic notice (which notice to the extent possible shall be given prior to the opening of the market) of the information required by Items 2 and 4(a) of Schedule 14D–9 and shall mail a copy of the Schedule to each national securities exchange where the class of securities is registered and listed for trading and, if the class is authorized for quotation in the NASDAQ interdealer quotation system, to the National Association of Securities Dealers, Inc. ("NASD").

(3) If such person is neither the subject company nor an affiliate of the subject company.

(i) Such person shall mail a copy of the schedule to the bidder at its principal office or at the address of the person authorized to receive notices and communications (which is set forth on the cover sheet of the bidder's Schedule 14D–1 filed with the Commission); and

(ii) Such person shall mail a copy of the Schedule to the subject company at its principal office.

(b) *Amendments.* If any material change occurs in the information set forth in the Schedule 14D–9 required by this section, the person who filed such Schedule 14D–9 shall:

(1) File with the Commission eight copies of an amendment on Schedule 14D–9 disclosing such change promptly, but not later than the date such material is first published, sent or given to security holders; and

(2) Promptly deliver copies and give notice of the amendment in the same manner as that specified in paragraph (a)(2) or paragraph (a)(3) of this section, whichever is applicable; and

(3) Promptly disclose and disseminate such change in a manner reasonably designed to inform security holders of such change.

(c) *Information Required in Solicitation or Recommendation.* Any solicitation or recommendation to holders of a class of securities referred to in section 14(d)(1) of the Act with respect to a tender offer for such securities shall include the name of the person making such solicitation or recommendation and the information required by Items 1, 2, 3(b), 4, 6, 7 and 8 of Schedule 14D–9 or a fair and adequate summary thereof: *Provided, however,* That such solicitation or recommendation may omit any of such information previously furnished to security holders of such class of securities by such person with respect to such tender offer.

(d) *Applicability.*

(1) Except as provided in paragraphs (d)(2) and (e) of this section, this section shall only apply to the following persons:

(i) The subject company, any director, officer, employee, affiliate or subsidiary of the subject company;

(ii) Any record holder or beneficial owner of any security issued by the subject company, by the bidder, or by any affiliate of either the subject company or the bidder; and

(iii) Any person who makes a solicitation or recommendation to security holders on behalf of any of the foregoing or on behalf of the bidder other than by means of a solicitation or recommendation to security holders which has been filed with the Commission pursuant to this section or Rule 14d–3.

(2) Notwithstanding paragraph (d)(1) of this section, this section shall not apply to the following persons:

(i) A bidder who has filed a Schedule 14D–1 pursuant to Rule 14d–3;

(ii) Attorneys, banks, brokers, fiduciaries or investment advisers who are not participating in a tender offer in more than a ministerial capacity and who furnish information and/or advice regarding such tender offer to their customers or clients on the unsolicited request of such customers or clients or solely pursuant to a contract or a relationship providing for advice to the customer or client to whom the information and/or advice is given.

(e) *Stop-Look-and-Listen Communications.* This section shall not apply to the subject company with respect to a communication by the subject company to its security holders which only:

(1) Identifies the tender offer by the bidder;

(2) States that such tender offer is under consideration by the subject company's board of directors and/or management;

(3) States that on or before a specified date (which shall be no later than 10 business days from the date of commencement of such tender offer) the subject company will advise such security holders of (i) whether the subject company recommends acceptance or rejection of such tender offer; expresses no opinion and remains neutral toward such tender offer; or is unable to take a position with respect to such tender offer and (ii) the reason(s) for the position taken by the subject company with respect to the tender offer (including the inability to take a position); and

(4) Requests such security holders to defer making determination whether to accept or reject such tender offer until they have been advised of the subject company's position with respect thereto pursuant to paragraph (e)(3) of this section.

(f) *Statement of Management's Position.* A statement by the subject company's of its position with respect to a tender offer which is required to be published or sent or given to security holders pursuant to Rule 14e–2 shall be deemed to constitute a solicitation or recommendation within the meaning of this section and section 14(d)(4) of the Act.

Rule 14d–100. Schedule 14D–1. Tender Offer Statement Pursuant to Section 14(d)(1) of the Securities Exchange Act of 1934

* * *

GENERAL INSTRUCTIONS

* * *

C. If the statement is filed by a partnership, limited partnership, syndicate or other group, the information called for by Items 2–7, inclusive, shall be given with respect to: (i) each partner of such partnership; (ii) each partner who is denominated as a general partner or who functions as a general partner of such limited partnership; (iii) each member of such syndicate or group; and (iv) each person controlling such partner or member. If the statement is filed by a corporation, or if a person referred to in (i), (ii), (iii), or (iv) of this Instruction is a corporation, the information called for by the above mentioned items shall be given with respect to: (a) each executive officer and director of such corporation; (b) each person controlling such corporation; and (c) each executive officer and director of any corporation ultimately in control of such corporation. A response to an item in the statement is required with respect to the bidder and to all other persons referred to in this instruction unless such item specifies to the contrary.

D. Upon termination of the tender offer, the bidder shall promptly file a final amendment to Schedule 14D–1 disclosing all material changes in the items of that Schedule and stating that the tender offer has terminated, the date of such termination and the results of such tender offer.

E. If the bidder, before filing this statement, has filed a Schedule 13D with respect to the acquisition of securities of the same class referred to in Item 1(a) of this statement, the bidder shall amend such Schedule 13D and may do so by means of this statement and amendments thereto, including the final amendment required to be filed by Instruction D: *Provided,* That the bidder indicated on the cover sheet of this statement that it is amending its Schedule 13D by means of this statement.

F. The final amendment required to be filed by Instruction D shall be deemed to satisfy the reporting requirements of section 13(d) of the Act with respect to all securities acquired by the bidder pursuant to the tender offer as reported in such final amendment.

G. For purposes of this statement, the following definitions shall apply:

(i) The term "bidder" means any person on whose behalf a tender offer is made; and

(ii) The term "subject company" means any issuer whose securities are sought by a bidder pursuant to a tender offer.

Item 1. Security and Subject Company

(a) State the name of the subject company and the address of its principal executive offices;

(b) State the exact title and the number of shares outstanding of the class of equity securities being sought (which may be based upon information contained in the most recently available filing with the Commission by the subject company unless the bidder has reason to believe such information is not current), the exact amount of such securities being sought and the consideration being offered therefor; and

(c) Identify the principal market in which such securities are traded and state the high and low sales prices for such securities in such principal market (or, in the absence thereof, the range of high and low bid quotations) for each quarterly period during the past two years.

Item 2. Identity and Background

If the person filing this statement or any person enumerated in Instruction C of this statement is a corporation, partnership, limited partnership, syndicate or other group of persons, state its name, the state or other place of its organization,its principal business, the address of its principal office and the information required by (e) and (f) of this Item. If the person filing this statement or any person enumerated in Instruction C is a natural person, provide the information specified in (a) through (g) of this Item with respect to such person(s).

(a) Name;

(b) Residence or business address;

(c) Present principal occupation or employment and the name, principal business and address of any corporation or other organization in which such employment or occupation is conducted;

(d) Material occupations, positions, offices or employments during the last 5 years, giving the starting and ending dates of each and the name, principal business and address of any business corporation or other organization in which such occupation, position, office or employment was carried on;

Instruction. If a person has held various positions with the same organization, or if a person holds comparable positions with multiple related organizations, each and every position need not be specifically disclosed.

(e) Whether or not, during the last 5 years, such person has been convicted in a criminal proceeding (excluding traffic violations or similar misdemeanors) and, if so, give the dates, nature of conviction, name and location of court, and penalty imposed or other disposition of the case;

Instruction. While a negative answer to this sub-item is required in this schedule, it need not be furnished to security holders.

(f) Whether or not, during the last 5 years, such person was a party to a civil proceeding of a judicial or administrative body of competent jurisdiction and as a result of such proceeding was or is subject to a judgment, decree or final order enjoining future violations of, or prohibiting activities subject to, federal or state securities laws or finding any violation of such laws; and, if so, identify and describe such proceeding and summarize the terms of such judgment, decree or final order; and

Instruction. While a negative answer to this sub-item is required in this schedule, it need not be furnished to security holders.

(g) Citizenship(s).

Item 3. Past Contracts, Transactions or Negotiations With the Subject Company

(a) Briefly state the nature and approximate amount (in dollars) of any transaction, other than those described in Item 3(b) of this schedule, which has occurred since the commencement of the subject company's third full fiscal year preceding the date of this schedule, between the person filing this schedule (including those persons enumerated in Instruction C of this schedule) and:

(1) the subject company or any of its affiliates which are corporations: *Provided, However,* That no disclosure need be made with respect to any transaction if the aggregate amount involved in such transaction was less than one percent of the subject company's consolidated revenues (which may be based upon information contained in the most recently available filing with the Commission by the subject company, unless the bidder has reason to believe otherwise) (i) for the fiscal year in which such transaction occurred or, (ii) for the portion of the current fiscal year which has occurred, if the transaction occurred in such year; and

(2) the executive officers, directors, or affiliates of the subject company which are not corporations if the aggregate amount involved in such transaction or in a series of similar transactions, including all periodic installments in the case of any lease or other agreement providing for periodic payments or installments, exceeds $40,000.

(b) Describe any contacts, negotiations or transactions which have occurred since the commencement of the subject company's third full fiscal year preceding the date of this schedule between the bidder or its subsidiaries (including those persons enumerated in Instruction C of this schedule) and the subject company or its affiliates concerning: a merger, consolidation or acquisition; a tender offer or other acquisition of securities; an election of directors; or a sale or other transfer of a material amount of assets.

Item 4. Source and Amount of Funds or Other Consideration

(a) State the source and the total amount of funds or other consideration for the purchase of the maximum number of securities for which the tender offer is being made.

(b) If all or any part of such funds or other consideration are or are expected to be, directly or indirectly, borrowed for the purpose of the tender offer:

(1) Provide a summary of each loan agreement or arrangement containing the identity of the parties, the term, the collateral, the stated and effective interest rates, and other material terms or conditions relative to such loan agreement; and

(2) Briefly, describe any plans or arrangements to finance or repay such borrowings, or if no such plans or arrangements have been made, make a statement to that effect.

(c) If the source of all or any part of the funds to be used in the tender offer is a loan made in the ordinary course of business by a bank as defined by section 3(a)(6) of the Act, the name of such bank shall not be made available to the public if the person filing the statement so requests in writing and files such request, naming such bank, with the Secretary of the Commission.

Item 5. Purpose of the Tender Offer and Plans or Proposals of the Bidder

State the purpose or purposes of the tender offer for the subject company's securities. Describe any plans or proposals which relate to or would result in:

(a) An extraordinary corporate transaction, such as a merger, reorganization or liquidation, involving the subject company or any of its subsidiaries;

(b) A sale or transfer of a material amount of assets of the subject company or any of its subsidiaries;

(c) Any change in the present board of directors or management of the subject company including, but not limited to, any plans or proposals to change the number or the term of directors or to fill any existing vacancies on the board;

(d) Any material change in the present capitalization or dividend policy of the subject company;

(e) Any other material change in the subject company's corporate structure or business, including, if the subject company is a registered closed-end investment company, any plans or proposals to make any changes in its investment policy for which a vote would be required by section 13 of the Investment Company Act of 1940;

(f) Causing a class of securities of the subject company to be delisted from a national securities exchange or to cease to be authorized to be quoted in an inter-dealer quotation system of a registered national securities association; or

(g) A class of equity securities of the subject company becoming eligible for termination of registration pursuant to section 12(g)(4) of the Act.

Item 6. Interest in Securities of the Subject Company

(a) State the aggregate number and percentage of the class represented by such shares (which may be based on the number of shares outstanding as contained in the most recently available filing with the Commission by the subject company unless the bidder has reasons to believe such information is not current), beneficially owned (identifying those shares for which there is a right to acquire) by each person named in Item 2 of this schedule and by each associate and majority-owned subsidiary of such person giving the name and address of any such associate or subsidiary.

(b) Describe any transaction in the class of securities reported on that was effected during the past 60 days by the persons named in response to paragraph (a) of this item or by any executive officer, director or subsidiary of such person.

Instructions: 1. The description of a transaction required by Item 6(b) shall include, but not necessarily be limited to: (1) the identity of the person covered by Item 6(b) who effected the transaction; (2) the date of the transaction; (3) the amount of securities involved; (4) the price per share; and (5) where and how the transaction was effected.

2. If the information required by Item 6(b) of this schedule is available to the bidder at the time this statement is initially filed with the Commission pursuant to Rule 14d–3(a)(1), such information should be included in such initial filing. However, if such information is not available to the bidder at the time of such initial filing, it shall be filed with the Commission promptly but in no event later than two business days after the date of such filing and, if material, shall be disclosed in a manner reasonably designed to inform security holders. The procedure specified by this instruction is provided for the purpose of maintaining the confidentiality of the tender offer in order to avoid possible misuse of inside information.

Item 7. Contracts, Arrangements, Understandings or Relationships With Respect to the Subject Company's Securities

Describe any contract, arrangement, understanding or relationship (whether or not legally enforceable) between the bidder (including those persons enumerated in Instruction C to this schedule) and any person with respect to any securities of the subject company (including, but not limited to, any contract, arrangement, understanding or relationship concerning the transfer or the voting of any of such securities, joint ventures, loan or option arrangements, puts or calls, guaranties of loans, guaranties against loss, or the giving or withholding of proxies) naming the persons with whom such contracts, arrangements, understandings or relationships have been entered into and giving the material provisions thereof. Include such information for any of such securities that are pledged or otherwise subject to a contingency, the occurrence of which would give another person the power to direct the voting or disposition of such securities, except that disclosure of standard default and similar provisions contained in loan agreements need not be included.

Item 8. Persons Retained, Employed or to Be Compensated

Identify all persons and classes of persons employed, retained or to be compensated by the bidder, or by any person on the bidder's behalf, to make solicitations or recommendations in connection with the tender offer and describe briefly the terms of such employment, retainer or arrangement for compensation.

Item 9.   Financial Statements of Certain Bidders

Where the bidder is other than a natural person and the bidder's financial condition is material to a decision by a security holder of the subject company whether to sell, tender or hold securities being sought in the tender offer, furnish current, adequate financial information concerning the bidder, *Provided,* That if the bidder is controlled by another entity which is not a natural person and has been formed for the purpose of making the tender offer, furnish current, adequate financial information concerning such parent.

Instructions.   1. The facts and circumstances concerning the tender offer, particularly the terms of the tender offer, may influence a determination as to whether disclosure of financial information is material.   However, once the materiality requirement is applicable, the adequacy of the financial information will depend primarily on the nature of the bidder.

In order to provide guidance in making this determination, the following types of financial information will be deemed adequate for purposes of this item for the type of bidder specified: (a) financial statements prepared in compliance with Form 10 as amended for a domestic bidder which is otherwise eligible to use such form; and (b) financial statements prepared in accordance with Item 17 of Form 20–F for a foreign bidder that is otherwise eligible to use such form.

2.   If the bidder is subject to the periodic reporting requirements of sections 13(a) or 15(d) of the Act, financial statements contained in any document filed with the Commission may be incorporated by reference in this schedule solely for the purposes of this schedule, *Provided,* That such financial statements substantially meet the requirements of this item; an express statement is made that such financial statements are incorporated by reference; the matter incorporated by reference is clearly identified by page, paragraph, caption or otherwise; and an indication is made where such information may be inspected and copies obtained.   Financial statements which are required to be presented in comparative form for two or more fiscal years or periods shall not be incorporated by reference unless the material incorporated by reference includes the entire period for which the comparative data is required to be given.

3.   If the bidder is not subject to the periodic reporting requirements of the Act, the financial statements required by this item need not be audited if such financial statements are not available or obtainable without unreasonable cost or expense and a statement is made to that effect disclosing the reasons therefor.

Item 10.   Additional Information

If material to a decision by a security holder whether to sell, tender or hold securities being sought in the tender offer, furnish information as to the following:

(a) Any present or proposed material contracts, arrangement, understandings or relationships between the bidder or any of its executive officers, directors, controlling persons or subsidiaries and the subject company or any of its executive officers, directors, controlling persons or subsidiaries (other than any contract, arrangement or understanding required to be disclosed pursuant to Items 3 or 7 of this schedule);

(b) To the extent known by the bidder after reasonable investigation, the applicable regulatory requirements which must be complied with or approvals which must be obtained in connection with the tender offer;

(c) The applicability of anti-trust laws;

(d) The applicability of the margin requirements of section 7 of the Act and the regulations promulgated thereunder;

(e) Any material pending legal proceedings relating to the tender offer including the name and location of the court or agency in which the proceedings are pending, the date instituted, the principal parties thereto and a brief summary of the proceedings; and

Instruction. In connection with this sub-item, a copy of any document relating to a major development (such as pleadings, an answer, complaint, temporary restraining order, injunction, opinion, judgment or order) in a material pending legal proceeding should be promptly furnished to the Commission on a supplemental basis.

(f) Such additional material information, if any, as may be necessary to make the required statements, in light of the circumstances under which they are made, not materially misleading.

Item 11. Material to Be Filed as Exhibits

Furnish a copy of:

(a) Tender offer material which is published, sent or given to security holders by or on behalf of the bidder in connection with the tender offer;

(b) Any loan agreement referred to in Item 4 of this schedule;

Instruction. The identity of any bank which is a party to a loan agreement need not be disclosed if the person filing the statement has requested that the identity of such bank not be made available to the public pursuant to Item 4 of this schedule.

(c) Any document setting forth the terms of any contracts, arrangements, understandings or relationships referred to in Item 7 or 10(a) of this schedule;

(d) Any written opinion prepared by legal counsel at the bidder's request and communicated to the bidder pertaining to the tax consequences of the tender offer;

(e) In an exchange offer where securities of the bidder have been or are to be registered under the Securities Act of 1933, the prospectus containing the information to be included therein by Rule 432 of that Act;

(f) If any oral solicitation of security holders is to be made by or on behalf of the bidder, any written instruction, form or other material which is furnished to the persons making the actual oral solicitation for their use, directly or indirectly, in connection with the tender offer.

* * *

Rule 14d–101. Schedule 14D–9

* * *

Item 1. Security and Subject Company

State the title of the class of equity securities to which this statement relates and the name and the address of the principal executive offices of the subject company.

Item 2. Tender Offer of the Bidder

Identify the tender offer to which this statement relates, the name of the bidder and the address of its principal executive offices or, if the bidder is a natural person, the bidder's residence or business address (which may be based on the bidder's Schedule 14D–1 filed with the Commission).

Item 3. Identity and Background

(a) State the name and business address of the person filing this statement.

(b) If material, describe any contract, agreement, arrangement or understanding and any actual or potential conflict of interest between the person filing this statement or its affiliates and: (1) the subject company, its executive officers, directors or affiliates; or (2) the bidder, its executive officers, directors or affiliates.

Instruction. If the person filing this statement is the subject company and if the materiality requirement of Item 3(b) is applicable to any contract, agreement, arrangement or understanding between the subject company or any affiliate of the subject company and any executive officer or director of the subject company, it shall not be necessary to include a description thereof in this statement, or in any solicitation or recommendation published, sent or given to security holders if such information, or information which does not differ materially from such information, has been disclosed in any proxy statement, report or other communication sent within one year of the filing date of this statement by the subject company to the then holders of the securities and has been filed with the Commission: *Provided,* That this statement and the solicitation or recommendation published, sent or given to security holders shall contain specific reference to such proxy statement, report or other communication and that a copy of the pertinent portion(s) thereof is filed as an exhibit to this statement.

Item 4. The Solicitation or Recommendation

(a) State the nature of the solicitation or the recommendation. If this statement relates to a recommendation, state whether the person filing this statement is advising security holders of the securities being sought by the bidder to accept or reject the tender offer or to take other action with respect to the tender offer and, if so, furnish a description of such other action being recommended. If the person filing this statement is the subject company and a recommendation is not being made, state whether the subject company is either expressing no opinion and is remaining neutral toward the tender offer or is unable to take a position with respect to the tender offer.

(b) State the reason(s) for the position (including the inability to take a position) stated in (a) of this Item.

Instruction. Conclusory statements such as "The tender offer is in the best interest of shareholders," will not be considered sufficient disclosure in response to Item 4(b).

Item 5. Persons Retained, Employed or to Be Compensated

Identify any person or class of persons employed, retained or to be compensated by the person filing this statement or by any person on its behalf, to make solicitations or recommendations to security holders and describe briefly the terms of such employment, retainer or arrangement for compensation.

Item 6. Recent Transactions and Intent With Respect to Securities

(a) Describe any transaction in the securities referred to in Item 1 which was effected during the past 60 days by the person(s) named in response to Item 3(a) and by any executive officer, director, affiliate or subsidiary of such person(s).

(b) To the extent known by the person filing this statement, state whether the persons referred to in Item 6(a) presently intend to tender to the bidder, sell or hold securities of the class of securities being sought by the bidder which are held of record or beneficially owned by such persons.

Item 7. Certain Negotiations and Transactions by the Subject Company

(a) If the person filing this statement is the subject company, state whether or not any negotiation is being undertaken or is underway by the subject company in response to the tender offer which relates to or would result in:

(1) An extraordinary transaction such as a merger or reorganization, involving the subject company or any subsidiary of the subject company;

(2) A purchase, sale or transfer of a material amount of assets by the subject company or any subsidiary of the subject company;

(3) A tender offer for or other acquisition of securities by or of the subject company; or

(4) Any material change in the present capitalization or dividend policy of the subject company.

Instruction. If no agreement in principle had yet been reached, the possible terms of any transaction or the parties thereto need not be disclosed if in the opinion of the Board of Directors of the subject company such disclosure would jeopardize continuation of such negotiations. In such event, disclosure that negotiations are being undertaken or are underway and are in the preliminary states will be sufficient.

(b) Describe any transaction, board resolution, agreement in principle, or a signed contract in response to the tender offer, other than one described pursuant to Item 3(b) of this statement, which relates to or would result in one or more of the matters referred to in Item 7(a)(1), (2), (3) or (4).

Item 8. Additional Information to Be Furnished

Furnish such additional information, if any, as may be necessary to make the required statements, in light of the circumstances under which they are made, not materially misleading.

Item 9. Material to Be Filed as Exhibits

Furnish a copy of:

(a) Any written solicitation or recommendation which is published or sent or given to security holders in connection with the solicitation or recommendation referred to in Item 4.

(b) If any oral solicitation or recommendation to security holders is to be made by or on behalf of the person filing this statement, any written instruction, or other material which is furnished to the persons making the actual oral solicitation or recommendation for their use, directly or indirectly, in connection with the solicitation or recommendation.

(c) Any contract, agreement, arrangement or understanding described in Item 3(b) or the pertinent portion(s) of any proxy statement, report or other communication referred to in Item 3(b).

*   *   *

REGULATION 14E

Rule 14e–1. Unlawful Tender Offer Practices

As a means reasonably designed to prevent fraudulent, deceptive or manipulative acts or practices within the meaning of section 14(e) of the Act, no person who makes a tender offer shall:

(a) Hold such tender offer open for less than twenty business days from the date such tender offer is first published or sent or given to security holders: *Provided, however,* That this paragraph shall not apply to a tender offer by the issuer of the class of securities being sought which is not made in anticipation of or in response to another person's tender offer for securities of the same class.

(b) Increase the offered consideration or the dealer's soliciting fee to be given in a tender offer unless such tender offer remains open for at least ten business days from the date that notice of such increase is first published, sent or given to security holders: *Provided, however,* That this paragraph shall not apply to a tender offer by the issuer of the class of securities being sought which is not made in anticipation of or in response to another person's tender offer for securities of the same class.

(c) Fail to pay the consideration offered or return the securities deposited by or on behalf of security holders promptly after the termination or withdrawal of a tender offer.

(d) Extend the length of a tender offer without issuing a notice of such extension by press release or other public announcement, which notice shall include disclosure of the approximate number of securities deposited to date and shall be issued no later than the earlier of (i) 9:00 a.m. Eastern time, on the next business day after the scheduled expiration date of the offer or (ii), if the class of securities which is the subject of the tender offer is registered on one or more national securities exchanges, the first opening of any one of such exchanges on the next business day after the scheduled expiration date of the offer.

Rule 14e–2. Position of Subject Company With Respect to a Tender Offer

(a) *Position of Subject Company.* As a means reasonably designed to prevent fraudulent, deceptive or manipulative acts or practices within the meaning of section 14(e) of the Act, the subject company, no later than 10 business days from the date the tender offer is first published or sent or given, shall publish, send or give to security holders a statement disclosing that the subject company:

(1) Recommends acceptance or rejection of the bidder's tender offer;

(2) Expresses no opinion and is remaining neutral toward the bidder's tender offer; or

(3) Is unable to take a position with respect to the bidder's tender offer.

Such statement shall also include the reason(s) for the position (including the inability to take a position) disclosed therein.

(b) *Material Change.* If any material change occurs in the disclosure required by paragraph (a) of this section, the subject company shall promptly publish, send or give a statement disclosing such material charge to security holders.

Rule 14e–3. Transactions in Securities on the Basis of Material, Nonpublic Information in the Context of Tender Offers

(a) If any person has taken a substantial step or steps to commence, or has commenced, a tender offer (the "offering person"), it shall constitute a fraudulent, deceptive or manipulative act or practice within the meaning of section 14(e) of the Act for any other person who is in possession of material information relating to such tender offer which information he knows or has reason to know is nonpublic and which he knows or has reason to know has been acquired directly or indirectly from (1) the offering person, (2) the issuer of the securities sought or to be sought by such tender offer, or (3) any officer, director, partner or employee or any other person acting on behalf of the offering person or such issuer, to purchase or sell or cause to be purchased or sold any of such securities or any securities convertible into or exchangeable for any such securities or any option or right to obtain or to dispose of any of the foregoing securities, unless within a reasonable time prior to any purchase or sale such information and its source are publicly disclosed by press release or otherwise.

(b) A person other than a natural person shall not violate paragraph (a) of this section if such person shows that:

(1) The individual(s) making the investment decision on behalf of such person to purchase or sell any security described in paragraph (a) or to cause any such security to be purchased or sold by or on behalf of others did not know the material, nonpublic information; and

(2) Such person had implemented one or a combination of policies and procedures, reasonable under the circumstances, taking into consideration the nature of the person's business, to ensure that individual(s) making investment decision(s) would not violate paragraph (a), which policies and procedures may include, but are not limited to, (i) those which restrict any purchase, sale and causing any purchase and sale of any such security or (ii) those which prevent such individual(s) from knowing such information.

(c) Notwithstanding anything in paragraph (a) to the contrary, the following transactions shall not be violations of paragraph (a) of this section:

(1) Purchase(s) of any security described in paragraph (a) by a broker or by another agent on behalf of an offering person; or

(2) Sale(s) by any person of any security described in paragraph (a) to the offering person.

(d)(1) As a means reasonably designed to prevent fraudulent, deceptive or manipulative acts or practices within the meaning of section 14(e) of the Act, it shall be unlawful for any person described in paragraph (d)(2) of this section to communicate material, nonpublic information relating to a tender offer to any other person under circumstances in which it is reasonably foreseeable that such communication is likely to result in a violation of this section *except* that this paragraph shall not apply to a communication made in good faith:

(i) To the officers, directors, partners or employees of the offering person, to its advisors or to other persons, involved in the planning, financing, preparation or execution of such tender offer;

(ii) To the issuer whose securities are sought or to be sought by such tender offer, to its officers, directors, partners, employees or advisors or to other persons, involved in the planning, financing, preparation or execution of the activities of the issuer with respect to such tender offer; or

(iii) To any person pursuant to a requirement of any statute or rule or regulation promulgated thereunder.

(d)(2) The persons referred to in paragraph (d)(1) of this section are:

(i) The offering person or its officers, directors, partners, employees or advisors;

(ii) The issuer of the securities sought or to be sought by such tender offer or its officers, directors, partners, employees or advisors;

(iii) Anyone acting on behalf of the persons in paragraph (d)(2)(i) or the issuer or persons in paragraph (d)(2)(ii); and

(iv) Any person in possession of material information relating to a tender offer which information he knows or has reason to know is nonpublic and which he knows or has reason to know has been acquired directly or indirectly from any of the above.

Rule 14f–1. Change in Majority of Directors

If, pursuant to any arrangement or understanding with the person or persons acquiring securities in a transaction subject to section 13(d) or 14(d) of the Act, any persons are to be elected or designated as directors of the issuer, otherwise than at a meeting of security holders, and the persons so elected or designated will constitute a majority of the directors of the issuer, then, not less than 10 days prior to the date any such person take office as a director, or such shorter period prior to that date as the Commission may authorize upon a showing of good cause therefor, the issuer shall file with the Commission and transmit to all holders of record of securities of the issuer who would be entitled to vote at a meeting for election of directors, information substantially equivalent to the information which would be required by Items 5(a), (d), (e), and (f), 6 and 7 of Schedule 14A of Regulation 14A to be transmitted if such person or persons were nominees for election as directors at a meeting of such security holders. Eight copies of such information shall be filed with the Commission.

* * *

*

APPENDIX B

FORM OF ACQUISITION AGREEMENT

PLAN OF REORGANIZATION

This Agreement, made this _____ day of _____, 19__, between Acquiring Corp., a Delaware corporation (hereinafter called "Acquiring"), Target Corp., a California corporation (hereinafter called "Target"), and Controlling Shareholder, a California resident (hereinafter called the "Shareholder"):

WITNESSETH:

WHEREAS, Target is a corporation duly organized, validly existing and in good standing under the laws of the State of California; and

WHEREAS, Acquiring is a corporation duly organized, validly existing and in good standing under the laws of the State of Delaware; and

WHEREAS, Acquiring will form a California corporation (hereinafter "Subsidiary") which shall be a wholly-owned subsidiary of Acquiring; and

WHEREAS, if the conditions for the merger contemplated herein are satisfied, Subsidiary will be merged into Target pursuant to Section 368(a) of the Internal Revenue Code of 1954, as amended; and

WHEREAS, the respective Boards of Directors of Acquiring and Target deem it advisable for the general welfare and advantage of the respective corporations and their respective shareholders that, subject to the terms and conditions herein contained and in accordance with the applicable laws of the State of California, Subsidiary merge (hereinafter sometimes called the "Merger") with and into Target, with Target being the surviving corporation (hereinafter sometimes called the "Surviving Corporation");

NOW, THEREFORE, in consideration of the premises and the mutual agreements, provisions, covenants and grants herein contained, the parties hereto hereby agree that if the conditions for the Merger contained herein are satisfied prior to the Merger, Subsidiary shall be merged into Target in accordance with the applicable laws of the State of California, and that the terms and conditions of the Merger and the mode of carrying it into effect are and shall be as hereinafter set forth:

I. COMPUTATION OF TARGET'S NET WORTH AND ACQUIRING'S NET WORTH

A. Acquiring shall cause a certified public accounting firm (the "Accountants") of its own selection, at its own expense, to audit the financial position of Target as of December 31, 19__. This audit shall be of the financial position of Target prior to giving effect to the sale of certain assets of Target constituting its "Southward Division," although all other references herein give effect to such sale having been consummated. In connection therewith, Acquiring and its representatives, and the Accountants, may make such investigation of the properties, books and records of Target and its legal and financial condition as Acquiring or the Accountants shall deem necessary and/or advisable to familiarize Acquiring and Subsidiary with said properties and other matters; such investigation shall not, however, affect the Shareholder's and Target's representations and warranties hereunder. The Shareholder and Target agree to permit Acquiring and said other parties to have full access to all premises occupied by and to all the books and records of Target, and the officers and employees of Target will be instructed to furnish them with such financial and operating data and other information with respect to the business and properties of Target as they shall from time to time reasonably request. The Shareholder and Target shall deliver to Acquiring unaudited interim financial statements of Target as they are prepared and shall cause such other reasonable financial information of Target to be prepared and delivered to Acquiring at any time during the term of this Agreement as Acquiring may request; provided, however, that the Shareholder and Target shall not be required to cause such interim financial information to be prepared more frequently than once each month. At any time during the term of this Agreement, but not more frequently than once each three months, Acquiring may, in its sole discretion and at its own expense, cause a firm of independent certified accountants to audit the financial position of Target.

B. The audit of the financial position of Target as of December 31, 19__, to be conducted by the Accountants, shall be conducted in accordance with generally accepted accounting principles consistently applied. A balance sheet (the "Balance Sheet") setting forth Target's financial position as of December 31, 19__, shall be prepared based on the audit, and certified by the Accountants, without exception. The Balance Sheet, so prepared, shall be a final determination of the financial position of Target as of the date thereof, and shall be conclusive for purposes of determining Target's Net Worth. Target's Net Worth shall be the amount of the shareholders' equity of Target as of December 31, 19__.

C. For purposes of this Agreement, Acquiring's Net Worth shall mean the amount of its stockholders' equity as of December 31, 19__, as presented on its unaudited financial statements as filed with the Securities and Exchange Commission on Form 10–Q. For purposes of this Agreement, Acquiring's Book Value Per Share shall be that quotient resulting from dividing Acquiring's Net Worth by the number of shares of Acquiring Common Stock which are issued and outstanding on December 31, 19__.

D. When Target's Net Worth and Acquiring's Net Worth and Book Value Per Share have been computed as provided in this Agreement, the Shareholder, Target and Acquiring shall execute Exhibit I to be attached hereto, acknowledging said Net Worth figures and Acquiring's Book Value Per Share.

II. *TERMS OF MERGER*

Subject to this Agreement being consummated and to the terms and conditions herein stated:

A.   At the Closing, all of the common stock of Target shall be converted as a result of the Merger into shares of Acquiring's Common Stock.   The number of shares of Acquiring's Common Stock which Shareholder will receive as a result of the Merger will be equal to the amount computed by dividing Target's Net Worth by Acquiring's Book Value Per Share and adding 15,000 shares thereto.   The shares of Acquiring Common Stock which are so computed to be due to Shareholder are hereinafter identified as the "Merger Shares."

B.   (1) The Shareholder hereby agrees that at the Closing, upon receipt of the Merger Shares, he will immediately deposit 15,000 of such Merger Shares into escrow for a period ending no later than 42 months after the Closing at which time the escrowed Merger Shares then remaining in escrow will be returned to him.

(2) The Shareholder agrees to enter into an escrow agreement substantially in the form of the escrow agreement attached hereto as Appendix A (hereinafter the "Escrow Agreement"), with National Bank (hereinafter "Depository"), which Escrow Agreement will provide that the 15,000 escrowed shares will be held subject to the following provisions:

(a) If during the first four full fiscal quarters of Target succeeding the Closing ("Year One"), the business operations which constituted Target on the date of the Closing (hereinafter the "Operations") shall experience net sales equal to or in excess of 115% of those experienced by the Operations in the twelve full months (the "Base Year") immediately preceding Year One and have pretax earnings (after elimination of all non-operating gains and losses) equal to or in excess of 3.4% of net sales, then 5,000 shares of Acquiring Common Stock placed in escrow by the Shareholder shall be released from the escrow and delivered to the Shareholder within 90 days of the end of Year One.

(b) If during the first four fiscal quarters of Target following Year One ("Year Two"), the Operations experienced net sales equal to or in excess of 132% of those experienced by the Operations in the Base Year, and pretax earnings (after elimination of non-operating gains and losses) equal to or in excess of 4.2% of such net sales, then 5,000 shares of Acquiring Common Stock placed in escrow by the Shareholder shall be released from the escrow and delivered to the Shareholder within 90 days of the end of Year Two.

(c) If during the four fiscal quarters of Target following Year Two ("Year Three"), the Operations shall experience net sales equal to or in excess of 152% of those experienced by the Operations in the Base Year, and pretax earnings (after elimination of non-operating gains and losses) equal to or in excess of 4.8% of such sales, then 5,000 shares of Acquiring Common Stock placed in escrow by the Shareholder shall be released from the escrow and delivered to the Shareholder within 90 days after the end of Year Three.

(d) Notwithstanding subsections II.B.(2)(a)—(c) above, in the event that any Merger Shares received by the Shareholder at the Closing remain in escrow after the end of Year Three, all of such shares shall be released from the escrow and delivered to the Shareholder within 90 days after the end of Year Three, if the Operations shall experience net sales in Year Three equal to or in excess of 152% of those experienced by the Operations in the Base Year, and the aggregate pretax earnings (after elimination of non-operating gains and losses) of the Operations in the Years One, Two and Three shall equal or exceed the sum of (i) 3.4% of the Year One's net sales, (ii) 4.2% of Year Two's net sales and (iii) 4.8% of Year Three's net sales.

(e) Those escrowed Merger Shares which are not released from escrow and delivered to Shareholder pursuant to Sections II.B.(2)(a) through II.B.(2)(d) shall be returned to Acquiring 42 months following the Closing. Prior to such date all voting and dividend rights in the escrowed Merger Shares shall belong to Shareholder, as stated in the Escrow Agreement. Dividends, whether in cash, stock or other securities or property (other than Acquiring Common Stock) paid on, or in respect of the escrowed Merger Shares, shall be retained by Shareholder. Dividends in Acquiring Common Stock and Acquiring Common Stock issued as a result of a stock split shall be delivered by Shareholder to the Depository to be held in escrow and distributed with the Acquiring Common Stock in respect of which it was issued.

(f) It is agreed that until the end of Year Three, Acquiring shall not charge any general or administrative expenses of Acquiring to the Surviving Corporation nor shall it be reimbursed by the Surviving Corporation for any expenses other than those directly incurred on the Surviving Corporation's behalf; *provided, however,* Acquiring shall be entitled to reasonable interest on any loans or advances made to the Surviving Corporation.

C. When this Agreement and the transaction contemplated hereby shall have been adopted, approved, executed, and an agreement of Merger filed in accordance with the laws of the State of California, the separate existence of Subsidiary shall cease and it shall be merged into

Target.   The date on which the Merger is effected shall be known as the "Closing Date".

D.   The laws which are to govern the Surviving Corporation are the laws of the State of California.   The Articles of Incorporation of Target as in effect on the Closing Date (unless otherwise set forth in the Agreement of Merger) shall be the Articles of Incorporation of the Surviving Corporation from and after the Closing, subject always to the right of the Surviving Corporation to amend its Articles of Incorporation in accordance with the laws of the State of California.

E.   The Bylaws of Target in effect immediately prior to the Closing Date shall be and remain the Bylaws of the Surviving Corporation until the same shall be altered, amended or repealed as provided therein or as provided by law.

F.   The directors and officers of Target on the Closing Date shall be the directors and officers of the Surviving Corporation immediately following the Merger.

G.   On, or prior to, the Closing Date, Acquiring will issue and deliver the Merger Shares to Subsidiary to be delivered to Shareholder upon surrender by the Shareholder to Acquiring of the certificates theretofore representing all of the outstanding shares of the common stock of Target.

H.   At the Closing, all of the common stock of Subsidiary shall be converted as a result of the Merger into 100 shares of Target common stock.

I.   In the event that, subsequent to the date of this Agreement but prior to the Closing, the outstanding shares of Acquiring Common Stock shall have been, without consideration, increased, decreased, changed into or exchanged for a different number or kind of shares of securities through reorganization, recapitalization, reclassification, stock dividend, stock split, reverse stock split, or other like changes in Acquiring's capitalization, then an appropriate and proportionate adjustment shall be made in the number and kind of shares to be issued to the Shareholder on the Closing Date and to be placed in escrow by the Shareholder.

III.   WARRANTIES, REPRESENTATIONS AND AGREE-MENTS OF THE SHAREHOLDER AND TARGET

A.   Target and the Shareholder jointly and severally represent, warrant and agree as follows:

(1) Target is a corporation duly organized, validly existing and in good standing under the laws of the State of California, with the power to own its property, to carry on its business as now being conducted, and to enter into and carry out the terms of this Agreement.

(2) Target is not qualified to do business as a foreign corporation in any jurisdiction; and neither the character of the properties

owned and leased by Target, nor the nature of the business conducted by Target makes qualification as a foreign corporation in any other jurisdiction necessary.

(3) The Shareholder is the lawful owner of, and has good and marketable title to, all of the outstanding capital stock of Target, free and clear of any mortgages, pledges, claims, liens, charges or encumbrances, or other rights in third persons to purchase any shares thereof.

(4) The authorized capital stock of Target consists of _____ shares of common stock, $1 par value, of which _____ shares are issued and outstanding, and no shares are held as treasury stock. All of the issued and outstanding shares of Target have been duly authorized and validly issued and are fully paid and non-assessable. There are no outstanding options, warrants, rights, calls, commitments, conversion rights, plans or other agreements of any character providing for the purchase of any authorized but unissued shares of the capital stock of Target. Prior to the Closing, Target will not issue any capital stock or authorize any increase in the number of shares of its authorized capital stock or issue any options, warrants, calls, commitments or rights to subscribe for or purchase any of its securities. Copies of the Articles of Incorporation, Bylaws and all minutes of Target are contained in the minute books of Target and such minute books and all stock books of Target will be delivered to Acquiring at the Closing.

(5) Each balance sheet delivered to Acquiring pursuant to this Agreement shall reflect all claims, debts or liabilities of Target which should be reflected thereon in accordance with generally accepted accounting principles. Without the prior written consent of Acquiring other than in the ordinary course of business or as otherwise permitted herein, Target will not incur, prior to the Closing, any indebtedness for money borrowed or incur any liabilities.

(6) All of Target's inventories, except for quantities deemed not to be material, of finished foods, work in process, raw materials and supplies are current, usable and merchantable and are not excessive or out of balance, are in the physical possession of Target and will be valued on the Balance Sheet and all financial statements furnished to Acquiring pursuant to this Agreement at the lower-of-cost-or-market (cost being computed on a "First-in, First-out" basis).

(7) Since November 30, 19__, Target has not issued, or declared or paid any dividend on, or declared or made any distribution on, or authorized the creation or issuance of, or effected any split-up or any recapitalization of any of its capital stock of any class, or, directly or indirectly, redeemed, purchased or otherwise acquired any of its outstanding stock or authorized or made any change in its Articles of Incorporation or agreed to take any such action and, prior to the Closing, Target will take no such action.

(8) Target has filed all requisite Federal income, payroll and excise tax returns and all appropriate state and local income, sales, payroll, personal property and franchise tax returns required to be filed by it and has paid all taxes and assessments (including interest or penalties) owned by it to the extent that such taxes and assessments are due. To the extent any subsequent tax liabilities have accrued but have not become payable, the full amounts thereof have been reflected as liabilities on the books and in the financial statements of Target as of the date of their accrual. In addition, Target has paid all taxes which would not require the filing of returns and which are required to be paid and which otherwise would be delinquent.

(9) Target does not own any real property. Except as noted on Schedule A,* Target has good and marketable title to all of its personal property, free and clear of all encumbrances, liens and charges of every kind and character. None of the personal property of Target is subject (i) to a contract for sale, except inventory to be sold in the ordinary course of business, or (ii) to mortgages, pledges, liens, encumbrances, security interests or charges of any kind of character except as herein disclosed or as set forth in Schedule A. Except as set forth on Schedule A, all buildings, structures, appurtenances, machinery and equipment owned or leased by Target are in good operating condition and in a state of good maintenance and repair, ordinary wear and tear excepted. There is no real or personal property currently used in the Operations which is not either leased or owned by Target, and all property owned or leased by Target is in its possession.

(10) Set forth on Schedule B * hereto is a list of all leases under which Target holds any real or personal property. Each lease set forth in such schedule is in full force and effect, all rents and additional rents due to date on each such lease have been paid; in each case the lessee has been in peaceable possession since the commencement of the original term of such lease and neither Target nor, to the best of its knowledge, any lessor is in default thereunder; no waiver, indulgence or postponement of the lessee's obligations thereunder has been granted by the lessor, or of the lessor's obligations by lessee; and there exists no event, occurrence, condition or act which, with the giving of notice, and lapse of time or the happening of any further event or condition would become a default by the lessee (or to the best of Target's knowledge any lessor) under any such lease. Target has not violated any of the terms of conditions under any such lease and all of the covenants to be performed by the lessee and lessor under each such lease have been fully performed.

(11) Set forth on Schedule C * hereto is a true and correct list of all obligations for indebtedness and all obligations not incurred

* Schedules A, B, and C have been omitted. [Ed.]

in the ordinary course of business stating the origin of the obligation, amount owed and the terms of payment.

(12) Set forth on Schedule D* hereto is a true and correct list of all policies of insurance on which Target is named as the insured party, including the amounts thereof, in force as at the date hereof, and such policies are in full force and effect. Target will continue to maintain the coverage afforded by such policies in full force and effect up to and including the Closing Date.

(13) Set forth on Schedule E* is a true and correct listing of all trade secrets, technical information, patents, patent rights, applications for patents, trademarks, trade names, copyrights, processes or formulae owned, possessed, licensed or used by Target in its business. Except as set forth in such schedule, none of such trademarks or trade names have been registered in, filed in, or issued by any governmental office. Except as noted on such schedule, to the best of Shareholder's and Target's knowledge, no such trademark or trade name infringes on others. Except as noted on such schedule, no such trademark or trade name is licensed by Target to, or used by Target, pursuant to a license from, any other person, firm or corporation in the United States or elsewhere. Except as set forth in Schedule E, Target has full right, title and ownership to its corporate name and to any and all other names under which it does business. Target possesses valid rights to use all trademarks, trade names, and licenses now used or necessary to conduct its business as presently being conducted.

(14) Except as set forth in Schedule F* hereto, there are no actions, suits or proceedings which have been served on Target or to Target's knowledge, threatened against or which affect Target, at law or in equity, by or before any Federal, state or municipal court or other governmental department, commission, board, bureau, agency or instrumentality. Target is not subject to any material liability by reason of a violation of any order, rule, or regulation of any Federal, state, municipal or other governmental agency, department, commission, bureau, board or instrumentality to which it is subject. To the best information and belief of the Shareholder, there exists no event, condition or other circumstance (relating particularly to the business of Target as contrasted with matters relating to its industry or of a regional, national or international character) which immediately or with a lapse of time will materially adversely affect the business of Target as presently conducted.

(15) Except as set forth in Schedule G* hereto, Target does not have any collective bargaining agreements with employees, employment agreements, compensation plans, employees' pension or retirement plans or pension trust, employees' profit sharing or bonus or stock purchase plans or any other similar agreements or plans

---

* Schedules D, E, F and G have been omitted. [Ed.]

(formal or informal). To the knowledge of Target and Shareholder, no party is in violation of any of the provisions of such agreements or plans. Target has not had any work stoppage due to concerted action by any of its employees and to the best of its knowledge none is threatened or contemplated. Between the date hereof and the Closing, Target will not, without the written consent of Acquiring, except in the ordinary course of business and consistent with prior practices, make or agree to make any increase in the rate of wages, salaries, bonuses, or other remuneration of any employee or employees, or become a party to any employment contract or arrangement with any of its officers or employees, or become a party to any contract or arrangement with any officers or employees providing for bonuses or profit sharing payments, severance pay or retirement benefits.

(16) Set forth in Schedule H* hereto is a true and correct list of all outstanding contracts, agreements or understanding to which Target is a party, except (i) those referred to elsewhere in this Section II, (ii) any contract, agreement or understanding involving an aggregate expenditure of less than $5,000 and (iii) purchase commitments for Target inventory which Target expects to sell within 30 days of receipt in the ordinary course of business. Neither Target nor to the best of its knowledge any other party to any such contract, agreement or understanding is in default under the terms of any such contract, agreement or understanding. Between the date hereof and the Closing, Target will not, without the written consent of Acquiring, make any changes or modifications in any such contracts, agreements or understanding, which result in an increase of Target's obligations by more than $2,000 for each such agreement or surrender any rights thereunder, or make any further additions to its property or further purchases of equipment except such changes or modifications, each in an amount less than $5,000, as are in the ordinary course of business or are necessary or appropriate to maintain its properties and equipment and except for the replacement of any trucks as are necessary or appropriate. Target is not a party to any continuing contract for the future purchase of materials, supplies or equipment in excess of the requirements for its business as now being conducted. Neither Target nor the Shareholder is subject to, or is a party to, any mortgage, lien, lease, agreement, contract, instrument, order, judgment or degree or any other restriction of any kind or character which would prevent the continued operation of the business of Target after the Closing on substantially the same basis as theretofore operated.

(17) Neither Target nor the Shareholder is subject to any order, judgment or decree with respect to Target's business or any of Target's assets or property, or to any charter, bylaw, mortgage, lease, agreement, instrument, order, judgment or decree which

---

* Schedule H has been omitted. [Ed.]

would prevent the consummation of any of the transactions contemplated hereunder, or compliance by Target or the Shareholder with the terms, conditions and provisions hereof.

(18) All outstanding accounts receivable (trade or other) of Target as will be set forth in the Balance Sheet and in Target's books and records, and in any other financial statements prepared by Target pursuant to the terms of this Agreement will be collectible, except to the extent of the reasonable reserve for bad debts to be set forth on said Balance Sheet, books and records, or other financial statements.

(19) Since December 31, 19__, the business, properties, or condition, financial or otherwise, of Target has not been materially adversely affected in any way as a result of any legislative or regulatory change, revocation of any license or right to do business, fire, explosion, accident, casualty, labor trouble, flood, drought, riot, storm, condemnation, or act of God or other public force or otherwise (whether or not covered by insurance).

(20) The copies of all leases, instruments, agreements or other documents that have been or will be delivered to Acquiring or Subsidiary pursuant to the terms of this Agreement are and will be complete and correct as of the date delivered and as of the Closing. Except as set forth in Schedule I,* the execution and delivery of this Agreement and the other agreements which are to be executed pursuant to this Agreement (all such agreements, including this Agreement, are sometimes collectively referred to as the "Executed Agreements"), and the performance of the obligations thereunder do not on the date hereof and will not hereafter violate any of the terms of provisions of any leases, instruments, agreements or other documents to which Target is a party and none require the consent of any third party to the transactions contemplated hereby.

(21) Target has maintained its books of account in accordance with generally accepted accounting principles applied on a consistent basis.

(22) In the negotiations leading up to the transactions contemplated by this Agreement, neither the Shareholder nor Target has retained or utilized the services of any broker or finder.

(23) During the period from the date hereof to and including the Closing, Target will conduct its business solely in the usual and ordinary manner and will refrain from any transaction not in the ordinary course of business or except as otherwise permitted herein unless the prior written consent of Acquiring to such transaction has been obtained.

(24) All actions and proceedings required by law to be taken either by Target or the Shareholder at or prior to the Closing in connection with the Executed Agreements and the transactions

---

* Schedule I has been omitted. [Ed.]

provided for therein shall be duly and validly taken on or prior to the Closing.

(25) To the knowledge of the Shareholder, no information necessary to make any of the representations and warranties herein contained not materially misleading has been withheld from or has not been disclosed to, Acquiring.

(26) The only officers and directors of Target are:

Name	**Position**
	President and Director
	Vice President, Secretary and Director
	Vice President, Sales
	Treasurer and Director
	Assistant Secretary and Director
	Director

(27) Target will give Acquiring written notice of all meetings (or actions in writing without a meeting) of Target's Board of Directors and/or its shareholder held (or taken) prior to the Closing at least ten days prior to such meeting (or the taking of actions without a meeting). The notice herein provided shall disclose the purpose of the meeting or the proposed action in writing without a meeting. Acquiring may at its discretion waive the ten days' notice requirement of this subsection. Target shall allow a representative of Acquiring to attend, as an observer, any meeting of its Board of Directors or of its shareholders. Promptly after preparation of the minutes for any of the above-described meetings or actions, Target shall cause a copy of such minutes to be forwarded to Acquiring.

(28) Target does not have any subsidiaries or affiliates or own any interest in any other business, corporation, joint venture, partnership or proprietorship.

B.   The Shareholder covenants, warrants and represents both as of the date hereof and as of the Closing Date, as follows:

(1) That, except as required in connection with his employment by Target, he will not disclose or use at any time any secret, confidential or proprietary information or knowledge pertaining to the business affairs of Target.

(2) That he has no claim against Target except for current salary, and claims disclosed in Schedule J * attached hereto.

(3) That he has full power, right and authority to enter into this Agreement and agrees to vote his shares of Target common stock in favor of the transactions contemplated by this Agreement.

* Schedule J has been omitted. [Ed.]

(4) Shareholder recognizes that among the intangible assets of Target is its goodwill. Until the Closing, Shareholder will utilize his best efforts to keep Target's business intact, to keep available to the Surviving Corporation the services of Target's present officers and employees, and to preserve for the Surviving Corporation the goodwill of Target's suppliers and customers and the goodwill of others with whom Target has business relations. Shareholder agrees that, for a period of three (3) years following the Closing Date, he will not, without the written consent of Acquiring or as an employee of Target, on his own behalf or as a partner, officer, executive, employee, agent, consultant, director, trustee, or shareholder (except as a shareholder of not more than 5% of the outstanding securities of a publicly held corporation) carry on a business of the type conducted by Target on the Closing Date or engage in any business which would be competitive with such business within any county in any state in which Target has carried on its business and so long as Target continues a like business therein.

IV. *WARRANTIES, REPRESENTATIONS AND AGREEMENTS OF ACQUIRING*

Acquiring represents, warrants and agrees as follows:

A. Acquiring is a corporation duly organized, validly existing and in good standing under the laws of the State of Delaware and has the corporate power to own its property and to carry on its business as now being conducted by it.

B. As of November 30, 19__, the authorized capital stock of Acquiring consisted of _____ shares of Common Stock, par value $1 per share, and _____ shares of Preferred Stock, par value $1 per share.

C. The Merger Shares when issued and delivered pursuant to this Agreement will be duly authorized, validly issued, fully paid and nonassessable Common Stock of Acquiring listed on the American Stock Exchange (or listed subject to notice of issuance), free and clear of all preemptive rights, and other claims, liens or encumbrances whatsoever.

D. All actions and proceedings required by law to be taken by Acquiring and Subsidiary at or prior to the Closing Date in connection with the Executed Agreements and the transactions provided for therein shall have been duly and validly taken on or prior to the Closing Date.

E. Acquiring's Board of Directors has approved the transactions contemplated by this Agreement.

F. Acquiring shall apply for a tax ruling at its expense that no gain will be realized as a result of the Merger or as a result of the release of shares from the escrow referred to in Article II.

G. In the event the Merger is not consummated, all written information furnished to Acquiring or its representatives with respect to Target shall be returned to Acquiring, and Acquiring shall keep confidential all non-public information obtained pursuant to the terms of this Agreement.

H. (1) Acquiring will at any time or times during the three years immediately following the Closing Date, upon the written request of the Shareholder and at his expense, file as soon as practicable a Registration Statement pursuant to the Securities Act of 1933 (the "Act"), and all requisite registrations or qualifications under any state securities laws, covering the sale by such Shareholder of all or part of the Acquiring Common Stock to be issued to him hereunder (and any additional shares distributed thereon in any stock dividend or stock split), and shall use its best efforts to have such Registration Statement made effective in order to permit a sale of such Common Stock upon terms of an offering to be supplied to Acquiring in writing. The Shareholder shall promptly pay and reimburse Target for all costs and expenses (or, if any other shareholder of Acquiring shall join in such registration as provided in subsection (3) below, each "selling shareholder" participating in such registration shall pay and reimburse Acquiring for his proportionate share of all costs and expenses) related to such registration (including legal, accounting and printing expenses), without regard to whether the Registration Statement is made effective or the proposed sale of Acquiring Common Stock is carried out.

(2) Acquiring agrees to notify the Shareholder in writing prior to the filing of any Registration Statement (including any Registration Statement filed pursuant to the provisions of subsection H(1)) during the three years immediately following the Closing Date. If so requested by the Shareholder without ten (10) days after receipt of such notice as aforesaid, Acquiring shall include in such registration all or such part of the shares of Target Common Stock received by the Shareholder hereunder as the Shareholder may request.

(3)(a) The covenants and obligations of Acquiring under subsections H(1) and/or H(2) are subject to the following conditions:

(i) Acquiring shall not be required to file more than one Registration Statement during any period of twelve consecutive calendar months.

(ii) The Shareholder shall deliver to Acquiring a statement in writing that he bona fide intends to sell the shares of Common Stock which he proposes to include in the Registration Statement.

(iii) The Shareholder shall cooperate with Acquiring in the preparation of the Registration Statement to the extent required to furnish information concerning the Shareholder therein.

(iv) With respect to any Registration Statement relating to any shares of Common Stock of the Shareholder, the Shareholder will indemnify Acquiring and each person, if any, who controls Acquiring within the meaning of the Act, in writing, in form and substance acceptable to counsel for Acquiring, against all expenses, claims, damages or liabilities to which Acquiring may become subject, under the Act or otherwise, insofar as such expenses, claims, damages or liabilities arise out of or are based upon any untrue statement or alleged untrue statement of any material fact contained in any Preliminary Prospectus, the Registration Statement, the final Prospectus or any amendment or supplement thereto, or arise out of or are based upon the omission or alleged omission to state therein a material fact required to be stated therein or necessary to make the statements therein not misleading, in each case to the extent, but only to the extent, that such untrue statement or alleged untrue statement or omission or alleged omission was made therein in reliance upon and in conformity with written information furnished to Acquiring by the Shareholder expressly for use in the preparation thereof.

(v) With respect to any Registration Statement relating to any shares of Common Stock of Shareholder, Acquiring will indemnify the Shareholder, each Underwriter of the shares of the Shareholder, and each person, if any, who controls the Shareholder or any such Underwriter within the meaning of the Act, in writing, in form and substance acceptable to counsel for Target, the Shareholder and such Underwriters, against all expenses, claims, damages or liabilities to which the Shareholder, any such Underwriter, or any such controlling person may become subject, under the act or otherwise, insofar as such expenses, claims, damages or liabilities arise out of or are based upon any untrue statement or alleged untrue statement of any material fact contained in any Preliminary Prospectus, the Registration Statement, the final Prospectus or any amendment or supplement thereto, or arise out of or are based upon the omission or alleged omission to state therein a material fact required to be stated therein or necessary to make the statements therein not misleading; provided, however, that (X) Acquiring shall not be liable to the Shareholder (or any controlling person of the Shareholder) in any such case to the extent that such expenses, claims, damages or liabilities arise out of or are based upon any untrue statement or alleged untrue statement or omission or alleged omission made therein in reliance upon and in conformity with written information furnished to Acquiring by such Shareholder expressly for use in the preparation thereof, and (Y) Acquiring shall not be liable to any Underwriter (or any controlling person of such Underwriter) in any such case to the extent that such expenses, claims, damages or liabilities arise out of or are based upon any untrue statement or omission or alleged omission made therein in reliance upon and in conformity with written information furnished to Acquiring by such Underwriter expressly for use in the preparation thereof.

Any such Underwriter, as a condition to obtaining the indemnity agreement referred to in this subparagraph (v), shall be required to indemnify Acquiring on the same terms as provided in the previous subparagraph (iv) in the case of the Shareholder in respect of the written information furnished by such Underwriter which is referred to in clause (Y) of the preceding paragraph.

(b) The covenants and obligations of Acquiring under subsection H(2) are subject to the following conditions:

(i) Acquiring shall not be required to include any of the Common Stock if, by reason of such inclusion, Acquiring shall be required to prepare and file a Registration Statement on a form other than that which Acquiring otherwise would use.

(ii) Acquiring shall not be required to include any Common Stock in such Registration Statement if any managing underwriter with respect to the Common Stock then being offered by Acquiring shall in good faith object to the inclusion therein of the Common Stock of the Shareholder.

(iii) The Shareholder shall offer and sell his Common Stock pursuant to such Registration Statement and the Prospectus forming a part thereof upon such terms and conditions and at such times as shall be agreed upon and consented to by any managing underwriter with respect to the Common Stock offered by Acquiring pursuant to such Registration Statement.

(iv) In the event that by reason of such inclusion of the Common Stock of the Shareholder in any Registration Statement the effective date of such Registration Statement is unduly delayed, Acquiring may thereupon amend any such Registration Statement and remove therefrom any of the Common Stock owned by the Shareholder previously included therein.

(v) Without regard to whether the Registration Statement relating to the proposed sale of any Common Stock of Acquiring is made effective or the proposed sale of such Common Stock is carried out: (x) if the Shareholder shall propose to sell Common Stock received by the Shareholder hereunder in conjunction with the proposed sale of Common Stock by Acquiring, then Acquiring shall pay the Shareholder's portion of the fees and expenses in connection with such Registration Statement, including without limitation, legal, accounting, and printing fees and expenses; except that the Shareholder shall pay his pro rata portion of the registration fees under the Act and the state securities laws, all of the underwriting discounts and commission with respect to the Common Stock of the Shareholder included in the Registration Statement, and all of the fees and expenses of counsel to the Shareholder, (y) if the Shareholder shall propose to sell any Common Stock of Acquiring received by the Shareholder hereunder in conjunction with the sale of such Common Stock by any other shareholder of Acquiring, each selling shareholder shall pay his proportionate share of all costs and expenses related to such registration (including legal, accounting and printing expenses), each such shareholder paying a percentage of such costs and expenses equal to the percentage of such shareholder's interest in the net proceeds of the sale of all of the Common Stock which are offered for sale in such registration.

V. *AGREEMENTS AND INDEMNIFICATION*

Target, and the Shareholder, jointly and individually, agree as follows:

A. The Shareholder agrees that, notwithstanding any investigation of the business and assets of Target made by or on behalf of Acquiring prior to the Closing, he will indemnify and hold harmless Target and Shareholder from and against any "Loss," which with respect to Target and Shareholder shall mean any claims, liabilities, losses, costs or damages, net of any taxes and future tax benefits or other recoverable sums, and actual expenses (including without limitation reasonable counsel fees incurred in litigation or otherwise) arising out of or sustained by Target or Shareholder directly or indirectly due to (i) breach of any warranty, representation or agreement of Target or Shareholder contained in this Agreement, or in any Certificate, Schedule, Exhibit, Appendix or writing attached hereto or required by this Agreement, or (ii) any liability, debts, claim, tax penalty, or loss of Target arising out of any transaction prior to the Closing Date which was required to be disclosed and was not fully disclosed pursuant to this Agreement, or (iii) any cost or expense which may be incurred by Target or Shareholder in curing any breach of warranty contained in the Executed Agreements.

B. The Shareholder and Target agree that (i) any expense incurred, settlement made or judgment paid by Acquiring or Target after December 31, 19__ which arose out of any action or inaction prior to January 1, 19__ (including those which are described in Exhibit F hereto) or which occurred at any time on or after January 1, 19__ and prior to the Closing (x) as to which it is probable that a claim will be asserted and (y) which was not disclosed to Acquiring as required by Sections VI.B. shall be a "Loss" as to which Target is indemnified under Section V.A. above; and (ii) any expense incurred, settlement made or judgment paid by Target or Acquiring after December 31, 19__ which arose out of any action or inaction of Target which occurred after December 31, 19__ shall not be a "Loss" as to which Acquiring is indemnified under Section V.A. above, unless such action or inaction occurred prior to the Closing Date, it is probable that a claim will be asserted with respect thereto, and Target has failed to disclose the facts surrounding such an event to Acquiring by the Closing Date.

C. In the event a claim is made against Target or Subsidiary in respect of which they are (or either of them is) indemnified hereunder, Target or Subsidiary shall notify the Shareholder of such claim. In case any action is brought against Target, Subsidiary or Acquiring and Acquiring shall notify the Shareholder of the commencement thereof, the Shareholder shall assume the defense thereof with counsel satisfactory to Acquiring. Acquiring shall have the right to employ separate counsel in any such action and participate in the defense thereof but the fees and expenses of such counsel shall be at the expense of Acquiring unless the Shareholder has authorized the employment of such counsel. The Shareholder shall have the right to settle any such action or judgment based on any such action and in such event the Shareholder shall pay the amount of such settlement. If the Shareholder shall fail to promptly defend such action, Acquiring may do so with attorneys of its own selection and the Shareholder shall be responsible and pay any settlement or judgment effected by Acquiring and attorneys' fees. Notwithstanding anything contained herein to the contrary, the Shareholder shall not be required to pay the first $25,000 of Losses (as defined in this Article V.).

VI. *CONDITIONS TO ACQUIRING'S AND SUBSIDIARY'S OBLIGATION TO CLOSE*

The obligations of Acquiring and Subsidiary to consummate the transactions herein contemplated shall be subject to the fulfillment on or prior to the Closing Date of the following:

A. (1) Target must have: (i) realized pretax earnings (after elimination of non-operating gains and losses) or at least the lesser of 2.2% of net sales or $220,000 in the six-month period preceding July 1, 19__; or (ii) not incurred a loss in the first quarter of 19__ and realized pretax earnings (after elimination of non-operating gains and losses) of at least the lesser of 2.2% of net sales or $220,000 in the six-month period preceding September 30, 19__; or (iii) realized pretax earnings (after elimination of non-operating gains and losses) of 1% of net sales in calendar year 19__; and have informed Acquiring in writing at least two weeks prior to the end of each of the above-referenced periods during which Target believes that it might satisfy the pretax earnings condition referred to above as to such period and given written notice to Acquiring of having met one of the earnings goals outlined in this Section VI.A.(1) within thirty (30) days of having first reached one of such goals (which notice hereby agrees to give).

(2) Notice from Target (for purposes of this Section VI.A.) shall include a balance sheet and statement of earnings of Target, which Acquiring, at its election may have audited by a firm of independent certified accountants in the same manner and subject to the same requirements as provided in Section I hereof. In the event Acquiring should desire to perform an audit, the conclusions of the

firm of certified public accountants selected by Acquiring to perform such audit as to whether the conditions set forth in this Section VI.A. have been met shall be conclusive and binding on the parties hereto. Provided that the conditions set forth in Sections VI and VII are met or waived, the Closing shall occur upon 72 hours notice from Target to Acquiring, but no later than ninety (90) days after receipt by Target of notice from Acquiring that the conditions of this Section VI.A. have first been met, or thirty (30) days from the delivery to Target and Acquiring of the above-referenced audity, whichever shall occur first.

(3) Notwithstanding the foregoing, in the event of Shareholder's death or permanent disability, the Closing will occur no later than one hundred twenty (120) days after receipt by Acquiring of notice of such death or evidence reasonably satisfactory to Acquiring of such permanent disability.

B. Contemporaneously with giving notice to Acquiring, Target shall have provided Acquiring with revised Schedules dated as of the last day of the applicable period referred to in Section VI.A.(1) hereof (the "Revised Schedules"), with material changes through such date duly noted, and the Revised Schedules shall not contain any disclosures which would constitute a violation of this Agreement unless any such disclosures have been approved in writing by Acquiring.

C. Acquiring shall have received from _____, counsel for Target and the Shareholder, a favorable opinion, dated the Closing Date, to the effect that (i) is a corporation duly organized and existing in good standing under the laws of the State of California; (ii) Target has the corporate power to carry on its business as then being conducted and, to the knowledge of such counsel, is not required to be qualified as a foreign corporation in any jurisdiction in which the character of the properties owned and/or leased by it or the nature of the business conducted by it makes such qualification necessary; (iii) the authorized and outstanding capital stock of Target is as represented in this Agreement, and all the issued shares have been duly and validly authorized and issued and are fully paid and non-assessable; (iv) neither the execution of this Agreement nor the consummation of the transactions contemplated herein will conflict with any provision of the Articles of Incorporation or Bylaws of Target or to the best of such counsel's knowledge (after having made due investigation with respect thereto), conflict with or result in a breach of any indenture, mortgage, deed of trust or other agreement to which Target or Shareholder is a party and which violation would have a material adverse effect on Target; (v) to the knowledge of such counsel (after having made due investigation with regard thereto), there are no outstanding options or agreements on the part of Target or the Shareholder to issue or sell any capital stock of Target; (vi) this Agreement, the Merger Agreement, the Escrow Agreement and the Employment Agreement have been duly executed and delivered to the extent required by Target and the Shareholder and, assuming valid execution by Target and Subsidiary, each of this Agreement, the Merger Agreement and the Employment Agreement is the legal, valid and binding obligation of Target and the Shareholder to the extent executed by it or him and all corporate action required pursuant to the terms of this Agreement has been taken; (vii) to the knowledge of such counsel, Target is not engaged in or threatened with any legal action or other proceeding, except such legal actions or proceedings as are disclosed on the Revised Schedules, nor has Target been charged with any presently pending violation of any Federal, state or local law or administrative regulation, which would materially adversely affect the financial condition, business, operations, prospects, properties or assets of Target; (viii) no stock transfer taxes are applicable to the transactions provided herein; (ix) all other actions and proceedings required by law, or any of the Executed Agreements, to be taken by Target or the Shareholder at or prior to the Closing Date in connection with the Executed Agreements and the transactions provided for therein have been duly and validly taken; (x) upon filing the Merger Agreement with the California Secretary of State, the Merger will be effective under and in compliance with the laws of the State of California; and (xi) as to such other matters incident to the transactions contemplated hereby as Acquiring may reasonably request at or prior to the Closing.

D. No action or proceeding before a court or any other governmental agency or body shall have been instituted or threatened to restrain or prohibit the Merger contemplated hereby.

E. The representations and warranties of Target and the Shareholder (and any written statement, certificate or schedule furnished pursuant to or in connection with this Agreement) shall have been correct when made and the information contained in the Revised Schedules shall be true on and as of the Closing Date with the same effect as though all such information had been given to Acquiring on and as of such date and each and all of the actions of Shareholder and to be performed on or before the Closing Date pursuant to the terms hereof shall have been duly performed; and Shareholder and Target shall have provided Acquiring with a certificate to that effect.

F. The Shareholder shall have entered into an Employment Agreement with Target in substantially the form attached hereto as Appendix B * and executed an investment letter in substantially the form attached hereto as Appendix C.*

G. Target and the owner of the building currently leased by Target in _____, California shall have entered into a lease in substantially the form of the existing lease covering that property, except that: (i) the original term shall end five years after the Closing Date; (ii) Lessee shall have a five year option to renew at same basic rent; and (iii) Lessee shall, if Lessor desires to sell the premises, have the option to purchase the premises for $1.2 million. Lessor shall give Lessee written notice of such desire and Lessee shall have 15 days to exercise

* Appendices B and C have been omitted.
[Ed.]

the option and an additional 30 days to consummate the transaction and to pay the purchase price.

H. All consents, if any, to the consummation of the transactions contemplated herein required in order to prevent a breach of or a default under the terms of any agreement to which Target or the Shareholder is a party or is bound shall have been obtained.

I. The parties shall have complied with all Federal and state securities laws applicable to the transactions contemplated by this Agreement.

J. The Shareholder shall have executed on the Closing Date a general release of all claims which such Shareholder may have to the date thereof against Target, Subsidiary and Acquiring, except claims for current salary, and rights and claims under this Agreement, the Employment Agreement, the lease referred to in Section VI.G., and claims disclosed to Acquiring prior to the Closing Date and consented to in writing by Acquiring.

K. Acquiring shall have received on the Closing Date certificates of good standing, qualification and tax certificates from the State of California.

L. Acquiring shall have received on the Closing Date certificates representing all the issued and outstanding shares and all treasury shares of Target.

M. Acquiring shall have received on the Closing Date the corporate minute books, seals and stock transfer books of Target and its predecessors (if any) certified by the corporate secretary of Target (in form and substance acceptable to Acquiring) as complete, true and correct.

N. Acquiring shall have received at the Closing copies of minutes of meetings of the shareholders and the Board of Directors of Target, certified by the corporate secretary of Target, unanimously approving and authorizing the Merger and the other transactions contemplated by this Agreement.

VII. *CONDITIONS TO TARGET'S OBLIGATION TO CLOSE*

The obligation of the Shareholder and Target to consummate the transactions herein contemplated shall be subject to the fulfillment on or prior to the Closing of the following conditions:

A. The Shareholder shall have received from _____, counsel for Acquiring, a favorable opinion, dated the Closing Date, in form and substance satisfactory to Target, the Shareholder and their counsel, to the effect that (i) Acquiring is a corporation duly organized, validly existing and in good standing under the laws of the State of Delaware and it has the corporate power to own its property and to carry on its business as it is now being conducted; (ii) Subsidiary is a corporation duly organized, validly existing and in good standing under the laws of the State of California; (iii) the shares of Acquiring Common Stock to be issued and delivered to the Shareholder pursuant to this Agreement have been duly and validly authorized and issued and upon consummation of the transactions contemplated herein will be fully paid and non-assessable; (iv) this Agreement and the transactions contemplated herein have been duly authorized by the Board of Directors of Acquiring and Subsidiary and, assuming valid execution by the Shareholder and Target, this Agreement is a valid and binding obligation of Acquiring and Subsidiary in accordance with its terms; (v) the Merger Shares have been listed, or approved for listing subject to official notice of issuance, on the American Stock Exchange; and (vi) the issuance of the Merger Shares is exempt from registration under the Act pursuant to Section 4(2) thereof.

B.   The representations and warranties made by Acquiring herein shall have been correct when made, and shall be deemed to have been repeated at the Closing Date and shall be true and correct as of such date.

C.   No action or proceeding before a court or any other governmental agency or body shall have been instituted or threatened by an agency of the United States Government to restrain or prohibit the Merger contemplated hereby.

D.   Shareholder shall have received a favorable tax ruling covering the matters referred to in Section IV.F.

E.   The parties shall have complied with all Federal and state securities laws applicable to the transactions contemplated by this Agreement.

F.   The Book Value Per Share of Acquiring Common Stock (determined in the same manner as set forth in Section I.C., but using updated information) as of the end of Acquiring's most recent financial quarter prior to the Closing Date shall not be less than Acquiring's Book Value Per Share on December 31, 19__.

VIII.   *CLOSING*

The Closing shall be held on the Closing Date at the office of Acquiring or its counsel. At the Closing, Acquiring, Target and Subsidiary shall consummate the Merger contemplated by this Agreement by filing an Agreement of Merger complying with the laws of the State of California relating to the merger of domestic corporations. At the Closing the Shareholder shall receive the Acquiring Shares to which he is entitled pursuant to Section II. hereof.

IX.   *TERMINATION*

This Agreement may be terminated and abandoned prior to the Closing Date:

A.   By mutual written consent of Acquiring, Target and the Shareholder.

B. By Acquiring if, by the Closing Date, the conditions set forth in Sections V and VI hereof shall not have been met or waived.

C. By Target or the Shareholder if, by the Closing Date, the conditions set forth in Sections V and VII hereof shall not have been met or waived.

D. By any party hereto if the Closing Date contemplated herein shall not have occurred on or before March 1, 19___.

X. *ADDITIONAL REPRESENTATIONS OF SHAREHOLDER*

The Shareholder hereby acknowledges:

A. That in his opinion he has such knowledge and experience in financial and business matters, and particularly the business conducted by Acquiring, that he is capable of evaluating the risks of the investment in Acquiring Common Stock contemplated by this Agreement.

B. That he is able to bear the economic risk of the investment in Acquiring Common Stock contemplated by this Agreement.

C. That the Merger Shares which Shareholder may receive are for his own account and not on behalf of other persons;

D. That Acquiring has furnished to Shareholder a copy of its annual report for the fiscal year ended _____, 19___ on Form 10–K, its quarterly report for the quarter ended _____, 19___ on Form 10–Q, its proxy statement dated _____, 19___, all as filed with the Securities and Exchange Commission, and its 19___ Annual Report to Stockholders and a description of Acquiring Common Stock. Acquiring has made available, and does hereby agree to continue to make available, any additional information which the Shareholder may wish to obtain to the extent Acquiring possesses such information or can acquire it without unreasonable effort or expense necessary to verify the accuracy of any information contained in the above-referenced documents and descriptions.

E. That he has been informed that he must continue to bear the economic risk of the investment in Acquiring Common Stock contemplated herein for an indefinite period because the Merger Shares will not have been registered under the Securities Act of 1933 and therefore will be subject to the restrictions set forth in subsection F below and cannot be sold unless they are subsequently registered under the Securities Act of 1933 or an exemption from such registration is available.

F. That the certificates representing the Merger Shares will contain a legend stating that the Acquiring Common Stock has not been registered under the Securities Act of 1933 and cannot be sold absent registration under such Act or an exemption therefrom and that stop transfer instructions will be given to the transfer agent for Acquiring prohibiting such transfer agent from transferring the Acquiring Common Stock without compliance with the provisions of the Securities Act of 1933.

G.   That he will be required as a condition to receiving his Acquiring Common Stock at the Closing (and thereafter) to execute an investment letter in the form of the letter attached hereto as Appendix C.

XI. *NOTICES*

Any notices or communication required or permitted hereunder shall be sufficiently given if sent by first class mail, postage prepaid, and if to the Target or the Shareholder addressed to: _____, California with a copy to _____, Attention: _____. If to Acquiring or Subsidiary addressed to it at _____, marked for the attention of _____, with a copy thereof to _____, Attention: _____.

XII. *HEIRS, LEGAL REPRESENTATIVES AND ASSIGNS*

This Agreement and the rights of the parties hereunder may not be assigned and shall be binding upon and shall inure to the benefit of the parties hereto and their heirs, legal representatives and successors.

XIII. *ENTIRE AGREEMENT*

This Agreement and the Schedules, Exhibits and Appendices attached hereto and to be attached hereto, and the documents delivered pursuant hereto constitute the entire agreement and understanding between Acquiring, Subsidiary, Target and the Shareholder and supersede any prior agreement and understanding relating to the subject matter of this Agreement.   No change, amendment, termination or attempted waiver of any of the provisions hereof shall be binding on Acquiring, Subsidiary, Target or Shareholder unless in writing and signed by the President or other senior officer of Acquiring, Subsidiary, or Target, as the case may be, and if such change affects the Shareholder, then if signed by the Shareholder.   Unless specifically otherwise herein provided or agreed to by Acquiring, Subsidiary, Target and the Shareholder in writing, no modification, waiver, termination, rescission, discharge or cancellation of this Agreement shall affect the right of Acquiring, Subsidiary, Target or the Shareholder to enforce any claim whether or not liquidated, which accrued prior to the date of such modification waiver, termination, rescission, discharge or cancellation of this Agreement, and no waiver of any provision or of any default under this Agreement shall affect the rights of Acquiring, Subsidiary, Target or the Shareholder thereafter to enforce said provision or to exercise any right or remedy in the event of any other default, whether or not similar.

XIV. *COUNTERPARTS*

This Agreement may be executed simultaneously in two or more counterparts, each of which shall be deemed an original and all of which together shall constitute but one and the same instrument.

XV. *EXPENSES*

Whether or not the transactions herein contemplated shall be consummated, Acquiring, Subsidiary and the Shareholder will each pay their own fees, expenses and disbursements and their counsels in connection with the subject matter of this Agreement or any of the Executed Agreements and any amendments thereto and all other costs and expenses incurred by it or him in performing and complying with all conditions to be performed by it or him under this Agreement or any of the Executed Agreements. Target will pay the fees, expenses and disbursements incurred by it and its counsel in connection with the subject of this Agreement or any of the Executed Agreements and any amendments thereto and all other costs and expenses incurred by it in performing and complying with all conditions to be performed by it under this Agreement, and any of the Executed Agreements.

XVI. *FURTHER ASSURANCES*

Upon reasonable request from time to time, the Shareholder shall execute and deliver all reasonably required documents and do all other acts which may be reasonably requested by Acquiring to implement and carry out the terms and conditions of the transaction contemplated by this Agreement, all such actions to be performed without further consideration, but at the expense of Acquiring, unless arising out of the default of the Shareholder. Except as prohibited by law, the Shareholder shall be required to furnish evidence against himself.

XVII. *MISCELLANEOUS*

A. Any party hereto may waive any provision contained in this Agreement for its benefit and such waiver shall not affect any of the other provisions hereof.

B. The singular shall include the plural and the plural shall include the singular; any gender shall include all other genders—all as the meaning and context of this Agreement shall require.

C. This Agreement shall be governed and regulated and the rights and liabilities of all parties hereto shall be construed in accordance with the laws of the State of California.

IN WITNESS WHEREOF, the undersigned parties have set their hands and seals as of the day and year first above written.

APPENDIX A

ESCROW AGREEMENT

AGREEMENT made as of this _____ day of _____, 19__, by and among _____ ("_____"), _____, a California resident ("Shareholder"), and _____ ("Depository") hereinafter referred to as "ESCROW AGREEMENT".

PRELIMINARY STATEMENT

Acquiring Corp. ("Acquiring") and the Shareholder have entered into a Plan of Reorganization for the conversion of all of the issued and outstanding shares of Target Corp., a California corporation ("Target") into shares of Acquiring's common stock, par value $1 ("Acquiring Common Stock"), dated _____ __, 19_ (the "Acquisition Agreement"), which Acquisition Agreement is incorporated herein by reference and made a part hereof. The parties have agreed that Shareholder will deposit certain of the Acquiring Common Stock received pursuant to the Acquisition Agreement (the "Merger Shares") in escrow in accordance with the provisions of Section II of the Acquisition Agreement.

NOW, THEREFORE, in consideration of the mutual covenants, representations and promises of the parties to this Escrow Agreement, the parties hereto agree as follows:

1. *DEPOSIT OF SHARES.* Shareholder will deliver to the Depository that portion of the Merger Shares referred to in Section II.B. of the Acquisition Agreement (i.e., 15,000 shares) at the time a place of Closing (as defined in the Acquisition Agreement).

Such shares as are delivered to Depository (the "Escrow Shares") shall be held and distributed by Depository as provided herein and in Section II of the Acquisition Agreement. The Escrow Shares will have attached thereto a stock power duly executed in blank by Shareholder, with signature guaranteed by a bank or trust company having an office or correspondent in New York City or by a broker or by a firm of brokers having membership in the New York Stock Exchange, in proper form to permit the transfer of the Shares represented thereby on the books of Acquiring.

The Escrow Shares shall continue to be registered in the name of Shareholder unless they are transferred to _____ in accordance with the terms of this Escrow Agreement.

For purposes of this Escrow Agreement:

(a) "Year One" is the four fiscal quarters of 19_ ending on _____. The "Base Year" is the twelve full months immediately preceding Year One. "Year Two" is the first four fiscal quarters of 19_ following Year One. "Year Three" is the first four fiscal quarters of 19_ following Year Two.

(b) The "Target Operations" are the business operations which constituted Target immediately prior to the Closing.

(c) "Pretax Earnings" are the pretax earnings of the Operations after elimination of all non-operating gains and losses, as computed by the public accounting firm which is the public accounting firm of _____ at the time of such computation (the "Accounts"). "Net Sales" are the net sales of the Operations (as determined by the Accountants) for the time period in question. Acquiring, Shareholder and Depository hereby agree that, for purposes of this Escrow Agreement, determinations of Net Sales and Pretax Earnings, as computed by the Accountants, shall be final and binding.

2. *THE TERM OF THE ESCROW.* The Depository (or its nominee) agrees to accept delivery of the certificates representing the Escrow Shares subject to the provisions of this Escrow Agreement, and to hold and distribute said shares during the period of this Escrow Agreement, all as herein provided.

3. *DELIVERY AND DISTRIBUTION OF ESCROW SHARES.* Within sixty days from the end of each Year (Year One, Year Two or Year Three), as appropriate, the Accountants shall compute and deliver to the Shareholder, Acquiring and to the Depository, a statement showing the Net Sales and the Pretax Earnings of the Operations for such Year. Within thirty days from the date of the receipt of such statements from the Accountants, the Depository shall distribute and deliver to Shareholder the number of Escrow Shares (if any) to which Shareholder may be entitled pursuant to this Escrow Agreement, and upon termination of this Escrow Agreement, the Depository shall distribute all of the Escrow Shares remaining in escrow and deliver same to Shareholder or Acquiring all in accordance with the following provisions:

(a) If during Year One the Target Operations shall experience Net Sales equal to or in excess of 115% of those experienced by the Target Operations in the Base Year and have Pretax Earnings equal to or in excess of 3.4% of such Net Sales, then 5,000 of the Escrow Shares shall be delivered to Shareholder.

(b) If during Year Two the Target Operations experience Net Sales equal to or in excess of 132% of those experienced by the Operations in the Base Year, and have Pretax Earnings equal to or in excess of 4.2% of such Net Sales, then 5,000 of the Escrow Shares shall be delivered to Shareholder.

(c) If during Year Three the Target Operations experience Net Sales equal to or in excess of 152% of those experienced by the Target Operations in the Base Year, and have Pretax Earnings equal to or in excess of 4.8% of such Net Sales, then 5,000 of the Escrow Shares shall be delivered to Shareholder.

(d) Notwithstanding Sections 3(a) through 3(c) above, in the event that any Escrow Shares remain in escrow after the end of Year Three, all remaining Escrow Shares shall be delivered to the Shareholder if the Target Operations shall experience Net Sales in Year Three equal to or in excess of 152% of those experienced by the Target Operations in the Base Year, and the aggregate Pretax Earnings of the Target Operations in the Years One, Two and Three shall equal or exceed the sum of (i) 3.4% of Year One's Net Sales (ii) 4.2% of Year Two's Net Sales, and (iii) 4.8% of Year Three's Net Sales. Those Escrow Shares which are not released from escrow and delivered to Shareholder pursuant to Sections 3(a) through 3(d) shall be returned to Acquiring 42 months following the Closing.

4. *DIVIDENDS AND OTHER DISTRIBUTIONS: VOTING.* Shareholder shall be entitled to retain all dividends, whether in cash, shares or other securities or property paid or distributed on or in respect of the Escrow Shares other than dividends payable in Common Stock. Shareholder agrees to deliver to Depository to be held in escrow subject to the term of this Escrow Agreement, all dividends in Acquiring Common Stock and all Acquiring Common Stock issued as a result of a stock split, together with stock powers duly executed in blank by Shareholder, with signature guaranteed by a bank or trust company having an office or correspondent in New York City or by a broker or by a firm of brokers having membership in the New York Stock Exchange, in proper form to permit the transfer of the Shares represented thereby on the books of Acquiring. All such shares shall be distributed by Depository in the same manner as the Escrow Shares in respect of which it was issued.

5. *FEES AND EXPENSES.* Acquiring shall bear and pay all expenses and charges of the Depository incurred in connection with this Escrow Agreement upon demand by the Depository.

6. *LIMITATION OF DEPOSITORY'S LIABILITY.* The Depository shall incur no liability in respect of any action taken or suffered by it in reliance upon any notice, direction, instruction, consent, statement or other paper or document believed by it to be genuine and duly authorized, nor for anything except its own willful misconduct or gross negligence. The Depository shall not be responsible for the validity or sufficiency of any shares or other securities which may be delivered to it hereunder. In all questions arising under this Escrow Agreement, the Depository may rely on the advice of counsel, and for anything done, omitted or suffered in good faith by the Depository shall not be liable to anyone.

Without limiting the generality of the foregoing provisions, the Depository shall be entitled to completely rely on the statements delivered to it by the Accountants and/or on the certification and direction of the President or any Vice-President of Acquiring, and shall not be liable for any error, misstatement, misinformation or misdirection in the Statements of the Accountants or the certification or direction of the President or any Vice-President of Acquiring.

7. *NOTICES.* All notices, instructions and other communications required or permitted to be given hereunder or necessary or convenient in connection herewith shall be in writing and shall be deemed to have been duly given if delivered personally or mailed first-class, postage prepaid, registered or certified mail, as follows:

If to the Depository:

If to Shareholder:

If to _____:

With copy to:

or to such other addresses as the Depository, Shareholder or shall designate in writing delivered to each other.

8. *GENERAL.* This Agreement shall be governed by and construed in accordance with the laws of the State of _____ and shall be binding upon and inure to the benefit of the parties hereto and their respective heirs, executors, administrators or other legal representatives, and their respective successors.

9. *ADDITIONAL DOCUMENTS.* Acquiring and the Shareholder agree to execute all other documents reasonably required by the Depository, in keeping with the meaning and intent of this Escrow Agreement and the Acquisition Agreement.

IN WITNESS WHEREOF, the parties hereto have set their hands and seals the day and year first above written.

INDEX

References are to Pages

†